TEXAS DISCOVERY

TEXAS DISCOVERY

A Practioner's Guide to Taking and Resisting Discovery Under the Texas Rules of Civil Procedure

Robert K. Wise
Kennon L. Wooten
Francesca A. Di Troia

2022

fastcase FULL COURT PRESS

First published in 2019.

Printed in the United States of America

1 2 3 4 5 6 7 8 9 0

ISBN 978-1-949884-69-2

Dedication

To Mr. Wise's parents, Rudy and Josephine Wise—gone, but never forgotten.

To Mr. Wise's daughters, Reagan and Riley. Without your support, I could not have written this book.

To Ms. Wooten's husband, Louie. Our partnership has enabled me to do many things I could not do alone. And to our daughter, Linden, whose love and laughter gave me the energy I needed to power through the long hours it took to complete this book.

To Ms. Di Troia's husband, Ethan, for endlessly supporting me in many new endeavors, including this book, and to our daughter, Elise, for occasionally allowing me to work on this book between playtimes.

Summary of Contents

Table of Contents

Acknowledgments

Mr. Wise thanks his paralegal, Emily Diebitsch, for her help and encouragement in writing this book.

Ms. Wooten thanks her partners, associates, and staff members at Scott Douglass & McConnico for encouraging her work on this book.

Mr. Wise, Ms. Wooten, and Ms. Di Troia thank and acknowledge the following University of Texas law students for their invaluable help in editing this book: Jacob Bishop, Tiffany Campbell, Lena Dennington, Lauren Doxey, David Gonzalez, Alex Gras, Anna Harris, Carly Stuart-Micocci, Sean Nanovic, David Oh, Abigail Oregeron, Meghan Romere, Jacob Sims, Matthew Streety, and Neal Whetstone. Special thanks and acknowledgment are due to Ms. Romere and Mr. Whetstone, whose participation in the book's editing far exceeded their original commitments.

The opinions in this book are the authors' own and not those of their law firms or the other attorneys in them.

About the Authors

Mr. Wise is a founding member of Lillard Wise Szygenda PLLC. Since completing his clerkship for the Hon. Paul C. Weick of the U.S. Court of Appeals for the Sixth Circuit, he has practiced law in Dallas, Texas, for more than forty years. A former equity partner in the international law firm of Hunton & Williams LLP, Mr. Wise left Hunton to form LWS, a boutique litigation firm focused on providing its clients with elite representation at reasonable rates. Mr. Wise's practice centers on trial and appellate litigation. He has tried many lawsuits and arbitrations and has argued many appeals primarily in both Texas federal appellate courts, including ones in the Texas and Oklahoma Supreme Courts. His practice areas include complex commercial litigation involving contract, misrepresentation, and breach of fiduciary duty claims, primarily in the energy, construction, and real estate industries; construction-defects litigation; accounting-malpractice defense; and complex personal-injury litigation.

Mr. Wise is an accomplished writer, having taught legal writing at the Dedman School of Law of Southern Methodist University and having published another book, *A Practitioner's Guide to Drafting and Responding to Written Discovery Under the Texas Rules of Civil Procedure* (published in 2014 by Texas Lawyer Books, an ALM publication) and many law review articles on different topics. He has given many presentations about discovery, including ones for the Dallas, Fort Worth, and Austin bar associations and a CLE on discovery for the University of Texas.

Mr. Wise consistently has been recognized as a "Super Lawyer" by the publishers of *Texas Super Lawyers* (Thompson Reuters Business), was named "Litigator of the Week" in the March 25, 2012 edition of the *Texas Lawyer* for beating the Federal Trade Commission in *FTC v. Financial Freedom Processing, Inc., et al.*, No. 3:10-CV-2446-N (N.D. Tex. Mar. 12, 2012), *aff'd*, No. 12-10520, 2013 U.S. App. LEXIS 16766 (5th Cir. Aug. 12, 2013), and "Appellate Lawyer of the Week" in the November 24, 2014 edition of the *Texas Lawyer* for preserving a summary-judgment in a multi-million dollar fire case, and received the Texas Bar Foundation's 2015 "Outstanding Law Review Article Award" for his 2014 St. Mary Law Journal article, *A Guide to Properly Using and Responding to Requests for Admission Under the Texas Discovery Rules.*

Ms. Wooten is a partner at Scott Douglass & McConnico LLP in Austin, Texas. Before joining the firm, she clerked for former Chief Justice Wallace B. Jefferson of the Supreme Court of Texas, worked at Baker Botts LLP, and served as the Rules Attorney for the Supreme Court of Texas. Ms. Wooten has represented a wide range of clients on both sides of the docket. Her practice focuses on general civil litigation and appeals.

Ms. Wooten's experience as Rules Attorney gave her a specialized understanding of local and statewide rules in Texas. In that position, she responded to public inquiries about rules, assisted with promulgating rules, and worked with the State Bar of Texas, committees, and task forces to address issues confronting Texas litigants. She has continued to focus on rule-related matters in private practice. She serves on the Texas Supreme Court Advisory Committee and the Texas Remote Proceedings Task Force, and she served on the Supreme Court of Texas Task Force for Rules in

Expedited Actions in 2011–2012 and, for over a decade, on the State Bar's Court Rules Committee.

Ms. Wooten's dedication to serving the community extends beyond rule-related work. For example, she is a member of the American Law Institute, the State Bar's Board of Directors, the Texas Access to Justice Commission, the State Bar's Pro Bono College, and the Editorial Board of *The Advocate* (a publication of the State Bar's Litigation Section). Previously, she served as the president of the Austin Bar Association, as the president of the Austin Young Lawyers Association, as a board member and secretary for the Texas Legal Services Center, as a member of the Texas Commission to Expand Civil Legal Services, and as Editor-in-Chief for *Austin Lawyer* (an Austin Bar publication).

Ms. Wooten is a frequent speaker at Continuing Legal Education events in Texas. She is a Chambers USA Band 1 recognized practitioner in general commercial litigation, and she has been named by *Austin Monthly* as one of Austin's Top Attorneys in Civil Litigation (in 2020–2021) and by Thomson Reuters as a "Texas Rising Star" (in 2008–2009 and 2013–2017) and a "Texas Super Lawyer" (in 2019–2021). She has received several awards, including a Litigation/Appellate Attorney Award from the Travis County Women Lawyers Association, a State Bar "Standing Ovation" Volunteer Award, and a Special Commendation of the Supreme Court of Texas and State Bar for work on rules.

Ms. Di Troia is "Of Counsel" at Savrick, Schumann, Johnson, McGarr, Kaminski, & Shirley, LLP in Austin, Texas, where she represents both plaintiffs and defendants in a wide variety of cases in both state and federal courts. She has authored briefs filed in the Texas Supreme Court and the United States Court of Appeals for the Fifth Circuit. Ms. Di Troia previously was an Assistant Attorney General in the Office of the Texas Attorney General. She an adjunct professor in the University of Texas Law School's Advocacy department and coaches mock trial as well.

Ms. Di Troia has spoken at many Continuing Legal Education events on a wide variety of topics, including sovereign immunity, discovery practices, and civility in dealings with opposing counsel. She is a member of the Barbara Jordan Inn of Court and has served on its board of directors in varying capacities since its inception. She also serves on the Board of Directors for the YMCA's Youth & Government Program and is active in Youth Justice Alliance, a non-profit dedicated to involving high-school students in pro bono litigation work.

User's Guide

Texas Rules of Civil Procedure, former Texas Rules of Civil Procedure, Federal Rules of Civil Procedure, and former Federal Rules of Civil Procedure are referred to respectively as "Texas Rule(s) __," former Texas(s) __, Federal Rule(s) __, and former Federal Rule(s) __.

Unpublished decisions are cited to both LEXIS and Westlaw when both citations are available, with only the LEXIS pages numbers provided.

In late 2020, the Texas Supreme Court amended many Texas discovery rules (i.e., Rules 190 and 192-98) as well as Texas Rules 47, "Claims for Relief," 99, "Issuance and Form of Citation," and 169, "Expedited Actions." Those amendments apply to cases filed on or after January 1, 2021, except for cases filed in justice court. The pre-amended version of those Rules continue to apply to cases filed before January 1, 2021.

The first two sections of each chapter of this book, other than Chapter 1, which does not relate to a specific discovery rule, respectively contain the current version of the Rule, all the official comments for the Rule, and a discussion of any changes made to the Rule by the 2021 amendments. The Appendix contains a copy of the pre-amended Texas discovery rules, Texas Rules 190-215.

CHAPTER 1

Introduction

"Discovery" is the "[c]ompulsory disclosure, at a party's request, of information that relates to the litigation."[1] It allows the parties to "'seek the truth, so that disputes may be decided by what the facts reveal, not by what facts are concealed.'"[2] Discovery's principal goals are to "provide[] notice of the evidence that the opposing party intends to present" and to "prevent trial by ambush."[3] Notwithstanding its laudatory purpose

---

1 *Discovery, Black's Law Dictionary* (11th ed. 2019); *accord* Bryan A. Garner, *A Dictionary of Modern Legal Usage* 239–40 (2d ed. 1995) (defining "discovery" as "disclosure by a party to an action, at the other party's instance, of facts or documents relevant to the lawsuit"); *see also Sec. Nat'l Bank v. Abbott Labs.*, 299 F.R.D. 595, 596 (N.D. Iowa 2014) (noting that "discovery" is "a process intended to facilitate the free flow of information between parties"), *rev'd on other grounds*, 800 F.3d 936 (8th Cir. 2015).

2 *In re Colonial Pipeline Co.*, 968 S.W.2d 938, 941 (Tex. 1998) (orig. proceeding) (quoting *Jampole v. Touchy*, 673 S.W.2d 569, 573 (Tex. 1984)), *disapproved of on other grounds by Walker v. Parker*, 827 S.W.2d 833, 842 (Tex. 1992) (orig. proceeding); *accord Crosstex Energy Servs., L.P. v. Pro Plus, Inc.*, *430* S.W.3d 384, 394 (Tex. 2014); *In re Alford Chevrolet-Geo*, 997 S.W.2d 173, 180 (Tex. 1999) (orig. proceeding); *In re State Farm Lloyds,* No. 02-20-00163-CV, 2020 Tex. App. LEXIS 7207, at *6–7, 2020 WL 5242414 (Tex. App.—Fort Worth Sept. 3, 2020, orig. proceeding) (mem. op.); *In re United Fire Lloyds,* 578 S.W.3d 572, 583 (Tex. App.—Tyler 2019, orig. proceeding) (mem. op.); *In re Box,* No. 13-16-00016-CV, 2016 Tex. App. LEXIS 1782, at *5, 2016 WL 747787 (Tex. App.—Corpus Christi Feb. 19, 2016, orig. proceeding) (mem. op.); *Nancarrow v. Whitmer,* 463 S.W.3d 243, 253 (Tex. App.—Waco 2015, no pet.); *In re VERP Inv., LLC,* 457 S.W.3d 255, 260 (Tex. App.—Dallas 2015, orig. proceeding).

3 *Best Indus. Unif. Supply Co. v. Gulf Coast Alloy Welding, Inc.*, 41 S.W.3d 145, 147 (Tex. App.—Amarillo 2000, pet. denied); *accord Penny v. El Patio, LLC,* 466 S.W.3d 914, 925 (Tex. App.—Austin 2015, pet. denied); *Ersek v. Davis & Davis, P.C.*, 69 S.W.3d 268, 271 (Tex. App.—Austin 2002, pet. denied); *see also Insignia Hosp. Grp., Inc. v. Jalaram Guru, LLC, No. 07-19-00057-CV,* 2020 Tex. App. LEXIS 4146, at *3, 2020 WL 2786676 (Tex. App.—Amarillo May 27, 2020, pet. denied) (mem. op.) (addressing discovery rules' purpose of preventing trial by ambush); *Black v. Watts,* 04-17-00489-CV, 2018 Tex. App. LEXIS 6186, at *12, 2018 WL 3747746 (Tex. App.—San Antonio Aug. 8, 2018, pet. denied) (mem. op.) (same).

and goals, discovery is "the bane of modern litigation."[4] By its very nature, it is intrusive and invasive.[5]

Discovery also is the largest cost in most civil actions—as much as 90 percent in complex cases[6]—and can be the most frustrating part of litigation because it often is mired in obstructionism.[7] As one judge noted: "Although the . . . discovery rules were

---

[4] *Rossetto v. Pabst Brewing Co.*, 217 F.3d 539, 542 (7th Cir. 2000) (Posner, C.J.); *see also Liguria Foods, Inc. v. Griffith Labs., Inc.*, 320 F.R.D. 168, 182 (N.D. Iowa 2017) ("Few practicing attorneys would be surprised that discovery was singled out as 'the primary cause for cost and delay,' and often 'can become an end in itself.'" (quoting Hon. Paul W. Grimm & David S. Yellin, *A Pragmatic Approach to Discovery Reform: How Small Changes Can Make a Big Difference in Civil Discovery*, 64 S.C.L. Rev. 495, 495–96 (2013))); *Fudali v. Napolitano*, 283 F.R.D. 400, 401 (N.D. Ill. 2012) ("While discovery may be the bane of modem litigation, parties and their counsel have an obligation to participate fully, fairly and cooperatively in that often needlessly contentious endeavor.").

[5] *Bond v. Utreras*, 585 F.3d 1061, 1067 (7th Cir. 2009); *Cusumano v. Microsoft Corp.*, 162 F.3d 708, 717 (1st Cir. 1998); *see also Flentye v. Kathrein*, No. 06 C 3492, 2007 U.S. Dist. LEXIS 74260, at *7, 2007 WL 2903128 (N.D. Ill. Oct. 2, 2007) ("[Discovery] is, like life itself, 'nasty [and] brutish. . . .' Unfortunately, it is not generally 'short.'" (quoting Hobbes, *Leviathan*, Ch. XIII)).

[6] Robert K. Wise, *Ending Evasive Responses to Written Discovery: A Guide for Properly Responding (and Objecting) to Interrogatories and Document Requests Under the Texas Discovery Rules*, 65 Baylor L. Rev. 510, 512 (2013); *see also, e.g., In re Nat'l Lloyds Ins. Co.*, 532 S.W.3d 794, 813 (Tex. 2017) (per curiam) (orig. proceeding) ("Especially in the context of multi-party litigation, costs are magnified by expanding the scope of discovery, and 'the costs of multi-party litigation can drive defendants to settle regardless of the merits.'" (quoting *In re Alford Chevrolet–Geo*, 997 S.W.2d 173, 180 (Tex. 1999) (orig. proceeding))); *Liguria Foods, Inc. v. Griffith Labs., Inc.*, 320 F.R.D. 168, 182 (N.D. Iowa 2017) ("[B]y some estimates, discovery costs now comprise between 50 and 90 percent of the total litigation costs in a case" and "[d]iscovery abuse also represents one of the principal causes of delay and congestion in the judicial system[.]" (quoting John H. Beisner, *Discovering A Better Way*, 60 Duke L.J. 547, 549 (2010))); *Steenbergen v. Ford Motor Co.*, 814 S.W.2d 755, 758 (Tex. App.—Dallas 1991, writ denied) ("It is well known that discovery costs are a major part of the overall expense of a trial."); Thomas E. Willging & Emery G. Lee III, *In Their Words: Attorney Views About Costs and Procedures in Federal Civil Litigation* 14 (Federal Judicial Center 2010) (noting that discovery is the "number one cost-driver and there isn't a close second" and that discovery costs increase five percent for every non-expert deposition, another five percent for each additional type of discovery, and another 11 percent for every expert-witness deposition).

[7] *See, e.g., In re Nat'l Lloyds Ins. Co.*, 532 S.W.3d 794, 813 (Tex. 2017) (per curiam) (orig. proceeding) ("'Discovery is often the most significant cost of litigation' and a potential 'weapon capable of imposing large and unjustifiable costs on one's adversary.'" (quoting *In re Alford Chevrolet-Geo*, 997 S.W.2d 173, 180 (Tex. 1999) (orig. proceeding) (citing Wayne D. Brazil, *Views From the Front Lines: Observations by Chicago Lawyers About the System of Civil Discovery*, 1980 Am. B. Found. Res. J. 219, 229, and Frank H. Easterbrook, *Discovery as Abuse*, 69 B.U.L. Rev. 635, 636 (1989))); *Garcia v. Peeples*, 734 S.W.2d 343, 347 (Tex. 1987) (orig. proceeding) ("Unfortunately, this goal of the discovery process is often frustrated by the adversarial approach to discovery. The 'rules of the game' encourage parties to hinder opponents by forcing them to utilize repetitive and expensive methods to find out the facts. The truth about relevant matters is often kept submerged beneath the surface of glossy denials and formal challenges to requests until an opponent unknowingly utters some magic phrase to cause the facts to rise.") (citation omitted); *Explanatory Statement Accompanying the 1999 Amendments to the Rules of Civil Procedure Governing Discovery*,

intended to facilitate discovery and refocus cases on the legal merits, 'the discovery process has supplanted trial as the most contentious stage in litigation.' Improper discovery responses necessarily add to the contentiousness of litigation, because they start with non-disclosure as their premise."[8]

Many practitioners are quick to dispute discovery requests, slow to produce information, and all-too-eager to object at every stage of the process. For example, in responding to written discovery (e.g., "requests for production and inspection of documents and tangible things, requests for entry onto property, interrogatories, and requests for admission"[9]), many practitioners interpose every objection imaginable even though courts and commentators resoundingly disapprove boilerplate objections.[10]

Order of Approval of the Revisions to the Texas Rules of Civil Procedure, Misc. Docket No. 98-9196 (Tex. Nov. 9, 1998) (recognizing that "discovery may be misused to deny justice . . . by driving up the costs of litigation until it is unaffordable and stalling resolution of cases"), printed at 61 Tex. Bar J. 1140, 1140 (Dec. 1998); *cf. Liguria Foods, Inc. v. Griffith Labs., Inc.*, 320 F.R.D. 168, 185 (N.D. Iowa 2017) ("Improper discovery responses necessarily add to the contentiousness of litigation, because they start with non-disclosure as their premise."); Frank H. Easterbrook, *Discovery as Abuse*, 69 B.U. L. Rev. 635, 636 (1989) ("Litigants with weak cases have little use for bringing the facts to light and every reason to heap costs on the adverse party. . . . The prospect of these higher costs leads the other side to settle on favorable terms.").

8 *Liguria Foods, Inc. v. Griffith Labs., Inc.*, 320 F.R.D. 168, 185 (D. Iowa 2017) (citation omitted) (quoting Mitchell London, *Resolving the Civil Litigant's Discovery Dilemma*, 26 Geo. J. Legal Ethics 837 (2013)).

9 Tex. R. Civ. P. 192.7(a) (defining "written discovery").

10 *See, e.g.*, Robert K. Wise, *Ending Evasive Responses to Written Discovery: A Guide for Properly Responding (and Objecting) to Interrogatories and Document Requests Under the Texas Discovery Rules*, 65 Baylor L. Rev. 510, 567–72 (2013) (discussing boilerplate objections and pointing out that they are improper under the Texas discovery rules); Matthew L. Jarvey, Note, *Boilerplate Discovery Objections: How They Are Used, Why They Are Wrong, and What We Can Do About Them*, 61 Drake L. Rev. 913, 915 (2013) ("One of the most rampant abuses of the discovery process is the use of boilerplate objections to discovery requests."); *cf. Tim Long Plumbing, Inc. v. Kinsale Ins. Co.*, No. 4:20-CV-00042, 2020 U.S. Dist. LEXIS 208897, at *8, 2020 WL 6559869 (E.D. Tex. Nov. 9, 2020) ("It is well-established that parties cannot make general or boilerplate objections to discovery requests." (citing *Heller v. City of Dall.*, 303 F.R.D. 466, 483 (N.D. Tex. 2014))); *Lopez v. Don Herring Ltd.*, 327 F.R.D. 567, 581 (N.D. Tex. 2018) ("Serving unsupported and boilerplate or stock objections does not preserve or accomplish anything other than waiver and subjecting the responding party to sanctions. . . ."); *Team Express Distrib., LLC v. Junction Sols., Inc.*, No. CVSA15CA-00994DAE, 2017 U.S. Dist. LEXIS 224336, at *4, 2017 WL 10820159 (W.D. Tex. Aug. 30, 2017) ("General or boilerplate objections are invalid, and [o]bjections to discovery must be made with specificity, and the responding party has the obligation to explain and support its objections." (quoting *Samsung Elecs. Am. Inc. v. Yang Kun "Michael" Chung*, 325 F.R.D. 578, 590 (N.D. Tex. 2017))); *Resendez v. Smith's Food & Drug Ctrs., Inc.*, No. 2:15-cv-00061-JAD-PAL, 2015 U.S. Dist. LEXIS 34038, at *5–6, 2015 WL 1186581 (D. Nev. Mar. 16, 2015) ("Federal courts have routinely held that boilerplate objections are improper."); *Heller v. City of Dall.*, 303 F.R.D. 466, 483–84 (N.D. Tex. 2014) ("So-called boilerplate or unsupported objections—even when asserted in response to a specific discovery request and not as part of a general list of generic objections preceding any responses to specific discovery requests—are likewise improper and ineffective and may rise (or fall) to the level of what the Fifth Circuit has described as 'an all-too-common example of the sort of "Rambo tactics"

Some practitioners engage in obstructionist discovery practice to grandstand for their clients, to intentionally obstruct the flow of clearly discoverable information, to win a war of attrition, or to intimidate and harass the opposing party. Others do it simply because it is how they were taught[11] or because they have a warped view of zealous advocacy.[12] As one discovery expert has written: "It would appear that there is something in the DNA of the American civil justice system that resists cooperation during discovery."[13] Irrespective of the reason, obstructionist discovery practice results in costly litigation and disregards the Texas Supreme Court's directive to use the Texas Rules of Civil Procedure "to obtain the just, fair, equitable, and impartial adjudication of the rights of litigants . . . *at the least expense* both to the litigants and to the state as may be practicable[.]"[14]

---

that have brought disrepute upon attorneys and the legal system.'" (quoting *McLeod, Alexander, Powel & Apffel, P.C. v. Quarles*, 894 F.2d 1482, 1484–86 (5th Cir. 1990))); *Russell v. Daiichi-Sankyo, Inc.*, No. CV 11-34-BLG-CSO, 2012 U.S. Dist. LEXIS 49161, at *3, 2012 WL 1161435 (D. Mont. Apr. 6, 2012) ("The recitation of 'boilerplate, shotgun-style objections' are not consistent with the requirements of discovery rules."); *Mancia v. Mayflower Textile Servs. Co.*, 253 F.R.D. 354, 364 (D. Md. 2008) (noting that "boilerplate objections that a request for discovery is 'overboard and unduly burdensome, and not reasonably calculated to lead to the discovery of material admissible in evidence,' persist despite a litany of decisions from courts, including this one, that such objections are improper unless based on particularized facts.") (citation omitted); *St. Paul Reinsurance Co. v. Com. Fin. Corp.*, 198 F.R.D. 508, 512 (N.D. Iowa 2000) (collecting cases and sanctioning lawyers for using boilerplate objections in response to production requests). See also Chapter 5, section 5-3:3 (discussing the impropriety of boilerplate objections).

11 *See, e.g., Liguria Foods, Inc. v. Griffith Labs., Inc.*, 320 F.R.D. 168, 181 (N.D. Iowa 2017) ("As to the question of why counsel for both sides had resorted to 'boilerplate' objections, counsel admitted that it had a lot to do with the way they were trained, the kinds of responses that they had received from opposing parties, and the 'culture' that routinely involved the use of such 'standardized' responses.").

12 As explained by leading commentators on discovery:

> The truth is that lawyers and clients avoid cooperating with their adversary during discovery—despite the fact that it is in their clear interest to do so—for a variety of inadequate and unconvincing reasons. They do not cooperate because they want to make the discovery process as expensive and punitive as possible for their adversary, in order to force a settlement to end the costs rather than having the case decided on the merits. They do not cooperate because they wrongly assume that cooperation requires them to compromise the legitimate legal positions that they have a good faith basis to hold. Lawyers do not cooperate because they have a misguided sense that they have an ethical duty to be oppositional during the discovery process—to "protect" their client's interests—often even at the substantial economic expense of the client. Clients do not cooperate during discovery because they want to retaliate against their adversary, or "get back" at them for the events that led to the litigation. But the least persuasive of the reasons for not cooperating during the discovery process is the entirely misplaced notion that the "adversary system" somehow prohibits it.

Hon. Paul W. Grimm & David S. Yellin, *A Pragmatic Approach to Discovery Reform: How Small Changes Can Make a Big Difference in Civil Discovery*, 64 S.C.L. Rev. 495, 525–26 (2013) (footnotes omitted); *see Liguria Foods, Inc. v. Griffith Labs., Inc.*, 320 F.R.D. 168, 182 (N.D. Iowa 2017) ("Unfortunately, experience has taught me that attorneys do not know or pay little attention to the discovery rules in the Federal Rules of Civil Procedure.").

13 Hon. Paul W. Grimm & David S. Yellin, *A Pragmatic Approach to Discovery Reform: How Small Changes Can Make a Big Difference in Civil Discovery*, 64 S.C.L. Rev. 495, 530 (2013).

14 Tex. R. Civ. P. 1 (emphasis added).

Obstructionist discovery practice persists in part because most practitioners simply accept it as inevitable and, more importantly, because courts often ignore it. By ignoring it, courts "reinforce—even incentivize—obstructionist tactics."[15]

This book's purpose is to provide a comprehensive guide to Texas discovery, primarily by focusing on each Texas discovery rule: Texas Rules of Civil Procedure 176 and 190–215.[16] Some of these rules—Texas Rules 190 and 192–198—were amended in

[15] *Sec. Nat'l Bank v. Abbott Labs.*, 299 F.R.D. 595, 597 (N.D. Iowa 2014), *rev'd on other grounds*, 800 F.3d 930 (8th Cir. 2015).

[16] The Texas discovery rules are Texas Rules of Civil Procedure 176 and 190–215.

The Texas discovery rules largely are based in part on the Federal discovery rules—Federal Rules 26–37 and 45. *See, e.g.*, *Final Approval of Amendments to Texas Rules of Civil Procedure 47, 99, 169, 190, 192, 193, 194, 195, 196, 197, and 198,* Misc. Docket No. 20-9153 (Tex. Dec. 23, 2020), *available at* https://www.txcourts.gov/supreme/administrative-orders/2020/ (noting, in comments to 2021 changes, that current Texas Rule 194 "is amended based on Federal Rule of Civil Procedure 26(a) to require disclosure of basic discovery automatically, without awaiting a discovery request[,]" and that new Texas Rules 195.5(c) and (d) "are based on Federal Rules of Civil Procedure 26(b)(4)(B) and (C)"); *Fireman's Fund Ins. Co. v. Com. Standard Ins. Co.*, 490 S.W.2d 818, 825 (Tex. 1972) (noting that former Texas Rule 169 governing requests for admission "was taken with minor textual changes from Federal Civil Rule 36 as it existed in 1941"); *In re Soc'y of Our Lady*, No. 13-19-00064-CV, 2019 Tex. App. LEXIS 6269, at *22 (Tex. App.—Corpus Christi July 23, 2019, orig. proceeding) (noting that the Texas Supreme Court held that the federal courts' construction of the analogous federal rule was 'helpful' to an analysis of our Texas rule" and applying federal court decisions in construing Texas Rule 204, regarding physical and mental examinations (citing *Coates v. Whittington*, 758 S.W.2d 749, 751 (Tex. 1988), *overruled in part by* Tex. R. Civ. P. 204.1)); *Texaco, Inc. v. Dominguez*, 812 S.W.2d 451, 455 (Tex. App.—San Antonio 1991, orig. proceeding) (noting that former Texas Rule 167 relating to production requests was based on Federal Rule 34); *In re Fina Oil & Chem. Co.*, No. 13-98-640-CV, 1999 Tex. App. LEXIS 1751, at *14–15, 1999 WL 33589153 (Tex. App.—Corpus Christi Mar. 11, 1999, orig. proceeding) (not designated for publication) (noting that former Texas "Rule 201(4) is patterned after Federal Rule of Civil Procedure 30(b)(6)"); *Hosp. Corp. of Am. v. Farrar*, 733 S.W.2d 393, 394–95 (Tex. App.—Fort Worth 1987, orig. proceeding) (equating former Texas Rule 201(4) to Federal Rule 30(b)(6)). Accordingly, federal cases are persuasive authority in construing the Texas discovery rules patterned after the federal ones. *See, e.g.*, *In re State Farm Lloyds*, 520 S.W.3d 595, 613 (Tex. 2017) ("To be sure, there are differences in language between the Texas rule and the federal rule. But as we affirmed in *In re Weekley Homes,* [295 S.W.3d 309, 316–17 (Tex. 2009) (orig. proceeding),] 'our rules as written are not inconsistent with the federal rules or the case law interpreting them,' even though they may not 'mirror the federal language.") (footnote omitted); *In re Weekley Homes, L.P.*, 295 S.W.3d 309, 316–17 (Tex. 2009) (orig. proceeding) (conceding that state discovery rules are not identical to federal rules, but "are not inconsistent," and "therefore we look to the federal rules for guidance"); *Farmers Grp., Inc. v. Lubin*, 222 S.W.3d 417, 425 (Tex. 2007) (looking to cases interpreting federal rules where Texas rules incorporate identical language); *In re Kimberly-Clark Corp.*, 228 S.W.3d 480, 486–88 (Tex. App.—Dallas 2007, orig. proceeding) (relying on federal cases in interpreting Texas Rule 196.7 regarding entry onto land); *In re Fina Oil & Chem. Co.*, No. 13-98-640-CV, 1999 Tex. App. LEXIS 1751, at *14–15, 1999 WL 33589153 (Tex. App.—Corpus Christi Mar. 11, 1999, orig. proceeding) (not designated for publication) (relying on federal cases in interpreting former Texas Rule 201(4) because it was "patterned after Federal Rule of Civil Procedure 30(b)(6)"); *Hosp. Corp. of Am. v. Farrar*, 733 S.W.2d 393, 394–95 (Tex. App.—Fort Worth 1987, orig. proceeding) (same); *Indep. Insulating Glass/Sw., Inc. v. Street*, 722 S.W.2d 798, 802 (Tex. App.—Fort Worth 1987, orig. proceeding) (relying on federal cases in interpreting former Texas

December 2020, with the amendments "apply[ing] to cases filed on or after January 1, 2021, except for those filed in justice court."[17] The former version of these rules "continue to govern procedures and limitations in cases filed before January 1, 2021."[18] As a result of that continued applicability, this book covers both the former and current versions of these amended rules.

This book's goal is to help all readers and ensure that the practitioners among them are never subject to the following admonishment:

> If there is a hell to which disputatious, uncivil, vituperative lawyers go, let it be one in which the damned are eternally locked in discovery disputes with other lawyers of equally repugnant attributes.[19]

Rules 167 and 168 regarding waiver of objections to production requests and interrogatories, respectively); *see also Rimmer v. State*, 392 S.W.3d 635, 639 (Tex. 2012) ("Because [Texas] Rule 42 is patterned after Federal Rule of Civil Procedure 23, federal decisions and authorities interpreting current federal class action requirements are instructive."); *cf. Tex. Dep't of Pub. Safety v. Caruana*, 363 S.W.3d 558, 566 n.1 (Tex. 2012) ("When the federal and Texas rules of evidence are similar, we look to federal case law and the Federal Advisory Committee Notes when interpreting the Texas rules.").

17 *Final Approval of Amendments to Texas Rules of Civil Procedure 47, 99, 169, 190, 192, 193, 194, 195, 196, 197, and 198,* Misc. Docket No. 20-9153, at 1 (Tex. Dec. 23, 2020), *available at* https://www.txcourts.gov/supreme/administrative-orders/2020/.

18 *Final Approval of Amendments to Texas Rules of Civil Procedure 47, 99, 169, 190, 192, 193, 194, 195, 196, 197, and 198,* Misc. Docket No. 20-9153, at 1 (Tex. Dec. 23, 2020), *available at* https://www.txcourts.gov/supreme/administrative-orders/2020/.

19 *Dahl v. City of Huntington Beach*, 84 F.3d 363, 364 (9th Cir. 1996) (quoting *Krueger v. Pelican Prod. Corp.*, No. CIV-87-2385-A (W.D. Okla. Feb. 24, 1989)).

CHAPTER 2

Discovery's Purpose and Discovery Control Plans and Limitations—Texas Rule 190

2-1 Text of Rule 190

RULE 190. DISCOVERY LIMITATIONS

190.1. Discovery Control Plan Required

Every case must be governed by a discovery control plan as provided in this Rule. A plaintiff must allege in the first numbered paragraph of the original petition whether discovery is intended to be conducted under Level 1, 2, or 3 of this Rule.

190.2. Discovery Control Plan—Expedited Actions and Divorces Involving $250,000 or Less (Level 1)

(a) **Application.** This subdivision applies to:

(1) any suit that is governed by the expedited actions process in Rule 169; and

(2) unless the parties agree that Rule 190.3 should apply or the court orders a discovery control plan under Rule 190.4, any suit for divorce not involving children in which a party pleads that the value of the marital estate is more than zero but not more than $ 250,000.

(b) **Limitations.** Discovery is subject to the limitations provided elsewhere in these rules and to the following additional limitations:

(1) **Discovery period.** All discovery must be conducted during the discovery period, which begins when the first initial disclosures are due and continues for 180 days

(2) **Total time for oral depositions.** Each party may have no more than 20 hours in total to examine and cross-examine all witnesses in oral depositions. The court may modify the deposition hours so that no party is given unfair advantage.

(3) **Interrogatories.** Any party may serve on any other party no more than 15 written interrogatories, excluding interrogatories asking a party only to identify or authenticate specific documents. Each discrete subpart of an interrogatory is considered a separate interrogatory.

(4) **Requests for production.** Any party may serve on any other party no more than 15 written requests for production. Each discrete subpart of a request for production is considered a separate request for production.

(5) **Requests for admissions.** Any party may serve on any other party no more than 15 written requests for admissions. Each discrete subpart of a request for admission is considered a separate request for admission.

(c) **Reopening discovery.** If a suit is removed from the expedited actions process in Rule 169 or, in a divorce, the filing of a pleading renders this subdivision no longer applicable, the discovery period reopens, and discovery must be completed within the limitations provided in Rules 190.3 or 190.4, whichever is applicable. Any person previously deposed may be redeposed. On motion of any party, the court should continue the trial date if necessary to permit completion of discovery.

190.3. Discovery Control Plan—By Rule (Level 2)

(a) **Application.** Unless a suit is governed by a discovery control plan under Rules 190.2 or 190.4, discovery must be conducted in accordance with this subdivision.

(b) **Limitations.** Discovery is subject to the limitations provided elsewhere in these rules and to the following additional limitations:

(1) **Discovery period.** All discovery must be conducted during the discovery period, which begins when the first initial disclosures are due and continues until:

(A) 30 days before the date set for trial, in cases under the Family Code; or

(B) in other cases, the earlier of

(i) 30 days before the date set for trial, or

(ii) nine months after the first initial disclosures are due.

(2) **Total time for oral depositions.** Each side may have no more than 50 hours in oral depositions to examine and cross-examine parties on the opposing side, experts designated by those parties, and persons who are subject to those parties' control. "Side" refers to all the litigants with generally common interests in the litigation. If one side designates more than two experts, the opposing side may have an additional six hours of total deposition time for each additional expert designated. The court may modify the deposition hours and must do so when a side or party would be given unfair advantage.

(3) **Interrogatories.** Any party may serve on any other party no more than 25 written interrogatories, excluding interrogatories asking a party only to identify or authenticate specific documents. Each discrete subpart of an interrogatory is considered a separate interrogatory.

190.4. Discovery Control Plan—By Order (Level 3)

(a) **Application.** The court must, on a party's motion, and may, on its own initiative, order that discovery be conducted in accordance with a discovery control plan tailored to the circumstances of the specific suit. The parties may submit an agreed order to the court for its consideration. The court should act on a party's motion or agreed order under this subdivision as promptly as reasonably possible.

(b) **Limitations.** The discovery control plan ordered by the court may address any issue concerning discovery or the matters listed in Rule 166, and may change any limitation on the time for or amount of discovery set forth in these rules. The discovery limitations of Rule 190.2, if applicable, or otherwise of Rule 190.3 apply unless specifically changed in the discovery control plan ordered by the court. The plan must include:

(1) a date for trial or for a conference to determine a trial setting;

(2) a discovery period during which either all discovery must be conducted or all discovery requests must be sent, for the entire case or an appropriate phase of it;

(3) appropriate limits on the amount of discovery; and

(4) deadlines for joining additional parties, amending or supplementing pleadings, and designating expert witnesses.

190.5. Modification of Discovery Control Plan

The court may modify a discovery control plan at any time and must do so when the interest of justice requires. Unless a suit is governed by the expedited actions process in Rule 169, the court must allow additional discovery:

(a) related to new, amended or supplemental pleadings, or new information disclosed in a discovery response or in an amended or supplemental response, if:

(1) the pleadings or responses were made after the deadline for completion of discovery or so nearly before that deadline that an adverse party does not have an adequate opportunity to conduct discovery related to the new matters, and

(2) the adverse party would be unfairly prejudiced without such additional discovery;

(b) regarding matters that have changed materially after the discovery cutoff if trial is set or postponed so that the trial date is more than three months after the discovery period ends.

190.6. Certain Types of Discovery Excepted

This rule's limitations on discovery do not apply to or include discovery conducted under Rule 202 ("Depositions Before Suit or to Investigate Claims"), or Rule 621a ("Discovery and Enforcement of Judgment"). But Rule 202 cannot be used to circumvent the limitations of this rule.

Comments to Texas Rule 190

Comment to 2021 change:

Rule 190.2 is amended to implement section 22.004(h-1) of the Texas Government Code. Under amended Rule 190.2, Level 1 discovery limitations now apply to a broader subset of civil actions: expedited actions under Rule 169, which is also amended to implement section 22.004(h-1) of the Texas Government Code, and divorces not involving children in which the value of the marital estate is not more than $250,000. Level 1 limitations are revised to impose a twenty-hour limit on oral depositions. Disclosure requests under Rule 190.2(b)(6) and Rule 194 are now replaced by required disclosures under Rule 194, as amended. The discovery periods under Rules 190.2(b)(1) and 190.3(b)(1) are revised to reference the required disclosures.

Comment to 2013 change:

Rule 190 is amended to implement section 22.004(h) of the Texas Government Code, which calls for rules to promote the prompt, efficient, and cost-effective resolution of civil actions when the amount in controversy does not exceed $100,000. Rule 190.2 now applies to expedited actions, as defined by Rule 169. Rule 190.2 continues to apply to divorces not involving children in which the value of the marital estate is not more than $50,000, which are otherwise exempt from the expedited actions process. Amended Rule 190.2(b) ends the discovery period 180 days after the date the first discovery request is served; imposes a fifteen-limit maximum on interrogatories, requests for production, and requests for admission; and allows for additional disclosures. Although expedited actions are not subject to mandatory additional discovery under amended Rule 190.5, the court may still allow additional discovery if the conditions of Rule 190.5(a) are met.

Comments to 1999 change:

1. This rule establishes three tiers of discovery plans and requires that every case be in one at all times. A case is in Level 1 if it is pleaded by the plaintiff so as to invoke application of Level 1, as provided by Rule 190.2(a). If a plaintiff does not or cannot plead the case in compliance with Rule 190.2(a) so as to invoke the application of Level 1, the case is automatically in Level 2. A case remains in Level 1 or Level 2, as determined by the pleadings, unless and until it is moved to Level 3. To be in Level 3, the court must order a specific plan for the case, either on a party's motion or on the court's own initiative. The plan may be one agreed to by the parties and submitted as an agreed order. A Level 3 plan may simply adopt Level 1 or Level 2 restrictions. Separate Level 3 plans for phases of the case may be appropriate. The initial pleading required by Rule 190.1 is merely to notify the court and other parties of the plaintiff's intention; it does not determine the applicable discovery level or bind the court or other parties. Thus, a plaintiff's failure to state in the initial pleading that the case should be in Level 1, as provided in Rule 190.1, does not alone make the case subject to Level 2 because the discovery level is determined by Rule 190.2. Likewise, a plaintiff's statement in the initial paragraph of the petition that the case is to be governed by Level 3 does not make Level 3 applicable, as a case can be in Level 3 only by court order. A plaintiff's failure to plead as required by Rule 190.1 is subject to special exception.

2. Rule 190.2 does not apply to suits for injunctive relief or divorces involving children. The requirement of an affirmative pleading of limited relief (e.g., "Plaintiff affirmatively pleads that he seeks only monetary relief aggregating $50,000 or less, excluding costs, pre-judgment interest and attorneys' fees") does not conflict with other pleading requirements, such as Rule 47 and Tex. *Rev. Civ. Stat. Ann. art. 4590i*, § 5.01. In a suit to which Rule 190.2 applies, the relief awarded cannot exceed the limitations of Level 1 because the purpose of the rule, unlike Rule 47, is to bind the pleader to a maximum claim. To this extent, the rule in *Greenhalgh v. Service Lloyds Ins. Co.*, 787 S.W.2d 938 (Tex. 1990), does not apply.

3. "Discrete subparts" of interrogatories are counted as single interrogatories, but not every separate factual inquiry is a discrete subpart. *See* Fed. R. Civ. P. 33(a). While not susceptible of precise definition, *see Braden v. Downey*, 811 S.W.2d 922, 927–928 (Tex. 1991), a "discrete subpart" is, in general, one that calls for information that is not logically or factually related to the primary interrogatory. The number of sets of interrogatories is no longer limited to two.

4. As other rules make clear, unless otherwise ordered or agreed, parties seeking discovery must serve requests sufficiently far in advance of the end of the discovery period that the deadline for responding will be within the discovery period. The court may order a deadline for sending discovery requests in lieu of or in addition to a deadline for completing discovery.

5. Use of forms of discovery other than depositions and interrogatories, such as requests for disclosure, admissions, or production of documents, are not restricted in Levels 1 and 2. But depositions on written questions cannot be used to circumvent the limits on interrogatories.

6. The concept of "side" in Rule 190.3(b)(2) borrows from Rule 233, which governs the allocation of peremptory strikes, and from Fed. R. Civ. P. 30(a)(2). In most cases there are only two sides—plaintiffs and defendants. In complex cases, however, there may be more than two sides, such as when defendants have sued third parties not named by plaintiffs, or when defendants have sued each other. As an example, if *P1* and *P2* sue *D1*, *D2*, and *D3*, and *D1* sues *D2* and *D3*, *Ps* would together be entitled to depose *Ds* and others permitted by the rule (*i.e.*, *Ds*' experts and persons subject to *Ds*' control) for 50 hours, and *Ds* would together be entitled to depose *Ps* and others for 50 hours. *D1* would also be entitled to depose *D2* and *D3* and others for 50 hours on matters in controversy among them, and *D2* and *D3* would together be entitled to depose *D1* and others for 50 hours.

7. Any matter listed in Rule 166 may be addressed in an order issued under Rule 190.4. A pretrial order under Rule 166 may be used in individual cases regardless of the discovery level.

8. For purposes of defining discovery periods, "trial" does not include summary judgment.

2-1:1 2021 Amendments to the Texas Rules of Civil Procedure

The 2021 amendments to the Texas Rules of Civil Procedure modified Texas Rule 190 in a few respects. First, the monetary threshold for cases in Level 1 was increased. Second, the number of oral-deposition hours allowed in Level 1 was increased. Third, the discovery-period computation for Level 1 and Level 2 cases was modified in light of the initial disclosures required under amended Texas Rule 194.2. Fourth, the requests-for-disclosure provision was removed from Texas Rule 190.1, because the initial disclosures are now the same for all three case levels.[1]

---

[1] Tex. R. Civ. P. 194.2 (regarding initial disclosures).

2-2 Discovery's Purpose

Discovery's purpose is to allow the parties to obtain full knowledge of the issues and facts before trial, with the goal being "'to seek the truth so that disputes are decided by what the facts reveal, not by what facts are concealed.'"[2] The Texas Supreme Court has emphasized that discovery is "the linchpin of the search for truth, as it makes a trial less of a game of blind man's bluff and more a fair contest with the issues and facts disclosed to the fullest practicable extent."[3] By enabling parties to obtain (and exchange) information and material regarding their claims and defenses before trial, the Texas discovery rules, in theory, eliminate "trial by ambush," cause actions to be resolved on their merits, and promote settlement by giving parties the information and material needed to fully and accurately evaluate their positions' merits.[4]

---

[2] *In re Colonial Pipeline Co.*, 968 S.W.2d 938, 941 (Tex. 1998) (orig. proceeding) (quoting *Jampole v. Touchy*, 673 S.W.2d 569, 573 (Tex. 1984) (orig. proceeding), *disapproved of on other grounds by Walker v. Packer*, 827 S.W.2d 833, 842 (Tex. 1992) (orig. proceeding)); *accord, e.g., Crosstex Energy Servs., L.P. v. Pro Plus, Inc.*, 430 S.W.3d 384, 394 (Tex. 2014); *In re Alford Chevrolet-Geo*, 997 S.W.2d 173, 180 (Tex. 1999) (orig. proceeding); *In re State Farm Lloyds*, No. 02-20-00163-CV, 2020 Tex. App. LEXIS 7207, at *6–7, 2020 WL 5242414 (Tex. App.—Fort Worth Sept. 3, 2020, orig. proceeding) (mem. op.); *In re United Fire Lloyds*, 578 S.W.3d 572, 583 (Tex. App.—Tyler 2019, orig. proceeding) (mem. op.); *In re Box*, No. 13-16-00016-CV, 2016 Tex. App. LEXIS 1782, at *5, 2016 WL 747787 (Tex. App.—Corpus Christi Feb. 19, 2016, orig. proceeding) (mem. op.); *Nancarrow v. Whitmer*, 463 S.W.3d 243, 253 (Tex. App.—Waco 2015, no pet.); *In re VERP Inv., LLC*, 457 S.W.3d 255, 260 (Tex. App.—Dallas 2015, orig. proceeding).

[3] *State v. Lowry*, 802 S.W.2d 669, 671 (Tex. 1991) (orig. proceeding) (quoting *United States v. Procter & Gamble Co.*, 356 U.S. 677, 682 (1958)), *quoted with approval in Crosstex Energy Servs., L.P. v. Pro Plus, Inc.*, 430 S.W.3d 384, 394 (Tex. 2014), *In re Swepi L.P.*, 103 S.W.3d 578, 587 (Tex. App.—San Antonio 2003, orig. proceeding), *and Collins v. Cleme Manor Apartments*, 37 S.W.3d 527, 532 (Tex. App.—Texarkana 2001, no pet.); *accord In re Alford Chevrolet-Geo*, 997 S.W.2d 173, 180 (Tex. 1999) (orig. proceeding) ("As the United States Supreme Court has noted, modern discovery and pretrial procedures serve the useful purpose of '[making] a trial less a game of blindman's bluff and more a fair contest with the basic issues and facts disclosed to the fullest practicable extent.'" (quoting *United States v. Procter & Gamble Co.*, 356 U.S. 677, 682 (1958))).

[4] Nathan L. Hecht & Robert H. Pemberton, *A Guide to the 1999 Texas Discovery Rules Revisions* § II.A (Nov. 11, 1998), https://www.adrr.com/law1/rules.htm; *see Mid Continent Lift & Equip., LLC v. J. McNeill Pilot Car Serv.*, 537 S.W.3d 660, 672–73 (Tex. App.—Austin 2017, no pet.) (describing the purposes of Texas's discovery rules as including "ensuring that parties receive notice of the witnesses and evidence their opponents intend to present at trial, thereby promoting realistic assessment of settlement prospects and preventing 'trial by ambush'" (citing cases)); *Best Indus. Unif. Supply Co. v. Gulf Coast Alloy Welding, Inc.*, 41 S.W.3d 145, 147 (Tex. App.—Amarillo 2000, pet. denied) (identifying two goals of discovery: "First, discovery provides the parties with notice of the evidence that the opposing party intends to present. . . . Second, the discovery process prevents trial by ambush."); *Ersek v. Davis & Davis, P.C.*, 69 S.W.3d 268, 271 (Tex. App.—Austin 2002, pet. denied) (same); *see also Insignia Hosp. Grp., Inc. v. Jalaram Guru, LLC*, No. 07-19-00057-CV, 2020 Tex. App. LEXIS 4146, at *3, 2020 WL 2786676 (Tex. App.—Amarillo May 27, 2020, pet. denied) (mem. op.) (addressing discovery rules' purpose of preventing trial by ambush); *Black v. Watts*, No. 04-17-00489-CV, 2018 Tex. App. LEXIS 6186, at *12, 2018 WL 3747746 (Tex. App.—San Antonio Aug. 8, 2018, pet. denied) (mem. op.) (same).

Unfortunately, innovations in computer word processing and photocopying that allow even litigants of modest means to bury their opponents in voluminous "boilerplate" discovery requests or objections—compounded by a weakening in professional ethics that in earlier times would have made discovery misuse or abuse unthinkable, and technological advancements in the 1990s (e.g., email and other computer use) that greatly increased the volume of documents and other things subject to discovery—made it clear to the Texas Supreme Court that unrestricted discovery could be, and was being, used to needlessly and improperly drive up litigation costs to extort settlements and hinder the timely disposition of actions.[5] Accordingly, in an effort to eliminate discovery's excesses while retaining its benefits, the Texas discovery rules were amended extensively in 1999 and introduced, for the first time, limits on the amount of, and time for, discovery by means of discovery-control plans and discovery levels, which are discussed in the following Chapters.[6] Discovery abuses continued under the 1999 rules.

Since 1999, the Texas Supreme Court has amended the discovery rules twice in an effort "to promote the prompt, efficient, and cost-effective resolution of civil actions[.]"[7] In 2013, the court introduced an expedited-actions process (in Texas Rule 169) and made it subject to Level 1 discovery.[8] Then, effective January 1, 2021, the court significantly expanded the types of cases subject to the expedited-actions

---

[5] Nathan L. Hecht & Robert H. Pemberton, *A Guide to the 1999 Texas Discovery Rules Revisions* § II.A (Nov. 11, 1998), https://www.adrr.com/law1/rules.htm; *see In re Alford Chevrolet-Geo*, 997 S.W.2d 173, 180 (Tex. 1999) (orig. proceeding) ("[D]iscovery is not only 'a tool for uncovering facts essential to accurate adjudication,' but also 'a weapon capable of imposing large and unjustifiable costs on one's adversary.' Discovery is often the most significant cost of litigation. Because the costs of compliance are usually borne solely by the replying party, a requesting party improves its bargaining position by maximizing those costs." (citations omitted) (quoting Frank H. Easterbrook, *Discovery as Abuse*, 69 B.U. L. Rev. 635, 636 (1989))); Frank H. Easterbrook, *Discovery as Abuse*, 69 B.U. L. Rev. 635, 636 (1989) ("Litigants with weak cases have little use for bringing the facts to light and every reason to heap costs on the adverse party. . . . The prospect of these higher costs leads the other side to settle on favorable terms.").

[6] Chapter 8, section 8-6 addresses how technological advancements continue to change the landscape of discoverable information and thereby necessitate clarification of, and changes to, discovery standards governing electronically stored information.

[7] *See generally* Misc. Docket No. 20-9153, *Final Approval of Amendments to Texas Rules of Civil Procedure 47, 99, 169, 190, 192, 193, 194, 195, 196, 197, and 198* (Dec. 23, 2020) (setting forth amendments and associated comments and, on page 6, referencing the legislative mandate in Section 22.004(h-1) of the Texas Government Code for the court to adopt rules "to promote the prompt, efficient, and cost-effective resolution of civil actions"); Misc. Docket No. 13-9022, *Final Approval of Rules for Dismissals and Expedited Actions* (Feb. 12, 2013) (setting forth amendments and associated comments, including comment 1 to Former Texas Rule 169, which references the legislative mandate in Section 22.004(h) of the Texas Government Code for the court to adopt rules "to promote the prompt, efficient, and cost-effective resolution of civil actions").

[8] *See* Misc. Docket No. 20-9153 at 7–13, *Final Approval of Amendments to Texas Rules of Civil Procedure 47, 99, 169, 190, 192, 193, 194, 195, 196, 197, and 198* (Dec. 23, 2020) (setting forth Former Texas Rule 169, in its original form, as well as the associated amendments to Texas discovery rules); *see also In re State Farm Mut. Auto. Ins. Co.*, 551 S.W.3d 858, 862 (Tex. App.—Amarillo 2018, orig. proceeding) (Texas Rule "169 establishes an 'expedited actions process' that allows most civil claimants to fast-track their claims. . . . Under this expedited process, limits are applied to discovery, continuances, challenges to experts,

process and made additional amendments to the Texas discovery rules "to promote the prompt, efficient, and cost-effective resolution of civil actions[.]"[9]

2-3 Discovery-Control Plans

Texas Rule 190 divides civil actions into three "levels" of "discovery control plans" (Level 1, Level 2, and Level 3),[10] requires every civil action to be in one level at all times[11] and controls the amount of, and time for, discovery at each level.[12] As discussed in detail in the following Chapters, Level 1 applies to cases governed by the expedited-actions process and to certain, specified divorce cases; Level 2 applies by "default" to all other civil cases; and Level 3 generally applies to high-dollar or complex cases, although it may be invoked in any civil case other than a civil case governed by the expedited-actions process in Texas Rule 169.

2-3:1 Level 1 Discovery-Control Plans

As of 2021, Level 1 applies to the following two types of actions: (1) an action "governed by the expedited actions process in [Texas] Rule 169;"[13] and (2) unless the parties agree to a Level 2 discovery-control plan or the court orders a Level 3 one, "any suit for divorce not involving children in which a party pleads that the value of the marital estate is more than zero but not more than $250,000."[14]

The "expedited-actions process" of Texas Rule 169 was amended in 2021 to apply to significantly higher-dollar cases than those covered by Former Texas Rule 169.[15] The rule now "applies to a suit in which all claimants, other than counter-claimants, affirmatively plead that they seek only monetary relief aggregating $250,000 or less, *excluding* interest, statutory or punitive damages and penalties, and attorney fees and

---

and time for presentation of evidence and argument at trial. The discovery limitations are identified in Rule 190.2. . . .") (citations omitted).

[9] *See* Misc. Docket No. 20-9153 at 4–20, ***Final Approval of Amendments to Texas Rules of Civil Procedure 47, 99, 169, 190, 192, 193, 194, 195, 196, 197, and 198*** (Dec. 23, 2020) (setting forth amendments to Texas Rule 169 and amendments to Texas discovery rules, and conveying, in associated comments, that the amendments at hand were intended, in part, "to promote the prompt, efficient, and cost-effective resolution of civil actions").

[10] Tex. R. Civ. P. 190.2–.4.

[11] Tex. R. Civ. P. 190.1 ("Every case must be governed by a discovery control plan."); Tex. R. Civ. P. 190 cmt. 1 to 1999 change ("This rule establishes three tiers of discovery plans and requires that every case be in one at all times."). However, Texas Rule 190's discovery limitations "on discovery do not apply to or include discovery conducted under [Texas] Rule 202 ('Depositions Before Suit or to Investigate Claims'), or [Texas] Rule 621a ('Discovery and Enforcement of Judgment'). But [Texas] Rule 202 cannot be used to circumvent the limitations of this rule." Tex. R. Civ. P. 190.6.

[12] Tex. R. Civ. P. 190.2-.4.

[13] Tex. R. Civ. P. 190.2(a)(1); *see also* Tex. R. Civ. P. 169(d)(1) ("Discovery [in expedited actions] is governed by [Texas] Rule 190.2.").

[14] Tex. R. Civ. P. 190.2(a)(2).

[15] Under Former Texas Rule 169(a)(1), "[t]he expedited actions process . . . applie[d] to a suit in which all claimants, other than counter-claimants, affirmatively plead[ed] that they [sought] only monetary relief aggregating $100,000 or less, *including* damages of any kind, penalties, costs, expenses, pre-judgment interest, and attorney fees." (Emphasis added.)

costs."[16] As with Former Texas Rule 169, however, the expedited-actions process still does not apply to any actions in which the plaintiffs seeks non-monetary relief (e.g., injunctive or declaratory relief). Nor does it apply to actions "exempt from [Texas] Rule 169's application by statute."[17] Thus, in the foregoing types of actions, Level 1 is never proper, even if the amount in controversy is less than $250,000. Rather, discovery in those actions will be governed by Level 2 or Level 3.

Like Texas Rules 169 and 190, Texas Rule 47 was amended in 2021 and now requires that an "original pleading which sets forth a claim for relief, whether an original petition, counterclaim, cross-claim or third party claim" (except in actions governed by the Family Code and in probate proceedings),[18] include "a statement that the party seeks:"

(1) only monetary relief of $250,000 or less, excluding interest, statutory or punitive damages and penalties, and attorney fees and costs;

(2) monetary relief of $250,000 or less and non-monetary relief;

(3) monetary relief over $250,000 but not more than $1,000,000;

(4) monetary relief over $1,000,000; or

(5) only non-monetary relief[.][19]

Texas Rule 47(c), in effect, requires plaintiffs to plead into, or out of, the expedited-actions process set forth in Texas Rule 169.[20] A party who fails to comply with Texas Rule 47(c) may not conduct discovery (i.e., serve discovery requests or discovery subpoenas or conduct oral depositions) until the party's pleading is amended to comply.[21] The expedited-actions process is mandatory, and any suit that falls within the definition of an "expedited action" is subject to the process,[22] including the Level 1 discovery-control plan under Texas Rule 190.2.[23]

As Level 1 can be chosen by plaintiffs alone, a defendant cannot force an action into a Level 1 discovery-control plan. Nonetheless, a defendant who believes that a particular action belongs in Level 1 can seek an agreement or a court order, including a Level 3 discovery-control plan, adopting Level 1 discovery limits.[24]

---

16 Tex. R. Civ. P. 169(a) (emphasis added).

17 Tex. R. Civ. P. 169 cmt. to 2021 change (citing Tex. Estates Code §§ 53.107, 1053.105 as a non-exhaustive list of examples).

18 Tex. R. Civ. P. 47(c); *see also* Tex. Estates Code § 53.107 (providing that Texas Rules 47(c) and 169 are inapplicable to probate proceedings).

19 Tex. R. Civ. P. 47(c)(1)–(5).

20 Tex. R. Civ. P. 47 cmt. to 2013 change ("The further specificity in paragraphs (c)(2)–(5) [of Texas Rule 47] is to provide information regarding the nature of cases filed and does not affect a party's substantive rights.").

21 Tex. R. Civ. P. 47.

22 Tex. R. Civ. P. 169 cmt 2 to 2013 change.

23 Tex. R. Civ. P. 169(d)(1), 190.2(a)(1).

24 Tex. R. Civ. P. 190 cmt. 1 to 1999 change. See also Chapter 2, section 2-4:4 (discussing modifying and changing discovery levels).

Level 1 has the least discovery of the three levels.[25] It allows each party: (1) a total of 20 deposition hours "to examine and cross-examine all witnesses in oral depositions;"[26] (2) to "serve on any other party no more than 15 written interrogatories[,]" including "discrete subpart[s]," but "excluding interrogatories asking a party only to identify or authenticate specific documents;"[27] (3) to "serve on any other party no more than 15 written requests for production[,]" including "discrete subpart[s];"[28] and (4) to "serve on any other party no more than 15 written requests for admissions[,]" including "discrete subpart[s]."[29]

Before the 2021 amendments, Level 1 provided one discovery device that was unavailable in Level 2 and Level 3 actions—a request for disclosure of "all documents, electronic information, and tangible items that the disclosing party has in its possession, custody, or control and may use to support its claims or defenses."[30] That language was struck as part of the 2021 amendments because initial disclosures are now generally required under Texas Rule 194.2 and include, among other things, the provision of "a copy—or a description by category and location—of all documents, electronically stored information, and tangible things that the responding party has in its possession, custody, or control, and may use to support its claims or defenses, unless the use would be solely for impeachment."[31]

Discovery in a Level 1 action "must be conducted during the discovery period, which begins when the first initial disclosures are due and continues for 180 days."[32] Written-discovery requests in a Level 1 action must be served no later than 30 days (and in some cases 31 or 33 days) before the discovery period ends.[33]

---

[25] The limitations can be modified by the parties' agreement or court order. Tex. R. Civ. P. 191.1. Further, an amended pleading might take the action out of Level 1. Tex. R. Civ. P. 169(c), 190.2(c). See also Chapter 2, section 2-3:4 (discussing modifying and changing discovery-control plans).

[26] Tex. R. Civ. P. 190.2(b)(2).

[27] Tex. R. Civ. P. 190.2(b)(3).

[28] Tex. R. Civ. P. 190.2(b)(4).

[29] Tex. R. Civ. P. 190.2(b)(5). Oddly, the number of depositions on written questions is not limited in a Level 1 action. Tex. R. Civ. P. 190.2(b). Nonetheless, such depositions "cannot be used to circumvent the limits on interrogatories." Tex. R. Civ. P. 190 cmt. 5 to 1999 change.

[30] This language was in Former Texas Rule 190.2(b)(6).

[31] Tex. R. Civ. P. 194.2(b)(6).

[32] Tex. R. Civ. P. 190.2(b)(1).

[33] Tex. R. Civ. P. 196.1(a) (production requests), 196.7(a) (requests or motions for entry on land or other property), 197.1 (interrogatories), 198.1 (requests for admission), 205.3(a) (nonparty subpoena to produce documents).

A deposition notice to a party or a person subject to a party's control that contains a production request also must be served at least 30 days before the discovery period ends because Texas Rule 199.2(b)(5) provides that such requests are governed by Texas Rules 193 and 196, and the latter rule provides for 30 days to respond to a production request. Tex. R. Civ. P. 196.2(a).

If such a deposition notice or a written-discovery request is served by mail, it must be served at least 33 days before the discovery period ends. *See* Tex. R. Civ. P. 21a(c). If it is served by fax after 5:00 p.m. local time of the recipient, it must be served at least 31 days before the discovery period ends. *See* Tex. R. Civ. P. 21a(b)(2).

2-3:2 Level 2 Discovery-Control Plans

Level 2 is the "default" discovery-control plan, applying to actions not in Level 1 and not subject to a court-ordered Level 3 discovery-control plan.[34] An action automatically is in Level 2 if the plaintiff does not, or cannot, plead the action in compliance with Texas Rule 190.2(a) to invoke Level 1 because an action cannot be in Level 3 until the court so orders on any party's motion or its own initiative.[35]

Level 2, like Level 1, has limits on the amount of deposition time and the number of interrogatories. Level 2, however, does not limit the number of production requests or requests for admission.[36] Whereas Level 1 allows each party to serve up to 15 interrogatories (including "discrete subpart[s,]" but "excluding interrogatories asking a party only to identify or authenticate specific documents") on any other party,[37] Level

---

[34] Tex. R. Civ. P. 190.3(a) ("Unless a suit is governed by a discovery control plan under [Texas] Rules 190.2 or 190.4, discovery must be conducted in accordance with this subdivision."); *see Pentland v. Pentland*, No. 03-19-00049-CV, 2020 Tex. App. LEXIS 10259, at *5, 2020 WL 7703073 (Tex. App.—Austin Dec. 29, 2020, no pet.) (mem. op.) (determining that a party's discovery requests were untimely under Level 2, which applied by default to the action at hand); *Buholtz v. Field*, No. 03-17-00232-CV, 2018 Tex. App. LEXIS 854, at *12, 2018 WL 700058 (Tex. App.—Austin Jan. 31, 2018, pet. denied) (mem. op.) ("In his petition, Buholtz indicated his intention to conduct discovery under Level 2, which is the default discovery level when there is no order adopting a discovery control plan, as appears to be the case here."); *Espinoza v. Odness*, No. 04-02-00729-CV, 2003 Tex. App. LEXIS 2794, at *6, 2003 WL 1712558 (Tex. App.—San Antonio Apr. 2, 2003, no pet.) (mem. op.) ("These time periods are based on the level two discovery plan time periods; because the petition did not specify a discovery control plan, the level two rules apply by default.").

[35] Tex. R. Civ. P. 190 cmt. 1 to 1999 change ("If a plaintiff does not or cannot plead the case in compliance with [Texas] Rule 190.2(a) so as to invoke the application of Level 1, the case is automatically in Level 2. A case remains in Level 1 or Level 2, as determined by the pleadings, unless and until it is moved to Level 3. To be in Level 3, the court must order a specific plan for the case, either on a party's motion or on the court's own initiative."); *see Estate of Grogan*, 595 S.W.3d 807, 823 (Tex. App.—Texarkana 2020, no pet.) ("When, as here, a suit is not governed by a Level I or Level III discovery control plan, discovery must be conducted in accordance with a Level II discovery plan."); *Shafer v. Shafer*, No. 09-12-00468-CV, 2014 Tex. App. LEXIS 11898, at *28, 2014 WL 5490933 (Tex. App.—Beaumont Oct. 30, 2014, no pet.) (mem. op.) ("Because the trial court did not enter an order adopting a specific discovery control plan, the default deadlines and limitations of Level 2 controlled this case."); *Payne v. J. Baker Corp.*, No. 02-12-00181-CV, 2013 Tex. App. LEXIS 6106, at *16, 2013 WL 2091774 (Tex. App.—Fort Worth May 16, 2013, no pet.) (mem. op.) ("Because the Homeowners did not affirmatively plead for the amount of monetary relief set out in [Texas R]ule 190.2, and the trial court has not ordered a discovery control plan, Level 2 discovery applied.") (footnote omitted); *Mulcahy v. Wal-Mart Stores, Inc.*, No. 02-10-00074-CV, 2010 Tex. App. LEXIS 9955, at *6, 2010 WL 5118199 (Tex. App.—Fort Worth Dec. 16, 2010, no pet.) (mem. op.) ("Mulcahy stated in her pleadings that discovery would be conducted under a level 3 discovery control plan, but the record does not show any court order adopting a level 3 control plan or any other discovery schedule. Accordingly, the default discovery deadlines of a level 2 discovery control plan applied."); *In re Kings Ridge Homeowners Ass'n*, 303 S.W.3d 773, 781 (Tex. App.—Fort Worth 2009, orig. proceeding) ("When a trial court does not sign an order adopting a Level 3 discovery control plan, the default discovery limitations of Level 1 (which does not apply here) or Level 2 apply.").

[36] *Compare* Tex. R. Civ. P. 190.2(b), *with* Tex. R. Civ. P. 190.3(b).

[37] Tex. R. Civ. P. 190.2(b)(3).

2 allows each party to serve up to 25 interrogatories (including "discrete subpart[s,]" but "excluding interrogatories asking a party only to identify or authenticate specific documents") on any other party.[38]

In a Level 2 action, deposition time is limited to 50 hours per "side."[39] This includes both the examination and cross-examination of the opposing sides' parties, experts, and other persons under their control.[40] The 50-hour limit does not apply to depositions of nonparty fact witnesses who are not under a party's control.[41] Moreover, if one side designates more than two experts, the opposing side has an additional six hours of deposition time for each additional expert designated that can be used to depose the expert(s) or any other witness.[42]

The discovery period in all Level 2 actions "begins when the first initial disclosures are due[.]"[43] For Level 2 actions under the Family Code, the discovery period "continues until . . . 30 days before the date set for trial[.]"[44] For other Level 2 actions, the discovery period "continues until . . . the earlier of (i) 30 days before the date set for trial, or (ii) nine months after the first initial disclosures are due."[45] Written discovery requests in a Level 2 action must be served no later than 30 days (and in some cases 31 or 33 days) before the discovery period ends.[46]

---

[38] Tex. R. Civ. P. 190.3(b)(3); *see also Estate of Flarity*, No. 09-19-00089-CV, 2020 Tex. App. LEXIS 7536, at *18, 2020 WL 5552140 (Tex. App.—Beaumont Sept. 17, 2020, pet. denied) (mem. op.) ("Under [Texas] Rule 190.3 . . ., the probate court had the right to count '[e]ach discrete subpart of an interrogatory' as a separate question when it calculated whether Joe's interrogatories complied with Rule 190.3."). What constitutes a "discrete subpart" and an "interrogatory asking a party only to identify or authenticate documents" is discussed in Chapter 9, section 9-4.

[39] Tex. R. Civ. P. 190.3(b)(2). ("'Side' refers to all the litigants with generally common interests in the litigation."). The "side" concept is borrowed from Texas Rule 223, which governs the allocation of preemptory strikes. Tex. R. Civ. P. 190 cmt. 6 to 1999 change.

[40] Tex. R. Civ. P. 190.3(b)(2).

[41] Tex. R. Civ. P. 190.3(b)(2). As in Level 1, there is no limit on the number of depositions on written questions in a Level 2 action. Tex. R. Civ. P. 190.2(b), 190.3(b). Nonetheless, such depositions "cannot be used to circumvent the limits on interrogatories." Tex. R. Civ. P. 190 cmt. 5 to 1999 change.

[42] Tex. R. Civ. P. 190.3(b)(2).

[43] Tex. R. Civ. P. 190.3(b)(1).

[44] Tex. R. Civ. P. 190.3(b)(1)(A).

[45] Tex. R. Civ. P. 190.3(b)(1)(B).

[46] Tex. R. Civ. P. 196.1(a) (production requests), 196.7(a) (requests or motions for entry on land or other property), 197.1 (interrogatories), 198.1 (requests for admission), 205.3(a) (nonparty subpoena to produce documents).

A deposition notice to a party or a person subject to a party's control that contains a production request also must be served at least 30 days before the discovery period ends because Texas Rule 199.2(b)(5) provides that such requests are governed by Texas Rules 193 and 196, and the latter rule provides for 30 days to respond to a production request. Tex. R. Civ. P. 196.2(a).

If such a deposition notice or a written-discovery request is served by mail, it must be served at least 33 days before the discovery period ends. *See* Tex. R. Civ. P. 21a(c). If it is served by fax after 5:00 p.m. local time of the recipient, it must be served at least 31 days before the discovery period ends. *See* Tex. R. Civ. P. 21a(b)(2).

2-3:3 Level 3 Discovery-Control Plans

Comparable to federal-court practice, Level 3 provides for a discovery-control plan "tailored to the circumstances of the specific suit."[47] It is designed for high-dollar or complex actions,[48] although a party in any type of action (other than an expedited action) may move for a Level 3 discovery-control plan.[49] A trial court "must" issue a Level 3 discovery-control plan "as promptly as reasonably possible" on the request of any party.[50] The court also may do so on its own initiative.[51] If a party is added to a Level 3 action after the discovery deadlines have expired, "the better practice" is for "all parties upon [joinder of the new party] to . . . submit . . . a modified or new agreed scheduling order to establish a new discovery period and deadlines."[52]

Although a Level 3 discovery-control plan is to be "tailored to the circumstances of the specific suit[,]"[53] a court can use a form order, provided it includes all four of the required elements discussed below,[54] or the parties can submit an agreed order for the court's consideration, again, provided the order contains the four required elements discussed below.[55] As mentioned above, if the parties submit such an order, the court "should act on [it] as promptly as reasonably possible."[56]

A Level 3 discovery-control plan must include the following four matters: "(1) a date for trial or for a conference to determine a trial setting; (2) a discovery period during which either all discovery must be conducted or all discovery requests must be sent for the entire case or an appropriate phase of it; (3) appropriate limits on the amount of discovery; and (4) deadlines for joining additional parties, amending or supplementing pleadings, and designating expert witnesses."[57] As made clear by the second and third requirements, a Level 3 plan can limit the time for, or amount of, discovery. The plan, however, need not address such matters because, before its entry,

---

[47] Tex. R. Civ. P. 190.4(a); *see also* Nathan L. Hecht & Robert H. Pemberton, *A Guide to the 1999 Texas Discovery Rules Revisions* § C-3 (Nov. 11, 1998), https://www.adrr.com/law1/rules.htm (describing "Level 3 court managed discovery" and noting that it calls for "discovery similar to current federal court practice").

[48] *Ramirez v. Allstate Vehicle & Prop. Ins. Co.*, No. 7:20-CV-00211, 2020 U.S. Dist. LEXIS 178964, at *30)–31, 2020 WL 5806436 (S.D. Tex. Sept. 29, 2020) ("Level 3 discovery 'is designed for complex cases involving greater damages and discovery than could be easily accommodated by the lower-level discovery control plans' . . . ." (quoting *Noyola v. State Farm Lloyds*, No. 7:13-CV-146, 2013 U.S. Dist. LEXIS 93449, at * 11 n.32, 2013 WL 3353963 (S.D. Tex. July 3, 2013))); *List v. PlazAmericas Mall Tex., LLC*, No. CV H-18-4810, 2019 U.S. Dist. LEXIS 19602, at *6, 2019 WL 480130, at *3 (S.D. Tex. Feb. 7, 2019) ("Under Texas law, Level 3 discovery is used in complicated cases involving a larger amount in controversy and requiring relatively extensive discovery.").

[49] *See* Nathan L. Hecht & Robert H. Pemberton, *A Guide to the 1999 Texas Discovery Rules Revisions* § C-3 (Nov. 11, 1998), https://www.adrr.com/law1/rules.htm. See also Chapter 2, section 2-3:1 (discussing the expedited-actions process).

[50] Tex. R. Civ. P. 190.4(a).

[51] Tex. R. Civ. P. 190.4(a).

[52] *In re Kings Ridge Homeowners Ass'n,* 303 S.W.3d 773, 7832 (Tex. App.—Fort Worth 2009, orig. proceeding).

[53] Tex. R. Civ. P. 190.4(a).

[54] Tex. R. Civ. P. 190 cmt. 1 to 1999 change.

[55] Tex. R. Civ. P. 190.4(a).

[56] Tex. R. Civ. P. 190.4(a).

[57] Tex. R. Civ. P. 190.4(b)(1)–(4).

the action automatically is in Level 1 or 2, depending on the pleadings, and if the plan fails to modify any discovery limitation existing under the applicable level, that limitation will control.[58] As explained by the Fort Worth Court of Appeals:

> The rule addressing level 3 discovery-control plans states that "[t]he court ***must***, on a party's motion, . . . order that discovery be conducted in accordance with a discovery control plan tailored to the circumstances of the specific suit." While the rule states that the court "must" enter a level 3 scheduling order on a party's motion, it does not require that the order provide deadlines different from those under a level 2 case; even under a level 3 scheduling order, the level 2 deadlines continue to apply "unless specifically changed in the discovery control plan ordered by the court." That decision is left to the trial court's discretion: "The discovery control plan ordered by the court . . . ***may*** change any limitation on the time for . . . discovery set forth in these rules."[59]

Thus, for example, if the plaintiff initially pleaded the action into Level 1 and the court later enters a Level 3 discovery-control plan that does not address the number of interrogatories, production requests, or requests for admission, the 15-number limit of Texas Rules 190.2(b)(3)–(5) will control.[60] Similarly, if the action was a Level 2 one before the Level 3 discovery-control plan's entry, and the plan does not address the number of interrogatories or deposition hours, the 25-interrogatory limit per party and the 50-hour-deposition-time limit per side of Texas Rules 190.3(b)(2)–(3) will control.

Importantly, a Level 3 discovery-control plan can be used both to limit or expand the amount of, and time for, discovery. Thus, a party who believes that Level 2 allows more discovery than the action needs can move for a Level 3 plan limiting the amount of discovery, and a Level 3 plan may provide for ***any*** amount of discovery, even Level 1's discovery limitations.[61]

As discussed in Chapter 4, section 4-3:4, for cases filed on or after September 1, 2015, Section 41.0115 of the Texas Civil Practice and Remedies Code prohibits

---

58 Tex. R. Civ. P. 190.4(b); ***see Estate of Grogan***, 595 S.W.3d 807, 824 (Tex. App.—Texarkana 2020, no pet.) (Texas "Rule 190.4 does not automatically set deadlines different from Level II deadlines, because they remain under Level II[] 'unless specifically changed in the discovery control plan ordered by the court.'" (quoting ***Border States Elec. Supply of Tex., Inc. v. Coast to Coast Elec., LLC***, No. 13-13-00118-CV, 2014 Tex. App. LEXIS 5681, at *31, 2014 WL 3953961 (Tex. App.—Corpus Christi May 29, 2014, pet. denied) (mem. op.), and ***Allen v. United of Omaha Life Ins. Co.***, 236 S.W.3d 315, 327 (Tex. App.—Fort Worth 2007, pet. denied))).

59 ***Allen v. United of Omaha Life Ins. Co.***, 236 S.W.3d 315, 327 (Tex. App.—Fort Worth 2007, pet. denied) (quoting Tex. R. Civ. P. 190.4(a)–(b)); ***accord Brescia v. Slack & Davis, L.L.P.***, No. 03-08-00042-CV, 2010 Tex. App. LEXIS 9204, at *9–10, 2010 WL 4670322 (Tex. App.—Austin Nov. 19, 2010, pet. denied) (mem. op.).

60 Tex. R. Civ. P. 190.4(b) ("The discovery limitations of [Texas] Rule 190.2, if applicable, or otherwise of [Texas] Rule 190.3 apply unless specifically changed in the discovery control plan ordered by the court."); ***Brescia v. Slack & Davis, L.L.P.***, No. 03-08-00042-CV, 2010 Tex. App. LEXIS 9204, at *10, 2010 WL 4670322 (Tex. App.—Austin Nov. 19, 2010, pet. denied) (mem. op.) ("[E]ven under a Level 3 scheduling order, Level 2 deadlines continue to apply 'unless specifically changed in the discovery control plan ordered by the court.'" (quoting Tex. R. Civ. P. 190.4(b))).

61 Tex. R. Civ. P. 190 cmt. 1 to 1999 change.

net-worth discovery in exemplary-damages cases absent a court order, after a hearing, authorizing such discovery:

(a) On the motion of a party and after notice and a hearing, a trial court may authorize discovery of evidence of a defendant's net worth if the court finds in a written order that the claimant has demonstrated a substantial likelihood of success on the merits of a claim for exemplary damages. Evidence submitted by a party to the court in support of or in opposition to a motion made under this subsection may be in the form of an affidavit or a response to discovery.

. . . .

(d) If a party requests net worth discovery under this section, the court shall presume that the requesting party has had adequate time for the discovery of facts relating to exemplary damages for purposes of allowing the party from whom net worth discovery is sought to move for summary judgment on the requesting party's claim for exemplary damages under Rule 166a(i), Texas Rules of Civil Procedure.[62]

Accordingly, trial courts and parties in actions in which exemplary damages are sought should consider whether the action should be a Level 3 one for discovery purposes and whether the action's discovery-control plan should have deadlines for filing a motion for net-worth discovery and the hearing on it and the relationship of such deadlines to any deadlines for summary judgment motions and hearings.

Written-discovery requests in a Level 3 action must be served no later than 30 days (and in some cases 31 or 33 days) before the discovery period ends.[63]

2-3:4 Choosing and Moving the Discovery Level and Modifying the Discovery-Control Plan

The first numbered paragraph of an original petition *must* state whether discovery is intended to be conducted under Level 1, 2, or 3.[64] This statement, however, is merely a

---

[62] Tex. Civ. Prac. & Rem. Code § 41.0115(a), (d).

[63] Tex. R. Civ. P. 196.1(a) (production requests), 196.7(a) (request or motion for entry on land or other property), 197.1 (interrogatories), 198.1 (requests for admission), 205.3(a) (nonparty subpoena to produce documents).

A deposition notice to a party or a person subject to a party's control that contains a production request also must be served at least 30 days before the discovery period ends because Texas Rule 199.2(b)(5) provides that such requests are governed by Texas Rules 193 and 196, and the latter rule provides for 30 days to respond to a production request. Tex. R. Civ. P. 196.2(a).

If such a deposition notice or a written-discovery request is served by mail, it must be served at least 33 days before the discovery period ends. *See* Tex. R. Civ. P. 21a(c). If it is served by fax after 5:00 p.m. local time of the recipient, it must be served at least 31 days before the discovery period ends. *See* Tex. R. Civ. P. 21a(b)(2).

[64] Tex. R. Civ. P. 190.1; *accord Brescia v. Slack & Davis, L.L.P.*, No. 03-08-00042-CV, 2010 Tex. App. LEXIS 9204, at *8, 2010 WL 4670322 (Tex. App.—Austin Nov. 19, 2010, pet. denied) (mem. op.) ("[P]laintiff must allege in the original petition whether discovery is intended to be conducted under Level 1, 2, or 3.").

nonbinding notice for the benefit of the court and the other parties.[65] It neither determines nor waives the applicable discovery level. Thus, a plaintiff's failure to choose Level 1 in its pleadings does not make the action a Level 2 one because the discovery level is determined by the pleadings' substantive allegations regarding the action's nature and the relief sought.[66] Thus, for example, if the original petition states that the discovery is intended to be conducted under Level 2, but seeks only monetary relief of $250,000 or less—excluding interest, statutory or punitive damages and penalties, and attorney fees and costs—the action is governed by Level 1.[67] However, if the plaintiff does not, or cannot, so plead the action (and thereby invoke Level 1's application), the action automatically is in Level 2.[68] In addition, a statement in an original petition's first paragraph that discovery is intended to be governed by Level 3 does not make Level 3 applicable because an action can be in Level 3 only by court order.[69]

A court must remove an action from the expedited-actions process, and, therefore, from Level 1, in two circumstances: (1) "on motion and a showing of good cause by any party;" or (2) "if any claimant, other than a counter-claimant, files a pleading or an amended or supplemental pleading that seeks" nonmonetary relief or monetary relief of more than $250,000.[70] A pleading, amended pleading, or supplemental pleading removing an action from the expedited-actions process cannot be filed without leave of court, unless it is filed before the earlier of 30 days after the discovery period is closed or 30 days before the date set for trial.[71] "Leave to amend may be granted only if good cause for filing the pleading outweighs any prejudice to an opposing party."[72] If an action is removed from the expedited-actions process, the court must reopen discovery.[73] Discovery must then be completed under Level 2 or Level 3, whichever is applicable.[74] Any person previously deposed may be deposed again.[75] On any party's motion, the court should continue the trial date if necessary to permit discovery's completion.[76]

---

65 Tex. R. Civ. P. 190 cmt. 1 to 1999 change ("The initial pleading required by [Texas] Rule 190.1 is merely to notify the court and other parties of the plaintiff's intention; it does not determine the applicable discovery level or bind the court or other parties."); *accord Brescia v. Slack & Davis, L.L.P.*, No. 03-08-00042-CV, 2010 Tex. App. LEXIS 9204, at *8, 2010 WL 4670322 (Tex. App.—Austin Nov. 19, 2010, pet. denied) (mem. op.).

66 See Chapter 2, section 2-3:1 (discussing Level 1 discovery-control plans).

67 Tex. R. Civ. P. 190 cmt. 1 to 1999 change ("[A] plaintiff's failure to state in the initial pleading that the case should be in Level 1, as provided in [Texas] Rule 190.1, does not alone make the case subject to Level 2 because the discovery level is determined by [Texas] Rule 190.2.").

68 See Chapter 2, section 2-3:2 (discussing Level 2 discovery-control plans).

69 Tex. R. Civ. P. 190 cmt. 1 to 1999 change ("[A] plaintiff's statement in the initial paragraph of the petition that the case is to be governed by Level 3 does not make Level 3 applicable, as a case can be in Level 3 only by court order."). See Chapter 2, section 2-3:2 (discussing the default application of Level 2 discovery-control plans and the court-order requirement for Level 3 discovery-control plans).

70 Tex. R. Civ. P. 169(c)(1)(A)–(B).

71 Tex. R. Civ. P. 169(c)(2).

72 Tex. R. Civ. P. 169(c)(2).

73 Tex. R. Civ. P. 169(c)(3) (citing Texas Rule 190.2(c)).

74 Tex. R. Civ. P. 190.2(c).

75 Tex. R. Civ. P. 190.2(c).

76 Tex. R. Civ. P. 190.2(c).

An action moves to Level 3 from Level 1 or Level 2 only if the trial court enters a Level 3 discovery-control plan.[77] There are three ways to obtain such a plan: (1) any party can move for one without regard to whether the action was previously subject to a Level 1 or Level 2 plan; (2) the parties can submit an agreed order for a Level 3 plan; or (3) the court can institute a Level 3 plan on its own initiative.[78] Although the court is not required to approve the particular Level 3 plan submitted by a party, the court must rule on the motion or agreed order as promptly as reasonably possible.[79]

A court can "modify a discovery-control plan at any time and must do so when the interest of justice requires."[80] "Unless a suit is governed by the expedited actions process in [Texas] Rule 169, the court must allow additional discovery:"

(a) related to new, amended or supplemental pleadings, or new information disclosed in a discovery response or in an amended or supplemental response, if:

(1) the pleadings or responses were made after the deadline for completion of discovery or so nearly before that deadline that an adverse party does not have an adequate opportunity to conduct discovery related to the new matters, and

(2) the adverse party would be unfairly prejudiced without such additional discovery; [or]

(b) regarding matters that have changed materially after the discovery cutoff if trial is set or postponed so that the trial date is more than three months after the discovery period ends.[81]

---

77 Tex. R. Civ. P. 190 cmt. 1 to 1999 change. See Chapter 2, section 2-3:2 (discussing the default application of Level 2 discovery-control plans and the court-order requirement for Level 3 discovery-control plans); Chapter 2, section 2-3:3 (discussing Level 3 discovery-control plans).

78 Tex. R. Civ. P. 190.4(a).

79 Tex. R. Civ. P. 190 cmt. 1 to 1999 change.

80 Tex. R. Civ. P. 190.5.

81 Tex. R. Civ. P. 190.5.

CHAPTER 3

Modifying Discovery Procedures; Conference Requirements; Signing Written-Discovery Requests; Responses and Objections; and Filing Requirements—Texas Rule 191

3-1 Text of Rule 191

RULE 191. MODIFYING DISCOVERY PROCEDURES AND LIMITATIONS; CONFERENCE REQUIREMENT; SIGNING DISCLOSURES, DISCOVERY REQUESTS, RESPONSES, AND OBJECTIONS; FILING REQUIREMENTS

191.1. Modification of Procedures

Except where specifically prohibited, the procedures and limitations set forth in the rules pertaining to discovery may be modified in any suit by the agreement of the parties or by court order for good cause. An agreement of the parties is enforceable if it complies with Rule 11 or, as it affects an oral deposition, if it is made a part of the record of the deposition.

191.2. Conference

Parties and their attorneys are expected to cooperate in discovery and to make any agreements reasonably necessary for the efficient disposition of the case. All discovery motions or requests for hearings relating to discovery must contain a certificate by the party filing the motion or request that a reasonable effort has been made to resolve the dispute without the necessity of court intervention and the effort failed.

191.3. Signing of Disclosures, Discovery Requests, Notices, Responses, and Objections

(a) **Signature required.** Every disclosure, discovery request, notice, response, and objection must be signed:

(1) by an attorney, if the party is represented by an attorney, and must show the attorney's State Bar of Texas identification number, address, telephone number, and fax number, if any; or

(2) by the party, if the party is not represented by an attorney, and must show the party's address, telephone number, and fax number, if any.

(b) **Effect of signature on disclosure.** The signature of an attorney or party on a disclosure constitutes a certification that to the best of the signer's knowledge, information, and belief, formed after a reasonable inquiry, the disclosure is complete and correct as of the time it is made.

(c) **Effect of signature on discovery request, notice, response, or objection.** The signature of an attorney or party on a discovery request, notice, response, or objection constitutes a certification that to the best of the signer's knowledge, information, and belief, formed after a reasonable inquiry, the request, notice, response, or objection:

(1) is consistent with the rules of civil procedure and these discovery rules and warranted by existing law or a good faith argument for the extension, modification, or reversal of existing law;

(2) has a good faith factual basis;

(3) is not interposed for any improper purpose, such as to harass or to cause unnecessary delay or needless increase in the cost of litigation; and

(4) is not unreasonable or unduly burdensome or expensive, given the needs of the case, the discovery already had in the case, the amount in controversy, and the importance of the issues at stake in the litigation.

(d) **Effect of failure to sign.** If a request, notice, response, or objection is not signed, it must be stricken unless it is signed promptly after the omission is called to the attention of the party making the request, notice, response, or objection. A party is not required to take any action with respect to a request or notice that is not signed.

(e) **Sanctions.** If the certification is false without substantial justification, the court may, upon motion or its own initiative, impose on the person who made the certification, or the party on whose behalf the request, notice, response, or objection was made, or both, an appropriate sanction as for a frivolous pleading or motion under Chapter 10 of the Civil Practice and Remedies Code.

191.4. Filing of Discovery Materials

(a) **Discovery materials not to be filed.** The following discovery materials must not be filed:

(1) discovery requests, deposition notices, and subpoenas required to be served only on parties;

(2) responses and objections to discovery requests and deposition notices, regardless on whom the requests or notices were served;

(3) documents and tangible things produced in discovery; and

(4) statements prepared in compliance with Rule 193.3(b) or (d).

(b) **Discovery materials to be filed.** The following discovery materials must be filed:

(1) discovery requests, deposition notices, and subpoenas required to be served on nonparties;

(2) motions and responses to motions pertaining to discovery matters; and

(3) agreements concerning discovery matters, to the extent necessary to comply with Rule 11.

(c) **Exceptions.** Notwithstanding paragraph (a)

(1) the court may order discovery materials to be filed;

(2) a person may file discovery materials in support of or in opposition to a motion or for other use in a court proceeding; and

(3) a person may file discovery materials necessary for a proceeding in an appellate court.

(d) **Retention requirement for persons.** Any person required to serve discovery materials not required to be filed must retain the original or exact copy of the materials during the pendency of the case and any related appellate proceedings begun within six months after judgment is signed, unless otherwise provided by the trial court.

(e) **Retention requirement for courts.** The clerk of the court shall retain and dispose of deposition transcripts and depositions upon written questions as directed by the Supreme Court.

191.5. Service of Discovery Materials

Every disclosure, discovery request, notice, response, and objection required to be served on a party or person must be served on all parties of record.

Comments to Texas Rule 191

Comments to 1999 change:

1. Rule 191.1 preserves the ability of parties by agreement and trial courts by order to adapt discovery to different circumstances. That ability is broad but not unbounded. Parties cannot merely by agreement modify a court order without the court's concurrence. Trial courts cannot simply "opt out" of these rules by form orders or approve or order a discovery control plan that does not contain the matters specified in Rule 190.4, but trial courts may use standard or form orders for providing discovery plans, scheduling, and other pretrial matters. In individual instances, courts may order, or parties may agree, to use discovery methods other than those prescribed in these rules if appropriate. Because the general rule is stated here, it is not repeated in each context in which it applies. Thus, for example, parties can agree to enlarge or shorten the time permitted for a deposition and to change the way a deposition is conducted, notwithstanding Rule 199.5, although parties could not agree to be abusive toward a witness.

2. Rule 191.2 expressly states the obligation of parties and their attorneys to cooperate in conducting discovery.

3. The requirement that discovery requests, notices, responses, and objections be signed also applies to documents used to satisfy the purposes of such instruments. An example is a statement that privileged material or information has been withheld, which may be separate from a response to the discovery request but is nevertheless part of the response.

3-2 2021 Amendments to the Texas Rules of Civil Procedure

The 2021 amendments to the Texas Rules of Civil Procedure did not modify Texas Rule 191 in any respect.

3-3 Modification: In General

Texas Rule 191.1 allows parties and courts to modify "the procedures and limitations set forth in the rules pertaining to discovery[,]" except "where specifically prohibited" from doing so.[1] For example, "[i]n individual instances, courts may order, or parties may agree, to use discovery methods other than those prescribed in [the Texas discovery rules] if appropriate."[2] Also by way of example, "parties can agree to enlarge or shorten the time permitted for a deposition and to change the manner in which a deposition is conducted, notwithstanding [Texas] Rule 199.5, although parties could not agree to be abusive toward a witness."[3]

The ability of parties and courts "to adapt discovery to different circumstances . . . is broad but not unbounded" under Texas Rule 191.1.[4] Distinct modification standards and limits apply to parties versus courts.

3-3:1 Modification by Parties

Under Texas Rule 191.1, "the procedures and limitations set forth in the rules pertaining to discovery may be modified in any suit by [an] agreement of the parties . . . [that] complies with [Texas] Rule 11 or, as it affects an oral deposition, . . . is made a part of the record at the deposition."[5] To comply with Texas Rule 11, the parties' agreement must "be in writing, signed[,] and filed with the papers as part of the record" or "be made in open court and entered of record."[6] For written agreements, "[Texas]

---

1 Tex. R. Civ. P. 191.1. See also Chapter 2, section 2-3:4 (discussing modifications to discovery-control plans).

2 Tex. R. Civ. P. 191 cmt. 1 to 1999 change.

3 Tex. R. Civ. P. 191 cmt. 1 to 1999 change.

4 Tex. R. Civ. P. 191 cmt. 1 to 1999 change.

5 Tex. R. Civ. P. 191.1; *see In re Does*, 337 S.W.3d 862, 865 (Tex. 2011) (per curiam) ("It is true that '[e]xcept where specifically prohibited, the procedures and limitations set forth in the rules pertaining to discovery may be modified in any suit by agreement of the parties[.]'" (quoting Tex. R. Civ. P. 191.1)); *In re BP Prods. N. Am., Inc.*, 244 S.W.3d 840, 845–46 (Tex. 2008) (Texas "Rule 191.1 provides that 'except where specifically prohibited' the parties may modify the 'rules pertaining to discovery' by agreement." (quoting Tex. R. Civ. P. 191.1)); *Glob. Supply Chain Sols., LLC v. Riverwood Sols., Inc.*, No. 05-18-00188-CV, 2019 Tex. App. LEXIS 7261, at *36, 2019 WL 3852661 (Tex. App.—Dallas Aug. 16, 2019, no pet.) (mem. op.) ("Global Supply argues that [Texas Rule] 195 governs expert designations and reports. But here, as the trial court explained at the hearing on the motion to strike, the parties agreed to a requirement that differed from the rules, as the rules expressly permit parties to do." (citations omitted) (citing Tex. R. Civ. P. 191.1)).

6 Tex. R. Civ. P. 11. *But see In re Estate of Powell*, No. 05-19-00689-CV, 2020 Tex. App. LEXIS 6134, at *9, 2020 WL 4462666 (Tex. App.—Dallas Aug. 4, 2020, no pet.) (mem. op.) ("The purpose of the [Texas Rule 11] is to relieve the courts of the necessity of resolving disputes over the terms of oral agreements relating to pending suits. As explained in [*Anderson v. Cocheu*, 176 S.W.3d 685, 688 (Tex. App.—Dallas 2005, pet. denied)], however, in enforcing [Texas R]ule 11 'the Texas Supreme Court has been mindful of the fact that the rule may be said to abridge the substantive right of persons to enter into oral contracts.'

Rule 11, like the statute of frauds, requires a 'written memorandum which is complete within itself in every material detail, and which contains all of the essential elements of the agreement,' so that the agreement 'can be ascertained from the writings without resorting to oral testimony.'"[7] Moreover, an agreement, to be enforceable under Texas Rule 191.1, must be made by all parties that are impacted by it[8] and either "made in

Consequently, courts have balanced the purpose of the rule with the ability to make oral agreements, resulting in recognition of certain equitable exceptions to [Texas R]ule 11's writing requirement.") (citations omitted); *Wal-Mart Stores Tex. LLC v. Shirey*, No. 14-18-00545-CV, 2020 Tex. App. LEXIS 945, at *7, 2020 WL 548323 (Tex. App.—Houston [14th Dist.] Feb. 4, 2020, pet. denied) (mem. op.) ("'[S]lavish adherence to the literal language of [Texas] Rule [11] is not required in all cases.'" (quoting *Kennedy v. Hyde*, 682 S.W.2d 525, 529 (Tex. 1984))).

[7] *In re Burlington Coat Factory Warehouse of McAllen, Inc.*, 167 S.W.3d 827, 829 n.1 (Tex. 2005) (quoting *Padilla v. LaFrance*, 907 S.W.2d 454, 460 (Tex. 1995)); *accord Shamrock Psychiatric Clinic, P.A. v. Tex. Dep't of Health & Human Servs.*, 540 S.W.3d 553, 561 (Tex. 2018); *see also Padilla v. LaFrance*, 907 S.W.2d 454, 460 (Tex. 1995) ("The written memorandum, however, need not be contained in one document."), *cited with approval in Shamrock Psychiatric Clinic, P.A. v. Tex. Dep't of Health & Human Servs.*, 540 S.W.3d 553, 561 (Tex. 2018); *Tomorrow Telecom, Inc. v. Johnson*, No. 07-19-00427-CV, 2021 Tex. App, LEXIS 1890, at *8, 2021 WL 937121 (Tex. App.—Amarillo Mar. 11, 2021, no pet.) (mem. op.) ("A valid [Texas] Rule 11 agreement must contain all essential terms of the agreement and must be 'complete within itself in every material detail.'" (quoting *Padilla v. La France*, 907 S.W.2d 454, 460 (Tex. 1995))); *Nguyen v. Nguyen*, No. 14-19-00913-CV, 2021 WL 786628 (Tex. App.—Houston [14th Dist.] Mar. 2, 2021, no pet.) (mem. op.) ("Essential terms [of a Texas Rule 11 agreement] are those terms that the parties 'would reasonably regard as vitally important elements of their bargain. . . .'" (quoting *Potcinske v. McDonald Prop. Invs., Ltd.*, 245 S.W.3d 526, 531 (Tex. App.—Houston [1st Dist.] 2007, no pet.))); *Clarent Energy Servs. Inc. v. Leasing Ventures, LLC*, No. 01-18-00821-CV, 2020 Tex. App. LEXIS 2159, at *19, 2020 WL 1173706 (Tex. App.—Houston [1st Dist.] Mar. 12, 2020, no pet.) (mem. op.) ("To be effective, a [Texas] Rule 11 agreement must consist of a written memorandum which is complete within itself in every material detail and which contains all the essential elements of the agreement."); *In re Schlumberger Tech. Corp.*, No. 11-19-00204-CV, 2019 WL 5617632 (Tex. App.—Eastland Oct. 24, 2019, orig. proceeding) (mem. op.) ("A series of letters or e-mails can establish a [Texas] Rule 11 agreement between the parties."); *Tolbert v. Kartye*, No. 12-18-00169-CV, 2019 Tex. App. LEXIS 2167, at *4–5, 2019 WL 1272687 (Tex. App.—Tyler Mar. 20, 2019, pet. denied) (mem. op.) (same); *Bandera Cnty. v. Hollingsworth*, 419 S.W.3d 639, 645 (Tex. App.—San Antonio 2013, no pet.) ("The writing need not be contained in one single document to satisfy the 'in writing' requirement; however, the writings must be complete in every material detail and must contain all of the essential elements of the agreement, so that the contract can be ascertained from the writings without resorting to oral testimony."); *Green v. Midland Mortg. Co.*, 342 S.W.3d 686, 691 (Tex. App.—Houston [14th Dist.] 2011, no pet.) (concluding that a series of emails and a Texas Rule 11 letter constituted a valid Rule 11 agreement).

[8] *See In re Does*, 337 S.W.3d 862, 865 (Tex. 2011) (per curiam) ("It is true that '[e]xcept where specifically prohibited, the procedures and limitations set forth in the rules pertaining to discovery may be modified in any suit by agreement of the parties. . . .' But PRK and Google were not the only parties to the proceeding. . . . PRK and Google could not modify the procedures prescribed by [Texas] Rule 202 by an agreement that did not include relators." (citation omitted) (quoting Tex. R. Civ. P. 191.1))); *see also Araiza v. Bumb*, No. 14-18-00633-CV, 2019 Tex. App. LEXIS 6886, at* 5, 2019 WL 3725554 (Tex. App.—Houston [14th Dist.] Aug. 8, 2019, no pet.) (mem. op.) ("[W]hile Caudillo's attorney could have signed on her behalf, there is no evidence that Caudillo's attorney signed or agreed in writing to the [R]ule 11

open court and entered of record"[9] or filed in the court record before "it is sought to be enforced."[10]

In explaining the bounds on parties' ability to modify discovery procedures and limitations, the Texas Supreme Court has made clear that "[p]arties cannot merely by agreement modify a court order without the court's concurrence."[11] Also, as Texas Rule 191.1 provides, parties cannot agree to a modification that is specifically prohibited by another rule.[12] Similarly, as Texas case law provides, parties cannot agree to a modification that is prohibited by statute.[13]

"Wherever possible, a trial court should give effect to agreements between the parties" that are enforceable under Texas Rule 191.1.[14] In explaining why this is so, the Texas Supreme Court reasoned: "Discovery agreements serve an important role in efficient trial management, permitting the parties to settle their disputes without

---

settlement agreement. On this record, Araiza failed to establish that a valid and binding [Texas R]ule 11 settlement agreement exists between Caudillo and appellees. Accordingly, the trial court did not abuse its discretion in refusing to enforce the alleged agreement. . . .") (citations omitted).

[9] Tex. R. Civ. P. 11; *see also* Tex. R. Civ. P. 191.1 ("An agreement of the parties is enforceable if it complies with [Texas] Rule 11. . . ."); *Castorena v. Castorena*, No. 13-18-00492-CV, 2020 Tex. App. LEXIS 8554, at *5, 2020 WL 6343335 (Tex. App.—Corpus Christi Oct. 29, 2020, no pet.) (mem. op.) ("'To be 'entered of record' includes the dictation of the agreement into the trial court record.'" (quoting *Kanan v. Plantation Homeowner's Ass'n Inc.*, 407 S.W.3d 320, 328 (Tex. App.—Corpus Christi 2013, no pet.))); *Bartee v. Bartee*, No. 11-18-00017-CV, 2020 Tex. App. LEXIS 914, at *23, 2020 WL 524909 (Tex. App.—Eastland Jan. 31, 2020, no pet.) (mem. op.) ("Under [Texas] Rule 11, an agreed property division constitutes an enforceable consent judgment—even if neither party signed the agreement—if the agreement is 'made in open court and entered of record.' Therefore, when the parties' agreement is evidenced by a party's attorney reciting the terms of the agreement to the court and the party confirming those terms, the agreement need not be in writing or signed." (citations omitted) (quoting Hahne v. Hahne, 663 S.W.2d 77, 79 (Tex. App.—Houston [14th Dist.] 1983, no writ))).

[10] *Padilla v. La France*, 907 S.W.2d 454, 461 (Tex. 1995) (Texas Rule 11's "purpose is satisfied so long as the agreement is filed before it is sought to be enforced."); *accord Wal-Mart Stores Tex. LLC v. Shirey*, No. 14-18-00545-CV, 2020 Tex. App. LEXIS 945, at *7–8, 2020 WL 548323 (Tex. App.—Houston [14th Dist.] Feb. 4, 2020, pet. denied) (mem. op.); *In re Caballero*, 441 S.W.3d 562, 572 (Tex. App.—El Paso 2014, orig. proceeding).

[11] Tex. R. Civ. P. 191 cmt. 1 to 1999 change.

[12] Tex. R. Civ. P. 191.

[13] *See Walker v. Pegasus Eventing, LLC*, No. 05-19-00252-CV, 2020 Tex. App. LEXIS 4492, at *22, 2020 WL 3248476 (Tex. App.—Dallas June 16, 2020, pet. denied) (mem. op.) ("Under the terms of section 27.004, parties may not, by agreement, extend the hearing date beyond ninety days after service of the motion, though the court may 'allow' discovery and conduct the hearing up to 120 days after service. To permit a [Texas] Rule 11 agreement to serve as an 'allow[ance]' of discovery by the court would circumvent the statutory restriction that parties may not agree to an extension beyond ninety days." (quoting Tex. Civ. Prac. & Rem. § 27.004(a))).

[14] *In re BP Prods. N. Am., Inc.*, 244 S.W.3d 840, 846 (Tex. 2008); *accord In re Guniganti*, No. 12-10-00199-CV, 2010 Tex. App. LEXIS 6624, at *6, 2010 WL 3232247 (Tex. App.—Tyler Aug. 17, 2010, orig. proceeding) (mem. op.); *Coon v. Umphrey*, No. 09-09-00264-CV, 2020 Tex. App. LEXIS 4492, at *22, 2009 WL 3030354 (Tex. App.—Beaumont Sept. 24, 2009, pet. dism'd) (mem. op.); *In re Jerry F.*, 294 S.W.3d 297, 299 (Tex. App.—Fort Worth 2009, orig. proceeding).

resort to judicial supervision. The [Texas] Rules of Civil Procedure encourage parties to reach agreements. When the parties conclude an agreement, the court should not lightly ignore their bargain."[15] Furthermore, "[a] court should be particularly reluctant to set aside a [Texas] Rule 191.1 agreement after one party has acted in reliance on the agreed procedure and performed its obligations under the agreement. An easy disregard for partially performed agreements would discourage parties from committing to discovery agreements for fear that the other party would avail itself of the benefit of the bargain and then attempt to avoid its own obligations."[16]

3-3:2 Modification by Court

Texas Rule 191.1 provides, in relevant part, that "[e]xcept where specifically prohibited, the procedures and limitations set forth in the rules pertaining to discovery may be modified in any suit by the agreement of the parties or by court order for good cause." Accordingly, "a trial court may modify discovery procedures and limitations for 'good cause'" under Texas Rule 191.1.[17] The good-cause standard gives trial courts a fair amount of discretion. For example, good cause may exist to reset a party's expert-designation deadline when another party discloses the nature and amount of its damages after the first party's expert-designation deadline has passed and within days of the end of the discovery period in a case.[18]

Another example would be a motion asking a trial court to compel a party to sign an authorization for the release of relevant documents in the possession of a nonparty, such as employment records, federal or state tax returns, emails, or a state or federal agency's records regarding the party, where it would be extremely time-consuming or impossible to obtain the document from the nonparty by subpoena. Typically, the authorization will be sought by means of a production request under Texas Rule 196.1. The Texas Supreme Court has not directly decided whether such a production request is proper under that Rule,[19] and the Texas courts of appeals have split on the question

---

[15] *In re BP Prods. N. Am., Inc.*, 244 S.W.3d 840, 846 (Tex. 2008) (citation omitted), ***quoted in*** *Walker v. Pegasus Eventing, LLC*, No. 05-19-00252-CV, 2020 Tex. App. LEXIS 4492, at *22, 2020 WL 3248476 (Tex. App.—Dallas June 16, 2020, pet. denied) (mem. op.). See also Chapter 3, section 3-4 (discussing conference and cooperation requirements).

[16] *In re BP Prods. N. Am., Inc.*, 244 S.W.3d 840, 846 (Tex. 2008) (citation omitted).

[17] *In re BP Prods. N. Am., Inc.*, 244 S.W.3d 840, 846 (Tex. 2009) (quoting Tex. R. Civ. P. 191.1); *see also El-Khalidi v. Arabian Am. Dev. Co.*, No. 09-16-00400-CV, 2017 Tex. App. LEXIS 10564, at *23, 2017 WL 5179967 (Tex. App.—Beaumont Nov. 9, 2017, pet. denied) (mem. op.) ("Rule 191.1 of the Texas Rules of Civil Procedure allows trial courts to control the order of discovery."); *In re Nat'l Lloyds Ins. Co.*, NO. 13-15-00390-CV, 2015 Tex. App. LEXIS 11299, at *13, 2015 WL 6759153 (Tex. App.—Corpus Christi Nov. 3, 2015, orig. proceeding) (mem. op.) ("To the extent that relator argues that the trial court abused its discretion in ordering production within two days, we note that the trial court has discretion to schedule discovery and may shorten or lengthen the time for making a response for good cause."). See also Chapter 2, section 2-4:3 (discussing case-specific discovery-control plans), section 2-4:4 (discussing modifications to discovery-control plans).

[18] *In re Bird*, No. 12-13-00031-CV, 2013 Tex. App. LEXIS 6716, at *5–6, 2013 WL 2407228 (Tex. App.—Tyler May 31, 2013, orig. proceeding) (mem. op.).

[19] The Texas Supreme Court twice has suggested that Texas Rule 196's predecessor, former Texas Rule 167, permitted a party to request an authorization. *See Groves v. Gabriel*, 874 S.W.2d 660, 661 (Tex. 1994) (holding, under the more restrictive pre-1999 Texas discovery rules, that the trial court abused its discretion in ordering the plaintiff to provide a medical-

with some holding that production requests for authorizations are proper under the Rule because they merely require the responding party to produce documents under its "control" and others holding that such requests are improper because they require the creation of a document (i.e., the authorization).[20]

---

records authorization because the authorization was overly broad and unaccompanied by a protective order, not because the trial court lacked authority to require the authorization, and stating: "[A] trial court's order compelling release of medical records should be restrictively drawn so as to maintain the privilege with respect to records or communications not relevant to the underlying suit."); *Mutter v. Wood,* 744 S.W.2d 600, 601 (Tex. 1988) (orig. proceeding) (same). In fact, in the latter case, the Texas Supreme Court cited a Dallas Court of Appeals' decision expressly holding that former Texas Rule 167 permits production requests for authorizations, *Martinez v. Rutledge,* 592 S.W.2d 398, 400 (Tex. App.—Dallas 1979, writ ref'd n.r.e.), ***cited with approval*** *Mutter v. Wood,* 744 S.W.2d 600, 601 (Tex. 1988) (orig. proceeding) (same).

20 ***Compare, e.g.,*** *Martinez v. Rutledge,* 592 S.W.2d 398, 400 (Tex. App.—Dallas 1979, writ ref'd n.r.e.) ("Plaintiff first complains that the court's order is unauthorized because it requires the creation of a document not in existence whereas [former Texas] Rule 167 requires a party to produce only designated documents or tangible things for inspection. . . . [W]e cannot agree that the rule compels this limited construction. The tangible thing here sought is the record which is in existence. The authorization is merely the means of acquiring that which is sought. We do not agree that the order required creation of a document and therefore overrule plaintiff's first point."), ***with, e.g.,*** *In re Guzman,* 19 S.W.3d 522 (Tex. App.—Corpus Christi May 4, 2000, orig. proceeding) ("Before the trial court, respondent contended that the action requested 'is well within the Court's discretion to order the production of these authorizations.' However, the signed authorizations were not in existence at the time of the hearing. The effect of the Court's order is to order relator to create the authorizations. The rules do not permit the trial court to force a party to create documents which do not exist, solely to comply with a request for production."). ***See also*** *In re Mitsubishi Heavy Indus. Am., Inc.,* 269 S.W.3d 679, 680 (Tex. App.—Dallas 2008, orig. proceeding) ("We begin by noting that it was within the trial court's discretion to order relators to sign an authorization" for "any document 'within the custody of the FAA, as herein limited, where the FAA is deferring a right of control of the document to (the plaintiffs) or where the FAA is treating the document as a proprietary document of (the plaintiffs).'" (citing *Mutter v. Wood,* 744 S.W.2d 600, 601 (Tex. 1988) (orig. proceeding), and *Martinez v. Rutledge,* 592 S.W.2d 398, 400 (Tex. App.—Dallas 1979, writ ref'd n.r.e.))); *In re Home State Cnty. Mut. Ins. Co.,* No. 12-06-00144-CV, 2006 Tex. App. LEXIS 9919, at *10 n.5, 2006 WL 3313683 (Tex. App.—Tyler Nov. 15, 2006, orig. proceeding) (mem. op.) (suggesting that authorizations are not permitted); *In re Shipmon,* 68 S.W.3d 815, 819–21 (Tex. App.—Amarillo 2001, orig. proceeding) (holding without any analysis of Texas Rule 196 that the trial court did not abuse its discretion in ordering the plaintiff to provide an employment-records authorization); *Batson v. Rainey,* 762 S.W.2d 717, 721 (Tex. App.—Houston [1st Dist.] 1988, orig. proceeding) (holding without any analysis of former Texas Rule 167 that the trial court properly ordered the plaintiff to provide a medical-records authorization) (citing *Mutter v. Wood,* 744 S.W.2d 600, 601 (Tex. 1988) (orig. proceeding))).

Federal courts likewise have split on the question in interpreting Federal Rule 34, the Rule on which Texas Rule 196 and its predecessor are modeled. *E.g., Hunters Run Gun Club, LLC v. Baker,* No. 17-176-SDD-EWD, 2019 U.S. Dist. LEXIS 20032, at *15 (M.D. La. 2019) ("It is clear that the courts in this circuit (and nationwide) have different views on whether they are empowered under Fed. R. Civ. P. 34(a) to order a party to sign an authorization or release that permits the requesting party to obtain documents such as cell phone records from non-parties."); *Scott v. City of Bismarck,* 328 F.R.D. 242, 246–50 (D.N.D. 2018) ("Unfortunately, the [federal] courts are seriously divided over this issue."); *Prado-Guajardo v. Perez,*

Irrespective of whether Texas Rule 196 permits a production request for authorizations, Texas Rule 191.1 clearly allows a trial court to order a party to sign one if the requesting party can establish good cause for the authorization (i.e., the documents sought are relevant and the authorization is more convenient than a subpoena). This is because nothing in the Texas discovery rules "specifically prohibit" a trial court from ordering a responding party to provide an authorization.[21] To the contrary, they clearly indicate that authorizations are permitted because the discovery rules expressly provide for medical authorizations.[22]

Texas Rule 191.1 prohibits discovery modifications that are specifically prohibited under the Texas discovery rules.[23] Moreover, Texas Rule 191.1 does not permit trial courts to "simply 'opt out' of [the Texas discovery R]ules by form orders or approve or order a [Level 3] discovery control plan that does not contain the matters specified in [Texas] Rule 190.4[.]"[24] "[B]ut trial courts may use standard or form orders for providing discovery plans, scheduling, and other pretrial matters" and may order the use of "discovery methods other than those prescribed in [the Texas discovery R]ules" when it is appropriate to do so.[25]

3-4 Conference and Cooperation Requirements

Texas Rule 191.2 provides that "[p]arties and their attorneys are expected to cooperate in discovery and to make any agreements reasonably necessary for the efficient disposition of the case."[26] To that end, the Rule contains the following conference

---

No. 2:16-cv-00546-GMN-VCF, 2017 U.S. Dist. LEXIS 114844, at *13, 17, 2017 WL 3130420 (D. Nev. 2017) (noting that federal "[c]ourts are divided about whether a party may be compelled to execute a signed records authorization or release under [Federal] Rule 34").

21 Tex. R. Civ. P. 191.1.

22 Tex. R. Civ. P. 194.2(j).

23 Tex. R. Civ. P. 191.1. See also Chapter 2, section 2-3:4 (discussing permissible modifications to discovery-control plans).

24 Tex. R. Civ. P. 191 cmt. 1 to 1999 change.

25 Tex. R. Civ. P. 191 cmt. 1 to 1999 change.

26 Tex. R. Civ. P. 191.2; *see In re Weekley Homes, L.P.*, 295 S.W.3d 309, 321 (Tex. 2009) (orig. proceeding) ("A fundamental tenet of our discovery rules is cooperation between parties and their counsel, and the expectation that agreements will be made as reasonably necessary for efficient disposition of the case." (citing Tex. R. Civ. P. 191.2)); *In re BP Prods. N. Am., Inc.*, 244 S.W.3d 840, 846 (Tex. 2008) ("The Rules of Civil Procedure encourage parties to reach discovery agreements."); *In re Alford Chevrolet-Geo*, 997 S.W.2d 173, 184 (Tex. 1999) ("As with all litigants, we expect class-action litigants to cooperate on discovery plans and make any agreements reasonably necessary for the efficient disposition of the case."); *In re Sw. Pub. Serv. Co.*, No. 13-19-00111-CV, 2020 Tex. App. LEXIS 3212, at *33 n.9, 2020 WL 1887762 (Tex. App.—Corpus Christi Apr. 16, 2020, orig. proceeding) (mem. op.) (same); *Eurecat US, Inc. v. Marklund*, 527 S.W.3d 367, 376 (Tex. App.—Houston [14th Dist.] 2017, no pet.) (same); *Clark v. Clark*, 546 S.W.3d 268, 273 (Tex. App.—El Paso 2017, no pet.) (mem. op.) (noting that under Texas Rule 191.2 "'[p]arties and their attorneys are expected to cooperate in discovery and to make any agreements reasonably necessary for the efficient disposition of the case'" and, "[t]o that end, all discovery motions must contain a certificate of conference stating that 'reasonable efforts' were used to resolve the pending dispute without the need for court intervention" (quoting Tex. R. Civ. P. 191.2)); *Low v. State*, No. 2-03-347-CV, 2005 Tex. App. LEXIS 3657, at *11–12, 2005 WL 1120013 (Tex. App.—Fort Worth May 12, 2005, no pet.) (mem. op.) ("The rules of civil procedure require

requirement: "All discovery motions or requests for hearings relating to discovery must contain a certificate by the party filing the motion or request that a reasonable effort has been made to resolve the dispute without the necessity of court intervention and the effort failed."[27] But Texas Rule 191.2 does not address the consequences of either a failure to confer or a failure to include a certificate of conference in the motion. It also does not explain what constitutes a "reasonable effort" to resolve a discovery dispute without court intervention.

3-4:1 Consequences of Not Including a Certificate of Conference

Because Texas Rule 191.2's certificate-of-conference requirement is "for the benefit of the trial court,"[28] it is "enforced at the option of the trial court."[29] Accordingly, an oppos-

---

a certificate of conference on all discovery motions or requests for hearings related to discovery. The purpose of the rule is to ensure that parties cooperate during the discovery process and make reasonable efforts to resolve discovery disputes without the necessity of court intervention.").

[27] Tex. R. Civ. P. 191.2 (emphasis added); *see, e.g., Goughnour v. Patterson, Tr. of Deborah Patterson Howard Tr.*, No. 12-17-00234-CV, 2019 Tex. App. LEXIS 1665, at *76, 2019 WL 1031575 (Tex. App.—Tyler Mar. 5, 2019, pet. denied) (mem. op.) ("[T]he rules of civil procedure require that all discovery motions contain a certificate of conference stating that reasonable efforts were used to resolve the pending dispute without the need for court intervention."); *Low v. State*, No. 2-03-347-CV, 2005 Tex. App. LEXIS 3657, at *11–12, 2005 WL 1120013 (Tex. App.—Fort Worth May 12, 2005, no pet.) (mem. op.) ("The rules of civil procedure require a certificate of conference on all discovery motions or requests for hearings related to discovery. The purpose of the rule is to ensure that parties cooperate during the discovery process and make reasonable efforts to resolve discovery disputes without the necessity of court intervention.").

[28] *Groves v. Gabriel*, 874 S.W.2d 660, 661 n.3 (Tex. 1994) (orig. proceeding); *accord In re Sw. Pub. Serv. Co.*, No. 13-19-00111-CV, 2020 Tex. App. LEXIS 3212, at *33 n.9, 2020 WL 1887762 (Tex. App.—Corpus Christi Apr. 16, 2020, orig. proceeding) (mem. op.); *Goughnour v. Patterson, Tr. of Deborah Patterson Howard Tr.*, No. 12-17-00234-CV, 2019 Tex. App. LEXIS 1665, at *76, 2019 WL 1031575 (Tex. App.—Tyler Mar. 5, 2019, pet. denied) (mem. op.).

[29] *Gunn v. Fuqua*, 397 S.W.3d 358, 371 (Tex. App.—Dallas 2013, pet. denied); *accord Groves v. Gabriel*, 874 S.W.2d 660, 661 n.3 (Tex. 1994) (per curiam) ("Groves also complains that Owens' motion to compel discovery did not contain the certificate of conference required under [former] Texas Rule of Civil Procedure 166b(7). Because this rule is for the benefit of the trial court, the court's failure to require a certificate of conference does not justify mandamus relief.") (citation omitted); *In re Sw. Pub. Serv. Co.*, No. 13-19-00111-CV, 2020 Tex. App. LEXIS 3212, at *33 n.9, 2020 WL 1887762 (Tex. App.—Corpus Christi Apr. 16, 2020, orig. proceeding) (mem. op.) (same); *Goughnour v. Patterson, Tr. of Deborah Patterson Howard Tr.*, No. 12-17-00234-CV, 2019 Tex. App. LEXIS 1665, at *76, 2019 WL 1031575 (Tex. App.—Tyler Mar. 5, 2019, pet. denied) (mem. op.) (same); *Cogsdil v. Jimmy Fincher Body Shop, LLC*, No. 07-17-00054-CV, 2018 Tex. App. LEXIS 9209, at *6, 2018 WL 5852772 (Tex. App.—Amarillo Nov. 8, 2018, no pet.) (mem. op.) ("This Court has held that 'rules requiring certificates of conference are for the trial court's benefit; thus, they may be enforced at the option of the trial court.'" (quoting *Fuentes v. Schooling*, No. 07-07-00118-CV, 2008 Tex. App. LEXIS 9001, at *9, 2008 WL 5083012 (Tex. App.—Amarillo Dec. 3, 2008. no pet.) (mem. op.))); *Centennial Psychiatric Assocs., LLC v. Cantrell*, Nos. 14-17-00391-CV, 14-17-00380-CV, 2017 Tex. App. LEXIS 11909, at *35 n.17, 2017 WL 6544283 (Tex. App.—Houston [14th Dist.] Dec. 21, 2017, no pet.) (mem. op.) ("While we do not vacate the sanction order based on Ryan's failure to confer with Centennial, we note that compliance

ing party should not rely solely on the lack of a certificate of conference to defeat a discovery motion or hearing request.[30] Its focus instead should be on the actual effort that was made to resolve the discovery dispute without court intervention.[31]

3-4:2 Assessing Effort to Resolve Discovery Disputes

No statewide standard exists for assessing whether parties have made a reasonable effort to resolve a discovery dispute. Instead, efforts are assessed on a court-by-court and case-by-case basis. Some courts have local rules that define or otherwise address what constitutes "reasonable efforts" and include form certificates of conference that

---

with [Texas R]ule 191.2 may have saved the time Ryan spent preparing his motion, the time the trial court spent considering the motion, and the time this court spent addressing it on appeal."); *Fuentes v. Schooling*, No. 07-07-0118-CV, 2008 Tex. App. LEXIS 9001, at *8–9, 2008 WL 5083012 (Tex. App.—Amarillo Dec. 3, 2008, no pet.) (mem. op.) (rejecting an allegation that the trial court abused its discretion in levying sanctions because the amended motion to quash lacked a certificate of conference as the procedural "rules requiring certificates of conference are for trial court's benefit[, and] may be enforced at the option of the trial court"); *Low v. State*, No. 2-03-347-CV, 2005 Tex. App. LEXIS 3657, at *12, 2005 WL 1120013 (Tex. App.—Fort Worth May 12, 2005, no pet.) (mem. op.) ("[T]he record shows that the State's reasonable efforts to resolve the discovery dispute failed, and the trial court did not abuse its discretion by assessing sanctions against Low despite the lack of a certificate of conference on the motion to compel."); *Academy Corp. v. Interior Buildout & Turnkey Constr., Inc.*, 21 S.W.3d 732, 743 (Tex. App.—Houston [14th Dist.] 2000, no pet.) (finding no error because the trial court did not require a certificate of conference for motions filed in her court). *But see Clark v. Clark*, 546 S.W.3d 268, 273–74 (Tex. App.—El Paso 2017, no pet.) (mem. op.) (noting that "[c]ourts are somewhat split on the import of [Texas Rule 191.2] and the predecessor rule" and identifying one case, *United Servs. Auto. Ass'n v. Thomas*, 893 S.W.2d 628, 630 (Tex. App.—Corpus Christi 1994, writ denied), in which a court vacated a sanction when the movant did not include a certificate of conference).

[30] *See, e.g., Groves v. Gabriel*, 874 S.W.2d 660, 661 n.3 (Tex. 1994) (per curiam) ("Groves also complains that Owens' motion to compel discovery did not contain the certificate of conference required under [former] Texas Rule of Civil Procedure 166b(7). Because this rule is for the benefit of the trial court, the court's failure to require [a] certificate of conference does not justify mandamus relief.") (citation omitted); *Tjernagel v. Roberts*, 928 S.W.2d 297, 300 (Tex. App.—Amarillo 1996, no writ) (same); *Int'l Surplus Lines Ins. Co. v. Wallace*, 843 S.W.2d 773, 776 (Tex. App.—Texarkana 1992, orig. proceeding) (same); *cf. Rice v. Hickerson*, No. 04-18-00694-CV, 2020 Tex. App. LEXIS 2461, at *31, 2020 WL 1443562 (Tex. App.—San Antonio Mar. 25, 2020, pet. denied) (mem. op.) ("The trial court found that Susan Rice failed to comply with [Texas] Rule 191.2 *and the totality of her conduct* abused the discovery process. We agree. . . . Having reviewed the entire record and applying the required two-part inquiry [for assessing sanctions], we conclude the trial court's sanctions order was appropriate or just.") (emphasis added).

[31] *See Low v. State*, No. 2-03-347-CV, 2005 Tex. App. LEXIS 3657, at *12, 2005 WL 1120013 (Tex. App.—Fort Worth May 12, 2005, no pet.) (mem. op.) ("[T]he record shows that the State's reasonable efforts to resolve the discovery dispute failed, and the trial court did not abuse its discretion by assessing sanctions against Low despite the lack of a certificate of conference on the motion to compel."); *cf. Alexander Interactive, Inc. v. Adorama, Inc.*, No. 12 Civ. 6608 (PKC) (JCF), 2013 U.S. Dist. LEXIS 170931, at *10, 2013 WL 6283511 (S.D.N.Y. Dec. 4, 2013) ("Nevertheless, [Federal] Rule 37 is satisfied as long as the parties have in fact met and conferred, even if they fail to submit a proper certification."); *Care Envtl. Corp. v. M2 Techs. Inc.*, No. 05 CV 1600, 2006 U.S. Dist. LEXIS 35396, at *10, 2006 WL 1517742 (E.D.N.Y. May 30, 2006) ("Thus, if the parties did meet and confer, they have satisfied [Federal] Rule 37's purpose even if the plaintiff does not submit a proper certification.").

must be included on discovery motions and hearing requests.[32] Some of those rules even extend the certificate-of-conference requirement to motions unrelated to discovery disputes.[33] In the absence of a local rule, "reasonableness" of the effort is the touchtone for conference requirements.

Generally, sending the opposing party a letter or email demanding certain action by a set deadline is unlikely to constitute a "reasonable effort" to resolve the discovery dispute "without court intervention," as required by Texas Rule 191.2.[34] Rather, to be

---

[32] For example, Local Rule 2.07 for the Dallas County Civil Courts has certificate-of-conference forms and provides: "Prior to the filing of a motion, counsel for the potential movant shall personally attempt to contact counsel for the potential respondent to hold or schedule a conference to resolve the disputed matters. Counsel for the potential movant shall make at least three attempts to contact counsel for the potential respondent. The attempts shall be made during regular business hours on at least two business days." Dallas Cnty. (Tex.) Civ. Ct. Loc. R. 2.07(a)–(c). Local Rule 3.2 for the Collin County district courts provides similarly: "Prior to the filing of a motion, counsel for the movant shall personally attempt to contact counsel for the respondent to hold or schedule a conference to resolve the disputed matters." Collin Cnty. (Tex.) Dist. Ct. Loc. R. 3.2. The rule continues: "Counsel for the movant shall use good faith efforts to contact opposing counsel and be prepared to outline such efforts for the Court." Collin Cnty. (Tex.) Dist. Ct. Loc. R. 3.2. Local Rule 3.3 then provides language for certificates of conference. Collin Cnty. (Tex.) Dist. Ct. Loc. R. 3.3.

[33] *See, e.g.*, Harris Cnty. (Tex.) Civ. Dist. Ct. Loc. R. 3.3.6 ("The certificates of conference required by the Texas Rules of Civil Procedure are extended to all motions, pleas and special exceptions except summary judgments, default judgments, agreed judgments, motions for voluntary dismissal or non-suit, post-verdict motions and motions involving service of citation."); Collin Cnty. (Tex.) Dist. Ct. Loc. R. 3.1, 3.4 (extending certificate-of-conference requirement to all pretrial disputes except dispositive motions, summary judgment motions, default motions, motions for voluntary dismissal or nonsuit, post-verdict motions, and motions involving service of citation); El Paso Cnty. (Tex.) Statutory Prob. Ct. Loc. R. 2(j) (addressing certificates of conference required for motions other than dispositive motions, stating that it is strictly enforced, providing examples of what does not suffice as a good-faith effort to resolve a contested matter or dispute, and providing certificate language).

[34] *Cf. Navarette v. C.R. Bard, Inc.*, No. 5:19-CV-01278-OLG, 2020 U.S. Dist. LEXIS 247508, at *3, 2020 WL 8092373 (W.D. Tex. Oct. 2, 2020) ("[T]he parties do not satisfy the conference requirements simply by requesting or demanding compliance, because the parties need to confer, deliberate, converse, or compare views with a goal of resolving the dispute."); *Am. Power Chassis, Inc. v. Jones*, No. 13-4134-KHV, 2018 U.S. Dist. LEXIS 239004, at *4, 2018 WL 4863623 (D. Kan. Jan. 19, 2018) ("The court finds that a single letter, sent by counsel for plaintiff, does not constitute a 'reasonable effort to confer' under D. Kan. Rule 37.2. Plaintiff's counsel makes no showing that he undertook any additional efforts to resolve the dispute beyond writing the letter. Merely repeating a position and requesting or demanding compliance with a discovery request does not satisfy a party's requirement to 'converse, confer, compare views, consult, and deliberate, or in good faith attempt to do so.' Accordingly, the court denies the motion."); *Reed v. Beverly Hills Porsche*, No. 6:17-CV-59, 2017 U.S. Dist. LEXIS 227319, at *2, 2017 WL 11495243 (W.D. Va. Nov. 22, 2017) ("Indeed, simply exchanging emails or letters, demanding compliance with discovery requests, or merely stating that the parties have met and conferred do not satisfy Rule 37(a)(1)."); *Merz N. Am., Inc. v. Cytophil, Inc.*, No. 5:15-CV-262-H-KS, 2017 U.S. Dist. LEXIS 158914, at *8, 2017 WL 4274856 (E.D.N.C. Sept. 26, 2017) ("Meet and confer requirements are not satisfied 'by requesting or demanding compliance with the requests for discovery" or by "mailing or faxing a letter to the opposing party." (quoting *Pro Fit Mgmt., Inc. v. Lady of Am. Franchise Corp.*, No. 08-CV-02662-JAR-DJW, 2011 U.S. Dist. LEXIS 133285,

safe, the movant's attorney should either meet or call the opposing attorney and discuss the issues and their potential resolution in good faith.[35]

---

at *3–4, 2011 WL 5825423 (D. Kan. Nov. 17, 2011))); *Gann v. N.-Cent. Ala. Reg'l Council of Gov'ts*, No. CV-13-S-270-NE, 2013 U.S. Dist. LEXIS 167610, at *16–17, 2013 WL 6190799 (N.D. Ala. Nov. 26, 2013) ("Plaintiff's act of merely sending a letter demanding compliance with his discovery requests by an arbitrary deadline does not satisfy the meet-and-confer requirement of [Federal] Rule 37(a)(1)."); *Bank v. Shamgochian*, 287 F.R.D. 397, 400 (S.D. Tex. 2012) ("Plaintiff's single letter unilaterally identifying flaws in Defendant's discovery responses and setting an arbitrary response deadline for Defendant would seem to be inadequate, as it does not equate to a good faith conferral or attempt to confer."); *Limtiaco v. Auction Cars.com, LLC*, No. 2:11-cv-00370-MMD-CWH, 2012 U.S. Dist. LEXIS 149172, at *6–7, 2012 WL 5179708 (D. Nev. Oct. 17, 2012) (concluding that sending several letters identifying perceived failings in the opposing party's discovery responses did not satisfy Federal Rule 37's meet-and-confer requirement); *Velazquez-Perez v. Developers Diversified Realty Corp.*, 272 F.R.D. 310, 312 (D. P.R. 2011) (holding that sending emails and letters to the defendant were insufficient to satisfy the meet-and-confer requirement); *Adams v. Austal*, U.S.A., No. 08-0155-KD-N, 2009 U.S. Dist. LEXIS 117084, at *3, 2009 WL 5066779 (S.D. Ala. Dec. 16, 2009) ("A single letter between counsel addressing a discovery dispute does not satisfy the duty to confer."); *Robinson v. Napolitano*, No. CIV. 08-4084, 2009 U.S. Dist. LEXIS 50025, at *7–11, 2009 WL 1586959 (D.S.D. June 4, 2009) (same); *Ross v. Citifinancial, Inc.*, 203 F.R.D. 239, 240 (S.D. Miss. 2001) (holding that meet-and-confer "prerequisite is not an empty formality" and "cannot be satisfied by including with the motion copies of correspondence that discuss the discovery at issue"); *Williams v. Bd. of Cnty. Comm'rs*, 192 F.R.D. 698, 699 (D. Kan. 2000) (clarifying that "sending unanswered correspondence to opposing counsel demanding discovery be produced by a specific deadline" does not satisfy duty to confer); *Cotracom Commodity Trading Co. v. Seaboard Corp.*, 189 F.R.D. 456, 459 (D. Kan. 1999) (holding that "parties do not satisfy the conference requirements simply by requesting or demanding compliance with the requests for discovery" by an arbitrary deadline); *Alexander v. FBI*, 186 F.R.D. 197, 199 (D.D.C. 1999) ("In short, the court notes that leaving a vague message late on a Friday afternoon with opposing counsel and filing the motion less than two hours later—without ever meeting and conferring, and without any legitimate reason for expediency—does not meet the requirements of Local Rule 108(m)."); *Soto v. City of Concord*, 162 F.R.D. 603, 623 (N.D. Cal. 1995) ("Sending a letter to the opposing party demanding compliance with a discovery request is not what this Court regards as an earnest attempt to 'meet and confer' on the issues. Rather, a live exchange of ideas and opinions is required."), *cited with approval in Moore v. Superway Logistics, Inc.*, No. 117CV01480DADBAM, 2019 U.S. Dist. LEXIS 90111, at *11, 2019 WL 2285392 (E.D. Cal. May 29, 2019).

At least one federal court has held that it is also insufficient to request or demand compliance via telephone. *See Eagle Railcar Servs.-Roscoe, Inc. v. NGL Crude Logistics, LLC*, No. 1:16-CV-0153-BL, 2018 U.S. Dist. LEXIS 85415, at *48, 2018 WL 2317696 (N.D. Tex. May 22, 2018) ("Counsel for Eagle states that during the February telephone call, he asked NGL to review its objections, withdraw and/or revise them, and indicate whether NGL has any responsive documents. That amounts to little more than simply requesting or demanding compliance with the discovery request—actions that do not constitute good faith efforts to confer.").

[35] *Cf. Elite Mitigation Servs. LLC v. Westchester Surplus Lines Ins. Co.*, 5:19-CV-381-TKW/MJF, 2020 U.S. Dist. LEXIS 195708, at *12 n.5, 2020 WL 6122557 (N.D. Fla. May 4, 2020) ("To date, the parties have filed over ten discovery motions, which is an excessive number. Frequently these motions were filed without the parties discussing matters telephonically or in person. Many of the issues likely could have been resolved if the parties would have discussed the relevant matters as opposed to merely sending emails. This court, therefore, will require the parties to confer telephonically.");

3-4:3 Consequences of Not Making a Reasonable Effort to Resolve Discovery Disputes

If a party files a motion to compel or for sanctions without first making a reasonable effort to resolve the discovery dispute at issue, the trial court has the discretion

---

Navarette v. C.R. Bard, Inc., No. 5:19-CV-01278-OLG, 2020 U.S. Dist. LEXIS 247508, at *3, 2020 WL 8092373 (W.D. Tex. Oct. 2, 2020) ("'Good faith' requires a genuine attempt to resolve the dispute and 'conferment' requires two-way communication which is necessary to genuinely discuss any issues and to avoid judicial recourse."); *Moore v. Superway Logistics, Inc.*, No. 117CV01480DADBAM, 2019 U.S. Dist. LEXIS 9011 at *12, 2019 WL 2285392 (E.D. Cal. May 29, 2019) ("There is no indication that the parties ever met and conferred telephonically or in person to resolve their dispute at any time before or after the motion was filed. The Court does not consider the parties' efforts to be a good faith attempt to resolve the parties' dispute prior to filing the motion or the Joint Statement re Discovery Disagreement and Plaintiffs' motion is therefore subject to denial for failure to adequately meet and confer."); *Aetna Inc. v. People's Choice Hosp., LLC*, No. SA-18-CV-00323-OLG, 2018 U.S. Dist. LEXIS 228072, at *11–12, 2018 WL 6220169 (W.D. Tex. June 18, 2018) "In many instances, letters or emails alone may not be sufficient to demonstrate that a good-faith effort was made to resolve the open issues." (citing cases); *Merz N. Am., Inc. v. Cytophil, Inc.*, No. 5:15-CV-262-H-KS, 2017 U.S. Dist. LEXIS 158914, at *8, 2017 WL 4274856 (E.D.N.C. Sept. 26, 2017) ("While not expressly required by [Federal] Rule 37 or this court's local rules, it is the undersigned's expectation that any discovery conference be conducted in person or telephonically absent exceptional circumstances. The parties are further encouraged to request a discovery conference with the court prior to filing any discovery motions."); *Kirschenman v. Auto-Owners Ins.*, 280 F.R.D. 474, 479 (D.S.D. 2012) (holding that a series of letters, email messages, and telephone calls constituted a good-faith effort to resolve discovery disputes informally); *Antonis v. Elecs. for Imaging, Inc.*, No. 07-cv-163-JL, 2008 U.S. Dist. LEXIS 6887, at *2–3, 2008 WL 169955 (D.N.H. Jan. 16, 2008) (noting that, "as a general principle, simply reiterating demands for production in a series of emails probably does not meet the requirement that the parties confer in good faith about discovery issues before invoking judicial remedies," but finding that repeated emails and phone calls between counsel is sufficient); *Care Envtl. Corp. v. M2 Techs. Inc.*, No. CV-05-1600 (CPS), 2006 U.S. Dist. LEXIS 35396, at *10, 2006 WL 1517742 (E.D.N.Y. May 30, 2006) (holding that a good-faith effort to confer had occurred because the parties exchanged emails and had a two-hour "substantive" telephone conversation).

Some federal courts require an in-person meeting or telephone call for there to have been a proper conference. *E.g., Martin v. Nev. Div. of Ins.*, No. 3:13-cv-00047-RCJ-WGC, 2014 U.S. Dist. LEXIS 65628, at *3, 2014 WL 1917703 (D. Nev. May 13, 2014) ("Writing a letter to opposing counsel with no attempt to meet personally . . . falls woefully short of the concept of 'personal consultation.'"); *Compass Bank v. Shamgochian*, 287 F.R.D. 397, 399 (S.D. Tex. 2012) (providing that the movant must "actually attempt a meeting or conference"); *Ellipso, Inc. v. Mann*, 460 F. Supp. 2d 99, 102 (D.D.C. 2006) (admonishing that counsel should, at minimum, pick up the telephone and speak to each other about discovery disputes before filing motions to compel); *Prescient Partners, L.P. v. Fieldcrest Cannon, Inc.*, No. 96 Civ. 7590 (DAB) (JCF), 1998 U.S. Dist. LEXIS 1826, at *7, 1998 WL 67672 (S.D.N.Y. Feb. 18, 1998) ("The meet-and-confer requirement mandates that parties actually 'meet, in person or by telephone.'") (citation omitted); *Shuffle Master, Inc. v. Progressive Games, Inc.*, 170 F.R.D. 166, 172 (D. Nev. 1996) (holding that "conferring" requires "a personal or telephonic consultation during which the parties engage in meaningful negotiations").

to deny the motion.[36] The order denying the motion, however, should be without prejudice, providing that the movant can refile its motion if the dispute cannot be resolved after a proper conference.[37]

---

[36] See note 29 and accompanying text. Federal courts consistently have denied discovery motions when the movant fails to comply with Federal Rule 37(a)(1)'s comparable conference requirement. *E.g., Avera v. United Airlines, Inc.*, 465 F. App'x 855, 859 (11th Cir. 2012) (holding that the magistrate judge did not abuse his discretion in denying the movant's motion to compel without prejudice because the movant failed to confer with the respondent before filing the motion as required by Federal Rule 37(a)(1)); *Robinson v. Potter,* 453 F.3d 990, 995 (8th Cir. 2006) ("Because Robinson cannot show the parties attempted to confer in good faith to resolve the discovery request, the district court did not abuse its discretion in denying the motion."); *Reed v. Beverly Hills Porsche,* No. 6:17-CV-59, 2017 U.S. Dist. LEXIS 227319, at *3, 2017 WL 11495243 (W.D. Va. Nov. 22, 2017) ("Plaintiff must meet the substance of what [Federal] Rule 37(a)(1) requires, at a minimum, to attempt to confer in good faith with Defendants in person or by telephone to resolve the dispute without involving the Court. I deny the motion to compel and require the parties to engage in a meaningful meet and confer not just because the Federal Rules so demand, but because communication between counsel is essential to making the discovery process work as designed.") (citations omitted); *Motley v. Host Hotels & Resorts, Inc.*, No. PX 15–2062, 2017 U.S. Dist. LEXIS 60307, at *15–16, 2017 WL 1406297 (D. Md. Apr. 20, 2017) ("Plaintiff provides only one undated e-mail correspondence from Defendants' counsel that simply reflects Defendants' due diligence in searching for documents in connection with the Plaintiff's deposition of a loss prevention officer. Plaintiff provides no proof of any additional attempts to confer and does not even attempt to meet this Court's requirements set forth in the Local Rules. Accordingly, Plaintiff's motion must fail.") (citations omitted); *Separzadeh v. Iconix Brand Grp., Inc.*, No. 15 Civ. 8643 (AT) (JCF), 2017 U.S. Dist. LEXIS 54617, at *2, 2017 WL 1330331 (S.D.N.Y. Apr. 10, 2017) ("Here, plaintiff's counsel acknowledges that he did not succeed in scheduling a conference with RAG's attorney prior to filing the motion, but contends that further delay would have caused his client some unspecified prejudice. This does not satisfy the meet-and-confer requirement; there has been not an adequate showing that 'temporal exigencies required speedy action' or that 'efforts at informal compromise would have been clearly futile.' And, while there was some discussion with counsel for Iconix, the specific issues raised in the plaintiff's motion do not appear to have been addressed in detail. This failure to conduct a meaningful conference is, by itself, grounds for denying the relief requested by the plaintiff." (citations omitted) (quoting *Prescient Partners, L.P. v. Fieldcrest Cannon, Inc.*, No. 96 Civ. 7590 (DAB)(JCF), 1998 U.S. Dist. LEXIS 1826, at *7, 1998 WL 67672 (S.D.N.Y. Feb. 18, 1998))); *Cavanaugh v. S. Cal. Permanente Med. Grp., Inc.*, 583 F. Supp. 2d 1109, 1139 (C.D. Cal. 2008) (denying motion to compel where moving party failed to include certification that the movant met and conferred in good faith); *Dimitric v. Tex. A&M Univ.*, No. G-06-107, 2007 U.S. Dist. LEXIS 103260, at *3, 2007 WL 1090982 (S.D. Tex. Apr. 9, 2007) ("Prior to filing this Motion, Dimitric did not confer. . . . For this reason, alone, his Motion should be denied."); *Shaw Grp. Inc. v. Zurich Am. Ins. Co.*, No. 12-257-JJB-RLB, 2014 U.S. Dist. LEXIS 122514, at *8, 2014 WL 4373197 (M.D. La. Sept. 3, 2014) ("Due to Zurich's failure to attach a [Federal] Rule 37 certification to its motion as is specifically required by the Rule, as well as its failure to meet and confer with all opposing counsel subject to the motion, the Motion to Compel is DENIED."); *Aponte-Navedo v. Nalco Chem. Co.*, 268 F.R.D. 31, 41 (D.P.R. 2010) ("Thus, plaintiffs' failure to comply with the meet and confer requirements constitutes sufficient reason to deny the motion to compel."). See also cases cited in notes 34–35.

[37] *Cf. Pendleton v. Jordan*, 3:20-CV-5297-BHS-DWC, 2021 U.S. Dist. LEXIS 44129, at *7, 2021 WL 871425 (W.D. Wash. Mar. 9, 2021) ("According to counsel for Defendants, no

Although "reasonable efforts" are required to resolve a discovery dispute informally in all but the most unusual of circumstances, a trial court has discretion to grant a discovery motion despite a failure to confer.[38] In construing comparable Federal Rule 37, "'[c]ourts have excused a failure to meet and confer where: (1) under the circumstances, the parties do not have time to attempt to reach an agreement; or

---

such meet and confer took place, and the record does not contain any certification by Plaintiff that it did. For these reasons, and because Plaintiff is proceeding pro se and it is unclear if the discovery he requests is relevant to the pending Motion for Summary Judgment, Plaintiff's second Motion to Compel is also denied without prejudice.") (citations omitted); *Hutten v. Serv. Ins. Co.*, No. 2:20-CV-45-FL, 2020 U.S. Dist. LEXIS 229769, at *22–23, 2020 WL 7232855 (E.D.N.C. Dec. 8, 2020) (denying plaintiffs' motion to compel without prejudice, in part because there was no documented good-faith effort to resolve the discovery dispute); *Zenteno v. Bank of Am., N.A.*, No. 8:17-CV-2591-T-02TGW, 2019 U.S. Dist. LEXIS 147956, at *3, 2019 WL 7482201 (M.D. Fla. Aug. 30, 2019) ("The responses to the requests for admission and the privilege log will therefore not be finally determined, and the motion is denied without prejudice due to failure to confer appropriately. . . . The answers to the interrogatories will therefore not be examined, and the motion is denied without prejudice due to failure to confer appropriately."); *Am. Home Assur. Co. v. KBEKbe Bldg. Corp.*, No. CCB-13-1941, 2015 U.S. Dist. LEXIS 4076, at *36, 2015 WL 348292 (D. Md. Jan. 13, 2015) ("For failure to confer, then, Watkins' motion to quash will be denied without prejudice."); *Cmty. Ass'n Underwriters of Am. v. Queensboro Flooring Corp.*, No. 3:10-CV-1559, 2014 U.S. Dist. LEXIS 51525, at *11–12, 2014 WL 1516152 (M.D. Pa. Apr. 15, 2014) ("The Pozarliks' [Federal] Rule 37 motions do not include any such certification, nor is there anything in the motions, briefs, or exhibits to suggest that counsel have met and conferred to address these issues. Indeed, given the broad scope of both motions, it appears that no good faith effort was made whatsoever to resolve or narrow the discovery disputes at issue prior to filing. In the absence of certification, or any other evidence, of a good faith effort to resolve these discovery disputes prior to seeking court intervention, the Court concludes that these motions must be denied, albeit without prejudice to renewal of these motions, in whole or in part, if the parties are unable to resolve or narrow these discovery disputes after conferring with one another in good faith."); *Alexander Interactive, Inc. v. Adorama, Inc.*, No. 12 Civ. 6608 (PKC) (JCF), 2013 U.S. Dist. LEXIS 170931, at *11, 2013 WL 6283511 (S.D.N.Y. Dec. 4, 2013) (noting that "the remedy when a plaintiff has not submitted a certification is to deny the motion without prejudice"); *Compass Bank v. Shamgochian*, 287 F.R.D. 397, 399–400 (S.D. Tex. 2012) (citing cases outlining efforts that "are insufficient to constitute a good faith conferral or attempt to confer," identifying the single, insufficient letter in the record, and denying a motion to compel without prejudice); *Stulting v. Grafton*, No. 03:11-cv-00411-HU, 2011 U.S. Dist. LEXIS 152939, at *17–18, 2011 WL 7153947 (D. Or. Dec. 14, 2011) ("The exchange of e-mail correspondence did not comply with either the spirit or the letter of the conferral rule. Good-faith conferral is warranted in all but the most unusual of circumstances. Ordinarily, when there has been a failure to confer, I will deny the motion without prejudice to refiling once counsel have conferred as required by the Local Rule.").

[38] *See, e.g., Clark v. Clark*, 546 S.W.3d 268, 273 (Tex. App.—El Paso 2017, no pet.) (mem. op.) (affirming order compelling discovery and imposing Texas Rule 215 monetary sanctions despite the appellants' complaint that the appellee did not meaningfully confer with them before filing the motion to compel). See also discussion at note 29.

(2) an attempt to compromise would have been clearly futile.'"[39] What constitutes exigent circumstances or a futility depends on the case's facts.[40]

---

[39] *Care Envtl. Corp. v. M2 Techs. Inc.*, No. 05 CV 1600, 2006 U.S. Dist. LEXIS 35396, at *9–10, 2006 WL 1517742 (E.D.N.Y. May 30, 2006) (quoting *Yoon v. Celebrity Cruises, Inc.*, No. 97 Civ. 3808 (DC), 1999 U.S. Dist. LEXIS 2779, at *17, 1999 WL 135222 (S.D.N.Y. Mar. 12, 1999)); *accord Elhannon LLC v. F.A. Bartlett Tree Expert Co.*, No. 2:14-cv-262, 2017 U.S. Dist. LEXIS 58693, at *30, 2017 WL 1382024 (D. Vt. Apr. 18, 2017); *Munive v. Town of Cicero*, No. 12 C 5481, 2016 U.S. Dist. LEXIS 182159, at *2, 2016 WL 8673072 (N.D. Ill. Oct. 14, 2016); *Prescient Partners, L.P. v. Fieldcrest Cannon*, No. 96 CV. 7590 (DAB) (JCF), 1998 U.S. Dist. LEXIS 1826, at *7–8, 1998 WL 67672 (S.D.N.Y. Feb. 18, 1998); *see Seaman v. Duke Univ.*, No. 1:15CV462, 2018 U.S. Dist. LEXIS 47118, at 19 n.11, 2018 WL 1441267 (M.D.N.C. Mar. 21, 2018) ("In addition, 'courts have implied a futility exception to the meet and confer requirement. For the futility exception to apply, however, a Court must find any attempt to meet and confer would have been futile; otherwise, a motion to compel must be denied for failure to follow the Rules.'" (quoting *Hurley by Hurley v. Potomac Edison Co.*, No. 3:07CV14, 2008 U.S. Dist. LEXIS 129354, at *11, 2008 WL 11344676 (N.D.W. Va. May 15, 2008))); *In re Sulfuric Acid Antitrust Litig.*, 231 F.R.D. 351, 356 (N.D. Ill. 2005) ("The doctrine of futility is as applicable in the context of [Federal] Rule 37 and Local Rule 37.2 as it is in any other."); *Coultas v. Payne*, No. 3:11-cv-45-AC, 2013 U.S. Dist. LEXIS 63886, at *3, 2013 WL 1870545 (D. Or. May 3, 2013) ("This court has recognized a futility exception to the conferral requirement."); *In re NASDAQ Market-Makers Antitrust Litig.*, No. 94 Civ. 3996, 1996 U.S. Dist. LEXIS 4969, at *2, 1996 WL 187409 (S.D.N.Y. Apr. 18, 1996) (excusing failure to confer in part because of imminence of deadlines for filing papers relating to class-certification motion); *Imperial Chems. Indus., PLC v. Barr Labs., Inc.*, 126 F.R.D. 467, 472 (S.D.N.Y. 1989) (excusing failure to comply with conference requirement of local rule given "exigencies of time"). *But see Smith v. Premiere Valet Servs. Inc.*, No. 219CV09888C-JCMAA, 2020 U.S. Dist. LEXIS 228465, at *20–21, 2020 WL 7034346 (C.D. Cal. Aug. 4, 2020) ("To the extent that Plaintiff's accusations of Defendant's counsel are intended to establish that it would have been futile for him to try to arrange this conference because Defendant's counsel have, in the past, refused to meet and confer by telephone, there is no futility exception to the meet and confer requirement."); *Whitaker v. Aviano*, LLC, No. 219CV07070RSWLMAA, 2020 U.S. Dist. LEXIS 152485, at *9, 2020 WL 4787999 (C.D. Cal. June 15, 2020) ("As a threshold matter, the Court is unaware of a futility exception to the Rule 37-1 meet-and-confer requirement, and Plaintiff points to no such authority."); *Bonner v. Cnty. of Los Angeles*, No. CV 15-8885 GW (SSX), 2017 U.S. Dist. LEXIS 225561, at *6, 2017 WL 10509044 (C.D. Cal. May 19, 2017) ("There is no futility exception to the meet and confer requirement.").

[40] *Cf. Bonumose Biochem, LLC v. Yi-Heng Zhang*, No. 3:17-CV-00033, 2018 U.S. Dist. LEXIS 231073, at *15, 2018 WL 10068638 (W.D. Va. Oct. 31, 2018) ("Federal district courts have broad discretion under [Federal] Rule 37 to determine whether a movant has adequately conferred with the opposing party prior to filing a motion to compel. In making such a determination, a court must consider the totality of the circumstances surrounding the discovery process.") (citations omitted); *Compare, e.g., Kunneman Properties LLC v. Marathon Oil Co.*, No. 17-CV-456-GKF-JFJ, 2020 U.S. Dist. LEXIS 113287, at *8–9, 2020 WL 3473659 (N.D. Okla. Apr. 24, 2020) ("Although the Court does not deny Plaintiffs' motion based solely on the failure to meet and confer, as Marathon recommends, the Court considers it a factor weighing against sanctions and disagrees with Plaintiffs' argument that conferring necessarily would have been futile."); *Blackburn v. Walmart Inc.*, No. EDCV182487DOCSPX, 2019 U.S. Dist. LEXIS 221951, at *2–3, 2019 WL 7171558 (C.D. Cal. July 18, 2019) ("Defendant argues the litigation history shows any attempt to meet and confer would have been futile, but the record indicates otherwise. In particular, the emails attached to the recent Walshok Declaration show very recent meet and confer efforts have been fruitful in reaching certain compromises. Those efforts should have been fully

exhausted before any motion was filed. Thus, the meet and confer requirement has not been satisfied and it should have been."); *Elhannon LLC v. F.A. Bartlett Tree Expert Co.*, No. 2:14-cv-262, 2017 U.S. Dist. LEXIS 58693, at *30–31, 2017 WL 1382024 (D. Vt. Apr. 18, 2017) ("In this case, the parties' filings indicate that counsel have approached each other with significant animosity, and that substantial challenges exist to narrowing discovery disputes. However, in light of Bartlett's representation that Elhannon promised to provide a list of outstanding discovery disputes after the parties' mediation but failed to do so, the parties' differences in this case cannot be solely attributed to Bartlett's uncooperative attitude. Thus, a meet-and-confer effort would not necessarily have been futile."), *U-Haul Co. of Nev., Inc. v. Gregory J. Kamer, Ltd.*, No. 2:12-cv-00231-KJD-CWH, 2013 U.S. Dist. LEXIS 132795, at *7–8, 2013 WL 5278523 (D. Nev. Sept. 17, 2013) ("Plaintiff has simply unilaterally declared that any meet and confer effort would have been futile. The undersigned does not accept the declaration of futility and finds that the failure to even provide the alleged 'meet and confer' letter lends further support to the conclusion that Plaintiff did not satisfy the meet and confer requirements prior to filing this motion. As such, the request to compel Wilcher's computer, SIM card, and to obtain information from Yahoo!(r) is denied."), *Remy Inc. v. Tecnomatic, S.P.A.*, No. 1:11-cv-00991-SEB-MJD, 2013 U.S. Dist. LEXIS 43205, at *9–10, 2013 WL 1311095 (S.D. Ind. Mar. 26, 2013) (rejecting an argument that conference was excused merely because the movant believed the other side would not have agreed to requested action), *and Robinson v. Napolitano*, No. Civ. 08-4084, 2009 U.S. Dist. LEXIS 50025, at *11–12, 2009 WL 1586959 (D.S.D. June 4, 2009) ("It is undisputed that the government did not confer in any way with Mr. Robinson between the time the government received his amended discovery answers on April 20 and the time the government filed its motion to compel on April 21st. Nor is there a 'track record' showing that conferment with Mr. Robinson would have been futile. Although progress has been made in fits and starts, every time in the past when the government conferred with Mr. Robinson, he addressed the government's concerns and provided additional information. When the government did confer with Mr. Robinson in the past, he was prompt to respond, as he did on April 13th and again on April 20th. There is no reason to believe that he would not have done so again had the government contacted Mr. Robinson after receiving his April 20th responses."), *with, e.g., Gov't Employees Ins. Co. v. Strut,* No. 19-CV-728-JLS-HBS, 2021 U.S. Dist. LEXIS 12248, at *16 n.3, 2021 WL 230902 (W.D.N.Y. Jan. 22, 2021) ("Plaintiffs assert that Defendant did not meet and confer on this issue. Even if true, the Court would excuse that failure under the circumstances."); *Bishop v. White,* No. 16 C 6040, 2020 U.S. Dist. LEXIS 194073, at *8–9, 2020 WL 6149567 (N.D. Ill. Oct. 20, 2020) ("Indeed, based on the briefs filed by both sides, it does not seem there are any issues raised that could have been, or still could be, avoided by a proper meet and confer. Granting Plaintiff's Motion for failure to comply with [Federal] Rule 37 and Local Rule 37.2 would therefore result in nothing more than the parties engaging in a futile meet and confer process and filing additional briefs that would be the same, or at least substantially similar, to what they already have filed. That does not seem to be a good use of anyone's time."); *O'Neal v. Las Vegas Metro. Police Dep't,* 217CV02765AP-GEJY, 2020 U.S. Dist. LEXIS 143119, at *4–5, 2020 WL 8617648 (D. Nev. Aug. 10, 2020) ("Here, Defendants demonstrate that efforts to meet and confer with Plaintiffs would have been futile. Defendants sent multiple notices of Plaintiffs' depositions that were ignored; Plaintiffs failed to respond to Defendants' Requests for Admissions; Plaintiffs have engaged in verbally abusive conduct when confronted with discovery processes; and, Plaintiffs have not responded to Defendants' instant Motion or Joinder. Based on these uncontested facts, there is no doubt that had Defendants attempted to meet and confer with Plaintiffs such attempts would have been futile."); *Leibovitz v. City of N.Y.*, No. 15 Civ. 546 (LGS)(HBP), 2017 U.S. Dist. LEXIS 15662, at *3–4, 2017 WL 462515 (S.D.N.Y. Feb. 3, 2017) ("Plaintiff failed to comply with the requirements of Fed. R. Civ.P. 37(a)(1) . . . . Nevertheless, plaintiff and the City's counsel have appeared before me several times and there is clearly personal friction between them. Given this friction, I conclude that attempting to enforce the meet-and-confer requirement would do nothing to advance the action. I shall, therefore, excuse

3-5 Signing and Certification Requirements

Texas Rule 191.3 requires a party's attorney or a *pro se* party to sign all written discovery requests, responses, and objections.[41] "The requirement that discovery requests, notices, responses, and objections be signed also applies to documents used to satisfy the purposes of such instruments. An example is a statement that privileged material or information has been withheld, which may be separate from a response to the discovery request but is nevertheless part of the response."[42]

A signature on a disclosure is a "certification that to the best of the signer's knowledge, information, and belief, formed after a reasonable inquiry, the disclosure is complete and correct as of the time it is made."[43] A signature on a discovery request, notice, response, objection, or privilege assertion also is "a certification that to the

---

plaintiff's failure to comply with the meet-and-confer requirement and proceed to the merits of the dispute."), *Coultas v. Payne*, No. 3:11-cv-45-AC, 2013 U.S. Dist. LEXIS 63886, at *4–5, 2013 WL 1870545 (D. Or. May 3, 2013) ("Where the court seeks to excuse the conferral requirement, it should evaluate whether the failure to confer prejudiced the non-moving party. However, where, as here, the parties have a pattern of interaction during the course of litigation that evidences the futility of conferral, conferral may be excused. Here, Coultas has repeatedly litigated an issue that the court has decided, and the State Defendants reasonably concluded that further conferral would have been futile. Furthermore, there is no evidence that failure to confer was prejudicial to Coultas and Coultas did oppose the motion after the fact. Accordingly, on these facts, the court excuses the State Defendants' failure to confer.") (citations omitted), *Bolger v. D.C.*, 248 F.R.D. 335, 343–44 (D.D.C. 2008) (excusing the movant's failure to confer because of the opposing party's repeated refusals to comply with both the movant's requests and the court's discovery orders), *Armstrong v. Amstead Indus.*, No. 01 C 2963, 2004 U.S. Dist. LEXIS 12427, at *8–9, 2004 WL 1497779 (N.D. Ill. July 1, 2004) ("Amsted first argues that plaintiffs' motion should be denied because it does not comport with Local Rule 37.2, which requires a statement from the movant that a consultation between the parties was unable to resolve the discovery dispute or at least that attempts to schedule a consultation were made but were unsuccessful due to no fault of the movant. Though plaintiffs' motion does not contain such a statement and apparently no consultation was attempted, we accept plaintiffs' contention that a meeting between the parties would have been fruitless, given plaintiffs' desired sanction."), *Reidy v. Runyon*, 169 F.R.D. 486, 490 (E.D.N.Y. 1997) (excusing a failure to confer because compromise was unlikely given defendant's history of noncompliance with court orders), *and Oleson v. Kmart Corp.*, 175 F.R.D. 570, 571 (D. Kan. 1997) (excusing movant's failure to confer before filing a motion to compel because it was apparent to the court, based on the number and tenor of discovery disputes that were the subject of the motion, that it was unlikely parties would have resolved their differences).

41 Tex. R. Civ. P. 191.3(a) ("Every disclosure, discovery request, notice, response, and objection must be signed: (1) by an attorney, if the party is represented by an attorney, and must show the attorney's State Bar of Texas identification number, address, telephone number, and fax number, if any; or (2) by the party, if the party is not represented by an attorney, and must show the party's address, telephone number, and fax number, if any."). Texas Rule 191.3(a) does not yet require the signature block to contain the attorney's or *pro se* party's email address. *Cf.* Tex. R. Civ. P. 57 (requiring a pleading's signature block to contain email addresses).

42 Tex. R. Civ. P. 191 cmt. 3 to 1999 change.

43 Tex. R. Civ. P. 191.3(b).

best of the signer's knowledge, information, and belief, formed after a reasonable inquiry, the request, notice, response, or objection:"

(1) is consistent with the rules of civil procedure and these discovery rules are warranted by existing law or a good faith argument for the extension, modification, or reversal of existing law;

(2) has a good faith factual basis;

(3) is not interposed for any improper purpose, such as to harass or to cause unnecessary delay or needless increase in the cost of litigation; and

(4) is not unreasonable or unduly burdensome or expensive, given the needs of the case, the discovery already had in the case, the amount in controversy, and the importance of the issues at stake in the litigation.[44]

This certification is broader than the general one under Texas Rule 13, which provides that "[t]he signatures of attorneys or parties constitute a certificate by them that they have read the pleading, motion, or other paper; that to the best of their knowledge, information, and belief formed after reasonable inquiry the instrument is not groundless and brought in bad faith or groundless and brought for the purpose of harassment."[45] Texas Rule 191.3's certification is similar to the certification for pleadings and motions required by Section 10.001 of the Texas Civil Practice and Remedies Code.[46]

The purpose of Texas Rule 191.3's certification is to deter discovery abuse by requiring the person making the certification to carefully consider the propriety of the discovery request, notice, response, objection, or privilege assertion before signing it. "If the certification is false without substantial justification, the court may, upon motion or its own initiative, impose on the person who made the certification, or the party on whose behalf the request, notice, response, or objection was made, or both,

---

[44] Tex. R. Civ. P. 191.3(c)(1)–(4).

[45] Tex. R. Civ. P. 13.

[46] Section 10.001 provides:

> The signing of a pleading or motion as required by the Texas Rules of Civil Procedure constitutes a certificate by the signatory that to the signatory's best knowledge, information, and belief, formed after reasonable inquiry:
>
> (1) the pleading or motion is not being presented for any improper purpose, including to harass or to cause unnecessary delay or needless increase in the cost of litigation;
>
> (2) each claim, defense, or other legal contention in the pleading or motion is warranted by existing law or by a nonfrivolous argument for the extension, modification, or reversal of existing law or the establishment of new law;
>
> (3) each allegation or other factual contention in the pleading or motion has evidentiary support or, for a specifically identified allegation or factual contention, is likely to have evidentiary support after a reasonable opportunity for further investigation or discovery; and
>
> (4) each denial in the pleading or motion of a factual contention is warranted on the evidence or, for a specifically identified denial, is reasonably based on a lack of information or belief.

Tex. Civ. Prac. & Rem. Code Ann. § 10.001.

an appropriate sanction as for a frivolous pleading or motion under Chapter 10 of the Civil Practice and Remedies Code."[47]

A written discovery request, notice, response, objection, or privilege assertion that is not signed "must be stricken unless it is signed promptly after the omission is called to the attention of the party making the request, notice, response, or objection."[48] A responding party served with an unsigned written discovery request or notice need not respond or take any other action with respect to it.[49] A clerical error, however, such as a failure to verify interrogatory answers that is remedied when discovered, is harmless and does not invalidate the answers.[50]

3-6 Filing Discovery Materials

Texas Rule 191.4(a) prohibits the filing of all discovery requests directed to parties and all discovery responses, objections, and privilege assertions by parties and non-parties,[51] subject to the following exceptions: "(1) the court may order discovery materials to be filed; (2) a person may file discovery materials in support of or in opposition to a motion or for other use in a court proceeding; and (3) a person may file discovery materials necessary for a proceeding in an appellate court."[52] However, under Texas Rule 191.4(b), "[t]he following discovery materials must be filed: (1)

---

[47] Tex. R. Civ. P. 191.3(e); *see also Polansky v. Berenji*, 393 S.W.3d 362, 370 (Tex. App.—Austin 2012, no pet.) ("A court may impose sanctions on its own initiative under civil practice and remedies code chapter 10, Texas Rules of Civil Procedure 13 and 191.3, and its own inherent power, but it first must provide notice and a show-cause hearing to the person to be sanctioned."). Section 10.004(c) of the Texas Civil Practice and Remedies Code provides for the following sanctions: "(1) a directive to the violator to perform, or refrain from performing, an act; (2) an order to pay a penalty into court; and (3) an order to pay to the other party the amount of the reasonable expenses incurred by the other party because of the filing of the pleading or motion, including reasonable attorney's fees." Tex. Civ. Prac. & Rem. Code Ann. § 10.004(c).

[48] Tex. R. Civ. P. 191.3(d).

[49] Tex. R. Civ. P. 191.3(d) ("A party is not required to take any action with respect to a request or notice that is not signed."); *cf. Ingram v. State*, No. 09-10-00346-CV, 2011 Tex. App. LEXIS 8767, at *6–7, 2011 WL 5299475 (Tex. App.—Beaumont July 14, 2011, pet. denied) (mem. op.) ("The requests for admission in the record do not bear Ingram's signature. When a party receives requests that are not signed, the Rules of Civil Procedure do not require the party to take any action. Because Ingram's requests for admission do not bear his signature, the trial court did not err by failing to consider them as having been deemed admitted.").

[50] *Warriner v. Warriner*, 394 S.W.3d 240, 250 (Tex. App.—El Paso 2012, no pet.).

[51] Tex. R. Civ. P. 191.4(a) ("The following discovery materials must not be filed: (1) discovery requests, deposition notices, and subpoenas required to be served only on parties; (2) responses and objections to discovery requests and deposition notices, regardless on whom the requests or notices were served; (3) documents and tangible things produced in discovery; and (4) statements prepared in compliance with Rule 193.3(b) or (d)."). Improperly filing discovery materials, however, does not invalidate the materials. *See, e.g., Black v. Watts*, No. 04-17-00489-CV, 2018 Tex. App. LEXIS 6186, at *14, 2018 WL 3747746 (Tex. App.—San Antonio Aug. 8, 2018, pet. denied) (mem. op.) (Texas "Rule 191.4's text requiring certain discovery requests not to be filed was intended to alleviate storage problems of district clerks' offices. There is nothing in the text or the history of the rule to support Black's contention that a 'violation' of the rule somehow invalidates the discovery request.") (citations omitted).

[52] Tex. R. Civ. P. 191.4(c).

discovery requests, deposition notices, and subpoenas required to be served on nonparties; (2) motions and responses to motions pertaining to discovery matters; and (3) agreements concerning discovery matters, to the extent necessary to comply with [Texas] Rule 11."[53]

Texas Rule 191.4(d) requires parties and nonparties to keep unfiled discovery requests and responses during the action's pendency and "any related appellate proceedings begun within six months after judgment is signed, unless otherwise provided by the trial court."[54]

3-7 Service of Discovery Materials

Texas Rule 191.5 provides that "[e]very disclosure, discovery request, notice, response, and objection required to be served on a party or person must be served on all parties of record."[55] Although not expressly required by the Rule, the service requirement logically applies to any documents used to satisfy the purpose of those listed in the Rule, such as documents containing privilege assertions.[56] However, it does not apply to documents or other tangible things produced in discovery.[57]

Under Texas Rule 21a, service is made by delivering a copy to the party to be served, or the party's duly authorized agent or attorney of record in the manner specified below:

(1) **Documents Filed Electronically.** A document filed electronically under [Texas] Rule 21 must be served electronically through the electronic filing manager if the email address of the party or attorney to be served is on file with the electronic filing manager. If the email address of the party or attorney to be served is not on file with the electronic filing manager, the document may be served on that party or attorney under subparagraph (2).

(2) **Documents Not Filed Electronically.** A document not filed electronically may be served in person, by mail, by commercial delivery service, by fax, by email, or by such other manner as the court in its discretion may direct.[58]

---

[53] Tex. R. Civ. P. 191.4(b); *see also In re Daugherty*, 558 S.W.3d 272, 277 (Tex. App.—Dallas 2018, orig. proceeding) ("As between the parties, discovery materials are only to be filed if they pertain to motions and responses to motions before the court or agreements concerning discovery matters.").

[54] Tex. R. Civ. P. 191.4(d) ("Any person required to serve discovery materials not required to be filed must retain the original or exact copy of the materials during the pendency of the case and any related appellate proceedings begun within six months after judgment is signed, unless otherwise provided by the trial court.").

[55] Tex. R. Civ. P. 191.5; *see In re de la Cerda*, No. 12-12-00149-CV, 2013 Tex. App. LEXIS 1065, at *4, 2013 WL 451830 (Tex. App.—Tyler Feb. 6, 2013, orig. proceeding) (mem. op.) (holding that the trial court did not abuse its discretion in denying the plaintiff's motion to compel disclosures when the request was served on the court's clerk rather than on the defendant).

[56] *Cf.* Tex. R. Civ. P. 191.3 & cmt. 3 to 1999 change.

[57] *See* Tex. R. Civ. P. 176.6 (allowing nonparty to produce its subpoenaed documents to requesting party and other parties at specified time and place), 196.2–.3 (allowing responding party to produce its documents to requesting party and other parties at specified time and place).

[58] Tex. R. Civ. P. 21a(a)(1)–(2).

In Level 1 and Level 2 cases filed before January 1, 2021, the discovery period began when the cases were filed, and parties could serve written discovery with their original pleadings.[59] This is not permitted in cases filed on or after January 1, 2021 because Texas Rule 192.2 provides that, "[u]nless otherwise agreed to by the parties or ordered by the court, a party cannot serve discovery on another party until after the other party's initial disclosures are due."[60] The reason for the change is that initial disclosures might obviate the need for certain discovery or at least narrow or otherwise impact its scope.

A failure to serve discovery in accordance with the rules will likely excuse the party to whom it is directed from responding to it.[61] The Texas discovery rules also require service of written discovery, notices, responses, objections, and privilege assertions on the person to whom they are addressed.[62] Under Texas Rules 196.1(c) and 205.3(c), discovery requests for a nonparty's medical or mental-health records must be served on the nonparty.[63]

[59] *See* Former Tex. R. Civ. P. 194.3(a), 196.2(a), 196.7(c)(1), 198.2(a).

[60] Tex. R. Civ. P. 192.2(a); *see also* ***Final Approval of Amendments to Texas Rules of Civil Procedure 47, 99, 169, 190, 192, 193, 194, 195, 196, 197, and 198,*** Misc. Docket No. 20-9153, at 1 (Tex. Dec. 23, 2020), available at https://www.txcourts.gov/supreme/administrative-orders/2020 ("The amendments [in this Order] apply to cases filed on or after January 1, 2021, except for those filed in justice court.").

[61] *E.g., Holmes v. Graham Mortg. Corp.*, 449 S.W.3d 257, 261–62 (Tex. App.—Dallas 2014, pet. denied) (holding that the trial court did not err in refusing to consider allegedly deemed admissions in connection with the defendant's summary judgment motion because the requests for admission were not properly served on the defendant); *Approximately $14,980.00 v. State*, 261 S.W.3d 182, 186 (Tex. App.—Houston [14th Dist.] 2005, no pet.) ("A party's duty to respond is dependent upon receipt of the requests. Where service is not perfected, the receiving party cannot be made to suffer the consequences of not answering or untimely answering.") (citation omitted); *Payton v. Ashton*, 29 S.W.3d 896, 898 (Tex. App.—Amarillo 2000, no pet.) (affirming the trial court's refusal to consider alleged deemed admissions because the requests were not properly served on the defendant).

[62] *See* Tex. R. Civ. P. 196.1(c) (production requests), 196.7(a) (requests and motions for entry on land or other property), 197.1 (interrogatories), 198.1 (requests for admission), 205.2 (notices for nonparty subpoenas for documents or depositions).

[63] Tex. R. Civ. P. 196.1(c), 205.3(c).

CHAPTER 4

Permissible Discovery; Forms, Sequence, and Scope of Discovery; Work Product; and Protective Orders—Texas Rule 192

4-1 Text of Rule 192

RULE 192. PERMISSIBLE DISCOVERY: FORMS AND SCOPE; WORK PRODUCT: PROTECTIVE ORDERS; DEFINITIONS

192.1. Forms of Discovery

Permissible forms of discovery are:

(a) required disclosures;

(b) requests for production and inspection of documents and tangible things;

(c) requests and motions for entry upon and examination of real property;

(d) interrogatories to a party;

(e) requests for admission;

(f) oral or written depositions; and

(g) motions for mental or physical examinations.

192.2. Timing and Sequence of Discovery

(a) **Timing.** Unless otherwise agreed to by the parties or ordered by the court, a party cannot serve discovery on another party until after the other party's initial disclosures are due.

(b) **Sequence.** The permissible forms of discovery may be combined in the same document and may be taken in any order or sequence.

192.3. Scope of Discovery

(a) **Generally.** In general, a party may obtain discovery regarding any matter that is not privileged and is relevant to the subject matter of the pending action, whether it relates to the claim or defense of the party seeking discovery or the claim or defense of any other party. It is not a ground for objection that the information sought will be inadmissible at trial if the information sought appears reasonably calculated to lead to the discovery of admissible evidence.

(b) **Documents and tangible things.** A party may obtain discovery of the existence, description, nature, custody, condition, location, and contents of documents and tangible things (including papers, books, accounts, drawings, graphs, charts, photographs, electronic or videotape recordings, data, and data compilations) that constitute or contain matters relevant to the subject matter of the action. A person is required to produce a document or tangible thing that is within the person's possession, custody, or control.

(c) **Persons with knowledge of relevant facts.** A party may obtain discovery of the name, address, and telephone number of persons having knowledge of relevant facts, and a brief statement of each identified person's connection with the case. A person has knowledge of relevant facts when that person has or may have knowledge of any discoverable matter. The person need not have admissible information or personal knowledge of the facts. An expert is "a person with knowledge of relevant facts" only if that knowledge was obtained first-hand or if it was not obtained in preparation for trial or in anticipation of litigation.

(d) **Trial witnesses.** A party may obtain discovery of the name, address, and telephone number of any person who is expected to be called to testify at trial. This paragraph does not apply to rebuttal or impeaching witnesses the necessity of whose testimony cannot reasonably be anticipated before trial.

(e) **Testifying and consulting experts.** The identity, mental impressions, and opinions of a consulting expert whose mental impressions and opinions have not been reviewed by a testifying expert are not discoverable. A party may discover the following information regarding a testifying expert or regarding a consulting expert whose mental impressions or opinions have been reviewed by a testifying expert:

(1) the expert's name, address, and telephone number;

(2) the subject matter on which a testifying expert will testify;

(3) the facts known by the expert that relate to or form the basis of the expert's mental impressions and opinions formed or made in connection with the case in which the discovery is sought, regardless of when and how the factual information was acquired;

(4) the expert's mental impressions and opinions formed or made in connection with the case in which discovery is sought, and any methods used to derive them;

(5) any bias of the witness;

(6) all documents, tangible things, reports, models, or data compilations that have been provided to, reviewed by, or prepared by or for the expert in anticipation of a testifying expert's testimony;

(7) the expert's current resume and bibliography.

(f) **Indemnity and insuring agreements.** Except as otherwise provided by law, a party may obtain discovery of the existence and contents of any indemnity or insurance agreement under which any person may be liable to satisfy part or all of a judgment rendered in the action or to indemnify or reimburse for payments made to satisfy the judgment. Information concerning the indemnity or insurance agreement is not by reason of disclosure admissible in evidence at trial.

(g) **Settlement agreements.** A party may obtain discovery of the existence and contents of any relevant portions of a settlement agreement. Information concerning a settlement agreement is not by reason of disclosure admissible in evidence at trial.

(h) **Statements of persons with knowledge of relevant facts.** A party may obtain discovery of the statement of any person with knowledge of relevant facts—a "witness statement"—regardless of when the statement was made. A witness statement is (1) a written statement signed or otherwise adopted or approved in writing by the person making it, or (2) a stenographic, mechanical, electrical, or other type of recording of a witness's oral statement, or any substantially verbatim transcription of such a recording. Notes taken during a conversation or interview with a witness are not a witness statement. Any person may obtain, upon written request, his or her own statement concerning the lawsuit, which is in the possession, custody or control of any party.

(i) **Potential parties.** A party may obtain discovery of the name, address, and telephone number of any potential party.

(j) **Contentions.** A party may obtain discovery of any other party's legal contentions and the factual bases for those contentions.

192.4. Limitations on Scope of Discovery

The discovery methods permitted by these rules should be limited by the court if it determines, on motion or on its own initiative and on reasonable notice, that:

(a) the discovery sought is unreasonably cumulative or duplicative, or is obtainable from some other source that is more convenient, less burdensome, or less expensive; or

(b) the burden or expense of the proposed discovery outweighs its likely benefit, taking into account the needs of the case, the amount in controversy, the parties' resources, the importance of the issues at stake in the litigation, and the importance of the proposed discovery in resolving the issues.

192.5. Work Product

(a) **Work product defined.** Work product comprises:

(1) material prepared or mental impressions developed in anticipation of litigation or for trial by or for a party or a party's representatives, including the party's attorneys, consultants, sureties, indemnitors, insurers, employees, or agents; or

(2) a communication made in anticipation of litigation or for trial between a party and the party's representatives or among a party's representatives, including the party's attorneys, consultants, sureties, indemnitors, insurers, employees, or agents.

(b) **Protection of work product**

(1) **Protection of core work product—attorney mental processes.** Core work product—the work product of an attorney or an attorney's

representative that contains the attorney's or the attorney's representative's mental impressions, opinions, conclusions, or legal theories—is not discoverable.

(2) **Protection of other work product.** Any other work product is discoverable only upon a showing that the party seeking discovery has substantial need of the materials in the preparation of the party's case and that the party is unable without undue hardship to obtain the substantial equivalent of the material by other means.

(3) **Incidental disclosure of attorney mental processes.** It is not a violation of subparagraph (1) if disclosure ordered pursuant to subparagraph (2) incidentally discloses by inference attorney mental processes otherwise protected under subparagraph (1).

(4) **Limiting disclosure of mental processes.** If a court orders discovery of work product pursuant to subparagraph (2), the court must—insofar as possible—protect against disclosure of the mental impressions, opinions, conclusions, or legal theories not otherwise discoverable.

(c) **Exceptions.** Even if made or prepared in anticipation of litigation or for trial, the following is not work product protected from discovery:

(1) information discoverable under Rule 192.3 concerning experts, trial witnesses, witness statements, and contentions;

(2) trial exhibits ordered disclosed under Rule 166 or Rule 190.4;

(3) the name, address, and telephone number of any potential party or any person with knowledge of relevant facts;

(4) any photograph or electronic image of underlying facts (e.g., a photograph of the accident scene) or a photograph or electronic image of any sort that a party intends to offer into evidence; and

(5) any work product created under circumstances within an exception to the attorney-client privilege in *Rule 503(d) of the Rules of Evidence.*

(d) **Privilege.** For purposes of these rules, an assertion that material or information is work product is an assertion of privilege.

192.6. Protective Orders

(a) **Motion.** A person from whom discovery is sought, and any other person affected by the discovery request, may move within the time permitted for response to the discovery request for an order protecting that person from the discovery sought. A person should not move for protection when an objection to written discovery or an assertion of privilege is appropriate, but a motion does not waive the objection or assertion of privilege. If a person seeks protection regarding the time or place of discovery, the person must state a reasonable time and place for discovery with which the person will comply. A person must comply with a request to the extent protection is not sought unless it is unreasonable under the circumstances to do so before obtaining a ruling on the motion.

(b) **Order.** To protect the movant from undue burden, unnecessary expense, harassment, annoyance, or invasion of personal, constitutional, or property rights, the court may make any order in the interest of justice and may—among other things—order that:

(1) the requested discovery not be sought in whole or in part;

(2) the extent or subject matter of discovery be limited;

(3) the discovery not be undertaken at the time or place specified;

(4) the discovery be undertaken only by such method or upon such terms and conditions or at the time and place directed by the court;

(5) the results of discovery be sealed or otherwise protected, subject to the provisions of Rule 76a.

192.7. Definitions

As used in these rules –

(a) *Written discovery* means required disclosures, requests for production and inspection of documents and tangible things, requests for entry onto property, interrogatories, and requests for admission.

(b) *Possession, custody, or control* of an item means that the person either has physical possession of the item or has a right to possession of the item that is equal or superior to the person who has physical possession of the item.

(c) A *testifying expert* is an expert who may be called to testify as an expert witness at trial.

(d) A *consulting expert* is an expert who has been consulted, retained, or specially employed by a party in anticipation of litigation or in preparation for trial, but who is not a testifying expert.

Comments to Texas Rule 192

Comments to 1999 change:

1. While the scope of discovery is quite broad, it is nevertheless confined by the subject matter of the case and reasonable expectations of obtaining information that will aid resolution of the dispute. The rule must be read and applied in that context. *See In re American Optical Corp.*, __ S.W.2d ___ (Tex. 1998) (per curiam); *K-Mart v. Sanderson*, 937 S.W.2d 429 (Tex. 1996) (per curiam); *Dillard Dept. Stores v. Hall*, 909 S.W.2d 491 (Tex. 1995) (per curiam); *Texaco, Inc. v. Sanderson*, 898 S.W.2d 813 (Tex. 1995) (per curiam); *Loftin v. Martin*, 776 S.W.2d 145, 148 (Tex. 1989).

2. The definition of documents and tangible things has been revised to clarify that things relevant to the subject matter of the action are within the scope of discovery regardless of their form.

3. Rule 192.3(c) makes discoverable a "brief statement of each identified person's connection with the case." This provision does not contemplate a narrative statement of the facts the person knows, but at most a few words describing the person's identity as relevant to the lawsuit (for instance, "treating physician," "eyewitness," "chief financial officer," "director," "plaintiff's mother and eyewitness to accident"). The rule is intended to be consistent with *Axelson, Inc. v. McIlhany*, 798 S.W.2d 550 (Tex. 1990).

4. Rule 192.3(g) does not suggest that settlement agreements in other cases are relevant or irrelevant.

5. Rule 192.3(j) makes a party's legal and factual contentions discoverable but does not require more than a basic statement of those contentions and does not require a marshalling of evidence.

6. The sections in former Rule 166b concerning land and medical records are not included in this rule. They remain within the scope of discovery and are discussed in other rules.

7. The court's power to limit discovery based on the needs and circumstances of the case is expressly stated in Rule 192.4. The provision is taken from Rule 26(b)(2) of the Federal Rules of Civil Procedure. Courts should limit discovery under this rule only to prevent unwarranted delay and expense as stated more fully in the rule. A court abuses its discretion in unreasonably restricting a party's access to information through discovery.

8. Work product is defined for the first time and its exceptions stated. Work product replaces the "attorney work product" and "party communication" discovery exemptions from former Rule 166b.

9. Elimination of the "witness statement" exemption does not render all witness statements automatically discoverable but subjects them to the same rules concerning the scope of discovery and privileges applicable to other documents or tangible things.

4-1:1 2021 Amendments to the Texas Rules of Civil Procedure

The 2021 amendments to the Texas Rules of Civil Procedure modified Texas Rule 192 in two respects. First, references to "requests for disclosure" (in former Texas Rules 192.1(a) and 192.7(a)) were replaced with references to "required disclosures," which were added to Texas Rule 194 as part of the 2021 amendments. Second, Texas Rule 192.2 was modified by adding subpart (a), providing: "Unless otherwise agreed to by the parties or ordered by the court, a party cannot serve discovery on another party until after the other party's initial disclosures are due."

4-2 Discovery Types, Timing, and Sequence

Texas Rule 192.1 identifies the seven permissible forms of discovery: "(a) required disclosures; (b) requests for production and inspection of documents and tangible things; (c) requests and motions for entry upon and examination of real property; (d) interrogatories; (e) requests for admission; (f) oral or written depositions; and (g) motions for mental or physical examinations."[1] A separate rule governs each form of discovery as well as discovery from nonparties.[2]

---

[1] Tex. R. Civ. P. 192.1.

[2] *E.g.*, Tex. R. Civ. P. 194 (required disclosures), 196 (production requests), 197 (interrogatories), 198 (requests for admission), 199 (oral depositions), 200 (depositions on written questions), 202 (depositions before suit or to investigate claims), and 205 (nonparty discovery requests).

The 2021 amendments added the following standard for discovery's timing: "Unless otherwise agreed to by the parties or ordered by the court, a party cannot serve discovery on another party until after the other party's initial disclosures are due."[3] The default requirement for initial disclosures to precede other forms of discovery recognizes that the content of a party's initial disclosures may negate the need for additional discovery in relation to that party, or affect the scope or nature of such additional discovery. Of course, initial disclosures are not required in every case[4] and, even when they are required, it might not make sense to begin with them (e.g., when a party is in poor health and needs to be deposed immediately).

Texas Rule 192.2(a)'s exceptions to the default requirement—by agreement or order—acknowledge that case-specific needs may warrant case-specific timing. Texas Rule 191.1 also allows modifications of default discovery procedures and limitations by agreement or order.[5] But, unlike Texas Rule 192.2(a), it states that the agreements generally must comply with Texas Rule 11 and that court-ordered modifications require "good cause."[6] An open question is whether those requirements apply to Texas Rule 192.2 agreements and orders. A plain, harmonious reading of Texas Rules 11, 191.1, and 192.2(a) suggests that Rule 192.2(a) agreements should comply with the requirements set forth in Texas Rule 191.1. The answer is less clear for the "good cause" requirement in Texas Rule 191.1. To err on the side of caution, when seeking an order under Texas Rule 192.2(a), a party should arm the court with good cause for the order sought.[7]

Other than initial disclosures, parties can use the forms of written discovery in any order or sequence and can combine them in the same document.[8] Thus, for example, a single document can contain any two or more of the following: (1) production requests, (2) interrogatories, (3) requests for admissions, and (4) deposition notices. Of course, a court, on motion, may issue an order prescribing discovery's sequence.[9] And a party wishing to establish a discovery sequence can move for a protective order prescribing such a sequence.[10]

---

[3] Tex. R. Civ. P. 192.2(a).

[4] *See* Tex. R. Civ. P. 194.2(d) (addressing proceedings exempt from initial disclosures).

[5] See Chapter 3, section 3–3 (discussing modifications to discovery procedures and limitations).

[6] Tex. R. Civ. P. 191.1.

[7] Anne M. Johnson, Kennon L. Wooten & Sarah A. Nocolas, ***Rules Update: What's New with the Texas Rules of Civil Procedure and Texas Rules of Appellate Procedure***, presented at 10th Annual State Bar of Tex. Advanced Trial Strategies CLE Course (Feb. 5, 2021).

[8] Tex. R. Civ. P. 192.2 ("The permissible forms of discovery may be combined in the same document and may be taken in any order or sequence.").

[9] Tex. R. Civ. P. 192.6(b)(4) (providing for protective orders that "the discovery be undertaken only by such method or upon such terms and conditions or at the time and place directed by the court").

[10] Tex. R. Civ. P. 192.6(b)(4) (providing for protective orders that "the discovery be undertaken only by such method or upon such terms and conditions or at the time and place directed by the court").

4-3 Discovery's Scope

4-3:1 In General

Although discovery's scope is largely within the trial court's discretion,[11] that discretion is limited by Texas Rule 192.3(a), which provides:

> In general, a party may obtain discovery regarding any matter that is not privileged and is relevant to the subject matter of the pending action, whether it relates to the claim or defense of the party seeking discovery or the claim or defense of any other party. It is not a ground for objection that the information sought will be inadmissible at trial if the information sought appears reasonably calculated to lead to the discovery of admissible evidence.[12]

Texas Rule 192.3(a)'s general provision relating to discovery's scope is virtually identical to that in former Texas Rule 166b.2(a), which, in turn, was modeled after former Federal Rule 26.[13] The crucial phrase in the definition—"relevant to the subject

---

[11] *E.g.*, *In re Nat'l Lloyds Ins. Co.*, 532 S.W.3d 794, 802 (Tex. 2017) (orig. proceeding); *In re State Farm Lloyds*, 520 S.W.3d 595, 604 (Tex. 2017) (orig. proceeding); *In re Graco Children's Prods., Inc.*, 210 S.W.3d 598, 600 (Tex. 2006) (orig. proceeding) (per curiam); *In re CSX Corp.*, 124 S.W.3d 149, 152 (Tex. 2003) (orig. proceeding) (per curiam); *In re Colonial Pipeline Co.*, 968 S.W.2d 938, 941 (Tex. 1998) (orig. proceeding) (per curiam).

[12] Tex. R. Civ. P. 192.3(a).

[13] In 2000, Federal Rule 26(b) was amended to provide a two-tiered discovery scope:

> Unless otherwise limited by court order, the scope of discovery is as follows: Parties may obtain discovery regarding any nonprivileged matter that is relevant to any party's claim or defense. . . . For good cause, the court may order discovery of any matter relevant to the subject matter involved in the action. Relevant information need not be admissible at the trial if the discovery appears to be reasonable calculated to lead to the discovery of admissible evidence[.]

Fed. R. Civ. P. 26(b)(1). Before its 2000 amendment, Federal Rule of Civil Procedure 26(b)(1) provided:

> Parties may obtain discovery regarding any matter, not privileged, which is relevant to the subject matter involved in the pending action, which it relates to the claim or defense of the party seeking discovery or to the claim or defense of any other party, including the existence, description, nature, custody, condition and location of any books, documents, or other tangible things and the identity and location of persons having knowledge of discoverable matter. The information sought need not be admissible at the trial if the information sought appears reasonable calculated to the discovery of admissible evidence.

Fed. R. Civ. P. 26(b)(1) (1999) (amended 2000); *see Sanyo Laser Prods., Inc. v. Arista Records, Inc.*, 214 F.R.D. 496, 498–99 (S.D. Ind. 2003) (comparing discovery's scope under the 2000 amendment to Federal Rule 26(b)(1) to the pre-2000 version of the Rule).

Federal Rule 26(b)(1) was dramatically amended effective December 1, 2015. The amended rule deletes "the 'reasonably calculated' phrase" and adds language requiring discovery to be relevant to the claims and defenses and "proportional to the needs of the case[.]" It also incorporates several factors that should be considered in determining whether a discovery request is proportional to the needs of the case, including the importance of the issues at stake in the case, the amount in controversy, the parties' relative access to relevant information, the parties' resources, the importance of the discovery in matter of the pending action"—has been construed broadly. For example, the United States Supreme Court has interpreted the comparable phrase in Federal Rule 26 "to encompass any matter that bears on, or that reasonably could lead to other matter that could bear on, any issue that is or may be in the case[,]" reasoning:

> Consistently with the notice-pleading system establish by the [Federal] Rules, discovery is not limited to issues raised by the pleadings, for discovery itself is designed to help define and clarify the issues. Nor is discovery limited to the merits of the case, for a variety of fact-oriented issues may arise during the litigation that are not related to the merits.[14]

In Texas, the crucial phrase—"relevant to the subject matter of the pending action"—has been interpreted in a similarly broad manner to encompass all information that "appears reasonably calculated to lead to the discovery of admissible evidence."[15] The Texas Supreme Court has provided this guidance:

---

resolving the issues, and whether the expense of the proposed discovery outweighs the likely benefit. Amended Federal Rule 26(b)(1) reads, in full:

> Unless otherwise limited by court order, the scope of discovery is as follows: Parties may obtain discovery regarding any nonprivileged matter that is relevant to any party's claim or defense and proportional to the needs of the case, considering the importance of the issues at stake in the action, the amount in controversy, the parties' relative access to relevant information, the parties' resources, the importance of the discovery in resolving the issues, and whether the burden or expense of the proposed discovery outweighs its likely benefit. Information within this scope of discovery need not be admissible in evidence to be discoverable.

Under Federal Rule 26(b)(1), information and materials are discoverable if they are (1) not privileged, (2) relevant to a claim or defense alleged in the action, and (3) proportional to the action's needs. Fed. R. Civ. P. 26(b)(1).

14 ***Oppenheimer Fund, Inc. v. Sanders***, 437 U.S. 340, 351 (1978) (citations omitted).

15 Tex. R. Civ. P. 192.3(a); *see, e.g.*, ***In re Turner,*** 591 S.W.3d 121, 126 (Tex. 2019) ("Generally, 'a party may obtain discovery regarding any matter that is not privileged and is relevant to the subject matter of the pending action.' Further, '[i]t is not a ground for objection that the information sought will be inadmissible at trial if the information sought appears reasonably calculated to lead to the discovery of admissible evidence.'" (citations omitted) (quoting Tex. R. Civ. P. 192.3(a)); ***In re N. Cypress Med. Ctr. Operating Co.***, 559 S.W.3d 128, 129 (Tex. 2018) ("Our procedural rules allow broad discovery of unprivileged information that is 'relevant to the subject matter of the pending action.' This includes information that may ultimately be inadmissible at trial so long as it 'appears reasonably calculated to lead to the discovery of admissible evidence.'" (citations omitted) (quoting Tex. R. Civ. P. 192.3(a)); ***In re Nat'l Lloyds Ins. Co.***, 532 S.W.3d 794, 808 (Tex. 2017) (orig. proceeding) ("The scope of discovery extends to any unprivileged information that is 'relevant to the subject matter' of the pending action, even if inadmissible at trial, so long as the information sought 'appears reasonably calculated to lead to the discovery of admissible evidence.'" (footnotes omitted) (quoting Tex. R. Civ. P. 192.3(a) and *Ford Motor Co. v. Castillo*, 279 S.W.3d 656, 664 (Tex. 2009))); ***In re Nat'l Lloyds Ins. Co.***, 449 S.W.3d 486, 488 (Tex. 2014) (orig. proceeding) (per curiam) (same); ***In re CSX Corp.***, 124 S.W.3d 149, 152 (Tex. 2003) (orig. proceeding) (per curiam) ("Our procedural rules define the general scope of discovery as any unprivileged information that is relevant to the subject of the action, even if it would be inadmissible at trial, as long as the information sought is 'reasonably calculated to lead to the discovery of admissible evidence.'" (quoting Tex. R. Civ. P. 192.3(a))); *Eli Lilly Co. v. Marshall*, 850 S.W.2d 155, 160 (Tex. 1993) ("To effectuate the truth-finding function of the legal system,

We broadly construe the phrase "relevant to the subject matter" to provide litigants the opportunity "to obtain the fullest knowledge of the facts and issues prior to trial." Evidence is relevant if "(a) it has any tendency to make a fact more or less probable than it would be without the evidence; and (b) the fact is of consequence in determining the action." Although the scope of discovery is broad, a request for information "must show a reasonable expectation of obtaining information that will aid the dispute's resolution."

The discovery guideposts can be summarized as follows: only relevant evidence is discoverable; relevant evidence that is privileged is not discoverable; relevant evidence that is not privileged is discoverable when (i) it is admissible or (ii) it is inadmissible but reasonably calculated to lead to the discovery of admissible evidence; and failing either of those admissibility criteria, the request for discovery may be denied even if the requested information is relevant and unprivileged.[16]

Under the Texas discovery rules, however, discovery is limited in two important respects. *First*, it is limited to the causes of action and defenses identified in the pleadings and cannot be used to develop new ones.[17]

---

discovery is not limited to what may be admissible at trial, but includes any information relevant to the pending subject matter that is reasonably calculated to lead to the discovery of admissible evidence."); *Lindsey v. O'Neill*, 689 S.W.2d 400, 402 (Tex. 1985) (orig. proceeding) (per curiam) (Under former Texas Rule 166b(2)(a), "the scope of discoverable information shall include 'any matter which is relevant to the subject matter in the pending action whether it relates to the claim or defense of the party seeking discovery or the claim or defense of any other party.' Discoverability is likewise not limited to admissible evidence, if the information sought appears reasonably calculated to lead to the discovery of admissible evidence." (quoting former Texas Rule 166b(2)(a))).

16 *In re Nat'l Lloyds Ins. Co.*, 532 S.W.3d 794, 808 (Tex. 2017) (orig. proceeding) (footnotes omitted) (quoting *Ford Motor Co. v. Castillo*, 279 S.W.3d 656, 664 (Tex. 2009), *Axelson, Inc. v. McIlhany*, 798 S.W.2d 550, 553 (Tex. 1990) (orig. proceeding), Tex. R. Evid. 401, and *In re CSX Corp.*, 124 S.W.3d 149, 152 (Tex. 2003) (orig. proceeding) (per curiam)).

17 *E.g., Dillard Dep't Stores, Inc. v. Hall*, 909 S.W.2d 491, 491–92 (Tex. 1995) (orig. proceeding) (per curiam) (holding that, in an action involving an alleged false arrest, discovery geared "to explor[ing] whether [the plaintiff] can in good faith allege racial discrimination" was an improper fishing expedition); *In re Walmart, Inc.*, 620 S.W.3d 851, 865 (Tex. App.—El Paso 2021, orig. proceeding) ("Because the scope of the language here permits the discovery of information that is irrelevant under the Families' pleaded theories and is not reasonably limited in scope, the trial court abused its discretion by allowing for overbroad discovery and essentially authorized a fishing expedition."); *In re Allstate Fire & Cas. Ins. Co.*, 617 S.W.3d 635, 643 (Tex. App.—Houston [14th Dist.] Jan. 7, 2021, orig. proceeding) ("Facts that may be of consequence to issues not raised by pleadings are not permissible areas of discovery. 'Discovery undertaken with the purpose of finding an issue, rather than in support of an issue already raised by the pleadings, would constitute an impermissible "fishing expedition" under [*In re Alford Chevrolet-Geo*, 997 S.W.2d 173, 180 (Tex. 1999)].'" (quoting *In re Am. Home Assur. Co.*, 88 S.W.3d 370, 376 (Tex. App.—Texarkana 2002, orig. proceeding))); *In re Brookshire Grocery Co.*, No. 12-06-00065-CV, 2006 Tex. App. LEXIS 6366, at *3, 2006 WL 2036569 (Tex. App.—Tyler July 21, 2006, orig. proceeding) (mem. op.) ("Parties must have some latitude in fashioning proper discovery requests. On the other hand, discovery may not be used as a fishing expedition to investigate new claims rather than to support existing claims.") (footnote omitted) (citations omitted); *In re Sears, Roebuck & Co.*, 123 S.W.3d 573, 578 (Tex. App.—Houston [14th Dist.] 2003, orig. proceeding) (defining an

Second, even though Texas Rule 192.3, unlike Federal Rule 26(b),[18] has not been amended to expressly require the requested discovery to be proportional to the action's needs, the Texas Supreme Court has recognized that "all discovery is subject to the proportionality overlay embedded in our discovery rules[.]"[19] Accordingly, proportionality always is a consideration in determining discovery's proper scope.

---

improper "fishing expedition" as "one aimed not as supporting existing claims but finding new ones"); ***In re Am. Home Assurance Co.***, 88 S.W.3d 370, 376 (Tex. App.—Texarkana 2002, orig. proceeding) (holding that "discovery undertaken with the purpose of finding an issue, rather than in support of an issue already raised by the pleadings, would constitute an impermissible 'fishing expedition' under the cases cited in [***In re Alford Chevrolet-Geo***, 997 S.W.2d 173 (Tex. 1999) (orig. proceeding)]").

18 See discussion in note 13.

19 ***In re State Farm Lloyds***, 520 S.W.3d 595, 599, 613–14 (Tex. 2017) (orig. proceeding); *see* ***In re Shipman***, 540 S.W.3d 562, 569–70 (Tex. 2018) (orig. proceeding) (per curiam) (quoting ***In re State Farm Lloyds***, 520 S.W.3d 595, 599 (Tex. 2017) (orig. proceeding), for the proposition that "all discovery is subject to the proportionality overlay embedded in our discovery rules[.]"); ***In re Wilcox***, No. 09-20-00271-CV, 2021 Tex. App. LEXIS 2042, at *10–11, 2021 WL 1031141 (Tex. App.—Beaumont Mar. 18, 2021, orig. proceeding) (per curiam) (mem. op.) ("The discovery ordered in this case lacks the proportionality and the restraint required by [***In re Shipman***, 540 S.W.3d 562 (Tex. 2018) (orig. proceeding)]. The trial court established some protocols for a third-party to search Wilcox's ESI, but in this business dispute, the trial court has ordered Wilcox to turn over his electronic devices and home computer, as well as his personal account and storage information to a third-party, and to allow intrusive discovery of personal electronic devices that contain vast amounts of information totally unrelated to any legitimate inquiry when it could have simply required Wilcox to run specific searches and produce responsive data narrowly tailored to the parties' dispute."); ***In re Methodist Primary Care Group***, 553 S.W.3d 709, 715 (Tex. App.—Houston [14th Dist.] 2018, orig. proceeding) (same); *cf.* Fed. R. Civ. P. 26(b)(1) (defining discovery's scope as encompassing "any nonprivileged matter that is relevant to any party's claim or defense and ***proportional to the needs of the case***" (emphasis added)). In ***In re State Farm Lloyds***, the Texas Supreme Court made clear that in adopting the proportionality test that it was keeping Texas discovery "procedures in line with their federal counterparts." ***In re State Farm Lloyds***, 520 S.W.3d 595, 613 (Tex. 2017) (orig. proceeding). Accordingly, even though the case involved electronic discovery, its proportionality analysis applies to all types of discovery. In that regard, the Texas Supreme Court recognized that the proportionality requirement derives primarily from Texas Rule 192.4, which, according to the Court, "expressly constrains the scope of discovery as to otherwise discoverable matters." ***In re State Farm Lloyds***, 520 S.W.3d 595, 604–05 (Tex. 2017) (orig. proceeding). Texas Rule 192.4 provides:

> The discovery methods permitted by these rules should be limited by the court if it determines, on motion or on its own initiative and on reasonable notice, that:
>
> (a) the discovery sought is unreasonably cumulative or duplicative, or is obtainable from some other source that is more convenient, less burdensome, or less expensive; or
>
> (b) the burden or expense of the proposed discovery outweighs its likely benefit, taking into account the needs of the case, the amount in controversy, the parties' resources, the importance of the issues at stake in the litigation, and the importance of the proposed discovery in resolving the issues.

Tex. R. Civ. P. 192.4.

"The proportionality inquiry requires case-by-case balancing in light of the following factors:" (1) the "[l]ikely benefit of the requested discovery";[20] (2) "[t]he needs of the case"; (3) "[t]he amount in controversy";[21] (4) "[t]he parties'

---

[20] With respect to this factor, the Texas Supreme Court noted:

> If the benefits of the requested form are negligible, nonexistent, or merely speculative, any enhanced efforts or expense attending the requested form of production is undue and sufficient to deny the requested discovery. In such cases, quantifying or estimating time and expenses would not be critical, as it may be when benefits clearly exist. At the opposite end of the spectrum, a particularized need for the proposed discovery will weigh heavily in favor of allowing discovery as requested but, depending on the force of other prudential concerns, may warrant cost-shifting for any "extraordinary steps" required.
>
> Courts should consider cumulative effects rather than viewing benefits and burdens in a vacuum. Here, for example, many similar cases arising from the same extreme weather event are currently pending against State Farm. The identification and retrieval process State Farm would have to develop for native-form production may be a ticket for one train only—exponentially increasing the burden when considered in the context of repeated litigation—or have broader utility, which could have a cumulatively reductive effect. The record does not tell us, but if there are likely uses for the identification and retrieval process beyond the instant mandamus cases, initial burden and expense may be substantially ameliorated, and if not, the burden and expense may be significantly enhanced.

In re State Farm Lloyds, 520 S.W.3d 595, 608 (Tex. 2017) (orig. proceeding) (footnotes omitted).

[21] In discussing this factor, the Advisory Committee Note to the 2015 Amendment to Federal Rule 26(b) points out:

> It also is important to repeat the caution that the monetary stakes are only one factor, to be balanced against other factors. The 1983 Committee Note recognized "the significance of the substantive issues, as measured in philosophic, social, or institutional terms. Thus the rule recognizes that many cases in public policy spheres, such as employment practices, free speech, and other matters, may have importance far beyond the monetary amount involved." Many other substantive areas also may involve litigation that seeks relatively small amounts of money, or no money at all, but that seeks to vindicate vitally important personal or public values.

Fed. R. Civ. P. 26, Advisory Committee Note to 2015 Amend. The Texas Supreme Court also noted:

> When the discovery rules were adopted, an explanatory guide explained an initial impetus for discovery constraints that rings just as true in today's electronic discovery frontier:
>
> > For four decades following adoption of the federal rules, discovery procedures were continually expanded. In the 1970's, however, it became apparent that unrestricted discovery could be used to undermine the cause of justice if litigants with resources and motive to do so could drive up the cost of litigation, effectively pricing their opponents out of court and delaying disposition. Innovations in computer word processing, facsimile transmissions, and photocopying quickly made it possible for litigants of even modest means to drive up litigation costs and by "burying" their opponents in voluminous "boilerplate" discovery requests or objections, often with little more than the touch of a button. Technological changes have greatly increased the volume of documents and things that can be discoverable in a lawsuit. These developments in discovery practice have been compounded by

resources";[22] (5) the "[i]mportance of the issues at stake in the litigation";[23] (6) "[t]he importance of the proposed discovery in resolving the litigation";[24] and (7) "[a]ny other articulable factor bearing on proportionality."[25]

The concept of "proportionality," however, does "not permit the opposing party to rely on boilerplate objections of disproportionality."[26] Rather, the responding party

---

> an unfortunate weakening of professional norms that in earlier times would have made misuse or abuse of discovery unthinkable.
>
> For these reasons, the amount in controversy plays a pivotal role in determining whether production in a specified form is justified given the burden or expense required to meet the demand

In re State Farm Lloyds, 520 S.W.3d 595, 610 (Tex. 2017) (orig. proceeding) (footnote omitted) (quoting Nathan L. Hecht & Robert H. Pemberton, *A Guide to the 1999 Texas Discovery Rules Revisions* (Nov. 11, 1998), available at: http://www.txcourts.gov/rules-forms/rules-standards).

22 In discussing this factor, the Texas Supreme Court noted:

> Whether the producing party has the means to fairly and realistically produce in the requested format is a significant proportionality consideration. An expense that is a drop in the bucket to one party, may be insurmountable to another. While this factor is important to the balancing inquiry "considerations of the parties' resources does not foreclose discovery requests addressed to an impecunious party, nor justify unlimited discovery requests addressed to a wealthy party." Rather, "'the court must apply the standards in an even-handed manner that will prevent use of discovery to wage a war of attrition or as a device to coerce a party, whether financially weak or affluent.'"

In re State Farm Lloyds, 520 S.W.3d 595, 610–11 (Tex. 2017) (orig. proceeding) (footnotes omitted) (quoting Fed. R. Civ. P. 26, Advisory Committee Note to 2015 Amend. (quoting Fed. R. Civ. P. 26, Advisory Committee Note to 1983 Amend.)).

23 In discussing this factor, the Texas Supreme Court noted:

> Legal disputes are always important to those who are litigating them. For one side, however, the precedential value may be more significant than the other, justifying an outlay of time and expenses that would otherwise be unwarranted. Likewise, "'many cases in public policy spheres, such as employment practices, free speech, and other matters, may have importance far beyond the monetary amount involved.' Many other substantive areas also may involve litigation that seeks relatively small amounts of money, or no money at all, but that seeks to vindicate vitally important personal or public values."

In re State Farm Lloyds, 520 S.W.3d 595, 611 (Tex. 2017) (orig. proceeding) (quoting Fed. R. Civ. P. 26, Advisory Committee Note to 2015 Amend.).

24 In discussing this factor, the Texas Supreme Court noted: "Discovery must bear at least a reasonable expectation of obtaining information that will aid the dispute's resolution. Reasonable discovery does not countenance a 'fishing expedition.'" *In re State Farm Lloyds*, 520 S.W.3d 595, 611 (Tex. 2017) (orig. proceeding) (quoting *In re Alford Chevrolet-Geo*, 997 S.W.2d 173, 181 (Tex. 1999) (orig. proceeding)).

25 *In re State Farm Lloyds*, 520 S.W.3d 595, 607–12 (Tex. 2017) (orig. proceeding). In discussing the seventh factor, the Texas Supreme Court noted: "Trial courts have flexibility to consider any articulable factor that informs this jurisprudential inquiry" (i.e., proportionality). *In re State Farm Lloyds*, 520 S.W.3d 595, 612 (Tex. 2017) (orig. proceeding).

26 *In re State Farm Lloyds*, 520 S.W.3d 595, 614–15 (Tex. 2017) (orig. proceeding) (footnote omitted). See also cases cited in note 27.

must object and support proportionality complaints with evidence if the parties cannot resolve a discovery dispute without court intervention, but the party seeking discovery must comply with proportionality limits on discovery requests and "may well need to . . . make its own showing of many or all of the proportionality factors." . . . Ultimately, the "court's responsibility, using all the information provided by the parties, is to consider [the proportionality] factors in reaching a case-specific determination of the appropriate scope of discovery."[27]

---

[27] *In re State Farm Lloyds*, 520 S.W.3d 595, 614 (Tex. 2017) (orig. proceeding) (footnotes omitted) (quoting *Carr v. State Farm Mut. Auto. Ins.*, 312 F.R.D. 459, 468–69 (N.D. Tex. 2015), and Fed. R. Civ. P. 26, Advisory Committee Note to 2015 Amend.); *cf. Hammler v. Franklin,* No. CV 18-5525-JGB (SP), 2020 U.S. Dist. LEXIS 245548, at *6–7, 2020 WL 7711832 (C.D. Cal. Dec. 11, 2020) (overruling "defendant's boilerplate relevance, overbreadth, and proportionality objections"); ***Oppenheimer v. Episcopal Communicators, Inc.,*** No. 1:19-CV-00282-MR, 2020 U.S. Dist. LEXIS 146398, at *6, 2020 WL 4732238 (W.D.N.C. Aug. 14, 2020) ("The Plaintiff's vagueness, ambiguousness, relevance, overbreadth, and proportionality objections are boilerplate objections. Such objections have been declared invalid by several courts.") (citing cases); *Jenkins v. Miller*, No. 2:12-CV-184, 2019 U.S. Dist. LEXIS 189290, at *7, 2019 WL 5561387 (D. Vt. Oct. 29, 2019) ("Formulaic 'boilerplate' language in a discovery objection on proportionality grounds cannot overcome the broad scope of discovery under [Federal] Rule 26."); *Deutsche Bank Nat'l Tr. Co. as Tr. for Ameriquest Mortgage Sec. Inc. v. Pink*, No. 7:18-CV-00020-O-BP, 2019 U.S. Dist. LEXIS 15732, at *13, 2019 WL 399533 (N.D. Tex. Jan. 31, 2019) (Federal "Rule 26(b) (1) is not 'intended to permit the opposing party to refuse discovery simply by making a boilerplate objection that it is not proportional.'" (quoting *Carr v. State Farm Mut. Auto. Ins. Co.*, 312 F.R.D 459, 468 (N.D. Tex. 2015))); *Bragel Int'l, Inc. v. Kohl's Dep't Stores*, No. CV 17-7414 RGK (SSX), 2018 U.S. Dist. LEXIS 224955, at *16, 2018 WL 7890682 (C.D. Cal. Nov. 14, 2018) ("[F]ollowing the 2015 amendments to [Federal] Rule 26, courts have also rejected boilerplate assertions that a discovery request is 'disproportionate' and require that 'objections based on proportionality' be 'explained with specificity.'" (quoting *Polycarpe v. Seterus, Inc.*, 2017 U.S. Dist. LEXIS 77808, at *9, 2017 WL 2257571 (M.D. Fla. May 23, 2017))); *Nat'l R.R. Passenger Corp. v. Cimarron Crossing Feeders, LLC*, No. 16-cv-1094-JTM-TJJ, 2017 U.S. Dist. LEXIS 173452, at *12, *2017 WL 4770702* (D. Kan. Oct. 19, 2017) (mem. op.) ("The party resisting discovery bears the burden to support its objections based upon proportionality; it cannot refuse discovery 'simply by making a boilerplate objection that [the discovery sought] is not proportional.'" (footnote omitted) (quoting Fed. R. Civ. P. 26, Advisory Committee Note to 2015 Amend.))); *First Am. Bankcard v. Smart Bus. Tech., Inc.*, No. 15–638 SECTION "N" (2), No. 15-638, 2017 U.S. Dist. LEXIS 79508, at *3–4, 2017 WL 2267149 (E.D. La. May 24, 2017) ("All objections are overruled. The limited responsive information provided in response to these interrogatories is deficient. Again, defendant has offered nothing more than a boilerplate proportionality objection, without providing any information concerning burden or expense that the court would expect to be within defendant's own knowledge."); *see also Amos v. Taylor*, 4:20-CV-7-DMB-JMV, 2020 U.S. Dist. LEXIS 224295, at *23, 2020 WL 7049848, at *7 (N.D. Miss. Dec. 1, 2020) ("Examples of boilerplate objections include 'Defendant objects to this Request, as it is overly broad and vague' and 'Defendant objects to this Request to the extent it seeks discovery of information that is irrelevant and not proportional to the needs of the case.'" (quoting *Tim Long Plumbing, Inc. v. Kinsale Ins. Co.*, No. 4:20-CV-42, 2020 U.S. Dist. LEXIS 208897, at *9, 2020 WL 6559869 (E.D. Tex. Nov. 9, 2020))); *Harvard v. Inch*, No. 4:19CV212-MW/CAS, 2020 U.S. Dist. LEXIS 26677, at *6, 2020 WL 701990 (N.D. Fla. Feb. 7, 2020) ("Boilerplate objections such as . . . 'not proportional to the needs of this case' . . ., without an explanation, do not inform this Court or Plaintiffs of the justification underlying Defendants' objections. That is to say, boilerplate objections beg the question—why, for example, is the request vague or ambiguous? Further, they do not provide Plaintiffs a reasonable roadmap to correct any defect in their requests before asserting their remedies through a motion to compel. That Defendants subsequently attempt to provide specific objections in its response to Plaintiffs' motion to compel is unavailing.").

To a large extent, what is discoverable is set forth in Texas Rule 192.3, which first defines discovery's scope generally and then sets forth specific matters that are within its scope: (1) "the existence, description, nature, custody, condition, location, and contents of documents and tangible things"; (2) "the name, address, and telephone number of persons having knowledge of relevant facts, and a brief statement of each identified person's connection to the case"; (3) "the name, address, and telephone number of any person who is expected to be called to testify at trial" other than "rebuttal or impeaching witnesses . . . whose testimony cannot be reasonably anticipated before trial"; (4) information regarding testifying experts and consulting experts whose mental impressions and opinions have been reviewed by testifying experts; (5) "the existence and contents of any indemnity or insurance agreement under which any person may be liable to satisfy part or all of a judgment rendered in the action or to indemnify or reimburse for payments made to satisfy the judgment"; (6) "the existence and contents of any relevant portions of settlement agreements"; (7) "witness statement[s]"; (8) "the name, address, and telephone number of any potential party"; and (9) "any other party's legal contentions and the factual bases for those contentions."[28] Because the first item is covered by Texas Rules 196 and 205, which respectively govern production requests to parties and nonparties,[29] it is addressed in the chapters relating to party and nonparty production requests, Chapters 8 and 13, respectively. Because the second and fourth through ninth items are matters that a party is required to disclose under Texas Rule 194, they are addressed in Chapter 6, the chapter relating to required disclosures.

The third item—trial witnesses—as well as certain other types of information and material, are discussed below.

4-3:2 Trial Witnesses

Texas Rule 192.3(d) provides for the discovery of the "name, address, and telephone number of any person who is expected to be called to testify at trial."[30] The Texas discovery rules clearly distinguish between persons having knowledge of relevant facts and trial witnesses, and the disclosure of one is not the disclosure of the other.[31]

---

[28] Tex. R. Civ. P. 192.3(b)–(j).

[29] Tex. R. Civ. P. 196, 205.3.

[30] Tex. R. Civ. P. 192.3(d).

[31] *Compare* Tex. R. Civ. P. 192.3(c), ***with*** Tex. R. Civ. P. 192.3(d); ***see also In re E.R.A.***, No. 09-20-00042-CV, 2021 Tex. App. LEXIS re 2026, at *13–14, 2021 WL 1031142 (Tex. App.—Beaumont Mar. 18, 2021, no pet.) (mem. op.) ("A party may obtain discovery of the name of persons who have knowledge of relevant facts when those persons have or may have knowledge of any discoverable matter. A party may also obtain discovery of the name of any person who is expected to testify at trial, excluding rebuttal or impeaching witnesses, the necessity of whose testimony cannot reasonably be anticipated before trial.") (citation omitted); *Carlton v. Stewart*, No. 05-05-00888-CV, 2006 Tex. App. LEXIS 2839, at *6 n.1, 2006 WL 894879 (Tex. App.—Dallas Apr. 7, 2006, pet. denied) (mem. op.) ("In *Daredia v. Nat'l Distribs.*, [No. 05-04-00307-C, 2005 Tex. App. LEXIS 3168, at *9 (Tex. App.—Dallas, Apr. 28, 2005, pet. denied) (mem. op.)], this Court recognized that the rules of civil procedure clearly distinguish between persons with knowledge of relevant facts and intended trial witnesses, and we concluded that the two categories could not be interchanged for discovery purposes."); *cf. Queensberry v. Volvo Grp. N. Am., Inc.*, 267 F.R.D. 475, 479–80 (W.D. Va. 2010) ("The plaintiffs argued that requiring the disclosure of these nineteen class members at any time prior to February 23, 2010, would be tantamount to requiring that they disclose witnesses before the court-ordered date. This argument confuses two

Consequently, a person who is not disclosed as a trial witness in response to an interrogatory asking the sponsoring party to identify its trial witnesses should be excluded absent the party's showing of good cause for the failure to disclose the person or a lack of unfair surprise or prejudice to the other parties.[32]

Several questions arise with respect to Texas Rule 192.3(d). *First,* is a rebuttal or impeachment witness a person who is expected to be called to testify at trial? Such a witness is such a person unless his or her testimony could not reasonably have been anticipated before trial.[33]

---

separate requirements under [Federal] Rule 26. The witness list, indeed, was submitted to the defendants on the date set by the court for pretrial disclosures, in accord with [Federal] Rule 26(a)(3). However, the plaintiffs still had an obligation to disclose these individuals as persons likely to have discoverable information under [Federal] Rule 26(a)(1). Performance of one of these rules cannot be substituted for the other because they serve different purposes. The objective of [Federal] Rule 26(a)(3) is to list, after all the information has been gathered and discovery is closed, the witnesses who will be called by a party at trial and allow the opposing party to properly prepare to examine those witnesses. The aim of [Federal] Rule 26(a)(1), on the other hand, is to identify at the outset those persons that may have any information relevant to the case in order to allow for a complete investigation by all parties, thus allowing parties to depose, interview, or subpoena documents of such individuals during the period of time set aside for discovery.").

[32] *E.g.*, *In re E.R.A.*, No. 09-20-00042-CV, 2021 Tex. App. LEXIS 2026, at *14–15, 2021 WL 1031142 (Tex. App.—Beaumont Mar. 18, 2021, no pet.) (mem. op.) ("[T]he record reflects C.A. did not identify Santos in disclosures or interrogatories, and C.A.'s counsel admitted that despite knowing about Santos's impeachment evidence for a few weeks before trial, he failed to file a motion for leave to disclose her late. Because the record shows that C.A. knew about the necessity of obtaining Santos's testimony before trial and did not meet his burden of establishing good cause for his failure to timely disclose, we conclude that the trial court did not err by excluding the testimony."); *Daredia v. Nat'l Distribs.*, No. 05-04-00307-CV, 2005 Tex. App. LEXIS 3168, at *9–10, 2005 WL 977828 (Tex. App.—Dallas Apr. 28, 2005, pet. denied) (mem. op.) (holding that a witness who was identified as a person having knowledge of relevant facts, but not a trial witness, should not have been allowed to testify because the responding party failed to establish good cause or a lack of unfair prejudice or surprise).

[33] Tex. R. Civ. P. 193.2(d); *see In re E.R.A.*, No. 09-20-00042-CV, 2021 Tex. App. LEXIS 2026, at *14–15, 2021 WL 1031142 (Tex. App.—Beaumont Mar. 18, 2021, no pet.) (mem. op.) ("[T]he record reflects C.A. did not identify Santos in disclosures or interrogatories, and C.A.'s counsel admitted that despite knowing about Santos's impeachment evidence for a few weeks before trial, he failed to file a motion for leave to disclose her late. Because the record shows that C.A. knew about the necessity of obtaining Santos's testimony before trial and did not meet his burden of establishing good cause for his failure to timely disclose, we conclude that the trial court did not err by excluding the testimony."); *Christian v. Oceanwide Am., Inc.*, No. 01-19-00557-CV, 2020 Tex. App. LEXIS 10451, at *9, 2020 WL 7775762 (Tex. App.—Houston [1st Dist.] Dec. 31, 2020, no pet.) (mem. op.) ("Not every person who ultimately testifies at trial must be predisclosed. Under [Texas] Rule 192.3(d), a party is not required to disclose in discovery the identity of 'rebuttal or impeaching witnesses the necessity of whose testimony cannot reasonably be anticipated before trial.' The Texas Supreme Court has held that an unexpected need for a rebuttal witness may, under certain circumstances, constitute good cause." (citation omitted) (quoting Tex. R. Civ. P. 192.3(d)); *Schlein v. Griffin,* No. 01-14-00799-CV, 2016 Tex. App. LEXIS 3715, at *29, 2016 WL 1456193 (Tex. App.—Houston [1st Dist.] Apr. 12, 2016, pet. denied) (mem. op.) ("A rebuttal witness still has to be disclosed if the need to call the witness reasonably should have been anticipated."); *Homeyer v. Farmer*, No. 10-11-00009-CV, 2011 Tex. App. LEXIS 9316, at *26, 2011 WL 6004338 (Tex. App.—Waco Nov. 23, 2011, no pet.) (mem. op.) (same);

Second, is it proper to identify trial witnesses by using collective description, such as "employees," "insureds," "adjusters," "clients," or "customers" of a party or other person, or to identify an entity, such as a corporation or partnership? It generally is improper to do either because the clear purpose of Texas Rule 193.2(d) is to allow the requesting party to identify the specific individuals who the responding party expects to use as trial witnesses.[34]

Third, as Texas Rule 192.3(d) only requires disclosure of the witness's "address and telephone number," a question exists regarding whether the responding party should disclose an individual's home or work address and telephone number. Because

---

Fowler v. Samuel, No. 09-08-00348-CV, 2010 Tex. App. LEXIS 787, at *14–15 (Tex. App.—Beaumont Feb. 4, 2010, no pet.) (mem. op.) (same); *In re Commitment of Marks,* 230 S.W.3d 241, 245–46 (Tex. App.—Beaumont 2007, no pet) (same); *Moore v. Mem'l Hermann Hosp. Sys.,* 140 S.W.3d 870, 875 (Tex. App.—Houston [14th Dist.] 2004, no pet.) (same).

34 *See W. Atlas Int'l, Inc. v. Randolph,* No. 13-02-00244-CV, 2005 Tex. App. LEXIS 2199, at *21–22, 2005 WL 673483 (Tex. App.—Corpus Christi Mar. 24, 2005, no pet.) (mem. op.) ("[Texas] Rules 193.1 and 194.2(e) . . . require that parties provide complete responses to written discovery and disclose 'the name, address and telephone number of persons having knowledge of relevant facts,' with a brief statement of their connection to the case. Identifying a general category of people, without naming individuals or providing specific contact information, is insufficient to satisfy this requirement.") (citation omitted); *cf. Hernandez-Torres v. Intercontinental Trading,* 158 F.3d 43, 49–50 (1st Cir. 1998) (holding that the trial court did not abuse its discretion in excluding two of the defendants' former employees as witnesses for the plaintiff because the plaintiff's disclosure only identified "employees or representatives of the defendants" and not specific employees' names); *Alston v. DIRECTV, Inc.,* 254 F. Supp. 3d 765, 779–80 (D.S.C. 2017) ("Here, the court begins by concluding that DirecTV's reference to 'witnesses identified by DirecTV in Arnold' in its September 29, 2016 supplemental disclosure and in its initial disclosure, which presumably contained the same reference, is not sufficient to identify Hill for purposes of [Federal] Rule 26(a)(1)(A)(i)."); *Knox v. Jones Group,* No. 115CV01738SEBTAB, 2016 U.S. Dist. LEXIS 143887, at *5, 2016 WL 6083526 (S.D. Ind. Oct. 18, 2016) ("The Court clarifies that Defendants must identify all individuals that belong in the three categories of witnesses listed in their initial disclosures."); *Pritchett v. Werner Enters.,* No. 12-0182-WS-C, 2014 U.S. Dist. LEXIS 196684, at *3 n.1 (S.D. Ala. Feb. 11, 2014) ("The parties must provide the specific names of the individuals they might use as witnesses. It is not sufficient to identify them through the use of a collective description, such as 'employees or representatives of the defendant.'" (quoting *Womack v. Smith,* No. 1:06-CV-2348, 2012 U.S. Dist. LEXIS 52212, at *28 (M.D. Pa. 2012) (quoting 6 *Moore's Federal Practice* § 26.22[4][a][i]) (2012))); *Bibolotti v. Am. Home Mortg. Servicing, Inc.,* No. 4:11-CV-472, 2013 U.S. Dist. LEXIS 69242, at *16, 2013 WL 2147949 (E.D. Tex. May 15, 2013) ("In their initial disclosures, Defendants designated only the 'Custodian of Records and/or Corporate Representatives' of AHMSI. The plain language of the rule clearly requires a party to disclose the names of individuals with discoverable information. Thus, Defendants' initial disclosures did not comply with the requirements of [Federal] Rule 26."); *Smith v. Pfizer, Inc.,* 265 F.R.D. 278, 283 (M.D. Tenn. 2010) (ruling that the plaintiff did not comply with Federal Rule 26(a)(1)(A)(i) by listing as witnesses "friends and family of the deceased" and "defendants' employees and representatives"); *Labadie v. Dennis,* No. 1:07-cv-480, 2008 U.S. Dist. LEXIS 103754, at *6, 2008 WL 5411901 (W.D. Mich. Dec. 23, 2008) ("Plaintiff lists generic categories of persons, such as 'all members of plaintiff's family,' or 'all investigating persons.' This is patently insufficient and amounts to a non-disclosure."); *In re Sambrano,* 440 B.R. 702, 706 (Bankr. W.D. Tex. 2010) ("The contested witnesses were not listed by name in Hartford's initial disclosures; the initial disclosures merely listed 'employees and agents of Hartford' as persons likely to have discoverable information relevant to the case. The plain language of the rule requires the disclosing party to list the names of these individuals requirement.") (citation omitted).

Texas Rule 192.3(d)'s obvious purpose is "to allow the opposing party to easily locate, interview, and depose the proposed witness[,]"[35] the responding party should be able to designate the individual's home address and telephone number, work address and telephone number, another address or telephone number, or a combination of the foregoing so long as the address and telephone number disclosed are ones at which the person easily can be found, contacted, and subpoenaed.[36] A court, however, should generally order the responding party to provide an identified trial witness's home address and telephone number if the requesting party claims that they are needed to enable it to conduct a thorough background check of the person because a person's home address and telephone number generally are not private or confidential information.[37]

---

[35] *In re C.S.*, 977 S.W.2d 729, 732 (Tex. App.—Fort Worth 1998, no writ) (construing former Texas Rule 166b(2)(d), which allowed discovery of persons having knowledge of relevant facts); *accord Matthews v. S&A Rest. Corp.*, No. 14-98-00172-CV, 2000 Tex. App. LEXIS 4629, at *16–17, 2000 WL 963372 (Tex. App.—Houston [14th Dist.] July 13, 2000, no pet.) (not designated for publication); *$23,900 v. State*, 899 S.W.2d 314, 316 (Tex. App.—Fort Worth 1995, no writ); *Varner v. Howe*, 860 S.W.2d 458, 464 (Tex. App.—El Paso 1993, no writ).

[36] *Cf. Matthews v. S&A Rest. Corp.*, No. 14-98-00172-CV, 2000 Tex. App. LEXIS 4629, at *16–17, 2000 WL 963372 (Tex. App.—Houston [14th Dist.] July 13, 2000, no pet.) (not designated for publication) ("Here, S & A listed the officer by business address and phone number. This was sufficient. A single phone call to the storefront location does not establish Matthews's inability to contact the officer. Thus, the trial court did not abuse its discretion in allowing the officer to testify."); *$23,900 v. State*, 899 S.W.2d 314, 316 (Tex. App.—Fort Worth 1995, no writ) (holding that, under former Texas Rule 166b(2)(d), a police officer was properly identified in an interrogatory answer because he could be contacted through the information provided even though it was not the officer's correct station); *Varner v. Howe*, 860 S.W.2d 458, 464 (Tex. App.—El Paso 1993, no writ) (holding that, under former Texas Rule 166b(2)(d), a witness was sufficiently identified in an interrogatory answer because her nickname and employer's address and telephone number were provided); *Amsav Grp. v. Am. Sav. & Loan*, 796 S.W.2d 482, 486 (Tex. App.—Houston [14th Dist.] 1990, writ denied) (holding that, under former Texas Rule 166b(2)(d), a witness was sufficiently identified in an interrogatory answer that merely referred the requesting party to deposition testimony in which the witness was identified).

[37] *Cf. Pinkney v. Meadville, Pa.*, No. 1:19-CV-167, 2020 U.S. Dist. LEXIS 73669, at *11, 2020 WL 1985037 (W.D. Pa. Apr. 27, 2020) ("[A] person's home address is not ordinarily a private fact sufficient to support an action for publication of private facts."); *Limon v. Circle K Stores Inc.*, No. 1:18-CV-01689-SKO, 2020 WL 1503448 (E.D. Cal. Mar. 30, 2020) ("In class action suits, the disclosure of names, addresses, and telephone numbers is commonly allowed, because such disclosure 'does not involve revelation of personal secrets, intimate activities, or similar private information, which have been found to be serious invasions of privacy.'" (quoting *Artis v. Deere & Co.*, 276 F.R.D. 348, 353 (N.D. Cal. 2011))); *Thrasher v. CMRE Fin. Servs., Inc.*, No. No. 14–CV–1540 BEN (NLS), 2015 U.S. Dist. LEXIS 34965, at *6, 2015 WL 1138469 (S.D. Cal. Mar. 13, 2015) ("The disclosure of phone numbers and names does not constitute a serious invasion of privacy and is commonplace in class actions."); *Townsend v. Hosp. Bd. of Dirs.*, No. 2:10-cv-59-FtM-29SPC, 2010 U.S. Dist. LEXIS 103064, at *1–4, 2010 WL 3702546 (M.D. Fla. Sept. 16, 2010) (overruling the defendant's confidentiality objection to providing the residential address and telephone numbers of persons with relevant knowledge because such information is "necessary and may be used by Plaintiff's counsel to conduct background investigations of these witnesses for deposition and trial"); *Khalilpour v. CELLCO P'ship*, No. C 09-02712 CW MEJ, 2010 U.S. Dist. LEXIS 43885, at *6, 2010 WL 1267749 (N.D. Cal. Apr. 1, 2010) ("The disclosure of names, addresses, social security numbers, and telephone numbers is a common practice in the class action context."); *Thurby v. Encore Receivable Mgmt.*, 251 F.R.D. 620, 622 (D.

It is clear, however, that a responding party cannot properly disclose its attorney's address and telephone number for itself or its employees,[38] and courts have rejected the argument that the use of such an address and telephone number is justified by a concern that the requesting party may contact the responding party or its employees in violation of the ethical rules.[39]

Because Texas Rule 192.3(d) allows parties to best allocate their limited deposition hours by deposing expected trial witnesses and because trial witnesses are ***not*** subject to disclosure under Texas Rule 194.2,[40] an interrogatory should be used to secure the information discoverable about trial witnesses.

Colo. 2008) (holding that, under Federal Rule 26(a)(1)(A)(i), the responding party has to provide the disclosed persons home addresses and telephone numbers because "personal contact information, such as 'birth dates, home addresses or telephone numbers, e-mail addresses, or driver's license numbers' are not usually held as private, and instead are 'regularly disclosed to friends, relatives, vendors, credit card companies, schools, children's sports teams, and the like[,]'" accordingly, "the personal identifying information at issue here is necessary to allow the plaintiffs to conduct thorough background investigations . . . and that such investigations may lead to the discovery of admissible evidence." (quoting *Estate of Rice ex rel. Garber v. City & Cnty. of Denver*, No. 07-cv-01571-MSK-BNB, 2008 U.S. Dist. LEXIS 42381, at *20–21 (D. Colo. May 27, 2008))).

[38] *Cf. Bowman v. Green Tree Serv., Inc.*, No. 3-12-CV-31, 2012 U.S. Dist. LEXIS 146472, at *4–5, 2012 WL 4849616 (N.D.W. Va. Oct. 11, 2012) (holding that it was improper to provide the responding attorney's address and telephone number for persons having knowledge of discoverable information); *Hartman v. Am. Red Cross*, No. 09-1302, 2010 U.S. Dist. LEXIS 46126, at *2–3, 2010 WL 1882002 (C.D. Ill May 11, 2010) (same); *Viveros v. Nationwide Janitorial Ass'n*, 200 F.R.D. 681, 684 (N.D. Ga. 2000) (same); *Dixon v. CertainTeed Corp.*, 164 F.R.D. 685, 689 (D. Kan. 1996) (same). *But see Gibbons v. Luby's Inc.*, No. 02-12-00202-CV, 2015 Tex. App. LEXIS 9234, at *69–72, 2015 WL 5116146 (Tex. App.—Fort Worth Aug. 31, 2015, pet. denied) (mem. op.) (deciding, after examining case-specific facts, that a trial court did not abuse its discretion by overruling a party's objections to the presentation of two witnesses' testimony by deposition on the basis that the other side failed to supplement its disclosures to correct the witnesses' names and provide their personal addresses, rather than the addresses of their employer's attorney).

[39] *Cf. Hartman v. Am. Red Cross*, No. 09-1302, 2010 U.S. Dist. LEXIS 46126, at *2–3, 2010 WL 1882002 (C.D. Ill 2010) ("It may very well be the case that current supervisors and managers are represented by defense counsel and may not be contacted directly by Plaintiff's counsel. That question is not before the Court at this time. The apparent basis for Defendant's position on this question is an unspoken concern that Plaintiff's counsel will contact represented employees. That hypothetical concern, however, does not justify unilateral disregard for the disclosures mandated by [Federal] Rule 26(a). The Court will not engage in speculation that counsel might not act in accord with legal ethics. If the time comes that a concrete ethical issue arises, counsel for both parties shall bring the matter to the Court's attention."); *Dixon v. CertainTeed Corp.*, 164 F.R.D. 685, 689 (D. Kan. 1996) ("CertainTeed expresses concern that counsel for plaintiff will contact its employees outside its presence. It may not pose its concern as cause to unilaterally disregard its duties of disclosure under [Federal] Rule 26(a). Nor will the court indulge in speculation that counsel will unethically use the disclosed information. The court expects counsel to abide by the canons of legal ethics. It assumes attorneys will be ethical, absent some evidence to show otherwise."). If the responding party is concerned that the requesting party will violate the ethical rules and improperly contact its employees or others, it should move for a protective order under Texas Rule 192.6.

[40] Tex. R. Civ. P. 194.2. See also Chapter 6, section 6-3:3 (discussing Texas Rule 194.2 required disclosures).

4-3:3 Income Tax Returns

Public policy disfavors discovery of income tax returns.[41] This policy is founded in provisions of the Internal Revenue Code providing that federal income tax returns are confidential communications between taxpayers and the government.[42]

---

[41] *See, e.g.*, *Sears, Roebuck & Co. v. Ramirez*, 824 S.W.2d 558, 559 (Tex. 1992) (orig. proceeding) (per curiam) (providing that mandamus' issuance was "guided by [the court's] reluctance to allow uncontrolled and unnecessary discovery of federal tax returns"); *In re Potashnik*, No. 05-19-01188-CV, 2020 Tex. App. LEXIS 3399, at *5, 2020 WL 1933796 (Tex. App.—Dallas Apr. 22, 2020, orig. proceeding) (mem. op.) ("Tax returns are treated differently from other types of financial records. This is because federal income tax returns are considered private and the protection of that privacy is of constitutional importance."); *In re Vaughan*, No. 13-18-00541-CV, 2019 Tex. App. LEXIS 1445, at *9, 2019 WL 962381 (Tex. App.—Corpus Christi Feb. 27, 2019, orig. proceeding) (mem. op.) ("The Texas Supreme Court has cautioned us that we must scrupulously examine discovery requests for income tax returns to balance privacy rights and the pursuit of justice. . . ." (citing *Sears, Roebuck & Co. v. Ramirez*, 824 S.W.2d 558, 559 (Tex. 1991) (orig. proceeding) (per curiam), and *Maresca v. Marks*, 362 S.W.2d 299, 301 (Tex. 1962) (orig. proceeding))); *In re 7677 Real St., LLC*, No. 01-16-00683-CV, 2017 Tex. App. LEXIS 9299, at *18, 2017 WL 4366033 (Tex. Civ. App.—Houston [1st Dist.] Oct. 3, 2017, orig. proceeding) (mem. op.) ("In financial-records production cases, the burden generally lies with the party seeking to prevent production to show that the records are not relevant or are subject to a privilege. But tax returns 'are treated differently than other types of financial records.' The reason for this difference is that the Texas Supreme Court is reluctant 'to allow uncontrolled and unnecessary discovery of federal income tax returns,' because federal income tax returns are considered private and the protection of that privacy is of constitutional importance." (citations omitted) (quoting *In re Beeson*, 378 S.W.3d 8, 12 (Tex. App.—Houston [1st Dist.] 2011, orig. proceeding), and *Sears, Roebuck & Co. v. Ramirez*, 824 S.W.2d 558, 559 (Tex. 1992))); *In re Howeth*, No. 03-17-00286-CV, 2017 Tex. App. LEXIS 5699, at *6, 2017 WL 2729680 (Tex. App.—Austin June 22, 2017, orig. proceeding) (mem. op.) ("As an initial matter, we note that different burdens apply to the production of the tax returns and the accountant documents. The party seeking discovery of tax returns has the burden of showing their materiality and relevance. On the other hand, '[t]he general rule in financial records production cases is that the burden on the discovery of financial records lies with the party seeking to prevent production.'" (citation omitted) (quoting *In re Patel*, 218 S.W.3d 911, 916 (Tex. App.—Corpus Christi 2007, orig. proceeding))); *In re Brewer Leasing, Inc.*, 255 S.W.3d 708, 714 (Tex. App.—Houston [1st Dist.] 2008, orig. proceeding) ("The reason tax returns are treated differently from other discovery of financial information is because federal income tax returns are considered private and the protection of that privacy is determined to be of constitutional importance."); *cf. Premium Serv. Corp. v. Sperry & Hutchinson Co.*, 511 F.2d 225, 229 (9th Cir. 1975) (holding that, although tax returns do not enjoy absolute privilege from discovery, there is a public policy against unnecessary disclosure to encourage taxpayers to file accurate forms); *Progressive N. Ins. Co. v. Sampson*, No. 10-CV-566-GKF-PJC, 2011 U.S. Dist. LEXIS 76486, at *5–6, 2011 WL 2748678 (N.D. Okla. July 14, 2011) ("Whether or not characterized as a 'qualified privilege,' federal and state courts recognize the confidential nature of tax returns and disfavor disclosure.").

[42] I.R.C. §§ 6103, 7213(a) (2016); *see Payne v. Howard*, 75 F.R.D. 465, 469–70 (D.D.C. 1977) (noting that courts broadly construe Internal Revenue Code provisions making federal tax returns confidential communications between taxpayer and government as expressing a federal policy against disclosing tax returns generally).

Income tax returns, however, are not absolutely privileged. Rather, "they are discoverable to the extent they are relevant and material to the issues presented in the lawsuit."[43] Income tax returns are not "material" if the information in them can be obtained from another source.[44] If part, but not all, of an income tax return is

---

[43] *Hall v. Lawlis*, 907 S.W.2d 493, 494 (Tex. 1995) (orig. proceeding) (per curiam); *accord In re Vaughan*, No. 13-18-00541-CV, 2019 Tex. App. LEXIS 1445, at *10, 2019 WL 962381 (Tex. App.—Corpus Christi Feb. 27, 2019, orig. proceeding) (mem. op.) (citing cases); *see also In re Brewer Leasing, Inc.*, 255 S.W.3d 708, 714 (Tex. App.—Houston [1st Dist.] 2008, orig. proceeding) ("[Federal] tax returns may be discovered only when the pursuit of justice . . . outweighs the protection of privacy.").

[44] *E.g., Sears, Roebuck & Co. v. Ramirez*, 824 S.W.2d 558, 559 (Tex. 1992) (orig. proceeding) (per curiam) ("Sears disclosed its net worth to Perez by providing its audited and certified annual reports. An affidavit by the Manager of Federal Income Tax Returns for Sears states that the annual reports accurately reflect Sears' net worth. There is no indication that Sears' annual reports do not accurately reflect its net worth. Under the facts of this case, discovery of federal income tax statements in addition to the annual reports is unnecessarily duplicative. There is no justification for requiring Sears to produce the same information in different form. Our opinion in this case is guided by our reluctance to allow uncontrolled and unnecessary discovery of federal income tax returns."); *In re Berridge Mfg. Co.*, No. 04-20-00462-CV, 2020 Tex. App. LEXIS 9885, at *5, 2020 WL 7365455 (Tex. App.—San Antonio Dec. 16, 2020, orig. proceeding) (mem. op.) ("If there are other adequate methods to ascertain net worth, the trial court should not allow discovery of tax returns."); *In re Potashnik*, No. 05-19-01188-CV, 2020 Tex. App. LEXIS 3399, at *5–6, 2020 WL 1933796 (Tex. App.—Dallas Apr. 22, 2020, orig. proceeding) (mem. op.) ("[F]ederal income tax returns are not material if the same information can be obtained from another source." (citing *In re Sullivan*, 214 S.W.3d 622, 624–25 (Tex. App.—Austin 2006, orig. proceeding))); *In re Vaughan*, No. 13-18-00541-CV, 2019 Tex. App. LEXIS 1445, at *10–11, 2019 WL 962381 (Tex. App.—Corpus Christi Feb. 27, 2019, orig. proceeding) (mem. op.) ("[B]ecause of the privacy interests inherent in these documents, income tax returns may not be discoverable when there are other adequate methods to determine net worth. Further, income tax returns may not be subject to discovery when they would be duplicative of other information regarding net worth that has already been produced.") (citations omitted); *In re 7677 Real St., LLC*, No. 01-16-00683-CV, 2017 Tex. App. LEXIS 9299, at *18, 2017 WL 4366033 (Tex. Civ. App.—Houston [1st Dist.] Oct. 3, 2017, orig. proceeding) (mem. op.) ("Materiality requires a finding that the same information cannot be obtained from an alternate source. The party seeking the production must show why the discovery it has conducted and other potential follow-up discovery cannot reveal the requested information. Materiality is not shown by merely expressing frustration with the produced discovery or distrust of the other party.") (citations omitted); *In re Williams*, 328 S.W.3d 103, 116 (Tex. App.—Corpus Christi 2010, orig. proceeding) (same); *In re Brewer Leasing, Inc.*, 255 S.W.3d 708, 714 (Tex. App.—Houston [1st Dist.] 2008, orig. proceeding) ("But tax returns may not be discovered when the corporation has provided audited and certified annual reports to show the net worth of the corporation because the tax returns are unnecessarily duplicative of the information already provided. Further, if there are other adequate methods to ascertain net worth, the trial court should not allow discovery of tax returns.") (citation omitted); *In re Sullivan*, 214 S.W.3d 622, 624–25 (Tex. App.—Austin 2006, orig. proceeding) ("Federal income tax returns are not material if the same information can be obtained from another source. This limitation, as several of our sister courts have recognized, requires the requesting party to show that whatever relevant information contained in the federal income tax returns cannot be obtained through another source, such as interrogatories and depositions.") (citations omitted).

relevant, discovery should be limited to the relevant part.[45] Generally, income tax returns are relevant to show income[46] and possibly lost profits.[47] They, however, do

---

In determining whether to compel production of tax returns, many federal courts apply a two-prong test that requires findings that "[(1)] the returns are relevant to the subject matter of the action, and [(2)] there is a compelling need for the tax returns because the information is not otherwise readily obtainable." *Progressive N. Ins. Co. v. Sampson*, No. 10-CV-566-GKF-PJC, 2011 U.S. Dist. LEXIS 76486, at *2, 2011 WL 2748678 (N.D. Okla. July 14, 2011); *accord Donald William Fairbanks Architect, P.C. v. Fairfield Cnty. Contrs. LLC*, No. 3:14CV1079 (JAM), 2014 U.S. Dist. LEXIS 174729, at *11, 2014 WL 7271933 (D. Conn. Dec. 18, 2014); *Sadofsky v. Fiesta Prods., LLC*, 252 F.R.D. 143, 149 (E.D.N.Y. 2008). Other federal courts "have held that the appropriate analysis is limited to whether the tax returns fall within the scope of [Federal] Rule 26(b)(1)." *Queen v. City of Bowling Green*, No. 1:16CV-00131-JHM, 2017 U.S. Dist. LEXIS 160425, at *18, 2017 WL 4355689 (W.D. Ky. Sept. 29, 2017) (mem. op.) (citing cases).

Tax returns of entities are entitled to the same protection as those of individuals. *In re Brewer Leasing, Inc.*, 255 S.W.3d 708, 715 (Tex. App.—Houston [1st Dist.] 2008, orig. proceeding).

[45] *Maresca v. Marks*, 362 S.W.2d 299, 301 (Tex. 1962) (orig. proceeding) (holding that "the trial judge abused his discretion in ordering relators to produce for respondent's inspection and copying their entire income tax returns for the years in question without separation of the relevant and material parts from the irrelevant and immaterial parts thereof"); *In re 7677 Real St., LLC*, No. 01-16-00683-CV, 2017 Tex. App. LEXIS 9299, at *20–21, 2017 WL 4366033 (Tex. Civ. App.—Houston [1st Dist.] Oct. 3, 2017, orig. proceeding) (mem. op.) ("For the protection of privacy, a trial court is required to segregate the relevant and material portions of the returns from the portions that are not."); *In re Howeth*, No. 03-17-00286-CV, 2017 Tex. App. LEXIS 5699, at *11–12, 2017 WL 2729680 (Tex. App.—Austin June 22, 2017, orig. proceeding) (mem. op.) ("Although we recognize that the trial court attempted to safeguard Howeth's privacy with its protective order, that order does not go far enough to balance the privacy concerns underlying the protection of tax returns with the pursuit of discoverable information. In this case, redaction of the tax returns and accountant documents is necessary to limit disclosure solely to the discoverable information outlined in the order."); *In re Sullivan*, 214 S.W.3d 622, 625 (Tex. App.—Austin 2006, orig. proceeding) ("Where federal income tax returns contain relevant and material information, redaction, as the trial court ordered, may be advisable or necessary to limit disclosure solely to that discoverable information."); *cf. Queen v. City of Bowling Green*, No. 1:16CV-00131-JHM, 2017 U.S. Dist. LEXIS 160425, at *17–18, 2017 WL 4355689 (W.D. Ky. Sept. 29, 2017) (compelling production of portions of the plaintiff's joint tax returns that related his income but allowing the redaction of his wife's "financial information" and his "investment income and losses, charitable donations, other deductions, and child care"); *Johnson v. Kraft Foods N. Am., Inc.*, 236 F.R.D. 535, 539–40, 546 (D. Kan. 2006) ("[T]he Court will allow Plaintiff to redact any information contained on the returns that relates solely to his spouse or his dependents, as there has been no showing that this information is relevant to Plaintiff's claim for damages.").

[46] *See In re Williams*, No. 07-00-0136-CV, 2000 Tex. App. LEXIS 2362, at *7–8, 2000 WL 369687 (Tex. App.—Amarillo Apr. 11, 2000, orig. proceeding) (not designated for publication); *cf. Bourne v. Arruda*, No. 10-cv-393-LM, 2012 U.S. Dist. LEXIS 45938, at *9–10, 2012 WL 1107694 (D.N.H. Apr. 2, 2012); *Progressive N. Ins. Co. v. Sampson*, No. 10-CV-566-GKF-PJC, 2011 U.S. Dist. LEXIS 76486, at *3, 2011 WL 2748678 (N.D. Okla. July 14, 2011).

[47] *In re Guniganti*, No. 12-10-00199-CV, 2010 Tex. App. LEXIS 6624, at *6–8, 2010 WL 3232247 (Tex. App.—Tyler Aug. 17, 2010, orig. proceeding) (mem. op.) (holding individual tax returns were relevant to a showing that net profits were distributed); *D/FW Comm. Roofing Co. v. Mehra*, 854 S.W.2d 182, 187–88 (Tex. App.—Dallas 1993, no writ) (holding that there

not show net worth.[48]

---

was factually sufficient evidence of lost profits when tax returns were part of the evidence presented to the jury).

Tax returns may be admissible for other purposes as illustrated by the following cases: *In re Howeth*, No. 03-17-00286-CV, 2017 Tex. App. LEXIS 5699, at *11–12, 2017 WL 2729680 (Tex. App.—Austin June 22, 2017, orig. proceeding) (mem. op.) (holding that tax returns were discoverable to show whether a partnership existed); *Smith v. MPIRE Holdings, LLC*, No. 3:08-0549, 2010 U.S. Dist. LEXIS 15426, at *3, 2010 WL 711797 (M.D. Tenn. Feb. 22, 2010) ("The complaint in this case alleges that the Manuel defendants swindled plaintiffs out of $200,000 by means of a bogus investment scheme involving MPIRE Holdings, LLC and MRT Holdings. Defendants have generally denied wrongdoing and involvement with or control of defendant entities. To the extent that their tax returns show any income from or other relationship with the other defendants, including MPIRE or MRT, the tax returns are relevant to issues in this case."); *Elipas v. Jedynak*, No. 07 C 3026, 2008 U.S. Dist. LEXIS 122898, at *10–11 (N.D. Ill. Oct. 3, 2008) ("The Jedynak Defendants' finances are at the heart of Plaintiffs' case alleging fraud and theft of investors' funds. Plaintiffs allege that Jedynak, Howard, and Cummings fraudulently induced Plaintiffs and other investors to purchase membership interests in UWT and then diverted the bulk of the investors' money to themselves for their own personal use. Plaintiffs claim Jedynak took proceeds from his fraudulent membership sales in UWT and transferred them to various Jedynak Entities to conceal the funds that he received from the Plaintiffs and other investors. Plaintiffs say that Jedynak, Howard, and Cummings have failed to explain or account for what happened to in excess of $20,000,000 they received from the sale of UWT membership interests. Information regarding the alleged money trail may be gleaned from the tax returns."); *Burket v. Hyman Lippitt, P.C.*, Nos. 05-CV-72110, 05-CV-72171, 05-CV-72221, 2007 U.S. Dist. LEXIS 54529, at *12, 2007 WL 2214302 (E.D. Mich. July 27, 2007) ("[T]ax returns may be relevant to issues other than income. At the heart of many of Defendant Hyman Lippitt's allegations are issues about foreign trusts, foreign and offshore entities and any possible distributions to or from these entities. The tax returns are relevant to these issues. Tax returns are also relevant to allegations of financial impropriety and fraud."); *Shearson Lehman Hutton, Inc. v. Lambros*, 135 F.R.D. 195, 198 (M.D. Fla. 1990) (holding that the defendant's tax returns relevant to the plaintiff's claims of financial impropriety and conversion); *Benchmark Design, Inc. v. BDC, Inc.*, No. 88-1007-FR, 1989 U.S. Dist. LEXIS 8240, at *3, 1989 WL 81618 (D. Ore. July 5, 1989) ("The tax returns of the individual defendants may help ascertain the extent and nature of financial dealings between the individual defendants. Tax returns are discoverable in order to determine the interconnections between interrelated parties."); *Credit Life Ins. Co. v. Uniworld Ins. Co.*, 94 F.R.D. 113, 121 (S.D. Ohio 1982) (holding that the defendant's tax returns were relevant to whether personal jurisdiction existed over the defendant and to the plaintiff's "alter ego" theory).

48 *Hall v. Lawlis*, 907 S.W.2d 493, 495 (Tex. 1995) (per curiam) (orig. proceeding); *In re House of Yahweh*, 266 S.W.3d 668, 674 (Tex. App.—Eastland 2008, orig. proceeding); *In re Brewer Leasing, Inc.*, 255 S.W.3d 708, 711 (Tex. App.—Houston [1st Dist.] 2008, orig. proceeding); *Chamberlain v. Cherry*, 818 S.W.2d 201, 205–06 (Tex. App.—Amarillo 1991, orig. proceeding); *see In re Garth*, 214 S.W.3d 190, 193–194 (Tex. App.—Beaumont 2007, orig. proceeding) (per curiam) ("Here, the trial court's order requiring the production of tax returns exceeded the court's discretion for two reasons. First, the trial court's order required the production of certain financial statements regarding the individual's net worth, therefore, additional information showing only assets would not be relevant. Second, Kaiser failed to show how the tax returns would evidence the net worth of these individuals. Absent a predicate showing of relevance on the issue of net worth, the returns are not subject to discovery."). *But see In re Vaughan*, No. 13-18-00541-CV, 2019 Tex. App. LEXIS 1445, at *11, 2019 WL 962381 (Tex. App.—Corpus Christi Feb. 27, 2019, orig. proceeding) (mem. op.)

"[W]hen a party objects to the production of tax returns, unlike the production of other financial records, the party seeking to obtain the tax returns has the burden to show that they are relevant and material to the issues in the case."[49]

4-3:4 Financial Information, Bank Records, Net-Worth Information

A party's financial information, bank records, and net worth seldom are relevant for discovery purposes absent special circumstances.[50] Such material, however, can be relevant when it implicates a specific element of a claim or defense asserted in the action or the responding party's damages.[51]

("As applicable to this original proceeding, income tax returns may be relevant to discovering net worth.").

49 *In re Potashnik,* No. 05-19-01188-CV, 2020 Tex. App. LEXIS 3399, at *6, 2020 WL 1933796 (Tex. App.—Dallas Apr. 22, 2020, orig. proceeding) (mem. op.); *accord In re Berridge Mfg. Co.,* No. 04-20-00462-CV, 2020 Tex. App. LEXIS 9885, at *5, 2020 WL 7365455 (Tex. App.—San Antonio Dec. 16, 2020, orig. proceeding) (mem. op.); *In re Stagner,* No. 01-18-00758-CV, 2020 Tex. App. LEXIS 630, at *15, 2020 WL 370565 (Tex. App.—Houston [1st Dist.] Jan. 23, 2020, orig. proceeding) (mem. op.); *In re Vaughan,* No. 13-18-00541-CV, 2019 Tex. App. LEXIS 1445, at *11, 2019 WL 962381 (Tex. App.—Corpus Christi Feb. 27, 2019, orig. proceeding) (mem. op.); *In re Ming Chu Chang,* No. 13-15-00352-CV, 2015 Tex. App. LEXIS 10382, at *13–14, 2015 WL 5895197 (Tex. App.—Corpus Christi Oct. 8, 2015, orig. proceeding) (mem. op.); *In re 7677 Real St., LLC,* No. 01-16-00683-CV, 2017 Tex. App. LEXIS 9299, at *18, 2017 WL 4366033 (Tex. Civ. App.—Houston [1st Dist.] Oct. 3, 2017, orig. proceeding) (mem. op.); *In re Beeson,* 378 S.W.3d 8, 12 (Tex. App.—Houston [1st Dist.] 2011, orig. proceeding); *In re Patel,* 218 S.W.3d 911, 918 (Tex. App.—Corpus Christi 2007, orig. proceeding); *In re Sullivan,* 214 S.W.3d 622, 624 (Tex. App.—Austin 2006, orig. proceeding).

50 *See In re Potashnik,* No. 05-19-01188-CV, 2020 Tex. App. LEXIS 3399, at *4–5, 2020 WL 1933796 (Tex. App.—Dallas Apr. 22, 2020, orig. proceeding) (mem. op.) ("With respect to net-worth discovery, generally, only financial documents pertaining to *current* net worth are relevant. In the context of pretrial net-worth discovery, allowed when exemplary damages are sought, financial records are generally restricted to a twelve-month period.") (citations omitted); *In re Ameriplan Corp.,* No. 05-09-01407-CV, 2010 Tex. App. LEXIS 31, at *2, 2010 WL 22825 (Tex. App.—Dallas Jan. 6, 2010, orig. proceeding) (mem. op.) (holding that, though the plaintiff was entitled to discovery of the defendant's current net worth, it was not entitled to certain documents including "income statements or old balance sheets"); *In re House of Yahweh,* 266 S.W.3d 668, 673–74 (Tex. App.—Eastland 2008, orig. proceeding) ("However, the trial court erred in failing to limit discovery to relators' current balance sheet because earlier balance sheets would not be relevant to relators' current net worth.").

51 *See, e.g., In re Potashnik,* No. 05-19-01188-CV, 2020 Tex. App. LEXIS 3399, at *5, 2020 WL 1933796 (Tex. App.—Dallas Apr. 22, 2020, orig. proceeding) (mem. op.) ("In the context of pretrial net-worth discovery, allowed when exemplary damages are sought, financial records are generally restricted to a twelve-month period. When there is an allegation of fraudulent transfers, however, broader discovery of financial documents may be appropriate to trace the purported moving of assets and money to deflate net worth.") (citations omitted); *In re Daybreak Cmty. Servs. Tex., LLC,* No. 10-19-00395-CV, 2020 Tex. App. LEXIS 1623, at *5, 2020 WL 958457 (Tex. App.—Waco Feb. 26, 2020, orig. proceeding) (mem. op.) ("A defendant's net worth is relevant in a suit involving exemplary damages. Conversely, 'when punitive damages clearly are not recoverable, information about net worth is not relevant and, as a result, not discoverable.'" (citations omitted) (quoting *In re Islamorada*

Unlike tax returns, "there are no constitutional rights to privacy affected by disclosure of banking records or in personal financial records."[52] The general rule that the responding party has the burden to establish that they are not discoverable on relevance or other grounds applicable to such records.[53] Relevancy, however, is never

---

Fish Co. Tex., L.L.C., 319 S.W.3d 908, 912 (Tex. App.—Dallas 2010, orig. proceeding))); *In re Vaughan*, No. 13-18-00541-CV, 2019 Tex. App. LEXIS 1445, at *8, 2019 WL 962381 (Tex. App.—Corpus Christi Feb. 27, 2019, orig. proceeding) (mem. op.) ("Medina contested Vaughan's net worth, which entitled him to 'conduct reasonable discovery concerning the judgment debtor's net worth.'" (citations omitted) (quoting Tex. R. App. P. 24.2(c)(2))); *In re Gonzalez*, No. 14-10-01186-CV, 2010 Tex. App. LEXIS 9831, at *4–5, 2010 WL 5132590 (Tex. App.—Houston [1st Dist.] Dec. 14, 2010, orig. proceeding) (mem. op.) (holding that the defendant's bank records were discoverable because they were relevant to the plaintiff's claim that the defendant received payment for the sale of certain Federal Express routes); *In re Manion*, No. 07-08-0318-CV, 2008 Tex. App. LEXIS 6813, at *8, 2008 WL 4180294 (Tex. App.—Amarillo Sept. 11, 2008, orig. proceeding) (mem. op.) (holding that "financial information for the period [the defendant] was Stallion Manager is relevant and discoverable" in action alleging that the defendant used his position for financial gain in violation of his fiduciary duties); *cf. Daval Steel Prods., Div. of Francosteel Corp. v. M/V Fakredine*, 951 F.2d 1357, 1367–68 (2d Cir. 1991) (holding that bank records were relevant and discoverable in connection with an "alter ego" claim).

52 *Neely v. Comm'n for Lawyer Discipline*, 302 S.W.3d 331, 341 (Tex. App.—Houston [14th Dist.] 2009, pet. denied); *accord In re Manion*, No. 07-08-0318-CV, 2008 Tex. App. LEXIS 6813, at *6, 2008 WL 4180294 (Tex. App.—Amarillo Sept. 11, 2008, orig. proceeding) (mem. op.) ("[I]t has previously been determined that there is no constitutionally protected privacy right in one's personal financial records."); *Martin v. Darnell*, 960 S.W.2d 838, 844 (Tex. App.—Amarillo 1997, orig. proceeding) (same); *cf. In re Marriott Int'l Customer Data Sec. Breach Litig.*, No. 19-MD-2879, 2020 U.S. Dist. LEXIS 235764, at *66, 2020 WL 7350432 (D. Md. Dec. 15, 2020) ("[C]ourts in the 4th Circuit have concluded that people have no privacy right that permits them to quash a subpoena directed to a bank or similar institution seeking the bank records pertaining to their account."); *Adeeko v. Chattanooga Metro. Airport Auth.*, No. 1:19-CV-113, 2020 U.S. Dist. LEXIS 50163, at *22, 2020 WL 1442875 (E.D. Tenn. Mar. 24, 2020) ("[C]ourts have held personal financial information . . . do not implicate fundamental privacy rights protected by the Fourteenth Amendment."). *But see Salinas v. Cornwell Quality Tools Co.*, No. EDCV192275JGBSPX, 2020 U.S. Dist. LEXIS 247356, at *15, 2020 WL 8028618 (C.D. Cal. Oct. 2, 2020) ("California courts have recognized that individuals have a right to privacy in their financial information."); *Hett v. Barron-Lunde*, 290 So. 3d 565, 570–71 (Fla. Dist. Ct. App. 2020) ("[Petitioner] correctly argues that personal financial information is afforded protection under the fundamental right to privacy found in Article I, section 23, of the Florida Constitution.").

53 *In re 7677 Real St., LLC*, No. 01-16-00683-CV, 2017 Tex. App. LEXIS 9299, at *18, 2017 WL 4366033 (Tex. Civ. App.—Houston [1st Dist.] Oct. 3, 2017, orig. proceeding) (mem. op.) ("In financial-records production cases, the burden generally lies with the party seeking to prevent production to show that the records are not relevant or are subject to a privilege."); *In re Jacobs*, 300 S.W.3d 35, 40 (Tex. App.—Houston [14th Dist.] 2009, orig. proceeding) (same); *In re Brewer Leasing*, Inc., 255 S.W.3d 708, 712 (Tex. App.—Houston [1st Dist.] 2008, orig. proceeding) (same); *In re Manion*, No. 07-08-0318-CV, 2008 Tex. App. LEXIS 6813, at *6, 2008 WL 4180294 (Tex. App.—Amarillo Sept. 11, 2008, orig. proceeding) (mem. op.) (same); *see In re Gonzalez*, No. 14-10-01186-CV, 2010 Tex. App. LEXIS 9831, at *3–4, 2010 WL 5132590 (Tex. App.—Houston [1st Dist.] Dec. 14, 2010, orig. proceeding) (mem. op.) ("[T]here are no constitutional rights to privacy affected by the disclosure of banking records.").

established merely because the requesting party wants to know the responding party's financial condition to determine if it can satisfy a judgment.[54]

Traditionally, in Texas, a party seeking exemplary damages could obtain discovery about its opponent's net worth as a matter of right.[55] This changed for actions filed on or after September 1, 2015, when certain amendments to Chapter 41 of the Texas Civil Practice & Remedies Code, governing damages, became effective.

"Net worth" is defined in the Chapter 41 as "the total assets of a person minus the total liabilities of the person on a date determined appropriate by the trial court."[56] Although Chapter 41 does not specify the "date" for the net-worth determination, Texas courts traditionally have held that a claimant is only entitled to discover documents showing *current* net worth, that is, "net worth as of the time the discovery is responded to, though net worth information should be updated through supplementation . . . if it changes materially between the service of the discovery response and the time of trial."[57]

---

[54] *Cf. Nowlin v. Lusk*, No. 11CV712S, 2014 U.S. Dist. LEXIS 10341, at *21, 2014 WL 298155 (W.D.N.Y. Jan. 28, 2014) ("Here, plaintiff has not shown that O'Flynn's (or the other requested defendants') assets are relevant to any claim or defense. . . . If he seeks this information to learn the ability of these defendants (in their individual capacities) to pay any judgment, that is not relevant to his claims. 'As a general rule, discovery concerning an adversary party's assets is not permitted during the course of the litigation unless it is relevant to the merits of a claim. Rather, such discovery is properly reserved for post-judgment proceedings, when a judgment creditor seeks the information necessary to permit it to enforce the judgment.' Thus, general discovery of O'Flynn's assets unrelated to a punitive damages claim is denied[.]" (quoting *Sequa Corp. v. Gelmin*, No. 91 Civ. 8675, 1995 U.S. Dist. LEXIS 9338, at *6 (S.D.N.Y. July 7, 1995))); *Metal Mgmt., Inc. v. Schiavone*, 514 F. Supp. 2d 227, 239–40 (D. Conn. 2007) (same); *Bahrain Telecomm. Co. v. Discoverytel, Inc.*, 476 F. Supp. 2d 176, 187–88 (D. Conn. 2007) (same); *Ranney-Brown Distrib., Inc. v. E.T. Barwick Indus., Inc.*, 75 F.R.D. 3, 5 (S.D. Ohio 1977) (same).

[55] *Lunsford v. Morris*, 746 S.W.2d 471, 473 (Tex. 1988) (orig. proceeding) ("Our rules of civil procedure do not require [a prima facie showing of entitlement to exemplary damages] before net worth can be discovered."), *disapproved of on other grounds by Walker v. Packer*, 827 S.W.2d 833, 842 (Tex. 1996) (orig. proceeding); *In re Jacobs*, 300 S.W.3d 35, 40–41 (Tex. App.—Houston [14th Dist.] 2009, orig. proceeding) ("[U]nder Texas law, a party seeking discovery of net-worth information need not satisfy any evidentiary prerequisite, such as making a prima facie show of entitlement to punitive damages, before discovery of net worth is permitted."); *In re House of Yahweh*, 266 S.W.3d 668, 673 (Tex. App.—Eastland 2008, orig. proceeding) ("Information regarding net worth is discoverable in cases for which exemplary damages may be awarded. A party seeking discovery of net worth is not required to make a prima facie showing of a right to recover exemplary damages before discovery is permitted.").

[56] Tex. Civ. Prac. & Rem. Code § 41.001(7-a).

[57] *In re Jacobs*, 300 S.W.3d 35, 44–45 & n.9 (Tex. App.—Houston [14th Dist.] 2009, orig. proceeding) (holding that a discovery order ordering the defendants to produce two years of net-worth information was overly broad because only their "current net worth [was] relevant[,] that is, their net worth as of the time the discovery [was] responded to, though net worth information should be updated through supplementation . . . if it changes materially between the service of the discovery response and the time of trial"); *see, e.g., In re Potashnik*, No. 05-19-01188-CV, 2020 Tex. App. LEXIS 3399, at *5, 2020 WL 1933796 (Tex. App.—Dallas Apr. 22, 2020, orig. proceeding) (mem. op.) ("With respect to net-worth discovery, generally, only financial documents pertaining to current net worth are relevant."); *In re*

In addition, Section 41.0115 of the Code establishes a protocol, as well as the threshold that must be met, for net-worth discovery. *First*, the statute permits a trial court to authorize such discovery only on a party's written motion to which the opposing party must be given an opportunity to respond.[58]

Second, the statute provides for "a hearing" on the written motion, which appears to prohibit a trial court from ruling on the motion on submission without the parties' consent.[59] It further provides that the evidence in support of, or in opposition to, the written motion "may be the form of an affidavit or a response to discovery."[60] Because the statute uses the permissive "may," rather than the mandatory "shall," and appears to require a hearing, it is unclear whether live testimony can be heard at the hearing.

Third, the statute prohibits net-worth discovery unless the court enters a "written order" finding that "the claimant has demonstrated a substantial likelihood of success on the merits of a claim for exemplary damages."[61] Although the statute does not define a "substantial likelihood of success on the merits of a claim for exemplary damages," the phrase should be given its plain or ordinary meaning.[62] For example, one of

---

Vaughan, No. 13-18-00541-CV, 2019 Tex. App. LEXIS 1445, at *8–9, 2019 WL 962381 (Tex. App.—Corpus Christi Feb. 27, 2019, orig. proceeding) (mem. op.) (same); *In re Ming Chu Chang*, No. 13-15-00352-CV, 2015 Tex. App. LEXIS 10382, at *11, 2015 WL 5895197 (Tex. Civ. App.—Corpus Christi Oct. 8, 2017, orig. proceeding) (mem. op.) ("Discovery regarding net worth must be narrowly crafted to show current net worth."); *In re Ameriplan Corp.*, No. 05-09-01407-CV, 2010 Tex. App. LEXIS 31, at *2, 2010 WL 22825 (Tex. App.—Dallas Jan. 6, 2010, orig. proceeding) (mem. op.) (holding that a discovery order directing the defendant to produce financial documents that did not show its current net worth was an abuse of discretion); *In re House of Yahweh*, 266 S.W.3d 668, 673 (Tex. App.—Eastland 2008, orig. proceeding) ("Information regarding net worth is discoverable in cases for which exemplary damages may be awarded. . . . The trial court ordered defendants to produce 'all documents that evidence or reflect [defendants'] net worth.' . . . However, the use of the word 'all' in [the request] may make it overly broad because [defendants] should only be required to produce documents sufficient to show their net worth."); *cf. Basra v. Ecklund Logistics, Inc.*, No. 8:16CV83, 2016 U.S. Dist. LEXIS 177395, at *10, 2016 WL 7413474 (D. Neb. Dec. 22, 2016) ("However, only Defendant's current financial status is relevant to the issue of punitive damages."); *United States v. Autumn Ridge Condo. Ass'n*, 265 F.R.D. 323 (N.D. Ind. 2009) (holding, in an action brought under the Fair Housing Act, that only information concerning the defendants' current financial status was relevant to the issue of punitive damages).

58 Tex. Civ. Prac. & Rem. Code § 41.0115(a).

59 Tex. Civ. Prac. & Rem. Code § 41.0115(a).

60 Tex. Civ. Prac. & Rem. Code § 41.0115(a).

61 Tex. Civ. Prac. & Rem. Code § 41.0115(a); *see also In re Boone*, 629 S.W.3d 372, 374 (Tex. App.—San Antonio 2020, orig. proceeding) ("[T]he trial court abused its discretion by ordering discovery of Boone's net worth without first finding that Hall demonstrated a substantial likelihood of success on the merits of his gross negligence claim."); *In re WTG Fuels, Inc.*, No. 11-19-00390-CV, 2020 Tex. App. LEXIS 280, at *7, 2020 WL 205254 (Tex. App.—Eastland Jan. 13, 2020, orig. proceeding) (mem. op.) (concluding that a trial judge could not exercise discretion to order discovery of a defendant's net worth because, in the order granting the motion to engage in such discovery, the judge "did not make a finding that Plaintiffs had demonstrated a substantial likelihood of success on the merits of their claim for gross negligence").

62 Tex. Gov't Code § 311.011(a)–(b) (providing that "[w]ords and phrases shall be read in context and construed according to the rules of grammar and common usage" and that

the requirements for the issuance of a temporary injunction under federal and many states' common law is "a substantial likelihood of success on the merits."[63] To establish a "substantial likelihood of success on the merits," the movant "is not required to prove [its] entitlement to summary judgment[.]"[64] Rather, it only is required to present a prima-facie case,[65] that is, it must produce enough evidence to permit the trier of fact to infer the facts needed to establish its right to exemplary damages (e.g., that the opposing was grossly negligent or committed fraud).

Fourth, the trial court must authorize only the "least burdensome method available" to obtain net-worth discovery.[66] Accordingly, the motion and response should, if possible, discuss the scope of the net-worth discovery. For example, if the opposing party has current financial statements prepared in the ordinary course of business showing its net worth, it should propose that discovery be limited to their production in its response.

Fifth, the statute presumes that the written motion seeking net-worth discovery will be entertained only after substantial discovery has been taken: "If a party requests net worth discovery under this section, the court shall presume that the requesting party has had adequate time for the discovery of facts relating to exemplary damages for purposes of allowing the party from whom net worth discovery is sought to move for summary judgment on the requesting party's claim for exemplary damages

---

"[w]ords and phrases that have acquired a technical or particular meaning, whether by legislative definition or otherwise, shall be construed accordingly"); *see also In re Tex. Educ. Agency*, 619 S.W.3d 679, 687, (Tex. 2021) ("We apply the plain meaning of statutory language unless (1) the Legislature has prescribed definitions, (2) the words have acquired a technical or particular meaning, (3) a contrary intention is apparent from the context, or (4) a plain-meaning construction leads to nonsensical or absurd results.") (footnote omitted); *Colorado Cnty. v. Staff*, 510 S.W.3d 435, 448 (Tex. 2017) (same). *But see In re Boone*, 629 S.W.3d 372, 376–77, (Tex. App.—San Antonio 2020, orig. proceeding) (assessing whether a party demonstrated a substantial likelihood of success on the merits of his exemplary-damages claim by analyzing whether the party met his ultimate burden of establishing, by clear and convincing evidence, the objective element of his gross-negligence claim for which he sought exemplary damages).

[63] *E.g., Big Tyme Invs., L.L.C. v. Edwards*, 985 F.3d 456, 463–64 (5th Cir. 2021) (noting to obtain a preliminary injunction the movant must establish "'a substantial likelihood of success on the merits'" (quoting *Speaks v. Kruse*, 445 F.3d 396, 399–400 (5th Cir. 2006))); *accord Texans for Free Enter. v. Ethics Comm'n*, 732 F.3d 535, 536–37 (5th Cir. 2013); *Byrum v. Landreth*, 566 F.3d 442, 445 (5th Cir. 2009).

[64] *Byrum v. Landreth*, 566 F.3d 442, 446 (5th Cir. 2009); *accord Tex. Voters All. v. Dall. Cnty.*, No. 4:20-CV-00775, 2020 U.S. Dist. LEXIS 193388, at *24–25, 2020 WL 6146248 (E.D. Tex. Oct. 20, 2020).

[65] 11A Charles Alan Wright, Arthur R. Miller & Mary Kay Kane, *Federal Practice and Procedure* § 2948.3 (3d ed. 2021) ("All courts agree that plaintiff must present a prima facie case but need not show a certainty of winning.") (footnote omitted).

[66] Tex. Civ. Prac. & Rem. Code § 41.0115(b) ("If a trial court authorizes discovery under Subsection (a), the court's order may only authorize use of the least burdensome method available to obtain the net worth evidence."); *accord e.g., In re Elara Signature Homes, Inc.*, 611 S.W.3d 62, 67–68 (Tex. App.—Beaumont 2020, orig. proceeding) ("Under Texas law, plaintiffs suing for punitive damages may discover evidence about a defendant's net worth, but they may do so only by using the least burdensome method that is available for that purpose.").

under Rule 166a(i), Texas Rules of Civil Procedure."[67] Accordingly, the movant should anticipate that a no-evidence or traditional summary-judgment motion will be filed in response to the motion and, by reason of the statute, is conceding that there has been sufficient time for discovery so that summary judgment on the issue of exemplary damages is appropriate from a timing perspective.

Finally, the statute limits the evidence an appellate court can consider in reviewing an order allowing or denying discovery of net-worth evidence to that evidence submitted to the trial court in support of, or in opposition to, the written motion seeking the discovery.[68]

Trial courts and parties, in actions in which exemplary damages are sought, should consider whether the action should be under Level 3 for discovery purposes and whether the action's discovery-control plan should have deadlines for the filing of a motion for net-worth discovery and the hearing on it and the relationship of such deadlines to the deadlines for summary judgment motions and hearings.[69]

Discovery of a party's financial information is often appropriate to support, or defend against, a claim for damages.[70] But interrogatories regarding damages, in many respects, are supplanted by Texas Rule 194.2(b)(4), which requires a party to disclose "the amount and any method of calculating economic damages."[71]

4-3:5 Impeachment Information

Information usable to impeach a witness at trial generally is discoverable.[72] For example, the identity of the person or party paying litigation expenses may be relevant to

---

[67] Tex. Civ. Prac. & Rem. Code § 41.0115(d).

[68] Tex. Civ. Prac. & Rem. Code § 41.0115(c) ("When reviewing an order authorizing or denying discovery of net worth evidence under this section, the reviewing court may consider only the evidence submitted by the parties to the trial court in support of or in opposition to the motion described by Subsection (a).").

[69] See Chapter 2, section 2-3:3 (discussing Level 3 discovery-control plans).

[70] *Cf. Sinclair Ref. Co. v. Jenkins Petroleum Process Co.*, 289 U.S. 689, 693 (1933) ("[D]iscovery is as appropriate for proof of a plaintiff's damages as it is for proof of other facts essential to his case."); *RTC v. Bright*, 157 F.R.D. 397, 399–401 (N.D. Tex. 1994) (holding that the plaintiff's documents relating to the value of a savings and loan association's properties were discoverable by the association's former directors and officers because the properties allegedly had "no value" at time of the association was placed in conservatorship).

[71] Tex. R. Civ. P. 194.2(b)(4). See also Chapter 6, section 6-3:3.4 (discussing damage disclosures).

[72] *E.g.*, Tex. R. Civ. P. 192.3(e)(5) (allowing discovery of information to show "any bias" of an expert witness); *In re Ford Motor Co.*, 427 S.W.3d 396, 397 (Tex. 2014) (orig. proceeding) (per curiam) (noting that Texas Rule 192.3(e) permits discovery about the bias of a testifying expert, while also recognizing that "discovery into the extent of an expert's bias is not without limits"); *Walker v. Packer*, 827 S.W.2d 833, 838–39 (Tex. 1992) (holding that discovery geared at showing an expert witness's bias is permissible); *In re GreCon, Inc.*, 542 S.W.3d 774, 785 (Tex. App.—Houston [14th Dist.] 2018, orig. proceeding) ("[S]ettlement agreements and offers may be discoverable for purposes other than to establish liability, such as to demonstrate bias or prejudice of a party or witness, or, to establish the existence of a promise or agreement made by nonparties to the settled lawsuit." (quoting *In re Univar USA, Inc.*, 311 S.W.3d 175, 182 (Tex. App.–Beaumont 2010, orig. proceeding))); *Liles*

v. Contreras, 547 S.W.3d 280, 289 (Tex. App.—San Antonio 2018, pet. denied) (same); ***In re DCP Midstream, L.P.***, No. 13-14-00502-CV, 2014 Tex. App. LEXIS 11092, at *29–30, 2014 WL 5019947 (Tex. App.—Corpus Christi Oct. 7, 2014, no pet.) (mem. op.) ("We conclude that those portions of the settlement agreement that are relevant to the existence or nonexistence of potential witness bias, such as those portions that reflect agreements to provide testimony, to provide cooperation, or to not cooperate with the nonsettling defendant, as a consideration for the settlement are relevant and are reasonably calculated to lead to the discovery of relevant impeachment or bias evidence."); ***In re K.L.***, 336 S.W.3d 286, 290–91 (Tex. App.—San Antonio 2010, orig. proceeding) (compelling the plaintiff to disclose her social security number so that the defendant could conduct a background investigation to find information that could impeach her credibility); ***In re Univar USA, Inc.***, 311 S.W.3d 175, 182–83 (Tex. App.—Beaumont 2010, orig. proceeding) (same); *cf.* ***Hickman v. Taylor***, 329 U.S. 495, 511 (1947) (holding that information that might be used for impeachment or corroboration is discoverable); ***Wishart v. Welkley***, No. 19-CV-6189-DGL-MJP, 2020 U.S. Dist. LEXIS 67013, at *6, 2020 WL 1891764 (W.D.N.Y. Apr. 16, 2020) ("Witness bias, and witness impeachment, are within the legitimate scope of discovery."); ***Elite Mitigation Servs., LLC v. Westchester Surplus Lines Ins. Co.***, No. 5:19-CV-381-TKW/MJF, 2020 WL 6122069, at *4 (N.D. Fla. Apr. 10, 2020) ("Various courts have noted that information regarding an expert witness's potential for bias is discoverable." (citing cases)); ***Murillo Modular Grp., Ltd.*** v. ***Sullivan***, No. 3:13-cv-3020-M, 2016 U.S. Dist. LEXIS 145308, at *26–30, 2016 WL 6139096 (N.D. Tex. Oct. 20, 2016) (mem. op.) ("Information relevant to a party's or likely witness's credibility may fall within [Federal] Rule 26(b)(1)'s scope. . . . Impeachment evidence is thus discoverable when relevant—in other words, when 'disclosure may reveal information affecting the credence afforded to a witness' trial testimony.' The impeachment evidence Plaintiff seeks is plainly discoverable here. Plaintiff seeks discovery relating to a sanctions order that was entered in a related case where Sullivan allegedly allowed Sal Murillo to sign a false affidavit. Any such allowance speaks to Sullivan's credibility as a witness since it 'demonstrate[s] a propensity for deception . . . in a context where there is a premium on veracity.' . . . While evidence discovered pursuant to these requests may prove to be inadmissible to the extent it improperly suggests guilt based on Sullivan's past actions, '[i]nformation within [its] scope of discovery need not be admissible in evidence to be discoverable[.]'" (quoting ***Davidson Pipe Co. v. Laventhol & Horwath***, 120 F.R.D. 455, 462 (S.D.N.Y. 2010), and Fed. R. Civ. P. 26(b)(1))); ***SEC v. Cuban***, No. 3:08-cv-2050-D, 2012 U.S. Dist. LEXIS 17000, at *3, 2012 WL 456532 (N.D. Tex. Feb. 10, 2012) (mem. op.) ("Cuban has at least shown that the nonprivileged portions of the SEC's investigative file for the investigation of Mamma.com, and documents pertaining to the relationship between the Mamma.com investigation and the investigation of Cuban, are relevant to the credibility of Mamma.com witnesses, including CEO Guy Faure . . ., and are therefore within the scope of [Federal] Rule 26(b)(1)."); ***Roehrig v. W.G. Tomko, Inc.***, No. 15–146, 2015 U.S. Dist. LEXIS 108094, *3–4 (W.D. Pa. Aug. 17, 2015) Where, as here, Plaintiff seeks to engage in questioning regarding Mr. Tomko's criminal conviction 'to explore potential grounds to challenge [Mr.] Tomko's credibility,' the Court believes that such questioning falls within the bounds of discoverable information and would, alternatively, deny Defendant's Motion for a Protective Order solely on this basis."); ***Deakins v. T.S. Pack***, No. 1:10–1396, 2012 U.S. Dist. LEXIS 9409, at *42, 2012 WL 242859 (S.D.W. Va. Jan. 25, 2012) ("The undersigned finds Plaintiffs' objections to Interrogatory Number 2 to be without merit. In their Complaint, Plaintiffs allege that Defendants used unnecessary and excessive force. The Court first finds that Plaintiffs' criminal histories are relevant to Plaintiffs' claims or Defendants' defenses. Specifically, Plaintiffs' criminal histories are relevant to Plaintiffs' credibility and the necessity of any force used by Defendants. Plaintiffs' conclusion that their criminal histories are not discoverable because the information is inadmissible under the Federal Rules of Evidence is incorrect. Thus, Plaintiffs' criminal histories are potentially admissible or may lead to the discovery of admissible evidence.") (citation omitted); ***Penn v. Knox Cnty.***, No. 2:11-cv-363-NT, 2012 U.S. Dist. LEXIS 67025, at *6, 2012 WL 1681974 (D. Me. May 14, 2012) ("Courts and leading commentators likewise have recognized that evidence bearing on a witness's credibility can be discoverable.").

the credibility of a witness, particularly a named party.[73] Similarly, the criminal record of an opposing party or a witness is relevant and discoverable because it may be useful for impeachment purposes.[74] And "any bias" of a testifying expert or discoverable consulting expert expressly is made discoverable by Texas Rule 192.3(e)(5).[75] Further, evidence of conduct or character of a party or witness that suggests the party or witness might be less than truthful is discoverable.[76] Finally, it appears that a party

---

[73] *Cf. Uinta Oil Ref. Co. v. Cont'l Oil Co.*, 226 F. Supp. 495, 500 (D. Utah 1964) (holding that an interrogatory requesting the names of the persons sharing the litigants' cost was proper).

[74] *E.g.*, Tex. R. Evid. 609(a) (allowing impeachment by evidence of conviction of a crime); *In re Freeman*, No. 03-99-00005-CV, 1999 Tex. App. LEXIS 1037, at *2–4, 1999 WL 76454 (Tex. App.—Austin Feb. 19, 1999, orig. proceeding) (per curiam) (mem. op.) (refusing to reverse a discovery order requiring the production of "a list of all criminal and civil lawsuits of which Freeman has been a party or witness in the last 10 years"); *cf. Andersen v. City of Chi.*, No. 16 C 1963, 2019 WL 423144, at *3 (N.D. Ill. Feb. 4, 2019) (concluding, in a civil rights action, that a witness's "criminal history records [were] relevant and discoverable"); *Deakins v. T.S. Pack*, No. 1:10-1396, 2012 U.S. Dist. LEXIS 9409, at *42–43, 2012 WL 242859 (S.D.W. Va. Jan. 25, 2012) (mem. op.) ("The Court first finds that Plaintiffs' criminal histories are relevant to Plaintiffs' claims or Defendants' defenses. Specifically, Plaintiffs' criminal histories are relevant to Plaintiffs' credibility and the necessity of any force used by Defendants."); *EEOC v. Luihn Food Sys., Inc.*, No. 5:09-CV-387-D, 2011 U.S. Dist. LEXIS 13911, at *15, 2011 WL 649749 (E.D.N.C. Feb. 11, 2011) ("The request for information on criminal histories is reasonably calculated to lead to discovery of admissible evidence."); *Harris v. United States*, 121 F.R.D. 652, 656 (W.D.N.C. 1988) (holding that, in an administrator's action to recover an estate's present monetary value, the heirs' criminal records were relevant for impeachment purposes); *Tisby v. Buffalo Gen. Hosp.*, 157 F.R.D. 157, 170 (W.D.N.Y. 1994) ("'Discovery is commonly allowed in which the discovering party seeks information with which to impeach witnesses for the opposition. Inquiry is routinely allowed about criminal convictions of a party or witness and similar matters that go to his credibility.'" (quoting *Coyne v. Houss*, 584 F. Supp. 1105, 1107 (E.D.N.Y. 1984))).

[75] Tex. R. Civ. P. 192.3(e)(5). See Chapter 7, section 7-4:6 for a discussion regarding discovery about an expert's bias.

[76] Tex. R. Evid. 608 (allowing impeachment with evidence of character and conduct of witness); *cf. Rodriguez v. U.S.*, No. 17-CV-00251-WMS-JJM, 2018 U.S. Dist. LEXIS 143729, at *3, 2018 WL 4026739 (W.D.N.Y. Aug. 23, 2018) ("Information showing that a person having knowledge of discoverable facts may not be worthy of belief is always relevant to the subject matter of the action. . . . Therefore, discovery is commonly allowed in which the discovering party seeks information with which to impeach witnesses for the opposition." (quoting Davidson Pipe Co. v. Laventhol & Horwath, 120 F.R.D. 455, 461 (S.D.N.Y. 1988))); *Hemphill v. State Farm Mut. Auto. Ins. Co.*, No. 2:13CV201-HSO-RHW, 2014 U.S. Dist. LEXIS 114404, at *3, 2014 WL 4101657 (S.D. Miss. Aug. 18, 2014) ("State Farm argues that the content of the document in dispute goes to the potential bias or prejudice of Rodney and Heather Taylor as witnesses. The rules of discovery are broad enough to encompass evidence that relates to witness credibility or bias. State Farm has identified a document that relates specifically to the potential bias of the Taylors as witnesses; therefore, the document is relevant and discoverable unless protected by some privilege." (citing *United States v. Abel*, 469 U.S. 45, 52 (1984) (holding that "[p]roof of bias is almost always relevant"))); *Davidson Pipe Co. v. Laventhol & Horwath*, 120 F.R.D. 455, 461 (S.D.N.Y. 1988) ("By its terms, Rule 26(b)(1) of the Federal Rules of Civil Procedure authorizes only that discovery 'which is relevant to the subject matter involved in the pending actions.' Occasionally courts have construed this language literally to foreclose discovery of information useful only for impeachment. But the far more common and logical analysis is that '[i]nformation showing that a person having knowledge of discoverable facts may not be worthy of belief is always relevant to the subject matter of the action.'") (citations omitted).

can discover at least certain types of information that an opponent plans to use for impeachment purposes against itself or its witnesses.[77]

4-3:6 Discoverable Information Need Not Be Admissible at Trial

Discovery of inadmissible information or material is permissible,[78] provided that the information or material is "relevant" (i.e., "(a) it has any tendency to make a fact more or

---

[77] *Cf. Chiasson v. Zapata Gulf Marine Corp.*, 988 F.2d 513, 517–18 & n.4 (5th Cir. 1993) (holding that surveillance tape of a personal-injury plaintiff is discoverable); *Driscoll v. Castellanos*, No. CV 19-527 JCH/KK, 2020 U.S. Dist. LEXIS 243615, at *16, 27, 2020 WL 7711869 (D.N.M. Dec. 29, 2020) (explaining that the fact "that Defendants may use an investigator's surveillance evidence solely for impeachment does not exempt that evidence from discovery," and finding that "the surveillance evidence to be produced [was] discoverable notwithstanding its work-product status"); *Washburn v. Lawrence Cnty. Bd. of Comm'rs*, No. 1:10-cv-464, 2012 U.S. Dist. LEXIS 75498, at *3–4 (S.D. Ohio May 31, 2012) (allowing discovery of surveillance tapes); *Iowa Ins. Inst. v. Core Grp.*, 867 N.W.2d 58, 71 (Iowa 2015) ("It is clear that surveillance materials are documents or tangible things, prepared in anticipation of litigation, by or for another party or that party's representative. We therefore agree with the prevailing view in jurisdictions following the federal definition of work product that surveillance materials are protected, lower-tier materials, at least initially. The consensus also seems to be that surveillance loses the status of protected work product once a determination is made that the surveillance will be used at trial."). *But see In re Weeks Marine, Inc.*, 31 S.W.3d 389, 391 (Tex. App.—San Antonio 2000, orig. proceeding) (per curiam) (holding that surveillance material was non-discoverable work product).

[78] Tex. R. Civ. P. 192.3(a); *see In re N. Cypress Med. Ctr. Operating Co.,* 559 S.W.3d 128, 131 (Tex. 2018) (orig. proceeding) ("[E]vidence need not be admissible to be discoverable so long as it 'appears reasonably calculated to lead to the discovery of admissible evidence.'" (quoting Tex. R. Civ. P. 192.3(a))); *In re Nat'l Lloyds Ins. Co.*, 532 S.W.3d 794, 808 (Tex. 2017) (orig. proceeding) ("The discovery guideposts can be summarized as follows: only relevant evidence is discoverable; relevant evidence that is privileged is not discoverable; relevant evidence that is not privileged is discoverable when (i) it is admissible or (ii) it is inadmissible but reasonably calculated to lead to the discovery of admissible evidence; and failing either of those admissibility criteria, the request for discovery may be denied even if the requested information is relevant and unprivileged."); *Jampole v. Touchy*, 673 S.W.2d 569, 573 (Tex. 1984) ("[D]iscovery is not limited to information that will be admissible at trial. To increase the likelihood that all relevant evidence will be disclosed and brought before the trier of fact, the law circumscribes a significantly larger class of discoverable evidence to include anything reasonably calculated to lead to the discovery of material evidence.") (citations omitted), *overruled on other grounds*, *Walker v. Packer*, 827 S.W.2d 833, 842 (Tex. 1992) (orig. proceeding); *In re Plains Pipeline, L.P.*, 618 S.W.3d 780, 789–90 (Tex. App.—El Paso 2020, orig. proceeding) ("Relevance for purposes of discovery is broader than relevance under the Texas Rules of Evidence. Information is relevant for discovery purposes even if it 'will be inadmissible at trial if the information sought appears reasonably calculated to lead to discovery of admissible evidence.'" (quoting *In re Kimberly-Clark Corp.*, 228 S.W.3d 480, 486 (Tex. App.—Dallas 2007, orig. proceeding))); *In re Cook*, No. 05-19-01283-CV, 2020 Tex. App. LEXIS 3999, at *5–6, 2020 WL 2552881 (Tex. App.—Dallas May 20, 2020, no pet.) (mem. op.) ("A party is typically entitled to obtain discovery on any matter that is not privileged and is relevant to the subject matter of the pending action. It is not a ground for objection that the information sought will be inadmissible at trial if the information sought appears reasonably calculated to lead to the discovery of admissible evidence. The phrases 'relevant to the subject matter' and 'reasonably calculated to lead to the discovery of admissible evidence' are to be liberally construed.") (citations omitted);

less probable than it would be without the evidence; and (b) the fact is of consequence in determining the action").[79] For example, inadmissible hearsay evidence is discoverable.[80] Evidence that would otherwise be inadmissible at trial because of its unduly prejudicial effect also is discoverable,[81] as is evidence such as settlement or insurance information for which a strong public policy exists against its admissibility at trial.[82] However, discovery that can only lead to inadmissible evidence is improper.[83]

In re Daybreak Cmty. Servs. Tex., LLC, No. 10-19-00395-CV, 2020 Tex. App. LEXIS 1623, at *4, 2020 WL 958457 (Tex. App.—Waco Feb. 26, 2020, orig. proceeding) (mem. op.) ("The rules governing discovery do not require as a prerequisite that the information sought be admissible evidence; it is enough that the information appears reasonably calculated to lead to the discovery of admissible evidence."); *In re United Fire Lloyds*, 578 S.W.3d 572, 578 (Tex. App.—Tyler 2019, orig. proceeding) (mem. op.) (same); *In re SSCP Mgmt., Inc.*, 573 S.W.3d 464, 469 (Tex. App.—Fort Worth 2019, orig. proceeding) (same); *In re Vaughan*, No. 13-18-00541-CV, *2019 Tex. App. LEXIS 1445, at *7*, 2019 WL 962381 (Tex. App.—Corpus Christi Feb. 27, 2019, orig. proceeding) (mem. op.) (same); *In re Sun Coast Rs., Inc.*, 562 S.W.3d 138, 146 (Tex. App.—Houston [14th Dist.] 2018, orig. proceeding) (same); *In re Allstate Ins. Co.*, 551 S.W.3d 798, 800 (Tex. App.—San Antonio 2018, orig. proceeding) (same); *In re Am. Power Conversion Corp.*, No. 04-12-00140-CV, 2012 Tex. App. LEXIS 9369, at *9, 2012 WL 5507111 (Tex. App.—San Antonio Nov. 14, 2012, orig. proceeding) (mem. op.) ("Without question, the scope of discovery exceeds the scope of admissible evidence, and a party need not prove information is admissible in order for the same to be discoverable.").

[79] Tex. R. Evid. 401; *see In re Nat'l Lloyds Ins. Co.*, 532 S.W.3d 794, 808 (Tex. 2017) (orig. proceeding) (defining relevance for discovery purposes by quoting Tex. R. Evid. 401); *accord In re Allstate Fire & Cas. Ins. Co.*, 617 S.W.3d 635, 643 (Tex. App.—Houston [14th Dist.] 2021, orig. proceeding); *In re Savoy*, 607 S.W.3d 120, 126 (Tex. App.—Austin 2020, orig. proceeding); *In re Vaughan,* No. 13-18-00541-CV, 2019 Tex. App. LEXIS 1445, at *7, 2019 WL 962381 (Tex. App.—Corpus Christi Feb. 27, 2019, orig. proceeding) (mem. op.); *In re Padilla,* No. 03-18-00477-CV, 2018 Tex. App. LEXIS 6832, at *3–4, 2018 WL 4087733 (Tex. App.—Austin Aug. 28, 2018, no pet.) (mem. op.).

[80] *Cf. Coleman v. Am. Red Cross*, 23 F.3d 1091, 1097 (6th Cir. 1994) (noting that discovery of hearsay evidence is permissible if it is possible that such evidence will lead to the discovery of admissible evidence); *Meier v. UHS of Del., Inc.*, No. 4:18-CV-00615, 2021 U.S. Dist. LEXIS 63721, at *12, 2021 WL 1226619 (E.D. Tex. Apr. 1, 2021) ("[T]he mere fact that evidence is hearsay does not prevent it from being discoverable."); *Schyvincht v. Menard, Inc.*, No. 18 CV 50286, 2019 U.S. Dist. LEXIS 114277, at *9–10, 2019 WL 3002961 (N.D. Ill. July 10, 2019) ("Hearsay is generally discoverable under Federal Rules of Civil Procedure."); *Freedom's Path at Dayton v. Dayton Metro. Hous. Auth.*, No. 3:16-CV-466, 2018 U.S. Dist. LEXIS 98851, at *10–11, 2018 WL 2948021 (S.D. Ohio June 13, 2018) ("Defendant's argument that Ms. Smith's testimony is not relevant because it would constitute inadmissible hearsay lacks merit for discovery purposes: 'Information within this scope of discovery need not be admissible in evidence to be discoverable.'" (quoting Fed. R. Civ. P 26(b) (1))).

[81] *Cf. Schuurman v. Town of N. Reading*, 139 F.R.D. 276, 277 (D. Mass. 1991) (allowing discovery of the plaintiff's probation records because objections regarding the evidence's tendency to prejudice or confuse the jury should be raised at trial rather than during discovery).

[82] *Cf. Thermal Design, Inc. v. Guardian Bldg. Prods., Inc.*, 270 F.R.D. 437, 438–39 (E.D. Wis. 2010) (pointing out that Federal Rule of Evidence 408 places "limits on the *admissibility* of settlement material rather than limits on their *discoverability*"); *McQuade v. Michael Gassner Mech. & Elec. Contractors, Inc.*, 587 F. Supp. 1183, 1190 (D. Conn. 1984) (allowing discovery of the contents of tapes of telephone calls in action seeking damages for illegally taping phone conversations even though the tapes' contents were potentially excludable from evidence and their disclosure was punishable under federal statute).

[83] *E.g., In re Nat'l Lloyds Ins. Co.*, 532 S.W.3d 794, 808 (Tex. 2017) (orig. proceeding) ("The discovery guideposts can be summarized as follows: only relevant evidence is discover-

4-4 Work Product

The work-product doctrine's primary purpose "'is to shelter the mental processes, conclusions, and legal theories of the attorney, providing a privileged area within which the lawyer can analyze and prepare his or her case.'"[84] The work-product privilege thus "preserves the rights of attorneys to thoroughly prepare cases for trial and to investigate both favorable and unfavorable aspects of their cases, while preventing attorneys from taking advantage of their opposing counsel's efforts."[85] In recognition of the fact that the privilege's "underlying purpose would be totally defeated if the . . . privilege were limited to documents that were prepared in the particular case for which discovery is sought[,]" the Texas Supreme Court has held that the "work product privilege [in Texas] is of continuing duration."[86]

---

able; relevant evidence that is privileged is not discoverable; relevant evidence that is not privileged is discoverable when (i) it is admissible or (ii) it is inadmissible but reasonably calculated to lead to the discovery of admissible evidence; and failing either of those admissibility criteria, the request for discovery may be denied even if the requested information is relevant and unprivileged."); *In re Hamilton*, No. 13-20-00254-CV, 2020 WL 5494503 (Tex. App.—Corpus Christi Sept. 10, 2020, orig. proceeding) (mem. op.) ("A party can seek discovery of unprivileged information that is relevant to the subject matter of the lawsuit, including inadmissible evidence, *as long as* the request is reasonably calculated to lead to the discovery of admissible evidence.") (emphasis added); *cf. U.S. v. Shalon,* No. 15 CR 333-LTS, 2020 U.S. Dist. LEXIS 219093, at *2, 2020 WL 6873447 (S.D.N.Y. Nov. 23, 2020) ("Even inadmissible evidence may be material *if* it could lead to the discovery of admissible evidence.") (emphasis added); *Ford Motor Co. v. Edgewood Props., Inc.*, 257 F.R.D. 418, 423–24 (D.N.J. 2009) ("[D]iscovery which can only lead to inadmissible evidence is prohibited by the plain language of [Federal] Rule 26 and would violate the command of [Federal] Rule 1 . . ., which requires that the [Federal] Rules be construed and administered to secure the just, speedy, and inexpensive determination of every action." (quoting *Steele v. Lincoln Fin. Grp.*, No. 05 C 7163, 2007 U.S. Dist. LEXIS 25587, at *14 (N.D. Ill. Apr. 3, 2007))).

[84] *In re Nat'l Lloyds Ins. Co.*, 532 S.W.3d 794, 803 (Tex. 2017) (orig. proceeding) (quoting *Owens–Corning Fiberglas Corp. v. Caldwell*, 818 S.W.2d 749, 750 (Tex. 1991) (orig. proceeding)); *accord In re Cook,* 597 S.W.3d 589, 601 (Tex. App.—Houston [14th Dist.] 2020, no pet.); *In re Bilfinger Westcon, Inc.*, No. 13-19-00466-CV, 2019 Tex. App. LEXIS 10807, at *30, 2019 WL 6795870 (Tex. App.—Corpus Christi Dec. 12, 2019, orig. proceeding) (mem. op.); *In re Bonding*, 522 S.W.3d 75, 86 (Tex. App.—Houston [1st Dist.] 2017, orig. proceeding); *In re Bexar Cnty. Crim. Dist. Attorney's Office*, 224 S.W.3d 182, 186 (Tex. 2007) (orig. proceeding); *In re Commitment of Smith*, No. 09-12-00001-CV, 2013 Tex. App. LEXIS 10286, at *5, 2013 WL 4279647 (Tex. App.—Beaumont Aug. 15, 2013, no pet.) (mem. op.); *In re McDaniel*, No. 14-13-00127-CV, 2013 Tex. App. LEXIS 4052, at *5, 2013 WL 1279454 (Tex. App.—Houston [14th Dist.] Mar. 28, 2013, orig. proceeding) (mem. op.); *In re Jefferson Cnty. Appraisal Dist.*, 315 S.W.3d 229, 233 (Tex. App.—Beaumont 2010, orig. proceeding).

[85] *In re Baytown Nissan Inc.*, 451 S.W.3d 140, 147 (Tex. App.—Houston [1st Dist.] 2014, orig. proceeding), *quoted in In re Bonding*, 522 S.W.3d 75, 86 (Tex. App.—Houston [1st Dist.] 2017, orig. proceeding); *accord In re Union Carbide Corp.*, No. 01-02-01153-CV, 2003 Tex. App. LEXIS 9683, at *14 (Tex. App.—Houston [1st Dist.] Nov. 13, 2003, orig. proceeding) (mem. op.); *see Wiley v. Williams*, 769 S.W.2d 715, 717 (Tex. App.—Austin 1989, orig. proceeding) ("The purpose of the work product privilege is to promote the adversary system by safeguarding the fruits of an attorney's trial preparations from the discovery efforts of the opponent.").

[86] *Owens–Corning Fiberglas Corp. v. Caldwell*, 818 S.W.2d 749, 751–52 (Tex. 1991) (orig. proceeding); *accord In re Bexar Cnty. Crim. Dist. Attorney's Office*, 224 S.W.3d 182, 186 (Tex.

The work-product privilege is firmly implanted in Texas jurisprudence, with its roots dating back to 1940. The privilege has evolved significantly since then, in part to reflect changes in Texas discovery procedures and in part to be more consistent with the federal work-product doctrine.

4-4:1 History of Work-Product Doctrine

The original Texas Rules of Civil Procedure, adopted in 1940 and effective in 1941, included a broad privilege that limited discovery as follows: "the rights herein granted shall not extend to the written communications passing between agents or representatives or the employees of either party to the suit, or communications between any party and his agents, representatives, or their employees, where made subsequent to the occurrence or transaction upon which the suit is based, and made in connection with the prosecution, investigation or defense of such claim or the circumstances out of which same has arisen."[87] Although this provision encompassed some of the information that is considered work product today, it did not use the term "work product" or address trial-preparation materials specifically;[88] perhaps for that reason, courts sometimes forget or ignore its role in the history of the work-product doctrine in Texas.[89]

2007) (orig. proceeding) ("The privilege continues indefinitely beyond the litigation for which the materials were originally prepared."); *Nat'l Union Fire Ins. Co.* v. *Valdez*, 863 S.W.2d 458, 460 (Tex. 1993) (orig. proceeding) ("The [work-product] exemption continues even after the litigation for which the work product was prepared concludes."); *Humphreys v. Caldwell*, 888 S.W.2d 469, 471 (Tex. 1994) (per curiam) ("It is irrelevant that many of [the] documents [at issue] were prepared in connection with [another suit] rather than the underlying suit since the work product privilege is of continuing duration."); *In re Bonding*, 522 S.W.3d 75, 88 (Tex. App.—Houston [1st Dist.] 2017, orig. proceeding) ("[W]e note that the Texas Supreme Court has held that the work product privilege is 'of continuing duration,' and that courts have interpreted this to mean the privilege is 'not applicable solely to the lawsuit in which it arises.'" (quoting *In re Baptist Hosps.*, 172 S.W.3d 136, 144 (Tex. App.—Beaumont 2005, orig. proceeding))); *see also In re Baptist Hosps.*, 172 S.W.3d 136, 144 (Tex. App.—Beaumont 2005, orig. proceeding) (relying on continuing duration of work-product privilege to conclude that "work product developed in anticipation of, and during, [a plaintiff's] litigation against [a defendant] extends to [a third party's] intervention against [the plaintiff] in the same suit"); *In re Mid-Century Ins. Co.*, 549 S.W.3d 730, 733 (Tex. App.—Waco 2017, orig. proceeding) (mem. op.) ("The work product privilege is not necessarily specific to the claim for which it is sought, but is specific for the claim for which it was created. Once it is created as work product in relation to a claim, it remains work product and protected by a privilege from disclosure from any claim, subject only to limited exceptions such as waiver.").

[87] Former Tex. R. Civ. P. 167, ***quoted in*** William V. Dorsaneo, III, *The History of Texas Civil Procedure*, 65 Baylor L. Rev. 713, 773 n.408 (2013).

[88] William V. Dorsaneo, III, *The History of Texas Civil Procedure*, 65 Baylor L. Rev. 713, 774 (2013).

[89] *See, e.g., In re Bexar Cnty. Crim. Dist. Attorney's Office*, 224 S.W.3d 182, 186 (Tex. 2007) (orig. proceeding) ("The United States Supreme Court first recognized the work-product doctrine 60 years ago in *Hickman v. Taylor*, 329 U.S. 495 (1947)."); *In re Bonding*, 522 S.W.3d 75, 85 (Tex. App.—Houston [1st Dist.] 2017, orig. proceeding) (same); *In re Baptist Hosps.*, 172 S.W.3d 136, 139 (Tex. App.—Beaumont 2005, orig. proceeding) (same). ***But see Nat'l Tank Co. v. Brotherton***, 851 S.W.2d 193, 201 (Tex. 1993) (recognizing that the privilege protecting communications between a party's representatives, "which in one form or

The United States Supreme Court laid the foundation for the modern-day work-product doctrine in 1947, in *Hickman v. Taylor*.[90] The question before the Court was "the extent to which a party may inquire into oral and written statements of witnesses, or other information, secured by an adverse party's counsel in the course of preparation for possible litigation after a claim has arisen."[91] The district court had ordered the production of written witness statements obtained by an attorney, a substantive statement of any fact concerning the case that the defendants had learned through oral statements to their attorney, and the attorney's memoranda containing witness statements.[92] The United States Circuit Court of Appeals for the Third Circuit reversed the district court's order because the information sought "was part of the 'work product of the lawyer' and hence privileged from discovery under the Federal Rules of Civil Procedure."[93]

In analyzing the issues before it, the United States Supreme Court noted that it was "dealing with an attempt to secure the production of written statements and mental impressions contained in the files and the mind of the attorney . . . without any showing of necessity or any indication or claim that denial of such production would unduly prejudice the preparation of petitioner's case or cause him any hardship or injustice."[94] The Court concluded that no "rule dealing with discovery contemplate[d] production under such circumstances."[95] It then provided the following rationale for protecting the information sought:

> [A] lawyer is an officer of the court and is bound to work for the advancement of justice while faithfully protecting the rightful interests of his clients. In performing his various duties, however, it is essential that a lawyer work with a certain degree of privacy, free from unnecessary intrusion by opposing parties and their counsel. Proper preparation of a client's case demands that he assemble information, sift what he considers to be the relevant from the irrelevant facts, prepare his legal theories and plan his strategy without undue and needless interference. That is the historical and the necessary way in which lawyers act within the framework of our system of jurisprudence to promote justice and to protect their clients' interests. This work is reflected, of course, in interviews, statements, memoranda, correspondence, briefs, mental impressions, personal beliefs, and countless other tangible and intangible ways—aptly though roughly termed by the Circuit Court of Appeals in this case as the "Work product of

---

another has been part of the Texas Rules of Civil Procedure since their adoption in 1941, is broad enough to protect ordinary work product").

90 *See In re Bexar Cnty. Crim. Dist. Attorney's Office*, 224 S.W.3d 182, 186 (Tex. 2007) (orig. proceeding) (addressing the history of work-product privilege); *Nat'l Tank Co.* v. *Brotherton*, 851 S.W.2d 193, 201 (Tex. 1993) ("The *Hickman* work product doctrine was codified in Fed. R. Civ. P. 26(b)(3) in 1970."); Fed. R. Civ. P. 26, Advisory Committee Note to 1970 Amend. ("In deciding the *Hickman* case, the Supreme Court appears to have expressed a preference in 1947 for an approach to the problem of trial preparation materials by judicial decision rather than by rule. Sufficient experience has accumulated, however, with lower court applications of the Hickman decision to warrant a reappraisal.").

91 *Hickman v. Taylor*, 329 U.S. 495, 497 (1947).

92 *Hickman v. Taylor*, 329 U.S. 495, 499 (1947).

93 *Hickman v. Taylor*, 329 U.S. 495, 499 (1947).

94 *Hickman v. Taylor*, 329 U.S. 495, 510 (1947).

95 *Hickman v. Taylor*, 329 U.S. 495, 499 (1947).

> the lawyer." Were such materials open to opposing counsel on mere demand, much of what is now put down in writing would remain unwritten. An attorney's thoughts, heretofore inviolate, would not be his own. Inefficiency, unfairness and sharp practices would inevitably develop in the giving of legal advice and in the preparation of cases for trial. The effect on the legal profession would be demoralizing. And the interests of the clients and the cause of justice would be poorly served.[96]

The Supreme Court was careful to say it was not protecting from disclosure "all written materials obtained or prepared by an adversary's counsel with an eye toward litigation" and that, "[w]here relevant and non-privileged facts remain hidden in an attorney's file and where production of those facts is essential to the preparation of one's case, discovery may properly be had."[97] But it also concluded that, because "the general policy against invading the privacy of an attorney's course of preparation is so well recognized and so essential to an orderly working of our system of legal procedure[,] . . . a burden rests on the one who would invade that privacy to establish adequate reasons to justify production through a subpoena or court order."[98] After analyzing the specific requests before it, the Supreme Court concluded: "If there should be a rare situation justifying production of these matters, petitioner's case is not of that type."[99]

When the Texas Supreme Court amended the Texas discovery rules in 1957, it went beyond *Hickman* by protecting "all post-occurrence investigations made in connection with the prosecution, investigation, or defense of the claims made in the action[,]" without requiring anticipation of litigation, and by providing an absolute investigative provision that "protected the underlying facts in addition to the investigatory memoranda that memorialized the facts."[100] But the term "work product" did not appear in the discovery rules, and thus a work-product privilege still was not expressly recognized in Texas.

The Texas discovery rules addressed "work product" by name for the first time in 1973, in former Texas Rule 186a, which exempted from disclosure (but did not define) "work product for an attorney."[101] Relatedly, former Texas Rule 186a also exempted from disclosure "witness statements" and the identity, "mental impressions and opinions of experts used solely for consultation" (i.e., consulting experts)[102]

Sweeping changes to the Texas discovery rules occurred in 1984, including the elimination of the aforementioned, broad privilege exempting investigative information

---

96 *Hickman v. Taylor*, 329 U.S. 495, 510–11 (1947) (citation omitted).

97 *Hickman v. Taylor*, 329 U.S. 495, 511 (1947).

98 *Hickman v. Taylor*, 329 U.S. 495, 512 (1947).

99 *Hickman v. Taylor*, 329 U.S. 495, 513–14 (1947) (affirming the court of appeals' judgment).

100 William V. Dorsaneo, III, *The History of Texas Civil Procedure*, 65 Baylor L. Rev. 713, 774 (2013) (citing former Texas Rules 167 and 186a).

101 William V. Dorsaneo, III, *The History of Texas Civil Procedure*, 65 Baylor L. Rev. 713, 775 (2013) (citing former Texas Rule 186a); *see also Nat'l Tank Co. v. Brotherton*, 851 S.W.2d 193, 201 (Tex. 1993) ("The specific work product exemption did not appear in the Texas Rules until 1973[.]").

102 William V. Dorsaneo, III, *The History of Texas Civil Procedure*, 65 Baylor L. Rev. 713, 775 (2013) (citing former Texas Rule 186a).

from disclosure.[103] Also as part of the 1984 amendments, the work-product privilege was moved from former Texas Rule 186a to former Texas Rule 166b, which provided a series of "investigative" privileges, including the attorney-work-product privilege, party-communication privilege, witness-statement privilege, and consulting-expert privilege.[104] Former Texas Rule 166b applied a "substantial need" and "undue hardship" exception to the party-communication and witness-statement privileges but *not* to the attorney-work-product or consulting-expert privilege.[105]

The Texas Supreme Court did not define "work product" in the 1984 rules. Rather, in case law, it held that the attorney-work-product privilege protected "documents prepared by attorneys or their agents in anticipation of litigation that contain the attorneys' mental processes, conclusions, or legal theories."[106] The court also adopted a two-prong test for assessing whether an investigation was conducted "in anticipation of litigation:" (1) an objective prong, which is satisfied if "a reasonable person would have concluded from the totality of the circumstances surrounding the investigation that there was a substantial chance that litigation would ensue;" and (2) a subjective prong, which is satisfied if "the party resisting discovery believed in good faith that there was a substantial chance that litigation would ensue and conducted the investigation for the purpose of preparing for such litigation."[107]

In discussing the objective prong, the Court explained that the "[s]ubstantial-chance-of-litigation" prong "does not refer to any particular statistical probability that litigation will occur[,]" but "simply means that litigation is 'more than merely an abstract possibility or unwarranted fear.'"[108] Also regarding the objective prong, the Court "did not require actual notice of the potential litigation for a party to anticipate litigation. Instead, [it] recognized that 'common sense dictates that a party may reasonably anticipate suit being filed . . . before the plaintiff manifests an intent to sue.'"[109]

---

103 William V. Dorsaneo, III, *The History of Texas Civil Procedure*, 65 Baylor L. Rev. 713, 778 (2013).

104 *See* Alex Wilson Albright, *The Texas Work Product Rule*, 27 The Advoc. (Tex.) 10, 10 (2004) (citing former Texas Rule 166(b)(3)).

105 *See* Alex Wilson Albright, *The Texas Work Product Rule*, 27 The Advoc. (Tex.) 10, 12 (2004) (citing former Texas Rule 166(b)(3)).

106 *In re Ford Motor Co.*, 988 S.W.2d 714, 719 (Tex. 1998) (citing *Humphreys v. Caldwell*, 888 S.W.2d 469, 471 (Tex. 1994), and *Nat'l Tank Co. v. Brotherton*, 851 S.W.2d 193, 200 (Tex. 1993)); *see also Nat'l Tank Co. v. Brotherton*, 851 S.W.2d 193, 201–03 (Tex. 1993) (noting that "work product" was not defined in Texas rules and relying on precedent from Texas courts of appeals, federal courts, and other state courts to "conclude that the term 'work product' as used in [former Texas] Rule 166b(3)(a) applie[d] only to materials prepared in anticipation of litigation").

107 *Nat'l Tank Co. v. Brotherton*, 851 S.W.2d 193, 207 (Tex. 1993); *see also Nat'l Tank Co. v. Brotherton*, 851 S.W.2d 193, 203–07 (Tex. 1993) (modifying the two-prong test of *Flores v. Fourth Court of Appeals*, 777 S.W.3d 38, 40–41 (Tex. 1989), and providing detailed analysis of policies and precedent before stating the modified two-prong test for assessing whether an investigation occurred in anticipation of litigation).

108 *Nat'l Tank Co. v. Brotherton*, 851 S.W.2d 193, 204 (Tex. 1993) (agreeing with and quoting dissenting justices' explanation).

109 *Trevino v. Ortega*, 969 S.W.2d 950, 956 (Tex. 1998) (quoting *Nat'l Tank Co. v. Brotherton*, 851 S.W.2d 193, 204 (Tex. 1993)).

Between 1987 and 1990, there were several amendments to the discovery rules concerning the party-communication and consulting-expert privileges.[110] Perhaps most notably, "[c]onsulting experts' identities, mental impressions and opinions, as well as any documents or tangible things containing them became discoverable under a new standard, which was intended to broaden discoverability, i.e., 'if the consulting expert's opinion or impressions have been reviewed by a testifying expert[,]'"[111] and the party-communication privilege "was amended to narrow the scope of the exemption for post-occurrence party communications by requiring the communication to be 'in connection with the prosecution, investigation or defense of the particular suit, or in anticipation of the prosecution or defense of the claims made a part of the pending litigation.'"[112]

Finally, in 1999, the Texas Supreme Court amended the discovery rules extensively again. In doing so, it eliminated the witness-statement privilege, moved the consulting-expert privilege to a separate provision, Texas Rule 192.3(e), combined the party-communication and attorney-work-product privileges into one work-product privilege set forth in Texas Rule 192.5, defined work product, incorporated different levels of protection for "core work product" versus "other [or noncore] work product," and added new procedures for asserting privileges.[113] The remainder of this Chapter focuses on the 1999 (i.e., current) version of the work-product privilege in the Texas rules but includes pre-1999 precedent that remains authoritative.

4-4:2 Definition and Protection of "Work Product" Under Work-Product Privilege

Texas Rule 192.5(a) defines "work product" as—

(1) material prepared or mental impressions developed in anticipation of litigation or for trial by or for a party or a party's representatives, and communications made in anticipation of litigation or for trial between or among a party and the

---

110 William V. Dorsaneo, III, *The History of Texas Civil Procedure*, 65 Baylor L. Rev. 713, 778 (2013).

111 William V. Dorsaneo, III, *The History of Texas Civil Procedure*, 65 Baylor L. Rev. 713, 778 (2013) (citing former Texas Rule 166b(3)(b)).

112 William V. Dorsaneo, III, *The History of Texas Civil Procedure*, 65 Baylor L. Rev. 713, 778–79 (2013) (citing former Texas Rule 166b(3)(d)).

113 *See* William V. Dorsaneo, III, *The History of Texas Civil Procedure*, 65 Baylor L. Rev. 713, 803 (2013); William V. Dorsaneo, III, *The History of Texas Civil Procedure*, 65 Baylor L. Rev. 713, 804 (2013) (noting that the discovery-rule amendments "were accompanied by amendments made to the attorney-client privilege under [Texas] Evidence Rule 503, . . . which greatly expanded the scope of the attorney-client privilege under the former 'control group' approach to a much broader 'subject matter' standard based on an expanded definition of who qualifies as a party's representatives"); Alex Wilson Albright, *The Texas Work Product Rule*, 27 The Advoc. (Tex.) 10, 10 (2004) (citing former Texas Rule 166(b)(3)); *see also* Tex. R. Civ. P. 192 cmt. 8 to 1999 change ("Work product is defined for the first time, and its exceptions stated. Work product replaces the 'attorney work product' and party communication' discovery exemptions from former [Texas] Rule 166b."); Tex. R. Civ. P. 192 cmt. 9 to 1999 change ("Elimination of the 'witness statement' exemption does not render all witness statements automatically discoverable but subjects them to the same rules concerning the scope of discovery and privileges applicable to other documents or tangible things.").

parties' representatives, including the party's attorneys, consultants, sureties, indemnitors, insurers, employees, or agents; or

(2) a communication made in anticipation of litigation or for trial between a party and the party's representatives or among a party's representatives, including the party's attorneys, consultants, sureties, indemnitors, insurers, employees, or agents.[114]

Texas Rule 192.5(b) then categorizes work product as "core work product" or "other [noncore] work product" and sets forth the different protection levels for the two categories:

(1) **Protection of core work product—attorney mental processes.** Core work product—the work product of an attorney or an attorney's representative that contains the attorney's or the attorney's representative's mental impressions, opinions, conclusions, or legal theories—is not discoverable.

(2) **Protection of other work product.** Any other work product is discoverable only upon a showing that the party seeking discovery has substantial need of the materials in the preparation of the party's case and that the party is unable without undue hardship to obtain the substantial equivalent of the material by other means.

(3) **Incidental disclosure of attorney mental processes.** It is not a violation of subparagraph (1) if disclosure ordered pursuant to subparagraph (2) incidentally discloses by inference attorney mental processes otherwise protected under subparagraph (1).

(4) **Limiting disclosure of mental processes.** If a court orders discovery of work product pursuant to subparagraph (2), the court must—insofar as possible—protect against disclosure of the mental impressions, opinions, conclusions, or legal theories not otherwise discoverable.[115]

Texas Rule 192.5(d) finally makes clear that "an assertion that material or information is work product is an assertion of privilege."[116]

---

[114] Tex. R. Civ. P. 192.5(a)(1)–(2); *see also In re Bexar Cnty. Crim. Dist. Attorney's Office*, 224 S.W.3d 182, 186 (Tex. 2007) (orig. proceeding) (asserting that the work-product privilege encompasses "more than just documents: it extends to an attorney's mental impressions, opinions, conclusions, and legal theories, as well as the selection and ordering of documents"); *In re Allstate Fire & Cas. Ins. Co.*, 617 S.W.3d 635, 647 (Tex. App.—Houston [14th Dist.] 2021, orig. proceeding) ("Work product includes 'material prepared or mental impressions developed' by [a party] and its counsel." (quoting Tex. R. Civ. P. 192.5(a)(1))); *In re Monsanto Co.*, 998 S.W.2d 917, 923 (Tex. App.—Waco 1999, orig. proceeding) (asserting that the "work product" definition "encompasses the 'attorney work product' and 'party communication[]' discovery exemptions in former [Texas] Rule 166b").

[115] Tex. R. Civ. P. 192.5(b)(1)–(4); *see also e.g.*, *Paxton v. City of Dall.*, No. 06-18-00095-CV, 2019 Tex. App. LEXIS 3868, at *8–9, 2019 WL 2119644 (Tex. App.—Texarkana May 15, 2019, pet. denied) (mem. op.) ("The level of protection [Texas] Rule 192.5 accords to work product depends on its classification as 'core work product' or 'other work product,' sometimes referred to as noncore work product.").

[116] Tex. R. Civ. P. 192.5(d).

4-4:2.1 Comparing Work-Product Privilege with Attorney-Client Privilege

In several respects, "[t]he work[-]product privilege is broader than the attorney-client privilege."[117] For example, the definition of a "party's representatives" for the work-product privilege in Texas Rule 192.5 is broader than the definition of a "client's representatives" for the attorney-client privilege in Texas Rule of Evidence 503.[118] In addition, the work-product privilege is broader than the attorney-client privilege because "it includes all communications made in preparation for trial, including an attorney's interviews with parties and non-party witnesses[,]"[119] and extends beyond communications to cover, for example, documents, the selection and ordering of documents, opinions, conclusions, legal theories, reports, and mental impressions.[120]

---

[117] *In re Bexar Cnty. Crim. Dist. Attorney's Office*, 224 S.W.3d 182, 186 (Tex. 2007) (orig. proceeding), *quoted in In re Nat'l Lloyds Ins. Co.*, 532 S.W.3d 794, 803 (Tex. 2017) (orig. proceeding); *accord In re WHC, LLC*, 570 S.W.3d 349, 353 (Tex. App.—El Paso 2018, orig. proceeding).

[118] Alex Wilson Albright, *The Texas Work Product Rule*, 27 The Advoc. (Tex.) 10, 10 (2004) (citing former Texas Rule 166(b)(3)); Tex. R. Evid. 503(a)(2)(A)–(B) ("A 'client's representative' is: (A) a person who has authority to obtain professional legal services for the client or to act for the client on the legal advice rendered; or (B) any other purpose who, to facilitate the rendition of professional legal services to the client, makes or receives a confidential communication while acting in the scope of employment for the client."); *see In re WHC, LLC*, 570 S.W.3d 349, 353 (Tex. App.—El Paso 2018, orig. proceeding) (Texas "Rule 192.5 protects an attorney's work product from discovery. The protection extends to materials developed and communications made in anticipation of litigation or for trial for or by a party or its representatives, including the party's attorneys, employees, and agents.") (citations omitted); *In re DISH Network, LLC*, 528 S.W.3d 177, 181 (Tex. App.—El Paso 2017, orig. proceeding) (same).

[119] *In re Bexar Cnty. Crim. Dist. Attorney's Office*, 224 S.W.3d 182, 186 (Tex. 2007) (orig. proceeding) (citing Tex. R. Evid. 503); *accord In re Cook*, 597 S.W.3d 589, 602 (Tex. App.—Houston [14th Dist.] 2020, orig. proceeding); *Reed v. Davis*, No. 06-16-00038-CV, 2017 Tex. App. LEXIS 2552, at *14 n.12, 2017 WL 1101141 (Tex. App.—Texarkana Mar. 24, 2017, orig. proceeding) (mem. op.); *In re Park Cities Bank*, 409 S.W.3d 859, 867 (Tex. App.—Tyler 2013, orig. proceeding).

[120] *See, e.g., In re York Risk Servs. Grp., Inc.*, No. 12-17-00210-CV, 2017 Tex. App. LEXIS 10942, at *9, 2017 WL 5622951 (Tex. App.—Tyler Nov. 22, 2017, orig. proceeding) (mem. op.) ("The work product privilege is broader than the attorney-client privilege because it includes all communications made in preparation for trial, such as an attorney's interviews with parties and nonparty witnesses, extends to an attorney's mental impressions, opinion, conclusions, and legal theories, and includes the selection and ordering of documents."); *In re Bonding*, 522 S.W.3d 75, 86 (Tex. App.—Houston [1st Dist.] 2017, orig. proceeding) ("The work product privilege exempts from discovery an attorney's documents, reports, communications, memoranda, mental impressions, conclusions, opinions, or legal theories 'if generated in anticipation of litigation.'" (quoting *In re Baytown Nissan Inc.*, 451 S.W.3d 140, 148 (Tex. App.—Houston [1st Dist.] 2014, orig. proceeding))); *In re Fairway Methanol LLC*, 515 S.W.3d 480, 490–91 (Tex. App.—Houston [14th Dist.] 2017, orig. proceeding) ("The work product privilege extends both to documents actually created by the attorney and to memoranda, reports, notes, or summaries prepared by other individuals for the attorney's use."); *State ex rel. Jimerson*, No. 12-14-00153-CV, 2015 Tex. App. LEXIS 1306, at *4–5, 2015 WL 602637 (Tex. App.—Tyler Feb. 11, 2015, orig. proceeding) (mem. op.) ("The work product privilege includes all communications made in preparation for trial or in anticipation of litigation, including an attorney's interviews with parties and nonparty witnesses,

The work-product privilege is also broader than the attorney-client privilege because it is held by the attorney and the client, whereas the attorney-client privilege is held only by the client.[121]

The work-product privilege, however, is narrower than the attorney-client privilege in certain respects because its protection of communications extends only to communications made "in anticipation of litigation or for trial."[122] As explained above, the privilege does not protect material or mental impressions unless they were "developed in anticipation of litigation or for trial."[123] Thus, whether litigation is anticipated is often a key inquiry in assessing whether the work-product privilege protects information being sought in discovery.

4-4:2.2 Anticipation of Litigation Needed to Trigger Work-Product Privilege

Although *National Tank* predates the extensive 1999 amendments to the work-product rules, its anticipation-of-litigation test remains valid[124] and has been extended beyond the investigation context in which it arose. Under current Texas law, litigation is anticipated when (1) "a reasonable person would have concluded from the totality of the circumstances that there was a substantial chance that litigation would

---

and extends to an attorney's mental impressions, opinion, conclusions, legal theories, and the selection and ordering of documents."); *In re Baytown Nissan Inc.*, 451 S.W.3d 140, 148 (Tex. App.—Houston [1st Dist.] 2014, orig. proceeding) ("[T]he work product privilege exempts an attorney's documents, reports, communications, memoranda, mental impressions, conclusions, opinions, or legal theories from discovery if generated in anticipation of litigation. The privilege also protects the mental impressions and strategy of the attorney.") (citation omitted); *In re Park Cities Bank*, 409 S.W.3d 859, 867 (Tex. App.—Tyler 2013, orig. proceeding) (explaining that the work-product privilege "covers more than just documents, extending to an attorney's mental impressions, opinion, conclusions, and legal theories . . . [and] . . . also includes the selection and ordering of documents") (citations omitted).

121 Alex Wilson Albright, *The Texas Work Product Rule*, 27 The Advoc. (Tex.) 10, 10 (2004) (citing former Texas Rule 166(b)(3)) (noting that [Texas] Rule 192.5, like Federal Rule 26(b)(3)(A), "encompasses all work product, whether it is a lawyer's or client's, an opinion or ordinary work product, or party communications"); *cf. In re Grand Jury Subpoenas*, 561 F.3d 408, 411 (5th Cir. 2009) ("Work product protections, unlike the attorney-client privilege, are held by the attorney as well as the client."); *In re Grand Jury Proceedings*, 43 F.3d 966, 972 (5th Cir. 1994) (same); *Zelaya v. H&F Transp., Inc.*, No. CV SA-16-CA-450-PM, 2016 U.S. Dist. LEXIS 196119, at *7, 2016 WL 11583012 (W.D. Tex. Oct. 28, 2016) (same); *Alpert v. Riley*, No. H-04-CV-3774, 2009 U.S. Dist. LEXIS 36612, at *35, 2009 WL 1226767 (S.D. Tex. Apr. 30, 2009) ("Under federal and Texas law, work-product protection belongs to both the client and the attorney, either of whom may assert it."); *see also In re Cook*, 597 S.W.3d 589, 602 (Tex. App.—Houston [14th Dist.] 2020, orig. proceeding) (recognizing a client's "right to assert the work product privilege to prevent discovery of the [client's] attorney's work product").

122 *Compare* Tex. R. Civ. P. 192.5(a)(1)–(2) (protecting communications made "in anticipation of litigation or for trial"), *with* Tex. R. Evid. 503(b) (protecting "confidential" communications "made to facilitate the rendition of professional legal services to the client").

123 Tex. R. Civ. P. 192.5(d).

124 Alex Wilson Albright, *The Texas Work Product Rule*, 27 The Advoc. (Tex.) 10, 11 (2004) (citing former Texas Rule 166(b)(3) and noting that "National Tank and its progeny remain valid law."). *National Tank's* two-prong test is discussed in Chapter 4, section 4-4:1.

ensue[,]" and (2) "the party asserting the work product privilege subjectively believed in good faith that there was a substantial chance that litigation would ensue."[125] In other words, "trial courts must look at the totality of the circumstances and decide whether a reasonable person in the party's position would have anticipated litigation and whether the party actually did anticipate litigation."[126]

---

[125] *In re Baytown Nissan Inc.*, 451 S.W.3d 140, 148 (Tex. App.—Houston [1st Dist.] 2014, orig. proceeding); *accord Paxton v. City of Dall.*, No. 06-18-00095-CV, 2019 Tex. App. LEXIS 3868, at *13–14, 2019 WL 2119644 (Tex. App.—Texarkana May 15, 2019, pet. denied) (mem. op.) ("A document is prepared in anticipation of litigation when it meets both the objective and subjective prongs of the . . . two-part test established by the Texas Supreme Court" in *National Tank Co. v. Brotherton*, 851 S.W.2d 193, 195 (Tex. 1993)); *Leander Indep. Sch. Dist. v. Office of Attorney Gen.*, No. 03-18-00243-CV, 2018 Tex. App. LEXIS 10322, at *13–14, 2018 WL 6581523 (Tex. App.—Austin Dec. 14, 2018, orig. proceeding) (mem. op.) (same); *In re Mid-Century Ins. Co.*, 549 S.W.3d 730, 734 (Tex. App.—Waco 2017, orig. proceeding) (mem. op.) ("An investigation is conducted in anticipation of litigation if it meets the two-prong test of [*Flores v. Fourth Court of Appeals*, 777 S.W.3d 38, 40–41 (Tex. 1989),] which includes both an objective prong and a subjective prong. Specifically, an investigation is conducted in anticipation of litigation if (1) 'a reasonable person would have concluded from the totality of the circumstances surrounding the investigation that there was a substantial chance that litigation would ensue' (the objective prong); and (2) 'the party resisting discovery believed in good faith that there was a substantial chance that litigation would ensue and conducted the investigation for the purpose of preparing for such litigation' (the subjective prong)." (citation omitted) (quoting *Nat'l Tank Co. v. Brotherton*, 851 S.W.2d 193, 207 (Tex. 1993))); *In re Bonding*, 522 S.W.3d 75, 87 (Tex. App.—Houston [1st Dist.] 2017, orig. proceeding) ("In determining whether communications were made 'in anticipation of litigation' for purposes of applying the work product privilege, courts consider not only whether a reasonable person would have concluded from the totality of the circumstances that there was a substantial chance that litigation would ensue, but also whether '*the party invoking the privilege* believes in good faith that there is a substantial chance that litigation will ensue.'" (quoting *Nat'l Tank Co. v. Brotherton*, 851 S.W.2d 193, 207 (Tex. 1993))); *In re Fairway Methanol LLC*, 515 S.W.3d 480, 490–92 (Tex. App.—Houston [14th Dist.] 2017, orig. proceeding) (applying the two-prong anticipation-of-litigation test to investigations); *In re Monsanto Co.*, 998 S.W.2d 917, 923 (Tex. App.—Waco 1999, orig. proceeding) (relying on *National Tank* in holding that litigation is anticipated "(1) whenever the circumstances would indicate to a reasonable person that there is a substantial chance of litigation, and (2) the party now asserting the privilege had a good faith belief that litigation would ensue"); *In re Maher*, 143 S.W.3d 907, 912 (Tex. App.—Fort Worth 2004, orig. proceeding) (relying on *National Tank* to assert that "[a] document is prepared in actual anticipation of litigation . . . if: (1) a reasonable person would have concluded from the totality of the circumstances that there was a substantial chance that litigation would ensue (the objective standard); and (2) the party resisting discovery believed in good faith that there was a substantial chance that litigation would ensue and prepared the document(s) for the purposes of preparing for such litigation (the subjective standard)").

[126] *Trevino v. Ortega*, 969 S.W.2d 950, 956 (Tex. 1998); *accord In re York Risk Servs. Grp., Inc.*, No. 12-17-00210-CV, 2017 Tex. App. LEXIS 10942, at *9–10, 2017 WL 5622951 (Tex. App.—Tyler Nov. 22, 2017, orig. proceeding) (mem. op.); *In re Bonding*, 522 S.W.3d 75, 86 (Tex. App.—Houston [1st Dist.] 2017, orig. proceeding); *Reed v. Davis*, No. 06-16-00038-CV, 2017 Tex. App. LEXIS 2552, at *14 n.12, 2017 WL 1101141 (Tex. App.—Texarkana Mar. 24, 2017, orig. proceeding) (mem. op.); *In re Park Cities Bank*, 409 S.W.3d 859, 867 (Tex. App.—Tyler 2013, orig. proceeding); *In re Toyota Motor Corp.*, 94 S.W.3d 819, 823 (Tex. App.—San Antonio 2002, orig. proceeding); *In re Monsanto Co.*, 998 S.W.2d 917, 924 (Tex. App.—Waco 1999, orig. proceeding).

As established by *National Tank*, "[a]ctual notice of a potential lawsuit is not required for a party to anticipate litigation[.]"[127] Moreover, "[a] 'substantial chance of litigation' does not 'refer to any particular statistical probability that litigation will occur' but 'simply means that litigation is more than merely an abstract possibility or unwarranted fear.'"[128] In this regard, "[a] party may reasonably anticipate suit being filed and prepare for the expected litigation before anyone manifests an intent to sue[,]"[129] and the circumstances surrounding an accident can be sufficient to trigger the privilege.[130]

On the other hand, "'[t]he mere fact that an accident has occurred is not sufficient to clothe all post-accident investigations . . . with a privilege.'"[131] Rather, the objective prong of the anticipation-of-litigation test will be satisfied only "[i]f a reasonable person would conclude from the severity of the accident and the other circumstances surrounding it that there was a substantial chance that litigation would ensue[.]"[132]

---

[127] *In re Park Cities Bank*, 409 S.W.3d 859, 867 (Tex. App.—Tyler 2013, orig. proceeding); *see Trevino v. Ortega*, 969 S.W.2d 950, 956 (Tex. 1998) ("Importantly, [in *Nat'l Tank Co. v. Brotherton*, 851 S.W.2d 193, 204 (Tex. 1993),] we did not require actual notice of the potential litigation for a party to anticipate litigation. Instead, we recognized that 'common sense dictates that a party may reasonably anticipate suit being filed . . . before the plaintiff manifests an intent to sue.'"); *In re Certain Underwriters at Lloyd's London*, 294 S.W.3d 891, 900 (Tex. App.—Beaumont 2009, orig. proceeding) (concluding that insurance carriers anticipated litigation when they evaluated whether policy covered a claim *before* they issued reservation-of-rights letter or denied the claim and *before* the policyholders filed suit because the carriers previously had retained the same lawyer to handle similar claims, the lawyer had advised the carriers to anticipate litigation before the communications at issue had occurred, and the lawyer's affidavit accurately described the communications at issue as being "confidential, in furtherance of his legal representation, and contain[ing] his 'legal advice, theories, opinions, conclusions, mental analyses, and evaluations regarding the claims'").

[128] *In re Fairway Methanol LLC*, 515 S.W.3d 480, 490 (Tex. App.—Houston [14th Dist.] 2017, orig. proceeding) (quoting *Nat'l Tank Co. v. Brotherton*, 851 S.W.2d 193, 204 (Tex. 1993)); *accord Paxton v. City of Dall.*, No. 06-18-00095-CV, 2019 Tex. App. LEXIS 3868, at *14, 2019 WL 2119644 (Tex. App.—Texarkana May 15, 2019, pet. denied) (mem. op.); *Leander Indep. Sch. Dist. v. Office of Attorney Gen.*, No. 03-18-00243-CV, 2018 Tex. App. LEXIS 10322, at *14, 2018 WL 6581523 (Tex. App.—Austin Dec. 14, 2018, orig. proceeding) (mem. op.).

[129] *In re Monsanto Co.*, 998 S.W.2d 917, 923 (Tex. App.—Waco 1999, orig. proceeding) (citing *Nat'l Tank Co. v. Brotherton*, 851 S.W.2d 193, 204 (Tex. 1993)); *accord In re Mid-Century Ins. Co.*, 549 S.W.3d 730, 734 (Tex. App.—Waco 2017, orig. proceeding) (mem. op.); *Reed v. Davis*, No. 06-16-00038-CV, 2017 Tex. App. LEXIS 2552, at *14 n.12 (Tex. App.—Texarkana Mar. 24, 2017, orig. proceeding) (mem. op.); *In re Fairway Methanol LLC*, 515 S.W.3d 480, 490 (Tex. App.—Houston [14th Dist.] 2017, orig. proceeding); *In re Park Cities Bank*, 409 S.W.3d 859, 867 (Tex. App.—Tyler 2013, orig. proceeding).

[130] *See, e.g.*, *In re Fairway Methanol LLC*, 515 S.W.3d 480, 490 (Tex. App.—Houston [14th Dist.] 2017, orig. proceeding) ("The Texas Supreme Court rejected the proposition 'that the circumstances surrounding an accident can never by themselves be sufficient to trigger the privilege. If a reasonable person would conclude from the severity of the accident and the other circumstances surrounding it that there was a substantial chance that litigation would ensue, then the objective prong . . . is satisfied.'" (citations omitted) (quoting *Nat'l Tank Co. v. Brotherton*, 851 S.W.2d 193, 204 (Tex. 1993))).

[131] *Nat'l Tank Co. v. Brotherton*, 851 S.W.2d 193, 204 (Tex. 1993) (quoting *Stringer v. Eleventh Court of Appeals*, 720 S.W.2d 801, 802 (Tex. 1986)).

[132] *Nat'l Tank Co. v. Brotherton*, 851 S.W.2d 193, 204 (Tex. 1993); *see Paxton v. City of Dall.*, No. 06-18-00095-CV, 2019 Tex. App. LEXIS 3868, at *14, 2019 WL 2119644 (Tex. App.—Texarkana May 15, 2019, pet. denied) (mem. op.) ("'If a reasonable person would conclude

The subjective prong of the anticipation-of-litigation test does not require a party "to be absolutely convinced that litigation will occur; it requires only a good faith belief that there is a substantial chance that litigation will ensue" and, in the case of an investigation, "'that the investigation actually be conducted for the purpose of preparing for litigation.'"[133] "However, [Texas] Rule 192.5 does not require that the sole . . . purpose of the material or communication be for preparing for litigation[.]"[134]

Texas courts have held that, as a general rule, "discovery regarding the methods of document collection and production invades the work-product privilege."[135] They also have held that "[c]ompelling an attorney of record involved in the litigation of the case to testify concerning the suit's subject matter generally implicates work product concerns"[136] and that "'[a]n attorney's litigation file goes to the heart of the privileged

---

from the severity of the accident and the other circumstances surrounding it that there was a substantial chance that litigation would ensue, then the objective prong' is satisfied." (quoting *Nat'l Tank Co. v. Brotherton*, 851 S.W.2d 193, 195 (Tex. 1993))); *In re Mid-Century Ins. Co.*, 549 S.W.3d 730, 734 (Tex. App.—Waco 2017, orig. proceeding) (mem. op.) ("A 'substantial chance of litigation' does not 'refer to any particular statistical probability that litigation will occur' but 'simply means that litigation is more than merely an abstract possibility or unwarranted fear.' The Texas Supreme Court rejected the proposition 'that the circumstances surrounding an accident can never by themselves be sufficient to trigger the privilege. If a reasonable person would conclude from the severity of the accident and the other circumstances surrounding it that there was a substantial chance that litigation would ensue, then the objective prong . . . is satisfied. It is not necessary that litigation be threatened or imminent, as long as the prospect of litigation is identifiable because of claims that have already arisen.'" (citations omitted) (quoting *Nat'l Tank Co. v. Brotherton*, 851 S.W.2d 193, 204–05 (Tex. 1993))).

133 *In re Mid-Century Ins. Co.*, 549 S.W.3d 730, 734 (Tex. App.—Waco 2017, orig. proceeding) (mem. op.) (quoting *Nat'l Tank Co. v. Brotherton*, 851 S.W.2d 193, 204 (Tex. 1993)); *accord Paxton v. City of Dall.*, No. 06-18-00095-CV, 2019 Tex. App. LEXIS 3868, at *15–16, 2019 WL 2119644 (Tex. App.—Texarkana May 15, 2019, pet. denied) (mem. op.); *In re Fairway Methanol LLC*, 515 S.W.3d 480, 490 (Tex. App.—Houston [14th Dist.] 2017, orig. proceeding); *In re Bonding*, 522 S.W.3d 75, 86 (Tex. App.—Houston [1st Dist.] 2017, orig. proceeding) ("The subjective portion of this test 'is properly satisfied if the party invoking the privilege believes in good faith that there is a substantial chance that litigation will ensue,' and the test does not require the party invoking the privilege 'to be absolutely convinced that litigation will occur.'" (quoting *Nat'l Tank Co. v. Brotherton*, 851 S.W.2d 193, 204 (Tex. 1993))).

134 *In re Mid-Century Ins. Co.*, 549 S.W.3d 730, 734 (Tex. App.—Waco 2017, orig. proceeding) (mem. op.).

135 *In re Arpin Am. Moving Sys., LLC*, 416 S.W.3d 927, 929 (Tex. App.—Dallas 2013, orig. proceeding) ("[D]iscovery regarding the methods of document collection and production invades the work-product privilege."); *In re Exxon Corp.*, 208 S.W.3d 70, 75–76 (Tex. App.—Beaumont 2006, orig. proceeding) (holding that plaintiffs' request "to depose an Exxon representative for the purpose of inquiring specifically into the process by which Exxon's representative responded to the requests for production . . . necessarily and almost exclusively concerns the 'mental impressions developed in anticipation of litigation or for trial by or for a party or a party's representatives' . . . subject to protection as work product").

136 *In re Baptist Hosps.*, 172 S.W.3d 136, 140 (Tex. App.—Beaumont 2005, orig. proceeding), *quoted in In re Baytown Nissan Inc.*, 451 S.W.3d 140, 149 (Tex. App.—Houston [1st Dist.] 2014, orig. proceeding); *see also In re Baptist Hosps.*, 172 S.W.3d 136, 145 (Tex. App.—Beaumont 2005, orig. proceeding) ("[C]ompelling a deposition of the opposing party's attorney of record concerning the subject matter of the litigation is inappropriate under most circumstances.").

work area guaranteed by the work product exemption.'"[137] Because such information, by its very nature, is prepared for trial, it should generally be shielded from discovery with little analysis under the anticipation-of-litigation test.

Other types of information are less susceptible to general rules. For example, courts have struggled to determine the proper treatment of information generated in the ordinary course of business.[138]

In *National Tank*, the Texas Supreme Court determined "there should be no bright-line ordinary course of business exception" for routine investigations.[139] The court held that the standard anticipation-of-litigation test applies to routine investigations and that, when such investigations occur for litigation *and* nonlitigation reasons, the primary motivating purpose underlying the practice determines its treatment:

> It may very well be that a party routinely investigates serious accidents because such accidents routinely give rise to litigation. As with other investigations, an investigation performed in the ordinary course of business is conducted in anticipation of litigation if it passes both prongs of the [anticipation-of-litigation] test. With regard to the subjective prong, the circumstances must indicate that the investigation was in fact conducted to prepare for potential litigation. The court therefore must consider the reasons that gave rise to the company's ordinary business practice. If a party routinely investigates accidents because of litigation and nonlitigation reasons, the court should determine the primary motivating purpose underlying the ordinary business practice.[140]

---

137 *In re Baptist Hosps.*, 172 S.W.3d 136, 140 (Tex. App.—Beaumont 2005, orig. proceeding) (quoting *State ex rel. Curry v. Walker*, 873 S.W.2d 379, 380 (Tex. 1994) (per curiam)); *accord Nat'l Union Fire Ins. Co. v. Valdez*, 863 S.W.2d 458, 460 (Tex. 1993).

138 *See Nat'l Tank Co. v. Brotherton*, 851 S.W.2d 193, 205–06 (Tex. 1993) (recognizing that a "fundamental problem that has plagued other courts is determining whether a 'routine' investigation is conducted in anticipation of litigation" and analyzing federal and other states' precedent to convey differing views on the ordinary-course-of-business exception).

139 *Nat'l Tank Co. v. Brotherton*, 851 S.W.2d 193, 206 (Tex. 1993).

140 *Nat'l Tank Co. v. Brotherton*, 851 S.W.2d 193, 206 (Tex. 1993) (emphasis added) (footnotes omitted); *see Henry P. Roberts Invs., Inc. v. Kelton*, 881 S.W.2d 952, 955 (Tex. App.—Corpus Christi 1994, no writ) ("With regard to the subjective prong of the test, the court must also examine the totality of the circumstances to test the good faith beliefs and intentions of the party resisting discovery. Although the party need not be absolutely convinced that litigation will occur, the investigation must actually be conducted for the purpose of preparing for such litigation. In order for the privilege to apply, preparation for litigation must be the primary motivating purpose underlying the investigation, even though nonlitigation factors may also be involved.") (citation omitted); *Henry P. Roberts Invs., Inc. v. Kelton*, 881 S.W.2d 952, 956 (Tex. App.—Corpus Christi 1994, no writ) ("[A]n insurer's anticipation that it may have to negotiate with a claimant over the payment of a claim does not itself trigger the privilege. An investigation made primarily for the purpose of analyzing or strengthening the insurer's bargaining position in that negotiation is also not protected as having been made in anticipation of litigation. Rather, before the insurer's investigations will be considered to have been made in 'anticipation of litigation,' there must be some reasonable basis to conclude that a lawsuit will be filed, and preparation for that lawsuit must have been the primary purpose for the investigation. We are not unaware of the difficulty of distinguishing whether any given claims investigation is conducted primarily 1) for the purpose of settling the claim or 2) for litigation expected to result from a failure to settle. Whether settlement or litigation is more likely often depends upon the results of the investigation and

This primary-motivating-purpose test has been extended beyond the "routine investigation" context in which it arose. For example, in a case not involving an investigation, the Fort Worth Court of Appeals, after pointing out that the work-product privilege "is not an umbrella for protecting materials gathered in the ordinary course of business," explained that it applies only "when preparation for litigation [is] *the primary motivating purpose underlying the creation of the document.* A document is not prepared 'in anticipation of litigation' if it is *in fact prepared for some other purpose.*"[141]

4-4:2.3 Scope of Protection for "Core" and "Noncore" Work Product

Subject to the narrow exceptions in Texas Rule 192.5(c), "[c]ore work product—the work product of an attorney or an attorney's representative that contains the attorney's or the attorney's representative's mental impressions, opinions, conclusions, or legal theories—is not discoverable."[142] The Texas Supreme Court has described core work product as "sacrosanct" and as providing "impermeable" protection against discovery.[143]

---

the insurance company's own post-investigation determinations about the validity of the claim. . . . If the primary motivating factor of the investigation is to determine whether the claim should be paid or settled and the potential lawsuit avoided, then it would not appear to meet the test set forth in *Brotherton*. On the other hand, if the insurance company has already determined that it will not settle the claim and seeks further investigation primarily for the purpose of preparing its case for the anticipated lawsuit, its investigation should be considered to have been undertaken in anticipation of litigation. When the insurer later seeks to shield its investigation from discovery as having been prepared in anticipation of litigation, we would expect it to detail and justify its emphasis on litigation rather than claim settlement as the primary purpose of the investigation.").

141 *In re Maher*, 143 S.W.3d 907, 912 (Tex. App.—Fort Worth 2004, orig. proceeding) (emphasis added); *accord Oyster Creek Fin. Corp. v. Richwood Invs., II, Inc.*, 957 S.W.2d 640, 646 (Tex. App.—Amarillo 1997, pet. denied); *Flores v. Fourth Court of Appeals*, 777 S.W.2d 38, 41 (Tex. 1989); *Henry P. Roberts Invs. v. Kelton*, 881 S.W.2d 952, 955 (Tex. App.—Corpus Christi 1994, no writ)); *see Oyster Creek Fin. Corp. v. Richwood Invs., II, Inc.*, 957 S.W.2d 640, 648 (Tex. App.—Amarillo 1997, pet. denied) ("[F]ollowing *Nat'l Tank* [*Co. v. Brotherton*, 851 S.W.2d 193, 206 (Tex. 1993)], we hold that calculations of principal and interest made by an attorney for his client in an effort to affect private collection of a note under threat of private foreclosure, do not constitute attorney 'work product.'").

142 Tex. R. Civ. P. 192.5(b)(1); *accord In re Nat'l Lloyds Ins. Co.*, 532 S.W.3d 794, 803–04 (Tex. 2017) (orig. proceeding) ("Core work product—work product that contains 'the mental impressions, opinions, conclusions, or legal theories' of an attorney or an attorney's representative—is not discoverable."); *In re Bexar Cnty., Crim. Dist. Attorney's Office*, 224 S.W.3d 182, 187 (Tex. 2007) (orig. proceeding) (recognizing that core work product may be discovered under the limited circumstances set forth in Texas Rule 192.5(c)); *Occidental Chem. Corp. v. Banales*, 907 S.W.2d 488, 490 (Tex. 1995) (orig. proceeding) (per curiam) ("With respect to an attorney's thought processes, we agree with OxyChem that the work product privilege is absolute, subject only to the narrow exceptions found in the Texas Rules of Civil Procedure." (citing former Texas Rule 166b(3)(a))); *see* Tex. R. Civ. P. 192.5(c) (identifying work-product exceptions).

143 *In re Bexar Cnty. Crim. Dist. Attorney's Office*, 224 S.W.3d 182, 187 (Tex. 2007) (orig. proceeding), *quoted in In re Allstate Fire & Cas. Ins. Co.*, 617 S.W.3d 635, 647 (Tex. App.—Houston [14th Dist.] 2021, orig. proceeding), *Paxton v. City of Dall.*, No. 06-18-00095-CV,

Examples of core work product include an attorney's litigation file;[144] "a litigation binder prepared by or at the direction of an attorney;"[145] notes and other writings evincing an attorney's thought processes, including the attorney's "strategy decisions and issue formulation;"[146] an attorney's complete set of billing records (e.g., billing invoices, payment logs, payment ledgers, payment summaries, documents showing flat rates, and audits);[147] deposition questions to an attorney, requesting the attorney's

2019 Tex. App. LEXIS 3868, at *9, 2019 WL 2119644 (Tex. App.—Texarkana May 15, 2019, pet. denied) (mem. op.), and *State ex rel. Jimerson*, No. 12-14-00153-CV, 2015 Tex. App. LEXIS 1306, at *5, 2015 WL 602637 (Tex. App.—Tyler Feb. 11, 2015, orig. proceeding) (mem. op.); *see Occidental Chem. Corp. v. Banales*, 907 S.W.2d 488, 490 (Tex. 1995) (orig. proceeding) (per curiam) ("With respect to an attorney's thought processes, . . . the work product privilege is absolute, subject only to the narrow exceptions found in the Texas Rules of Civil Procedure.").

144 *See, e.g., Nat'l Union Fire Ins. Co. v. Valdez*, 863 S.W.2d 458, 460 (Tex. 1993) ("An attorney's litigation file goes to the heart of the privileged work area guaranteed by the work product exemption. The organization of the file, as well as the decision as to what to include in it, necessarily reveals the attorney's thought processes concerning the prosecution or defense of the case."), *cited with approval in In re Nat'l Lloyds Ins. Co.*, 532 S.W.3d 794, 804–05 (Tex. 2017) (orig. proceeding); *accord In re York Risk Servs. Grp., Inc.*, No. 12-17-00210-CV, 2017 Tex. App. LEXIS 10942, at *26, 2017 WL 5622951 (Tex. App.—Tyler Nov. 22, 2017, orig. proceeding) (mem. op.) ("'An attorney's litigation file goes to the heart of the privileged work area guaranteed by the work product exemption. [A]n attorney's selection and ordering of documents in anticipation of litigation is protected work product, even where the individual documents are not privileged[.]'" (quoting *Nat'l Union Fire Ins. Co. v. Valdez*, 863 S.W.2d 458, 460–61 (Tex. 1993) (orig. proceeding))). *But see Nat'l Union Fire Ins. Co. v. Valdez*, 863 S.W.2d 458, 461 (Tex. 1993) ("Our decision today does not prevent a party from requesting specific documents or categories of documents relevant to issues in a pending case, even though some or all of the documents may be contained in an attorney's files. It does, however, prevent a party from requesting the entire file, which is almost certain to encompass numerous irrelevant and immaterial documents, such as transmittal letters and pleadings already on file with the court, as well as privileged information.").

145 *In re Toyota Motor Corp.*, 94 S.W.3d 819, 825 (Tex. App.—San Antonio 2002, orig. proceeding) ("PTM–0081 is clearly a litigation binder prepared by or at the direction of an attorney, and despite the fact that certain documents contained therein may be subject to discovery in response to appropriate requests, the binder as a whole should be protected as work product. . . . The trial court abused its discretion in ordering production of the binder.") (footnote omitted) (citation omitted).

146 *Occidental Chem. Corp. v. Banales*, 907 S.W.2d 488, 490 (Tex. 1995); *see also Humphreys v. Caldwell*, 888 S.W.2d 469, 471 (Tex. 1994) (orig. proceeding) (per curiam) (concluding that memoranda and correspondence prepared by attorney in connection with litigation was "attorney-work product" and that trial court abused its discretion in ordering production of an entire claims file containing such "product").

147 *In re Nat'l Lloyds Ins. Co.*, 532 S.W.3d 794, 805 (Tex. 2017) (orig. proceeding) (quoting *Nat'l Union Fire Ins. Co. v. Valdez*, 863 S.W.2d 458, 461 (Tex. 1993) ("A request for all billing invoices, payment logs, payment ledgers, payment summaries, documents showing flat rates, and audits is analogous to the request in [*Nat'l Union Fire Ins. Co. v. Valdez*, 863 S.W.2d 458, 460 (Tex. 1993),] for an attorney's entire litigation file. These billing records—which are generated in anticipation of litigation and trial—are 'almost certain to encompass numerous irrelevant and immaterial documents.'"); *accord Morrison v. State*, 575 S.W.3d 1, 12 (Tex. App.—Texarkana 2019, no pet.). *But see In re Nat'l Lloyds Ins. Co.*, 532 S.W.3d 794, 806 (Tex. 2017) (orig. proceeding) (quoting Tex. R. Civ. P. 192.5(b)(2)) ("Our holding does not prevent a more narrowly tailored request for information relevant to an issue in a

mental impressions of the attorney's conversation with a witness about claims in the case in which discovery is sought;[148] a jury consultant's discussions with a party's attorneys, as well as notes documenting such discussions, that reflect the mental impressions and legal theories of the party's attorneys;[149] an attorney's memoranda analyzing potential claims to assert against parties;[150] and an investigative report that (1) is prepared after the investigator learns that an attorney is involved in the matter at hand and that litigation could occur as a result, and (2) summarizes witnesses' statements and identifies inconsistencies in them.[151]

Although noncore work product is more susceptible to discovery, parties seeking such work product still have a heavy burden of proof. To obtain noncore work product through discovery, a party must prove that it (1) "has substantial need of the materials in the preparation of [its] case," and (2) "is unable without undue hardship to obtain the substantial equivalent of the material by other means[.]"[152] Texas precedent

---

pending case that does not invade the attorney's strategic decisions or thought processes. Nor does our holding preclude a party from seeking noncore work product 'upon a showing that the party seeking discovery has substantial need of the materials in the preparation of the party's case and that the party is unable without undue hardship to obtain the substantial equivalent of the material by other means.'").

148 *See, e.g.*, *In re Baytown Nissan Inc.*, 451 S.W.3d 140, 149 (Tex. App.—Houston [1st Dist.] 2014, orig. proceeding) (concluding that "[o]ther questions requesting factual details" relating to conversation between attorney and witness were "non-core work product").

149 *In re Jefferson Cnty. Appraisal Dist.*, 315 S.W.3d 229, 234 (Tex. App.—Beaumont 2010, orig. proceeding) ("Discovery of the jury consultant's discussions with JCAD's legal counsel, including notes of such discussions, may reflect the mental impressions and legal theories of JCAD's counsel. Therefore, such information goes to the core of the work product doctrine and is not discoverable.").

150 *In re AEP Tex. Cent. Co.*, 128 S.W.3d 687, 692 (Tex. App.—San Antonio 2003, orig. proceeding) (holding that an attorney's memoranda analyzing potential claims contained the attorney's mental impressions, opinions, and legal theories and was core work product protected by the work-product privilege).

151 *See In re Weeks Marine, Inc.*, 31 S.W.3d 389, 391 (Tex. App.—San Antonio 2000, orig. proceeding) ("While a redacted form of the report may have been discoverable, the total report [was] privileged as core work product.").

152 Tex. R. Civ. P. 192.5(b)(2) (emphasis added); *see also In re Nat'l Lloyds Ins. Co.*, 532 S.W.3d 794, 804 (Tex. 2017) (orig. proceeding) ("A trial court may order disclosure of noncore work product . . . only if the requesting party shows substantial need and undue hardship."); *In re Bexar Cnty. Crim. Dist. Attorney's Office*, 224 S.W.3d 182, 188 (Tex. 2007) (orig. proceeding) (referring to "heavy burden" of showing substantial need and undue hardship); *In re Allstate Fire & Cas. Ins. Co.*, 617 S.W.3d 635, 647–48 (Tex. App.—Houston [14th Dist.] 2021, orig. proceeding) ("Any work product other than core work product is discoverable only upon a showing that the party seeking it has substantial need of the material and 'is unable without undue hardship to obtain the substantial equivalent of the material by other means.'" (quoting Tex. R. Civ. P. 192.5(b)(2))); *Paxton v. City of Dall.*, No. 06-18-00095-CV, 2019 Tex. App. LEXIS 3868, at *9, 2019 WL 2119644 (Tex. App.—Texarkana May 15, 2019, pet. denied) (mem. op.) (same); *In re Small*, 346 S.W.3d 657, 668 (Tex. App.—El Paso 2009, orig. proceeding) (asserting that party seeking discovery of non-core work product "labors under a heavy burden to show both that a substantial need for the materials exists and that materials equivalent to those sought cannot be obtained without substantial hardship"); *In re Mid-Century Ins. Co.*, 549 S.W.3d 730, 735 (Tex. App.—Waco, 2017, orig. proceeding) (mem. op.) ("A party seeking to obtain documents through this exception bears a heavy burden to prove its applicability. . . . As the party seeking discovery of non-core work

regarding the need-and-hardship exception is limited but informative.[153]

In *In re Bexar County Criminal District Attorney's Office*, the Texas Supreme Court addressed both prongs of the need-and-hardship exception and determined that neither had been met. Regarding its first prong, the court made clear that establishing "substantial need" requires more than asserting that the work product sought will improve the party's odds of winning the litigation at hand.[154] The Court reasoned that "[s]ubstantial need is not merely substantial desire."[155]

---

product, Cobb labors under a heavy burden to show both that a substantial need for the materials exists and that materials equivalent to those sought cannot be obtained without substantial hardship.") (citations omitted); *State ex rel. Jimerson*, No. 12-14-00153-CV, 2015 Tex. App. LEXIS 1306, at *4–19, 2015 WL 602637 (Tex. App.—Tyler Feb. 11, 2015, orig. proceeding) (mem. op.) (noting the "heavy burden" established with establishing entitlement to noncore work product and concluding, "[a]fter viewing the record as a whole" that a party had "not satisfied its burden of showing that it [had] a substantial need for the County Attorney's testimony to prove its claim for malicious prosecution"); *In re O'Quinn*, No. 04-08-00019-CV, 2008 Tex. App. LEXIS 2712, at *12, 2008 WL 1733256 (Tex. App.—San Antonio Apr. 16, 2008, orig. proceeding) (mem. op.) (holding that a party failed to meet the "heavy burden" by making "broad assertion that he had a substantial need for the documents to address witness credibility and memory" and by failing to "argue or show that he was unable without undue hardship to obtain the substantial equivalent of the documents by other means"); *Flores v. Fourth Court of Appeals*, 777 S.W.3d 38, 42 (Tex. 1989) (discussing the need-and-hardship exception in former Texas Rule 166(b)(3)(e) and in Federal Rule of Civil Procedure 26(b)(3), and noting its role in "further[ing] the purpose of discovery—to prevent trial by ambush").

[153] Because the need-and-hardship exception originated in *Hickman v. Taylor*, which was codified in Federal Rule of Civil Procedure 26(b)(3)(A)–(B), federal precedent also provides useful guidance. *E.g., Barr v. City of Sinton*, 295 S.W.3d 287, 296 n.42 (Tex. 2009) (citing *Nat'l Tank Co. v. Brotherton*, 851 S.W.2d 193, 202 (Tex. 1993), for proposition that federal law is instructive because the work-product doctrine is similar in Texas and federal courts); *Dillard Dep't Stores, Inc. v. Sanderson*, 928 S.W.2d 319, 321 (Tex. App.—Beaumont 1996, orig. proceeding) (noting dearth of Texas authority on need-and-hardship exception and relying on federal cases holding that "[i]ssues of credibility and failing memory . . . satisfy the substantial need and undue hardship exception under Fed. R. Civ. P. 26(b)(3)" to conclude that trial court did not abuse its discretion in ordering production of witness's prior statement to counsel).

[154] *In re Bexar Cnty. Crim. Dist. Attorney's Office*, 224 S.W.3d 182, 188 (Tex. 2007); *accord In re Mid-Century Ins. Co.*, 549 S.W.3d 730, 735 (Tex. App.—Waco 2017, orig. proceeding) (mem. op.).

[155] *In re Bexar Cnty. Crim. Dist. Attorney's Office*, 224 S.W.3d 182, 188 (Tex. 2007) (orig. proceeding); *accord In re Mid-Century Ins. Co.*, 549 S.W.3d 730, 735 (Tex. App.—Waco 2017, orig. proceeding) (mem. op.) ("Improving Cobb's odds of winning is not enough [to meet the substantial-need element]; substantial need is not merely substantial desire. . . . Additionally, a 'substantial need' is not established by evidence that Cobb could not prove her cause of action without the materials requested.") (citations omitted); *In re Fairway Methanol LLC*, 515 S.W.3d 480, 493 (Tex. App.—Houston [14th Dist.] 2017, orig. proceeding) ("A party seeking to obtain documents through this exception bears a heavy burden to prove its applicability. Improving a civil litigant's odds of winning is not enough; substantial need is not merely substantial desire.") (citations omitted); *In re Small*, 346 S.W.3d 657, 668 (Tex. App.—El Paso 2009, orig. proceeding) (concluding that party's statement establishing nothing more than party's desire to obtain non-core work product was insufficient to satisfy burden of proving "substantial need").

Regarding the exception's second prong, the Supreme Court explained: "[Texas] Rule 192.5 strikes a sensible balance, recognizing that a lawyer's thoughts are his own and that a party cannot invade every nook and cranny of a lawyer's case preparation, particularly when the 'essence' of what the party seeks has already been revealed to him or is readily available."[156] The Court then held that (1) the plaintiff did not establish "substantial need" for privileged District Attorney (DA) testimony in a malicious-prosecution suit merely by asserting that he needed the testimony to prove causation, and (2) because a prosecution file that the DA's Office had produced to the plaintiff was the "substantial equivalent" of the testimony sought, the plaintiff had not met the exception's hardship prong.[157] Its analysis of the hardship prong was facilitated by the facts that the prosecution file was extensive, the plaintiff "ha[d] already taken a deposition on written questions of the DA's custodian of records in order to establish that the prosecution file contain[ed] records of regularly conducted activity under [Texas Rule of Evidence] 803(6)[,]" and the plaintiff had conceded that the file contained "all the evidence he need[ed]" to prove malice in his malicious-prosecution suit.[158]

In *State v. Lowry*,[159] the Texas Supreme Court addressed both prongs of the need-and-hardship exception applicable to the party-communication and witness-statement privileges under former Texas Rule 166b(3), concluding that they had been met.[160] In that case, the question was whether defendant insurers were entitled to obtain from the Attorney General of Texas (the AG) certain documents about the AG's investigation of the defendant insurers under the Texas Free Enterprise Trust Act.[161] The documents at issue included materials gathered by the AG pursuant to his Civil Investigative Demands (CID) power, such as "depositions, written interrogatory questions and answers, as well as related exhibits."[162]

Regarding substantial need, the Supreme Court reasoned: "[A]ll of the information sought to be discovered was gathered by the State during the investigation that led to the filing of this antitrust enforcement action. The State has refused to provide materials requested by the insurers that could lead to evidence supporting their defense. It is difficult for the insurers to make a more particularized showing of need for these

---

156 *In re Bexar Cnty. Crim. Dist. Attorney's Office*, 224 S.W.3d 182, 189 (Tex. 2007) (orig. proceeding) (citing *Hickman v. Taylor*, 329 U.S. 495, 509 (1947)).

157 *Hickman v. Taylor*, 329 U.S. 495, 509 (1947); *see In re Small*, 346 S.W.3d 657, 657 (Tex. App.—El Paso 2009, orig. proceeding) (relying on *In re Bexar Cnty. Crim. Dist. Attorney's Office*, 224 S.W.3d 182, 188 (Tex. 2007), in holding that "a 'substantial need' is not established by evidence that the party could not prove his cause of action without the materials" sought).

158 *In re Bexar Cnty. Crim. Dist. Attorney's Office*, 224 S.W.3d 182, 188 (Tex. 2007) (orig. proceeding) ("The DA's Office, however, has already provided [the plaintiff] with the substantial equivalent of testimony: it has, pursuant to the subpoena duces tecum, turned over its entire prosecution file, which contains notes related to the investigation, sheriff's department complaint reports, [a defendant's] affidavit to the sheriff's department detailing [the plaintiff's] alleged threat [against him], and [the DA's] log of conversations with [the other defendant] that ultimately prompted [the DA] to dismiss the [underlying] criminal charges [against the plaintiff].").

159 *See State v. Lowry*, 802 S.W.2d 669 (Tex. 1991).

160 *See State v. Lowry*, 802 S.W.2d 669, 673 (Tex. 1991).

161 *State v. Lowry*, 802 S.W.2d 669, 670 (Tex. 1991).

162 *State v. Lowry*, 802 S.W.2d 669, 671 (Tex. 1991).

documents, the contents of which are unknown to them."[163] Regarding undue hardship, the Court noted that the defendant insurers urged, and the State apparently did not dispute, "the extreme difficulty and burden of replicating the investigative materials [the State had] amassed."[164] After concluding that, even if the insurers "could somehow retrace their opponent's investigative path with any hope of finding all the information that had been assembled against them, the defendants should not be put to the expense and delay of that exercise[,]"[165] the Supreme Court held that the "trial judge properly ordered production" of the materials.[166]

A party seeking to demonstrate the need-and-hardship exception bears "a particularly heavy burden when a discovery request seeks to compel the deposition of [an opposing] party's attorney."[167] Two courts of appeals have likened an effort to compel such a deposition to an effort to compel production of an attorney's litigation file, stating: "'As with compelling production of opposing counsel's litigation file, compelling a deposition of the opposing party's attorney of record concerning the subject matter of the litigation is inappropriate under most circumstances'" because it "'seriously disrupts the counsel's functioning as an advocate and may create a false impression that the advocate was improperly involved in the underlying issues in the litigation.'"[168] Both courts have thus heightened the burden required to justify an order compelling the deposition of an opposing party's attorney of record.

In *In re Baytown*, the Houston (First) Court of Appeals engrafted on the need-and-hardship exception "the two-part test provided in *Hickman* for exemption from privilege requiring that (1) the information be 'hidden in the attorney's file' and (2) the facts sought to be discovered must be 'essential to the preparation of one's case.'"[169] The court then concluded that the information sought through the deposition of the opposing party's attorney, "far from being hidden, [was] readily available" through the other party to the conversation that would be the focus of the deposition.[170] Thus, the court held that there was "no indication in the record of a substantial need for [the attorney's] testimony" about the conversation and that the "trial court erred in compelling [the attorney] to testify about [it]."[171]

---

[163] *State v. Lowry*, 802 S.W.2d 669, 673 (Tex. 1991).

[164] *State v. Lowry*, 802 S.W.2d 669, 673 (Tex. 1991).

[165] *State v. Lowry*, 802 S.W.2d 669, 673 (Tex. 1991).

[166] *State v. Lowry*, 802 S.W.2d 669, 673 (Tex. 1991).

[167] *In re Baytown Nissan Inc.*, 451 S.W.3d 140, 149 (Tex. App.—Houston [1st Dist.] 2014, orig. proceeding).

[168] *In re Baytown Nissan Inc.*, 451 S.W.3d 140, 149–50 (Tex. App.—Houston [1st Dist.] 2014, orig. proceeding) (quoting *In re Baptist Hosps.*, 172 S.W.3d 136, 145 (Tex. App.—Beaumont 2005, orig. proceeding)).

[169] *In re Baytown Nissan Inc.*, 451 S.W.3d 140, 150 (Tex. App.—Houston [1st Dist.] 2014, orig. proceeding) (quoting *Hickman v. Taylor*, 329 U.S. 495, 511 (1947), and *Marshall v. Hall*, 943 S.W.2d 180, 183 (Tex. App.—Houston [1st Dist.] 1997, no writ), which applied two-part *Hickman* test to deny discovery of attorney's employee's notes reflecting the interview of a witness to the car accident at issue).

[170] *In re Baytown Nissan Inc.*, 451 S.W.3d 140, 150 (Tex. App.—Houston [1st Dist.] 2014, orig. proceeding).

[171] *In re Baytown Nissan Inc.*, 451 S.W.3d 140, 150 (Tex. App.—Houston [1st Dist.] 2014, orig. proceeding).

In *In re Baptist Hospitals*, the Beaumont Court of Appeals coupled the need-and-hardship exception with the discovery limits imposed in Texas Rule 192.4, holding: "Generally, even when discovery of non-core work product is permitted because of substantial need and undue hardship [under Texas Rule 192.5(b)(2)], a trial court should not order a deposition of an attorney of record on the subject matter of the litigation without requiring a showing that less intrusive discovery methods are unavailable to obtain the information sought."[172] In doing so, the court, after identifying several other potential (non-lawyer) sources of the information that a party was seeking though the deposition of the opposing party's attorney,[173] concluded that the party had failed to show "that it [had] substantial need of the facts known by [the attorney] for the preparation of its case and that it [was] unable without undue hardship to obtain the substantial equivalent of the material by other means."[174] The court also held that, because the trial court's "order compelling the deposition of the attorney of record [did] not limit its scope in any way or otherwise protect against disclosure of work product[,]" the trial abused its discretion in entering it.[175]

Finally, in *In re Burroughs*, the Beaumont Court of Appeals followed *In re Baptist Hospitals*, holding that the trial court abused its discretion in ordering the oral deposition of a nonparty's attorney.[176] The attorney had represented the nonparty in underlying proceedings to recover insurance proceeds for personal injury and property damage suffered during an automobile accident.[177] In a later action by one of the drivers involved in the accident (Lawson) against one of the other drivers involved in the accident (Todd), the third driver involved in the accident (Biehle) was deposed as a nonparty fact witness.[178] In an effort to impeach Biehle's testimony, Lawson sought to depose Biehle's attorney (Burroughs).[179]

In a mandamus proceeding brought after the trial court denied Burroughs' motion to quash the deposition notice,[180] the court of appeals held that the trial court had abused its discretion in compelling Burroughs' deposition because (1) "Lawson made no showing that less intrusive discovery methods were unavailable to obtain the discovery sought[,]" and (2) the "trial court's order compelling Burroughs to present himself for the oral deposition contained no limitation as to subject matter and failed to protect against disclosure of attorney work product" as required by Texas Rule 192.5(b)(2).[181] In reaching its conclusions, the court noted that the "work product

[172] *In re Baptist Hosps.*, 172 S.W.3d 136, 145 (Tex. App.—Beaumont 2005, orig. proceeding); *see also In re Baptist Hosps.*, 172 S.W.3d 136, 145–50 (Tex. App.—Beaumont 2005, orig. proceeding) (identifying written discovery requests as potentially less intrusive and asserting that, "[i]f, as a last resort, the advocate's oral deposition is to be ordered, the area of questions permitted should be specified and a protective order entered, to protect against the disclosure of core work product and other privileged information").

[173] *In re Baptist Hosps.*, 172 S.W.3d 136, 144–45 (Tex. App.—Beaumont 2005, orig. proceeding).

[174] *In re Baptist Hosps.*, 172 S.W.3d 136, 145. (Tex. App.—Beaumont 2005, orig. proceeding).

[175] *In re Baptist Hosps.*, 172 S.W.3d 136, 145 (Tex. App.—Beaumont 2005, orig. proceeding).

[176] *In re Burroughs*, 203 S.W.3d 858, 859 (Tex. App.—Beaumont 2006, orig. proceeding).

[177] *In re Burroughs*, 203 S.W.3d 858, 859 (Tex. App.—Beaumont 2006, orig. proceeding).

[178] *In re Burroughs*, 203 S.W.3d 858, 859 (Tex. App.—Beaumont 2006, orig. proceeding).

[179] *In re Burroughs*, 203 S.W.3d 858, 859 (Tex. App.—Beaumont 2006, orig. proceeding).

[180] *In re Burroughs*, 203 S.W.3d 858, 859 (Tex. App.—Beaumont 2006, orig. proceeding).

[181] *In re Burroughs*, 203 S.W.3d 858, 859 (Tex. App.—Beaumont 2006, orig. proceeding).

privilege is of continuing duration" and thus that it was "appropriate to extend [its] holding in *In re Baptist Hospitals* to the facts and circumstances" at issue.[182]

As with the attorney-client privilege, the work-product privilege can be waived through offensive use.[183] Such a waiver "'should not lightly be found'"; indeed, it "requires each of the following elements: (1) the party asserting the privilege must seek affirmative relief; (2) the privileged information must be such that, if believed by the fact finder, would probably be outcome determinative; and (3) disclosure of the confidential information must be the only means by which the aggrieved party may obtain the evidence."[184]

Finally, the Texas Supreme Court has made clear that "factual information is not exempt from discovery by mere inclusion with protected documents."[185] For example, "a document is not privileged simply because it is contained in an attorney's files[,]"[186] and the work-product doctrine does not preclude a party from "requesting specific documents or categories of documents relevant to issues in a pending case, even though some or all of the documents may be contained in an attorney's files."[187]

---

182 *In re Burroughs*, 203 S.W.3d 858, 860. (Tex. App.—Beaumont 2006, orig. proceeding).

183 *See, e.g., In re Nat'l Lloyds Ins. Co.*, 532 S.W.3d 794, 807 (Tex. 2017) (orig. proceeding) ("We acknowledge that an opposing party may waive its work-product privilege through offensive use—perhaps by relying on its billing records to contest the reasonableness of opposing counsel's attorney fees or to recover its own attorney fees."); *Nat'l Union Fire Ins. Co. v. Valdez*, 863 S.W.2d 458, 461 (Tex. 1993) (orig. proceeding) ("We recognized in *Ginsberg v. Fifth Court of Appeals*, 686 S.W.2d 105 (Tex. 1985) (orig. proceeding), that a privilege may be waived by offensive use. . . . Although *Ginsberg* concerned the psychotherapist-patient privilege, we have recently applied the offensive waiver principle to the attorney-client privilege, as well as indicating that it applies to the work-product privilege.") (citations omitted); *In re Bonding*, 522 S.W.3d 75, 89–90 (Tex. App.—Houston [1st Dist.] 2017, orig. proceeding) (reciting the standards for offensive-use waiver and concluding that, even if the emails at issue in the case did constitute privileged work product, the plaintiffs waived the privilege through their offensive use of the emails in question).

184 *Nat'l Union Fire Ins. Co. v. Valdez*, 863 S.W.2d 458, 461 (Tex. 1993) (orig. proceeding) (quoting *Republic Ins. Co. v. Davis*, 856 S.W.2d 158, 163 (Tex. 1993) (orig. proceeding)).

185 *In re Nat'l Lloyds Ins. Co.*, 532 S.W.3d 794, 807 (Tex. 2017) (orig. proceeding); *see Leede Oil & Gas, Inc. v. McCorkle*, 789 S.W.2d 686, 687 (Tex. App.—Houston [1st Dist.] 1990, orig. proceeding) (per curiam) ("The work product privilege protects the mental impressions and strategy of the attorney, not facts of the case."); *cf. Deamus v. State*, No. 05-15-01182-CR, 2017 Tex. App. LEXIS 8029, at *25, 2017 WL 3599771 (Tex. App.—Dallas Aug. 22, 2017, no pet.) (mem. op.) ("Work product protects an attorney's thoughts and impressions, rather than the underlying factual information.").

186 *Nat'l Union Fire Ins. Co. v. Valdez*, 863 S.W.2d 458, 460 (Tex. 1993) (orig. proceeding); *see also Owens–Corning Fiberglas Corp. v. Caldwell*, 818 S.W.2d 749, 750 n.2 (Tex. 1991) (orig. proceeding) ("While an attorney must be allowed to work with a degree of privacy, the protection granted under the work product doctrine does not extend to facts the attorney may acquire."); *cf. Hickman v. Taylor*, 329 U.S. 495, 511 (1947) ("We do not mean to say that all written materials obtained or prepared by an adversary's counsel with an eye toward litigation are necessarily free from discovery in all cases. Where relevant and non-privileged facts remain hidden in an attorney's file and where production of those facts is essential to the preparation of one's case, discovery may properly be had.").

187 *Nat'l Union Fire Ins. Co. v. Valdez*, 863 S.W.2d 458, 461 (Tex. 1993) (orig. proceeding) ("[A] party may not cloak a document with the attorney-client privilege simply by forwarding it to his or her attorney. Similarly, a file memorandum is not necessarily attorney work

4-4:3 Exceptions to Work-Product Privilege

Texas Rule 192.5(c) sets forth five exceptions to the work-product privilege:

Even if made or prepared in anticipation of litigation or for trial, the following is not work product protected from discovery:

(1) information discoverable under [Texas] Rule 192.3 concerning experts, trial witnesses, witness statements, and contentions;

(2) trial exhibits ordered disclosed under [Texas] Rule 166 or [Texas] Rule 190.4;

(3) the name, address, and telephone number of any potential party or any person with knowledge of relevant facts;

(4) any photograph or electronic image of underlying facts (e.g., a photograph of the accident scene) or a photograph or electronic image of any sort that a party intends to offer into evidence; and

(5) any work product created under circumstances within an exception to the attorney-client privilege in Rule 503(d) of the [Texas] Rules of Evidence [i.e., the crime-fraud exception to the attorney-client privilege].[188]

---

product, even though prepared by a lawyer.") (citations omitted); *accord In re York Risk Servs. Grp., Inc.*, No. 12-17-00210-CV, 2017 Tex. App. LEXIS 10942, at *26, 2017 WL 5622951 (Tex. App.—Tyler Nov. 22, 2017, orig. proceeding) (mem. op.) ("A party may request specific documents or categories of documents relevant to issues in a pending case, even when some or all of the documents may be contained in an attorney's file. . . . '[A] document is not privileged simply because it is contained in an attorney's files.'" (quoting *Nat'l Union Fire Ins. Co. v. Valdez*, 863 S.W.2d 458, 460 (Tex. 1993) (orig. proceeding))).

188 Tex. R. Civ. P. 192.5(c)(1)–(5); *see In re Nat'l Lloyds Ins. Co.*, 532 S.W.3d 794, 803, 814 (Tex. 2017) (orig. proceeding) ("Certain matters are expressly excluded from the definition of 'work product,' however, and are not protected from discovery even if made or prepared in anticipation of litigation or for trial. . . . [T]he work-product privilege does not apply to 'information discoverable under [Texas] Rule 192.3 concerning experts, trial witnesses, witness statements, and contentions.' Thus, the tactical decision to designate counsel as a testifying witness provides the opposing party with the means to access information and attorney work product not otherwise available under the general scope of discovery." (footnotes omitted) (quoting Tex. R. Civ. P. 192.5(c)(1))); *In re Christus Spohn Hosp. Kleberg*, 222 S.W.3d 434, 438 (Tex. 2007) (orig. proceeding) ("It is true, as the Hospital claims and Palmer does not dispute, that the Northcutt documents constitute work product under [Texas] Rule 192.5, and that work product is carefully protected from discovery under our rules. However, [Texas] Rule 192.5(c)(1) specifically states that work product loses its protected status when it is provided to a testifying expert[.]") (citations omitted); *In re Sting Soccer Grp., LP*, No. 05-17-00317-CV, 2017 Tex. App. LEXIS 11197, at *14, 2017 WL 5897454 (Tex. App.—Dallas Nov. 30, 2017, orig. proceeding) (mem. op.) ("[Discovery requests seeking a party's legal or factual contentions are excepted from the work product doctrine and cannot be protected from discovery even if they otherwise fit the definition of work product. Because work product is not a proper objection to contention interrogatories, the trial court had no discretion and could only overrule Vola's work product objections.") (citations omitted); *In re Tex. Windstorm Ins. Ass'n*, No. 14-16-00677-CV, 2016 Tex. App. LEXIS 13178, at *6 (Tex. App.—Houston [14th Dist.] Dec. 13, 2016, orig. proceeding) (mem. op.) (explaining that "'information discoverable under [Texas R]ule 192.3 concerning experts, trial witnesses, witness statements, and contentions' are not work product protected from discovery[,]" and that "[t]he work-product privilege is not applicable to requests for disclosure pursuant

Texas Rule of Evidence 503(d) provides that the attorney-client "privilege does not apply" if: (1) "the lawyer's services were sought or obtained to enable or aid anyone to commit or plan to commit what the client knew or reasonably should have known to be a crime or fraud;" (2) "the communication is relevant to an issue between parties claiming through the same deceased client;" (3) "the communication is relevant to an issue of breach of duty by a lawyer to the client or by a client to the lawyer;" (4) "the communication is relevant to an issue concerning an attested document to which the lawyer is an attesting witness;" or (5) "the communication: (A) is offered in an action between clients who retained or consulted a lawyer in common; (B) was made by any of the clients to the lawyer; and (C) is relevant to a matter of common interest between the clients."[189]

4-5 Protective Orders

Texas Rule 192.6 provides for protective orders. Under it, "[a] person from whom discovery is sought, and any other person affected by the discovery request, may move . . . for an order protecting that person from the discovery sought."[190] Because the Rule refers to "persons," not "parties," a nonparty has standing to seek protection when it is affected by the discovery request.[191] Moreover, a party responding to a

to [Texas R]ule 194.2(f)(4)." (quoting Tex. R. Civ. P. 192.5(c)(1))); *Maverick Cnty. v. R.R. Comm'n*, No. 03-14-00257-CV, 2015 Tex. App. LEXIS 12971, at *12, 2015 WL 9583873 (Tex. App.—Austin Dec. 29, 2015, pet. denied) (mem. op.) ("Documents shared with these contracting experts [were] not protected by the attorney-client or work product privileges") (footnotes omitted); *see also In re Bilfinger Westcon, Inc.*, No. 13-19-00466-CV, 2019 Tex. App. LEXIS 10807, at *31–32, 2019 WL 6795870 (Tex. App.—Corpus Christi Dec. 12, 2019, orig. proceeding) (mem. op.) (noting that "[c]ertain matters are expressly excluded from the definition of 'work product,' . . . and are not protected from discovery even if made or prepared in anticipation of litigation or for trial[,]" and rejecting as "nonsensical" a party's claim that a trial court violated the work-product privilege by requiring the party to identify documents responsive to an opposing party's production requests).

189 Tex. R. Evid. 503(d)(1)-(5); *see also In re Cook*, 597 S.W.3d 589, 603 (Tex. App.—Houston [14th Dist.] 2020, orig. proceeding) ("The purpose of the crime fraud exception to the attorney-client privilege is 'to assure that the seal of secrecy between lawyer and client does not extend to communications made for the purpose of getting advice for the commission of a fraud or crime.'" (quoting *U.S. v. Zolin*, 491 U.S. 554, 563 (1989))); *Stanton v. Gloersen*, No. 05-16-00214-CV, 2016 Tex. App. LEXIS 12726, at *12–13 n.14, 2016 WL 7166550 (Tex. App.—Dallas Nov. 30, 2016, pet. denied) (mem. op.) ("Generally, a client of an attorney has a privilege to refuse to disclose and to prevent any other person from disclosing 'confidential communications made to facilitate the rendition of professional legal services to the client' between certain designated individuals. However, the privilege does not apply '[i]f the lawyer's services were sought or obtained to enable or aid anyone to commit or plan to commit what the client knew or reasonably should have known to be a crime or fraud.' The crime-fraud exception applies with the same force to a claim that information is protected as attorney work-product." (citations omitted) (quoting Tex. R. Evid. 503(d)(1))).

190 Tex. R. Civ. P. 192.6(a).

191 *See, e.g.*, *In re Garza*, 544 S.W.3d 836, 842 (Tex. 2018) (orig. proceeding) (per curiam) (The "use of 'and' [in Texas Rules 176.6(e) and 192.6(a)] means that *both* the potential deponent and any other person affected by the discovery request are entitled to seek protection by filing motions for protection."); *In re Univ. of Tex.*, No. 04-20-00439-CV, 2021 Tex. App. LEXIS 365, at *10 n.3, 2021 WL 185529 (Tex. App.—San Antonio Jan. 20, 2021, orig. proceeding) (mem. op.) ("A party to a suit may seek nonparty production of documents in

discovery request can seek a protective order to protect a nonparty's privileged, proprietary, or confidential information.[192]

"A person should not move for protection when an objection to written discovery or an assertion of privilege is appropriate. . . ."[193] This provision relates to parties *only* and requires them to comply with Texas Rule 193 in interposing objections to written discovery and production requests in a deposition notice.[194] Its purpose is twofold: "First, it clarifies that persons should not move for a protective order when an objection is appropriate. Second, it attempts to avoid creating a 'trap' for the unwary or 'breeding satellite litigation' regarding whether a protective order or an objection was the appropriate vehicle for seeking relief from discovery."[195]

Although the filing of a motion for protective order when an objection should have been interposed "does not waive the objection or assertion of privilege[,]"[196] the motion only preserves those objections made in it. In other words, any objection

---

the nonparty's possession, and a nonparty may move for a protective order."); *Envtl. Procedures, Inc. v. Guidry*, 282 S.W.3d 602, 635 n.54 (Tex. App.—Houston [14th Dist.] 2009, pet. denied) ("A nonparty may seek relief from a trial court regarding discovery sought from the nonparty by parties in a case pending in the trial court."); *In re Does 1-10*, 242 S.W.3d 805, 812 (Tex. App.—Texarkana 2007, orig. proceeding) (holding that a nonparty had standing to move for a protective order under Texas Rules 192.6(a)–(b) to prevent the release of his name and information by an Internet service provider); *In re Shell E&P, Inc.*, 179 S.W.3d 125, 129–30 (Tex. App.—San Antonio 2005, orig. proceeding) (holding that a nonparty could seek protection of its confidential documents that one party had obtained in a previous lawsuit involving the nonparty, but which were still subject to protective order from the previous suit); *see In re Kuntz*, 124 S.W.3d 179, 184 n.4 (Tex. 2003) (noting in *dicta* that a nonparty document owner could seek to protect its documents from production).

192 *In re CI Host, Inc.*, 92 S.W.3d 514, 517 (Tex. 2002) (orig. proceeding) ("Our discovery rules do not require notice to third parties so that they might have an opportunity to be heard on their own objections. Yet, we are loath to allow CI Host to unilaterally waive its customers' privacy rights by its failing to adhere to the discovery rules. It therefore falls upon the trial court to give serious consideration to these interests.") (citation omitted); *In re United Fire Lloyds*, 578 S.W.3d 572, 579 (Tex. App.—Tyler 2019, orig. proceeding) (mem. op.) ("[T]he rules demonstrate that Inner Pipe [a party] had standing to both object to and seek protection from the discovery propounded on the four non-parties."); *In re R.C.K.*, No. 09-16-00132-CV, 2016 Tex. App. LEXIS 6138, at *5, 2016 WL 3197585 (Tex. App.—Beaumont June 9, 2016, orig. proceeding) (per curiam) (mem. op.) (concluding that a party had standing to object to, and seek protection from, the production by third parties of the party's medical records); *In re Christus Health Se. Tex.*, 167 S.W.3d 596, 601–03 (Tex. App.—Beaumont 2005, orig. proceeding) (ordering the trial court to review documents produced by a hospital to protect the privilege of its emergency-room patients).

193 Tex. R. Civ. P. 192.6(a).

194 Nonparties responding to discovery subpoenas can either move for protection or object. *See* Tex. R. Civ. P. 176.6. See also Chapter 13, section 13-4:4 (discussing responses to nonparty document subpoenas).

195 *In re Park Cities Bank*, 409 S.W.3d 859, 876, 878 (Tex. App.—Tyler 2013, orig. proceeding) (quoting Nathan L. Hecht & Robert H. Pemberton, *A Guide to the 1999 Texas Discovery Rules Revisions* § E-5 (Nov. 11, 1998), http://www.txcourts.gov/rules-forms/rules-standards).

196 Tex. R. Civ. P. 192.6(a); *In re Park Cities Bank*, 409 S.W.3d 859, 878 (Tex. App.—Tyler 2013, orig. proceeding).

not made in the motion is waived. This principle is illustrated by the Tyler Court of Appeals' opinion in *In re Park Cities Bank*.[197]

In that case, the defendants, rather than objecting to the plaintiff's production requests, filed a motion for protective order with respect to them.[198] After the motion was denied, they interposed objections to the requests that had not been asserted in the motion.[199] The plaintiff then moved to compel, arguing that the defendants waived the new objections by not asserting them in the motion.[200] After being ordered to produce all nonprivileged documents, the defendants filed a petition for a writ of mandamus claiming that the trial court abused its discretion in overruling their new objections under Texas Rule 193.6(e)'s no-waiver provision.[201] The Tyler Court of Appeals disagreed:

> Relators' argument suggests that filing a motion for a protective order provides an exception to [Texas Rule 193.2(e)] that "[a]n objection that is not made within the time required . . . is waived unless the court excuses the waiver for good cause shown." However, nothing in the language of either rule persuades us that this is the correct interpretation. Moreover, Relators have not directed us to any authority supporting this interpretation, nor have we been able to locate any such authority. Indeed, the express language of [Texas] Rule 192.6(a) is that "the objection" is not waived. We interpret "the objection" to mean the complaint that was asserted by a motion for protection when an objection was appropriate. This reading is consistent with the plain language of the rule and does not limit the application of [Texas] Rule 193.2(e). [Texas] Rule 192.6(a) does not aid Relators.[202]

If, however, a motion for protective order is proper (e.g., when the responding party seeks protection from an entire set of production requests, interrogatories, or requests for admission because they are unduly burdensome, unreasonably cumulative or duplicative of other discovery, or disproportionate the case's needs), the motion is denied, and the party is ordered to respond to the discovery, the responding party has *not* waived its specific objections to individual discovery requests and can assert them.[203]

To be consistent with Texas Rule 193's requirements regarding partial objections to discovery requests,[204] Texas Rule 192.6(a) also provides that, "[i]f a person seeks

---

[197] *In re Park Cities Bank*, 409 S.W.3d 859 (Tex. App.—Tyler 2013, orig. proceeding).

[198] *In re Park Cities Bank*, 409 S.W.3d 859, 865 (Tex. App.—Tyler 2013, orig. proceeding).

[199] *In re Park Cities Bank*, 409 S.W.3d 859, 865, 877–78 (Tex. App.—Tyler 2013, orig. proceeding).

[200] *In re Park Cities Bank*, 409 S.W.3d 859, 878 (Tex. App.—Tyler 2013, orig. proceeding).

[201] *In re Park Cities Bank*, 409 S.W.3d 859, 876, 878 (Tex. App.—Tyler 2013, orig. proceeding).

[202] *In re Park Cities Bank*, 409 S.W.3d 859, 878 (Tex. App.—Tyler 2013, orig. proceeding) (citations omitted) (quoting Tex. R. Civ. P. 192.6(a), 193.2(e)).

[203] *See* Tex. R. Civ. P. 177.6(d)–(e), 192.6, 193.4.

[204] Tex. R. Civ. P. 193.2(b) ("A party must comply with as much of the request to which the party has made no objection unless it is unreasonable under the circumstances to do so before obtaining a ruling on the objection. If the responding party objects to the requested time or place of production, the responding party must state a reasonable time and place for complying with the request and must comply at that time and place without further request or order."). See also Chapter 5, section 5-3 (discussing objections to written discovery).

protection regarding the time or place of discovery, the person must state a reasonable time and place for discovery with which the person will comply. A person must comply with a request to the extent protection is not sought unless it is unreasonable under the circumstances to do so before obtaining a ruling on the motion."[205] A party, however, should not file a motion for protection with respect to a production request on the ground that the time or place for production is unreasonable because it can object on that basis.[206] Moreover, a responding party should rarely file a motion for protective order with respect to individual written-discovery requests because objections can be interposed with respect to them. Rather, such a motion generally is proper only when the responding party believes that an entire set of written-discovery requests is improper and protection is needed (e.g., a set of requests for admission contains so many requests that they are disproportionate to the case's needs or that responding to them would be unduly burdensome or expensive).

Unlike Texas Rules 196.2(b), 197.2(b), 198.2(b), and 176.6(d)—which respectively govern responses to production requests, interrogatories, requests for admission, and subpoenas requesting the production of documents and tangible things—there are no provisions in Texas Rules 199, 200, or 176.6 that allow a party or nonparty to object to a deposition notice or subpoena for an oral deposition or a deposition upon written questions. Rather, any objection to such a deposition notice or subpoena should be made by filing a motion for protective order or to quash.[207]

---

[205] Tex. R. Civ. P. 192.6(a).

[206] *See* Tex. R. Civ. P. 193.2(b) ("If the responding party objects to the requested time or place of production, the responding party must state a reasonable time and place for complying with the request and must comply at that time and place without further request or order.").

[207] *See* Tex. R. Civ. P. 176.6(e) ("A person commanded to appear at a deposition . . . and any other person affected by the subpoena, may move for a protective order under [Texas] Rule 192.6(b)—before the time specified for compliance—either in the court in which the action is pending or in a district court in the county where the subpoena was served."), 199.4 ("A party or witness may object to the time and place designated for an oral deposition by motion for protective order or by motion to quash the notice of deposition."); *In re Garza*, 544 S.W.3d 836, 841 (Tex. 2018) (orig. proceeding) (per curiam) ("[The rules permit potential deponents to seek protection for themselves. . . ."); *In re Baylor Univ.*, No. 01-20-00439-CV, 2020 Tex. App. LEXIS 9200, at *13–14, 2020 WL 6878411 (Tex. App.—Houston [1st Dist.] Nov. 24, 2020, orig. proceeding) (mem. op.) ("[T]he person noticed for deposition has the right to protection 'from undue burden, unnecessary expense, harassment or annoyance, or invasion of personal, constitutional, or property rights.'" (quoting *Crown Cent. Petroleum Corp. v. Garcia*, 904 S.W.2d 125, 127 (Tex. 1995))); *In re Hamilton*, No. 13-20-00254-CV, 2020 Tex. App. LEXIS 7378, at *8, 2020 WL 5494503 (Tex. App.—Corpus Christi Sept. 10, 2020, orig. proceeding) (mem. op.) (same); *In re Perry*, No. 13-18-00676-CV, 2019 Tex. App. LEXIS 3176, at *9, 2019 WL 1723509 (Tex. App.—Corpus Christi Apr. 18, 2019, orig. proceeding) (mem. op.) (same); *cf. Beach Mart, Inc. v. L&L Wings, Inc.*, 302 F.R.D. 396, 406 (E.D.N.C. 2014) ("[T]here is no provision in the rules which provides for a party whose deposition is noticed to serve objections so as to be able to avoid providing the requested discovery until an order compelling discovery is issued. . . . The proper procedure to object to a [Federal] Rule 30(b)(6) deposition notice is not to serve objections on the opposing party, but to move for a protective order."); *Fort Worth Emps. Ret. Fund v. J.P. Morgan Chase & Co.*, No. 09 Civ. 3701 (JPO) (JCF), 2013 U.S. Dist. LEXIS 173006, at *7–8, 2013 WL 6439069 (S.D.N.Y. Dec. 9, 2013) ("The weight of the authority holds that a party believing it has received a flawed 30(b)(6) notice may not merely rest upon its objections, but must move for a protective order. . . . This principle applies not only to objections that

A motion for a protective order must be filed "within the time permitted for response to the discovery" (i.e., before the response date),[208] which makes Rule 192.6 consistent with Texas Rule 193.2(a) governing objections.[209] A person who fails to timely move for protection generally waives its objection to the discovery request.[210]

Unlike under federal discovery practice, a party or nonparty who files a motion for protective order need not comply with the discovery request, deposition notice, or subpoena until the trial court rules on the motion.[211] Accordingly, the party seeking the discovery or deposition should secure a ruling on the motion as quickly as possible.

---

go to the notice in its entirety, but also to those that define the scope of the [Federal Rule] 30(b)(6) deposition."); ***Robinson v. Quicken Loans, Inc.***, No. 3:12-cv-00981, 2013 U.S. Dist. LEXIS 59127, at *9 (S.D.W. Va. Apr. 25, 2013) (mem. op.) (same).

An exception to this rule relates to document requests. If the deposition notice or subpoena contains a production request, the party or nonparty can file objections to it. Tex. R. Civ. P. 199.2(b)(5) (incorporating Texas Rule 196's procedures with respect to production requests for deposition notices served on a party or a person subject to a party's control), 200.1(b) ("The notice [for a deposition upon written questions] also may include a request for production of documents as permitted by [Texas] Rule 199.2(b)(5), the provisions of which will govern the request, service, and response."), 176.6(d) ("A person commanded to produce and permit inspection or copying of designated documents and things may serve on the party requesting issuance of the subpoena—before the time specified for compliance—written objections to producing any or all of the designated materials. A person need not comply with the part of a subpoena to which objection is made as provided in this paragraph unless ordered to do so by the court. The party requesting the subpoena may move for such an order at any time after an objection is made.").

[208] Tex. R. Civ. P. 192.6(a); ***accord In re Park Cities Bank***, 409 S.W.3d 859, 877 (Tex. App.—Tyler 2013, orig. proceeding) ("A party from whom discovery is sought may move for a protective order within the time for the response."); *see* Tex. R. Civ. P. 176.6(e) ("A person commanded to appear at a deposition, hearing, or trial, or to produce and permit inspection and copying of designated documents and things, and any other person affected by the subpoena, may move for a protective order under [Texas] Rule 192.6(b)—before the time specified for compliance—either in the court in which the action is pending or in a district court in the county where the subpoena was served.").

[209] ***E.g., In re Grecon, Inc.***, 542 S.W.3d 774, 780 (Tex. App.—Houston [14th Dist.] 2018, orig. proceeding) ("[M]otions for protection are generally required to be filed before the deadline to respond to the discovery request."). See also Chapter 5, section 5-3 (discussing objections to written discovery).

[210] ***In re Grecon, Inc.***, 542 S.W.3d 774, 780–81 (Tex. App.—Houston [14th Dist.] 2018, orig. proceeding) (holding that a plaintiff who failed to file timely a motion for protective order with respect to a former Texas Rule 194.2(h) request for disclosure waived his claim that the settlement agreements at issue were not relevant); ***Bohmfalk v. Linwood***, 742 S.W.2d 518, 520 (Tex. App.—Dallas 1987, no writ) (holding that a party waived inadequate notice regarding a deposition because he did not move for protection regarding it). See also Chapter 5, section 5-3 (discussing objections to written discovery).

[211] This is clearly the case for nonparties because Texas Rule 176.6(e) provides: "A person need not comply with the part of a subpoena from which protection is sought under this paragraph unless ordered to do so by the court. The party requesting the subpoena may seek such an order at any time after the motion for protection is filed." Oddly, Texas Rule 192.6 does not contain similar language. It does, however, provide that "[a] person must comply with a request to the extent protection is not sought unless it is unreasonable under the circumstances to do so before obtaining a ruling on the motion." Tex. R. Civ. P. 192.6(a). Thus, the implication is that the moving party need not comply with the portion of the

Even though Texas Rule 192.6, unlike its predecessor, former Texas Rule 166b(5), does not expressly require the movant to specify the grounds for the protective order or to show good cause for its entry, the movant still has such burdens under longstanding Texas jurisprudence:

> The party seeking to avoid discovery must show a particular, specific, and demonstrable injury by facts sufficient to justify a protective order, and the trial court may not grant a protective order limiting discovery unless the party seeking such protection has met this burden. Thus, the party resisting discovery is not free to make conclusory statements that the requested discovery is unduly burdensome or unnecessarily harassing, but, instead, must produce some evidence supporting its request for a protective order.[212]

---

discovery request or deposition notice for which protection is sought until the trial court rules on the motion.

The federal rule is the opposite (i.e., the movant must secure a ruling on its protective order before the time of compliance with the discovery request or deposition notice). *E.g., Batt v. Kimberly-Clark Corp.*· 438 F. Supp. 2d 1315, 1318 (N.D. Okla. 2006) (holding that the mere filing motion for protective order is insufficient to stay a deposition and that "Defendant was required to take some action to stay the deposition until the parties, with or without the Court's assistance, could resolve the dispute. This could have been done even without a formal motion. Local Rule 37.2 provides a simple mechanism to invoke the Court's aid. Even only hours before the May 23 deposition, Defendant could have enlisted the Court's assistance by telephone, but did not do so. Thus, under the law, Defendant is in the wrong."); *Goodwin v. City of Boston*, 118 F.R.D. 297, 298 (D. Mass. 1988) ("The filing of a motion to quash or a motion for protective order does not automatically operate to stay a deposition or other discovery. When it appears that a Court is not going to be able to decide a motion to quash or a motion for protective order before the date set for a deposition, counsel for the movant should contact counsel for the party noticing the deposition and attempt to reach an agreement staying the deposition until after the Court acts on the motion to quash and/or the motion for a protective order. If agreement cannot be reached, it is incumbent on counsel for the movant to file a motion to stay the deposition until the Court acts on the motion to quash and/or for a protective order and to alert the clerk to the need for immediate action on the motion to stay. Certainly nothing less is required here.").

212 *In re Liberty Mut. Ins. Co.*, No. 14-09-00086-CV, 2009 Tex. App. LEXIS 1234, at *15, 2009 WL 441897 (Tex. App.—Houston [1st Dist.] Feb. 24, 2009, orig. proceeding) (mem. op.) (citations omitted); *accord Masinga v. Whittington*, 792 S.W.2d 940, 940 (Tex. 1990) (orig. proceeding); *Garcia v. Peeples*, 734 S.W.2d 343, 345 (Tex. 1987) (orig. proceeding); *Grass v. Golden*, 153 S.W.3d 659, 662–63 (Tex. App.—Tyler 2004, orig. proceeding); *In re Alford Chevrolet-Geo*, 997 S.W.2d 173, 181 (Tex. 1999) (orig. proceeding); *In re Eurecat US, Inc.*, 425 S.W.3d 577, 582–83 (Tex. App.—Houston [14th Dist.] 2014, orig. proceeding); *Blankinship v. Brown*, 399 S.W.3d 303, 312 (Tex. App.—Dallas 2013, pet. denied).

Although Federal Rule 26(c), which governs protective orders under the federal discovery rules, expressly requires the movant to show "good cause" for a protective order, its "good cause" requirement is substantially the same as the Texas requirement. *E.g., Rosas v. Alice's Tea Cup, LLC*, 127 F. Supp. 3d 4, 9 (S.D.N.Y. 2015) ("If the evidence sought is relevant, 'the burden is upon the party seeking non-disclosure or a protective order to show good cause.' Good cause is established by 'demonstrating a particular need for protection.' Moreover, 'the appropriateness of protective relief from discovery depends upon a balancing of the litigation needs of the discovering party and any countervailing protectible interests of the party from whom discovery is sought.'" (quoting *Penthouse Int'l, Ltd. v. Playboy Enters.*, 663 F.2d 371, 391 (2d Cir. 1981), *Cipollone v. Liggett Grp., Inc.*, 785 F.2d 1108,

Texas Rule 192.6(b) sets forth the following nonexclusive bases for a protective order with respect to written discovery: "[t]o protect the movant from undue burden, unnecessary expense, harassment, annoyance, or invasion of personal, constitutional, or property rights."[213] In deciding whether a protective order is appropriate, a trial court balances the parties' interests.[214] The balancing test is codified in Texas Rule

---

1121 (3d Cir. 1986), and *Apex Oil Co. v. DiMauro*, 110 F.R.D. 490, 496 (S.D.N.Y. 1985))); *Voice Domain Techs., LLC v. Apple, Inc.*, No. 13-40138-TSH, 2014 U.S. Dist. LEXIS 143903, at *4–5, 2014 WL 5106413 (D. Mass. Oct. 8, 2014) ("The burden is on the party seeking the more restrictive protective order to show good cause under [Federal] Rule 26(c). To show good cause, the party seeking the protective order must demonstrate a particular need for protection; '[b]road allegations of harm, unsubstantiated by specific examples or articulated reasons, do not satisfy the [Federal] Rule 26(c) test.'" (quoting *Cipollone v. Liggett Grp., Inc.*, 785 F.2d 1108, 1121 (3d Cir. 1986))); *Hall v. New Orleans City,* No. 13-2463 SECTION "B" (3), 2014 U.S. Dist. LEXIS 134289, at *6–7, 2014 WL 4792185 (E.D. La. Sept. 24, 2014) ("In other words, the party seeking the protective order must show good cause by demonstrating a particular need for protection. To establish good cause, a party seeking a protective order must set forth particular and specific demonstrations of fact, as distinguished from stereotyped and conclusory statements. Broad allegations of harm, unsubstantiated by specific examples or articulated reasoning, do not satisfy the [Federal] Rule 26(c) test. Moreover, the alleged harm must be significant, not a mere trifle."). In fact, the Texas test is based on the federal one. *E.g., Masinga v. Whittington*, 792 S.W.2d 940, 942 (Tex. 1990) ("While Texas courts have not written on the proof necessary to obtain a [former Texas] Rule 166b-4 [now Rule 166b(5)] protective order, federal courts have dealt with the issue pursuant to Fed. R. Civ. P. 26(c). In *United States v. Garrett*, 571 F.2d 1323[, 1326 n.3] (5th Cir. 1978), the court noted that a movant must show 'a particular and specific demonstration of fact as distinguished from stereotyped conclusory statements.' Sweeping predictions of injury and '[b]road allegations of harm, unsubstantiated by specific examples of articulated reasoning,' do not justify a protective order. Though the Texas and federal rules are not identical, these requirements of an articulated and demonstrable injury, as opposed to conclusory allegations, apply to motions for protective orders under [former Texas Rule 166b-4." (citations omitted) (quoting *Cipollone v. Liggett Grp., Inc.*, 785 F.2d 1108, 1121 (3rd Cir. 1986))); *accord Garcia v. Peeples*, 734 S.W.2d 343, 345 (Tex. 1987) (same); *see In re Collins*, 286 S.W.3d 911, 919 (Tex. 2009) (setting forth the test for a protective order under Texas Rule 193.6 and quoting *Masinga v. Whittington*, 792 S.W.2d 940, 940 (Tex. 1990), which relied on the federal test)); *In re Alford Chevrolet-Geo*, 997 S.W.2d 173, 181 (Tex. 1999) (orig. proceeding) (setting forth the test for a protective order under Texas Rule 193.6 and citing *Garcia v. Peeples*, 734 S.W.2d 343, 345 (Tex. 1987), which relied on the federal test).

213 Tex. R. Civ. P. 192.6(b); *see In re Alford Chevrolet-Geo*, 997 S.W.2d 173, 181 (Tex. 1999) (orig. proceeding) ("[A] court may 'in the interest of justice,' issue a protective order to 'protect the movant from undue burden, unnecessary expense, harassment, annoyance, or invasion of personal, constitutional, or property rights.' The new discovery rules explicitly encourage trial courts to limit discovery when 'the burden or expense of the proposed discovery outweighs its likely benefit, taking into account the needs of the case, the amount in controversy, the parties' resources, the importance of the issues at stake in the litigation, and the importance of the proposed discovery in resolving the issues.'" (quoting Tex. R. Civ. P. 192.6(b), 192.4(b))); *Sells v. Drott*, 330 S.W.3d 696, 706 (Tex. App.—Tyler 2010, pet. denied) ("The rules of civil procedure dictate that the court must provide protection from undue burden caused by issuance of a subpoena or by discovery methods." (citing Tex. R. Civ. P. 176.7, 192.4, 192.6(b))).

214 *Garcia v. Peeples*, 734 S.W.2d 343, 348 (Tex. 1987) (orig. proceeding) (holding that the trial court should have balanced the parties' competing needs before granting a protective

192.4(b),[215] which provides that discovery "should be limited" if the court determines that "the burden or expense of the proposed discovery outweighs its likely benefit, taking into account the needs of the case, the amount in controversy, the parties' resources, the importance of the issues at stake in the litigation, and the importance of the proposed discovery in resolving the issues" (i.e., a proportionality analysis).[216] The court can "also consider harm that the resisting party might suffer as a result of the discovery."[217]

Texas Rule 192.6(b) lists the following types of orders a trial court can issue to protect a party or other affected person from such matters:

(1) the requested discovery not be sought in whole or in part;

(2) the extent or subject matter of discovery be limited;

(3) the discovery not be undertaken at the time or place specified;

(4) the discovery be undertaken only by such method or upon such terms and conditions or at the time and place directed by the court; [and]

(5) the results of discovery be sealed or otherwise protected, subject to the provisions of Texas Rule 76a.[218]

A trial court is not limited to protective orders of the types listed in Texas Rule 192.6(b). Rather, it can make any order that justice requires to protect a party or other affected person from annoyance, embarrassment, oppression, undue burden, or expense.[219] Thus, a court has discretion to fashion a protective order to fit the action's facts and circumstances. For example, in an action to recover disability benefits for

---

order); *Eurecat US, Inc. v. Marklund*, 527 S.W.3d 367, 376 (Tex. App.—Houston [14th Dist.] 2017, no pet.) (same); *see In re State Farm Lloyds*, 520 S.W.3d 595, 603–15 (Tex. 2017) (orig. proceeding) (discussing "proportionality" with respect to discovery's scope).

215 *Eurecat US, Inc. v. Marklund*, 527 S.W.3d 367, 376 (Tex. App.—Houston [14th Dist.] 2017, no pet.) ("The trial court's balancing test is codified in Texas Rule 192.4(b)."); *In re State Farm Lloyds*, 520 S.W.3d 595, 604–05 (Tex. 2017) (orig. proceeding) ("As a counterbalance rested in concerns about 'unwarranted delay and expense,' [Texas] Rule 192.4 expressly constrains the scope of discovery as to otherwise discoverable matters. . . . To put it succinctly, 'the simple fact that requested information is discoverable . . . does not mean that discovery must be had.'" (quoting *Nicholas v. Wyndham Int'l, Inc.*, 373 F.3d 537, 543 (4th Cir. 2004))).

216 Tex. R. Civ. P. 192.4(b).

217 *Eurecat US, Inc. v. Marklund*, 527 S.W.3d 367, 376 (Tex. App.—Houston [14th Dist.] 2017, no pet.); *accord* Tex. R. Civ. P. 192.6(b) (authorizing protective orders to protect against "undue burden, unnecessary expense, harassment, annoyance, or invasion of personal, constitutional, or property rights"); *In re Weekley Homes, L.P.*, 295 S.W.3d 309, 322–23 (Tex. 2009) (orig. proceeding) (in granting a protective order, considering the harm the party resisting discovery might suffer "from revealing private conversations, trade secrets, and privileged or otherwise confidential communications").

218 Tex. R. Civ. P. 192.6(b).

219 Tex. R. Civ. P. 192.6(b) (providing that "the court may make any order in the interest of justice and may—among other things—order [one of the Rule's five specified things]"); *accord In re Berrenberg*, 605 S.W.3d 922, 927 (Tex. App.—El Paso 2020, orig. proceeding); *In re Bilfinger Westcon, Inc.*, No. 13-19-00466-CV, 2019 Tex. App. LEXIS 10807, at *8–9, 2019 WL 6795870 (Tex. App.—Corpus Christi Dec. 12, 2019, no pet.) (mem. op.); *In re Soc'y of Our Lady of Most Holy Trinity*, 622 S.W.3d 1, 12 (Tex. App.—Corpus Christi 2019, orig. proceeding).

psychiatric disorders, a federal court entered a protective order allowing the plaintiff to proceed in pseudonym because of a strong probability that he would be stigmatized in the community and would suffer irreparable harm to his professional reputation if his name were revealed.[220]

A court will deny a protective order if the movant fails to establish that it is needed to protect against annoyance, embarrassment, oppression, undue burden or expense, or to prevent an invasion of a personal, constitutional, or property right. For example, one federal court refused to issue a protective order precluding disclosure of the plaintiff's diary in a sexual-harassment action because the plaintiff had already disclosed intimate details of her sexual relationship with the professor she claimed had sexually harassed her.[221] In the same vein, another federal court refused to issue a protective order prohibiting the public dissemination of a mayor's videotaped deposition in a civil-rights action against the mayor and city, even though the plaintiff's counsel's stated purpose in distributing the videotape was to publicly embarrass the mayor in the eyes of his constituents, because any discomfort on the part of the mayor was outweighed by the right of public access to "this important component of the litigation process."[222]

Although a trial court is specifically authorized to issue a protective order that disclosure or discovery not be had, courts seldom order that discovery not be taken at all.[223] Instead, discovery is expected to go forward, with the parties asserting their objections to particular matters during discovery. As noted by Comment 7 to the 1999 change to Texas Rule 192: "Courts should limit discovery under this rule only to prevent unwarranted delay and expense as stated more fully in the rule. A court abuses its discretion in unreasonably restricting a party's access to information through discovery."[224] A trial court also abuses its discretion when it limits discovery in the absence of evidence or other information showing circumstances justifying a protective order.[225]

---

220 *Doe v. Provident Life & Accident Ins. Co.*, 176 F.R.D. 464, 470 (E.D. Pa. 1997) (also finding that the defendant failed to establish that its ability to prepare for trial would be prejudiced by maintaining the plaintiff's anonymity).

221 *Topol v. Trs. of Univ. of Pa.*, 160 F.R.D. 476, 477 (E.D. Pa. 1995).

222 *Flaherty v. Seroussi*, 209 F.R.D. 295, 299 (N.D.N.Y. 2001).

223 *Global Servs., Inc. v. Bianchi*, 901 S.W.2d 934, 938 (Tex. 1995) (original proceeding); *cf. Campos v. Webb Cnty.*, 288 F.R.D. 134, 137 (S.D. Tex. 2012) (observing that protective orders completely prohibiting depositions are rarely granted); *N.F.A. Corp. v. Riverview Narrow Fabrics, Inc.*, 117 F.R.D. 83, 84 (M.D.N.C. 1987) (same); *see In re Allstate Cnty. Mut. Ins. Co.*, 85 S.W.3d 193, 196 (Tex. 2002) (orig. proceeding) ("[D]enial of discovery 'going to the heart of a party's case may render the appellate remedy inadequate.'").

224 Tex. R. Civ. P. 192 cmt. 7 to 1999 change.

225 *See In re Alford Chevrolet-Geo*, 997 S.W.2d 173, 181 (Tex. 1999) (orig. proceeding) ("A party resisting discovery . . . cannot simply make conclusory allegations that the requested discovery is unduly burdensome or unnecessarily harassing. The party must produce some evidence supporting its request for a protective order."); *accord In re Marshall*, 617 S.W.3d 670, 675 (Tex. App.—San Antonio 2021, orig. proceeding); *In re Garrison Prop. & Cas. Ins. Co.*, 12-20-00190-CV, 2020 Tex. App. LEXIS 8409, at *15, 2020 WL 6164982 (Tex. App.—Tyler Oct. 21, 2020, orig. proceeding) (mem. op.); *In re Liberty Cnty. Mut. Ins. Co.*, 606 S.W.3d 866, 874 (Tex. App.—Houston [14th Dist.] 2020, orig. proceeding); *In re Bilfinger Westcon, Inc.*, No. 13-19-00466-CV, 2019 Tex. App. LEXIS 10807, at *36–37, 2019 WL 6795870 (Tex. App.—Corpus Christi Dec. 12, 2019, orig. proceeding) (mem. op.); *In re Mustang Asset Recovery, Ltd.*, No. 05-19-01036-CV, 2019 Tex. App. LEXIS 10605, at *6, 2019 WL 6649056

(Tex. App.—Dallas Dec. 6, 2019, orig. proceeding) (mem. op.); *see also In re Cook*, No. 05-19-01283-CV, 2020 Tex. App. LEXIS 3999, at *7–8, 2020 WL 2552881 (Tex. App.—Dallas May 20, 2020, orig. proceeding) (mem. op.) (noting that "litigants are not required to produce evidence in support of their request for protection" whenever such "evidence is not necessary to determine the discoverability of requested information," but concluding that the trial court abused its discretion in issuing a blanket protective order barring deposition questioning that was not facially irrelevant); *Turner v. Williams*, No. 01-17-00494-CV, 2019 Tex. App. LEXIS 1404, at *30, 2019 WL 922057 (Tex. App.—Houston [1st Dist.] Feb. 26, 2019, no pet.) (mem. op.) ("A trial court abuses its discretion by limiting discovery in the absence of some evidence supporting the request for a protective order."); *In re Issuance of Subpoenas Depositions of Bennett*, 502 S.W.3d 373, 381 (Tex. App.—Houston [14th Dist.] 2016, no pet.) ("Because Bennett, Clark, and Lowe did not meet their burden of establishing the depositions would cause undue burden, unnecessary expense, harassment, annoyance, or invasion of personal, constitutional or property rights, the trial court abused its discretion to the extent it restricted their depositions based on [Texas] Rule 192.6(b).").

CHAPTER 5

Written Discovery: Response, Objection, Privilege Assertion; Amending or Supplementing Responses; Failure to Timely Respond; Presumption of Authenticity—Texas Rule 193

5-1 Text of Rule 193

RULE 193. WRITTEN DISCOVERY: RESPONSE; OBJECTION; ASSERTION OF PRIVILEGE; SUPPLEMENTATION AND AMENDMENT; FAILURE TO TIMELY RESPOND; PRESUMPTION OF AUTHENTICITY

193.1. Responding to Written Discovery; Duty to Make Complete Response

A party must respond to written discovery in writing within the time provided by court order or these rules. When responding to written discovery, a party must make a complete response, based on all information reasonably available to the responding party or its attorney at the time the response is made. The responding party's answers, objections, and other responses must be preceded by the request or required disclosure to which they apply.

193.2. Objecting to Written Discovery

(a) **Form and time for objections.** A party must make any objection to written discovery in writing—either in the response or in a separate document—within the time for response. The party must state specifically the legal or factual basis for the objection and the extent to which the party is refusing to comply with the request.

(b) **Duty to respond when partially objecting; objection to time or place of production.** A party must comply with as much of the request to which the party has made no objection unless it is unreasonable under the circumstances to do so before obtaining a ruling on the objection. If the responding party objects to the requested time or place of production, the responding party must state a reasonable time and place for complying with the request and must comply at that time and place without further request or order.

(c) **Good faith basis for objection.** A party may object to written discovery only if a good faith factual and legal basis for the objection exists at the time the objection is made.

(d) **Amendment.** An objection or response to written discovery may be amended or supplemented to state an objection or basis that, at the time the objection or response initially was made, either was inapplicable or was unknown after reasonable inquiry.

(e) **Waiver of objection.** An objection that is not made within the time required, or that is obscured by numerous unfounded objections, is waived unless the court excuses the waiver for good cause shown.

(f) **No objection to preserve privilege.** A party should not object to a request for written discovery on the grounds that it calls for production of material or information that is privileged but should instead comply with Rule 193.3. A party who objects to production of privileged material or information does not waive the privilege but must comply with Rule 193.3 when the error is pointed out.

193.3. Asserting a Privilege

A party may preserve a privilege from written discovery in accordance with this subdivision.

(a) **Withholding privileged material or information.** A party who claims that material or information responsive to written discovery is privileged may withhold the privileged material or information from the response. The party must state—in the response (or an amended or supplemental response) or in a separate document—that:

(1) information or material responsive to the request or required disclosure has been withheld,

(2) the request or required disclosure to which the information or material relates, and

(3) the privilege or privileges asserted.

(b) **Description of withheld material or information.** After receiving a response indicating that material or information has been withheld from production, a party seeking discovery may serve a written request that the withholding party identify the information and material withheld. Within 15 days of service of that request, the withholding party must serve a response that:

(1) describes the information or materials withheld that, without revealing the privileged information itself or otherwise waiving the privilege, enables other parties to assess the applicability of the privilege, and

(2) asserts a specific privilege for each item or group of items withheld.

(c) **Exemption.** Without complying with paragraphs (a) and (b), a party may withhold a privileged communication to or from a lawyer or lawyer's representative or a privileged document of a lawyer or lawyer's representative

(1) created or made from the point at which a party consults a lawyer with a view to obtaining professional legal services from the lawyer in the prosecution or defense of a specific claim in the litigation in which discovery is requested or required, and

(2) concerning the litigation in which the discovery is requested or required.

(d) **Privilege not waived by production.** A party who produces material or information without intending to waive a claim of privilege does not waive that claim under these rules or the Rules of Evidence if—within 10 days or a shorter time ordered by the court, after the producing party actually discovers that such production was made—the producing party amends the response, identifying the material or information produced and stating the privilege asserted. If the producing party thus amends the response to assert a privilege, any party who has obtained the specific material or information must promptly return the specified material or information and any copies pending any ruling by the court denying the privilege.

193.4. Hearing and Ruling on Objections and Assertions of Privilege

(a) **Hearing.** Any party may at any reasonable time request a hearing on an objection or claim of privilege asserted under this rule. The party making the objection or asserting the privilege must present any evidence necessary to support the objection or privilege. The evidence may be testimony presented at the hearing or affidavits served at least seven days before the hearing or at such other reasonable time as the court permits. If the court determines that an *in camera* review of some or all of the requested discovery or required disclosure is necessary, that material or information must be segregated and produced to the court in a sealed wrapper within a reasonable time following the hearing.

(b) **Ruling.** To the extent the court sustains the objection or claim of privilege, the responding party has no further duty to respond to that request or required disclosure. To the extent the court overrules the objection or claim of privilege, the responding party must produce the requested or required material or information within 30 days after the court's ruling or at such time as the court orders. A party need not request a ruling on that party's own objection or assertion of privilege to preserve the objection or privilege.

(c) **Use of material or information withheld under claim of privilege.** A party may not use—at any hearing or trial—material or information withheld from discovery under a claim of privilege, including a claim sustained by the court, without timely amending or supplementing the party's response to that discovery.

193.5. Amending or Supplementing Responses to Written Discovery

(a) **Duty to amend or supplement.** If a party learns that the party's response to written discovery was incomplete or incorrect when made, or, although complete and correct when made, is no longer complete and correct, the party must amend or supplement the response:

(1) to the extent that the written discovery sought the identification of persons with knowledge of relevant facts, trial witnesses, or expert witnesses, and

(2) to the extent that the written discovery sought other information, unless the additional or corrective information has been made known to the other parties in writing, on the record at a deposition, or through other discovery responses.

(b) **Time and form of amended or supplemental response.** An amended or supplemental response must be made reasonably promptly after the party discovers the necessity for such a response. Except as otherwise provided by these rules, it is presumed that an amended or supplemental response made less than 30 days before trial was not made reasonably promptly. An amended or supplemental response must be in the same form as the initial response and must be verified by the party if the original response was required to be verified by the party, but the failure to comply with this requirement does not make the amended or supplemental response untimely unless the party making the response refuses to correct the defect within a reasonable time after it is pointed out.

193.6. Failing to Timely Respond—Effect on Trial

(a) **Exclusion of evidence and exceptions.** A party who fails to make, amend, or supplement a discovery response, including a required disclosure, in a timely manner may not introduce in evidence the material or information that was not timely disclosed, or offer the testimony of a witness (other than a named party) who was not timely identified, unless the court finds that:

(1) there was good cause for the failure to timely make, amend, or supplement the discovery response; or

(2) the failure to timely make, amend, or supplement the discovery response will not unfairly surprise or unfairly prejudice the other parties.

(b) **Burden of establishing exception.** The burden of establishing good cause or the lack of unfair surprise or unfair prejudice is on the party seeking to introduce the evidence or call the witness. A finding of good cause or of the lack of unfair surprise or unfair prejudice must be supported by the record.

(c) **Continuance.** Even if the party seeking to introduce the evidence or call the witness fails to carry the burden under paragraph (b), the court may grant a continuance or temporarily postpone the trial to allow a response to be made, amended, or supplemented, and to allow opposing parties to conduct discovery regarding any new information presented by that response.

193.7. Production of Documents Self-Authenticating

A party's production of a document in response to written discovery authenticates the document for use against that party in any pretrial proceeding or at trial unless—within 10 days or a longer or shorter time ordered by the court, after the producing party has actual notice that the document will be used—the party objects to the authenticity of the document, or any part of it, stating the specific basis for objection. An objection must be either on the record or in writing and must have a good faith factual and legal basis. An objection made to the authenticity of only part of a document does not affect the authenticity of the remainder. If objection is made, the party attempting to use the document should be given a reasonable opportunity to establish its authenticity.

Comments

Comments to 1999 change:

1. This rule imposes a duty upon parties to make a complete response to written discovery based upon all information reasonably available, subject to objections and privileges.

2. An objection to written discovery does not excuse the responding party from complying with the request to the extent no objection is made. But a party may object to a request for "all documents relevant to the lawsuit" as overly broad and not in compliance with the rule requiring specific requests for documents and refuse to comply with it entirely. *See Loftin v. Martin*, 776 S.W.2d 145 (Tex. 1989). A party may also object to a request for a litigation file on the ground that it is overly broad and may assert that on its face the request seeks only materials protected by privilege. *See National Union Fire Ins. Co. v. Valdez*, 863 S.W.2d 458 (Tex. 1993). A party who objects to production of documents from a remote time period should produce documents from a more recent period unless that production would be burdensome and duplicative should the objection be overruled.

3. This rule governs the presentation of all privileges including work product. It dispenses with objections to written discovery requests on the basis that responsive information or materials are protected by a specific privilege from discovery. Instead, the rule requires parties to state that information or materials have been withheld and to identify the privilege upon which the party relies. The statement should not be made prophylactically, but only when specific information and materials have been withheld. The party must amend or supplement the statement if additional privileged information or material is found subsequent to the initial response. Thus, when large numbers of documents are being produced, a party may amend the initial response when documents are found as to which the party claims privilege. A party need not state that material created by or for lawyers for the litigation has been withheld as it can be assumed that such material will be withheld from virtually any request on the grounds of attorney-client privilege or work product. However, the rule does not prohibit a party from specifically requesting the material or information if the party has a good faith basis for asserting that it is discoverable. An example would be material or information described by Rule 503(d)(1) of the Rules of Evidence.

4. Rule 193.3(d) is a new provision that allows a party to assert a claim of privilege to material or information produced inadvertently without intending to waive the privilege. The provision is commonly used in complex cases to reduce costs and risks in large document productions. The focus is on the intent to waive the privilege, not the intent to produce the material or information. A party who fails to diligently screen documents before producing them does not waive a claim of privilege. This rule is thus broader than Tex. R. Evid. 511 and overturns *Granada Corp. v. First Court of Appeals*, 844 S.W.2d 223 (Tex. 1992), to the extent the two conflict. The 10-day period allowed for an amended response (which may be shortened by the court) does not run from the production of the material or information but from the party's first awareness of the mistake. To avoid complications at trial, a party may identify prior to trial the documents intended to be offered, thereby triggering the obligation to assert any overlooked privilege under this rule. A trial court may also order this procedure.

5. This rule imposes no duty to supplement or amend deposition testimony. The only duty to supplement deposition testimony is provided in Rule 195.6.

6. Any party can request a hearing in which the court will resolve issues brought up in objections or withholding statements. The party seeking to avoid discovery has the burden of proving the objection or privilege.

7. The self-authenticating provision is new. Authentication is, of course, but a condition precedent to admissibility and does not establish admissibility. *See Tex. R. Evid.*

901(a). The 10-day period allowed for objection to authenticity (which period may be altered by the court in appropriate circumstances) does not run from the production of the material or information but from the party's actual awareness that the document will be used. To avoid complications at trial, a party may identify prior to trial the documents intended to be offered, thereby triggering the obligation to object to authenticity. A trial court may also order this procedure. An objection to authenticity must be made in good faith.

5-1:1 2021 Amendments to Texas Rules of Civil Procedure

The 2021 amendments to the Texas Rules of Civil Procedure modified Texas Rules 193.1, 193.3, 193.4, and 193.6 by adding references to required disclosures, which were added to the Texas Rules in 2021 and are addressed in Chapter 6. The amendments also modified Texas Rule 193.3(d) by clarifying that, when the Rule's snap-back procedure is implemented to retrieve inadvertently produced privileged material or information, "any party who has obtained the specific material or information" (not just the party who requested such material or information) "must promptly return the specified material or information and any copies pending any ruling by the court denying the privilege."

5-2 Responses to Written-Discovery Requests and Required Disclosures

Texas Rule 193.1 sets forth a party's general obligations regarding written-discovery requests. It requires a written response within the time provided by the pertinent rule governing the discovery type or by court order.[1] Generally, in cases filed on or after January 1, 2021, a party must make required disclosures by the deadlines set forth in Texas Rules 194.2(a) (initial disclosures), 194.4(b) (pretrial disclosures), and 195.2 (expert disclosures) unless the time is extended or otherwise modified by the parties' agreement or by court order,[2] except that initial disclosures and pretrial disclosures are not required in certain proceedings.[3] A party must generally respond to written-discovery requests within thirty days after their service unless the time is extended due to the manner of service, by the parties' agreement, or by court order.[4]

---

[1] Tex. R. Civ. P. 193.1 ("A party must respond to written discovery in writing within the time provided by court order or these rules."); *see, e.g.*, ***Sharp v. Broadway Nat'l Bank***, 784 S.W.2d 669, 671 (Tex. 1990) (holding that oral identification of witnesses was improper); ***Zaatari v. City of Austin***, 615 S.W.3d 172, 186 (Tex. App.—Austin 2019, pet. denied) (stating Texas Rule 193.1's requirement for a party to "respond to written discovery in writing within the time provided by court order or [the Texas discovery] rules").

[2] Tex. R. Civ. P. 194.2(a) (initial disclosures), 194.4(b) (pretrial disclosures), 195.2 (expert disclosures).

[3] *See* Tex. R. Civ. P. 194.2(d) (listing proceedings exempt from initial disclosures), 194.4(c) (listing proceedings exempt from pretrial disclosures). See Chapter 6 for a thorough discussion of required disclosures.

[4] *See* Tex. R. Civ. P. 196.2(a) (production requests), 196.7(c)(1) (request for entry on land or other property), 197.2(a) (interrogatories), 198.2(a) (requests for admission); *see* ***$2,424.21 in U.S. Currency v. State,*** No. 02-18-00303-CV, 2019 Tex. App. LEXIS, at *8–9, 2019 WL 3244495 (Tex. App.—Fort Worth July 18, 2019, no pet.) (mem. op.) (listing Texas discovery rules containing 30-day response deadlines); ***In re Nat'l Lloyds Ins. Co.***, No. 13-14-00713-CV, 2015 Tex. App. LEXIS 5509, at *20, 2015 WL 3751701 (Tex. App.—Corpus Christi May 29,

Moreover, "[t]he responding party's answers, objections, and other responses must be preceded by the request or required disclosure to which they apply."[5]

Perhaps most importantly, a responding party is affirmatively required to "make a complete response, based on all information reasonably available to the responding party or its attorney at the time the response is made."[6] In addition, Texas Rule 193.5 requires a responding party to supplement incomplete or incorrect written-discovery responses "reasonably promptly" after discovering the original response's deficiency.[7] Finally, Texas Rule 193.6(a) provides that both a failure to amend or supplement discovery and a failure to "make . . . a discovery response, including a required disclosure, in a timely manner" may prevent the responding party from using the information or material at trial.[8]

These provisions are intended to require parties to provide complete written-discovery responses as early in the action as possible. Nothing in Texas Rule 193's comments explains when "information" is "reasonably available" under Texas

---

2015, orig. proceeding) (mem. op.) ("In general, the rules require the responding party to serve a written response, including any objections to written discovery, within thirty days after service of a request for production."); *In re Summersett*, 438 S.W.3d 74, 80 n.4 (Tex. App.—Corpus Christ 2013, orig. proceeding) ("Responses to requests for production are due within 30 days after the date of service."); *Izen v. Sjostrom*, No. 14-06-00142-CV, 2007 Tex. App. LEXIS 2586, at *5–6, 2007 WL 968841 (Tex. App.—Houston [14th Dist.] Apr. 3, 2007, no pet.) (mem. op.) ("A party has thirty days to respond to a request for production and an interrogatory request."). Under former Texas Rule 193.4, which applies to cases filed before January 1, 2021, a responding party is generally required to "serve a written response on the requesting party within 30 days after service of the request[.]"

A written-discovery request can provide more than thirty days to respond, but it cannot provide less than thirty days. Depending on the type of service (mail or fax), the party may have an additional one or three days to respond. Tex. R. Civ. P. 21a(b)–(c). In such circumstances (1) three days are added if the request is served by mail, Tex. R. Civ. P. 21a(c), and (2) one day is, added if the request is received by fax after 5:00 p.m. local time of the recipient, Tex. Rule Civ. P. 21a(b)(2); *In re Summersett*, 438 S.W.3d 74, 80 n.4 (Tex. App.—Corpus Christ 2013, orig. proceeding) (noting that, if the written-discovery request is served by mail, the responding party has thirty-three days to respond).

Although Texas Rule 21a(a)(2) permits discovery requests (and responses) to be served by email, unlike with respect to the other forms of service (e.g., mail, personal delivery, commercial delivery, and fax), nothing in Texas Rule 21a(b) specifies when service by email is complete. Presumably, it is complete on transmission of the document to the receiving party. *Cf.* Tex. R. Civ. P. 21(b)(3) ("Electronic service is complete on transmission of the document to the serving party's electronic filing service provider."); Fed. R. Civ. P. 5(b)(2)(E) (providing that "[a] paper is served under this rule by . . . sending it by electronic means if the person consented in writing—in which event service is complete upon transmission, but is not effective if the serving party learns that it did not reach the person to be served").

5 Tex. R. Civ. P. 193.1.

6 Tex. R. Civ. P. 193.1.

7 Tex. R. Civ. P. 193.5(b) ("An amended or supplemental response must be made reasonably promptly after the party discovers the necessity for such a response.").

8 Tex. R. Civ. P. 193.6(a) ("A party who fails to make, amend, or supplement a discovery response in a timely manner may not introduce in evidence the material or information that was not timely disclosed, or offer the testimony of a witness (other than a named party) who was not timely identified[.]").

Rule 193.1,[9] and no Texas case addresses that question.[10] But federal courts interpreting comparable federal written-discovery rules provide useful guidance.

What information and material is "reasonably available" depends largely on the responding party's obligation of reasonable inquiry (i.e., the search the party must conduct to respond to a discovery request) and what information and material is under its control.

5-2:1 Reasonable Inquiry with Respect to Disclosures, Interrogatories, and Requests for Admission

A reasonable-inquiry obligation applies to a party providing required disclosures and responding to interrogatories and requests for admission.[11] What constitutes a reasonable inquiry is case-specific,[12] but some general principles exist. For example, federal

---

[9] Comment 1 to the 1999 change to Texas Rule 193 merely reiterates the requirement: "This rule imposes a duty upon parties to make a complete response to written discovery based upon all information reasonably available, subject to objections and privileges." Tex. R. Civ. P. 193 cmt. 1 to 1999 change.

[10] Instead, Texas courts have addressed whether information is "reasonably available" on a case-by-case basis, without applying any general, guiding principles. In *Zaatari v. City of Austin*, for example, the court assessed whether the State met its obligation to disclose information pertaining to owners of short-term rentals, such that the State could use affidavits of certain owners as part of its summary-judgment evidence. 615 S.W.3d 172, 185–86 (Tex. App.—Austin 2019, pet. denied). The court concluded that the State met its obligation, reasoning that, before the close of discovery, the State had identified owners generally as persons with knowledge of relevant facts and that, when doing so, "the State had not yet had time to identify from [a recently disclosed list of the names of all short-term rental licensees] the specific witnesses that it intended to rely on and the evidence those witnesses would provide." *Zaatari v. City of Austin*, 615 S.W.3d 172, 186 (Tex. App.—Austin 2019, pet. denied).

[11] *Cf. Hawthorne v. Bennington*, No. 316CV00235RCJCLB, 2020 U.S. Dist. LEXIS 120755, at *12, 2020 WL 3884426 (D. Nev. July 8, 2020) ("Although the Rule does not define 'reasonable inquiry' or 'readily available,' courts have held that '[a] party's duty of reasonable inquiry in responding to requests for admissions is similar to its duty in answering interrogatories.'" (quoting *FDIC v. Halpern*, 271 F.R.D. 191, 193 (D. Nev. 2010))); *Jones v. Zimmer*, No. 2:12-cv-01578-JAD-NJK, 2014 U.S. Dist. LEXIS 167750, at *13, 2014 WL 6772916 (D. Nev. Dec. 2, 2014) ("[B]efore making such a response [to a request for admission], the responding party must undertake a reasonable inquiry into readily obtainable information from persons and/or documents within the responding party's relative control. This reasonable inquiry requirement is similar to the duty owed in answering interrogatories."); *Erie Ins. Prop. & Cas. Co. v. Johnson*, 272 F.R.D. 177, 183–84 (S.D. W. Va. 2010) ("[A] party's duty of reasonable inquiry in responding to a request for admission is similar to its duty in answering an interrogatory."); *FDIC v. Halpern*, 271 F.R.D. 191, 193 (D. Nev. 2010) (same). See Chapter 3, section 3-5 for a discussion of the reasonable-inquiry requirement as it pertains to signatures on disclosures and discovery requests, notices, responses, and objections.

[12] As held by one court in discussing what constitutes a reasonable inquiry with respect to a response to a request for admission: "What constitutes 'reasonable inquiry' and what material is 'readily obtainable' is a relative matter that depends upon the facts of each case." *T. Rowe Price Small-Cap Fund, Inc. v. Oppenheimer & Co.*, 174 F.R.D. 38, 43 (S.D.N.Y. 1997), ***quoted with approval in Stephenson v. Family Sols. of Ohio, Inc.***, No. 1:18CV2017, 2021 U.S. Dist. LEXIS 32377, at *8 n.2, 2021 WL 681403 (N.D. Ohio Feb. 22, 2021), *Hawthorne*

courts have held that "a reasonable inquiry is limited to inquiry of documents and persons 'readily available' and within the responding party's control."[13] This requires the responding party to review its readily available documents and inquire of its officers, employees, agents, attorneys, and others subject to its control "who conceivably, but in realistic terms, may have information which may lead to or furnish the necessary

---

v. Bennington, No. 316CV00235RCJCLB, 2020 U.S. Dist. LEXIS 120755, at *12, 2020 WL 3884426 (D. Nev. July 8, 2020), *and ABKCO Music, Inc. v. Sagan*, No. 15 Civ. 4025 (ER) (HBP), 2017 U.S. Dist. LEXIS 120171, at *9–10, 2017 WL 3236443 (S.D.N.Y. July 31, 2017)); *accord Tomaszewski v. Allstate Ins. Co.*, No. 19-CV-0080, 2021 U.S. Dist. LEXIS 64699, at *9, 2021 WL 1238894 (E.D. Pa. Apr. 2, 2021) ("[T]here is no bright line rule defining the limits of a 'reasonable inquiry.'" (quoting *Haggie v. Coldwell Banker Real Estate Corp.*, Nos. 4:04CV111-M-A, *et al.*, 2007 U.S. Dist. LEXIS 35665, at *36, 2007 WL 1452495 (N.D. Miss. Nov. 15, 2017))); *Breuder v. Bd. of Trustees*, No. 15 CV 9323, 2021 U.S. Dist. LEXIS 56943, at *23, 2021 WL 1165089 (N.D. Ill. Mar. 25, 2021) ("What qualifies as a 'reasonable inquiry' depends on the facts of the case."); *Jones v. Zimmer*, No. 2:12-cv-01578-JAD-NJK, 2014 U.S. Dist. LEXIS 167750, at *13, 2014 WL 6772916 (D. Nev. Dec. 2, 2014 ("[B]efore making such a response, the responding party must undertake a reasonable inquiry into readily obtainable information from persons and/or documents within the responding party's relative control. . . . What constitutes a 'reasonable' inquiry depends on the circumstances of each particular case.")) (citations omitted); *In re Gulf Oil/Cities Serv. Tender Offer Litig.*, Nos. 87 Civ. 5253 (MBM), 87 CIV 8982 (MBM), 1990 U.S. Dist. LEXIS 5009, at *5, 1990 WL 657537 (S.D.N.Y. May 2, 1990) ("The extent of the obligation of reasonable inquiry turns on the practicalities of the case."); *Dubin v. E.F. Hutton Grp. Inc.*, 125 F.R.D. 372, 374 (S.D.N.Y. 1989) ("However, the standard of 'reasonable inquiry' under [Federal] Rule 36 is a relative standard depending on the particular facts of each case. [Federal] Rule 36 makes clear that determination of what constitutes 'reasonable inquiry' in a given case is committed to the sound discretion of the motion court, in this instance, the Magistrate.").

13 *JZ Buckingham Invests., LLC v. U.S.*, 77 Fed. Cl. 37, 47 (Ct. Cl. 2007) (discussing responses to requests for admission); *accord Odom v. Roberts*, 337 F.R.D. 347, 351 (N.D. Fla. 2020) ("'Reasonable inquiry' includes a reasonable effort 'to secure information that is readily obtainable from persons and documents within the responding party's relative control. . . .'" (quoting *Henry v. Champlain Enters., Inc.*, 212 F.R.D. 73, 78 (N.D.N.Y. 2003), and *T. Rowe Price Small-Cap Fund, Inc. v. Oppenheimer & Co.*, 174 F.R.D. 38, 43 (S.D.N.Y. 1997))); *Duncan v. Nunez*, No. 1:17-CV-1623-P, 2019 U.S. Dist. LEXIS 194260, at *5–6, 2019 WL 5861997 (W.D. La. Nov. 7, 2019) ("'Reasonable inquiry' means an 'inquiry of documents and persons readily available and within the responding party's control.' A reasonable inquiry includes both (1) an investigation of officers, administrators, agents and employees who conceivably and realistically may have information that may lead to a necessary and appropriate response, and (2) a review of relevant documents and regulations.'" (citations omitted) (quoting *Dickie Brennan & Co., Inc. v. Lexington Ins. Co.*, No. 09-CV-3866, 2010 WL 11538525 (E.D. La. Feb. 10, 2010)); *Lieber v. Wells Fargo Bank, N.A.*, No. 1:16 CV 2868, 2017 U.S. Dist. LEXIS 144910, at *8, 2017 WL 3923128 (N.D. Ohio Sept. 7, 2017) ("Generally, courts are in agreement that a 'reasonable inquiry' is limited to review and inquiry of those persons and documents that are within the responding party's control."); *ABKCO Music, Inc. v. Sagan*, No. 15 Civ. 4025 (ER) (HBP), 2017 U.S. Dist. LEXIS 120171, at *9–10, 2017 WL 3236443 (S.D.N.Y. July 31, 2017) ("Generally, a 'reasonable inquiry' is limited to review and inquiry of those persons and documents that are within the responding party's control."); *see Costa v. Kerzner Int'l Resorts, Inc.*, 277 F.R.D. 468, 470 (S.D. Fla. 2011) ("Furthermore, as with [Federal] Rule 34, a party must provide information in response to a [Federal] Rule 33 interrogatory if such information is under its control."). The meaning of "control" is discussed in Chapter 8, section 8-4:3.1.

and appropriate response."[14] As noted by one federal court: "When answering interrogatories, '[a] party is charged with knowledge of what its agents know, or what is in records available to it, or even, for purposes of [Federal] Rule 33, information others have given it on which it intends to rely in its suit.' A party responding to interrogatories 'cannot meet its discovery obligations by sticking its head in the sand and refusing to look for the answers and then saying it does not know the answer.'"[15] In other

---

[14] *Odom v. Roberts*, 337 F.R.D. 347, 351–52 (N.D. Fla. 2020) (quoting *T. Rowe Price Small-Cap Fund, Inc. v. Oppenheimer & Co., Inc.*, 174 F.R.D. 38 43 (S.D.N.Y. 1997)); *accord Murrey v. City of L.A.*, No. CV 19-2501 FMO (AS), 2020 U.S. Dist. LEXIS 79959, at *8–9, 2020 WL 2065019 (C.D. Cal. Feb. 21, 2020); *Gevas v. Dunlop*, No. 18 C 6556, 2020 U.S. Dist. LEXIS 27829, at *14, 2020 WL 814875 (N.D. Ill. Feb. 19, 2020); *Idaho Waste Sys., Inc. v. U.S. Air Force*, No. 1:18-CV-229-BLW, 2019 U.S. Dist. LEXIS 173016, at *6–7, 2019 WL 4777286 (D. Idaho Sept. 30, 2019); *CX Reinsurance Co. Ltd. v. Homewood Realty Inc.*, No. CV JFM-15-3136, 2018 U.S. Dist. LEXIS 11209, at *6, 2018 WL 2118545 (D. Md. Jan. 31, 2018); *Noble v. Gonzalez*, No. 1:07-cv-01111-LJO-GSA-PC, 2013 U.S. Dist. LEXIS 121252, at *52 (E.D. Cal. Aug. 26, 2013); *Iron Workers Local No. 60 Annuity Pension Fund v. Solvay Iron Works, Inc.*, No. 5:15-CV-0054 (BKS/DEP), 2017 U.S. Dist. LEXIS 61394, at *9–10, 2017 WL 1458772 (N.D.N.Y. Apr. 24, 2017); *Paramount Fin. Commc'ns, Inc.* v. *Broadridge Inv'r Commc'n Sos., Inc.*, No. 15-405, 2017 U.S. Dist. LEXIS 16802, at *12–13, 2017 WL 495784 (E.D. Pa. Feb. 7, 2017); *BNSF Ry. v. Gilster-Mary Lee Corp.*, No. 15-cv-250-JPG-SCW, 2017 U.S. Dist. LEXIS 28984, at *4–5, 2017 WL 9531979 (S.D. Ill. Jan. 18, 2017); *Montes v. Pinnacle Propane, LLC*, No. 16-cv-0126 JCH/SMV, 2016 U.S. Dist. LEXIS 144369, at *4, 2016 WL 9819527 (D.N.M. Oct. 18, 2016); *Flint v. City of Milwaukee*, No. 14-CV-333-JPS, 2014 U.S. Dist. LEXIS 151436, *11, 2014 WL 5431153 (E.D. Wis. Oct. 24, 2014).

Of course, it is improper for a party to refuse to fully answer a required disclosure, interrogatory, or request for admission simply because it does not maintain the data it needs to review in the format requested. *Cf. Health Grades, Inc. v. MDX Med., Inc.*, No. 11-cv-00520-RM-BNB, 2014 U.S. Dist. LEXIS 802, at *8–9, 2014 WL 30001 (D. Colo. Jan. 3, 2014) (interrogatories); *L.H. v. Schwarzenegger*, No. 2:06-cv-2042-LKK-GGH, 2007 U.S. Dist. LEXIS 73752, at *17–18, 2007 WL 2781132 (E.D. Cal. Sept. 21, 2007) (interrogatories).

[15] *Health Grades, Inc. v. MDX Med., Inc.*, No. 11-cv-00520-RM-BNB, 2014 U.S. Dist. LEXIS 802, at *8–9, 2014 WL 30001 (D. Colo. Jan. 3, 2014) (quoting *Okla. v. Tyson Foods, Inc.*, 262 F.R.D. 617, 629 (N.D. Okla. 2009), and *In re Indep. Servs. Org. Antitrust Litig.*, 168 F.R.D. 651, 653 (D. Kan. 1996)); *accord Odom v. Roberts*, 337 F.R.D. 347, 351–52 (N.D. Fla. 2020) ("'[I]f the information is held by the responding party or by an individual or entity with which the responding party maintains a relationship that enables it readily to procure the required information, then that party may be expected to seek out the information and respond substantively to the request for admission.' Sifting through data provided in the discovery process generally is considered part of a reasonable inquiry." (citations omitted) (quoting *Fed. Deposit Ins. Corp. v. Halpern*, 271 F.R.D. 191, 194 (D. Nev. 2010))); *Crowther v. City of Fontana*, No. 517CV01457MWFSK, 2018 U.S. Dist. LEXIS 225900, at *2, 2018 WL 6016289 (C.D. Cal. Sept. 10, 2018) (providing that a party was "required to engage in a reasonable inquiry into readily obtainable information before answering that it cannot admit or deny a fact"); *U.S. v. All Assets Held at Bank Julius Baer & Co.*, No. CV 04-798 (PLF/GMH), 2018 WL 8867711, at *9 (D.D.C. Jan. 19, 2018) (Federal "Rule 33 requires a responding party to 'compile information within his control' and provide 'all information available to him.'" (quoting *Huthnance v. District of Columbia*, 255 F.R.D. 285, 292–93 (D.D.C. 2008))); *Colony Ins. Co. v. Kuehn*, No. 2:10-cv-01943-KJD-GWF, 2011 U.S. Dist. LEXIS 106884, at *10, 2011 WL 4402738 (D. Nev. Sept. 20, 2011) ("A party is generally charged with knowledge of what its agents know, or what is in records available to it, or even information others have given to it on which it intends to rely in its suit. A party cannot limit its interrogatory answers

words, "a party must identify potentially 'key players' in the litigation 'who [are] likely to have relevant information' and then ensure that these key players turn over all of the relevant material in their possession."[16]

Thus, in the case of an organizational party, such as a corporation, partnership, limited-liability company, or unincorporated association, the duty to provide information reasonably available includes information reasonably imputed to the party, including information possessed by its officers, employees, partners, managers, members, agents, and others under its control.[17] For example, a corporation answering

---

to matters within its own knowledge and ignore information immediately available to it or under its control."); *Stark-Romero v. Nat'l R.R. Passenger Co.*, 275 F.R.D. 551, 558 (D.N.M. 2011) ("A reasonable inquiry means that a party has to ask their counsel, and if their counsel knows the answer, they need to use that information to admit or deny."); *Okla. v. Tyson Foods, Inc.*, 262 F.R.D. 617, 629 (N.D. Okla. 2009) ("Further, a corporation's response to interrogatories is not limited to information maintained in the ordinary course of business. The corporation 'must furnish the information available to the party.'" (quoting Fed. R. Civ. P. 33(b)(1)(B))); *U.S. ex. rel. Englund v. L.A. Cty.*, 235 F.R.D. 675, 685 (E.D. Cal. 2006) (holding that the duty of a responding party to make a "reasonable inquiry" "is limited to persons and documents within the responding party's control (e.g., its employees, partners, corporate affiliates, etc.)"); *Herrera v. Scully*, 143 F.R.D. 545, 548 (S.D.N.Y. 1992) ("Reasonable inquiry includes investigation and inquiry of any of defendant's officers, administrators, agents, employees, servants, enlisted or other personnel, who conceivably, but in realistic terms, may have information which may lead to or furnish the necessary and appropriate response. In this connection, relevant documents and regulations must be reviewed as well." (quoting *Diederich v. Dep't of Army*, 132 F.R.D. 614, 619 (S.D.N.Y. 1990))); *see T. Rowe Price Small-Cap Fund, Inc. v. Oppenheimer & Co.*, Inc., 174 F.R.D. 38, 43 (S.D.N.Y. 1997) (noting that, in responding to requests for disclosure, a party "may not give lack of information or knowledge as a reason for failure to admit or deny [a request for admission] unless he has made [a reasonable] inquiry" into the matter at hand); *CherCo Props., Inc. v. Law, Snakard & Gambill, P.C.*, 985 S.W.2d 262, 267–68 (Tex. App.—Fort Worth 1999, no writ) (holding that a reasonable inquiry required the plaintiff corporation to ask its sole shareholder for information needed to answer requests for admission).

16 *Newill v. Campbell Transp. Co.*, No. 2:12-cv-1344, 2013 U.S. Dist. LEXIS 160903, at *15, 2013 WL 6002349 (Nov. 12, 2013) (quoting *Zubulake v. UBS Warburg LLC*, 229 F.R.D. 422, 432 (S.D.N.Y. 2004)).

17 *Cf. Odom v. Roberts*, 337 F.R.D. 347, 352 (N.D. Fla. 2020) ("[I]n the case of a business or corporation, reasonable inquiry includes investigation and inquiry of the answering party's 'officers, administrators, agents, employees, servants, enlisted or other personnel, who conceivably, but in realistic terms, may have information which may lead to or furnish the necessary and appropriate response.'" (quoting *T. Rowe Price Small-Cap Fund, Inc. v. Oppenheimer & Co.*, 174 F.R.D. 38, 42 (S.D.N.Y. 1997))); *Thomas v. Cate*, 715 F. Supp. 2d 1012, 1032 (E.D. Cal. 2010 ("[Federal] Rule 33 imposes a duty on the responding party to secure all information available to it. Where an interrogatory is directed at a party that is a governmental entity, [Federal] Rule 33(b)(1)(B) requires the party to furnish information 'available' to an officer or agent of the governmental entity.") (citations omitted); *Goodrich Corp. v. Emhart Indus.*, No. EDCV 04-00759-VAP (SSx), 2005 U.S. Dist. LEXIS 17190, at *8 (C.D. Cal. June 10, 2005) ("A corporation responding to interrogatories must provide not only the information contained in its own files and possessed by its own employees, but also all information under its control."); *Weddington v. Consol. Rail Corp.*, 101 F.R.D. 71, 74 (N.D. Ind. 1984) (holding that a corporation had a duty to discover information from its employees); *Twentieth Century Fox Film Corp. v. Marvel Enters.*, No. 01 Civ. 3016 (AGS)(HBP), 2002 U.S. Dist. LEXIS 14682, at *10, 2002 WL 1835439 (S.D.N.Y. Aug. 6, 2002) ("A corporation responding to interrogatories must provide

interrogatories must provide information within the knowledge of any of its employees and others under its control who conceivably, but realistically, could have responsive information.[18] An unincorporated association must provide information known to its members and others under its control who conceivably, but realistically, could have responsive information.[19]

The reasonable-inquiry requirement for required disclosures, interrogatories, and requests for admission also requires the responding party to make a good-faith effort to refresh its recollection about matters about which it previously had knowledge.[20]

---

not only the information contained in its own files and possessed by its own employees, it must also provide all information under its control. 'A party served with interrogatories is obliged to respond by furnishing such information as is available to the party. [Defendant] therefore is obliged to respond to the interrogatories not only by providing the information it has, but also the information within its control or otherwise obtainable by it.'" (citation omitted) (quoting *In re Auction Houses Antitrust Litig.*, 196 F.R.D. 444, 445 (S.D.N.Y. 2000))); *Trane Co. v. Klutznick*, 87 F.R.D. 473, 476 (W.D. Wis. 1980) ("In each of these instances, the courts held that an official answering the interrogatories for a corporation had an affirmative duty to search out all information under the control of the corporation and could not evade answering the interrogatories based on his own limited knowledge. Although this rule of law is based, in part, on the theory that a corporation's knowledge is an amalgamation of the knowledge of each individual officer or employee, it is equally grounded on the theory that a party cannot plead personal ignorance as an excuse for not answering interrogatories if indeed the information is within his control."); *Int'l Ass'n of Machinists, Dist. 169 v. Amana Refrigeration, Inc.*, 90 F.R.D. 1, 2 (E.D. Tenn. 1978) ("[T]he answering agent must consult with other members of the organization who are in possession of the information sought to be discovered and then answer."); *Weddington v. Consol. Rail Corp.*, 101 F.R.D. 71, 75 (N.D. Ind. 1984) (holding that a corporation had a duty to discover information from its employees); *cf. Wiand v. Wells Fargo Bank*, No. 8:12-CV-557-T-27EAJ, 2013 U.S. Dist. LEXIS 174768, at *10–11, 2013 WL 12156100 (M.D. Fla. Dec. 13, 2013) ("A principal is deemed to have control over documents in the possession of its agent."); *Jans ex rel. Jans v. The GAP Stores, Inc.*, No. 6:05-cv-1534-Orl-31JGG, 2006 U.S. Dist. LEXIS 67266, at *7–8, 2006 WL 2691800 (M.D. Fla. Sept. 20, 2006) (finding that a party had control over documents from prior litigation held by its attorney because an attorney is the client's agent).

18 *Cf. Weddington v. Consol. Rail Corp.*, 101 F.R.D. 71, 74 (N.D. Ind. 1984); *Trane Co. v. Klutznick*, 87 F.R.D. 473, 476 (W.D. Wis. 1980).

19 *Int'l Ass'n of Machinists, Dist. 169 v. Amana Refrigeration, Inc.*, 90 F.R.D. 1, 2 (E.D. Tenn. 1978).

20 *See, e.g., McPeak v. Tex. Dep't of Pub. Safety*, 346 S.W.2d 138, 140 (Tex. Civ. App.—Dallas 1961, no writ) (In an appeal from the revocation of his driver's license, the plaintiff's answer "I don't remember" to requests for admission regarding his prior traffic offenses was evasive because "[h]ere by the exercise of ordinary diligence, plaintiff could have inspected the records of the city of Dallas or made other inquiry which would have revealed his convictions of offenses inquired about. The facts . . . indicate clearly that appellant made no effort to ascertain the facts requested to be admitted, nor did he give any reasons for not doing so, and, therefore, his answers are clearly waived."); *cf. Breuder v. Bd. of Trustees*, 15 CV 9323, 2021 U.S. Dist. LEXIS 56943, at *24–25, 2021 WL 1165089 (N.D. Ill. Mar. 25, 2021) ("[T]he fact that the Individual Defendants believe that their recollection can be refreshed indicates that there are materials or persons who can refresh their recollection. The Court finds that the Individual Defendants have a duty to reasonably inquire of those materials or persons to refresh their recollections before submitting their amended responses to the RFAs."); *A. Farber & Partners v. Garber*, 237 F.R.D. 250, 256 (C.D. Cal. 2006) (holding that the defendants' failure "to make a reasonable inquiry to obtain information is especially galling when they claim they do

Although the responding party generally is not required "to interview or subpoena records from independent third parties" to respond to required disclosure, interrogatories, or requests for admission,[21] "'[u]nder certain circumstances, parties may be

---

'not recall'—since that response clearly implies that, at one time, they possessed the necessary information to respond to the requests for admission and have now chosen not to refresh their recollections").

[21] *U.S. ex rel. Englund v. L.A. Cnty.*, 235 F.R.D. 675, 685 (E.D. Cal. 2006), ***quoted with approval in*** *McGee v. Poverello House*, No. 118CV000768LJOSAB, 2019 U.S. Dist. LEXIS 109892, at *15–16, 2019 WL 2725342 (E.D. Cal. July 1, 2019), ***and*** *Damian v. Int'l Metals Trading & Invs., Ltd.*, No. 1:16-CV-20343-DMM, 2017 U.S. Dist. LEXIS 108596, at *8, 2017 WL 2992200 (S.D. Fla. July 13, 2017); ***accord*** *Tomaszewski v. Allstate Ins. Co.*, No. 19-CV-0080, 2021 U.S. Dist. LEXIS 64699, at *10, 2021 WL 1238894 (E.D. Pa. Apr. 2, 2021) (Reasonable inquiry "'does not require the responding party to interview or subpoena records from independent third parties in order to admit or deny a Request for Admission.'" (quoting *Haggie v. Coldwell Banker Real Estate Corp.*, Nos. 4:04CV111-M-A, *et al.*, 2007 U.S. Dist. LEXIS 35665, at *36, 2007 WL 1452495 (N.D. Miss. Nov. 15, 2017))); *Berry v. Office of the Fayette Cnty. Sheriff*, No. 5: 14-356-DCR, 2015 U.S. Dist. LEXIS 82352, at *6, 2015 WL 3916126 (E.D. Ky. June 25, 2015) ("The Sheriff's Office argues that the plaintiffs could have made a 'simple request pursuant to the Kentucky Open Records Act to the Defendant' to reveal the accuracy of the paystubs. Notwithstanding this option, Federal Rule 36 does not place this type of burden on the plaintiffs. The reasonable inquiry standard does not require the plaintiffs to acquire discovery on the defendant's behalf or collect information from third parties outside their immediate control for the purpose of responding to requests for admissions. Instead, a reasonable inquiry is limited to an inquiry of 'persons and documents within the responding party's control (e.g., its employees, partners, corporate affiliates, etc.).'" (quoting *Petro v. Jones*, No. 11-151-GFVT, 2014 U.S. Dist. LEXIS 31664, at *13, 2014 WL 970113 (E.D. Ky. Mar. 12, 2014))); *Bernstein v. Principal Life Ins. Co.*, No. 09 Civ. 4925 (CM) (HBP), 2010 U.S. Dist. LEXIS 127733, at *9–11, 2010 WL 4922093 (S.D.N.Y. Dec. 2, 2010) ("Plaintiffs correctly point out that requests 14, 17, 32, 33, 55, 56, 57, 66, 78 and 79 relate to either the conduct of third parties or the knowledge or motivation of third parties. A party's obligation to respond to a request for an admission does not usually encompass an obligation to interview non-parties or otherwise seek information from non-parties. . . . Accordingly, plaintiffs' failure to admit or deny these requests is appropriate."); *Haggie v. Coldwell Banker Real Estate Corp.*, No. 4:404CV111-M-A, 2007 U.S. Dist. LEXIS 35666, at *14–16, 2007 WL 1452495 (N.D. Miss. May 15, 2007) ("Under [Federal] Rule 36, a defendant's duty to make a 'reasonable inquiry' should not require the defendant to make judgments or put itself in the shoes of another unrelated defendant. In other words, a real estate company is not required to expend time, energy, and money to inquire as to the veracity of a request for admission regarding information that the bank, its employees, a mortgage lender, its employees, or an appraiser may have had or what those individuals may have thought or done in the course of closing a loan for the sale of a specific property. Instead, the court concludes that the defendant, Coldwell Banker, is responsible for responding only to requests for admission that relate directly to its corporate entity, its agents or employees and their acts, omissions, or impressions and not those of third parties or individuals or information outside its control. This does not mean that the defendant should not make every effort to respond to requests for admission completely and truthfully, but simply that the defendant is not under a duty to conclusively establish facts that it or its agents, partners, employees, corporate affiliates, etc., are without knowledge or evidence to determine."); *T. Rowe Price Small-Cap Fund, Inc. v. Oppenheimer & Co.*, 174 F.R.D. 38, 44 (S.D.N.Y. 1997) ("[I]t far exceeds the reasonable inquiry provision of [Federal] Rule 36 to require defendant to subpoena FDIC documents in Chicago, perhaps litigating the subpoena, travel to Chicago to review large volumes of documents and incur whatever additional expenses may be

required to inquire of third parties to properly respond to requests to admit.' Such circumstances exist where, for example, the respondent and the third party have parallel interests and have been closely cooperating in discovery in related cases, where respondent can respond by getting information from co-defendants without extraordinary expense or effort, where 'there is some identity of interest manifested, such as by both being parties to the litigation, a present or prior relationship of mutual concerns, or their active cooperation in the litigation, and when there is no manifest or potential conflict between the party and the third party,' where the third party is the respondent's family member, or where the third party is a former employee without any adverse interest to the respondent."[22] Generally, a reasonable inquiry also

---

involved in their production. Thus, to the extent various admissions called for admissions as to matters at the Bank of which Oppenheimer had no knowledge, as to which there may have been relevant information in the FDIC documents, it was appropriate to respond that it has made reasonable inquiry and it was unable to admit or deny the requests.").

[22] *BNSF Ry. v. Gilster-Mary Lee Corp.*, No. 15-cv-250-JPG-SCW, 2017 U.S. Dist. LEXIS 28988, *3–5, 2017 WL 781540 (S.D. Ill. Mar. 1, 2017) (citations omitted) (quoting *Hanley v. Como Inn, Inc.*, No. 99 C 1486, 2003 U.S. Dist. LEXIS 7130, at *4 (N.D. Ill. Apr. 28, 2003), and *Uniden Am. Corp.* v. *Ericsson Inc.*, 181 F.R.D. 302, 304 (M.D.N.C. 1998)); *accord Breuder v. Bd. of Trustees*, No. 15 CV 9323, 2021 U.S. Dist. LEXIS 56943, at *24, 2021 WL 1165089 (N.D. Ill. Mar. 25, 2021) ("[C]ourts have 'found that a party must make inquiry of a third party when there is some identity of interest manifested, such as both being parties to the litigation, a present or prior relationship of mutual concerns, or active cooperation in litigation, and when there is no manifest or potential conflict between the party and the person of whom inquiry will be made.'" (quoting *SEC v. Stifel*, No. 11-C-0755, 2016 U.S. Dist. LEXIS 113012, at *5, 2016 WL4471859 (E.D. Wis. Aug. 24, 2016))); *Ross v. Gossett*, No. 3:15-CV-309-SMY-MAB, 2021 U.S. Dist. LEXIS 30063, at *27 n.10, 2021 WL 632963 (S.D. Ill. Feb. 18, 2021) (citing cases in which inquiry of third parties was required); *ABKCO Music, Inc. v. Sagan*, No. 15CIV4025ERHBP, 2017 U.S. Dist. LEXIS 120171, at *9, 2017 WL 3236443 (S.D.N.Y. July 31, 2017) (same); *Wellin v. Wellin*, Nos. 2:13-CV-1831-DCN, 2:13-CV-3595-DCN, 2:14-CV-4067-DCN, 2015 U.S. Dist. LEXIS 135107, at *28, 2015 WL 5785709 (D.S.C. July 31, 2015) (quoting *T. Rowe Price Small-Cap Fund Inc. v. Oppenheimer & Co.*, 174 F.R.D. 38, 42 (S.D.N.Y. 1997)) ("Generally, a 'reasonable inquiry' is limited to review and inquiry of those persons and documents that are within the responding party's control. Under certain circumstances, however, parties may be required to inquire of third parties to properly respond to requests for admission. Reasonable inquiry includes investigation and inquiry of any of [a party's] officers, administrators, agents, employees, servants, enlisted or other personnel, who conceivably, but in realistic terms, may have information which may lead to or furnish the necessary and appropriate response."); *Inventio AG v. ThyssenKrupp Ams. Corp.*, No 08-874-RGA, 2013 U.S. Dist. LEXIS 116680, at *9–10, 2013 WL 12133902 (D. Del. July 29, 2013) ("[A] plain reading of the [Federal] Rule indicates that a responding party has a duty to inquire as to all documents and information readily available, whether in the party's possession or not. At a minimum, this would include a reasonable inquiry of Inventio's agents and other third parties within the party's control who have (or had in the past) identical interests to Inventio."); *Erie Ins. Prop. & Cas. Co. v. Johnson*, 272 F.R.D. 177, 183–84 (S.D. W. Va. 2010) (holding that "the defendant insurer should have asked its insurance agent about answers and the failure to do so did not constitute reasonable inquiry"); *JZ Buckingham Invests., LLC v. U.S.*, 77 Fed. Cl. 37, 47 (Ct. Cl. 2007) ("[A] 'reasonable inquiry' may encompass inquiry of a third party if there is an 'identity of interest' between the responding party and the third party—i.e., when they are both parties to, or actively cooperating, in the litigation or when they have a present or prior relationship of mutual concern—not if there is a manifest or potential conflict between the responding party and the third party."); *A. Farber & Partners v. Garber*, 237 F.R.D. 250, 256 (C.D. Cal. 2006)

requires the responding party to review deposition testimony, witness statements, and interviews.[23] However, it is not bound by a third party's testimony or statements when the third party is hostile or when the responding party has evidence that is contrary to the third party's testimony.[24]

(holding that a reasonable inquiry "includes, at a minimum, an inquiry of the other defendants represented by the same counsel"); *Uniden Am. Corp. v. Ericsson Inc.*, 181 F.R.D. 302, 304 (M.D. N.C. 1998) ("The Court finds that a party must make inquiry of a third party when there is some identity of interest manifested, such as by both being parties to the litigation, a present or prior relationship of mutual concerns, or their active cooperation in the litigation[.]"); *T. Rowe Price Small-Cap Fund, Inc. v. Oppenheimer & Co.*, 174 F.R.D. 38, 43 (S.D.N.Y. 1997) (holding that a reasonable inquiry may require inquiry of information readily available from a non-hostile third party); *In re Gulf Oil/Cities Serv. Tender Offer Litig.*, Nos. 87 Civ. 5253 (MBM), 87 CIV 8982 (MBM),1990 U.S. Dist. LEXIS 5009, at *8–13 (S.D.N.Y. May 2, 1990) (holding that the plaintiff must consult a nonparty's counsel to confirm data derived from figures produced by the nonparty because the plaintiff and nonparty had parallel interests and had been closely cooperating in discovery in two related cases); *Al Jundi v. Rockefeller*, 91 F.R.D. 590, 594–95 (W.D.N.Y. 1981) (holding that, "where without extra expense or effort," a defendant may be able to respond based on information secured from co-defendants and their counsel, such efforts must be made); *see Keralink Int'l, Inc. v. Stradis Healthcare, LLC*, CV CCB-18-2013, 2021 WL 1198150, at *5 (D. Md. Mar. 30, 2021) (A reasonable inquiry generally "does not 'require a respondent to ascertain from persons, known to him and to the court to be hostile or interested in the outcome of the suit, facts upon which to predicate a sworn response.'" (quoting *CX Reinsurance Co. v. Johnson*, No. RWT-15-3132, 2018 U.S. Dist. LEXIS 11209, at *6, 2018 WL 10075929, at *2 (D. Md. Jan. 24, 2018))); *Odom v. Roberts*, 337 F.R.D. 347, 352 (N.D. Fla. 2020) ("A reasonable inquiry generally includes requesting information from co-defendants and their counsel.").

23 *Cf. Odom v. Roberts*, 337 F.R.D. 347, 352 (N.D. Fla. 2020) ("A review of a deposition transcript also would be part of a 'reasonable inquiry.'"); *Caruso v. Coleman Co.*, No. 93-CV-6733, 1995 U.S. Dist. LEXIS 7934, at *4 (E.D. Pa. June 7, 1995) (Federal "Rule 36(a)s requirement of 'reasonable inquiry' does extend to third parties, if there exists sworn deposition testimony of such third party."); *Diederich v. Dep't of Army*, 132 F.R.D. 614, 620 (S.D.N.Y. 1990) (same); *see Apostol v. Landau*, 86 C 8070, 1994 U.S. Dist. LEXIS 3772, at *3, 1994 WL 110172 (N.D. Ill. Mar. 29, 1994) ("Ordinarily, a reasonable inquiry would require that counsel interview available witnesses, and review relevant documents—especially those in his client's possession."). *But see Reitz v. Creighton*, No. 15 C 1854, 2019 U.S. Dist. LEXIS 195669, at *7–8, 2019 WL 5798680 (N.D. Ill. Nov. 7, 2019) (concluding that a party did not have to review deposition transcripts to satisfy the "reasonable inquiry" requirement for requests for admission because "it is unnecessary to demand a party admit or deny what is contained in a deposition. The witness either said what is quoted or he didn't").

24 *Cf. T. Rowe Price Small-Cap Fund, Inc. v. Oppenheimer & Co.*, 174 F.R.D. 38, 44–45 (S.D.N.Y. 1997) (footnote omitted) (citations omitted); *see Uniden Am. Corp. v. Ericsson Inc.*, 181 F.R.D. 302, 304 (M.D. N.C. 1998) (holding that, if a nonparty has given deposition testimony regarding the matter, the responding party "can be compelled via [Federal] Rule 36 to admit or deny, that is to indicate whether it will introduce contrary evidence."); *Kendrick v. Sullivan*, No. 83-3175 (CRR), 1992 U.S. Dist. LEXIS 18270, at *44–45 (D.D.C. May 5, 1992) ("The court agrees with plaintiff that it need not admit facts testified to by hostile third parties, since plaintiff was entitled to have trial judge determine the weight and credibility of the testimony."); *In re Gulf Oil/Cities Serv. Tender Offer Litig.*, Nos. 87 Civ. 5253 (MBM), 87 CIV 8982 (MBM), 1990 U.S. Dist. LEXIS 5009, at *15–16 (S.D.N.Y. May 2, 1990) ("Although party need not be bound by witness's version of events if there is reason to question it, particularly based upon the interest or hostility of the witness, this case is distinguishable because facts are not in genuine dispute and are available from nonparty whose interests

Further, individuals and organizations generally have an obligation to obtain relevant information that is readily available to them from nonparties under their control,[25] such as information from entities owned or controlled by them[26] or their

---

are identified with the responding party."); *Dulansky v. Iowa-Ill. Gas & Elec. Co.*, 92 F. Supp. 118, 123 (S.D. Iowa 1950) (holding that a defendant was only obligated to notice the sworn testimony of its former employee in responding to a request for admission and specifically concluding that the defendant was not obligated to inquire any further of that employee).

25 *Cf. Odom v. Roberts*, 337 F.R.D. 347, 352 (N.D. Fla. 2020) (A reasonable "inquiry also may 'require venturing beyond the parties to the litigation and include, under certain limited circumstances, non-parties, but surely not strangers' unconnected to the case. [Federal] Rule 36 does not impose a duty on an answering party to subpoena records or conduct a broad investigation beyond documents within its control or which it easily could obtain." (quoting *Henry v. Champlain Enters., Inc.*, 212 F.R.D. 73, 78 (N.D.N.Y. 2003))); *Gevas v. Dunlop*, No. 18 C 6556, 2020 U.S. Dist. LEXIS 27829, at *14, 2020 WL 814875 (N.D. Ill. Feb. 19, 2020) ("An answering party may not rely solely on its lack of personal knowledge when responding to requests to admit. Consequently, a party may be required to contact third persons who are readily available, such as the party's 'officers, administrators, agents, employees, servants, enlisted or other personnel, who conceivably, but in realistic terms, may have information which may lead to or furnish the necessary and appropriate response.'" (citations omitted) (quoting *Taborn v. Unknown Officers*, No. 00C652, 2001 WL 138909, at *1 (N.D. Ill. Feb. 16, 2001))).

26 *Cf. U.S. v. Int'l Union of Petroleum & Indus. Workers, AFL-CIO*, 870 F.2d 1450, 1452 (9th Cir. 1989) ("A corporation must produce documents possessed by a subsidiary that the parent corporation owns or controls."); *Frieri v. Sysco Corp.*, No. 3:16-cv-01432-JLS-NLS, 2017 U.S. Dist. LEXIS 124425, at *7, 2017 WL 3387713 (S.D. Cal. Aug. 4, 2017) ("A parent may be properly compelled to respond to interrogatories that include information available from its subsidiaries."); *Goodrich Corp. v. Emhart Indus.*, No. EDCV 04-00759-VAP (SSx), 2005 U.S. Dist. LEXIS 17190, at *8–9, 2005 WL 6440828 (C.D. Cal. June 10, 2005) ("A corporation responding to interrogatories must provide not only the information contained in its own files and possessed by its own employees, but also all information under its control. Accordingly, 'when the parent is served with an interrogatory, it is no defense to claim that the information is within the possession of a wholly owned subsidiary, because such a corporation is owned and controlled by such interrogee.'" (quoting *Westinghouse Credit Corp. v. Mountain States Mining & Milling Co.*, 37 F.R.D. 348, 349 (D. Col. 1965))); *Twentieth Century Fox Film Corp. v. Marvel Enters.*, No. 01 Civ. 3016 (AGS) (HBP), 2002 U.S. Dist. LEXIS 14682, at *12–13, 2002 WL 1835439 (S.D.N.Y. Aug. 6, 2002) ("Numerous courts have concluded that a parent corporation has a sufficient degree of ownership and control over a wholly-owned subsidiary that it must be deemed to have control over documents located with that subsidiary. This principle applies where the subsidiary is not owned directly but, rather, is owned by an intermediate corporation that is itself a wholly-owned corporation of the parent corporation.") (citations omitted); *Cotracom Commodity Trading Co. v. Seaboard Corp.*, 189 F.R.D. 655, 663 (D. Kan. 1999) (agreeing with the "principle" that "that a parent must produce all the documents of its wholly-owned subsidiary"); *see Starlight Int'l Inc. v. Herlihy*, 186 F.R.D. 626, 634–35 (D. Kan. 1999) (holding that the "sole owner, officer, and director" of an entity that was a "member of the joint venture" with a defendant in the case "has a sufficient nexus with [the defendants] to attribute documents in his possession to be under their joint control" and that "members of a joint venture also have a legal right to obtain information of the venture on demand"); *see Imagine Auto. Grp. v. Boardwalk Motor Cars, Ltd.*, 430 S.W.3d 620, 641 (Tex. App.—Dallas 2014, pet. denied) (holding that the CEO and a principal of a company had possession, custody, or control of the company's documents); *In re Summersett*, 438 S.W.3d 74, 82 (Tex. App.—Corpus Christ 2013, orig. proceeding) (holding

designated, retained-testifying experts.[27]

Finally, if the responding party would have to obtain the information needed to respond to discovery in order to prepare for trial, the party should obtain the information in connection with discovery if it is reasonably and readily available.[28]

5-2:2 Reasonable Inquiry with Respect to Production Requests

The reasonable-inquiry requirement with respect to requests for production is like that for other written discovery. The keys are "control" and "reasonable availability."[29]

---

that the president and chief medical officer of a hospital had possession, custody, or control of documents relating to his employment by the hospital even though he claimed that the documents were those of the hospital); *Valley Forge Ins. Co. Relator v. Jones*, 733 S.W.2d 319, 321–22 (Tex. App.—Texarkana 1987, no writ) (ordering a controlling shareholder to produce documents of the corporations he owned because they were under his control).

[27] *Cf. Odom v. Roberts*, 337 F.R.D. 347, 352 (N.D. Fla. 2020) (Federal "Rule 36 does not require a party to retain an expert witness simply to answer a request for admission, but if a party already has retained an expert in a particular field, or an opposing party offers to make its expert available at no cost, consultation with such an expert could be encompassed within a 'reasonable inquiry.'" (citing *McKinney/Pearl Rest. Partners, L.P. v. Metro. Life Ins. Co.*, 322 F.R.D. 235, 253 (N.D. Tex. 2016), and *Lumpkin v. Meskill*, 64 F.R.D. 673, 679 (D. Conn. 1974))).

[28] *Cf. Procaps S.A. v. Patheon Inc.*, No. 12-24356-CIV-GOODMAN, 2015 U.S. Dist. LEXIS 47104, at *6–7, 2015 WL 1608807 (S.D. Fla. Apr. 10, 2015) ("Significantly, an 'interrogatory will not be held objectionable as calling for research if the interrogated party would gather the information in the preparation of its own case.'" (quoting 8B Charles Alan Wright, Arthur R. Miller & Richard L. Marcus, Federal Practice and Procedure § 2174 (3d ed. 2014))); *Dixie v. Virga*, No. 2:12-cv-2626-MCE-DAD, 2015 U.S. Dist. LEXIS 11429, at *27, 2015 WL 412298 (E.D. Cal. Jan. 29, 2015) ("[I]f the responding party would necessarily have to gather the requested information to prepare its own case, objections that it is too difficult to obtain the information for the requesting party are not honored." (quoting *L.H. v. Schwarzenegger*, No. 2:06-cv-2042-LKK-GGH, 2007 U.S. Dist. LEXIS 73752, at *9–10 (E.D. Cal. Sept. 21, 2007))); *In re Gulf Oil/Cities Serv. Tender Offer Litig.*, Nos. 87 Civ. 5253 (MBM), 87 CIV 8982 (MBM),1990 U.S. Dist. LEXIS 5009, at *8–9, 1990 WL 657537 (S.D.N.Y. May 2, 1990) ("[P]laintiffs will obviously be required to obtain this information as part of their trial preparation if they are to meet Gulf's assertion at trial that Cities misrepresented its oil reserves during the tender offer period. It necessarily follows that it would not be unreasonable to require plaintiffs to obtain such data at this stage in order to serve the purpose embodied in [Federal] Rule 36 of narrowing the scope of contested issues and proof at trial."); *Flour Mills, Inc. v. Pace*, 75 F.R.D. 676, 680 (D. Okla. 1977) ("An interrogatory will not be held objectionable as calling for research if it relates to details alleged in the pleading of the interrogated party, about which it presumably has information, or if the interrogated party would gather the information in the preparation of its own case.").

[29] See Chapter 8, section 8-4:3.1 (discussing when documents are within a party's possession, custody, or control within the meaning of Texas Rule 192.3(b), which defines the phrase "possession, custody, or control").

As one federal court explained: "[P]rior to responding to a request for production of documents under [Federal] Rule 34, a party must undertake a reasonable search to determine whether it has any responsive documents in its possession, custody, or control. Consistent with these requirements, after a litigation hold is issued, a party must identify potentially 'key players' in the litigation 'who [are] likely to have relevant information' and then ensure that these key players turn over all of the relevant material in their possession."[30] The party generally also must obtain documents that

---

[30] *Newill v. Campbell Transp. Co.*, No. 2:12-cv-1344, 2013 U.S. Dist. LEXIS 160903, at *15, 2013 WL 6002349 (Nov. 12, 2013) (quoting *Zubulake v. UBS Warburg LLC*, 229 F.R.D. 422, 432 (S.D.N.Y. 2004)); *accord Anderson v. Cryovac, Inc.*, 862 F.2d 910, 929 (1st Cir. 1988) ("[O]nce a proper discovery request has been seasonably propounded, we will not allow a party sentiently to avoid its obligations by . . . failing to examine records within its control."); *Hawkins v. Kroger Co.*, 15CV2320-JM (BLM), 2019 U.S. Dist. LEXIS 161210, at *27, 2019 WL 4416132 (S.D. Cal. Sept. 16, 2019) ("'[A] party has an obligation to conduct a reasonable inquiry into the factual basis of his responses to discovery. Based on that inquiry, a party responding to a request for production "is under an affirmative duty to seek that information reasonably available" to it and make an appropriate production of responsive documents.'" (quoting *Hartline v. Nat'l Univ.*, 2018 U.S. Dist. LEXIS 28853, at *9, 2018 WL 1014611 (E.D. Cal. Feb. 22, 2018))); *Robinson v. City of Ark. City*, No. 10-1431-JAR-GLR, 2012 U.S. Dist. LEXIS 23806, at *14 (D. Kan. Feb. 24, 2012) ("To adequately respond to a request for production, the respondent must 'conduct a reasonable search for responsive documents.' Parties, along with their employees and attorneys, have a duty to act 'competently, diligently, and ethically' with respect to discharging discovery obligations. This requires a joint effort 'to identify all employees likely to have been authors, recipients or custodians of documents' responsive to the requests for production. A party does not 'meet its discovery obligations by sticking its head in the sand and refusing to look for [documents].'" (quoting *FTC v. Affiliate Strategies, Inc.*, No. 09-4104-JAR, 2011 U.S. Dist. LEXIS 7689, at *12 n.22 (D. Kan. Jan. 26, 2011), *Cardenas v. Dorel Juvenile Grp., Inc.*, No. 04-2478-KHV-DJW, 2006 U.S. Dist. LEXIS 37465, at *23 (D. Kan. June 1, 2006), and *In re Indep. Servs. Org. Antitrust Litig.*, 168 F.R.D. 651, 653 (D. Kan. 1996))); *Cache La Poudre Feeds, LLC v. Land O'Lakes, Inc.*, 244 F.R.D. 614, 626 (D. Colo. 2007) ("[Federal] Rule 34 also imposed on Defendants an affirmative duty to seek information reasonably available through Land O'Lakes' employees, agents and others subject to their control."); *In re Indep. Servs. Org. Antitrust Litig.*, 168 F.R.D. 651, 653 (D. Kan. 1996) (holding that a party cannot meet its discovery obligations by "sticking its head in the sand and refusing to look for the answer and then saying it does not know the answer;" a corporation must "speak to those employees who may have responsive information"); *see In re Summersett*, 438 S.W.3d 74, 81 (Tex. App.—Corpus Christ 2013, orig. proceeding) ("Because the discovery rules often apply to reach information not within a party's physical possession, a party may often not have actual knowledge of the existence of information or documents in the possession of others 'but may be nevertheless obligated to gain knowledge of them.' Thus, in evaluating the scope of a given request to produce, the duty to produce is not always satisfied by producing the documents in the party's immediate physical possession but 'may often extend to documents in the possession of persons or entities who are not parties to the suit.'" (quoting *In re Certain Underwriters at Lloyd's London*, 294 S.W.3d 891, 903 (Tex. App.—Beaumont 2009, orig. proceeding))).

are readily available from nonparties under its control, such as entities owned or controlled by them.[31] Obligations for affiliates are case-specific.[32]

5-3 Objections to Written-Discovery Requests in General

Texas Rule 193.2 sets forth the obligations and procedures for objecting to written-discovery requests.[33] An objection must be made in writing within the time allowed for the response to the request—usually thirty days after the written-discovery request's

---

[31] *Cf. U.S. v. Int'l Union of Petroleum & Indus. Workers, AFL-CIO*, 870 F.2d 1450, 1452 (9th Cir. 1989) ("A corporation must produce documents possessed by a subsidiary that the parent corporation owns or controls."); *Waymo LLC v. Uber Techs., Inc.*, No. 3:17-cv-00939, 2017 U.S. Dist. LEXIS 213567, *35–36, 2017 WL 6501798 (N.D. Cal. Dec. 15, 2017) ("A party responding to . . . a [production] request must 'then make a reasonable inquiry to determine whether the responsive documents exist[.]' That requirement carries with it 'an affirmative duty to seek that information reasonably available to it from its employees, agents, or others subject to its control.'" (quoting *Ujhelyi v. Vilsack*, No. C 12-04282 JSW, 2014 U.S. Dist. LEXIS 142087, at *13, 2014 WL 4983550 (N.D. Cal. Oct. 6, 2014), and *A. Farber & Partners, Inc. v. Garber*, 234 F.R.D. 186, 189 (C.D. Cal. 2006))); *In re Namenda Direct Purchaser Antitrust Litig.*, No. 15CIV7488CMJCF, 2017 U.S. Dist. LEXIS 139983, at *18, 2017 WL 3822883 (S.D.N.Y. Aug. 30, 2017) ("A domestic corporation has been found to have control over documents held by its foreign parent or subsidiary."); *Twentieth Century Fox Film Corp. v. Marvel Enters.*, No. 01 Civ. 3016 (AGS) (HBP), 2002 U.S. Dist. LEXIS 14682, at *12–13, 2002 WL 1835439 (S.D.N.Y. Aug. 8, 2002 ("Numerous courts have concluded that a parent corporation has a sufficient degree of ownership and control over a wholly-owned subsidiary that it must be deemed to have control over documents located with that subsidiary. This principle applies where the subsidiary is not owned directly but, rather, is owned by an intermediate corporation that is itself a wholly-owned corporation of the parent corporation."(citations omitted) (quoting *Dietrich v. Bauer*, 95 Civ. 7051 (RWS), 2000 U.S. Dist. LEXIS 11729, at *8–10, 2000 WL 1171132 (S.D.N.Y. Aug. 16, 2000))); *Cotracom Commodity Trading Co. v. Seaboard Corp.*, 189 F.R.D. 655, 663 (D. Kan. 1999) (agreeing with the "principle" that "that a parent must produce all the documents of its wholly-owned subsidiary"); *Starlight Int'l Inc. v. Herlihy*, 186 F.R.D. 626, 634–35 (D. Kan. 1999) (holding that the "sole owner, officer, and director" of an entity that was a "member of the joint venture" with a defendant in the case "has a sufficient nexus with [the defendants] to attribute documents in his possession to be under their joint control" and that "members of a joint venture also have a legal right to obtain information of the venture on demand"). *But cf. Acosta v. La Piedad Corp.*, 894 F.3d 947, 952 (8th Cir. 2018) ("In most circumstances, a corporation does not have control over documents in the possession of its shareholders.").

[32] *Cf. In re Zantac (Ranitidine) Products Liab. Litig.*, No. 20-MD-2924, 2021 U.S. Dist. LEXIS 76346, at *18, 2021 WL 1522449 (S.D. Fla. Apr. 16, 2021) ("Whether documents are in a party's control under [Federal] Rule 34 is broadly construed. 'The burden is on the party seeking discovery to establish that the opposing party has "control" over documents held by an affiliate.'" (citation omitted) (quoting *Costa v. Kerzner Int'l Resorts, Inc.*, 277 F.R.D. 468, 473 n. 2 (S.D. Fla. 2011))); *Sanho Corp. v. KaiJet Tech. Int'l Ltd., Inc.*, No. 1:18-CV-05385-SDG, 2021 U.S. Dist. LEXIS 76346, at *18, 2020 WL 4346881 (N.D. Ga. July 29, 2020) ("A party seeking documents held by a corporate affiliate may establish the 'legal right to obtain documents requested upon demand' if the 'affiliated corporate entities . . . have actually shared responsive information and documents in the normal course of their business dealings.'" (quoting *Sergeeva v. Tripleton Int'l Ltd.*, 834 F.3d 1194, 1201 (11th Cir. 2016))).

[33] *See generally* Tex. R. Civ. P. 193.2.

service.[34] Generally, the failure to object timely to a written-discovery request, no matter how improper, waives the objection.[35] There are, however, two exceptions to this rule.

---

[34] Tex. R. Civ. P. 193.2(a) ("A party must make any objection to written discovery in writing—either in the response or in a separate document—within the time for the response."); *accord In re City Info Experts, LLC*, No. 01-20-00364-CV, 2020 Tex. App. LEXIS 8584, at *32, 2020 WL 6435782 (Tex. App.—Houston [1st Dist.] Nov. 3, 2020, orig. proceeding) (mem. op.) (reciting Texas Rule 193.2(a)'s requirements); *In re Yamin*, No. 14-20-00280-CV, 2020 Tex. App. LEXIS 6676, at *10, 2020 WL 4873021 (Tex. App.—Houston [14th Dist.] Aug. 20, 2020, orig. proceeding) (mem. op.) (applying Texas Rules 176.6(d) and 193.2(a) to conclude that objections to a subpoena duces tecum were timely because "[t]he subpoena stated: 'RECORDS NEEDED BY 2/15/20.' The Yamins made their objections on February 12, 2020, before Hardy was required to produce the tax returns and documents related to the returns"); *In re Park Cities Bank*, 409 S.W.3d 859, 876 (Tex. App.—Tyler 2013, orig. proceeding) ("In general, the rules require the responding party to serve a written response, including any objections to written discovery, within 30 days after service of a request for production."); *Izen v. Sjostrom*, No. 14-06-00142-CV, 2007 Tex. App. LEXIS 2586, at *5–6, 2007 WL 968841 (Tex. App.—Houston [14th Dist.] Apr. 3, 2007, no pet.) (mem. op.) ("A party has 30 days to respond to a request for production and an interrogatory request. A party may respond to a discovery request by providing the information, objecting to the request, or asserting a privilege.") (citations omitted). Texas's discovery rules set forth the default 30-day response deadline for parties to respond various types of discovery. *See* Tex. R. Civ. P. 194.2(a) (initial disclosures), 196.2 (requests for production or inspection), 196.7(c) (request for entry upon property), 197.2(a) (interrogatories), 198.2(a) (requests for admission).

[35] Tex. R. Civ. P. 193.2(e) ("An objection that is not made within the time required . . . is waived unless the court excuses the waiver for good cause shown."); *In re Nat'l Lloyds Ins. Co.*, 507 S.W.3d 219, 223 (Tex. 2016) (orig. proceeding) (per curiam) ("If an objection is not made within the time required, it 'is waived unless the court excuses the waiver for good cause shown.'" (quoting Tex. R. Civ. P. 193.2(e))); *In re City Info Experts, LLC*, No. 01-20-00364-CV, 2020 Tex. App. LEXIS 8584, at *35–37, 2020 WL 6435782 (Tex. App.—Houston [1st Dist.] Nov. 3, 2020, orig. proceeding) (mem. op.) (holding that the trial court did not abuse its discretion in ordering a party to respond to discovery without asserting objections, considering that the party had not responded, much less objected, to the discovery in a timely manner); *In re Flores*, No. 13-20-00105-CV, 2020 Tex. App. LEXIS 3283, at *13, 2020 WL 1951540 (Tex. App.—Corpus Christi Apr. 17, 2020, orig. proceeding) (mem. op.) (concluding that a party failed to preserve complaints on a basis that was not asserted in the party's objections); *In re GreCon, Inc.*, 542 S.W.3d 774, 780 (Tex. App.—Houston [14th Dist.] 2018, orig. proceeding) ("[C]ivil litigants must plead and prove their entitlement to protection from discovery in a timely fashion." (citing Texas Rules 192.6, 193.2, 193.3, 193.4 and *In re Gore*, 251 S.W.3d 696, 700 (Tex. App.—San Antonio 2007, orig. proceeding))); *In re Lowery*, No. 05-14-01509-CV, 2014 Tex. App. LEXIS 13633, at *7–8, 2014 WL 8060585 (Tex. App.—Dallas Dec. 18, 2014, orig. proceeding) (mem. op.) ("Failure to object within the required time period waives the objection unless the trial court excuses the waiver for good cause shown."); *In re Park Cities Bank*, 409 S.W.3d 859, 876 (Tex. App.—Tyler 2013, orig. proceeding) (same); *In re HEB Grocery Co.*, 345 S.W.3d 497, 501 (Tex. App.—Houston [14th Dist.] 2012, orig. proceeding) (holding that a failure to object to a production request as unduly burdensome in the trial court waived the objection); *In re Soto*, 270 S.W.3d 732, 734–35 (Tex. App.—Amarillo 2008, orig. proceeding) (holding that the responding parties waived their privilege objection because it was not timely asserted); *Reynolds v. Murphy*, 188 S.W.3d 252, 260 (Tex. App.—Fort Worth 2006, pet. denied) ("An objection that is not made within the time required by the discovery rules or court order . . . is waived unless the court excuses the waiver for good cause shown.").

First, under Texas Rule 193.2(e), a court can excuse the failure to assert a timely and proper objection for "good cause shown."[36] Unfortunately, no cases define "good cause shown" under that Rule or its predecessor, former Texas Rule 166(b)(4).[37] In the context of the withdrawal or amendment of an admission under Texas Rule 198.3,[38] "[g]ood cause is established by showing that the failure [to properly answer] was an accident or mistake, not intentional or the result of conscious indifference."[39] There is no reason why a more exacting standard should apply under Texas Rule 193.2(e).[40]

An objection to a written-discovery request also may be waived by a response that answers the objected-to portion of the request fully or by producing all of the objected-to documents, *cf. Berlinger v. Wells Fargo, N.A.*, No. 2:11-cv-459-FtM-99SPC, 2012 U.S. Dist. LEXIS 26650, at *12–13, 2012 WL 695836 (M.D. Fla. Mar. 1, 2012); *Anderson v. Hansen*, No. 1:09-cv-01924-LJO-MJS (PC), 2012 U.S. Dist. LEXIS 131010, at *18–19, 2012 WL 4049979 (E.D. Cal. Sept. 13, 2012), or by not asserting the objection in response to a motion to compel, *In re Waste Mgmt. of Tex., Inc.*, 392 S.W.3d 861, 870 (Tex. App.—Texarkana 2013, orig. proceeding) (mem. op.); *cf. Herrmann v. Rain Link, Inc.*, No. 11-1123-RDR, 2012 U.S. Dist. LEXIS 50553, at *3, 2012 WL 1207232 (D. Kan. Apr. 11, 2012); *Martin K. Eby Constr. Co. v. OneBeacon Ins. Co.*, No. 08-1250-MLB-KGG, 2012 U.S. Dist. LEXIS 43141, at *17 n.1, 2012 WL 1080801 (D. Kan. Mar. 29, 2012); *FTC v. Affiliate Strategies, Inc.*, No. 09-4104-JAR, 2011 U.S. Dist. LEXIS 7689, at *18 n.24, 2011 WL 251449 (D. Kan. Jan. 26, 2011).

36 Tex. R. Civ. P. 193.2(e). See also the authorities cited in note 35.

37 In *Remington Arms Co. v. Canales*, 837 S.W.2d 624, 625 (Tex. 1992) (orig. proceeding), however, the Texas Supreme Court held that inadvertence of counsel was insufficient to prevent the waiver of a discovery objection under former Texas Rule 166(b)(4)'s good-cause exception.

38 Texas Rule 198.3 allows a court to "permit the party to withdraw or amend the admission if," the party, among other things, "shows good cause for the withdrawal or amendment[.]" Tex. R. Civ. P. 198.3(a). See also Chapter 10, section 10-7 (discussing withdrawal, supplementation, or amendment of responses to requests for admission).

39 *E.g., Wheeler v. Green*, 157 S.W.3d 439, 442 (Tex. 2005) (per curiam); *In re City Info Experts, LLC*, No. 01-20-00364-CV, 2020 Tex. App. LEXIS 8584, at *23–24, 2020 WL 1951540, 2020 WL 6435782, at *10 (Tex. App.—Houston [1st Dist.] Nov. 3, 2020, orig. proceeding) (mem. op.); *In re TT-Fountains of Tomball, Ltd.*, No. 01-15-00817-CV, 2016 WL 3965117 (Tex. App.—Houston [1st Dist.] July 21, 2016, orig. proceeding) (mem. op.). See also Chapter 10, section 10-7 (discussing withdrawal, supplementation, or amendment of responses to requests for admission).

40 Federal courts, in making a good-cause determination in connection with a failure to timely object to discovery, often apply a balancing test that weighs the following factors: (1) the delay's length; (2) the reason for the delay; (3) whether the responding party was dilatory or acted in bad faith; (4) whether the requesting party has been prejudiced by the failure; (5) the burdensomeness of the discovery request; and (6) whether waiver would impose an excessively harsh result on the responding party. *E.g., Doerr v. Abplanalp*, No. 619CV1194ORL40LRH, 2020 U.S. Dist. LEXIS 221449, at *8–9, 2020 WL 6870912 (M.D. Fla. Sept. 3, 2020); *In re Outlaw Labs., LP Litig.*, No. 18CV840 GPC (BGS), 2020 U.S. Dist. LEXIS 60008, at *26–27, 2020 WL 1674552 (S.D. Cal. Apr. 6, 2020); *Salman v. Balderas*, No. CV 18-10966, 2019 U.S. Dist. LEXIS 234392, at *8–9, 2019 WL 11005040 (E.D. La. Aug. 2, 2019); *Lam v. City & Cnty. of San Francisco*, No. 4:10-cv-04641-PJH (LB), 2015 U.S. Dist. LEXIS 96994, at *8–9, 2015 WL 4498747 (N.D. Cal. July 15, 2015); *Clewis v. Medco Health Sols., Inc.*, No. 3:12-cv-5208-L, 2013 U.S. Dist. LEXIS 137206, at *6–7, 2013 WL 5354574 (N.D. Tex. Sept. 25, 2013); *Enron Corp. Savs. Plan v. Hewitt Assocs., L.L.C.*, 258 F.R.D. 149, 156–57 (S.D. Tex. 2009); *Hall v. Sullivan*, 231 F.R.D. 468, 474 (D. Md. 2005). This is an excellent approach that Texas courts should consider following.

Second, a party may amend or supplement a written-discovery response to state additional objections that were "inapplicable or . . . unknown" at the time of the response "after reasonable inquiry."[41] The reasonable-inquiry requirement precludes a party from interposing new objections in an amended or supplemental response that were omitted from the original response intentionally or by inadvertence or oversight. Thus, new objections are proper when, for example, documents or information that was not reasonably available when the discovery request was first answered make a previously unmade objection applicable to the documents or information.[42] The responding party has the burden of proving that the new objection was inapplicable or unknown when the original response was served.

The responding party must have "a good faith factual and legal basis" for each objection to a written-discovery request "at the time the objection is made."[43] The objection's legal or factual basis also must be stated specifically.[44] Thus, a responding party who objects to a request because it is overbroad, unduly burdensome, vague, ambiguous, or unreasonably cumulative or duplicative should explain why it suffers from each asserted malady.[45] Moreover, an objection "that is obscured by numerous unfounded objections[] is waived unless the court excuses the waiver for good cause shown."[46] These provisions' purpose is to eliminate the practice of interposing

---

41 Tex. R. Civ. P. 193.2(d); *accord In re Nat'l Lloyds Ins. Co.*, Nos. 13-14-00713-CV, 13-14-00714-CV, 2015 Tex. App. LEXIS 5509, at *20–21, 2015 WL 3751701 (Tex. App.—Corpus Christi May 29, 2015, orig. proceeding) (mem. op.) ("[A]n objection may be amended or supplemented to state an objection that was inapplicable or unknown after reasonable inquiry when the original objection was made."), *rev'd on other grounds* 507 S.W.3d 219 (Tex. 2016) (orig. proceeding) (per curiam); *In re Park Cities Bank*, 409 S.W.3d 859, 877 (Tex. App.—Tyler 2013, orig. proceeding) (same).

42 Robert K. Wise, *Ending Evasive Responses to Written Discovery: A Guide for Properly Responding (and Objecting) to Interrogatories and Document Requests Under the Texas Discovery Rules*, 65 Baylor L. Rev. 510, 562 (2013).

43 Tex. R. Civ. P. 193.2(c); *accord In re Master Flo Valve Inc.*, 485 S.W.3d 207, 220 (Tex. App.—Houston [14th Dist.] 2016, no pet.) (orig. proceeding) ("A party may object to written discovery if a good faith legal and factual basis for the objection exists at the time the objection is made."); *In re Park Cities Bank*, 409 S.W.3d 859, 877 (Tex. App.—Tyler 2013, orig. proceeding) (same).

44 Tex. R. Civ. P. 193.2(a) ("The party must state specifically the legal or factual basis for the objection and the extent to which the party is refusing to comply with the request."); *cf.* Fed R. Civ. P. 33(b)(4) ("The grounds for objecting to an interrogatory must be stated with specificity."); Fed R. Civ. P. 34(b)(2)(B) ("For each item or category, the response [to a production request] must either state that inspection and related activities will be permitted as requested or state with specificity the grounds for objecting to the request, including the reasons."); Fed R. Civ. P. 36(a)(5) ("The grounds for objecting to a request [for admission] must be stated.").

45 *In re Park Cities Bank*, 409 S.W.3d 859, 877 (Tex. App.—Tyler 2013, orig. proceeding) ("[A] responding party who objects to a request for production because is it overbroad, unduly burdensome, vague, ambiguous, or unreasonably cumulative or duplicative should explain why the discovery request suffers from each asserted deficiency." (citing Robert K. Wise, *Ending Evasive Responses to Written Discovery: A Guide for Properly Responding (and Objecting) to Interrogatories and Document Requests Under the Texas Discovery Rules*, 65 Baylor L. Rev. 510, 512 (2013))). As discussed in Chapter 5, section 5-3:3, an objection that merely recites objections without any explanation of them is an impermissible boilerplate objection.

46 Tex. R. Civ. P. 193.2(e); *accord De Anda v. Jason C. Webster, P.C.*, No. 14-17-00020-CV, 2018 Tex. App. LEXIS 5727, at *19–20, 2018 WL 3580579 (Tex. App.—Houston [14th Dist.] July 26,

boilerplate, hypothetical, or prophylactic objections to obfuscate what information or material is being withheld or to prevent a waiver of objections.[47]

In addition, in interposing an objection, the responding party, under Texas Rule 193.2(a), must state the extent to which it is refusing to comply with the written-discovery request[48] and generally must comply with that part of the request to which there is no objection.[49] In other words, if a request is objectionable only in part (e.g.,

---

2018, pet. denied) (mem. op.) ("[M]any of Webster's objections were unfounded. We therefore conclude that Webster waived his objections to De Anda's discovery requests." (citing Tex. R. Civ. P. 193.2e))); *In re Park Cities Bank*, 409 S.W.3d 859, 877 (Tex. App.—Tyler 2013, orig. proceeding) ("[A]n objection that is obscured by numerous unfounded objections is waived unless the court excuses the waiver for good cause shown.").

47 *In re Park Cities Bank*, 409 S.W.3d 859, 877 (Tex. App.—Tyler 2013, orig. proceeding) ("A primary goal of all of the groups considering discovery reform in anticipation of revising the former discovery rules was to rid the system of prophylactic objections. As a result, [Texas] Rule 193 requires a good faith legal and factual basis at the time the objection is made. Additionally, an objection that is obscured by numerous unfounded objections is waived unless the court excuses the waiver for good cause shown. These two provisions eliminate the perceived need for, and the practice of making, prophylactic objections to prevent a waiver of discovery objections." (citing Robert K. Wise, *Ending Evasive Responses to Written Discovery: A Guide for Properly Responding (and Objecting) to Interrogatories and Document Requests Under the Texas Discovery Rules*, 65 Baylor L. Rev. 510, 512 (2013)), and Nathan L. Hecht & Robert H. Pemberton, *A Guide to the 1999 Texas Discovery Rules Revisions* F-3 (Nov. 11, 1998), https://www.txcourts.gov/rules-forms/rules-standards)); *see De Anda v. Jason C. Webster, P.C.*, No. 14-17-00020-CV, 2018 Tex. App. LEXIS 5727, at *19–20, 2018 WL 3580579, at *7 (Tex. App.—Houston [14th Dist.] July 26, 2018, pet. denied) (mem. op.) ("With respect to De Anda's interrogatories and requests for production, Webster lodged the same global, prophylactic string of objections quoted above to every interrogatory and request for production. . . . . Having reviewed De Anda's interrogatories and requests for production, we conclude they sought relevant information and documents. In sum, many of Webster's objections were unfounded. We therefore conclude that Webster waived his objections to De Anda's discovery requests.") (citations omitted). See also Chapter 5, section 5-3:2 (discussing "general" and "subject-to" objections) and section 5-3:3 (discussing boilerplate objections).

48 Tex. R. Civ. P. 193.2(a) ("The party must state specifically the legal or factual basis for the objection and the extent to which the party is refusing to comply with the request."); *accord Unifund CCR Partners v. Weaver*, 262 S.W.3d 796, 798 (Tex. 2008) ("To constitute a valid objection, a party 'must state specifically the legal or factual basis for the objection and the extent to which the party is refusing to comply with the request.'" (quoting Tex. R. Civ. P. 193.2(a))).

49 Tex. R. Civ. P. 193.2(b) ("A party must comply with as much of the request to which the party has made no objection unless it is unreasonable under the circumstances to do so before obtaining a ruling on the objection."); *see In re Vaughan*, No. 13-18-00541-CV, 2019 Tex. App. LEXIS 1445, at *3 n.2, 2019 WL 962381 (Tex. App.—Corpus Christi Feb. 27, 2019, orig. proceeding) (mem. op.) ("The Texas Rules of Civil Procedure required Vaughan to 'comply with as much of the request to which the party has made no objection unless it is unreasonable under the circumstances to do so before obtaining a ruling on the objection.'" (quoting Tex. R. Civ. P. 193.2(b))); *In re Brookfield Infrastructure Grp., LLC*, No. 13-17-00486-CV, 2018 Tex. App. LEXIS 2492, at *12, 2018 WL 1725467 (Tex. App.—Corpus Christi Apr. 9, 2018, orig. proceeding) (mem. op.) (same); *In re Nat'l Lloyds Ins. Co.*, Nos. 13-14-00713-CV, 13-14-00714-CV, 2015 Tex. App. LEXIS 5509, at *20 (Tex. App.—Corpus Christi May 29, 2015, orig. proceeding) (mem. op.) (same); *In re Park Cities Bank*, 409 S.W.3d 859, 877 (Tex. App.—Tyler 2013, orig. proceeding) (same).

because its scope is overly broad), the responding party must respond to as much of the request as it deems is proper.[50]

Although Texas Rule 193.2(e)'s purpose is to allow discovery to proceed despite objections, it does not prohibit a responding party from objecting to a written-discovery request in its entirety.[51] To the contrary, as Comment 2 to the 1999 change to Texas Rule 193 recognizes, a discovery request might be wholly objectionable.[52] For example, if the responding party's documents are organized in a way that requires the same search regardless of the request's scope, the responding party can wait until the parties or court resolve the scope issues to produce any documents.[53] Of course, the responding party may choose to provide some information in response to the discovery request as a tactical matter in hope that the requesting party will be satisfied or that the court, in connection with a motion to compel, will look more favorably on a partial response than on no response.[54]

5-3:1 Proper and Improper Objections to Written-Discovery Requests

Most practitioners do not realize that besides objections regarding scope (i.e., that the discovery request, in whole or in part, seeks irrelevant information or material, or information or material not reasonably calculated to lead to the discovery of admissible evidence), the proper objections to interrogatories and production requests, for the most part, are set forth in the Texas discovery rules. For example, Texas Rule 192.6, which sets the bases for the entry of a protective order, also sets forth proper objections to interrogatories and production requests: "undue burden, unnecessary expense, harassment, annoyance, or invasion of personal, constitutional, or property rights[.]"[55] Similarly, Texas Rule 192.4, which addresses limitations on discovery's scope, defines undue burden and unnecessary expense[56] and sets forth other proper

---

50 Tex. R. Civ. P. 193 cmt. 2 to 1999 change ("An objection to written discovery does not excuse the responding party from complying with the request to the extent no objection is made. . . . A party who objects to a production of documents from a remote time period should produce documents from a more recent period unless that production would be burdensome and duplicative should the objection be overruled.").

51 *E.g.*, Tex. R. Civ. P. 193 cmt. 2 to 1999 change ("But a party may object to a request for 'all documents relevant to the lawsuit' as overly broad and not in compliance with the rule requiring specific requests for documents and refuse to comply with it entirely. A party may also object to request for a litigation file on the ground that it is overly broad and . . . seeks only materials protected by privilege.").

52 Tex. R. Civ. P. 193 cmt. 2 to 1999 change.

53 Tex. R. Civ. P. 193.2(b), 193 cmt. 2 to 1999 change.

54 Robert K. Wise, *Ending Evasive Responses to Written Discovery: A Guide for Properly Responding (and Objecting) to Interrogatories and Document Requests Under the Texas Discovery Rules*, 65 Baylor L. Rev. 510, 563 (2013).

55 Tex. R. Civ. P. 192.6(b).

56 Tex. R. Civ. P. 192.4(b); *see* Tex. R. Civ. P. 192.4(b) (providing that discovery "should be limited by the court if it determines . . . that . . . the discovery sought . . ., is obtainable from some other source that is more convenient, less burdensome, or less expensive"); Tex. R. Civ. P. 176.7 ("A party causing a subpoena to issue must take reasonable steps to avoid imposing undue burden or expense on the person served."). See also Chapter 13, section 13-4:4 (discussing responses to nonparty document subpoenas).

objections—the discovery is "unreasonably cumulative or duplicative[.]"[57] Other than the few objections discussed in the immediately following chapters, proper and improper objections to production requests, interrogatories, requests for admission, and nonparty document subpoenas are discussed in Chapter 8, section 8-5, Chapter 9, section 9-5:3, Chapter 10, section 10-5:8, and Chapter 13, section 13-4:4, respectively. As provided in Texas Rule 194.5 and discussed in Chapter 6, section 6-3:4.1, no objections are permitted with respect to disclosure requests (in cases filed before January 1, 2021) or required disclosures (in cases filed on or after January 1, 2021).

5-3:2 General and "Subject-to" or "Without Waiving" Objections Are Generally Improper

Many practitioners, even the most sophisticated and experienced ones, use one of two evasive methods in responding to written-discovery requests. The first method is to have a section at the beginning of the response entitled "general objections" that contains every imaginable objection—such as overly broad, unduly burdensome, irrelevant, vague, ambiguous, harassing, cumulative, duplicative, and privilege[58]—followed

---

[57] Tex. R. Civ. P. 192.4(a).

[58] Robert K. Wise, *Ending Evasive Responses to Written Discovery: A Guide for Properly Responding (and Objecting) to Interrogatories and Document Requests Under the Texas Discovery Rules*, 65 Baylor L. Rev. 510, 567 (2013). The objections in the "General Objections" section typically contain language like the following:

General Objections

1. [Responding party] objects to each document request *to the extent* that it is overly broad.
2. [Responding party] objects to each document request *to the extent* that it is unduly burdensome.
3. [Responding party] objects to each document request *to the extent* that it seeks documents that are neither relevant or nor reasonably calculated to lead to the discovery of admissible evidence.
4. [Responding party] objects to each document request *to the extent* it is vague and ambiguous.
5. [Responding party] objects to each document request *to the extent* it is harassing, cumulative, or duplicative.
6. [Responding party] objects to each document request to the extent it seeks the production of documents within the attorney-client, work product, or other privilege.

Robert K. Wise, *Ending Evasive Responses to Written Discovery: A Guide for Properly Responding (and Objecting) to Interrogatories and Document Requests Under the Texas Discovery Rules*, 65 Baylor L. Rev. 510, 567 n.223 (2013); *see Walls v. Ford Motor Co.*, No. 1:20CV98, 2021 U.S. Dist. LEXIS 82757, at *27–31, 2021 WL 1723154 (M.D.N.C. Apr. 30, 2021) (quoting responding party's general objections); *see SPV-LS, LLC v. Transamerica Life Ins. Co.*, No. CIV 14-4092, 2017 U.S. Dist. LEXIS 33213, at *17–18, 2017 WL 899882 (D.S.D. Mar. 6, 2017) (same). Often the general objections also contain an improper catch-all objection, such as "[responding party] objects to each document request *to the extent* it exceeds the scope of discovery permitted by Texas Rule 196, 197, or 198 [as applicable]." Robert K. Wise, *Ending Evasive Responses to Written Discovery: A Guide for Properly Responding (and Objecting) to Interrogatories and Document Requests Under the Texas Discovery Rules*, 65 Baylor L. Rev. 510, 567 n.223 (2013); *cf. Team Contrs., L.L.C. v. Waypoint NOLA, L.L.C.*, No. 16-1131 SECTION "E" (2), 2017 U.S. Dist. LEXIS 118653, at *7, 2017 WL 3216582 (E.D. La. July 28, by a separate section with answers to each written-discovery request that incorporate all of the general objections by reference "to the extent" they apply to the specific request.[59] The second method is to include in each written-discovery response a litany of prophylactic, boilerplate objections,[60] such as those set forth above, and then

---

2017) ("Waypoint's discovery requests are subject to the limitations and protections of the Federal Rules of Civil Procedure—it is unnecessary for Catlin to object generally on this basis."); *Berenson v. Adm'rs of the Tulane Educ. Fund*, No. 17-329 SECTION "R" (2), 2017 U.S. Dist. LEXIS 118651, at *3, 2017 WL 3216584 (E.D. La. July 28, 2017) (same); *SPV-LS, LLC v. Transamerica Life Ins. Co.*, No. CIV 14-4092, 2017 U.S. Dist. LEXIS 33213, at *18–19, 2017 WL 899882 (D.S.D. Mar. 6, 2017) (overruling a general objection that "objects to every interrogatory, and to every introductory 'definition' or 'instruction,' that seeks to impose obligations beyond those required by the Federal Rules of Civil Procedure, as reasonably interpreted and supplemented by local court rules").

Courts have criticized generalized "to the extent" qualifiers. *E.g.*, *Walls v. Ford Motor Co.*, No. 1:20CV98, 2021 U.S. Dist. LEXIS 82757, at *32–33, 2021 WL 1723154 (M.D.N.C. Apr. 30, 2021) (concluding that a litany of boilerplate objections asserted "to the extent" they applied to requests, and incorporated into responses to requests, did not bind the court and could not work to limit the responding party's responsibility under the discovery rules); *Smash Tech., LLC v. Smash Sols., LLC*, 335 F.R.D. 438, 447 (D. Utah 2020) ("[T]he 'to the extent that' moniker does not satisfy the specificity requirement because the objecting party is not even definitively contending that there is an actual, objection-worthy problem in the request. 'To the extent that' is a feeble 'maybe' objection behind which the objector lacks the resolve to definitively state whether something actually occurred that warrants objecting. It is the equivalent of saying, 'I am not sure that this request is worthy of objection, but if it is, then I object.' . . . [T]he generalized 'to the extent that' objection . . . lacks the requisite specificity to comply with [Federal] Rules 33 and 34."); *Reed Auto of Overland Park, LLC v. Landers McLarty Olathe KS, LLC*, No. 19-02510-JWB-KGG, 2020 U.S. Dist. LEXIS 157291, at *6, 2020 WL 5118103 (D. Kan. Aug. 31, 2020) ("Responses using the 'to the extent' qualifier are equally 'improper and confusing [in] nature. . . . .'" (quoting *Benney v. Midwest Health, Inc.*, No. 17-2548-HLT-KGG, 2019 U.S. Dist. LEXIS 116669, at *45, 2019 WL 3066425 (D. Kan. July 12, 2019))); *Advanced Exports, LLC v. Seabrook Wallcoverings, Inc.*, No. CV 18-830, 2018 U.S. Dist. LEXIS 138414, at *2, 2018 WL 3917939 (E.D. Pa. Aug. 16, 2018) ("Objections qualified by the noncommittal 'to the extent that' language leave AEL, and now this Court, without any idea whether documents were withheld. [Federal] Rule 34(b)(2)(B) provides that a party seeking discovery, such as AEL, is entitled to know that.").

59 Robert K. Wise, *Ending Evasive Responses to Written Discovery: A Guide for Properly Responding (and Objecting) to Interrogatories and Document Requests Under the Texas Discovery Rules*, 65 Baylor L. Rev. 510, 568 (2013). For example, the response to each written-discovery request may be: "[Responding party] incorporates each General Objection to the extent it applies. Subject to and without waiving the general objections, responsive non-privileged documents will be produced at a mutually convenient time and place." Robert K. Wise, *Ending Evasive Responses to Written Discovery: A Guide for Properly Responding (and Objecting) to Interrogatories and Document Requests Under the Texas Discovery Rules*, 65 Baylor L. Rev. 510, 568 n.224 (2013). Worse, the discovery response, after incorporating the general objections by reference, may contain specific objections, many of which repeat one or more general objections. Robert K. Wise, *Ending Evasive Responses to Written Discovery: A Guide for Properly Responding (and Objecting) to Interrogatories and Document Requests Under the Texas Discovery Rules*, 65 Baylor L. Rev. 510, 568 n.224 (2013).

60 Boilerplate objections are defined and discussed in Chapter 5, section 5-3:3.

"subject to and without waiving" the objections state, for example, that "non-privileged responsive documents will be produced."[61]

These methodologies have three purposes—one nefarious and two benign.[62] The nefarious purpose is pure gamesmanship—to hide damaging information or material behind a wall of objections.[63] The benign purposes are to protect against the possibility that an answer might be found to be inadequate or that an objection has been waived.[64] Both methodologies are improper.[65]

First, they violate Texas Rule 193.2(c) because they are hypothetical, and hypothetical objections are impermissible under the Rule, which limits objections to those for which "a good faith factual and legal basis . . . exists *at the time* the objection is made."[66]

Second, general objections and "subject-to" or "without waiving" objections violate Texas Rule 193.2(a)—which requires the responding party to "state . . . the extent to which the party is refusing to comply with the request" and to "state specifically the . . . factual basis for the objection"—because they are nonspecific and "hide the ball" with respect to what information or material is being provided and what

---

[61] Robert K. Wise, *Ending Evasive Responses to Written Discovery: A Guide for Properly Responding (and Objecting) to Interrogatories and Document Requests Under the Texas Discovery Rules,* 65 Baylor L. Rev. 510, 568 (2013). An example of this type of response is: "Objection, this document request is vague, ambiguous, overly broad, unduly burdensome, harassing, and seeks documents that are neither relevant nor reasonably calculated to lead to the discovery of admissible evidence. Subject to and without waiving these objections, responsive non-privileged documents will be produced at a mutually convenient time and place." Robert K. Wise, *Ending Evasive Responses to Written Discovery: A Guide for Properly Responding (and Objecting) to Interrogatories and Document Requests Under the Texas Discovery Rules,* 65 Baylor L. Rev. 510, 568 n.225 (2013); *accord Duffy v. Lawrence Mem'l Hosp.*, No. 2:14-cv-2256-SAC-TJJ, 2016 U.S. Dist. LEXIS 176848, at *6–7, 2016 WL 7386413 (D. Kan. Dec. 21, 2016) (describing a subject-to objection as one that "begins with objections and then states the following: 'Subject-to and without waiving these objections, ...'").

[62] Robert K. Wise, *Ending Evasive Responses to Written Discovery: A Guide for Properly Responding (and Objecting) to Interrogatories and Document Requests Under the Texas Discovery Rules,* 65 Baylor L. Rev. 510, 568 (2013).

[63] Robert K. Wise, *Ending Evasive Responses to Written Discovery: A Guide for Properly Responding (and Objecting) to Interrogatories and Document Requests Under the Texas Discovery Rules,* 65 Baylor L. Rev. 510, 568 (2013).

[64] Robert K. Wise, *Ending Evasive Responses to Written Discovery: A Guide for Properly Responding (and Objecting) to Interrogatories and Document Requests Under the Texas Discovery Rules,* 65 Baylor L. Rev. 510, 568 (2013); *see Liguria Foods, Inc. v. Griffith Labs., Inc.*, 320 F.R.D. 168, 181 (D. Iowa 2017) ("I believe that one of the attorneys hit the nail squarely on the head when he asserted that such responses (referring to those using general or boilerplate objections) arise, at least in part, out of 'lawyer paranoia' not to waive inadvertently any objections that might protect the parties they represent.").

[65] Robert K. Wise, *Ending Evasive Responses to Written Discovery: A Guide for Properly Responding (and Objecting) to Interrogatories and Document Requests Under the Texas Discovery Rules,* 65 Baylor L. Rev. 510, 568 (2013).

[66] Tex. R. Civ. P. 193.2(c) (emphasis added); *In re Park Cities Bank,* 409 S.W.3d 859, 877 (Tex. App.—Tyler 2013, orig. proceeding) (explaining that "general" objections are improper under Texas Rule 193.2(c)); Robert K. Wise, *Ending Evasive Responses to Written Discovery: A Guide for Properly Responding (and Objecting) to Interrogatories and Document Requests Under the Texas Discovery Rules,* 65 Baylor L. Rev. 510, 568 (2013).

information or material is being withheld and why.[67] In fact, both methodologies have been condemned by courts for this very reason. As explained by one federal court in holding that "subject-to" and "without waiving" objections are improper:

> The practice of including "subject to" or "without waiving" statements after objections is an age-old habit comparable to belts and suspenders. This practice is "manifestly confusing (at best) and misleading (at worse), and has no basis at all in the Federal Rules of Civil Procedure." Such an objection and answer "leaves the requesting [p]arty uncertain as to whether the question has actually been fully answered," and "wondering as to the scope of the documents or information that will be provided as responsive."
>
> [Federal] Rule 34 does not allow this kind of hedging. [Federal] Rule 34 allows a party either to "state that inspection and related activities will be permitted as required" or to "state with specificity the grounds for objecting to the request." If a party chooses to object to part of a request, the party "must specify the part and permit inspection of the rest." A response that states "subject to the foregoing" is not specific enough as to either (1) the completeness of the answer or (2) the availability of documents for inspection. The Court finds that Defendants' inclusion of "subject to the foregoing" is not supported by the federal rules and goes against the purposes of a just, speedy, and inexpensive resolution.[68]

---

[67] Tex. R. Civ. P. 193.2(a); *see* Robert K. Wise, *Ending Evasive Responses to Written Discovery: A Guide for Properly Responding (and Objecting) to Interrogatories and Document Requests Under the Texas Discovery Rules*, 65 Baylor L. Rev. 510, 568–69 (2013).

[68] *RealPage, Inc. v. Enter. Risk Control, LLC*, No. 4:16-CV-00737, 2017 U.S. Dist. LEXIS 46270, at *6–7, 2017 WL 1165688 (E.D. Tex. Mar. 29, 2017) (quoting *KeyCorp v. Holland*, No. 3:16-cv-1948-D, 2016 U.S. Dist. LEXIS 147926, at *34, 2016 WL 6277813 (N.D. Tex. Oct. 26, 2016), *Consumer Elecs. Ass'n v. Compras & Buys Magazine, Inc.*, No. 08-21085-CIV-UNGARO/SIMONTON, 2008 U.S. Dist. LEXIS 80465, at *8, 2008 WL 4327253 (S.D. Fla.), and *Broom, Clarkson, Lanphier & Yamamoto v. Kountze*, No. 8:14CV206, 2015 U.S. Dist. LEXIS 157449, at *24–25 (D. Neb. Nov. 18, 2015))Sept. 18, 2008), *Heller v. City of Dall.*, 303 F.R.D. 466, 487 (N.D. Tex. 2014), and Fed. R. Civ. P. 34(b)(2)(B)); *accord Smash Tech., LLC v. Smash Sols., LLC*, 335 F.R.D. 438, 446 (D. Utah 2020) ("[T]o meet the specificity requirements of [Federal] Rules 33 and 34, an objecting party must do more than rattle off a litany of trite phrases or make an objection 'subject to' other trite phrases located elsewhere in the discovery response. Instead, the objecting party must explain how each objection applies to each specific discovery request."); *Hannah v. Armor Corr. Health Servs., Inc.*, No. 8:19-CV-596-T-60SPF, 2020 U.S. Dist. LEXIS 121546, at *4, 2020 WL 3895369 (M.D. Fla. July 10, 2020) ("A response that is made subject to an objection 'preserves nothing and wastes the time and resources of the parties and the court.' While still common, 'such practice leaves the requesting [p]arty uncertain as to whether the question has actually been fully answered or whether only a portion of the question has been answered.'" (citations omitted) (quoting *Tanner v. Liberty Mut. Fire Ins. Co.*, No. 6:19-cv-585-Orl-37TBS, 2019 U.S. Dist. LEXIS 62231, at *3, 2019 WL 1569565 (M.D. Fla. Apr. 11, 2019), *Martin v. Zale Del., Inc.*, No. 8:08-CV-47-T-27EAJ, 2008 U.S. Dist. LEXIS 105215, at *4, 2008 WL 5255555 (M.D. Fla. Dec. 15, 2008), and *Consumer Elecs. Ass'n v. Compras & Buys Mag., Inc.*, No. 08-21085-CIV, 2008 U.S. Dist. LEXIS 80465, at *7, 2008 WL 4327253 (S.D. Fla. Sept. 18, 2008))); *Maint. Enters., LLC v. Orascom E&C USA, Inc.*, No. 316CV00014SMRCFB, 2018 WL 6380781 (S.D. Iowa Mar. 30, 2018) ("[S]imply stating that a response is 'subject to' one or more general objections does not satisfy the 'specificity' requirement, because, for example, it leaves the propounding party unclear about which of the numerous general objections is purportedly

applicable as well as whether the documents or answers provided are complete, or whether responsive documents are being withheld." (quoting *Liguria Foods, Inc. v. Griffith Labs., Inc.*, 320 F.R.D. 168, 187 (N.D. Iowa 2017))); *Fergin v. Westrock Co.*, No. 8:16CV26, 2017 U.S. Dist. LEXIS 197617, at *12–13, 2017 WL 5990129 (D. Neb. Dec. 1, 2017) ("Magnum did provide some answers and responses to interrogatories and production of documents, 'subject to' and 'without waiving' its objections. Both [Federal] Rule 33, which pertains to interrogatories, and [Federal] Rule 34, which pertains to requests for production of documents, require objections to be stated with specificity. '[S]imply stating that a response is "subject to" one or more general objections does not satisfy the "specificity" requirement, because, for example, it leaves the propounding party unclear about which of the numerous general objections is purportedly applicable as well as whether the documents or answers provided are complete, or whether responsive documents are being withheld.' 'Although it is common practice for a party to respond to discovery requests subject to and without waiving objections, such responses prevent the requesting party from knowing whether all information has been provided.'" (quoting *Liguria Foods, Inc. v. Griffith Labs., Inc.*, 320 F.R.D. 168, 187 (N.D. Iowa 2017), and *Broom, Clarkson, Lanphier & Yamamoto v. Kountze*, No. 8:14CV206, 2015 U.S. Dist. LEXIS 157449, at *24–25, 2015 WL 7302226 (D. Neb. Nov. 18, 2015))); *Duffy v. Lawrence Mem'l Hosp.*, No. 2:14-cv-2256-SAC-TJJ, 2016 U.S. Dist. LEXIS 176848, at *7, 2016 WL 7386413 (D. Kan. Dec. 21, 2016) ("[O]bjections followed by an answer 'preserve nothing and serve only to waste the time and resources of both the Parties and the Court.' As another court noted, 'answering subject to an objection lacks any rational basis. There is either a sustainable objection to a question or request or there is not. In this case, Defendant's conditional objections leave the reader confused as to whether the answers are complete and all requested documents are identified. [Federal] Rules 33 and 34 demand an answer to an interrogatory, a statement that inspection or production will be permitted as requested, or an objection. The discovery rules contemplate no other response." (quoting *Sprint Commc'ns Co., L.P. v. Comcast Cable Commc'ns, LLC*, Nos. 11-2684-JWL, 11-2685-JWL, 11-2686-JWL, 2014 U.S. Dist. LEXIS 16938, at *9, 2014 WL 545544 (D. Kan. Feb. 11, 2014))); *Heller v. City of Dall.*, 303 F.R.D. 466, 487 (N.D. Tex. 2014) ("Having reflected on it, the Court agrees with judges in this circuit and other jurisdictions that the practice of responding to interrogatories and documents requests 'subject to' and/or 'without waiving' objections is 'manifestly confusing (at best) and misleading (at worse), and has no basis at all in the Federal Rules of Civil Procedure.' As another court has observed, when a party 'respond[s] to [a] discovery request, subject to or without waiving such objection,' '[s]uch objection and answer . . . leaves the requesting [p]arty uncertain as to whether the question has actually been fully answered or whether only a portion of the question has been answered.' (quoting *Consumer Elecs. Ass'n v. Compras & Buys Magazine, Inc.*, No. 08-21085-CIV-UNGARO/SIMONTON, 2008 U.S. Dist. LEXIS 80465, at *7, 2008 WL 4327253 (S.D. Fla. Sept. 18, 2008))); *Curtis v. Time Warner Entm't-Advance/Newhouse P'ship*, No. 3:12-cv-2370-JFA, 2013 U.S. Dist. LEXIS 68115, at *7, 2013 WL 2099496 (D.S.C. May 13, 2013) ("The parties shall not recite a formulaic objection followed by an answer to the request. It has become common practice for a party to object on the basis of any of the above reasons and then state that, 'notwithstanding the above,' the party will respond to the discovery request, subject to or without waiving such objection. Such an objection and answer preserves nothing and serves only to waste the time and resources of both the parties and the court. Further, such practice leaves the requesting party uncertain as to whether the question has actually been fully answered or whether only a portion of the question has been answered."); *see In re Park Cities Bank*, 409 S.W.3d 859, 878 (Tex. App.—Tyler 2013, orig. proceeding) (holding general objections to production requests are improper: "Relators contend that their objections are not waived because they filed general objections and reserved the right to assert specific objections if the trial court denied their motion for protective order and required them to respond to Anderton's RFPs. However, prophylactic objections are now prohibited by the rules of procedure.").

Another federal court has reasoned similarly in condemning the use of general objections that are not tethered to any specific discovery request:

Many other cases overrule, strike, or condemn "subject-to" and "without waiver" objections, including the following: *Martley v. City of Basehor*, No. 19-2138-DDC-GEB, 2021 U.S. Dist. LEXIS 62153, at *40–41, 2021 WL 1210013 (D. Kan. Mar. 31, 2021); *Bilek v. Nat'l Cong. of Employers, Inc.*, No. 18 C 3083, 2021 U.S. Dist. LEXIS 53, at *21, 2021 WL 25543 (N.D. Ill. Jan. 4, 2021); *Reed Auto of Overland Park, LLC v. Landers McLarty Olathe KS, LLC*, No. 19-02510-JWB-KGG, 2020 U.S. Dist. LEXIS 157291, at *4–6, 2020 WL 5118103 (D. Kan. Aug. 31, 2020); *Handloser v. HCL Am., Inc.*, No. 19CV01242LHKVKD, 2020 U.S. Dist. LEXIS 152304, at *17–19, 2020 WL 4923971 (N.D. Cal. Aug. 21, 2020); *Centennial Bank v. Graham*, No. 8:19-CV-415-T-35SPF, 2020 U.S. Dist. LEXIS 83387, at *3–4, 2020 WL 2425732 (M.D. Fla. May 12, 2020); *Otto Brands, LLC v. Otto's Express Car Wash, LLC*, No. 3:19CV572/TKW/EMT, 2020 U.S. Dist. LEXIS 185118, at *17–19, 2020 WL 5845739 (N.D. Fla. Feb. 19, 2020); *Gibson v. JetBlue Airways Corp.*, No. 618CV1742ORL40TBS, 2019 U.S. Dist. LEXIS 119420, at *12 n.1, 2019 WL 3243285 (M.D. Fla. July 18, 2019); *City of Scranton v. Streetscapes*, No. 18-CV-4035-HLT-TJJ, 2019 U.S. Dist. LEXIS 66068, at *5–8, 2019 WL 1745419 (D. Kan. Apr. 18, 2019); *Hands on Chiropractic PL v. Progressive Select Ins. Co.*, No. 618CV192ORL37DCI, 2018 U.S. Dist. LEXIS 223752, at *17–18, 2018 WL 6983622 (M.D. Fla. Nov. 20, 2018); *Bragel Int'l, Inc. v. Kohl's Dep't Stores*, No. CV 17-7414 RGK (SSX), 2018 U.S. Dist. LEXIS 224955, at *16, 2018 WL 7890682 (C.D. Cal. Nov. 14, 2018); *Halleen v. Belk, Inc.*, No. 4:16-CV-55, 2018 U.S. Dist. LEXIS 131836, at *7–8, 2018 WL 3735579 (E.D. Tex. Aug. 6, 2018); *Lopez v. Don Herring Ltd.*, 327 F.R.D. 567, 581 (N.D. Tex. 2018); *Springer v. Gen. Atomics Aeronautical Sys.*, No. 16cv2331-BTM(KSC), 2018 U.S. Dist. LEXIS 9032, at *3–5, 2018 WL 490745 (S.D. Cal. Jan. 18, 2018); *Mt. Hawley Ins. Co.* v. *Adell Plastics, Inc.*, No. 17-00252-JKB, 2017 U.S. Dist. LEXIS 134721, at *6–7, 2017 WL 3621184 (D. Md. Aug. 22, 2017); *RealPage, Inc. v. Enter. Risk Control, LLC*, No. 4:16-CV-00737, 2017 U.S. Dist. LEXIS 46270, at *6–7, 2017 WL 1165688 (E.D. Tex. Mar. 29, 2017); *Gondola v. USMD PPM, LLC*, 223 F. Supp. 3d 575, 584 (N.D. Tex. 2016); *Duffy v. Lawrence Mem'l Hosp.*, No. 2:14-cv-2256-SAC-TJJ, 2016 U.S. Dist. LEXIS 176848, at *7, 2016 WL 7386413 (D. Kan. Dec. 21, 2016); *Dillon v. BMO Harris Bank, N.A.*, No. 1:13cv897, 2015 U.S. Dist. LEXIS 147372, at *33–34, 2015 WL 6619972 (M.D.N.C. Oct. 30, 2015); *Rivera v. Volvo Cars of N. Am., LLC*, No. CIV 13-0397 KG/KBM, 2015 U.S. Dist. LEXIS 179213, at *12–13, 2015 WL 11089501 (D.N.M July 20, 2015); *Aprile Horse Transp., Inc. v. Prestige Delivery Sys.*, No. 5:13-CV-15-GNS-LLK, 2015 U.S. Dist. LEXIS 86379, at *5–6, 2015 WL 4068457 (W.D. Ky. July 2, 2015); *Russell v. Daiichi-Sankyo, Inc.*, No. CV 11-34-BLG-CSO, 2012 U.S. Dist. LEXIS 49161, at *10, 2012 WL 1161435 (D. Mont. Apr. 6, 2012); *Leisure Hospitality, Inc. v. Hunt Props., Inc.*, No. 09-CV-272-GKF-PJC, 2010 U.S. Dist. LEXIS 93680, at *9–10, 2010 WL 3522444 (N.D. Okla. Sept. 8, 2010); *Robinson v. City of Ark. City*, No. 10-1431-JAR-GLR, 2012 U.S. Dist. LEXIS 23806, at *21–22, 2012 WL 603576 (D. Kan. Feb. 24, 2012); *Myers v. Goldco, Inc.*, No. 4:08cv8-RH/WCS, 2008 U.S. Dist. LEXIS 37089, at *2–3, 2008 WL 1995131 (N.D. Fla. May 6, 2008).

One federal judge highlighted the impropriety of these objections by citing extensive authority in support of this statement: "[F]ailing to follow the Federal Rules' and case law's requirements for specificity in objecting and responding and answering, as well as correspondingly answering or responding 'subject to' and 'without waiving' those objections, is improper, as the undersigned and many other judges in this circuit and elsewhere have now made clear for several years." *State Auto. Mut. Ins. Co. v. Freehold Mgmt., Inc.*, No. 3:16-CV-2255-L, 2018 U.S. Dist. LEXIS 123283, at *40–41, 2018 WL 3548866 (N.D. Tex. July 24, 2018) (citing cases); *accord Firebirds Int'l, LLC v. Firebird Rest. Grp., LLC*, No. 3:17-CV-2719-B, 2018 U.S. Dist. LEXIS 123283, at *40–41, 2018 WL 3655574 (N.D. Tex. July 16, 2018) ("The failures to follow the Federal Rules' requirements for specificity in objecting and responding and answering, and answering or responding 'subject to and without waiving objections,' are practices that attorneys must stop, as the undersigned and many other judges in this circuit and elsewhere have now made clear for several years.") (citing cases).

Defendant's "General Objections" and "General Statements" contained in its Amended Objections do not relate to any particular discovery request and, in fact, are nothing more than boilerplate, designed to obfuscate. It is impossible to tell which, if any, of these General Objections or General Statements would actually be relied upon with respect to any particular interrogatory. They are not specific nor [sic] appropriate and are, therefore, stricken.[69]

---

[69] *Barb v. Brown's Buick, Inc.*, No. 1:09cv785, 2010 U.S. Dist. LEXIS 8655, at *1–2 (E.D. Va. Feb. 2, 2010); *accord Mullenix v. Univ. of Tex.*, No. 1-19-CV-1203-LY, 2021 U.S. Dist. LEXIS 79965, at *9, 2021 WL 1647760 (W.D. Tex. Apr. 26, 2021) ("'It is well-established that parties cannot make general or boilerplate objections to discovery requests.' Examples of these general objections include: 'Defendant objects to this Request, as it is overly broad and vague' and 'Defendant objects to this Request to the extent it seeks discovery of information that is irrelevant and not proportional to the needs of the case.'" (citations omitted) (quoting *Tim Long Plumbing, Inc. v. Kinsale Ins. Co.*, No. 4:20-CV-00042, 2020 U.S. Dist. LEXIS 208897, at *4, 2020 WL 6559869 (E.D. Tex. Nov. 9, 2020))); *O.L. v. City of El Monte*, No. 220CV00797RGKJDEX, 2021 U.S. Dist. LEXIS 58722, at *76, 2021 WL 926105 (C.D. Cal. Jan. 11, 2021) ("To the extent Plaintiff asserts general objections, without evidentiary support, such as overbreadth, undue burden, oppressive, vague, compound, etc., such objections are overruled as unsupported."); *Daniels v. G4S Secure Sols. USA, Inc.*, No. 820CV00283JGBJDEX, 2021 U.S. Dist. LEXIS 78127, at *35, 2021 WL 1537040 (C.D. Cal. Jan. 21, 2021) ("[T]he Court, although declining to 'strike' general objections, does not consider them incorporated into specific responses unless, as required by [Federal] Rule 33(b)(4), they are stated 'with specificity' in the particular response."); *Sobol v. Imprimis Pharms.*, No. 16-14339, 2017 U.S. Dist. LEXIS 184478, at *11 (E.D. Mich. Oct. 26, 2017) ("'[I]ncorporating all of the General Objections into each response violates [Federal] Rule 34(b)(2)(B)'s specificity requirement as well as [Federal] Rule 34(b)(2)(C)'s requirement to indicate whether any responsive materials are withheld on the basis of an objection.' In fact, boilerplate objections are legally meaningless and amount to a waiver of an objection. Since Imprimis effectively failed to object to RFPD 7 and 11 in a timely manner, it waived any objections." (quoting *Fischer v. Forrest*, No. 14 CIV 1304-PAE-AJP, 2017 U.S. Dist. LEXIS 28102, at *7 (S.D.N.Y. Feb. 28, 2017))); *Neogenix Oncology, Inc. v. Gordon*, No. CV 14-4427 (JFB) (AKT), 2017 U.S. Dist. LEXIS 155429, at *7–8 (E.D.N.Y. Sept. 22, 2017) ("Any objection interposed [to a request for admission] must be directed at and specifically related to a particular request. Thus, '[g]eneral objections without any reference to a specific request to admit are meritless.'" (quoting *Henry v. Champlain Enters., Inc.*, 212 F.R.D. 73, 78 (N.D.N.Y. 2003))); *Team Contrs., L.L.C. v. Waypoint NOLA, L.L.C.*, No. 16-1131 SECTION "E" (2), 2017 U.S. Dist. LEXIS 118653, at *5–7 (E.D. La. July 28, 2017) ("[T]he court will ignore the 'General Objections' asserted in Catlin's responses. If Catlin has a specific objection to a particular request, it must state the objection 'with specificity.' Catlin's 'General Objections' fail to comply with the specificity requirements of the applicable rules and only obfuscate and confuse both Waypoint and the court concerning what objections Catlin is actually making, what information it has actually produced and whether a complete response has been made. 'In every respect these objections are textbook examples of what federal courts have routinely deemed to be improper objections.'" (citations omitted) (quoting Fed. R. Civ. P. 33(b)(4), 34(b)(2)(B) and *St. Paul Reinsurance Co., Ltd. v. Commercial Fin. Corp.*, 198 F.R.D. 508, 512 (N.D. Iowa 2000))).

Many other cases overrule, strike, or condemn general objections, including the following: *Walls v. Ford Motor Co.*, No. 1:20CV98, 2021 U.S. Dist. LEXIS 82757, at *32–34, 2021 WL 1723154 (M.D.N.C. Apr. 30, 2021); *Avenatti v. Gree USA, Inc.*, No. 220CV00354JPHMJD, 2021 U.S. Dist. LEXIS 52969, at *4–7, 15-16, 17, 2021 WL 1034392 (S.D. Ind. Mar. 17, 2021); *Lloyd v. Whirlpool Corp.*, No. 19 C 6225, 2020 U.S. Dist. LEXIS 247554, at *13–14, 2020 WL 8115869 (N.D. Ill. Oct. 27, 2020); *Star Well Servs., Inc. v. W. Oilfields Supply Co.*, No.

CIV-19-672-R, 2020 U.S. Dist. LEXIS 125522, at *2–4, 2020 WL 4018809 (W.D. Okla. July 16, 2020); *Dortch v. Wells Fargo Bank, N.A.*, No. 4:18-CV-00452, 2020 U.S. Dist. LEXIS 46501, at *8, 2020 WL 1289431 (E.D. Tex. Mar. 18, 2020); *Ecolab Inc. v. Int'l Chem. Corp.*, No. 618CV1910ORL41GJK, 2020 U.S. Dist. LEXIS 3728, at *8, 2020 WL 109693 (M.D. Fla. Jan. 8, 2020); *Four Fibers, L.L.C. v. Keps Techs., Inc.*, No. 2:18-CV-13867, 2019 U.S. Dist. LEXIS 205930, at *3–4, 2019 WL 6339814 (E.D. Mich. Nov. 27, 2019); *Ortega v. N.M. Legal Aid, Inc.*, No. CV 18-111 MV/KK, 2019 U.S. Dist. LEXIS 197593, at *6–8, 2019 WL 6042207 (D.N.M. Nov. 14, 2019); *Zurich Am. Ins. Co. v. Hardin*, No. 8:14-CV-775-T-23AAS, 2019 U.S. Dist. LEXIS 117097, at *13, 2019 WL 3082608 (M.D. Fla. July 15, 2019); *MD Helicopters, Inc. v. Aerometals, Inc.*, No. 2:16-CV-02249 TLN AC, 2019 U.S. Dist. LEXIS 81400, at *10, 2019 WL 2103408 (E.D. Cal. May 14, 2019); *Morgan v. Wesley Med. Ctr. LLC*, No. 18-2158-KHV-KGG, 2019 U.S. Dist. LEXIS 78382, at *3–7, 2019 WL 2067363 (D. Kan. May 9, 2019); *Atkins v. AT&T Mobility Servs., LLC*, No. 2:18-CV-00599, 2019 U.S. Dist. LEXIS 227963, at *20–26, 2019 WL 8017851 (S.D.W. Va. Apr. 25, 2019); *Johnston v. Transocean Offshore Deepwater Drilling, Inc.*, No. CV 18-491, 2019 U.S. Dist. LEXIS 61608, at *2–3, 2019 WL 1558040 (E.D. La. Apr. 10, 2019); *Flynn v. Mfrs. & Trades Tr. Co.*, No. 17-CV-04806-WB, 2018 U.S. Dist. LEXIS 183025, at *2–3, 2018 WL 5296371 (E.D. Pa. Oct. 25, 2018); *Ceuric v. Tier One, LLC*, 325 F.R.D. 558, 561 (W.D. Pa. 2018); *Wittmann v. Unum Life Ins. Co. of Am.*, No. CV 17-9501, 2018 U.S. Dist. LEXIS 68145, at *7–8, 2018 WL 1912163 (E.D. La. Apr. 23, 2018); *Huawei Techs. Co., Ltd. v. Yiren Huang*, No. 4:17-CV-893, 2018 U.S. Dist. LEXIS 231689, at *6–8, 2018 WL 10127426 (E.D. Tex. Apr. 4, 2018); *Team Contrs., L.L.C. v. Waypoint NOLA, L.L.C.*, No. 16-1131 SECTION "E" (2), 2017 U.S. Dist. LEXIS 118653, at *5–7, 2017 WL 3216582 (E.D. La. July 28, 2017); *Berenson v. Adm'rs of the Tulane Educ. Fund*, No. 17-329 SECTION "R" (2), 2017 U.S. Dist. LEXIS 118651, at *2–4, 2017 WL 3216584 (E.D. La. July 28, 2017); *SPV-LS, LLC v. Transamerica Life Ins. Co.*, No. CIV 14-4092, 2017 U.S. Dist. LEXIS 33213, at *17–19, 2017 WL 899882 (D.S.D. Mar. 6, 2017); *Polycarpe v. Seterus, Inc.*, No. 6:16-cv-1606-orl-37TBS, 2017 U.S. Dist. LEXIS 77808, at *3–5, 2017 WL 2257571 (M.D. Fla. May 23, 2017); *Terrell v. IRS (In re Terrell)*, 569 B.R. 881, 887–88 (Bankr. W.D. Okla. 2017); *Gonzalez v. Volkswagen Grp. of Am., Inc.*, No. A-14-CV-574-LY-ML, 2015 U.S. Dist. LEXIS 114376, at *4–5, 2015 WL 5097271 (W.D. Tex. Aug. 28, 2015); *Heller v. City of Dall.*, 303 F.R.D. 466, 483 (N.D. Tex. 2014); *Weems v. Hodnett*, No. 10-cv-1452, 2011 U.S. Dist. LEXIS 80746, at *3–4 (W.D. La. July 25, 2011); *Morgenstern v. Fox TV Stations*, No. 08-0562, 2010 U.S. Dist. LEXIS 15874, at *14–15, 2010 WL 678113 (E.D. Pa. Feb. 23, 2010); *DL v. D.C.*, 251 F.R.D. 38, 43 (D.D.C. 2008); *Interland, Inc. v. Bunting*, No. 1:04-CV-444-ODE, 2005 U.S. Dist. LEXIS 36112, at *29, 2005 WL 2414990 (N.D. Ga. Mar. 31, 2005); *Henry v. Champlain Enters., Inc.*, 212 F.R.D. 73, 78 (N.D.N.Y. 2003).

In some cases, courts have looked past general objections because they were not the only complaint about discovery requests. *See, e.g., Estate of Gabriel Strickland v. Nev. Cnty.*, No. 2:21-CV-00175 MCE AC, 2021 WL 2003119 (E.D. Cal. May 19, 2021) ("General or boilerplate objections, without explanation, are not prohibited but are insufficient as a sole basis for an objection or privilege claim."); *Daniels v. G4S Secure Sols. USA, Inc.*, No. 820CV00283JGBJDEX, 2021 U.S. Dist. LEXIS 78127, at *11, 2021 WL 1537040 (C.D. Cal. Jan. 21, 2021) ("Although general objections are disfavored, G4S, Guarino, and King nevertheless provided substantive responses and/or specific objections to discovery requests at issue in its responses. The Court therefore declines to find G4S, Guarino, or King's responses insufficient based on the assertion of general objections alone."); *Smith v. Bank of Am., N.A.*, No. CV 14-6668-DSF (PLAx), 2019 U.S. Dist. LEXIS 222618, at *12–13, 2019 WL 7188571 (C.D. Cal. Sept. 20, 2019) (declining to strike general objections where responding party restated applicable objections in substantive responses); *BBC Grp. NV LLC v. Island Life Rest. Grp. LLC*, 2019 U.S. Dist. LEXIS 222618, at *12–13, 2019 WL 2326212 (W.D. Wash. May 31, 2019) (declining to strike a party's general objections where the party provided specific responses in addition to general objections and apparently used the general objections "in an attempt to preserve certain objections").

Third, general and subject-to objections violate Texas Rule 191.3(c)'s certification requirement:

> The signature of an attorney or party on a discovery request, notice, response, or objection constitutes a certification that to the best of the signer's knowledge, information, and belief, formed after a reasonable inquiry, the request, notice, response, or objection:
>
> (1) is consistent with the rules of civil procedure and these discovery rules and warranted by existing law or a good faith argument for the extension, modification, or reversal of existing law;
>
> (2) has a good faith factual basis; [and]
>
> (3) is not interposed for any improper purpose.[70]

Fourth, even the benign rationales for such objections—to prevent a later ruling that a discovery response was inadequate or that an objection has been waived—are inapplicable. The excuse that general or subject-to objections prevent discovery responses from being found to be insufficient or incomplete at a later date is nonsensical because, under Texas Rule 193.5(a), a party must amend or supplement an incomplete or incorrect response to a discovery request and because, under Texas Rule 197.3, "[a]n answer to an interrogatory inquiring about [the opposing party's contentions or damages] that has been amended or supplemented is not admissible and may not be used for impeachment."[71] The excuse that such objections are needed to prevent a waiver of applicable objections has no merit because Texas Rule 193.2(d) allows a responding party to amend a response to state an objection not made initially if the objection either was "inapplicable or was unknown after reasonable inquiry" when the original response was made.[72]

Accordingly, general and subject-to objections such as the ones discussed above are improper and trial courts should strike them, ruling that each general or subject-to objection has been waived.[73] For example, in ***In re Park Cities Bank***, the defendants filed a motion for protective order claiming, among other things, that the plaintiff's production requests were objectionable because they were "overly broad, unduly burdensome, harassing, seek documents that are not relevant nor reasonably calculated to lead to the discovery of admissible evidence, constitute an impermissible fishing expedition, require [the defendants] to marshal their evidence, invade [the defendants'] right to privacy as guaranteed by the United States Constitution

---

70 Tex. R. Civ. P. 191.3(c); *cf. High Point Sarl v. Sprint Nextel Corp.*, No. 09-2269-CM-DJW, 2011 U.S. Dist. LEXIS 103118, at *33–36, 2011 WL 4036424 (D. Kan. Sept. 12, 2011) (sanctioning the responding party for interposing "general objections" because they violate Federal Rule 26(g)), the federal counterpart to Texas Rule 191.3(c).

71 Tex. R. Civ. P. 193.5(a), 197.3.

72 Tex. R. Civ. P. 193.2(d).

73 Tex. R. Civ. P. 193.2(e); ***In re Park Cities Bank***, 409 S.W.3d 859, 877 (Tex. App.—Tyler 2013, orig. proceeding); Robert K. Wise, *Ending Evasive Responses to Written Discovery: A Guide for Properly Responding (and Objecting) to Interrogatories and Document Requests Under the Texas Discovery Rules*, 65 Baylor L. Rev. 510, 571 (2013)). Such a ruling is required even if one of the series of prophylactic, boilerplate "general" or "subject-to" objections has merit because, under Texas Rule 193.2(e), "[a]n objection . . . that is obscured by numerous unfounded objections, is waived[.]" Tex. R. Civ. P. 193.2(e). See also the cases cited in notes 68–69.

and Texas Constitution, seek documents that are confidential, proprietary, and trade secrets, seek documents that are privileged attorney-client communications and attorney work product, among other things."[74] The defendants also "purported to 'reserve the right to assert specific objections to each request for production should the Court deny this motion and require [them] to substantively respond to [the plaintiff's] discovery requests.'"[75]

After the trial court denied the motion and held that the defendants had waived their objections to the production requests, the defendants sought a writ of mandamus.[76] In denying the writ, the Tyler Court of Appeals held that general objections, like those interposed by the defendants, were improper and waived any meritorious ones:

> [Defendants] contend that their objections are not waived because they filed general objections and reserved the right to assert specific objections if the trial court denied their motion for protective order and required them to respond to [Plaintiff's] RFPs. However, prophylactic objections are now prohibited by the rules of procedure. . . .
>
> The discovery rules specify the content of objections to written discovery, the time for making those objections, and the penalty for failing to do so. Prophylactic general objections . . . are not permitted under [Texas] Rule 193. Thus, a determination that prophylactic general objections satisfy [Texas] Rule 193 would be contrary to the rule's plain language and would reinstate the practice of filing prophylactic general objections to avoid waiver. The trial court properly declined to make such a ruling and therefore disregarded [Defendants'] general objections. . . . The trial court did not abuse its discretion by ruling that [Defendants] waived their objections.[77]

In addition to the general and subject-to objections set forth above, many practitioners include a variety of nonspecific objections in an introductory section of the discovery response containing objections, such as the following:

1. Defendant objects to Plaintiff's production requests and interrogatories, definitions, and instructions to the extent they exceed or seek to impose discovery obligations on Defendant that exceed and conflict with the nature and scope of discovery permitted under the Texas Rules of Civil Procedure.
2. Defendant makes no admissions of any nature, and no admissions may be implied by, or inferred from, these objections and responses. Nothing contained in any response shall be deemed to be an admission, concession, or waiver by Defendant as to the relevance, materiality, or admissibility of any information provided in response to Plaintiffs' discovery requests.

---

74 *In re Park Cities Bank*, 409 S.W.3d 859, 877 (Tex. App.—Tyler 2013, orig. proceeding).

75 *In re Park Cities Bank*, 409 S.W.3d 859, 877–78 (Tex. App.—Tyler 2013, orig. proceeding).

76 *In re Park Cities Bank*, 409 S.W.3d 859, 877–78 (Tex. App.—Tyler 2013, orig. proceeding).

77 *In re Park Cities Bank*, 409 S.W.3d 859, 878 (Tex. App.—Tyler 2013, orig. proceeding). See also cases cited in notes 68–69.

3. Defendant objects to Plaintiff's discovery requests to the extent they purport to require it to identify or produce information or documents that are not within this its possession, custody or control. Defendant will identify or produce nonprivileged information or documents that are presently in its possession, custody, or control.
4. Defendant reserves the right to supplement its responses if any additional information or documents are discovered.[78]

These types of objections are improper because they are nonspecific and unnecessarily regurgitate (or misstate) well-establish discovery or evidentiary principals. As noted by one federal court in holding that they are improper:

> As to the particular general objections that Defendant raised in this case, the objection to all requests to the extent that they exceed or conflict with the scope of permissible discovery is an off-the-shelf and decidedly non-specific objection that gains the responding party nothing without tying it to a particular discovery request and explaining precisely how that request exceeds or conflicts with the scope of permissible discovery. And the Court agrees with Plaintiffs' counsel that disavowing interrogatory responses as "admissions of any nature," flies in the face of [Federal] Rule 33(c)'s provision that "[a]n answer to an interrogatory may be used to the extent allowed by the Federal Rules of Evidence." Finally, any statement reserving the "right" to supplement discovery responses "merely reflects an already existing duty, pursuant to Fed. R. Civ. P. 26(e)."[79]

One type of general objection, however, is permissible—a general objection stated in a clear and discernible manner and based on the facts of the action, such as an objection to all interrogatories or production requests asking for information before a certain date or relating to certain products or facilities. This type of general objection is acceptable because repeating the objection in multiple responses is pointless and there is no uncertainty regarding what information or material is being withheld and why.[80]

---

[78] *See, e.g.*, *Heller v. City of Dall.*, 303 F.R.D. 466, 482–83 (N.D. Tex. 2014) (containing objections 1-2 and 4); *Chapman v. Hiland Operating, LLC*, No. 1:13-cv-052, 2014 U.S. Dist. LEXIS 54318, *4–5, 2014 WL 1513977 (D.N.D. Apr. 16, 2014) (containing objections 1-3).

[79] *Heller v. City of Dall.*, 303 F.R.D. 466, 484 (N.D. Tex. 2014) (citation omitted) (quoting Fed. R. Civ. P. 33(c) and *Zapata v. IBP, Inc.*, No. 93-2366-EEO, 1995 U.S. Dist. LEXIS 6436, at *4, 1995 WL 293931 (D. Kan. May 10, 1995)); *accord Chapman v. Hiland Operating, LLC*, No. 1:13-cv-052, 2014 U.S. Dist. LEXIS 54318, at *3–5, *8, 2014 WL 1513977 (D.N.D. Apr. 16, 2014).

[80] *Cf. Bursztein v. Best Buy Stores, L.P.*, No. 20CV00076ATKHP, 2021 U.S. Dist. LEXIS 92978, at *17, 2021 WL 1961645 (S.D.N.Y. May 17, 2021) ("[C]ourts in this District have previously said that general objections should rarely be used, unless the objections specifically apply to each document request at issue."); *Amos v. Taylor*, No. 4:20-CV-7-DMB-JMV, 2020 U.S. Dist. LEXIS 224295, at *26–27, 2020 WL 7049848 (N.D. Miss. Dec. 1, 2020) ("[W]here the general objections are connected both to the facts of this case and specific discovery requests, they are proper. When they are disconnected from either the facts or the discovery requests, they are improper."); *CBF Industria de Gusa S/A v. AMCI Holdings, Inc.*, No. 13CV2581PKCJLC, 2019 U.S. Dist. LEXIS 124326, at *31, 2019 WL 3334503 (S.D.N.Y. July 25, 2019) ("'General objections should rarely be used . . . unless each such objection applies to each document request (e.g., objecting to produce privileged material).'"

5-3:3 Boilerplate Objections Are Improper

Boilerplate objections "merely state[] the legal grounds for the objection without (1) specifying how the discovery request is deficient [or] (2) specifying how the objecting party would be harmed if it were forced to respond to the request. For example, a boilerplate objection might state that a discovery request is irrelevant or overbroad without taking the next step to explain why. These objections are taglines, completely 'devoid of any individualized factual analysis.'"[81]

Boilerplate objections typically underlie the improper general and subject-to objections discussed in Chapter 5, section 5-3:2. They also can be standalone objections pursuant which a responding party objects to a written-discovery request in its entirety.

Standalone boilerplate objections are improper under the Texas discovery rules.[82] This is made clear by Texas Rule 193.2(a), which requires that "[t]he party must state *specifically* the . . . factual basis for the objection[.]"[83] In fact, one of the purposes

---

(quoting *Fischer v. Forrest*, No. 14-CV-1304 (PAE) (AJP), 2017 U.S. Dist. LEXIS 28102, at *7, 2017 WL 773694 (S.D.N.Y. Feb. 28, 2017))); *Polycarpe v. Seterus, Inc.*, No. 6:16-cv-1606-orl-37TBS, 2017 U.S. Dist. LEXIS 77808, at *4, 2017 WL 2257571 (M.D. Fla. May 23, 2017) (Federal Rules 33 and 34 "leave no place for so-called 'General Objections' to interrogatories and requests for production except in those rare cases where the same objection specifically applies to every interrogatory or request."); *Berlinger v. Wells Fargo, N.A.*, No. 2:11-cv-459-FtM-99SPC, 2012 U.S. Dist. LEXIS 26650, at *12–13, 2012 WL 695836 (M.D. Fla. Mar. 1, 2012) ("'General or blanket objections should be used only when they apply to every discovery request at issue.' Otherwise, 'specific objections should be matched to specific' interrogatories or requests for production." (quoting *Desoto Health & Rehab., L.L.C. v. Phila. Indem. Ins. Co.*, No. 2:09-cv-599-FtM-99SPC, 2010 U.S. Dist. LEXIS 61503, at *2–3 (M.D. Fla. June 10, 2010))).

81 *Liguria Foods, Inc. v. Griffith Labs., Inc.*, 320 F.R.D. 168, 170 n.1 (N.D. Iowa Mar. 13, 2017) (quoting Matthew L. Jarvey, *Boilerplate Discovery Objections: How They Are Used, Why They Are Wrong, and What We Can Do About Them*, 61 Drake L. Rev. 913, 914–16 (2013)); *accord Wesley Corp. v. Zoom T.V. Prods., LLC*, No. 17-10021, 2018 U.S. Dist. LEXIS 5068, at *9–12, 2018 WL 372700 (E.D. Mich. Jan. 11, 2018); *In re Haynes*, 577 B.R. 711, 723–25 (Bankr. E.D. Tenn. 2017); *see Amos v. Taylor*, No. 4:20-CV-7-DMB-JMV, 2020 U.S. Dist. LEXIS 224295, at *23, 2020 WL 7049848 (N.D. Miss. Dec. 1, 2020) ("Boilerplate objections are those that utilize 'standardized text' or 'ready-made or all-purpose language.'" (quoting *Tim Long Plumbing, Inc. v. Kinsale Ins. Co.*, No. 4:20-CV-42, 2020 U.S. Dist. LEXIS 208897, at *9, 2020 WL 6559869 (E.D. Tex. Nov. 9, 2020))); *Holcombe v. Advanced Integration Tech.*, No. 4:17-CV-00522, 2018 U.S. Dist. LEXIS 135493, at *9, 2018 WL 3819974 (E.D. Tex. Aug. 10, 2018) ("'Boilerplate' means 'standardized text' or 'ready-made or all-purpose language.'" (quoting *Boilerplate, Merriam-Webster Collegiate Dictionary* (11th ed. 2007); *Boilerplate, Black's Law Dictionary* (10th ed. 2014))).

82 As discussed in Chapter 5, section 5-3:2, general and subject-to objections are generally improper largely because they almost always are based on boilerplate objections. Boilerplate objections also are improper under the federal discovery rules. See cases cited in note 88.

83 Tex. R. Civ. P. 193.2(a) (emphasis added); *accord In re Park Cities Bank*, 409 S.W.3d 859, 877 (Tex. App.—Tyler 2013, orig. proceeding); *see In re K & L Auto Crushers, LLC*, 627 S.W.3d 239, 253 (Tex. 2021) (orig. proceeding) ("[A] party resisting discovery must do more than 'make conclusory allegations that the requested discovery is unduly burdensome.'" (quoting *In re Alford Chevrolet-Geo*, 997 S.W.2d 173, 181 (Tex. 1999) (orig. proceeding))); *In re Alford Chevrolet-Geo*, 997 S.W.2d 173, 181 (Tex. 1999) (orig. proceeding) ("A party resisting discovery . . . cannot simply make conclusory allegations that the requested discovery is

of the 1999 amendments to the Texas discovery rules was to eliminate boilerplate objections.[84]

Although no Texas case directly condemns boilerplate objections, one Texas court of appeals has held that a responding party waived his objections to discovery requests by "lodg[ing] the same global, prophylactic string of objections[,]" which the court considered "unfounded," to each of the requests.[85] In addition, a Texas court of appeals analyzing Texas Rule 193.2(a)'s "specificity" requirement has stated that "a responding party who objects to a request for production because is it overbroad, unduly burdensome, vague, ambiguous, or unreasonably cumulative or duplicative should explain why the discovery request suffers from each asserted deficiency."[86] Federal courts construing similar language in Federal Rules 33(b)(4) and

---

unduly burdensome or unnecessarily harassing. The party must produce some evidence supporting its request for a protective order.").

Boilerplate objections generally are prophylactic, that is, they are interposed by the responding party out of an abundance of caution to prevent the waiver of objections that might prove later to be appropriate. To the extent that they are interposed for this purpose, the objections violate Texas Rule 193.2(c), which requires "a good faith factual and legal basis for the objection exists *at the time the objection is made.*" Tex. R. Civ. P. 193.2(c) (emphasis added); *see In re Park Cities Bank*, 409 S.W.3d 859, 877 ((Tex. App.—Tyler 2013, orig. proceeding) (explaining that prophylactic objections are improper for this reason).

[84] Nathan L. Hecht & Robert H. Pemberton, *A Guide to the 1999 Texas Discovery Rules Revisions* § F.3 (Nov. 11, 1998) ("Under the former discovery rules, objections and privilege claims against a discovery request had to be asserted within the time for responding or else they were waived. This frequently led parties, out of an abundance of caution, to assert voluminous prophylactic objections that, as discovery progressed, often proved to be unnecessary and unfounded. These types of objections obscured the true state of facts underlying the objections and responses—thus defeating the purposes of discovery—and gave rise to unnecessary expense as parties had to seek hearings, enter [Texas] Rule 11 agreements, or take other measures simply to discern which of their opponent's objections were 'real.' [Texas] Rule 193 eliminates the perceived need for these practices by requiring parties to object or assert privileges only to the extent that a good faith factual and legal basis for the objection or privilege claim exists and could be ascertained after reasonable inquiry at the time the objection or claim is made."), https://www.txcourts.gov/rules-forms/rules-standards/; Nathan L. Hecht & Robert H. Pemberton, *A Guide to the 1999 Texas Discovery Rules Revisions* § F.3 (Nov. 11, 1998) ("The new restrictions on prophylactic objections, coupled with the affirmative duty to respond, will help eliminate the abuse of parties 'burying' the truth behind an avalanche of all objections that conceivably could be applicable (and/or are available as forms on the party's word processing systems."), https://www.txcourts.gov/rules-forms/rules-standards/; *see In re Park Cities Bank*, 409 S.W.3d 859, 877 (Tex. App.—Tyler 2013, orig. proceeding) ("A primary goal of all of the groups considering discovery reform in anticipation of revising the former discovery rules was to rid the system of prophylactic objections.").

[85] *De Anda v. Jason C. Webster, P.C.*, No. 14-17-00020-CV, 2018 Tex. App. LEXIS 5727, at *19–20, 2018 WL 3580579 (Tex. App.—Houston [14th Dist.] July 26, 2018, pet. denied) (mem. op.).

[86] *In re Park Cities Bank*, 409 S.W.3d 859, 876 (Tex. App.—Tyler 2013, orig. proceeding) (citing Robert K. Wise, *Ending Evasive Responses to Written Discovery: A Guide for Properly Responding (and Objecting) to Interrogatories and Document Requests Under the Texas Discovery Rules*, 65 Baylor L. Rev. 510, 563 (Spring 2013)).

34(b)(2)(B)[87] uniformly hold that their "specificity" requirements outlaw boilerplate objections. As explained by one federal court:

> The key requirement in both [Federal] Rules 33 and 34 is that objections require "specificity." . . . "[T]he mere statement by a party that the interrogatory [or request for production] was overly broad, burdensome, oppressive and irrelevant is not adequate to voice a successful objection"; "[o]n the contrary, the party resisting discovery must show specifically how . . . each interrogatory [or request for production] is not relevant or how each question is overly broad, burdensome or oppressive." In other words, "merely assert[ing] boilerplate objections that the discovery sought is vague, ambiguous, overbroad, unduly burdensome, etc. . . . without specifying how each [interrogatory or] request for production is deficient and without articulating the particular harm that would accrue if [the responding party] were required to respond to [the proponent's] discovery requests" simply is not enough.[88]

---

[87] Federal Rule 33(b)(4) requires that objections to interrogatories be made "with specificity," Fed. R. Civ. P. 33(b)(4). Federal Rule 34(b)(2)(B) similarly requires that objections to production requests "state with specificity the grounds for objecting to the request[,]" Fed. R. Civ. P. 34(b)(2)(B).

[88] *In re Haynes*, 577 B.R. 711, 723–24 (Bankr. E.D. Tenn. 2017) (quoting *Liguria Foods, Inc. v. Griffith Labs., Inc.*, 320 F.R.D. 168, 185 (D. Iowa 2017), and *St. Paul Reinsurance Co., Ltd. v. Commercial Fin. Corp.*, 198 F.R.D. 508, 511–12 (N.D. Iowa 2000)); *accord McLeod, Alexander, Powel & Apffel, P.C. v. Quarles*, 894 F.2d 1482, 1485 (5th Cir. 1990) ("[T]o say an interrogatory was overly broad, burdensome, oppressive and irrelevant [is] not adequate to voice a successful objection to an interrogatory."); *Josephs v. Harris Corp.*, 677 F.2d 985, 992 (3d Cir. 1982) (quoting *Roesberg v. Johns-Manville Corp.*, 85 F.R.D. 292, 296–97 (E.D.Pa.1980)) ("[T]he mere statement by a party that the interrogatory was 'overly broad, burdensome, oppressive and irrelevant' is not adequate to voice a successful objection to an interrogatory. On the contrary, the party resisting discovery 'must show specifically how . . . each interrogatory is not relevant or how each question is overly broad, burdensome or oppressive.'" Pa. 1980))); *Hall v. Marriott Int'l, Inc.*, No. 319CV01715JLSAHG, 2021 U.S. Dist. LEXIS 90870, at *12–13, 2021 WL 1906464 (S.D. Cal. May 12, 2021) ("The party resisting discovery must specifically detail the reasons why each request is irrelevant or otherwise objectionable, and may not rely on boilerplate, generalized, conclusory, or speculative arguments. Where 'the responding party provides a boilerplate or generalized objection, said 'objections are inadequate and tantamount to not making any objection at all.'" (citation omitted) (quoting *Bess v. Cate*, No. 07cv1989-JAM-JFM, 2008 U.S. Dist. LEXIS 100253, at *12, 2008 WL 5100203 (E.D. Cal. Nov. 26, 2008))); *Crespo v. Nat'l R.R. Passenger Corp.*, No. 2:19-CV-275-JTM-JEM, 2021 U.S. Dist. LEXIS 67529, at *4, 2021 WL 1291769 (N.D. Ind. Apr. 7, 2021) ("The burden an objecting party carries cannot be met by 'a reflexive invocation of the same baseless, often abused litany that the requested discovery is vague, ambiguous, overly broad, unduly burdensome or that it is neither relevant nor reasonably calculated to lead to the discovery of admissible evidence.'" (quoting *Cunningham v. Smithkline Beecham*, 255 F.R.D. 474, 478 (N.D. Ind. 2009))); *Smash Tech., LLC v. Smash Sols., LLC*, 335 F.R.D. 438, 441 (D. Utah 2020) ("The amendments to the Federal Rules of Civil Procedure themselves along with cases too numerous to cite here have all declared an ignominious end to the tradition of boilerplate objections.") (citing cases); *Liguria Foods, Inc. v. Griffith Labs., Inc.*, 320 F.R.D. 168, 184–85 (D. Iowa 2017) ("The key requirement in both [Federal] Rules 33 and 34 is that objections require 'specificity.' As I explained a decade-and-a-half ago, 'the mere statement by a party that the interrogatory [or request for production] was overly broad, burdensome, oppressive and irrelevant is not adequate to voice a successful objection'; '[o]n the contrary,

the party resisting discovery must show specifically how . . . each interrogatory [or request for production] is not relevant or how each question is overly broad, burdensome or oppressive.' In other words, 'merely assert[ing] boilerplate objections that the discovery sought is vague, ambiguous, overbroad, unduly burdensome, etc. . . . without specifying how each [interrogatory or] request for production is deficient and without articulating the particular harm that would accrue if [the responding party] were required to respond to [the proponent's] discovery requests' simply is not enough." (quoting *St. Paul Reinsurance Co. v. Commercial Fin. Corp.*, 198 F.R.D. 508, 511–12 (D. Iowa 2000))).

Many other cases hold that boilerplate objections are improper, including the following: *Boegh v. Harless*, No. 518CV00123TBRLLK, 2021 U.S. Dist. LEXIS 91502, at *4–5, 2021 WL 1923365 (W.D. Ky. May 13, 2021); *Altima Diagnostic Imaging Solutions, Inc. v. The JDIS Grp., LLC*, No. 3:19-CV-2102-M-BK, 2021 U.S. Dist. LEXIS 92957, at *4, 2021 WL 1940206 (N.D. Tex. May 12, 2021); *HealthEdge Software, Inc. v. Sharp Health Plan*, No. 19-CV-11020-ADB, 2021 U.S. Dist. LEXIS 88061, at *10–11, 2021 WL 1821358 (D. Mass. May 6, 2021); *Zean v. eFinancial, LLC*, No. 19-CV-2958 (NEB/TNL), 2021 U.S. Dist. LEXIS 83805, at *7–9, 2021 WL 1732261 (D. Minn. May 3, 2021); *Walls v. Ford Motor Co.*, No. 1:20CV98, 2021 U.S. Dist. LEXIS 82757, at *15–16, 32–33, 42, 2021 WL 1723154 (M.D.N.C. Apr. 30, 2021); *Vera Bradley Designs, Inc. v. Aixin Li*, No. 20 C 2550, 2021 U.S. Dist. LEXIS 53365, at *4–8, 2021 WL 1088323 (N.D. Ill. Mar. 22, 2021); *Phoenix Process Equip. Co. v. Capital Equip. & Trading Corp.*, No. 3:16-CV-00024-CHB, 2021 U.S. Dist. LEXIS 51651, at *33–34, 2021 WL 1062553 (W.D. Ky. Mar. 19, 2021); *Cunningham v. Concentrix Sols. Corp.*, No. 4:20-CV-661, 2021 U.S. Dist. LEXIS 48667, at *12–13, 2021 WL 982717 (E.D. Tex. Mar. 16, 2021); *Carter v. Swift Transp. Co. of Arizona, LLC*, No. EDCV201383VAPKKX, 2021 U.S. Dist. LEXIS 42395, at *8, 2021 WL 843191 (C.D. Cal. Mar. 5, 2021); *Shayler v. Yacoub*, No. CV 20-01882 RAO, 2020 U.S. Dist. LEXIS 251694, at *4–6, 2020 WL 8812454 (C.D. Cal. Dec. 23, 2020) (citing *A. Farber & Partners, Inc. v. Garber*, 234 F.R.D. 186, 188 (C.D. Cal. 2006)); *Twin Falls NSC, LLC v. S. Idaho Ambulatory Surgery Ctr., LLC*, No. 1:19-CV-00009-DCN, 2020 U.S. Dist. LEXIS 168764, at *29–30, 2020 WL 5523384 (D. Idaho Sept. 14, 2020); *Annie Oakley Enters. Inc. v. Amazon.com, Inc.*, No. 119CV01732JMSMJD, 2020 U.S. Dist. LEXIS 141480, at *2–3, 2020 WL 4571742 (S.D. Ind. Aug. 7, 2020); *Watkins v. Bigwood*, No. 18-CV-63035, 2020 U.S. Dist. LEXIS 163199, at *4–5, 2020 WL 5367325 (S.D. Fla. Sept. 8, 2020); *Carboline Co. v. A-1 Indus. Maint., Inc.*, No. 4:19 CV 1721 CDP, 2020 U.S. Dist. LEXIS 116457, at *5, 2020 WL 3605295 (E.D. Mo. July 2, 2020); *Otto Brands, LLC v. Otto's Express Car Wash, LLC*, No. 3:19CV572/TKW/EMT, 2020 U.S. Dist. LEXIS 185118, at *11–12, 2020 WL 5845739 (N.D. Fla. Feb. 19, 2020); *LADS Network Sols., Inc. v. Agilis Sys., LLC*, No. 4:19-CV-00011-AGF, 2019 U.S. Dist. LEXIS 190781, at *7–9, 2019 WL 5696147 (E.D. Mo. Nov. 4, 2019); *Zurich Am. Ins. Co. v. Hardin*, No. 8:14-CV-775-T-23AAS, 2019 U.S. Dist. LEXIS 117097, at *12–14, 2019 WL 3082608 (M.D. Fla. July 15, 2019); *Atkins v. AT&T Mobility Servs., LLC*, No. 2:18-CV-00599, 2019 U.S. Dist. LEXIS 227963, at *20–26, 2019 WL 8017851 (S.D.W. Va. Apr. 25, 2019); *Holcombe v. Advanced Integration Tech.*, No. 4:17-CV-00522, 2018 U.S. Dist. LEXIS 135493, at *7, 2018 WL 3819974 (E.D. Tex. Aug. 10, 2018); *Halleen v. Belk, Inc.*, No. 4:16-CV-55, 2018 U.S. Dist. LEXIS 131836, at *6–8, 2018 WL 3735579 (E.D. Tex. Aug. 6, 2018); *Coleman v. Lennar Corp.*, No. 18-MC-20182, 2018 U.S. Dist. LEXIS 214354, at *7–8, 2018 WL 3672251 (S.D. Fla. June 14, 2018); *Hayse v. City of Melvindale*, No. CV 17-13294, 2018 U.S. Dist. LEXIS 240302, at *18–19, 2018 WL 11176493 (E.D. Mich. Apr. 10, 2018); *Duracell U.S. Operations, Inc. v. JRS Ventures, Inc.*, No. 17 C 3166, 2018 U.S. Dist. LEXIS 17920, at *13–15, 2018 WL 704686 (N.D. Ill. Feb. 5, 2018); *Wesley Corp. v. Zoom T.V. Prods., LLC*, No. 17-10021, 2018 U.S. Dist. LEXIS 5068, at *9–12, 2018 WL 372700 (E.D. Mich. Jan. 11, 2018); *Springer v. Gen. Atomics Aeronautical Sys.*, No. 16cv2331-BTM(KSC), 2018 U.S. Dist. LEXIS 9032, at *3–5, 2018 WL 490745 (S.D. Cal. Jan. 18, 2018); *Ctr. for Individual Rights v. Chevaldina*, No. 16-20905-Civ-KING/TORRES, 2017 U.S. Dist. LEXIS 195871, at *9–13, 2017 WL 5891679 (S.D. Fla. Nov. 29, 2017); *In re Abilify (Aripiprazole) Prods. Liab. Litig.*, No. 3:16-md-2734, 2017 U.S. Dist. LEXIS 161660, at *17, 2017 WL 4399198 (N.D. Fla. Sept. 29, 2017); *Amerisure Ins. Co. v. Auchter Co.*, No.

Besides violating Texas Rule 193.2(a), boilerplate objections are improper because their lack of specificity obstructs and delays the discovery process by preventing the opposing party from properly evaluating the objections' merits,[89] thereby making it more likely that an unnecessary motion to compel will be filed. The objections lack of specificity also impedes a court's ability to evaluate them in ruling on a motion to compel.[90]

"The use of boilerplate objections is rampant, notwithstanding that there appear to be no published or unpublished decisions that allow or condone boilerplate objections."[91] "They are 'often the result of a local "culture" of protectionist discovery responses, even though such responses are contrary to the decisions of every court to address them.'"[92] So how does a responding party avoid making boilerplate objections and what should a trial court do when faced with them?

3:16-cv-407-J-39JRK, 2017 U.S. Dist. LEXIS 186609, at *6, 2017 WL 3712917 (M.D. Fla. July 7, 2017); *RealPage, Inc. v. Enter. Risk Control, LLC*, No. 4:16-CV-00737, 2017 U.S. Dist. LEXIS 46270, at *8, 2017 WL 1165688 (E.D. Tex. Mar. 29, 2017); *Tadlock v. Arctic Cat Sales, Inc.*, No. 15-766-JJB-EWD, 2017 U.S. Dist. LEXIS 38429, at *22, 2017 WL 1032516 (M.D. La. Mar. 17, 2017); *Arrow Enter. Computing Sols., Inc. v. BlueAlly, LLC*, No. 5:15-CV-00037-FL, 2016 U.S. Dist. LEXIS 107930, at *5, 2016 WL 4287929 (E.D.N.C. Aug. 15, 2016); *Ramos v. Town of East Hartford*, No. 3:16-cv-166 (VLB), 2016 U.S. Dist. LEXIS 174860, at *5, 2016 WL 7340282 (D. Conn. Dec. 19, 2016); *Buskirk v. Wiles*, No. 3:15-03503, 2016 U.S. Dist. LEXIS 168081, at *3–4, 2016 WL 7118288 (S.D.W. Va. Dec. 6, 2016); *KeyCorp v. Holland*, No. 3:16-cv-1948-D, 2016 U.S. Dist. LEXIS 147926, at *33–34, 2016 WL 6277813 (N.D. Tex. Oct. 26, 2016); *Heller v. City of Dall.*, 303 F.R.D. 466, 483–84 (N.D. Tex. 2014); *Enron Corp. Sav. Plan v. Hewitt Assocs., L.L.C.*, 258 F.R.D. 149, 159 (S.D. Tex. 2009).

89 *Cf. TIGI Linea Corp. v. Prof'l Prods. Grp., LLC*, No. 419CV00840RWSKPJ, 2021 U.S. Dist. LEXIS 92071, 2021 WL 1947341 (E.D. Tex. May 14, 2021) ("'Summary objections are rejected because broad-based, non-specific objections are almost impossible to assess on their merits, and fall woefully short of the burden that must be borne by a party making an objection to an interrogatory of [sic] document request.'" (quoting *Young v. Braum's, Inc.*, Nos. 5:19-cv-161, 5:20-cv-178, 5:20-cv-179, 2021 U.S. Dist. LEXIS 75795, at *21, 2021 WL 1413128 (E.D. Tex. Jan. 8, 2021) (cleaned up))); *Miccosukee Tribe of Indians v. Cypress*, No. 12-22439-CIV-COOKE/MCALILEY, 2013 U.S. Dist. LEXIS 189729, at *6, 2013 WL 10740706 (S.D. Fla. June 28, 2013) ("Specificity is required in objections because without it both the requesting party and the Court lacks sufficient information to understand the scope of the objection, and to fairly consider whether the objection has merit."); *DL v. D.C.*, 251 F.R.D. 38, 43 (D.D.C. 2008) (noting that Federal Rule 34(b)(2)(B)'s specificity "requirement enables the requesting party to evaluate and determine whether to challenge the objection raised"); *see Panola Land Buyers Ass'n v. Shuman*, 762 F.2d 1550, 1559 (11th Cir. 1985) (explaining that objections must be "plain enough and specific enough so that the court can understand in what way the discovery is alleged to be objectionable"); *Duracell U.S. Operations, Inc. v. JRS Ventures, Inc.*, No. 17 C 3166, 2018 U.S. Dist. LEXIS 17920, at *13–15, 2018 WL 704686 (N.D. Ill. Feb. 5, 2018) (noting that boilerplate objection result in "the needless imposition of costs on the opposing party").

90 See cases cited in note 89.

91 *In re Haynes*, 577 B.R. 711, 722 (Bankr. E.D. Tenn. 2017); *accord RealPage, Inc. v. Enter. Risk Control, LLC*, No. 4:16-CV-00737, 2017 U.S. Dist. LEXIS 46270, at *8, 2017 WL 1165688 (E.D. Tex. Mar. 29, 2017); *Liguria Foods, Inc. v. Griffith Labs., Inc.*, 320 F.R.D. 168, 184–85 (D. Iowa 2017). See also cases cited in note 88.

92 *Duracell U.S. Operations, Inc. v. JRS Ventures, Inc.*, No. 17 C 3166, 2018 U.S. Dist. LEXIS 17920, at *13–15, 2018 WL 704686 (N.D. Ill. Feb. 5, 2018) (quoting *Liguria Foods, Inc. v. Griffith Labs., Inc.*, 320 F.R.D. 168, 190 (N.D. Iowa 2017)).

A responding party avoids a boilerplate objection by providing a brief explanation for each objection. For example, instead of baldly objecting to—

- a production request as "irrelevant" or "overly broad," the responding party should explain why the request is overly broad or why the requested material is irrelevant (e.g., the request covers too many years or products or facilities other than those at issue in the action);[93]
- an interrogatory as "vague" or "ambiguous," the responding party not only should identify the words or phrases in the interrogatory that are vague or ambiguous, but also should explain why they are such (i.e., why they are reasonably susceptible of more than one meaning and why the responding party cannot use the word's or phrase's ordinary or other meaning in responding to the interrogatory);[94]
- a production request as unduly burdensome or unnecessarily expensive, the responding party should explain the undue burden or unnecessary expense (i.e., identify the approximate number of documents, emails, or locations that will have to be searched or produced or the approximate cost of searching for and producing the materials);[95]

---

93 Of course, in such an instance, the responding party should also agree to produce all responsive documents related to the time period, products, or facilities that it believes are relevant. Tex. R. Civ. P. 193.2(b) ("A party must comply with as much of the request to which the party has made no objection unless it is unreasonable under the circumstances to do so before obtaining a ruling on the objection."); Tex. R. Civ. P. 193 cmt. 2 to 1999 change ("An objection to written discovery does not excuse the responding party from complying with the request to the extent no objection is made. . . . A party who objects to a production of documents from a remote time period should produce documents from a more recent period unless that production would be burdensome and duplicative should the objection be overruled."). See also Chapter 5, section 5-3 (discussing objections generally).

94 *Cf. Samsung Elecs. Am., Inc. v. Chung*, 321 F.R.D. 250, 289 (N.D. Tex. 2017) ("The Court has previously explained that a 'party objecting to discovery as vague or ambiguous has the burden to show such vagueness or ambiguity'; that '[a] party objecting on these grounds must explain the specific and particular way in which a request is vague'; that '[t]he responding party should exercise reason and common sense to attribute ordinary definitions to terms and phrases utilized in interrogatories. If necessary to clarify its answers, the responding party may include any reasonable definition of the term or phrase at issue'; and that, '[i]f a party believes that the request is vague, that party [should] attempt to obtain clarification [by conferring with the requesting party] prior to objecting on this ground.' A vague and ambiguous objection does not justify a complete refusal to respond or answer unless a request is so vague or ambiguous as to be incapable of reasonable interpretation and prohibit a response." (quoting *Heller v. City of Dall.*, 303 F.R.D. 466, 491–92 (N.D. Tex. 2014))). See also Chapter 8, section 8-5:7 (discussing vague-and-ambiguous objections to production requests), and Chapter 9, section 9-5:3.7 (discussing vague-and-ambiguous objections to interrogatories).

95 *See In re Alford Chevrolet-Geo*, 997 S.W.2d 173, 181 (Tex. 1999) (orig. proceeding) ("A party resisting discovery . . . cannot simply make conclusory allegations that the requested discovery is unduly burdensome or unnecessarily harassing. The party must produce some evidence supporting its request for a protective order."). See also Chapter 8, section 8-5-6 (discussing undue-burden-and expense objections to production requests), Chapter 9, section 9-5:3.7 (discussing undue-burden-and expense objections to interrogatories), and

- an interrogatory as unduly cumulative or duplicative, the responding party should identify the other discovery which the interrogatory duplicates.[96]

Texas Rule 193.2(e) dictates how a court should deal with boilerplate objections. Because it provides that "an objection that is obscured by numerous unfounded objections[] is waived unless the court excuses the waiver for good cause shown[,]"[97] a court faced with boilerplate objections to a discovery request generally should (1) deem *all* objections to the request waived (even non-boilerplate and meritorious ones),[98] (2) order the responding party to answer the discovery request with-

---

Chapter 10, section 10-5:8.6 (discussing vague-and-ambiguous objections to requests for admission).

96 *Cf. Alexander v. FBI*, 194 F.R.D. 299, 302 (D.D.C. 2000) (rejecting unreasonably cumulative and duplicative objection because responding party failed to identify duplicative documents already produced). See also Chapter 8, section 8-5:8 (discussing unduly-cumulative-or-duplicative objections to production requests), Chapter 9, section 9-5:3.8 (discussing unduly-cumulative-or-duplicative objections to interrogatories), and Chapter 10, section 10-5:8.7 (discussing unduly-cumulative-or-duplicative objections to requests for admissions).

97 Given that Texas Rule 193.2(d) allows a party to amend a written-discovery response to state an objection not initially made if the objection "either was inapplicable or was unknown after reasonable inquiry[,]" Tex. R. Civ. P. 193.2(d), it is difficult to imagine how a boilerplate objection can be made in good faith.

98 *See, e.g.*, *De Anda v. Jason C. Webster, P.C.*, No. 14-17-00020-CV, 2018 Tex. App. LEXIS 5727, at *20, 2018 WL 3580579 (Tex. App.—Houston [14th Dist.] July 26, 2018, pet. denied) (mem. op.) ("[M]any of Webster's objections were unfounded. We therefore conclude that Webster waived his objections to De Anda's discovery requests." (citing Tex. R. Civ. P. 193.2e))).

Most federal courts strike or overrule boilerplate objections, holding that the responding party has waived them irrespective of whether one of them has merit. As explained by one court: "Failure to state objections specifically in conformity with the [Federal] Rules will be regarded as a waiver of those objections." *Mills v. E. Gulf Coal Preparation Co.*, 259 F.R.D. 118, 132 (S.D.W. Va. 2009); *accord Gaddis v. City of Detroit*, 2:18-CV-13763, 2020 U.S. Dist. LEXIS 76550, at *8, 2020 WL 2085068 (E.D. Mich. Apr. 30, 2020); *Hands on Chiropractic PL v. Progressive Select Ins. Co.*, No. 618CV192ORL37DCI, 2018 U.S. Dist. LEXIS 223752, at *18–19, 2018 WL 6983622 (M.D. Fla. Nov. 20, 2018); *Holcombe v. Advanced Integration Tech.*, No. 4:17-CV-00522, 2018 U.S. Dist. LEXIS 135493, at *9–10, 2018 WL 3819974 (E.D. Tex. Aug. 10, 2018); *Lopez v. Don Herring Ltd.*, 327 F.R.D. 567, 592 (N.D. Tex. 2018); *Halleen v. Belk, Inc.*, No. 4:16-CV-55, 2018 U.S. Dist. LEXIS 131836, at *7–8, 2018 WL 3735579 (E.D. Tex. Aug. 6, 2018); *Liguria Foods, Inc. v. Griffith Labs., Inc.*, 320 F.R.D. 168, 185 (D. Iowa 2017); *Ctr. for Individual Rights v. Chevaldina*, No. 16-20905-Civ-KING/TORRES, 2017 U.S. Dist. LEXIS 195871, at *9–13, 2017 WL 5891679 (S.D. Fla. Nov. 29, 2017); *RealPage, Inc. v. Enter. Risk Control, LLC*, No. 4:16-CV-00737, 2017 U.S. Dist. LEXIS 46270, at *8, 2017 WL 1165688 (E.D. Tex. Mar. 29, 2017); *Tadlock v. Arctic Cat Sales, Inc.*, No. 15-766-JJB-EWD, 2017 U.S. Dist. LEXIS 38429, at *22, 2017 WL 1032516 (M.D. La. Mar. 17, 2017); *KeyCorp v. Holland*, No. 3:16-cv-1948-D, 2016 U.S. Dist. LEXIS 147926, at *33–34, 2016 WL 6277813 (N.D. Tex. Oct. 26, 2016); *Sabol v. Brooks*, 469 F. Supp. 2d 324, 328 (D. Md. 2006); *Terrell v. IRS (In re Terrell)*, 569 B.R. 881, 887–89 (Bankr. W.D. Okla. 2017).

As explained by another federal court, if objections "are not applied with sufficient specificity to enable this Court to evaluate their merits . . . this Court will overrule the objections in their entirety." *DL v. D.C.*, 251 F.R.D. 38, 43 (D.D.C. 2008); *see Springer v. Gen. Atomics Aeronautical Sys.*, No. 16cv2331-BTM(KSC), 2018 U.S. Dist. LEXIS 9032, at *3–5, 2018 WL 490745 (S.D. Cal. Jan. 18, 2018) (overruling boilerplate objections because they "are inadequate and tantamount to not making any objection at all"); *Adelman v. Boy Scouts* out objection, and (3) impose appropriate sanctions under Texas Rule 215.[99] If the responding party has withdrawn the boilerplate objections in response to a motion to compel, the court nonetheless, in ruling on the motion, can impose monetary sanctions against the responding party under Texas Rule 215 to compensate the moving party for its expenses in obtaining the objections' withdrawal and to deter the use of boilerplate objections in the future. As one federal court has explained:

---

of Am., 276 F.R.D. 681, 688 (S.D. Fla. 2011) ("[B]oilerplate objections [are] legally inadequate or meaningless."); *In re Abilify (Aripiprazole) Prods. Liab. Litig.*, No. 3:16-md-2734, 2017 U.S. Dist. LEXIS 161660, at *17, 2017 WL 4399198 (N.D. Fla. Sept. 29, 2017) ("[T]o the extent Plaintiffs challenge the boilerplate objections, Plaintiffs' objection is sustained and the Court will deem the boilerplate objections to be a nullity."); *Nissan N. Am., Inc. v. Johnson Elec. N. Am., Inc.*, No. 09-CV-11783, 2011 U.S. Dist. LEXIS 16006, at *4, 2011 WL 1002835 (E.D. Mich. Feb. 17, 2011) ("Boilerplate or generalized objections are tantamount to no objection at all[.]"). *But see Perez v. U.S.*, No. 13cv1417-WQH-BGS, 2016 U.S. Dist. LEXIS 8993, at *3–7, 2016 WL 304877 (S.D. Cal. Jan. 25, 2016) (rejecting an argument that boilerplate objections are "automatically" waived as a matter of law).

99 *Cf. Lopez v. Don Herring Ltd.*, 327 F.R.D. 567, 581 (N.D. Tex. 2018) ("Serving unsupported and boilerplate or stock objections does not preserve or accomplish anything other than waiver and subjecting the responding party to sanctions."), *quoted with approval in Altima Diagnostic Imaging Sols., Inc. v. The JDIS Grp., LLC*, No. 3:19-CV-2102-M-BK, 2021 U.S. Dist. LEXIS 92957, at *4, 2021 WL 1940206 (N.D. Tex. May 12, 2021), *and MCR Oil Tools, LLC v. Spex Offshore, Ltd.*, No. 3:18-CV-731-X-BK, 2020 U.S. Dist. LEXIS 191138, at *10, 2020 WL 5984424 (N.D. Tex. May 27, 2020); *Mich. Auto. Ins. Placement Facility v. New Grace Rehabiliation Ctr., PPC*, No. 417CV11007TGBDRG, 2019 U.S. Dist. LEXIS 13511, at *10, 2019 WL 355654 (E.D. Mich. Jan. 29, 2019) ("Failure to make properly drawn objections, or reassertion of boilerplate objections, will result in sanctions."); *Hayse v. City of Melvindale*, No. CV 17-13294, 2018 U.S. Dist. LEXIS 240302, at *19, 2018 WL 11176493 (E.D. Mich. Apr. 10, 2018) ("[G]enerally, defendants' reliance on boilerplate objections is improper and could expose them to sanctions."); *Springer v. Gen. Atomics Aeronautical Sys.*, No. 16cv2331-BTM(KSC), 2018 U.S. Dist. LEXIS 9032, at *5, 2018 WL 490745 (S.D. Cal. Jan. 18, 2018) ("If General Atomics continues to include general, boilerplate, unsupported, and/or non-specific objections in its supplemental responses, the Court will overrule the objections and consider imposing monetary sanctions."); *Wesley Corp. v. Zoom T.V. Prods., LLC*, No. 17-10021, 2018 U.S. Dist. LEXIS 5068, at *13, 2018 WL 372700 (E.D. Mich. Jan. 11, 2018) ("The court agrees that in light of Defendants' conduct in discovery, and in light of the need to deter future use of boilerplate objections, a sanction in the form of attorney fees is warranted."); *Kristensen v. Credit Payment Servs.*, No. 2:12-cv-0528-APG-PAL, 2014 U.S. Dist. LEXIS 165489, at *18, 2014 WL 6675748 (D. Nev. Nov. 25, 2014) (imposing monetary sanctions against the defendant for interposing boilerplate discovery objections); *Blemaster v. Sabo*, No. 2:16-cv-04557 JWS, 2017 U.S. Dist. LEXIS 178498, at *13, 2017 WL 4843241 (D. Ariz. Oct. 25, 2017) ("The court finds that the Sabos' boilerplate objections are objectively unreasonable, asserted without a reasonable inquiry into the facts. In light of this discovery violation, the court will order the Sabos' counsel to pay the reasonable attorney's fees and costs that Blemaster incurred in challenging these objections."); *Marine Lumber Co. v. Precision Moving & Storage, Inc.*, No. 16-00365 LEK-RLP, 2017 U.S. Dist. LEXIS 130944, at *14–15, 2017 WL 3568668 (D. Hawaii Aug. 16, 2017) (imposing monetary sanctions for use of boilerplate discovery objections); *Moser v. Holland*, No. 2:14-cv-02188-KJM-AC, 2016 U.S. Dist. LEXIS 13797, at *10–11, 2017 WL 462515 (E.D. Cal. Feb. 3, 2016) (same); *St. Paul Reinsurance Co. v. Commercial Fin. Corp.*, 198 F.R.D. 508, 515–18 (N.D. Iowa 2000) (same). See Chapter 14, section 14-3 for a discussion of discovery sanctions.

> I realize my judicial colleagues, especially state trial court judges, are overwhelmed with cases, deluged with discovery matters, likely sick and tired of them, and lack the resources needed to deal with them in as timely a manner as they aspire to. In my view, the imposition of increasingly severe sanctions will help solve the problems. Lawyers are advocates and trained to push the envelope—rightly so. Judges need to push back, get our judicial heads out of the sand, stop turning a blind eye to the "boilerplate" discovery culture and do our part to solve this cultural discovery "boilerplate" plague. Like Chief Justice Ketchum [of the West Virginia Supreme Court], I am convinced that "[s]tiff sanctions by judges for each violation would have a dramatic effect on these unauthorized boilerplate objections. The word would spread quickly, and the practice would suddenly stop."[100]

5-3:4 Disproportionality Objections Are Proper

The 2015 amendments to Federal Rule 26, the Rule governing discovery's scope, modified the definition of permissible discovery by expressly incorporating into Federal Rule 26(b)(1) the concept of proportionality that previously was set forth in Federal Rule 25(b)(2)(C)(iii), the Rule governing protective orders.[101] Thus, Federal Rule 26(b)(1) now provides:

> Unless otherwise limited by court order, the scope of discovery is as follows: Parties may obtain discovery regarding any nonprivileged matter that is relevant to any party's claim or defense and proportional to the needs of the case, considering the importance of the issues at stake in the action, the amount in controversy, the parties' relative access to relevant information, the parties' resources, the importance of the discovery in resolving the issues, and whether the burden or expense of the proposed discovery outweighs its likely benefit. Information within this scope of discovery need not be admissible in evidence to be discoverable.[102]

Under Federal Rule 26(b)(1), challenged discovery is first examined for relevancy and, if it seeks materials or information relevant to a party's claim or defense, it is then weighed against the six proportionality factors set forth in the Rule (i.e., "the

---

100 *Liguria Foods, Inc. v. Griffith Labs., Inc.*, 320 F.R.D. 168, 191 (D. Iowa 2017) (quoting Chief Justice Menis E. Ketchum, II, *Impeding Discovery: Eliminating Worthless Interrogatory Instructions and Objections*, 2012 W. Va. L. Rev. 18, 19 (2012)); *accord Wesley Corp. v. Zoom T.V. Prods., LLC*, No. 17-10021, 2018 U.S. Dist. LEXIS 5068, at *9–12, 2018 WL 372700 (E.D. Mich. Jan. 11, 2018) ("Courts and commentators have called on courts to deter boilerplate objections by imposing sanctions with their inherent power and under Federal Rule of Civil Procedure 26.").

101 Fed. R. Civ. P. 26, Advisory Committee Note to the 2015 Amend.; Fed. R. Civ. P. 26(b)(1). *See also O'Garra v. Northwell Health Sys. Inc.*, No. CV 16-2191 (DRH) (AYS), 2018 U.S. Dist. LEXIS 9746, at *5–6 (E.D.N.Y. Jan. 22, 2018) (explaining the 2015 amendments to Federal Rule 26(b)(1)); *Reibert v. CSAA Fire & Cas. Ins. Co.*, No. 17-CV-350-CVE-JFJ, 2018 U.S. Dist. LEXIS 860, at *10–11 & n.4 (N.D. Okla. Jan. 3, 2018) (same); *Small v. Welldyne, Inc.*, No. 5:16-CV-00062-BO, 2017 U.S. Dist. LEXIS 88210, at *3–4, 2017 WL 2484181 (E.D.N.C. June 8, 2017) (same).

102 Fed. R. Civ. P. 26(b)(1).

importance of the issues at stake in the action, the amount in controversy, the parties' relative access to relevant information, the parties' resources, the importance of the discovery in resolving the issues, and whether the burden or expense of the proposed discovery outweighs its likely benefit").[103] If the requested material or information is not relevant to a party's claim or defense, it is not discoverable, regardless of its proportionality. As explained by one federal court: "'Proportionality focuses on the marginal utility of the discovery sought.' Thus, [p]roportionality and relevance are 'conjoined' concepts; the greater the relevance of the information in issue, the less likely its discovery will be found to be disproportionate, and vice versa."[104]

---

[103] Fed. R. Civ. P. 26(b)(1); *Dixon v. Spurlin*, No. 1:18-CV-00133, 2020 U.S. Dist. LEXIS 212909, at *21–22, 2020 WL 6707325 (W.D. La. Nov. 13, 2020); *Ayo v. Dunn*, No. CV 17-526-SDD-EWD, 2018 WL 4896723 (M.D. La. Oct. 9, 2018); *Dumas v. O'Reilly Auto. Stores, Inc.*, No. 16-262-BAJ-EWD, 2017 U.S. Dist. LEXIS 91130, at *4–6, 2017 WL 2573956 (W.D. La. June 14, 2017); *Small v. Welldyne, Inc.*, No. 5:16-CV-00062-BO, 2017 U.S. Dist. LEXIS 88210, at *3–4, 2017 WL 2484181 (E.D.N.C. June 8, 2017); *cf. TIGI Linea Corp. v. Pro. Prods. Grp., LLC*, No. 419CV00840RWSKPJ, 2021 U.S. Dist. LEXIS 92071, at *8, 2021 WL 1947341 (E.D. Tex. May 14, 2021) ("Under [Federal] Rule 26(b)(1), discoverable matter must be both relevant and proportional to the needs of the case—which are related but distinct requirements." (quoting *Samsung Elecs. Am., Inc. v. Chung*, 321 F.R.D. 250, 279 (N.D. Tex. 2017))); *Dancy v. Lanxess Corp.*, No. 19-CV-02690-SHL-TMP, 2020 WL 5262311 (W.D. Tenn. Sept. 3, 2020) ("The party seeking discovery is obligated to demonstrate relevance. Upon a showing of relevance, the burden shifts to the party opposing discovery to show, with specificity, why the requested discovery is not proportional to the needs of the case.") (citations omitted); *Motorola Sols., Inc. v. Hytera Commc'n Corp.*, No. 17 C 1973, 2019 U.S. Dist. LEXIS 110281, at *9 n.2, 2019 WL 2774126 (N.D. Ill. July 2, 2019) ("Of course, the threshold inquiry is always relevancy. If the evidence is not relevant it is not discoverable."); *Bonumose Biochem, LLC v. Yi-Heng Zhang*, No. 3:17-cv-00033, 2018 U.S. Dist. LEXIS 231074, at *6, 2018 WL 10068639 (W.D. Va. Sep. 10, 2018) ("[T]he party asserting that the information requested is not relevant, and, therefore, not discoverable, bears the burden of establishing that the information is not relevant." (quoting *Kidwiler v. Progressive Paloverde Ins. Co.*, 192 F.R.D. 193, 199 (N.D. W. Va. 2000))); *In re State Farm Lloyds*, 520 S.W.3d 595, 614 (Tex. 2017) (orig. proceeding) (stating that the 2015 amendment to Federal Rule 26 "is directed to changing the existing 'mindset' that relevance is enough, restoring proportionality as the 'collective responsibility' of the parties and the court") (footnotes omitted) (citations omitted).

[104] *Royal Park Invs. v. Deutsche Bank Nat'l Tr. Co.*, No. 14-CV-04394(AJN)(BCM), 2018 U.S. Dist. LEXIS 24417, at *23 (S.D.N.Y. Feb. 9, 2018) (quoting *Vaigasi v. Solow Mgmt. Corp.*, No. 11 Civ. 5088 (RMB) (HBP), 2016 U.S. Dist. LEXIS 18460, at *43 (S.D.N.Y. Feb. 16, 2016)); *accord ValveTech, Inc. v. Aerojet Rocketdyne, Inc.*, No. 17-CV-6788-FPG-MJP, 2021 U.S. Dist. LEXIS 30219, at *3, 2021 WL 630910 (W.D.N.Y. Feb. 18, 2021); *B.T. by & through Jackson v. Battle*, 1:18-CV-00919-JPB, 2020 U.S. Dist. LEXIS 244997, at *2, 2020 WL 7864336 (N.D. Ga. Dec. 31, 2020); *Purugganan v. AFC Franchising, LLC*, No. 3:20-CV-00360 (KAD), 2020 U.S. Dist. LEXIS 147827, at *3, 2020 WL 4818362 (D. Conn. Aug. 17, 2020); *Runton v. Brookdale Senior Living, Inc.*, No. 17-60664-CIV, 2018 U.S. Dist. LEXIS 31375, at *5, 2018 WL 1083493 (S.D. Fla. Feb. 27, 2018); Hon. Elizabeth D. Laporte & Jonathan M. Redgrave, *A Practical Guide to Achieving Proportionality under New Federal Rule of Procedure 26*, 9 Fed. Ct. L. Rev. 19, 53 (Fall 2015) ("[T]he application of the concept of proportionality often turns on how 'central' (or relevant) the proposed discovery may be to overcome any number of objections that are associated with the discovery at issue.").

In the "old days" (i.e., before the Federal Rule 26(b)(1)'s amendment in 2015), a responding party in a federal case, who believed that discovery was disproportionate to the case's needs, would either object to the discovery as unduly burdensome and/or unnecessarily expensive or file a motion for protective order on those bases. After Federal Rule 26(b)(1)'s amendment, responding parties in federal cases began interposing "proportionality" objections in their discovery responses.[105]

Although the Texas discovery rule defining discovery's scope, Texas Rule 192.3(a),[106] has not been amended to include "proportionality," the Texas Supreme Court, relying on Texas Rules 194.2 and 196.4, has made clear that "all discovery is subject to the proportionality overlay. . . ."[107] It also has made clear that parties can object to discovery requests as disproportionate to the case's needs,[108] and identified

---

105 *E.g., Stancu v. Hyatt Corp./Hyatt Regency*, Nos. 3:17-cv-675-L-BN, 3:17-cv-2918-L, 2018 U.S. Dist. LEXIS 23981, at *12–13, 2018 WL 888909 (N.D. Tex. Feb. 14, 2018) (production requests); *Levin v. Johnson & Johnson*, No. CV 16-6631 (JFB)(AYS), 2017 U.S. Dist. LEXIS 192090, at *8–15, 2017 WL 5592684 (E.D.N.Y. Nov. 20, 2017) (interrogatories); *Small v. WellDyne, Inc.*, No. 5:16-CV-00062-BO, 2017 U.S. Dist. LEXIS 88210, at *3–4, 2017 WL 2484181 (E.D.N.C. June 8, 2017) ("WellDyne claims, as a general matter, that the Estate's discovery requests are not proportional to the needs of the case."); *RealPage, Inc. v. Enter. Risk Control, LLC*, No. 4:16-CV-00737, 2017 U.S. Dist. LEXIS 46270, at *8, 2017 WL 1165688 (E.D. Tex. Mar. 29, 2017) (production requests).

106 Texas Rule 192.3(a) provides:

> In general, a party may obtain discovery regarding any matter that is not privileged and is relevant to the subject matter of the pending action, whether it relates to the claim or defense of the party seeking discovery or the claim or defense of any other party. It is not a ground for objection that the information sought will be inadmissible at trial if the information sought appears reasonably calculated to lead to the discovery of admissible evidence.

Tex. R. Civ. P. 192.3(a). This rule is modeled after an earlier version of Federal Rule 26(b)(1). See Chapter 4, section 4-3:1 (discussing the origin of Texas Rule 192.3(a), as well as discovery's scope under it generally).

107 *In re State Farm Lloyds*, 520 S.W.3d 595, 599 (Tex. 2017) (orig. proceeding); *accord In re Shipman*, 540 S.W.3d 562, 569–70 (Tex. 2018) (orig. proceeding) (per curiam); *In re Wilcox*, No. 09-20-00271-CV, 2021 Tex. App. LEXIS 2042, at *8, 2021 WL 1031141 (Tex. App.—Beaumont Mar. 18, 2021, orig. proceeding) (per curiam) (mem. op.); *In re State Farm Lloyds*, No. 02-20-00163-CV, 2020 Tex. App. LEXIS 7207, at *7 2020 WL 5242414 (Tex. App.—Fort Worth Sept. 3, 2020, orig. proceeding) (mem. op.); *In re Preventative Pest Control Hous., LLC*, 580 S.W.3d 455, 460 (Tex. App.—Houston [14th Dist.] 2019, orig. proceeding); *see In re USAA Gen. Indem. Co.*, 624 S.W.3d 782, 788 (Tex. 2021) ("We have described [Texas] Rule 192.4 as encompassing a 'proportionality standard that requires' a case-by-case balancing of jurisprudential considerations.'" (quoting *In re K & L Auto Crushers*, 627 S.W.3d 239, 253 (Tex. 2021) (orig. proceeding), and *In re State Farm Lloyds*, 520 S.W.3d 595, 599 (Tex. 2017) (orig. proceeding))); *see also In re Muller*, 612 S.W.3d 701, 706 (Tex. App.—Amarillo 2020, orig. proceeding) (citing *In re State Farm Lloyds*, 520 S.W.3d 595, 599 (Tex. 2017) (orig. proceeding), as support for the proposition that "the trial court could have reasonably determined that the requested discovery [at issue in the case] was not proportional to the needs of the case or that the burden or expense of production outweigh[ed] its likely benefit").

108 *In re State Farm Lloyds*, 520 S.W.3d 595, 614 (Tex. 2017) (orig. proceeding) ("The opposing party must object and support proportionality complaints with evidence if the parties cannot resolve a discovery dispute without court intervention[.]" (footnotes omitted))).

the following proportionality factors: (1) "the likely benefit of the requested discovery"; (2) "the needs of the case"; (3) "the amount in controversy"; (4) "the parties' resources"; (5) "the importance of the issues at stake in the litigation"; (6) "the importance of the proposed discovery in resolving the litigation"; and (7) "any other articulable factor bearing on proportionality."[109]

Because the burden and expense of responding to a discovery request necessarily are part of the proportionality analysis and because it generally is easier to object to discovery requests than to move for protection with respect to them, Texas practitioners, in appropriate circumstances, can, and should, interpose proportionality objections to discovery requests. In doing so, however, they should keep in mind that "[p]roportionality determinations are made on a case-by-case basis,"[110] and as with other discovery objections: (1) a proportionality objection must be specific (i.e., boilerplate proportionality objections are improper);[111] and (2) the objecting party has the

---

Although *State Farm Lloyds* involved a dispute over the form in which electronically-stored information must be produced, the Texas Supreme Court's proportionality was analysis not limited only to electronic discovery. *See In re State Farm Lloyds,* 520 S.W.3d 595, 599, 604–15 (Tex. 2017) (orig. proceeding).

The propriety of proportionality objections under the Texas discovery rules also is supported by Texas Rule 191.3(c)(4), which provides: "The signature of an attorney or party on a discovery request, notice, response, or objection constitutes a certification that to the best of the signer's knowledge, information, and belief, formed after a reasonable inquiry, the request, notice, response, or objection: . . . (4) is not unreasonable or unduly burdensome or expensive, given the needs of the case, the discovery already had in the case, the amount in controversy, and the importance of the issues at stake in the litigation."

109 *In re State Farm Lloyds*, 520 S.W.3d 595, 607–12 (Tex. 2017) (orig. proceeding); *see In re K & L Auto Crushers, LLC*, 627 S.W.3d 239m 252 (Tex. 2021) (orig. proceeding) (stating that "proportionality requires a fact-intensive, complex balancing of many relevant factors, particularly where discovery is sought from non-parties whom trial courts 'must' protect from undue burden or expense in answering subpoenas" (quoting Tex. R. Civ. P. 176.7)).

110 *In re USAA Gen. Indem. Co.*, 624 S.W.3d 782, 792 (Tex. 2021).

111 *E.g., Generation Brands, LLC v. Decor Selections, LLC,* No. 19 C 6185, 2021 U.S. Dist. LEXIS 37599, at *6–7, 2021 WL 780485 (N.D. Ill. Mar. 1, 2021) ("Apart from the fact that the concept of proportionality is not particularly new, like other concepts, it is not self-defining; it requires a common sense and experiential assessment. . . . In short, simply choosing to contend that something is not proportional is not enough. After all, here, as in all contexts, merely saying so doesn't make it so." (citing cases) (footnote omitted)); *Smash Tech., LLC v. Smash Sols., LLC,* 335 F.R.D. 438, 446 (D. Utah 2020) overuling boilerplate proportionality objection); *Hammler v. Franklin,* No. CV 18-5525-JGB (SP), 2020 U.S. Dist. LEXIS 245548, at *7, 2020 WL 7711832 (C.D. Cal. Dec. 11, 2020) (overruling "defendant's boilerplate relevance, overbreadth, and proportionality objections"); *Tim Long Plumbing, Inc. v. Kinsale Ins. Co.*, No. 4:20-CV-00042, 2020 U.S. Dist. LEXIS 208897, at *9, 2020 WL 6559869 (E.D. Tex. Nov. 9, 2020) ("A party may not 'refuse discovery simply by making a boilerplate objection that is not proportional.'" (quoting Fed. R. Civ. P. 26, Advisory Committee Notes to 2015 Amend.)); *Jenkins v. Miller,* No. 2:12-CV-184, 2019 U.S. Dist. LEXIS 189290, at *7, 2019 WL 5561387 (D. Vt. Oct. 29, 2019) ("Formulaic 'boilerplate' language in a discovery objection on proportionality grounds cannot overcome the broad scope of discovery under [Federal] Rule 26."); *Off Lease Only, Inc. v. Lakeland Motors, LLC,* No. 618CV1555ORL37DCI, 2019 U.S. Dist. LEXIS 182075, at *3, 2019 WL 5265219 (M.D. Fla. June 5, 2019) ("With respect to Plaintiff's objection that the request is not proportionate to the needs of the

burden to prove disproportionality,[112] but the requesting party, "to prevail on a motion to compel, may well need to make its own showing of many or all of the proportionality factors, . . . in opposition to the resisting party's showing."[113]

---

case, that objection is boilerplate and, as a result, is waived."); *Bragel Int'l, Inc. v. Kohl's Dep't Stores*, No. CV 17-7414 RGK (SSX), 2018 U.S. Dist. LEXIS 224955, at *16, 2018 WL 7890682 (C.D. Cal. Nov. 14, 2018) ("In keeping with this requirement, following the 2015 amendments to [Federal] Rule 26, courts have also rejected boilerplate assertions that a discovery request is 'disproportionate' and require that 'objections based on proportionality' be 'explained with specificity.'" (quoting *Polycarpe v. Seterus, Inc.*, No: 6:16–cv–1606–Orl–37TBS, 2017 U.S. Dist. LEXIS 77808, at *10, 2017 WL 2257571 (M.D. Fla. May 23, 2017))); *Holcombe v. Advanced Integration Tech.*, No. 4:17-CV-00522, 2018 U.S. Dist. LEXIS 135493, at *8, 2018 WL 3819974 (E.D. Tex. Aug. 10, 2018) ("A party may not 'refuse discovery simply by making a boilerplate objection that it is not proportional.'" (quoting Fed. R. Civ. P. 26, Advisory Committee Notes to 2015 Amend.))); *Small v. WellDyne, Inc.*, No. 5:16-CV-00062-BO, 2017 U.S. Dist. LEXIS 88210, at *3–4, 2017 WL 2484181 (E.D.N.C. June 8, 2017) ("WellDyne claims, as a general matter, that the Estate's discovery requests are not proportional to the needs of the case. But it does not provide any support for this assertion. Although the 2015 Amendments to the [Federal] Civil Rules were enacted to bring greater attention to the importance of proportionality in the discovery process, they do 'not . . . permit the opposing party to refuse discovery simply by making a boilerplate objection that it is not proportional.' A party raising a proportionality objection must include specific details in its objection that explain why the request is improper." (quoting Fed. R. Civ. P. 26, Advisory Committee Notes to 2015 Amend.)); *First Am. Bankcard, Inc. v. Smart Bus. Tech., Inc.*, No. CV 15-638, 2017 U.S. Dist. LEXIS 79508, at *3, 2017 WL 2267149 (E.D. La. May 24, 2017) (rejecting disproportionality objection because the "defendant has offered nothing more than a boilerplate proportionality objection, without providing any information concerning burden or expense that the court would expect to be within defendant's own knowledge"); *RealPage, Inc. v. Enter. Risk Control, LLC*, No. 4:16-CV-00737, 2017 U.S. Dist. LEXIS 46270, at *8, 2017 WL 1165688 (E.D. Tex. Mar. 29, 2017) (same); *see In re State Farm Lloyds*, 520 S.W.3d 595, 614 (Tex. 2017) (orig. proceeding) (noting that the "2015 amendments to the [F]ederal [R]ules . . . do not permit the opposing party to rely on boilerplate objections of disproportionality").

112 *In re USAA Gen. Indem. Co.*, 624 S.W.3d 782, 792 (Tex. 2021) ("Parties 'must "support [such] proportionality complaints with evidence"' and may not rely on conclusory allegations." (quoting *In re K & L Auto Crushers, LLC*, 627 S.W.3d 239, 253 (Tex. 2021) (orig. proceeding))); *cf.* Fed. R. Civ. P. 26, Advisory Committee Note to 2015 Amend. ("Restoring the proportionality calculation to [Federal] Rule 26(b)(1) does not . . . place on the party seeking discovery the burden of addressing all proportionality considerations."); *Seastrunk v. Entegris, Inc.*, No. 3:16-cv-2795-L, 2017 U.S. Dist. LEXIS 206901, at *17–18, 2017 WL 6406627 (N.D. Tex. Dec. 15, 2017) ("But a party seeking to resist discovery on these grounds still bears the burden of making a specific objection and showing that any discovery request that is relevant to any party's claim or defense fails the proportionality calculation mandated by [Federal] Rule 26(b) by coming forward with specific information to address—insofar as that information is available to it—the importance of the issues at stake in the action, the amount in controversy, the parties' relative access to relevant information, the parties' resources, the importance of the discovery in resolving the issues, and whether the burden or expense of the proposed discovery outweighs its likely benefit."); *Small v. Welldyne, Inc.*, No. 5:16-CV-00062-BO, 2017 U.S. Dist. LEXIS 88210, at *3–4, 2017 WL 2484181 (E.D.N.C. June 8, 2017) (same).

113 *Stancu v. Hyatt Corp./Hyatt Regency*, No. 3:17-cv-675-L-BN, 2018 U.S. Dist. LEXIS 23981, at *11, 2018 WL 888909 (N.D. Tex. Feb. 14, 2018).

5-4 Privilege Objections and Assertions

5-4:1 In General

Discovery is not permitted as to privileged matters.[114] The reference in the discovery rules to privilege is to evidentiary privilege. A privilege's scope during the discovery stage is the same as its scope at trial.

Privilege, however, is not a proper objection to a written-discovery request. Texas Rule 193.2(f) provides that "[a] party should *not* object to a request for written discovery on the grounds that it calls for production of material that is privileged but should instead comply with [Texas] Rule 193.3."[115] Texas Rule 193.3(a), in turn, requires a responding party, who withholds privileged information or material, to make a withholding statement (1) advising that information or material "responsive to the request or required disclosure" is being withheld as privileged, (2) identifying the specific privilege(s) asserted, and (3) identifying the individual requests or required disclosures to which the withheld information or material relates.[116] Texas Rule 193.3 "governs

---

[114] Tex. R. Civ. P. 192.3(a) ("In general, a party may obtain discovery regarding *any matter that is not privileged* and is relevant to the subject matter of the pending action, whether it relates to the claim or defense of the party seeking discovery or the claim or defense of any other party." (emphasis added)).

[115] Tex. R. Civ. P. 193.2(f) (emphasis added); *accord In re WHC, LLC*, 570 S.W.3d 349, 353 (Tex. App.—El Paso 2018, orig. proceeding) (citing Texas Rule 193.2(f) for the proposition that "a party should not object to a written request for discovery on the grounds that it calls for production of privileged materials or information but should instead comply with [Texas] Rule 193.3"); *De Anda v. Jason C. Webster, P.C.*, No. 14-17-00020-CV, 2018 WL 3580579, at *7 (Tex. App.—Houston [14th Dist.] July 26, 2018, pet. denied) (mem. op.) (citing Texas Rule 193.2(f) for the proposition that "the rules prohibit objections based on privilege"); *In re Graco Children's Prods., Inc.*, 173 S.W.3d 600, 605 (Tex. App.—Corpus Christi 2005, orig. proceeding) ("[N]o objection needs to be made to preserve a privilege[.]"); *In re Christus Health Se. Tex.*, 167 S.W.3d 596, 599 (Tex. App.—Beaumont 2005, orig. proceeding) (same); *In re Anderson*, 163 S.W.3d 136, 140 (Tex. App.—San Antonio 2005, orig. proceeding) (same); *In re Shipmon*, 68 S.W.3d 815, 822 (Tex. App.—Amarillo 2001, orig. proceeding) (same); *In re Monsanto Co.*, 998 S.W.2d 917, 924 (Tex. App.—Waco 1999, orig. proceeding) (same). Nor should a party seek a protective order with respect to privileged material. *In re Shipmon*, 68 S.W.3d 815, 822 (Tex. App.—Amarillo 2001, orig. proceeding).

[116] Tex. R. Civ. P. 193.3(a)(1)-(3); *see* Tex. R. Civ. P. 193 cmt. 3 to 1999 change (noting that withholding statements "should not be made prophylactically, but only when specific information and materials have been withheld"). Texas Rule 193.3(a)'s language regarding required disclosures was added as part of the 2021 amendments that took effect on January 1, 2021. Before those amendments took effect, several courts construed the Rule's requirements in relation to discovery requests. *See Marteny v. Coon*, No. 09-19-00019-CV, 2020 Tex. App. LEXIS 7702, at *17, 2020 WL 5666567 (Tex. App.—Beaumont Sept. 24, 2020, orig. proceeding) (mem. op.) (Texas "Rule 193.3 provides that a party claiming privilege may withhold privileged material but '*must* state' in its response or in a separate document that: '(1) information or material responsive to the request has been withheld, (2) the request to which the information or material relates, and (3) the privilege or privileges asserted.'" (quoting Tex. R. Civ. P. 193.3(a))); *In re Atl. Sounding Co.*, No. 14-18-00523-CV, 2018 Tex. App. LEXIS 2492, at *12, 2018 WL 4116837 (Tex. App.—Houston [14th Dist.] Aug. 28, 2018, orig. proceeding) (mem. op.) (quoting the withholding standards in former Texas Rule 193.3(a)); *In re Brookfield Infrastructure Grp., LLC*, No. 13-17-00486-CV, 2018 Tex. App. LEXIS 2492, at *26, 2018 WL 1725467 (Tex. App.—Corpus Christi Apr. 9, 2018, orig. proceeding) (mem.

the presentation of all privileges[,] including work product."[117] The withholding statement required under Texas Rule 193.3 may be in the original discovery "response (or an amended or supplemented response) or in a separate document[.]"[118]

A failure to follow Texas Rule 193.3's procedure, however, does not waive privilege.[119] Rather, a privilege objection is sufficient to preserve the privilege claim if the "error" is not pointed out.[120] But once the error is pointed out, the responding party must assert privilege in accordance with Rule 193.3 or waive it.[121]

Significantly, a withholding statement is required only when the responding party is answering the discovery request, in whole or in part. If an objection is interposed to the entire request (e.g., the request is overly broad, unduly burdensome, vague, ambiguous, or unreasonably cumulative or duplicative of other discovery) and the responding party is refusing to comply with ***any*** part of it, a withholding statement is unnecessary.[122] Similarly, if the responding party objects only to part of the request,

---

op.) ("If a party chooses to withhold, then that party must disclose that responsive material has been withheld, identify the requests to which the material is responsive, and identify the privilege or privileges asserted."); ***In re York Risk Servs. Grp., Inc.***, No. 12-17-00210-CV, 2017 Tex. App. LEXIS 10942, at *10, 2017 WL 5622951 (Tex. App.—Tyler Nov. 22, 2017, orig. proceeding) (mem. op.) ("The party [asserting privilege] must state: (1) that information or material responsive to the request has been withheld, (2) the request to which the information or material relates, and (3) the privilege or privileges asserted."); ***In re Sw. Airlines Co.***, No. 02-12-00179-CV, 2012 Tex. App. LEXIS 5613, at *6–7, 2012 WL 2864507 (Tex. App.—Fort Worth July 12, 2012, orig. proceeding) (mem. op.) (Texas "Rule 193.3 requires that a party who claims that material or information responsive to written discovery is privileged state in the response to discovery or in a separate document: (1) that information or material responsive to the request has been withheld; (2) the request to which the information or material relates; and (3) the privilege or privileges asserted."); ***In re Anderson***, 163 S.W.3d 136, 140 (Tex. App.—San Antonio 2005, orig. proceeding) (same).

117 Tex. R. Civ. P. 193 cmt. 3 to 1999 change.

118 Tex. R. Civ. P. 193.3(a).

119 Tex. R. Civ. P. 193.2(f).

120 Tex. R. Civ. P. 193.2(f); ***see In re Learjet Inc.***, 59 S.W.3d 842, 846 (Tex. App.—Texarkana 2001, orig. proceeding) (holding that a failure to follow Texas Rule 193.3's procedure did not waive privilege because the objection was made before the party produced the documents and at a time when the trial court could rule on the privilege assertion); ***In re Graco Children's Prods., Inc.***, 173 S.W.3d 600, 604 (Tex. App.—Corpus Christi 2005, orig. proceeding) ("The rules specifically instruct counsel not to object to written discovery based on privileges. Nevertheless, counsel for Relator made such an objection. Although the objection was inappropriate, the rules specify that an objection to written discovery based on privilege will not waive a privilege, as long as the party complies with [Texas R]ule 193.3(a)."); ***In re Monsanto Co.***, 998 S.W.2d 917, 924 n.5 (Tex. App.—Waco 1999, orig. proceeding) ("[A]n objection is apparently sufficient to preserve the claim of privilege if the 'error' is not pointed out.").

121 Tex. R. Civ. P. 193.2(f); ***see In re Univ. of Tex. Health Ctr.***, 33 S.W.3d 822, 826 (Tex. 2000) (orig. proceeding) ("[T]he Health Center's objections and motions made it clear that documents would not be produced and the basis for the objections, and thus, the Health Center did not waive any privileges under [Texas] Rule 193."); ***In re Monsanto Co.***, 998 S.W.2d 917, 924 n.5 (Tex. App.—Waco 1999, orig. proceeding) ("Once the error is pointed out, the objecting party must assert the privilege in compliance with [Texas] Rule 193.3.").

122 ***In re Lincoln Elec. Co.***, 91 S.W.3d 432, 437 (Tex. App.—Beaumont 2007, orig. proceeding) ("In keeping with the overall spirit of non-waiver apparent in the applicable discovery rules set out above, however, we prefer to emphasize the words 'as required by these rules . . .,'

it must provide a withholding statement only for that portion of the request for which it is complying. If the trial court later overrules the objection and orders a response, the responding party, in connection with its response, must make a withholding statement for any responsive information or material withheld as privileged.[123]

A failure to assert a privilege with respect to responsive information or material within the time allowed for the response should result in the privilege's waiver unless the responding party establishes that there was good cause for the failure under Texas Rule 193.2(e) or the objection was either inapplicable or unknown after reasonable inquiry when the response was served under Texas Rule 193.2(d).[124]

---

which, we believe, permits a responding party the opportunity to make 'objections' to such things as vagueness, overbreadth, relevance, etc., under [Texas] Rule 193.2, have these 'objections' ruled upon, and then make any assertions of privilege under [Texas] Rule 193.3 at a later time. Indeed, an 'objection' to the scope of discovery would be governed by [Texas] Rule 192.3, entitled 'Scope of Discovery,' and explicitly excludes irrelevant and privileged matters.")) (citations omitted).

[123] *See* Tex. R. Civ. P. 193 cmt. 2 to 1999 change; Tex. R. Civ. P. 193.3(a) (allowing a withholding statement with an amended or a supplemental response).

[124] *E.g.*, Tex. R. Civ. P. 196.2(b) (providing that a response to a production request "must state objections and assert privileges as required by these rules"), 197.2(b) (providing that responses to interrogatories "must include the party's answers to the interrogatories and may include objections and assertions of privilege as required under these rules"), 198.2(b) ("Unless the responding party states an objection or asserts a privilege, the responding party must specifically admit or deny the request or explain in detail the reasons that the responding party cannot admit or deny the request."); *see Izen v. Sjostrom*, No. 14-06-00142-CV, 2007 Tex. App. LEXIS 2586, at *5–6 (Tex. App.—Houston [14th Dist.] Apr. 3, 2007, no pet.) (mem. op.) ("A party has 30 days to respond to a request for production and an interrogatory request. A party may respond to a discovery request by providing the information, objecting to the request, or asserting a privilege.") (citations omitted); *In re Anderson*, 163 S.W.3d 136, 142 (Tex. App.—San Antonio 2005, orig. proceeding) ("Because the City failed to assert its privilege in accordance with [Texas R]ule 193.3(a), the trial court erred in denying Anderson's motion to compel[.]"); *Valdez v. Progressive Cnty. Mut. Ins. Co.*, No. 04-11-00254-CV, 2011 Tex. App. LEXIS 9773, at *11–12 (Tex. App.—San Antonio Dec. 14, 2011, no pet.) (mem. op.) ("We hold that even if Valdez had a valid Fifth Amendment or other constitutional privilege to refuse production of his tax returns, he waived these rights by failing to timely object in writing to the discovery request on this basis.").

In *In re Graco Children's Prods., Inc.*, 173 S.W.3d 600, 605 (Tex. App.—Corpus Christi 2005, orig. proceeding), the court, in *dicta*, noted that "[a]lthough the time limit for objecting to written discovery is 30 days from the date of service, no objection needs to be made to preserve a privilege and the rules set no time-limit for asserting a privilege." Several courts, based on this *dictum*, have held that the discovery rules set no time limit for asserting a privilege. *E.g.*, *In re Park Cities Bank*, 409 S.W.3d 859, 870 (Tex. App.—Tyler 2013, orig. proceeding); *In re Williams*, No. 10-08-000364-CV, 2009 Tex. App. LEXIS 1561, at *7 (Tex. App.—Waco Mar. 4, 2009, orig. proceeding) (mem. op.).

Graco and its progeny, however, are wrong. Although Texas Rule 193.3 does not set forth a time limit for asserting privilege, the rules relating to production requests, interrogatories, and requests for admissions make clear that responses must include objections and privilege assertions. *See* Tex. R. Civ. P. 196.2(b) (providing that a response to a production request "must state objections and assert privileges as required by these rules"), 197.2(b) (providing that responses to interrogatories "must include the party's answers to the interrogatories and may include objections and assertions of privilege as required under these rules"), 198.2(b) (providing that "[u]nless the responding party states an objection

After receiving the withholding statement, a requesting party desiring to pursue information or documents to which a privilege has been claimed "may serve a written request that the withholding party identify the information and material withheld."[125] The responding party, within fifteen days after receiving the request, must serve a response—commonly called a privilege log—that "(1) describes the information or materials withheld that, without revealing the privileged information itself or otherwise waiving the privilege, enables other parties to assess the applicability of the privilege, and (2) asserts a specific privilege for each item or group of items withheld."[126]

---

or asserts a privilege, the responding party must specifically admit or deny the request or explain in detail the reasons that the responding party cannot admit or deny the request"). Thus, a failure to timely assert the privilege generally waives the privilege.

[125] Tex. R. Civ. P. 193.3(b); *see Marteny v. Coon*, No. 09-19-00019-CV, 2020 Tex. App. LEXIS 7702, at *17, 2020 WL 5666567, at *7 (Tex. App.—Beaumont Sept. 24, 2020, orig. proceeding) (mem. op.) ("After receiving a response indicating material has been withheld from production, the party seeking discovery may serve a written request that the withholding party identify the information and material withheld." (citing Tex. R. Civ. P. 193.3(b))); *In re Brookfield Infrastructure Grp., LLC*, No. 13-17-00486-CV, 2018 Tex. App. LEXIS 2492, at *26, 2018 WL 1725467 (Tex. App.—Corpus Christi Apr. 9, 2018, orig. proceeding) (mem. op.) ("The party seeking discovery may then serve a written request asking the withholding party to identify the withheld information and material."); *In re Sw. Airlines Co.*, No. 02-12-00179-CV, 2012 Tex. App. LEXIS 5613, at *7, 2012 WL 2864507 (Tex. App.—Fort Worth July 12, 2012, orig. proceeding) (mem. op.) ("The party seeking discovery may then serve a written request that the withholding party identify the information and material withheld[.]"); *In re Monsanto Co.*, 998 S.W.2d 917, 924 (Tex. App.—Waco 1999, orig. proceeding) (same).

[126] Tex. R. Civ. P. 193.3(b); *accord In re Living Ctrs. of Tex., Inc.*, 175 S.W.3d 253, 261 (Tex. 2005) (orig. proceeding) ("Upon request, the withholding party must serve a privilege log describing the withheld materials, without revealing privileged information, and asserting a specific privilege for each withheld item."); *In re E.I. DuPont de Nemours & Co.,* 136 S.W.3d 218, 222 (Tex. 2004) (orig. proceeding) (per curiam) (noting that "'privilege log' is the commonly used term for a response pursuant to Texas Rule of Procedure 193.3(b)"); *Marteny v. Coon*, No. 09-19-00019-CV, 2020 Tex. App. LEXIS 7702, at *17–18, 2020 WL 5666567, at *7 (Tex. App.—Beaumont Sept. 24, 2020, orig. proceeding) (mem. op.) ("'Within fifteen days of receiving a request, the withholding party 'must serve a response that: (1) describes the information or materials withheld that, without revealing the privileged information itself or otherwise waiving the privilege, enables other parties to assess the applicability of the privilege, and (2) asserts a specific privilege for each item or group of items withheld.'" (quoting Tex. R. Civ. P. 193.3(b))); *In re Atl. Sounding Co.*, No. 14-18-00523-CV, 2018 Tex. App. LEXIS 6880, at *3, 2018 WL 4116837 (Tex. App.—Houston [14th Dist.] Aug. 28, 2018, orig. proceeding) (mem. op.) ("Upon request, the withholding party must serve a privilege log describing the withheld materials, without revealing the privileged information, and asserting a specific privilege for each withheld item."); *In re Brookfield Infrastructure Grp., LLC*, No. 13-17-00486-CV, 2018 Tex. App. LEXIS 2492, at *26–27, 2018 WL 1725467 (Tex. App.—Corpus Christi Apr. 9, 2018, orig. proceeding) (mem. op.) ("Within fifteen days, 'the withholding party must serve a response' describing the withheld material or information, 'without divulging the privileged information itself or waiving the privilege,' but in a manner that 'enables other parties to assess the applicability of the privilege.' The response must also assert 'a specific privilege for each item or group of items withheld.' This response identifying withheld items is commonly called a privilege log." (citations omitted) (quoting Tex. R. Civ. P. 193.3(b))); *In re York Risk Servs. Grp., Inc.*, No. 12-17-00210-CV, 2017 Tex. App. LEXIS 10942, at *10, 2017 WL 5622951 (Tex. App.—Tyler Nov. 22, 2017, orig. proceeding) (mem. op.) ("Upon request, the withholding party must serve a privilege log that (1) describes the information or mate-

Even if a withholding party has not asserted privilege properly under Texas Rule 193.3(a), the requesting party still should request a privilege log before challenging the privilege assertions.[127]

Although Texas Rule 193.3 only generally identifies the information that must be in a privilege log, it is clear that such a log must set forth the privilege asserted and provide sufficient information about the allegedly privileged material or information to allow the trial court and requesting party to assess the privilege assertion's validity.[128]

---

rials withheld that, without revealing the privileged information itself or otherwise waiving the privilege, (2) enables other parties to assess the applicability of the privilege, and (3) asserts a specific privilege for each item or group of items withheld."); ***In re Lumbermen's Underwriting Alliance***, 421 S.W.3d 289, 293 (Tex. App.—Texarkana 2014, orig. proceeding) ("The purpose of a privilege log is to identify the material that has been withheld and the specific privilege or privileges under which it was withheld so that the claim of privilege may be evaluated."); ***In re Lumbermen's Underwriting Alliance***, 421 S.W.3d 289, 296 (Tex. App.—Texarkana 2014, orig. proceeding) ("We find that the trial court abused its discretion in not requiring the production of a privilege log so that the claim of privilege could be properly asserted."); ***In re Sw. Airlines Co.***, No. 02-12-00179-CV, 2012 Tex. App. LEXIS 5613, at *7, 2012 WL 2864507 (Tex. App.—Fort Worth July 12, 2012, orig. proceeding) (mem. op.) ("The party seeking discovery may then serve a written request that the withholding party identify the information and material withheld, and within 15 days of service of that request, the withholding party must serve a response that: (1) describes the information or materials withheld that, without revealing the privileged information itself or otherwise waiving the privilege, enables other parties to assess the privilege's applicability, and (2) asserts a specific privilege for each item or group of items withheld."); ***In re Monsanto Co.***, 998 S.W.2d 917, 924 (Tex. App.—Waco 1999, orig. proceeding) (same).

It is not uncommon for a written-discovery request to instruct the responding party to serve a privilege-log with its discovery response. Such a request is objectionable because Texas Rule 193.3(b) expressly provides that a party is entitled to request the log only "[a]fter receiving a response indicating that material or information has been withheld from production." ***In re Lumbermen's Underwriting Alliance***, 421 S.W.3d 289, 293 (Tex. App.—Texarkana 2014, orig. proceeding) (emphasis added). ***But see In re Christus Health Se. Tex.***, 167 S.W.3d 596, 599 (Tex. App.—Beaumont 2005, orig. proceeding) (suggesting that privilege-log request contained in a production request triggered the responding party's obligation to provide one).

[127] ***In re TIG Ins. Co.***, 172 S.W.3d 160, 169–70 (Tex. App.—Beaumont 2005, orig. proceeding) (holding that, because the movant had not requested a privilege log as required by Texas Rule 193.3(b), issues regarding certain documents' work-product status had not been properly raised and the trial court erred in overruling the privilege assertions).

[128] Tex. R. Civ. P. 193.3(b)(1) (requiring a privilege log to describe withheld information or documents in a way that "allows the other parties to assess the applicability of the privilege"); ***Marteny v. Coon***, No. 09-19-00019-CV, 2020 Tex. App. LEXIS 7702, at *1–20, 2020 WL 5666567 (Tex. App.—Beaumont Sept. 24, 2020, orig. proceeding) (mem. op.) (The defendants' "privilege log was a single page, and while it provided broad classes of documents, it did not provide descriptions of the specific documents withheld by identifying the authors, the dates, or the recipients. It also did not provide date ranges for the documents withheld and failed to identify which requests the withheld materials were responsive to. . . . Considering the deficient privilege log and [the defendants'] failure to make a prima facie case for the applicability of the asserted privileges, we determine the trial court abused its discretion by refusing to rule on [the plaintiff's] motion to compel.") (footnotes omitted) (citations omitted); ***In re Christus Health Se. Tex.***, 167 S.W.3d 596, 599 (Tex. App.—Beaumont 2005, orig. proceeding) ("[T]he description of the information or material withheld must

For documents, a privilege log ordinarily is sufficient if it provides the document's Bates number, if any; its author(s); addressee(s) and other recipients; its date; its type or nature (e.g., letter, email, memorandum, etc.), the privilege asserted; and the document's general subject matter (unless doing so would waive the privilege).[129] Because

---

be specific enough that the requesting party can identify each document withheld and assess the applicability of that privilege."); *In re Anderson*, 163 S.W.3d 136, 140–41 (Tex. App.—San Antonio 2005, orig. proceeding) (same); *In re Monsanto Co.*, 998 S.W.2d 917, 924 (Tex. App.—Waco 1999, orig. proceeding) (same); *see In re Maher*, 143 S.W.3d 907, 914 (Tex. App.—Fort Worth 2004, orig. proceeding) ("[T]he privilege log RPI ultimately filed pursuant to the trial court's order does not begin to meet the requirements of [Texas] Rule 193.3. The log states, for example, 'internal computer records, claim activity logs and file notes as work product made in anticipation of litigation with an anticipation of litigation date of July 9, 2001' as an item withheld. RPI's other four claims of privilege in its log, which are asserted to withhold all of the documents requested in all of Relator's 26 requests for production, are equally broad and nonspecific. Without any indication, at the very least, of the author and the date the records, logs, and notes were created, the privilege log does not allow Relator or the trial court to assess the applicability of the privilege."); *In re Rental Servs. Corp.*, No. 2-06-338-CV, 2006 Tex. App. LEXIS 10502, at *5 (Tex. App.—Fort Worth Dec. 7, 2006, orig. proceeding) (mem. op.) (holding that a privilege log was deficient because it was so vague that it did not allow the court and opposing counsel to assess the privileges' applicability); *In re Monsanto Co.*, 998 S.W.2d 917, 925, 930 (Tex. App.—Waco 1999, orig. proceeding) (reviewing privilege logs that identified "each document by 'Bates number,' number of pages, date, document title, document type, document traits, author/source (if known), and recipient(s) (if applicable); identified the person receiving a copy of the document; and identified the privilege(s) asserted as to each document" and concluding that the privilege logs "fairly describe[d] the documents and [complied] with [Texas] Rule 193.3(b)").

[129] *See In re E.I. DuPont de Nemours & Co.*, 136 S.W.3d 218, 225–26 (Tex. 2004) (orig. proceeding) (per curiam) (describing how to establish a prima-facie case of privilege with a privilege log and the affidavits needed if the log is challenged); *In re Maher*, 143 S.W.3d 907, 914 (Tex. App.—Fort Worth 2004, orig. proceeding) ("Without any indication, at the very least, of the author and the date the records, logs, and notes were created, the privilege log does not allow Relator or the trial court to assess the applicability of the privilege."); *cf. Orchestrate HR, Inc. v. Blue Cross & Blue Shield of Kan., Inc.*, No. 19-CV-4007-HLT-TJJ, 2020 U.S. Dist. LEXIS 240179, at *7–8, 2020 WL 7626536 (D. Kan. Dec. 22, 2020) (providing a list of information that "courts have required" privilege logs to include); *Schaeffer v. City of Chi.*, No. 19 C 7711, 2020 U.S. Dist. LEXIS 239755, at *8–9, 2020 WL 7395217 (N.D. Ill. Dec. 15, 2020) ("[A] privilege log must be detailed enough to enable any other party to assess the applicability of the privilege asserted and should include: (1) the name and capacity of each individual from whom or to whom a document and any attachments were sent or otherwise disclosed (including which persons are lawyers); (2) the date of the document and any attachments; (3) the type of document; (4) the Bates numbers of the documents; (5) the nature of the privilege asserted; and (6) a description of the subject matter contained in the document in sufficient detail to determine if legal advice was sought or received or if the document constitutes attorney work product."); *Chaudhry v. Angell*, No. 1:16-CV-01243-SAB, 2020 U.S. Dist. LEXIS 229529, at *25–26, 2020 WL 7182083 (E.D. Cal. Dec. 7, 2020) ("A privilege log has been held sufficient to establish the attorney-client privilege where it identifies '(a) the attorney and client involved, (b) the nature of the document, (c) all persons or entities shown on the document to have received or sent the document, (d) all persons or entities known to have been furnished the document or informed of its substance, and (e) the date the document was generated, prepared, or dated.'" (quoting *Skyline Wesleyan Church v. Cal. Dep't of Managed Health Care*, 322 F.R.D. 571, 584 (S.D. Cal. 2017))); *Kizer*

there is no presumption that a person identified on a privilege log properly received the privileged material or information,[130] the log should identity which persons are lawyers, lawyer representatives, clients, or client representatives subject to the privilege asserted and provide sufficient information about the identified persons to allow the court and requesting party to assess the privilege's assertion.

5-4:2 Exemption for Litigation Material

Texas Rule 193.3(c) provides that a responding party need not make a withholding statement or include on a privilege log "a privileged communication to or from a lawyer or lawyer's representative or a privileged document of a lawyer or lawyer's representative (1) created or made from the point at which a party consults a lawyer with a view to obtaining professional legal services from the lawyer in the prosecution or defense of a specific claim in the litigation in which discovery is requested, and (2) concerning the litigation in which the discovery is requested."[131]

---

v. N. Am. Transp. Servs., LLC, No. CIV-18-846-D, 2020 U.S. Dist. LEXIS 197485, at *4, 2020 WL 6263733 (W.D. Okla. Oct. 23, 2020) ("Generally, a privilege log is adequate if it identifies with particularity the documents withheld, [] their date of creation, author, title or caption, addressee and [] recipient, and general nature or purpose for creation." (quoting *Zander v. Craig Hosp.*, 743 F. Supp. 2d 1225, 1232 (D. Colo. 2010))); *Evanston Ins. Co* (quoting *Zander v. Craig Hosp.*, 743 F. Supp. 2d 1225, 1232 (D. Colo. 2010)). v. *Tracey Portee Murphy*, No. CV-19-04954-PHX-MTL, 2020 U.S. Dist. LEXIS 189586, at *8–9, 2020 WL 6048206 (D. Ariz. Oct. 13, 2020) ("A privilege log containing the following information is sufficient to establish this prima facie showing: '(1) the author(s); (2) the nature or type of document; (3) the names of all individuals who were shown, sent, received, or informed of the substance of the document; (4) the date of the document; and (5) the subject matter of the document.'" (quoting *MJG Enters., Inc. v. Cloyd*, No. 2:10-cv-00086-TMB, 2012 U.S. Dist. LEXIS 198058, at *5–6, 2012 WL 12964345 (D. Ariz. Oct. 30, 2012); *Bad Moms, LLC v. STX Fin., LLC*, No. 17-CV-62510, 2018 U.S. Dist. LEXIS 149005, at *12 n.4, 2018 WL 4184535 (S.D. Fla. Aug. 31, 2018) ("[A] proper privilege log should contain the following information regarding the challenged entries: (1) the name and job title or capacity of the author of the document; (2) the name and job title or capacity of each recipient of the document; (3) the date the document was prepared and, if different, the date(s) on which it was sent to or shared with persons other than the author(s); (4) the title and description of the document; (5) the subject matter addressed in the document; (6) the purpose(s) for which it was prepared or communicated; and (7) the specific basis for the claim that it is privileged."). Of course, the withheld document's description should not provide so much information that it waives the privilege.

130 *See In re E.I. DuPont de Nemours & Co.*, 136 S.W.3d 218, 225 (Tex. 2004) (orig. proceeding) (per curiam) ("There is no presumption that documents are privileged, and there is no presumption that a party listed on the privilege log is an authorized person under the rule governing the privilege.").

131 Tex. R. Civ. P. 193.3(c); *see In re Topletz*, No. 05-20-00634-CV, 2020 Tex. App. LEXIS 8197, at *10, 2020 WL 6073877 (Tex. App.—Dallas Oct. 15, 2020, orig. proceeding) (mem. op.) ("[P]rivileged documents of a lawyer 'concerning the litigation in which the discovery is requested' are exempt from the privilege log requirement." (quoting Tex. R. Civ. P. 193.3(c))); *In re Brookfield Infrastructure Grp., LLC*, No. 13-17-00486-CV, 2018 Tex. App. LEXIS 2492, at *27, 2018 WL 1725467 (Tex. App.—Corpus Christi Apr. 9, 2018, orig. proceeding) (mem. op.) ("[A] party is not required to file a privilege log for communications or documents to or from its attorney or for privileged documents of a lawyer or lawyer's representative."); *In re Lumbermen's Underwriting Alliance*, 421 S.W.3d 289, 293 (Tex.

As evidenced by its plain language, this exemption does not apply to communications that predate the lawsuit and that were not created or made for the purpose of obtaining legal services in it.[132] Moreover, it does not encompass the work product of a party's non-lawyer representatives in the litigation at hand.[133] Although Texas Rule 193.3(c) does not define "lawyer's representative," the term is used in Texas Rule of Evidence 503, which governs the attorney-client privilege and defines "lawyer's representative" as: "(A) one employed by the lawyer to assist the lawyer in the rendition of professional legal services; or (B) an accountant who is reasonably necessary for the lawyer's rendition of professional legal services."[134] There is no logical reason why this definition should not apply to "lawyer's representative" as used in Texas Rule 193.3(c).

Because Texas Rule 193.3(c) requires a document to be that "of the lawyer or the lawyer's representative," it clearly does not apply to a document that is simply given to the lawyer or a lawyer's representative by the client. This is because "a document is not privileged simply because it is contained in an attorney's files. There is no specific privilege . . . for 'documents in an attorney's files.' Thus, a party may not cloak a document with the attorney-client privilege simply by forwarding it to his or her attorney."[135]

App.—Texarkana 2014, orig. proceeding) ("Some privileged information is entitled to more procedural protection than other such information. For instance, even though other privileged information may exist, only communications to or from a lawyer or lawyer's representative or privileged documents of a lawyer or lawyer's representative are exempt from the privilege log disclosure."). It is assumed that such materials will be withheld under the attorney-client and work-product privileges. Tex. R. Civ. P. 193 cmt. 3 to 1999 change.

[132] *See* Tex. R. Civ. P. 193.3(c); ***In re Brookfield Infrastructure Grp., LLC***, No. 13-17-00486-CV, 2018 Tex. App. LEXIS 2492, at *29, 2018 WL 1725467 (Tex. App.—Corpus Christi Apr. 9, 2018, orig. proceeding) (mem. op.) ("Brookfield is not exempted from the privilege log requirement for privileged communications with its attorneys that were not obtained for obtaining professional legal services 'in the prosecution or defense of a specific claim in the litigation in which discovery is requested,' and 'concerning the litigation in which the discovery is requested.'" (quoting Tex. R. Civ. P. 193.3(c))); ***In re Anderson***, 163 S.W.3d 136, 142 (Tex. App.—San Antonio 2005, orig. proceeding) ("The memorandum was created before this litigation arose. It was not created for the purpose of obtaining professional legal services in the defense of Anderson's suit [i.e., the suit before the court] . . . . We, therefore, hold that [Texas R]ule 193.3(c)'s exemption does not apply to the memorandum at issue."). ***In re Anderson*** makes clear that a responsive, privileged document that has been withheld should be logged unless the [Texas] Rule 193.3(c)'s exemption clearly applies to the document. *See* ***In re Anderson***, 163 S.W.3d 136, 142 (Tex. App.—San Antonio 2005, orig. proceeding) ("And, because the exemption in paragraph (c) does not apply, to assert its privilege, the City was required to comply with paragraph (a), which it did not do. . . . Because the City failed to assert its privilege in accordance with [Texas R]ule 193.3(a), the trial court erred in denying Anderson's motion to compel production of the memorandum." (footnotes omitted)).

[133] *See* ***In re Lumbermen's Underwriting Alliance***, 421 S.W.3d 289, 293 (Tex. App.—Texarkana 2014, orig. proceeding) ("MWC is correct in arguing that it has no obligation to produce a privilege log for attorney (or the attorney's representatives) communications or documents, but is incorrect in asserting that all of the work product of MWC's nonattorney representatives is exempt from the privilege log requirement.").

[134] Tex. R. Evid. 503(a)(4).

[135] *Nat'l Union Fire Ins. Co. v. Valdez*, 863 S.W.2d 458, 460 (Tex. 1993).

Finally, Texas Rule 193.3(c)'s exemption "does not prohibit a party from specifically requesting the material or information [that does not have to be logged] if the party has a good faith basis for asserting that it is discoverable."[136]

5-4:3 Inadvertent Production

Texas Rule 193.3(d) is the "snap-back" provision, which allows a party to recover inadvertently produced privileged information or documents.[137] Under it, a party that produces privileged information or material, in response to a written-discovery request, without intending to waive privilege, does not do so, if it amends the discovery response with ten days after discovering the information's or material's production.[138] The ten-day period allowed for an amended response does not run from

---

[136] Tex. R. Civ. P. 193 cmt. 3 to 1999 change (providing that an "example would be material or information described by Rule 503(d)(1) of the Rules of Evidence"—the crime-fraud exception); *see In re Brookfield Infrastructure Grp., LLC*, No. 13-17-00486-CV, 2018 Tex. App. LEXIS 2492, at *28, 2018 WL 1725467 (Tex. App.—Corpus Christi Apr. 9, 2018, orig. proceeding) (mem. op.) (A comment to Texas Rule 193 "states that 'the [R]ule does not prohibit a party from specifically requesting the [exempted] material or information if the party has a good faith basis for asserting that it is discoverable'" (quoting Tex. R. Civ. P. 193 cmt. 3 to 1999 change)); *In re Park Cities Bank*, 409 S.W.3d 859, 869 (Tex. App.—Tyler 2013, orig. proceeding) (noting that the crime-fraud exception applies to the attorney-client and work-product privileges).

[137] *In re City of Dickinson*, 568 S.W.3d 642, 649 (Tex. 2019) (orig. proceeding) (Texas "Rule 193.3(d) provides a party who has inadvertently produced privileged material a means to preserve the privilege."); *In re FEDD Wireless LLC.*, 567 S.W.3d 470, 476 (Tex. App.—Houston [14th Dist.] 2019, orig. proceeding) (Texas Rule 193.3(d), the snap-back provision, "was 'designed to protect the inadvertent disclosure of privileged material in order to reduce the cost and risk involved in document production'" and "applies with respect to" any information inadvertently disclosed in state-court cases, not just documents produced in response to written discovery requests (footnote omitted) (citation omitted) (quoting *In re Christus Spohn Hosp. Kleberg*, 222 S.W.3d 434, 437 (Tex. 2007) (orig. proceeding))); *In re Tex. Windstorm Ins. Ass'n*, No. 14-16-00677-CV, 2016 Tex. App. LEXIS 13178, at *11–12, 2016 WL 7234466 (Tex. App.—Houston [14th Dist.] Dec. 13, 2016, orig. proceeding) (mem. op.) ("The purpose of the snap-back rule is to protect the inadvertent disclosure of privileged material to reduce the cost and risk involved in document production. 'The snap-back provision has typically been applied when a party inadvertently produces privileged documents to an opposing party.'" (citation omitted) (quoting *In re Christus Spohn Hosp. Kleberg*, 222 S.W.3d 434, 438–39 (Tex. 2007) (orig. proceeding))); *see In re Living Ctrs. of Tex., Inc.*, 175 S.W.3d 253, 260 (Tex. 2005) (orig. proceeding) ("Under the current rules of discovery, inadvertent disclosure does not automatically waive a claim of privilege."); *In re JDN Real Estate-McKinney L.P.*, 211 S.W.3d 907, 917–18 (Tex. App.—Dallas 2006, orig. proceeding) (mem. op.) (pointing out that Texas Rule 193.3(d) is "known as the 'snap-back rule' [and] contemplates that, on occasion, certain materials or information may be inadvertently produced to an opposing party without any intent on the part of the producing party to waive a claim of privilege"); *In re Parnham*, 263 S.W.3d 97, 105 (Tex. App.—Houston [1st Dist.] 2006, orig. proceeding) (mem. op.) (same).

[138] Tex. R. Civ. P. 193.3(d) ("A party who produces material or information without intending to waive a claim of privilege does not waive that claim under these rules or the Rules of Evidence if—within ten days or a shorter time ordered by the court, after the producing party actually discovers that such production was made—the producing party amends the response, identifying the material or information produced and stating the privilege asserted. If the producing party thus amends the response to assert a privilege, the request-

the production of the material or information but rather from the responding party's actual awareness of its mistake and may be shortened by the trial court.[139]

Comment 4 to the 1999 change to Texas Rule 193 explains that "[t]he focus is on the intent to waive the privilege, not the intent to produce the material or information. A party who fails to diligently screen documents before producing them does not waive a claim of privilege."[140] However, a court might find that a responding party who intentionally fails to screen its documents for privilege at all intended to produce privileged ones.[141] Of course, a prudent attorney should carefully review his or her client's documents to ensure that privileged material is not produced because Texas Rule 193.3(d) "does not specifically restrict the use of the information by the recipient party" before it is snapped-back.[142] Thus, regaining possession of the privileged document or information might not undo the damage resulting from its production in the first instance.

---

ing party must promptly return the specified material or information and any copies pending any ruling by the court denying the privilege."); *see In re City of Dickinson*, 568 S.W.3d 642, 649 (Tex. 2019) (orig. proceeding) (Texas Rule 193.3(d) "allows parties to recover privileged material so long as they amend their response to the discovery request and identify the privileged material within ten days of its inadvertent disclosure. Critically, the material must be protected by a recognized privilege for the snap-back provision to apply.") (citation omitted); *In re FEDD Wireless LLC.*, 567 S.W.3d 470, 476 (Tex. App.—Houston [14th Dist.] 2019, orig. proceeding) (same); *In re Certain Underwriters at Lloyd's London*, 294 S.W.3d 891, 906–08 (Tex. App.—Beaumont 2009, orig. proceeding) (holding that there is no privilege waiver when a party timely makes a snap-back request); *Warrantech Corp. v. Comput. Adapters Servs., Inc.*, 134 S.W.3d 516, 524–25 (Tex. App.—Fort Worth 2004, no pet.) (holding that a party did not waive its privilege even though it first discovered inadvertently produced document during trial); *In re AEP Tex. Cent. Co.*, 128 S.W.3d 687, 690, 693–94 (Tex. App.—San Antonio 2003, orig. proceeding) (holding that there was no privilege waiver when a party requested the return of a privileged document within 10 days after discovering its production).

139 Tex. R. Civ. P. 193 cmt. 4 to the 1999 change; *see In re Certain Underwriters at Lloyd's London*, 294 S.W.3d 891, 903 (Tex. App.—Beaumont 2009, orig. proceeding) (rejecting a "should-have-known" test).

140 Tex. R. Civ. P. 193 cmt. 4 to the 1999 change. *Compare In re Certain Underwriters at Lloyd's London*, 294 S.W.3d 891, 903 (Tex. App.—Beaumont 2009, orig. proceeding) (allowing the snap-back of privileged documents), *In re JDN Real Estate-McKinney L.P.*, 211 S.W.3d 907, 917–21 (Tex. App.—Dallas 2006, orig. proceeding) (same), *and Warrantech Corp. v. Comput. Adapters Servs., Inc.*, 134 S.W.3d 516, 524–25 (Tex. App.—Fort Worth 2004, no pet.) (same), *with In re Carbo Ceramics Inc.*, 81 S.W.3d 369, 376–77 (Tex. App.—Houston [14th Dist.] 2002, orig. proceeding) (not allowing the snap-back of a privileged document because the privileged document's production was intentional and the alleged inadvertence was the result of a trial-strategy change).

141 *Warrantech Corp. v. Comput. Adapters Servs., Inc.*, 134 S.W.3d 516, 524–25 (Tex. App.—Fort Worth 2004, no pet.) (suggesting that the complete failure to screen documents would result in a waiver of any privileges).

142 *See In re Christus Spohn Hosp. Kleberg*, 222 S.W.3d 434, 439 (Tex. 2007) (orig. proceeding) (holding that the snap-back provision "does not provide authority for disqualification of counsel who review inadvertently disclosed materials during the course of discovery")); *In re Parnham*, No. 01-06-00236-CV, 2006 Tex. App. LEXIS 8252, *20, 22–24 (Tex. App.—Houston [1st Dist.] 2006, orig. proceeding) (mem. op.) (same).

To avoid last-minute snap-back privilege assertions at trial in a case filed before January 1, 2021, the requesting party "may identify prior to trial the documents intended to be offered, thereby triggering the [10-day period for the responding party] to assert any overlooked privilege. . . . A trial court may also order this procedure" on its own initiative.[143] In addition, Texas Rule 194.4 now requires the parties in cases filed on or after January 1, 2021, to "promptly file the following information [30 days before trial] about the evidence that it may present at trial other than solely for impeachment": . . . "an identification of each document or other exhibits, including summaries of other evidence—separately identifying those items the party expects to offer and those it may offer if the need arises."[144] Accordingly, the filing of the trial exhibit list will trigger the 10-day period to snap-back any inadvertently produced material.

Texas Rule 193.3(d) allows parties to retrieve privileged information or documents obtained from an opponent from another source that does not have the right to waive the privilege.[145] It generally does not allow parties to retrieve privileged information or materials inadvertently produced to either a testifying expert or a discoverable consulting expert because a party is generally required to disclose all documents provided to such experts;[146] however, it does allow parties to retrieve inadvertently produced privileged communications between an attorney and a client or client representative who is offering expert testimony in a case.[147]

---

143 Tex. R. Civ. P. 193 cmt. 4 to 1999 change; *see In re JDN Real Estate-McKinney L.P.*, 211 S.W.3d 907, 917–18 (Tex. App.—Dallas 2006, orig. proceeding); *Warrantech Corp. v. Comput. Adapters Servs., Inc.*, 134 S.W.3d 516, 524–25 (Tex. App.—Fort Worth 2004, no pet.).

144 Tex. R. Civ. P. 194.4(a)–(b).

145 *In re Certain Underwriters at Lloyd's London*, 294 S.W.3d 891, 903 (Tex. App.—Beaumont 2009, orig. proceeding) (allowing an insurance company to snap-back privileged documents produced by its third-party claims adjuster). *But see In re Ortuno*, No. 14-08-00227-CV, 2008 Tex. App. LEXIS 3396, at *5, 2009 WL 2339800 (Tex. App.—Houston [14th Dist.] May 6, 2008, orig. proceeding) (mem. op.) (per curiam) (holding that Texas Rule 193.3 could not be used to snap-back the production of a patient's privileged medical record because it had been produced by a nonparty to the suit—a hospital).

146 *In re Christus Spohn Hosp. Kleberg*, 222 S.W.3d 434, 440–41 (Tex. 2007) (orig. proceeding) ("[W]e conclude that [Texas] Rules 192.3(e)(6) and 192.5(c)(1) prevail over [Texas] Rule 193.3(d)'s snap-back provision so long as the expert intends to testify at trial despite the inadvertent document production. That is, once privileged documents are disclosed to a testifying expert, and the party who designated the expert continues to rely upon that designation for trial, the documents may not be retrieved even if they were inadvertently produced.").

A party may nonetheless snap-back privileged documents given to a testifying expert if they could not, by their nature, have influenced the expert's opinion. *In re Christus Spohn Hosp. Kleberg*, 222 S.W.3d 434, 441 (Tex. 2007) (orig. proceeding) (reasoning that such documents do "not evoke the concerns the expert-disclosure rule was designed to prevent and the policy concerns underlying the rule's disclosure requirement would presumably never arise"). But the Texas Supreme Court has stated that "a party seeking snap-back under such circumstances would bear a heavy burden in light of the disclosure rule's underlying purpose." *In re Christus Spohn Hosp. Kleberg*, 222 S.W.3d 434, 441 (Tex. 2007) (orig. proceeding).

147 *In re City of Dickinson*, 568 S.W.3d 642, 649 (Tex. 2019) (orig. proceeding) (holding that the Texas "discovery rules do not operate to waive the attorney–client privilege whenever a client or its representative offers expert testimony" and, in turn, that Texas Rule "193.3(d)'s

The party snapping-back the privileged information or document has the burden of proving that the snap-back was timely and proper. As with other procedural requirements relating to privileges, a party will lose its right to snap-back inadvertently produced privileged documents and thereby waive its privilege if it does not comply with Texas Rule 193.3(d)'s requirements.[148]

The snap-back provision typically is "applied when a party inadvertently produces privileged documents to an opposing party."[149] Texas courts of appeals are divided on whether the provision applies to nonparties.

---

snap-back provision [is] a proper remedy" when privileged communications with the client-expert are inadvertently produced and need to be returned to preserve privilege).

[148] *See, e.g.*, ***Cooper v. First Fin. Bank, N.A.***, No. 05-19-00569-CV, 2020 Tex. App. LEXIS 8482, at *23, 2020 WL 6304994 (Tex. App.—Dallas Oct. 28, 2020, pet. denied) (mem. op.) (rejecting a party's suggestion that Texas Rule 193.3(d) could be invoked for a document that the party had "knowingly presented" to the trial court in multiple filings "years ago"); ***In re FEDD Wireless LLC.***, 567 S.W.3d 470, 476 (Tex. App.—Houston [14th Dist.] 2019, orig. proceeding) (after explaining that "[a] snap-back motion or amendment that is filed more than ten days after the movant discovers that a privileged document has been produced is untimely," holding that a party's untimely filed snap-back request waived any privilege claim regarding the document subject to the motion); ***In re Samson Lone Star, LLC***, No. 06-10-00050-CV, 2010 Tex. App. LEXIS 6464, at *7–8, 2010 WL 3008670 (Tex. App.—Texarkana Aug. 3, 2010, orig. proceeding) (mem. op.) (holding that a trial court acted within its discretion in denying a snap-back motion filed over eight months after the party discovered the inadvertent production of privileged documents); *cf.* ***In re Certain Underwriters at Lloyd's London***, 294 S.W.3d 891, 906 (Tex. App.—Beaumont 2009, orig. proceeding) (Texas "Rule 193.3(d)'s requirement of 'actual discovery' focuses the inquiry on whether the party holding the privilege intended to waive it. By establishing a standard of actual knowledge, evidence that a party should have known privileged documents were produced is insufficient under [Texas] Rule 193.3(d) to adequately support a trial court's implied finding that the waiver of a privilege occurred."); ***In re O'Quinn***, No. 04-08-00019-CV, 2008 Tex. App. LEXIS 2712, at *6, 2008 WL 1733256 (Tex. App.—San Antonio Apr. 16, 2008, orig. proceeding) (mem. op.) ("When the producing party timely notifies the requesting party of the inadvertently produced material or information, and amends its response to assert the privilege, the requesting party must promptly return the material or information and any copies pending the trial court's ruling on the claim of privilege.").

[149] ***In re Christus Spohn Hosp. Kleberg***, 222 S.W.3d 434, 439 (Tex. 2007) (orig. proceeding) (applying snap-back provision when plaintiff's counsel inadvertently produced privileged documents to defendant's counsel and concluding that the provision "does not provide authority for disqualification of counsel who review inadvertently disclosed materials during the course of discovery"); ***Warrantech Corp. v. Comp. Adapters Servs.***, 134 S.W.3d 516, 525 (Tex. App.—Forth Worth 2004, no pet.) (applying the snap-back provision to hold that a party's inadvertent production of a privileged letter to opposing counsel did not waive privilege); ***In re AEP Tex. Cent. Co.***, 128 S.W.3d 687, 693–94 (Tex. App.—San Antonio 2003, orig. proceeding) (applying the snap-back provision to hold that a privileged legal memo inadvertently produced by a party's counsel to opposing counsel had to be returned); ***In re O'Quinn***, No. 04-08-00019-CV, 2008 Tex. App. LEXIS 2712, at *12–13, 2008 WL 1733256 (Tex. App.—San Antonio Apr. 16, 2008, orig. proceeding) (mem. op.) (holding that the trial court abused its discretion by failing to order a party to return non-core work product inadvertently produced by an opposing party that had complied with the snap-back procedures of Texas Rule 193.3(d)); ***see In re Tex. Windstorm Ins. Ass'n***, 549 S.W.3d 592, 598–99 (Tex. App.—Houston [14th Dist.] 2016, orig. proceeding) (mem. op.) ("The purpose of the snap-back rule is to protect the inadvertent disclosure of privileged material to reduce the cost and risk involved in document production. 'The snap-back provision has typically been

In *In re Certain Underwriters at Lloyd's London*, the Beaumont Court of Appeals allowed a party to snap-back work product that its consultant produced to the opposing party.[150] In that case, the insurance-carrier defendants hired an adjusting firm to investigate and adjust a policyholder's corrosion claim.[151] In response to a subpoena duces tecum, the adjusting firm produced to the policyholders' attorney a file containing, among other things, its vice-president's handwritten notes concerning conversations about the claim during meetings with the defendants' counsel.[152]

The policyholders declined to return the notes, arguing, among other things, that they were not subject to the snap-back provision because, the provision "by its terms, does not apply when a nonparty to the lawsuit produces the documents."[153] The Beaumont Court of Appeals disagreed, concluding "that the term 'party who produces,' as used in Texas Rule 193.3(d), was not intended to limit the right of a party to file objections to a nonparty's production of privileged documents."[154]

In reaching its conclusion, the court rejected a contrary conclusion by the Houston (14th District) Court of Appeals in *In re Ortuno*.[155] In that case, the court addressed whether the plaintiff could snap-back a consulting expert's report that the consulting expert's employer, Texas Children's Hospital, produced to the defendant in response to a deposition upon written questions.[156] The court held that the report could not be snapped back "[b]ecause the producing entity was not a party to this lawsuit and therefore outside the scope of [Texas] Rule 193.3(d)."[157] But the court left open the possibility that the plaintiff could seek a protective order from the trial court, to prevent "the disclosure or use of the already-produced report."[158]

---

applied when a party inadvertently produces privileged documents to an opposing party.'" (citation omitted) (quoting *In re Christus Spohn Hosp. Kleberg*, 222 S.W.3d 434, 439 (Tex. 2007) (orig. proceeding))).

150 *See In re Certain Underwriters at Lloyd's London*, 294 S.W.3d 891, 901–05 (Tex. App.—Beaumont 2009, orig. proceeding).

151 *In re Certain Underwriters at Lloyd's London*, 294 S.W.3d 891, 896 (Tex. App.—Beaumont 2009, orig. proceeding).

152 *In re Certain Underwriters at Lloyd's London*, 294 S.W.3d 891, 896–98 (Tex. App.—Beaumont 2009, orig. proceeding).

153 *In re Certain Underwriters at Lloyd's London*, 294 S.W.3d 891, 897, 901 (Tex. App.—Beaumont 2009, orig. proceeding).

154 *In re Certain Underwriters at Lloyd's London*, 294 S.W.3d 891, 905 (Tex. App.—Beaumont 2009, orig. proceeding); *see In re Certain Underwriters at Lloyd's London*, 294 S.W.3d 891, 902–05 (Tex. App.—Beaumont 2009, orig. proceeding) (supporting its conclusion with analysis of "the history of [Texas] Rule 193.3(d), the broad reach of the rules of privilege [including the work-product privilege] to information possessed by parties and nonparties, the structure of the rules of discovery to allow discovery to reach information in the possession of both parties and nonparties, and the remedial purpose of [Texas] Rule 193.3").

155 *In re Certain Underwriters at Lloyd's London*, 294 S.W.3d 891, 905 (Tex. App.—Beaumont 2009, orig. proceeding) (disagreeing with conclusion reached in *In re Ortuno*, No. 14-08-00227-CV, 2008 Tex. App. LEXIS 3396, at *4–5, 2008 WL 2339800 (Tex. App.—Houston [14th Dist.] May 6, 2008, orig. proceeding) (mem. op.)).

156 *In re Ortuno*, No. 14-08-00227-CV, 2008 Tex. App. LEXIS 3396, at *1–2, 2008 WL 2339800 (Tex. App.—Houston [14th Dist.] May 6, 2008, orig. proceeding) (mem. op.).

157 *In re Ortuno*, No. 14-08-00227-CV, 2008 Tex. App. LEXIS 3396, at *4–5, 2008 WL 2339800 (Tex. App.—Houston [14th Dist.] May 6, 2008, orig. proceeding) (mem. op.).

158 *In re Ortuno*, No. 14-08-00227-CV, 2008 Tex. App. LEXIS 3396, at *5–6, 2008 WL 2339800 (Tex. App.—Houston [14th Dist.] May 6, 2008, orig. proceeding) (mem. op.).

As part of the 2021 amendments to Texas's discovery rules, Texas Rule 193.3(d) was revised to clarify that "*any party*" who receives material or information subject to a snap-back request "must promptly return the specified material or information and any copies pending any ruling by the court denying the privilege."[159] This change ensures that parties who did not request the material or information but nevertheless receive it must return it to the producing party.

5-5 Hearings and Rulings on Privilege Objections and Assertions

Texas Rule 193.4 provides for hearings and rulings on objections and privilege assertions made pursuant to Texas Rules 193.2 and 193.3. Either the requesting or responding party can request a hearing on an objection or privilege assertion.[160] If neither party requests one, the requesting party waives the objected-to discovery.[161] Thus, once objections or privileges have been asserted, the requesting party effectively has the burden of securing a hearing to resolve any dispute regarding them.[162] To secure a hearing on privilege assertions, however, the requesting party does not have to specify its rationale for challenging the assertions; a general challenge to them is sufficient to entitle the requesting party to a hearing.[163]

The responding party almost always has the burden of proving an objection's or a privilege's applicability.[164] And it must present any evidence necessary to support the

---

159 Tex. R. Civ. P. 193.3(d) (emphasis added).

160 Tex. R. Civ. P. 193.4(a); *see Hagan v. Pennington*, No. 05-18-00010-CV, 2019 Tex. App. LEXIS 5101, at *46, 2019 WL 2521719 (Tex. App.—Dallas June 19, 2019, no pet.) (mem. op.) ("Once a party has asserted a claim of privilege, the trial court may, upon the request of any party, conduct a hearing to determine whether the discovery should be disallowed."); *In re AEP Tex. Cent. Co.*, 128 S.W.3d 687, 690 (Tex. App.—San Antonio 2003, orig. proceeding) ("[Texas] Rule 193.4(a) authorizes either the requesting or objecting party to request a hearing on objections to discovery."); *In re Born*, No. 01-01-00971-CV, 2002 Tex. App. LEXIS 3279, at *6, 2002 WL 937663 (Tex. App.—Houston [1st Dist.] May 9, 2002, orig. proceeding) (mem. op.) (same).

161 *Balay v. Gamble*, No. 01-10-00017-CV, 2011 Tex. App. LEXIS 4576, at *19, 2011 WL 2435929 (Tex. App.—Houston [1st Dist.] June 16, 2011, no pet.) (mem. op.); *Roberts v. Whitfill*, 191 S.W.3d 348, 361 n.3 (Tex. App.—Waco 2006, no pet.).

162 *Trahan v. Lone Star Title Co.*, 247 S.W.3d 269, 282–83 (Tex. App.—El Paso 2007, pet. denied) ("[T]he case law indicates that as a general rule, only failure to obtain a pretrial ruling on discovery disputes constitutes a waiver of a claim for sanctions based on that conduct."); *Klein & Assocs. Political Relations v. Port Arthur Indep. Sch. Dist.*, 92 S.W.3d 889, 894 (Tex. App.—Beaumont 2002, pet. denied) ("The Texas Supreme Court has explained that 'because the party requesting discovery is in the best position to evaluate its need for information . . ., the orderly administration of justice will be better served by placing responsibility for obtaining a hearing on discovery matters on the party requesting discovery.'" (quoting *McKinney v. Nat'l Union Fire Ins. Co.*, 772 S.W.2d 72, 75 (Tex. 1989))).

163 *In re E.I. DuPont de Nemours & Co.*, 136 S.W.3d 218, 226–27 (Tex. 2004) (orig. proceeding) (per curiam) (rejecting argument that plaintiffs' global challenge to privilege assertions was insufficient to place those assertions at issue, reasoning in part that Texas Rule 193.4(a) "does not contain a requirement that the party seeking discovery specify their rationale for objecting to each document before requesting a hearing").

164 *See State v. Lowry*, 802 S.W.2d 669, 671 (Tex. 1991) (orig. proceeding) ("The burden is on the party seeking to avoid discovery to plead the basis for exemption or immunity and

objection or privilege.[165] "The evidence may be testimony presented at the hearing or affidavits served at least seven days before the hearing or at such other reasonable

---

to produce evidence supporting that claim."); *In re DISH Network, LLC*, 528 S.W.3d 177, 181 (Tex. App.—El Paso 2017, orig. proceeding) ("The party resisting discovery bears the burden of proving an applicable privilege."); *In re Univar USA, Inc.*, 311 S.W.3d 175, 180 (Tex. App.—Beaumont 2010, orig. proceeding) ("[T]he general rule is that a party resisting discovery has the burden to plead and prove the basis for its objections."); *In re Rogers*, 200 S.W.3d 318, 321–22 (Tex. App.—Dallas 2006, orig. proceeding) ("In the trial court, the party objecting to discovery bears the burden of proving the request is outside the rules' guidelines."); *In re AEP Tex. Cent. Co.*, 128 S.W.3d 687, 690 (Tex. App.—San Antonio 2003, orig. proceeding) ("If a hearing is held, the party who has objected or asserted a privilege must present any evidence necessary to support the objection or privilege.").

165 *See In re Marshall*, 617 S.W.3d 670, 676 (Tex. App.—San Antonio 2021, orig. proceeding) ("As to any claim of attorney-client privilege, 'the party asserting a privilege from discovery [has] the burden to produce evidence concerning its applicability. This may be accomplished by testimony or affidavit evidence sufficient to establish a prima facie case for the privilege.' . . . 'Texas law recognizes that a party asserting privilege may initiate its claim and establish a prima facie case of privilege by submitting evidence short of tendering each and every document.'" (citations omitted) (quoting *In re Stephens Inc.*, 579 S.W.3d 438, 445 (Tex. App.—San Antonio 2019, orig. proceeding), and *In re Living Centers of Tex., Inc.*, 175 S.W.3d 253, 261 (Tex. 2005) (orig. proceeding))); *Marteny v. Coon*, No. 09-19-00019-CV, 2020 Tex. App. LEXIS 7702, at *18, 2020 WL 5666567 (Tex. App.—Beaumont Sept. 24, 2020, orig. proceeding) (mem. op.) ("There is no presumption that documents are privileged. The party asserting a privilege has the burden to produce evidence concerning the privilege's applicability. Simply listing a specific privilege in a response or a privilege log does not preserve the privilege. '[I]n addition to the privilege log, the party resisting discovery must establish a prima facie case for the privilege by testimony or affidavit.'" (citations omitted) (quoting *In re Park Cities Bank*, 409 S.W.3d 859, 868 (Tex. App.—Tyler 2013, orig. proceeding))); *In re United Fire Lloyds*, 578 S.W.3d 572, 580–81 (Tex. App.—Tyler 2019, no pet.) (mem. op.) ("A party objecting or asserting a privilege must present any evidence necessary to support the objection or privilege."); *In re Atl. Sounding Co.*, No. 14-18-00523-CV, 2018 Tex. App. LEXIS 6880, at *3, 2018 WL 4116837 (Tex. App.—Houston [14th Dist.] Aug. 28, 2018, orig. proceeding) (mem. op.) (same); *In re NCAA*, 543 S.W.3d 487, 491 (Tex. App.—Dallas 2018, no pet.) (same); *In re York Risk Servs. Grp., Inc.*, No. 12-17-00210-CV, 2017 Tex. App. LEXIS 10942, at *10, 2017 WL 5622951 (Tex. App.—Tyler Nov. 22, 2017, orig. proceeding) (mem. op.) ("The party asserting a privilege has the burden to produce evidence concerning the applicability of the privilege."); *In re Rescue Concepts, Inc.*, 556 S.W.3d 331, 339 (Tex. App.—Houston [1st Dist.] 2017, orig. proceeding) ("To properly assert a claim of privilege, a party must plead the particular privilege, produce evidence to support the privilege through affidavits or testimony, and produce the documents for an in camera inspection, if the trial court determines review is necessary."); *In re Waste Mgmt. of Tex., Inc.*, No. 13-11-00197-CV, 2011 Tex. App. LEXIS 7192, at *14 n.5, 2011 WL 3855745 (Tex. App.—Corpus Christi Aug. 31, 2011, orig. proceeding) (mem. op.) ("[T]his court and others have placed the burden of proof regarding relevance, or lack thereof, on the party seeking to avoid discovery."); *In re Exmark Mfg. Co.*, 299 S.W.3d 519, 524 (Tex. App.—Corpus Christi 2009, orig. proceeding) ("The party objecting to discovery must present any evidence necessary to support its objection. . . . When it is not self-evident that the discovery order is overly broad, the party resisting discovery bears the burden of offering evidence to provide its objection."); *In re Gen. Elec. Railcar Servs. Corp.*, No. 09-03-530 CV, 2004 Tex. App. LEXIS 630, at *5–6, 2003 WL 23189458 (Tex. App.—Beaumont Jan. 22, 2004, orig. proceeding) (mem. op.) ("If, in responding to the discovery request, it becomes apparent that the discovery is unduly burdensome, the party responding should present information concerning the burden to the trial court.").

time as the court permits."[166] But proof is not always necessary to sustain certain objections, such as ones that a written-discovery request is overbroad or irrelevant.[167] If the objection can be determined from the discovery request's face, a trial court does not abuse its discretion in ruling on them without conducting a hearing about them.[168]

The party asserting a privilege must first make a prima facie showing of privilege.[169] This only requires "the minimum quantum of evidence necessary to support a

---

[166] Tex. R. Civ. P. 193.4(a); *see In re Atl. Sounding Co.*, No. 14-18-00523-CV, 2018 Tex. App. LEXIS 6880, at *3–4, 2018 WL 4116837 (Tex. App.—Houston [14th Dist.] Aug. 28, 2018, orig. proceeding) (mem. op.) ("Evidence may be presented by affidavit or by testimony at the hearing.").

[167] *In re Union Pac. Res. Co.*, 22 S.W.3d 338, 341 (Tex. 1999) (orig. proceeding) (holding that evidence was not needed to establish that settlement agreements were not relevant); *In re Topletz*, No. 05-20-00634-CV, 2020 Tex. App. LEXIS 8197, at *10, 2020 WL 6073877 (Tex. App.—Dallas Oct. 15, 2020, orig. proceeding) (mem. op.) ("[N]either the rules of civil procedure nor case law requires evidence in support of an assertion relating to discovery when evidence is unnecessary to decide the matter."); *In re CAR Fin. Servs., Inc.*, No. 02-20-00157-CV, 2020 Tex. App. LEXIS 5735, at *12, 2020 WL 4213839 (Tex. App.—Fort Worth July 23, 2020, no pet.) ("[A]lthough a party objecting to discovery must present evidence supporting its objections when 'necessary,' the rules do not require a party to present supporting evidence if the discovery requests are overbroad as a matter of law." (citations omitted) (quoting Tex. R. Civ. P. 193.4, 199.6)); *In re Hyundai Motor Co.*, No. 12-19-00417-CV, 2020 Tex. App. LEXIS 2475, at *5–6, 2020 WL 1445303 (Tex. App.—Tyler Mar. 25, 2020, orig. proceeding) (mem. op.) ("The party objecting to discovery 'must present any evidence necessary to support the objection.'" (quoting Tex. R. Civ. P. 193.4(a))); *In re Young*, 410 S.W.3d 542, 551 (Tex. App.—Beaumont 2013, no pet.) (holding that the responding party did not need evidence to establish a relevance objection); *In re Badgerow*, No. 14-12-00239-CV, 2012 Tex. App. LEXIS 2879, at *7–8, 2012 WL 1253273 (Tex. App.—Houston [14th Dist.] Apr. 12, 2012, orig. proceeding) (mem. op.) ("The objections in this case, on grounds of relevance and overbreadth, can be determined from the face of the pleadings without evidence. We conclude that the trial court did not abuse its discretion in ruling on the motion to quash without conducting a hearing.").

[168] *In re Young*, 410 S.W.3d 542, 551 (Tex. App.—Beaumont 2013, no pet.); *In re Badgerow*, No. 14-12-00239-CV, 2012 Tex. App. LEXIS 2879, at *7–8, 2012 WL 1253273 (Tex. App.—Houston [14th Dist.] Apr. 12, 2012, orig. proceeding) (mem. op.).

[169] *See, e.g.*, Tex. R. Civ. P. 193.4(a) ("The party . . . asserting the privilege must present any evidence necessary to support the . . . privilege."); *In re Nat'l Lloyds Ins. Co.*, 532 S.W.3d 794, 804 (Tex. 2017) (orig. proceeding) ("The party asserting a privilege in opposition to a discovery request 'must establish by testimony or affidavit a prima facie case for the privilege[.]'" (quoting *In re Mem'l Hermann Hosp. Sys.*, 464 S.W.3d 686, 698 (Tex. 2015) (orig. proceeding)); *In re Mem'l Hermann Hosp. Sys.*, 464 S.W.3d 686, 698 (Tex. 2015) (orig. proceeding) ("Pleading and producing evidence establishing the existence of a privilege is the burden of the party seeking to avoid discovery. The party asserting the privilege must establish by testimony or affidavit a prima facie case for the privilege.") (footnote omitted); *In re E.I. DuPont de Nemours & Co.*, 136 S.W.3d 218, 223 (Tex. 2004) (orig. proceeding) (per curiam) ("The party who seeks to limit discovery by asserting a privilege has the burden of proof."); *Huie v. DeShazo*, 922 S.W.2d 920, 926 (Tex. 1996) (orig. proceeding) ("The party resisting discovery bears the burden of proving any applicable privilege."); *Marteny v. Coon*, No. 09-19-00019-CV, 2020 Tex. App. LEXIS 7702, at *18, 2020 WL 5666567, at *7 (Tex. App.—Beaumont Sept. 24, 2020, orig. proceeding) (mem. op.) ("The party asserting a privilege has the burden to produce evidence concerning the privilege's applicability."); *In re Brookfield Infrastructure Grp., LLC*, No. 13-17-00486-CV, 2018 Tex. App. LEXIS 2492, at *27, 2018 WL 1725467 (Tex. App.—Corpus Christi Apr. 9, 2018, orig. proceeding) (mem. op.) ("The mere listing of a specific privilege in a response or a privilege log does not prove that privilege. Therefore, in

rational inference that the allegation is in fact true."[170] In some cases, the subject "documents themselves may constitute sufficient evidence to make a prima facie showing of attorney-client or work product privilege."[171] But most often, a prima facie case is established by a privilege log and evidence in the form of testimony or an affidavit.[172]

---

addition to the privilege log, the party resisting discovery must establish a prima facie case for the privilege by testimony or affidavit.") (citations omitted); *In re Rescue Concepts, Inc.*, 556 S.W.3d 331, 339 (Tex. App.—Houston [1st Dist.] Sept. 19, 2017, orig. proceeding) ("The burden to make a prima facie showing of the privilege is on the party seeking to shield information from discovery, and the party has the obligation to prove, by competent evidence, that the privilege applies to the information sought."); *In re DISH Network, LLC*, 528 S.W.3d 177, 181 (Tex. App.—El Paso 2017, orig. proceeding) ("The party asserting a privilege must establish by testimony or affidavit a *prima facie* case for the privilege."); *In re Park Cities Bank*, 409 S.W.3d 859, 868 (Tex. App.—Tyler 2013, orig. proceeding) ("The burden is on the party asserting a privilege from discovery to produce evidence concerning the applicability of the privilege. The mere listing of a specific privilege in a response or a privilege log does not prove that privilege.") (citation omitted); *In re BP Prods. N. Am. Inc.*, 263 S.W.3d 106, 111–12 (Tex. App.—Houston [1st Dist.] 2006, orig. proceeding) ("There is no presumption that documents are privileged, and the party seeking to resist discovery bears the burden of pleading and proving an applicable privilege. To meet its burden, the party seeking to assert a privilege must make a prima facie showing of the applicability of a privilege by first asserting the privilege.") (citation omitted); *In re Anderson*, 163 S.W.3d 136, 141 (Tex. App.—San Antonio 2005, orig. proceeding) ("Because there is no presumption that documents are privileged, the party who seeks to limit discovery by asserting the privilege has the burden of proof."); *In re Christus Health Se. Tex.*, 167 S.W.3d 596, 599 (Tex. App.—Beaumont 2005, orig. proceeding) (same); *In re Maher*, 143 S.W.3d 907, 913 (Tex. App.—Fort Worth 2004, orig. proceeding) (noting further that "prima facie case is required to prevent trial judges from being compelled to inspect untold numbers of documents").

170 *In re E.I. DuPont de Nemours & Co.*, 136 S.W.3d 218, 223 (Tex. 2004) (orig. proceeding) (per curiam) (quoting *Tex. Tech. Univ. Health Sciences Ctr. v. Apodaca*, 876 S.W.2d 402, 407 (Tex. App.—El Paso 1994, writ denied)); *accord In re Nat'l Lloyds Ins. Co.*, 532 S.W.3d 794, 804 (Tex. 2017) (orig. proceeding); *In re Goin*, No. 06-17-00047-CV, 2017 Tex. App. LEXIS 6351, at *6–7, 2017 WL 2961478 (Tex. App.—Texarkana July 12, 2017, orig. proceeding) (mem. op.); *In re Park Cities Bank*, 409 S.W.3d 859, 868 (Tex. App.—Tyler 2013, orig. proceeding); *In re BP Prods. N. Am. Inc.*, 263 S.W.3d 106, 114 (Tex. App.—Houston [1st Dist.] 2006, orig. proceeding); *In re Christus Health Se. Tex.*, 167 S.W.3d 596, 599 (Tex. App.—Beaumont 2005, orig. proceeding); *In re Maher*, 143 S.W.3d 907, 913 (Tex. App.—Fort Worth 2004, orig. proceeding).

171 *In re E.I. DuPont de Nemours & Co.*, 136 S.W.3d 218, 223 (Tex. 2004) (orig. proceeding) (per curiam); *accord In re Nat'l Lloyds Ins. Co.*, 532 S.W.3d 794, 804 (Tex. 2017) (orig. proceeding); *In re Atl. Sounding Co.*, No. 14-18-00523-CV, 2018 Tex. App. LEXIS 6880, at*4, 2018 WL 4116837 (Tex. App.—Houston [14th Dist.] Aug. 28, 2018, orig. proceeding) (mem. op.) *In re Mid-Century Ins. Co.*, 549 S.W.3d 730, 733 (Tex. App.—Waco 2017, orig. proceeding) (mem. op.); *In re Park Cities Bank*, 409 S.W.3d 859, 868 (Tex. App.—Tyler 2013, orig. proceeding); *In re Christus Health Se. Tex.*, 167 S.W.3d 596, 600 (Tex. App.—Beaumont 2005, orig. proceeding).

172 Tex. R. Civ. P. 193.4(a); *see In re Living Ctrs. of Tex., Inc.*, 175 S.W.3d 253, 261 (Tex. 2005) (orig. proceeding) ("In addition to the privilege log, a prima facie case for the privilege must be established by testimony or affidavit. A prima facie case is required to prevent trial judges from being compelled to inspect untold numbers of documents."); *In re York Risk Servs. Grp., Inc.*, No. 12-17-00210-CV, 2017 Tex. App. LEXIS 10942, at *10–11, 2017 WL 5622951 (Tex. App.—Tyler Nov. 22, 2017, orig. proceeding) (mem. op.) ("In addition to providing a privilege log, the party resisting discovery must provide testimony or affidavits establishing a prima facie case for the privilege."); *In re Mid-Century Ins. Co.*, 549 S.W.3d

An affidavit does not need to address each document individually to make a prima facie showing that the documents are privileged.[173] But an affidavit has "no probative value if it merely presents global allegations that documents come within the asserted privilege."[174]

If a party asserting a privilege makes a prima facie showing of privilege and tenders the withheld documents to the trial court, the court must conduct an in camera inspection of them before ruling on the motion to compel their production.[175] A trial court that refuses to conduct an in camera inspection abuses its discretion when the inspection is critical to a privilege claim's evaluation.[176] But the court

---

730, 733 (Tex. App.—Waco 2017, orig. proceeding) (mem. op.) ("Generally, this prima facie showing [of privilege] is made by serving a privilege log identifying the withheld documents and, if a hearing is held, by presenting evidence supporting the privilege."); *In re Goin*, No. 06-17-00047-CV, 2017 Tex. App. LEXIS 6351, at *6–7, 2017 WL 2961478 (Tex. App.—Texarkana July 12, 2017, orig. proceeding) (mem. op.) ("The party asserting a privilege from discovery has the burden to produce evidence concerning its applicability. Generally, this is accomplished by testimony or affidavit evidence sufficient to establish a prima facie case for the privilege.") (citations omitted); *In re Park Cities Bank*, 409 S.W.3d 859, 868 (Tex. App.—Tyler 2013, orig. proceeding) ("[I]n addition to the privilege log, the party resisting discovery must establish a prima facie case for the privilege by testimony or affidavit."); *In re Anderson*, 163 S.W.3d 136, 141 (Tex. App.—San Antonio 2005, orig. proceeding) ("The party asserting the privilege must present necessary evidence at the hearing by testimony or affidavit. . . . Only after the party asserting a privilege has made a prima facie case—provided the proper privilege log and presented evidence supporting the privilege at the hearing—does the requesting party have the burden to show the court which specific documents or groups of documents it believes require an in camera inspection."); *In re Maher*, 143 S.W.3d 907, 913 (Tex. App.—Fort Worth 2004, orig. proceeding) ("The privilege log is not proof; a prima facie case for the privilege must be proved by evidence necessary to support the privilege.").

173 *In re E.I. DuPont de Nemours & Co.*, 136 S.W.3d 218, 223–24 (Tex. 2004) (orig. proceeding) (per curiam) ("[A]n affidavit, even if it addresses groups of documents rather than each document individually, has been held to be sufficient to make a prima facie showing of attorney-client and/or work product privilege.").

174 *In re E.I. DuPont de Nemours & Co.*, 136 S.W.3d 218, 224 (Tex. 2004) (orig. proceeding) (per curiam); *accord In re BP Prods. N. Am. Inc.*, 263 S.W.3d 106, 113 (Tex. App.—Houston [1st Dist.] 2006, orig. proceeding) ("An affidavit is conclusory if it provides no factual bases for the applicability of the privileges asserted.").

175 *In re E.I. DuPont de Nemours & Co.*, 136 S.W.3d 218, 223 (Tex. 2004) (orig. proceeding) (per curiam); *In re Brookfield Infrastructure Grp., LLC*, No. 13-17-00486-CV, 2018 Tex. App. LEXIS 2492, at *27, 2018 WL 1725467 (Tex. App.—Corpus Christi Apr. 9, 2018, orig. proceeding) (mem. op.); *In re BP Prods. N. Am. Inc.*, 263 S.W.3d 106, 112 (Tex. App.—Houston [1st Dist.] 2006, orig. proceeding); *In re JDN Real Estate—McKinney L.P.*, 211 S.W.3d 907, 925–26 (Tex. App.—Dallas 2006, orig. proceeding).

176 *In re Silver*, 540 S.W.3d 530, 539 (Tex. 2018) (orig. proceeding) ("A trial court can review documents *in camera* if necessary to determine whether a privilege applies. When such a review is critical to the determination of a privilege claim, the trial court abuses its discretion when it fails to conduct an adequate *in camera* inspection.") (citation omitted); *accord In re Living Ctrs. of Tex., Inc.*, 175 S.W.3d 253, 261 (Tex. 2005) (orig. proceeding); *In re E.I. DuPont de Nemours & Co.*, 136 S.W.3d 218, 223 (Tex. 2004) (orig. proceeding) (per curiam); *Hagan v. Pennington*, No. 05-18-00010-CV, 2019 Tex. App. LEXIS 5101, at *46, 2019 WL 2521719 (Tex. App.—Dallas June 19, 2019, no pet.) (mem. op.); *see In re Atl. Sounding Co.*, No. 14-18-00523-CV, 2018 Tex. App. LEXIS 6880, at *5, 2018 WL 4116837 (Tex. App.—

has discretion to determine the quantity of documents it needs to review to assess privileges.[177]

"To the extent the court sustains the objection or privilege claim, the responding party has no further duty to respond to the request[.]"[178] However, to the extent the objection or privilege claim is overruled, the responding party must produce the requested documents or provide the requested information within thirty days after the court's ruling or at such time as the court orders.[179] Mandamus relief is appropriate when a trial "court erroneously orders disclosure of privileged information"[180] or discovery that exceeds the scope permitted under the Texas discovery rules.[181]

Houston [14th Dist.] Aug. 28, 2018, orig. proceeding) (mem. op.) ("The trial court had no evidence available other than the documents to which relators claimed the attorney-client and work-product privileges applied. Relator repeatedly offered to tender the documents to the trial court for an in camera review. Under these circumstances, the trial court was obligated to conduct an in camera review before granting the motion to compel and abused its discretion by failing to do so.").

[177] *In re Living Ctrs. of Tex., Inc.*, 175 S.W.3d 253, 261 (Tex. 2005) (orig. proceeding).

[178] Tex. R. Civ. P. 193.4(b).

[179] Tex. R. Civ. P. 193.4(b); *accord In re Treatment Equip. Co.*, No. 02-19-00202-CV, 2019 Tex. App. LEXIS 6267, at *15, 2019 WL 3295633 (Tex. App.—Fort Worth July 23, 2019, orig. proceeding) (mem. op.).

[180] *In re Bexar Cnty. Crim. Dist. Attorney's Office*, 224 S.W.3d 182, 185 (Tex. 2007) (orig. proceeding) ("We grant mandamus relief when the trial court has abused its discretion and a party has no adequate appellate remedy. . . . [W]e have repeatedly held that appeal is inadequate when a court erroneously orders disclosure of privileged information.") (footnotes omitted) (citation omitted); *accord In re Silver,* 540 S.W.3d 530, 538 (Tex. 2018) (orig. proceeding) ("Mandamus relief is appropriate when the trial court abuses its discretion, and no adequate appellate remedy exists to correct the abuse. A trial court abuses its discretion when it compels the production of privileged documents. Moreover, when the trial court orders production of privileged information, the party claiming the privilege has no adequate appellate remedy.") (citation omitted); *In re Nat'l Lloyds Ins. Co.*, 532 S.W.3d 794, 803 (Tex. 2017) (orig. proceeding) ("Mandamus relief is appropriate when . . . a trial court compels production of irrelevant information or information that is relevant but privileged."); *In re Christus Santa Rosa Health Sys.*, 492 S.W.3d 276, 279 (Tex. 2016) (orig. proceeding) ("If the trial court issues an erroneous order requiring the production of privileged documents, the party claiming the privilege is left without an adequate appellate remedy. If the documents at issue are alleged to be privileged, 'mandamus is appropriate if we conclude that they are privileged and have been improperly ordered disclosed.'" (citations omitted) (quoting *In re Living Ctrs. of Tex., Inc.*, 175 S.W.3d 253, 256 (Tex. 2005) (orig. proceeding))); *In re Mem'l Hermann Hosp. Sys.*, 464 S.W.3d 686, 697–98 (Tex. 2015) (orig. proceeding) ("'Mandamus is proper when the trial court erroneously orders the disclosure of privileged information because the trial court's error cannot be corrected on appeal.'" (quoting *In re DuPont de Nemours & Co.*, 136 S.W.3d 218, 222 (Tex. 2004) (orig. proceeding) (per curiam))); *In re Ford Motor Co.*, 211 S.W.3d 295, 297–98 (Tex. 2006) (orig. proceeding) (per curiam) ("We consider Ford's request for mandamus relief under a well-settled standard: mandamus is proper when the trial court has abused its discretion by committing a clear error of law for which appeal is an inadequate remedy. Moreover, as we have repeatedly held, appeal is inadequate when a trial court erroneously orders the production of confidential information or privileged documents.") (citations omitted).

[181] *See, e.g., In re Weekley Homes, L.P.*, 295 S.W.3d 309, 322 (Tex. 2009) (orig. proceeding) ("Mandamus relief is available when the trial court compels production beyond the permissible bounds of discovery."); *In re Allstate Cnty. Mut. Ins. Co.*, 227 S.W.3d 667, 668

An interesting question is how a court faced with a proper objection to a partially objectionable written-discovery request should proceed. In such a case, the court has two options: it can either narrow the request or sustain the objection in its entirety.[182] In most instances in which the discovery request is only partially objectionable, the appropriate course is to narrow the request so that is proper. As one federal court explained:

> It is within the discretion of a court ruling on a motion to compel to narrow the requests rather than sustain the responding party's objections to them in toto. In doing so, the court effectively sustains an objection that the requests are vague, ambiguous, or overbroad in part, and overrules it in part.[183]

This approach is consistent with Texas Rule 193.2(a), which allows parties to object to written-discovery requests in part,[184] and Texas Rule 192.6(b)(4), which allows a court to enter a protective order that "the discovery be undertaken only . . . upon such terms and conditions . . . directed by the court[.]"[185] It also is consistent with the interests of judicial economy because it will prevent the requesting party from serving additional interrogatories and production requests to obtain the information or material and the expense, time, and delay associated with a second motion to compel when the responding party invariably interposes the same objections to the new discovery.[186]

(Tex. 2007) (orig. proceeding) (per curiam) (same); *In re Graco Children's Prods., Inc.*, 210 S.W.3d 598, 600 (Tex. 2006) (orig. proceeding) (per curiam) (same); *In re CSX Corp.*, 124 S.W.3d 149, 152 (Tex. 2003) (orig. proceeding) (per curiam) (same).

182 *See, e.g., Francis v. Bryant*, No. CV F 04 5077 REC SMS P, 2006 U.S. Dist. LEXIS 21211, at *5–12, 2006 WL 947771 (E.D. Cal. Apr. 10, 2006) (sustaining objections to discovery requests as overbroad and irrelevant); *Wiley v. Williams*, 769 S.W.2d 715, 716–17 (Tex. App.—Austin 1989, orig. proceeding) (sustaining a privileged objection to a discovery request).

183 *Green v. Baca*, 219 F.R.D. 485, 490 (C.D. Cal. 2003); *accord Robinson v. Adams*, No. 1:08-cv-01380-AWI-BAM PC, 2012 U.S. Dist. LEXIS 41165, at *6, 2012 WL 1027921 (E.D. Cal. Mar. 26, 2012) ("It is well within the discretion of the court in ruling on a motion to compel to narrow the request rather than sustaining the responding parties [sic] objections."); *In re Control Data Corp. Sec. Litig.*, No. 3-85-1341, 1987 U.S. Dist. LEXIS 16829, at *10 (D. Minn. Dec. 10, 1987) ("In order to resolve a discovery dispute, the court may properly narrow the scope of a discovery request."); *see In re Alford Chevrolet-Geo*, 997 S.W.2d 173, 191–92 (Tex. 1999) (orig. proceeding) (Hecht, J., concurring in part, dissenting in part) ("When a party's attempted reach exceeds its legal grasp, we routinely limit the reach; we do not amputate the hand.").

184 Tex. R. Civ. P. 193.2(a) ("The party must state . . . the extent to which the party is refusing to comply with the request.").

185 Tex. R. Civ. P. 192.6(b)(4).

186 Robert K. Wise, *Ending Evasive Responses to Written Discovery: A Guide for Properly Responding (and Objecting) to Interrogatories and Document Requests Under the Texas Discovery Rules*, 65 Baylor L. Rev. 510, 566 (2013). The Beaumont Court of Appeals appears to have rejected this approach. *E.g., In re Master Flo Valve Inc.*, 485 S.W.3d 207, 214 (Tex. App.—Houston [14th Dist.] 2016, orig. proceeding) ("It is not this court's responsibility to remedy this defect[,] a production request that was overly broad because it had no time limit]. 'The burden to propound discovery complying with the rules of discovery should be on the party propounding the discovery, and not on the courts to redraft overly broad discovery so that, as re-drawn by the court, the requests comply with the discovery rules.' We

Finally, a party who withholds information or documents from discovery under an objection or privilege claim, even one that has been sustained by the trial court, cannot use the information or documents at any hearing or trial "without timely amending or supplementing the party's response to that discovery to reveal the withheld information."[187]

5-6 Amendment and Supplementation

Texas Rule 193.5(a) governs a party's duty to amend or supplement written-discovery responses.[188] It requires a responding party to amend or supplement two types of discovery responses: (1) responses to written discovery that sought the identification of persons with knowledge of relevant facts, trial witnesses, or expert witnesses; and (2) written-discovery responses on all other matters, unless the other parties have been made aware of the corrective or additional information in writing, on the record at a deposition, or through other discovery responses.[189] Thus, under the Rule, amendment or supplementation is always necessary for written discovery that seeks identification of persons with knowledge of relevant facts or trial and expert witnesses. But

---

therefore direct the trial court to vacate the part of its order that requires Master Flo to fully respond to request no. 14." (citation omitted) (quoting *In re TIG Ins. Co.*, 172 S.W.3d 160, 168 (Tex. App.—Beaumont 2005, orig. proceeding))); *In re Family Dollar Stores of Tex., LLC*, No. 09-11-00432-CV, 2011 Tex. App. LEXIS 8782, at *9–10, 2011 WL 5299578 (Tex. App.—Beaumont Sept. 19, 2011, orig. proceeding) (mem. op.) ("The burden to propound discovery that complies with the rules of procedure is placed on the party propounding the discovery. . . . [T]hat burden should not be transferred to the courts to redraft a party's discovery requests."); *In re Premcor Ref. Grp., Inc.*, No. 09-09-00222-CV, 2009 Tex. App. LEXIS 5850, at *11, 2009 WL 2253290 (Tex. App.—Beaumont June 8, 2009, orig. proceeding) (mem. op.) (per curiam) ("We believe that the remedy for a party's overbroad discovery request lies principally with the discovery's draftsman as we have stated: 'The burden to propound discovery complying with the discovery rules should be on the party and not on the courts to redraft overbroad discovery. We again decline to transfer the burden to properly draft narrowly tailed discovery to the courts and direct the trial court to enter the ruling that is should have entered at the hearing and to sustain Valero's objection.'"); *In re Mobil Oil Corp.*, No. 09-06-392 CV, 2006 Tex. App. LEXIS 9187, at *5, 2006 WL 3028063 (Tex. App.—Beaumont Oct. 26, 2006, orig. proceeding) (mem. op.) (per curiam) ("The requesting part has the responsibility to tailor its discovery requests; the tailoring is not the responsibility of the court or the responding party."); *In re TIG Ins. Co.*, 172 S.W.3d 160, 168 (Tex. App.—Beaumont 2005, orig. proceeding) (per curiam) ("The burden to propound discovery complying with the rules of discovery should be on the party propounding the discovery and not on the court to re-draft overly broad discovery so that redrawn by the court the requests compel with the discovery rules."); *In re Sears, Roebuck & Co.*, 146 S.W.3d 328, 333 (Tex. App.—Beaumont 2004, orig. proceeding) (per curiam) ("[A] responding party does not have the burden to tailor a reasonable request for the requesting party.").

187 Tex. R. Civ. P. 193.4(c).

188 The duty to amend or supplement does not apply to deposition testimony other than expert deposition testimony. Tex. R. Civ. P. 193 cmt. 5 to 1999 change ("This rule imposes no duty to supplement or amend deposition testimony. The only duty to supplement deposition testimony is provided in [Texas] Rule 195.6, [which relates to experts].").

189 Tex. R. Civ. P. 193.5(a). A party who has admitted a request for admission cannot withdraw or qualify the admission without leave of court. Tex. R. Civ. P. 198.3. See also Chapter 10, section 10-7 (discussing withdrawal, supplementation, or amendment of responses to requests for admission).

amendment or supplementation is required for other discovery responses only when the responding party has not otherwise provided the information or documents to the requesting party in writing or on the record at a deposition.[190]

Once a requesting party ceases to be part of the action (e.g., through settlement or dismissal), the remaining parties have no duty to supplement written discovery served by the former party because the duty to respond to discovery requests is owed only to the party who served them.[191] And in multi-party litigation, a non-requesting party is entitled to rely on responses to another active party's written-discovery requests. Accordingly, a failure to amend or supplement nonetheless may result in an exclusionary sanction when an undisclosed witness or other evidence is offered only against a party who did not request the information.[192]

Texas Rule 193.5 refers to both "amending" and "supplementing" written-discovery responses[193] but does not explain the difference between them or specify when one, rather than the other, is required. Legally, an "amended response" is one that wholly replaces an earlier one, whereas a "supplemental response" is one that provides additional information to the earlier one without replacing it in its entirety.[194] Because Texas Rule 193.5's predecessor, former Texas Rule 166b(6), only provided for supplemental discovery responses, care should be taken in labeling subsequent discovery responses because an opposing party can argue that the introduction of "amended responses" to the discovery lexicon was intentional and necessarily means that such a response is one that entirely replaces the earlier one. If so, objections made in an earlier response that are omitted in an amended one arguably have been waived and information disclosed in an earlier response that is omitted in an amended one arguably should be excluded under Texas Rule 193.6 as having not been timely disclosed.

The duty to amend or supplement written-discovery responses arises when "a party learns that the party's response to written discovery was incomplete or incorrect when made, or, although complete and correct when made, is no longer complete and correct[.]"[195] The amendment or supplementation must occur "reasonably

---

[190] *See, e.g.*, *Munoz v. Castillo*, No. 13-18-00451-CV, 2020 Tex. App. LEXIS 2960, at *34, 2020 WL 1856476 (Tex. App.—Corpus Christi Apr. 9, 2020) (mem. op.) ("[A]lthough Castillo's discovery response was inadequate, he was under no obligation to supplement it because 'the additional or corrective information has been made known to the other parties . . . on the record at a deposition. . . .'" (quoting Tex. R. Civ. P. 193.5(2))).

[191] *Austin Ranch Enters., Inc. v. Wells*, 760 S.W.2d 703, 710 (Tex. App.—Fort Worth 1988, writ denied).

[192] *See Ticor Title Ins. Co. v. Lacy*, 803 S.W.2d 265, 266 (Tex. 1991) (holding that in multi-party litigation, one party may rely on the discovery answers of the other parties).

[193] Tex. R. Civ. P. 193.5.

[194] *See* Tex. R. Civ. P. 62, 64, 65, 69 (explaining the difference between amended and supplemental pleadings).

[195] Tex. R. Civ. P. 193.5(a); *accord Estate of Toarmina*, No. 05-15-00073-CV, 2016 Tex. App. LEXIS 6239, at *4, 2016 WL 3267253 (Tex. App.—Dallas June 13, 2016, pet. denied) (mem. op.) ("If a party learns that his response to written discovery is no longer complete and correct, the party must amend or supplement the response."); *Magro v. Magro*, No. 01-19-00701-CV, 2020 Tex. App. LEXIS 9650, at *45, 2020 WL 7251864 (Tex. App.—Houston [1st Dist.] Dec. 10, 2020, no pet.) (mem. op.) ("Parties have a duty to amend or supplement incomplete or incorrect responses to written discovery."); *VSDH Vaquero Venture, Ltd. v. Gross*, No. 05-19-00217-CV, 2020 WL 3248481, at *4 (Tex. App.—Dallas June 16, 2020, no pet.) (mem. op.) ("Under Texas Rule . . . 193.5, a party is under a duty to supplement its

promptly after the party discovers the necessity for such a response."[196] Thus, Texas Rule 193.5(b) requires a responding party to supplement continuously, rather than waiting until thirty days before trial, as under former Texas Rule 166b(6).[197] The 30-day requirement is still the final deadline for amendment or supplementation because Texas Rule 193.5(b) "presume[s] that an amended or supplemental response made less than 30 days before trial was not made reasonably promptly."[198] But the opposite presumption does *not* apply—amending or supplementing written discovery more than thirty days before trial is not presumed to be timely.[199] Thus, a supplemental or

---

discovery responses if the party knows the responses are incomplete or are no longer true unless the additional or corrective information has been made known to the other parties in writing, on the record at a deposition, or through other discovery responses."); *see LoCascio v. Mongrain*, No. 07-18-00280-CV, 2019 Tex. App. LEXIS 8795, at *25, 2019 WL 6525795 (Tex. App.—Amarillo Sept. 30, 2019, no pet.) (mem. op.) (Texas "Rule 193.5(a) imposes a duty on a party to supplement a discovery response that is incomplete.").

196 Tex. R. Civ. P. 193.5(b); *accord In re Dawson*, 550 S.W.3d 625, 630 (Tex. 2018) ("[T]he rules don't allow a party to drag its feet—the supplemental or amended response must be provided 'reasonably promptly after the party discovers the necessity for such a response.'" (quoting Tex. R. Civ. P. 193.5(b))); *In re Bertrand*, 602 S.W.3d 691, 696 (Tex. App.—Fort Worth 2020, no pet.) (Texas Rule "[193.5](b) provides, in pertinent part, that an amended or supplemental response must be made 'reasonably promptly' after the party discovers the necessity for amendment or supplementation."); *Consol. Reinforcement, L.P. v. Cheraif*, No. 04-18-00443-CV, 2019 Tex. App. LEXIS 4371, at *10, 2019 WL 2272890 (Tex. App.—San Antonio May 29, 2019, no pet.) (mem. op.) (same); *Estate of Toarmina*, No. 05-15-00073-CV, 2016 Tex. App. LEXIS 6239, at *4, 2016 WL 3267253 (Tex. App.—Dallas June 13, 2016, pet. denied) (mem. op.) (same); *see Liles v. Contreras*, 547 S.W.3d 280, 290 (Tex. App.—San Antonio 2018, pet. denied) ("R&G waited almost four months to provide Contreras with the settlement agreement and only after Contreras made an addition request, which she was not required to do. The trial court could have found the almost four month delay in supplementation was not reasonably prompt.").

197 *See, e.g.*, *In re Sun Coast Res., Inc.*, 562 S.W.3d 138, 156 n.5 (Tex. App.—Houston [14th Dist.] 2018, no pet.) (noting that a party "has a continuing duty to supplement its discovery responses").

198 Tex. R. Civ. P. 193.5(b); *accord Sohani v. Sunesara*, 546 S.W.3d 393, 408 (Tex. App.—Houston [1st Dist.] 2018, no pet.) ("The party must make an amended or supplemental response 'reasonably promptly after the party discovers the necessity for such a response,' and it is presumed that an amended or supplemental response made less than thirty days before trial was not made reasonable promptly." (quoting Tex. R. Civ. P. 193.5(b))); *Yarbrough v. ELC Energy, LLC*, No. 12-15-00303-CV, 2017 Tex. App. LEXIS 4950, at *24, 2017 WL 2351357 (Tex. App.—Tyler May 31, 2017, no pet.) (mem. op.) ("[I]it is presumed that an amended or supplemental response made less than thirty days before trial was not made reasonably promptly[.]").

199 *See In re Seas*, 13-17-00685-CV, 2018 Tex. App. LEXIS 1035, at *6, 2018 WL 740306 (Tex. App.—Corpus Christi Feb. 6, 2018, no pet.) (mem. op.) ("While there is a presumption that a supplement made less than thirty days before trial is untimely, there is no opposite presumption that a supplement made more than thirty days before trial is timely."); *In re Staff Care, Inc.*, 422 S.W.3d 876, 881 (Tex. App.—Dallas 2014, no pet.) ("Staff Care argues that its amended and supplemental disclosures were timely because they were made within the discovery period and more than 30 days prior to the date for trial. But there is no presumption that an amended disclosure made more than 30 days prior to trial is timely."); *Navarrete v. Williams*, 342 S.W.3d 116, 122 (Tex. App.—El Paso 2011, no pet.) ("Ms. Navarrete contends that because a discovery supplement made less than 30 days before trial is presumed to be untimely, that the opposite presumption must also apply. We disagree. If the opposite

amended written-discovery response made within thirty days of the discovery deadline can be found not to have been made reasonably promptly so that the evidence or witness properly is excluded.[200]

Additionally, information supplied in an amended or supplemental written-discovery response can itself give rise to the duty to amend or supplement. Thus, for example, a case decided under former Texas Rule Texas 166b(6) held that a defendant whose supplemented fact-witnesses list, which was served ten days before trial and which included an incorrect address for a new witness, had to show good cause not only for the late supplementation, but also for the failure to correct the faulty supplemental response.[201]

Finally, Texas Rule 193.5(b) provides that "[a]n amended or supplemental response must be in the same form as the initial response and must be verified by the party if the original response was required to be verified by the party, but the failure to comply with this requirement does not make the amended or supplemental response untimely unless the party making the response refuses to correct the defect within a reasonable time after it is pointed out."[202]

5-7 Consequences of Failing to Timely Respond, Amend, or Supplement

Under Texas Rule 193.6, a party's failure "to make, amend, or supplement" a written discovery response, including a required disclosure, in a timely manner will prevent the party from introducing in evidence the undisclosed material or information and from using the testimony of an undisclosed witness (other than named parties), unless the responding party shows "good cause" for the failure to disclose or the failure "will not unfairly surprise or unfairly prejudice the other

---

presumption had been intended, it would have been included in the language of the provision. Because no such language appears in the provision, we conclude the trial court did not abuse its discretion by excluding Plaintiff's Exhibits 10, 15, 16, and 17.") (citation omitted); ***Snider v. Stanley***, 44 S.W.3d 713, 715 (Tex. App.—Beaumont 2001, pet. denied) (noting that, although Texas Rule 193.5(b) includes a presumption that a supplement made less than 30 days before trial is untimely, there is no opposite presumption that supplement made more than 30 days before trial is timely).

200 ***E.g., In re Staff Care, Inc.***, 422 S.W.3d 876, 882–83 (Tex. App.—Dallas 2014, no pet.) (holding that, because the defendant's Texas Rule 194.2(d) damage disclosure request had been pending for more than two years, the trial court did not abuse its discretion in holding that an amended damage disclosure disclosing for the first time the plaintiff's damage theory and calculations a few days before the discovery cutoff was not made "reasonably promptly" as required by Texas Rule 193.5(b)); ***Hatch v. Tex. Prop. & Cas. Ins. Guar. Ass'n***, No. 01-06-00631-CV, 2007 Tex. App. LEXIS 5499, at *15–16, 2007 WL 2011041 (Tex. App.—Houston [1st Dist.] July 12, 2007, no pet.) (mem. op.) (holding that a supplementation of an expert disclosure made two business days before trial was not made "reasonably promptly"); ***Ersek v. Davis & Davis, P.C.***, 69 S.W.3d 268, 271 n.2 (Tex. App.—Austin 2002, pet. denied) (holding that the plaintiff's supplementation of his expert disclosure made eight months after the original response and two months after his expert-designation deadline was not made reasonably promptly).

201 ***Ramos v. Champlin Petroleum Co.***, 750 S.W.2d 873, 875, 877 (Tex. App.—Corpus Christi 1988, writ denied).

202 Tex. R. Civ. P. 193.5(b).

parties."[203] Texas Rule 193.6's purposes are "to promote responsible assessment of settlement[,] . . . prevent trial by ambush[,]"[204] and "give the other party the

[203] Tex. R. Civ. P. 193.6(a)-(b); *accord Fort Brown Villas III Condo. Ass'n v. Gillenwater*, 285 S.W.3d 879, 881 (Tex. 2009) (per curiam) ("Under Texas Rule 193.6, discovery that is not timely disclosed and witnesses that are not timely identified are inadmissible as evidence."); *Hsu v. Conterra Servs., LLC*, 01-20-00182-CV, 2021 Tex. App. LEXIS 1813, at *8–9, 2021 WL 921672 (Tex. App.—Houston [1st Dist.] Mar. 11, 2021, no pet.) (mem. op.) (same); *Paniagua v. Weekley Homes, LLC*, No. 05-19-00439-CV, 2021 Tex. App. LEXIS 265 at *25, 2021 WL 118663 (Tex. App.—Dallas Jan. 13, 2021, pet. filed) (mem. op.) (same); *Martinez Jardon v. Pfister*, 593 S.W.3d 810, 826 (Tex. App.—El Paso 2019, no pet.) ("A party who fails to make a timely discovery response may not introduce in evidence the material that was not timely disclosed, unless it makes a showing of good cause and lack of unfair surprise or prejudice to the opposing party."); *In re A.C.*, No. 02-18-00129-CV, 2018 Tex. App. LEXIS 8656 at *23, 2018 WL 5273931 (Tex. App.—Fort Worth Oct. 24, 2018, pet. denied) (mem. op.) (same); *Arshad v. Am. Express Bank, FSB*, 580 S.W.3d 798, 808 (Tex. App.—Houston [14th Dist.] 2019, no pet.) (noting that the "[R]ule mandating exclusion of witness testimony for failure to disclose witness does not apply to a named party" and that "[t]his court has held that a trial court may not exclude the testimony of a corporate representative at trial, even if the corporation fails to disclose the representative as a witness in its discovery responses") (citing cases); *Sadeghian v. Wright*, No. 06-18-00062-CV, 2019 Tex. App. LEXIS 354 at *13, 2019 WL 255741 (Tex. App.—Texarkana Jan. 18, 2019, pet. denied) (mem. op.) ("[T]he parenthetical reference '(other than a named party)' 'essentially states that named parties can testify at trial even if they do not list themselves as a fact witness in response to requests for disclosure[, but] . . . does not state or imply that parties are not required to respond to interrogatories or other types of discovery requests.'" (quoting *Cornejo v. Jones*, No. 05-12-01256-CV, 2014 Tex. App. LEXIS 966, at *6, 2014 WL 316607 (Tex. App.—Dallas Jan. 29, 2014, no pet.) (mem. op.))); *Mid Continent Lift & Equip., LLC v. J. McNeill Pilot Car Serv.*, 537 S.W.3d 660, 670–77 (Tex. App.—Austin 2017, no pet.) (affirming the trial court's exclusion of an expert on attorneys' fees who was designated late); *Ashmore v. JMS Constr., Inc.*, No. 05-15-00537-CV, 2016 Tex. App. LEXIS 13201, at *21, 2016 WL 7217256 (Tex. App.—Dallas Dec. 13, 2016, no pet.) (mem. op.) (same); *Estate of Toarmina*, No. 05-15-00073-CV, 2016 Tex. App. LEXIS 6239, at *4–5, 2016 WL 3267253 (Tex. App.—Dallas June 13, 2016, pet. denied) (mem. op.) (same); *Beinar v. Deegan*, 432 S.W.3d 398, 405 (Tex. App.—Dallas 2014, no pet.) (same); *Miller v. Carter*, No. 05-11-00193-CV, 2012 Tex. App. LEXIS 7255, at *5–6, 2012 WL 3679200 (Tex. App.—Dallas Aug. 28, 2012, pet. denied) (mem. op.) (same); *Dyer v. Cotton*, 333 S.W.3d 703, 717 (Tex. App.—Houston [1st Dist.] 2010, no pet.) (same); *see W. Atlas Int'l, Inc. v. Randolph*, No. 13-02-00244-CV, 2005 Tex. App. LEXIS 2199, at *21–23, 2005 WL 673483 (Tex. App.—Corpus Christi Mar. 24, 2005, no pet.) (mem. op.) (holding that a trial court did not abuse its discretion in excluding witnesses who were not properly identified in response to an interrogatory asking for the identity of the plaintiff's trial witnesses).

[204] *In re A.C.*, No. 02-18-00129-CV, 2018 Tex. App. LEXIS 8656, at *23, 2018 WL 5273931 (Tex. App.—Fort Worth Oct. 24, 2018, pet. denied) (mem. op.) (quoting *Alvarado v. Farah Mfg. Co.*, 830 S.W.2d 911, 914 (Tex. 1992)); *accord Insignia Hosp. Grp., Inc. v. Jalaram Guru, LLC*, No. 07-19-00057-CV, 2020 Tex. App. LEXIS 4146, at *13, 2020 WL 2786676 (Tex. App.—Amarillo May 27, 2020, pet. denied) (mem. op.); *In re Marriage of Keys*, No. 06-19-00018-CV, 2019 Tex. App. LEXIS 8814, at *15, 2019 WL 4865671 (Tex. App.—Texarkana Oct. 3, 2019, no pet.) (mem. op.); *Corey v. Rankin*, No. 14-17-00752-CV, 2018 Tex. App. LEXIS 9224, at *15, 2018 WL 5914531 (Tex. App.—Houston [14th Dist.] Nov. 13, 2018, no pet.) (mem. op.); *Ramirez v. Welch*, No. 05-16-00681-CV, 2018 Tex. App. LEXIS 6101, at *7, 2018 WL 3725254 (Tex. App.—Dallas Aug. 6, 2018, no pet.) (mem. op.); *Tijerina v. Wysong*, No. 14-15-00188-CV, 2017 Tex. App. LEXIS 1015, at *15, 2017 WL 506779 (Tex. App.—Houston [14th Dist.] Feb. 7, 2017, no pet.) (mem. op.); *Tex. Mun. League Intergovernmental Risk Pool v. Burns*, 209 S.W.3d 806, 817 (Tex. App.—Fort Worth 2006, no pet.); *Dyer v. Cotton*, 333 S.W.3d 703, 717 (Tex. App.—Houston [1st Dist.]

opportunity to prepare rebuttal to expert testimony."[205] Despite recognizing that the exclusion of evidence under Texas Rule 193.6 is a harsh consequence,[206] the courts have held that it is not a "death-penalty sanction."[207]

2010, no pet.); *Didur-Jones v. Family Dollar, Inc.*, No. 2-09-069-CV, 2009 Tex. App. LEXIS 8999, at *9, 2009 WL 3937477 (Tex. App.—Fort Worth Nov. 19, 2009, pet. denied) (mem. op.); *In re Kings Ridge Homeowners Ass'n*, 303 S.W.3d 773, 783 (Tex. App.—Fort Worth 2009, orig. proceeding); *Harris Cnty. v. Inter Nos, Ltd.*, 199 S.W.3d 363, 368 (Tex. App.—Houston [1st Dist.] 2006, no pet.); *see Martinez v. Pluma ex rel. A.C.V.*, No. 01-19-00411-CV, 2020 Tex. App. LEXIS 9977, at *12, 2020 WL 7391699 (Tex. App.—Houston [1st Dist.] Dec. 17, 2020, no pet.) (mem. op.) (stating purposes as protecting parties from surprise and preventing trial by ambush).

205 *F 1 Constr., Inc. v. Banz*, No. 05-19-00717-CV, 2021 Tex. App. LEXIS 401, at *5, 2021 WL 194109 (Tex. App.—Dallas Jan. 20, 2021, no pet.) (mem. op.); *accord In re D.W.G.K.*, 558 S.W.3d 671, 680 (Tex. App.—Texarkana 2018, pet. denied) ("The purposes of [Texas] Rule 193.6 are threefold: (1) to promote responsible assessment of settlement, (2) to prevent trial by ambush, and (3) to give the other party the opportunity to prepare rebuttal to expert testimony." (citing cases)); *VSDH Vaquero Venture, Ltd. v. Gross*, No. 05-19-00217-CV, 2020 Tex. App. LEXIS 4488, at *12–13, 2020 WL 3248481 (Tex. App.—Dallas June 16, 2020, no pet.) (mem. op.) (same); *In re D.C.*, No. 06-18-00114-CV, 2019 Tex. App. LEXIS 4865, at *32 n.12, 2019 WL 2455622 (Tex. App.—Texarkana June 13, 2019, no pet.) (mem. op.) (same).

206 *TierOne Converged Networks, Inc. v. Parman*, No. 05-12-00026-CV, 2013 Tex. App. LEXIS 8380 at *8, 2013 WL 3477346 (Tex. App.—Dallas July 9, 2013, pet. denied) (mem. op.) (stating that "the exclusion of the evidence is a harsh consequence"); *Dyer v. Cotton*, 333 S.W.3d 703, 717 (Tex. App.—Houston [1st Dist.] 2010, no pet.) (same); *State v. Target Corp.*, 194 S.W.3d 46, 50 n.4 (Tex. App.—Waco 2006, no pet.) ("not[ing] that the obvious purpose of [Texas] Rule 193.6(c) is to alleviate the harshness of the exclusion of evidence by vesting the trial court with discretion to grant a continuance in situations where a party . . . files a motion to exclude an opponent's critical evidence on the eve of trial").

207 *E.g.*, *F 1 Constr., Inc. v. Banz*, No. 05-19-00717-CV, 2021 Tex. App. LEXIS 401, at *4, 2021 WL 194109 (Tex. App.—Dallas Jan. 20, 2021, no pet.) (mem. op.) (rejecting a party's characterization of the exclusion of evidence as a death-penalty sanction, reasoning, among other things, that sanctions for discovery abuse under Texas Rule 215 are discretionary, whereas the Texas Rule 193.6 penalty is mandatory); *Sadeghian v. Wright*, No. 06-18-00062-CV, 2019 Tex. App. LEXIS 354, at *24 n.6, 2019 WL 255741 (Tex. App.—Texarkana Jan. 18, 2019, pet. denied) (mem. op.) ("'[A] trial court's imposition of the automatic . . . exclusion mandated by rule 193.6 is not a death-penalty sanction and is not reviewed as such.'" (quoting *Santana v. Santana*, No. 02-15-00140-CV, 2016 Tex. App. LEXIS 628, at *9 n.4, 2016 WL 278781 (Tex. App.—Fort Worth Jan. 21, 2016, no pet.) (mem. op.))); *Black v. Watts*, No. 04-17-00489-CV, 2018 Tex. App. LEXIS 6186, at *17, 2018 WL 3747746 (Tex. App.—San Antonio Aug. 8, 2018, pet. denied) (mem. op.) (same); *Amudo v. Amudo*, No. 01-17-00318-CV, 2018 WL 3059729, at *5 (Tex. App.—Houston [1st Dist.] June 21, 2018, no pet.) (mem. op.) ("The exclusion of evidence under [Texas] Rule 193.6, as here, 'is a matter of admissibility rather than a sanction for discovery abuse.'" (quoting *In re J.A.M., Jr.*, No. 04-11-00165-CV, 2012 Tex. App. LEXIS 3630 at *17, 2012 WL 1648215 (Tex. App.—San Antonio May 9, 2012, pet. denied) (mem. op.))); *Ashmore v. JMS Constr., Inc.*, No. 05-15-00537-CV, 2016 Tex. App. LEXIS 13201, at *21, 2016 WL 7217256 (Tex. App.—Dallas Dec. 13, 2016, no pet.) (mem. op.) ("Ashmore characterizes the trial court's decision to strike the disclosure responses as an imposition of death penalty sanctions. Once again, Ashmore confuses a consequence for his failure to file timely disclosure responses with a discovery sanction. As stated above, the sixth (last) scheduling order had a March 7, 2013 deadline for serving amended or supplemented discovery responses. Ashmore had the burden to establish good cause for the untimely response or lack of unfair surprise or unfair prejudice. If Ashmore failed to meet this burden, then under rule 193.6, the trial court's decision to strike the responses should be affirmed.") (citation omitted); *Lee v. Wal-Mart*, No. 11-14-00078-CV, 2016 Tex. App. LEXIS 2805, at *6–7, 2016 WL 1072644 (Tex. App.—Eastland Mar. 17, 2016, no pet.) (mem. op.) (holding that striking of the plaintiff's

Because Texas Rule 193.6 addresses the duty to *respond* to discovery, it is not triggered without a discovery request or a disclosure requirement necessitating a response.[208] Thus, for example, a party cannot use the Rule to justify the automatic exclusion of material or information at trial not produced before trial, if the party did not serve any discovery requests seeking the material or information and the material's or information's production was not otherwise prompted by required disclosures.[209]

Texas Rule 193.6's evidentiary exclusion applies equally to trial and summary judgment proceedings.[210] Accordingly, a trial court may exclude summary judgment

---

expert's summary judgment affidavit because the expert had not been timely disclosed was not a death-penalty sanction); *In re Staff Care, Inc.*, 422 S.W.3d 876, 882 (Tex. App.—Dallas 2014, no pet.) ("Staff Care also argues that the striking of its amended disclosure responses constituted a 'death penalty' discovery sanction, and that therefore, the trial court was required to consider lesser sanctions before granting defendants' motion to strike. We disagree."). *But see In re G.N.H.*, No. 11-05-00405-CV, 2006 Tex. App. LEXIS 9492, at *7, 2006 WL 3094354 (Tex. App.—Eastland Nov. 2, 2006, no pet.) (mem. op.) ("To the extent that the trial court's ruling [under Texas Rule 193.6] constituted an exclusion of evidence, it was comparable to a death penalty or dismissal because it destroyed Rossler's opportunity for a decision on the merits of the bill of review.").

Death-penalty sanctions are discussed in Chapter 14, section 14-3:2.

208 *See In re E.l.A.V.*, No. 08-18-00052-CV, 2019 Tex. App. LEXIS 9589, at *7, 2019 WL 5616970 (Tex. App.—El Paso Oct. 31, 2019, no pet.) (Texas "Rule 193.6 involves a party's duty to respond to a written discovery request. This obviously contemplates that there be a discovery request requiring a response before evidence may be excluded for failure to produce.") (citations omitted); *In re Methodist Primary Care Grp.*, 553 S.W.3d 709, 721 (Tex. App.—Houston [14th Dist.] 2018, orig. proceeding) ("[A] party cannot be compelled to produce (or sanctioned for failing to produce) that which it has not been requested to produce." (quoting *In re Lowe's Cos., Inc.*, 134 S.W.3d 876, 880 n.7 (Tex. App.—Houston [14th Dist.] 2004, orig. proceeding))).

209 *See In re E.l.A.V.*, No. 08-18-00052-CV, 2019 Tex. App. LEXIS 9589, at *7, 2019 WL 5616970 (Tex. App.—El Paso Oct. 31, 2019, no pet.) ("In this case, Father objected that the exhibits were not produced prior to trial, but he has not identified any discovery request seeking those documents and the appellate record does not contain any such request. Because Father has failed to establish that Mother had a duty to produce the exhibits prior to trial, we cannot conclude that the trial court abused its discretion by not excluding them pursuant to [Texas] Rule 193.6.").

210 *Fort Brown Villas III Condo. Ass'n v. Gillenwater*, 285 S.W.3d 879, 882 (Tex. 2009) (per curiam) ("Because we have already held that evidentiary rules apply equally in trial and summary judgment proceedings, we also hold that the evidentiary exclusion under [Texas] Rule 193.6 applies equally."); *accord Barron as Tr. of 3001 Decatur Tr. v. Fort Worth Transp. Auth.*, No. 02-19-00274-CV, 2021 Tex. App. LEXIS 2703, at *8, 8 n.12, 2021 WL 1323415 (Tex. App.—Fort Worth Apr. 8, 2021, no pet.) (mem. op.); *Sadeghian v. Wright*, No. 06-18-00062-CV, 2019 Tex. App. LEXIS 354, at *21 n.7, 2019 WL 255741 (Tex. App.—Texarkana Jan. 18, 2019, pet. denied) (mem. op.); *City of Hous. v. Ellis*, 01-17-00423-CV, 2018 Tex. App. LEXIS 6904, at *5–7, 2018 WL 4087415 (Tex. App.—Houston [1st Dist.] Aug. 28, 2018, no pet.) (mem. op.); *Black v. Watts*, No. 04-17-00489-CV, 2018 Tex. App. LEXIS 6186, at *8–10, 2018 WL 3747746 (Tex. App.—San Antonio Aug. 8, 2018, pet. denied) (mem. op.); *Yarbrough v. ELC Energy, LLC*, No. 12-15-00303-CV, 2017 Tex. App. LEXIS 4950, at *2–6 (Tex. App.—Tyler May 31, 2017, no pet.) (mem. op.); *Beinar v. Deegan*, 432 S.W.3d 398, 405 (Tex. App.—Dallas 2014, no pet.); *see Hagan v. Pennington*, No. 05-18-00010-CV, 2019 Tex. App. LEXIS 5101, at *22, 2019 WL 2521719 (Tex. App.—Dallas June 19, 2019, no pet.) (mem. op.) ("The rules requiring an expert to be designated before any testimony from that expert can be admitted apply in summary judgment proceedings, such that a non-designated expert's

evidence, including expert evidence, that was not provided in response to written discovery before the summary judgment hearing.[211] Texas Rule 193.6, however, is inapplicable to non-merits hearings.[212]

Although the evidentiary exclusion is automatic[213] and a motion for sanctions or to

---

affidavit cannot be considered as summary judgment evidence absent a showing of good cause or a lack of unfair surprise or prejudice."); *LSREF2 Apex (TX) II, LLC v. Blomquist*, No. 05-14-00851-CV, 2015 Tex. App. LEXIS 7845, at *4–8, 2015 WL 4554522 (Tex. App.—Dallas July 29, 2015, no pet.) (mem. op.) (relying on Texas Rule 193.6 to hold that a trial court did not abuse its discretion in striking summary judgment response documents that were not timely produced in response to discovery requests).

[211] *See, e.g., Black v. Watts*, No. 04-17-00489-CV, 2018 Tex. App. LEXIS 6186, at *12–13, 2018 WL 3747746 (Tex. App.—San Antonio Aug. 8, 2018, pet. denied) (mem. op.) ("We find no abuse of discretion by the trial court in determining that Black had not met his burden to show admission of evidence from an undisclosed, untimely designated expert in the summary judgment proceeding would not unfairly surprise or prejudice Harris and Watts."); *Didur-Jones v. Family Dollar, Inc.*, No. 2-09-069-CV, 2009 Tex. App. LEXIS 8999, at *7, 2009 WL 3937477 (Tex. App.—Fort Worth Nov. 19, 2009, pet. denied) (mem. op.) ("Under [Texas R]ule 193.6, discovery that is not timely disclosed is inadmissible as evidence."); *Duerr v. Brown*, 262 S.W.3d 63, 76 (Tex. App.—Houston [14th Dist.] 2008, no pet.) (upholding the striking of a party's expert evidence in connection with a summary judgment motion because it was not timely disclosed); *Carbonara v. Tex. Stadium Corp.*, 244 S.W.3d 651, 657 (Tex. App.—Dallas 2008, no pet.) (same); *Ersek v. Davis & Davis, P.C.*, 69 S.W.3d 268, 271–72 (Tex. App.—Austin 2002, pet. denied) (same); *Blake v. Dorado*, 211 S.W.3d 429, 432 (Tex. App.—El Paso 2006, no pet.) ("Evidence that would be inadmissible at trial due to the proponent's failure to timely answer or supplement a request for production is also inadmissible in a summary judgment proceeding.").

[212] *In re Toyota Motor Corp.*, 191 S.W.3d 498, 501 (Tex. App.—Waco 2006, orig. proceeding) ("[Texas] Rule 193.6 does not operate to exclude an undisclosed expert's testimony from a preliminary hearing not on the merits. Thus, we hold that Respondent did not abuse his discretion by refusing to exclude Gaines's testimony from the hearing on the motion to quash the deposition notices.") (citation omitted); *Monsanto Co. v. Davis*, 24 S.W.3d 773, 785 (Tex. App.—Waco 2000, pet. dism'd w.o.j.) (holding that Texas Rule 193.6 was inapplicable to a class-certification hearing).

[213] Tex. R. Civ. P. 193.6(a) ("A party who fails to make, amend, or supplement a discovery response, including a required disclosure, in a timely manner *may not* introduce in evidence the material or information that was not timely disclosed, or offer the testimony of a witness (other than a named party) who was not timely identified[.]" (emphasis added)); *accord Argueta v. Guiterrez ex rel. M.C.*, No. 14-19-00794-CV, 2021 Tex. App. LEXIS 3007, at *5, 2021 WL 1567716 (Tex. App.—Houston [14th Dist.] Apr. 22, 2021, no pet.) (mem. op.); *F 1 Constr., Inc. v. Banz*, No. 05-19-00717-CV, 2021 Tex. App. LEXIS 401, at *3–5, 2021 WL 194109 (Tex. App.—Dallas Jan. 20, 2021, no pet.) (mem. op.); *VSDH Vaquero Venture, Ltd. v. Gross*, No. 05-19-00217-CV, 2020 Tex. App. LEXIS 4488, at *11–12, 2020 WL 3248481 (Tex. App.—Dallas June 16, 2020, no pet.) (mem. op.); *LoCascio v. Mongrain*, No. 07-18-00280-CV, 2019 Tex. App. LEXIS 8795, at *25, 2019 WL 6525795 (Tex. App.—Amarillo Sept. 30, 2019, no pet.) (mem. op.); *In re D.C.*, No. 06-18-00114-CV, 2019 Tex. App. LEXIS 4865, at *31–32, 2019 WL 2455622 (Tex. App.—Texarkana June 13, 2019, no pet.) (mem. op.); *McPherson v. Rudman*, No. 05-16-00719-CV, 2018 Tex. App. LEXIS 4601, at *14–15, 2018 WL 3062447 (Tex. App.—Dallas June 21, 2018, no pet.) (mem. op.); *Ashmore v. JMS Constr.*, Inc., No. 05-15-00537-CV, 2016 Tex. App. LEXIS 13201, at *18–19, 2016 WL 7217256 (Tex. App.—Dallas Dec. 13, 2016, no pet.) (mem. op.); *Lee v. Wal-Mart,* No. 11-14-00078-CV, 2016 Tex. App. LEXIS 2805, at *6, 2016 WL 1072644 (Tex. App.—Eastland Mar. 17, 2016) (mem. op.); *Dyer v. Cotton*, 333 S.W.3d 703, 717 (Tex. App.—Houston [1st Dist.] 2010, no pet.); *White v.*

compel generally is not a prerequisite to its application,[214] a requesting party should not lie behind the log and claim that ambiguities or minor deficiencies in written-discovery responses require the exclusion of the testimony or other evidence. Rather, the better practice is for a requesting party, who believes that a response is deficient, to move to compel a proper one.[215]

Moreover, Texas Rule 193.6(c) allows a trial court, rather than excluding the evidence or witness, to grant either a continuance or a temporary postponement to allow immediate supplementation and any needed additional discovery.[216] Thus, the Rule

---

Perez, No. 2-09-251-CV, 2010 Tex. App. LEXIS 150, at *3–4, 2010 WL 87469 (Tex. App.—Fort Worth Jan. 7, 2010, pet. denied) (mem. op.) (same).

214 *Cornejo v. Jones*, No. 05-12-01256-CV, 2014 Tex. App. LEXIS 966, at *9, 2014 WL 316607 (Tex. App.—Dallas Jan. 29, 2014, no pet.) (mem. op.) ("A motion to compel, however, is not a prerequisite to the exclusion of evidence under [Texas R]ule 193.6(a)."); *White v. Perez*, No. 2-09-251-CV, 2010 Tex. App. LEXIS 150, at *4–5, 2010 WL 87469 (Tex. App.—Fort Worth Jan. 7, 2010, pet. denied) (mem. op.) ("[N]o motion for sanctions or motion to compel is required to trigger [Rule 193.6's] application."). But see cases cited in note 214.

215 *See, e.g., Goldman v. Olmstead*, 414 S.W.3d 346, 365 n.5 (Tex. App.—Dallas 2013, pet. denied) (denying exclusion of the plaintiff's attorney's testimony regarding attorney's fees because "the Goldmans could have filed a motion to compel under rule 215 of the Texas Rules of Civil Procedure to obtain more specific information, but failed to do so"); *Roman v. Cuprum S.A. de C.V*, No. 13-10-00165-CV, 2012 Tex. App. LEXIS 2553, at *9–10, 2012 WL 1073251 Tex. App.—Corpus Christi Mar. 29, 2012, no pet.) (mem. op.) (denying exclusion of an expert witness's testimony because "if Roman believed that Cuprum's [expert] disclosures were insufficiently specific, she could have moved to compel additional disclosure or she could have taken the opportunity to depose Dr. Knox. Roman chose to do neither of those things.") (citation omitted); *$27,877.00 Current Money v. State*, 331 S.W.3d 110, 120 (Tex. App.—Fort Worth 2010, pet. denied) ("We have said before that failure to respond to a request for the mental impressions and opinions of the expert is a complete failure to respond, triggering the automatic exclusion under [Texas] Rule 193.6, not just an incomplete answer, which the Texas Supreme Court has held requires a pretrial objection or a pretrial motion to compel or for sanctions[.]" (citing *State Farm Fire & Cas. Co. v. Morua*, 979 S.W.2d 616, 619–20 (Tex. 1998))); *Van Heerden v. Van Heernden*, 321 S.W.3d 869, 876 n.2 (Tex. App—Houston [14th Dist.] 2010, no pet.) ("Casper did not complain about Anne's disclosures until trial. If he believed he needed more information . . ., he should have moved to compel. . . . The discovery rules are not meant to be used as weapons in an ambush.").

216 Tex. R. Civ. P. 193.6(c) ("Even if the party seeking to introduce the evidence or call the witness fails to carry the burden under paragraph (b), the court may grant a continuance or temporarily postpone the trial to allow a response to be made, amended, or supplemented, and to allow opposing parties to conduct discovery regarding any new information presented by that response."); *accord Saum v. Am. Express Nat'l Bank*, No. 02-19-00415-CV, 2021 Tex. App. LEXIS 2071, at *31–32, 2021 WL 1034146 (Tex. App.—Fort Worth Mar. 18, 2021, pet. denied); (mem. op.) *Insignia Hosp. Grp., Inc. v. Jalaram Guru, LLC*, No. 07-19-00057-CV, 2020 Tex. App. LEXIS 4146, at *7–11, 2020 WL 2786676 (Tex. App.—Amarillo May 27, 2020, pet. denied) (mem. op.); *see Sundance Energy, Inc. v. NRP Oil & Gas LLP*, No. 01-18-00340-CV, 2019 Tex. App. LEXIS 7223 at *26, 2019 WL 3819523 (Tex. App.—Houston [1st Dist.] Aug. 15, 2019, pet. denied) (mem. op.) ("[W]e cannot conclude that the trial court's offer of a continuance was insufficient to remedy any unfair prejudice to Sundance. Accordingly, having refused the trial court's offer a continuance pursuant to Texas Rule . . . 193.6(c), Sundance cannot now argue that it suffered unfair prejudice by the admission of NRP's attorney's fees evidence."); *Amudo v. Amudo*, No. *Sadeghian v. Wright*, No. 06-18-00062-CV, 2019 Tex. App. LEXIS 354, at *11–12, 2019 WL 255741 (Tex. App.—Texarkana Jan. 18, 2019, pet. denied) (mem. op.) (addressing a party's failure to request a

provides great flexibility to the court.[217] The Rule also does not prohibit imposing appropriate sanctions for discovery abuse, if exclusion is not ordered. For example, the court might combine a postponement or continuance with a monetary sanction to compensate the other parties for any delay or added expense.

To exclude an undisclosed witness or other evidence, the opposing party must make a timely objection, either in a pretrial motion to exclude or when the witness or evidence is offered in a summary judgment proceeding or at trial.[218] Once the objection is made, the party offering the witness or evidence has the burden to establish good cause or lack of surprise or unfair prejudice, which must be supported by the record.[219]

---

continuance and concluding that, because the party did not avail himself of the safeguard against automatic exclusion, the trial court did not abuse its discretion by following Texas Rule 193.6 to exclude undesignated witnesses and evidence of previously undisclosed matters); *Orbison v. Ma-Tex Rope Co., Inc.*, 553 S.W.3d 17, 39 (Tex. App.—Texarkana 2018, pet. denied) ("In this case, the trial court offered the remedy provided in [Texas] Rule 193.6(c), but Appellants refused to continue the trial. In similar circumstances, several of our sister courts of appeals have found a waiver of any complaint under [Texas] Rule 193.6.") (citing cases); *Ashmore v. JMS Constr., Inc.*, No. 05-15-00537-CV, 2016 Tex. App. LEXIS 13201, at *21, 2016 WL 7217256 (Tex. App.—Dallas Dec. 13, 2016, no pet.) (mem. op.) ("While a trial court has the discretion to permit a continuance to allow for additional discovery, it is not obligated to do so."); *Estate of Toarmina*, No. 05-15-00073-CV, 2016 Tex. App. LEXIS 6239, at *5, 2016 WL 3267253 (Tex. App.—Dallas June 13, 2016, pet. denied) (mem. op.) ("Even if the party seeking to introduce the evidence or call the witness fails to show good cause or lack of unfair surprise, the court may grant a continuance or temporarily postpose the trial to allow a response to be made or allow opposing parties to conduct discovery regarding any new information presented."); *Cunningham v. Columbia / St. David's Healthcare Sys., L.P.*, 185 S.W.3d 7, 11, 15 (Tex. App.—Austin 2005, no pet.) ("In determining whether the court abused its discretion in denying the continuance, we consider 'the length of time the case has been on file, the materiality and purpose of the discovery sought, and whether the party seeking the continuance has exercised due diligence to obtain the discovery sought.'" (quoting *Joe v. Two Thirty Nine J.V.*, 145 S.W.3d 150, 161 (Tex. 2004))).

[217] *Mid Continent Lift & Equip., LLC v. J. McNeill Pilot Car Serv.*, 537 S.W.3d 660, 676–77 (Tex. App.—Austin 2017, no pet.) (holding that a trial court has no affirmative obligation to grant a continuance or temporary postponement and that the party seeking exclusion of the evidence has no obligation to request a continuance or temporary postponement).

[218] *See, e.g., Clark v. Trailways, Inc.*, 774 S.W.2d 644, 647 (Tex. 1989) (holding that error is waived when a party fails to object to a non-disclosed witness's testimony); *Argueta v. Guiterrez ex rel. M.C.*, No. 14-19-00794-CV, 2021 Tex. App. LEXIS 3007, at *6, 2021 WL 1567716 (Tex. App.—Houston [14th Dist.] Apr. 22, 2021, no pet.) (mem. op.) ("A [Texas] Rule 193.6 challenge must be raised in the trial court and a ruling must be secured to preserve the issue for appellate review."); *Petroleum Workers Union of the Republic of Mex. v. Gomez*, 503 S.W.3d 9, 36 (Tex. App.—Houston [14th Dist.] 2016, no pet.) ("The Union did not raise a timely objection based on [Texas] Rule 193.6 or timely request an instruction to the jury or a mistrial."); *Beinar v. Deegan*, 432 S.W.3d 398, 402 (Tex. App.—Dallas 2014, no pet.) ("As a prerequisite to presenting a complaint for appellate review, the record must show the complaint was made to the trial court by a timely request, objection, or motion." (citing Tex. R. App. P. 33.1(a)); *City of Paris v. McDowell*, 79 S.W.3d 601, 607 (Tex. App.—Texarkana 2000, no pet.) (same); *Atl. Richfield Co. v. Misty Prods., Inc.*, 820 S.W.2d 414, 421 (Tex. App.—Houston [14th Dist.] 1991, writ denied) (same).

[219] Tex. R. Civ. P. 193.6(b) ("The burden of establishing good cause or the lack of unfair surprise or unfair prejudice is on the party seeking to introduce the evidence or call the witness. A

The good-cause exception permits a trial court to excuse a failure to comply with discovery in difficult or impossible circumstances.[220] The Texas Supreme Court has held that "[c]ounsel should not be excused from the requirements of the rule without a strict showing of good cause."[221]

The following factors, standing alone, do not constitute good cause: inadvertence of counsel, lack of surprise, and the uniqueness or importance of the evidence at

---

finding of good cause or of the lack of unfair surprise or unfair prejudice must be supported by the record."); *accord Fort Brown Villas III Condo. Ass'n v. Gillenwater*, 285 S.W.3d 879, 881 (Tex. 2009) (per curiam); *Argueta v. Guiterrez ex rel. M.C.*, No. 14-19-00794-CV, 2021 Tex. App. LEXIS 3007, at *5–7, 2021 WL 1567716 (Tex. App.—Houston [14th Dist.] Apr. 22, 2021, no pet.) (mem. op.); *Christian v. Oceanwide Am., Inc.*, No. 01-19-00557-CV, 2020 Tex. App. LEXIS 10451, at *9–10, 2020 WL 7775762 (Tex. App.—Houston [1st Dist.] Dec. 31, 2020, no pet.) (mem. op.); *LoCascio v. Mongrain*, No. 07-18-00280-CV, 2019 Tex. App. LEXIS 8795, at *25, 2019 WL 6525795 (Tex. App.—Amarillo Sept. 30, 2019, no pet.) (mem. op.); *Arshad v. Am. Express Bank, FSB*, 580 S.W.3d 798, 807 (Tex. App.—Houston [14th Dist.] 2019, no pet.); *Ramirez v. Welch*, No. 05-16-00681-CV, 2018 Tex. App. LEXIS 6101, at *4–7, 2018 WL 3725254 (Tex. App.—Dallas Aug. 6, 2018, no pet.) (mem. op.); *Cornejo v. Jones*, No. 05-12-01256-CV, 2014 Tex. App. LEXIS 966, at *8–9, 2014 WL 316607 (Tex. App.—Dallas Jan. 29, 2014, no pet.) (mem. op.); *PopCap Games, Inc. v. MumboJumbo, LLC*, 350 S.W.3d 699, 718 (Tex. App.—Dallas 2011, pet. denied); *Good v. Baker*, 339 S.W.3d 260, 271 (Tex. App.—Texarkana 2011, pet. denied); *Dyer v. Cotton*, 333 S.W.3d 703, 717 (Tex. App.—Houston [1st Dist.] 2010, no pet.); *In re Kings Ridge Homeowners Ass'n, Inc.*, 303 S.W.3d 773, 783 (Tex. App.—Fort Worth 2009, orig. proceeding); *Perez v. Embree Constr. Grp., Inc.*, 228 S.W.3d 875, 884 (Tex. App.—Austin 2007, pet. denied); *see Magro v. Magro*, 01-19-00701-CV, 2020 Tex. App. LEXIS 9650, at *46, 2020 WL 7251864 (Tex. App.—Houston [1st Dist.] Dec. 10, 2020, no pet.) (mem. op.) ("The trial court has broad discretion to determine whether the party has met this burden [of showing good cause or lack of unfair surprise or prejudice], but the trial court's determination must be supported by the record."); *Anani v. Abuzaid*, No. 05-16-01364-CV, 2018 Tex. App. LEXIS 4141, at *23, 2018 WL 2926660 (Tex. App.—Dallas June 7, 2018, no pet.) (mem. op.) ("The record as a whole can be taken into consideration when making the determination of whether a party is unfairly surprised or prejudiced or whether there is good cause to allow testimony from a witness who was not timely disclosed.").

[220] *See Franke v. Palau*, No. 01-18-00424-CV, 2019 Tex. App. LEXIS 4264, at *12–13, 2019 WL 2220112 (Tex. App.—Houston [1st Dist.] May 23, 2019, no pet.) (mem. op.) ("Good cause exists when circumstances make timely disclosure or designation difficult or impossible."); *PopCap Games, Inc. v. MumboJumbo, LLC*, 350 S.W.3d 699, 718 (Tex. App.—Dallas 2011, pet. denied) ("The good-cause exception allows a trial judge to excuse a party's failure to comply with discovery obligations in difficult or impossible circumstances."); *accord F 1 Constr., Inc. v. Banz*, No. 05-19-00717-CV, 2021 Tex. App. LEXIS 401, at*4–6, 2021 WL 194109 (Tex. App.—Dallas Jan. 20, 2021, no pet.) (mem. op.); *see Dyer v. Cotton*, 333 S.W.3d 703, 717 (Tex. App.—Houston [1st Dist.] 2010, no pet.) ("Although exclusion of testimony is a harsh consequence for failure to timely disclose or supplement, the good cause exception allows the trial court to excuse the failure to comply in 'difficult or impossible circumstances.'" (quoting *Alvarado v. Farah Mfg. Co.*, 830 S.W.2d 911, 914 (Tex. 1992))); *Keystone Architects v. Lanai Dev., L.L.C.*, No. 13-05-542-CV, 2008 Tex. App. LEXIS 1469, at *16, 2008 WL 523272 Tex. App.—Corpus Christi Feb. 28, 2008, no pet.) (mem. op.) (same).

[221] *Alvarado v. Farah Mfg. Co.*, 830 S.W.2d 911, 915 (Tex. 1992) (construing predecessor rule); *accord Franke v. Palau*, No. 01-18-00424-CV, 2019 Tex. App. LEXIS 4264, at *12, 2019 WL 2220112 (Tex. App.—Houston [1st Dist.] May 23, 2019, no pet.) (mem. op.) ("A party who relies on the good-cause exception must make a strict showing.").

issue.[222] In *Alvarado v. Farah Manufacturing Co.*, the Texas Supreme Court explained why these factors do not constitute good cause:

> The reasons in each instance are intuitive. If inadvertence of counsel, by itself, were good cause, the exception would swallow up the rule, for there would be few cases in which counsel would admit to making a deliberate decision not to comply with the discovery rules. Determining whether a party is really surprised by an offer of testimony not formally identified in discovery is difficult. The better prepared counsel is for trial, the more likely he is to have anticipated what evidence may be offered against his client, and the less likely he is to be surprised. It would hardly be right to reward competent counsel's diligent preparation by excusing his opponent from complying with the requirements of the rules. . . . Finally, if good cause could be shown simply by establishing the unique importance of the evidence to the presentation of the case, only unimportant evidence would ever be excluded, and the rule would be pointless.
>
> To relax the good cause standard in [former Texas] Rule 215.5 would impair its purpose. Counsel should not be excused from the requirements of the rule without a strict showing of good cause.[223]

Also, insufficient to establish good cause for the late designation of experts is the incompetence of a party's prior counsel and prior expert witness.[224] But a party's good-faith efforts to locate a potential witness or inability to anticipate the use of a witness's testimony at trial may support a finding of good cause for failure to timely disclose the witness.[225]

---

222 *Franke v. Palau*, No. 01-18-00424-CV, 2019 Tex. App. LEXIS 4264, at *13, 2019 WL 2220112 (Tex. App.—Houston [1st Dist.] May 23, 2019, no pet.) (mem. op.); *see Alvarado v. Farah Mfg. Co.*, 830 S.W.2d 911, 915 (Tex. 1992) ("We have repeatedly addressed what factors, standing alone, are not in themselves good cause. Included among these are inadvertence of counsel, lack of surprise, and uniqueness of the excluded evidence.") (citations omitted) (construing former Texas Rule 215.5); *F1 Constr., Inc. v. Banz*, No. 05-19-00717-CV, 2021 Tex. App. LEXIS 401, at *5, 2021 WL 194109 (Tex. App.—Dallas Jan. 20, 2021, no pet.) (mem. op.) (same); *PopCap Games, Inc. v. MumboJumbo, LLC*, 350 S.W.3d 699, 718 (Tex. App.—Dallas 2011, pet. denied) (same); *Harris Cnty. v. Inter Nos, Ltd.*, 199 S.W.3d 363, 367 (Tex. App.—Houston [1st Dist.] 2006, no pet.); *see Robinson v. Lubbering*, No. 03-09-00655-CV, 2011 Tex. App. LEXIS 1592, at *20–22, 2011 WL 749197 (Tex. App.—Austin Mar. 30, 2011, no pet.) (mem. op.) (holding that good cause was not established because plaintiff failed to timely seek discovery needed to provide proper damage disclosure); *O'Dell v. Wright*, 320 S.W.3d 505, 511–12 (Tex. App.—Fort Worth 2010, no pet.) ("Inadvertence [of counsel] alone will not constitute good cause for the failure to timely make, amend, or supplement a discovery response.").

223 *Alvarado v. Farah Mfg. Co.*, 830 S.W.2d 911, 915 (Tex. 1992) (citation omitted); *see Sprague v. Sprague*, 363 S.W.3d 788, 800 (Tex. App.—Houston [14th Dist.] 2012, pet. denied) ("Inadvertence of counsel is not good cause for failure to adhere to discovery deadlines.").

224 *See PopCap Games, Inc. v. MumboJumbo, LLC*, 350 S.W.3d 699, 718 (Tex. App.—Dallas 2011, pet. denied) (relying on the fact that inadvertence of counsel is not a good cause for the late designation of new experts to conclude that the incompetence of an original counsel and an original expert also are not good cause).

225 *See, e.g.*, *Clark v. Trailways, Inc.*, 774 S.W.2d 644, 647 (Tex. 1989) ("Lira's testimony falls short of indicating Clark's good faith efforts to locate Lira or her inability to anticipate the

In assessing whether the admission of undisclosed or untimely disclosed evidence will unfairly surprise or prejudice other parties, courts "focus on whether the evidence will cause unfair surprise or prejudice, and not on whether the '*issue*' to which the evidence is directed will unfairly surprise or prejudice the other parties."[226] The existence of unfair surprise or prejudice tends to be a fact-specific determination.[227]

---

use of his testimony at trial, which could otherwise support a finding of good cause to permit the testimony of an unidentified witness."); *Spurck v. Tex. Dept. of Family & Protective Servs.*, 396 S.W.3d 205, 216 (Tex. App.—Austin 2013, no pet.) ("[W]hen a party learns about the existence of witness during trial, the party may have good cause for failing to disclose the witness's identity to opposing counsel. . . . This is not a per se rule. If, for example, the party offering a witness would have learned about the witness's existence earlier if the party had conducted a reasonable investigation, the witness could be excluded based on lack of good cause.") (citation omitted); *Dyer v. Cotton*, 333 S.W.3d 703, 717 (Tex. App.—Houston [1st Dist.] 2010, no pet.) ("The Texas Supreme Court has previously indicated that a party's good faith efforts at locating a potential witness can support a finding of good cause.").

226 *PopCap Games, Inc. v. MumboJumbo, LLC*, 350 S.W.3d 699, 718 (Tex. App.—Dallas 2011, pet. denied) (emphasis added); *accord Franke v. Palau*, No. 01-18-00424-CV, 2019 Tex. App. LEXIS 4264 at *13, 2019 WL 2220112 (Tex. App.—Houston [1st Dist.] May 23, 2019, no pet.) (mem. op.) ("As to unfair surprise and prejudice, the inquiry focuses on whether the particular evidence will cause unfair surprise or prejudice, not whether the general issue or subject matter to which the evidence relates will unfairly surprise or prejudice the other parties."); *Lopez v. La Madeleine of Tex., Inc.*, 200 S.W.3d 854, 862 (Tex. App.—Dallas 2006, no pet.) ("Although it might be possible that untimely supplemented or amended discovery responses could cause surprise concerning the issues in a case, [Texas R]ule 193.6(a) relates to the discovery of evidence; its principal purpose—and most common application—is to protect a party from surprise concerning the existence of undisclosed evidence—not issues."), *quoted with approval in El-Rayes v. Lee*, No. 05-19-00881-CV, 2020 Tex. App. LEXIS 10395 at *7, 2020 WL 7767939 (Tex. App.—Dallas Dec. 30, 2020, no pet.) (mem. op.).

227 *See, e.g.*, *Estate of Trickett*, No. 13-19-00154-CV, 2020 Tex. App. LEXIS 8431, at *24, 2020 WL 6164324 (Tex. App.—Corpus Christi Oct. 22, 2020, pet. filed) (mem. op.) ("[A] party on appeal should not be heard to complain of the admission of improper evidence offered by the other side, when he, himself, introduced the same evidence or evidence of a similar character."); *VSDH Vaquero Venture, Ltd. v. Gross*, No. 05-19-00217-CV, 2020 Tex. App. LEXIS 4488, at *13, 2020 WL 3248481 (Tex. App.—Dallas June 16, 2020, no pet.) (mem. op.) ("Courts have found abuses of discretion in excluding late-disclosed witnesses or evidence when prior independent disclosure of materially the same information negated unfair surprise or unfair prejudice." (citing cases)); *Chang v. Denny*, No. 05-17-01457-CV, 2019 Tex. App. LEXIS 7586, at *32, 2019 WL 3955765 (Tex. App.—Dallas Aug. 22, 2019, pet. denied) (mem. op.) ("[W]ithin her disclosure on her damage calculation, Denny disclosed that she had been unable to work since 2012 and 'is permanently disabled.' Given this information, we reject any notion that Dr. Chang was somehow ambushed at trial with evidence of Denny's disability."); *Consol. Reinforcement, L.P. v. Cheraif*, No. 04-18-00443-CV, 2019 Tex. App. LEXIS 4371, at *11–12, 2019 WL 2272890 (Tex. App.—San Antonio May 29, 2019, no pet.) (mem. op.) ("Because the record establishes Cheraif's supplemental responses to interrogatories identified his trial attorney as a witness, the trial court did not abuse its discretion in determining CRI would not be unfairly surprised or prejudiced by allowing Cheraif's trial attorney to testify regarding attorney's fees."); *Lee v. Glob. Stainless Supply, Inc.*, No. 01-17-00865-CV, 2018 Tex. App. LEXIS 10639, at *21, 2018 WL 6684854 (Tex. App.—Houston [1st Dist.] Dec. 20, 2018, pet. denied) (mem. op.) (analyzing the facts to conclude that "the trial court reasonably could have concluded that [Texas] Rule 193.6's exception for no unfair

But some general rules apply. For example, the "fact that a party needs an expert to establish its cause of action does not establish that other parties will not be unfairly surprised by the late designation of an expert."[228] Moreover, "[o]ffering other parties an opportunity to depose a late-designated expert also does not ensure the absence of unfair surprise or prejudice."[229] In addition, the fact that the trial court could have reopened discovery or granted a short postponement to ameliorate any unfair prejudice or prejudice is not dispositive of the issue.[230] Finally, consistent with Texas Rule

---

surprise or prejudice applied" to authorize the admission of opinions of an accounting firm that had not been designated as an expert); *In re A.C.*, No. 02-18-00129-CV, 2018 Tex. App. LEXIS 8656, at *23, 2018 WL 5273931 (Tex. App.—Fort Worth Oct. 24, 2018, pet. denied) (mem. op.) ("The trial court ruled that TDFPS's witnesses could testify after clarifying that the disclosures were, at most, six days late (or eighty-four days before trial) and after TDFPS's counsel explained that Mother knew what the witness would testify about. On this record, the trial court could have reasonably concluded that TDFPS met its burden to show that Mother sustained no unfair surprise or prejudice."); *Ramirez v. Welch*, No. 05-16-00681-CV, 2018 Tex. App. LEXIS 6101, at *20, 2018 WL 3725254 (Tex. App.—Dallas Aug. 6, 2018, no pet.) (mem. op.) ("We conclude that there is some evidence supporting the trial court's implicit finding that Welch's discovery violations did not unfairly surprise or unfairly prejudice Ramirez, if that is how the trial court decided this case."); *Mintz v. Julye Nesbitt Carew, M.D., P.A.*, No. 05-16-00997-CV, 2018 Tex. App. LEXIS 1194, at *17, 2018 WL 833371 (Tex. App.—Dallas Feb. 13, 2018, pet. denied) (mem. op.) ("Mintz's argument that there was no surprise or prejudice to Carew or Chestnut fails because the material he cites contains numerous, different amounts and methods of calculating damages."); *Miller v. Kennedy & Minshew, Prof'l Corp.*, 142 S.W.3d 325, 349 (Tex. App.—Fort Worth 2003, pet. denied) (holding that the trial court did not abuse its discretion in allowing expert testimony of individuals disclosed as fact witnesses, but not as expert witnesses, in discovery responses "because of the length of time [the requesting party] had known of the substance of their testimony and because [the requesting party's] experts had devoted so much time to attacking their valuation reports").

228 *PopCap Games, Inc. v. MumboJumbo, LLC*, 350 S.W.3d 699, 718 (Tex. App.—Dallas 2011, pet. denied); *accord Franke v. Palau*, No. 01-18-00424-CV, 2019 Tex. App. LEXIS 4264, at *13, 2019 WL 2220112 (Tex. App.—Houston [1st Dist.] May 23, 2019, no pet.) (mem. op.); *see Cunningham v. Columbia / St. David's Healthcare Sys., L.P.*, 185 S.W.3d 7, 14 (Tex. App.—Austin 2005, no pet.) ("'A party should not have to anticipate the disclosure of a material witness merely because his or her testimony would be vital to the case. The discovery rules were revised to make that sort of anticipation unnecessary.'" (quoting *Matagorda Cnty. Hosp. Dist. v. Burwell*, 94 S.W.3d 75, 83 (Tex. App.—Corpus Christi 2002, no pet.))); *Ersek v. Davis & Davis, P.C.*, 69 S.W.3d 268, 272 (Tex. App.—Austin 2002, pet. denied) ("Ersek contends that Davis & Davis was not unfairly surprised or prejudiced because an expert witness was required to establish this cause of action and because Ersek offered Davis & Davis open access to depose the expert witness. We do not find these arguments persuasive.").

229 *PopCap Games, Inc. v. MumboJumbo, LLC*, 350 S.W.3d 699, 718 (Tex. App.—Dallas 2011, pet. denied); *accord Franke v. Palau*, No. 01-18-00424-CV, 2019 Tex. App. LEXIS 4264, at *13, 2019 WL 2220112 (Tex. App.—Houston [1st Dist.] May 23, 2019, no pet.) (mem. op.).

230 *Mid Continent Lift & Equip., LLC v. J. McNeill Pilot Car Serv.*, 537 S.W.3d 660, 676–77 (Tex. App.—Austin 2017, no pet.) ("In a final argument advanced by Mid Continent, it posits that McNeill could have suffered no unfair surprise and unfair prejudice because the discovery rules provided means for McNeill to seek to reopen discovery in response to Mid Continent's untimely designation—specifically, [Texas] Rule 190.5, which allows for reopening of discovery where an adverse party would be 'unfairly prejudiced' by a pleading filed after or near the end of the discovery period, and subsection (c) of [Texas] Rule

193.6's purposes, some courts have held that "to establish the absence of unfair surprise or prejudice, the party seeking to call an untimely disclosed witness or introduce untimely disclosed evidence must establish that the other party had enough evidence to reasonably assess settlement, to avoid trial by ambush, and to prepare rebuttal to expert testimony."[231]

On appeal, a trial court's exclusion or admission of testimony or other evidence is reviewed for an abuse of discretion.[232] The erroneous admission or exclusion of the testimony or other evidence is reversible "only if the error probably though not necessarily resulted in [the rendition of] an improper judgment."[233] Accordingly,

---

193.6, which affords trial courts, in lieu of automatic exclusion when not finding unfair surprise and unfair prejudice, the option of permitting late disclosure and postponing trial to allow responsive discovery. Mid Continent further insists that McNeill had an affirmative duty to seek additional discovery under these provisions, and extracts from case law the proposition that '[t]here is no unfair prejudice or surprise when a party chooses to ignore opportunities to mitigate any purported unfair prejudice.' The authorities Mid Continent cites for that proposition, however, have involved circumstances where a party has declined a trial court's offer of additional discovery under subsection (c) or failed to timely move to exclude under [Texas] Rule 193.6. Neither is the situation here. As applied to this case, Mid Continent's argument would effectively invert its burden of proof under the unfair-surprise and unfair-prejudice exception to [Texas] Rule 193.6, if not effectively read [Texas] Rule 193.6's automatic exclusion out of the civil discovery rules entirely. We must instead evaluate the district court's exercise of discretion under the rules as written.").

231 *F 1 Constr., Inc. v. Banz*, No. 05-19-00717-CV, 2021 Tex. App. LEXIS 401, at *5, 2021 WL 194109 (Tex. App.—Dallas Jan. 20, 2021, no pet.) (mem. op.); *accord In re D.W.G.K.*, 558 S.W.3d 671, 680 (Tex. App.—Texarkana 2018, pet. denied); *VSDH Vaquero Venture, Ltd. v. Gross*, No. 05-19-00217-CV, 2020 Tex. App. LEXIS 4488, at *12, 2020 WL 3248481 (Tex. App.—Dallas June 16, 2020, no pet.) (mem. op.).

232 *Fort Brown Villas III Condo. Ass'n v. Gillenwater*, 285 S.W.3d 879, 881 (Tex. 2009) (per curiam) ("A trial court's exclusion of an expert who has not been properly designated can be overturned only upon a finding of abuse of discretion." (quoting *Mentis v. Barnard*, 870 S.W.2d 14, 16 (Tex. 1994))); *PopCap Games, Inc. v. MumboJumbo, LLC*, 350 S.W.3d 699, 718 (Tex. App.—Dallas 2011, pet. denied) (same); *Perez v. Embree Constr. Grp., Inc.*, 228 S.W.3d 875, 884 (Tex. App.—Austin 2007, pet. denied) (same); *see Nat'l Liab. & Fire Ins. Co. v. Allen*, 15 S.W.3d 525, 527–28 (Tex. 2000) ("On appeal, we review a trial court's evidentiary decisions by an abuse of discretion standard."); *Argueta v. Guiterrez ex rel. M.C.*, No. 14-19-00794-CV, 2021 Tex. App. LEXIS 3007, at *6, 2021 WL 1567716 (Tex. App.—Houston [14th Dist.] Apr. 22, 2021, no pet.) (mem. op.) (same); *F 1 Constr., Inc. v. Banz*, No. 05-19-00717-CV, 2021 Tex. App. LEXIS 401, at *5 2021 WL 194109 (Tex. App.—Dallas Jan. 20, 2021, no pet.) (mem. op.) (same); *Paniagua v. Weekley Homes, LLC*, No. 05-19-00439-CV, 2021 Tex. App. LEXIS 265, at*26, 2021 WL 118663 (Tex. App.—Dallas Jan. 13, 2021, pet. filed) (mem. op.) (same); *Black v. Watts*, No. 04-17-00489-CV, 2018 Tex. App. LEXIS 6186, at *10–11, 2018 WL 3747746 (Tex. App.—San Antonio Aug. 8, 2018, pet. denied) (mem. op.) (same); *Spurck v. Tex. Dept. of Family & Protective Servs.*, 396 S.W.3d 205, 214 (Tex. App.—Austin 2013, no pet.); *Harris Cnty. v. Inter Nos, Ltd.*, 199 S.W.3d 363, 367 (Tex. App.—Houston [1st Dist.] 2006, no pet.) (same); *see Hsu v. Conterra Servis. LLC*, No. 01-20-00182-CV, 2021 Tex. App. LEXIS 1813, at *8, 2021 WL 921672 (Tex. App.—Houston [1st Dist.] Mar. 11, 2021, no pet.) (mem. op.) ("The burden of establishing good cause or lack of unfair surprise and unfair prejudice is on the party seeking to call the witness. The trial court has broad discretion to determine whether the party has carried this burden.") (citation omitted).

233 *Nissan Motor Co. Ltd. v. Armstrong*, 145 S.W.3d 131, 144 (Tex. 2004) ("Erroneous admission of evidence requires reversal only if the error probably though not necessarily resulted in

"[r]eversible error does not ordinarily exist for erroneous exclusion or admission of evidence which is not controlling on a material issue dispositive of the case."[234]

5-8 Presumption of Authenticity[235]

Texas Rule 193.7 provides for self-authentication of documents produced by the parties in response to discovery requests.[236] Under the Rule, a party need not establish a document's authenticity through other discovery or evidence before using the document against the party producing it at a hearing or trial unless that party objects to its authentication by a specific, good-faith objection.[237] The Rule is particularly useful with respect to emails, whose authors or completeness may be difficult to verify. But

---

[the rendition of] an improper judgment."); *accord Kia Motors Corp. v. Ruiz*, 432 S.W.3d 865, 883 (Tex. 2014); *see* Tex. R. App. P. 44.1(a)(1)-(2) ("No judgment may be reversed on appeal on the ground that the trial court made an error of law unless the court of appeals concludes that the error complained of: (1) probably caused the rendition of an improper judgment; or (2) probably prevented the appellant from properly presenting the case to the court of appeals.").

[234] *Elliott v. Elliott*, 21 S.W.3d 913, 922 (Tex. App.—Fort Worth 2000, pet. denied) (citing *Gee v. Liberty Mut. Fire Ins. Co.*, 765 S.W.2d 394, 395 (Tex. 1989)); *accord Guijarro v. Charles P. Johnson, Inc.*, No. 13-19-00268-CV, 2021 Tex. App. LEXIS 2262, at *28, 2021 WL 1133614 (Tex. App.—Corpus Christi Mar. 25, 2021, no pet.) (mem. op.); *Warner Bros. Entm't, Inc. v. Jones*, 538 S.W.3d 781, 817 (Tex. App.—Austin 2017), *aff'd*, 611 S.W.3d 1 (Tex. 2020); *Perez v. Embree Const. Grp., Inc.*, 228 S.W.3d 875, 884 (Tex. App.—Austin 2007, pet. denied).

[235] This subchapter addresses how and to what extent documents are authenticated by virtue of their production. Self-authentication also is addressed by Texas Rule of Evidence 902, which is beyond the scope of this book.

[236] To be admissible into evidence, information or material not only must be relevant but it must be "authentic." To authenticate evidence means to identify it by a competent witness's testimony (or otherwise as permitted by rules of evidence) to be what the proponent claims it is. Tex. R. Evid. 901(a) ("To satisfy the requirement of authenticating or identifying an item of evidence, the proponent must produce evidence sufficient to support a finding that the item is what the proponent claims it is."); *see Fleming v. Wilson*, 610 S.W.3d 18, 20 (Tex. 2020) (per curiam) (Texas "Rule [of Evidence] 901 requires the proponent to 'produce evidence sufficient to support a finding that the item is what the proponent claims it is' and then provides a non-exclusive list of examples of such evidence." (quoting Tex. R. Evid. 901(a))).

[237] Tex. R. Civ. P. 193.7 ("A party's production of a document in response to written discovery authenticates the document for use against that party in any pretrial proceeding or at trial unless . . . the party objects to the authenticity of the document, or any part of it[.]"); *see Choice Asset Mgmt., Inc. v. CIT Tech. Fin. Servs., Inc.*, No. 07-12-00304-CV, 2013 Tex. App. LEXIS 11584, at *7, 2013 WL 5039340 (Tex. App.—Amarillo Sept. 11, 2013, no pet.) (mem. op.) ("[A] party's own production of evidence in response to written discovery authenticates the document for use against the producing party, unless that party objects to its authentication by 'stating the specific basis for the objection.'" (quoting Tex. R. Civ. P. 193.7)); *Blanche v. First Nationwide Mortg. Corp.*, 74 S.W.3d 444, 451 (Tex. App.—Dallas 2002, no pet.) ("Under [Texas R]ule 193.7, '[a] party's production of a document in response to written discovery authenticates the document for use against that party in any pretrial proceeding or at trial' unless the party who produced the document files a timely objection to the document's authenticity. The clear purpose of this rule is to alleviate the burden on a party receiving documents through discovery from proving the authenticity of those documents when they are used against the party who produced them." (quoting Tex. R. Civ. P. 193.7)).

the Rule cannot be used to authenticate emails or any other documents that were not produced "in response to written discovery[.]"[238]

Because Texas Rule 193.7 only provides for the document's self-authentication when it is used against the party producing the document, in a multi-party action, the party using the document must authentic it independently for use against non-producing parties. Moreover, a party cannot use the Rule to authentic documents that it has produced in discovery.[239]

Although Texas Rule 193.7 presumes that documents produced by a party are authentic for use against the party, it permits the producing party to make authenticity objections to those documents. Any objection must (1) be in writing or on the record, (2) be specific, (3) have a good faith factual and legal basis, and (4) be made

---

The mere fact that a document is relevant and authentic may be insufficient for its admission into evidence. Thus, a party also should ensure that all foundational questions needed for the document's admission into evidence exist—for example, that it is a party admission or a business record.

238 Tex. R. Civ. P. 193.7; *accord LocumTenens.com, LLC v. Hanna*, No. 14-18-00739-CV, 2020 Tex. App. LEXIS 1549, at *8, 2020 WL 897362 (Tex. App.—Houston [14th Dist.] Feb. 25, 2020, no pet.) (mem. op.) ("Because nothing in the record shows that [the plaintiff] produced the Purported Agreement in response to written discovery, [the defendant] did not authenticate the Purported Agreement under [Texas] Rule 193.7."); *Albert Lee Giddens, APLC v. Cuevas*, 14-16-00772-CV, 2017 Tex. App. LEXIS 8816, at *9, 2017 WL 4159263 (Tex. App.—Houston [14th Dist.] Sept. 19, 2017, no pet.) (mem. op.) ("Appellees also assert that the prior judgment was authenticated against Intervenor under [Texas R]ule 193.7 because, according to appellees, Intervenor produced it to Cuevas. We disagree. Nothing in the record tends to establish that Intervenor produced this document in response to written discovery in this case."); *see In re Sting Soccer Grp., LP*, 05-17-00317-CV, 2017 WL 5897454, at *7 (Tex. App.—Dallas Nov. 30, 2017, no pet.) (mem. op.) ("Texas law does not allow a party to evade discovery requests by simply asserting that the other party already has the information. Not only do such requests ensure that the parties have the same basic documents, requiring your opponent to produce certain documents enables the party seeking discovery to activate the automatic authentication rights provided by [Texas] Rule 193.7.") (citation omitted).

239 *See Brown v. Tarbert, LLC*, 616 S.W.3d 159, 166 (Tex. App.—Houston [14th Dist.] 2020, pet. denied) ("Even assuming the document was 'produced' as contemplated by [Texas] Rule 193.7, the Browns are the producing party, so the document is not authenticated for their use, but rather for the opposing parties' use."); *Tex. Black Iron, Inc. v. Arawak Energy Int'l Ltd.*, 566 S.W.3d 801, 812–13 (Tex. App.—Houston [14th Dist.] 2018, pet. denied) ("'A party cannot authenticate a document for use in its own favor by merely producing it in response to a discovery request.'" (quoting *Polmounter v. Keystone Food Prods.*, No. 14-05-00560-CV, 2006 Tex. App. LEXIS 7954, at *10–11, 2006 WL 2548239 (Tex. App.—Houston [14th Dist.] Sept. 5, 2006, no pet.) (mem. op.))); *Gunville v. Gonzales*, 508 S.W.3d 547, 562 (Tex. App.—El Paso 2016, no pet.) (same); *Gilbert v. Gen. Motors Corp.*, No. 2-05-00243-CV, 2006 Tex. App. LEXIS 5363, at *12–13 (Tex. App.—Fort Worth June 22, 2006, no pet.) (mem. op.) (same); *Blanche v. First Nationwide Mortg. Corp.*, 74 S.W.3d 444, 452 (Tex. App.—Dallas 2002, no pet.) (same).

One of the best ways to establish a document's authenticity is to send requests for admission to the opposing party asking it to admit that the document (irrespective of whether it is the requesting party's, an opposing party's, or a nonparty's document) is authentic. See Chapter 10, section 10-2:2.3 (discussing the use of requests for admission to establish documents' genuineness).

within ten days after the party obtains actual knowledge that another party will use the document in a hearing or trial, unless the trial court lengthens or shortens that time period.[240] The objection procedure's practical effect is that a party need not evaluate its documents' authenticity before producing them, but rather can wait until it is notified that particular documents will be used in a hearing or trial.

Authenticity objections are proper not only when the producing party has a specific, good-faith basis for disputing a document's authenticity, but also when it lacks sufficient knowledge to determine whether the document is authentic. For example, parties often produce documents created by others and about which they have little knowledge. An authenticity objection to such documents is proper.

Because the producing party does not have to assert authenticity objections until after it knows that a document will be used in a hearing or trial, there is a risk of "ambushing" the party seeking to use the document. Texas Rule 193.7 ameliorates this risk in two ways. *First*, it allows the party seeking to use the document a "reasonable opportunity to establish authenticity."[241] *Second*, as suggested by Comment 7 to the 1999 change to the Rule, to avoid authenticity issues at trial, "a party may identify prior to trial the documents intended to be offered, thereby triggering the obligation to object to authenticity. A trial court may also order this procedure."[242] Thus, a party in a case filed before January 1, 2021, should request that the action's pretrial order require the parties to exchange exhibit lists.[243]

The exhibit lists' exchange will trigger the producing party's obligation to object the authenticity of its documents on the opposing party's list.[244] If the producing party

---

[240] Tex. R. Civ. P. 193.7 ("A party's production of a document in response to written discovery authenticates the document for use against that party in any pretrial proceeding or at trial unless—within ten days or a longer or shorter time ordered by the court, after the producing party has actual notice that the document will be used—the party objects to the authenticity of the document, or any part of it, stating the specific basis for objection. An objection must be either on the record or in writing and must have a good faith factual and legal basis[.]"); *see Rodriguez v. City of Poteet*, No. 04-13-00274-CV, 2014 Tex. App. LEXIS 2136, at *8, 2014 WL 769286 (Tex. App.—San Antonio Feb. 26, 2014, no pet.) (mem. op.) ("When a party produces a document in response to written discovery, however, the document is self-authenticated for use against that party in any pretrial proceeding or at trial unless the party objects to the authenticity of the document, either on the record or in writing, within ten days of becoming actually aware that the document will be used. The objecting party must state a 'specific basis' for the objection." (quoting Tex. R. Civ. P. 193.7)); *Choice Asset Mgmt., Inc. v. CIT Tech. Fin. Servs.*, No. 07-12-00304-CV, 2013 Tex. App. LEXIS 11584, at *7, 2013 WL 5039340 (Tex. App.—Amarillo Sept. 11, 2013, no pet.) (mem. op.) ("The written objections tendered by Choice below were non-specific and bereft of allusion to any factual basis. The same omissions appear in its brief here. So, Choice failed to preserve its error and illustrate that the trial court erred in rejecting its complaint.").

[241] Tex. R. Civ. P. 193.7; *Rodriguez v. City of Poteet*, No. 04-13-00274-CV, 2014 Tex. App. LEXIS 2136, at *8–9, 2014 WL 769286 (Tex. App.—San Antonio Feb. 26, 2014, no pet.) (mem. op.) ("Following an objection, the party attempting to use the document 'should be given a reasonable opportunity to establish its authenticity." (quoting Tex. R. Civ. P. 193.7)).

[242] Tex. R. Civ. P. 193.7 cmt. 7 to 1999 change.

[243] In cases filed after January 1, 2021, Texas Rule 194 requires the parties to file exhibits lists thirty days before trial. Tex. R. Civ. P. 194.4(a)(2), (b).

[244] Tex. R. Civ. P. 193.7 cmt. 7 to 1999 change. The exhibit list will also trigger the ability to snap-back any inadvertently produced privileged document under Texas Rule 193.3(d).

fails to object to its documents' authenticity within ten days after the list's service, its listed documents will be deemed authentic for use against the party at trial. However, if the producing party objects to their authenticity, the party seeking to use the documents must be given a reasonable opportunity to establish the document's authenticity even if discovery has closed or a continuance is required.[245]

Many practitioners attempt to invoke Texas Rule 193.7's self-authentication provision by including in a pleading or a notice a statement to the effect that all documents produced by the opposing party will be deemed authentic for use against the producing party. For example, in *Merrell v. Wal-Mart Stores, Inc.*, Wal-Mart received a notice, styled "Notice of Self Authentication Pursuant to Rule 193.7, Tex. R. Civ. P.," that stated: "Please take notice that the documents you produced in response to all parties' Request for Production of Documents are authenticated pursuant to Rule 193.7, TEX. R. CIV. P., and will be used by Plaintiff at any trial or hearing."[246] Although the sufficiency of the notice was not decided on appeal because Wal-Mart "waived any complaints by not objecting to the specificity of the notice in the trial court[,]"[247] such a notice clearly is insufficient to trigger authenticity objections because the Rule's objection procedure contemplates a specific list of documents to which good-faith objections can be made. Nonetheless, until there is definitive authority holding that such a notice is improper, a party who receives such a notice should object to it within ten days after its service.

Texas Rule 176.6(c) adopts Texas Rule 193.7 with respect to nonparty documents, providing: "A nonparty's production of a document authenticates the document for use against the nonparty to the same extent as a party's production of a document is authenticated for use against the party under Rule 193.7."[248]

Texas Rule 193.3(d)'s "snap-back" provision is discussed in Chapter 5, section 5-4:3.

245 *Rodriguez v. City of Poteet*, No. 04-13-00274-CV, 2014 Tex. App. LEXIS 2136, at *9–10, 2014 WL 769286 (Tex. App.—San Antonio Feb. 26, 2014, no pet.) (mem. op.) (holding that, in a summary judgment proceeding, the nonmovant can request continuance to authenticate summary judgment evidence challenged by the movant).

246 *Merrell v. Wal-Mart Stores, Inc.*, 276 S.W.3d 117, 130 (Tex. App.—Texarkana 2008), *rev'd on other grounds*, 313 S.W.3d 837 (Tex. 2010).

247 *Merrell v. Wal-Mart Stores, Inc.*, 276 S.W.3d 117, 131 (Tex. App.—Texarkana 2008) ("Assuming, without deciding, the rule contains a specificity requirement, Wal-Mart has waived any error. The [plaintiffs] filed the notice of self-authentication approximately seventeen months before summary judgment. If Wal-Mart had any complaints concerning the notice, it should have raised those complaints in the trial court at a time when any deficiency could have been remedied."), *rev'd on other grounds*, 313 S.W.3d 837 (Tex. 2010).

248 Tex. R. Civ. P. 176.6(c).

CHAPTER 6

Disclosures—Texas Rule 194

6-1 Text of Rule 194

RULE 194. REQUIRED DISCLOSURES

194.1. Duty to Disclose; Production

(a) **Duty to Disclose.** Except as exempted by Rule 194.2(d) or as otherwise agreed by the parties or ordered by the court, a party must, without awaiting a discovery request, provide to the other parties the information or material described in Rule 194.2, 194.3, and 194.4.

(b) **Production.** If a party does not produce copies of all responsive documents, electronically stored information, and tangible things with the response, the response must state a reasonable time and method for the production of these items. The responding party must produce the items at the time and in the method stated, unless otherwise agreed by the parties or ordered by the court, and must provide the requesting party a reasonable opportunity to inspect them.

194.2. Initial Disclosures

(a) **Time for Initial Disclosures.** A party must make the initial disclosures within 30 days after the filing of the first answer or general appearance unless a different time is set by the parties' agreement or court order. A party that is first served or otherwise joined after the filing of the first answer or general appearance must make the initial disclosures within 30 days after being served or joined, unless a different time is set by the parties' agreement or court order.

(b) **Content.** Without awaiting a discovery request, a party must provide to the other parties:

(1) the correct names of the parties to the lawsuit;

(2) the name, address, and telephone number of any potential parties;

(3) the legal theories and, in general, the factual bases of the responding party's claims or defenses (the responding party need not marshal all evidence that may be offered at trial);

(4) the amount and any method of calculating economic damages;

(5) the name, address, and telephone number of persons having knowledge of relevant facts, and a brief statement of each identified person's connection with the case;

(6) a copy—or a description by category and location—of all documents, electronically stored information, and tangible things that the responding party has in its possession, custody, or control, and may use to support its claims or defenses, unless the use would be solely for impeachment;

(7) any indemnity and insuring agreements described in Rule 192.3(f);

(8) any settlement agreements described in Rule 192.3(g);

(9) any witness statements described in Rule 192.3(h);

(10) in a suit alleging physical or mental injury and damages from the occurrence that is the subject of the case, all medical records and bills that are reasonably related to the injuries or damages asserted or, in lieu thereof, an authorization permitting the disclosure of such medical records and bills;

(11) in a suit alleging physical or mental injury and damages from the occurrence that is the subject of the case, all medical records and bills obtained by the responding party by virtue of an authorization furnished by the requesting party;

(12) the name, address, and telephone number of any person who may be designated as a responsible third party.

(c) **Content in Certain Suits Under the Family Code**

(1) In a suit for divorce, annulment, or to declare a marriage void, a party must, without awaiting a discovery request, provide to the other party the following, for the past two years or since the date of marriage, whichever is less:

(A) all deed and lien information on any real property owned and all lease information on any real property leased;

(B) all statements for any pension plan, retirement plan, profit-sharing plan, employee benefit plan, and individual retirement plan;

(C) all statements or policies for each current life, casualty, liability, and health insurance policy; and

(D) all statements pertaining to any account at a financial institution, including banks, savings and loans institutions, credit unions, and brokerage firms.

(2) In a suit in which child or spousal support is at issue, a party must, without awaiting a discovery request, provide to the other party:

(A) information regarding all policies, statements, and the summary description of benefits for any medical and health insurance coverage that is or would be available for the child or the spouse;

(B) the party's income tax returns for the previous two years or, if no return has been filed, the party's Form W-2, Form 1099, and Schedule K-1 for such years; and

(C) the party's two most recent payroll check stubs.

(d) **Proceedings Exempt from Initial Disclosure.** The following proceedings are exempt from initial disclosure, but a court may order the parties to make particular disclosures and set the time for disclosure:

(1) an action for review on an administrative record;

(2) a forfeiture action arising from a state statute;

(3) a petition for habeas corpus;

(4) an action under the Family Code filed by or against the Title IV-D agency in a Title IV-D case;

(5) a child protection action under Subtitle E, Title 5 of the Family Code;

(6) a protective order action under Title 4 of the Texas Family Code;

(7) other actions involving domestic violence; and

(8) an action on appeal from a justice court.

194.3. Testifying Expert Disclosures

In addition to the disclosures required by Rule 194.2, a party must disclose to the other parties testifying expert information as provided by Rule 195.

194.4. Pretrial Disclosures

(a) **In General.** In addition to the disclosures required by Rule 194.2 and 194.3, a party must provide to the other parties and promptly file the following information about the evidence that it may present at trial other than solely for impeachment:

(1) the name and, if not previously provided, the address, and telephone number of each witness—separately identifying those the party expects to present and those it may call if the need arises;

(2) an identification of each document or other exhibits, including summaries of other evidence—separately identifying those items the party expects to offer and those it may offer if the need arises.

(b) **Time for Pretrial Disclosures.** Unless the court orders otherwise, these disclosures must be made at least 30 days before trial.

(c) **Proceedings Exempt from Pretrial Disclosure.** An action arising under the Family Code filed by or against the Title IV-D agency in a Title IV-D case is exempt from pretrial disclosure, but a court may order the parties to make particular disclosures and set the time for disclosure.

194.5. No Objection or Assertion of Work Product

No objection or assertion of work product is permitted to a disclosure under this rule.

194.6. Certain Responses Not Admissible

A disclosure under Rule 194.2(b)(3) and (4) that has been changed by an amended or supplemental response is not admissible and may not be used for impeachment.

Comments

Comments to 2021 change:

Rule 194 is amended to implement section 22.004(h-1) of the Texas Government Code. Rule 194 is amended based on Federal Rule of Civil Procedure 26(a) to require disclosure of basic discovery automatically, without awaiting a discovery request. A party is not excused from making its disclosures because it has not fully investigated the case or because it challenges the sufficiency of another party's disclosures or because another party has not made its disclosures. As with other written discovery responses, required disclosures must be signed under Rule 191.3, complete under Rule 193.1, served under Rule 191.5, and timely amended or supplemented under Rule 193.5.

Comments to 2004 change:

Rule 194.2(l) is added as required by changes in chapter 33 of the Texas Civil Practice and Remedies Code. The amendment applies in all cases filed on or after July 1, 2003, in which a request under Rule 194.1 is made after May 1, 2004.

Comments to 1999 change:

1. Disclosure is designed to afford parties basic discovery of specific categories of information, not automatically in every case, but upon request, without preparation of a lengthy inquiry, and without objection or assertion of work product. In those extremely rare cases when information ordinarily discoverable should be protected, such as when revealing a person's residence might result in harm to the person, a party may move for protection. A party may assert any applicable privileges other than work product using the procedures of Rule 193.3 applicable to other written discovery. Otherwise, to fail to respond fully to a request for disclosure would be an abuse of the discovery process.

2. Rule 194.2(c) and (d) permit a party further inquiry into another's legal theories and factual claims than is often provided in notice pleadings. So-called "contention interrogatories" are used for the same purpose. Such interrogatories are not properly used to require a party to marshal evidence or brief legal issues. Paragraphs (c) and (d) are intended to require disclosure of a party's basic assertions, whether in prosecution of claims or in defense. Thus, for example, a plaintiff would be required to disclose that he or she claimed damages suffered in a car wreck caused by defendant's negligence in speeding and would be required to state how loss of past earnings and future earning capacity was calculated but would not be required to state the speed at which defendant was allegedly driving. Paragraph (d) does not require a party, either a plaintiff or a defendant, to state a method of calculating non-economic damages, such as for mental anguish. In the same example, defendant would be required to disclose his or her denial of the speeding allegation and any basis for contesting the damage calculations.

3. Responses under Rule 194.2(c) and (d) that have been amended or supplemented are inadmissible and cannot be used for impeachment, but other evidence of changes in position is not likewise barred.

6-1:1 2021 Amendments to Texas Rules of Civil Procedure

The 2021 amendments to the Texas Rules of Civil Procedure modified Texas Rule 194 in several significant ways. First, "requests for disclosure" were replaced by three types of "required disclosures": (1) initial disclosures; (2) testifying expert disclosures; and (3) pretrial disclosures.[1] With some exceptions set forth in Texas Rule 194, a party must provide these required disclosures without waiting for a discovery request. Second, the 2021 amendments added a new initial disclosure that is modeled after Federal Rule of Civil Procedure 26(a)(1)(a)(ii). Texas Rule 194.2(b)(6) now requires disclosure of "a copy—or a description by category and location—of all documents, electronically stored information, and tangible things that the responding party has in its possession, custody, or control, and may use to support its claims or defenses, unless the use would be solely for impeachment[.]"[2] Third, both pretrial disclosures and specific family-law disclosures were added to the Rule. Fourth, details regarding testifying-expert disclosures were moved from Texas Rule 194 to Texas Rule 195.5. Default deadlines for initial disclosures and pretrial disclosures are set forth in Texas Rules 194.2(a) and 194.4(b), respectively, while default deadlines for expert disclosures are set forth in Texas Rule 195.5.

In the order approving the 2021 amendments, the Texas Supreme Court stated that "[t]he amendments apply to cases filed on or after January 1, 2021, except for those filed in justice court[,]" and that former discovery rules "continue to govern procedures and limitations in cases filed before January 1, 2021."[3] Accordingly, until all cases filed before January 1, 2021 are fully resolved, requests for disclosure will remain a legitimate form of written discovery in Texas state-court proceedings. For that reason, this chapter addresses both requests for disclosure under former Texas Rule 194 and required disclosures under amended Texas Rule 194.

6-2 Disclosures in General

Former Texas Rule 194 generally governs requests for disclosure[4]—written requests to obtain one or more of a laundry list of twelve categories of basic information set

---

[1] *See* Tex. R. Civ. P. 194.1(a) (referencing required disclosures under Texas Rules 194.2, 194.3, and 194.4); Tex. Civ. P. 194.2 (addressing initial disclosures); Tex. R. Civ. P. 194.3 (addressing testifying-expert disclosures); Tex. R. Civ. P. 194.4 (addressing pretrial disclosures).

[2] Tex. R. Civ. P. 194.2(b)(6); *cf.* Fed. R. Civ. P. 26(a)(1)(A)(ii) (requiring the same disclosure).

[3] *Final Approval of Amendments to Texas Rules of Civil Procedure 47, 99, 169, 190, 192, 193, 194, 195, 196, 197, and 198*, Misc. Docket No. 20-9153, at 1, ¶ 2 (Tex. Dec. 23, 2020), *available at* https://www.txcourts.gov/supreme/administrative-orders/2020/.

[4] An interesting question is: What is the proper plural form of "request for disclosure?" Among the variations are requests for disclosure, request for disclosures, and requests for disclosures. *E.g.*, *Bonsmara Nat. Beef Co., LLC v. Hart of Tex. Cattle Feeders, LLC*, 603 S.W.3d 385, 407 (Tex. 2020) ("requests for disclosure"); *LaLonde v. Gosnell*, 593 S.W.3d 212, 227 (Tex. 2019) ("requests for disclosures"); *In re Dawson*, 550 S.W.3d 625, 627 (Tex. 2018) (orig. proceeding) (per curiam) ("request for disclosures"); Tex. R. Civ. P. 194 ("requests for disclosure"). The first—"requests for disclosure"—is the proper plural form of the discovery device. *Webster's Third International Dictionary of the English Language Unabridged* 25a (Phillip Babcock Gove et al. eds., 3d ed. 2002) ("Three-word compounds consisting of an initial noun plus prepositional phrase hyphened or open customarily pluralize the initial

forth in Texas Rule 194.2.[5] Disclosure requests provide inexpensive, basic discovery without the delay relating to objections or work-product assertions.[6] Although the discovery device is borrowed from Federal Rule 26(a),[7] former Texas Rule 194 is different from the federal rule in two important respects. First, unlike the federal rule, former Texas Rule 194 disclosures are not mandatory;[8] rather, they are request driven.[9] Second, the information that must be disclosed is different under the two Rules.[10]

---

noun: . . . coats of mail[.]"); Bryan A. Garner, *A Dictionary of Modern Legal Usage* 669–70 (3d ed. 2009) (describing the proper plural form of a compound noun).

5 Tex. R. Civ. P. 194.2. Former Texas Rule 190.2(b)(6)—for Level 1 discovery—sets forth a category of documents subject to disclosure in "expedited actions" governed by Texas Rule 169 and in divorce cases "not involving children in which a party pleads that the value of the marital estate is more than zero but not more than $50,000[.]" Former Tex. R. Civ. P. 190.2(b)(6), which provided that "a party may request disclosure of all documents, electronic information, and tangible items that the disclosing party has in its possession, custody, or control and may use to support its claims or defenses." This disclosure is discussed in. See–Chapter 6, section 6-3:3.12. In addition to former Texas Rules 190.2(b)(6) and 194, former Texas Rules 190, 191, 192, 193, 195, and 215 relate to disclosure requests.

Disclosure requests cannot be served on nonparties. *In re I.E.Z.*, No. 09-09-00499-CV, 2010 Tex. App. LEXIS 6695, at *12 (Tex. App.—Beaumont Aug. 19, 2010, no pet.) (mem. op.) (holding that disclosure requests can be served only on parties); Former Tex. R. Civ. P. 194.1 ("A *party* may obtain disclosure from *another party* of the information or material listed in [Texas] Rule 194.2 by serving the *other party*[.]") (emphasis added). They, however, can be served on parties whose interests are not adverse. *See* Former Tex. R. Civ. P. 194.1; *cf. Ferrara v. U.S.*, No. 90 Civ. 0972 (DNE), 1992 U.S. Dist. LEXIS 601, at *3 (S.D.N.Y. Jan. 23, 1992) ("The [Federal] Rule does not limit discovery only to parties that have a hostile stance toward each other in the litigation.").

6 Tex. R. Civ. P. 194 cmt. 1 to 1999 change ("Disclosure is designed to afford parties basic discovery of specific categories of information, not automatically in every case, but upon request, without preparation of a lengthy inquiry, and without objection or assertion of work product.").

7 Federal Rule 26(a) provides for (1) initial disclosures, which require the disclosing party to identify the persons with "discoverable information" that it may use to support its claims or defenses, identify or produce documents that it may use to support its claims or defenses, provide a damage computation, and produce relevant insurance agreements, Fed. R. Civ. P. 26(a)(1); (2) disclosure of expert testimony, which requires the disclosing party to identify and provide a report or information about its experts, Fed. R. Civ. P. 26(a)(2); and (3) pretrial disclosures, which require the disclosing party to disclose its trial witnesses and exhibits, Fed. R. Civ. P. 26(a)(3).

8 *Compare* Former Tex. R. Civ. P. 190.2(b)(6) ("[A] party may request disclosure of . . . ."), Former Tex. R. Civ. P. 194.1 ("A party may obtain disclosure from another party . . . by serving the other party . . . the following request. . . ."), *and* Tex. R. Civ. P. 194 cmt. 1 to 1999 change (explaining that disclosures must be requested), *with* Fed. R. Civ. P. 26(a) (providing that a party "must" disclose).

9 Disclosures were not mandatory under the former Texas discovery rules because research showed that many Texas state-court actions settle without discovery. Alex Wilson Albright, *New Discovery Rules: The Texas Supreme Court Advisory Committee's Proposal*, 15 Rev. Litig. 275, 277 (1996). Accordingly, it was believed that making disclosures mandatory would increase litigation costs. Alex Wilson Albright, *New Discovery Rules: The Texas Supreme Court Advisory Committee's Proposal*, 15 Rev. Litig. 275, 286 (1996).

10 *Compare* Former Tex. R. Civ. P. 190.2(b)(6), and Former Tex. R. Civ. P. 194.2, *with* Fed. R. Civ. P. 26(a). The information and materials that are subject to disclosure are discussed in Chapter 6, section 6-3:3.

As noted above, the 2021 amendments to the Texas Rules of Civil Procedure brought Texas's disclosure rules more in line with the federal disclosure rules. First, like Federal Rules 26(a)(1)–(a)(3), Texas Rules 194.1–194.4 now require initial disclosures, testifying-expert disclosures, and pretrial disclosures, with some exceptions that are set forth in the Rules and discussed in subchapter 6-3:3 below.[11] Second, disclosure provisions in Federal Rule 26 have been carried over to Texas Rule 194. For example, like Federal Rule 26(a)(1)(A)(ii), Texas Rule 194.2(b)(6) now requires disclosure of "a copy—or a description by category and location—of all documents, electronically stored information, and tangible things that the responding party has in its possession, custody, or control, and may use to support its claims or defenses, unless the use would be solely for impeachment[.]"[12] And Texas Rule 194.2(d) exempts certain state-court proceedings from initial-disclosure requirements, as Federal Rule 26(a)(1)(B) does for certain federal-court proceedings.[13] In addition, the pretrial-disclosures provisions in Federal Rule 26(a)(3)(A)(i) and (iii) have been carried over to Texas Rule 194.4(a)(1)–(2), and, in both sets of rules, the default deadline for pretrial disclosures is "30 days before trial."[14] Finally, as discussed in Chapter 7, section 7-4:3, expert-disclosure provisions in Federal Rules 26(a)(2)(iv)–(vi) and 26(b)(4)(B)–(C) have been carried over to Texas Rules 195.5(a)(4)(C)–(E), 195.5(c)(1)–(3), and 195.5(d).[15]

Differences remain between Texas's disclosure rules and the federal disclosure rules. For example, the initial disclosures required under Texas Rule 194.2(b) differ in several ways from the initial disclosures required under Federal Rule 26(a)(1).[16] In addition, the deadlines for initial disclosures and expert disclosures are different under the two sets of rules.[17] But, differences notwithstanding, to the extent that the

---

[11] *Compare* Tex. R. Civ. P. 194.1 ("Except as exempted by [Texas] Rule 194.2(d) or as otherwise agreed by the parties or ordered by the court, a party must, without awaiting a discovery request, provide to the other parties the information or material described in [Texas] Rule 194.2, 194.3, and 194.4."), Tex. R. Civ. P. 194.2 (initial disclosures), Tex. R. Civ. P. 194.3 (testifying-expert disclosures), *and* Tex. R. Civ. P. 194.4 (pretrial disclosures), *with* Fed. R. Civ. P. 26(a)(1) (addressing initial disclosures that "must" be made "[e]xcept as exempted by [Federal] Rule 26(a)(1)(B)), Fed. R. Civ. P. 26(a)(2) (addressing what "a party must disclose" in relation to experts), *and* Fed. R. Civ. P. 26(a)(3) (addressing pretrial disclosures that a party "must" provide).

[12] Tex. R. Civ. P. 194.2(b)(6) (mirroring Federal Rule 26(a)(1)(A)(ii) in all respects except one—the Texas Rule refers to "the responding party," while the Federal Rule refers to "the disclosing party").

[13] *Compare* Tex. R. Civ. P. 194.2(d), *with* Fed. R. Civ. P. 26(a)(1)(B).

[14] *Compare* Tex. R. Civ. P. 194.4(b), *with* Fed. R. Civ. P. 26(a)(3)(B).

[15] Texas Rule 194.3 refers to Texas Rule 195.5 for details relating to expert disclosures. *See* Tex. R. Civ. P. 194.3 ("In addition to the disclosures required by [Texas] Rule 194.2, a party must disclose to the other parties testifying expert information as provided by [Texas] Rule 195.").

[16] *Compare* Tex. R. Civ. P. 194.2(b)–(c), *with* Fed. R. Civ. P. 26(a)(1)(A).

[17] *Compare* Tex. R. Civ. P. 194.2(a) ("A party must make the initial disclosures within 30 days after the filing of the first answer or general appearance unless a different time is set by the parties' agreement or court order. A party that is first served or otherwise joined after the filing of the first answer or general appearance must make the initial disclosures within 30 days after being served or joined, unless a different time is set by the parties' agreement or court order."), *and* Tex. R. Civ. P. 195.2 ("Unless otherwise ordered by the court, a party must designate experts—that is, furnish information described in Rule 195.5(a)—by the following dates: (a) with regard to all experts testifying for a party seeking affirmative

Texas disclosure rules track language in the corresponding federal disclosure rules, federal cases interpreting the federal disclosure rules offer helpful guidance for Texas courts and practitioners when addressing questions related to disclosures.[18]

6-3 Procedure

6-3:1 Form of Disclosure Requests and Required Disclosures

Former Texas Rule 194.1 specifies the disclosure request's form. It provides, in relevant part: "A party may obtain disclosure from another party of the information or material listed in [Texas] Rule 194.2 *by serving the other party . . . the following request*: 'Pursuant to [Texas] Rule 194, you are requested to disclose, within 30 days of service of this request, the information or material described in Rule [state rule, e.g., 194.2, or 194.2(a), (c), and (f), or 194.2(d)-(g)].'"[19] Accordingly, a disclosure request should contain the former Rule's exact language except that it may provide more than thirty days to respond[20] and must provide at least fifty days to respond if the request is served on the defendant before the defendant's answer date.[21] For cases filed before

---

relief, 90 days before the end of the discovery period; (b) with regard to all other experts, 60 days before the end of the discovery period."), ***with*** Fed. R. Civ. P. 26(a)(1)(C) ("A party must make the initial disclosures at or within 14 days after the parties' [Federal] Rule 26(f) conference unless a different time is set by stipulation or court order, or unless a party objects during the conference that initial disclosures are not appropriate in this action and states the objection in the proposed discovery plan. In ruling on the objection, the court must determine what disclosures, if any, are to be made and must set the time for disclosure."), ***and*** Fed. R. Civ. P. 26(a)(2)(D) ("A party must make these [expert] disclosures at the times and in the sequence that the court orders. Absent a stipulation or a court order, the disclosures must be made: (i) at least 90 days before the date set for trial or for the case to be ready for trial; or (ii) if the evidence is intended solely to contradict or rebut evidence on the same subject matter identified by another party under [Federal] Rule 26(a)(2)(B) or (C), within 30 days after the other party's disclosure.").

18 Anne M. Johnson, Kennon L. Wooten & Sarah A. Nicolas, ***Rules Update: What's New with the Texas Rules of Civil Procedure and Texas Rules of Appellate Procedure***, presented at 10th Annual State Bar of Tex. Advanced Trial Strategies CLE Course (Feb. 5, 2021). The Texas Supreme Court has recognized that federal cases construing the comparable federal rules provide guidance for the construction of the Texas rule. ***See, e.g., In re State Farm Lloyds***, 520 S.W.3d 595, 613 (Tex. 2017) ("To be sure, there are differences in language between the Texas rule and the federal rule. But as we affirmed in ***In re Weekley Homes L.P.***, 295 S.W.3d 309, 316–17 (Tex. 2009) (orig. proceeding)], 'our rules as written are not inconsistent with the federal rules or the case law interpreting them,' even though they may not 'mirror the federal language.'") (footnote omitted); ***In re Weekley Homes***, 295 S.W.3d 309, 316–17 (Tex. 2009) (orig. proceeding) (conceding that state discovery rules are not identical to federal rules, but "are not inconsistent," and "therefore we look to the federal rules for guidance"); ***Farmers Grp., Inc. v. Lubin***, 222 S.W.3d 417, 425 (Tex. 2007) (looking to cases interpreting federal rules where Texas rules incorporate identical language).

19 Former Tex. R. Civ. P. 194.1 (emphasis added).

20 A disclosure request can provide more than thirty days for a response. It cannot, however, require less than thirty days. ***See*** Former Tex. R. Civ. P. 194.1, 194.3.

21 ***See*** Former Tex. R. Civ. P. 194.3. The time to respond to a former Texas Rule 194.2(f) request for disclosure regarding testifying experts in a case filed before January 1, 2021, is governed by former Texas Rule 195.2.

January 1, 2021, a disclosure request also should refer to Former Texas Rule 190.2(b)(6) in an action under Level 1.[22]

Former Texas Rules 190.2(b)(6) and 194 do not require disclosure requests to be made in any particular type of document or at any particular time. Thus, they can be made in the requesting party's initial pleading,[23] in a formal discovery request entitled "Request(s) for Disclosure," in a formal discovery request that combines disclosure requests with other written-discovery requests (e.g., interrogatories, production requests, or requests for admission),[24] or even in a letter to the responding party's attorney that is signed and served pursuant to Texas Rule 21a.[25]

As provided by Texas Rule 194.1(a), in cases filed on or after January 1, 2021, a party generally must make required disclosures "without awaiting a discovery request[.]"[26] In other words, required disclosures do not necessitate a discovery request at all, much less a discovery request in a particular form. Indeed, in cases in which required disclosures apply and the number of discovery requests is limited (e.g., in Level 1 actions), parties should not use any of their limited discovery requests to seek information or material that they are entitled to receive as a matter of course pursuant to Texas Rules 194.2, 194.3, and 194.4—which govern initial disclosures, testifying-expert disclosures, and pretrial disclosures, respectively.

In cases exempt from initial disclosures, however, an interesting question is whether a party may seek disclosures from another party and, if so, in what form. Because the rules authorize courts to order parties to make particular disclosures in cases exempt from initial disclosures,[27] it is clear that parties can seek court-ordered initial disclosures in such cases and that a court can specify the form for any disclosure it requires. In the absence of a court order, parties can simply agree to make particular initial disclosures in cases exempt from required disclosures, and can agree further to the form of their agreed-upon disclosures.[28] In addition, in cases exempt from initial disclosures, nothing in the rules precludes a party from using

---

22 *See* Former Tex. R. Civ. P. 190.2(b)(6).

23 If the request is made in a pleading, the pleading's style should mention it (*e.g.*, "Plaintiff's Original Petition and Request for Disclosure" or "Defendant's Special Exceptions, Answer, Counterclaim, and Request for Disclosure").

24 Former Tex. R. Civ. P. 192.2 ("The permissible forms of discovery may be combined in the same document[.]"). If the same discovery request contains disclosure requests and other types of written-discovery requests, the document's title should refer to each type of discovery (*e.g.*, "Plaintiff's Request for Disclosure, First Interrogatories, and First Production Requests").

25 Service of discovery material is discussed in Chapter 3, section 3-6.

26 Tex. R. Civ. P. 194.1(a) ("Except as exempted by Rule 194.2(d) or as otherwise agreed by the parties or ordered by the court, a party must, without awaiting a discovery request, provide to the other parties the information or material described in [Texas] Rule 194.2, 194.3, and 194.4.").

27 *See* Tex. R. Civ. P. 194.2(d) (listing the proceedings that are exempt from initial disclosures but providing that "a court may order the parties to make particular disclosures and set the time for disclosure"); Tex. R. Civ. P. 194.4 (listing the proceedings that are exempt from pretrial disclosures but providing that "a court may order the parties to make particular disclosures and set the time for disclosure").

28 *See, e.g.*, Tex. R. Civ. P. 191.1 ("*Except where specifically prohibited, the procedures and limitations set forth in the rules pertaining to discovery may be modified in any suit by the agreement of the parties* or by court order for good cause. An agreement of the parties is enforceable if

other types of written discovery (e.g., requests for production or interrogatories) to request information or material encompassed by the initial-disclosure provision of Texas Rule 194.2 because the information and documents covered by the Rule are discoverable under Texas Rule 192.3, which governs discovery's scope. If a party uses a different type of written discovery to seek such information or material, the party should follow all requirements, including form requirements, that are applicable to the chosen type of discovery.

6-3:2 Timing of Disclosure Requests and Required Disclosures

For a case filed before January 1, 2021, disclosure requests can be served any time after the case's filing,[29] and generally must be served no later than thirty days (and in some cases thirty-one or thirty-three days) before the discovery period ends.[30] Thus, in cases filed before January 1, 2021, a disclosure request can be served with the party's initial pleading and, as discussed in Chapter 6, section 6-3.1, it even can be included in the pleading. The request should set forth when the response is due, usually thirty days after service, if the request is served after the defendant answers, but at least fifty days after service, if served before the defendant answers.[31] As with other written-discovery requests, a party served with an unsigned disclosure request need not respond or take any action with respect to the disclosure request.[32] And, a disclosure request that is not properly served need not be answered.[33]

---

it complies with [Texas] Rule 11 or, as it affects an oral deposition, if it is made a part of the record of the deposition.") (emphasis added).

[29] *See, e.g.*, Former Tex. R. Civ. P. 190.2(b)(1), 190.3(b)(1).

[30] Former Tex. R. Civ. P. 194.1. If the requests are served by mail, they must be served at least thirty-three days before the discovery period ends. Tex. R. Civ. P. 21a(c). If they are served by fax after 5:00 p.m. local time of the recipient, the requests must be served at least thirty-one days before the discovery period ends. Tex. R. Civ. P. 21a(b)(2).

[31] Former Tex. R. Civ. P. 194.3.

[32] Tex. R. Civ. P. 191.3(d) ("A party is not required to take any action with respect to a request or notice that is not signed.").

[33] *See In re de la Cerda*, No. 12-12-00149-CV, 2013 Tex. App. LEXIS 1065, at *4, 2013 WL 451830 (Tex. App.—Tyler Feb. 6, 2013, orig. proceeding) (mem. op.) (holding that a trial court did not abuse its discretion in denying the plaintiff's motion to compel disclosures when the request was served on the court's clerk rather than on the defendant); *cf. Ordonez v. Solorio*, 480 S.W.3d 56, 62 (Tex. App.—El Paso 2015, no pet.) ("Service on an attorney before that attorney becomes the party's attorney of record is not valid service under [Texas] Rule 21a, and a request for admissions so served is neither properly served under [Texas] Rule 198.1 nor deemed admitted under [Texas] Rule 198.2(c)."); *Holmes v. Graham Mortg. Corp.*, 449 S.W.3d 257, 261–62 (Tex. App.—Dallas 2014, pet. denied) (holding that the trial court did not err in refusing to consider allegedly deemed admissions in connection with the defendant's summary judgment motion because the requests for admission were not properly served on the defendant); ***Approximately $14,900.00 v. State***, 261 S.W.3d 182, 186 (Tex. App.—Houston [14th Dist.] 2005, no pet.) ("A party's duty to respond is dependent upon receipt of the requests. Where service is not perfected, the receiving party cannot be made to suffer the consequences of not answering or untimely answering.") (citation omitted); *Payton v. Ashton*, 29 S.W.3d 896, 898 (Tex. App.—Amarillo 2000, no pet.) (affirming the trial court's refusal to consider alleged deemed admissions because the requests were not properly served on the defendant).

For a case filed on or after January 1, 2021 and subject to required disclosures, the Texas discovery rules provide deadlines to make each type of required disclosure. But the deadlines are not rigid; they can be modified by agreement or by court order.

Under Texas Rule 194.2(a), "[a] party must make the initial disclosures within 30 days after the filing of the first answer or general appearance unless a different time is set by the parties' agreement or court order[,]" and "[a] party that is first served or otherwise joined after the filing of the first answer or general appearance must make the initial disclosures within 30 days after being served or joined, unless a different time is set by the parties' agreement or court order."[34] By default, the discovery period for Level 1 and 2 cases is set with reference to initial disclosures—it "begins ***when the first initial disclosures are due*** and continues for 180 days" for Level 1 cases[35] and, for Level 2 cases, it "***begins when the first initial disclosures are due*** and continues until: (A) 30 days before the date set for trial, in cases under the Family Code; or (B) in other cases, the earlier of (i) 30 days before the date set for trial, or (ii) nine months ***after the first initial disclosures are due***."[36] The Rule's language does not specify whether the referenced "due" date is the default deadline under Texas Rule 194.2(a) or any modified deadline set by agreement or by court order. Thus, to err on the side of caution and avoid uncertainty, if initial-disclosure deadlines in a Level 1 or 2 case are modified by agreement or by court order, the discovery period should also be modified by agreement (as permitted by Texas Rule 191.1) or by court order (as permitted by Texas Rules 190.5 and 191.1).[37] In addition, because a party generally "cannot serve discovery on another party until after the other party's initial disclosures are due[,]" if initial-disclosure deadlines are extended by agreement or by court order, there should be consideration of whether to allow service of other discovery before the initial disclosures are due.[38] When considering that possibility, however, practitioners should keep in mind why initial disclosures are due first by default—the content of initial disclosures may negate the need for certain additional discovery or at least affect that discovery's nature or appropriate scope in a case.[39]

Under Texas Rule 194.3 "a party must disclose to the other parties testifying expert information as provided by [Texas] Rule 195."[40] Texas Rule 195.2, in turn, provides that, "[u]nless otherwise ordered by the court, a party must designate experts—that is, furnish information described in [Texas] Rule 195.5(a)—by the following dates: (a) with regard to all experts testifying for a party seeking affirmative relief, 90 days before the end of the discovery period; (b) with regard to all other experts, 60 days before the end of the discovery period."[41] If the default initial-disclosure deadline is

---

34 Tex. R. Civ. P. 194.2(a).

35 Tex. R. Civ. P. 190.2(b)(1) (emphasis added).

36 Tex. R. Civ. P. 190.3(b)(1) (emphasis added).

37 Tex. R. Civ. P. 190.5, 191.1, 194.2(a).

38 Texas Rule 192.2(a) expressly allows modification of the default restriction. *See* Tex. R. Civ. P. 192.2(a) ("***Unless otherwise agreed to by the parties or ordered by the court,*** a party cannot serve discovery on another party until after the other party's initial disclosures are due.") (emphasis added).

39 *See* Anne M. Johnson, Kennon L. Wooten & Sarah A. Nicolas, ***Rules Update: What's New with the Texas Rules of Civil Procedure and Texas Rules of Appellate Procedure***, presented at 10th Annual State Bar of Tex. Advanced Trial Strategies CLE Course (Feb. 5, 2021).

40 Tex. R. Civ. P. 194.3.

41 Tex. R. Civ. P. 195.2.

modified and the discovery period is impacted as a result, parties should consider whether there is a need to modify the default testifying-expert-disclosure deadline, as well. If such a need is perceived, a court order modifying that should be obtained.[42]

Finally, Texas Rule 194.4(b) provides that—by default—pretrial "disclosures must be made at least 30 days before trial."[43] As with the default testifying-expert-disclosure deadline, a court order is required to modify the default pretrial-disclosure deadline.[44] But, unlike all of the other required disclosures, pretrial disclosures must be filed with the court in addition to being served on the case's other parties.[45]

6-3:3 Contents of a Disclosure Requests and Required Disclosures

Former Texas Rule 194.2 generally sets forth the information and material that can be obtained by disclosure requests in cases filed before January 1, 2021, under Level 1, 2, and 3 discovery control plans. It allows a party to request disclosure "of any or all" of the following:

(a) the correct names of the parties to the lawsuit;

(b) the name, address, and telephone number of any potential parties;

(c) the legal theories and, in general, the factual bases of the responding party's claims or defenses (the responding party need not marshal all evidence that may be offered at trial);

(d) the amount and any method of calculating economic damages;

(e) the name, address, and telephone number of persons having knowledge of relevant facts, and a brief statement of each identified person's connection with the case;

(f) for any testifying expert:

   (1) the expert's name, address, and telephone number;

   (2) the subject matter on which the expert will testify;

   (3) the general substance of the expert's mental impressions and opinions and a brief summary of the basis for them, or if the expert is not retained by, employed by, or otherwise subject to the control of the responding party, documents reflecting such information;

   (4) if the expert is retained by, employed by, or otherwise subject to the control of the responding party:

---

42 *See* Tex. R. Civ. P. 195.2 (requiring a court order to modify default testifying-expert-disclosure deadlines).

43 Tex. R. Civ. P. 194.4(b).

44 Tex. R. Civ. P. 194.4(b) ("Unless the court orders otherwise, these disclosures must be made at least 30 days before trial.").

45 Tex. R. Civ. P. 194.4(a) ("In addition to the disclosures required by [Texas] Rule 194.2 and 194.3, a party must provide to the other parties ***and promptly file*** the following information about the evidence that it may present at trial other than solely for impeachment. . . .") (emphasis added).

(A) all documents, tangible things, reports, models, or data compilations that have been provided to, reviewed by, or prepared by or for the expert in anticipation of the expert's testimony; and

(B) the expert's current resume and bibliography;

(g) any indemnity and insuring agreements described in [Texas] Rule 192.3(f);

(h) any settlement agreements described in [former Texas] Rule 192.3(g);

(i) any witness statements described in [former Texas] Rule 192.3(h);

(j) in a suit alleging physical or mental injury and damages from the occurrence that is the subject of the case, all medical records and bills that are reasonably related to the injuries or damages asserted or, in lieu thereof, an authorization permitting the disclosure of such medical records and bills;

(k) in a suit alleging physical or mental injury and damages from the occurrence that is the subject of the case, all medical records and bills obtained by the responding party by virtue of an authorization furnished by the requesting party;

(l) the name, address, and telephone number of any person who may be designated as a responsible third party.[46]

In addition to the foregoing, in Level 1 cases filed before January 1, 2021,[47] "a party may request disclosure of all documents, electronic information, and tangible items that the disclosing party has in its possession, custody, or control and may use to support its claims or defenses."[48]

Except for certain information about testifying experts, which—in a case filed before January 1, 2021—can only be obtained by use of a disclosure request, depositions, and expert reports as permitted by former Texas Rule 195,[49] the information and materials discoverable pursuant to former Texas Rules 190.2(b)(6) and 194.2 also can

---

[46] Former Tex. R. Civ. P. 194.2.

[47] Former Tex. R. Civ. P. 190.2(a).

[48] Former Tex. R. Civ. P. 190.2(b)(6). "A request for disclosure made pursuant to [Former Texas Rule 190.2(b)(6)] is not considered a request for production," Former Tex. R. Civ. P. 190.2(b)(6), and, therefore, does not count against the fifteen-production-request limit of Texas Rule 190.2(b)(4) in a Level 1 action.

[49] *In re Nat'l Lloyds Ins. Co.*, 532 S.W.3d 794, 814 (Tex. 2017) (Former Texas "'Rule 195 addresses the methods for obtaining such information, limiting testifying-expert discovery to that acquired through disclosures, expert reports, and oral depositions of expert witnesses.' To minimize undue expense and curb discovery abuse, [former Texas] Rule 195 does not provide for interrogatories or requests for production like the discovery requests at issue here." (footnotes omitted) (quoting *In re Ford Motor Co.*, 427 S.W.3d 396, 397 (Tex. 2014) (per curiam))); Former Tex. R. Civ. P. 195.1 ("A party may request another party to designate and disclose information concerning testifying-expert witnesses only through a disclosure request under [Texas] Rule 194 and through depositions and reports as permitted by this rule."). As discussed in Chapter 7, sections 7-4:1 and 7-5, respectively, production requests under Texas Rules 176 or 205 can be used to obtain documents from non-retained testifying experts and interrogatories, production requests under Texas Rules 176 or 205, and requests for admission can be used to obtain information about discoverable consulting-expert witnesses.

Expert disclosures are discussed in Chapter 6, section 6-3:3.14 and Chapter 7, section 7-4:3.

be obtained through depositions, interrogatories, and production requests. Because the number of deposition hours, interrogatories, and production requests are limited in Level 1 cases,[50] because the number of deposition hours and interrogatories are limited in Level 2 cases,[51] and because, even in Level 3 cases, the number of deposition hours and interrogatories likely will be limited, disclosure requests always should be used in cases filed before January 1, 2021 to obtain the information permitted by former Texas Rule 190.2(b)(6) and former Texas Rules 194.2(a)–(e) and (g)–(k) in Level 1 cases and former Texas Rules 194.2(a)–(e) and (l) in Level 2 and 3 cases. Because, in a pre-2021 case, a disclosure request is the only type of written discovery that can be used to obtain certain information about another party's testifying experts, a former Texas Rule 194.2(f) disclosure request should always be used in such a case to obtain information about such experts irrespective of the case's discovery level.

Although all of Texas Rule 194's content provisions were renumbered as part of the 2021 amendments, there were only a handful of substantive revisions to them. The revised requirements, along with the preexisting, carry-over requirements, are discussed in the following sections of this Chapter. The substantive revisions can be summarized generally as follows: (1) like Federal Rule 26(a)(1)(A)(ii), Texas Rule 194.2(b)(6) now requires disclosure of "a copy—or a description by category and location—of all documents, electronically stored information, and tangible things that the responding party has in its possession, custody, or control, and may use to support its claims or defenses, unless the use would be solely for impeachment;"[52] (2) new disclosures, listed in Texas Rules 194.2(c), are required for certain suits under the Texas Family Code;[53] (3) details regarding testifying-expert disclosures were moved from Texas Rule 194 to Texas Rule 195.5, which is now referenced in Texas Rule 194.3;[54] and (4) pretrial-disclosures provisions in Federal Rule 26(a)(3)(A)(i) and (iii) were added to Texas Rule 194.4(a)(1)–(2).[55]

Many of Texas Rule 194's former and current categories call for information and materials specifically discoverable under Texas Rule 192.3, which governs discovery's scope and was not modified by the 2021 amendments. For example:

- Former Texas Rule 194.2(b)—now Texas Rule 194.2(b)(2)— requires disclosure of "the name, address, and telephone number of any potential parties[,]" which also is discoverable under Texas Rule 192.3(i).[56]

---

[50] *See* Tex. R. Civ. P. 190.2(b)(2)-(4) (limiting deposition hours, interrogatories, and production requests).

[51] Tex. R. Civ. P. 190.3(b)(2)-(3) (limiting each "side" to fifty deposition hours and each "party" to twenty-five interrogatories in Level 2 actions).

[52] Tex. R. Civ. P. 194.2(b)(6) (mirroring Federal Rule 26(a)(1)(A)(ii) in all respects except one—the Texas Rule refers to "the responding party," while the Federal Rule refers to "the disclosing party").

[53] *See* Tex. R. Civ. P. 194.2(c)(1) (addressing initial disclosures required "[i]n a suit for divorce, annulment, or to declare a marriage void"), Tex. R. Civ. P. 194.2(c)(2) (addressing initial disclosures required "[i]n a suit in which child or spousal support is at issue").

[54] *See* Tex. R. Civ. P. 194.3 ("In addition to the disclosures required by [Texas] Rule 194.2, a party must disclose to the other parties testifying expert information as provided by [Texas] Rule 195.").

[55] *Compare* Tex. R. Civ. P. 194.4(b), *with* Fed. R. Civ. P. 26(a)(3)(B).

[56] See Chapter 6, section 6-3.3.2.

- Former Texas Rule 194.2(c)—now Texas Rule 194.2(b)(3)— requires disclosure of "the legal theories and, in general, the factual bases of the responding party's claims or defenses," which also is discoverable under Texas Rule 192.3(j).[57]
- Former Texas Rule 194.2(e)—now Texas Rule 194.2(b)(5)— requires disclosure of "the name, address, and telephone number of persons having knowledge of relevant facts, and a brief statement of each identified person's connection with the case[,]" which also is discoverable under Texas Rule 192.3(c).[58]
- Former Texas Rule 194.2(f)—now Texas Rule 195.5(a), which is referenced in Texas Rule 194.3—requires the disclosure of certain information about testifying experts, which is discoverable in part under Texas Rule 192.3(e).[59]
- Former Texas Rule 194.2(g)—now Texas Rule 194.2(b)(7)— requires disclosure of "any indemnity and insuring agreements described in [Texas] Rule 192.3(f)."[60]
- Former Texas Rule 194.2(h)—now Texas Rule 194.2(b)(8)— requires disclosure of "any settlement agreements described in [Texas] Rule 192.3(g)."[61]
- Former Texas Rule 194.2(i)—now Texas Rule 194.2(b)(9)— requires disclosure of "any witness statements described in [Texas] Rule 192.3(h)."[62]

Each of the discoverable categories of information and material referenced above is discussed in the following sections of this Chapter—both in relation to (1) requests for disclosure, applicable in cases filed before January 1, 2021, and (2) required disclosures, applicable in cases filed on or after January 1, 2021.

6-3:3.1 The Parties' Correct Names

Former Texas Rule 194.2(a)—now Texas Rule 194.2(b)(1)—requires the disclosure of "the correct names of the parties to the lawsuit[.]"[63] This information enables the party receiving it to determine whether the correct party has sued or been sued, whether a party has sued or been sued in the correct capacity, and whether a party has sued or been sued in the correct name.

6-3:3.2 Potential Parties

Former Texas Rule 194.2(b)—now Texas Rule 194.2(b)(2)—requires the disclosure of "the name, address, and telephone numbers of any potential parties."[64] Nothing

---

57 See Chapter 6, section 6-3.3.3.
58 See Chapter 6, section 6-3.3.5.
59 See Chapter 6, section 6-3:3.14 and Chapter 7, section 7-4:3.
60 See Chapter 6, section 6-3.3.7.
61 See Chapter 6, section 6-3.3.8.
62 See Chapter 6, section 6-3.3.9.
63 Former Tex. R. Civ. P. 194.2(a); Tex. R. Civ. P. 194.2(b)(1).
64 Former Tex. R. Civ. P. 194.2(b); Tex. R. Civ. P. 194.2(b)(2); *accord Port of Corpus Christi, LP v. Port of Corpus Christi Auth. of Nueces Cnty.*, No. 13-19-00304-CV, 2021 Tex. App. LEXIS 1120, at *22, 2021 WL 499067 (Tex. App.—Corpus Christi Feb. 11, 2021, no pet.) (mem. op.) (noting that plaintiffs "were not permitted to conduct any jurisdictional discovery, and [that] identifying the appropriate official [to seek to enjoin via an *ultra vires* claim], whomever that may be, [could] be easily ascertained through discovery" under former Texas Rule 194.2(b), and remanding to the trial court for further proceedings); *In re Morse*, 153

in either version of that Rule or in Texas Rule 192.3(i), which generally provides for such discovery,[65] defines "potential party," and there are no cases defining the term in this context. The word "potential" means "[c]apable of coming into being; possible if the necessary conditions exist[.]"[66] Because undefined words in procedural rules are typically given their plain or ordinary meaning,[67] under former Texas Rule 194.2(b) and current Texas Rule 194.2(b)(2), a responding party must identify any person or entity that possibly could be a party (e.g., a plaintiff, defendant, or third-party defendant).[68] Thus, for example: (1) in a premises-liability action, a defendant should disclose the names of other individuals or entities with an ownership interest in the property at issue; (2) in a medical-malpractice case, the defendant should

---

S.W.3d 578, 581 (Tex. App.—Amarillo 2004, orig. proceeding) ("Considering that relators were entitled to the disclosure of the names and addresses of the shareholders or former shareholders as potential parties and based on the above standard of review, we conclude the trial court abused its discretion in denying the motion to compel the requested disclosures."); *Helfand v. Coane*, 12 S.W.3d 152, 157 n.3 (Tex. App.—Houston [1st Dist.] 2000, pet. denied) ("We reject Coane's argument that Helfand was not entitled to discovery for the mere purpose of determining who another defendant is or may be. Under our discovery rules, past and present, a party is entitled to discovery regarding potential parties to a lawsuit." (citing Former Tex. R. Civ. P. 192.3(i), 192.5(c)(3), and 194.2(b))).

[65] Tex. R. Civ. P. 192.3(i) ("A party may obtain discovery of the name, address, and telephone number of any potential party.").

[66] *Black's Law Dictionary* 1287 (11th ed. 2019); *accord The American Heritage Dictionary of the English Language* 1417 (3d ed. 1992) (defining "potential" as, among other things, "[h]aving possibility, capability, or power").

[67] *E.g., In re Silver*, 540 S.W.3d 530, 534 (Tex. 2018) (orig. proceeding) ("[W]hen determining a rule's meaning we typically rely on the ordinary meaning of the words used, unless the text or relevant definitions indicate a different meaning. When determining the ordinary meaning of a word, we frequently consult dictionaries.") (citation omitted); *In re Bridgestone Ams. Tire Operations, LLC*, 459 S.W.3d 565, 569 (Tex. 2015) (orig. proceeding) ("When we analyze Texas's procedural rules, we apply the same rules of construction that govern the interpretation of statutes. That is, we look first to the rule's language and construe it according to its plain meaning.") (citation omitted); *In re Sw. Pub. Serv. Co.*, No. 13-19-00111-CV, 2020 Tex. App. LEXIS 3212, at *26 n.6, 2020 WL 1887762 (Tex. App.—Corpus Christi Apr. 16, 2020, orig. proceeding) (mem. op.) ("We look first to the rule's language and construe it according to its plain meaning."); *Equistar Chems., LP v. ClydeUnion DB, Ltd.*, 579 S.W.3d 505, 524 (Tex. App.—Houston [14th Dist.] 2019, pet. denied) ("We interpret statutes and rules alike by looking to their language and construing them according to their plain meaning."); *Robles v. Rivera*, No. 05-17-00733-CV, 2018 Tex. App. LEXIS 4724, at *5, 2018 WL 3120858 (Tex. App.—Dallas June 26, 2018, pet. denied) (mem. op.) ("We give words used in the rules their ordinary meaning unless the text or relevant definitions indicate a different meaning."); *Assignees of Best Buy v. Combs*, 395 S.W.3d 847, 864 (Tex. App.—Austin 2013, pet. denied) ("When construing rules of civil procedure, we apply the same rules of construction that we use when interpreting statutes. If the rule's language is unambiguous, we must interpret it according to its plain meaning, giving meaning to the language consistent with other provisions in the rule. We typically give undefined terms in a statute their ordinary meaning[.]") (citations omitted).

[68] The way the term has been used in cases supports this construction. *See, e.g., Wulchin Land, L.L.C. v. Ellis*, No. 13-18-00156-CV, 2020 Tex. App. LEXIS 2275, at *30–31, 2020 WL 1303230 (Tex. App.—Corpus Christi Mar. 19, 2020, pet. denied) (mem. op.) (referencing the identification of a potential party in a pleading that referred to the party as an "additional party defendant" that would be joined if the party did not take an action described in the pleading).

disclose the names of other healthcare providers for the plaintiff; and (3) in a suit against a general or limited partnership, the partnership should identify the names of its general partners.

Another issue regarding "potential party" disclosures relates to the address and telephone number that must be disclosed for the potential party. For example, it is unclear whether the responding party should disclose an individual's home or work address and telephone number. Similarly, for an entity that has multiple offices, it is unclear which address and telephone number should be disclosed.

Because Texas Rules 193.2(i), former Texas Rule 194.2(b), and current Texas Rule 194.2(b)(2) are in the singular—they only require the disclosure of the potential party's "address[] and telephone number"—and because Texas Rule 193.2(i)'s purpose is to allow the opposing party to easily locate the potential party,[69] for an individual, the responding party can designate the individual's home address and telephone number, work address and telephone number, another address and telephone number, or any combination of the foregoing at which the party normally can be found and served with process.[70] However, if the party receiving the disclosure claims that the home address and telephone number of a potential party are needed for a proper investigation of the party, a court should order the responding party to provide them.[71]

In contrast, for an entity, the responding party should provide the address and telephone number of either the entity's principal office in Texas or the business location with the most significant relationship to the facts in the case at hand. It is clear, however, that a responding party should not provide the potential party's attorney's address and telephone number.[72]

6-3:3.3 Legal Theories and Factual Bases for Claims and Defenses

Former Texas Rule 194.2(c)—now Texas Rule 194.2(b)(3)—requires the disclosure of the responding party's "legal theories, and, in general, the factual bases for [its] claims or defenses[.]"[73] This disclosure corresponds to Texas Rule 193.2(j), which allows contention discovery.[74]

As with a contention interrogatory answer, the responding party, in a contention disclosure, "need not marshal all evidence that may be offered at trial"[75] or "brief legal issues."[76] Rather, the Rule's purpose is to provide the responding "party's basic

---

69 See discussion in note 120 and accompanying text.

70 See discussion in note 121 and accompanying text.

71 See discussion in note 122 and accompanying text.

72 See discussion in notes 123–125 and accompanying text.

73 Former Tex. R. Civ. P. 194.2(c); Tex. R. Civ. P. 194.2(b)(3).

74 Tex. R. Civ. P. 192.3(j) ("A party may obtain discovery of any other party's legal contentions and the factual bases for those contentions.").

75 Former Tex. R. Civ. P. 194.2(c); Tex. R. Civ. P. 194.2(b)(3).

76 Tex. R. Civ. P. 194 cmt. 2 to 1999 change (Former Texas "Rule 194.2(c) and (d) permit a party further inquiry into another's legal theories and factual claims than is often provided in notice pleadings. So-called 'contention interrogatories' are used for the same purpose. Such interrogatories are not properly used to require a party to marshal evidence or brief legal issues. Paragraphs (c) and (d) are intended to require disclosure of a party's basic assertions,

assertions, whether in prosecution of claims or in defense."[77]

Unfortunately, there is no precise answer regarding the level of detail needed for a proper contention disclosure. Rather, this depends on the action's nature and complexity. Because the principal purpose of contention disclosures is to provide basic information about legal and factual contentions early in the case so that the party receiving the disclosure can plan and focus its discovery or determine that discovery is unnecessary, two things are clear. First, a proper disclosure cannot merely reference the responding party's pleadings. Thus, for example, a plaintiff's disclosure should not refer the requesting party to the plaintiff's petition no matter how detailed,[78] and a defendant's

---

whether in prosecution of claims or in defense."); *see also* Tex. R. Civ. P. 192 cmt. 5 (stating that "the responding party need not marshal all evidence that may be offered at trial").

[77] Tex. R. Civ. P. 194 cmt. 2 to 1999 change. Texas Rules 194 and 197 prohibit interrogatories from "requir[ing] the responding party to marshal all of its available proof or the proof it intends to offer at trial." Tex. R. Civ. P. 197.1; Tex. R. Civ. P. 194.2 cmt. 2 to 1999 change (stating that contention interrogatories "are not properly used to require a party to marshal evidence or brief legal issues"); Tex. R. Civ. P. 197 cmt. 1 to 1999 change ("[I]nterrogatories that ask a party to state all legal and factual assertions are improper. . . . [I]nterrogatories may be used to ascertain basic legal and factual claims and defenses, but may not be used to force a party to marshal evidence."). But neither Rule explains what constitutes evidence marshalling. Cases, however, make clear that "[m]arshaling means '[a]rranging all of a party's evidence in the order that it will be presented at trial.'" *Sheffield Dev. Co. v. Carter & Burgess, Inc.*, No. 02-11-00204-CV, 2012 Tex. App. LEXIS 10599, at *17, 2012 WL 6632500 (Tex. App.—Fort Worth Dec. 21, 2012, pet. dism'd) (mem. op.) (quoting *Black's Law Dictionary* 1063 (9th ed. 2009)); *accord In re Sting Soccer Grp., LP*, No. 05-17-00317-CV, 2017 Tex. App. LEXIS 11197, at *13, 2017 WL 5897454 (Tex. App.—Dallas Nov. 30, 2017, orig. proceeding) (mem. op.); *Cmty. Initiatives, Inc. v. Chase Bank of Tex.*, 153 S.W.3d 270, 280 (Tex. App.—El Paso 2004, no pet.); *Bubbajunk.com, Inc. v. Momentum Software, Inc.*, No. 03-03-00590-CV, 2004 Tex. App. LEXIS 3741, at *4 n.1, 2004 WL 904081 (Tex. App.—Austin Apr. 29, 2004, pet. denied) (mem. op.) (citing *In re Mohawk Rubber Co.*, 982 S.W.2d 494, 498 (Tex. App.—Texarkana 1998, orig. proceeding)). Also of note, a recent case holds that a party is not required to list arbitration in response to a request for disclosure under former Texas Rule 194.2(c) to preserve the right to enforce an arbitration agreement, reasoning that "[a]rbitration is not a legal theory; it is part of the alternative dispute resolution process." *Holt Tex., Ltd. v. Rubio*, No. 13-19-00206-CV, 2020 Tex. App. LEXIS 2096, at *12, 2020 WL 1181253 (Tex. App.—Corpus Christi Mar. 12, 2020, no pet.) (mem. op.).

[78] *Cf. Anderson v. UPS, Inc.*, No. 09-2526-KHV-DJW, 2010 U.S. Dist. LEXIS 123878, at *22, 2010 WL 4822564 (D. Kan. Nov. 22, 2010) ("[C]ourts typically hold that referring the propounding party to other pleadings, or incorporating by reference portions of other pleadings such as the complaint, is insufficient to answer an interrogatory.") (footnote omitted); *Hawn v. Shoreline Towers Phase I Condo. Ass'n*, No. 3:07cv97/RV/EMT, 2007 U.S. Dist. LEXIS 58032, at *6–7, 2007 WL 2298009 (N.D. Fla. Aug. 9, 2007) ("[I]t is insufficient to answer an interrogatory by merely referencing allegations of a pleading."); *Williams v. Sprint/United Mgmt. Co.*, 235 F.R.D. 494, 501 (D. Kan. 2006) ("Plaintiffs may not answer the interrogatory by generally referring Defendant to the pleadings filed in this case. . . ."); *Davidson v. Goord*, 215 F.R.D. 73, 77 (W.D.N.Y. 2003) ("Nor it is [sic] permissible to refuse to provide answers to interrogatories . . . on the ground that information sought can be gleaned from the requested party's pleading. . . . As answers to interrogatories . . . must be in a form suitable for use at trial, it is insufficient to answer by merely referencing allegations of a pleading."); *DiPietro v. Jefferson Bank*, 144 F.R.D. 279, 282 (E.D. Pa. 1992) ("[T]he fact that plaintiff's complaint is sworn does not make it any more acceptable to answer an interrogatory solely by referencing paragraphs of that sworn complaint."); *Stabilus v. Haynsworth,*

disclosure should neither refer the requesting party to the defendant's answer nor re-urge a general denial.[79]

Second, although a contention disclosure need not contain exacting detail, a plaintiff's disclosure should identify each cause of action and state the basic facts underlying it. Similarly, a defendant's disclosure should (1) deny the factual allegations underlying each cause of action and state the basic facts underlying the denial, and (2) identify each affirmative defense and the basic facts underlying it. This conclusion is supported by Texas Rule 194's commentary, which provides the following example of a proper disclosure under former Texas Rule 194.2(c):

> [F]or example, a plaintiff would be required to disclose that he or she claimed damages suffered in a car wreck caused by defendant's negligence in speeding . . ., but would not be required to state the speed at which defendant was allegedly driving. . . . In the same example, defendant would be required to disclose his or her denial of the speeding allegation[.][80]

A more detailed inquiry into the responding party's contentions should be made through depositions and interrogatories. Accordingly, former Texas Rule 194.2(c)—now Texas Rule 194.2(b)(3)—should be used to obtain basic information concerning the responding party's contentions, and depositions and interrogatories should be used to obtain any additional needed detail about them.

Oftentimes, a contention disclosure served early in a case will claim that the responding party needs further discovery to make a proper disclosure. Such a response is improper because a plaintiff asserting a cause of action must have some factual basis for asserting it when filing suit and a defendant must have some basis for contesting it when answering.[81] Thus, the responding party has an obligation, when

---

Baldwin, Johnson & Greaves, P.A., 144 F.R.D. 258, 263–64 (E.D. Pa. 1992) ("[P]laintiff's [interrogatory] response is to 'See plaintiff's Complaint.' Plaintiff cannot avoid answering interrogatories by referring the defendant to the complaint, no matter how detailed."); *King v. E.F. Hutton & Co.*, 117 F.R.D. 2, 6 (D.D.C. 1987) ("Nor is it an adequate response to say that the information is reflected in the complaint, no matter how detailed[.]").

79 *See LaBeth v. Pasadena Bayshore Hosp., Inc.*, No. 14-10-01237-CV, 2012 Tex. App. LEXIS 254, at *5, 2012 WL 113050 (Tex. App.—Houston [14th Dist.] Jan. 12, 2012, pet. denied) (mem. op.) (suggesting that the defendant's reference to its general denial was improper); *cf. Morock v. Chautauqua Airlines, Inc.*, No. 8:07-cv-210-T-17-MAP, 2007 U.S. Dist. LEXIS 88532, at *6, 2007 WL 4247767 (M.D. Fla. Dec. 3, 2007) (holding that answering an interrogatory by referring the requesting party to the responding answer is "deficient"). See also cases cited in note 47.

80 Tex. R. Civ. P. 194 cmt. 2 to 1999 change. A disclosure in a simple breach-of-contract case would be similar. The plaintiff should (1) identify the specific contract allegedly breached, (2) identify the contractual obligation or provision breached, and (3) describe generally how the obligation or provision was breached. Conversely, the defendant should (a) state whether it is denying the breach and, if so, the basic facts supporting its denial, such as why the obligation or provision at issue was not breached, and (b) disclose each affirmative defense and the basic facts underlying it.

81 Tex. Civ. Prac. & Rem. Code § 10.001(3) ("The signing of a pleading or motion as required by the Texas Rules of Civil Procedure constitutes a certificate by the signatory that to the signatory's best knowledge, information, and belief, formed after reasonable inquiry: . . . (3) each allegation or other factual contention in the pleading . . . has evidentiary support

it makes a contention disclosure, to disclose the best information then available concerning each of its causes of action or defenses, however limited and susceptible to change it may be.[82]

Unlike most other written-discovery responses, a contention disclosure "that has been changed by an amended or supplemental response is not admissible and may not be used for impeachment."[83] The obvious purpose of this prohibition is to encourage parties to be transparent and describe their contentions early in the case without fear of having an early, candid disclosure come back to haunt them.

Although a failure to disclose a cause of action or defense set forth in the responding party's pleadings does not waive the cause of action or defense,[84] the responding

---

or, for a specifically identified allegation or factual contention, is likely to have evidentiary support after a reasonable opportunity for further investigation or discovery. . . ."); *see* Tex. R. Civ. P. 13 ("The signatures of attorneys or parties constitute a certificate by them that they have read the pleading . . .; that to the best of their knowledge, information, and belief formed after reasonable inquiry the instrument is not groundless and brought in bad faith or groundless and brought for the purpose of harassment."); *cf. Firetrace USA, LLC v. Jesclard*, No. CV-07-2001-PHX-ROS, 2009 U.S. Dist. LEXIS 2972, at *6, 2009 WL 73671 (D. Ariz. Jan. 9, 2009) ("Defendants, who asserted affirmative defenses in their Answer, must have contemplated a [Federal] Rule 11 basis in law or fact when they asserted these defenses and should be required to reveal this [Federal] Rule 11 basis, as well as other presently-known facts on the matter, when responding to Plaintiffs' contention interrogatories, regardless of how much discovery has transpired."); *U.S. ex rel. O'Connell v. Chapman Univ.*, 245 F.R.D. 646, 649 (C.D. Cal. 2007) ("Requiring a party to answer contention interrogatories is 'consistent with Rule 11 of the Federal Rules of Civil Procedure, [which requires that] plaintiffs must have some factual basis for the allegations in their complaint.'" (quoting *Cooperman v. One Bancorp* (*In re One Bancorp Sec. Litig.*), 134 F.R.D. 4, 8 (D. Me. 1991))).

82 Tex. R. Civ. P. 193.1 ("When responding to written discovery, a party must make a complete response, based on all information reasonably available to the responding party or its attorney at the time the response is made."). See also discussion in notes 96–97 and accompanying text.

83 Tex. R. Civ. P. 194.6.

84 *E.g.*, *In re J.N.*, No. 02-17-00179-CV, 2017 Tex. App. LEXIS 8544, at *7, 2017 WL 3910910 (Tex. App.—Sept. 7, 2017, no pet.) (mem. op.) ("[P]roperly pled claims for affirmative relief, as opposed to withheld evidence, are not abandoned or waived by a party's failure to expressly identify those claims in a response to a request for disclosure." (quoting *Concept Gen. Contracting, Inc. v. Asbestos Maint. Servs.*, 346 S.W.3d 172, 180 (Tex. App.—Amarillo 2011, pet. denied))); *Bundren v. Holly Oaks Townhomes Ass'n*, 347 S.W.3d 421, 431 (Tex. App.—Dallas 2011, pet. denied) ("While, absent proof of good cause or lack of unfair surprise or prejudice, the failure to completely respond to discovery requests results in the automatic exclusion of non-disclosed evidence, 'properly pled claims for affirmative relief, as opposed to withheld evidence, are not abandoned or waived by a party's failure to expressly identify those claims' in response to a discovery request." (quoting *Concept Gen. Contracting, Inc. v. Asbestos Maint. Servs., Inc.*, 346 S.W.3d 172, 179–80 (Tex. App.—Amarillo 2011, pet. denied))); *Killam Ranch Props., Ltd. v. Webb Cty.*, No. 04-08-00105-CV, 2008 Tex. App. LEXIS 8682, at *4–5, 2008 WL 4958452 (Tex. App.—San Antonio Nov. 19, 2008, no pet.) (mem. op.) ("A request for recovery of attorney's fees, stated in an answer, is a claim for affirmative relief. Killam Ranch has not provided this court with any authority suggesting that the County abandoned its claim for attorney's fees by failing to respond, or fully respond, to Killam Ranch's discovery requests under [Texas R]ules 194.2(c) and (d). The only authorities cited by Killam Ranch involved situations where the appellate courts held the trial court did not err in excluding evidence based on failures to comply with discovery. These

party, under Texas Rule 193.6, should be precluded from offering evidence about the cause of action or defense at trial or in response to a summary judgment motion if it failed to disclose the general factual bases for the cause of action or defense absent a showing of good cause for the failure or a lack of unfair surprise or unfair prejudice from it.[85]

6-3:3.4 Damages

Former Texas Rule 194.2(d)—now Texas Rule 194.2(b)(4)—requires disclosure of "the amount and any method of calculating economic damages."[86] Thus, by its express terms, the Rule does not relate to non-economic or exemplary damages.[87] Nothing in

---

cases in no way suggest a party *abandons* a claim by failing to respond to a [Texas R]ule 194.2(c) discovery request. There is nothing in the case law linking a failure to respond to discovery to an abandonment of a claim.") (citations omitted).

[85] *E.g.*, *Hardin v. Lella*, No. 03-14-00607-CV, 2015 Tex. App. LEXIS 11315, at *5–7, 2015 WL 6830598 (Tex. App.—Austin Nov. 4, 2015, no. pet.) (mem. op.) (in affirming a summary judgment to collect on a promissory note, holding that the trial court did not abuse its discretion in allowing the defendant to amend his petition on the day of the summary judgment hearing to assert novation as a defense, but precluding him from adducing any summary judgment evidence in support of the defense because it was not disclosed in his former Texas Rule 194.2(c) disclosure); *Holland v. Friedman & Feiger*, No. 05-12-01714-CV, 2014 Tex. App. LEXIS 12892, at *21, 2014 WL 6778394 (Tex. App.—Dallas Dec. 2, 2014, pet. denied) (mem. op.) ("Under [former Texas R]ule 194.2(c), appellees were entitled to disclosure of the Hollands' legal theories and the factual basis of their claims. We conclude the Hollands' failure to disclose they either suffered or were seeking mental anguish damages did not comply with [former Texas R]ule 194.2(c)."); *Grimes v. State*, No. 03-04-00154-CV, 2005 Tex. App. LEXIS 6963, at *14–15, 2005 WL 2043842 (Tex. App.—Austin Aug. 26, 2005, no pet.) (mem. op.) ("Last, Grimes asserts that the Railroad Commission erred because it failed to consider whether Endeavor still had a good faith claim to the Hill '30-A' Lease. In Grimes's response to the . . . discovery request for disclosure [under former Texas Rule 194], he failed to identify this ground as a legal basis for his opposition to the permit. The discovery request for disclosure required Grimes to disclose all of his legal theories and underlying factual bases. A party who fails to make, amend, or supplement a discovery response in a timely manner may not introduce in evidence the material or information that was not timely disclosed. It was therefore proper for the Railroad Commission to exclude evidence related to this legal theory at trial because Grimes failed to supplement his disclosure to include this theory in a timely manner."); *Jackson v. Maul*, No. 04-02-00873-CV, 2003 Tex. App. LEXIS 8614, at *2–5, 2003 WL 22295332 (Tex. App.—San Antonio Oct. 8, 2003, no pet.) (mem. op.) (affirming the trial court's order precluding the plaintiff from presenting evidence about the defendant's negligence because the plaintiff's disclosure under former Texas Rule 194.2(c) only identified the categories of damages sustained by the plaintiff and failed to provide the general factual bases for the defendant's alleged negligence). See also Chapter 5, section 5-7 (discussing the consequences under Texas Rule 193.6 for failing to timely respond, supplement, or amend written discovery responses).

[86] Former Tex. R. Civ. P. 194.2(d); Tex. R. Civ. P. 194.2(b)(4).

[87] *Levine v. Steve Scharn Custom Homes, Inc.*, 448 S.W.3d 637, 653 (Tex. App.—Houston [1st Dist.] 2014, pet. denied) ("The Levines argue that SSCHI was 'legally precluded' from recovering on its defamation claim because SSCHI failed to disclose their method and amount of damages pursuant the Levines' request for disclosure. [Former Texas] Rule 194.2(d) requires a plaintiff to disclose to a defendant who requests it 'the amount and any method of calculating economic damages.' This rule only concerns economic damages. It

the Rule defines "economic damages."[88] In other contexts, however, "economic damages" have been defined as "compensatory damages intended to compensate a claimant for actual economic or pecuniary loss" other than exemplary damages,[89] whereas,

---

is undisputed that SSCHI sought and obtained only non-economic damages.") (citations omitted).

"'Exemplary damages' means any damages awarded as a penalty or by way of punishment but not for compensatory purposes. Exemplary damages are neither economic nor noneconomic damages. 'Exemplary damages' includes punitive damages." Tex. Civ. Prac. & Rem. Code § 41.001(5).

[88] Comment 2 to the 1999 change to former Texas Rule 194 identifies "mental anguish" as an example of non-economic damages. Tex. R. Civ. P. 194 cmt. 2 to 1999 change.

[89] Tex. Civ. Prac. & Rem. Code § 41.001(4) (defining "economic damages" for purposes of exemplary damages); *accord* Tex. Bus. & Comm. Code § 17.45(11) (defining "economic damages" for purposes of the Deceptive Trade Practices-Consumer Protection Act as "compensatory damages for pecuniary loss, including costs of repair and replacement. The term does not include exemplary damages or damages for physical pain and mental anguish, loss of consortium, disfigurement, physical impairment, or loss of companionship and society."); Tex. Prop. Code § 27.001(6) (defining "economic damages" for purposes of the Residential Construction Liability Act as "compensatory damages for pecuniary loss proximately caused by a construction defect. The term does not include exemplary damages or damages for physical pain and mental anguish, loss of consortium, disfigurement, physical impairment, or loss of companionship and society."); *see also Hsu v. Conterra Servs., LLC*, No. 01-20-00182-CV, 2021 Tex. App. LEXIS 1813, at *6, 2021 WL 921672 (Tex. App.—Houston [1st Dist.] Mar. 11, 2021, no pet.) (mem. op.) ("Economic damages are generally understood to constitute compensation for pecuniary loss." (citing Tex. Civ. Prac. & Rem. Code § 41.001(4) and Tex. Bus. & Com. Code § 17.45(11))); Robert K. Wise, *Negligent Misrepresentation in Texas: The Misunderstood Tort*, 40 Tex. Tech. L. Rev. 845, 901 (2008) ("Pecuniary, or economic loss, has been broadly defined by Texas courts. Generally, the term has been defined to include money and everything that can be valued in money. *Black's Law Dictionary* defines pecuniary loss as a 'loss of money or of something having monetary value.' In other words, a loss that affects a plaintiff's pocketbook, as opposed to a personal injury or a physical injury to property." (footnotes omitted) (quoting *Black's Law Dictionary* 964 (8th ed. 2004))).

"Examples of pecuniary or economic losses include the difference between the value paid and the value received in a transaction, the cost of settling a lawsuit, the value of a lost cause of action against a third party, damages incurred in preparation for the use of an article, and lost profits and other types of consequential damages. Pecuniary or economic loss does not include damages for physical injury, physical pain and suffering, mental or emotional pain or anguish, loss of consortium, injury to reputation, or physical injury to property." Robert K. Wise, *Negligent Misrepresentation in Texas: The Misunderstood Tort*, 40 Texas Tech. L. Rev. 845, 901 (2008) (footnote omitted); *accord Golden Eagle Archery, Inc. v. Jackson*, 116 S.W.3d 757, 763 (Tex. 2003) ("When someone suffers personal injuries, the damages fall within two broad categories—economic and non-economic damages. Traditionally, economic damages are those that compensate an injured party for lost wages, lost earning capacity, and medical expenses. Non-economic damages include compensation for pain, suffering, mental anguish, and disfigurement. 'Hedonic' damages are another type of non-economic damages and compensate for loss of enjoyment of life."); *Cotton Patch Café, Inc. v. Micros Sys., Inc.*, No. MJG-09-3242, 2012 U.S. Dist. LEXIS 168494, at *14–15, 2012 WL 5986773 (D. Md. Nov. 27, 2012) ("In Texas, 'economic loss' has been defined as 'damages for inadequate value, costs of repair and replacement of the defective product, or consequent loss of profits—without any claim of personal injury or damage to other property . . . as well as the diminution in the value of the product because it is inferior in quality and "non-economic damages" have been defined as "damages awarded for the purpose of compensating a claimant for physical pain and suffering, mental or emotional pain or anguish, loss of consortium, disfigurement, physical impairment, loss of companionship and society, inconvenience, loss of enjoyment of life, injury to reputation, and all other nonpecuniary losses of any kind other than exemplary damages."[90] The foregoing definition of "economic damages" should apply to former Texas Rule 194.2(d)—now Texas Rule 194.2(b)(4).[91]

Because attorneys' fees awarded pursuant to a contractual provision, fee-shifting statute, or common-law exception to the "American Rule" about attorney's fees (e.g., the "common-fund" or "bad-faith" exceptions) are not economic damages, they need not be disclosed in a damage disclosure.[92] However, if the fees are part of the

---

does not work for the general purposes for which it was manufactured and sold.'" (quoting *Entergy Gulf States, Inc. v. Akrotex, Inc.*, 40 S.W.3d 201, 204 (Tex. App.—Beaumont 2001, no pet.) (quoting *2314 Lincoln Park W. Condo. Ass'n v. Mann, Gin, Ebel & Frazier, Ltd.*, 555 N.E.2d 346, 348 (Ill. 1990))); *City of Alton v. Sharyland Water Supply Corp.*, 277 S.W.3d 132 (Tex. App.—Corpus Christi 2009) (same), *aff'd and rev'd in part on other grounds*, 354 S.W.2d 407 (Tex. 2011).

90 Tex. Civ. Prac. & Rem. Code § 41.001(12); *see also* Tex. Bus. & Comm. Code § 17.45(11) (defining economic damages for purposes of the Deceptive Trade Practices-Consumer Protection Act); Tex. Prop. Code § 27.001(6) (defining "economic damages" for purposes of the Residential Construction Liability Act).

91 *See, e.g., Hsu v. Conterra Servs., LLC*, No. 01-20-00182-CV, 2021 Tex. App. LEXIS 1813, at *6–7, 2021 WL 921672 (Tex. App.—Houston [1st Dist.] Mar. 11, 2021, no pet.) (mem. op.) (relying on the definitions of "economic damages" in Tex. Civ. Prac. & Rem. Code § 41.001(4) and Tex. Bus. & Com. Code § 17.45(11) to assert that "[e]conomic damages are generally understood to constitute compensation for pecuniary loss" and concluding that "[p]rejudgment interest is a type of damages" with a compensatory purposes and, therefore, that former Texas Rule 194.2(d) requires a party "to disclose the method of calculating its prejudgment interest"); *Chang v. Denny*, No. 05-17-01457-CV, 2019 Tex. App. LEXIS 7586, at *32, 2019 WL 3955765 (Tex. App.—Dallas Aug. 22, 2019, pet. denied) ("In her supplemental response, [the plaintiff] disclosed the amount of damages she was seeking, which included her lost earning capacity in the past and in the future, and provided a calculation. This information was responsive to the particular request for disclosure [under former Texas Rule 194.2(d)] . . . ."); *Grant v. Sw. Elec. Power Co.*, 20 S.W.3d 764, 770 (Tex. App.—Texarkana 2000) (noting that "[t]he term economic damages is a term of art with a specific legal meaning" and then applying the definition of such damages in Section 41.001(4) of the Texas Civil Practice and Remedies Code to the determination of whether an electric utility's damages limitation reasonably limited the recovery), *aff'd and rev'd in part on other grounds*, 73 S.W.3d 211 (Tex. 2002).

92 *E.g., Tex. Vein & Vascular v. Martinez*, No. 13-14-00176-CV, 2015 Tex. App. LEXIS 9393, at *16, 2015 WL 5233342 (Tex. App.—Corpus Christi Sept. 3, 2015, pet. denied) (mem. op.) (noting that "attorney fees are not economic damages subject to disclosure"); *Safeco Sur. v. J.P. Sw. Concrete, Inc.*, No. 01-12-00672-CV, 2013 Tex. App. LEXIS 13314, at *28–29, 2013 WL 5820619(Tex. App.—Houston [1st Dist.] Oct. 29, 2013, no pet.) (mem. op.) ("[W]here, as here, attorney's fees are not sought as an element of damages, they are not economic damages and are therefore not required to be disclosed in accordance with [former Texas R]ule 194.2(d)."); *Goldman v. Olmstead*, 414 S.W.3d 346, 365 n.5 (Tex. App.—Dallas 2013, no pet.) ("[T]he calculation of the amount of attorney's fees incurred by a party is not an economic damage that is required to be disclosed in response to a request for disclosure."); *Jespersen v. Sweetwater Ranch Apartments*, 309 S.W.3d 644, 660–61 (Tex. App.—Dallas 2012, no pet.) (same); *Carter v. Flowers*, No. 02-10-00226-CV, 2011 Tex. App. LEXIS 7829, at *16,

plaintiff's damages (e.g., in a case in which an insurer or indemnitor breaches its duty to defend), they must be disclosed.[93]

Under former Texas Rule 194.2(d)—now Texas Rule 194.2(b)(4)—it is improper for a responding party, who is seeking damages, simply to provide a "lump-sum statement" of the damages it allegedly sustained. Rather, it must disclose each category or type of damages for each cause of action, its amount, and how the amount was calculated.[94] As explained by the commentary to Texas Rule 194, "a plaintiff would be

---

2011 WL 4502203 (Tex. App.—Fort Worth Sept. 29, 2011, no pet.) (mem. op.) (same); *Shafer v. Gulliver*, No. 14-09-00646-CV, 2010 Tex. App. LEXIS 9021, at *33, 2010 WL 4545164 (Tex. App.—Houston [14th Dist.] Nov. 12, 2010, no pet.) (mem. op.) (same).

[93] *See C.A. Walker Constr. Co. v. J.P. Sw. Concrete, Inc.*, No. 01-07-00904-CV, 2009 Tex. App. LEXIS 2228, at *19–20, 2009 WL 884754 (Tex. App.—Houston [1st Dist.] Apr. 2, 2009, no pet.) (mem. op.) (reversing a damage award because the plaintiff's damage disclosure, among other things, did not disclose that it was seeking to recover attorneys' fees paid to a third party in another lawsuit); *Shafer v. Gulliver*, No. 14-09-00646-CV, 2010 Tex. App. LEXIS 9021, at *33–34 & n.12, 2010 WL 4545164 (Tex. App.—Houston [14th Dist.] Nov.12, 2010, no pet.) (mem. op.) (distinguishing between a situation in which a party claims attorneys' fees as damages and one in which it claims them under a fee-shifting statute).

[94] *Cf. Silicon Knights, Inc. v. Epic Games, Inc.*, No. 5:07-CV-275-D, 2012 U.S. Dist. LEXIS 63707, at *10–11, 2012 WL 1596722 (E.D.N.C. May 7, 2012) ("Not surprisingly, SK argues that, independent of the Lloyd Report, it complied with [Federal] Rules 26(a)(1)(A)(iii) and 26(e). First, SK notes that it stated in its initial and first supplemental initial disclosures that it expected its damages for the various claims in its complaint to be 'several million dollars . . . .' SK then argues that these statements were adequate damages computations. However, a [Federal] Rule 26(a)(1)(A)(iii) disclosure must include 'more than a lump sum statement of the damages allegedly sustained.' Instead, the rule 'contemplates some analysis,' including an analysis of the damages sought as to each claim. SK's statements that it expected its damages to be 'several million dollars' lack precision and analysis. Accordingly, SK did not satisfy its [Federal] Rule 26(a)(1)(A)(iii) obligation with these statements." (citations omitted) (quoting *City & Cnty. of S.F. v. Tutor-Saliba Corp.*, 218 F.R.D. 219, 221 (N.D. Cal. 2003))); *Frontline Med. Assocs., Inc. v. Coventry Health Care*, 263 F.R.D. 567, 569 (C.D. Cal. 2009) ("Plaintiff's complaint alleged damages under three causes of action for breach of contract, violation of fair procedure, and interference with prospective economic advantage. Plaintiff's initial disclosure, therefore, should disclose a computation of each category of damages attributable to each cause of action.") (citations omitted); *City & Cnty. of S.F. v. Tutor-Saliba Corp.*, 218 F.R.D. 219, 221–22 (N.D. Cal. 2003) ("[T]he plaintiff should provide more than a lump sum statement of the damages allegedly sustained. As one treatise explained: 'The meaning of "category" of damages is not clear. Presumably, however, it requires more than merely the broad types of damages ("wrongful death," or "property damage," "bodily injury," etc.). To make the disclosure obligation meaningful, a more detailed specification of damages is apparently required: For example, in a personal injury case, the nature and extent of any injuries suffered must be disclosed, including amounts claimed for "general" damages (pain, suffering or disfigurement) as well as "special" damages (medical bills, lost wages, cost of repairing damaged property, etc.).' Moreover, the 'computation' of damages required by [Federal] Rule 26(a)(1)(C) contemplates some analysis . . . . On the other hand, disclosing a precise figure for damages without a method of calculation may be sufficient in cases where other evidence is developed *e.g.* in the context of a preliminary hearing, and it is appropriate to defer further specification to *e.g.* development of expert testimony. The Court concludes that Plaintiff should provide its assessment of damages in light of the information currently available to it in sufficient detail so as to enable each of the multiple Defendants in this case to understand the contours of its potential exposure and make informed decisions as to settlement and discovery. More spe-

cifically, in this case, Plaintiffs' aggregation of *e.g.* compensatory damages for all claims, all contracts, and all defendants does not permit each Defendant to know the extent of its liability since the SAC alleges breaches and fraud with respect to six different contracts, each of them involving some defendants but not others. Nor are the Defendants able to discern how the compensatory damages claimed are distributed among the contracts. It would be useful to know, for instance, for both discovery organization as well as for settlement discussions, whether the bulk of damages are attributable to one or two contracts. Nor are Defendants able to discern from Plaintiffs' initial disclosure which portion of the compensatory damages are attributable to breach of contract, fraud, and RICO claims. Because the merits analysis and assessment of likelihood of success may vary among the claims, knowing what portion of the damages are attributed to each claim would assist the parties in putting a settlement value on the case. Providing this information, even if based on tentative early information, would advance the litigation without imposing a significant burden on the Plaintiffs. The Court notes the fact that Plaintiffs disclose a very specific dollar amount ($42,284,757.00) for compensatory and other damages indicates that they have already engaged in a detailed calculation of damages. While the Court does not yet mandate disclosure of precise calculations given that many of the documents which are likely to inform the calculation remain in Defendants' hands and some level of expert analysis may be required, the Court contemplates that Plaintiffs will update its disclosure and provide greater detail as to its calculations as discovery progresses." (footnotes omitted) (citations omitted) (quoting Rutter Group, ***Federal Civil Procedure Before Trial*** § 11:166 (2001))); ***see also, e.g.***, ***Bullard v. Roadway Exp.***, 3 F. App'x 418, 420 (6th Cir. 2001) (holding that, in a claim for lost wages, there should be some information relating to hours worked and pay rate); ***Advanced Training Grp. Worldwide, Inc. v. Proactive Techs. Inc.***, No. 19-CV-505, 2020 U.S. Dist. LEXIS 141855, at *11, 2020 WL 4574493 (E.D. Va. Aug. 7, 2020) ("For a party to satisfy its obligations under [Federal] Rule 26, a party must provide a computation of its damages. District courts have therefore correctly held that, where a party only discloses a lump sum or merely refers to documents from which the opposing party can presume damages, the disclosing party has not met its obligation.") (citing cases); ***Grouse River Outfitters Ltd. v. Oracle Corp.***, No. 16-CV-02954-LB, 2019 U.S. Dist. LEXIS 112869, at *2, 2019 WL 2929867 (N.D. Cal. July 8, 2019) ("'Computation of each category of damages,' as used in [Federal] Rule 26, 'contemplates some analysis beyond merely setting forth a lump sum amount for a claimed element of damages.'" (quoting ***Silver State Broad., LLC v. Beasley FM Acquisition***, No. 2:11-CV-01789-APG-CWH, 2016 U.S. Dist. LEXIS 8904, at *6, 2016 WL 320110 (D. Nev. Jan. 25, 2016))); ***Fabick, Inc. v. FABCO Equip., Inc.***, No. 16-cv-172-wmc, 2017 U.S. Dist. LEXIS 198963, at *15, 2017 WL 6001869 (W.D. Wis. Dec. 4, 2017) ("[P]laintiff does not attempt to argue that its initial disclosure, dated November 30, 2016, was adequate, nor could it since the disclosure only lists categories of damages without any attempt at a 'computation.'"); ***Easton v. Asplundh Tree Experts Co.***, No. C16-1694RSM, 2017 U.S. Dist. LEXIS 189168, at *10, 2017 WL 5483769 (W.D. Wash. Nov. 15, 2017) (precluding the plaintiff from offering evidence of actual damages because, "[a]t no point in this litigation did plaintiff quantify—even roughly—the amount of actual damages she suffered as a result of her layoff. . . . However, making certain documents available and promising that someone (in this case Plaintiff) will testify regarding damages is not a 'computation' and fails to apprise Defendant of the extent of its exposure in this case."); ***Silvagni v. Wal-Mart Stores, Inc.***, No. 2:16-cv-00039-JCM-NJK, 2017 U.S. Dist. LEXIS 181543, at *2–3, 2017 WL 5100162 (D. Nev. Nov. 2, 2017) ("As the word 'computation' contemplates, a proper damages disclosure must provide 'some analysis beyond merely setting forth a lump sum amount for a claimed element of damages.' . . . In this case, Plaintiff has disclosed a claim for future lumbar surgery in the amount of $213,000. . . . [H]owever, Plaintiff never disclosed how she arrived at that figure and is merely relying on that lump sum as her disclosure. That lump sum is not a computation, as required by [Federal] Rule 26. As a result, Defendant has shown that Plaintiff failed to comply with her disclosure obligations with respect to her damages claim for future lumbar surgery." (citations omitted) (quoting ***Allstate Ins. Co. v. Nassiri***, No.

required to disclose that he or she claimed damages suffered in a car wreck caused by defendant's negligence in speeding, and would be required to state how loss of past earnings and future earning capacity was calculated[.]"[95]

Oftentimes, a damage disclosure, like a contention disclosure, served early in a case will claim that the responding party needs further discovery to make a proper disclosure. Such a response is improper because a party claiming damages must have some evidence that an injury occurred and some basis for calculating its alleged damages before filing suit.[96] Thus, the responding party has an obligation, when it makes its damage disclosure, to disclose the best information then available concerning its damages, however limited and susceptible to change it may be. As noted by one federal court in compelling the plaintiffs to disclose the amount and method of calculation of their damages under the comparable federal disclosure rule, Federal Rule 26(a)(1)(A)(iii):

> Plaintiff's computation of damages is nothing more than a regurgitation of its prayer for relief in its complaint. Such a computation does not, even at this early stage of the case, comply with the requirements of [Federal] Rule 26(a)(1)(A)(iii). . . . A party is not excused from making its disclosures because it has not fully investigated the case or because it challenges the sufficiency of another party's disclosures or because another party has not made its disclosures.
>
> In *City and County of San Francisco v. Tutor-Saliba Corporation*, 218 F.R.D. 219, 221 (N.D. Cal. 2003), the court . . . stated that a plaintiff should provide its computation of damages in light of the information currently available to it in sufficient detail so as to enable the defendants to understand the contours of their potential exposure and make informed decisions regarding settlement and discovery. The court further stated that the word "computation" contemplates some analysis beyond merely setting forth a lump sum amount for a claimed element of damages. A computation of damages may not need to be detailed early

---

2:08-cv-00369-JCM-GWF, 2011 U.S. Dist. LEXIS 79866, at *14, 2011 WL 2977127 (D. Nev. July 21, 2011))); ***Sulaiman v. Biehl & Biehl***, No. 15 C 04518, 2016 U.S. Dist. LEXIS 136677, at *25, 2016 WL 5720476 (N.D. Ill. Sept. 30, 2016) (mem. op.) ("If Sulaiman was claiming actual damages, he was required by [Federal] Rule 26(a)(1)(A)(iii) to disclose, and compute, those damages. Sulaiman does not contest that actual damages are an element of an ICFA claim and fails to identify any evidence of actual damages that he suffered as a result of the conduct he claims violated the ICFA. Accordingly, he failed to meet the disclosure requirements of [Federal] Rule 26(a)(1)(A)(iii)."); ***Frontline Med. Assocs. v. Coventry Health Care***, 263 F.R.D. 567, 570 (C.D. Cal. 2009) (holding that (1) initial disclosures regarding reputational harm were "clearly deficient" because the plaintiff stated only that its damages were based on lost referrals.).

[95] Tex. R. Civ. P. 194.2 cmt. 2 to 1999 change. See also cases cited in notes 89, 91.

[96] Tex. Civ. Prac. & Rem. Code § 10.001(3) ("The signing of a pleading or motion as required by the Texas Rules of Civil Procedure constitutes a certificate by the signatory that to the signatory's best knowledge, information, and belief, formed after reasonable inquiry: . . . (3) each allegation or other factual contention in the pleading or motion has evidentiary support or, for a specifically identified allegation or factual contention, is likely to have evidentiary support after a reasonable opportunity for further investigation or discovery[.]"); Tex. R. Civ. P. 13 ("The signatures of attorneys or parties constitute a certificate by them that they have read the pleading, motion, or other paper; that to the best of their knowledge, information, and belief formed after reasonable inquiry the instrument is not groundless and brought in bad faith or groundless and brought for the purpose of harassment.").

in the case before all relevant documents or evidence has been obtained by the plaintiff. As discovery proceeds, however, the plaintiff is required to supplement its initial damages computation to reflect the information obtained through discovery. . . .

Plaintiff argues that it cannot provide a more specific damages computation at this time because its damages will substantially be based on recovery of the profits that Defendant has obtained through its interference with Plaintiff's current or prospective contractual and business relations. Plaintiff states that once it has obtained all the necessary information through discovery, its damages expert(s) will evaluate the data and prepare a damages computation. The Court understands that precise calculation of Plaintiff's alleged damages may need to await future expert analysis. Plaintiff alleges, however, that Defendant has interfered with its current or prospective contractual and business relations. Unless this allegation is wholly speculative, Plaintiff must have some knowledge of the contractual or business relationships that have been interrupted, and should be able to provide some estimates of value of those contracts or relationships in order to provide a preliminary computation of its damages. If Plaintiff does not presently have information that its contractual or business relationships have, in fact, been damaged by Defendant's alleged conduct, then it should so state.[97]

---

[97] *LT Game Int'l Ltd. v. Shuffle Master, Inc.*, No. 2:12-cv-01216-GMN-GWF, 2013 U.S. Dist. LEXIS 11835, at *15–18, 2013 WL 321659 (D. Nev. Jan. 28, 2013) (citations omitted); *accord Agena v. Cleaver-Brooks, Inc.*, No. CV 19-00089 DKW-WRP, 2020 U.S. Dist. LEXIS 223764, at *12, 2020 WL 6888725 (D. Haw. July 31, 2020) (Federal "Rule 26(a) requires that Plaintiffs must disclose the information they current possess regarding their claimed damages. The fact that expert testimony will be required as this litigation proceeds does not excuse Plaintiffs from complying with their initial disclosure obligations.") (citations omitted); *Johnson v. Hooters, Inc.*, No. 218CV01381RFBBNW, 2020 U.S. Dist. LEXIS 250507, at *9, 2020 WL 8614574 (D. Nev. Apr. 16, 2020) ("Courts recognize that a 'computation of damages may not need to be detailed early in the case before all relevant documents or evidence has been obtained by the plaintiff.' But a party's initial disclosures should provide 'the best information then available to it concerning that claim, however limited and potentially changing it may be.'" (citations omitted) (quoting *LT Game Int'l Ltd. v. Shuffle Master, Inc.*, No. 2:12-cv-01216-GMN, 2013 U.S. Dist. LEXIS 11835, at *16, 2013 WL 321659 (D. Nev. Jan. 28, 2013), and *Moore's Federal Practice* § 26.22 [4][c][i] (3d ed. 2016))); *Schedler v. FieldTurf USA, Inc.*, 3:16-CV-344-PK, 2018 U.S. Dist. LEXIS 224884, at *31, 2018 WL 7132502 (D. Or. Sept. 11, 2018) ("The level of specificity for the damages computation varies depending on the stage of the litigation and the claims at issue. 'A party must make its initial disclosures based on the information then reasonably available to it.'" (quoting Fed. R. Civ. P. 26(a)(1)(E))); *Port Auth. Police Benevolent Ass'n, Inc. v. Port Auth.*, No. 15CV3526KMWSDA, 2018 U.S. Dist. LEXIS 8987, at *7–8, 2018 WL 485980, at *3 (S.D.N.Y. Jan. 19, 2018) ("PAPBA's second explanation for not properly disclosing its damages is that, because its damages were ongoing, PAPBA could not have fully disclosed them in 2015. This explanation fails because, even if PAPBA could not have provided a final computation of damages at the start of this litigation, PAPBA still could have provided an estimate of the damages it had incurred as of 2015. PAPBA violated [Federal] Rule 26(a)(1) by not providing any computation at all.") (citation omitted); *LW Air I, L.L.C. v. Air 7, L.L.C.*, No. 3:16-CV-00546-L, 2017 U.S. Dist. LEXIS 176073, at *2, 2017 WL 3209398 (N.D. Tex. Apr. 20, 2017) ("'A party claiming damages has the obligation, when it makes its initial disclosures, to disclose to the other parties the best information then available to it concerning that claim, however limited and potentially changing it may be.'" (quoting *Tendeka, Inc. v. Glover*, No. H-13-1764, 2015 U.S. Dist.

A defendant must disclose "any basis for contesting the damage calculation."[98] Thus, if it believes that the plaintiff's damages are overstated or improperly calculated, it should disclose that fact and the bases for it. And, if the defendant intends to provide its own damage calculation at trial, it should disclose both the damages' amount and its calculation.

A failure to make a proper damage disclosure timely (e.g., by failing to clearly identify each category or type of economic damages, its dollar amount, or how the dollar amount was calculated) generally will result in the exclusion of any evidence offered by the party regarding that damages category or type irrespective of whether the responding party is seeking or contesting damages at trial or in response to a sum-

---

LEXIS 60977, at *41–42, 2015 WL 2212601 (S.D. Tex. May 11, 2015), and *Joseph v. Las Vegas Metro. Police Dep't*, No. 2:09-CV-0966-HDM-LRL, 2010 U.S. Dist. LEXIS 93145, at *6, 2010 WL 3238992, (D. Nev. Aug. 13, 2010))); ***Johnstech Int'l Corp. v. Jf Microtechnology SDN BHD***, No. 14-cv-02864-JD, 2016 U.S. Dist. LEXIS 104380, at *4–5, 2016 WL 4182402 (N.D. Cal. Aug 8, 2016) ("While the courts have declined to take a rigid approach to the specificity required for initial disclosures about damages, it has been abundantly clear for some time that at least some facts and figures, however tentative, need to be provided; simply saying 'you owe me' is not enough. And yet, all JFM said in its initial disclosures for damages was just that. Even as late as its final supplemental disclosures, which it served just before the close of discovery, JFM's 'computations' of special damages consisted of nothing more than cursory and unadorned statements like '[a]ll monies lost . . . as a result of business lost by JF Microtechnology as the result of the false letter' and '[a]ll profits earned as a result of the unlawful diversion of business' from JFM to Johnstech. The 'computation' for general damages managed to be even less informative: '[m]onies to compensate' for 'shame, mortification and hurt feelings resulting from the false letter.' Needless to say, JFM did not provide or even identify any evidence or documentation in support of these hazy generalizations. In effect, JFM never disclosed at any time in the litigation a useful valuation of its counterclaim damages as [Federal] Rule 26(a) requires. That is an unacceptable default.") (citations omitted); ***Stemrich v. Zabiyaka***, No. 1:12-CV-1409, 2013 U.S. Dist. LEXIS 113674, at *5–6, 2013 WL 4080310 (M.D. Pa. Aug. 13, 2013) ("[T]he timing requirements of [Federal] Rule 26(a)(1)(C) cannot be avoided if the receiving party insists on compliance. Here, Defendants so insist. As such, Plaintiffs must disclose the best information available related to the damages claim, even if that information is subject to change.") (citations omitted); ***Dunstan v. Wal-Mart Stores E., L.P.***, No. 3:07-cv-713-J-32TEM, 2008 U.S. Dist. LEXIS 38125, at *3–4, 2008 WL 2025313 (M.D. Fla. 2008) ("'Plaintiffs should be able to make a good faith estimate of damages and methods of calculations based on the information available at this stage of the litigation, while reserving the right to amend their calculations.' Moreover, [Federal] Rule 26(e) provides a duty to supplement prior disclosures and amend discovery responses as appropriate during the course of litigation. If estimates are made which might be subject to revision after the deposition of Dr. Hatten, as Plaintiffs contend, that is entirely permissible, but the requirements of [Federal] Rule 26 cannot be avoided. Defendant is entitled to such information in order to prepare for any settlement discussions, mediation and trial of this cause." (citation omitted) (quoting *Leblanc v. Unifund CCR Partners, G.P.*, No. 8:06-cv-1216-T-TBM, 2007 U.S. Dist. LEXIS 62141, at *3, 2007 WL 2446900 (M.D. Fla. Aug. 23, 2007))); ***see In re Staff Care, Inc.***, 422 S.W.3d 876, 881 (Tex. App.—Dallas 2014, no pet.) (Former Texas "Rule 194.3 required Staff Care to initially respond to the request for disclosures within 30 days and Staff Care had no reason to delay providing in its response economic damages because Staff Care could not be impeached if it later amended its economic damages disclosures as the case progressed.").

[98] Tex. R. Civ. P. 194.2 cmt. 2 to 1999 change.

mary judgment motion, unless the disclosing party can show there was good cause for the failure or it will not unfairly surprise or unfairly prejudice the other parties.[99]

A damage disclosure that has been amended or supplemented is inadmissible and cannot be used for impeachment.[100] Again, the obvious purpose of this prohibition is to encourage parties to be transparent and provide information about damages and their calculation early in the action without fear of having an early, candid disclosure coming back to haunt them.

6-3:3.5 Persons Having Knowledge of Relevant Facts

Former Texas Rule 194.2(e)—now Texas Rule 194.2(b)(5)—requires the disclosure of "the name, address, and telephone number of persons having knowledge of relevant facts, and a brief statement of each identified person's connection with the case."[101]

---

[99] Tex. R. Civ. P. 193.6; *Mintz v. Carew*, No. 05-16-00997-CV, 2018 Tex. App. LEXIS 1194, at *13–14, 2018 WL 833371 (Tex. App.—Dallas Feb. 13, 2018, pet. denied) (mem. op.) (affirming the trial court's exclusion of the plaintiff's "fraud damages" because neither his disclosure nor any other discovery response calculated them); *Veal v. CBREI/USA Hollister DST*, No. 14-16-00051-CV, 2017 Tex. App. LEXIS 8738, at *7, 2017 WL 4080249 (Tex. App.—Houston [14th Dist.] Sept. 14, 2017, no pet.) (mem. op.) ("Because Veal did not show good cause for failing to timely supplement his disclosure of damages during discovery, we hold that the trial court did not abuse its discretion in excluding Veal's evidence regarding damages."); *Heat Shrink Innovations, LLC v. Med. Extrusion Techs.-Tex., Inc.*, No. 02-12-00512-CV, 2014 Tex. App. LEXIS 11494, at *11–16, 2014 WL 5307191 (Tex. App.—Fort Worth Oct. 16, 2014, pet. denied) (mem. op.) (reversing an award of lost profits because the plaintiff did not disclose how they were calculated); *In re Staff Care, Inc.*, 422 S.W.3d 876, 881 (Tex. App.—Dallas 2014, no pet.) (excluding the plaintiff's damage calculation because an amended damage disclosure was untimely); *Harris Cnty. v. Inter Nos., Ltd.*, 199 S.W.3d 363, 368 (Tex. App.—Houston [1st Dist.] 2011, pet. denied) (excluding the county's calculation of condemned property's value because it failed to supplement its damage disclosure to reflect a change in the calculation's underlying assumptions); *Robinson v. Lubbering*, No. 03-09-00655-CV, 2011 Tex. App. LEXIS 1592, at *10, 2011 WL 749197 (Tex. App.—Austin Mar. 2, 2011, no pet.) (mem. op.) (holding insufficient a damage disclosure that read: "Plaintiff seeks his damages proximately caused by [defendant's] breach of contract, together with reasonable attorneys' fees, economic and exemplary damag-es. The exact amount of those damages are unknown at this time."); *Elkins v. Capital One Bank*, No. 05-06-01539-CV, 2009 Tex. App. LEXIS 605, at *15–16, 2008 WL 223849 (Tex. App.—Dallas Jan. 29, 2008, pet. denied) (mem. op.) (excluding statutory damages because they were not disclosed); *Keystone Architects v. Lanai Dev., L.L.C.*, No. 13-05-542-CV, 2008 Tex. App. LEXIS 1469, at *16, 2008 WL 523272 (Tex. App.—Corpus Christi Feb. 28, 2008, no pet.) (mem. op.) (holding insufficient a damage disclosure that read: "Plaintiffs are still in the process of calculating damages and will supplement this response as required by the rules."). See also Chapter 5, section 5-7 (discussing the consequences under Texas Rule 193.6 for failing to timely respond, supplement, or amend written discovery responses).

[100] Former Tex. R. Civ. P. 194.6; Tex. R. Civ. P. 194.6; *see In re Staff Care, Inc.*, 422 S.W.3d 876, 881 (Tex. App.—Dallas 2014, no pet.) ("[Former Texas] Rule 194.3 required Staff Care to initially respond to the request for disclosures within 30 days and Staff Care had no reason to delay providing in its response economic damages because Staff Care could not be impeached if it later amended its economic damages disclosures as the case progressed.").

[101] Former Tex. R. Civ. P. 194.2(e); Tex. R. Civ. P. 194.2(b)(5).

6-3:3.5a Identifying Persons Having Knowledge of Relevant Facts

Although former Texas Rule 194.2—now Texas Rule 194.2(b)(5)—does not define "persons having knowledge of relevant facts," Texas Rule 192.3(c), which permits such discovery generally,[102] provides that "[a] person has knowledge of relevant facts when that person has or may have knowledge of any discoverable matter. The person need not have admissible information or personal knowledge of the facts."[103] Thus, even when the responding party has little or no use for a person's testimony because, for example, the responding party believes that the testimony will be adverse to its position or that the person lacks credibility—the person must be disclosed.[104] "Persons having knowledge of relevant facts" include, among others, parties[105] and their spouses and other relatives, eyewitnesses, employers, co-workers, treating physicians and other healthcare providers, and non-retained experts (e.g., police officers, firemen, and other first responders).

Texas Rule 192.3(c) specifically provides that a testifying or consulting expert is "a person having knowledge of relevant facts" if the expert's "knowledge was obtained first-hand or if it was not obtained in preparation for trial or in anticipation of litigation."[106] Neither the Rule nor the case on which it is based, *Axelson, Inc. v. McIlhany*,[107] defines "first-hand" knowledge. Nonetheless, it is clear that the Texas Supreme Court in *Axelson* was referring to personal knowledge (i.e., facts the expert learned through the expert's personal involvement in the incident or transaction underlying the action), not to "second-hand" knowledge (i.e., facts the expert learned through oral or written communications from others or from the expert's engagement with respect to the action).[108] For example,

---

[102] Tex. R. Civ. P. 192.3(c) ("A party may obtain discovery of the name, address, and telephone number of persons having knowledge of relevant facts, and a brief statement of each identified person's connection with the case.").

[103] Tex. R. Civ. P. 192.3(c); *see In re Team Transp., Inc.*, 996 S.W.2d 256, 259 (Tex. App.—Houston [14th Dist.] 1999, orig. proceeding) ("A person with knowledge of relevant facts need not have personal knowledge of the facts.").

[104] *Ashmore v. JMS Constr., Inc.*, 05-15-00537-CV, 2016 Tex. App. LEXIS 13201, at *24, 2016 WL 7217256 (Tex. App.—Dallas Dec. 13, 2016, no pet.) (mem. op.) (Texas "[R]ule 194.2(e) requires the disclosure of potential witnesses, not just favorable witnesses.").

[105] Under former Texas Rule 166b(2)(d), which governed discovery of the identity of persons having knowledge of relevant facts who might testify at trial, parties were not exempt from the disclosure requirement in response to an appropriate discovery request. *Ceasar v. Rodriguez*, No. 01-02-00027-CV, 2003 Tex. App. LEXIS 749, at *9, 2003 WL 164463 (Tex. App.—Houston [1st Dist.] Jan. 23, 2003, no pet.) (mem. op.). This no longer is the case because Texas Rule 193.6 specifically exempts named parties from the requirement that witnesses be identified in discovery as a prerequisite to testifying at trial. Tex. R. Civ. P. 193.6(a) ("A party who fails to make, amend, or supplement a discovery response in a timely manner may not . . . offer the testimony of a witness (other than a named party) who was not timely identified[.]"). Nonetheless, the better practice is to identify parties as persons having knowledge of relevant facts and trial witnesses.

[106] Tex. R. Civ. P. 192.3(c). This portion of Texas Rule 192.3(c) "is intended to be consistent with *Axelson, Inc. v. McIlhany*, 798 S.W.2d 550 (Tex. 1990)." Tex. R. Civ. P. 192 cmt. 3 to 1999 change. In *Axelson*, the Texas Supreme Court held that the "factual knowledge and opinions acquired by an individual who is an expert and an active participant in the events material to the lawsuit are discoverable." *Axelson, Inc. v. McIlhany*, 798 S.W.2d 550, 554 (Tex. 1990).

[107] *Axelson, Inc. v. McIlhany*, 798 S.W.2d 550 (Tex. 1990).

[108] *Axelson, Inc. v. McIlhany*, 798 S.W.2d 550, 554 (Tex. 1990).

an expert who was consulted before litigation was anticipated is not a consulting-only expert[109] and must be disclosed as a person having knowledge of relevant facts. Similarly, a person who otherwise qualifies as an expert, but who acquired relevant information as "an active participant in the events material to the lawsuit," such as an employee involved in the incident or transaction underlying the action, is not a consulting-only expert[110] and must be disclosed as a person with knowledge of relevant facts.

In contrast, when an expert examines a photograph of the accident scene or interviews witnesses to the accident, the expert is not discoverable as a "person with knowledge of relevant facts."[111] Also not discoverable is an expert who visits, inspects, or photographs the accident scene or examines, inspects, or conducts tests or experiments on the product, soil, water, or other thing at issue in the action, if the activity was done solely in preparation for trial or in anticipation of litigation.[112]

Several questions arise with respect to Texas Rule 194.2(e) disclosures. *First*, is a rebuttal or impeachment witness a "person having knowledge of relevant facts?" Such a witness is such a person unless his or her testimony could not reasonably have been anticipated before trial.[113]

---

109 *See Lindsey v. O'Neill*, 689 S.W.2d 400, 402 (Tex. 1985).

110 *Axelson, Inc. v. McIlhany*, 798 S.W.2d 550, 554 (Tex. 1990).

111 *Axelson, Inc. v. McIlhany*, 798 S.W.2d 550, 554–55 (Tex. 1990).

112 *See In re Commitment of Terry*, No. 09-15-00053-CV, 2015 Tex. App. LEXIS 9570, at *7–9 (Tex. App.—Beaumont Sept. 10, 2015, no pet.) (mem. op.) (holding that the defendant was not entitled to discovery from a psychiatrist for the state who examined the defendant because "the record suggest that Dr. Self participated in the events giving rise to the initiation of civil commitment proceedings. Because Dr. Self did not gain factual information by virtue of any involvement relating to the events giving rise to the litigation, we conclude that Dr. Self was not a dual capacity witness and the trial court did not abuse its discretion by refusing to order disclosure"); *In re McDaniel*, No. 14-13-00127-CV, 2013 Tex. App. LEXIS 4052, at *10–11, 2013 WL 1279454 (Tex. App.—Houston [14th Dist.] Mar. 28, 2013, no pet.) (mem. op.) (holding that tests by a consulting expert on the product at issue were not discoverable); *In re Fast-Track Constr., Inc.*, 307 S.W.3d 526, 527 (Tex. App.—Dallas 2010, orig. proceeding) (holding that "destructive" soil tests by a consulting expert were not discoverable). *But see In re Energy Transfer Partners, L.P.*, No. 12-08-00422, 2009 Tex. App. LEXIS 3763, at *12 n.3, 2009 WL 1028056 (Tex. App.—Tyler Apr. 15, 2009, orig. proceeding) (mem. op.) (holding that raw data from sound tests conducted by a consulting expert were discoverable).

113 *E.g., In re E.R.A.*, No. 09-20-00042-CV, 2021 Tex. App. LEXIS 2026, at *13–14, 2021 WL 1031142 (Tex. App.—Beaumont Mar. 18, 2021, no pet.) (mem. op.) ("A party may obtain discovery of the name of persons who have knowledge of relevant facts when those persons have or may have knowledge of any discoverable matter. A party may also obtain discovery of the name of any person who is expected to testify at trial, excluding rebuttal or impeaching witnesses, the necessity of whose testimony cannot reasonably be anticipated before trial.") (citations omitted); *In re Commitment of Sells*, No. 09-15-00172-CV, 2016 Tex. App. LEXIS 3916, at *25, 2016 WL 1469059 (Tex. App.—Beaumont Apr. 14, 2016, pet. denied) (mem. op.) ("The mere fact that a witness is called 'in rebuttal' does not mean that the witness does not have to be disclosed. A rebuttal witness should be disclosed if the need to call that witness reasonably should have been anticipated.") (citations omitted); *Schlein v. Griffin*, No. 01-14-00799-CV, 2016 Tex. App. LEXIS 3715, at *29, 2016 WL 1456193 (Tex. App.—Houston [1st Dist.] Apr. 12, 2016, no pet.) (mem. op.) ("A rebuttal witness still has to be disclosed if the need to call the witness reasonably should have been anticipated."); *Homeyer v. Farmer*, No. 10-11-00009-CV, 2011 Tex. App. LEXIS 9316, at *26, 2011

Second, is it proper to identify persons by use of a collective description, such as "employees," "insureds," "adjusters," "clients," or "customers" of a party or other person or to simply identify an entity, such as a corporation or partnership? Even though the word "'[p]erson' includes corporation, organization, government or governmental subdivision or agency, business trust, estate, trust, partnership, association, and any other legal entity[,]"[114] it generally is improper to do either because the clear purpose of former Texas Rule 194.2(e)—now Texas Rule 194.2(b)(5)—is to allow the requesting party to identify potential deponents and trial witnesses.[115] The exception to this rule is when the responding party does not know the names of the entity's

---

WL 6004338 (Tex. App.—Waco Nov. 23, 2011, no pet.) (mem. op.) ("If the rebuttal witness's testimony could reasonably have been anticipated, then the witness is not exempt from the scope of written discovery."); ***In re Marks.***, 230 S.W.3d 241, 245–46 (Tex. App.—Beaumont 2007, no pet) (same); ***Moore v. Mem'l Hermann Hosp. Sys.***, 140 S.W.3d 870, 875 (Tex. App.—Houston [14th Dist.] 2004, no pet.) (same).

114 Tex. Gov't Code § 311.005.

115 ***W. Atlas Int'l, Inc. v. Randolph***, No. 13-02-00244-CV, 2005 Tex. App. LEXIS 2199, at *21–22, 2005 WL 673483 (Tex. App.—Corpus Christi Mar. 24, 2005, no pet.) (mem. op.) ("[Texas] Rule[] 193.1 and [former Texas Rule] 194.2(e) . . . require that parties provide complete responses to written discovery and disclose 'the name, address and telephone number of persons having knowledge of relevant facts,' with a brief statement of their connection to the case. Identifying a general category of people, without naming individuals or providing specific contact information, is insufficient to satisfy this requirement.") (citation omitted); *cf.* ***Hernandez-Torres v. Intercontinental Trading***, 158 F.3d 43, 49–50 (1st Cir. 1998) (holding that the trial court did not abuse its discretion in excluding two of the defendants' former employees as witnesses for the plaintiff because the plaintiff's disclosure only identified "employees or representatives of the defendants" and not specific employees' names); ***Brinkman v. Ryan***, No. CV1502027PHXROSBSB, 2017 U.S. Dist. LEXIS 225160, at *3, 2017 WL 11453550 (D. Ariz. Nov. 21, 2017) ("As Defendant notes, Plaintiff's initial disclosure is inadequate. First, aside from a single witness, Plaintiff did not disclose the names of individuals likely to have discoverable information. Plaintiff did identify some individuals by vague references to titles or functions, but he failed to disclose 'the subjects of [the] information' that they are likely to possess." (quoting Fed. R. Civ. P. 26)); ***Meeker v. Life Care Ctrs. of Am., Inc.***, No. 14-CV-02101-WYD-NYW, 2015 U.S. Dist. LEXIS 94060, at *10, 2015 WL 4400533 (D. Colo. July 20, 2015) ("Rule 26(a)(1) of the Federal Rules of Civil Procedure requires disclosure of 'the name' of 'each individual' the party may use to support its claims or defenses. The rule is not satisfied by a categorical description such as (as provided in the instant case by the Life Care Defendants) 'one or more representatives.'" (citations omitted) (quoting Fed. R. Civ. P. 26(a)(1))); ***Bibolotti v. Am. Home Mortg. Servicing, Inc.***, No. 4:11-CV-472, 2013 U.S. Dist. LEXIS 69242, at *16, 2013 WL 2147949 (E.D. Tex. May 15, 2013) (mem. op.) ("In their initial disclosures, Defendants designated only the 'Custodian of Records and/or Corporate Representatives' of AHMSI. The plain language of the rule clearly requires a party to disclose the names of individuals with discoverable information. Thus, Defendants' initial disclosures did not comply with the requirements of [Federal] Rule 26."); ***Smith v. Pfizer, Inc.***, 265 F.R.D. 278, 283 (M.D. Tenn. 2010) (ruling that the plaintiff did not comply with Federal Rule 26(a)(1)(A)(i) by listing as witnesses "friends and family of the deceased" and "defendants' employees and representatives"); ***Labadie v. Dennis***, No. 1:07-cv-480, 2008 U.S. Dist. LEXIS 103754, at *6, 2008 WL 5411901 (W.D. Mich. Dec. 23, 2008) ("Plaintiff lists generic categories of persons, such as 'all members of plaintiff's family,' or 'all investigating persons.' This is patently insufficient and amounts to a non-disclosure."); ***In re Sambrano***, 440 B.R. 702, 706 (Bankr. W.D. Tex. 2010) ("The contested witnesses were not listed by name in Hartford's initial disclosures; the initial disclosures merely listed 'employees and agents of Hartford' as persons likely to have discoverable information relevant to the case.

officers, directors, employees, or agents that have knowledge of relevant facts or if the responding party intends to use a representative of the entity to testify on its behalf.[116] Of course, if the responding party learns during discovery which officers, directors, employees, or agents of the entity have knowledge of relevant facts or which one will be the entity's representative at trial or a deposition, it should timely supplement its disclosure.[117] For example, the Austin Court of Appeals held a Texas court held that the State of Texas met its disclosure obligation by identifying witnesses as "individuals who currently hold, or were previously granted, Short-Term Rental (STR) permits by [the City], and the individuals who testified at any public hearing on short-term rental regulations"—at a time when "the State had not yet had time to identify from [a list of the names of such individuals] the specific witnesses that it intended to rely on and the evidence those witnesses would provide"—and by supplementing its disclosures to identify the witnesses three months after learning their identities and approximately six months before the hearing at which the witnesses' declarations were offered as evidence.[118]

Third, as Texas Rules 192.3(c) and Texas Rule 194.2(b)(5)—former Texas Rule 194.2(e)—only require disclosure of the person's "address and telephone" number, a question exists regarding whether the responding party should disclose an individual's home or work address and telephone number. Although federal courts in

---

The plain language of the rule requires the disclosing party to list the names of these individuals.") (citation omitted).

In the same vein, a disclosure that merely references all persons disclosed by the other party or parties is similarly improper. *Cf. Andrews v. CBOCS W., Inc.*, No. 09-cv-1025-WDS-SCW, 2011 U.S. Dist. LEXIS 17505, at *5–6, 2011 WL 722606 (S.D. Ill. Feb. 23, 2011) (holding that the defendant's disclosure identifying "[a]ll persons identified by Plaintiff" was insufficient).

[116] *Cf. Jones v. RealPage, Inc.*, No. 3:19-CV-2087-B, 2020 U.S. Dist. LEXIS 193404, at *7, 2020 WL 6149969 (N.D. Tex. Oct. 19, 2020) ("Jones asserts that RealPage's failure to list the names of the specific representatives until the close of discovery 'robb[ed]' her of the ability to take discovery of these witnesses. . . . To start, as RealPage points out, other district courts facing this issue have concluded that listing 'corporate representatives,' or something similar, in initial disclosures can be sufficient to comply with [Federal Rule 26(a) . . . . The same thing occurred here. Jones herself identified both GDS and Marietta in her own initial disclosures. More significantly, . . . RealPage's initial disclosures and supplemental initial disclosures adequately notified Jones that RealPage intended to call the representatives of GDS and Marietta to oppose class certification. Yet, . . . Jones did not notice a [Federal] Rule 30(b)(6) deposition for either of them or otherwise seek additional discovery related to these representatives once she was aware that they had discoverable information. Jones provides no explanation for this failure. Thus, Jones's complaints that she was 'robb[ed]' of time needed to take the depositions of these representatives fall short.") (citations omitted) (citing *Krawczyk v. Centurion Capital Corp.*, No. 06-C-6273, 2009 U.S. Dist. LEXIS 12204, at *18–19, 2009 WL 395458 (N.D. Ill. Feb. 18, 2009)); *see also Hunter v. Time Warner Cable Inc.*, No. 15-CV-6445 (JPO), 2019 U.S. Dist. LEXIS 137495, at *22, 2019 WL 3812063 (S.D.N.Y. Aug. 14, 2019) ("In the context of this motion for class certification, the identification of the corporate entities from which Time Warner would seek representatives as witnesses in the September 28, 2018 supplemental disclosures was sufficient to put Plaintiffs on notice of these witnesses.").

[117] *Cf. Bibolotti v. Am. Home Mortg. Servicing, Inc.*, No. 4:11-CV-472, 2013 U.S. Dist. LEXIS 69242, at *16, 2013 WL 2147949 (E.D. Tex. May 15, 2013) (mem. op.).

[118] *Zaatari v. City of Austin*, 615 S.W.3d 172, 185–87 (Tex. App.—Austin 2019, pet. denied).

interpreting the comparable federal disclosure rule, Federal Rule 26(a)(1)(A)(i),[119] have held that the person's home address and telephone number should be disclosed, if they are available,[120] this does not appear to be required under the Texas discovery rules. Because the purpose of Texas Rule 192.3(c) and former Texas Rule 194.2(e)—now Texas Rule 194.2(b)(5)—is "to allow the opposing party to easily locate, interview, and depose the proposed witness[,]"[121] the responding party should be able to designate the individual's home address and telephone number, work address and telephone number, another address or telephone number, or a combination of the foregoing as long as the address and telephone number disclosed are ones at which the person easily can be found, contacted, and served with a subpoena.[122] A court, however, should order the responding party to provide the disclosed person's home address and telephone number if the requesting party claims that they are needed for a proper background check of the person because a person's home address and

---

119 Fed. R. Civ. P. 26(a)(1)(A)(i).

120 *E.g., Rodriguez v. Christus Spohn Health Sys. Corp.*, No. C-09-95, 2011 U.S. Dist. LEXIS 114062, at *4, 2011 WL 13351118 (S.D. Tex. Oct. 3, 2011) (mem. op.) ("The decisions interpreting [Federal] Rule 26 make it clear that the home addresses and telephone numbers, if known, are required to be produced."); *Hartman v. Am. Red Cross*, No. 09-1302, 2010 U.S. Dist. LEXIS 46126, at *2, 2010 WL 1882002 (C.D. Ill May 11, 2010) (same); *Fausto v. Credigy Servs. Corp.*, 251 F.R.D. 427, 429 (N.D. Cal. 2008) (same); *Thurby v. Encore Receivable Mgmt.*, 251 F.R.D. 620, 621 (D. Colo. 2008) (same); *Viveros v. Nationwide Janitorial Ass'n.*, 200 F.R.D. 681, 684 (N.D. Ga. 2000) (same); *Dixon v. CertainTeed Corp.*, 164 F.R.D. 685, 689 (D. Kan. 1996) (same).

121 *In re C.S.*, 977 S.W.2d 729, 732 (Tex. App.—Fort Worth 1998, no writ) (construing former Texas Rule 166b(2)(d), which allowed discovery of persons having knowledge of relevant facts), *cited with approval in Gibbons v. Luby's Inc.*, No. 02-12-00202-CV, 2015 Tex. App. LEXIS 9234, at *70–71 n. 119, 2015 WL 5116146 (Tex. App.—Fort Worth Aug. 31, 2015, pet. denied) (mem. op.); *accord $23,900 v. State*, 899 S.W.2d 314, 316 (Tex. App.—Fort Worth 1995, no writ) (same); *Varner v. Howe*, 860 S.W.2d 458, 464 (Tex. App.—El Paso 1993, no writ) (same).

122 *Cf. In re C.S.*, 977 S.W.2d 729, 732–33 (Tex. App.—Fort Worth 1998, pet. denied) (holding that, under former Texas Rule 166b(2)(d), even though a complete street address for a witness was not disclosed, under the facts of the case, the trial court could reasonably have concluded that the witness could have been easily located with the information provided, and therefore the witness had been sufficiently identified); *$23,900 v. State*, 899 S.W.2d 314, 316 (Tex. App.—Fort Worth 1995, no writ) (holding that, under former Texas Rule 166b(2)(d), a police officer was properly identified in an interrogatory answer because he could be contacted through the information provided even though it was not the officer's correct station); *Varner v. Howe*, 860 S.W.2d 458, 464 (Tex. App.—El Paso 1993, no writ) (holding that, under former Texas Rule 166b(2)(d), a witness was sufficiently identified in an interrogatory answer because her nickname and employer's address and telephone number were provided); *Amsav Grp. v. Am. Sav. & Loan*, 796 S.W.2d 482, 486 (Tex. App.—Houston [14th Dist.] 1990, writ denied) (holding that, under former Texas Rule 166b(2)(d), a witness was sufficiently identified in an interrogatory answer that merely referred the requesting party to deposition testimony in which the witness was identified); *see also Gibbons v. Luby's Inc.*, No. 02-12-00202-CV, 2015 Tex. App. LEXIS 9234, at *70–72 n. 119, 2015 WL 5116146 (Tex. App.—Fort Worth Aug. 31, 2015, pet. denied) (mem. op.) (holding that the trial court did not err in allowing two defense witnesses to testify even though the defendant provided it attorney's address and telephone number for them in its disclosure because "[b]oth witnesses were deposed, and [the plaintiff's] attorney attended the depositions. And [the plaintiff] introduced excerpts of [one of the witness's] deposition in her case in chief.").

telephone number generally are not private or confidential information.[123] It is clear, however, that a responding party cannot properly disclose its attorney's address and telephone number for itself or its employees,[124] and federal courts uniformly have rejected the argument that the use of such an address and telephone number is justified by a concern that the requesting party may contact the responding party or its employees in violation of the ethical rules[125] or because there is an inordinately large

---

[123] *Cf. Thurby v. Encore Receivable Mgmt.*, 251 F.R.D. 620, 622 (D. Colo. 2008) (holding that (1) under Federal Rule 26(a)(1)(A)(i), the responding party had to provide the disclosed persons' home addresses and telephone numbers because "personal contact information, such as 'birth dates, home addresses or telephone numbers, e-mail addresses, or driver's license numbers' are not usually held as private, and instead are 'regularly disclosed to friends, relatives, vendors, credit card companies, schools, children's sports teams, and the like[,]'" and (2) "the personal identifying information at issue here is necessary to allow the plaintiffs to conduct thorough background investigations . . . and that such investigations may lead to the discovery of admissible evidence" (quoting *Estate of Rice ex rel. Garber v. City & Cnty. of Denver*, No. 07-cv-01571-MSK-BNB, 2008 U.S. Dist. LEXIS 42381, at *20–21, 2008 WL 2228702 (D. Colo. May 27, 2008))).

[124] *Cf. Daniels v. Hyster-Yale Grp., Inc.*, 5:19-CV-00531-FL, 2020 U.S. Dist. LEXIS 83421, at *15–16, 2020 WL 2334088 (E.D.N.C. May 11, 2020) ("In the context of initial disclosures, courts have repeatedly held that because of [Federal Rule 26's] specific instruction to turn over an individual's address and telephone number, a responding party does not comply with the Federal Rules when they fail to provide this information and, instead, say that the person can be contacted through counsel for a party.") (citing cases); *Tamas v. Family Video Movie Club, Inc.*, 304 F.R.D. 543, 545 (N.D. Ill. 2015) ("[Federal] Rule 26(a) requires a party to voluntarily disclose to other parties 'the name and, if known, the address and telephone number of each individual likely to have discoverable information—along with the subjects of that information—that the disclosing party may use to support its claims or defenses.' 'Numerous courts have held that this obligation is satisfied only by producing individual addresses for individual witnesses; disclosure of an attorney's address or an employer's address is not sufficient.'" (quoting *Hartman v. Am. Red Cross*, No. 09-1302, No. 2010 U.S. Dist. LEXIS 46126, at *2, 2010 WL 1882002 (C.D. Ill. May 11, 2010))); *Bowman v. Green Tree Serv., Inc.*, 3-12-CV-31, 2012 U.S. Dist. LEXIS 146472, at *4–5 (N.D.W. Va. Oct. 11, 2012) (holding that it was improper to provide the responding attorney's address and telephone number for persons having knowledge of discoverable information); *Viveros v. Nationwide Janitorial Ass'n*, 200 F.R.D. 681, 684 (N.D. Ga. 2000) (same); *Dixon v. CertainTeed Corp.*, 164 F.R.D. 685, 689 (D. Kan. 1996) (same).

[125] *E.g., Edmondson v. Brennan & Clark, Ltd.*, No. 4:18-CV-11, 2019 U.S. Dist. LEXIS 51113, at *2–3, 2019 WL 1375780 (N.D. Ind. Mar. 26, 2019) ("Defendants state that because the employees are represented, they should only be contacted through counsel, so they provided counsel's contact information. However, courts have held that the 'hypothetical' concern that counsel may contact represented individuals does not relieve a party's obligation under [Federal] Rule 26(a) to provide contact information." (citing cases)); *Hartman v. Am. Red Cross*, No. 09-1302, 2010 U.S. Dist. LEXIS 46126, at *2–3 (C.D. Ill. May 11, 2010) ("It may very well be the case that current supervisors and managers are represented by defense counsel and may not be contacted directly by Plaintiff's counsel. That question is not before the Court at this time. The apparent basis for Defendant's position on this question is an unspoken concern that Plaintiff's counsel will contact represented employees. That hypothetical concern, however, does not justify unilateral disregard for the disclosures mandated by [Federal] Rule 26(a). The Court will not engage in speculation that counsel might not act in accord with legal ethics. If the time comes that a concrete ethical issue arises, counsel for both parties shall bring the matter to the Court's attention."); *Dixon v. CertainTeed Corp.*, 164 F.R.D. 685, 689 (D. Kan. 1996) ("CertainTeed expresses

number of persons with knowledge of relevant facts.[126]

Finally, as discussed in Chapter 4, section 4-3:2, Texas Rule 192.3(d) provides for the discovery of the "name, address, and telephone number of any person who is expected to be called to testify at trial."[127] The Texas discovery rules distinguish between persons having knowledge of relevant facts and trial witnesses, and the disclosure of a person as one with knowledge of relevant facts is insufficient to constitute a disclosure of the person as a trial witness.[128] Consequently, a person who is not disclosed as a trial witness in response to an interrogatory asking the sponsoring party to identify such witnesses should be excluded even if the person was disclosed as a person having knowledge of relevant facts absent the party's showing of good cause for the failure to disclose the witness or lack of unfair surprise or prejudice to the other parties.[129] And the identification of a person on a pretrial witness list is not a substitute for a timely disclosure under former Texas Rule 194.2(e)—now Texas Rule

---

concern that counsel for plaintiff will contact its employees outside its presence. It may not pose its concern as cause to unilaterally disregard its duties of disclosure under [Federal] Rule 26(a). Nor will the court indulge in speculation that counsel will unethically use the disclosed information. The court expects counsel to abide by the canons of legal ethics. It assumes attorneys will be ethical, absent some evidence to show otherwise."). If the responding party is concerned that the requesting party will violate the ethical rules and improperly contact its employees or other persons, it should ask the requesting party not to engage in such contact and, as appropriate, move for a protective order, sanctions, or disqualification.

[126] *E.g.*, *Tamas v. Family Video Movie Club, Inc.*, 304 F.R.D. 543, 545 (N.D. Ill. 2015) (rejecting an argument that the requirement does not apply if a large number of persons are identified: "It is true that the cases cited apply to smaller numbers of individuals, but Defendant does not cite any case law to support its argument that when the number of individuals disclosed is numerous, the rule on providing known addresses and telephone numbers no longer applies. Moreover, it was Defendant that made the decision to identify 3,300 individuals, averaging 50 people for each opt-in discovery plaintiff, as 'likely to have discoverable information.'").

[127] Tex. R. Civ. P. 192.3(d).

[128] *Carlton v. Stewart*, No. 05-05-00888-CV, 2006 Tex. App. LEXIS 2839, at *6 n.1, 2006 WL 894879 (Tex. App.—Dallas Apr. 7, 2006, pet. denied) (mem. op.) ("In *Daredia v. Nat'l Distribs.*, [No. 05-04-00307-C, 2005 Tex. App. LEXIS 3168, at *9, 2005 WL 977828 (Tex. App.—Dallas, Apr. 28, 2005, pet. denied) (mem. op.)], this Court recognized that the rules of civil procedure clearly distinguish between persons with knowledge of relevant facts and intended trial witnesses, and we concluded that the two categories could not be interchanged for discovery purposes."); *cf. Rizvi v. Am. Express Nat'l Bank*, No. 02-19-00197-CV, 2020 Tex. App. LEXIS 5222, at*15–17, 2020 WL 3969585 (Tex. App.—Fort Worth June 18, 2020, no pet.) (mem. op.) (concluding that a party identified a trial witness sufficiently by disclosing the individual—as one of 12 assistant custodians of record—in response to a request for disclosure under former Texas Rule 194.2(e) and by incorporating that disclosure of 12 individuals with knowledge of relevant facts into an answer to an interrogatory asking the party to identify everyone whom it expected to call to testify at trial).

[129] *Daredia v. Nat'l Distribs.*, No. 05-04-00307-CV, 2005 Tex. App. LEXIS 3168, at *9–10, 2005 WL 977828 (Tex. App.—Dallas Apr. 28, 2005, pet. denied) (mem. op.) (holding that a witness who was identified as a person having knowledge of relevant facts, but not as a trial witness, should not have been allowed to testify because the sponsoring party failed to establish good cause or lack of unfair prejudice or surprise). Because the identity of trial witnesses is not subject to disclosure under former Texas Rule 194.2 (now Texas Rule 194.2(b)(5)), a party should obtain this information by means of an interrogatory.

194.2(b)(5)—because the pretrial witness list comes after the close of fact discovery and shortly before trial.[130] Again, such a witness should be excluded from testifying at trial absent the party's showing of good cause for the failure to disclose the witness as a person with knowledge of relevant facts or lack of unfair surprise or prejudice to the other parties.

6-3:3.5b The Person's Connection to the Case

As noted above, former Texas Rule 194.2(e)—now Texas Rule 194.2(b)95)—also requires the responding party to provide a brief description of each disclosed person's "connection to the case."[131] Although the Rule does not describe what constitutes a sufficient description of the person's "connection to the case," Comment 3 to the 1999 change to Texas Rule 193.2, which allows such discovery generally, explains that "[t]his provision does not contemplate a narrative statement of the facts the person knows, but at most a few words describing the person's identity as relevant to the lawsuit" and gives the following examples: "treating physician," "eyewitness," "chief financial officer," "director," "plaintiff's mother and eyewitness to accident."[132] Consistent with the comment, Texas courts have held that, in a divorce and child-custody action, the descriptions "Petitioner's father" and "Petitioner's sister" were sufficient[133] and that in an action to terminate parental rights the description "social worker" was sufficient.[134] In addition, in a recent breach-of-contrast case involving credit-card debt, the description of "being 'familiar with the maintenance of Plaintiff's account records[,]'" coupled with the job title "Assistant Custodian of Records," was sufficient for a custodian of records who testified at trial.[135]

---

130 *Cf. Phillip M. Adams & Assocs. v. Winbond Elecs. Corp.*, No. 1:05-CV-64 TS, 2010 U.S. Dist. LEXIS 84655, at *11, 2010 WL 3239331 (D. Utah Aug. 16, 2010); *see Queensberry v. Volvo Grp. N. Am., Inc.*, 267 F.R.D. 475, 479–80 (W.D. Va. 2010) ("The plaintiffs argued that requiring the disclosure of these nineteen class members at any time prior to February 23, 2010, would be tantamount to requiring that they disclose witnesses before the court-ordered date. This argument confuses two separate requirements under [Federal] Rule 26. The witness list, indeed, was submitted to the defendants on the date set by the court for pretrial disclosures, in accord with [Federal] Rule 26(a)(3). However, the plaintiffs still had an obligation to disclose these individuals as persons likely to have discoverable information under [Federal] Rule 26(a)(1). Performance of one of these rules cannot be substituted for the other because they serve different purposes. The objective of [Federal] Rule 26(a)(3) is to list, after all the information has been gathered and discovery is closed, the witnesses who will be called by a party at trial and allow the opposing party to properly prepare to examine those witnesses. The aim of [Federal] Rule 26(a)(1), on the other hand, is to identify at the outset those persons that may have any information relevant to the case in order to allow for a complete investigation by all parties, thus allowing parties to depose, interview, or subpoena documents of such individuals during the period of time set aside for discovery.").

131 Tex. R. Civ. P. 194.2(e).

132 Tex. R. Civ. P. 192 cmt. 3 to 1999 change.

133 *Van Heerden v. Van Heerden*, 321 S.W.3d 869, 876 (Tex. App.—Houston [14th Dist.] 2010, no pet.).

134 *L.B. v. Tex. Dep't of Family & Protective Servs.*, No. 03-09-00429-CV, 2010 Tex. App. LEXIS 2518, at *22 n.16, 2010 WL 1404608 (Tex. App.—Austin Apr. 9, 2010, no pet.) (mem. op.).

135 *Rizvi v. Am. Express Nat'l Bank*, No. 02-19-00197-CV, 2020 Tex. App. LEXIS 5222, at *15–17, 2020 WL 3969585 (Tex. App.—Fort Worth June 18, 2020, no pet.) (mem. op.).

If a party fails to disclose any of the information required by former Texas Rule 194.2(e) (now Texas Rule 194.2(b)(5)), the person's testimony generally will be excluded at trial or in connection with a summary judgment motion under Texas Rule 193.6's automatic exclusion rule unless the disclosing party can show there was good cause for the failure or it will not unfairly surprise or unfairly prejudice the other parties.[136]

---

136 *E.g., El-Rayes v. Lee*, No. 05-19-00881-CV, 2020 Tex. App. LEXIS 10395, at *6–8, 2020 WL 7767939 (Tex. App.—Dallas Dec. 30, 2020, no pet.) (mem. op.) (holding that the trial court did not abuse its discretion in allowing the testimony of an individual whom a party did not identify as a potential witness until just over a week before trial began because, among other reasons, the late disclosure did not unfairly surprise the other party as he had already disclosed the person); *Hunters Mill Ass'n v. Beres*, No. 04-17-00044-CV, 2017 Tex. App. LEXIS 8673, at *7, 2017 WL 4014619 (Tex. App.—San Antonio Sept. 13, 2017, no. pet.) (mem. op.) (holding that the trial court did not abuse its discretion in allowing a witness who was not disclosed as a person with knowledge of relevant facts from testifying and that "the fact that a party needs a particular witness to establish its cause of action does not establish the other party will not be unfairly surprised by the late designation of the witness. Stated differently, the fact that Hunters Mill needed Thomas's testimony to support its claim does not excuse it from complying with the rules of civil procedure.") (citations omitted); *Dunne v. Brinker Tex., Inc.*, No. 05-16-00496-CV, 2017 Tex. App. LEXIS 7647, at *7–10, 2017 WL 3431465 (Tex. App.—Dallas Aug. 10, 2017, pet. denied) (mem. op.) (affirming the trial court's striking of the plaintiff's pleadings after he failed to comply with an order compelling him to disclose persons with knowledge of relevant facts); *Ashmore v. JMS Constr., Inc.*, No. 05-15-00537-CV, 2016 Tex. App. LEXIS 13201, at *24–26, 2016 WL 7217256 (Tex. App.—Dallas Dec. 13, 2016, no pet.) (mem. op.) (holding that the trial court did not abuse its discretion in excluding a witness who was not timely disclosed as a person with knowledge of relevant facts); *Gibbs v. Bureaus Inv. Grp. Portfolio No. 14, LLC*, 441 S.W.3d 764, 767 (Tex. App.—El Paso 2014, no pet.) ("Bureaus' failure to disclose Verhines as a fact witness during pretrial discovery, absent a showing of good cause or lack of surprise or prejudice, triggers the automatic exclusion sanctions of [Texas] Rule 193.6."); *Perez v. Embree Constr. Grp., Inc.*, 228 S.W.3d 875, 884 (Tex. App.—Austin 2007, pet. denied) (noting that even a "[f]ailure to include a witness's address in discovery responses may be considered grounds for exclusion of the witness's testimony"); *Fertic v. Spencer*, 247 S.W.3d 242, 246–47 (Tex. App.—El Paso 2007, pet. denied) (excluding fact and expert witnesses who were not timely disclosed); *W. Atlas Int'l, Inc. v. Randolph*, No. 13-02-00244-CV, 2005 Tex. App. LEXIS 2199, at *19–24, 2005 WL 673483 (Tex. App.—Corpus Christi Mar. 24, 2005, no pet.) (mem. op.) (holding that the trial court did not abuse its discretion in excluding two witnesses because the plaintiffs failed to provide the proper contact information for one and failed to disclose the name of the other); *Beam v. A.H. Chaney, Inc.*, 56 S.W.3d 920, 922 (Tex. App.—Fort Worth 2001, pet. denied) (excluding a fact witness's testimony because his address and connection to the case were not disclosed); *cf. Boothe v. Hausler*, 766 S.W.2d 788 (Tex. 1989) (holding that, under former Texas Rule 215(5), the trial court erred in allowing a witness to testify, absent a showing of good cause, because the defendant's interrogatory response failed to provide the witness's address). See also Chapter 5, section 5-7 (discussing the consequences under Texas Rule 193.6 for failing to timely respond, supplement, or amend written discovery responses). *But see also Magro v. Magro*, No. 01-19-00701-CV, 2020 Tex. App. LEXIS 9650, at *46–48, 2020 WL 7251864 (Tex. App.—Houston [1st Dist.] Dec. 10, 2020, no pet.) (mem. op.) (holding that, although a party did not identify four individuals in response to a disclosure request under former Texas Rule 194.2(e), the trial court did not err in admitting their testimony at trial because the best interest of a child was at stake in the case and the witnesses' testimony shed light on the best interest of the child).

6-3:3.6 Materials That May Be Used to Support the Disclosing Party's Claims or Defenses

Former Texas Rule 190.2(b)(6), which applies only to Level 1 cases filed before January 1, 2021, requires disclosure of "all documents, electronic information, and tangible items that the disclosing party has in its possession, custody, or control and may use to support its claims or defenses."[137] Former Rule 190.2(b)(6) was based on Federal Rule 26(a)(1)(A)(ii), which requires the provision of "a copy—or a description by category and location—of all documents, electrically stored information, and tangible things that the disclosing party has in its possession, custody, or control and may use to support its claims or defenses, unless the use would be solely for impeachment[.]"[138]

Like former Texas Rule 190.2(b)(6), Texas Rule 194.2(b)(6)—which applies to cases filed on or after January 1, 2021—is based on Federal Rule 26(a)(1)(A)(ii). But there are two significant differences between the two Texas rules. First, Texas Rule 194.2(b)(6) tracks Federal Rule 26(a)(1)(A)(ii) even more closely than former Rule 190.2(b)(6) did, requiring the provision of "a copy—or a description by category and location—of all documents, electronically stored information, and tangible things that the disclosing party has in its possession, custody, or control, and may use to support its claims or defenses, unless the use would be solely for impeachment."[139] Second, unlike former Texas Rule 190.2(b)(6)'s limited applicability in Level 1 cases upon a party's request, Texas Rule 194.2(b)(6) applies by default, "[w]ithout awaiting a discovery request," in all civil cases other than those exempt from initial-disclosure requirements under Texas Rule 194.2(d): "(1) an action for review on an administrative record; (2) a forfeiture action arising from a state statute; (3) a petition for habeas corpus; (4) an action under the Family Code filed by or against the Title IV-D agency in a Title IV-D case; (5) a child protection action under Subtitle E, Title 5 of the Family Code; (6) a protective order action under Title 4 of the Texas Family Code; (7) other actions involving domestic violence; and (8) an action on appeal from a justice court."[140]

Under both former Texas Rule 190.2(b)(6) and Texas Rule 194.2(b)(6), the focus is on documents, electronically stored information, and tangible things that the disclosing party "may" use. Thus, a disclosing party need not disclose damaging or unfavorable documents, electronically stored information, or tangible things that the disclosing party does *not* intend to use merely because such material may be relevant to

---

137 Former Tex. R. Civ. P. 190.2(b)(6).

138 Fed. R. Civ. P. 26(a)(1)(A)(ii).

139 *Compare* Tex. R. Civ. P. 194.2(b)(6) (requiring the provision of "a copy—or a description by category and location—of all documents, electronically stored information, and tangible things that the disclosing party has in its possession, custody, or control, and may use to support its claims or defenses, unless the use would be solely for impeachment"), *with* Fed. R. Civ. P. 26(a)(1)(A)(ii) (requiring the provision of "a copy—or a description by category and location—of all documents, electronically stored information, and tangible things that the responding party has in its possession, custody, or control, and may use to support its claims or defenses, unless the use would be solely for impeachment").

140 Tex. R. Civ. P. 194.2(d); *see also* Tex. R. Civ. P. 194.2(b) (listing initial disclosures "a party must provide to other parties" "[w]ithout awaiting a discovery request," including the one set forth in Texas Rule 194.2(b)(6)).

the action's subject matter, claims, or defenses.[141] The disclosing party, however, does not have to be "one hundred percent sure" that it will use the material before it must disclose the material.[142]

"Use" should be construed broadly to include use during pretrial proceedings as well as trial. Accordingly, the disclosing party should disclose documents, electronically stored information, and tangible things that it may use at any stage of the case at hand, even material that is limited solely to uncontroverted or background facts. The document-disclosure rule is not limited to documents that the disclosing party might use at trial. Consequently, if the party anticipates that it might use a document in connection with a preliminary-injunction hearing, a summary judgment motion, or even a deposition, it must disclose it.[143] It also should disclose documents that it might use to establish uncontroverted background facts. In other words, because the potential penalty for failing to produce the documents, electronically stored information, or tangible things generally is the material's exclusion at trial,[144] the prudent course is to disclose all documents, electronically stored information, and tangible things that the disclosing party anticipates it might: (1) use to support its allegations, claims, or defenses, including uncontroverted background facts; (2) use to support a denial or rebuttal of another party's allegations, claims, or defenses; (3) use in depositions and other aspects of discovery (other than to frame a written-discovery response); or (4) use in connection with motions bearing on the case's merits (e.g., summary judgment motions or temporary injunction applications).

---

[141] *Cf. Guinnane v. Dobbins*, No. CV 19-85-M-DWM, 2020 U.S. Dist. LEXIS 147114, at *7, 2020 WL 4734897 (D. Mont. Aug. 14, 2020) (providing that, under Federal Rule 26(a)(1)(A)(ii), the disclosure "obligation is limited . . . to information supporting the disclosing party's claims and defenses"); *Goonewardena v. N.Y. Workers Comp. Bd.*, 258 F. Supp. 3d 326, 349 n.11 (S.D.N.Y. 2017) ("By its terms, [Federal] Rule 26(a)(1)(A)(ii) only requires the disclosure of 'documents, electronically stored information, and tangible things that the *disclosing party* . . . may use to support *its* claims or defenses.' The advisory committee notes to the Rule's 2000 amendment clarify that '[a] party is no longer obligated to disclose witnesses or documents, whether favorable or unfavorable, that it does not intend to use.'" (citations omitted) (quoting Fed. R. Civ. P. 26(a)(1)(A)(ii) and Fed. R. Civ. P. 26, Advisory Comm. Notes).

[142] *Cf. Baldus v. Members of the Wis. Gov't Accountability Bd.*, Nos. 11-CV-562 JPS-DPW-RMD, 11-CV-1011 JPS-DPW-RMD, 2011 U.S. Dist. LEXIS 138827, at *6, 2011 WL 6003185 (E.D. Wis. Nov. 30, 2011) (construing Federal Rule 26(a)(1)(A)(i)) (quoting *Frazier v. Layne Christensen Co.*, 370 F. Supp. 2d 823, 828 (W.D. Wis. 2005)), *vacated in part on other grounds*, 380 F. Supp. 2d 989 (W.D. Wis. 2005)).

[143] *Cf. Martino v. Kiewit N.M. Corp.*, 600 F. App'x 908, 910-11 (5th Cir. 2015) (affirming the trial court's striking of a contract not disclosed in connection with a summary judgment motion); *Denman Tire Corp. v. Compañia Hulera Tornel, S.A. de C.V.*, No. DR-12-CV-027-AM-VRG, 2013 U.S. Dist. LEXIS 202070, at *4–5 (W.D. Tex. Feb. 13, 2013) (noting that a party is required to identify documents and witnesses it may use in connection with a motion), *vacated on other grounds*, 2014 U.S. Dist. LEXIS 199693, 2014 WL 12564118 (W.D. Tex. Mar. 31, 2014); Fed. R. Civ. P. 26, Advisory Comm. Notes to 2000 amend. ("'Use' includes any use at a pretrial conference, to support a motion, or at trial. The disclosure obligation is also triggered by intended use in discovery, apart from use to respond to a discovery request; use of a document to question a witness during a deposition is a common example.").

[144] Tex. R. Civ. P. 193.6.

The fact that a document is publicly available or in the possession of the other parties does not excuse a failure to disclose it.[145] The only documents that a disclosing party might use in the case that it does not have to disclose are documents that it will use "solely for impeachment."[146] If a document is both substantive and impeachment evidence, it must be disclosed:

> "Substantive evidence is that which is offered to establish the truth of a matter to be determined by the trier of fact." "Impeachment evidence, on the other hand, is that which is offered to 'discredit a witness . . . to reduce the effectiveness of [her] testimony by bringing forth evidence which explains why the jury should not put faith in [her] or [her] testimony.'"
>
> [S]ome evidence serves both substantive and impeachment functions and thus should not be treated as "solely" impeachment evidence. [Federal] Rule 26(a)(1)'s automatic disclosure requirement "was adopted to end two evils that had threatened civil litigation: expensive and time-consuming pretrial discovery techniques and trial-by-ambush." "A too expansive reading of the impeachment exception 'could cause a resurgence of these evils."[147]

Because the only documents that the disclosing party does not have to disclose are ones that will be used solely for impeachment, it must disclose documents that might be used solely in rebuttal, if the need to use the document reasonably can be anticipated before trial.[148]

---

[145] *Cf. Martino v. Kiewit N.M. Corp.*, 600 F. App'x 908, 911 (5th Cir. 2015) (per curiam) ("[E]ven if a document is publicly available or in the opposing party's possession, a party must still disclose it under [Federal] Rule 26(a)(1)(A) to provide notice of evidence central to its claims or defenses."); *Shatsky v. Syrian Arab Rep.*, 312 F.R.D. 219, 223–24 (D.D.C. 2015) (same); *Robert Kubicek Architects & Assocs. v. Bosley*, No. CV11-2112 PHX DGC, 2013 U.S. Dist. LEXIS 34722, at *3–4 (D. Ariz. Mar. 13, 2013) (rejecting argument that a disclosing party does not have to disclose documents in the possession of the opposing party because it "misapprehends the purpose of [Federal] Rule 26(a)(1)(A)(ii)[,]" which "is not merely to apprise the opposing party of the existence of documents; it is to tell the opposing party which documents may be used at trial. The fact that a party has documents in its possession does nothing to inform that party that the opposing party may use them at trial.").

[146] Tex. R. Civ. P. 194.1(b).

[147] *Olivarez v. Geo Grp., Inc.*, 844 F.3d 200, 204 (5th Cir. 2016) (citations omitted) (quoting Chiasson v. *Zapata Gulf Marine Corp.*, 988 F.2d 513, 517 (5th Cir. 1993), and *Standley v. Edmonds-Leach*, 783 F.3d 1276, 1283 (D.C. Cir. 2015)); *accord Cooper v. City of Chi.*, No. 16 C 3519, 2018 U.S. Dist. LEXIS 140556, at *13–14, 2018 WL 3970141 (N.D. Ill. Aug. 20, 2018); *Robert Kubicek Architects & Assocs. v. Bosley*, No. CV11-2112 PHX DGC, 2013 U.S. Dist. LEXIS 34722, at *5–6 (D. Ariz. Mar. 13, 2013).

[148] *Cf. In re E.R.A.*, No. 09-20-00042-CV, 2021 Tex. App. LEXIS 2026, at *13–14, 2021 WL 1031142 (Tex. App.—Beaumont Mar. 18, 2021, no pet.) (mem. op.) ("A party may obtain discovery of the name of persons who have knowledge of relevant facts when those persons have or may have knowledge of any discoverable matter. A party may also obtain discovery of the name of any person who is expected to testify at trial, excluding rebuttal or impeaching witnesses, the necessity of whose testimony cannot reasonably be anticipated before trial.") (citations omitted); *In re Commitment of Sells*, No. 09-15-00172-CV, 2016 Tex. App. LEXIS 3916, at *25, 2016 WL 1469059 (Tex. App.—Beaumont Apr. 14, 2016, pet. denied) (mem. op.) ("The mere fact that a witness is called 'in rebuttal' does not mean that the witness does not have to be disclosed. A rebuttal witness should be disclosed if the need to call that witness reasonably

The disclosing party, in addition to describing the categories of documents, also needs to state where the documents are located.[149] For example, stating that the certain documents are in the possession of the disclosing party's attorney and that others are in its Dallas office should be sufficient.

Several questions arise with respect to document disclosures under the current document-disclosure rule, Texas Rule 194.2(b)(6). The first is whether copies of documents have to be produced under Texas Rule 194.2(b)(6).[150] The answer to this question is unclear. Although the Rule gives the disclosing party the option of producing copies of its documents or describing them "by category and location"[151] and although federal cases construe the federal version of the rule literally,[152] an argument

---

should have been anticipated.") (citations omitted); *Schlein v. Griffin*, No. 01-14-00799-CV, 2016 Tex. App. LEXIS 3715, at *29, 2016 WL 1456193 (Tex. App.—Houston [1st Dist.] Apr. 12, 2016, no pet.) (mem. op.) ("A rebuttal witness still has to be disclosed if the need to call the witness reasonably should have been anticipated."); *Homeyer v. Farmer*, No. 10-11-00009-CV, 2011 Tex. App. LEXIS 9316, at *26, 2011 WL 6004338 (Tex. App.—Waco Nov. 23, 2011, no pet.) (mem. op.) ("If the rebuttal witness's testimony could reasonably have been anticipated, then the witness is not exempt from the scope of written discovery."); *In re Marks.*, 230 S.W.3d 241, 245–46 (Tex. App.—Beaumont 2007, no pet) (same); *Moore v. Mem'l Hermann Hosp. Sys.*, 140 S.W.3d 870, 875 (Tex. App.—Houston [14th Dist.] 2004, no pet.) (same).

[149] Tex. R. Civ. P. 194.2(b)(6); *cf. Cervantes v. Zimmerman*, No. 17-cv-1230-BAS-NLS, 2019 U.S. Dist. LEXIS 64423, at *15–16, 2019 WL 1598219 (S.D. Cal. Apr. 15, 2019) ("Plaintiffs expressly disclosed 'photos, videos, and media stories' as a category of documents in their possession on which they might rely. Plaintiffs, however, conspicuously failed to describe any location, let alone that Goodman possessed such documents, in violation of [Federal] Rule 26(a).") (citation omitted); *Renfroe v. Quality Loan Serv. Corp.*, No. 2:17-CV-00194-SMJ, 2017 U.S. Dist. LEXIS 219973, at *9, 2017 WL 8777463 (E.D. Wash. Oct. 26, 2017) ("Defendants' initial disclosures identified only the 'loan file' and did not describe the location of the file. This disclosure is insufficient under [Federal] Rule 26.").

[150] Under former Texas Rule 194.2, materials generally have to be produced because the Rule did not give the disclosing party the option to state a time and method for their production and because former Texas Rule 194.4 generally required the party to serve materials with the response. Former Tex. R. Civ. P. 194.4 ("Copies of documents and other tangible items ordinarily must be served with the response. . . .").

[151] Tex. R. Civ. P. 194.2(b)(6).

[152] *E.g.*, *Amiri v. Omni Excavators, Inc.*, No. 18-586 (RMC), 2019 U.S. Dist. LEXIS 188636, at *6–7, 2019 WL 5653622 (D.D.C. October 31, 2019) ("The commentary further explains that [Federal] Rule 26(a)(1)(ii), which relates to documents used to support a party's claims or defenses, 'does not require production of any documents.' Only a description of documents by category and location is required. The commentary states that '[i]f . . . only the description [of documents] is provided, the other parties are expected to obtain the documents desired by proceeding under [F]ederal Rule 34 or through informal requests.'" (citations omitted) (quoting Fed. R. Civ. P. 26, Advisory Comm. Notes to 1993 Amend.))); *Edmondson v. Brennan & Clark, Ltd., LLC*, No. 4:18-CV-11, 2019 U.S. Dist. LEXIS 51113, at *4, 2019 WL 1375780 (N.D. Ind. Mar. 26, 2019) ("Plaintiff provides no basis to conclude that any document was wrongly omitted, or that Defendants were obligated to precisely describe such a document in their initial disclosures. Defendants described categories of documents, as permitted by the rule; they were not required to identify each document."); *Dhaliwal v. Singh*, No. 1:13-cv-00484-LJO-SKO, 2014 U.S. Dist. LEXIS 89670, at *14 (E.D. Cal. 2014) ([Federal] Rule 26(a)(1)(A)(ii) does not require the actual *production* of documents. Rather, it requires only that the disclosing party provide 'a copy—*or a description*

can be made that Texas Rule 194.1(b) nonetheless requires the party to produce the described documents because it provides, in relevant part, that "[i]f a party does not produce copies of all responsive documents, electronically stored information, and tangible things with the response, the response must state a reasonable time and method for the production of these items."[153] The authors, however, do not believe that production is required because (1) Texas Rule 194.1(b) properly can read as referring to the other initial-disclosure rules that *expressly* require the production of documents—Texas Rules 194.2(b)(7)-(11), which require the disclosing party to produce indemnity and insuring agreements, settlement agreements, witness statements, and medical records—and (2) reading Texas Rule 194.1(b) to require a disclosing party to produce the described documents makes the document-disclosure rule's option to describe them meaningless.[154]

The second question regarding the current document-disclosure rule is: if the disclosing party elects to describe the documents, what degree of specificity is needed in describing them? Unfortunately, there is no definitive answer as very few cases have considered the question. Although the disclosing party does not need to make a list of its documents, the description should be detailed and specific enough to allow the opposing party to draft a production request for each category or type of document described in the disclosure.[155]

---

by category and location—of all documents. . . ." (quoting Fed. R. Civ. P. 26(a)(1)(A)(ii))); *Ning Shing v. Howard Berger Co.*, Civ. No. 97-604 (WGB), 1998 U.S. Dist. LEXIS 11142, at *7 (D.N.J. 1998) ("[T]he Court does not read Fed. R. Civ. P. 26(a)(1)(B) to require actual production of tangible things as part of initial disclosure. The plain language of the rule only requires 'a copy of, or a description by category and location of' documents, data and tangible things. Ning Shing's disclosure of photos and drawings therefore satisfies the Rule's requirements.").

153 Tex. R. Civ. P. 194.1(b).

154 *Cameron v. Terrell & Garrett*, 618 S.W.2d 535, 540 (Tex. 1981) ("It is a rule of statutory construction that every word of a statute must be presumed to have been used for a purpose."); *Morter v. State*, 551 S.W.2d 715, 718 (Tex. Crim. App. 1977) ("Every word of a statute is presumed to have been used for a purpose, and a cardinal rule of statutory construction requires that each sentence, clause, phrase[,] and word be given effect if reasonably possible." (quoting *Eddins-Walcher Butane Co. v. Calvert*, 298 S.W.2d 93, 96 (Tex. 1957))).

155 *Cf. Amiri v. Omni Excavators, Inc.*, No. 18-586 (RMC), 2019 U.S. Dist. LEXIS 188636, at *6–7, 2019 WL 5653622 (D.D.C. October 31, 2019) (Although 'an itemized listing of each exhibit is not required,' descriptions of documents should be sufficiently detailed to 'enable opposing parties (1) to . . . [decide] which documents might need to be examined, at least initially, and (2) to frame their document requests in a manner likely to avoid squabbles resulting from the wording of the requests.'" (quoting *City of Chi v. Purdue Pharma L.P.*, No. 14-CV-4361, 2017 U.S. Dist. LEXIS 103048, at *10–11 (N.D. Ill. Mar. 3, 2017))). *Compare Dhaliwal v. Singh*, No. 1:13-cv-00484-LJO-SKO, 2014 U.S. Dist. LEXIS 89670, at *21–23, 2014 WL 2957310 (E.D. Cal. June 30, 2014) (concluding that the following categories of documents were "vague and insufficient:" (1) "[l]oan documents (including amendments, revisions, etc.);" (2) [c]orrespondence between Plaintiffs and Nirmal Singh and/or Defendants that pertain to payments, the loan, investment, operations of the Defendants and other matters;" (3) [a]ccounting records regarding the Defendants;" (4) "[f]inancial records and reports of Defendants"); *N. Am. Lubricants Co. v. Terry*, No. CIV S-11-1284 KJM GGH, 2011 U.S. Dist. LEXIS 133672, at *13–15, 2011 WL 5828232 (E.D. Cal. Nov. 19, 2011) ("NALC's listing of 'business files for NALC' and 'business files for United Petroleum' is wholly insufficient and amounts to abuse of the discovery process. Those terms are so broad as to be meaningless and do not provide defendants with any notice as to which documents, or at

The final question regarding the current document-disclosure rule is: how does a party deal with an over disclosure of documents? That is, the disclosing party has made a document dump. In such event, a motion to compel a proper disclosure should be filed.[156]

6-3:3.7 Insuring and Indemnity Agreements

Former Texas Rule 194.2(g)—now Texas Rule 19.2(b)(7)—requires the disclosure of "any indemnity and insuring agreements described in [Texas] Rule 192.3(f)."[157] Texas Rule 192.3(f), in turn, provides, in relevant part:

> Except as otherwise provided by law, a party may obtain discovery of the existence and contents of any indemnity or insurance agreement under which any person may be liable to satisfy part or all of a judgment rendered in the action or to indemnify or reimburse for payments made to satisfy the judgment. . . .[158]

The key phrase in Texas Rule 192.3(f) is "may be liable." This phrase requires the production of an insurance or indemnity agreement whenever it is possible, however remote, that the agreement either could satisfy all or part of the action's judgment or indemnify or reimburse any payments made to satisfy the judgment.[159]

---

least which categories of documents, NALC may use to support its claims."), *with Foster v. Costco Wholesale Corp.*, No. ED CV 17-2229 FMO (SPx), 2019 U.S. Dist. LEXIS 230636, at *6–8, 2019 WL 8640647 (C.D. Cal. Dec. 27, 2019) ("Plaintiff, relying on *North American Lubricants Company v. Terry*, No. CIV S-11-1284 KJM GGH, 2011 U.S. Dist. LEXIS 133672, at *13–15, 2011 WL 5828232 (E.D. Cal. Nov. 19, 2011)], contends that defendant's disclosures were 'vague and insufficient.' The court disagrees. In *Terry*, the plaintiff in a trade secret, misappropriation, and unfair competition action filed against its former employees (and others) listed 'business files' as a category in its initial disclosures. The court found this 'insufficient' because that term was 'so broad as to be meaningless and d[id] not provide defendants with any notice as to which documents, or at least which categories of documents, [plaintiff could] use to support its claims.' Here, unlike in *Terry*, defendant identified six distinct categories of documents that were specific to plaintiff's claims.").

156 *Cf. City of Chi. v. Purdue Pharma L.P.*, No. 14 CV 4361, 2017 U.S. Dist. LEXIS 103048, at *9 "'(N.D. Ill. Mar. 3, 2017) ("[Federal] Rule 26(a)(1)(A)(i) requires the identification only of persons whom a party may use to support its claims or defenses, not everyone with knowledge about the subject matter' . . . Applying the above principles to the parties' disclosures, . . . the City must now reduce the list to include only those individuals on whom it may rely in supporting its claims or defenses against Defendants. . . .").

157 Former Tex. R. Civ. P. 194.2(g); Tex. R. Civ. P. 194.2(b)(7).

158 Tex. R. Civ. P. 192.3(f). This rule is substantially the same as the federal disclosure rule about insurance and indemnity agreements, Federal Rule 26(a)(1)(A)(iv). *See* Fed. R. Civ. P. 26(a)(1)(A)(iv) (requiring "for inspection and copying as under [Federal] Rule 34, any insurance agreement under which an insurance business may be liable to satisfy all or part of a possible judgment in the action or to indemnify or reimburse for payments made to satisfy the judgment.").

159 *Cf. Bell v. Nusil Tech. LLC*, No. 120CV0061NONEJLT, 2020 U.S. Dist. LEXIS 209481, at *12, 2020 WL 6565258 (E.D. Cal. Nov. 9, 2020) ("[P]arties must produce all policies under which they may be liable to satisfy a possible judgment, even if they dispute liability under the policies."); *Ceraldi v. Strumpf*, No. 3:17 CV 1628 (JCH), 2019 U.S. Dist. LEXIS 186757, at *5, 2019 WL 5558472 (D. Conn. Oct. 29, 2019) ("The defendants' unilateral assertion that the insurance coverage is irrelevant does not suffice. In the absence of identifying 'a specific

Under Texas Rule 192.3(f), former Texas Rule 194.2(g), and Texas Rule 194.2(b)(7), the disclosing party must produce a complete copy of the relevant insurance or

---

prejudice which would arise from the disclosure of their existing policies[,]' the defendants must produce the insurance documents responsive to this request." (quoting *Tzanetis v. Weinstein & Riley, P.S.*, No. 3:09 CV 413 (WWE) (HBF), 2009 U.S. Dist. LEXIS 118387, at *3, 2009 WL 5128892 (D. Conn. Dec. 18, 2009))); *McCullar v. Pecos Valley of N.M., LLC*, No. CV 19-03 SMV/CG, 2019 U.S. Dist. LEXIS 100701, at *4, 2019 WL 11585161 (D.N.M. June 17, 2019) ("[P]arties must produce all policies under which they may be liable to satisfy a possible judgment, even if they dispute liability under the policies."); *Merriweather v. United Parcel Serv., Inc.*, No. 3:17-CV-349-CRS-LLK, 2018 WL 3572527, at *8 (W.D. Ky. July 25, 2018) ("Although there is no indication that the claims would be in excess of Defendant UPS' five-million-dollar policy, there is likewise no indication that a judgment would not be in excess of Defendant UPS' five-million-dollar policy. The phrase 'may be liable' indicates that regardless of whether there is actual liability, the mere potential of satisfying a judgment requires the production of the insurance agreement under [Federal] Rule 26."); *Pape v. Law Offices of Frank N. Peluso, P.C.*, No. 3:13 CV 63 (JGM), 2015 U.S. Dist. LEXIS 136742, at *5, 2016 WL 755602 (D. Conn. Oct. 7, 2015) ("As U.S. Magistrate Judge Marilyn D. Go held eleven years ago, in light of the mandatory language of [Federal] Rule 26(a)(1)(A)(iv), when a defense attorney asserts that the claims at issue fall within an exclusion in a defendant's insurance policy, a 'plaintiff is not limited to counsel's say-so in making this determination.'" (quoting *Calabro v. Stone*, 224 F.R.D. 532, 533 (E.D.N.Y. 2004))); *Jo Ann Howard & Assocs., P.C. v. Cassity*, No. 4:09CV01252 ERW, 2015 U.S. Dist. LEXIS 95322, at *8–10, 2015 WL 13359780 (E.D. Mo. July 22, 2015) (rejecting the defendant's claim that it properly failed to produce insurance policies "because the insurance carriers had not acknowledged coverage, and even if they had, [the defendant] had incurred a $107 million loss on an unrelated claim against the same polices so there would be no insurance left for Plaintiffs' claims," and reasoning that "[Federal] Rule 26(a)(1)(A)(iv) is clear; a party is required to disclose any insurance policy which *may* cover the claims at issue. [The defendant] made its own determination as to whether it believed the insurance policies would apply. This suggests the policies *may* cover the claims at issue even if [the defendant] believed they ultimately would not. [The defendant] should have disclosed the policies."); *Pellegrin v. Montco Oilfield Contrs., LLC*, No. 14-2161 SECTION: "S" (1), 2015 U.S. Dist. LEXIS 75722, at *25, 2015 WL 3651159 (E.D. La. June 11, 2015) (holding that the magistrate judge did not err in ordering the defendant to produce its excess policy because it was "not unreasonable to conclude" that the plaintiff's claim could exceed the limits of the primary policy); *Garcia v. Techtronic Indus. N. Am.*, Nos. 2:13-cv-05884 (MCA) (JAP), 3:14-cv-00840 (KM) (JAD), 2:14-cv-04697 (KM) (JAD), 2015 U.S. Dist. LEXIS 53249, at *9–10, 2015 WL 1880544 (D.N.J. Apr. 21, 2015) ("Although there is no indication that the claims would be in excess of Defendants' self-insured retention, there is likewise no indication that a judgment would not be in excess of Defendants' self-insured retention. The phrase 'may be liable' indicates that regardless of whether there is actual liability, the mere potential of satisfying a judgment requires the production of the insurance agreement under [Federal] Rule 26. . . . Defendants have not provided the Court with any evidence that the damages Plaintiffs seek are in any way capped and, therefore, the Court will not issue a ruling as if it were."); *Regalado v. Techtronic Indus. N. Am., Inc.*, No. 3:13-cv-4267-L, 2015 U.S. Dist. LEXIS 177983, at *3–6, 2015 WL 10818616 (N.D. Tex. Feb. 24, 2015) (rejecting the defendants' argument that they properly withheld from production their excess insurance policy because Federal Rule 26(a)(1)(A)(iv) requires production of "any insurance agreement that could possibly apply to require the insurance business—however unlikely it may be—to satisfy all or part of a possible judgment in a case"); *Gov't Benefits Analysis, Inc. v. Gradient Ins. Brokerage, Inc.* No. 10-2558-KHV-DJW, 2012 U.S. Dist. LEXIS 113223, at *7–10, 2012 WL 3292850 (D. Kan. Aug. 13, 2012) (rejecting the defendants' argument that they did not have to produce their insurance policies because they had reviewed them and determined that none of them indemnity agreement, not only the insurance agreement's declarations page, "relevant" portions of the indemnity or insurance agreement, or a description of the agreement's coverage.[160] Although no Texas case has considered the question, "[m]ost

---

provided coverage for the plaintiffs' claims and that the policies should be produced so that the plaintiffs' could make their own determinations regarding coverage).

[160] *Compare* Tex. R. Civ. P. 192.3(f) (providing for the discovery of the "contents of any indemnity or insurance agreement"), ***with*** Tex. R. Civ. P. 192.3(g) (providing for the discovery of the "contents of any ***relevant portions*** of a settlement agreement" (emphasis added)). *Cf. Van Schoick v. Acad. LTD*, No. 120CV00255CEACHS, 2021 U.S. Dist. LEXIS 76087, at *5–6, 2021 WL 1526384 (E.D. Tenn. Apr. 19, 2021) ("Defendant has not denied that it had an insurance agreement in place which may be used to satisfy all or part of a potential judgment in this case. Indeed, by producing a Declarations Page, Defendant has admitted that such an insurance agreement was in place. Defendant should have produced the insurance policy as part of it duty to provide initial disclosures."); ***Hoffman v. MJC Am., Ltd***, No. 4:18-CV-04169-LLP, 2019 U.S. Dist. LEXIS 173578, at *20, 2019 WL 4933526 (D.S.D. Oct. 7, 2019) ("The Hoffmans assert that because the policy produced by MJC and Gree USA lacks a copy of the declarations page, the disclosure is incomplete and inadequate. . . . [T]he court agrees."); *Schmidt v. Shifflett*, No. 1:18-CV-00663-KBM-LF, 2019 U.S. Dist. LEXIS 132547, at *3, 2019 WL 3573507 (D.N.M. Aug. 6, 2019) ("Both [Federal] Rule 26 and the governing case law require disclosure of the entire insurance policy."); ***Robin v. Weeks Marine***, No. 17–1539 SECTION: "E"(1), 2017 U.S. Dist. LEXIS 122360, at *5–6, 2017 WL 3311243 (E.D. La. Aug. 3, 2017) ("The primary issue at this time is the production of unredacted insurance policies requested by Mr. Robin. . . . The text of [Federal Rule 26(a)(1)(iv)] does not suggest that disclosure of such agreements may be limited in any way. . . . While there may still be some truth to the Wood court's observation that '[b]y allowing discovery of insurance limits, the court would be shifting the emphasis of the litigation from how much the plaintiff was damaged to how much the defendant can pay,' the amendment of the Federal Rules of Civil Procedure to require production of insurance liability policies makes clear that such agreements are discoverable. The Court finds that the unredacted insurance policies must be disclosed.") (citation omitted); ***Meredith v. United Collection Bureau, Inc.***, No. 1:16 CV 1102, 2016 U.S. Dist. LEXIS 156214, at *18, 2016 WL 6649279 (N.D. Ohio Nov. 10, 2016) ("Federal Rule of Civil Procedure 26(a)(1)(A)(iv) requires a party to produce any insurance agreement that might afford coverage in a particular case. Defendant produced only three pages of its $10,000,000 insurance policy and argues that these are sufficient to allow plaintiff to determine whether insurance coverage is available in this case. Defendant has cited no legal authority that would allow it to produce only those portions of its policy that it deems relevant."); ***Garcia v. Techtronic Indus. N. Am.***, Nos. 2:13-cv-05884 (MCA) (JAP), 3:14-cv-00840 (KM) (JAD), and 2:14-cv-04697 (KM) (JAD), 2015 U.S. Dist. LEXIS 53249, at *10–11, 2015 WL 1880544 (D.N.J. Apr. 21, 2015) (concluding that Federal Rule 26(a)(1)(A)(iv)'s production requirement is not satisfied by production of set declaration page); *Capozzi v. Atwood Oceanics, Inc.*, No. 08-776, 2009 U.S. Dist. LEXIS 91911, at *7, 2009 WL 3055321 (W.D. La. Sept. 20, 2009) (Federal Rule 26(a)(1)(A)(iv) "does not allow a party to designate which parts of an insurance agreement are relevant or not. The rule is very clear that 'any insurance agreement under which an insurance business may be liable' is to be produced, without awaiting any discovery request. Aramack has cited no authority for its position that it need only disclose the portions of its insurance policies it deems relevant."); ***Wolk v. Green***, No. C06-5025 BZ, 2008 U.S. Dist. LEXIS 67759, at *6, 2008 WL 298757 (N.D. Cal. Feb. 1, 2008) ("Defendant has repeatedly refused to disclose a complete copy of his liability insurance policy, and insists that the declarations page is sufficient to satisfy Federal Rule of Civil Procedure 26(a)(1)(A)(iv) (formerly [Federal] Rule 26(1)(D)). However, the plain language of the rule requires a party to disclose, and to provide for inspection, 'any insurance agreement,' not just the declarations page of the policy."); ***Boyer v. Riverhead Cent. Sch. Dist.***, No. CV 05-4955 (SJF) (AKT), 2006 U.S. Dist. LEXIS 93917, at *4–7, 2006

federal courts across the country that have examined this issue . . . have determined that the reference in Federal Rule 26(a)(1)(A)(iv) to 'any insurance agreement' includes reinsurance agreements[,]"[161] that is, "a contract by which one insurer insures the risks of another insurer."[162]

Insurance and indemnity agreements are discoverable because they assist the complaining party in determining the action's settlement value.[163] The fact that they are discoverable, however, does not make them admissible.[164] In this regard, such agreements are inadmissible to prove liability at trial.[165]

Texas Rule 192.3(f) only requires the production of the relevant insurance or indemnity agreements and not the production of other related insurance

---

WL 3833040 (E.D.N.Y. Dec. 29, 2006) (holding that summaries of insurance coverage were insufficient under former Federal Rule 26(a)(1)(D)); *Gaines-Hanna v. Farmington Pub. Sch. Dist.*, No. 04-CV-74910-DT, 2006 U.S. Dist. LEXIS 14885, at *9–10, 2006 WL 891434 (E.D. Mich. Mar. 31, 2006) (holding that the defendant's disclosure of its insurance carriers' names, the policy numbers, and an assurance that the coverage was adequate to cover any judgment was insufficient to satisfy the requirements of former Federal Rule 26(a)(1)(D)); *Henderson v. Zurn Indus., Inc.*, 131 F.R.D. 560, 563 (S.D. Ind. 1990) ("[D]efendant's attempt to limit discovery to the policy limits is contrary to the express mandate of [former Federal Rule 26(b)(2)].").

161 *Certain Underwriters at Lloyd's v. AMTRAK*, No. 14-CV-4717 (FB), 2016 U.S. Dist. LEXIS 64088, at *58, 2016 WL 2858815 (E.D.N.Y. May 16, 2016) (collecting cases); *see also Estate of Brown v. Lambert*, No. 15-CV-1583-DMS-WVG, 2020 U.S. Dist. LEXIS 117235, at *10, 2020 WL 3606392 (S.D. Cal. July 2, 2020) ("The vast majority of cases analyzing the discoverability of reinsurance agreements, rather than documents related to or arising from reinsurance agreements, favors the disclosure of Defendants' reinsurance policy here.") (collecting cases); *SavaSeniorCare, LLC v. Starr Indem. & Liab. Co.*, No. 1:18-CV-1991-SDG, 2019 U.S. Dist. LEXIS 232874, at *5, 2019 WL 9806574 (N.D. Ga. Oct. 31, 2019) ("There is no general [Federal] Rule 26 exception to the production of a reinsurance contract and courts have largely concluded that such contracts are discoverable.") (collecting cases).

162 *Certain Underwriters at Lloyd's v. AMTRAK*, No. 14-CV-4717 (FB), 2016 U.S. Dist. LEXIS 64088 at *20, 2016 WL 2858815 (quoting *N. River Ins. Co. v. Ace Am. Reinsurance Co.*, 361 F.3d 134, 137 (2d Cir. 2004)).

163 *In re Dana Corp.*, 138 S.W.3d 298, 303-04 (Tex. 1994) (orig. proceeding) (per curiam); *Carroll Cable Co. v. Miller*, 501 S.W.2d 299, 299 (Tex. 1973) (per curiam); *cf. Hoffman v. MJC Am., Ltd*, No. 4:18-CV-04169-LLP, 2019 U.S. Dist. LEXIS 173578, at *20–21, 2019 WL 4933526 (D.S.D. Oct. 7, 2019) ("Disclosure of insurance coverage enables counsel for both sides to make the same realistic appraisal of the case, so that settlement and litigation strategy are based on knowledge and not speculation." (quoting *Zed Lee v. Moana Pa'akai, Inc.*, NO. 14-00316 DKW-RLP, 2015 WL 12781707 (D. Haw. Apr. 15, 2015))).

164 Tex. R. Civ. P. 192.3(f) ("Information concerning the indemnity or insurance agreement is not by reason of disclosure admissible in evidence at trial.").

165 Tex. R. Evid. 411 ("Evidence that a person was or was not insured against liability is not admissible to prove whether the person acted negligently or otherwise wrongfully. But the court may admit this evidence for another purpose, such as proving a witness's bias or prejudice or, if disputed, proving agency, ownership, or control."); *In re Essex Ins. Co.*, 450 S.W.3d 524, 527 n.4 (Tex. 2014) (orig. proceeding) (per curiam) ("Texas law has long recognized the prejudice that results from the admission of evidence of liability insurance that covers an insured defendant."); *In re Foremost Ins. Co.*, 986 S.W.2d 770, 772 (Tex. App.—Corpus Christi 1998, orig. proceeding) (holding that a defendant "has a substantial right to have her liability decided without mention of insurance").

documents.[166] It, however, does not preclude such other discovery if it is otherwise relevant or reasonably calculated to lead to the discovery of admissible information.[167] Reservation-of-rights letters, however, generally are not discoverable.[168] Nor is

---

166 *In re Dana Corp.*, 138 S.W.3d 298, 303 (Tex. 1994) (orig. proceeding) (per curiam) ("Interpretation and application of the analogous federal rule supports our conclusion that [Texas] Rule 192.3(f) neither prohibits nor requires the discovery of more than an insurance agreement's existence and contents."); *cf. Sea Salt, LLC v. Bellerose*, No. 2:18-CV-00413-JAW, 2020 U.S. Dist. LEXIS 154147, at *4, 2020 WL 5032466 (D. Me. Aug. 25, 2020) (Federal Rule 26(a)(1)(A)(iv) "does not reference any insurance-related documents other than the insurance agreement. Furthermore, the Advisory Committee note states that the Rule 'provides that liability *insurance policies* be made available for inspection and copying.' Indeed, other courts have relied upon the plain language of the Rule to conclude that other insurance-related documents, including reservation-of-rights letters, are not discoverable." (citations omitted) (quoting Fed. R. Civ. P. 26 Advisory Comm. Note to 1983 Amendments (emphasis added))); *Jump v. Montgomery Cty.*, No. 13-cv-3084, 2015 U.S. Dist. LEXIS 97176, at *5, 2015 WL 4530522 (C.D. Ill. July 27, 2015) ("The requirement to produce any insurance agreement is limited to the agreement. [Federal Rule 26(a)(1)[(A)(iv)] does not require the production of any other document related to insurance" other than the relevant insurance policy); *Excelsior Coll. v. Frye*, 233 F.R.D. 583, 586 (S.D. Cal. 2006) ("[Former Federal] Rule 26(a)(1)(D), merely requires the disclosure of an insurance policy or other agreement that gives rise to an insurer's obligation to indemnify or hold its insured harmless for a judgment, and does not require the production of all agreements relating to insurance, as Plaintiff posits."); *Honeywell Int'l Inc. v. ICM Controls Corp.*, No. 11-cv-569 (JNE/TNL), 2013 U.S. Dist. LEXIS 169064, at *34, 2013 WL 6169671 (D. Minn. Nov. 22, 2013) ("Where the requested insurance-related discovery is 'not relevant or reasonably calculated to lead to the discovery of admissible evidence,' a party need only produce what is required under Fed. R. Civ. P. 26(a)(1)(A)(iv)." (quoting *Gulf Ins. Co. v. Skyline Displays Inc.*, No. 02-cv-3503 (DSD/SRN), 2003 U.S. Dist. LEXIS 26511, at 9-10 (D. Minn. Oct. 20, 2003))).

167 *In re Dana Corp.*, 138 S.W.3d 298, 302 (Texas 1994) (orig. proceeding) (per curiam) ("[Texas] Rule 193.2(f) does not foreclose discovery of insurance information beyond that identified in the rule; however we also conclude that the plain language of [Texas] Rule 192.3(f) by itself, does not provide a sufficient basis to order discovery beyond the 'existence and contents' of the policies. . . . [A] party may discover information beyond an insurance agreement's existence and contents only if the information is otherwise discoverable under our scope-of-discovery rules."); *cf. Phillips v. Clark Cnty. Sch. Dist.*, No. 2:10-cv-02068-GMN-GWF, 2012 U.S. Dist. LEXIS 5309, at *13–14, 2012 WL 135705 (D. Nev. Jan. 18, 2012) (holding that an insurance policy's drafting history was discoverable and relevant to the interpretation of an ambiguous insurance policy provision); *Henns v. Mony Life Ins. Co. of Am*, No. 5:11-cv-55-Oc-37TBS, 2011 U.S. Dist. LEXIS 125631, at *12–14, 2011 WL 5358423 (MD. Fla. Oct 31, 2011) (ordering production of insurance applications); *Bartlett v. Allstate Life Ins. Co.*, No. 92-101-FR, 1992 U.S. Dist. LEXIS 14792, at *4–7, 1992 WL 252119 (D. Ore. Sept. 28, 1992) (ordering production of the applications of all Louisiana residents who had applied for life insurance within the past year and who represented on the application that he or she had been charged with driving while intoxicated within the three months before the application's filing).

168 *In re Madrid*, 242 S.W.3d 563, 568 (Tex. App.—El Paso 2007, orig. proceeding) (holding that a reservation-of-rights letter was not discoverable under (1) Texas Rule 192.3(f) because it was not part of the insurance policy, or (2) Texas Rule 192.3(a) because it was not relevant to any claim or defense); *cf. Sea Salt, LLC v. Bellerose*, No. 2:18-CV-00413-JAW, 2020 U.S. Dist. LEXIS 154147, at *3–5, 2020 WL 5032466 (D. Me. Aug. 25, 2020) (holding that a reservation-of-rights letter was not discoverable); *Midwest Feeders, Inc. v. Bank of Franklin*, No. 5:14cv78-DCB-MTP, 2016 U.S. Dist. LEXIS 179327, at *11–12, 2016 WL 7422561 (S.D.

information about the remaining amount of insurance coverage.[169]

6-3:3.8 Settlement Agreements

Former Texas Rule 194.2(h)—now Texas Rule 194.2(b)(8)—requires the disclosure of "any settlement agreements described in [Texas] Rule 192.3(g)."[170] Texas Rule 192.3(g), in turn, permits the discovery of the "existence and contents of ***any relevant portions*** of a settlement agreement."[171]

Generally, the relevant portions of a settlement agreement in a pending action are (1) those containing the consideration paid by the settling party because they are relevant to the determination of any non-settling defendant's settlement credit after trial and to the question of a settlement demand's reasonableness,[172] and (2) those requiring the settling party either to provide testimony or other cooperation to the other party or not to cooperate with a non-settling party because they are relevant to bias.[173]

Miss. June 28, 2016) (holding that a reservation-of-rights letter was undiscoverable work product).

169 *In re Dana Corp.*, 138 S.W.3d 298, 302–04 (Tex. 1994) (orig. proceeding) (per curiam).

170 Former Tex. R. Civ. P. 194.2(h); Tex. R. Civ. P. 194.2(b)(8).

171 Tex. R. Civ. P. 192.3(g) (emphasis added); *accord In re DCP Midstream, L.P.*, No. 13-14-00502-CV, 2014 Tex. App. LEXIS 11092, at *14, 2014 WL 5019947 (Tex. App.—Corpus Christi Oct. 7, 2014, orig. proceeding) (mem. op.).

172 *In re Grecon, Inc.*, 542 S.W.3d 774, 782–84, 786 (Tex. App.—Houston [14th Dist.] 2018, orig. proceeding) (holding that (1) settlement agreements with other defendants are relevant to establish non-settling defendant's settlement credit and rejecting argument that the plaintiff did not have to produce them until after he prevailed at trial, and (2) "[a] non-settling defendant should be entitled to make its own independent assessment of its settlement credits to evaluate a settlement offer to avoid trial"); *In re DCP Midstream, L.P.*, No. 13-14-00502-CV, 2014 Tex. App. LEXIS 11092, at *15, 2014 WL 5019947 (Tex. App.—Corpus Christi Oct. 7, 2014, orig. proceeding) (mem. op.) ("Courts 'routinely' order production of settlement agreements that are relevant to a claim or defense of a party. Settlement agreements are relevant and necessary to determine the amount of settlement credits to which a defendant is entitled under the common law's 'one satisfaction' rule that a plaintiff should not be compensated twice for the same injury. Settlement agreements are also relevant under the Texas Civil Practice and Remedies Code in determining settlement credits.") (citations omitted); *In re Univar USA, Inc.*, 311 S.W.3d 175, 179 (Tex. App.—Beaumont 2010, orig. proceeding) ("[T]he settlement agreements containing the dollar amounts of a claimant's settlements are relevant to a remaining nonsettling defendant in at least two ways; first, to determine the amount of its settlement credit after a trial is completed, and second, before trial, to determine whether any settlement demand being made is reasonable when compared to the likely outcome of a trial."); *see* Tex. R. Evid. 408(b) (noting that a settlement agreement need not be excluded from evidence when offered to prove "a party's or witness's bias, prejudice, or interest").

173 *Liles v. Contreras*, 547 S.W.3d 280, 289–90 (Tex. App.—San Antonio 2018, pet. denied) ("Settlement agreements are discoverable for many reasons, including demonstrating bias or prejudice of a party or potential witness. . . . Although Rule 408 of the Texas Rules of Evidence generally precludes the admission of settlement agreements, such agreements may be admissible to prove a party's or witness's bias or prejudice.") (citations omitted); *In re Grecon, Inc.*, 542 S.W.3d 774, 785 (Tex. App.—Houston [14th Dist.] 2018, orig. proceeding) (holding that settlement agreements are relevant to show bias and that a non-settling defendant "should have the opportunity to examine the [s]ettlement [a]greements to determine whether they contain anything that would raise issues of

As with an indemnity or insurance agreement, the disclosing party should produce the actual settlement agreement, redacted to remove the non-relevant provisions.[174]

A settlement agreement in another action is discoverable if it is relevant to issues in the pending action.[175] The dollar amount of a settlement in another action, however, generally is neither relevant nor discoverable.[176]

Even though a settlement agreement may be discoverable, it is not admissible to prove or disprove liability at trial.[177]

---

witness bias or prejudice"); *In re DCP Midstream, L.P.*, No. 13-14-00502-CV, 2014 Tex. App. LEXIS 11092, at *15, 2014 WL 5019947 (Tex. App.—Corpus Christi Oct. 7, 2014, orig. proceeding) (mem. op.) ("[S]ettlement agreements and offers may be discoverable to demonstrate bias or prejudice of a party or witness or to establish the existence of a promise or agreement made by nonparties to the settled lawsuit.") (citations omitted); *In re Univar USA, Inc.*, 311 S.W.3d 175, 182 (Tex. App.—Beaumont 2010, orig. proceeding) ("[F]airness should allow a nonsettling party to evaluate whether a given settlement agreement potentially affects the prospective testimony of witnesses at a trial, an argument Univar advanced in the trial court and in its petition seeking a writ of mandamus. With respect to witness bias, we note that settlement agreements and offers may be discoverable for purposes other than to establish liability, such as to demonstrate bias or prejudice of a party or witness, or, to establish the existence of a promise or agreement made by nonparties to the settled lawsuit."); Tex. R. Evid. 408(b) (noting that a settlement agreement need not be excluded from evidence when offered to prove "a party's or witness's bias, prejudice, or interest").

174 *Liles v. Contreras*, 547 S.W.3d 280, 289 (Tex. App.—San Antonio 2018, pet. denied) (mem. op.) (Former Texas "Rule 192.3(g) requires a party responding to a request for disclosure to disclose not just the existence of a settlement agreement, but the contents of it. . . . Merely disclosing the names of the parties to the settlement, the amount, and that court approval was pending did not disclose 'the contents' of the settlement agreement so as to allow Contreras's counsel, among other things, to determine whether there might be bias or prejudice by the settling parties based on the agreement.").

175 *Ford Motor Co. v. Leggat*, 904 S.W.2d 643, 649 (Tex. 1995); *In re Frank A. Smith Sales*, 32 S.W.3d 871, 874 (Tex. App.—Corpus Christi 1990, orig. proceeding).

176 *Ford Motor Co. v. Leggat*, 904 S.W.2d 643, 649 (Tex. 1995); *Palo Duro Pipeline Co. v. Cochran*, 785 S.W.2d 455, 457 (Tex. App.—Houston [14th Dist.] 1990, orig. proceeding); *see* Tex. R. Evid. 408 ("Evidence of the following is not admissible either to prove or disprove the validity or amount of a disputed claim: (1) furnishing, promising, or offering—or accepting, promising to accept, or offering to accept—a valuable consideration in compromising or attempting to compromise the claim; and (2) conduct or statements made during compromise negotiations about the claim."). In *Collier Servs. Corp. v. Salinas*, 812 S.W.2d 372, 377 (Tex. App.—Corpus Christi 1991, orig. proceeding), the court of appeals properly allowed discovery of a settlement amount because it was relevant to the plaintiff's post-judgment efforts to uncover assets on which to execute.

177 Tex. R. Civ. P. 192.3(g) ("Information concerning the settlement agreement is not by reason of disclosure admissible in evidence at trial."); Tex. R. Evid. 408(a) (providing that settlement agreements are "not admissible to prove or disprove the validity or amount of a disputed claim"); *Ford Motor Co. v. Leggat*, 904 S.W.2d 643, 649 (Tex. 1995) (holding that settlement agreements are not admissible to prove liability); *see also Lewis v. ACCC Ins. Co.*, No. 14-19-00197-CV, 2020 Tex. App. LEXIS 6105, at *14, 2020 WL 4461338 (Tex. App.—Houston [14th Dist.] Aug. 4, 2020, no pet.) (mem. op.) ("A settlement agreement is neither an agreement to pay damages nor an admission of liability; to the contrary, a 'settlement agreement does nothing more than buy peace.'" (quoting *State Farm Cnty. Mut. Ins. Co. of Tex. v. Ollis*, 768 S.W.2d 722, 723 (Tex. 1989) (per curiam))).

6-3:3.9 Witness Statements

Former Texas Rule 194.2(i)—now Texas Rule 194.2(b)(9)—requires the disclosure of "any witness statements described in [Texas] Rule 192.3(h)."[178] Texas Rule 192.3(h), in turn, permits "discovery of the statement of any person having knowledge of relevant facts—a 'witness statement'—regardless of when the statement was made."[179]

Texas Rule 192.3(h) defines a witness statement as "(1) a written statement signed or otherwise adopted or approved in writing by the person making it, or (2) a stenographic, mechanical, electrical, or other type of recording of a witness's oral statement, or any substantially verbatim transcription of such a recording[,]" but makes clear that "[n]otes taken during a conversation or interview with a witness are not a witness statement."[180]

Generally, witness statements, irrespective of when they were made, must be produced and are not shielded from discovery by the work-product privilege.[181] For example, a letter written by an employee who witnessed the accident to the party's insurer describing how the accident occurred is a discoverable "witness statement."[182] So is an insurance company's recording of a telephone call with its insured about the accident.[183] In fact, one court properly held that edited and unedited versions of videotaped witness statements used during mediation were discoverable.[184] A witness statement, however, is protected from discovery if it falls within a privilege other than the work-product privilege, such as the attorney-client privilege or the Fifth Amendment privilege against self-incrimination.[185]

---

178 Former Tex. R. Civ. P. 194.2(i); Tex. R. Civ. P. 194.2(b)(9).

179 Tex. R. Civ. P. 192.3(h).

180 Tex. R. Civ. P. 192.3(h).

181 *See* Tex. R. Civ. P. 192.5(c)(1) (providing that witness statements are not work product); *In re Nat'l Lloyds Ins. Co.*, 532 S.W.3d 794, 803 (Tex. 2017) (orig. proceeding) ("Certain matters are expressly excluded from the definition of 'work product[]' . . . and are not protected from discovery even if made or prepared in anticipation of litigation or for trial. The carve-outs include 'information discoverable under [Texas] Rule 192.3 concerning experts, trial witnesses, witness statements, and contentions.'" (footnote omitted) (citations omitted) (quoting Tex. R. Civ. P. 192.5(c)(1))); *Spohn Hosp. v. Mayer*, 72 S.W.3d 52, 62 (Tex. App.—Corpus Christi 2001) ("Information discoverable under [Texas R]ule 192.3, including witness statements, is not work product protected from discovery, even if prepared in anticipation of litigation."), *rev'd on other grounds*, 104 S.W.3d 878 (Tex. 2003).

182 *In re Team Transp., Inc.*, 996 S.W.2d 256, 259 (Tex. App.—Houston [14th Dist.] 1999, orig. proceeding).

183 *In re Jimenez*, 4 S.W.3d 894, 896 (Tex. App.—Houston [1st Dist.] 1999, orig. proceeding).

184 *In re Learjet Inc.*, 59 S.W.3d 842, 846 (Tex. App.—Texarkana 2001, orig. proceeding).

185 Tex. R. Civ. P. 192 cmt. 9 to 1999 change ("Elimination of the 'witness statement' exemption does not render all witness statements automatically discoverable but subjects them to the same rules concerning the scope of discovery and privileges applicable to other documents or tangible things."); *In re ExxonMobil Corp.*, 97 S.W.3d 353, 360 (Tex. App.—Houston [14th Dist.] 2003, orig. proceeding) (holding that a witness statement in a document protected by the attorney-client privilege is not discoverable); *In re Fontenot*, 13 S.W.3d 111, 113–14 (Tex. App.—Fort Worth 2000, orig. proceeding) (holding that the plaintiff's written narrative and claim questionnaire given to his attorney was not discoverable because it was protected by the attorney-client privilege).

6-3:3.10 Medical Records and Bills

Former Texas Rules 194.2(j) and (k)—now Texas Rules 194.2(b)(10) and (11)—are mirror-image provisions applicable in actions "alleging physical or mental injury and damages from the occurrence that is the subject of the case[.]"[186] The first Rule requires the injured party to produce "all medical records and bills that are reasonably related to the injuries or damages asserted or, in lieu thereof, an authorization permitting the disclosure of such medical records and bills[.]"[187] The second Rule requires the non-injured party to produce "all medical records and bills obtained by the disclosing party by virtue of an authorization furnished by the requesting party[.]"[188] Under former Texas Rule 192.4(j)—now Texas Rule 194.2(b)(10)—it is the requesting, non-injured party who has the option of requesting either the medical authorization or the injured, disclosing party's documents.[189]

6-3:3.11 Responsible Third Parties

Former Texas Rule 194.2(l)—now Texas Rule 194.2(b)(12)—requires the disclosure of "the name, address, and telephone number of any person who may be designated as a responsible third party."[190] A responsible third party is defined as:

> any person who is alleged to have caused or contributed to causing in any way the harm for which recovery of damages is sought, whether by negligent act or omission, by any defective or unreasonably dangerous product, by other conduct or activity that violates an applicable legal standard, or by any combination of these. The term "responsible third party" does not include a seller eligible

---

186 Former Tex. R. Civ. P. 194.2(j)–(k); Tex. R. Civ. P. 194.2(b)(10)–(11).

187 Former Tex. R. Civ. P. 194.2(j); Tex. R. Civ. P. 194.2(b)(10).

188 Former Tex. R. Civ. P. 194.2(k); Tex. R. Civ. P. 194.2(b)(11).

189 *In re Soto*, 270 S.W.3d 732, 734 (Tex. App.—Amarillo 2008, orig. proceeding) ("[T]he option belongs to the party requesting disclosure, not the one responding to it. If a legitimate authorization is sought, then the respondent cannot unilaterally comply with the request by simply delivering selected medical records."); *see Navarrete v. Williams*, 342 S.W.3d 116, 122 (Tex. App.—El Paso 2011, no pet.) ("Ms. Navarrete cites to [former Texas] Rule 194.2(j), for the proposition that a disclosure request of medical information or records may be answered with such a release, and, in essence, concludes that no further response or supplementation is necessary. We disagree with Ms. Navarrete's interpretation of this provision.").

190 Former Tex. R. Civ. P. 194.2(l); Tex. R. Civ. P. 194.2(b)(12); *see In re Dawson*, 550 S.W.3d 625, 629–30 (Tex. 2018) (orig. proceeding) (per curiam) (analyzing disclosures provided in response to a request under former Texas Rule 194.2(l) and concluding that they were insufficient, reasoning that "[t]he only response [Defendant] gave to that request before limitations ran was 'Defendant will supplement'" and that "[e]ven after limitations had passed, [Defendant] disclosed only [the purported responsible third party's] name and phone number; the record does not show it ever provided his address"); *Sanchez v. Castillo*, No. 05-18-01033-CV, 2020 Tex. App. LEXIS 1867, at *13–14, 2020 WL 1042519 (Tex. App.—Dallas Mar. 4, 2020, no pet.) (mem. op.) (Former Texas "Rule 194.2 obligates a defendant, upon a request from the plaintiff, to disclose, among other things, the name, address, and telephone number of 'any person who may be designated as a responsible third party.' The response must be complete 'based on all information reasonably available' at the time." (citations omitted) (quoting Former Tex. R. Civ. P. 194.2(l); Tex. R. Civ. P. 193.1)).

for indemnity under Section 82.002 [of the Texas Civil Practice and Remedies Code].[191]

For a number of years, Section 33.004 of the Texas Civil Practice and Remedies Code allowed a plaintiff to assert a claim against a person designated as a responsible third party by a defendant even if the claim would otherwise have been barred by limitations, as long as the plaintiff brought the claim within sixty days after the responsible third party's designation.[192] The Texas Legislature closed this perceived loophole in 2011 by repealing that provision.[193] In its place, Section 33.004 was amended to provide that "[a] defendant may not designate . . . a responsible third party . . . after the [statute of limitations] . . . has expired" on the plaintiff's claim unless the defendant has "timely" disclosed that person in its discovery responses.[194] A designation

---

[191] Tex. Civ. Prac. & Rem. Code Ann. § 33.011(6); *see also Sanchez v. Castillo*, 05-18-01033-CV, 2020 Tex. App. LEXIS 1867, at *4, 2020 WL 1042519 (Tex. App.—Dallas Mar. 4, 2020, no pet.) (mem. op.) ("The Texas Civil Practice and Remedies Code permits defendants to designate responsible third parties. Consistent with the tenet of tort law that a party's liability arises from its own injury-causing conduct, the designation's purpose is to hold each party 'responsible [only] for [the party's] own conduct causing injury.'" (quoting *MCI Sales & Serv., Inc. v. Hinton*, 329 S.W.3d 475, 505 (Tex. 2010))); *In re CVR Energy, Inc.*, 500 S.W.3d 67, 73 (Tex. App.—Houston [1st Dist.] 2016, orig. proceeding) ("[A] defendant may be precluded from designating a responsible third party if it had an obligation to disclose the person earlier but did not do so and the statute of limitations has run on the plaintiff's claim against the late-disclosed party[.]").

[192] Act of June 11, 2003, 78th Leg., R.S., ch. 204, § 4.04, 2003 Tex. Gen. Laws 847, 856, *repealed by* Act of May 30, 2011, 82d Leg., R.S., ch. 203, §§ 5.01-.02, 2011 Tex. Gen. Laws 757, 759.

[193] Act of May 30, 2011, 82d Leg., R.S., ch. 203, §§ 5.01–.02, 2011 Tex. Gen. Laws 757, 759 (codified as Tex. Civ. Prac. & Rem. Code § 33.004(d)).

[194] Tex. Civ. Prac. & Rem. Code § 33.004(d); Former Tex. R. Civ. P. 194.2(l); *see In re Mobile Mini, Inc.*, 596 S.W.3d 781, 786–87 (Tex. 2020) (orig. proceeding) (per curiam) (describing the legislative history of Section 33.004 of the Civil Practice and Remedies Code and the interplay between Section 33.004 and former Rule 194.2(l)—now Texas Rule 194.2(b)(12))); *In re Bertrand*, 602 S.W.3d 691, 696–99, 705–06 (Tex. App.—Fort Worth 2020, orig. proceeding) (same); *see In re Dawson*, 550 S.W.3d 625, 628 (Tex. 2018) (orig. proceeding) (per curiam) ("Under Chapter 33 of the Texas Civil Practice and Remedies Code, a defendant may not designate a responsible third party after limitations has expired 'if the defendant has failed to comply with its obligations, if any, to timely disclose that the person may be designated as a responsible third party.'" (quoting Tex. Civ. Prac. & Rem. Code Ann. § 33.004(d))); *In re MAF Indus., Inc.*, No. 13-20-00255-CV, 2020 Tex. App. LEXIS 8432, at *14–15, 2020 WL 6158248 (Tex. App.—Corpus Christi Oct. 19, 2020, orig. proceeding) (mem. op.) (same); *In re VB Harlingen Holdings*, No. 13-1900131-CV, 2019 Tex. App. LEXIS 5443, at *20–22, 2019 WL 2707978 (Tex. App.—Corpus Christi June 27, 2019, orig. proceeding) (mem. op.) (same); *In re VB Harlingen Holdings*, No. 13-19-00131-CV, 2019 WL 2707978, at *8 (Tex. App.—Corpus Christi June 27, 2019, orig. proceeding) (mem. op.) ("We conclude that the trial court did not abuse its discretion denying [the defendant's] motion for leave to designate [a responsible third party] after the statute of limitations had expired as to [the plaintiff's] claims because [the defendant] failed to 'comply with its obligations . . . to timely disclose that the person may be designated as a responsible third party under the Texas Rules of Civil Procedure.'" (quoting Tex. Civ. Prac. & Rem. Code Ann. § 33.004(d))); *cf. Magna Equities II, LLC v. Heartland Bank*, No. H-17-1479, 2018 U.S. Dist. LEXIS 31971, at *13, 2018 WL 1135482 (S.D. Tex. Feb. 28, 2018) (noting that the limitation in Section 33.004(d) of the Texas Civil Practice & Remedies Code "seeks to address a defendant's interest in identifying nonparties who may have some culpability while recognizing that a

after the statute of limitations has expired, however, is timely if (1) the plaintiff sues immediately before the limitations period runs and the defendant's disclosure is not due until after the period expired,[195] or (2) if the responsible third party is a former

---

plaintiff has time limitations on pursuing its claims against parties not already included in its suit." (quoting *Vasquez v. Tristar Prods.*, No. B: 15-108, 2017 U.S. Dist. LEXIS 218714, at *4, 2017 WL 7038196 (S.D. Tex. May 22, 2017))).

Two interesting questions are whether the responsible third-party statute, Section 33.004 of the Texas Civil Practices and Remedies Code, applies in a federal diversity action governed by Texas law, and, if so, whether a defendant can designate a responsible third party after limitations has run on the plaintiff's claim against that party if the defendant had not previously disclosed the responsible third party's existence. The second question arises because, under Section 33.004(d), a defendant generally cannot designate a responsible third party after limitations has run unless it has timely disclosed that person "under the Texas Rules of Civil Procedure[,]" Tex. Civ. Prac. & Rem. Code § 33.004(d), and there is no federal discovery rule comparable to former Texas Rule 194.2(l)—now Texas Rule 194.2(b)(12)—requiring the disclosure of responsible third parties. *See Morris v. AirCon Corp.*, No. 9:16-cv-35, 2017 U.S. Dist. LEXIS 110310, at *11–12, 2017 WL 2927478 (E.D. Tex. June 15, 2017) ("GreCon is correct that the Federal Rules of Civil Procedure, either under Rule 26 or otherwise, do not require a party to disclose who it believes may be a responsible third party."); *Switzer v. Beach*, No. 1:18-CV-66, 2018 U.S. Dist. LEXIS 230758, at *5–7, 2018 WL 9869730 (E.D. Tex. July 16, 2018) (same).

Although the Fifth Circuit has not answered either question, with respect to the first question, "the prevailing view among district courts is that the procedure for designation of responsible third parties is Texas state substantive law." *Morris v. AirCon Corp.*, No. 9:16-cv-35, 2017 U.S. Dist. LEXIS 110310, at *6, 2017 WL 2927478 (E.D. Tex. June 15, 2017); *accord Oliva v. USA Truck, Inc.*, No. 3:18-CV-2814-E, 2019 U.S. Dist. LEXIS 225736, at *16–19, 2019 WL 7756355 (N.D. Tex. Nov. 15, 2019); *Ramos v. Beltran*, No. 5:15-CV-1042-RP, 2016 U.S. Dist. LEXIS 175595, at *3, 2016 WL 8234983 (W.D. Tex. Dec. 20, 2016).

There is, however, no consensus with respect to the answer to the second question. Some district courts hold that a responsible third party can be named after limitations has run even though the defendant had not previously disclosed the party's existence, *e.g.*, *Spencer v. BMW of N. Am., LLC*, No. 5:14-CV-869-DAE, 2015 U.S. Dist. LEXIS 43463, at *7, 2015 WL 1529773 n.3 (W.D. Tex. Apr. 2, 2015) ("Since there is no federal counterpart for responsible third parties, there would be no disclosure requirement under federal law, in which case Defendants had no timely disclosure obligations with which they would have had to comply under § 33.004(d)."); *see Webber, LLC v. Symons Corp.*, No. 4:12-CV-181-A, 2013 U.S. Dist. LEXIS 188131, at *6, 2013 WL 3356291 (N.D. Tex. July 3, 2013) (noting that "[a] plausible argument can be made that the Texas rules of procedure mentioned above are not applicable in this federal court litigation, with the consequence that Dayton cannot be deemed to have failed to comply with any obligation of disclosure under the Texas Rules of Civil Procedure because it had no such obligation."), whereas others hold that the defendant must have timely disclosed the responsible third party before limitations ran, *e.g.*, *Magna Equities II., LLC v. Heartland Bank*, No. H-17-1479, 2018 U.S. Dist. LEXIS 31971, at *21–22, 2018 WL 1135482 (S.D. Tex. Feb. 28, 2018). Accordingly, until the Fifth Circuit decides the issue, a plaintiff in a federal diversity case governed by federal law should serve an interrogatory asking the defendant to identify any responsible third parties and a defendant, who anticipates designating one, should disclose the responsible third party's identity to the plaintiff at the earliest possible time, even if no responsible third-party interrogatory has been served.")

[195] *See, e.g.*, *In re Mobile Mini, Inc.*, 596 S.W.3d 781, 786–87 (Tex. 2020) (orig. proceeding) (per curiam) ("Because a timely disclosure in accordance with the Texas Rules of Civil Procedure is all that is required of the defendant under the statute, requiring an earlier disclosure in suits filed mere days before the expiration of the statute of limitations is repug-

defendant in the action who was dismissed by the plaintiff after the limitations period expired.[196]

The amended statute and the Rule eliminate the possibility of a plaintiff colluding with a defendant to have it designate a responsible third party to allow the plaintiff to revive a time-barred claim. Although the statute tries to prevent defendants from delaying the designation of responsible third parties to prejudice the plaintiff (e.g., where the limitations period expires during a defendant's delay),[197] there will undoubtedly be instances in which plaintiffs will file suit shortly before limitations runs, and any claim against responsible third parties will be too late, even if the latter are designated promptly. In these situations, plaintiffs will simply have to face a trial in which the defendant points to the "empty chair" that previously would have been occupied by the responsible third party.

Mandamus relief may be available if a trial court erroneously denies a motion to designate a responsible third party.[198] "[A]n adequate appellate remedy is ordinarily

---

nant to the statutory language, unfairly burdens defendants, and skews the legislatively determined balance of interests."); *In re MAF Indus., Inc.*, No. 13-20-00255-CV, 2020 Tex. App. LEXIS 8432, at *14–15, 2020 WL 6158248 (Tex. App.—Corpus Christi Oct. 19, 2020, orig. proceeding) (mem. op.) ("Here, MAF properly filed its first amended motion for leave to designate Paramount LLC as a responsible third party. . . . Further, because MAF's duty to disclose responsible third parties did not arise until after the limitations period expired [which occurred nine days after MAF was served with the plaintiff's original petition], the timing of its disclosure is immaterial to the issue of timeliness under § 33.004(d). As such, the trial court's denial of MAF's motion was an improper application of the law, and, therefore, an abuse of discretion.") (citations omitted); *In re Bertrand*, 602 S.W.3d 691, 704 (Tex. App.—Fort Worth 2020, orig. proceeding) ("This case is an application of the principle discussed in [*In re Mobile Mini, Inc.*, 596 S.W.3d 781 (Tex. 2020) (orig. proceeding) (per curiam)]. Plaintiffs did not file suit until shortly before limitations ran against the potential responsible third parties. Their requests for disclosure to the defendants were served with the original petitions, and responses were not required to be served under the Rules of Civil Procedure until after plaintiffs' limitations against the responsible third parties had expired. As in *Mobile Mini*, defendants were not required to respond until after limitations expired. Therefore, it was the plaintiffs' conduct in the timing of their suit filing and service of discovery which failed to create a duty to disclose potential responsible third parties by the defendants before limitations expired.") (citations omitted); *In re Bustamante*, 510 S.W.3d 732, 736–37 (Tex. App.—San Antonio 2016, orig. proceeding) (holding that a defendant's designation of a responsible third party was "timely" because its response to the disclosure was not due until after limitations expired: "[W]e read section 33.004(d) to require a defendant to disclose a potential responsible third party before the expiration of the statute of limitations, if that is possible. In this case, Bustamante did not fail to comply with his obligation to timely disclose Riojas and CBE as potential responsible third parties because it was impossible for Bustamante to make a disclosure before the statute of limitations ran. The statute of limitations ran one day after this suit was filed.").

196 *In re CVR Energy, Inc.*, 500 S.W.3d 67, 78 (Tex. App.—Houston [1st Dist.] 2016, orig. proceeding).

197 *In re Bertrand*, 602 S.W.3d 691, 702 (Tex. App.—Fort Worth 2020, orig. proceeding) ("[T]he objective of Section 33.004(d) is to prevent defendants from surreptitiously delaying disclosure of responsible third parties until after limitations has expired and then disclosing to deprive plaintiffs of an opportunity to make a timely claim against them.").

198 *E.g., In re Mobile Mini, Inc.*, 596 S.W.3d 781, 783 (Tex. 2020) (orig. proceeding) (per curiam) ("The court of appeals denied Mobile Mini's mandamus petition without substan-

lacking because allowing a case to proceed to trial without a properly requested responsible-third-party designation 'would skew the proceedings, potentially affect the outcome of the litigation, and compromise the presentation of [a party's] defense in ways unlikely to be apparent in the appellate record.'"[199] Accordingly, a party seeking mandamus relief "ordinarily need only establish that the trial court abused its discretion in denying a timely filed motion to designate a responsible third party to demonstrate entitlement to mandamus relief."[200] The Texas Supreme Court has indicated that mandamus relief may also be available when a trial court erroneously grants a defendant's motion to designate a responsible third party, depending on the case's facts.[201]

6-3:3.12 Content Required in Certain Suits Under the Texas Family Code

As part of the 2021 amendments to the Texas discovery rules, the Texas Supreme Court added Texas Rule 194.2(c), which sets forth particular initial disclosures

---

tive comment, but we hold that Mobile Mini is entitled to mandamus relief because the trial court abused its discretion in denying Mobile Mini's motion [to designate an entity as a responsible third party] and Mobile Mini lacks an adequate appellate remedy."); *In re Coppola*, 535 S.W.3d 506, 509–10 (Tex. 2017) (orig. proceeding) (per curiam) (citing multiple cases to support the proposition that "a majority of our intermediate appellate courts have held that when a timely filed motion to designate a responsible third party is erroneously denied, no adequate remedy by appeal ordinarily exists" and "conditionally grant[ing] the petition for writ of mandamus and direct[ing] the trial court to vacate its order denying" a party's motion to designate responsible third parties); *see also In re MAF Indus., Inc.*, No. 13-20-00255-CV, 2020 Tex. App. LEXIS 8432, at *4, 2020 WL 6158248 (Tex. App.—Corpus Christi Oct. 19, 2020, orig. proceeding) (mem. op.) ("The Texas Supreme Court has held that mandamus may be appropriate to review an order denying a defendant's motion to designate a responsible third party.") (citing cases); *In re Bertrand*, 602 S.W.3d 691, 706 (Tex. App.—Fort Worth 2020, orig. proceeding) ("The Supreme Court has already established that there is no adequate remedy at law when a trial court denies a timely filed motion for leave to designate a responsible third party.") (citing cases).

199 *In re Mobile Mini, Inc.*, 596 S.W.3d 781, 788 (Tex. 2020) (orig. proceeding) (per curiam) (quoting *In re Coppola*, 535 S.W.3d 506, 509 (Tex. 2017) (orig. proceeding) (per curiam)); *accord see also In re Bertrand*, 602 S.W.3d 691, 695 (Tex. App.—Fort Worth 2020, orig. proceeding) ("[T]here is no adequate remedy at law when a trial court denies a timely filed motion for leave to designate a responsible third party under Texas Civil Practice and Remedies Code Section 33.004(a).").

200 *In re MAF Indus., Inc.*, No. 13-20-00255-CV, 2020 Tex. App. LEXIS 8432, at *4–5, 2020 WL 6158248 (Tex. App.—Corpus Christi Oct. 19, 2020, orig. proceeding) (mem. op.) (citing cases).

201 *In re Dawson*, 550 S.W.3d 625, 630 (Tex. 2018) (orig. proceeding) (per curiam) ("[E]ven though mandamus is not an equitable remedy, equitable principles largely govern its issuance. And 'what's sauce for the goose is sauce for the gander.' We held in *In re Coppola* [, 535 S.W.3d 506, 510 (Tex. 2017) (orig. proceeding) (per curiam),] that, 'ordinarily,' a defendant is entitled to mandamus relief when a trial court erroneously prevents it from designating a responsible third party. So it seems equitable and right—at least under these facts—that a plaintiff get the same relief when a trial court erroneously grants a defendant leave to so designate." (citations omitted) (quoting *Lewis v. Peoples Sav. & Loan Ass'n*, 463 S.W.2d 284, 287 (Tex. Civ. App.—Austin 1971, writ ref'd n.r.e.), then *In re Coppola*, 535 S.W.3d 506, 510 (Tex. 2017) (orig. proceeding) (per curiam))).

required for certain suits brought under the Texas Family Code.[202] Under Texas Rule 194.2(c)(1), "[i]n a suit for divorce, annulment, or to declare a marriage void, a party must, without awaiting a discovery request, provide to the other party the following, for the past two years or since the date of marriage, whichever is less: (A) all deed and lien information on any real property owned and all lease information on any real property leased; (B) all statements for any pension plan, retirement plan, profit-sharing plan, employee benefit plan, and individual retirement plan; (C) all statements or policies for each current life, casualty, liability, and health insurance policy; and (D) all statements pertaining to any account at a financial institution, including banks, savings and loans institutions, credit unions, and brokerage firms."[203] And, under Texas Rule 194.2(c)(2), "[i]n a suit in which child or spousal support is at issue, a party must, without awaiting a discovery request, provide to the other party: (A) information regarding all policies, statements, and the summary description of benefits for any medical and health insurance coverage that is or would be available for the child or the spouse; (B) the party's income tax returns for the previous two years or, if no return has been filed, the party's Form W-2, Form 1099, and Schedule K-1 for such years; and (C) the party's two most recent payroll check stubs."[204]

As of the date of this publication, these initial disclosures have not been analyzed in any Texas opinion. They also have no federal analogue. Thus, their plain language is the best interpretive guide for them at this juncture.

6-3:3.13 Proceedings Exempt from Initial Disclosures

The 2021 amendments to the Texas discovery rules generally exempt certain types of proceedings from initial-disclosure requirements. Specifically, Texas Rule 194.2(d) generally exempts the following:

(1) an action for review on an administrative record;

(2) a forfeiture action arising from a state statute;

(3) a petition for habeas corpus;

(4) an action under the Family Code filed by or against the Title IV-D agency in a Title IV-D case;

(5) a child protection action under Subtitle E, Title 5 of the Family Code;

(6) a protective order action under Title 4 of the Texas Family Code;

(7) other actions involving domestic violence; and

(8) an action on appeal from a justice court.[205]

Importantly, however, the Rule makes clear that "a court may order the parties to make particular disclosures and set the time for disclosure[.]"[206] In other words, the fact that initial disclosures do not apply in a proceeding by default does not mean that they will not be applied, in whole or in part, via court order. In addition, even if

---

202 Tex. R. Civ. P. 194.2(c).
203 Tex. R. Civ. P. 194.2(c)(1).
204 Tex. R. Civ. P. 194.2(c)(2).
205 Tex. R. Civ. P. 194.2(d)(1)–(8).
206 Tex. R. Civ. P. 194.2(d)(1)–(8).

there is no ordered disclosure, there is no reason why parties in the proceedings set forth above cannot agree to exchange certain disclosures and set the time for those disclosures.[207] Finally, in the absence of a court order or an agreement for disclosures, a party in a proceeding exempt from initial-disclosure requirements can simply use other forms of discovery to seek the information that would otherwise be available via initial disclosures.[208]

6-3:3.14 Testifying Expert Disclosures

For litigation purposes, an "expert" is a person, who through education, training, or experience has developed skill or knowledge in a subject sufficient to allow the person to render an opinion that will assist the fact finder.[209] The Texas discovery rules recognize two general types of experts: "testifying experts" and "consulting experts."[210]

A "testifying expert" is an expert "who may be called to testify as an expert witness at trial."[211] There are two types of testifying experts: (1) experts who are retained by, employed by, or otherwise in the control of the party (retained-testifying experts) and (2) experts who are not retained by, employed by, or otherwise in the control of the party (non-retained-testifying experts),[212] which typically are treating or emergency-room physicians or nurses, police officers, firemen, and other first responders.

A "consulting expert" is an expert "who has been consulted, retained, or specifically employed by a party in anticipation of litigation or in preparation for trial, but who is not a testifying expert."[213] There also are two types of consulting experts: consulting experts whose mental impressions and opinions have not been reviewed by a testifying expert (a consulting-only expert), and those whose mental impressions and opinions have been reviewed by a testifying expert.[214]

---

[207] *See* Tex. R. Civ. P. 191.1 ("Except where specifically prohibited, the procedures and limitations set forth in the rules pertaining to discovery may be modified in any suit by the agreement of the parties. . . .").

[208] *See* Tex. R. Civ. P. 192.1 (listing the permissible forms of discovery).

[209] Tex. R. Evid. 702 ("A witness who is qualified as an expert by knowledge, skill, experience, training, or education may testify in the form of an opinion or otherwise if the expert's scientific, technical, or other specialized knowledge will help the trier of fact to understand the evidence or to determine a fact in issue."); *see In re Nat'l Lloyds Ins. Co.*, 532 S.W.3d 794, 815 (Tex. 2017) (orig. proceeding) ("'The line between who is a [Texas] Rule [of Evidence] 702 expert witness and who is a [Texas] Rule [of Evidence] 701 [fact] witness is not always bright.' But when a witness is properly disclosed and designated as an expert and the main substance of the witness's testimony is based on specialized knowledge, skill, experience, training, and education, 'the testimony will generally be expert testimony within the scope of [Federal] Rule [of Evidence] 702.'" (footnotes omitted) (quoting *Reid Rd. Mun. Util. Dist. No. 2 v. Speedy Stop Food Stores, Ltd.*, 337 S.W.3d 846, 851 (Tex. 2011))).

[210] Tex. R. Civ. P. 192.7(c)–(d).

[211] Tex. R. Civ. P. 192.7(c).

[212] *See* Tex. R. Civ. P. 195.5(a) (setting forth the disclosure requirements for the two types of testifying experts).

[213] Tex. R. Civ. P. 192.7(d).

[214] Testifying or consulting experts can also be fact witnesses (i.e., dual-capacity witnesses) if they have knowledge of relevant facts that "was obtained first-hand or [that] . . . was not obtained in preparation for trial or in anticipation of litigation." Tex. R. Civ. P. 192.3(c). Such experts must be disclosed as persons with knowledge of relevant facts under Texas Rule

Often the identity of a person who otherwise would qualify as an expert because of the person's knowledge, skill, experience, training, or education must be disclosed as person having knowledge of relevant facts and cannot be shielded from discovery as a consulting-only expert. This is because to be a consulting-only expert, the person must have been consulted, retained, or specially employed *solely* in anticipation of litigation or in preparation for trial.[215] For example, an expert who was consulted before litigation was anticipated is not a consulting-only expert and the expert's identity, impressions, and opinions are discoverable if they are relevant to the action.[216]

Additionally, a person who otherwise qualifies as an expert, but who acquired relevant information as "an active participant in the events material to the lawsuit" is not a consulting-only expert.[217] For example, a person who gains factual information due to the person's involvement in the incident or transaction underlying the action cannot qualify as consulting-only expert—even if the person acquired some information through consulting—because the consultation is not the sole basis of the person's information. Accordingly, a party's employee whose duties involve the action's subject matter ***never*** qualifies as a consulting-only expert because the employee was not employed as an expert solely in anticipation of litigation or in preparation for trial.[218] But an employee who lacks personal knowledge of the facts relevant to the action and who is assigned to assist the employer or its attorneys in connection with the action can qualify as a consulting-only expert.[219]

Former Texas Rule 194.2(f)—now Texas Rule 194.3—*only* requires disclosures about *testifying* experts.[220] Whereas former Rule 194.2(f) set forth the specific disclosures required for testifying experts, Texas Rule 194.3 simply states: "In addition to the disclosures required by Rule 194.2, a party must disclose to the other parties testifying expert information as provided by Rule 195."[221] Because the details regarding testifying-expert disclosures are now in Texas Rule 195.5 (rather than Texas Rule 194.2), the discussion of those disclosures is provided in Chapter 7, section 7.4.3, rather than in this Chapter.

6-3:3.15 Pretrial Disclosures

The 2021 amendments to the Texas discovery rules added pretrial disclosures as a component of required disclosures. Specifically, except as provided in Texas Rule 194.4(c), Texas Rule 194.4(a) requires "a party must provide to the other parties and promptly file the following information about the evidence that it may present at trial other than solely for impeachment: (1) the name and, if not previously provided, the address, and telephone number of each witness—separately identifying those the

---

194.2(c) and can be deposed about their knowledge that either is first-hand or that was not obtained in their role as a consulting expert. See Chapter 6, section 6-3:3.5a for a discussion of when an expert is a dual-capacity witness.

215 Tex. R. Civ. P. 192.7(d). See also notes 106–112 and accompanying text.

216 *Lindsey v. O'Neill*, 689 S.W.2d 400, 402 (Tex. 1985).

217 *Axelson, Inc. v. McIlhany*, 798 S.W.2d 550, 554 (Tex. 1990). See also notes 106–112 and accompanying text.

218 *Axelson, Inc. v. McIlhany*, 798 S.W.2d 550, 554 (Tex. 1990).

219 *Axelson, Inc. v. McIlhany*, 798 S.W.2d 550, 554 (Tex. 1990).

220 Former Tex. R. Civ. P. 194.2(f); Tex. R. Civ. P. 194.3.

221 Tex. R. Civ. P. 194.3.

party expects to present and those it may call if the need arises; [and] (2) an identification of each document or other exhibits, including summaries of other evidence—separately identifying those items the party expects to offer and those it may offer if the need arises."[222]

Under Texas Rule 194.4(c), "[a]n action arising under the Family Code filed by or against the Title IV-D agency in a Title IV-D case is exempt from pretrial disclosure, but a court may order the parties to make particular disclosures and set the time for disclosure."[223] In addition, the parties can agree to make pretrial disclosures.[224]

6-3:4 Responding to Disclosure Requests and Making Required Disclosures

For a case filed before January 1, 2021, a party must respond to a disclosure request within thirty days after its service[225] unless the time is extended due to the manner of service, by the parties' agreement, or by court order,[226] except that (1) "a defendant served with a request before the defendant's answer is due need not respond until 50 days after service of the request," and (2) a response to a request for an expert disclosure under former Texas Rule 194.2(f) is due within the time provided by former Texas Rule 195.[227] Under former Texas Rule 195, which applies to cases filed before

---

[222] Tex. R. Civ. P. 194.4(a).

[223] Tex. R. Civ. P. 194.4(c).

[224] Tex. R. Civ. P. 191.1 ("Except where specifically prohibited, the procedures and limitations set forth in the rules pertaining to discovery may be modified in any suit by the agreement of the parties. . . .").

[225] Former Tex. R. Civ. P. 194.3; *accord In re Grecon, Inc.*, 542 S.W.3d 774779 (Tex. App.—Houston [14th Dist.] 2018, orig. proceeding) ("As to the response to the request for disclosure, [Former Texas] Rule 194.3 provides that "[t]he responding party must serve a written response on the requesting party within 30 days after service of the request[.]" (quoting former Tex. R. Civ. P. 194.3)).

[226] *See* Tex. R. Civ. P. 193.1 ("A party must respond to written discovery within the time provided by court order or these rules."). Three days are added to the response date if the production request is served by mail. Tex. R. Civ. P. 21a(c). One day is added if it is received by fax after 5:00 p.m. local time of the recipient. Tex. R. Civ. P. 21a(b)(2).

[227] Former Tex. R. Civ. P. 194.3(a)–(b); *accord In re Smith*, No. 01-19-00014-CV, 2020 Tex. App. LEXIS 7184, at *9, 2020 WL 5269417 (Tex. App.—Houston [1st Dist.] Sept. 3, 2020) (mem. op.) ("Pursuant to [former Texas] Rule 194.3, the party responding to the request for disclosure 'must serve a written response on the requesting party within 30 days after service of the request, except that: (a) a defendant served with a request before the defendant's answer is due need not respond until 50 days after service of the request, and (b) a response to a request under [former Texas] Rule 194.2(f) is governed by [former Texas] Rule 195.'" (quoting Former Tex. R. Civ. P. 194.3)); *In re Bertrand*, 602 S.W.3d 691, 696 (Tex. App.—Fort Worth 2020, orig. proceeding) ("When requests for disclosure are served before the defendant's answer to the petition is due, such as here, where they were served with the citation and petition, the defendant 'need not respond' until 50 days after the service of the request." (quoting Former Tex. R. Civ. P. 194.3)); *Black v. Watts*, No. 04-17-00489-CV, 2018 Tex. App. LEXIS 6186, at *8, 2018 WL 3747746 (Tex. App.—San Antonio Aug. 8, 2018, pet. denied) (mem. op.) ("Pursuant to [former Texas] Rule 194.3, the party responding to the request for disclosure 'must serve a written response on the requesting party within 30 days after service of the request, except that: (a) a defendant served with a request before the defendant's answer is due need not respond until 50 days after service of

January 1, 2021, an expert disclosure is due, unless otherwise ordered by the court, ninety days before the end of the discovery period with regard to all experts testifying for a party seeking affirmative relief and sixty days before the end of that period with respect to all other testifying experts.[228]

For a case filed on or after January 1, 2021, the general deadlines for required disclosures—initial disclosures, testifying-expert disclosures, and pretrial disclosures—are set forth in Texas Rules 194.2(a), 195.2(a)–(b), and 194.4(b), respectively.[229] For additional information relating to deadlines for required disclosures, see Chapter 6, section 6-3:2.

The response to a disclosure request must be in writing[230] and preceded by the request.[231] The party's attorney or a pro se party must sign the response to a disclosure request and the required disclosures.[232] Unlike interrogatory answers, however, the responses need not be verified.[233] If the response to a disclosure request or the

---

the request, and (b) a response to a request under Rule 194.2(f) is governed by Rule 195.'" (quoting Former Tex. R. Civ. P. 194.3)).

228 Former Tex. R. Civ. P. 195.2 ("Unless otherwise ordered by the court, a party must designate experts—that is, furnish the information required by Texas Rule 194.2(f)—by the later of the following two dates: "30 days after the request is served, or—(a) with regard to all experts testifying for a party seeking affirmative relief, 90 days before the end of the discovery period; (b) with regard to all other experts, 60 days before the end of the discovery period."). See also Chapter 7, section 7-4:1 (discussing expert-disclosure requests and designating experts).

229 Tex. R. Civ. P. 194.2(a) ("A party must make the initial disclosures within 30 days after the filing of the first answer or general appearance unless a different time is set by the parties' agreement or court order. A party that is first served or otherwise joined after the filing of the first answer or general appearance must make the initial disclosures within 30 days after being served or joined, unless a different time is set by the parties' agreement or court order."); Tex. R. Civ. P. 194.3 ("In addition to the disclosures required by [Texas] Rule 194.2, a party must disclose to the other parties testifying expert information as provided by [Texas] Rule 195."); Tex. R. Civ. P. 195.2(a)–(b) ("Unless otherwise ordered by the court, a party must designate experts—that is, furnish information described in [Texas] Rule 195.5(a)—by the following dates: (a) with regard to all experts testifying for a party seeking affirmative relief, 90 days before the end of the discovery period; (b) with regard to all other experts, 60 days before the end of the discovery period."); Tex. R. Civ. P. 194.4(b) ("Unless the court orders otherwise, these [pretrial] disclosures must be made at least 30 days before trial.").

230 Former Tex. R. Civ. P. 194.3; *Vingcard A.S. v. Merrimac Hospitality Sys., Inc.*, 59 S.W.3d 847, 855 (Tex. App.—Fort Worth 2001, pet. denied) ("[Texas] Rule 194.3 requires the responding party to serve a written response on the requesting party."). Oral information is not a substitute for written answers. *See, e.g., Sharp v. Broadway Nat'l Bank*, 784 S.W.2d 699, 671 (Tex. 1990) (holding that oral identification of witnesses was insufficient).

231 Tex. R. Civ. P. 193.1 ("The responding party's answers, objections, and other responses must be preceded by the request to which they apply.").

232 Tex. R. Civ. P. 191.3(a) ("Every disclosure, discovery request, notice, response, and objection must be signed: (1) by an attorney, if the party is represented by an attorney, and must show the attorney's State Bar of Texas identification number, address, telephone number, and fax number, if any; or (2) by the party, if the party is not represented by an attorney, and must show the party's address, telephone number, and fax number, if any."); *see also* Tex. R. Civ. P. 194 cmt. to 2021 change ("As with other written discovery responses, required disclosures must be signed under [Texas] Rule 191.3. . . .").

233 *See* Tex. R. Civ. P. 191.3.

required disclosure is not properly signed, it "must be stricken unless it is signed promptly after the omission is called to the attention of the [requesting or responding] party[.]"[234] Disclosures can be used only against the disclosing party at trial or a hearing.[235]

In a case filed before January 1, 2021, copies of documents and other tangible things (i.e., a testifying expert's reviewed and relied upon documents, resume, and bibliography, relevant insurance policies and indemnity agreements, relevant portions of settlement agreements, the medical authorization or medical records and bills, statements of witnesses, and the documents the disclosing party may use to support its claims or defenses) must be served with the response unless they are voluminous, in which case the response must state a reasonable time and place for their production and the disclosing party must provide the requesting party a reasonable opportunity to inspect them.[236] In a case filed on or after January 1, 2021, responsive documents, electronically stored information, and tangible things ordinarily must be produced with the required disclosure to which they relate; however, if a party does not produce these items "with the response, the response must state

---

[234] Tex. R. Civ. P. 191.3(d).

[235] *Cf. Vodicka v. Lahr*, No. 03-10-00126-CV, 2012 Tex. App. LEXIS 4557, at *29 n.10, 2012 WL 2075713 (Tex. App.—Austin June 6, 2012, no pet.) (mem. op.) (holding that one party's interrogatory answer was not proper summary judgment evidence against another defendant); *Buck v. Blum*, 130 S.W.3d 285, 290 (Tex. App.—Houston [14th Dist.] 2004, no pet.) ("[A] party's answers to interrogatories can only be used against that party and not against another party, including a codefendant."). Nor can a party rely on its own disclosures as evidence. *Cf. Maxwell v. Willis*, 316 S.W.3d 680, 685–86 (Tex. App.—Eastland 2010, no pet.) (holding that the trial court erred in relying on the moving party's own interrogatory answer in granting the party summary judgment); *Zarzosa v. Flynn*, 266 S.W.3d 614, 619 (Tex. App.—El Paso 2008, no pet.) (holding that a party's interrogatory answers did not raise a fact issue in response to a summary judgment motion even though the opposing party put them into evidence); *Garcia v. Nat'l Eligibility Express, Inc.*, 4 S.W.3d 887, 890–91 (Tex. App.—Houston [1st Dist.] 1999, no pet.) (holding that a party's own interrogatory answers are incompetent summary judgment evidence). However, in a multi-party pre-January 1, 2021, case, any party may use the responding party's disclosures against the responding party, thereby obviating the need for redundant disclosure requests. *Cf. Ticor Title Ins. Co. v. Lacy*, 803 S.W.2d 265, 266 (Tex. 1991).

[236] Former Tex. R. Civ. P. 194.4 ("Copies of documents and other tangible items ordinarily must be served with the response. But if the responsive documents are voluminous, the response must state a reasonable time and place for the production of documents. The responding party must produce the documents at the time and place stated, unless otherwise agreed by the parties or ordered by the court, and must provide the requesting party a reasonable opportunity to inspect them."); *accord In re Grecon, Inc.*, 542 S.W.3d 774, 779 (Tex. App.—Houston [14th Dist.] 2018, orig. proceeding) ("Under [former Texas] Rule 194.4, the responding party 'ordinarily must' serve documents and other tangible items with the response, and 'must produce the documents at the time and place stated, unless otherwise agreed by the parties ordered by the court[.]'" (quoting Former Tex. R. Civ. P. 194.4)); *RDJRLW, Inc. v. Miller*, No. 02-17-00132-CV, 2017 Tex. App. LEXIS 5494, at *18, 2017 WL 2590568 (Tex. App.—Fort Worth June 15, 2017, no pet.) (mem. op.) ("Copies of [the testifying expert's] documents and other tangible items must be served with the response, but if the responsive documents are voluminous, the response must state a reasonable time and place for their production.").

a reasonable time and method for the production of these items."[237] In addition, as provided in Texas Rule 194.1(b), the party making the required disclosure "must produce the items at the time and in the method stated, unless otherwise agreed by the parties or ordered by the court, and must provide the requesting party a reasonable opportunity to inspect them."[238]

Perhaps most importantly, under Texas Rule 193.1, the disclosing party "must make a complete response, based on all information reasonably available to the disclosing party or its attorney at the time the response is made."[239] As discussed in detail in Chapter 5, sections 5-2 and 5-2:1, nothing in Texas Rule 193 or the other discovery rules explains when "information" is "reasonably available." As also pointed out in those sections, what information and material are reasonably available depends in large measure on the disclosing party's obligation of reasonable inquiry (i.e., how extensive a search the disclosing party must make to respond to the discovery request). This, of course, depends on the facts of each action. The principles regarding reasonable inquiry with respect to disclosure respects are discussed in Chapter 5, sections 5-2:1.[240]

Disclosures, like other discovery responses, are not filed with the trial court,[241] but must be served on all parties to the action.[242] In addition, the parties "must retain the original or exact copy of [the disclosures] during the pendency of the case and any related appellate proceedings begun within six months after judgment is signed, unless otherwise provided by the trial court."[243]

6-3:4.1 Privilege Objections and Assertions

"No objection or assertion of work product is permitted to a request [for disclosure under former Texas Rule 194]."[244] Likewise, "[n]o objection or assertion of work prod-

---

237 Tex. R. Civ. P. 194.1(b).

238 Tex. R. Civ. P. 194.1(b).

239 Tex. R. Civ. P. 193.1; *see also* Tex. R. Civ. P. 194 cmt. to 2021 change ("As with other written discovery responses, required disclosures must be . . . complete under [Texas] Rule 191.3. . . .").

240 The "reasonable inquiry" requirement for disclosures is the same as that for interrogatory answers and responses to requests for admission. See Chapter 5, section 5-2:1 (discussing the reasonable inquiry requirement for disclosures, interrogatory answers, and requests for admission).

241 Tex. R. Civ. P. 191.4(a) (providing that discovery requests and responses are not filed); *accord Nat'l Family Care Life Ins. v. Fletcher*, 57 S.W.3d 662, 667 n.6 (Tex. App.—Beaumont 2001, pet. denied) (noting that disclosures are not filed).

242 Tex. R. Civ. P. 191.5; *see also* Tex. R. Civ. P. 194 cmt. to 2021 change ("As with other written discovery responses, required disclosures must be . . . served under [Texas] Rule 191.5. . . .").

243 Tex. R. Civ. P. 191.4(d).

244 Former Tex. R. Civ. P. 194.5; *accord In re Grecon, Inc.*, 542 S.W.3d 774, 779 (Tex. App.—Houston [14th Dist.] 2018, orig. proceeding) ("No objection is permitted to a request for disclosure. . . . This method is intended to streamline the discovery process as to the matters covered by requests for disclosure."); *In re Fed. Corp.*, No. 13-16-00219-CV, 2016 Tex. App. LEXIS 11816, at *25–26, 2016 WL 4578411 (Tex. App.—Corpus Christi Nov. 1, 2016, orig. proceeding) (mem. op.) (holding that objections are not permitted to requests for disclosure); *In re DCP Midstream, L.P.*, No. 13-14-00502-CV, 2014 Tex. App. LEXIS 11092,

uct is permitted to a required disclosure" under amended Texas Rule 194.[245] However, "[i]n those extremely rare cases when information ordinarily discoverable should be protected, such as when revealing a person's residence might result in harm to the person, a party may move for protection. A party may assert any applicable privileges other than work product using the procedures of [Texas] Rule 193.3 applicable to other written discovery."[246] Thus, if the disclosure will require the disclosing party to reveal information protected by a privilege other than the work-product privilege, such as the attorney-client or Fifth Amendment privilege against self-incrimination, a privilege assertion is proper.[247]

---

at *18–19, 2014 WL 5019947 (Tex. App.—Corpus Christi Oct. 7, 2014, orig. proceeding) (mem. op.) ("The Texas Rules of Civil Procedure expressly prohibit objections to requests for disclosure. Instead, in 'those extremely rare cases when information ordinarily discoverable should be protected,' a party is allowed to file a motion for a protective order pursuant to [Texas] Rule 192.6." (quoting Tex. R. Civ. P. 194 cmt. 1 to 1999 change); *In re Univar USA, Inc.*, 311 S.W.3d 175, 180 (Tex. App.—Beaumont 2010, orig. proceeding) (same).

[245] Tex. R. Civ. P. 194.5; *accord In re Grecon, Inc.*, 542 S.W.3d 774, 779 (Tex. App.—Houston [14th Dist.] 2018, orig. proceeding) ("No objection is permitted to a request for disclosure. . . . This method is intended to streamline the discovery process as to the matters covered by requests for disclosure."); *In re Fed. Corp.*, No. 13-16-00219-CV, 2016 Tex. App. LEXIS 11816, at *25–26, 2016 WL 4578411 (Tex. App.—Corpus Christi Nov. 1, 2016, orig. proceeding) (mem. op.) (holding that objections are not permitted to requests for disclosure); *In re DCP Midstream, L.P.*, No. 13-14-00502-CV, 2014 Tex. App. LEXIS 11092, at *18–19, 2014 WL 5019947 (Tex. App.—Corpus Christi Oct. 7, 2014, orig. proceeding) (mem. op.) ("The Texas Rules of Civil Procedure expressly prohibit objections to requests for disclosure. Instead, in 'those extremely rare cases when information ordinarily discoverable should be protected,' a party is allowed to file a motion for a protective order pursuant to [Texas] Rule 192.6." (quoting Tex. R. Civ. P. 194 cmt. 1 to 1999 change); *In re Univar USA, Inc.*, 311 S.W.3d 175, 180 (Tex. App.—Beaumont 2010, orig. proceeding) (same).

[246] Tex. R. Civ. P. 194 cmt. 1 to 1999 change; *accord In re Grecon, Inc.*, 542 S.W.3d 774, 779 (Tex. App.—Houston [14th Dist.] 2018, orig. proceeding) ("In those 'extremely rare cases' when settlement agreements ordinarily covered by the mandatory disclosure rule ought to be withheld, the responding party may file a motion for protection."); *In re Fed. Corp.*, No. 13-16-00219-CV, 2016 Tex. App. LEXIS 11816, at *25–26 (Tex. App.—Corpus Christi Nov. 1, 2016, orig. proceeding) (mem. op.) ("Even though we acknowledge that requests for disclosure B-L would require responses that would arguably be overbroad at this stage of the case, the rules provide that the proper remedy is to seek a protective order pursuant to Texas Rule of Civil Procedure 192.6."); *In re DCP Midstream* 2014 Tex. App. LEXIS 11092, at *19 (Tex. App.—Corpus Christi Oct. 7, 2014, orig. proceeding) (mem. op.) (same); *In re Univar. USA, Inc.*, 311 S.W.3d 175, 180 (Tex. App.—Beaumont 2010, orig. proceeding) (same). See also Chapter 5, section 5-4 (discussing privilege assertions).

[247] *See, e.g., In re City of Dickinson, 568 S.W.3d 642, 647 (Tex. 2019)* (orig. proceeding) ("Two other provisions confirm that [former Texas] Rule 194.2 does not require disclosure of testifying-expert materials that are also attorney–client privileged. First, [former Texas] Rule 194.3(b) provides that a response to a request for disclosure must disclose the requested information under [former Texas] Rule 194.2(f) 'unless otherwise ordered by the court.' This provision indicates that the rules do not invariably require disclosure, allowing the trial court to limit or relieve any disclosure obligations under [former Texas] Rule 194.2. Second, the official comments to Rule 194 explain that a responding party may assert any privilege to a Rule 194.2 request except work product. . . ." (citations omitted) (quoting Former Tex. R. Civ. P. 194.3(b), 195.2(a))); *In re Does 1-10*, 242 S.W.3d 805, 821–23 (Tex. App.—Texarkana 2007, orig. proceeding) (suggesting that the First Amendment may apply to Texas Rule 194.2(a) and (e) disclosures of potential parties and persons having knowledge

6-3:4.2 Amending and Supplementing Disclosures

As with other written discovery responses, disclosures must be timely amended or supplemented.[248] However, as discussed in Chapter 6, sections 6-3:3.3 and 6-3:3.4, a contention or damages disclosure that has been amended is inadmissible and cannot be used for impeachment.[249]

6-3:4.3 Failing to Respond, Partial Responses, and Late Responses

A failure to respond fully or timely to a disclosure request, like a failure to make required disclosures, is "an abuse of the discovery process,"[250] and may result in sanctions under Texas Rule 215.3.[251] In addition, as discussed in Chapter 5, section 5-7, under Texas Rule 193.6, a failure to timely or fully respond to a disclosure request will prevent the disclosing party from introducing the undisclosed evidence or using the testimony of an undisclosed witness at trial unless it shows "good cause" for the failure to disclose or the failure "will not unfairly surprise or unfairly prejudice the other parties."[252] The exclusion of witnesses or other evidence under Texas Rule 193.6,

---

of relevant facts); *In re Hinterlong*, 109 S.W.3d 611, 624 (Tex. App.—Fort Worth 2003, orig. proceeding) ("While the identity of a potential party or witness's identity is generally discoverable, section 414.009 of the crime stoppers statute[, Tex. Gov't Code Ann. § 414.009,] specifically prohibits disclosure of the identity of a crime stoppers tipster. Consequently, the identity of a crime stoppers tipster is privileged and beyond the scope of relevant, nonprivileged discovery authorized by [Texas Rule] 192.3[(e)].") (footnote omitted).

248 Tex. R. Civ. P. 193.5; *see also* Tex. R. Civ. P. 194 cmt. to 2021 change ("As with other written discovery responses, required disclosures must be . . . timely amended or supplemented under [Texas] Rule 193.5."). See also Chapter 5, section 5-6 (discussing supplementing and amending written discovery responses).

249 Former Tex. R. Civ. P. 194.6; Tex. R. Civ. P. 194.6.

250 Tex. R. Civ. P. 194 cmt. 1 to 1999 change, *quoted with approval in In re City of Dickinson*, 568 S.W.3d 642, 647 (Tex. 2019) (orig. proceeding); *accord In re Grecon, Inc.*, 542 S.W.3d 779 (Tex. App.—Houston [14th Dist.] 2018, orig. proceeding) ("If a party does not move for protection or assert any applicable privileges by the thirty-day deadline for responding to the request, a failure to 'respond fully' to a request for disclosure is considered an 'abuse of the discovery process.'" (quoting Tex. R. Civ. P. 194 cmt. 1 to 1999 change)); *In re Morse*, 153 S.W.3d 578, 581 (Tex. App.—Amarillo 2004, orig. proceeding) ("Under [Texas] Rule 194.3, the responding party must serve a written response within 30 days, and according to comment 1, if a party does not move for protection or assert any applicable privileges, failure to 'respond fully to a request for disclosure would be an abuse of the discovery process.'").

251 Tex. R. Civ. P. 215.3 ("If the court finds a party is abusing the discovery process in seeking, making or resisting discovery . . . or [that a response or answer] is unreasonably frivolous or made for purposes of delay, then the court in which the action is pending may, after notice and hearing, impose any appropriate sanction authorized by paragraphs (1), (2), (3), (4), (5), and (8) of [Texas] Rule 215.2(b).").

252 Tex. R. Civ. P. 193.6; *accord Fort Brown Villas III Condo. Ass'n v. Gillenwater*, 285 S.W.3d 879, 881 (Tex. 2009) ("Under Texas Rule 193.6, discovery that is not timely disclosed and witnesses that are not timely identified are inadmissible as evidence."); *Saum v. Am. Express Nat'l Bank*, No. 02-19-00415-CV, 2021 Tex. App. LEXIS 2071, at *24–25, 2021 WL 1034146 (Tex. App.—Fort Worth Mar. 18, 2021, pet. denied) (mem. op.) ("The rules of civil procedure provide that a party may not 'offer the testimony of a witness (other than a named party) who was not timely identified' unless the court finds one of two things—(1) 'there was good cause for the failure to timely make, amend, or supplement the discovery

while harsh, is not a "death-penalty sanction."[253]

---

response; or (2) the failure to timely make, amend, or supplement the discovery response will not unfairly surprise or unfairly prejudice the other parties.'" (quoting Tex. R. Civ. P. 193.6(a))); *Hsu v. Conterra Servs., LLC*, 01-20-00182-CV, 2021 Tex. App. LEXIS 1813, at *8–9, 2021 WL 921672 (Tex. App.—Houston [1st Dist.] Mar. 11, 2021, no pet.) (mem. op.) (same). See also Chapter 5, section 5-7 (discussing the consequences under Texas Rule 193.6 for failing to timely respond, supplement or amend written discovery responses).

[253] *E.g*, *F 1 Constr., Inc. v. Banz*, No. 05-19-00717-CV, 2021 Tex. App. LEXIS 401, at *4, 2021 WL 194109 (Tex. App.—Dallas Jan. 20, 2021, no pet.) (mem. op.) (rejecting a party's characterization of the exclusion of evidence as a death-penalty sanction, reasoning in part that sanctions for discovery abuse under Texas Rule 215 are discretionary, whereas the Texas Rule 193.6 penalty is mandatory); *Sadeghian v. Wright*, No. 06-18-00062-CV, 2019 Tex. App. LEXIS 354, at *24 n.6, 2019 WL 255741 (Tex. App.—Texarkana Jan. 18, 2019, pet. denied) (mem. op.) ("'[A] trial court's imposition of the automatic . . . exclusion mandated by rule 193.6 is not a death-penalty sanction and is not reviewed as such.'" (quoting *Santana v. Santana*, No. 02-15-00140-CV, 2016 Tex. App. LEXIS 628, at *4–5 n.4, 2016 WL 278781 (Tex. App.—Fort Worth Jan. 21, 2016, no pet.) (mem. op.))); *Black v. Watts*, No. 04-17-00489-CV, 2018 Tex. App. LEXIS 6186, at *7, 2018 WL 3747746 (Tex. App.—San Antonio Aug. 8, 2018, pet. denied) (mem. op.) ("It is clear from the record that the exclusion of Black's expert witness under [Texas] Rule 193.6(a) was a matter of admissibility rather than a sanction for discovery abuse."); *Amudo v. Amudo*, No. 01-17-00318-CV, 2018 WL 3059729 (Tex. App.—Houston [1st Dist.] June 21, 2018, no pet.) (mem. op.) ("The exclusion of evidence under [Texas] Rule 193.6, as here, 'is a matter of admissibility rather than a sanction for discovery abuse.'" (quoting *In re J.A.M., Jr.*, No. 04-11-00165-CV, 2012 Tex. App. LEXIS 3630, at *17, 2012 WL 1648215 (Tex. App.—San Antonio May 9, 2012, pet. denied) (mem. op.))); *Ashmore v. JMS Constr., Inc.*, No. 05-15-00537-CV, 2016 Tex. App. LEXIS 13201, at *19–20, 2016 WL 7217256 (Tex. App.—Dallas Dec. 13, 2016, no pet.) (mem. op.) ("Ashmore characterizes the trial court's decision to strike the disclosure responses as an imposition of death penalty sanctions. Once again, Ashmore confuses a consequence for his failure to file timely disclosure responses with a discovery sanction. As stated above, the sixth (last) scheduling order had a March 7, 2013 deadline for serving amended or supplemented discovery responses. Ashmore had the burden to establish good cause for the untimely response or lack of unfair surprise or unfair prejudice. If Ashmore failed to meet this burden, then under [Texas R] ule 193.6, the trial court's decision to strike the responses should be affirmed.") (citation omitted); *Lee v. Wal-Mart*, No. 11-14-00078-CV, 2016 Tex. App. LEXIS 2805, at *6–7, 2016 WL 1072644 (Tex. App.—Eastland Mar. 17, 2016, no pet.) (mem. op.) (holding that striking the plaintiff's expert's summary judgment affidavit because the expert had not been timely disclosed was not a death-penalty sanction); *In re Staff Care, Inc.*, 422 S.W.3d 876, 882 (Tex. App.—Dallas 2014, orig. proceeding) ("Staff Care also argues that the striking of its amended disclosure responses constituted a 'death penalty' discovery sanction, and that therefore, the trial court was required to consider lesser sanctions before granting defendants' motion to strike. We disagree."). *But see In re G.N.H.*, No. 11-05-00405-CV, 2006 Tex. App. LEXIS 9492, at *7, 2006 WL 3094354 (Tex. App.—Eastland Nov. 2, 2006, no pet.) (mem. op.) ("To the extent that the trial court's ruling [under Texas Rule 193.6] constituted an exclusion of evidence, it was comparable to a death penalty or dismissal because it destroyed Rossler's opportunity for a decision on the merits of the bill of review.").

"Among the sanctions available under [Texas] Rule 215.2 are orders striking out pleadings or parts thereof, dismissing with or without prejudice the actions or proceedings or any part thereof, and rendering a judgment by default against the disobedient party. These sanctions, that adjudicate a claim and preclude presentation of the merits of the case, are often referred to as death penalty sanctions." *Shops at Legacy (Inland) Ltd. P'ship v. Fine Autographs & Memorabilia Retail Stores, Inc.*, 418 S.W.3d 229, 232 (Tex. App.—Dallas 2013,

6-3:4.4 Use of Disclosures

Disclosures, like interrogatory answers, can be used only against the disclosing party at trial, during a hearing, or in connection with a summary judgment motion.[254] Like interrogatories, to constitute evidence, they must be introduced into evidence at the trial or hearing, or be properly included in the summary judgment record.

---

pet. denied) (internal quotations omitted). Such sanctions are discussed in Chapter 14, section 14-3:2.

[254] *Cf. Monreal v. Dotsy,* No. 05-14-00682-CV, 2016 Tex. App. LEXIS 8834, at *7, 2016 WL 4276283 (Tex. App.—Dallas Aug. 15, 2016, no pet.) (mem. op.) ("Under [Texas R]ule 197.3, a party's answers to interrogatories can only be used against that party. They may not be used against another party, including a co-defendant.") (citation omitted); *Vodicka v. Lahr*, No. 03-10-00126-CV, 2012 Tex. App. LEXIS 4557, at *29 n.10, 2012 WL 2075713 (Tex. App.—Austin June 6, 2012, no pet.) (mem. op.) (holding that one party's interrogatory answer was not proper summary judgment evidence against another defendant); *Maxwell v. Willis*, 316 S.W.3d 680, 685–86 (Tex. App.—Eastland 2010, no pet.) (holding that the trial court erred in relying on the moving party's own interrogatory answer in granting the party summary judgment); *Zarzosa v. Flynn*, 266 S.W.3d 614, 619 (Tex. App.—El Paso 2008, no pet.) (holding that a party's interrogatory answers did not raise a fact issue in response to a summary judgment motion even though the opposing party put them into evidence); *Buck v. Blum*, 130 S.W.3d 285, 290 (Tex. App.—Houston [14th Dist.] 2004, no pet.) ("[A] party's answers to interrogatories can only be used against that party and not against another party, including a codefendant."). Nor can a party rely on its own disclosures as evidence. *Cf. Morgan v. Anthony*, 27 S.W.3d 928, 929 (Tex. 2000) ("Generally, a party cannot rely on its own answer to an interrogatory as summary judgment evidence."); *Gonzales v. Williams,* No. 11-17-00130-CV, 2019 Tex. App. LEXIS 5450, at *13, 2019 WL 2710046 (Tex. App.—Eastland June 28, 2019, no pet.) (mem. op.) (same); *Gilmore v. Rotan*, No. 11-16-00253-CV, 2018 Tex. App. LEXIS 7705, at *8, 2018 WL 4496232 (Tex. App.—Eastland Sept. 20, 2018, no pet.) (mem. op.) (same); *Dalehite v. Nauta*, 79 S.W.3d 243, 245 (Tex. App.—Houston [14th Dist.] 2002, pet. denied) (same); *Sympson v. Mor-Win Prods.*, 501 S.W.2d 362, 364 (Tex. App.—Fort Worth 1973, no writ) ("[S]elf-serving answers to an adversary's requests for admissions [sic] can be used only against him."); *Gilmer v. Macy's Retail Hldgs.*, No. 06-3020 (JBS), 2009 U.S. Dist. LEXIS 4937, at *31–32, 2009 WL 140518 (D.N.J. Jan. 20, 2009) ("More fundamentally, a litigant 'may not introduce statements from its own answers to interrogatories or requests for admission as evidence because such answers typically constitute hearsay when used in this manner." (quoting *Underberg v. U.S.*, 362 F. Supp. 2d 1278, 1283 (D.N.M. 2005).

CHAPTER 7

Expert Discovery—Texas Rule 195

7-1 Text of Texas Rule 195

RULE 195. DISCOVERY REGARDING TESTIFYING EXPERT WITNESSES

195.1. Permissible Discovery Tools

A party may obtain information concerning testifying expert witnesses only through disclosure under this rule and through depositions and reports as permitted by this rule.

195.2. Schedule for Designating Experts

Unless otherwise ordered by the court, a party must designate experts—that is, furnish information described in Rule 195.5(a)—by the following dates:

(a) with regard to all experts testifying for a party seeking affirmative relief, 90 days before the end of the discovery period;

(b) with regard to all other experts, 60 days before the end of the discovery period.

195.3. Scheduling Depositions

(a) **Experts for Party Seeking Affirmative Relief.** A party seeking affirmative relief must make an expert retained by, employed by, or otherwise in the control of the party available for deposition as follows:

(1) **If No Report Furnished.** If a report of the expert's factual observations, tests, supporting data, calculations, photographs, and opinions is not produced when the expert is designated, then the party must make the expert available for deposition reasonably promptly after the expert is designated. If the deposition cannot—due to the actions of the tendering party—reasonably be concluded more than 15 days before the deadline for designating other experts, that deadline must be extended for other experts testifying on the same subject.

(2) **If Report Furnished.** If a report of the expert's factual observations, tests, supporting data, calculations, photographs, and opinions is produced when the expert is designated, then the party need not make the expert available for deposition until reasonably promptly after all other experts have been designated.

(b) **Other Experts.** A party not seeking affirmative relief must make an expert retained by, employed by, or otherwise in the control of the party available for deposition reasonably promptly after the expert is designated and the experts testifying on the same subject for the party seeking affirmative relief have been deposed.

195.4. Oral Deposition

In addition to the information disclosed under Rule 195.5(a), a party may obtain discovery concerning the subject matter on which the expert is expected to testify, the expert's mental impressions and opinions, the facts known to the expert (regardless of when the factual information was acquired) that relate to or form the basis of the testifying expert's mental impressions and opinions, and other discoverable matters, including documents not produced in disclosure, only by oral deposition of the expert and by a report prepared by the expert under this rule.

195.5. Expert Disclosures and Reports

(a) **Disclosures.** Without awaiting a discovery request, a party must provide the following for any testifying expert:

(1) the expert's name, address, and telephone number;

(2) the subject matter on which the expert will testify;

(3) the general substance of the expert's mental impressions and opinions and a brief summary of the basis for them, or if the expert is not retained by, employed by, or otherwise subject to the control of the responding party, documents reflecting such information;

(4) if the expert is retained by, employed by, or otherwise subject to the control of the responding party:

(A) all documents, tangible things, reports, models, or data compilations that have been provided to, reviewed by, or prepared by or for the expert in anticipation of the expert's testimony;

(B) the expert's current resume and bibliography;

(C) the expert's qualifications, including a list of all publications authored in the previous 10 years;

(D) except when the expert is the responding party's attorney and is testifying to attorney fees, a list of all other cases in which, during the previous four years, the expert testified as an expert at trial or by deposition; and

(E) a statement of the compensation to be paid for the expert's study and testimony in the case.

(b) **Expert Reports.** If the discoverable factual observations, tests, supporting data, calculations, photographs, or opinions of an expert have not been recorded and reduced to tangible form, the court may order these matters reduced to tangible form and produced in addition to the deposition.

(c) **Expert Communications Protected.** Communications between the party's attorney and any testifying expert witness in the case are protected from discovery, regardless of the form of the communications, except to the extent that the communications:

(1) relate to compensation for the expert's study or testimony;

(2) identify facts or data that the party's attorney provided and that the expert considered in forming the opinions to be expressed; or

(3) identify assumptions that the party's attorney provided and that the expert relied on in forming the opinions to be expressed.

(d) **Draft Expert Reports and Disclosures Protected.** A draft expert report or draft disclosure required under this rule is protected from discovery, regardless of the form in which the draft is recorded.

195.6. Amendment and Supplementation

A party's duty to amend and supplement written discovery regarding a testifying expert is governed by Rule 193.5. If an expert witness is retained by, employed by, or otherwise under the control of a party, that party must also amend or supplement any deposition testimony or written report by the expert, but only with regard to the expert's mental impressions or opinions and the basis for them.

195.7. Cost of Expert Witnesses

When a party takes the oral deposition of an expert witness retained by the opposing party, all reasonable fees charged by the expert for time spent in preparing for, giving, reviewing, and correcting the deposition must be paid by the party that retained the expert.

Notes and Comments

Comment to 2021 change:

Rule 195 is amended to reflect changes to Rule 194. Amended Rule 195.5(a) lists the disclosures for any testifying expert, which are now required without awaiting a discovery request, that were formerly listed in Rule 194(f). Amended Rule 195.5(a) also includes three new disclosures based on Federal Rule of Civil Procedure 26(a)(2)(B). New Rules 195.5(b) and (c) [sic] are based on Federal Rules of Civil Procedure 26(b)(4)(B) and (C) and are added to clarify protections available.

Comments to 1999 change:

1. This rule does not limit the permissible methods of discovery concerning consulting experts whose mental impressions or opinions have been reviewed by a testifying expert. *See* Rule 192.3(e). Information concerning purely consulting experts, of course, is not discoverable.

2. This rule and Rule 194 do not address depositions of testifying experts who are not retained by, employed by, or otherwise subject to the control of the responding party, nor the production of the materials identified in Rule 192.3(e)(5) and (6) relating to such experts. Parties may obtain this discovery, however, through Rules 176 and 205.

3. In scheduling the designations and depositions of expert witnesses, the rule attempts to minimize unfair surprise and undue expense. A party seeking affirmative relief must either produce an expert's report or tender the expert for deposition before an opposing party is required to designate experts. A party who does not wish to incur the expense of a report may simply tender the expert for deposition, but a party who wishes an expert to have the benefit of an opposing party's expert's opinions before being deposed may trigger designation by providing a report. Rule 191.1 permits a trial court, for good cause, to modify the order or deadlines for designating and deposing experts and the allocation of fees and expenses.

7-1:1 2021 Amendments to the Texas Rules of Civil Procedure

The 2021 amendments add required disclosures to Texas Rule 195.5(a) and protect certain communications and draft expert reports from discovery in Texas Rules 195.5(c) and (d), respectively. The disclosures set forth in Texas Rule 195.5(a)(1)–(a)(4)(B) are the same as the disclosures set forth in former Texas Rule 194.2(f). The new disclosures in Texas Rules 195.5(a)(4)(C)–(E) are modeled after Federal Rule 26(a)(2)(B)(iv)–(vi), and the protections from discovery in Texas Rules 195.5(c)–(d) are modeled after Federal Rules 26(b)(4)(B)–(C). Texas Rules 195.1, 195.2, and 195.4 have been modified slightly to reflect the fact that expert disclosures are required by Texas Rules 194.3 and 195.5(a).

7-2 Expert Discovery in General

Texas Rule 195 is the principal rule governing discovery about expert witnesses. The other discovery rules specifically relating to discovery about them are Texas Rules 192.3(e), regarding discovery's scope, 192.7(c), defining "testifying expert," 192.7(d), defining "consulting expert," and 194.3, providing that "a party must disclose to the other parties testifying expert information as provided by [Texas] Rule 195."

7-3 Types of Experts

For litigation purposes, an "expert" is a person, who through education, training, or experience has developed skill or knowledge in a subject sufficient to allow the person to render an opinion that will assist the factfinder.[1] The Texas discovery rules recognize two general types of experts: "testifying experts" and "consulting experts."[2]

"A *testifying expert* is an expert who may be called to testify as an expert witness at trial."[3] There are two types of testifying experts: (1) testifying experts who are retained by, employed by, or otherwise in the control of the party (retained-testifying experts); and (2) testifying experts who are not retained by, employed by, or otherwise in the control of the party (non-retained-testifying experts).[4] The experts in the latter category are typically treating or emergency-room physicians and nurses, police officers, firemen, and other first responders.

---

[1] Tex. R. Evid. 702 ("A witness who is qualified as an expert by knowledge, skill, experience, training, or education may testify in the form of an opinion or otherwise if the expert's scientific, technical, or other specialized knowledge will help the trier of fact to understand the evidence or to determine a fact in issue."); *see In re Nat'l Lloyds Ins. Co.*, 532 S.W.3d 794, 815 (Tex. 2017) (orig. proceeding) ("'The line between who is a [Texas] Rule [of Evidence] 702 expert witness and who is a [Texas] Rule [of Evidence] 701 [fact] witness is not always bright.' But when a witness is properly disclosed and designated as an expert and the main substance of the witness's testimony is based on specialized knowledge, skill, experience, training, and education, 'the testimony will generally be expert testimony within the scope of Rule 702.'" (footnotes omitted) (quoting *Reid Rd. Mun. Util. Dist. No. 2 v. Speedy Stop Food Stores, Ltd.*, 337 S.W.3d 846, 850–52 (Tex. 2011))).

[2] Tex. R. Civ. P. 192.7(c)–(d).

[3] Tex. R. Civ. P. 192.7(c).

[4] *See* Tex. R. Civ. P. 195.5(a) (setting forth the disclosure requirements for the two types of testifying experts).

"A *consulting expert* is an expert who has been consulted, retained, or specifically employed by a party in anticipation of litigation or in preparation for trial, but who is not a testifying expert."[5] There are two types of consulting experts: (1) consulting experts whose mental impressions and opinions have not been reviewed by a testifying expert (a consulting-only expert); and (2) those whose mental impressions and opinions have been reviewed by a testifying expert.[6]

Often the identity of a person who otherwise would qualify as an expert because of the person's knowledge, skill, experience, training, or education must be disclosed as person having knowledge of relevant facts and cannot be shielded from discovery as a consulting-only expert. This is because to be a consulting-only expert, the person must have been consulted, retained, or specially employed *solely* in anticipation of litigation or in preparation for trial.[7] For example, an expert who was consulted before litigation was anticipated is not a consulting-only expert and the expert's identity, impressions, and opinions are discoverable if they are relevant to the action.[8]

Additionally, a person who otherwise qualifies as an expert, but who acquired relevant information as "an active participant in the events material to the lawsuit" is not a consulting-only expert.[9] For example, a person who gains factual information due to the person's involvement in the incident or transaction underlying the action cannot qualify as consulting-only expert—even if the person acquired some information through consulting—because the consultation is not the sole basis of the person's information. Accordingly, a party's employee whose duties involve the action's subject matter *never* qualifies as a consulting-only expert because the employee was not employed as an expert solely in anticipation of litigation or in preparation for trial.[10] However, an employee who lacks personal knowledge of the facts relevant to the action and who is assigned to assist the employer or its attorneys in connection with the action can qualify as a consulting-only expert.[11]

Texas Rule 195.5 *only* requires disclosures about *testifying* experts.[12] The rule replaces and eliminates interrogatories concerning such experts. The identity and mental impressions of a consulting-only expert are not discoverable,[13] whereas the

---

[5] Tex. R. Civ. P. 192.7(d).

[6] Consulting-only experts also can be fact witnesses if they have knowledge of relevant facts that "was obtained first-hand or . . . was not obtained in preparation for trial or in anticipation of litigation." Tex. R. Civ. P. 192.3(c). Such experts must be disclosed as persons with knowledge of relevant facts under Texas 194.2(b)(5) and can be deposed about their knowledge that is first-hand or was not obtained in their role as a consulting expert. See Chapter 6, section 6-3:3.5a for a discussion of when a consulting-only expert is a fact witness.

[7] Tex. R. Civ. P. 192.7(c).

[8] *Lindsey v. O'Neill*, 689 S.W.2d 400, 402 (Tex. 1985).

[9] *Axelson, Inc. v. McIlhany*, 798 S.W.2d 550, 554 (Tex. 1990). See also Chapter 6, section 6-3:3.5a.

[10] *Axelson, Inc. v. McIlhany*, 798 S.W.2d 550, 554 (Tex. 1990).

[11] *Axelson, Inc. v. McIlhany*, 798 S.W.2d 550, 554 (Tex. 1990).

[12] Tex. R. Civ. P. 195.5; *see also* Tex. R. Civ. P. 194.3 ("In addition to the disclosures required by [Texas] Rule 194.2, a party must disclose to the other parties *testifying* expert information as provided by [Texas] Rule 195.") (emphasis added).

[13] Tex. R. Civ. P. 192.3(e) ("The identity, mental impressions, and opinions of a consulting expert whose mental impressions and opinions have not been reviewed by a testifying expert are not discoverable."); *Aguilar v. Trujillo*, 162 S.W.2d 839, 847 n.5 (Tex. App.—El Paso 2005, pet. denied) (same).

identity, mental impressions, and opinions of a consulting expert whose mental impressions and opinions have been reviewed by a testifying expert are discoverable.[14] The discovery methods to obtain such information and documents depend on whether the expert is a retained-testifying expert, a non-retained-testifying expert, or a consulting expert whose mental impressions or opinions have been reviewed by an expert.[15] Information about consulting-only experts is not discoverable.[16]

7-4 Discovery Concerning Testifying Experts

For cases filed on or after January 1, 2021, Texas Rules 195.1, 195.4, and 195.5 identify the only discovery methods that can be used to obtain information from testifying experts: (1) the required disclosures under Texas Rule 195.5(a);[17] (2) oral depositions;[18]

---

[14] Tex. R. Civ. P. 192.3(e) ("A party may discover the following information . . . regarding a consulting expert whose mental impressions or opinions have been reviewed by a testifying expert[.]"). The same information that is discoverable from testifying experts is discoverable from non-consulting-only experts. Tex. R. Civ. P. 192.3(e).

[15] See Chapter 7, section 7-4 (discussing discovery concerning testifying experts) and Chapter 7, section 7-5 (discussing discovery concerning consulting experts whose mental impressions and opinions have been reviewed by a testifying expert).

[16] Tex. R. Civ. P. 192.3(e) ("The identity, mental impressions, and opinions of a consulting expert whose mental impressions and opinions have not been reviewed by a testifying expert are not discoverable."); Tex. R. Civ. P. 195 cmt. 1 to 1999 change ("Information concerning purely consulting experts, of course, is not discoverable."); ***In re City of Georgetown***, 53 S.W.3d 328, 334 (Tex. 2001) ("The rules of civil procedure delineate a category for consulting experts whose mental impressions and opinions have not been reviewed by a testifying expert. The rules expressly provide that a party is not required to disclose the identity, mental impressions, and opinions of consulting experts.") (citation omitted); ***Paxton v. City of Dall.***, No. 06-18-00095-CV, 2019 Tex. App. LEXIS 3868, at *20, 2019 WL 2119644 (Tex. App.—Texarkana May 15, 2019, pet. denied) (mem. op.) (same); ***In re Alexander***, No. 09-12-00236-CV, 2013 Tex. App. LEXIS 6529, at *3–4, 2013 WL 2444184 (Tex. App.—Beaumont May 30, 2013, pet. denied) (mem. op.) (same); ***Rodriguez-Aguero v. Tex. Med. Bd.***, No. 03-09-00262-CV, 2010 Tex. App. LEXIS 3220, at *19, 2010 WL 1730023 (Tex. App.—Austin Apr. 30, 2010, no pet.) (mem. op.) (same); ***see Spectrum Healthcare Res., Inc. v. McDaniel***, 306 S.W.3d 249, 253–54 (Tex. 2010) ("Under the Texas Rules of Civil Procedure, a retained testifying expert's report is always discoverable, but a retained consulting-only expert's report generally is not.").

[17] For case filed before January 1, 2021, disclosures relating to testifying experts are available upon request pursuant to former Texas Rule 194.2(f).

[18] Texas Rule 195.4 provides that, "[i]n addition to the information disclosed under [Texas] Rule 195.5(a), a party may obtain discovery concerning the subject matter on which the expert is expected to testify, the expert's mental impressions and opinions, the facts known to the expert . . . that relate to or form the basis of the testifying expert's mental impressions and opinions, and other discoverable matters, including documents not produced in disclosure, ***only by oral deposition of the expert***[.]" Tex. R. Civ. P. 195.4 (emphasis added). However, Comment 2 to the 1999 change to Texas Rule 195 provides, in relevant part that "[t]his rule and [former Texas] Rule 194 do not address depositions of testifying experts who are not retained by, employed by, or otherwise subject to the control of the responding party[.]" Tex. R. Civ. P. 195 cmt. 2 to 1999 change. Thus, although retained-testifying experts only can be deposed by oral deposition, non-retained-testifying experts can be deposed either by oral deposition or upon written question.

and (3) expert reports.[19] Because these methods are not mutually exclusive, a party can use all of them to obtain discovery about retained-testifying experts. Interrogatories, production requests, requests for admission, and depositions upon written questions, however, *cannot* be used to obtain discovery about retained-testifying experts.[20]

The discovery methods that can be used to obtain discovery from non-retained-testifying experts are the same as those that can be used to obtain discovery from retained-testifying experts[21] with two exceptions—non-retained-testifying experts can also be deposed upon written questions[22] and can be served with a production request under Texas Rules 176 and 205, including for information unobtainable via Texas Rule 195.5(a)(4).[23]

7-4:1 Designating Testifying Experts

Texas Rule 195.2 sets forth a schedule for testifying-expert designations, which can be modified by court order or by the parties' agreement.[24] As amended effective January 1, 2021, it provides:

> [A] party must designate experts—that is, furnish information described in [Texas] Rule 195.5(a)—by the following dates:
>
> (a) with regard to all experts testifying for a party seeking affirmative relief, 90 days before the end of the discovery period;

---

[19] Tex. R. Civ. P. 195.1 ("A party may obtain information concerning testifying expert witnesses only through disclosure under this rule and through depositions and reports as permitted by this rule."); ***accord In re Nat'l Lloyds Ins. Co.,*** 532 S.W.3d 794, 814 (Tex. 2017) (orig. proceeding) ("[Texas] Rule 195 addresses the methods for obtaining such information, limiting testifying-expert discovery to that acquired through disclosures, expert reports, and oral depositions of expert witnesses." (footnote omitted) (quoting ***In re Ford Motor Co.,*** 427 S.W.3d 396, 397 (Tex. 2014) (orig. proceeding))).

[20] ***In re Nat'l Lloyds Ins. Co.,*** 532 S.W.3d 794, 814 (Tex. 2017) (orig. proceeding) (pointing out that Texas Rule 195 "does not provide for interrogatories or requests for production" with respect to retained-testifying experts); ***In re Segner,*** 441 S.W.3d 409, 412–13 (Tex. App.—Dallas 2013, orig. proceeding) (noting that a party cannot serve a production request in conjunction with a deposition notice on a retained-testifying expert).

[21] Tex. R. Civ. P. 195.1, 195.4, 195.5.

[22] See discussion in note 18.

[23] Tex. R. Civ. P. 195 cmt. 2 to 1999 change ("This rule and [former Texas] Rule 194 do not address . . . the production of the materials identified in [Texas] Rule 192.3(e)(5) and (6) relating to [non-retained-testifying] experts. Parties may obtain this discovery, however, through [Texas] Rules 176 and 205.").

[24] ***See*** Tex. R. Civ. P. 191.1 ("Except where specifically prohibited, the procedures and limitations set forth in the rules pertaining to discovery may be modified in any suit by the agreement of the parties or by court order for good cause. An agreement of the parties is enforceable if it complies with [Texas] Rule 11 or, as it affects an oral deposition, if it is made a part of the record of the deposition."); Tex. R. Civ. P. 195 cmt. 3 to 1999 change (Texas "Rule 191.1 permits a trial court, for good cause, to modify the order or deadlines for designating and deposing experts.").

(b) with regard to all other experts, 60 days before the end of the discovery period.[25]

The designation deadline for "experts testifying for a party seeking affirmative relief" (e.g., a plaintiff, counter-plaintiff, cross-plaintiff, or third-party plaintiff) applies only to experts testifying specifically in support of a claim for relief, and not to all experts that a party seeking affirmative relief may use. Thus, for example, in an action in which the defendant has filed a counterclaim, both the plaintiff and the defendant must designate experts on their respective claims and counterclaims within the 90-day period and can designate their experts on defensive issues within the 60-day period.

Although Texas Rule 195.2 does not specifically deal with "dual-purpose" experts (i.e., experts who will testify about both affirmative claims for relief and defensive issues), its language suggests that both deadlines apply to such experts depending on their opinions. In other words, the expert's opinions on affirmative claims and defensive issues would be due within the 90-day deadline and 60-day deadline, respectively.

Texas Rule 195.2 does not provide for the designation of rebuttal experts. Consequently, if the parties anticipate using them, the better and most prudent practice is to provide a deadline for their designation in a scheduling or other order or a Texas Rule 11 agreement.

An interesting question is: What happens when the party who designated an expert later decides the expert's opinions and testimony could do it more harm than good, or otherwise wants to de-designate the expert?[26] This so-called "Red Rover" issue[27] arises often in civil litigation.

Texas Law permits a testifying expert to be "de-designated" as long as it is not part of "a bargain between adversaries to suppress testimony" or for some other improper purpose.

---

[25] Tex. R. Civ. P. 195.2; *see W. Inland Energy, Inc. v. Rockwater Energy Sols., Inc.*, No. 11-19-00219-CV, 2021 Tex. App. LEXIS 4392, at *13, 2021 WL 2277810 (Tex. App.—Eastland June 4, 2021, pet. denied) (mem. op.) ("Unless otherwise ordered by the court, a party seeking affirmative relief must designate all testifying experts no later than ninety days before the end of the applicable discovery period."); *Plunkett v. Christus St. Michael Health Sys.*, No. 06-16-00010-CV, 2016 Tex. App. LEXIS 13427, at *9–10, 2016 WL 7335872 (Tex. App.—Texarkana Dec. 19, 2016, pet. denied) (mem. op.) ("The sponsor of an expert's testimony must timely disclose 'the general substance of the expert's mental impressions and opinions and a brief summary of the basis for them. . . .' Unless the court orders otherwise, disclosure pursuant to this Rule must generally be accomplished by the later of thirty days after the service of the disclosure request or sixty days before the discovery period ends." (quoting [former] Tex. R. Civ. P. 194.2(f)(3))).

[26] A party may also want to de-designate a testifying expert is because the party has provided privileged information to the expert that it does not want produced. Such a de-designation is permissible as discussed in Chapter 7, section 7-4:5.

[27] *Pope v. State,* 207 S.W.3d 352, 361 n. 29 (Tex. Crim. App. 2006) (citing Stephen D. Easton, *"Red Rover, Red Rover, Send That Expert Right Over": Clearing the Way for Parties to Introduce the Testimony of Their Opponents' Expert Witnesses*, 55 SMU L. Rev. 1427, 1439 (2002)). "The term 'Red Rover' refers to the children's playground game in which one team 'calls over' a member of the opposing team who must try to break through the hand-holding members of the calling team. If that person cannot break through the human chain, he becomes a member of the calling team." *Pope v. State*, 207 S.W.3d 352, 361 n.29 (Tex. Crim. App. 2006) (citing Stephen D. Easton, *"Red Rover, Red Rover, Send That Expert Right Over": Clearing the Way for Parties to Introduce the Testimony of Their Opponents' Expert Witnesses*, 55 SMU L. Rev. 1427, 1437 n.49 (2002)).

> The policy underlying the discovery rules is to seek the truth so that disputes may be decided by facts that are revealed rather than concealed. . . . The protection afforded by the consulting expert privilege is intended to be only a shield to prevent a litigant from taking undue advantage of his adversary's industry and effort, not a sword to be used to thwart justice or to defeat the salutary objects of discovery.[28]

7-4:2 Depositions of Testifying Experts

Depositions are one of the discovery methods that can be used with respect to testifying experts.[29] As discussed above, retained-testifying experts can be deposed only by an oral deposition, whereas a non-retained testifying expert can be deposed either by an oral deposition or a deposition upon written question.[30] In addition, the deposition notice for a non-retained-testifying expert, unlike that for a retained testifying expert, also can contain production requests.[31]

A testifying expert's deposition can cover the matters in Texas Rule 192.3(e).[32] Absent agreement or contrary court order, Texas Rule 199.5(c)'s six-hour time limit applies to expert depositions.[33]

---

[28] *In re Christus Spohn Hosp. Kleberg*, No. 13-07-405-CV, 2007 Tex. App. LEXIS 7801, at *6–7, 2007 WL 2812149 (Tex. App.—Corpus Christi Sept. 26, 2007, orig. proceeding) (mem. op.) (citations omitted) (quoting *Castellanos v. Littlejohn*, 945 S.W.2d 236, 240 (Tex. App.—San Antonio 1997, orig. proceeding))); *accord In re Robins & Morton Grp.*, No. 04-16-0045-CV, 2016 Tex. App. LEXIS 4649, at *9, 2016 WL 2584526 (Tex. App.—San Antonio May 4, 2016, orig. proceeding) (mem. op.) ("Texas law permits a testifying expert to be 'de-designated' so long as it is not part of 'a bargain between adversaries to suppress testimony' or for some other improper purpose." (quoting *Castellanos v. Littlejohn*, 945 S.W.2d 236 240(Tex. App.—San Antonio 1997, orig. proceeding))); *In re Doctors' Hosp. of Laredo, Ltd.*, 2 S.W.3d 504, 506 (Tex. App.—San Antonio 1999, orig. proceeding) (same); *see Tom L. Scott, Inc. v. McIlhany*, 798 S.W.2d 556, 560 (Tex. 1990) (holding, in a multi-plaintiff action, that the settling plaintiffs' assignment of their experts to the defendants and their designation as the defendants' consulting experts as a settlement condition was impermissible because it was an improper bargain between adversaries to suppress evidence); *Harnischfeger Corp. v. Stone*, 814 S.W.2d 263, 265 (Tex. App.—Houston [14th Dist.] 1991, orig. proceeding) (holding that the defendant could not designate the same expert as a testifying expert in one case and as a consulting-only expert in a companion case).

[29] *See* Tex. R. Civ. P. 195.1 & cmt. 1 to 1999 change; Tex. R. Civ. P. 195.4.

[30] See discussion in note 18.

[31] Tex. R. Civ. P. 195 cmt. 2 to 1999 change ("This rule and [former Texas] Rule 194 do not address . . . the production of the materials identified in [Texas] Rule 192.3(e)(5) and (6) relating to [non-retained-testifying] experts. Parties may obtain this discovery, however, through [Texas] Rules 176 and 205.").

[32] *See* Tex. R. Civ. P. 195.4 (noting that, in an oral deposition, "a party may obtain discovery concerning the subject matter on which the expert is expected to testify, the expert's mental impressions and opinions, the facts known to the expert (regardless of when the factual information was acquired) that relate to or form the basis of the testifying expert's mental impressions and opinions, and other discoverable matters, including documents not produced in disclosure, only by oral deposition of the expert and by a report prepared by the expert under this rule").

[33] Tex. R. Civ. P. 199.5(c) ("No side may examine or cross-examine an individual witness for more than six hours.").

Texas Rule 195.3 sets out the scheduling sequence for depositions of retained-testifying experts.[34] It distinguishes between depositions of experts of a party seeking affirmative relief and those of a party who is not seeking affirmative relief.[35] For a party seeking affirmative relief (e.g., a plaintiff, counter-plaintiff, cross-plaintiff, or third-party plaintiff),[36] Texas Rule 195.3 has different schedules depending on whether an expert report has been produced.

The Rule generally requires that a retained-testifying expert of a party seeking affirmative relief, who has not produced an expert report, be produced for deposition "reasonably promptly after the expert is designated."[37] "Designation" occurs when the

---

[34] Texas Rule 195.3 provides:

(a) **Experts for party seeking affirmative relief.** A party seeking affirmative relief must make an expert retained by, employed by, or otherwise in the control of the party available for deposition as follows:

(1) **If no report furnished.** If a report of the expert's factual observations, tests, supporting data, calculations, photographs, and opinions is not produced when the expert is designated, then the party must make the expert available for deposition reasonably promptly after the expert is designated. If the deposition cannot—due to the actions of the tendering party—reasonably be concluded more than 15 days before the deadline for designating other experts, that deadline must be extended for other experts testifying on the same subject.

(2) **If report furnished.** If a report of the expert's factual observations, tests, supporting data, calculations, photographs, and opinions is produced when the expert is designated, then the party need not make the expert available for deposition until reasonably promptly after all other experts have been designated.

(b) **Other experts.** A party not seeking affirmative relief must make an expert retained by, employed by, or otherwise in the control of the party available for deposition reasonably promptly after the expert is designated and the experts testifying on the same subject for the party seeking affirmative relief have been deposed.

Tex. R. Civ. P. 195.3.

[35] Tex. R. Civ. P. 195.3(a)–(b).

[36] A party can be both a "party seeking affirmative relief" and another party (e.g., a plaintiff and counter-defendant, a defendant and counter-plaintiff, a defendant and third-party plaintiff, or a defendant and cross-plaintiff).

[37] Tex. R. Civ. P. 195.3(a)(1); ***Duerr v. Brown***, 262 S.W.3d 63, 75 (Tex. App.—Houston [14th Dist.] 2008, no pet.) ("Because Lyon provided no report, Duerr was obligated to make Lyon available for deposition 'reasonably promptly' after designating him." (quoting Tex. R. Civ. P. 195.3); ***Facundo v. Solis***, No. 03-05-00059-CV, 2006 Tex. App. LEXIS 318, at *6, 2006 WL 66467 (Tex. App.—Austin Jan. 12, 2006, no pet.) (mem. op.) (Texas "Rule 195.3(a)(2), titled 'Scheduling Depositions,' states that if a party seeking affirmative relief has retained and designated an expert who has not yet furnished a report, the expert must be made available for deposition reasonably promptly after he is designated."); ***Vaughn v. Ford Motor Co.***, 91 S.W.3d 387, 389 (Tex. App.—Eastland 2002, pet. denied) (Texas "[r]ule 195.3 mandates that, where no expert report is furnished at the time of designation, a party seeking affirmative relief 'must make the expert available for deposition reasonably promptly after the expert is designated.' The comment to [Texas] Rule 195 provides that a party seeking affirmative relief 'must either produce an expert's report or tender the expert for deposition before an opposing party is required to designate experts.'" (footnote omitted) (quoting Tex. R. Civ. P. 195.3(a)(1) & cmt. 3 to 1999 change)).

information required by the expert-disclosure rule, Texas Rule 195.5(a), is provided.[38] If, however, the party provides an expert report, which must include the expert's "factual observations, tests, supporting data, calculations, photographs, and opinions,"[39] the expert need not be produced "for deposition until reasonably promptly after all other experts have been designated."[40] Thus, a party needs to balance an expert report's cost against the value of postponing the expert's deposition until after the other parties designate their experts.[41]

If the retained-testifying expert's deposition, "due to the actions of the tendering party," cannot "reasonably be concluded more than 15 days before the deadline for designating other retained-testifying experts, that deadline must be extended[, under Texas Rule 195.3(a)(1),] for other experts testifying on the same subject."[42] Although not expressly required by the Rule, a party needing such an extension of time, as a matter of prudence, should move for one before the deadline that would otherwise have applied to its expert designations.

Under Texas Rule 195.3(b), a party not seeking affirmative relief need not make its retained-testifying experts available for deposition until "reasonably promptly" after (1) it has designated such experts, and (2) "the experts testifying on the same subject for the party seeking affirmative relief have been deposed."[43] Literally applied, this limitation appears to allow a party to avoid producing its retained-testifying expert for deposition by failing to depose the retained-testifying experts of the party seeking affirmative relief. But any argument for such a construction should be rejected as

---

38 Tex. R. Civ. P. 195.2 ("Unless otherwise ordered by the court, a party must designate experts—that is, furnish information described in [Texas] Rule 195.5(a)."). For cases filed before January 1, 2021, former Texas Rule 195.2 still applies and provides that designation occurs when information requested under former Texas Rule 194.2(f) is furnished. *See* Former Tex. R. Civ. P. 195.2 ("[A] party must designate experts—that is, furnish information requested under [former Texas] Rule 194.2(f)—by the later of the following two dates: 30 days after the request is served, or—(a) with regard to all experts testifying for a party seeking affirmative relief, 90 days before the end of the discovery period; (b) with regard to all other experts, 60 days before the end of the discovery period.").

39 Tex. R. Civ. P. 195.3(a)(1); *accord* Tex. R. Civ. P. 195.5(b).

40 Tex. R. Civ. P. 195.3(a)(2); ***King v. Cirillo***, 233 S.W.3d 437, 441 (Tex. App.—Dallas 2007, pet. denied) ("Under [Texas R]ule 195, the parties have the option of providing at the time of the designation of the expert under [former Texas R]ule 194 'a report of the expert's factual observations, tests, supporting data, calculations, photographs, and opinions.' If no report is produced at the time of designation, the party must make the expert available for deposition 'reasonably promptly after the expert is designated.' If the report is produced at the time of designation, then the expert does not have to be made available for deposition 'until reasonably promptly after all other experts have been designated.'" (quoting Tex. R. Civ. P. 195.3(a)(1)–(2))).

41 Tex. R. Civ. P. 195 cmt. 3 to 1999 change ("A party who does not wish to incur the expense of a report may simply tender the expert for deposition, but a party who wishes an expert to have the benefit of an opposing party's expert's opinions before being deposed may trigger designation by providing a report.").

42 Tex. R. Civ. P. 195.3(a)(1); *see* ***Vaughn v. Ford Motor Co.***, 91 S.W.3d 387, 392 (Tex. App.—Eastland 2002, pet. denied) (noting this remedy in holding that the trial court abused its discretion in striking experts under Texas Rule 215 because the plaintiff failed to make them available for deposition reasonably promptly after their designation).

43 Tex. R. Civ. P. 195.3(b).

gamesmanship, and, under Texas Rule 191.1, the trial court should modify the limitation and order the retained-testifying expert's deposition at an appropriate time.

Neither Texas Rule 195.2 nor any other procedural rule specifies the time for making non-retained-testifying experts available for deposition. Accordingly, such experts can be deposed, subject to the constraints on the conduct of discovery from nonparties, at any time during the applicable discovery period after their designation.

With respect to retained-testifying experts, the party hiring the expert generally must pay "all reasonable fees charged by the expert for time spent in preparing for, giving, reviewing, and correcting the deposition[.]"[44] For good cause, however, a trial court can modify this allocation of fees.[45] Neither Texas Rule 195 nor any other discovery rule requires the party who deposes a non-retained-testifying expert to pay the expert a "reasonable fee" for giving his deposition.[46]

7-4:3 Expert Disclosures and Reports

Texas Rule 195.5(a) sets forth the disclosures required for testifying expert witnesses in cases filed on or after January 1, 2021.[47] The general purpose of these disclosures is "to give the opposing party sufficient information about the expert's opinions to prepare to cross-examine the expert and to prepare expert rebuttal evidence."[48]

Texas Rule 195.5(a) provides as follows:

> Without awaiting a discovery request, a party must provide the following for any testifying expert:
>
> (1) the expert's name, address, and telephone number;

---

[44] Tex. R. Civ. P. 195.7. It is unclear whether a non-retained testifying expert can charge a fee for appearing at a deposition, and neither Texas Rule 195.7 nor any other discovery rule specifies which party pays such fees. Presumably, the party taking the deposition must pay them.

[45] Tex. R. Civ. P. 195 cmt. 3 to 1999 change (Texas "Rule 191.1 permits a trial court, for good cause, to modify . . . the allocation of fees and expenses.").

[46] Texas Rule 176.7 allows a trial court to "impose reasonable conditions on compliance with a subpoena, including compensating the witness for undue hardship." The mere fact that a non-retained-testifying expert is required to appear for a deposition without compensation beyond the statutory-witness fee is not "undue hardship."

[47] *See* Tex. R. Civ. P. 194.3 ("In addition to the disclosures required by [Texas] Rule 194.2, a party must disclose to the other parties testifying expert information as provided in [Texas] Rule 195.").

[48] *See Bexar Cnty. Appraisal Dist. v. Abdo*, 399 S.W.3d 248, 256 (Tex. App.—San Antonio 2012, no pet.) (construing former Texas Rule 194.2(f)) (quoting *Miller v. Kennedy & Minshew, P.C.*, 142 S.W.3d 325, 348 (Tex. App.—Fort Worth 2003, pet. denied)); *accord Garcia v. Roth Constr., Inc.*, No. 13-18-00458-CV, 2020 Tex. App. LEXIS 5688, at *30, 2020 WL 4218715 (Tex. App.—Corpus Christi July 23, 2020, pet. denied) (mem. op.); *Babaria v. City of Southlake*, No. 02-14-00068-CV, 2016 Tex. App. LEXIS 454, at *10, 2016 WL 287523 (Tex. App.—Fort Worth Jan. 14, 2016, pet. denied) (mem. op.) (same); *Roman v. Cuprum S.A. de C.V.*, No. 13-10-00165-CV, 2012 Tex. App. LEXIS 2553, at *5, 2012 WL 1073251 (Tex. App.—Corpus Christi Mar. 29, 2012, no pet.) (mem. op.) (also noting that expert "disclosures and expert reports not only prevent trial by ambush, but affect the opposing party's preparation for trial").

(2) the subject matter on which the expert will testify;

(3) the general substance of the expert's mental impressions and opinions and a brief summary of the basis for them, or if the expert is not retained by, employed by, or otherwise subject to the control of the responding party, documents reflecting such information;

(4) if the expert is retained by, employed by, or otherwise subject to the control of the responding party:

(A) all documents, tangible things, reports, models, or data compilations that have been provided to, reviewed by, or prepared by or for the expert in anticipation of the expert's testimony;

(B) the expert's current resume and bibliography;

(C) the expert's qualifications, including a list of all publications authored in the previous 10 years;

(D) except when the expert is the responding party's attorney and is testifying to attorney fees, a list of all other cases in which, during the previous four years, the expert testified as an expert at trial or by deposition; and

(E) a statement of the compensation to be paid for the expert's study and testimony in the case.[49]

As noted in section 7-1:1 above, the disclosures in Texas Rule 195.5(a)(1)–(4)(B) are the same as the disclosures in former Texas Rule 194.2(f), whereas the disclosures in Texas Rules 195.5(a)(4)(C)–(E) are modeled after those in Federal Rule 26(a)(2)(B)(iv)–(vi).[50]

As with former Texas Rule 194.2(f), some of Texas Rule 195.5(a)'s provisions apply to retained and non-retained-testifying experts,[51] while others apply only to retained-testifying experts.[52] Specifically, the disclosures in Texas Rule 195.5(a)(1)–(3) are required for testifying experts generally, while those in Texas Rule 195.5(a)(4) are only required for retained-testifying experts (i.e., those "retained by, employed by, or otherwise subject to the control of the responding party").[53] Texas Rules 195.5(a)(4)(C)–(E) list the retained-testifying-expert disclosures that are new to the 2021 Texas discovery rules and address the following three topics, respectively: (1) the expert's qualifications; (2) other cases in which the expert has testified; and (3) the expert's compensation.[54] These disclosures are modeled after Federal Rule 26(a)(2)(B)(iv)–(vi)[55] with one principal difference—Texas Rule 195.5(a)(4)(D), unlike Federal Rule

49 Tex. R. Civ. P. 195.5(a).

50 Tex. R. Civ. P. 195 cmt. to 2021 change ("Amended [Texas] Rule 195.5(a) also includes three new disclosures based on Federal Rule . . . 26(a)(2)(B).").

51 *See* Tex. R. Civ. P. 195.5(a)(1)–(3); *see also* Former Tex. R. Civ. P. 194.2(f)(1)–(3) (containing same disclosures).

52 *See* Tex. R. Civ. P. 195.5(a)(4); *see also* Former Tex. R. Civ. P. 194.2(f)(4) (containing some of the same disclosures).

53 *See generally* Tex. R. Civ. P. 195.5(a).

54 Tex. R. Civ. P. 195.5(a).

55 *Compare* Tex. R. Civ. P. 195.5(a)(4)(C)–(E) (for retained testifying experts, requiring disclosure of "(C) the expert's qualifications, including a list of all publications authored in the previous 10 years; (D) except when the expert is the responding party's attorney and

26(a)(2)(B)(v), does not require "the responding party's attorney" who "is testifying to attorney fees" to provide a list of cases in which the attorney has testified.[56] Both Texas Rule 195.5(a)(4)(C) and Federal Rule 26(a)(2)(B)(iv) require disclosure of a retained-testifying "expert's qualifications, ***including*** a list of all publications authored in the previous 10 years."[57] Other than the publication list, neither rule specifies what information needs to be disclosed about such an expert's qualifications. Finally, both Texas Rule 195.5(a)(4)(E) and Federal Rule 26(a)(2)(B)(vi) require disclosure of "a statement of the compensation to be paid for the study and testimony in the case."[58]

With respect to a non-retained-testifying expert (e.g., an emergency-room physician or a fireman, police officer, or other first responder), the responding party need not produce the documents specified in Texas Rule 195.5(a)(4) and the requesting party must resort to other discovery devices to obtain them (e.g., a Texas Rule 205 production request or a deposition notice with a production request under Texas Rules 176 and 205).[59] Also, with respect to such an expert, the responding party need not provide all of the information specified by Texas Rule 195.5(a)(3). Instead, it can produce "documents reflecting such information."[60] For example, the responding party can produce a treating doctor's records or a police officer's accident or other report setting forth the doctor's or officer's mental impressions and opinions and the bases for them in lieu of a description of them in the disclosure. Thus, for non-retained-testifying experts, Texas Rule 195.5(a) assumes that the party is relying on the opinions in the expert's documents and the party may produce them. If there are no such documents, if the responding party does not have copies of them, or if the expert's documents do not set forth the expert's mental impressions and opinions and the bases

---

is testifying to attorney fees, a list of all other cases in which, during the previous four years, the expert testified as an expert at trial or by deposition; and (E) a statement of the compensation to be paid for the expert's study and testimony in the case"), ***with*** Fed. R. Civ. P. 26(a)(2)(B)(iv)–(vi) (requiring the written report of a "witness . . . retained or specially employed to provide expert testimony in the case or [a witness] whose duties as the party's employee regularly involve giving expert testimony" to contain, among other things "(iv) the witness's qualifications, including a list of all publications authored in the previous 10 years; (v) a list of all other cases in which, during the previous 4 years, the witness testified as an expert at trial or by deposition; and (vi) a statement of the compensation to be paid for the study and testimony in the case").

[56] ***Compare*** Tex. R. Civ. P. 195.5(a)(4)(D) (for retained testifying experts, requiring disclosure of "a list of all other cases in which, during the previous four years, the expert testified as an expert at trial or by deposition" "except when the expert is the responding party's attorney and is testifying to attorney fees"), ***with*** Fed. R. Civ. P. 26(a)(2)(B)(v) (requiring the written report of a "witness . . . retained or specially employed to provide expert testimony in the case or [a witness] whose duties as the party's employee regularly involve giving expert testimony" to contain, among other things "a list of all other cases in which, during the previous 4 years, the witness testified as an expert at trial or by deposition").

[57] Tex. R. Civ. P. 195.5(a)(4)(C) (emphasis added); ***accord*** Fed. R. Civ. P. 26(a)(2)(B)(iv).

[58] Tex. R. Civ. P. 195.5(a)(4)(E); ***accord*** Fed. R. Civ. P. 26(a)(2)(B)(vi).

[59] Tex. R. Civ. P. 195 cmt. 2 to 1999 change ("This rule and [former Texas] Rule 194 do not address depositions of testifying experts who are not retained by, employed by, or otherwise subject to the control of the responding party, nor the production of the materials identified in [Texas] Rule 192.3(e)(5) and (6) relating to such experts. Parties may obtain this discovery, however, through [Texas] Rules 176 and 205.").

[60] Tex. R. Civ. P. 195.5(a)(3).

for them, the responding party should set forth the expert's mental impressions and opinions in the disclosure.

It is important to note that Texas Rule 195.5(a)'s disclosure requirement applies to rebuttal experts.[61] It also is important to note that the information that has to be disclosed under the Rule is narrower than the information discoverable from testifying experts generally under Texas Rule 192.3(e), the rule regarding the scope of expert discovery.[62] For example, Texas Rule 192.3(e) permits discovery of "any bias of the witness[,]"[63] whereas Texas Rule 195.5(a) does not require disclosure of the testifying expert's bias. Similarly, whereas Texas Rules 192.3(e)(3) and (4) respectively allow

---

[61] *Press Energy Servs. LLC v. Ruiz*, No. 08-19-00179-CV, 2021 Tex. App. LEXIS 5706, at *28–30, 2021 WL 3013313 (Tex. App.—El Paso July 16, 2021, no pet.) (holding the trial court did not abuse its discretion when refusing to allow rebuttal testimony from a witness that was not timely disclosed); *Christian v. Oceanwide Am., Inc.*, No. 01-19-00557-CV, 2020 Tex. App. LEXIS 10451, at *10, 2020 WL 7775762 (Tex. App.—Houston [1st Dist.] Dec. 31, 2020, no pet.) (mem. op.) ("A rebuttal witness must be disclosed if the need for testimony on that issue reasonably should have been anticipated."); *City of Brownsville v. Ahumada*, No. 13-14-00265-CV, 2015 Tex. App. LEXIS 6858, at *6, 2015 WL 4116731 (Tex. App—Corpus Christi July 2, 2015, no pet.) (mem. op.) (holding that rebuttal expert testimony that reasonably can be anticipated is not exempt from former Texas Rule 193.2(f)'s disclosure requirement); *Prevallet v. Prevallet*, No. 02-12-00260-CV, 2014 Tex. App. LEXIS 288, at *34–35, 2014 WL 92793 (Tex. App.—Fort Worth Jan. 9, 2014, no pet.) (mem. op.) (same); *In re Marks.*, 230 S.W.3d 241, 245–46 (Tex. App.—Beaumont 2007, no pet) (affirming the trial court's exclusion of an undisclosed rebuttal expert); *Moore v. Mem'l Hermann Hosp. Sys., Inc.*, 140 S.W.3d 870, 875 (Tex. App.—Houston [14th Dist.] 2004, no pet.) (same).

[62] Texas Rule 192.3(e) provides, in relevant part:

> A party may discover the following information regarding a testifying expert or regarding a consulting expert whose mental impressions or opinions have been reviewed by a testifying expert:
>
> (1) the expert's name, address, and telephone number;
>
> (2) the subject matter on which a testifying expert will testify;
>
> (3) the facts known by the expert that relate to or form the basis of the expert's mental impressions and opinions formed or made in connection with the case in which the discovery is sought, regardless of when and how the factual information was acquired;
>
> (4) the expert's mental impressions and opinions formed or made in connection with the case in which discovery is sought, and any methods used to derive them;
>
> (5) any bias of the witness;
>
> (6) all documents, tangible things, reports, models, or data compilations that have been provided to, reviewed by, or prepared by or for the expert in anticipation of a testifying expert's testimony;
>
> (7) the expert's current resume and bibliography.
>
> Tex. R. Civ. P. 192.3(e).

Texas Rule 195.2 does not provide for the designation of rebuttal experts. Consequently, if the parties anticipate using them, the better and most prudent practice is to provide a deadline for their designation in a scheduling order or other order or a Texas Rule 11 agreement.

[63] Tex. R. Civ. P. 192.3(e)(5).

discovery of "the facts known by the expert that relate to or form the basis of the expert's mental impressions and opinions formed or made in connection with the case in which the discovery is sought, regardless of when and how the factual information was acquired" and "the expert's mental impressions and opinions formed or made in connection with the case in which discovery is sought, and any methods used to derive them,"[64] Texas Rule 195.5(a)(3) only requires the disclosure of "the general substance of the [testifying] expert's mental impressions and opinions and a brief summary of the basis for them."[65] Thus, a requesting party normally should depose a testifying expert and obtain a report from retained-testifying experts. And, if a party wants to explore a testifying expert's bias, it generally can so only in a deposition.[66]

Because Texas Rule 195.5(a)(4)(A) requires the responding party to produce "all documents . . . that have been provided to . . . [a retained-testifying] expert in anticipation of the expert's testimony[,]" privileged documents inadvertently given to a such an expert generally must be produced.[67] "If a party is concerned about the discovery of

---

64 Tex. R. Civ. P. 192.3(e)(3)–(4).

65 Tex. R. Civ. P. 195.5(a)(3).

66 *In re Ford Motor Co.*, 427 S.W.3d 396, 397–98 (Tex. 2014) (per curiam) (orig. proceeding) (directing the trial court to vacate an order requiring depositions of the defendant's retained testifying expert witnesses' employers to show the experts' bias in favor of the defendant and other car manufactures); *see In re Vaco*, No. 10-20-00229-CV, 2021 Tex. App. LEXIS 3932, at *7, 2021 WL 2022065 (Tex. App.—Waco May 19, 2021, orig. proceeding) (mem. op.) ("Discovery of bias evidence is what is expressly permitted by the rule, but a document request has never been a proper discovery tool to conduct a fishing expedition, particularly to try to find impeachment evidence limited to bias."); *In re State Farm Lloyds*, No. 02-20-00163-CV, 2020 Tex. App. LEXIS 7207, at *15–16, 2020 WL 5242414 (Tex. App.—Fort Worth Sept. 3, 2020, orig. proceeding) (mem. op.) (holding the trial court abused its discretion by ordering the defendant to produce engineering reports issued by a consultant for all claims over a five-year period because it was not relevant to show bias); *In re Interinsurance Exch.*, No. 01-14-00979-CV, 2016 Tex. App. LEXIS 268, at *9–10, 2016 WL 144784 (Tex. App.—Houston [1st Dist.] Jan. 12, 2016, orig. proceeding) (mem. op.) (holding that the trial court abused its discretion in ordering defendant insurer's retained-testifying expert to produce every report for the defendant for a twelve-year period because the expert had already testified about his work for the defendant in his deposition); *In re Cent. N. Constr., LLC*, No. 05-14-00178-CV, 2014 Tex. App. LEXIS 4010, at *7 (Tex. App.—Dallas Apr. 10, 2014, orig. proceeding) (mem. op.) ("Generally, although an expert witness may be questioned regarding payment received for his work as an expert witness, pre-trial discovery sought only to establish financial interest for impeachment purposes is not allowed."); *In re Weir*, 166 S.W.3d 861, 864 (Tex. App.—Beaumont 2005, orig. proceeding) (per curiam) ("Proof of bias may be offered to impeach the credibility of a witness. . . . Generally, an expert witness may be questioned regarding payment received for his work as an expert witness. However, pretrial discovery of all of a witness's accounting and financial records, solely for the purpose of impeachment, may be denied.") (citations omitted). See also Chapter 7, section 7-4:6 (discussing discovery of an expert's bias).

67 *In re Christus Spohn Hosp. Kleberg*, 222 S.W.3d 434, 440–41 (Tex. 2007) ("[W]e conclude that [Texas] Rules 192.3(e)(6) and 192.5(c)(1) prevail over [Texas] Rule 193.3(d)'s snap-back provision so long as the expert intends to testify at trial despite the inadvertent document production. That is, once privileged documents are disclosed to a testifying expert, and the party who designated the expert continues to rely upon that designation for trial, the documents may not be retrieved even if they were inadvertently produced."). Nonetheless, a party may snap-back such documents if they could not by their nature have influenced the expert's opinion or if the expert is de-designated. *In re Christus Spohn Hosp.*

its privileged information through expert discovery, the party may designate another expert in the first place or, presumably, withdraw a currently designated expert and name another."[68]

If a party fails to disclose the information required by Texas Rule 195.5(a), the expert's testimony generally will be excluded at trial under Texas Rule 193.6's automatic-exclusion rule unless the disclosing party can show there was good cause for the failure or it will not unfairly surprise or unfairly prejudice the other parties.[69]

Kleberg, 222 S.W.3d 434, 441 (Tex. 2007) ("Of course, inadvertently produced material that could not by its nature have influenced the expert's opinion does not evoke the concerns the expert-disclosure rule was designed to prevent and the policy concerns underlying the rule's disclosure requirement would presumably never arise. In that event, there would be nothing to prevent the snap-back rule's application, although we note that a party seeking snap-back under such circumstances would bear a heavy burden in light of the disclosure rule's underlying purpose.").

[68] *In re Nat'l Lloyds Ins. Co.*, 532 S.W.3d 794, 814 n. 89 (Tex. 2017); *see In re Jourdanton Hosp. Corp.*, No. 04-14-00356-CV, 2014 Tex. App. LEXIS 8209, at *14–15, 2014 WL 3745447 (Tex. App.—San Antonio July 30, 2014) (mem. op.) ("Here, the Hospital de-designated Castillo promptly. . . . In addition to providing an affidavit testifying that the Report was not provided to her in anticipation of any expert testimony she might give, Castillo is no longer a testifying expert witness. Therefore, the Investigation Report remains privileged.").

[69] Tex. R. Civ. P. 193.6; *Press Energy Servs. LLC v. Ruiz*, No. 08-19-00179-CV, 2021 Tex. App. LEXIS 5706, at *28–30, 2021 WL 3013313 (Tex. App.—El Paso July 16, 2021, no pet.) (holding the trial court did not abuse its discretion when refusing to allow rebuttal testimony from a witness that was not timely disclosed); *Barron as Tr. of 3001 Decatur Tr. v. Fort Worth Transp. Auth.*, No. 02-19-00274-CV, 2021 Tex. App. LEXIS 2703, at *9–10, 2021 WL 1323415 (Tex. App.—Fort Worth Apr. 8, 2021, pet. denied) (mem. op.) (holding the trial court did not abuse its discretion by excluding expert testimony that was disclosed 251 days after the disclosure deadline and the offering party made no showing of good cause or lack of unfair surprise); *OIC Holdings, LLC v. Gleason*, No. 05-18-00029-CV, 2019 Tex. App. LEXIS 3863, at *21–22, 2019 WL 2098616 (Tex. App.—Dallas May 14, 2019, no pet.) (mem. op.) ("Oregon Ice Cream offered no evidence of the lack of unfair surprise or unfair prejudice. The trial court ruled before trial that the reasonableness and necessity of attorney's fees would be submitted to the jury. It was not until after trial began that the parties stipulated to submit all attorney's fees issues to the trial judge after the jury's verdict. The Gleasons made that agreement in light of the pleadings and designations of experts at that time. Given that OIC and the Gleasons timely designated their expert witnesses and Oregon Ice Cream did not, the Gleasons were entitled to prepare for trial with the assurance that Oregon Ice Cream would not call an undesignated expert on its own behalf. The mere fact that an expert would be required to support a claim for attorney's fees, and thus should have been anticipated by the Gleasons, is insufficient to show the lack of unfair surprise or prejudice."); *Lawson v. Collins*, No. 03-17-00003-CV, 2017 Tex. App. LEXIS 8843, at *21–22, 2017 WL 4228728 (Tex. App.—Austin Sept. 20, 2017, no pet.) (mem. op.) (holding the trial court did not abuse its discretion in excluding an affidavit of an undisclosed expert in connection with a no-evidence summary judgment hearing); *RDJRLW, Inc. v. Miller*, No. 02-17-00132-CV, 2017 Tex. App. LEXIS 5494, at *22, 2017 WL 2590568 (Tex. App.—Fort Worth June 15, 2017, no pet.) (mem. op.) ("We conclude that the trial court was within its discretion to exclude RDJ's expert based solely on RDJ's failure to produce or make available the expert's working file[.]"); *Red Ball Oxygen Co.* v. *Sw. R.R. Car Parts Co.*, 523 S.W.3d 288, 298 (Tex. App.—Tyler 2017, no pet.) (affirming judgment denying the plaintiff attorneys' fees because it did not timely designate an expert to testify about their reasonableness); *Bailey v. Respironics, Inc.*, No. 05-11-01057-CV, 2014 Tex. App. LEXIS 8003, at *21–22, 2014 WL 3698828 (Tex. App.—Dallas July 23, 2014, no pet.) (mem. op.) ("Bailey disclosed that Reese was

'expected to testify generally about the ventilator and its role in the incident made the basis of this lawsuit.' Bailey did not disclose, as requested by Respironics and as required by [former Texas R]ule 194.2(f), the subject matter on which Reese would testify; the general substance of Reese's mental impressions and opinions and a brief summary of the basis for them; and all documents, tangible things, reports, models or data compilations that had been provided to, reviewed by, or prepared by Reese in anticipation of his testimony. The purpose of [Texas R]ule 194.2(f) is to give the opposing party sufficient information about the expert's opinions to prepare to cross examine the expert and to prepare expert rebuttal evidence. Bailey's vague disclosure of the substance of Reese's testimony did not comply with the requisites of [Texas R]ule 194.2(f). . . . Because Bailey missed the deadline for designating Reese as an expert and failed to meet the requirements of [Texas R]ule 194.2(f), we conclude the trial court did not abuse its discretion in excluding Reese's affidavit."); *In re T.K.D-H*, 439 S.W.3d 473, 477 (Tex. App.—San Antonio 2014, no pet.) ("Here, Jose provided Ries's name and contact information, but he did not provide any of the other information required by [Texas] Rule 194.2(f). Therefore, even if his disclosure was filed on or before the discovery deadline, the disclosure did not comply with the requi-sites of [Texas] Rule 194.2(f)." (quoting *Miller v. Kennedy & Minshew, P.C.*, 142 S.W.3d 325, 348 (Tex. App.—Fort Worth 2003, pet. denied))); *In re B.L.B.*, No. 13-13-00594-CV, 2014 Tex. App. LEXIS 5447, at *15–16, 2014 WL 2158132 (Tex. App.—Corpus Christi May 22, 2014, no pet.) (mem. op.) ("In this case, it is undisputed that S.B. failed to properly identify her counsel (or anyone else) as an expert on attorney's fees in response to M.B.'s request for disclosure. Furthermore, at trial, S.B. failed to establish, and in fact, did not even attempt to establish, good cause or lack of unfair surprise or prejudice to M.B. . . . Instead, the trial court expressly stated that its reason for allowing S.B.'s attorney to testify over M.B.'s objection was that there was no case law that S.B.'s attorney was 'considered an expert for his own attorney's fees' and thus he did not need to be designated. We believe this was incorrect."); *Bexar Cty. Appraisal Dist. v. Abdo*, 399 S.W.3d 248, 256–57 (Tex. App.—San Antonio 2012, no pet.) (excluding the District's expert because its expert disclosure only vaguely stated expert may testify "about what is and what is not useable land and/or what is or is not in the floodplain" "and/or matters associated therewith"); *In re M.H.*, 319 S.W.3d 137, 146 (Tex. App.—Waco 2010, no pet.) (concluding that an expert should not have been permitted to testify because the Department's expert disclosure did "not in any manner identify or disclose: (1) 'the general substance of the expert's mental impressions and opinions'; (2) 'a brief summary of the basis for them' (with regard to [a retained expert]); or (3) documents reflecting such a summary with regard to the non-retained experts"); *Baker v. Energy Transfer Co.*, No. 10-09-00214-CV, 2011 Tex. App. LEXIS 8304, at *3, 2011 WL 4978287 (Tex. App.—Waco Oct. 19, 2011, pet. denied) (mem. op.) ("A failure to properly designate expert witnesses results in the automatic exclusion of the expert testimony unless the offering party demonstrates good cause for the failure or a lack of unfair surprise."); *Perez v. Embree Constr. Grp., Inc.*, 228 S.W.3d 875, 884 (Tex. App.—Austin 2007, pet. denied) (same); *Carlton v. Stewart*, No. 05-05-00888-CV, 2006 Tex. App. LEXIS 2839, at *5–6 (Tex. App.—Dallas Apr. 7, 2006, pet. denied) (mem. op.) (affirming the exclusion of the plaintiff's treating physician because the plaintiff never disclosed that he would testify on causation); *see $27,877.00 Current Money v. State*, 331 S.W.3d 110, 120 (Tex. App.—Fort Worth 2010, pet. denied) ("We have said before that failure to respond to a request for the mental impressions and opinions of the expert is a complete failure to respond, triggering the automatic exclusion under [Texas] Rule 193.6, not just an incomplete answer, which the Texas Supreme Court has held requires a pretrial objection or a pretrial motion to compel or for sanctions[.]"). *But see Kim v. Sanchez*, No. 02-12-00465-CV, 2014 Tex. App. LEXIS 10055, at *10 (Tex. App.—Fort Worth Sept. 4, 2014, pet. denied) (mem. op.) ("In response to Kim's request for disclosure of any expert witness, Sanchez stated the following: 'Mr. Moore is expected to testify regarding the reasonable and necessary attorney fees that were necessary in prosecuting this case and in rebuttal to any attorney fee testimony offered by an expert on behalf of Defendant.' A disclosure identifying an attorney's fees expert that states that the expert will be testifying about the reasonableness and necessity

Under former Texas Rule 194.4, which still applies to cases filed before January 1, 2021, documents responsive to testifying-expert disclosures under former Texas Rule 194.2(f) "must be served with the response, but if the responsive documents are voluminous, the response must state a reasonable time and place for their production."[70] For cases filed on or after January 1, 2021, Texas Rule 194.1 applies to testifying-expert disclosures under Texas Rule 195.5(a) and provides: "If a party does not produce copies of all responsive documents, electronically stored information, and tangible things with the response, the response must state a reasonable time and method for the production of these items. The responding party must produce the items at the time and in the method stated, unless otherwise agreed by the parties or ordered by the court, and must provide the requesting party a reasonable opportunity to inspect them."[71] Notwithstanding this flexible standard, the better practice is serve response documents with testifying-expert disclosure.

Under Texas Rule 195.5(b), a party can move the trial court to order the opposing party's expert to produce a report: "If the discoverable factual observations, tests, supporting data, calculations, photographs, or opinions of an expert have not been recorded and reduced to tangible form, the court may order these matters reduced to tangible form and produced in addition to the deposition."[72] As a general matter, a party should obtain such a report before it deposes retained-testifying expert.

The information required to be in the expert report is more limited than the general scope of expert discovery under Texas Rule 192.3(e). For example, an expert report need not disclose "the facts known by the expert that relate . . . to the expert's . . . mental impressions and opinions," the "methods" used to derive the expert's mental

---

of attorney's fees sought is sufficient to give the 'general substance' of that expert's anticipated testimony, especially when, as here, the responding party is seeking fees for representation during the entire litigation, which are not determinable at the time of disclosure. Accordingly, we conclude and hold that the trial court did not abuse its discretion by allowing Sanchez's counsel to testify regarding his attorney's fees. We overrule Kim's fourth issue."). See generally Chapter 5, section 5-7 (discussing the consequences under Texas Rule 193.6 for failing to timely respond, supplement, or amend written discovery responses).

[70] Former Tex. R. Civ. P. 194.4; *RDJRLW, Inc. v. Miller*, No. 02-17-00132-CV, 2017 Tex. App. LEXIS 5494, at *18, 2017 WL 2590568 (Tex. App.—Fort Worth June 15, 2017, no pet.) (mem. op.); *accord* former Tex. R. Civ. P. 194.4 ("Copies of documents and other tangible items ordinarily must be served with the response. But if the responsive documents are voluminous, the response must state a reasonable time and place for the production of documents."); *In re Grecon, Inc.*, 542 S.W.3d 774, 779 (Tex. App.—Houston [14th Dist.] 2018, orig. proceeding) ("Under [Texas] Rule 194.4, the responding party 'ordinarily must' serve documents and other tangible items with the response, and 'must produce the documents at the time and place stated, unless otherwise agreed by the parties ordered by the court[.]'" (quoting former Tex. R. Civ. P. 194.4)).

[71] Tex. R. Civ. P. 194.1(b).

[72] Tex. R. Civ. P. 195.5(b). Absent a court order or Rule 11 agreement, there is no obligation to provide an expert report. *Willie v. Comm'n for Lawyer Discipline*, No. 14-13-00872-CV, 2015 Tex. App. LEXIS 2466, at *58, 2015 WL 1245965 (Tex. App.—Houston [14th Dist.] Mar. 17, 2015, pet. denied) (mem. op.) ("Contrary to Willie's assertion, nothing in [Texas] Rule 195.3 'imposes a duty to designate experts and furnish an expert report;' thus, the Commission did not fail to timely produce an expert report under [Texas] Rule 195.3.") (quoting Texas Rule 195.3).

impressions or opinions, or any "bias" of the expert.[73] Thus, there is certain information that is discoverable only through a testifying expert's deposition.

Texas Rule 195.5 does not expressly state whether a report can be obtained from a non-retained-testifying expert. Because such an expert is not within the designating party's control, and often may be uncooperative or even hostile to that party, a trial court generally abuses its discretion if it orders the designating party to obtain a report from such an expert. This conclusion is supported by Texas Rule 205, which generally governs nonparty discovery and which does not authorize expert reports from nonparties.[74]

7-4:4 Protected Communications and Material

Perhaps the most important amendment to Texas Rule 195 relates to the testifying-expert-witness information and materials that are protected from discovery and disclosure in cases filed on or after January 1, 2021. In such cases, under Texas Rule 195.5(c), all communications—whether in a telephone call, meeting, in person, a letter, a text message, or email—between a testifying expert and the party's attorney are exempt from discovery unless the communications "(1) relate to compensation for the expert's study or testimony; (2) identify facts or data that the party's attorney provided and that the expert considered in forming the opinions to be expressed; or (3) identify assumptions that the party's attorney provided and that the expert relied on in forming the opinions to be expressed."[75] This exemption, while fairly broad in scope, is limited to communications between "*the party's attorney* and *any testifying witness* in the case" (whether retained or non-retained).[76] Consequently, *communications*

---

[73] *Compare* Tex. R. Civ. P. 192.3(e), *with* Tex. R. Civ. P. 195.5(a), Tex. R. Civ. P. 195.3(a)(1), *and* Tex. R. Civ. P. 195.5(b).

[74] *See* Tex. R. Civ. P. 205.

[75] Tex. R. Civ. P. 195.5(c)(1)–(3); *cf. Republic of Ecuador v. For Issuance of a Subpoena Under 28 U.S.C. Sec. 1782(a)*, 735 F.3d 1179, 1187 (10th Cir. 2013) ("[Federal]Rule 26(b)(4), especially subdivision (C), restores the core understanding that the work-product doctrine solely protects the inner workings of an attorney's mind."); *Allstate Ins. Co. v. Electrolux Home Prods.*, Inc., 840 F.Supp.2d 1072, 1080 (N.D. Ill. 2012) (holding that discoverable factual information includes material that the expert "considered" "means something broader than 'relied upon,' but something less than material simply in the background knowledge of the expert."); *Euclid Chem. Co. v. Vector Corrosion Techs., Inc.*, No. 1:05CV80, 2007 U.S. Dist. LEXIS 38720, at *12–14, 2007 WL 1560277 (N.D. Ohio May 29, 2007) ("[T]he courts have embraced an objective test that defines 'considered' as anything received, reviewed, read, or authored by the expert, before or in connection with the forming of his opinion, if the subject matter relates to the facts or opinions expressed. All ambiguities must be resolved in favor of discovery.").

[76] Tex. R. Civ. P. 195.5(c) (emphasis added); *cf. Hernandez v. Office of the Comm'r of Baseball*, 335 F.R.D. 45, 106 Fed. R. Serv. 3d 1157 (S.D.N.Y. 2020) (holding that an expert's memorandum, setting forth methodology for evaluating comments was not communication to attorney, and thus was not protected by rule because memorandum was not created at request of the attorney, and expert stated that he prepared the memorandum for himself in anticipation of deposition); *Benson v. Rosenthal*, No. 15-782, 2016 U.S. Dist. LEXIS 33909, at *20, 2016 WL 1046126 (E.D. La. Mar. 16, 2016) ("[C]ommunications between a testifying expert and a <u>non</u>-attorney are <u>not</u> protected from discovery by [Federal] Rule 26(b)(4), and must be produced, or at least logged.") (emphasis in original); *Burkhead & Scott, Inc. v. City of Hopkinsville*, No. 5:12-CV-00198-TBR, 2014 U.S. Dist. LEXIS 166374, at *3, 2014 WL 6751205

between the expert and the party or its employees or other agents are not exempt from discovery.

Under Texas Rule 195.5(d) in all cases filed on or after January 1, 2021, draft expert disclosures and reports are not discoverable.[77] This means that the party's attorney can review, edit, and comment on the draft disclosures and reports of the party's testifying experts freely, without disclosing the feedback to the other side. Because Texas Rule 195.5(c) does not protect communications between the party's expert and anyone other than the party's attorney, however, it stands to reason that any feedback by non-covered persons is discoverable.

7-4:5 Inadvertent Disclosure of Privilege Materials to Testifying Experts

A party is entitled to "all documents, tangible things, reports, models, or data compilations that have been provided to, reviewed by, or prepared by or for [a retained-testifying] expert in anticipation of a testifying expert's testimony[.]"[78] These materials

(W.D. Ky. Dec. 1, 2014) ("Emails without an attorney recipient or sender are not privileged, nor are emails to or from non-parties."); *In re Application of Republic of Ecuador,* 280 F.R.D. 506, 514 (N.D. Cal. 2012), aff'd sub nom. *Republic of Ecuador v. Mackay*, 742 F.3d 860 (9th Cir. 2014) ("Communications between Kelsh and his assistants and Chevron's attorneys are expressly protected as work product under [Federal] Rule 26(b)(4)(C). Because the term 'expert' includes assistants of the expert, such internal communications, as well as those between Kelsh's assistants and Chevron attorneys, are protected work product."); *United States v. Sierra Pac. Indus.*, No. CIV S-09-2445 KJM EF, 2011 U.S. Dist. LEXIS 60372, at *18–26, 2011 WL 2119078 (E.D. Cal. May 26, 2011) (explaining that Federal Rule 26(b)(4) applied only to experts who were required to provide a report and not to employee experts whose disclosure is more limited).

[77] Tex. R. Civ. P. 195.5(d); *cf. Sioux Steel Co. v. Prairie Land Millwright Servs., Inc.*, No. 16 C 2212, 2020 U.S. Dist. LEXIS 97260, at *17–18, 2020 WL 2900834 (N.D. Ill. 2020) ("The final category of documents on the privilege log consists of drafts of Meyer's expert report and expert declaration. These are expressly protected from disclosure by [Federal] Rule 26(b)(4)(B), which covers 'drafts of any report or disclosure required under Rule 26(a)(2), regardless of the form in which the draft is recorded.'"); *Maldonado-Rodriguez v. Grupo HIMA San Pablo, Inc.*, 326 F.R.D. 367, 100 Fed. R. Serv. 3d 1581 (D.P.R. 2018) (holding that a medical expert's unsigned draft report was an attorney-expert communication under Fed R. Civ. P. 26(b)(4)(C) and thus protected from discovery); *Davita Healthcare Partners, Inc. v. United States*, 128 Fed. Cl. 584, 591 (2016) ("Spreadsheets, graphs, presentations, and charts are protected under [Federal] Rule 26(b)(4)(B), so long as the documents were prepared by the testifying expert to be included in draft expert reports."); *United States ex rel. Wall v. Vista Hospice Care*, 319 F.R.D. 498 (N.D. Tex. 2016) (extending work-product protection to drafts of expert reports); *Deangelis v. Corzine*, No. 1:11-CV-07866-VM-JCF, 2016 U.S. Dist. LEXIS 1856, at *35, 2016 WL 93862 (S.D.N.Y. Jan. 7, 2016) ("The documents were prepared not simply to aid Mr. Markham in drafting his report, but rather to form part of the report itself and were in fact included in preliminary versions of that report. They are, in short, drafts of his report.").

[78] Tex. R. Civ. P. 192.3(e)(6); *accord* Tex. R. Civ. P. 195.5(a)(4)(A) (requiring a party to disclosure for experts retained by, employed by, or otherwise under a party's control "all documents, tangible things, reports, models, or data compilations that have been provided to, reviewed by, or prepared by or for the expert in anticipation of the expert's testimony"); *see In re Christus Spohn Hosp. Kleberg*, 222 S.W.3d 434, 438 (Tex. 2007) (orig. proceeding) ("To avoid the discovery disputes that frequently arose over what material an expert may or may

are discoverable irrespective of who prepared them and irrespective of whether the expert relied on them or even read them.[79] Accordingly, as a general rule, everything provided to, reviewed by, or prepared by or for a testifying expert is discoverable, except to the extent that the materials are protected from discovery under Texas Rule 195.5(c)–(d) in cases filed on or after January 1, 2021.[80]

If a party discloses privileged material to its retained-testifying expert, the materials are discoverable and generally cannot be "snapped back" under Texas Rule 193.3(d). As explained by the Texas Supreme Court:

> In light of these important policy concerns that underlie the expert-disclosure rule, we conclude that [Texas] Rules 192.3(e)(6) and 192.5(c)(1) prevail over [Texas] Rule 193.3(d)'s snap-back provision so long as the expert intends to testify at trial despite the inadvertent document production. That is, once privileged documents are disclosed to a testifying expert, and the party who designated the expert continues to rely upon that designation for trial, the documents may not be retrieved even if they were inadvertently produced.[81]

Notwithstanding this general rule, if the privileged material could not, by its nature, have influenced the testifying expert's opinion, it can be snapped back:

> Of course, inadvertently produced material that could not by its nature have influenced the expert's opinion does not evoke the concerns the expert-disclosure rule was designed to prevent and the policy concerns underlying the rule's disclosure requirement would presumably never arise. In that event, there would be nothing to prevent the snap-back rule's application, although we note that a party seeking snap-back under such circumstances would bear a heavy burden in light of the disclosure rule's underlying purpose.[82]

Instead of attempting to snap-back the privileged material, the party, to preserve its privilege, may be able to de-designate the expert and name a new one. As explained by the Texas Supreme Court:

> An attorney who discovers that privileged documents have been inadvertently provided to a testifying expert may presumably withdraw the expert's

---

not have relied upon, the rule was amended in 1999 to include more expansive language. In addition to documents 'prepared by or for the expert,' the rule now mandates discovery of documents 'that have been provided to, [or] reviewed by' a testifying expert." (quoting Tex. R. Civ. P. 192.3(e)(6))).

[79] *In re Christus Spohn Hosp. Kleberg*, 222 S.W.3d 434, 438 (Tex. 2007) ("The Hospital's argument that the Northcutt documents were prepared by or for the Hospital rather than by or for the expert, and that Menzies did not read them in any event, erroneously ignores [Texas Rule 192.3(e)(6)'s] disjunctive language. Whether or not the documents were actually 'read' by or prepared for Menzies, they were clearly 'provided to' the Hospital's testifying expert and thus fall within [Texas] Rule 192.3(e)(6)'s plain language.").

[80] *See* Tex. R. Civ. P. 192.3(e)(6); former Tex. R. Civ. P. 194.2(f)(4)(A); Tex. R. Civ. P. 195.5(a)(4)(A), (c)–(d).

[81] *In re Christus Spohn Hosp. Kleberg*, 222 S.W.3d 434, 440–41 (Tex. 2007).

[82] *In re Christus Spohn Hosp. Kleberg*, 222 S.W.3d 434, 441 (Tex. 2007).

> designation and name another. Although such a course may entail additional expense and perhaps delay, these concerns do not outweigh countervailing concerns that require full disclosure from an expert who will testify. If leave of court is necessary for an alternative designation—when, for example, the expert designation deadline has passed—courts should carefully weigh the alternatives available to prevent what may be akin to a death-penalty sanction for the party forced to trial without a necessary expert.[83]

However, if the testifying expert is a party or its employee, with whom communications would normally be shielded by attorney-client privilege, snapping back any inadvertently disclosed material is appropriate.[84]

7-4:6 Discovery of an Expert's Bias

"Bias, in its usual meaning, is an inclination toward one side of an issue rather than to the other."[85] Proof of an expert's bias can be offered to impeach a testifying expert's credibility.[86] Accordingly, discovery of an expert's bias is expressly permitted by Texas Rule 192.3(e)(5).[87] The Texas Supreme Court, however, has made clear that expansive discovery regarding expert bias is improper because "concerns about allowing overly expansive discovery about testifying experts that can 'permit witnesses to be subjected to harassment and might well discourage reputable experts' from participating in the litigation process."[88] Accordingly, the Texas Supreme Court and Texas courts of appeals consistently have held that depositions of, and production requests to, third

---

[83] *In re Christus Spohn Hosp. Kleberg*, 222 S.W.3d 434, 445 (Tex. 2007); *accord In re Nat'l Lloyds Ins. Co.*, 532 S.W.3d 794, 814 n.89 (Tex. 2017) (orig. proceeding) ("If a party is concerned about the discovery of its privileged information through expert discovery, the party may designate another expert in the first place or, presumably, withdraw a currently designated expert and name another."); *In re Jourdanton Hosp. Corp.*, No. 04-14-00356-CV, 2014 Tex. App. LEXIS 8209, at *11–15, 2014 WL 3745447 (Tex. App.—San Antonio July 30, 2014, orig. proceeding) (mem. op.) (holding that privilege was not waived with respect to a document provided to a testifying expert who had been de-designated properly).

[84] *In re City of Dickinson*, 568 S.W.3d 642, 646 (Tex. 2019).

[85] *Cantu v. Comm'n for Lawyer Discipline*, No. 13-16-00332-CV, 2020 Tex. App. LEXIS 9434, at *79, 2020 WL 7064806 (Tex. App.—Corpus Christi Dec. 3, 2020, no pet.) (mem. op.); *accord In re Interinsurance Exch.*, No. 01-14-00979-CV, 2016 Tex. App. LEXIS 268, at *5, 2016 WL 144784 (Tex. App.—Houston [1st Dist.] Jan. 12, 2016, orig. proceeding) (mem. op.).

[86] *Cantu v. Comm'n for Lawyer Discipline*, No. 13-16-00332-CV, 2020 Tex. App. LEXIS 9434, at *79, 2020 WL 7064806 (Tex. App.—Corpus Christi Dec. 3, 2020, no pet.) (mem. op.) ("Proof of bias on the part of an expert witness may be offered to impeach the expert's credibility."); *In re Interinsurance Exch.*, No. 01-14-00979-CV, 2016 Tex. App. LEXIS 268, at *5, 2016 WL 144784 (Tex. App.—Houston [1st Dist.] Jan. 12, 2016, orig. proceeding) (mem. op.) (same); *In re Weir*, 166 S.W.3d 861, 864 (Tex. App.—Beaumont 2005, orig. proceeding) (per curiam) ("Proof of bias may be offered to impeach the credibility of a witness. . . . Generally, an expert witness may be questioned regarding payment received for his work as an expert witness.") (citations omitted); *see* Tex. R. Evid. 613(b) (setting forth how a witness can be questioned about his or her bias or interest).

[87] Tex. R. Civ. P. 192.3(e)(5) ("A party may discover the following information regarding a testifying expert or regarding a consulting expert whose mental impressions or opinions have been reviewed by a testifying expert: . . . (5) any bias of the witness[.]").

[88] *In re Ford Motor Co.*, 427 S.W.3d 396, 397 (Tex. 2014) (orig. proceeding) (per curiam) (quoting *Ex parte Shepperd*, 513 S.W.2d 813, 816 (Tex. 1974) (orig. proceeding)).

parties for the purpose of discovering evidence of a testifying expert's bias generally are overbroad and impermissible if the expert readily can be questioned about the matter during a deposition.[89] However, "[w]here there is other extrinsic evidence of

[89] In *In re Ford Motor*, the Texas Supreme Court held that the employers of defendants' two testifying experts did not have to appear for depositions to provide "detailed financial and business information for all cases the companies have handled for Ford or any other automobile manufacturer from 2000 to 2011," *In re Ford Motor Co.*, 427 S.W.3d 396, 397 (Tex. 2014) (per curiam), because the experts' bias was established by their deposition testimony:

> Indeed, the most probative information regarding the bias of a testifying expert comes from the expert herself. In this case, for example, Harley testified that only 5% of the cases she handles are for plaintiffs and that she has never testified against an automobile manufacturer. Similarly, Mauldin testified that historically about 50% of Carr Engineering's work is done for Ford. Moreover, Mauldin admitted that in park-to-reverse cases, he has never testified that a vehicle has a design defect. Mauldin's deposition in this case also revealed that he worked at Ford for several years before becoming a consultant at Carr Engineering.

In re Ford Motor Co., 427 S.W.3d 396, 398 (Tex. 2014) (per curiam); *accord In re Cent. N. Constr., LLC*, No. 05-14-00178-CV, 2014 Tex. App. LEXIS 4010, at *3–4, *7, 2014 WL 1410548 (Tex. App.—Dallas Apr. 10, 2014, orig. proceeding) (mem. op.) (following *Ford Motor* and holding that the defendant's retained-testifying expert's employer did not have "to disclose the dollar amount of gross revenues received by [it] from insurance companies, their policy holders, manufacturers and their attorneys, separately for the years 2009 through 2013 and . . . for the same time period the dollar amount of gross revenues received by [it] from each insurance company, policy holder or their counsel involved in this case" because "[g]enerally, although an expert witness may be questioned regarding payment received for his work as an expert witness, pre-trial discovery sought only to establish financial interest for impeachment purposes is not allowed"); *see In re Vaco*, No. 10-20-00229-CV, 2021 Tex. App. LEXIS 3932, at *7, 2021 WL 2022065 (Tex. App.—Waco May 19, 2021, orig. proceeding) (mem. op.) ("Discovery of bias evidence is what is expressly permitted by the rule, but a document request has never been a proper discovery tool to conduct a fishing expedition, particularly to try to find impeachment evidence limited to bias."); *In re State Farm Lloyds*, No. 02-20-00163-CV, 2020 Tex. App. LEXIS 7207, at *15–16, 2020 WL 5242414 (Tex. App.—Fort Worth Sept. 3, 2020, orig. proceeding) (mem. op.) (holding that the trial court abused its discretion by ordering the defendant to produce engineering reports issued by a consultant for all claims over a five-year period because it was not relevant to show bias); *In re Interinsurance Exch.*, No. 01-14-00979-CV, 2016 Tex. App. LEXIS 268, at *9–10, 2016 WL 144784 (Tex. App.—Houston [1st Dist.] Jan. 12, 2016, orig. proceeding) (mem. op.) (following *Ford Motor* and holding that trial court abused its discretion in ordering the defendant insurer's testifying expert to produce all of his other reports for the defendant over a twelve-year period because the expert had testified about them in his deposition); *In re Siroosian*, 449 S.W.3d 920, 924–25 (Tex. App.—Fort Worth 2014, orig. proceeding) (following *Ford Motor* and holding that the plaintiff's treating chiropractor did not have to answer deposition questions about (1) the software used by, and the collections, revenues, and billings of, his employer' or (2) his personal political contributions because it was not reasonably calculated to reveal any bias); *In re Weir*, 166 S.W.3d 861, 865 (Tex. App.—Beaumont 2005, orig. proceeding) (per curiam) (holding that a retained-testifying expert did not have to testify about his personal financial information because there was other evidence of his bias), *cited with approval in In re Ford Motor Co.*, 427 S.W.3d 396, 397 (Tex. 2014) (per curiam); *Olinger v. Curry*, 926 S.W.2d 832, 834–35 (Tex. App.—Fort Worth 1996, orig. proceeding) (holding that the trial court abused its discretion in ordering the production of a retained-testifying expert's tax returns because the expert had admitted during his deposition that 90 percent of his services were provided to defendants in litigation), *cited with approval in In re Ford Motor Co.*, 427 S.W.3d 396, 397 (Tex. 2014) (per curiam).

bias discovered after the expert's deposition that puts the expert's credibility in doubt, discovery beyond the expert's deposition might be permissible."[90]

7-4:7 Amending and Supplementing Testifying Expert Discovery

Texas Rule 193.5, concerning amending and supplementing responses to written discovery, applies to Texas Rule 195.5(a) expert disclosures.[91] Accordingly, a party must supplement its expert disclosure "reasonably promptly" after it learns new information.[92] In addition, "[i]f an expert witness is retained by, employed by, or otherwise within a party's control, that party must also amend or supplement any deposition testimony or written report by the expert, but only with regard to the expert's mental impressions or opinions and the basis for them."[93] Although Rule 195.6 refers to

---

[90] *In re Cent. N. Constr., LLC,* No. 05-14-00178-CV, 2014 Tex. App. LEXIS 4010, at *8 (Tex. App.—Dallas Apr. 10, 2014, orig. proceeding) (mem. op.).

[91] Tex. R. Civ. P. 195.6 ("A party's duty to amend and supplement written discovery regarding a testifying expert is governed by [Texas] Rule 193.5."). Texas Rule 193.5's amendment and supplementation requirement is discussed generally in Chapter 5, section 5-6.

[92] Tex. R. Civ. P. 193.5(b) ("An amended or supplemental response must be made reasonably promptly after the party discovers the necessity for such a response. Except as otherwise provided by these rules, it is presumed that an amended or supplemental response made less than 30 days before trial was not made reasonably promptly."); *see Garcia v. Roth Constr., Inc.*, No. 13-18-00458-CV, 2020 Tex. App. LEXIS 5688, at *29–30, 2020 WL 4218715, (Tex. App.—Corpus Christi July 23, 2020, pet. denied) (mem. op.) ("When an expert changes her opinion about a material issue after being deposed, the party must supplement discovery."); *Whallon v. City of Hous.*, 462 S.W.3d 146, 169 (Tex. App.—Houston [1st Dist.] 2015, no pet.) ("Supplemental discovery related to a testifying expert should be made 'reasonably promptly after the party discovers the necessity for such a response.' There is a presumption that supplementation less than 30 days before trial is not made 'reasonably promptly.'" (quoting Tex. R. Civ. P. 193.5(b))); *Kingsley Props., LP v. San Jacinto Title Servs. of Corpus Christi, LLC,* 501 S.W.3d 344, 353 (Tex. App.—Corpus Christi 2016, no pet.) ("If a party learns that its written discovery responses regarding a testifying expert were or have become incomplete or incorrect, the party must supplement the response, unless the additional or corrective information has been made known to the other parties.").

A failure to supplement or amend expert discovery can lead to the exclusion of the expert's testimony at trial under Texas Rule 193.6. *E.g., City of Brownsville v. Ahumada*, No. 13-14-00265-CV, 2015 Tex. App. LEXIS 6858, at *5, 2015 WL 4116731 (Tex. App.—Corpus Christi July 2, 2015, no pet.) (mem. op.) ("A trial court can exclude an expert from testifying where there was an inadequate disclosure regarding the expert designation. . . . An expert is not permitted to testify to undisclosed opinions at trial without a showing that there was good cause for the failure to timely make, amend, or supplement the disclosures or that the failure to supplement will not unfairly surprise or prejudice the other party.") (citations omitted); *VingCard A.S. v. Merrimac Hosp. Sys., Inc.*, 59 S.W.3d 847, 856 (Tex. App.—Fort Worth 2001, pet. denied) (holding that the trial court did not abuse its discretion in excluding an expert from testifying where there was an inadequate disclosure regarding the expert designation and no showing of good cause, lack of surprise, or lack of prejudice). See also Chapter 5, section 5-7 (discussing the consequences of failing to timely respond, supplement, or amend written discovery).

[93] Tex. R. Civ. P. 195.6; *see Kingsley Props., LP v. San Jacinto Title Servs. of Corpus Christi, LLC,* 501 S.W.3d 344, 353 (Tex. App.—Corpus Christi 2016, no pet.) ("A party must also

amending or supplementing "any deposition testimony or written report,"[94] a party should amend or supplement both types of discovery even though the supplementation of only one of them might preclude the opposing party from excluding the evidence under the "unfair surprise" or "unfair prejudice" standard of Texas Rule 193.6 for the exclusion of evidence.

There is no supplementation or amendment obligation for certain information. "[F]actual observations, tests, supporting, [and] data calculations" need not be supplemented.[95] And, in some instances, even a "change in an expert's opinion does not require supplementation. For example, an expert may refine calculations or perfect a report through the time of trial. An expert may also change an opinion without supplementation if the opinion is an 'expansion on an already disclosed subject.' However, a party may not present a material alteration of an expert's opinion at trial that would constitute a surprise attack."[96]

---

supplement incomplete or incorrect deposition testimony by a retained expert, but only with regard to the expert's mental impressions or opinions and the basis for them."). The deposition testimony of a non-retained-testifying expert does not have to be supplemented. Tex. R. Civ. P. 195.6, 205.

94 Tex. R. Civ. P. 195.6 (emphasis added).

95 *See* Tex. R. Civ. P. 195.6 (limiting amendment and supplementation requirements to "expert's mental impressions or opinions and the basis for them"). Because the line between "mental impressions," which must be supplemented, and "factual observations," is a fine one, prudence dictates that counsel err on the side of providing supplementation or amendment.

96 *Pilgrim's Pride Corp. v. Smoak*, 134 S.W.3d 880, 902 (Tex. App.—Texarkana 2004, pet. denied) (citation omitted)(quoting *Navistar Int'l Transp. Corp. v. Crim Truck & Tractor Co.*, 883 S.W.2d 687, 691 (Tex. App.—Texarkana 1994, writ denied)); accord *Exxon Corp. v. W. Tex. Gathering Co.*, 868 S.W.2d 299, 304 (Tex. 1993) ("Our rules do not prevent experts from refining calculations and perfecting reports through the time of trial. The testimony of an expert should not be barred because a change in some minor detail of the person's work has not been disclosed a month before trial."); *Garcia v. Roth Constr., Inc.*, No. 13-18-00458-CV, 2020 Tex. App. LEXIS 5688, at *34–35, 2020 WL 4218715, (Tex. App.—Corpus Christi July 23, 2020, pet. denied) (mem. op.) (holding that the trial court abused its discretion by excluding a non-retained treating physician's supplemental affidavit when the opinion "was only an expansion of information that she revealed during her deposition."); *JLG Trucking LLC v. Garza*, 461 S.W.3d 554, 559–60 (Tex. App.—San Antonio 2013) (mem op.) ("Although Cortez recalculated Garza's future earning capacity based on information that she was steadily working toward completing her accounting degree, his methodology and the formula he used to make his calculations did not change."), *rev'd on other grounds*, 466 S.W.3d 157 (Tex. 2015); *Norfolk S. Ry. v. Bailey*, 92 S.W.3d 577, 581–82 (Tex. App.—Austin 2002, no pet.) ("In some instances, the change in an expert's opinion does not require supplementation. For example, an expert may refine calculations or perfect a report up until the time of trial. An expert also may change an opinion without supplementation if the opinion is an 'expansion of an already disclosed subject.' However, a party may not present a material alteration of an expert's opinion at trial that would constitute a surprise attack. The purpose of requiring timely disclosure of a material change in an expert's opinion is to give the other party an opportunity to prepare a rebuttal. . . . [A]lthough we find no cases directly on point about admitting a change in testimony based on the progression of asbestosis, Dr. Darcey's revised diagnosis falls somewhere between a refinement in calculations and an expansion of an already disclosed subject, both of which are admissible without the need for supplementation. We therefore conclude that the district court acted within the bounds of its discretion when it denied Norfolk Southern's motion to strike Dr. Darcey's testimony about his revised diagnosis." (citations omitted) (quoting *Navistar Int'l*

Nothing in Texas Rule 193.6 explains how to supplement or amend deposition testimony. Presumably, it can be done in any manner that communicates the new information, such as a letter or a statement on the record during another deposition in the action.[97]

7-5 Discovery Concerning Consulting Experts

As previously noted, Texas Rule 195 relates only to testifying experts.[98] Also as previously noted, discovery concerning a consulting-only expert is impermissible.[99]

Broad discovery, however, is available concerning a consulting expert whose mental impressions or opinions have been reviewed by a testifying expert.[100] The scope of such discovery is governed by Texas Rule 192.3(e) and, under that Rule, is the same as that for testifying experts.[101] In other words, a party is entitled to obtain the same information concerning a testifying expert and a consulting expert whose mental impressions or opinions have been reviewed by a testifying expert. And, although Texas Rule 195 limits the discovery methods concerning testifying experts, it does not limit the methods concerning consulting experts whose mental impressions or opinions have been reviewed by a testifying expert.[102] Rather, discovery concerning such consulting experts can be obtained by the methods permitted with respect to witnesses other than testifying experts. Thus, for example, interrogatories, although impermissible with respect to testifying experts, can be used with respect to consulting experts whose mental impressions or opinions have been reviewed by a testifying expert (and should be used with respect to such consulting experts because Texas Rule 195.5(a)'s disclosure obligation does not apply to them).

Transp. Corp. v. Crim Truck & Tractor Co., 883 S.W.2d 687, 691 (Tex. App.—Texarkana 1994, writ denied))); *Koko Motel, Inc. v. Mayo*, 91 S.W.3d 41, 51 (Tex. App.—Amarillo 2002, pet. denied) (holding that the trial court did not abuse its discretion in allowing an expert to testify by applying different data into his old methodology or formulas to voice an alternate opinion). *But see Kingsley Props., LP v. San Jacinto Title Servs. of Corpus Christi, LLC*, 501 S.W.3d 344, 353–54 (Tex. App.—Corpus Christi 2016, no pet.) (after pointing out that "[t]he discovery rules do not prevent experts from refining calculations and perfecting reports through the time of trial," holding that the trial court did not abuse its discretion in excluding defendant's expert's testimony because the defendant failed to supplement its disclosures or the expert's deposition testimony to indicate that the expert was relying on city ordinances not previously disclosed (quoting *Exxon Corp. v. W. Tex. Gathering Co.*, 868 S.W.2d 299, 304 (Tex. 1993))).

97 *See* Tex. R. Civ. P. 193.5(a)(2) (noting that there is no supplementation obligation if the information "has been made known to the other parties in writing [or] on the record at a deposition").

98 See Chapter 7, section 7-3 to -4.

99 See note 16 and accompanying text.

100 *See* Tex. R. Civ. P. 192.3(e) (providing for the scope of expert discovery); *see* Tex. R. Civ. P. 195 cmt. 1 to 1999 change ("This rule does not limit the permissible methods of discovery concerning consulting experts whose mental impressions or opinions have been reviewed by a testifying expert.").

101 Tex. R. Civ. P. 192.3(e).

102 Tex. R. Civ. P. 195 cmt. 1 to 1999 change ("This rule does not limit the permissible methods of discovery concerning consulting experts whose mental impressions or opinions have been reviewed by a testifying expert.").

Moreover, as discussed in Chapter 6, section 6-3:3.5a, a consulting expert who has first-hand knowledge of relevant facts or acquired knowledge of relevant facts other than in consultation about the action is not a consulting-only expert immune from discovery. Rather, such a person can be deposed regarding that knowledge.[103]

---

[103] A party's employee can be a consulting-only expert, but generally only if the employee was not employed in the area that is the subject of the action, has no first-hand knowledge of facts, and was assigned to the area specifically to assist the employer in anticipation of litigation or preparation for trial.

CHAPTER 8

Production Requests—Texas Rule 196

8-1 Text of Rule 196

RULE 196. REQUESTS FOR PRODUCTION AND INSPECTION TO PARTIES; REQUESTS AND MOTIONS FOR ENTRY UPON PROPERTY

196.1. Request for Production and Inspection to Parties

(a) **Request.** A party may serve on another party—no later than 30 days before the end of the discovery period—a request for production or for inspection, to inspect, sample, test, photograph and copy documents or tangible things within the scope of discovery.

(b) **Contents of request.** The request must specify the items to be produced or inspected, either by individual item or by category, and describe with reasonable particularity each item and category. The request must specify a reasonable time (on or after the date on which the response is due) and place for production. If the requesting party will sample or test the requested items, the means, manner and procedure for testing or sampling must be described with sufficient specificity to inform the producing party of the means, manner, and procedure for testing or sampling.

(c) **Requests for production of medical or mental health records regarding nonparties**

(1) **Service of request on nonparty.** If a party requests another party to produce medical or mental health records regarding a nonparty, the requesting party must serve the nonparty with the request for production under Rule 21a.

(2) **Exceptions.** A party is not required to serve the request for production on a nonparty whose medical records are sought if:

(A) the nonparty signs a release of the records that is effective as to the requesting party;

(B) the identity of the nonparty whose records are sought will not directly or indirectly be disclosed by production of the records; or

(C) the court, upon a showing of good cause by the party seeking the records, orders that service is not required.

(3) **Confidentiality.** Nothing in this rule excuses compliance with laws concerning the confidentiality of medical or mental health records.

196.2. Response to Request for Production and Inspection

(a) **Time for response.** The responding party must serve a written response on the requesting party within 30 days after service of the request.

(b) **Content of response.** With respect to each item or category of items, the responding party must state objections and assert privileges as required by these rules, and state, as appropriate, that:

(1) production, inspection, or other requested action will be permitted as requested;

(2) the requested items are being served on the requesting party with the response;

(3) production, inspection, or other requested action will take place at a specified time and place, if the responding party is objecting to the time and place of production; or

(4) no items have been identified—after a diligent search—that are responsive to the request.

196.3. Production

(a) **Time and place of production.** Subject to any objections stated in the response, the responding party must produce the requested documents or tangible things within the person's possession, custody or control at either the time and place requested or the time and place stated in the response, unless otherwise agreed by the parties or ordered by the court, and must provide the requesting party a reasonable opportunity to inspect them.

(b) **Copies.** The responding party may produce copies in lieu of originals unless a question is raised as to the authenticity of the original or in the circumstances it would be unfair to produce copies in lieu of originals. If originals are produced, the responding party is entitled to retain the originals while the requesting party inspects and copies them.

(c) **Organization.** The responding party must either produce documents and tangible things as they are kept in the usual course of business or organize and label them to correspond with the categories in the request.

196.4. Electronic or Magnetic Data

To obtain discovery of data or information that exists in electronic or magnetic form, the requesting party must specifically request production of electronic or magnetic data and specify the form in which the requesting party wants it produced. The responding party must produce the electronic or magnetic data that is responsive to the request and is reasonably available to the responding party in its ordinary course of business. If the responding party cannot—through reasonable efforts—retrieve the data or information requested or produce it in the form requested, the responding party must state an objection complying with these rules. If the court orders the responding party to comply with the request, the court must also order that the requesting party pay the reasonable expenses of any extraordinary steps required to retrieve and produce the information.

196.5. Destruction or Alteration

Testing, sampling or examination of an item may not destroy or materially alter an item unless previously authorized by the court.

196.6. Expenses of Production

Unless otherwise ordered by the court for good cause, the expense of producing items will be borne by the responding party and the expense of inspecting, sampling, testing, photographing, and copying items produced will be borne by the requesting party.

196.7. Request or Motion for Entry upon Property

(a) **Request or motion.** A party may gain entry on designated land or other property to inspect, measure, survey, photograph, test, or sample the property or any designated object or operation thereon by serving—no later than 30 days before the end of any applicable discovery period—

(1) a request on all parties if the land or property belongs to a party, or

(2) a motion and notice of hearing on all parties and the nonparty if the land or property belongs to a nonparty. If the identity or address of the nonparty is unknown and cannot be obtained through reasonable diligence, the court must permit service by means other than those specified in Rule 21a that are reasonably calculated to give the nonparty notice of the motion and hearing.

(b) **Time, place, and other conditions.** The request for entry upon a party's property, or the order for entry upon a nonparty's property, must state the time, place, manner, conditions, and scope of the inspection, and must specifically describe any desired means, manner, and procedure for testing or sampling, and the person or persons by whom the inspection, testing, or sampling is to be made.

(c) **Response to request for entry.**

(1) **Time to respond.** The responding party must serve a written response on the requesting party within 30 days after service of the request.

(2) **Content of response.** The responding party must state objections and assert privileges as required by these rules, and state, as appropriate, that:

(A) entry or other requested action will be permitted as requested;

(B) entry or other requested action will take place at a specified time and place, if the responding party is objecting to the time and place of production; or

(C) entry or other requested action cannot be permitted for reasons stated in the response.

(d) **Requirements for order for entry on nonparty's property.** An order for entry on a nonparty's property may issue only for good cause shown and only if the land, property, or object thereon as to which discovery is sought is relevant to the subject matter of the action.

Comments to Texas Rule 196

Comments to 1999 change:

1. "Document and tangible things" are defined in Rule 192.3(b).
2. A party requesting sampling or testing must describe the procedure with sufficient specificity to enable the responding party to make any appropriate objections.
3. A party requesting production of magnetic or electronic data must specifically request the data, specify the form in which it wants the data produced, and specify any extraordinary steps for retrieval and translation. Unless ordered otherwise, the responding party need only produce the data reasonably available in the ordinary course of business in reasonably usable form.
4. The rule clarifies how the expenses of production are to be allocated absent a court order to the contrary.
5. The obligation of parties to produce documents within their possession, custody or control is explained in Rule 192.3(b).
6. Parties may request production and inspection of documents and tangible things from nonparties under Rule 205.3.
7. Rule 196.3(b) is based on Tex. R. Evid. 1003.
8. Rule 196.1(c) is merely a notice requirement and does not expand the scope of discovery of a nonparty's medical records.

8-1:1 2021 Amendments to the Texas Rules of Civil Procedure

The 2021 amendments generally prohibit a party from serving "discovery on another party until after the other party's initial disclosures are due."[1] Accordingly, as part of the 2021 amendments, the Texas Supreme Court struck the part of former Texas Rules 196.2(a) and 196.7(c)(1) providing that "a defendant served with a [discovery] request before the defendant's answer is due need not respond until 50 days after service of the request."[2] Apart from this change, the 2021 amendments did not modify Texas Rule 196.

8-2 Production Requests in General

Texas Rule 196 governs requests for the production, inspection, sampling, photographing, and copying of documents and tangible things.[3] As with other written-discovery

---

[1] Tex. R. Civ. P 192.2(a) ("Unless otherwise agreed to by the parties or ordered by the court, a party cannot serve discovery on another party until after the other party's initial disclosures are due.").

[2] Former Tex. R. Civ. P. 196.2(a), 196.7(c)(1).

[3] Tex. R. Civ. P. 196.1(a) ("A party may serve on another party . . . a request for production or for inspection, to inspect, sample, test, photograph and copy documents or tangible things[.]"). The other discovery rules relating to production requests are Texas Rules 190, 191, 192, 193, 199.2(5), and 215. Under Texas Rule 199.2(5), a deposition notice can require

requests, production requests must be served no later than thirty days (and in some cases thirty-one or thirty-three days) before the discovery period ends[4] but not until after the responding party's initial disclosures are due.[5]

Production requests can seek the inspection, sampling, testing, photographing, or copying of any documents or tangible things within discovery's scope.[6] Given Texas Rule 196.1's use of the broad term "tangible things," it is difficult to imagine anything that cannot be required to be produced, tested, or sampled under appropriate circumstances. For example, one federal court, under Federal Rule 34, on which Texas Rule 196 is based, ordered a dead body exhumed and produced[7] and others have ordered DNA testing[8] and handwriting exemplars or fingerprints.[9]

---

a party to produce documents at its deposition. Such requests are governed by Texas Rule 196. Although a Texas Rule 196 production request cannot be served on nonparties, documents and tangible things can be obtained from them under Texas Rule 205.3(a). Tex. R. Civ. P. 205.3(a); *see* Tex. R. Civ. P. 196.1(a). See also Chapter 13 (discussing nonparty-document subpoenas).

4 Tex. R. Civ. P. 196.1(a); *e.g., Sohani v. Sunesara*, 546 S.W.3d 393, 408 (Tex. App.—Houston [1st Dist.] 2018, no pet.) ("No later than thirty days before the end of the discovery period, a party may serve on another party a request for production of documents within the scope of discovery.").

If the production request is served by mail, it must be served at least thirty-three days before the discovery period's end. *See* Tex. R. Civ. P. 21a(c). If it is served by fax after 5:00 p.m. local time of the recipient, the request must be served at least thirty-one days before the discovery period ends. *See* Tex. R. Civ. P. 21a(b)(2). Texas Rule 196.7 governs requests and motions for entry upon parties' and nonparties' real property. See Chapter 8, section 8-7 (discussing such requests and motions).

5 Tex. R. Civ. P. 192.2(a) ("Unless otherwise agreed to by the parties or ordered by the court, a party cannot serve discovery on another party until after the other party's initial disclosures are due.").

6 Tex. R. Civ. P. 196.1(a).

7 *Zalatuka v. Metro. Life Ins. Co.*, 108 F.2d 405, 405 (7th Cir. 1939); *see Wilstein v. San Tropai Condo. Master Ass'n*, 189 F.R.D. 371, 382 (N.D. Ill. 1999) ("For purposes of discovery, 'it is difficult to imagine any document or thing which could not be ordered produced under appropriate circumstances.' As [one leading] treatise notes, even dead bodies can be ordered produced." (quoting 4A *Moore's Federal Practice* § 34.09 (1983))).

8 *E.g., McGrath v. Nassau Health Care Corp.*, 209 F.R.D. 55, 61 (E.D.N.Y. 2002).

9 *E.g., Harris v. Athol-Royalston Reg'l Sch. Dist. Comm.*, 200 F.R.D. 18, 20–21 (D. Mass. 2001) (handwriting exemplars and citing cases); *Alford v. Ne. Ins. Co., Inc.*, 102 F.R.D. 99, 101 (N.D. Fla. 1984) (fingerprints).

Other courts have ordered the following items produced: (1) business records, *In re Rogers*, 200 S.W.3d 318, 322 (Tex. App.—Dallas 2006, orig. proceeding); *Federal Sav. & Loan Ins. Corp. v. Commonwealth Land Title Ins. Co.*, 130 F.R.D. 507, 509 (D.D.C. 1990); (2) tax returns, *Hall v. Lawlis*, 907 S.W.2d 493, 494–95 (Tex. 1995) (orig. proceeding) (per curiam); *Scott v. Arex, Inc.*, 124 F.R.D. 39, 41 (D. Conn. 1989); (3) social-security records, *Grove v. Aetna Cas. & Sur. Co.*, 855 F. Supp. 113, 116 (W.D. Pa. 1993); (4) bank records, *In re Gonzalez*, No. 14-10-01186-CV, 2010 Tex. App. LEXIS 9831, at *4–5, 2010 WL 5132590 (Tex. App.—Houston [14th Dist.] Dec. 14, 2010, orig. proceeding) (mem. op.); *Daval Steel Prods., Div. of Francosteel Corp. v. M/V Fakredine*, 951 F.2d 1357, 1367–68 (2d Cir. 1991); (5) photographs, *Terry v. Lawrence*, 700 S.W.2d 912, 913–14 (Tex. 1985) (orig. proceeding); *Daniels v. Nat'l R.R. Passenger Corp.*, 110 F.R.D. 160, 161 (S.D.N.Y. 1986); (6) movies and videotapes, *Food Lion, Inc. v. Capital Cities / ABC, Inc.*, 165 F.R.D. 454, 457 (M.D.N.C. 1996); (7) drawings, *Fin. Bldg. Consultants, Inc. v. Am. Druggists Ins. Co.*, 91 F.R.D. 59, 60 (N.D. Ga. 1981); (8) employment records,

Each production request must specify the items to be produced or inspected individually or by category and, further, describe each item or category with "reasonable particularity."[10] "Reasonable particularity," however, is not susceptible of a precise definition.[11] It depends on whether a reasonable person would know what documents or things are called for by the request.[12] The degree of specificity required depends on

---

Tri-State Wholesale Associated Grocers, Inc. v. Barrerra, 917 S.W.2d 391, 399 (Tex. App.—El Paso 1996, writ dism'd by agr.); *Cason v. Builders Firstsource-Se. Grp., Inc.*, 159 F. Supp. 2d 242, 248 (W.D.N.C. 2001); (9) contracts, *Chamberlain v. Cherry*, 818 S.W.2d 201, 204 (Tex. App.—Amarillo 1991, orig. proceeding); *Carey-Can., Inc. v. Cal. Union Ins. Co.*, 118 F.R.D. 242, 244–45 (D.D.C. 1986); (10) deposition transcripts, *In re Domestic Air Transp. Antitrust Litig.*, 142 F.R.D. 354, 355–56 (N.D. Ga. 1992); *Biben v. Card*, 119 F.R.D. 421, 429–30 (W.D. Mo. 1987); (11) fingerprints, *Harris v. Athol-Royalston Reg'l Sch. Dist. Comm.*, 206 F.R.D. 30, 33 (D. Mass. 2002); *Alford v. Ne. Ins. Co.*, 102 F.R.D. 99, 101 (N.D. Fla. 1984); (12) vaccine samples, *Williams v. Am. Cyanamid*, 164 F.R.D. 608, 611 (D.N.J. 1995); (13) diaries, *Merrill v. Waffle House, Inc.*, 227 F.R.D. 467, 472 (N.D. Tex. 2005); and (14) scientific-research data, *Simon v. G.D. Searle & Co.*, 119 F.R.D. 680, 681 (D. Minn. 1987).

[10] Tex. R. Civ. P. 196.1(b) ("The request must specify the items to be produced or inspected, either by individual item or by category, and describe with reasonable particularity each item and category."); *accord Loftin v. Martin*, 776 S.W.2d 145, 148 (Tex. 1989) (orig. proceeding) (holding that production requests "must be specific . . . and must recite precisely what is wanted"), *disapproved of on other grounds by Walker v. Packer*, 827 S.W.2d 833, 842 (Tex. 1992) (orig. proceeding); *In re Treatment Equip. Co.*, No. 02-19-00202-CV, 2019 Tex. App. LEXIS 6267, at *10, 2019 WL 3295633 (Tex. App.—Fort Worth July 23, 2019, orig. proceeding) (mem. op.) ("The [Texas] rules also dictate the contents of those requests: they 'must specify the items to be produced' and describe each item 'with reasonable particularity.'" (quoting Tex. R. Civ. P. 196.1(b))); *In re Belmore*, No. 05-04-01035-CV, 2004 Tex. App. LEXIS 8160, at *12, 2004 WL 1983597 (Tex. App.—Dallas, Sept. 8, 2004, orig. proceeding) (mem. op.) (holding that production requests must describe "with reasonable particularity" each item or category sought); *cf.* Fed. R. Civ. P. 34(b)(1)(A) ("The request . . . must describe with reasonable particularity each item or category of items to be inspected.").

[11] *Cf. Mallinckrodt Chem. Works v. Goldman, Sachs & Co.*, 58 F.R.D. 348, 353 (S.D.N.Y. 1973) ("'[R]easonable particularity' . . . is not susceptible to exact definition. What is reasonably particular is dependent upon the facts and circumstances in each case."), *quoted with approval in Lopez v. Chertoff*, No. CV 07-1566-LEW, 2009 U.S. Dist. LEXIS 50419, at *5, 2009 WL 1575214 (E.D. Cal. June 2, 2009).

[12] *Cf. Avanos Med. Sales, LLC v. Medtronic Sofamor Danek USA, Inc.*, No. 19-CV-02754-JPM-TMP, 2021 U.S. Dist. LEXIS 41670, at *21, 2021 WL 848177 (W.D. Tenn. Mar. 5, 2021) ("To determine if a request fails for reasonable particularity, district courts within the Sixth Circuit consider 'whether the request places the party upon reasonable notice of what is called for and what is not.'" quoting *Pan v. Kohl's Dep't Stores, Inc.*, No. 2:12-CV-1063, 2015 U.S. Dist. LEXIS 92001, at *5, 2015 WL 4346218 (S.D. Ohio July 15, 2015))); *Lopez v. Don Herring Ltd.*, 327 F.R.D. 567, 575 (N.D. Tex. 2018) (same); *Singh v. Hancock Nat. Res. Grp., Inc.*, No. 1:15-cv-01435 LJO JLT, 2016 U.S. Dist. LEXIS 179974, at *3, 2016 WL 7474886 (E.D. Cal. Dec. 28, 2016) (same); *Hager v. Graham*, 267 F.R.D. 486, 493 (N.D.W. Va. 2010) ("The test for reasonable particularity is whether the request places the party upon reasonable notice of what is called for and what is not. Therefore, the party requesting the production of documents must provide sufficient information to enable [the party to whom the request is directed] to identify responsive documents. This test, however, is a matter of degree depending on the circumstances of the case." (citations omitted) (quoting *Kidwiler v. Progressive Paloverde Ins. Co.*, 192 F.R.D. 193, 202 (N.D.W. Va. 2000))); *U.S. v. Nat'l Steel Corp.*, 26 F.R.D. 607, 610 (S.D. Tex. 1960) ("The goal [of particularity] is that the description be sufficient to apprise a man of ordinary intelligence which documents are required.").

the requesting party's knowledge about the documents or things sought as well as the action's progress when the request is made. Thus, a request served early in an action generally can be less precisely drafted than one served after substantial discovery has been taken.[13]

Each production request must specify a reasonable time and place for the production or inspection on or after the date when the written response to the request is due.[14] In other words, the request should generally set a deadline for the response (typically thirty days after service), as well as the place and time of production or inspection (for documents, typically thirty days after service at the requesting party's attorney's office; for testing or sampling, typically thirty days after service at the tangible thing's location).[15]

If the requesting party intends to test or sample the requested item, the requesting party must also specify the testing's or sampling's manner and its means and procedure with "sufficient specificity" to allow the responding party to make appropriate objections.[16] Absent the parties' agreement, the requested testing, sampling, or examination may not destroy or materially alter an item without prior court approval.[17]

Production requests, like all other written-discovery requests, must be signed by either the party's attorney or a pro se party.[18] If they are not properly signed, they "must be stricken unless [they are] signed promptly after the omission is called to the attention of the [requesting] party[.]"[19] Moreover, a responding party need not respond to a production request that is not signed.[20]

---

[13] *Cf. Taylor v. Fla. Atl. Univ.*, 132 F.R.D. 304, 305 (S.D. Fla. 1990) (holding that the categories of documents were set forth "with as much reasonable particularity as can be expected at this stage of discovery"), ***aff'd sub nom.***, *Taylor v. Popovich*, 976 F.2d 743 (11th Cir. 1992).

[14] Tex. R. Civ. P. 196.1(b).

[15] *See* Tex. R. Civ. P. 196.1(b), 196.2(a). A production request can provide more than thirty days to either respond or produce the documents or tangible things. It cannot, however, require less than thirty days. Tex. R. Civ. P. 196.2(a); ***In re Treatment Equip. Co.***, No. 02-19-00202-CV, 2019 Tex. App. LEXIS 6267, at *11, 2019 WL 3295633 (Tex. App.—Fort Worth July 23, 2019, orig. proceeding) (mem. op.) ("The responding party has at least thirty days to either object or assert a privilege to the requests or to answer them."); *see* ***Sohani v. Sunesara***, 546 S.W.3d 393, 408 (Tex. App.—Houston [1st Dist.] 2018, no pet.) ("The responding party must serve a written response to the request within thirty days after service of the request."). Notwithstanding the general practice of setting production deadlines for responding parties, there is no reason why the production request cannot specify production and inspection at a time and place convenient for the responding party, leaving it to the responding party to designate the time and place in its response. *See* Tex. R. Civ. P. 196.3(a).

[16] Tex. R. Civ. P. 196.1(b).

[17] Tex. R. Civ. P. 196.5.

[18] Tex. R. Civ. P. 191.3(a). See also Chapter 3, section 3-5 (discussing signing of written-discovery requests).

[19] Tex. R. Civ. P. 191.3(d).

[20] Tex. R. Civ. P. 191.3(d) ("A party is not required to take any action with respect to a request or notice that is not signed."); *cf.* ***Ingram v. State***, No. 09-10-00346-CV, 2011 Tex. App. LEXIS 8767, at *6–7, 2011 WL 5299475 (Tex. App.—Beaumont November 3, 2011, pet. denied) (mem. op.) ("The requests for admission in the record do not bear Ingram's signature. When a party receives requests that are not signed, the Rules of Civil Procedure do not require the party to take any action. Because Ingram's requests for admission do not bear

Like other written-discovery requests, production requests are not filed,[21] but must be served on all parties to the action.[22] In addition, the parties "must retain the original or exact copy of [the request] during the pendency of the case and any related appellate proceedings begun within six months after judgment is signed, unless otherwise provided by the trial court."[23]

8-3 Number of Production Requests

The action's discovery control plan, rather than Texas Rule 196, governs the number of production requests.[24] Level 1 actions are limited to fifteen production requests, including "discrete subparts."[25] In contrast, the Texas discovery rules do not limit either the number of production requests or the number of sets of production requests in Level 2 and 3 actions.[26]

As pointed out above, in a Level 1 action, the limit on the number of production requests includes "[e]ach discrete subpart."[27] Although nothing in Texas Rule 190 or its comments explains what constitutes a discrete subpart for a production request, Comment 3 to Texas Rule 190 explains what constitutes one for an interrogatory: "While not susceptible of precise definition, a 'discrete subpart' is, in general, one that calls for information that is not logically or factually related to the primary interrogatory." The test should be same as that with respect to interrogatories.[28]

Despite the absence of an express limit on the number of production requests in Level 2 and 3 actions, the discovery control plan in a Level 3 action can limit their number.[29] In addition, Texas Rules 192.4 and 192.6 allow a court to limit their number in both Level 2 and 3 actions by means of a protective order when: (1) the requests are "unreasonably cumulative or duplicative" of other discovery requests,[30] harassing, or invasive of personal, constitutional, or property rights;[31] (2) the information "sought is obtainable from some other source that is more convenient, less burdensome, or less expensive";[32] or (3) "the burden or expense of the proposed discovery outweighs its likely benefit, taking into account the needs of the case, the amount in controversy, the parties' resources, the importance of the issues at stake in the litigation, and the

---

his signature, the trial court did not err by failing to consider them as having been deemed admitted.").

21 Tex. R. Civ. P. 191.4(a)(1)–(2).

22 Tex. R. Civ. P. 191.5.

23 Tex. R. Civ. P. 191.4(d).

24 Tex. R. Civ. P. 190. Texas Rule 190 provides for three levels of discovery: Levels 1, 2, and 3. See Chapter 2, section 2-3 (discussing the discovery levels generally).

25 Tex. R. Civ. P. 190.2(b)(4). There is no limitation on the number of sets for production requests in a Level 1 action so long as the total number of requests does not exceed fifteen. *See* Tex. R. Civ. P. 190.2(b)(4).

26 Tex. R. Civ. P. 190.3–190.4, 196.

27 Tex. R. Civ. P. 190.2(b)(4).

28 See Chapter 9, section 9-4 (discussing what constitutes a discrete interrogatory subpart).

29 Tex. R. Civ. P. 190.4(b). See also Chapter 2, section 2-3:3 (discussing Level 3 discovery-control plans).

30 Tex. R. Civ. P. 192.4(a).

31 Tex. R. Civ. P. 192.6(b).

32 Tex. R. Civ. P. 192.4(a).

importance of the proposed discovery in resolving the issues."[33] In addition, a court can limit the number of production requests if they are disproportionate to the case's needs.[34]

8-4 Responding to Production Requests

8-4:1 In General

A party must respond in writing to a production request within thirty days after its service[35] unless the time is extended due to the manner of service, by the parties' agreement, or by court order.[36] Each response must be preceded by the request[37] and may include objections and assertions of privilege as allowed by Texas Rule 193.[38]

There are four proper responses to the substance of a production request: (1) a response agreeing to produce the requested items; (2) a response objecting to the request in its entirety; (3) a response objecting to the request in part, for example, because it is overbroad as to time, place, or subject matter;[39] or (4) a response stating

---

33 Tex. R. Civ. P. 192.4(b); *see also* Tex. R. Civ. P. 192.6(b) (allowing a protective order to protect "the movant from undue burden, unnecessary expense, harassment, annoyance, or invasion of personal, constitutional, or property rights").

The third basis for a protective order is the proportionality inquiry recognized by the Texas Supreme Court in *In re State Farm Lloyds*, 520 S.W.3d 595, 607–12 (Tex. 2017) (orig. proceeding). As discussed in Chapter 5, section 5-3:4, a responding party can object to a production request in its entirety or individual production requests on proportionality grounds.

34 *See In re State Farm Lloyds*, 520 S.W.3d 595, 607–12 (Tex. 2017) (orig. proceeding) (setting forth the following seven proportionality factors: (1) the likely benefit of the requested discovery; (2) the needs of the case; (3) the amount in controversy; (4) the parties' resources; (5) the importance of the issues at stake in the litigation; (6) the importance of the proposed discovery in resolving the litigation; and (7) any other articulable factor bearing on proportionality). Proportionality is discussed in Chapter 5, section 5-3:4.

35 Tex. R. Civ. P. 196.2(a).

36 *See* Tex. R. Civ. P. 193.1 ("A party must respond to written discovery in writing within the time provided by court order or these rules."). Three days are added to the response date if the production request is served by mail. Tex. R. Civ. P. 21a(c). One day is added if it is served by fax after 5:00 p.m. local time of the recipient. Tex. R. Civ. P. 21a(b)(2).

If the production request is contained in a deposition notice for a party or a person under a party's control, the receiving party must be given at least thirty days to respond to the request and produce documents. Tex. R. Civ. P. 199.2(b)(5) ("When the witness is a party or subject to the control of a party, document requests under this subdivision are governed by [Texas] Rules 193 and 196.").

37 Tex. R. Civ. P. 193.1 ("The responding party's answers, objections, and other responses must be preceded by the request to which they apply.").

38 Tex. R. Civ. P. 193.1. Objections and privilege assertions are discussed generally in Chapter 5, sections 5-3 and 5-4, respectively.

39 As discussed in Chapter 5, section 5-3, if the production request is objected to only in part, the responding party must clearly indicate the extent to which the request is objected and state what it will produce in response to the request. *See also* Tex. R. Civ. P. 193.2(b) ("A party must comply with as much of the request to which the party has made no objection unless it is unreasonable under the circumstances to do so before obtaining a ruling on the objection.").

that no responsive documents have been identified after a diligent search.[40] Thus, a response that relevant nonprivileged documents will be produced "to *the extent* they exist" is improper.[41] So are responses that merely promise to produce the requested

---

[40] Under Texas Rule 196.2(b)(4), if the responding party has no responsive documents, it must state that "no items have been identified—after diligent search—that are responsive to the request." Tex. R. Civ. P. 196.2(b)(4); *cf. Kinetic Concepts, Inc. v. ConvaTec Inc.*, 268 F.R.D. 226, 240–41 (M.D.N.C. 2010) (same); ("As one court has summarized it: '[T]here are only three appropriate responses to a request for production of documents: (1) an objection to the scope, time, method and manner of the requested production; (2) an answer agreeing to the requested scope, time, place, and manner of production; or (3) or [sic] a response offering a good faith, reasonable alternative production, which is definite in scope, time, place or manner.' Although '[a] party may file a hybrid answer, which objects to some of the requested production, while answering the unobjectionable portions,' 'a response to a request for production of documents which merely promises to produce the requested documents at some unidentified time in the future, without offering a specific time, place and manner, is not a complete answer as required by [Federal] Rule 34(b) and, therefore, pursuant to [the provision now codified at [Federal] Rule 37(a)(4)] is treated as a failure to answer or respond.'" (quoting *Jayne H. Lee, Inc. v. Flagstaff Indus. Corp.*, 173 F.R.D. 651, 656 & n.14 (D. Md. 1997))), *cited with approval in NOA, LLC v. Khoury*, No. 5:14-CV-114-FL, 2016 U.S. Dist. LEXIS 112108, at *17–18, 2016 WL 4444770 (E.D.N.C. Aug. 23, 2016).

[41] *Cf. Klaassen v. Atkinson*, No. 13-2561-DDC, 2016 U.S. Dist. LEXIS 72598, at *9, 2016 WL 3087809 (D. Kan. June 2, 2016) (mem. op.) ("[A] party may not unilaterally withhold information or documents that are responsive to a discovery request by stating that 'all relevant, non-privileged' responsive information or documents have been, or will be, produced." (quoting *Johnson v. Kraft Foods N.A., Inc.*, 236 F.R.D. 535, 541 (D. Kan. 2006))); *Armor Screen Corp. v. Storm Catcher, Inc.*, No. 07-81091-Civ-Ryskamp/Vitunac, 2009 U.S. Dist. LEXIS 63538, at *9–10, 2009 WL 291160 (S.D. Fla. Feb. 5, 2009) ("As to requests 1, 3, 9, 10, 12, 17 and 20, Plaintiff responds by objecting, but then states that 'subject to and without waiving the foregoing objection, [Plaintiff] will make responsive documents, to the extent they exist, available for inspection.' This response does not constitute a clear response and provides no reasonable means for Defendant to know precisely whether and which responsive documents exist. [Federal] Rule 34(b)(2)(B) requires Plaintiff, as the responding party to either state that an inspection will be permitted *or* object with reasons . . . but not both.") (emphasis added); *Innovative Piledriving Prods., LLC v. Unisto Oy*, No. 1:04-CV-453, 2005 U.S. Dist. LEXIS 23652, at *5–6, 2005 WL 8169578 (N.D. Ind. Oct. 14, 2005) ("[E]ven if IPP/HMC has no documents to produce in response to a request, Unisto is at least entitled to a response stating as much. Accordingly, IPP/HMC is ORDERED to execute an affidavit by October 31, 2005, (1) stating that after diligent search there are no responsive documents in its 'possession, custody or control,' . . ., and (2) describing its efforts to locate documents responsive to the requests at issue in Unisto's motion to compel.") (citations omitted); *Fresenius Med. Care Holding Inc. v. Baxter Int'l, Inc.*, 224 F.R.D. 644, 656 (N.D. Cal. 2004) ("[The defendant] responds [to the plaintiff's motion to compel by asserting] that it 'is not withholding any non-privileged, relevant responsive documents' . . ., [however,] [the defendants'] assertion that it is not withholding any non-privileged documents is clearly limited by its unilateral designation of relevance. . . . [The defendant] must produce all non-privileged responsive documents. . . ."); *Mercer v. Allegheny Ludlum Corp.*, 125 F.R.D. 43, 46 (S.D.N.Y. 1989) ("[Non-party] Goldman Sachs, through its counsel, answers [plaintiffs' motion to enforce a subpoena requesting documents] in essence that counsel have looked at the Goldman Sachs files; that they have given to plaintiffs' counsel everything relevant to the issues; and that plaintiffs must be content with that declaration. . . . [T]his is not sufficient. . . . Plaintiffs are not, in my judgment, required to accept the disclaimer of non-relevance from Goldman Sachs or its counsel in respect of documents

documents at some unspecified time in the future or that promise to continue to search for records and supplement responses in the future.[42]

In addition, under Texas Rule 196.2(b), the responding party "must" specifically state in the written response to each production request whether it is objecting to the time and place for the production or inspection set forth in the production request.[43] In doing so, the responding party must state one of three things.

First, if the time and place of the production is acceptable to the responding party and it intends to produce the items then and there, the written response must state that "production, inspection, or other requested action will be permitted as requested."[44]

Second, if the responding party desires to serve its documents with its written response, the response must state that "the requested items are being served on the requesting party with the response."[45]

Third, if the responding party objects to the time or place of the production specified in the production request, the written response must state that "production, inspection, or other requested action will take place at a specified time and place."[46] In other

---

which to date they have not been permitted to inspect."). See also Chapter 5, section 5-3:2 (discussing the inappropriateness of "subject-to" objections to written discovery requests).

42 Tex. R. Civ. P. 196.2(b) (setting forth the permissible responses to a production request); *cf. Source Network Sales & Mkg., LLC v. Jiangsu Mega Motor Co.*, No. 3:16-cv-1202-B-BK, 2017 U.S. Dist. LEXIS 221494, at *6, 2017 WL 7596913 (N.D. Tex. May 15, 2017) ("Mega's promise to search for responsive documents simply reiterates its ongoing duty to supplement under [Federal] Rule 26(e), and is not an adequate response."); *Comcast Cable Commc'ns, L.L.C. v. BT Americas, Inc.*, No. 12-CV-1712-M, 2013 U.S. Dist. LEXIS 195145, at *1, 2013 WL 12129283 (N.D. Tex. July 10, 2013) ("Nor is Defendants' promise to continue to search for documents and supplement their responses an adequate response to Plaintiffs' proper discovery request. *See Kinetic Concepts, Inc. v. ConvaTec Inc.*, 268 F.R.D. 226, 246–47 (M.D. N.C. 2010) (vague assurances that properly requested documents will be produced constitutes 'a completely inadequate response')"); *Autoridad De Carreteras Y Transportacion v. Transcore Atl., Inc.*, 319 F.R.D. 422, 434 (D.P.R. 2016) ("[A] response to a request for production of documents which merely promises to produce the requested documents at some unidentified time in the future, without offering a specific time, place and manner is not a complete answer as required by [Federal] Rule 34(b)." (quoting *Jayne H. Lee, Inc. v. Flagstaff Indus. Corp.*, 173 F.R.D. 651, 656 (D. Md. 1997))); *NOA, LLC v. Khoury*, No. 5:14-CV-114-FL, 2016 U.S. Dist. LEXIS 112108, at *17–18, 2016 WL 4444770 (E.D.N.C. Aug. 23, 2016) (same); *Kinetic Concepts, Inc. v. Convatec Inc.*, 268 F.R.D. 226, 240 (M.D.N.C. 2010) (same). It is also "improper to state . . . that production will be made at some unspecified time in the future," for example, stating that the items will be produced at a mutually agreeable time and place. *Mezu v. Morgan State Univ.*, 269 F.R.D. 565, 574 (D. Md. 2010); *accord Autoridad De Carreteras Y Transportacion v. Transcore Atl., Inc.*, 319 F.R.D. 422, 434 (D.P.R. 2016); *Martinez v. Neiman Marcus Grp., Inc.*, No. 3:05-CV-0422-P, 2005 U.S. Dist. LEXIS 19694, at *17, 2005 WL 2179137 (N.D. Tex. Sept. 7, 2005) (mem. op.); *Jayne H. Lee, Inc. v. Flagstaff Indus. Corp.*, 173 F.R.D. 651, 656 (D. Md. 1997).

43 Tex. R. Civ. P. 196.2(b).

44 Tex. R. Civ. P. 196.2(b)(1).

45 Tex. R. Civ. P. 196.2(b)(2).

46 Tex. R. Civ. P. 196.2(b)(3).

words, the response must state both the objection and the solution[47] (i.e., the responding party must state exactly when and where it will produce the items, and then must produce them at that time and place without further request or order).[48] Except in the rare case where the time or place of production is of unusual importance, this usually is satisfactory and the production will occur without court intervention.[49]

Responses to production requests, like all other written-discovery responses, must be signed by either the party's attorney or a pro se party.[50] Unlike interrogatory answers, however, the responses need not be verified.[51] If the responses are not properly signed, they "must be stricken unless it is signed promptly after the omission is called to the attention of the [responding] party[.]"[52]

Perhaps most importantly, under Texas Rule 193.1, the responding party "must make a complete response, based on all information reasonably available to the responding party or its attorney at the time the response is made."[53] As discussed in Chapter 5, section 5-2:2, nothing in Texas Rules 193 and 196 or the other discovery rules explains when "information" is "reasonably available." As also pointed out in those chapters, what material is reasonably available depends in large measure on the responding party's obligation of reasonable inquiry (i.e., how extensive a search the responding party must make to respond to the discovery request) and on whether the material is in the responding party's possession, custody, or control.[54] This, in turn, depends on the facts of each action.

Like other written-discovery responses, responses to production requests are not filed,[55] but must be served on all parties to the action.[56] In addition, the parties "must retain the original or exact copy of [the responses] during the pendency of the case and any related appellate proceedings begun within six months after judgment is signed, unless otherwise provided by the trial court."[57]

8-4:2 Motion for Protective Order

In appropriate situations, the responding party, rather than responding to a production request can move for a protective order pursuant to Texas Rule 192.6 if (1)

---

[47] Tex. R. Civ. P. 193.2(b) ("If the responding party objects to the requested time and place of production, the responding party must state a reasonable time and place for complying with the request and must comply at that time and place without further request or order."), 196.3 ("[T]he responding party must produce the requested documents or tangible things . . . at either the time and place requested or the time and place stated in the response, unless otherwise agreed to by the parties or ordered by the court[.]").

[48] Tex. R. Civ. P. 193.2(b), 196.3.

[49] *Jayne H. Lee, Inc. v. Flagstaff Indus. Corp.*, 173 F.R.D. 651, 655 (D. Md. 1997) (quoting Charles A. Wright et al., *Federal Practice and Procedure* § 2207 (3d. ed. 2010)).

[50] Tex. R. Civ. P. 191.3(a). See also Chapter 3, section 3–5 (discussing signing of written-discovery responses).

[51] Tex. R. Civ. P. 191.3.

[52] Tex. R. Civ. P. 191.3(d).

[53] Tex. R. Civ. P. 193.1.

[54] "Possession, custody, and control" is discussed in Chapter 8, section 8-4:3.1.

[55] Tex. R. Civ. P. 191.4(a)(1)–(2).

[56] Tex. R. Civ. P. 191.5.

[57] Tex. R. Civ. P. 191.4(d).

the requests subject the answering party to "undue burden, unnecessary expense, harassment, annoyance, or invasion of personal, constitutional, or property rights,"[58] or (2) are disproportionate to the case's needs.[59] The most typical situation in which such a motion will be proper is when the requests are so voluminous that responding to them will be unduly burdensome, unnecessarily expensive, or disproportionate to the case's needs.[60] In such a case, the court must balance the legitimate needs of the requesting party with the burden or expense on the responding party considering the factors in Texas Rule 192.4.[61]

8-4:3 Production or Inspection

The responding party must produce documents and tangible things within its "possession, custody or control" at either the time and place requested or the alternate time and place set forth in its written response.[62] It also must provide the requesting party a reasonable opportunity to inspect its documents and tangible things.[63] Unless the court finds good cause to shift the costs, the responding party is responsible for the cost of producing the items, and the requesting party is responsible for the cost of inspecting, sampling, photographing, and copying them.[64]

Copies rather than original documents may be produced unless either "a question is raised as to the authenticity of the original" or, under the circumstances, "it would be unfair to produce copies in lieu of originals."[65] For example, a party may request the production of an original document to determine if there are handwritten notes on it that are illegible or difficult to read on the copy or to determine if the notes are in different color ink, which would suggest that they were made at different times.

---

58 Tex. R. Civ. P. 192.6.

59 *In re State Farm Lloyds*, 520 S.W.3d 595, 599 (Tex. 2017) (orig. proceeding) ("[A]ll discovery is subject to the proportionality overlay. . . . ."); *In re Shipman*, 540 S.W.3d 562, 569–70 (Tex. 2018) (orig. proceeding) (per curiam) (same); *see In re Muller*, 612 S.W.3d 701, 706 (Tex. App.—Amarillo 2020, orig. proceeding) (citing *In re State Farm Lloyds*, 520 S.W.3d 595, 599 (Tex. 2017) (orig. proceeding), as support for the statement that "the trial court could have reasonably determined that the requested discovery [at issue in the case] was not proportional to the needs of the case or that the burden or expense of production outweigh[ed] its likely benefit"). Proportionality is discussed in Chapter 5, section 5-3:4.

60 See notes 33–34 and accompanying text.

61 *In re State Farm Lloyds*, 520 S.W.3d 595, 607–12 (Tex. 2017) (orig. proceeding) (setting forth the following seven proportionality factors: (1) the likely benefit of the requested discovery; (2) the needs of the case; (3) the amount in controversy; (4) the parties' resources; (5) the importance of the issues at stake in the litigation; (6) the importance of the proposed discovery in resolving the litigation; and (7) any other articulable factor bearing on proportionality). See also Chapter 4, section 4-5 (discussing protective orders), and Chapter 5, section 5-3:4 (discussing proportionality).

62 Tex. R. Civ. P. 196.3(a).

63 Tex. R. Civ. P. 196.3(a).

64 Tex. R. Civ. P. 196.6; *see Tolbert v. Taylor*, 629 S.W.3d 318, 333–34 (Tex. App.—Houston [14th Dist.] 2020, pet. granted) (holding the trial court abused its discretion by requiring the requesting party to pay for the cost of production without a showing of good cause).

65 Tex. R. Civ. P. 196.3(b).

The responding party must produce the documents or things either "as they are kept in the usual course of business or organize and label them to correspond with the categories in the request."[66] Although this directive and the one requiring the responding party to produce documents and things in its "possession, custody, or control"[67] are seemingly simple and straightforward, questions exist regarding both, which are discussed in the following chapters.

8-4:3.1 Possession, Custody, or Control

As noted above, to be subject to production or inspection under Texas Rule 196, the documents or tangible things sought must be within the responding party's "possession, custody, or control." Because the terms are in the disjunctive, only one of the requirements must be met.[68]

A responding party cannot be compelled to produce items that it neither has nor controls.[69] A document that does not exist is not within a party's possession, custody,

---

[66] Tex. R. Civ. P. 196.3(c); *see In re Bilfinger Westcon, Inc.*, No. 13-19-00466-CV, 2019 Tex. App. LEXIS 10807, at *29, 2019 WL 6795870 (Tex. App.—Corpus Christi Dec. 12, 2019, orig. proceeding) (mem. op.) (holding that the trial court did not abuse its discretion by ordering the responding party "to *either* 'identify each tangible item responsive to each' request for production or 'by general categories of documents,'" and noting that the order "was less burdensome than required by the rules") (emphasis added); *In re Exmark Mfg. Co.*, 299 S.W.3d 519, 531 (Tex. App.—Corpus Christi 2009, orig. proceeding) ("Under Texas Rule of Civil Procedure 196.3(c), 'the responding party must either produce documents and tangible things as they are kept in the usual course of business or organize and label them to correspond with the categories in the request.'" (quoting Tex. R. Civ. P. 196.3(c))). Merely producing a mass of disorganized documents does not comply with either of Texas Rule 196.3(c)'s alternatives. *See In re F.C. Holdings, Inc.*, 349 S.W.3d 811, 816 (Tex. App.—Tyler 2011, orig. proceeding) (stating that the party's "failure to organize and identify those pages" in responses to requests for production violated the rules of civil procedure); *cf. Cooper Vision, Inc. v. CIBA Vision Corp.*, No. 2:06CV149, 2007 U.S. Dist. LEXIS 57111, at *13, 2007 WL 2264848 (E.D. Tex. Aug. 6, 2007) (mem. op.) ("[S]imply placing documents in boxes and making them available does not conform to [Federal R]ule [34]."); *Wagner v. Dryvit Sys., Inc.*, 208 F.R.D. 606, 610 (D. Neb. 2001) ("[P]roducing large amounts of documents in no apparent order does not comply with a party's obligation under [Federal] Rule 34."); *Wagner v. Dryvit Sys., Inc.*, 208 F.R.D. 606, 610–11 (D. Neb. 2001) (same); *Stiller v. Arnold*, 167 F.R.D. 68, 71 (N.D. Ind. 1996) ("Producing 7,000 pages of documents in no apparent order does not comply with a party's obligation under [Federal] Rule 34(b).").

[67] Tex. R. Civ. P. 192.3(b).

[68] *Cf. Soto v. City of Concord*, 162 F.R.D. 603, 619 (N.D. Cal. 1995) ("'The phrase "possession, custody or control" is in the disjunctive and only one of the numerated requirements need be met.'" quoting *Cumis Ins. Soc'y, Inc. v. S.*–Coast Bank, 610 F. Supp. 193, 196 (N.D. Ind. 1985))); *see Morris v. Lowe's Home Ctrs., Inc.*, No. 1:10CV388, 2012 U.S. Dist. LEXIS 44422, at *20, 2012 WL 1073405 (M.D.N.C. Mar. 29, 2012) (mem. op.) ("Plaintiff notes that she has produced the 'records which she has in [her] possession,' the obligations under [Federal] Rule 34(a)(1) are broader, requiring the production of documents 'in the responding party's possession, custody, or control[.]' . . . Accordingly, 'Plaintiff has not discharged [her] obligation to produce responsive documents by stating that [she] has no such documents in [her] possession.'") (quoting Fed. R. Civ. P. 34(a)(1) and *EEOC v. Luihn Food Sys., Inc.*, No. 5:09-CV-387-D, 2011 U.S. Dist. LEXIS 13911, at *17, 2011 WL 649749 (E.D.N.C. Feb. 11, 2011)).

[69] *See In re Preventative Pest Control Hous., LLC*, 580 S.W.3d 455, 460 (Tex. App.—Houston [14th Dist.] 2019, orig. proceeding) ("Under Texas procedure, litigants are not required to produce documents or tangible things unless those items lie within their possession, custody,

or control.[70] Thus, a responding party cannot be required to produce a document that no longer exists or that never existed.[71] Nor can it be ordered to create a document

---

or control."); *In re Methodist Primary Care Grp.*, 553 S.W.3d 709, 722 (Tex. App.—Houston [14th Dist.] 2018, orig. proceeding) ("A party may not be compelled to produce documents that are not within its 'possession, custody, or control' as set forth in Texas Rule of Civil Procedure 192.7(b). That a party may have access to the documents is insufficient; the party must have a legal right to possession of the documents."); *cf. Estate of Logan v. City of S. Bend*, No. 3:19-CV-495-DRL-MGG, 2020 U.S. Dist. LEXIS 46347, at *9, 2020 WL 1284742 (N.D. Ind. Mar. 17, 2020) ("Moreover, no person or party, including the City, can produce what it does not control or possess."); *Parris v. Pappas*, No. 3:10CV1128 (WWE), 2017 U.S. Dist. LEXIS 122282, at *4–6, 2017 WL 3314001 (D. Conn. Aug. 3, 2017) ("It is well-established that 'a party is not obliged to produce . . . documents that it does not possess or cannot obtain.'" (quoting *Shcherbakovskiy v. Da Capo Al Fine, Ltd.*, 490 F.3d 130, 138 (2d Cir. 2007))); *N.Y. ex rel. Boardman v. Nat'l R.R. Passenger Corp.*, 233 F.R.D. 259, 267–68 (N.D.N.Y. 2006) (denying motion to compel because one New York state agency does not have control of another agency's documents); *Hagemeyer N. Am., Inc. v. Gateway Data Sciences Corp.*, 222 F.R.D. 594, 598 (E.D. Wis. 2004) ("A party need not produce documents or tangible things that are not in existence or within its control."); *Burton Mech. Contractors, Inc. v. Foreman*, 148 F.R.D. 230, 236 (N.D. Ind. 1992) (denying a motion to compel because the requesting party failed to show that the pertinent documents were in the responding party's possession, custody, or control).

70 *See In re Colonial Pipeline Co.*, 968 S.W.2d 938, 942 (Tex. 1998) (orig. proceeding) (holding that the defendants could not be ordered to prepare an inventory of documents); *McKinney v. Nat'l Union Fire Ins. Co.*, 772 S.W.2d 72, 73 n.2 (Tex. 1989) (explaining that a production request "cannot be used to force a party to make lists or reduce information to tangible form"); *Chavira v. Quarry Hills Mgmt., LLC*, 458 S.W.3d 561, 568 (Tex. App.—El Paso 2014, pet. denied) ("In fact, a discovery request can only seek a document that is in a party's possession, custody or control; it cannot compel a party to create a document where none exists."); *In re Family Dollar Stores of Tex., LLC*, No. 09-11-00432-CV, 2011 Tex. App. LEXIS 8782, at *4–5, 2011 WL 5299578 (Tex. App.—Beaumont Nov. 3, 2011, orig. proceeding) (per curiam) (mem. op.) ("We conclude that requiring a [responding] party to reduce raw data from an electronic database to a paper report or to a list in an electronic form requires [the party] to make a list that does not currently exist. Because [Texas] Rule 196.1 does not allow one party to require that others make lists, the . . . amended discovery order is broader than the scope of discovery permitted[.]") (citation omitted); *In re Jacobs*, 300 S.W.3d 35, 47 (Tex. App.—Houston [14th Dist.] 2009, orig. proceeding) (refusing to require the defendant-employee to create an affidavit concerning his net worth); *In re Guzman*, 19 S.W.3d 522, 525 (Tex. App.—Corpus Christi May 4, 2000, orig. proceeding) ("The [Texas discovery] rules do not permit the trial court to force a party to create documents which do not exist, solely to comply with a request for production.").

71 *See In re Preventative Pest Control Hous., LLC*, 580 S.W.3d 455, 460 (Tex. App.—Houston [14th Dist.] 2019, orig. proceeding) ("[P]arties cannot be forced to create documents that do not exist for the sole purpose of complying with a request for production."); *In re Sun Coast Res., Inc.*, 562 S.W.3d 138, 144 (Tex. App.—Houston [14th Dist.] 2018, orig. proceeding) ("We agree that a party cannot be compelled to produce documents that do not exist."); *Cline v. Guar. Bond Bank*, 404 S.W.2d 139, 142 (Tex. App.—Texarkana 2013, no pet.) ("We are unwilling to conclude that a trial court can abuse its discretion by refusing to order the Bank to produce a cashier's check that apparently does not exist."); *Gilmore v. SCI Tex. Funeral Servs., Inc.*, 234 S.W.3d 251, 263 n.12 (Tex. App.—Waco 2007, pet. denied) ("If a particular item has been lost or destroyed before a request for production is served, it is no longer in the party's possession and its non-production necessarily cannot constitute a discovery violation."); *cf. Clark v. Thomas*, 706 Fed. Appx. 358, 359 (9th Cir. Dec. 12, 2017) ("The district court did not abuse its discretion in denying Clark's motions to compel the production of photographs and for sanctions because the record contains no

that does not exist.[72]

---

evidence that the photographs existed."); *EMP Indus., Inc. v. KECO Inc.*, No. 8:17-CV-869-T-02JSS, 2018 U.S. Dist. LEXIS 223376, at *7, 2018 WL 7494607 (M.D. Fla. Nov. 28, 2018) ("The Court cannot compel production of documents that do not exist."); *Moss v. Princip*, No. 3:14-CV-3088-BF, 2017 U.S. Dist. LEXIS 160687, at *4, 2017 WL 2879694 (N.D. Tex. June 1, 2017) ("A court simply cannot compel Defendants to produce documents not in their possession or control. 'A party or non-party cannot produce what it does not have [a]nd, so, [c]learly, the court cannot compel [a party or non-party] to produce non-existent documents.'" (footnote omitted) (quoting *ORIX USA Corp. v. Armentrout*, No. 3:16-mc-63-N-BN, 2016 U.S. Dist. LEXIS 100617, at *12–13, 2016 WL 4095603 (N.D. Tex. Aug. 1, 2016) (mem. op.))); *Belanus v. Dutton*, No. CV 12-00065-H-DLC, 2017 U.S. Dist. LEXIS 42623, at *50–51, 2017 WL 1102727 (D. Mont. Mar. 23, 2017) ("A party is not required to create items to disclose in discovery. Rule 34 of the Federal Rules of Civil Procedure only requires a party to produce documents that already exist. A party responding to a [Federal] Rule 34 document request cannot be compelled to prepare or create new documents. The rules of discovery do not require a party to create or generate responsive materials (in this case, photographs) but only to produce and allow inspection of 'items in the responding parties' possession, custody, or control.'" (citations omitted) (quoting *Seed Research Equip. Sols., LLC v. Gary W. Clem, Inc.*, No. 09-1282-EFM-KGG, 2011 U.S. Dist. LEXIS 99087, at *4, 2011 WL 3880895 (D. Kan. Sept. 1, 2011) (mem. op.))); *Payne v. Forest River, Inc.*, No. 13-679-JJB-RLB, 2015 U.S. Dist. LEXIS 52706, at *12, 2015 WL 1912851 (M.D. La. Apr. 22, 2015) ("The court cannot order the production of documents that no longer exist or, despite a diligent search, cannot be found in the possession, custody, or control of a party.") (footnote omitted); *Steil v. Humana Kan. City, Inc.*, 197 F.R.D. 445, 448 (D. Kan. 2000) (holding that, under Federal Rule 34, a response that there are "no documents" was a proper response to a production request because a party cannot be compelled to produce documents that do not exist). Of course, if the document was improperly destroyed, the responding party may be subject to sanctions, a spoliation instruction, or both sanctions and such an instruction.

The rule that a party is not required to create documents in response to a production request does not excuse a party from searching existing databases for relevant information. Courts recognize that requiring a party to create computer programs to search an existing database for relevant information is different from requiring it to create a non-existent document. For example, in *Apple Inc. v. Samsung Electronics Co.*, the federal court explained: "While this court has held that a party should not [be] required to create completely new documents, that is not the same as requiring a party to query an existing dynamic database for relevant information. Courts regularly require parties to produce reports from dynamic databases, holding that 'the technical burden . . . of creating a new dataset for the instant litigation does not excuse production.'" *Apple Inc. v. Samsung Elecs. Co.*, No. 12-CV-0630-LHK (PSG), 2013 U.S. Dist. LEXIS 116493, at *33–34, 2013 WL 4426512 (N.D. Cal. Aug. 14, 2013) (footnotes omitted) (quoting *In re EBay Seller Antitrust Litig.*, No. C 07-1882 JF (RS), 2009 U.S. Dist. LEXIS 132817, at *7–8, 2009 WL 3613511 (N.D. Cal. Oct. 28, 2009)); *accord IQVIA, Inc. v. Veeva Sys., Inc.*, No. 2:17-CV-00177-CCC-MF, 2019 U.S. Dist. LEXIS 198652, at *21, 2019 WL 6044938 (D.N.J. Nov. 14, 2019); *Meredith v. United Collection Bureau, Inc.*, 319 F.R.D. 240, 243 (N.D. Ohio 2017); *Crocs, Inc. v. Effervescent, Inc.*, Nos. 06-cv-00605-PAB-KMT, 16-cv-02004-PAB-KMT, 12-cv-02096-PAB-BNB, 2017 U.S. Dist. LEXIS 184498, at *11–12, 2017 WL 3888502 (D. Colo. Feb. 8, 2017); *Gonzales v. Google, Inc.*, 234 F.R.D. 674, 683 (N.D. Cal. 2006).

[72] See cases cited in notes 70 and 71. In the same vein, a party cannot be compelled to produce, or sanctioned for failing to produce, documents or things that it has not been requested to produce. *E.g.*, *In re Preventative Pest Control Houston, LLC*, 580 S.W.3d 455, 460 (Tex. App.—Houston [14th Dist.] 2019, orig. proceeding) ("The [Texas] rules do not permit a trial court to order parties to create documents for the purposes of discovery."); *In re Master Flo Valve Inc.*, 485 S.W.3d 207, 218 (Tex. App.—Houston [14th Dist.] 2016, orig. proceeding) ("A party

A motion to compel generally should be denied when the responding party asserts

cannot be compelled to produce that which has not been requested."); *In re Exmark Mfg. Co.*, 299 S.W.3d 519, 531 (Tex. App.—Corpus Christi 2009, orig. proceeding) (same); *In re Lowe's Cos.*, 134 S.W.3d 876, 880 n.7 (Tex. App.—Houston [14th Dist.] 2004, orig. proceeding) (same).

An interesting question, and one not directly answered by Texas Rule 196 or any other Texas discovery rule, is whether a trial court can order a responding party to sign authorizations so that the requesting party can obtain relevant non-medical documents from nonparties, such income-tax returns, bank or credit-card records, or emails stored by an Internet Service Provider. Although Texas cases suggest that a court properly can enter such an order—*e.g.*, *Mutter v. Wood,* 744 S.W.2d 600, 601 (Tex. 1988) (suggesting that trial court had authority to require the plaintiff to sign an authorization to obtain to obtain the plaintiff's medical records); *In re Mitsubishi Heavy Indus. Am.*, 269 S.W.3d 679, 680 (Tex. App.—Dallas 2008, orig. proceeding) ("We begin by noting that it was within the trial court's discretion to order relators to sign an authorization" permitting the release of proprietary documents pertaining to the aircraft at issue in the files and databases of the FAA or within the FAA's custody or control.); *In re Shipmon*, 68 S.W.3d 815, 819–21 (Tex. App.—Amarillo 2001, orig. proceeding) (holding that the trial court did not abuse its discretion in ordering the plaintiff to sign an authorization allowing the defendant to obtain her employment records); *Martinez v. Rutledge*, 592 S.W.2d 398, 400 (Tex. App.—Dallas 1979, writ ref'd n.r.e.) (affirming sanctions dismissing action because the plaintiff failed to provide an authorization for her medical records); *but see In re Home State Cnty. Mut. Ins. Co.*, No. 12-06-00144-CV, 2006 Tex. App. LEXIS 9919, at *8, 2006 WL 3313683 (Tex. App.—Tyler Nov. 15, 2006, orig. proceeding) (mem. op.) (holding that the trial court properly denied a production request asking the plaintiff to sign an authorization for medical records in a *Stower* because Texas Rule 196 did not expressly permit authorizations and Texas Rule 194.2(b)(1)) was limited to medical authorizations in personal-injury cases); *In re Guzman*, 19 S.W.3d 522, 524–25 (Tex. App.—Corpus Christi May 4, 2000, orig. proceeding) (holding that the trial court abused its discretion in ordering the defendant to provide authorizations, which did not exist, so that the plaintiff could obtain the defendant's "drivers history, medical history, employment history and worker's compensation claims," reasoning that the order improperly required the creation of a document)—they do not provide any detailed reasoning for their conclusions.

Federal courts are divided on the issue. The better reasoning is that such authorizations are proper because they merely facilitate the production of existing documents under the responding party's control. *E.g.*, *Scott v. City of Bismarck*, 328 F.R.D. 242, 246–48, (D.N.D. 2018) (discussing the split of authority and holding that Federal Rules 34 and 37 empower courts to compel parties to sign written releases or authorization forms consenting to the production of various types documents); *Prado-Guajardo v. Perez*, No. 2:16-cv-00546-GMN-VCF, 2017 U.S. Dist. LEXIS 114844, at *11–13, 2017 WL 3130420 (D. Nev. July 24, 2017) (same); *Mir v. L-3 Commc'ns Integrated Sys., L.P.*, 319 F.R.D. 220, 226–31 (N.D. Tex. 2016) (same); *see SEC v. N. Star Fin., LLC*, No. GJH-15-1339, 2017 U.S. Dist. LEXIS 167926, at *10, 2017 WL 4539296 (D. Md. Oct. 10, 2017) (mem. op.) ("It is well-established that courts may compel parties to sign consent forms authorizing the release of their emails where those parties refused to produce the emails through discovery.").

In any event such authorizations, if not available under Texas Rule 196, should be available under Texas Rule 191.1, which provides, in pertinent part: "Except where specifically prohibited, the procedures and limitations set forth in the rules pertaining to discovery may be modified in any suit . . . by court order for good cause." Tex. R. Civ. P. 191.1 (emphasis added). The official commentary to the Rule explains that it "preserves the ability of . . . trial courts by order to adapt discovery to different circumstances. . . . In individual instances, courts may order . . . discovery methods other than those prescribed in these rules if appropriate." Tex. R. Civ. P. 199 cmt. 1 to 1999 Change (emphasis added). Nothing in the Texas discovery rules "specifically prohibit" a trial court from ordering a person to sign an authorization for the release relevant documents in a third party's possession. To that the requested documents do not exist or are not in its possession, custody, or control unless there is evidence suggesting the contrary.[73] If, however, it appears either

---

the contrary, the discovery rules clearly indicate that such authorizations are permitted because they expressly allow for medical authorizations, *see* Tex. R. Civ. P. 194.2(b)(11). *Accord In re Flores*, No. 13-20-00105-CV, 2020 Tex. App. LEXIS 3283, at *13 n.4 (Tex. App.—Corpus Christi Apr. 17, 2020, orig. proceeding) (mem. op.) (suggesting that authorizations are proper under Rule 191.1.).

As noted above, Texas Rule 194.2(b)(11) governs medical authorizations and allows a party to obtain a medical authorization in actions "alleging physical or mental injury and damages from the occurrence that is the subject of the case[.]" Tex. R. Civ. P. 194.2(b)(11); *In re Soto*, 270 S.W.3d 732, 734 (Tex. App.—Amarillo 2008, orig. proceeding) ("[T]he option belongs to the party requesting disclosure, not the one responding to it. If a legitimate authorization is sought, then the respondent cannot unilaterally comply with the request by simply delivering selected medical records."); *see Navarrete v. Williams*, 342 S.W.3d 116, 122 (Tex. App.—El Paso 2011, no pet.) ("Ms. Navarrete cites to [Former Texas] Rule 194.2(j), for the proposition that a disclosure request of medical information or records may be answered with such a release, and, in essence, concludes that no further response or supplementation is necessary. We disagree with Ms. Navarrete's interpretation of this provision."). This disclosure requirement is discussed in Chapter 6, section 6-3:3.10.

73 *In re Sun Coast Res., Inc.*, 562 S.W.3d 138, 144 (Tex. App.—Houston [14th Dist.] 2018, orig. proceeding) (holding the trial court abused its discretion when it ordered a party to produce documents when the record did not contain any evidence that could support a finding that the responsive documents existed but were not produced); *cf. Williams v. Wetzel*, No. 1:17-CV-79, 2019 U.S. Dist. LEXIS 41283, at *5, 2019 WL 1206061 (M.D. Pa. Mar. 14, 2019) ("[O]ne other immutable rule defines the court's discretion when ruling on motions to compel discovery. It is clear that the court cannot compel the production of things that do not exist. Nor can the court compel the creation of evidence by parties who attest that they do not possess the materials sought by an adversary in litigation."); *Mason Tenders Dist. Council v. Phase Constr. Servs.*, 318 F.R.D. 28, 42 (S.D.N.Y. 2016) ("Generally, 'a party's good faith averment that the items sought simply do not exist, or are not in his possession, custody, or control should resolve the issue of failure of production since one "cannot be required to produce the impossible. In the face of a denial by a party that it has possession, custody, or control of documents, the discovering party must make an adequate showing to overcome the assertion."'") In other words, Plaintiffs must cite to specific evidence to challenge Defendants' assertions that no additional responsive documents exist." (quoting *Menard v. Chrysler Grp. LLC*, No. 14 CV 6325 (VB), 2015 U.S. Dist. LEXIS 127814, at *7, 2015 WL 5472724 (S.D.N.Y. July 2, 2015), and *Golden Trade S.r.L. v. Lee Apparel Co.*, 143 F.R.D. 514, 525 n. 7 (S.D.N.Y. 1992))); *FTC v. Affiliate Strategies, Inc.*, No. 09-4104-JAR, 2011 U.S. Dist. LEXIS 7689, at *14, 2011 WL 251449 (D. Kan. Jan. 26, 2011) ("WPS's counsel is an officer of the court and without further evidence to the contrary, the undersigned will accept counsel's representation that all response documents have been produced.") (footnote omitted); *Margel v. E.G.L. Gem Lab Ltd.*, No. 04 Civ. 1514 (PAC) (HBP), 2008 U.S. Dist. LEXIS 41754, at *8–9, 2008 WL 2224288 (S.D.N.Y. May 29, 2008) ("Litigants commonly suspect that they are not getting all the documents they have requested and that an adversary is holding something back. That suspicion, however, will not sustain the imposition of sanctions. 'Under ordinary circumstances, a party's good faith averment that the items sought simply do not exist, or are not in his possession, custody or control, should resolve the issue of failure of production. . . .' Since defendants do not cite any specific evidence impugning plaintiffs' assertions that their production is complete, there is no basis for a finding of misconduct on the part of the plaintiffs or an award of sanctions." (quoting *Zervos v. S.S. Sam Hous.*, 79 F.R.D. 593, 595 (S.D.N.Y. 1978))); *Sonnino v. Univ. of Kan. Hosp. Auth.*, 220 F.R.D. 633, 640 (D. Kan. 2004) ("The Court cannot compel a party to produce documents that do not exist or that are not in that party's possession, custody, or control.

that the requested documents or things may exist or that they are within the possession, custody, or control of the responding party, the responding party must do more than simply provide an unsworn assertion to the contrary.[74]

"Possession, custody, or control" of an item is defined by Texas Rule 192.7 to "mean[] that the person either has physical possession of the item or has a right to possession of the item that is equal or superior to the person who has physical possession of the item."[75] Mere access to documents, however, does not constitute possession, custody,

---

Plaintiff has not provided the Court with information sufficient to lead the Court to question the veracity of the Hospital Defendants' statement that no additional responsive documents exist. The Court thus has no basis upon which to compel the Hospital Defendants to produce any additional documents. . . .") (footnote omitted).

[74] *Cf. Norman v. Young*, 422 F.2d 470, 473 (10th Cir. 1970) (holding that the requesting party established a prima facie case regarding existence and control by virtue of the requested documents' nature, and the responding party failed to properly deny their existence); *Mason Tenders Dist. Council v. Phase Constr. Servs.*, 318 F.R.D. 28, 43 (S.D.N.Y. 2016) ("[B]ecause Plaintiffs have cited to specific evidence that challenges Defendants' blanket assertion that no additional documents exist, the burden now shifts to Defendants to show *specifically* where they have searched and why these documents are not, in fact, within their custody, possession, or control."); *Schwartz v. Mktg. Publ'g Co.*, 153 F.R.D. 16, 21 (D. Conn. 1994) (granting a motion to compel because the responding party failed to swear to the lack of possession, custody, or control); *Comeau v. Rupp*, 810 F. Supp. 1127, 1166 (D. Kan. 1992) (holding that, because the FDIC was in a superior position to gain access to documents, naked averment that particular documents were not in its possession was insufficient).

[75] Tex. R. Civ. P. 192.7(b); *accord In re Sun Coast Res., Inc.*, 562 S.W.3d 138, 144 (Tex. App.—Houston [14th Dist.] 2018, orig. proceeding) (holding the trial court abused its discretion by requiring production of an at-will employee's personal text messages without an employment contract granting an employer a right to possess said text messages because the employer's "possession, custody, or control"); *In re Summersett*, 438 S.W.3d 74, 82 (Tex. App.—Corpus Christ 2013, orig. proceeding) (denying mandamus relief on an order compelling discovery of documents where relator was the president of a company and had an equal or greater right to non-confidential employee documents).

The federal discovery rules do not define "possession, custody, or control." Federal courts often define "control" as "the legal right to obtain the documents on demand." *Gerling Int'l Ins. Co. v. Comm'r*, 839 F.2d 131, 140 (3d Cir. 1988); *accord 7-UP Bottling Co. v. Archer Daniels Midland Co.* (*In re Citric Acid Litig.*), 191 F.3d 1090, 1107 (9th Cir. 1999); *Searock v. Stripling*, 736 F.2d 650, 653 (11th Cir. 1984); *Meridian Labs., Inc. v. OncoGenerix USA, Inc.*, 333 F.R.D. 131, 135 (N.D. Ill. 2019); *Parris v. Pappas*, No. 3:10CV1128 (WWE), 2017 U.S. Dist. LEXIS 122282, at *4, 2017 WL 3314001 (D. Conn. Aug. 3, 2017); *Frye v. CSX Transp., Inc.*, No. 14-cv-11996, 2016 U.S. Dist. LEXIS 62770, at *11–12, 2016 WL 2758268 (E.D. Mich. May 12, 2016) ("The Sixth Circuit and other courts have consistently held that 'documents are deemed to be within the "possession, custody or control" for purposes of [Federal] Rule 34 if the party has *actual* possession, custody or control, *or has the legal right to obtain the documents on demand*.' . . . But '[t]he relationship between the party and the person or entity having actual possession of the document is central in each case. The party must be able to command release of the documents by the person or entity in actual possession.'" (quoting *In re Bankers Tr. Co.*, 61 F.3d 465, 469 (6th Cir. 1995), and *Gen. Envtl. Sci. Corp. v. Horsfall*, Nos. 92-4110, 92-4111, 92-4112, 92-4113, 92-4114, 1994 U.S. App. LEXIS 13398, at *32 n.15, 1994 WL 228256 (6th Cir. May 25, 1994))).

Some federal courts, however, have adopted a more expansive notion of "control," holding that it extends to circumstances where a party has the "practical ability to obtain the documents from a nonparty to the action." *Flagg v. City of Detroit*, 252 F.R.D. 346, 353 n.16 (E.D. Mich. 2008) (quoting *Bank of N.Y. v. Meridien BIAO Bank Tanzania Ltd.*, 171 F.R.D. 135, 146 or control.[76] Accordingly, when documents are owned by another, it is error to require

(S.D.N.Y. 1997)); *accord Moretti v. Hertz Corp.*, No. CV 14-469-LPS, 2018 U.S. Dist. LEXIS 168609, at *3–4, 7–8, 13–14, 2018 WL 4693473 (D. Del. Sept. 30, 2018); *Toussie v. Allstate Ins. Co.*, Nos. 14 CV 2705 (FB) (CLP); 15 CV 5235 (ARR) (PK), 2017 U.S. Dist. LEXIS 174251, at *9, 2017 WL 4773374 (E.D.N.Y. Oct. 20, 2017); *Harper v. City of Dall.*, No. 3:14-cv-2647-M, 2017 U.S. Dist. LEXIS 137322, at *53–54, 2017 WL 3674830 (N.D. Tex. Aug. 25, 2017); *In re Barnwell Enters.*, 265 F. Supp. 3d 1, 16 (D.D.C. 2017); *First Am. Bankcard v. Smart Bus. Tech., Inc.*, No. 15-638 SECTION "N" (2), 2017 U.S. Dist. LEXIS 79508, at *6–9, 2017 WL 2267149 (E.D. La. May 24, 2017). *But see Robinson v. Moskus*, 491 F. Supp. 3d 359, 364 (C.D. Ill. 2020) ("This dissection of the cases addressing the proper standard to apply when considering whether a party has 'possession, custody, or control' of a document in the hands of a third-party demonstrates the following: Where a party and non-party are not corporate affiliates, '[t]he test is whether the party has a legal right to control or obtain' the documents requested; a party's 'practical ability' to obtain the documents is irrelevant absent a legal right to do so." (quoting *In re Folding Carton Antitrust Litigation*, 76 F.R.D. 420, 423 (N.D. Ill. 1977))); *7-UP Bottling Co. v. Archer Daniels Midland Co. (In re Citric Acid Litig.)*, 191 F.3d 1090, 1107–08 (9th Cir. 1999) (expressly rejecting the practical-ability test). The test is inconsistent with Texas Rule 192.7's definition of possession, custody, or control because the Rule focuses on the party's "right to possession" of the documents rather than on the party's "ability" to obtain them.

76 *In re Kuntz*, 124 S.W.3d 179, 184 (Tex. 2003) (orig. proceeding) ("Hal's mere access to the relevant letters of recommendation does not constitute 'physical possession' of the documents under the definition of 'possession, custody, or control' set forth in Texas Rule of Civil Procedure 192.7(b)."); *see In re Univ. of Tex. at San Antonio*, No. 04-20-00439-CV, 2021 Tex. App. LEXIS 365, at *9–10 (Tex. App.—San Antonio Jan. 20, 2021, orig. proceeding) (mem. op.) (holding an employer does not have constructive possession or a greater right to obtain an employee's confidential medical records); *In re Sun Coast Res., Inc.*, 562 S.W.3d 138, 159 n. 16 (Tex. App.—Houston [14th Dist.] 2018, (orig. proceeding) ("It is the right to *possess* the item that counts. Mere access to a document does not equate to possession, custody, or control."); *In re Shell E&P, Inc.*, 179 S.W.3d 125, 131 (Tex. App.—San Antonio 2005, orig. proceeding) (holding that an attorney has mere access to, rather than possession, custody, or control of, an opposing party's confidential documents obtained pursuant to discovery in another lawsuit); *cf. Wiwa v. Royal Dutch Petroleum Co.*, 392 F.3d 812, 821 (5th Cir. 2004) ("The phrase 'to which he has access' is overbroad; it would require the retrieval of documents from Nigeria—documents not under Oteri's custody, control, or possession, but to which he could conceivably have access by virtue of his prior position with Shell."); *U.S. v. Kent (In re Grand Jury Subpoena)*, 646 F.2d 963, 969 (5th Cir. 1981) ("[The employee's] subpoena, if upheld, would be illegal because it would direct her to produce documents not in her possession, custody, or control. Because [the employee] had mere access, her compliance with the subpoena would have required that she illegally take exclusive possession of [her employer's] documents and deliver them to the grand jury."); *Coventry Capital US LLC v. EEA Life Settlements Inc.*, 334 F.R.D. 68, 73 (S.D.N.Y. 2020) ("A party that lacks a contractual right to obtain a third-party's documents, however, may nonetheless be found to have control over the third-party's documents based on a demonstrated ability to access those documents in the ordinary course of business."); *Dotson v. Edmonson*, No. 16-15371 SECTION: "E"(1), 2017 U.S. Dist. LEXIS 159571, at *10–18, 2017 WL 4310676 (E.D. La. Sept. 28, 2017) (holding that an employee who is a party to litigation cannot be compelled to produce his non party employer's documents simply because he has the ability to access them, but not the authority to disclose them); *Love v. N.J. Dep't of Corr.*, No. 2:15-CV-4404-SDW-SCM, 2017 U.S. Dist. LEXIS 128905, at *12–13, 2017 WL 3477864 (D.N.J. Aug. 11, 2017) ("Many employees have some responsibility to create records or reports for their employer. If a party possesses copies of their employer's records at home or outside of their workplace, they are obligated to produce responsive records. If instead, the employee merely has access to his employer's records at work, such access alone does not equate with possession, custody, or control over the records. The same applies to a government employee

a party with mere access to them to produce them.[77]

Legal ownership of the requested documents or tangible things, however, is not determinative. A responding party who has actual possession or custody of a document or thing is required to produce it even if belongs to a nonparty[78] or even if it is located beyond the court's jurisdiction.[79] In fact, legal restrictions limiting a party's ability to obtain certain documents or to disclose them to others will not necessarily preclude a finding that the party has possession, custody, or control over those documents.[80]

---

who 'cannot on his own initiative remove government files and provide them to a third party.'" (quoting *Lowe v. Dist. of Columbia.*, 250 F.R.D. 36, 38 (D.D.C. 2008))); *Cordero v. Warren*, No. 12-2136 (MAS) (DEA), 2016 U.S. Dist. LEXIS 183793, at *5, 2016 WL 8199305 (D.N.J. Oct. 4, 2016) ("It is axiomatic that a party is not required to produce documents that are not in its possession, custody, or control. The Court rejects Plaintiff's argument that Defendants, as employees of the NJDOC, can simply 'access [NJDOC's] database' themselves to retrieve this information. As such, Plaintiff's motion is denied as to this document request.").

77 See cases cited in note 76.

78 *In re Rogers*, 200 S.W.3d 318, 322 (Tex. App.—Dallas 2006, orig. proceeding) (ordering a responding party to produce documents relating to a nonparty and corporations and partnerships in his possession); *cf. In re Bankers Tr. Co.*, 61 F.3d 465, 469–70 (6th Cir. 1995) (holding that Federal Reserve regulations prohibiting disclosure of confidential documents in responding party's possession were invalid when they conflicted with a discovery order); *Vicuna v. O.P. Schuman & Sons, Inc.*, 298 F. Supp. 3d 419, 435 (E.D.N.Y. 2017) (noting that "it is not dispositive whether Schuman 'owned' these documents in the strictest sense. What is important is that the documents were under the sole possession and control of Schuman and its employees during all pertinent times"); *Pilkington N. Am., Inc. v. Smith*, No. 11-176-BAJ-DLD, 2012 U.S. Dist. LEXIS 50877, at *5, 2012 WL 1205526 (M.D. La. Apr. 11, 2012) ("'[Federal] Rule 34 is broadly construed and documents within a party's control are subject to discovery, even if owned by a nonparty.'" (quoting *Autery v. SmithKline Beecham Corp.*, 2010 U.S. Dist. LEXIS 146713, at *5, 2010 WL 1489968 (W.D. La. April 13, 2010))); *Allen v. Woodford*, No. CV-F-05-1104 OWW LJO, 2007 U.S. Dist. LEXIS 11026, at *5, 2007 WL 309945 (E.D. Cal. Jan. 30, 2007) ("A party having actual possession of documents must allow discovery even if the documents belong to someone else; legal ownership of the documents is not determinative.").

A nonparty has the right to seek protection from its documents' disclosure. Tex. R. Civ. P. 192.6(a) ("[A] person affected by the discovery request, may move . . . for an order protecting that person from the discovery sought."); *see In re Kuntz*, 124 S.W.3d 179, 184 n.4 (Tex. 2003) (orig. proceeding) (stating that the third-party owner of the documents "may move for a protective order"); *In re Shell E&P, Inc.*, 179 S.W.3d 125, 129–30 (Tex. App.—San Antonio 2005, orig. proceeding) (same). See also Chapter 4, section 4-5 (discussing protective orders).

79 *Cf. In re Hulley Enters., Ltd.*, 358 F. Supp. 3d 331, 345 (S.D.N.Y. 2019), *aff'd sub nom. In re Hulley Enters. Ltd.*, 400 F. Supp. 3d 62 (S.D.N.Y. 2019) ("Given that section 1782 expressly provides that any discovery shall be taken 'in accordance with the Federal Rules of Civil Procedure,' we conclude that Congress intended that any order providing for discovery under section 1782 should accord with the procedures mandated by the Federal Rules of Civil Procedure in all respects. This includes the requirement that a party produce any documents within its possession and control, even those documents located in a foreign country."); *Novelty, Inc. v. Mt. View Mktg, Inc.*, 265 F.R.D. 370, 377 (S.D. Ind. 2009) ("'The fact that . . . documents are situated in a foreign country does not bar their discovery.'" (quoting *Cooper Indus., Inc. v. British Aerospace, Inc.*, 102 F.R.D. 918, 920 (S.D.N.Y.1984))); *Hunter Douglas, Inc. v. Comfortex Corp.*, No. M8-85 (WHP), 1999 U.S. Dist. LEXIS 101, at *10, 1999 WL 14007 (S.D.N.Y. Jan. 11, 1999) ("[T]he mere fact that the subpoenaed documents are in Canada does not exempt them from discovery.").

80 *Cf. Societe Internationale Pour Participations Industrielles et Commerciales, S.A. v. Rogers*, 357 U.S. 197, 205–06 (1958) (affirming that, under Federal Rule 34, a discovery order

Conversely, actual possession of the document or thing is unnecessary if the party has control of it. As explained by the Texas Supreme Court:

> The phrase "possession, custody, or control" . . . includes not only actual physical possession, but constructive possession, and the right to obtain possession from a third party, such as an agent or representative. The right to obtain possession is a legal right based upon the relationship between the party from whom a document is sought and the person who has actual possession of it.[81]

Thus, a responding party may be required to produce a document that it has the legal right to obtain even though it does not have a copy of the document in its possession. For example, a responding party can be compelled to produce documents or things in the possession of a third party if it has the contractual or other legal

---

requiring the responding party, who had control of documents, to produce them despite Swiss penal law that limited the party's ability to produce the documents); *Giorgi Glob. Holdings, Inc. v. Smulski*, No. CV 17-4416, 2020 U.S. Dist. LEXIS 89369, at *2–3, 2020 WL 2571177 (E.D. Pa. May 21, 2020) (same); *Nat'l Union Fire Ins. Co. v. Midland Bancor, Inc.*, 159 F.R.D. 562, 566–67 (D. Kan. 1994) (compelling a bank, under Federal Rule 34, to produce bank-examination reports even though reports were owned by FDIC and its regulations provided that the reports remained its property and could be released only with its consent); *Japan Halon Co. v. Great Lakes Chem. Corp.*, 155 F.R.D. 626, 627–29 (N.D. Ind. 1993) (holding, under Federal Rule 34, that the responding party had control of documents in the possession of its parent corporations even though Japanese law limited its right to demand the documents from them).

When the responding party asserts foreign law as a bar to production, federal courts perform a comity analysis to determine the weight to be given to the foreign jurisdiction's law and consider the following factors: (1) the importance of the documents or information requested to the litigation; (2) the degree of specificity of the request; (3) whether the information originated in the United States; (4) the availability of alternative means of retrieving the information; and (5) the extent to which noncompliance with the request would undermine important interests in the United States, or compliance with the request would undermine important interests of the state where the information is located. *E.g., Société Nationale Industrielle Aérospatiale v. U.S. Dist. Ct. for the S.D. Iowa*, 482 U.S. 522, 544 n.28 (1987); *NIKE, Inc. v. Wu*, 349 F. Supp. 3d 346, 364 (S.D.N.Y. 2018); *Tiffany (NJ) LLC v. Qi Andrew*, 276 F.R.D. 143, 151 (S.D.N.Y. 2011) (citing Restatement (Third) of Foreign Relations Law § 442(1)(c) (1987)).

[81] *GTE Commc'ns Sys. Corp. v. Tanner*, 856 S.W.2d 725, 729 (Tex. 1993) (orig. proceeding) (construing former Texas Rule 166b(2)); *accord In re Univ. of Tex. at San Antonio*, No. 04-20-00439-CV, 2021 Tex. App. LEXIS 365, at *9, 2021 WL 185529 (Tex. App.—San Antonio Jan. 20, 2021, orig. proceeding) (mem. op.) ("The party seeking production has the burden of proving that the relator has constructive possession or the right to obtain possession of the requested documents."); *In re Summersett*, 438 S.W.3d 74, 82 (Tex. App.—Corpus Christ 2013, orig. proceeding) ("Summersett does not need 'individual personal possession, custody, or control' to be required to produce documents under the rules of civil procedure, rather, the law requires only that he have either actual physical possession or constructive possession, or the right to obtain possession from a third party such as an agent or representative."); *cf. First Am. Bankcard v. Smart Bus. Tech., Inc.*, No. 15-638 SECTION "N" (2), 2017 U.S. Dist. LEXIS 79508, at *7, 2017 WL 2267149 (E.D. La. May 24, 2017) ("Typically, what must be shown to establish control over documents in the possession of a non-party is that there is a relationship, either because of some affiliation, employment or statute, such that a party is able to command release of certain documents by the non-party person or entity in actual possession." (quoting *Duarte v. St. Paul Fire & Marine Ins. Co.*, No. EP-14-CV-305-KC, 2015 U.S. Dist. LEXIS 161254, at *15, 2015 WL 7709433 (W.D. Tex. Sept. 25, 2015))).

right to obtain the documents.[82] Similarly, a party has possession, custody, or control

---

[82] *Cf. Anderson v. Cryovac, Inc.*, 862 F.2d 910, 928–29 (1st Cir. 1988) (holding that a seller had control of a report prepared for the purchaser and maintained in the purchaser's possession by virtue of a provision in the sales contract requiring the purchaser to make its records available to the seller); *Chamber of Commerce of U.S. of Am. v. City of Seattle*, 334 F.R.D. 440, 441 (W.D. Wash. 2020) ("'[A] party may be ordered to produce a document in the possession of a non-party entity if that party has a legal right to obtain the document or has control over the entity who is in possession of the document.'" (quoting *Campos-Eibeck v. C R Bard Inc.*, 2020 U.S. Dist. LEXIS 30189, at *4–5, 2020 WL 835305 (S.D. Cal. Feb 20, 2020))); *Robinson v. Moskus*, 491 F. Supp. 3d 359, 361 (C.D. Ill. 2020) ("Rather, a party to whom a request for production is made must have the 'legal right to obtain the documents sought to be produced . . . even in the absence of actual possession.'" (quoting *Burton Mech. Contractors, Inc. v. Foreman*, 148 F.R.D. 230, 236 (N.D. Ind. 1992))); *Williams v. Angie's List, Inc.*, No. 1:16-cv-00878-WTL-MJD, 2017 U.S. Dist. LEXIS 54270, at *6–11, 2017 WL 1318419 (S.D. Ind. Apr. 10, 2017) (holding that control "is certainly broad enough to encompass a contractual right to obtain documents"); *DRFP, LLC v. Republica Bolivariana de Venezuela*, No. 2:04-cv-793, 2014 U.S. Dist. LEXIS 165585, at *4–6, 2014 WL 6687137 (S.D. Ohio Nov. 26, 2014) ("[Federal Rule] 34(a) allows a party to ask for, and requires a party to produce for inspection and copying, documents within the responding party's 'possession, custody, or control.' . . . The language in ¶1.3 of the 2004 agreement, read straightforwardly, gives Skye the legal right to request documents from Gruppo Triad, and imposes a corresponding legal duty on Gruppo Triad to produce them."); *Libertarian Party of Ohio v. Husted*, No. 2:13-cv-953, 2014 U.S. Dist. LEXIS 111338, at *4, 2014 WL 3928293 (S.D. Ohio Aug. 12, 2014) (noting that a party has control over documents to which it has an "explicit contractual right"); *Tetra Techs., Inc. v. Hamilton*, No. CIV-07-1186-M, 2008 U.S. Dist. LEXIS 60094, at *2, 2008 WL 3307150 (W.D. Okla. Aug. 7, 2008) ("Plaintiff's Request for Production No. 9 provides: 'Produce the complete phone records since April 16, 2007, for the personal cellular phone used by you for business-related purposes.' Defendant's supplemental response provides: 'Hamilton does not and did not maintain copies of cell phone bills and has no such documents in his possession to produce in response to this Request.' 'Courts have universally held that documents are deemed to be within the possession, custody or control if the party has actual possession, custody or control or has the legal right to obtain the documents on demand.' As the subscriber/user of the cell phone service, the Court finds defendant has the legal right to obtain the cell phone records requested in Request for Production No. 9. The Court, accordingly, finds that defendant should be compelled to produce said phone records." (citations omitted) (quoting *Starlight Int'l Inc. v. Herlihy*, 186 F.R.D. 626, 635 (D. Kan. 1999))); *Washam v. Evans*, No. 2:10-CV-00150 JLH, 2011 U.S. Dist. LEXIS 70704, at *2–3, 2011 WL 2559850 (E.D. Ark. June 29, 2011) ("'A party may be ordered to produce a document in the possession of a non-party entity if that party has a legal right to obtain the document or has control over the entity who is in possession of the document.' Courts have held that a party has control over his medical records because, by either granting or denying consent, he may determine who shall have access to them." (quoting *Soto v. City of Concord*, 162 F.R.D. 603, 619 (N.D. Cal. 1995))); *Engel v. Town of Roseland*, No. 3:06 CV 430, 2007 U.S. Dist. LEXIS 73645, at *10–11, 2007 WL 2903196 (N.D. Ind. Oct. 1, 2007) ("A party can have a legal right to obtain documents from another person or entity that the party does not otherwise control. Thus, as recognized in the cases cited by Magistrate Judge Nuechterlein, because a party has a statutory right to inspect his or her own tax returns, and when, as is most likely the case, a person has a contractual right to obtain copies of his or her bank statements, the party is in control of those documents and must produce them in response to a request under [Federal Rule] 34.") (citation omitted); *Dorocon, Inc. v. Burke*, No. 02-2556 (CKK), 2005 U.S. Dist. LEXIS 38839, at *53 (D.D.C. Nov. 1, 2005) ("[Federal] Rule 34(a) obligates parties to turn over documents such as bank and credit card statements covered by discovery requests given that they enjoy constructive possession of such documents."); *In re Legato Sys., Inc. Sec. Litig.*, 204 F.R.D. 167, 170 (N.D. Cal. 2001) (holding that a corporate CEO had control over the transcript of his testimony before the SEC in a formal investigative proceeding because a SEC regulation gave him the right to obtain it).

over material in the possession of its officers, directors, employees, or agents;[83]

---

[83] *See State v. Lowry*, 802 S.W.2d 669, 673–74 (Tex. 1991) (orig. proceeding) (holding that the Texas Attorney General had to produce documents in the possession, custody, and control of his entire office and not just the antitrust division); *In re Topletz*, No. 05-19-00327-CV, 2019 Tex. App. LEXIS 8249, at *11–12, 2019 WL 4302254 (Tex. App.—Dallas Sept. 11, 2019, orig. proceeding) (mem. op.) ("Under the terms of the trust, relator, as beneficiary, has the right to access the documents at any time during regular business hours and the right to obtain prepared summary information in the form of a profit and loss statement and balance sheet toward the end of each fiscal year. Thus . . . the relator has a right to access and no contractual impediment to production. As beneficiary of the trust, relator has the right to obtain possession from the trustee who is his agent. Thus, we conclude appellant has constructive possession of the trust's financial documents and tax returns as was recognized by his former counsel who agreed to produce the documents.") (cleaned up); *cf. In re Barnwell Enters.*, 265 F. Supp. 3d 1, 16 (D.D.C. 2017) ("Courts have repeatedly found that employers have control over their employees and can be required to produce documents in their employees' possession." (quoting *Chevron Corp. v. Salazar*, 275 F.R.D. 437, 447–49 (S.D.N.Y. 2011))); *Waymo LLC v. Uber Techs., Inc.*, No. 17-cv-00939-WHA (JSC), 2017 U.S. Dist. LEXIS 108165, at *7–8, 2017 WL 2972806 (N.D. Cal. 2017) (N.D. Cal. July 12, 2017) ("Otto Trucking must produce responsive documents in the custody, control or possession of its officers, namely, Mr. Ron, Ms. Morgan or Mr. Bentley. It cannot hide responsive documents simply because these officers' work for Otto Trucking was done using their personal email accounts, especially since they are all current Otto Trucking officers. It is thus unsurprising that Otto Trucking does not cite a single case that supports that remarkable proposition. The cases Otto Trucking does cite are all inapposite; none involve a corporation refusing to produce documents involving corporation business in the possession, custody or control of the corporation's officers. To accept Otto Trucking's argument would mean that it could not compel its current officers to produce Otto Trucking's own trade secrets to Otto Trucking merely because the officers conducted Otto Trucking business with their personal email accounts. Nonsense."); *Blanton v. Torrey Pines Prop. Mgmt.*, No. 15-CV-0892 W (NLS), 2017 U.S. Dist. LEXIS 80777, at *16, 2017 WL 2291752 (S.D. Cal. May 24, 2017) ("A party responding to a [Federal] Rule 34 production request . . . 'is under an affirmative duty to seek that information reasonably available to [it] from [its] employees, agents, or others subject to [its] control.'" (quoting *Gray v. Faulkner*, 148 F.R.D. 220, 223 (N.D. Ind. 1992))); *Avalos v. Carpenter*, No. 1:15-cv-00369-LJO-JLT (PC), 2017 U.S. Dist. LEXIS 11878, at *6, 2017 WL 387243 (E.D. Cal. Jan. 27, 2017) ("[A] party may be required to produce documents turned over to an agent, such as its attorney or insurer."); *Montesa v. Schwartz*, No. 12 Civ. 6057 (CS) (JCM), 2015 U.S. Dist. LEXIS 193847, at *11 (S.D.N.Y. Mar. 6, 2015) ("[B]ecause a corporation may be required to produce its officers' and employees' documents, the Defendant District must produce its board members' and agents' documents."); *CA, Inc. v. AppDynamics, Inc.*, No. CV 13-2111 (WFK) (SIL), 2014 U.S. Dist. LEXIS 201721, at *8, 2014 WL 12860591 (E.D.N.Y. Sept. 8, 2014) ("In the context of a corporation's documents in the possession of an officer or director, the issue is whether the documents were created in connection with the officer's functions as a corporate employee. If so, the corporation has a proprietary interest in them and the officer has a fiduciary duty to turn them over on demand."); *Libertarian Party v. Husted*, No. 2:13-cv-953, 2014 U.S. Dist. LEXIS 111338, at *4, 2014 WL 3928293 (S.D. Ohio Aug. 12, 2014) ("An agency theory is one example of the type of relationship which gives a party—typically the principal— legal control over documents possessed by the agent."); *Schaaf v. SmithKline Beecham Corp.*, 233 F.R.D. 451, 455 (E.D.N.C. 2005) (holding that an employer had control over an employee's work-related documents, whether located at office or in her home); *Miniace v. Pac. Mar. Ass'n*, No. C 04-03506 SI, 2006 U.S. Dist. LEXIS 17127, at *7–8, 2006 WL 335389 (N.D. Cal. Feb. 13, 2006) ("PMA argues that its outside directors are not employees and that they therefore fall outside of PMA's control. This argument, however, overlooks the simple fact that a director may be removed from the Board. The Court finds that this easily satisfies the standard for control over the current members of the

A business-entity party generally does not have possession, custody, or control of documents in the possession of its parent or sibling entities.[88] Nonetheless, federal courts frequently require such an entity to produce documents possessed by its parent[89] or affiliates.[90] Although the cases are highly fact specific, certain factors have been reviewed by the federal courts to determine whether the party from whom documents are sought has sufficient control, including (1) whether the alter ego doctrine would justify piercing the corporate veil, (2) the nonparty's connection to the transaction at issue, (3) whether and to what degree the nonparty will receive the benefit of any judgment in the action, (4) the ability of the party to the action to obtain the documents when it wants them, and (5) whether by stock ownership or otherwise, one entity effectively controls the other.[91] It is doubtful that this test applies under the

---

control' of the served party if 'the party has actual possession, custody, or control, or has the legal right to obtain the documents on demand.' Accordingly, a party may be required to produce documents turned over to an agent, such as its attorney or insurer." (quoting *In re Bankers Tr. Co.*, 61 F.3d 465, 469 (6th Cir. 1995))); *Innovative Piledriving Prods., LLC v. Unisto Oy*, No. 1:04-CV-453, 2005 U.S. Dist. LEXIS 23652, at *3, 2005 WL 8169578 (N.D. Ind. Oct. 14, 2005) (same); *Henderson v. Zurn Indus., Inc.*, 131 F.R.D. 560, 567 (S.D. Ind. 1990) (same). See also cases cited in note 83.

[88] *In re U-Haul Int'l, Inc.*, 87 S.W.3d 653, 657 (Tex. App.—San Antonio 2002, orig. proceeding) (reversing sanctions against a responding party for failing to produce its affiliates' documents).

[89] *Cf. Japan Halon Co. v. Great Lakes Chem. Corp.*, 155 F.R.D. 626, 627–29 (N.D. Ind. 1993) (foreign parent corporation); *Mountain Ledge Corp., Inc. v. N. Am. Philips Corp.*, 109 F.R.D. 134, 138 (S.D.N.Y. 1986) (same); *Camden Iron & Metal, Inc. v. Marubeni Am. Corp.*, 138 F.R.D. 438, 441–44 (D.N.J. 1991) (same).

[90] *Cf. Steele Software Sys., Corp. v. DataQuick Info. Sys., Inc.*, 237 F.R.D. 561, 564–65 (D. Md. 2006); *Uniden Am. Corp. v. Ericsson Inc.*, 181 F.R.D. 302, 307 (M.D.N.C. 1998); *Cooper Indus., Inc. v. British Aerospace, Inc.*, 102 F.R.D. 918, 919–20 (S.D.N.Y. 1984).

[91] *Cf. FM Generator, Inc. v. MTU Onsite Energy Corp.*, No. 14-14354-DJC, 2016 U.S. Dist. LEXIS 189539, at *7, 2016 WL 8902603 (D. Mass. Aug. 25, 2016) ("Where documents are in the possession of the corporate parent, but are sought from the subsidiary, a court must look to the specific nature of the transactional relationship between the subsidiary and the parent company when determining whether control exists. Courts have found control to exist where: (1) the alter ego doctrine . . . warrants piercing the corporate veil; (2) the subsidiary was an agent of the parent in the transaction giving rise to the lawsuit; (3) the relationship is such that the agent-subsidiary can secure documents of the principal-parent to meet its own business needs and documents helpful for use in litigation; (4) there is access to documents when the need arises in the ordinary course of business; and (5) subsidiary was marketer and servicer of parent's product . . . in the U.S." (quoting *Pitney Bowes, Inc. v. Kern Int'l., Inc.*, 239 F.R.D. 62, 66–67 (D. Conn. 2006))); *Uniden Am. Corp. v. Ericsson Inc.*, 181 F.R.D. 302, 306 (M.D.N.C. 1998) (same); *see also In re Zantac (Ranitidine) Products Liab. Litig.*, No. 20-MD-2924, 2021 U.S. Dist. LEXIS 76346, at *33–34, 2021 WL 1522449 (S.D. Fla. Apr. 16, 2021) ("The Court can distill multiple relevant factors which guide whether the evidentiary record supports a finding that a party has control over a third-party entity's documents: These factors focus on the other corporation's actual control or inferred control, including any 'complicity' in storing or withholding documents. They include (a) commonality of ownership, (b) exchange or intermingling of directors, officers or employees of the two corporations, (c) exchange of documents between the corporations in the ordinary course of business, (d) any benefit or involvement by the non-party corporation in the transaction, and (e) involvement of the non-party corporation in the litigation."); *Princeton Digital Image Corp. v. Konami Digital Entm't Inc.*, 316 F.R.D. 89, 91 (D.N.J. 2016) ("In cases where a litigating company's sister corporation possesses the desired documents, the U.S. Court of Appeals for the Third Circuit has set out two pathways for a finding of the requisite control under [Federal] Rule 34(a). In *Gerling Int'l Ins. Co. v. Comm'r of Internal Revenue*, 839 F.2d 131,

Texas discovery rules because Texas Rule 192.7 defines "possession, custody, or control" in terms of a "right to possession,"[92] whereas the test applied by federal courts is more akin to the party's "practical ability" to obtain the documents, which is a more expansive test.[93]

The burden of establishing control over the requested documents or things is on the requesting party.[94] However, once it demonstrates that the responding party has a

---

140–41 (3d Cir. 1988), the Third Circuit explained that in such situations, control has been found only where (1) 'the sister corporation was found to be the alter ego of the litigating entity[;]' or (2) 'the litigating corporation had acted with its sister in effecting the transaction giving rise to suit and is litigating on its behalf[.]' As for circumstances that would satisfy the second scenario, the *Gerling* Court cited to a decision from this Court that served a representative 'example' thereof, *Afros S.P.A. v. Krauss-Maffei Corp.*, 113 F.R.D. 127 (D. Del. 1986), and went on to observe that '[w]here the relationship is thus such that the agent-subsidiary can secure documents of the principal-parent to meet its own business needs and documents helpful for use in the litigation, the courts will not permit the agent-subsidiary to deny control for purposes of discovery by an opposing party.'") (footnote omitted); *see also Costa v. Kerzner Int'l. Resorts, Inc.*, 277 F.R.D. 468, 471 (S.D. Fla. 2011) ("Control . . . does not require that a party have legal ownership or actual physical possession of the documents at issue," but merely requires that a party has the "right, authority, or practical ability to obtain the materials sought on demand."); *Japan Halon Co. v. Great Lakes Chem. Corp.*, 155 F.R.D. 626, 628–29 (N.D. Ind. 1993) (noting "extreme closeness" of the plaintiff and its parent corporations and that the parents would benefit from any award to the plaintiff); *Camden Iron & Metal, Inc. v. Marubeni Am. Corp.*, 138 F.R.D. 438, 443–44 (D.N.J. 1991) (finding that, because a parent played significant role in the transaction at issue, there was sufficient control even though the parent and wholly owned subsidiary maintained separate corporate formalities); *Mountain Ledge Corp. v. N. Am. Philips Corp.*, 109 F.R.D. 134, 138 (S.D.N.Y. 1986) (finding of control was supported by the defendants' ability to "easily obtain" the documents when it was in their interest to do so); *Cooper Indus., Inc. v. British Aerospace, Inc.*, 102 F.R.D. 918, 919–20 (S.D.N.Y. 1984) (finding that it was "inconceivable that defendant would not have access to these documents and the ability to obtain them for its usual business").

[92] Tex. R. Civ. P. 192.7.

[93] See discussion in note 75.

[94] *In re Summersett*, 438 S.W.3d 74, 81 (Tex. App.—Corpus Christ 2013, orig. proceeding) ("The party seeking production has the burden of proving that the relator has constructive possession or the right to obtain possession of the requested documents."); *In re U-Haul Int'l*, 87 S.W.3d 653, 656 (Tex. App.—San Antonio 2002, orig. proceeding) ("The plaintiffs had the burden of proving UHI had constructive possession or the right to obtain possession of the requested documents from Republic."); *see GTE. Commc'ns Sys. Corp. v. Tanner*, 856 S.W.2d 725, 729 (Tex. 1993) (orig. proceeding) ("Likewise, there is no evidence that GCSC had constructive possession of the document or a right to compel its production. Plaintiffs adduced no evidence regarding the corporate relationship between GTFL and GCSC, or any right of the latter to control the former. In fact, the only testimony regarding control was James' speculation regarding the ability of GCSC's parent to control its subsidiaries, assuming both GCSC and GTFL were subsidiaries of the same parent. There is no evidence that GCSC ever actually did exercise control of any type over GTFL."); *cf. Norman v. Young*, 422 F.2d 470, 472–73 (10th Cir. 1970) ("There is no doubt that the moving party is charged with establishing possession, custody or control[.]"); *St. Pierre v. Dearborn Nat'l Life Ins. Co.*, No. EP-19-CV-00223-DCG, 2020 U.S. Dist. LEXIS 194546, at *6–7, 2020 WL 6122555 (W.D. Tex. Apr. 14, 2020) ("The party seeking discovery bears the burden to show that the opposing party has possession, custody, or control over the discovery requested. Here, Plaintiff has failed to meet her burden. Plaintiff's interrogatories and RFPs ask Defendant to provide her discovery from the City without showing how this discovery is

legal right to obtain the requested documents, the burden shifts to responding party to show why it lacks control.[95]

8-4:3.2 Usual Course of Business or Organized and Labeled to Correspond with the Categories in the Request

Two questions exist with respect to the directive that documents be produced as they are maintained in the "usual course of business or organize[d] and label[ed] . . . to correspond with the categories in the request."[96] First, when are documents "kept in the usual course of business"? Second, does the decision regarding which alternative to use lie exclusively with the producing party?

8-4:3.2a Documents Are "Kept in the Usual Course of Business" When the Litigant Functions in the Manner of a Commercial Enterprise or the Documents Result from "Regularly Conducted Activity"

To determine what constitutes an appropriate production of records as they are kept in the "usual course of business," it is first necessary to define the term. Unfortunately, neither Texas Rule 196.3(c) nor any case construing it does so. One federal court, in interpreting the term "usual course of business," as used in Federal Rule 34,[97] has explained:

---

reasonably available to Defendant or how Defendant has possession, custody, or control over it. Plaintiff's only argument is that Defendant and the City have a close working relationship and that the City was represented by Defendant's counsel while it was still a party to this case. But Defendant has no duty to respond on behalf of the City—a non-party—or to request discovery from the City on behalf of Plaintiff. Moreover, Plaintiff does not cite to any authority supporting its argument that a mere contractual relationship between a party and a non-party makes discovery from the non-party reasonably available or that it affords the litigant party possession, custody, or control over it."); *Parris v. Pappas*, No. 3:10CV1128 (WWE), 2017 U.S. Dist. LEXIS 122282, at *4, 2017 WL 3314001 (D. Conn. Aug. 3, 2017) (noting that the moving party is charged with establishing possession, custody or control); *Mt. Hawley Ins. Co. v. Felman Prod., Inc.*, 269 F.R.D. 609, 620 (S.D. W. Va. 2010) (same); *N.Y. ex rel. Boardman v. Nat'l R.R. Passenger Corp.*, 233 F.R.D. 259, 268 (N.D.N.Y. 2006) (same).

95 *Greater N.Y. Taxi Ass'n v. City of N.Y.*, No. 13 Civ. 3089 (VSB) (JCF), 2017 U.S. Dist. LEXIS 146655, at *7–8, 2017 WL 4012051 (S.D.N.Y. Sept. 11, 2017) ("When the party resisting discovery denies possession or control, '[t]he discovering party bears the burden of establishing control.'" (quoting *SEC v. Strauss*, No. 09 Civ. 4150, 2009 U.S. Dist. LEXIS 101227, at *20, 2009 WL 3459204 (S.D.N.Y. Oct. 28, 2009))); *In re Nat'l Century Fin. Enters., Inc. Fin. Inv. Litig.*, No. 2:03-md-1565, 2009 U.S. Dist. LEXIS 92237, at *31, 2009 WL 10687963 (S.D. Ohio Sept. 1, 2009) ("The fact remains, however, that it was Pharos' burden to demonstrate that the email was not in its possession, custody, or control, and it failed to do so."); *Banff Ltd. v. Ltd., Inc.*, No. 93 Civ. 2514 (CSH) (RLE), 1994 U.S. Dist. LEXIS 1779, at *5, 1994 WL 66069 (S.D.N.Y. Feb. 18, 1994) ("[Federal Rule 34] requires a party to produce things which are in its 'possession, custody or control.' Items which have been lost cannot be deemed to fit this description. The party claiming this situation would, of course, have the burden of demonstrating that the items are lost or should be considered lost.").

96 Tex. R. Civ. P. 196.3(c).

97 The term is not defined in Federal Rule 34 or its Advisory Committee Note. *Ries v. Ardinger (In re Adkins Supply, Inc.)*, 555 B.R. 579, 592–94 (Bankr. N.D. Tex. 2016) ("Unfortunately, the phrase 'in the usual course of business' is not defined in the Rules or the advisory notes, and there are no records of Congress debating the term."); *SEC v. Collins & Aikman*

> [T]he option of producing documents "as they are kept in the usual course of business" under [Federal] Rule 34 requires the producing party to meet either of two tests. *First*, this option is available to commercial enterprises or entities that function in the manner of commercial enterprises. *Second*, this option may also apply to records resulting from "regularly conducted activity." Where a producing party's activities are not "routine and repetitive" such as to require a well-organized record-keeping system—in other words when the records do not result from an "ordinary course of business"—the party must produce documents according to the sole remaining option under [Federal] Rule 34: "organize[d] and label[ed] . . . to correspond to the categories in the request."
>
> The logic of [Federal] Rule 34 supports this limitation. When records do not result from "routine and repetitive" activity, there is no incentive to organize them in a predictable system. The purpose of the Rule is to facilitate production of records in a useful manner and to minimize discovery costs; thus it is reasonable to require litigants who do not create and/or maintain records in a "routine and repetitive" manner to organize the records in a usable fashion prior to producing them.[98]

In other words, the "usual-course-of-business" production method is not limited to commercial enterprises. Thus, courts have found that entities that function in the same manner as a commercial enterprise, such as the federal or state governmental agencies or bodies, can satisfy that requirement.[99]

Corp., 256 F.R.D. 403, 412 n.44 (S.D.N.Y. 2009) (same); *Williams v. Taser Int'l, Inc.*, No. 1:06-CV-0051-RWS, 2006 U.S. Dist. LEXIS 47255, at *23, 2006 WL 1835437 (N.D. Ga. June 30, 2006) (same); *Cardenas v. Dorel Juvenile Grp., Inc.*, 230 F.R.D. 611, 618 (D. Kan. 2005) (same).

[98] *SEC v. Collins & Aikman Corp.*, 256 F.R.D. 403, 412–13 (S.D.N.Y. 2009) (footnotes omitted); *accord Ries v. Ardinger (In re Adkins Supply, Inc.)*, 555 B.R. 579, 592–93 (Bankr. N.D. Tex. 2016).

[99] *U.S. v. Talmage*, No. 1:16-cv-19-DN-PMW, 2017 U.S. Dist. LEXIS 88251, at *10–11, 2017 WL 2483797 (D. Utah June 8, 2017) ("The 'usual course of business' method outlined in [Federal] Rule 34 is not limited to commercial entities. Courts have found that entities which function in the same manner as a commercial enterprise, like the federal government, may satisfy [Federal] Rule 34 by demonstrating that its document production is produced in the same manner as it is kept in the usual course of business."); *accord Traverse v. Gutierrez Co.*, No. CV 18-10175-DJC, 2019 U.S. Dist. LEXIS 238304, at *2–3, 2019 WL 12291348 (D. Mass. Aug. 15, 2019) ("The option of producing records as 'they are kept in the usual course of business' is only available to (1) commercial enterprises or entities that function in the manner of commercial enterprises and (2) records resulting from 'regularly conducted activity.'"); *Perez v. U.S.*, No. 13cv1417-WQH-BGS, 2016 U.S. Dist. LEXIS 8993, at *13–14, 2016 WL 304877 (S.D. Cal. Jan. 25, 2016) ("The government acts like a commercial entity in many instances, such as 'purchasing equipment from defense contractors, selling maps to backpackers, and executing contracts to construct buildings.' Therefore, it is reasonable to assume that the training of Border Patrol agents, and the investigation into use of force incidents, is likewise routine in nature for the government. Presumptively, such records are created and 'Maintained in an efficient fashion such that production as they are kept in the ordinary course of business' and comply with the requirements of [Federal] Rule 34." (quoting *SEC v. Collins & Aikman Corp.*, 256 F.R.D. 403, 412 (S.D.N.Y. 2009))); *SEC v. Collins & Aikman Corp.*, 256 F.R.D. 403, 412–13 (S.D.N.Y. 2009) (same, but holding

Moreover, documents in storage are only maintained "in the ordinary course of business" if they were stored in the same way they were used in the business or they have been used with regularity since they were placed in storage.[100]

8-4:3.2b The Responding Party Generally Decides the Manner of Production

A party who chooses to produce its documents as they are maintained in the ordinary course of business has the burden of proving that fact.[101] This may be proved from

---

that a SEC investigation—"which is by its very nature not routine or repetitive—cannot fall within the scope of the 'usual course of business'").

100 *Cf. Fifth Third Bank v. KCII Insure Servs.*, No. 11-cv-2101 CM/DJW, 2011 U.S. Dist. LEXIS 136160, at *14–16, 2011 WL 5920949 (D. Kan. Nov. 28, 2011) (holding that stored documents were not produced as they were kept in the usual course of business because the producing parties "provided no evidence as to how the documents were kept in the usual course of business while the business was operational. They have made no meaningful attempt to demonstrate that the documents currently stored in the warehouse are being kept in the same manner as they were kept before the business ceased operations."); *Mizner Grand Condo. Ass'n v. Traveler's Prop. Cas. Co. of Am.*, 270 F.R.D. 698, 701 (S.D. Fla. 2010) ("[T]he fact that an organization regularly stores documents as part of its business operations does not mean that production of *any* documents in storage automatically satisfies [Federal] Rule 34."); *In re Sulfuric Acid Antitrust Litig.*, 231 F.R.D. 351, 363 (N.D. Ill. 2005) (holding that records sent to a storage facility were not used with regularity and were only kept in the "usual course of '*storage*' because documents had no relation to day-to-day business operations and were not organized as they were used in the ordinary course of business") (emphasis added); *Ries v. Ardinger (In re Adkins Supply, Inc.)*, 555 B.R. 579, 593–94 (Bankr. N.D. Tex. 2016) ("Defendants have provided no evidence to the Court that the current manner of storage in a warehouse meets the usual course of business option. They have made only the bare assertion that '[t]he documents were produced in the manner in which they were kept.' Accordingly, that option is foreclosed, and it is reasonable that the rules require defendants to 'organize and label [the documents] to correspond to the categories in the request.'" (quoting Fed. R. Civ. P. 34(b)(2)(E)(i))). *But see In re RFC*, No. 13-3451 (SRN/HB), 2017 U.S. Dist. LEXIS 91645, at *2–6, 2017 WL 2572371 (D. Minn. June 14, 2017) (holding that documents of a bankrupt entity in storage were produced in the ordinary course of business); *Hagemeyer N. Am., Inc. v. Gateway Data Scis. Corp.*, 222 F.R.D. 594, 598 (E.D. Wisc. 2004) (same); *Devon Mobile Commc'ns Liquidating Tr. v. Adelphia Commc'ns Corp.*, 338 B.R. 546, 551 (Bankr. S.D.N.Y. 2005) (same).

101 *Texaco, Inc. v. Dominguez*, 812 S.W.2d 451, 457–58 (Tex. App.—San Antonio 1991, orig. proceeding) (holding that, under former Texas Rule 167(a)(1), it was the burden of the producing party to show that documents were produced in the usual course of business and a mere assertion that they were so produced is not sufficient to carry that burden); *cf. Pinnacle Bank v. Tradesman Brewing Co., Inc.*, No. CV 2:20-837-RMG, 2020 U.S. Dist. LEXIS 200215, at *7, 2020 WL 6305331 (D.S.C. Oct. 27, 2020) ("'A party who takes the option of producing documents in the usual course of its business bears the burden of demonstrating that the documents were produced in this manner.'") (quoting *CTL Eng'g of W. Va., Inc. v. Ms Consultants, Inc.*, No. 3:14-CV-90, 2015 U.S. Dist. LEXIS 199187, at *9, 2015 WL 12751694, at *3 (N.D.W. Va. Jan. 30, 2015); *Traverse v. Gutierrez Co.*, No. CV 18-10175-DJC, 2019 U.S. Dist. LEXIS 238304, at *2, 2019 WL 12291348 (D. Mass. Aug. 15, 2019) ("The producing party bears the burden of showing that the documents were produced as they were kept in the usual course of business."); *Ashmore v. Allied Energy, Inc.*, No. 8:14-cv-00227-JMC, 2016 U.S. Dist. LEXIS 65204, at *10, 2016 WL 2898007 (D.S.C. May 18, 2016) ("[I]f a party elects to produce documents 'as they are kept in the usual course of

the document production itself. If it is not readily apparent from the production, the producing party must do more than merely represent to the court and the requesting party that the documents have been produced as they are maintained in the ordinary course of business.[102] Rather, the responding party must "provide 'some modicum of information' regarding how documents are ordinarily kept in the course of business, which would ideally include 'the identity of the custodian or person from whom the documents were obtained, . . . assurance that the documents have been produced in the order in which they are maintained, and a general description of the filing system from which they were recovered.'"[103] A court faced with an absence of any evidence that documents were produced as they were kept in the usual course of business

---

business,' the producing party 'bear[s] the burden of showing that the documents were in fact produced in that manner.'" (quoting *Williams v. Taser Int'l, Inc.*, No. 1:06-CV-0051-RWS, 2006 U.S. Dist. LEXIS 47255, at *25, 2006 WL 1835437 (N.D. Ga. June 30, 2006))); *SEC v. Collins & Aikman Corp.*, 256 F.R.D. 403, 409 (S.D.N.Y. 2009) (same); *In re Sulfuric Acid Antitrust Litig.*, 231 F.R.D. 351, 363 (N.D. Ill. 2005) (same); *Johnson v. Kraft Foods N. Am., Inc.*, 236 F.R.D. 535, 540–41 (D. Kan. 2006) (same).

As one federal court explained: "If the producing party produces documents in the order in which they are kept in the usual course of business, the [Federal] Rule imposes no duty to organize and label the documents, provide an index of the documents produced, or correlate the documents to the particular request to which they are responsive." *MGP Ingredients, Inc., v. Mars, Inc.*, No. 06-2318-JWL-DJW, 2007 U.S. Dist. LEXIS 76853, at *10, 2007 WL 3010343 (D. Kan. Oct. 15, 2007); *see Rychner v. Cont'l Res., Inc.*, 1:19-CV-071, 2021 WL 2211110, at *5 (D.N.D. June 1, 2021) ("Having reviewed the record, the court concludes that Continental has produced the documents in substantially the same manner in which they were kept. Any unwieldiness of Continental's production is mitigated by the provision of indexes by Continental to guide the Rychners. The indexes organize the documents by Bates stamp and description. They also appear to sort the production of electronic communications by date. With this information, the Rychners should, with reasonable effort, be able to discern which documents are responsive to which requests. The documents were produced electronically and should therefore be searchable. Accordingly, the court finds that the manner of Continental's production comports with requirements of Fed. R. Civ. P. 34(b)(2)(E)(i)."); *accord 3M Co. v. Kanbar,* No. CO6-01225 JW (HRL), 2007 U.S. Dist. LEXIS 45232, at *6, *9, 2007 WL 1725448 (N. D. Cal. June 14, 2007); *In re G-I Holdings Inc.*, 218 F.R.D. 428, 439 (D.N.J. 2003).

102 *Cf. Century Jets Aviation LLC v. Alchemist Jet Air LLC*, 08 Civ. 9892, 2011 U.S. Dist. LEXIS 20540, at *10, 2011 WL 724734 (S.D.N.Y. Feb. 7, 2011) ("[T]he disclosing party must provide at least some information about how documents are organized in the party's ordinary course of business."); *SEC v. Collins & Aikman Corp.*, 256 F.R.D. 403, 409 (S.D.N.Y. 2009) ("A party choosing to produce documents as maintained in the ordinary course of business 'bears the burden of demonstrating that the documents made available were in fact produced consistent with that mandate.'" (quoting *Pass & Seymour, Inc. v. Hubbell Inc.*, 255 F.R.D. 331, 334 (N.D.N.Y. 2008))); *GP Indus., LLC v. Bachman*, No. 8:06CV50, 2008 U.S. Dist. LEXIS 90292, at *11, 2008 WL 1733606 (D. Neb. Apr. 10, 2008) (same); *Johnson v. Kraft Foods N. Am., Inc.*, 236 F.R.D. 535, 540–41 (D. Kan. 2006) (same); *Cardenas v. Dorel Juvenile Grp., Inc.*, 230 F.R.D. 611, 618 (D. Kan. 2005) (same).

103 *Mizner Grand Condo. Ass'n v. Traveler's Prop. Cas. Co. of Am.*, 270 F.R.D. 698, 701 (S.D. Fla. 2010) (quoting *Pass & Seymour, Inc. v. Hubbel, Inc.*, 255 F.R.D. 331, 337 (N.D.N.Y. 2008)); *accord Synventive Molding Sols., Inc. v. Husky Injection Molding Sys., Inc.*, 262 F.R.D. 365, 370–71 & n.9 (D. Vt. 2009).

can order the party producing documents "to identify which documents satisfy which request."[104]

It is unclear, however, whether the decision regarding which of the alternatives to use lies exclusively with the responding party. No Texas case has directly considered the question,[105] and federal courts interpreting the identical federal rule are divided on the issue.[106] The best approach is to allow the responding party to choose which of the two alternative methods of production to use, unless its system for organizing and maintaining documents is so deficient as to undermine the production's usefulness under the maintained-in-the-ordinary-course-of-business alternative.[107]

---

104 *Texaco, Inc. v. Dominguez*, 812 S.W.2d 451, 458 (Tex. App.—San Antonio 1991, orig. proceeding); *accord In re Hite*, No.12-18-00121-CV, 2018 Tex. App. LEXIS 4035, at *2, 7–8, 2018 WL 2715300 (Tex. App.—Tyler June 6, 2018, orig. proceeding) (mem. op.) (holding that the trial court did not abuse its discretion by ordering a party to re-produce his documents "by the request to which they apply" because they were wholly disorganized); *In re Bilfinger Westcon, Inc.*, No. 13-19-00466-CV, 2019 Tex. App. LEXIS 10807, at *27–28, 2019 WL 6795870 (Tex. App.—Corpus Christi Dec. 12, 2019, orig. proceeding) (mem. op.) (same); *cf. Johnson v. Kraft Foods N. Am., Inc.*, 236 F.R.D. 535, 541 (D. Kan. 2006) ("[T]he Court finds that Plaintiff has not met his burden to establish that he produced these documents 'as they are kept in the usual course of business.' Because Plaintiff did not do so, he should have organized and labeled them to correspond with the categories in each request. . . ."); *In re Sulfuric Acid Antitrust Litig.*, 231 F.R.D. 351, 363–64 (N.D. Ill. 2005) (same); *Synventive Molding Sols., Inc. v. Husky Injection Molding Sys., Inc.*, 262 F.R.D. 365, 371 (D. Vt. 2009) (same).

105 One Texas case suggests that the decision does not belong exclusively to that responding party, *Texaco, Inc. v. Dominguez*, 812 S.W.2d 451, 457–58 (Tex. App.—San Antonio 1991, orig. proceeding), whereas another holds as follows:

> [A] trial court cannot sanction a party for failing to organize responsive material according to the method its opponent prefers when the discovery response complies with an alternate method permitted under the rules. Because the state's response to the Porretto's request for production does not violate the discovery rules, the trial court abused its discretion in imposing sanctions.

Tex. Gen. Land Office v. Porretto, 369 S.W.3d 276, 290 (Tex. App.—Houston [1st Dist.] 2011), *aff'd in part and rev'd in part on other grounds*, 448 S.W.3d 343 (Tex. 2014).

106 *Cf. Innovative Piledriving Prods., LLC v. Unisto Oy*, No. 1:04-CV-453, 2005 U.S. Dist. LEXIS 14745, at *3, 2005 WL 8169577 (N.D. Ind. July 21, 2005) ("[I]t is not entirely clear whether the producing party has the exclusive option to determine which of the two methods will be used."). *Compare, e.g., MGP Ingredients, Inc., v. Mars, Inc.*, No. 06-2318-JWL-DJW, 2007 U.S. Dist. LEXIS 76853, at *10, 2007 WL 3010343 (D. Kan. Oct. 15, 2007) ("The Rule is phrased in the disjunctive, and the producing party may choose either of the two methods for producing the documents."), *and In re G-I Holdings Inc.*, 218 F.R.D. 428, 439 (D. N.J. 2003) ("The plain phrasing of [Federal] Rule 34(b) reveals that the producing party has the option of presenting information in one of two ways."), *with, e.g., Bd. of Educ. v. Admiral Heating & Ventilating, Inc.*, 104 F.R.D. 23, 36 (N.D. Ill. 1984) (stating that the defendant's reading of [Federal] Rule 34(b) giving it the choice of method of response is incorrect, as it "inserts a period (the British 'full stop') too early in [Federal] Rule 34(b)").

107 *Cf. W Holding Co. v. Chartis Ins. Co.*, 293 F.R.D. 68, 71 (D.P.R. 2013) ("The 'usual course of business' alternative is only available when by the documents' natural organization makes finding critical documents reasonably possible. For that reason, responding government agencies sometimes cannot rely on this modality; investigation documents often lack meaningful organization, in contrast to an agency's routine administrative records.") (citations omitted); *Mizner Grand Condo. Ass'n v. Traveler's Prop. Cas. Co. of Am.*, 270 F.R.D. 698, 701 (S.D. Fla. 2010) ("In this case, Mizner's production is so disorganized that

This conclusion is supported by several factors. Initially, Texas Rule 196.3(c) is based on Federal Rule 34(b). Federal Rule 34(b) was amended in 1980 to provide for production as the documents are maintained in the ordinary course of business to prevent a producing party from shuffling materials to make them harder to find.[108] Moreover, the responding party has the burden to select and produce the items requested rather than dumping large quantities of unrelated material on the requesting party along with the documents requested.[109]

Finally, requiring that the requested materials be segregated according to the requests often would impose a difficult and unnecessary burden on the responding party. The categories are devised by the requesting party and often overlap or are so elastic that the responding party may have difficulty determining which documents respond to which requests. Not only does such a segregation serve no substantial purpose, but it also becomes quite burdensome when a substantial number of documents

---

it is insufficient under [Federal] Rule 34(b)(2)(E)(i) . . . . In order to obtain documents responsive to its requests, Travelers would therefore have to examine and sort through each individual file folder. This is a task that [Federal] Rule 34(b)(2)(E)(i) clearly assigns to the producing party, whether it is completed in the usual course of business or in response to a specific request."); *Williams v. Taser Int'l, Inc.*, No. 1:06-CV-0051-RWS, 2006 U.S. Dist. LEXIS 47255, at *23–24, 2006 WL 1835437 (N.D. Ga. June 30, 2006) ("[T]he Court makes clear that while Taser has the option to produce documents as they are kept in the ordinary course of business, . . . [w]ere the Court to conclude that the filing system utilized was so disorganized as to prevent Plaintiffs from making a meaningful review of the requested documents, the Court would not hesitate to compel Taser to organize and specifically label documents as responsive to Plaintiffs' requests."); *Innovative Piledriving Prods., LLC v. Unisto Oy*, No. 1:04-CV-453, 2005 U.S. Dist. LEXIS 23652, at *2–4, 2005 WL 8169578 (N.D. Ind. Oct. 14, 2005) ("[T]he best approach . . . generally allows the producing party to choose which of the two alternative methods of production to use except when some special factor justifies allowing the requesting party to select the method, such as when the method chosen places an unreasonable burden on the party seeking production.").

[108] Fed. R. Civ. P. 34, Advisory Committee Note to 1980 Amend. (noting that the committee was advised that it was not rare for "parties deliberately to mix critical documents with others in the hope of obscuring significance"); *see Texaco, Inc. v. Dominguez*, 812 S.W.2d 451, 457 (Tex. App.—San Antonio 1991, orig. proceeding) ("A federal court has noted that the purpose of the 1980 amendment to [Federal Rule] 34(b), which contains the same language as the provision in [former Texas Rule] 167(1)(f), 'was aimed at forestalling such abuses as the deliberate mixing of critical documents with others in the hope of obscuring significance.'" (quoting *Bd. of Educ. v. Admiral Heating & Ventilating, Inc.*, 104 F.R.D. 23, 36 (N.D. Ill. 1984))); *Rychner v. Cont'l Res., Inc.*, No. 1:19-CV-071, 2021 U.S. Dist. LEXIS 102175, at *13–14, 2021 WL 2211110 (D.N.D. June 1, 2021) ("This rule is intended to prevent parties from hiding 'a needle in a haystack' and to minimize the costs associated with discovery.").

[109] *Cf., Rothman v. Emory Univ.*, 123 F.3d 446, 455 (7th Cir. 1997) (sanctioning the responding party for producing unrelated, non-responsive documents); *Williams v. Taser Int'l, Inc.*, No. 1:06-CV-0051-RWS, 2006 U.S. Dist. LEXIS 47255, at *24, WL 1835437 (N.D. Ga. June 30, 2006) ("Moreover, were the Court to conclude that Taser had been 'overly generous' in identifying responsive documents so as to unduly burden Plaintiffs in their search of those documents, the Court would similarly require Taser to organize and label documents as responsive to Plaintiffs' requests.").

are involved and even worse can invite claims of the very sort of "hiding" materials that the Rule was intended to prevent.[110]

8-5 Objections

Texas Rule 193.2 sets forth the obligations and procedures for objecting to written-discovery requests, such as production requests.[111] The general principles relating to objections are discussed in Chapter 5, section 5-3. Proper and improper production-request objections are discussed in the following sections of this Chapter.

8-5:1 General, Subject-to, and Boilerplate Objections

As discussed in Chapter 5, sections 5-3:2 and 5-3:3, respectively, "general" and "subject-to" objections to production requests[112] generally are improper and boilerplate objections to them are always improper.[113]

8-5:2 Proportionality

As discussed in Chapter 5, section 5-3:4, a lack of "proportionality" to the case's needs can be asserted as an objection to a production request in its entirety or to an individual production request.[114]

---

110 *MGP Ingredients, Inc., v. Mars, Inc.*, No. 06-2318-JWL-DJW, 2007 U.S. Dist. LEXIS 76853, at *10, 2007 WL 3010343 (D. Kan. Oct. 15, 2007) ("[I]mposing such a duty could result in undue burden on the producing party.").

111 Tex. R. Civ. P. 193.2.

112 "General objections" occur when the responding party includes a section at the beginning of its response entitled "general objections," which contains every imaginable objection, such as overbreadth, undue burden, relevance, vagueness, ambiguity, harassment, cumulativeness, duplicativeness, and privilege, which are then incorporated by reference "to the extent" they apply in each response to the individual production request to the pertinent discovery request. See Chapter 5, section 5-3:2 (discussing "general" objections). "Subject-to" objections occur when the responding party sets forth in the response to each individual production request a litany of prophylactic, boilerplate objections, such as those set forth above, and then, "subject to and without waiving" the objections, says nonprivileged responsive documents will be produced. See Chapter 5, section 5-3:2 (discussing "subject-to" objections).

113 A boilerplate objection is an objection that "merely states the legal grounds for the objection without (1) specifying how the discovery request is deficient and (2) specifying how the objecting party would be harmed if it were forced to respond to the request. For example, a boilerplate objection might state that a discovery request is irrelevant or overly broad without taking the next step to explain why. These objections are taglines, completely devoid of any individualized factual analysis." *Liguria Foods, Inc. v. Griffith Labs., Inc.*, 320 F.R.D. 168, 170 n.1 (N.D. Iowa 2017) (quoting Matthew L. Jarvey, *Boilerplate Discovery Objections: How They Are Used, Why They Are Wrong, and What We Can Do About Them*, 61 Drake L. Rev. 913, 914–16 (2013)). They often are used in general and subject-to objections. See Chapter 5, Section 5-3:2 (discussing general and subject-to objections).

114 The proportionality factors are (1) the likely benefit of the requested discovery; (2) the needs of the case; (3) the amount in controversy; (4) the parties' resources; (5) the importance of the issues at stake in the litigation; (6) the importance of the proposed discovery in resolving the litigation; and (7) any other articulable factor bearing on proportionality).

8-5:3 Privilege

Under the Texas discovery rules, unlike under the federal discovery rules, privilege is not a proper objection to a production request. Texas Rule 193.2(f) provides "[a] party should *not* object to a request for written discovery on the grounds that it calls for production of material that is privileged but should instead comply with [Texas] Rule 193.3."[115] In addition, an objection that the production of documents according to responsive request requires the party to reveal privileged work-product is also improper.[116] Privilege assertions under Texas Rule 193.3 are discussed at length in Chapter 5, section 5-4.

8-5:4 Scope Objections: Relevance and Not Reasonably Calculated to Lead to the Discovery of Admissible Evidence

If a production request seeks material that neither is relevant to the action's subject matter nor reasonably calculated to lead to the discovery of admissible evidence, the responding party should object on those grounds. Discovery's scope (i.e., information that is relevant or reasonably calculated to lead to the discovery of admissible evidence) is discussed in Chapter 4, section 4-3, and Chapter 6, section 6-3:3.

An interesting question is whether a responding party can redact otherwise responsive documents because those documents contain irrelevant material. Although no Texas case has directly considered the question,[117] federal courts generally hold that such redactions are improper.[118]

In re State Farm Lloyds, 520 S.W.3d 595, 607–12 (Tex. 2017) (orig. proceeding). See also Chapter 5, section 5-3:3 (discussing boilerplate objections).

115 Tex. R. Civ. P. 193.2(f) (emphasis added); *see In re Graco Children's Prods., Inc.*, 173 S.W.3d 600, 605 (Tex. App.—Corpus Christi 2005, orig. proceeding) ("[N]o objection needs to be made to preserve a privilege[.]"); *In re Christus Health Se. Tex.*, 167 S.W.3d 596, 599 (Tex. App.—Beaumont 2005, orig. proceeding) (same); *In re Anderson*, 163 S.W.3d 136, 140 (Tex. App.—San Antonio 2005, orig. proceeding) (same); *In re Shipmon*, 68 S.W.3d 815, 822 (Tex. App.—Amarillo 2001, orig. proceeding) (same); *In re Monsanto Co.*, 998 S.W.2d 917, 924 (Tex. App.—Waco 1999, orig. proceeding) (same).

116 As the Corpus Christi Court of Appeals explained: "Relator's contention is nonsensical. If we were to accept relator's premise, then all parties who have responded to requests for production by the 'organization and label' method as opposed to 'the ordinary course of business' have revealed attorney work product." *In re Bilfinger Westcon, Inc.*, No. 13-19-00466-CV, 2019 Tex. App. LEXIS 10807, at *30–32, 2019 WL 6795870 (Tex. App.—Corpus Christi, orig. proceeding) (mem. op.).

117 In *Trishe Res., Inc. v. Hilliard Energy, Ltd.*, No. 11-18-00086-CV, 2019 Tex. App. LEXIS 8164, at *10–12, 2019 WL 4232226 (Tex. App.—Eastland Sept. 6, 2019, pet. denied), the court held that the trial court did not abuse its discretion in imposing discovery sanctions against a party who redacted documents to remove relevant information from them.

118 *Ewalt v. GateHouse Media Ohio Holding II, Inc.*, No. 2:19-CV-4262, 2020 U.S. Dist. LEXIS 148829, at *4–6, 2020 WL 4782860 (S.D. Ohio Aug. 18, 2020) ("Defendant Gatehouse argued such redactions [to the produced documents] were appropriate because 'Plaintiffs are seeking discovery regarding absent class members' and suggested that such redactions would protect 'personally identifying information and other information of a personal nature.' The court responded: '[T]hat argument ignores the real issue: whether or not the parties can redact irrelevant information from otherwise relevant documents. In the Court's view, the Federal Rules of Civil Procedure provide no support for the redaction of

irrelevant information. "Redaction is an inappropriate tool for excluding alleged irrelevant information from documents that are otherwise responsive to a discovery request. It is a rare document that contains only relevant information. And irrelevant information within a document that contains relevant information may be highly useful to providing context for the relevant information." The Court declines to adopt Defendant's proposal accordingly.'") (citations omitted); *Aronstein v. Mass. Mut. Life Ins. Co.*, No. 15-12864-MGM, 2017 U.S. Dist. LEXIS 100867, at *16–18, 2017 WL 2818993 (D. Mass. June 29, 2017) ("[A]s the parties are aware, this court is already on record as being of the view that '[r]edactions of documents that are responsive and contain some relevant information should be limited to redactions of privileged information when, as in this case, there is a protective order restricting the use and dissemination of . . . sensitive information.' It remains the court's view that the weight of authority on this issue is on Aronstein's side. MassMutual's position that courts ordering the production of unredacted documents generally have done so for case specific reasons is not consistent with case law. To the contrary, many courts that have ordered the production of redacted information have relied primarily on the principles that Federal Rule of Civil Procedure 34 'requires documents to be produced as they are kept in the ordinary course of business and that "[t]here is no express or implied support" in the Rules of Civil Procedure for a procedure allowing 'a party [to] scrub responsive documents of nonresponsive information.' . . . To the extent MassMutual has made redactions to documents it produced on the grounds that the redacted information was not relevant, those documents should be produced to Aronstein in unredacted form except in instances where the redactions are of privileged material." (quoting *Sexual Minorities v. Lively*, No. 3:12-30051-MAP, 2015 U.S. Dist. LEXIS 104636, at *16–17, 2015 WL 4750931 (D. Mass. Aug. 10, 2015), and *Beverage Distribs., Inc. v. Miller Brewing Co.*, Nos. 2:08-cv-827, 2:08-cv-931, 2:08-cv-1112, 2:08-cv-1131, 2:08-cv-1136, 2010 U.S. Dist. LEXIS 50732, at *12 (S.D. Ohio Apr. 28, 2010))); *Engage Healthcare Commc'ns, LLC v. Intellisphere, LLC*, No. 12-cv-00787(FLW)(LHG), 2017 U.S. Dist. LEXIS 135101, at *10–14, 2017 WL 3624262 (D.N.J. Apr. 26, 2017) ("The majority of the cases cited by the parties, as well as those independently located by the Special Master, clearly state that unilateral redactions based on one party's subjective view of relevancy are improper. Aside from the number of courts that have rejected the position that a party has a unilateral right to redact information, the Special Master is satisfied that the underlying rationale in reaching those decisions is sound. Analysis of Fed. R. Civ. P. 34, which governs the production of documents between parties, is instructive. Nothing in that rule either expressly or impliedly authorizes a party to unilaterally redact documents. If anything, the Rule contemplates that a party cannot do so. For instance, the plain language of Fed. R. Civ. P. 34(a) permits a party to request that its adversary 'produce and permit the requesting party . . . to inspect [any responsive documents] in the responding party's possession custody or control[.]' In turn, 'the responding party may state that it will produce copies of documents . . . instead of permitting inspection.' The language of the rule plainly intimates that the copy of the document produced would be identical to the document to be inspected. If portions of a document produced did not contain the same content as the document had it been inspected, then it would not be a true copy, and would defeat the purpose of an inspection." (footnote omitted) (citations omitted) (quoting Fed. R. Civ. P. 34(b)(2)(B))); *Toyo Tires & Rubber Co., Ltd v. CIA Wheel Grp.*, No. SA CV 15-00246-DOC (DFMx), 2016 U.S. Dist. LEXIS 184189, at *6 (C.D. Cal. Feb. 23, 2016) ("[T]he Court agrees with Toyo that CIA may not redact otherwise responsive documents because those documents contain irrelevant material."); *Orion Power Midwest, L.P. v. Am. Coal Sales Co.*, No. 2:05-cv-555, 2008 U.S. Dist. LEXIS 76366, at *4–5, 2008 WL 4462301 (W.D. Pa. Sept. 30, 2008) ("Defendants' novel interpretation of their discovery obligations is not supported by the text of [Federal Rule] 34 and would open a fertile new field for discovery battles. [Federal] Rule 34 talks about production of 'documents,' as opposed to the relevant information contained in those documents. It is at least implicit that the duty to 'produce documents as they are kept in the usual course of business' includes the substantive contents of those

8-5:5 Overbreadth

Texas courts often use the term "overly broad" or "overbroad" in describing objectionable production requests.[119] Basically, an overbroad request is one that seeks irrelevant information.[120] A production request is overly broad when it encompasses time periods, activities, locations, or products that are not relevant to the action's subject matter.[121] For example:

---

documents. Certainly, a party that seeks to 'inspect' a document would anticipate being able to inspect the entire document. This interpretation of [Federal] Rule 34 is consistent with the guidance in [Federal Rule] 1 that the Rules be construed to advance the just, speedy and inexpensive determination of cases. There is no express or implied support for the insertion of another step in the process (with its attendant expense and delay) in which a party would scrub responsive documents of non-responsive information. In sum, the Court cannot countenance Defendants' 'redaction campaign.'").

119 *E.g.*, *In re K & L Auto Crushers, LLC*, 627 S.W.3d 239, 252-52 (Tex. 2021) (orig. proceeding); *In re Graco Children's Prods., Inc.*, 210 S.W.3d 598, 600–01 (Tex. 2006) (orig. proceeding) (per curiam); *In re CSX Corp.*, 124 S.W.3d 149, 152–53 (Tex. 2003) (orig. proceeding); *In re Alford Chevrolet-Geo*, 997 S.W.2d 173, 180 n.1 (Tex. 1999) (orig. proceeding); *Texaco, Inc. v. Sanderson*, 898 S.W.2d 813, 815 (Tex. 1995) (orig. proceeding) (per curiam). An overbreadth objection generally is a surrogate for an objection that the discovery request seeks information or documents that either are not relevant or are not reasonably calculated to lead to the discovery of admissible evidence. *See, e.g., In re Graco Children's Prods., Inc.*, 210 S.W.3d 598, 600 (Tex. 2006) (orig. proceeding) (per curiam).

120 *In re K & L Auto Crushers, LLC*, 627 S.W.3d 239, 253 (Tex. 2021) (orig. proceeding)); *In re Allstate Cnty. Mut. Ins. Co.*, 227 S.W.3d 667, 670 (Tex. 2007) (orig. proceeding) (per curiam) ("Overbroad requests for irrelevant information are improper whether they are burdensome or not, so the defendants were not required to detail what they might encompass.").

121 *E.g.*, *In re K & L Auto Crushers, LLC*, 627 S.W.3d 239, 253 (Tex. 2021) (orig. proceeding)) ("[D]iscovery requests and orders are overbroad if they are not properly 'tailored with regard to time, place, or subject matter' or otherwise require production of information that is not reasonably calculated to lead to the discovery of admissible evidence." (quoting *In re Nat'l Lloyds Ins. Co.*, 507 S.W.3d 219, 226 (Tex. 2016) (per curiam))); *In re CSX Corp.*, 124 S.W.3d 149, 152–53 (Tex. 2003) (orig. proceeding) ("Discovery orders requiring document production from an unreasonably long period of time or from distant or unrelated locations are impermissibly overbroad."); *In re Alford Chevrolet-Geo*, 997 S.W.2d 173, 180 n.1 (Tex. 1999) (orig. proceeding) ("We have identified as overbroad those requests encompassing time periods, products, or activities beyond those at issue in the case—in other words, matters of questionable relevancy to the case at hand."); *In re Walmart, Inc.*, 620 S.W.3d 851, 858 (Tex. App.—El Paso 2021, orig. proceeding) ("For instance, a discovery order that requires document production over an unreasonably long time-period or from distant and unrelated locales is impermissibly overbroad and subject to mandamus correction."); *In re Skyhawk Sec.*, LLC, No. 09-20-00146-CV, 2020 Tex. App. LEXIS 852, at *15, 2021 WL 377691 (Tex. App.—Beaumont Feb. 4, 2021, orig. proceeding) (mem. op.) (holding that the trial court abused its discretion by ordering a non party to produce documents that were not tailored and limited to information pertinent to the lawsuit or geographical region); *In re UV Logistics, LLC*, No. 12-20-00196-CV, 2021 Tex. App. LEXIS 723, at *7, 2021 WL 306205 (Tex. App.—Tyler Jan. 29, 2021, orig. proceeding) (mem. op.) ("A discovery request is overbroad when it encompasses time periods, activities, or products that are not relevant to the case in which the discovery is sought."); *In re Toyota Motor Sales, U.S.A., Inc.*, No. 05-18-00582-CV, 2018 Tex. App. LEXIS, *11, 2018 WL 2979855 (Tex. App.—Dallas June 14, 2018, orig. proceeding) (mem. op.) (finding the trial court abused its discretion by ordering the defendant to identify all folders and subfolders within databases and all papers maintained in its

- A production request for about 20,000 pages of documents relating to products not at issue in the action was overbroad.[122]
- Production requests in a "simple" false-arrest case for all lawsuits, claims, or incident reports for a five-year period in all 227 stores owned by the defendant alleging false arrest, civil rights violation, and excessive use of force were "overly broad as a matter of law."[123]

---

technical library, because it requires the production of irrelevant information, not limited by time, and places a disproportionate burden on the defendant); *In re NCAA*, 543 S.W.3d 487, 491–92 (Tex. App.—Dallas 2018, orig. proceeding) ("Discovery orders requiring document production from an unreasonably long time period, from distant and unrelated locales, or related to products never used by the plaintiff are often found to be impermissibly overbroad. . . . Allowing discovery involving other products, similar injuries, or similar conditions is not improper, however, if there is a connection between the issues in the case and the discovery ordered."); *In re BNSF Ry.*, No. 09-07-538 CV, 2008 Tex. App. LEXIS 634, at *4, 2007 WL 4822488 (Tex. App.—Beaumont Jan. 31, 2008, orig. proceeding) (mem. op.) ("A discovery request that is unlimited as to time, place or subject matter is overbroad as a matter of law."); *In re BP Prods. N. Am., Inc.*, No. 01-06-00140-CV, 2006 Tex. App. LEXIS 7861, at *6–7, 2006 WL 2522217 (Tex. App.—Houston [1st Dist.] Sept. 1, 2006, orig. proceeding) (mem. op.) ("We agree that Request 81 is overbroad because there are no limits as to time, location, and subject matter on what type of documents provided to the Baker Panel are sought.").

122 *In re Graco Children's Prods., Inc.*, 210 S.W.3d 598, 600–01 (Tex. 2006) (orig. proceeding) (per curiam); *see In re Am. Optical Corp.*, 988 S.W.2d 711, 713 (Tex. 1998) (per curiam) (orig. proceeding) (holding that a discovery order requiring the defendant to produce every document generated in relation to asbestos products was overbroad in an action alleging defective respiratory-protection products); *Gen. Motors Corp. v. Lawrence*, 651 S.W.2d 732, 734 (Tex. 1983) (orig. proceeding) (holding that discovery requests concerning the necks in all GM vehicle models were overbroad in an action involving an allegedly defective fuel-filler design in a particular truck model); *In re Daimler Trucks N. Am. LLC*, No. 09-20-00145-CV, 2020 Tex. App. LEXIS 9638, at *7–12, 2020 WL 7251471 (Tex. App.—Beaumont Dec. 10, 2020, orig. proceeding) (mem. op.) (holding that a discovery order requiring the defendant produce documents not related to the specific truck axel at issue was an abuse of discretion); *In re Am. Power Conversion Corp.*, No. 04-12-00140-CV, 2012 Tex. App. LEXIS 9369, at *14–16, 2012 WL 5507111 (Tex. App.—San Antonio Nov. 14, 2012, orig. proceeding) (mem. op.) (holding that production requests seeking documents related to a different product line than the one at issue were overbroad); *In re Valvoline Co.*, No. 01-10-00208-CV, 2010 Tex. App. LEXIS 3696, at *4–5, 2010 WL 2025825 (Tex. App.—Houston [1st Dist.] May 14, 2010, orig. proceeding) (mem. op.) ("[Defendant] asserts that the trial court improperly compelled discovery relating to Ashland products that had not been identified by [plaintiff] as products that [decedent] had used."); *In re BNSF Ry.*, No. 09-07-538 CV, 2008 Tex. App. LEXIS 634, at *7–8, 2007 WL 4822488 (Tex. App.—Beaumont Jan. 31, 2008, orig. proceeding) (mem. op.) ("The discovery request requests are not reasonably tailored. They are not limited to ergonomic issues related to knee issues or to employee conditions related to plaintiff's employment as a brakeman, switchman and conductor. Several requests seek documents related to back injuries.").

123 *Dillard Dep't Stores, Inc. v. Hall*, 909 S.W.2d 491, 492 (Tex. 1995) (orig. proceeding) (per curiam); *see In re Allstate Cnty. Mut. Ins. Co.*, 227 S.W.3d 667, 669 (Tex. 2007) (orig. proceeding) (per curiam) (finding that discovery requests seeking information and documents about, among other things, "every court order finding that Allstate wrongfully adjusted the value of a damaged vehicle" were improper because they "are overbroad as to time, location, and scope, and could easily have been more narrowly tailored to the dispute at hand");

- Where the "plaintiff could have worked at [the defendant's] factory for two years,

---

In re C & J Energy Servs. Inc., No. 13-20-00503-CV, 2021 Tex. App. LEXIS 3455, at *28–29, 2021 WL 1748090 (Tex. App.—Corpus Christi May 4, 2021, orig. proceeding) (mem. op.) (holding that requests for documents relating to oil well with no temporal limitation were overbroad); *In re HEB Grocery Co.*, 375 S.W.3d 497, 501 (Tex. App.—Houston [14th Dist.] 2012, orig. proceeding) (noting that "Texas courts often characterize premises liability discovery that is not limited to the premises at issue as overbroad" and holding, in a simple slip-and-fall case, that the plaintiff's production requests relating to incidents at all 23 HEB Houston area stores were overbroad); *In re Family Dollar Stores of Tex., LLC*, No. 09-11-00432-CV, 2011 Tex. App. LEXIS 8782, at *6–7, 2011 WL 5299578 (Tex. App.—Beaumont Nov. 3, 2011, orig. proceeding) (mem. op.) (holding that production requests seeking documents about every injury at the defendant's stores involving merchandise falling off a shelf were overbroad as a matter of law because "the discovery could have been easily narrowed to require production for a relevant geographic area of claims involving merchandise that fell off shelves of a similar design as the one involved in the incident"); *In re EOG Res., Inc.*, No. 10-10-00455-CV, 2011 Tex. App. LEXIS 969, at *2, 4–5, 2011 WL 455280 (Tex. App—Waco Feb. 9, 2011, orig. proceeding) (mem. op.) (holding that discovery requests seeking information and documents about policies for the use and installation of all trailers in any geographic region where the defendant did business for a period of ten years was overly broad because it was not limited in geographic scope and to the same type of trailer that the plaintiff was in when it shifted during a storm and injured him).

However, broad requests still must be analyzed within the context of the pleadings. As the Corpus Christi Court of Appeals noted: "[A] discovery order that covered a 10-year period might be too broad under some circumstances, but there is certainly nothing too broad as a matter of law about all discovery orders covering 10 years." *In re HEB Grocery Co.*, No. 13-10-00533-CV, 2010 Tex. App. LEXIS 9014, at *7 n.3, 2010 WL 4523765 (Tex. App.—Corpus Christi Nov. 8, 2010, orig. proceeding) (mem. op.). In *HEB Grocery*, the plaintiff, who was injured by another shopper driving a motorized cart provided by the defendants, requested all incident reports related to motorized vehicles ridden by customers inside the defendant's stores for the years 2004 through November 2009. *In re HEB Grocery Co.*, No. 13-10-00533-CV, 2010 Tex. App. LEXIS 9014, at *5–6, 2010 WL 4523765 (Tex. App.—Corpus Christi Nov. 8, 2010, orig. proceeding) (mem. op.). The court, in allowing the discovery, reasoned:

> [T]he instant case concerns allegations of negligence based . . . on its nationwide policy decisions regarding the provision and utilization of mechanized electronic carts for customers. Thus, unlike *Dillard Department Stores* [*v. Hall*, 909 S.W.2d 491 (Tex. 1995) (orig. proceeding),] and *K Mart* [*Corp. v. Sanderson*, 937 S.W.2d 429 (Tex. 1996) (orig. proceeding) (per curiam)], the discovery sought in this case is relevant to the specific allegations at issue in the lawsuit.
>
> . . . Moreover, HEB has not presented argument or evidence indicating that the policies and procedures vary from store to store and, accordingly, has failed to show that other locations are not relevant.

In re HEB Grocery Co., No. 13-10-00533-CV, 2010 Tex. App. LEXIS 9014, at *14–15, 2010 WL 4523765 (Tex. App.—Corpus Christi Nov. 8, 2010, orig. proceeding) (mem. op.); *see also In re H.E.B. Grocery Co., L.P.*, No. 13-14-00023-CV, 2014 Tex. App. LEXIS 1777, at *9–15, 2014 WL 700749 (Tex. App.—Corpus Christi Feb. 18, 2014, orig. proceeding) (mem. op.) (in a premises liability lawsuit arising out of a trip and fall over a parking corral in the parking lot of the defendant's grocery store, holding that the trial court did not abuse its discretion in ordering the production of incident reports for trip-and-fall accidents in the parking lot of the same store for the past three years even though the reports did not involve cart corrals because the plaintiff broadly alleged that the relator was negligent and failed to

1998–1999," a production request that "went back to 1948" was overbroad.[124]

- A discovery order requiring an electric utility to produce all documents regarding all lawsuits involving its electrical poles, power lines, guy wires, or anchors for the five years preceding the accident was overbroad because it was not limited to accidents like the one at issue, which involved an allegedly rotten utility pole.[125]

---

use ordinary care in maintaining the premises in a reasonably safe condition and free of hazards).

124 *In re Reynolds Metal Co.*, No. 14-04-00001-CV, 2004 Tex. App. LEXIS 3405, at *5–6, 10, 2004 WL 794535 (Tex. App.—Houston [14th Dist.] Apr. 15, 2004, orig. proceeding) (mem. op.); *see Texaco, Inc. v. Sanderson*, 898 S.W.2d 813, 815 (Tex. 1995) (orig. proceeding) (per curiam) ("While plaintiffs are entitled to discover evidence of defendants' safety policies and practices as they relate to the circumstances involved in their allegations, a request for all documents authored by Sexton on the subject of safety, without limitation as to time, place, or subject matter is overbroad."); *In re UPS Ground Freight, Inc.*, 12-19-00412-CV, 2020 Tex. App. LEXIS 1746, at *10–11, 2020 WL 975357, (Tex. App.—Tyler Feb. 28, 2020, orig. proceeding) (mem. op.) ("Here, the passage of time results in a sliding scale of relevance where information provided by previous employees becomes too attenuated from [Defendant's] situation to be of use. The likelihood that employees and test results from eleven years prior to the accident that is the focus of this litigation would shed any light on this case is too small to justify discovery. [Plaintiff's] request could be more narrowly tailored to include only relevant matters pertinent to a more appropriate time period."); *In re AWC Frac Valves, Inc.*, No. 09-13-00247-CV, 2013 Tex. App. LEXIS 10303, at *12, 2013 WL 4314377 (Tex. App.—Beaumont Aug. 15, 2013, orig. proceeding) (per curiam) (mem. op.) ("[C]oncluding that request 21 is overly broad because it asks that Apache produce documents in areas of business that differ from those defined by [the] non-competition agreement [at issue]."); *In re Atchison, Topeka & Santa Fe Ry. Co.*, No. 09-98-095 CV, 1998 Tex. App. LEXIS 2888, at *3, 1998 WL 241221 (Tex. App.—Beaumont May 14, 1998, orig. proceeding) (per curiam) (not designated for publication) ("ATSF has over 200 railroad facilities and sites in the U.S. [The decedent] was an employee from 1952 to 1969 at the Newton, Kansas site and worked in the backshop of it. The order covers all years before 1983. While plaintiff is entitled to discover evidence of asbestos related injuries, a discovery request asking for all documents that indicate in any way that individuals claimed injury to their lungs from asbestos at any ATSF facility with no limit as to time, place, or subject matter is simply overly broad.").

125 *In re Oncor*, 313 S.W.3d 910, 910 (Tex. App.—Dallas 2010, orig. proceeding); *see also In re Fed. Corp.*, No. 13-16-00219-CV, 2016 Tex. App. LEXIS 11816, at *15–16, 2016 WL 6519110 (Tex. App.—Corpus Christi Nov. 1, 2016, orig. proceeding) (mem. op.) (holding production requests and interrogatories served in connection with the defendant's special appearance that sought information about the defendant's activities in states other than Texas were "overbroad because information on [the defendant's] activities which are not directed at Texas is not 'directly relevant' to the subject matter of its special appearance"); *In re Hernandez*, No. 14-11-00408-CV, 2011 Tex. App. LEXIS 7981, at *9–10, 2011 WL 4600706 (Tex. App.—Houston [14th Dist.] Oct. 6, 2011, orig. proceeding) (mem. op.) (holding, in a malpractice action alleging that the plaintiffs' settlement was inferior to other settlements, that production requests seeking information about all settlements obtained by the defendant-attorney were overbroad because the "discovery is not tailored to discover information about similarly situated clients"); *In re Halliburton Energy Servs., Inc.*, No. 01-11-00358-CV, 2011 Tex. App. LEXIS 7974, at *10–13, 2011 WL 4612726 (Tex. App.—Houston [1st Dist.] Oct. 4, 2011, orig. proceeding) (mem. op.) (holding, in a contract action alleging that the defendant-client had agreed to use the plaintiff-attorney for its Louisiana and Gulf of Mexico offshore cases, personal-injury cases, workers-compensation disputes and routine matters, that a discovery order ordering the production of "all documents evidencing fees paid to outside counsel for legal matters originating in Louisiana or the Gulf of Mexico regions

- A discovery order ordering a defendant insurer to produce documents related to insurance claims other than the plaintiff's claim was overbroad.[126]
- A discovery order ordering the NCAA "to produce documents for a 67-year time period (1950 to present) regarding any head trauma suffered by student athletes in any NCAA sport" was overly broad because it was not limited to the type of head trauma sustained by the plaintiff's decedent—"concussive and

since July 1, 2007" was overbroad); *In re GMAC Direct Ins. Co.*, No. 09-10-00493-CV, 2010 Tex. App. LEXIS 10336, at *3–4 (Tex. App.—Beaumont Dec. 30, 2010, orig. proceeding) (mem. op.) ("The Carlsons contend they were harmed by the Relators' 'deliberate business practice of fraudulently adjusting property-damage claims in an outcome-oriented manner so as to minimize the amounts they paid out under the homeowners' policies they issued.' Thus, they argue, their requests are designed to produce evidence of a company-wide business practice for which the Carlsons may recover statutory additional damages and exemplary damages. Rather than tailor the request to include the electronic information actually used in adjusting the Carlsons' claim, the request asks for any electronically-stored information regarding any property damage without regard to time or geographical location. The tenuous connection to the Carlsons' claim is that if an analysis of the data shows that it is somehow 'skewed' in favor of the insurance company, then the Carlsons might be able to use that information to establish exemplary damages. This is precisely the sort of fishing expedition that harvests vast amounts of tenuous information along with the pertinent information that was used in adjusting the Carlsons' claim.").

[126] *In re Nat'l Lloyds Ins. Co.*, 449 S.W.3d 486, 489–90 (Tex. 2014) (orig. proceeding) (per curiam); *accord In re Methodist Primary Care Grp.*, No. 14-17-00299-CV, 2017 Tex. App. LEXIS 7687, at *9–11, 2017 WL 3480292 (Tex. App.—Houston [14th Dist.] Aug. 14, 2017, orig. proceeding) (mem. op.) (in an action claiming that the defendant interfered with the plaintiff's prospective business relationship by hiring two of the plaintiff's doctors, holding that production requests seeking financial information related to the defendant's seventy-eight other doctors was overly broad); *In re Tex. Windstorm Ins. Ass'n*, No. 09-16-00331-CV, 2016 Tex. App. LEXIS 11914, at *3–5, 2016 WL 6518614 (Tex. App.—Beaumont Nov. 3, 2016, original proceeding) (per curiam) (mem. op.) (holding that a discovery order requiring defendants to produce "all photographs and damage estimates on Hurricane Rita claims that they adjusted or investigated on property located within a one mile radius of the property that is the subject of the unfair claims settlement suit" was overbroad); *see In re Nat'l Lloyds Ins. Co.*, 507 S.W.3d 219, 222, 224–26 (Tex. 2016) (orig. proceeding) (holding that a discovery order requiring the production of defendant insurer's management reports and related emails was overbroad because the reports and emails were unrelated to the handling of the plaintiffs' insurance claims); *In re Walmart, Inc.*, 620 S.W.3d 851, 858 (Tex. App.—El Paso 2021, orig. proceeding) ("For instance, a discovery order that requires document production over an unreasonably long time-period or from distant and unrelated locales is impermissibly overbroad and subject to mandamus correction."); *In re Mem'l Hermann Health Sys.*, 607 S.W.3d 913, 920 (Tex. App.—Houston [14th Dist.] 2020, orig. proceeding, no pet.) ("[C]ompelling production of documents evidencing reimbursement rates with private insurers, Medicare, and Medicaid for services not received by [the plaintiff] is impermissibly overbroad."); *In re Toyota Motor Sales, U.S.A.*, Inc., No. 05-18-00582-CV, 2018 Tex. App. LEXIS, *11, 2018 WL 2979855 (Tex. App.—Dallas June 14, 2018, orig. proceeding) (mem. op.) (concluding that the trial court abused its discretion by ordering the defendant to identify all folders and subfolders within databases and all papers maintained in its technical library, because it required the production of irrelevant information, was overbroad in its reach, and placed a disproportionate burden on the defendant).

sub-concussive blows to the head and to the brain diseases and injuries that may result from such blows."[127]

- A discovery order requiring the plaintiff "to produce all Facebook, Google Account, and cell phone information including posts, likes, pictures, groups, ads, 'pokes,' location history, login information, passwords, emails, etc., no matter how mundane or remote, regardless of the topic, content, or subject" was overboard.[128]
- A discovery order requiring a California company produce jurisdictional discovery encompassing "communications by parties other than Relators regarding matters other than the relationship between Relators, Texas, and the [plaintiff's] claims in [the] lawsuit" were overly broad.[129]

The volume of responsive information or material does not necessarily make a production request overbroad.[130] Similarly, a request that is reasonably limited to

---

[127] *In re NCAA*, 543 S.W.3d 487, 493 (Tex. App.—Dallas 2018, orig. proceeding). The court in *In re NCAA*, however, concluded that neither that the discovery order's "temporal scope" nor its scope as to "all sports" was overbroad. As to its temporal scope, the court reasoned that it was "not overbroad considering the nature of the injury and the claims and defenses asserted. For example, [the plaintiff] allege[d] that her husband's injuries were progressive and argue[d] that the NCAA owed continuing duties to [him] and other players to inform them of research developments and new information related to the development and treatment of concussion-related injuries even after they sustained injuries playing for an NCAA team. [The plaintiff] also allege[d] that the NCAA may have known of the ramifications of these injuries on student-athletes for years, and possibly decades, before and after [her husband] played football at the University of Texas. . . . Discovery for the extended time period provide[d the plaintiff] the opportunity to discover what the NCAA knew and when the NCAA knew it regarding the cause, treatment, and prevention of her husband's injuries. Discovery of such information [was] not overreaching and [was] reasonably calculated to lead to the discovery of relevant, admissible evidence." *In re NCAA*, 543 S.W.3d 487, 493 (Tex. App.—Dallas 2018, orig. proceeding). As to the scope of the sports about which discovery was ordered, the court reasoned that "[i]nformation known to the NCAA regarding concussive and non-concussive blows to the head and the impact of those injuries on NCAA athletes [was] discoverable regardless of whether the NCAA obtained the information from studying brain injuries in soccer players, hockey players, football players, or athletes in other sports because the injury, not the sport, is the proper inquiry." *In re NCAA*, 543 S.W.3d 487, 496 (Tex. App.—Dallas 2018, orig. proceeding).

[128] *In re UV Logistics, LLC*, No. 12-20-00196-CV, 2021 Tex. App. LEXIS 723, at *9–12, 2021 WL 306205 (Tex. App.—Tyler Jan. 29, 2021, orig. proceeding) (mem. op.).

[129] *In re Perl*, No. 05-20-00170-CV, 2020 Tex. App. LEXIS 4157, at *18, 2020 WL 2847533 (Tex. App.—Dallas June 2, 2020, orig. proceeding) (mem. op.).

[130] *In re Alford Chevrolet-Geo*, 997 S.W.2d 173, 180–81 n.1 (Tex. 1999) (orig. proceeding) ("[I]t is clear that the sheer volume of a discovery request does not in itself render the request irrelevant or overbroad as a matter of law."); *In re Waste Mgmt. of Tex., Inc.*, 392 S.W.3d 861, 870 (Tex. App.—Texarkana 2013, orig. proceeding) (same); *In re Am. Home Assurance Co.*, 88 S.W.3d 370, 374 (Tex. App.—Texarkana 2002, orig. proceeding) (same); *In re Whiteley*, 79 S.W.3d 729, 734 (Tex. App.—Corpus Christi 2002, orig. proceeding) (same). The volume of information or material, however, may make the discovery request disproportionate to the case's needs, unduly burdensome, or unnecessarily expensive. See Chapter 5, section 5-3:4 (discussing proportionality), and Chapter 8, section 8-5:6 (discussing undue-burden and unnecessary-expense objections).

activities, locations, or products may be overbroad if it not limited to a reasonable time period or vice-versa.[131]

A central consideration in determining overbreadth is whether the production request could have been more narrowly tailored.[132] However, a reasonably tailored production request is not overbroad merely because it may include some information of doubtful relevance, and the parties have some latitude in fashioning proper discovery requests.[133]

The responding party is not required to show that responding to an overbroad production request is burdensome because such requests are improper whether they are burdensome or not.[134] Oftentimes no evidence is needed to establish overbreadth.[135]

---

[131] *See, e.g., In re Valvoline Co.*, No. 01-10-00208-CV, 2010 Tex. App. LEXIS 3696, at *16, 2010 WL 2025825 (Tex. App.—Houston [1st Dist.] May 14, 2010, orig. proceeding) (mem. op.).

[132] *E.g., In re Allstate Cnty. Mut. Ins. Co.*, 227 S.W.3d 667, 669 (Tex. 2007) (orig. proceeding) (per curiam); *In re CSX Corp.*, 124 S.W.3d 149, 153 (Tex. 2003) (orig. proceeding) (per curiam); *In re Am. Optical Corp.*, 988 S.W.2d 711, 713 (Tex. 1998) (orig. proceeding); *In re Marshall*, No. 04-20-00450-CV, Tex. App. LEXIS 593, at *7, 2021 WL 260242 (Tex. App.—San Antonio Jan. 27, 2021, orig. proceeding); *In re Mem'l Hermann Health Sys.*, 607 S.W.3d 913, 918 (Tex. App.—Houston [14th Dist.] 2020, orig. proceeding); *In re Toyota Motor Sales,* U.S.A., Inc., No. 05-18-00582-CV, 2018 Tex. App. LEXIS, *11, 2018 WL 2979855 (Tex. App.—Dallas June 14, 2018, orig. proceeding) (mem. op.); *In re Fed. Corp.*, No. 13-16-00219-CV, 2016 Tex. App. LEXIS 11816, at *5, 2016 WL 6519110 (Tex. App.—Corpus Christi Nov. 1, 2016, orig. proceeding) (mem. op.); *In re R.C.K.*, No. 09-16-00132-CV, 2016 Tex. App. LEXIS 6138, at *4, 2016 WL 3197585 (Tex. App.—Beaumont June 9, 2016, orig. proceeding) (per curiam) (mem. op.); *In re Nat'l Lloyds Ins. Co.*, No. 13-15-00390-CV, 2015 Tex. App. LEXIS 11299, *15 n.3, 2015 WL 6759153 (Tex. App.—Corpus Christi Nov. 3, 2015, orig. proceeding) (mem. op.); *In re Halliburton Energy Servs., Inc.*, No. 01-11-00358-CV, 2011 Tex. App. LEXIS 7974, at *9, 2011 WL 4612726 (Tex. App.—Houston [1st Dist.] Oct. 4, 2011, orig. proceeding) (mem. op.); *In re Hernandez*, No. 14-11-00408-CV, 2011 Tex. App. LEXIS 7981, at *10, 2011 WL 4600706 (Tex. App.—Houston [14th Dist.] Oct. 6, 2011, orig. proceeding) (mem. op.); *In re Waste Mgmt. of Tex., Inc.*, No. 13-11-00197-CV, 2011 Tex. App. LEXIS 7192, at *23, 2011 WL 3855745 (Tex. App.—Corpus Christi Aug. 31, 2011, orig. proceeding) (mem. op.).

[133] *E.g., In re Nat'l Lloyds Ins. Co.*, 449 S.W.3d 486, 488 (Tex. 2014) (orig. proceeding) (per curiam); *In re Am. Optical Corp.*, 988 S.W.2d 711, 713 (Tex. 1998) (orig. proceeding); *Texaco, Inc. v. Sanderson*, 898 S.W.2d 813, 815 (Tex. 1995); *In re Waste Mgmt. of Tex., Inc.*, No. 13-11-00197-CV, 2011 Tex. App. LEXIS 7192, at *23, 2011 WL 3855745 (Tex. App.—Corpus Christi Aug. 31, 2011, orig. proceeding) (mem. op.); *In re MHCB (USA) Leasing & Fin. Corp.*, No. 01-06-00075-CV, 2006 Tex. App. LEXIS 3515, at *23, 2006 WL 1098922 (Tex. App.—Houston [1st Dist.] Apr. 27, 2006, orig. proceeding) (mem. op.).

[134] *E.g., In re Nat'l Lloyds Ins. Co.*, 449 S.W.3d 486, 488 (Tex. 2014) (orig. proceeding) (per curiam); *In re Allstate Cnty. Mut. Ins. Co.*, 227 S.W.3d 667, 669 (Tex. 2007) (orig. proceeding) (per curiam); *In re R.C.K.*, No. 09-16-00132-CV, 2016 Tex. App. LEXIS 6138, at *4, 2016 WL 3197585 (Tex. App.—Beaumont June 9, 2016, orig. proceeding) (per curiam); *In re Waste Mgmt. of Tex., Inc.*, No. 13-11-00197-CV, 2011 Tex. App. LEXIS 7192, at *23, 2011 WL 3855745 (Tex. App.—Corpus Christi Aug. 31, 2011, orig. proceeding) (mem. op.).

[135] *In re Allstate Cnty. Mut. Ins. Co.*, 227 S.W.3d 667, 669 (Tex. 2007) (orig. proceeding) (per curiam); *In re Waste Mgmt. of Tex., Inc.*, 392 S.W.3d 861, 873 (Tex. App.—Texarkana 2013, orig. proceeding); *ISK Biotech Corp. v. Lindsay,* 933 S.W.2d 565, 568 (Tex. App.—Houston [1st Dist.] 1996, no pet.).

8-5:6 Undue Burden or Unnecessary Expense

The mere fact that locating and producing the material responsive to a production request may be burdensome or expensive is insufficient.[136] It is only when producing the material is ***unduly*** burdensome or ***unnecessarily*** expensive that the request is objectionable.[137] As explained by one federal court:

> All discovery requests are a burden on the party who must respond thereto. Unless the task of producing or answering is unusual, undue or extraordinary, the general rule requires the entity answering or producing the documents to bear that burden. Where the requested material is relevant and necessary to the discovery of evidence, a protective order should not be entered merely because compliance with a request for production would be costly or time consuming.[138]

"Undue burden" or "unnecessary expense" is shorthand for the standard found in Texas Rule 192.4, which is that a trial court "should" limit discovery if "the discovery sought is obtainable from some other source that is more convenient, less burdensome, or less expensive"[139] or "the burden or expense of the proposed discovery

---

136 Tex. R. Civ. P. 192.6(b) (providing for a protective order "to protect the movant from undue burden, unnecessary expense"); ***In re Bilfinger Westcon, Inc.***, No. 13-19-00466-CV, 2019 Tex. App. LEXIS 10807, at *36, 2019 WL 795870 (Tex. App.—Corpus Christi Dec. 12, 2019, orig. proceeding) ("The fact that a discovery request is burdensome is not enough to justify protection; 'it is only undue burden that warrants nonproduction.'" (quoting ***ISK Biotech Corp. v. Lindsay***, 933 S.W.2d 565, 568 (Tex. App.—Houston [1st Dist.] 1996, no pet.))); ***In re State Farm Lloyds***, 520 S.W.3d 595, 647, 657 (Tex. App.—Corpus Christi 2015, orig. proceeding) (mem. op.) ("[A] party's failure to comply with a discovery request is not excused because the request is burdensome; it is only an 'undue burden' that warrants nonproduction."); ***Forward v. Hous. Auth.***, 864 S.W.2d 167, 169 (Tex. App.—Tyler 1993, no writ) (same); ***In re Energas Co.***, 63 S.W.3d 50, 55 (Tex. App.—Amarillo 2001, orig. proceeding) (same); *cf.* ***McGuire v. Cooper***, No. 8:16CV04, 2016 U.S. Dist. LEXIS 180361, at *6 (D. Neb. Dec. 30, 2016) ("[G]enerally '[a]ll discovery requests are a burden on the party who must respond thereto. Unless the task of producing or answering is unusual, undue or extraordinary, the general rule requires the entity answering or producing the documents to bear that burden.'" (quoting ***Cont'l Ill. Nat'l Bank & Tr. Co. v. Caton***, 136 F.R.D. 682, 684–85 (D. Kan. 1991))); ***Maples v. Safeway, Inc.***, No. 5:14-CV-05082-JLV, 2016 U.S. Dist. LEXIS 112135, at *13 (D.S.D. Aug. 23, 2016) (same).

137 See authorities cited in note 134.

138 ***Cont'l Ill. Nat'l Bank & Tr. Co. v. Caton***, 136 F.R.D. 682, 684–85 (D. Kan. 1991) (citation omitted); ***accord*** Tex. R. Civ. P. 192.6(b) (providing for a protective order "to protect the movant from undue burden, unnecessary expense"). See also authorities cited in note 134.

139 Tex. R. Civ. P. 192.4(a); ***accord In re Weekly Homes, L.P.***, 295 S.W.3d 309, 317 (Tex. 2009) (orig. proceeding) ("[B]oth the federal rule and ours require trial courts to weigh the benefits of production against the burden when the requested information is not reasonably available in the ordinary course of business."); ***In re Waste Mgmt. of Tex., Inc.***, No. 13-11-00197-CV, 2011 Tex. App. LEXIS 7192, at *33, 2011 WL 3855745 (Tex. App.—Corpus Christi Aug. 31, 2011, orig. proceeding) (mem. op.) ("Under the rules of civil procedure, discovery should be limited if it . . . is obtainable from some other source that is more convenient, less burdensome or expensive."); ***In re Harris***, 315 S.W.3d 685, 696 (Tex. App.—Houston [1st Dist.] 2010, orig. proceeding) ("[T]he discovery rules explicitly encourage trial courts to limit discovery when the burden or expense of the proposed discovery outweighs its likely benefit, taking into account the needs of the case, the amount in controversy, the parties' resources, the importance of the issues at stake in the litigation, and the importance of the

outweighs its likely benefit, taking into account the needs of the case, the amount in controversy, the parties' resources, the importance of the issues at stake in the litigation, and the importance of the proposed discovery in resolving them."[140] In other words, the determination of whether a production request is unduly burdensome or unnecessarily expensive is not solely dependent on the inconvenience or expense of gathering the responsive information or producing the responsive material. To the contrary, the inconvenience and expense must be weighed against the other factors set forth in Texas Rule 192.4.[141]

Although the responding party has the burden of pleading and proving undue burden or unnecessary expense, very rarely does a responding party attempt to describe the nature of the undue burden or why producing the requested material is unnecessarily expensive. To prove undue burden or unnecessary expense, the responding party must do more than make a conclusory assertion that producing the requested material would be unduly burdensome or unnecessarily expensive.[142] Rather, it must adduce evidence establishing the undue burden or unnecessary expense or that the material is obtainable from a more convenient source or in a less burdensome or expensive manner.[143] Although most practitioners tend to equate undue burden and

---

proposed discovery in resolving the issues." (quoting *In re Alford Chevrolet-Geo*, 997 S.W.2d 173, 181 (Tex. 1999) (orig. proceeding))).

140 Tex. R. Civ. P. 192.4(b); *accord In re K & L Auto Crushers, LLC*, 627 S.W.3d 239, 253 (Tex. 2021) (orig. proceeding); *In re Weekly Homes, L.P.*, 295 S.W.3d 309, 317 (Tex. 2009) (orig. proceeding); *In re Waste Mgmt. of Tex., Inc.*, No. 13-11-00197-CV, 2011 Tex. App. LEXIS 7192, at *33, 2011 WL 3855745 (Tex. App.—Corpus Christi Aug. 31, 2011, orig. proceeding) (mem. op.); *In re Harris*, 315 S.W.3d 685, 696 (Tex. App.—Houston [1st Dist.] 2010, orig. proceeding).

141 Tex. R. Civ. P. 192.4(b).

142 In re *K & L Auto Crushers, LLC*, 627 S.W.3d 239, 253 (Tex. 2021) (orig. proceeding) ("But a party resisting discovery must do more than 'make conclusory allegations that the requested discovery is unduly burdensome.'" (quoting *In re Alford Chevrolet-Geo*, 997 S.W.2d 173, 181 (Tex. 1999) (orig. proceeding))); *In re State Farm Lloyds*, 02-20-00163-CV, 2020 Tex. App. LEXIS 7207, at *17–18, 2020 WL 5242414 (Tex. App.—Fort Worth Sept. 3, 2020, orig. proceeding) (mem. op.) ("State Farm put on uncontroverted evidence that it would take at least 706 hours to review the subject files at a cost of $26,298.50. And pursuant to their original petition, the [plaintiffs] were seeking damages 'in an amount greater than $100,000 but no more than $200,000.' Given the negligible relevance of the sought discovery . . ., coupled with the uncontroverted evidence of the great time and expense State Farm would expend in obtaining the sought discovery, and given the amount in controversy in the case, the trial court clearly abused its discretion by ordering production of the engineering reports."); *In re Toyota Motor Sales, U.S.A., Inc.*, No. 05-18-00582-CV, 2018 Tex. App. LEXIS, *11, 2018 WL 2979855 (Tex. App.—Dallas June 14, 2018, orig. proceeding) (mem. op.) (concluding that the trial court abused its discretion by ordering the defendant to identify all folders and subfolders within databases and all papers maintained in its technical library, because it requires the production of irrelevant information, is overbroad in its reach, and places a disproportionate burden on the defendant); *In re Sting Soccer Grp., LP*, No. 05-17-00317-CV, 2017 Tex. App. LEXIS 11197, at *19–20, 2017 WL 5897454 (Tex. App.—Dallas Nov. 30, 2017, orig. proceeding) (mem. op.).

143 *In re Alford Chevrolet-Geo*, 997 S.W.2d 173, 181 (Tex. 1999) (orig. proceeding) ("A party resisting discovery . . . cannot simply make conclusory allegations that the requested discovery is unduly burdensome or unnecessarily harassing. The party must produce some evidence supporting its request for a protective order."); *In re Marshall*, No. 04-20-00450-CV, Tex. App. LEXIS 593, at *7, 2021 WL 260242 (Tex. App.—San Antonio Jan. 27,

unnecessary expense with the number of hours of search time or the number of boxes of documents or the number of emails that must be reviewed, undue burden also includes the difficulty of the search process, including the interference with ongoing business activities and the number of diverse geographic locations and personnel that must be contacted, the commercial sensitivity of the material, privacy issues, and personal embarrassment.[144]

An undue burden or unnecessary expense objection is improper if the burden or expense is the result of the party's "own conscious, discretionary decisions."[145] Thus, for example, a responding party cannot rely on problems in retrieving material

---

2021, orig. proceeding) ("The party resisting discovery cannot simply make conclusory allegations that the requested discovery is unduly burdensome or unnecessarily harassing but must produce some evidence supporting its request for a protective order."); *In re United Fire Lloyds*, 578 S.W.3d 572, 581 (Tex. App.—Tyler 2019, orig. proceeding, no pet.) (mem. op.) ("Absent evidence demonstrating that the requested discovery is unduly burdensome or harassing, Respondent could not make an informed judgment on whether to limit discovery or place the cost for complying with the discovery."); *In re Sting Soccer Grp., LP*, No. 05-17-00317-CV, 2017 Tex. App. LEXIS 11197, at *19–20 (Tex. App.—Dallas Nov. 30, 2017, orig. proceeding) (mem. op.) ("Vola's objections that the requests for production are overbroad, burdensome, and an improper fishing expedition should not have been sustained by the trial court because Vola presented no evidence to support those objections. Here, Vola presented no arguments or evidence to support these objections. Because the trial court below was neither presented with arguments nor actual evidence to support these objections before ruling to limit discovery, the trial court abused its discretion in sustaining these objections.") (citation omitted); *In re Master Flo Valve Inc.*, 485 S.W.3d 207, 271 n.2 (Tex. App.—Houston [14th Dist.] Jan. 26, 2016, orig. proceeding) ("A party resisting discovery cannot simply make conclusory allegations that the requested discovery is unduly burdensome. 'The party must produce some evidence supporting its request for a protective order.' Any party who seeks to exclude matters from discovery on grounds that the requested information is unduly burdensome or costly has the affirmative duty to prove the work necessary to comply with discovery." (citation omitted) (quoting *In re Alford Chevrolet-Geo*, 997 S.W.2d 173, 181 (Tex. 1999) (orig. proceeding))); *In re Jinsun LLC*, No. 14-15-00568-CV, 2015 Tex. App. LEXIS 9011, at *13 (Tex. App.—Houston [14th Dist.] Aug. 27, 2015, orig. proceeding) (mem. op.) (same); *In re Univ. Gen. Hosp., LP*, No. 14-12-00280-CV, 2012 Tex. App. LEXIS 2799, at *6–7 (Tex. App.—Houston [14th Dist.] Apr. 10, 2012, orig. proceeding) (mem. op.) (same).

144 Robert K. Wise, *Ending Evasive Responses to Written Discovery: A Guide for Properly Responding (and Objecting) to Interrogatories and Document Requests Under the Texas Discovery Rules*, 65 Baylor L. Rev. 510, 590 (2013).

145 *In re K & L Auto Crushers, LLC*, 627 S.W.3d 239, 253 (Tex. 2021) (orig. proceeding)) ("[W]here a responding party's own conscious, discretionary decision, such as how it chooses to store and organize its materials, causes discovery to be burdensome, the burden is not considered 'undue.'"); *accord In re Waste Mgmt. of Tex., Inc.*, No. 13-11-00197-CV, 2011 Tex. App. LEXIS 7192, at *33–34, 2011 WL 3855745 (Tex. App.—Corpus Christi Aug. 31, 2011, orig. proceeding) (mem. op.) (quoting *ISK Biotech Corp. v. Lindsay*, 933 S.W.2d 565, 568–69 (Tex. App.—Houston [1st Dist.] 1996, orig. proceeding)); *In re HEB Grocery Co.*, No. 13-10-00533-CV, 2010 Tex. App. LEXIS 9014, at *5 (Tex. App.—Corpus Christi Nov. 8, 2010, orig. proceeding) (mem. op.).

resulting from the haphazard way it maintains its records.[146] An undue burden or unnecessary expense objection also is improper if the responding party would have to gather the material in the preparation of its own case.[147]

8-5:7 Vagueness, Ambiguity, or Lack of Specificity

An objection to a production request because it lacks specificity or is ambiguous or vague is proper.[148] Contrary to the belief of many practitioners, these are distinct objections.

By definition a production request that lacks specificity violates Texas Rule 196.1(b)'s "reasonable particularity" requirement.[149] A production request, for example, lacks specificity if it does not describe either a specific document or item, such as a person's birth certificate, bank records, financial statements, or a specific contract,

---

[146] *In re Waste Mgmt. of Tex., Inc.*, No. 13-11-00197-CV, 2011 Tex. App. LEXIS 7192, at *33–34, 2011 WL 3855745 (Tex. App.—Corpus Christi Aug. 31, 2011, orig. proceeding) (mem. op.) ("A discovery request will not result in an undue burden when the burdensomeness of responding to it is the result of the responding party's own 'conscious, discretionary decisions.'"); *ISK Biotech Corp. v. Lindsay*, 933 S.W.2d 565, 568–69 (Tex. App.—Houston [1st Dist.] 1996, orig. proceeding) (same); *see In re Luna*, No. 13-16-00467-CV, 2016 Tex. App. LEXIS 12011, at *23 (Tex. App.—Corpus Christi Nov. 7, 2016, orig. proceeding) (mem. op.) ("We further note that many of the costs that State Farm estimates for the proposed deposition are the result of State Farm's own internal policies or procedures, and a discovery request will not result in an undue burden when the burdensomeness of responding to it is the result of the responding party's own 'conscious, discretionary decisions.'" (quoting *ISK Biotech Corp. v. Lindsay*, 933 S.W.2d 565, 569 (Tex. App.—Houston [1st Dist.] 1996, no writ))); *cf. Miller UK Ltd. v. Caterpillar, Inc.*, No. 10 C 3770, 2013 U.S. Dist. LEXIS 16505, at *18 (N.D. Ill. Feb. 7, 2013) (mem. op.) ("[I]f it really is so tremendously taxing for Caterpillar to search its records, it is difficult to sympathize because the situation is one of Caterpillar's own creation, and it must bear the consequences of a system it has chosen."); *Wagner v. Dryvit Sys., Inc.*, 208 F.R.D. 606, 610–11 (D. Neb. 2001) ("To the contrary, producing large amounts of documents in no apparent order does not comply with a party's obligation under [Federal] Rule 34. The fact that a corporation has an unwieldy record keeping system which requires it to incur heavy expenditures of time and effort to produce requested documents is an insufficient reason to prevent disclosure of otherwise discoverable information."); *Kozlowski v. Sears Roebuck & Co.*, 73 F.R.D. 73, 76 (D. Mass. 1976) ("To allow a defendant whose business generates massive records to frustrate discovery by creating an inadequate filling system [here, by not creating an adequate indexing system], and then claiming undue burden, would defeat the purposes of the discovery rules.").

[147] *Cf. Labrier v. State Farm Fire & Cas. Co.*, 314 F.R.D. 637, 642 (W.D. Mo. 2016) (compelling discovery because the defendant "would need to gather information anyway, which is further reason for State Farm being required to incur this expense"); *Asberry v. Cate*, No. 2: 11-cv-2462 KJM KJN P, 2014 U.S. Dist. LEXIS 46334, at *8 (E.D. Cal. Mar. 31, 2014) ("[I]f the responding party would necessarily have to gather the requested information to prepare its own case, objections that it is too difficult to obtain the information for the requesting party are not honored."); *Bell v. Woodward Governor Co.*, No. 03 C 50190, 2005 U.S. Dist. LEXIS 4451, at *7 (N.D. Ill. Feb. 7, 2005) (mem. op.) ("[W]hen the responding party will need to research the same information requested to prepare their own case, courts are more inclined to require parties to compile information for the other side.").

[148] *Cf. City of Seattle v. Prof'l Basketball Club, LLC*, No. CO7-1620MJP, 2008 U.S. Dist. LEXIS 108533, at *8 (W.D. Wash. Feb. 25, 2008).

[149] See notes 10–13 and accompanying text.

letter, memorandum, or report, or a specific category of items, such as documents relating to a specific allegation, claim, or defense in a pleading, a type of damage, activity, or communication.[150] Thus, a request for "all notes, records, memorandum, documents, and communications made that [plaintiff] contends 'support its allegations'" is fatally nonspecific.[151] Similarly, a request for "all Documents on which [a Defendant] will rely on to support any defense" fails to describe documents with reasonable particularity.[152]

A production request is vague or ambiguous when the request's wording is such that it is uncertain what information or documents have been sought.[153] However,

---

150 *Loftin v. Martin*, 776 S.W.2d 145, 148 (Tex. 1989) (orig. proceeding) (holding that a request that does not identify any particular class or type of documents was vague, ambiguous, and overbroad), *disapproved of on other grounds by Walker v. Packer*, 827 S.W.2d 833, 842 (Tex. 1992) (orig. proceeding).

151 *Loftin v. Martin*, 776 S.W.2d 145, 148 (Tex. 1989) (orig. proceeding) (holding that a request that does not identify any particular class or type of documents was vague, ambiguous, and overbroad), *disapproved of on other grounds by Walker v. Packer*, 827 S.W.2d 833, 842 (Tex. 1992) (orig. proceeding); *In re Master Flo Valve Inc.*, 485 S.W.3d 207, 218 (Tex. App.—Houston [14th Dist.] Jan. 26, 2016, orig. proceeding) (holding that a request for "all documents, communications, tangible or intangible evidence relating in any way to defendants' claims, defenses, or alleged damages" was "vague and overbroad"); *Warriner v. Warriner*, 394 S.W.3d 240, 251 (Tex. App.—El Paso 2012, no pet.) (holding that a production request requesting "[a]ll documents which constitute or contain matter relevant to the subject matter of this lawsuit" was fatally nonspecific); Tex. R. Civ. P. 193 cmt. 2 to 1999 change ("[A] party may object to a request for 'all documents relevant to the lawsuit' as overly broad and not in compliance with the rule requiring specific requests for documents and refuse to comply with it entirely.") (citing *Loftin v. Martin*, 776 S.W.2d 145 (Tex. 1989)); *cf. Garcia v. O'Rafferty*, No. 1:14-cv-00476-BAM (PC), 2017 U.S. Dist. LEXIS 38945, at *16–17 (E.D. Cal. Mar. 17, 2017) (holding that a request for "[a]ny and all information and discovery documents related to this action that is in your possession" did not describe with reasonable particularity the category of documents to be produced); *Crom, LLC v. Preload, LLC*, No. 1:16-cv-238-WTH-GRJ, 2017 U.S. Dist. LEXIS 85071, at *7–8 (N.D. Fla. June 2, 2017) ("Mrs. Bacon's requests for production 3 and 17 seek 'all documents supporting, or relating to any of [Crom's] factual claims or defenses,' and '[a]ll documents and/or electronic data that support, refute, or relate to the allegations in paragraphs 26, 27, 28, 29 of the Amended Complaint.' . . . Crom argues, however, that these requests are overly broad because they do not request a discrete category of documents that can be identified and assembled by a layperson. The Court agrees that these requests are overly broad. Mrs. Bacon's requests for production 3 and 17 are essentially 'contention requests' that simply refer to claims and various allegations and seek production of documents related to those claims and allegations.").

152 *In re EOG Res., Inc.*, No. 10-10-00455-CV, 2011 Tex. App. LEXIS 969, at *5–6, 2011 WL 455280 (Tex. App.—Waco Feb. 9, 2011, orig. proceeding) (mem. op.). In *In re EOG Resources. Inc.*, the court also held that a production request seeking "all Documents relating to the damages claimed by Plaintiffs in this case" was fatally nonspecific. *In re EOG Res., Inc.*, No. 10-10-00455-CV, 2011 Tex. App. LEXIS 969, at *5–6, 2011 WL 455280 (Tex. App.—Waco Feb. 9, 2011, orig. proceeding) (mem. op.). The authors disagree with this holding and believe such a production request is sufficiently specific.

153 *Black's Law Dictionary* 93, 1689 (11th ed. 2019) (defining "ambiguity" and "ambiguous" as "[a]n uncertainty of meaning or intention" and "vague" as "imprecise . . . [and] uncertain"); *Merriam-Webster.com Dictionary*, https://www.merriam-webster.com/dictionary/ambiguous (last visited July 21, 2021) (defining "ambiguous" as "doubtful or uncertain or

the fact that a word or phrase is undefined does not necessarily make the request vague or ambiguous. Rather, a responding party should use common sense when interpreting words and phrases used in production requests, giving them their ordinary meanings, their specialized meaning used in the industry at issue, defining them as the opposing party has defined or used them in its pleadings, or providing its own definition of the term or phrase.[154]

One of the ultimate ironies is that most vague and ambiguous objections are wholly Delphic because they fail to explain why the discovery request suffers from the alleged malady. Thus, the objections leave both the requesting party and the court guessing as to why the request is unclear. Such a bald objection does not meet Texas Rule 193.2(a)'s specificity requirement for objections.

To properly object to a production request in its entirety as lacking specificity or as vague or ambiguous, the responding party should explain why the request lacks specificity or is vague or ambiguous. For example, it should not only identify the words or phrases in the request that are vague or ambiguous, but also should explain why they are such. That is, why they are reasonably susceptible of more than one meaning and why the responding party cannot use the word's or phrase's ordinary or other meaning in responding to the discovery request.

"capable of being understood in two or more possible senses or ways"); *Merriam-Webster.com Dictionary*, https://www.merriam-webster.com/dictionary/vague (last visited July 21, 2021) (defining "vague" as "not clearly expressed: stated in indefinite term" or "not having precise meaning").

154 *Cf. In re Swepi L.P.*, 103 S.W.3d 578, 590 (Tex. App.—San Antonio, 2003, orig. proceeding) ("[S]ometimes the lack of a definition can render an interrogatory vague that is not the case here. . . . The terms Shell has used to describe these claims are easily defined in the context of the lawsuit."); *see* Tex. R. Civ. P. 192.3 (requiring the responding party to "blue pencil" a partially objectionable discovery request); *cf. Lopez v. Don Herring Ltd.*, 327 F.R.D. 567, 580 (N.D. Tex. 2018) ("[A] 'party objecting to discovery as vague or ambiguous has the burden to show such vagueness or ambiguity'; that '[a] party objecting on these grounds must explain the specific and particular way in which a request is vague'; that '[t]he responding party should exercise reason and common sense to attribute ordinary definitions to terms and phrases utilized in interrogatories' and, '[i]f necessary to clarify its answers, . . . may include any reasonable definition of the term or phrase at issue'; and that, '[i]f a party believes that the request is vague, that party [should] attempt to obtain clarification [by conferring with the requesting party] prior to objecting on this ground.'" (quoting *Heller v. City of Dall.*, 303 F.R.D. 466, 491–92 (N.D. Tex. 2014))); *Samsung Elecs. Am., Inc. v. Chung*, 321 F.R.D. 250, 289 (N.D. Tex. 2017) (same); *Vlasich v. Fishback*, No. 1:05-cv-016150-LJO-GSA-PC, 2009 U.S. Dist. LEXIS 43098, at *12–13 (E.D. Cal. May 11, 2009) ("These phrases are not so overbroad, vague, and ambiguous that defendant could not, in good faith, frame an intelligent reply using wording clarifying what defendant believes is meant."); *Heartland Surgical Specialty Hosp., LLC v. Midwest Div., Inc.*, No. 05-2164-MLB-DWB, 2007 U.S. Dist. LEXIS 16816, at *33, 41–42 (D. Kan. Mar. 8, 2007) ("The words objected to as vague and ambiguous ('knowledge and information') have an understandable meaning in the common, everyday usage of the words.").

Even if a responding party is unsure of the definition of a word or phrase, rather than objecting to the request in its entirety, the party should object to the term as vague or ambiguous, explain why it is vague or ambiguous, define it appropriately and respond to the request using its definition.

8-5:8 Unreasonably Cumulative or Duplicative

Cumulative discovery refers to discovery that tends to prove the same point,[155] whereas duplicative discovery is discovery that duplicates or is substantively identical to earlier discovery.[156] A court generally will not limit discovery merely because it is somewhat cumulative or duplicative.[157] Rather, the discovery must be unreasonably so,[158] and can be unreasonably cumulative or duplicative of the same or a different type of discovery. Generally, however, a production request is likely to be cumulative or duplicative only of other production requests or of initial disclosures required by Texas Rule 194.2(b)(6)–(11).[159]

---

155 *Merriam-Webster.com Dictionary*, https://www.merriam-webster.com/dictionary/cumulative (last visited July 21, 2021) (defining "cumulative," in part, as "tending to prove the same point"); Bryan A. Garner, *A Dictionary of Modern Legal Usage* 239–40 (2nd ed. 1995) ("[C]umulative, in its general lay sense, means 'composed of successively added parts; acquiring or increasing in force or cogency in successive additions'" and "*[c]umulative* is used of evidence in the sense of 'tending to prove the same point that other evidence has already been offered to prove.'"); *see also Black's Law Dictionary* 636 (11th ed. 2019) (defining "cumulative evidence" as "[a]dditional evidence that supports a fact established by the existing evidence (esp. that which does not need further support)").

156 *Merriam-Webster.com Dictionary*, https://www.merriam-webster.com/dictionary/duplicative (last visited July 21, 2021) (defining "duplicative" as "repeat"); *Black's Law Dictionary* 578 (11th ed. 2019) (defining "duplicative" as "having or characterized by having identical content"); *accord* Bryan A. Garner, *A Dictionary of Modern Legal Usage* 300 (2nd ed. 1995) (same).

157 Tex. R. Civ. P. 192.4(a) (allowing a court to limit discovery when "the discovery sought is *unreasonably* cumulative or duplicative") (emphasis added).

158 Tex. R. Civ. P. 192.4; *cf. In re USAA Gen. Indem. Co.*, 624 S.W.3d 782, 792 (Tex. 2021) (orig. proceeding) ("[W]hile discovery from USAA will likely be cumulative to some extent of information that can be gleaned from other sources, we cannot conclude on this record that it is unreasonably so. . . ."); *Uniram Tech., Inc. v. Monolithic Sys. Tech., Inc.*, No. C 04-1268 VRW (MEJ), 2007 U.S. Dist. LEXIS 24869, at *6 (N.D. Cal. Mar. 23, 2007) ("[T]he question here is not whether topic 1 is duplicative of the June 2006 deposition, but whether topic 1 is *unreasonably* duplicative."); *Van Wagenen v. Consol. Rail Corp.*, 170 F.R.D. 86, 87 (N.D.N.Y. 1997) (holding that requests seeking the admission of the truth of various sentences taken from a document, the authenticity of which had already been admitted, were unreasonably duplicative and cumulative); *Aramburu v. Boeing Co.*, 885 F. Supp. 1434, 1444 (D. Kan. 1995) (holding that when information already provided by the defendant-employer should have been enough for the plaintiff-employee to make a preliminary determination as to whether the employer treated the employee's ethnic group differently, employee could not compel employer to cull information from 1,700 personnel files, even though files might contain some relevant information).

159 Texas Rules 194.2(b)(6)–(11) provide for the disclosure of the following: "(6) a copy—or a description by category and location—of all documents, electronically stored information, and tangible things that the responding party has in its possession, custody, or control, and may use to support its claims or defenses, unless the use would be solely for impeachment; (7) any indemnity and insuring agreements described in [Texas] Rule 192.3(f); (8) any settlement agreements described in [Texas] Rule 192.3(g); (9) any witness statements described in Rule 192.3(h); (10) in a suit alleging physical or mental injury and damages from the occurrence that is the subject of the case, all medical records and bills that are reasonably related to the injuries or damages asserted or, in lieu thereof, an authorization permitting the disclosure of such medical records and bills; [and] (11) in a suit alleging physical or mental injury and damages from the occurrence that is the subject of the case,

To establish that a production request is unreasonably cumulative or duplicative, the responding party must specifically identify the other production requests or required disclosures to which the objected-to request is unreasonably cumulative or duplicative.[160]

8-5:9 Expert Opinion

Under the Texas discovery rules, there are three discovery procedures that can be used to secure information about or from a retained-testifying expert: (1) a required disclosure; (2) an expert report; and (3) an oral deposition.[161] Consequently, a party cannot use a production request to obtain documents about or from a retained-testifying expert.[162] Accordingly, an objection that a production request improperly seeks documents about or from a retained-testifying expert is a proper one.[163]

8-5:10 Marshalling Evidence

Many practitioners object to production requests asking for "all," "each," or "every" document regarding a subject, claim, defense, or allegation because they improperly require the responding party to marshal its evidence. A marshalling-evidence objection, however, is *not* a proper objection to such a production request.[164]

---

all medical records and bills obtained by the responding party by virtue of an authorization furnished by the requesting party[.]" Tex. R. Civ. P. 194.2(b)(6)–(11).

160 *Cf. Wye Oak Tech., Inc. v. Republic of Iraq*, No. 1:10-cv-01182-RCL, 2018 U.S. Dist. LEXIS 159096, at *3 (D.D.C. 2018) ("By simply objecting to Wye Oak's request without referring to the specific documents that were previously produced, defendants have not met their burden of demonstrating that Wye Oak's request is in fact 'unreasonably cumulative or duplicative.'"); *Kickapoo Tribe of Indians v. Nemaha Brown Watershed Joint Dist. No. 7*, 294 F.R.D. 610, 614 (D. Kan. 2013) (same); *Alexander v. FBI*, 194 F.R.D. 299, 302 (D.D.C. 2000) (same).

161 Tex. R. Civ. P. 195.1, 195.5; *In re Nat'l Lloyds Ins. Co.*, 532 S.W.3d 794, 814 (Tex. 2017) (orig. proceeding) ("[Texas] Rule 195 does not provide for interrogatories or requests for production[.]") (footnotes omitted); *In re Segner*, 441 S.W.3d 409, 412–13 (Tex. App.—Dallas 2013, orig. proceeding) (noting that a party cannot serve a production request in conjunction with a deposition notice on a retained-testifying expert). See also Chapter 7, section 7-4 (discussing discovery concerning testifying experts).

The discovery methods that can be used to obtain discovery from non-retained-testifying experts are the same as those that can be used to obtain discovery from retained-testifying experts with two exceptions—non-retained-testifying experts can be deposed on written questions and can be served with a production request under Texas Rules 176 or 205. Tex. R. Civ. P. 195.1, 195.4, 195.5 & cmt. 2. See also Chapter 7, section 7-4 (discussing discovery concerning testifying experts).

"Information concerning purely consulting experts, of course, is not discoverable." Tex. R. Civ. P. 195 cmt. 1 to 1999 change. See also Chapter 7, section 7-5 (discussing discovery concerning consulting physis). In contrast, all discovery methods, including, production requests, can be used to obtain information about, or from, a consulting expert whose mental impressions or opinions have been reviewed by a testifying expert. Tex. R. Civ. P. 195 cmt. 1 to 1999 change. See also Chapter 7, section 7-5 (discussing discovery concerning consulting experts).

162 See authorities cited in note 161.

163 See authorities cited in note 161.

164 *In re Sting Soccer Grp., LP*, No. 05-17-00317-CV, 2017 Tex. App. LEXIS 11197, at *18 (Tex. App.—Dallas Nov. 30, 2017, orig. proceeding) (mem. op.) ("'Marshalling the evidence' is not

Unlike Texas Rule 197, which provides that interrogatories cannot be used "to require the responding party to marshal all of its available proof[,]"[165] nothing in Texas Rule 196 or its commentary contains a specific prohibition on "marshalling."[166] To the contrary, it is common for a production request to ask for "all documents concerning, relating to, or referring to" specific matters, claims, defenses, or allegations. Such requests are perfectly appropriate if they are specific enough (i.e., they are limited by time, location, or scope or to a type or class of documents).[167] As explained by the Dallas Court of Appeals:

> [R]equests for production may properly ask a party to provide "all," "each," or "every" document pertaining to a relevant, narrow subject of the litigation. "Marshalling the evidence" is not considered a valid objection to a request for production because, unlike the rule of civil procedure regarding interrogatories and requests for disclosure, the rules regarding requests for production does not include any language concerning the marshalling of evidence.[168]

---

considered a valid objection to a request for production because, unlike the rule of civil procedure regarding interrogatories and requests for disclosure, the rules regarding requests for production does not include any language concerning the marshalling of evidence.").

165 Tex. R. Civ. P. 197.1.

166 *See* Tex. R. Civ. P. 196.

167 *In re Allstate Cnty. Mut. Ins. Co.*, 227 S.W.3d 667, 669 (Tex. 2007) (orig. proceeding) (per curiam) ("A request for 'any and all' documents is not overly broad if limited by time, location, or scope or if it is restricted to a type or class of documents."); *In re Sting Soccer Grp., LP*, No. 05-17-00317-CV, 2017 Tex. App. LEXIS 11197, at *18 (Tex. App.—Dallas Nov. 30, 2017, orig. proceeding) (mem. op.) (same); *In re Patel*, 218 S.W.3d 911, 915 (Tex. App.—Corpus Christi 2007, orig. proceeding) (same); *Davis v. Pate*, 915 S.W.2d 76, 78 (Tex. App.—Corpus Christi 1996, orig. proceeding) (same); *Chamberlain v. Cherry*, 818 S.W.2d 201, 204 (Tex. App.—Amarillo 1991, orig. proceeding) ("[Former Texas] Rule 167 permits a party to request production of particular classes or types of documents but does not permit fishing expeditions for documents not of a particular type or class. In the present case, relators did request production of particular types of documents. For example, relators' first request for production asked Hogan for 'any and all lease agreements between yourself and [relators] regarding any portion of the subject property since 1974.' As another example, relators' twelfth request sought production of 'any and all leases or rental agreements, deposit agreements, and related documents concerning or pertaining to all or part of the property subject of this suit for the period since July 31, 1989.' These requests comply with [former Texas] Rule 167's mandate that requests for production must 'set forth the items to be inspected either by individual item or by category . . . with reasonable particularity.' The mere fact that the requests asked for 'any and all' such documents did not poison the requests." (quoting former Texas Rule 167(1)(c))). See also case cited in note 168.

168 *In re Sting Soccer Grp., LP*, No. 05-17-00317-CV, 2017 Tex. App. LEXIS 11197, at *18, 2017 WL 5897454 (Tex. App.—Dallas Nov. 30, 2017, orig. proceeding) (mem. op.) (citing Robert K. Wise, *Ending Evasive Responses to Written Discovery: A Guide for Properly Responding (and Objecting) to Interrogatories and Document Requests Under the Texas Discovery Rules*, 65 Baylor L. Rev. 510, 598 (2013)).

A request for "all documents concerning, relating to, or referring to" specific matters, claims, defenses, or allegations also are not objectionable as requiring "legal conclusions." *In re Sting Soccer Grp., LP*, No. 05-17-00317-CV, 2017 Tex. App. LEXIS 11197, at *18–19 (Tex. App.—Dallas Nov. 30, 2017, orig. proceeding) (mem. op.) ("[T]he rules permit parties to seek discovery supporting its adversary's specific factual and legal contentions. The requests at issue here simply asked Vola to produce documents it possessed that supported

8-5:11 Supernumerary Objections

There is no express limit on the number of production requests in Level 2 and 3 actions. A responding party faced with an excessive number of production requests in such actions, however, is not without remedy. If it believes that the requesting party is abusing discovery by serving too many production requests, it can move for a protective order that either limits the number of requests or orders that it need not respond to requests already served.[169] In ruling on such a motion, the court is to be guided by the proportionality considerations contained in Texas Rule 192.4.[170]

In contrast, in a Level 1 action, a responding party faced with too many production requests is in a much different and better position. It cannot, however, simply refuse to answer the entire set of production requests—it should answer the first fifteen production requests and interpose a supernumerary objection to the rest.[171] Responding to a supernumerary production request

---

the specific allegations in Vola's petition. Such requests are not objectionable for seeking legal conclusions.") (citations omitted).

[169] Tex. R. Civ. P. 192.6(b).

[170] *See In re Waste Mgmt. of Tex., Inc.*, No. 13-11-00197-CV, 2011 Tex. App. LEXIS 7192, at *33, 2011 WL 3855745 (Tex. App.—Corpus Christi Aug. 31, 2011, orig. proceeding) (mem. op.) ("Under the rules of civil procedure, discovery should be limited if it . . . is obtainable from some other source that is more convenient, less burdensome or expensive."); *In re Harris*, 315 S.W.3d 685, 696 (Tex. App.—Houston [1st Dist.] 2010, orig. proceeding) ("[T]he discovery rules 'explicitly encourage trial courts to limit discovery when the burden or expense of the proposed discovery outweighs its likely benefit, taking into account the needs of the case, the amount in controversy, the parties' resources, the importance of the issues at stake in the litigation, and the importance of the proposed discovery in resolving the issues.'" (quoting *In re Alford Chevrolet-Geo*, 997 S.W.2d 173, 181 (Tex. 1999) (orig. proceeding))). See also Chapter 4, section 4-5 (discussing protective orders), and Chapter 5, section 5-3:4 (discussing proportionality).

[171] *See* Tex. R. Civ. P. 192.6(a) ("A person should not move for protection when an objection to written discovery . . . is appropriate."); Tex. R. Civ. P. 193.2 ("The party must state specifically the legal or factual basis for the objection and the extent to which the party is refusing to comply with the request."); *cf. Childs v. Argenbright*, 927 S.W.2d 647, 652 (Tex. App.—Tyler 1992, no writ) (holding that, under former Texas Rule 168, which allowed no more than thirty interrogatory answers, the responding party should answer the first thirty questions); *Owens v. Wallace*, 821 S.W.2d 746, 749 (Tex. App.—Tyler 1992, orig. proceeding) (same); *cf. Osucha v. Alden State Bank*, No. 17CV1026V, 2019 U.S. Dist. LEXIS 214744, at *8–9, 2019 WL 6783289 (W.D.N.Y. Dec. 12, 2019) ("The party asked to respond to Interrogatories need not answer more than 25 posed and can choose merely to answer the first 25 (including distinct subparts that would total 25)."); *Mondragon v. Scott Farms, Inc.*, 329 F.R.D. 533, 541 (E.D.N.C. 2019) ("When a party is confronted with what it believes to be an excessive number of interrogatories, the appropriate course of action is to either move for a protective order before answering any interrogatories or 'answer up to the numerical limit and object to the remainder without answering.'"); *EEOC v. State of Mex.*, No. 15-879 KG/KK, 2016 U.S. Dist. LEXIS 139049, *8–9, 2016 WL 9777238 (D.N.M. Sept. 30, 2016) (mem. op.) ("In [the] future, should a party to this matter believe that a supernumerary objection is warranted, that party is instructed to 'either seek a protective order and not answer the requests at issue[,] or answer up to the numerical limit and object to the remaining requests without answering.' This procedure will prevent the objecting party from randomly (or strategically) choosing which interrogatories to answer, but, absent a motion for protective order, will also allow the party serving discovery to receive responses to some portion of its requests." (quoting *Lowery v. Cnty. of Riley*,

waives the objection.[172]

No. 04-3101-JTM-DWB, 2009 U.S. Dist. LEXIS 19957, at *11, 2009 WL 648928 (D. Kan. Mar. 12, 2009))); *Avila v. Mohave Cnty.*, No. 3:14-CV-8124-HRH, 2015 U.S. Dist. LEXIS 148956, at *26, 2015 WL 6660187 (D. Ariz. Nov. 2, 2015) (citing cases) (holding that the proper method for challenging a party's excessive interrogatories is to answer the requests chronologically until the allotted number is exhausted); *Rowell v. NCO Fin. Sys.*, No. 13-2514-CM, 2014 U.S. Dist. LEXIS 70095, at *11–12, 2014 WL 2154422 (D. Kan. May 22, 2014) ("Plaintiff did not follow the court's procedure for a party making a supernumerary objection. When such a situation arises, the objecting party is to either seek a protective order and not answer the requests at issue or answer up to the numerical limit and object to the remaining requests without answering. Instead, plaintiff chose to selectively apply this objection out of order and respond to some requests subject to that objection, but not others. This is improper. '[T]he responding party is not entitled to randomly select which of the . . . interrogatories it will answer[.]'" (quoting *Lowery v. Cnty. of Riley*, No. 04-3101-JTM-DWB, 2009 U.S. Dist. LEXIS 19957, at *11, 2009 WL 648928 (D. Kan. Mar. 12, 2009))); *Serigne v. Preveau*, No. 11-3160 SECTION: "R" (4), 2013 U.S. Dist. LEXIS 60004, at *6–8, 2013 WL 1789520 (E.D. La. Apr. 26, 2013) ("Where analysis of 'subparts' yields more than 25 interrogatories, courts have found that a party to whom excessive interrogatories had been propounded had an obligation to respond to the 'first' 25 Interrogatories which constitute discrete questions, and strike the rest."); *Paananen v. Celloc P'ship*, No. C08-1042 RSM, 2009 U.S. Dist. LEXIS 98997, at *12 (W.D. Wash. Oct. 8, 2009) ("[T]he best rule, and the one this Court applies here, is that a responding party must answer the first 25 interrogatories."). The reason why courts do not allow the responding party to choose which production requests to respond to is because "[s]uch a rule will allow the responding party to 'selectively respond to the [production requests] and thereby strategically omit the most prejudicial [documents].'" *Paananen v. Celloc P'ship*, No. C08-1042 RSM, 2009 U.S. Dist. LEXIS 98997, at *12, 2009 WL 3327227 (W.D. Wash. Oct. 8, 2009) (quoting *Herdlein Techs. Inc. v. Century Contractors, Inc.*, 147 F.R.D. 103, 104 (W.D.N.C. 1993)).

172 *Cf. Childs v. Argenbright*, 927 S.W.2d 647, 652 (Tex. App.—Tyler 1992, no writ) (holding that a supernumerary objection was waived when the responding party interposed substantive objections to the excessive interrogatories); *cf. Mondragon v. Scott Farms, Inc.*, 329 F.R.D. 533, 541–42 (E.D.N.C., 2019) ("Scott has selectively answered interrogatories beyond what it contends is the 25-interrogatory limit. By doing so, it has waived any objection that it had to the number of interrogatories that Plaintiffs served on it. Thus, the motion to compel shall be granted and, to the extent Scott did not respond to certain interrogatories on the basis of this objection, it shall do so."); *Engage Healthcare Commc'ns, LLC v. Intellisphere, LLC*, No. 12-cv-00787(FLW)(LHG), 2017 U.S. Dist. LEXIS 83068, at *24–25, 2017 WL 2371834 (D.N.J. Feb. 10, 2017) ("Here, Plaintiffs have answered and/or objected to the April 2013 Interrogatories, which number 18. In response to the October 2013 Interrogatories, which number 10, Plaintiffs did not object on the grounds that they, together with the April 2013 Interrogatories, exceeded the 25-interrogatory limit, and thus waived that objection."); *Paananen v. Celloc P'ship*, No. C08-1042 RSM, 2009 U.S. Dist. LEXIS 98997, at *12, 2009 WL 3327227 (W.D. Wash. Oct. 8, 2009) ("If [the responding party] answers more, the numerousity objection is waived as to those interrogatories that were answered."); *Allahverdi v. Regents of Univ. of N. Mex.*, 228 F.R.D.696, 698 (D.N.M. 2005) ("When a party believes that another party has asked too many interrogatories . . . [, t]he responding party should not answer some and object to the ones to which it does not want to respond."); *Capacchione v. Charlotte-Mecklenburg Schs.*, 182 F.R.D. 486, 492 (W.D.N.C. 1998) ("Yet, CMS, by responding to Interrogatories 21–25 without moving for a protective order, waived any objection on grounds of the 20 interrogatory limit. As stated by this Court: 'The responding party must object *(to the Court)* to the number of interrogatories before responding in order to rely on this rule.'" (quoting *Herdlein Techs. Inc. v. Century Contractors, Inc.*, 147 F.R.D. 103, 104 (W.D.N.C. 1993))).

Just as the responding party is not allowed to pick and choose which supernumerary production requests to answer, the requesting party cannot circumvent its violation by voluntarily withdrawing selected supernumerary requests. The operative word in Texas Rule 190.2(b)(4) is "serve" and every production request served counts against the numerical limit.[173] So do production requests to which objections have been interposed, and a requesting party cannot withdraw them.[174]

Finally, when the responding party believes that too many production requests have been asked in a Level 1 action, the better rule is that it need not interpose its substantive objections to the supernumerary requests unless and until the supernumerary objections are resolved adversely to it. Otherwise, the responding party would have to answer and object, which is contrary to the very purpose of the supernumerary objection in the first instance.[175]

8-5:12 The Requested Information or Material Is in the Requesting Party's or a Nonparty's Possession

Oftentimes a responding party will object to a production request because the material already is in the requesting party's possession or is equally available from a nonparty or a public source. Such an objection is almost always improper because the requesting party is entitled to ascertain what documents and other material the responding party has and to review the material to determine if they are the same as those in its or another person's possession and whether they have any notes or other markings on them. As noted by the Dallas Court of Appeals in rejecting such an objection:

---

[173] *Cf. Walker v. Lakewood Condo. Owners Ass'n*, 186 F.R.D. 584, 586–88 (C.D. Cal. 1999) ("Contrary to FHF's argument, neither [Federal] Rule 33(a) nor Local Rule 8.2.1, expressly or implicitly, state that only interrogatories that are served and answered count against the numerical limit. Indeed, the use of the term 'serve' in both [Federal] Rule 33(a) and Local Rule 8.2.1 is absolute and unqualified. Nor do either of these rules state or reasonably suggest that interrogatories disintegrate and vanish as if they were never served when timely objections, but not answers, are made pursuant to [Federal] Rule 33(b). Moreover, FHF's suggested interpretation also conflicts with [Federal] Rule 33(b)'s express terms authorizing a party served with interrogatories to respond with either objections or answers. FHF's argument is also flawed because it ignores that, in the context of [Federal] Rule 33(a), Local Rule 8.2.1, and the Rules pertaining to discovery, the term 'serve' is more than just an active verb; it is a term of art.") (citation omitted); *see McClellan v. Kern Cnty. Sheriff's Office*, No. 1:10-cv-0386-LJO-MJS (PC), 2015 U.S. Dist. LEXIS 131685, at *2, 2015 WL 5732077 (E.D. Cal. Sept. 29, 2015) ("Fed. R. Civ. P. 33(a)(1) limits to 25 the number of interrogatories one party may serve on another. An interrogatory need not be answered, but merely served and properly objected to, in order to count against the numerical limit.").

[174] *Cf. Walker v. Lakewood Condo. Owners Ass'n*, 186 F.R.D. 584, 588 (C.D. Cal. 1999) (construing Federal Rule 33(a)(1) relating to interrogatories).

[175] *Cf. Peach v. City of Kewanee*, No. 05-4012, 2006 U.S. Dist. LEXIS 77379, at *6, 2006 WL 8443111 (C.D. Ill. Oct. 23, 2006) ("In order to give meaningful teeth to the numeric limitation [on interrogatories] imposed by the Rule, this second line of cases defers the obligation to respond and object until [the supernumerary] objection is resolved. This second line of cases makes sense."); *see Herdlein Techs. Inc. v. Century Contractors, Inc.*, 147 F.R.D. 103, 104 (W.D.N.C. 1993) ("The responding party must object (to the Court) to the number of interrogatories before responding in order to rely on this rule.").

Vola's objection that the information sought is equally available is an invalid objection. Texas law does not allow a party to evade discovery requests by simply asserting that the other party already has the information. Not only do such [production] requests ensure that the parties have the same basic documents, requiring your opponent to produce certain documents enables the party seeking discovery to activate the automatic authentication rights provided by [Texas] Rule 193.7.[176]

[176] *In re Sting Soccer Grp., LP*, No. 05-17-00317-CV, 2017 Tex. App. LEXIS 11197, at *19, 2017 WL 5897454 (Tex. App.—Dallas Nov. 30, 2017, orig. proceeding) (mem. op.); *see In re Ochoa*, No. 12-04-00163-CV, 2004 Tex. App. LEXIS 4866, at *5, 2004 WL 1192444 (Tex. App.—Tyler May 28, 2004, orig. proceeding) (mem. op.) ("Plaintiffs contend that they do not have to answer contention interrogatories because defendants have equal access to their medical records and should be able to determine any prior pre-existing injuries. The rules contain no such limit on the use of contention interrogatories."); *cf. Traverse v. Gutierrez Co.*, No. CV 18-10175-DJC, 2019 U.S. Dist. LEXIS 238304, at *4, 2019 WL 12291348 (D. Mass. Aug. 15, 2019) ("A party must produce requested material within its possession, custody, or control even if it is already in the possession of the requesting party."); *Kruger v. Cogent Commc'ns, Inc.*, No. 14-1744 (EGS), 2016 U.S. Dist. LEXIS 153044, at *13–15 n.2, 2016 WL 11121058 (D.D.C. Oct. 24, 2016) ("The objection made to request 26 that the request calls for 'production of documents in the possession of Defendant' is inadequate because 'a responding party is required to produce documents in its possession, custody, or control regardless of whether the requesting party is already in possession of the requested documents.'" (quoting *Puerto Rico Med. Emergency Grp., Inc. v. Iglesia Episcopal Puertorriqueña, Inc.*, 318 F.R.D. 224, 230 (D.P.R. 2016))); *Med. Protective Co. v. Am. Int'l Specialty Lines Ins. Co.*, No. 1:13-CV-357, 2014 U.S. Dist. LEXIS 141557, at *8, 2014 WL 4979394 (N.D. Ind. Oct. 6, 2014) ("Nor is MedPro's argument that many of these documents are already in AISLIC's (or its coverage counsel's) possession effective. '[I]t is not a proper objection to discovery to suggest that the other party already has the information or that it is available elsewhere.'" (quoting *Jones v. Chase Manhattan Bank USA, NA*, No. 1:07-cv-58, 2007 U.S. Dist. LEXIS 82616, at *5, 2007 WL 3286854 (N.D. Ind. Nov. 5, 2007))); *Anderson v. Neb. Med. Ctr.*, No. 8:12CV390, 2013 U.S. Dist. LEXIS 168778, at *5, 2013 WL 6197094 (D. Neb. Nov. 27, 2013) ("These documents are clearly relevant to this employment discrimination action. Defendant maintains that it has no obligation to produce these materials because Plaintiff should already have them in his possession. This assertion has no merit. Although these documents may have been provided to Plaintiff during his employment, this fact does not relieve Defendant of the duty to produce the documents if they are in Defendant's possession."); *Gomez v. Tyson Foods, Inc.*, No. 8:08CV21, 2012 U.S. Dist. LEXIS 106274, at *11, 2012 WL 3111897 (D. Neb. July 31, 2012) ("[A] party is required to produce documents in its possession, custody, or control, regardless of whether it believes the requesting party already has those documents."); *Kenneth v. Nationwide Mut. Fire Ins. Co.*, No. 03-CV-521F (Consent), 2007 U.S. Dist. LEXIS 83973, at *51, 2007 WL 3533887 (W.D.N.Y. Nov. 13, 2007) ("A requested party may not refuse to respond to the requesting party's discovery request on the ground that the requested information is in the possession of the requesting party.").

The one exception to this rule is when the responding party establishes that producing the requested materials would be unduly burdensome or expensive and that obtaining the information or material from a nonparty or public source is more convenient or less burdensome or expensive. See Chapter 4, section 4-5 (discussing protective orders).

8-5:13 Fishing Expedition

A commonly used objection with respect to production requests is that the request constitutes a "fishing expedition." This objection derives from *Loftin v. Martin*, in which the Texas Supreme Court, in holding that certain production requests were improper, reasoned:

> Unlike interrogatories and depositions, [former Texas] Rule 167[, which governed production requests,] is not a fishing rule. It cannot be used simply to explore. You are permitted to fish under deposition procedures, but not under [former Texas] Rule 167. The Motion for Discovery must be specific, must establish materiality, and must recite precisely what is wanted. The Rule does not permit general inspection of the adversary records.[177]

Although since *Loftin*, the Texas Supreme Court has rejected the "notion that any discovery device can be used to 'fish,'"[178] and several courts have attempted to define what constitutes a "fishing expedition,"[179] the "fishing expedition" objection is nothing

---

[177] *Loftin v. Martin*, 776 S.W.2d 145, 148 (Tex. 1989) (orig. proceeding), ***disapproved of on other grounds by Walker v. Parker***, 827 S.W.2d 833, 842 (Tex. 1992) (orig. proceeding). Since *Loftin*, the Texas Supreme Court repeatedly has decried "fishing expeditions." *E.g., In re State Farm Lloyds*, 520 S.W.3d 595, 611 (Tex. 2017) (orig. proceeding) ("Discovery must bear at least a reasonable expectation of obtaining information that will aid the dispute's resolution. Reasonable discovery does not countenance a 'fishing expedition.'" (quoting *In re Alford Chevrolet-Geo*, 997 S.W.2d 173, 181 (Tex. 1999) (orig. proceeding))); *In re CSX Corp.*, 124 S.W.3d 149, 153 (Tex. 2003) (orig. proceeding) ("A request to identify all safety employees for over a 30-year period even though plaintiff never worked for relators or their parent company for that length of time is the type of fishing expedition this Court has repeatedly struck down."); *In re Alford Chevrolet-Geo*, 997 S.W.2d 173, 180–81 (Tex. 1999) (orig. proceeding) (noting that "discovery may not be used as a fishing expedition"); *In re Am. Optical Corp.*, 988 S.W.2d 711, 713 (Tex. 1998) ("This court has repeatedly emphasized that discovery may not be used as a fishing expedition."); *K Mart Corp. v. Sanderson*, 937 S.W.2d 429, 431 (Tex. 1996) (orig. proceeding) ("We reject the notion that any discovery device can be used to 'fish.'"); *Texaco, Inc. v. Sanderson*, 898 S.W.2d 813, 815 (Tex. 1995) (orig. proceeding) ("Parties must have some latitude in fashioning proper discovery requests. The request in this case is not close. It is not merely an impermissible fishing expedition, it is an effort to dredge the lake in hope of finding a fish."); *Dillard Dep't Stores, Inc. v. Hall*, 909 S.W.2d 491, 492 (Tex. 1995) (per curiam) (orig. proceeding) ("This is the very kind of fishing expedition that is not allowable[.]").

[178] *K Mart Corp. v. Sanderson*, 937 S.W.2d 429, 431 (Tex. 1996) (orig. proceeding).

[179] *In re Steadfast Ins. Co.*, No. 01-09-00235-CV, 2009 Tex. App. LEXIS 3556, at *7, 2009 WL 1424634 (Tex. App.—Houston [1st Dist.] May 18, 2009, orig. proceeding) (mem. op.) ("A party embarks on a fishing expedition when it submits discovery requests that are 'not narrowly tailored and are overly broad.'"); *In re Sears, Roebuck & Co.*, 123 S.W.3d 573, 578 (Tex. App.—Houston [14th Dist.] 2003, orig. proceeding) (defining a "fishing expedition" as "one aimed not at supporting existing claims but finding new ones"); *In re Am. Home Assur. Co.*, 88 S.W.3d 370, 376 (Tex. App.—Texarkana 2002, orig. proceeding) (holding that "discovery undertaken with the purpose of finding an issue, rather than in support of an issue already raised by the pleadings, will constitute an impermissible 'fishing expedition'"); *see Dillard Dep't Stores, Inc. v. Hall*, 909 S.W.2d 491, 492 (Tex. 1995) (orig. proceeding) (per curiam) (holding that, because the plaintiff sought the document discovery to explore the viability of an allegation of racial discrimination, he had embarked on an improper "fishing expedition").

more than a colorful and wholly imprecise way of objecting to the discovery request's scope (i.e., it either seeks irrelevant information or documents or seeks information or documents not reasonably calculated to lead to the discovery of admissible evidence). As such, it really is not a proper objection.

8-5:14 The Responding Party's Failure to Provide Discovery

It is improper to refuse to respond to production requests because the requesting party has withheld discovery. As explained by one court:

> The argument advanced by plaintiffs here that, in essence, "two wrongs make a right" in the discovery context, has been rejected by this court before. The existence of a discovery dispute as to one matter does not justify withholding other discovery. The proper method of resolution when counsel believes that discovery is inadequate is to file a motion to compel. Counsel "may not retaliate and hold [discovery] hostage."[180]

8-5:15 Harassment

Although a "harassment" objection is clearly a proper one,[181] it is difficult to envision a situation in which such an objection is a proper one to a production request. First, the

---

180 *Estate of Broccolino v. McKesson Corp.*, No. WDQ-05-0438, 2006 U.S. Dist. LEXIS 97220, at *5, 2006 WL 5217766 (D. Md. Feb. 23, 2006) (citations omitted) (quoting *Jayne H. Lee, Inc. v. Flagstaff Indus. Corp.*, 173 F.R.D. 651, 657 (D. Md. 1997)); *accord A.R. v. Dudek*, No. 12-60460-CIV-ZLOCH/HUNT, 2015 U.S. Dist. LEXIS 179554, at *21 (S.D. Fla. Oct. 9, 2015); *Kinetic Concepts, Inc. v. Convatec Inc.*, 268 F.R.D. 226, 242 n.23 (M.D.N.C. 2010); *Covad Commc'ns Co. v. Revonet, Inc.*, 258 F.R.D. 17, 23–24 (D.D.C. 2009); *Mahoney v. Kempton*, 142 F.R.D. 32, 33 (D. Mass. 1992); *see In re UV Logistics, LLC*, 12-20-00196-CV, 2021 Tex. App. LEXIS 723, at *8, 2021 WL 306205 (Tex. App.—Tyler Jan. 29, 2021, orig. proceeding) (mem. op.) (refusing to deny mandamus review of a discovery because of "Relators' alleged discovery abuse prior to the orders at issue in this mandamus proceeding, which includes violating a Rule 11 agreement, deleting relevant records after receiving Gentry's preservation letter, and generally stonewalling Gentry's prior discovery requests").

Under Texas Rule 215.2(b)(1), one of the sanctions available to a trial court is "an order disallowing any further discovery of any kind or a particular kind by the disobedient party." Tex. R. Civ. P. 215.2(b)(1). For a discussion when such an order is proper, see *Global Servs., Inc. v. Bianchi*, 901 S.W.2d 934, 938 (Tex. 1995) (orig. proceeding). See also Chapter 14, section 14-4:1 (discussing sanctions orders).

181 *E.g.*, Tex. R. Civ. P. 191.3(c)(3) (by signing written-discovery requests, the attorney certifies that the discovery was not sought for the purpose of harassment), 192.6(b) (allowing a party to ask for protection from harassing discovery), 215.3 (providing that harassing discovery is a ground for sanctions); *Alexson, Inc. v. McIlhany*, 798 S.W.2d 550, 553 (Tex. 1990) (orig. proceeding) ("The scope of discovery is also limited by the legitimate interest of the opposing party to avoid overbroad requests, harassment or the disclosure of privileged information."); *Jampole v. Touchy*, 673 S.W.2d 569, 573 (Tex. 1984) (orig. proceeding) (same), *disapproved of on other grounds by Walker v. Parker*, 827 S.W.2d 833, 842 (Tex. 1992) (orig. proceeding); *In re John Crane, Inc.*, No. 01-03-00698-CV, 2003 Tex. App. LEXIS 9684, at *5, 2003 WL 22682613 (Tex. App.—Houston [1st Dist.] Nov. 13, 2003, orig. proceeding) (mem. op.) ("A party resisting discovery, however, cannot simply make conclusory

definition of harassment does not readily lend itself to production requests. "Harassment" is defined as "[w]ords, conduct, or action (usu. repeated or persistent) that, being directed at a specific person, annoys, alarms, or causes substantial emotional distress in that person and serves no legitimate purpose."[182] Thus, what constitutes harassment is generally subjective because what annoys or alarms one person may not annoy or alarm another.

Second, and more importantly, a production request that seeks documents that are relevant or reasonably calculated to lead to the discovery of admissible evidence generally cannot be harassing.[183] As one Texas court has explained: "[W]e have already concluded, however, that these discovery requests were reasonably calculated to lead to the discovery of admissible evidence; a request that meets that criterion is manifestly not . . . 'sought solely for the purposes of harassment.'"[184]

Even a production request that seeks documents that are relevant or reasonably calculated to lead to the discovery of admissible evidence may be improper because it either is disproportionate to action's needs, unduly burdensome, unnecessarily expensive, or unreasonably cumulative or duplicative of other discovery.[185] Thus, even if the responding party believes that a production request's sole purpose is to "harass," such an objection should be denied unless the request seeks documents that are neither relevant nor reasonably calculated to lead to the discovery of admissible evidence, is disproportionate, unduly burdensome, unnecessarily expensive, or unreasonably cumulative or duplicative. It is those objections, rather than a harassment objection, that should be interposed.

8-5:16 Invasion of Protected Rights

A production request that improperly invades a party's personal, constitutional, or property rights is objectionable.[186]

---

allegations that the requested discovery is unduly burdensome or unnecessarily harassing."); *In re State Farm Lloyds*, No. 04-98-00018, 1998 Tex. App. LEXIS 2072, at *11, 1998 WL 161260 (Tex. App.—San Antonio Apr. 8, 1998, orig. proceeding) (not designated for publication) ("The right to broad discovery is limited by the opposing party's right to be free from harassment and the burden of overly broad requests.").

182 *Black's Law Dictionary* 784 (11th ed. 2019); *accord Merriam-Webster.com Dictionary,* https://www.merriam-webster.com/dictionary/harass (last visited July 28, 2021) (defining "harass" as "to annoy persistently").

183 *ISK Biotech Corp. v. Lindsay*, 933 S.W.2d 565, 568 (Tex. App.—Houston [1st Dist.] 1996, orig. proceeding).

184 *ISK Biotech Corp. v. Lindsay*, 933 S.W.2d 565, 568 (Tex. App.—Houston [1st Dist.] 1996, orig. proceeding).

185 *See* Tex. R. Civ. P. 192.6(b); *In re Alford Chevrolet-Geo*, 997 S.W.2d 173, 180–81 (Tex. 1999) (orig. proceeding); *In re Am. Home Assur. Co.*, 88 S.W.3d 370, 372–73 (Tex. App.—Texarkana 2002, orig. proceeding).

186 Tex. R. Civ. P. 192.6(b) (authorizing protection from a discovery request that invades a "personal, constitutional, or property right"); *see In re Baylor Univ.*, 01-20-00439-CV, 2020 Tex. App. LEXIS 9200, at *13, 2020 WL 6878411, (Tex. App.—Houston [1st Dist.] Nov. 24, 2020, orig. proceeding) (mem. op.) ("[T]he person noticed for deposition has the right to protection 'from undue burden, unnecessary expense, harassment or annoyance, or invasion of personal, constitutional, or property rights.'" (quoting *Crown Cent. Petroleum Corp. v. Garcia*, 904 S.W.2d 125, 127 (Tex. 1995))); *In re Hamilton*, 13-20-00254-CV, 2020 Tex.

8-5:17 A Claim's or Defense's Invalidity

With one exception, an objection to a production request on the ground that the cause of action or defense to which it relates is invalid is only proper when the cause of action or defense has been dismissed pursuant to special exception, dismissal motion, or summary judgment.[187] In the same vein, "a party cannot refuse to produce a requested document or information simply because it is relevant to a claim or defense on which the producing party believes that it will prevail."[188] In other words, "as long as the parties request information or documents relevant to the claims at issue in the case, and such requests are tendered in good faith and are not unduly burdensome, discovery shall proceed."[189]

App. LEXIS 7378, at *8, 2020 WL 5494503, (Tex. App.—Corpus Christi Sept. 10, 2020, orig. proceeding) (same)*;* *In re Cook*, 05-19-01283-CV, 2020 Tex. App. LEXIS 3999, at *7, 2020 WL 2552881, (Tex. App.—Dallas May 20, 2020, orig. proceeding) (mem. op.) (same); *In re H.E.B. Grocery Co.*, No. 13-14-00023-CV, 2014 Tex. App. LEXIS 1777, at *18–22, 2014 WL 700749 (Tex. App.—Corpus Christi Feb. 18, 2014, orig. proceeding) (mem. op.) ("As a general rule, the party who seeks to limit discovery by asserting a privilege has the burden of producing evidence to support its assertions. . . . This rule applies when a party asserts privacy rights as a ground for limiting discovery. A party asserting that privacy rights protect information from disclosure must present evidence showing 'a particular, articulated and demonstrable injury.'" (quoting *In re Crestcare Nursing & Rehab. Ctr.*, 222 S.W.3d 68, 73 (Tex. App.—Tyler 2006, orig. proceeding))); *In re Does 1-10*, 242 S.W.3d 805, 812 (Tex. App.—Texarkana 2007, orig. proceeding) ("One of the reasons to ask [for a protective order] is to protect the movant from 'invasion of personal, constitutional, or property rights'." (quoting Tex. R. Civ. P. 192.6(b))); *cf. Soto v. City of Concord*, 162 F.R.D. 603, 616 (N.D. Cal. 1995) ("Federal Courts ordinarily recognize a constitutionally based right of privacy that can be raised in response to discovery requests."). See also Chapter 4, section 4-3:3 (discussing the discoverability of income tax returns).

187 *Lunsford v. Morris*, 746 S.W.2d 471, 473 (Tex. 1988) (orig. proceeding) (holding that, because discovery is based on matters relevant to the claims pleaded, a party need not prove a claim before being entitled to discovery on it), *disapproved of on other grounds by Walker v. Parker*, 827 S.W.2d 833, 842 (Tex. 1992) (orig. proceeding); *In re Citizens Supporting Metro Solutions, Inc.*, No. 14-07-00190-CV, 2007 Tex. App. LEXIS 8550, at *8–9, 2007 WL 4277850 (Tex. App.—Houston [14th Dist.] Oct. 18, 2007, orig. proceeding) (mem. op.) (holding that "the scope of discovery is measured by the live pleadings regarding the pending claims and, as here, where the trial court has not ruled on the merits of any of the claims, then the scope of discovery in the mandamus proceeding will be based on the pleadings"); *In re Rogers*, 200 S.W.3d 318, 324 (Tex. App.—Dallas 2006, orig. proceeding) (holding that, when a petition was "broadly pleaded" and had not been "challenged or narrowed through special exceptions or any other pleading vehicle," the responding party "cannot attempt to limit the scope of discovery through objection").

188 *Michael Fergin v. Westrock Co.*, No. 8:16CV26, 2017 U.S. Dist. LEXIS 197617, at *10–11, 2016 WL 11472113 (D. Neb. Dec. 1, 2017) (quoting *Heller v. City of Dall.*, 303 F.R.D. 466, 489 (N.D. Tex. 2014)); *accord Third Pentacle, LLC v. Interactive Life Forms, LLC*, No. 3:10cv00238, 2012 U.S. Dist. LEXIS 1391, at *9, 2012 WL 27473 (S.D. Ohio Jan. 5, 2012) (Even if a party "presently holds a strong belief in the merits of [the party's] litigation positions, [the party's] strong belief—whether ultimately justified or not—provides no basis for avoiding [the party's] discovery obligations created by the Federal Rules of Civil Procedure.").

189 *Michael Fergin v. Westrock Co.*, No. 8:16CV26, 2017 U.S. Dist. LEXIS 197617, at *11, 2016 WL 11472113 (D. Neb. Dec. 1, 2017) (quoting *St. Paul Reinsurance Co., Ltd. v. Commercial Fin. Corp.*, 198 F.R.D. 508, 511 (N.D. Iowa 2000)).

The exception to this rule is an exemplary damages claim. Under Chapter 41 of the Texas Civil Practice and Remedies Code, net-worth discovery is prohibited unless the court enters a "written order" finding that "the claimant has demonstrated a substantial likelihood of success on the merits of a claim for exemplary damages."[190]

8-5:18 Confidentiality

An objection to a production request on the ground that it seeks "confidential" or "proprietary" material generally is improper.[191] In fact, the Texas Supreme Court has held that "discovery cannot be denied because of an asserted proprietary interest in the requested document when a protective order would sufficiently preserve the interest."[192] Rather, the proper way for a responding party to deal with its contractual and other "confidentiality" obligations is to produce any allegedly confidential documents pursuant to a protective order's terms.[193]

---

[190] Tex. Civ. Prac. & Rem. Code § 41.0115(a). Discovery regarding a party's net worth for exemplary-damages purposes is discussed in Chapter 4, section 4-3:4.

[191] Texas Rule of Evidence 507 creates a privilege for trade secrets, which are "any formula, pattern, device or compilation of information which is used in one's business and presents an opportunity to obtain an advantage over competitors who do not know or use it." Tex. R. Evid. 507; *see Comput. Assocs. Int'l v. Altai, Inc.*, 918 S.W.2d 453, 455 (Tex. 1996) ("A trade secret is any formula, pattern, device or compilation of information which is used in one's business and presents an opportunity to obtain an advantage over competitors who do not know or use it."). The privilege, however, is not an absolute one: "The party asserting the trade secret privilege has the burden of proving that the discovery information sought qualifies as a trade secret. If the resisting party meets its burden, the burden shifts to the party seeking the trade secret discovery to establish that the information is necessary for a fair adjudication of its claim." *In re Cooper Tire & Rubber Co.*, 313 S.W.3d 910, 915 (Tex. App.—Houston [14th Dist.] 2010, orig. proceeding) (citations omitted); *accord In re Bass*, 113 S.W.3d 735, 738 (Tex. 2003) (orig. proceeding); *In re Sw. Airlines Co.*, No. 02-12-00179-CV, 2012 Tex. App. LEXIS 5613, at *7 (Tex. App.—Fort Worth July 12, 2012, orig. proceeding) (mem. op.); *see* Tex. R. Evid. 507 ("A person has a privilege . . . to refuse to disclose . . . a trade secret owned by the person, if the allowance of the privilege will not tend to conceal fraud or otherwise work injustice.").

[192] *Jampole v. Touchy*, 673 S.W.2d 569, 574–75 (Tex. 1984) (orig. proceeding), *disapproved of on other grounds by Walker v. Parker*, 827 S.W.2d 833, 842 (Tex. 1992) (orig. proceeding).

[193] *E.g.*, *In re K & L Auto Crushers, LLC*, 627 S.W.3d 239, 256 (Tex. 2021) (orig. proceeding)) ("As we have noted, a protective order can help reduce the potential harm of disclosure. Even if the requested documents contain confidential information or trade secrets, the providers have not shown that an appropriate protective order will not address their concerns. If the trial court denied the motion for reconsideration on the ground that the requested documents contain confidential information or trade secrets, the court should have considered whether it could permit this discovery while protecting the information, yet the record contains no suggestion that the court ever did so. To the extent the court denied the discovery on this ground, we conclude the court abused its discretion."); *In re N. Cypress Med. Ctr. Operating Co., Ltd.*, 559 S.W.3d 128, 137 (Tex. 2018) (orig. proceeding) ("Nothing in the record indicates that the trial court is unwilling to issue a protective order in the event North Cypress requests and demonstrates its entitlement to one. Nor does North Cypress explain why, in the event it is entitled to a protective order, such relief would be insufficient to address its concerns. Accordingly, we decline to grant mandamus relief on the ground that the contracts contain confidential and proprietary information."); *In re Cont'l Ins. Co.*, 994 S.W.2d 423, 426 (Tex. App.—Waco 1999) ("Individuals cannot protect relevant information from discovery by confidentiality provisions in contracts, even settlement agreements.

8-5:19 Assumes Facts Not in Evidence

On occasion, a responding party will object to request for production because it assumes facts not in evidence or calls for speculation. Such objections generally are improper because (1) this is a trial objection, (2) a responding party has a duty of reasonable inquiry in responding to production requests, (3) an opposing party is entitled to discovery regarding "any matter that is not privileged and is relevant to the subject matter of the pending action" or that "appears reasonably calculated to lead to the discovery of relevant evidence."[194] In other words, the objection is contrary to the purpose of discovery, which is to learn facts.

The private agreement between two individuals does *not* override the discovery rules. The rules of civil procedure specifically allow for a method to produce relevant information to the opposing party in litigation while at the same time keep the information confidential.") (emphasis added), ***mandamus granted on other grounds sub nom., In re Union Pac. Res. Co.***, 22 S.W.3d 338, 341 (Tex. 1999); ***Jampole v. Touchy***, 673 S.W.2d 569, 574–75 (Tex. 1984) (orig. proceeding) ("[I]f the documents were relevant, any proprietary interest could be safeguarded by a protective order."), ***disapproved of on other grounds by Walker v. Parker***, 827 S.W.2d 833, 842 (Tex. 1992) (orig. proceeding); ***see In re DCP Midstream, L.P.***, No. 13-14-00502-CV, 2014 Tex. App. LEXIS 11092, at *17–18, 2014 WL 5019947 (Tex. App.—Corpus Christi Oct. 7, 2014, orig. proceeding) (mem. op.) ("Texas has a public policy of encouraging the peaceful resolution of disputes through voluntary settlement and orderly dispute resolution. . . . However, the fact that a settlement agreement contains a confidentiality provision does not render the agreement or its contents undiscoverable as a matter of law. Accordingly, the confidentiality provisions of the agreement do not insulate the settlement agreement from discovery if the discovery is otherwise warranted.") (citations omitted); ***cf. Shutrump v. Safeco Ins. Co. of Am.***, No. 17-CV-0022-CVE-TLW, 2017 U.S. Dist. LEXIS 132053, at *6–7, 2017 WL 3579211 (N.D. Okla. Aug. 18, 2017) ("[P]laintiff and Mercury argue that the file is privileged because it contains a settlement agreement that is subject to a confidentiality agreement. '[C]onfidentiality does not equate to privilege,' and 'the mere fact that the settling parties agree to maintain the confidentiality of their agreement does not serve to shield the agreement from discovery.'" (quoting ***DIRECTV, Inc. v. Puccinelli***, 224 F.R.D. 677, 685 (D. Kan. 2004))); ***EEOC v. Thorman & Wright Corp.***, 243 F.R.D. 426, 430 (D. Kan. 2007) ("[A]s this Court previously has held, 'a concern for protecting confidentiality does not equate to privilege.' With that said, a party may request the court enter a protective order pursuant to [Federal Rule] 26(c) as a means to protect such confidential information." (footnote omitted) (quoting ***DIRECTV, Inc. v. Puccinelli***, 224 F.R.D. 677, 682 (D. Kan. 2004))); ***Tinkers & Chance v. Leapfrog Enters.***, No. 2:05-CV-349, 2006 U.S. Dist. LEXIS 10115, at *6–7, 2006 WL 462601 (E.D. Tex. Feb. 23, 2006) (mem. op.) ("[T]his Court will order the production of all relevant documents and evidence, without regard to any private non-disclosure agreement between the parties. Any confidential matter shall be produced under a protective order.").

A nonparty owner of documents containing confidential information has the right to seek protection from the information's disclosure. Tex. R. Civ. P. 192.6(a) ("[A]ny other person affected by the discovery request may move . . . for an order protecting that person from the discovery sought."); ***In re Does 1-10***, 242 S.W.3d 805, 812 (Tex. App.—Texarkana 2007, orig. proceeding) (holding that an anonymous blogger had standing to challenge a discovery order compelling his internet service provider to disclose his name to the plaintiff in a defamation suit).

194 Tex. R. Civ. P. 192.3(a); ***see Sprint Communs. Co. v. Charter Communs.***, No. 20-cv-2161-JWB-TJJ, 2021 U.S. Dist. LEXIS 66408, at *8, 2021 WL 1265135 (D. Kan. Apr. 6, 2021) ("Individual Defendants also object to this RFP as assuming facts not in evidence 'regarding the purported "loss" or "deletion" of information.' The Court overrules this objection as

8-6 Electronic Discovery

In 1999, Texas became the first state in the nation to adopt a rule—Texas Rule 194.6—that expressly and exclusively addresses data or information existing in electronic or magnetic form ("electronically stored information" or "ESI") as a distinct category of discoverable information. Texas Rule 194.6 predated the Federal Rule amendments in that regard by more than six years. Without the guidance of any existing rules on the discovery of ESI and with very few cases pertaining to ESI, the Texas Rule 196.4 sets forth the requirements for requesting ESI, responding to such requests, and issuing orders requiring more than reasonable efforts to produce requested ESI:[195] It provides:

> To obtain discovery of data or information that exists in electronic or magnetic form, the requesting party must specifically request production of electronic or magnetic data and specify the form in which the requesting party wants it produced. The responding party must produce the electronic or magnetic data that is responsive to the request and is reasonably available to the responding party in its ordinary course of business. If the responding party cannot—through reasonable efforts—retrieve the data or information requested or produce it in the

---

an improper objection to Sprint's discovery request.") (footnotes omitted); *Two Rivers Pipeline & Constr. Co. v. Cimarex Energy Co.*, No. PE:19-CV-00049-DC-DF, 2020 U.S. Dist. LEXIS 206472, at *13–14, 2020 WL 6379302 (W.D. Tex. Sept. 14, 2020) ("Two Rivers objects to Cimarex's RFP Nos. 36-38, 40-46, and 51 as assuming facts not in evidence. Cimarex asserts that federal courts have rejected this objection. As noted by the Western District of Texas, '[a]ssuming facts not in evidence may be the basis for an objection during trial or some other evidentiary hearing. This, however, is discovery.'" (quoting *Vickers v. JP Morgan Chase N.A.*, SA-12-CA-31-XR, 2013 U.S. Dist. LEXIS 208157, at *26 & n.99, 2013 WL 12134153 (W.D. Tex. Feb. 22, 2013))); *see also Cf. Sutton v. Mgmt. & Training Corp.*, No. 1:13-cv-1344 - AWI-JLT, 2015 U.S. Dist. LEXIS 11399, at *15–16, 2015 WL 402024 (E.D. Cal. 2015) ("As an initial matter, the objection that an interrogatory 'assumes facts not in evidence' is not proper in the course of discovery."); *McGrath v. Cosco, Inc.*, No. 98-cv-1502, 1999 U.S. Dist. LEXIS 5893, at *3, 1999 WL 269920 (E.D. Pa. Apr. 21, 1999) ("That an interrogatory assumes facts not in evidence is not a valid objection in the context of discovery."); *see also Vickers v. JP Morgan Chase N.A.*, No. SA-12-CA-31-XR, 2013 U.S. Dist. LEXIS 208157, at *26–27 (W.D. Tex. 2013) ("JPMC's objections, 'assumes facts not in evidence, and assumes that such recording is required,' do not appear to be sufficient to avoid providing a further response, as the purpose of discovery is to learn facts.") (footnote omitted); *Richards v. Convergys Corp.*, Nos. 2:05-CV-00790-DAK, 2:05-CV-00812 DAK, 2006 U.S. Dist. LEXIS 63567, at *4–5 (D. Utah Sept. 5, 2006) (rejecting speculation and assumes-facts-not-in-evidence objections to an interrogatory because the responding "has a duty to make a reasonable inquiry for information in its possession"); *Baker v. Cnty. of Missaukee*, No. 1:09-cv-1059, 2013 U.S. Dist. LEXIS 154072, at *19, 2013 WL 5786899 (W.D. Mich. Oct. 28, 2013) ("Plaintiff is correct that defendant's objection to request [for admission] 8 on the ground that it 'assumes facts not in evidence' is meritless. This trial objection has no place in discovery practice and is overruled."); *Michilin Prosperity Co. v. Fellowes Mfg. Co.*, No. 04-1025 (RWR/JMF), 2006 U.S. Dist. LEXIS 32064, at *3, 2006 WL 1441575 (D.D.C. May 23, 2006) (rejecting a speculation objection to requests for admission because "to the extent that the requests may call for factual speculation, Michilin should have stated that it was unable to admit or deny and then explained why it could not truthfully admit or deny the request").

[195] *See* Nathan L. Hecht, *Taking Point on E-Discovery: Texas Rule of Civil Procedure* 196.4, 51 THE ADVOC. (Tex.) 18 (2010) (analyzing the history and text of Texas Rule 196.4).

form requested, the responding party must state an objection complying with these rules. If the court orders the responding party to comply with the request, the court must also order that the requesting party pay the reasonable expenses of any extraordinary steps required to retrieve and produce the information.[196]

Although Texas Rule 196.4 has not been amended since its adoption, Texas case law has construed it to keep Texas's electronic-discovery standards consistent with the more rapidly developing federal standards.[197] Thus, even though Texas Rule 196.4's

---

[196] Tex. R. Civ. P. 196.4. ESI is explicitly included in discovery's scope under the Texas discovery rules: "A party may obtain discovery of the existence, description, nature, custody, condition, location, and contents of documents and tangible things (including papers, books, accounts, drawings, graphs, charts, photographs, *electronic or videotape recordings, data, and data compilations*) that constitute or contain matters relevant to the subject matter of the action." Tex. R. Civ. P. 192.3(b) (emphasis added); *see id.* R. 194.2(b) (requiring a party to disclosure "a copy—or a description by category and location—of all documents, electronically stored information, and tangible things that the responding party has in its possession, custody, or control, and may use to support its claims or defenses, unless the use would be solely for impeachment") (emphasis added).

[197] Federal Rules 26 and 34 include provisions pertaining to discovery of ESI. The former rule requires each party, in its initial disclosures, to disclose, among other information, ESI the party may use to support its claims or defenses and that is reasonably available to it as part of the party's initial disclosures. Fed. R. Civ. P. 26(a)(1)(A)(ii), (E).

Federal Rule 26(b)(2)(B), which addresses limitations on the scope of discovery relating to ESI, provides:

> A party need not provide discovery of [ESI] from sources that the party identifies as not reasonably accessible because of undue burden or cost. On motion to compel discovery or for a protective order, the party from whom discovery is sought must show that the information is not reasonably accessible because of undue burden or cost. If that showing is made, the court may nonetheless order discovery from such sources if the requesting party shows good cause, considering the limitations of [Federal] Rule 26(b)(2)(C). The court may specify conditions for the discovery.

Federal Rule 26(b)(2)(C), which governs when a court must limit discovery's frequency or extent, was amended in 2015. Previously, one instance in which a discovery limitation was mandatory was when "the burden or expense of the proposed discovery outweighs its likely benefit, considering the needs of the case, the amount in controversy, the parties' resources, the importance of the issues at stake in the action, and the importance of the discovery in resolving the issues." This language is repeated verbatim in Texas Rule 192.4(b). As a result of the 2015 amendments to Federal Rule 26(b)(2)(C), however, this limitation is no longer in Federal Rule 26(b)(2)(C). Instead, Federal Rule 26(b)(2)(C) now requires a limitation when "the proposed discovery is outside the scope permitted by [Federal] Rule 26(b)(1)." Fed. R. Civ. P. 26(b)(2)(C)(iii). Interestingly, the Rule's former language now is included in Federal Rule 26(b)(1), which states: "Unless otherwise limited by court order, the scope of discovery is as follows: Parties may obtain discovery regarding any non-privileged matter that is relevant to any party's claim or defense and proportional to the needs of the case, considering the importance of the issues at stake in the action, the amount in controversy, the parties' relative access to relevant information, the parties' resources, the importance of the discovery in resolving the issues, and whether the burden or expense of the proposed discovery outweighs its likely benefit. Information within this scope of discovery need not be admissible in evidence to be discoverable."

Federal Rule 34(a)(1)(A), which governs production requests, allows a party to serve a request for "any designated documents or [ESI]—including writings, drawings, graphs, text differs somewhat from the text in Federal Rules 26 and 34 that addresses ESI, federal case law on the comparable Federal Rule text is instructive for electronic-discovery disputes in Texas proceedings.

8-6:1 Electronic Discovery Procedure

Although Texas Rule 196.4 applies to the discovery of all ESI, and such discovery is now commonplace in civil litigation, it took ten years for a case involving Texas Rule 196.4's application to reach the Texas Supreme Court.

The seminal Texas Supreme Court opinion about the Rule's scope and procedure is *In re Weekley Homes, L.P.*[198] In that case, the Court considered the trial court's discovery order requiring four employees of a defendant to produce their

---

charts, photographs, sound recordings, images, and other data or data compilations—stored in any medium from which information can be obtained either directly or, if necessary, after translation by the responding party into a reasonably usable form."

Federal Rule 34(b)(2)(E) governs the procedure for producing documents or ESI. Consistent with Texas Rule 196.3(c), Federal Rule 34(b)(2)(E)(i) provides that a responding party "must produce documents as they are kept in the usual course of business or must organize and label them to correspond to the categories in the request." Fed. R. Civ. P. 34(b)(2)(E)(i). Unlike the Texas Rules, however, Federal Rule 34(b)(2)(E)(ii) also provides a default form for production of ESI in the absence of a specified form—if the discovery request does not specify a form for producing ESI, "a party must produce it in a form or forms in which it is ordinarily maintained or in a reasonably usable form or forms." Fed. R. Civ. P. 34(b)(2)(E)(ii). The responding party is not, however, required to produce the same ESI in more than one form. Fed. R. Civ. P. 34(b)(2)(E)(iii).

Based on the similarities between the Texas Rules and the Federal Rules, Texas state courts have looked to federal decisions for guidance when considering electronic-discovery issues. *See, e.g., In re State Farm Lloyds*, 520 S.W.3d 595, 612–13 (Tex. 2017) (orig. proceeding) ("Our application of proportionality principles in this context aligns electronic-discovery practice under the Texas Rules of Civil Procedure with electronic-discovery practice under the Federal Rules of Civil Procedure. . . . To be sure, there are differences in language between [Texas Rule 196.4] and [Federal Rule 34]. But as we affirmed in *In re Weekley Homes*, [295 S.W.3d 309, 317 (Tex. 2009) (orig. proceeding),] 'our rules as written are not inconsistent with the federal rules or the case law interpreting them,' even though they may not 'mirror the federal language.' In this regard, we observe the proportionality principles under the federal rules similarly limit discovery of otherwise discoverable information. [Federal] Rule 26 delineates the scope of discovery as inherently limited by proportionality. . . . The factors expressly identified as limitations on the scope of discovery [in Federal Rule 26] accord with the proportionality analysis we have explicated under our discovery rules, keeping our procedures in line with their federal counterparts.") (footnotes omitted) (citations omitted); *In re Weekley Homes, L.P.*, 295 S.W.3d 309, 317 (Tex. 2009) (orig. proceeding) ("[B]oth the federal rule and ours require trial courts to weigh the benefits of production against the burdens imposed when the requested information is not reasonably available in the ordinary course of business. We see no difference in the considerations that would apply when weighing the benefits against the burdens of electronic-information production; therefore we look to the federal rules for guidance."); *In re Waste Mgmt. of Tex., Inc.*, 392 S.W.3d 861, 874 (Tex. App.—Texarkana 2013, orig. proceeding) ("The Texas Supreme Court has instructed that the Texas Rules governing electronic discovery are sufficiently similar to the Federal Rules for Texas courts to 'look to the federal rules for guidance.'").

198 *In re Weekley Homes, L.P.*, 295 S.W.3d 309 (Tex. 2009) (orig. proceeding).

computer hard drives to a forensic expert to image, copy, and search for deleted emails.[199] The Court ultimately held that mandamus relief was appropriate because the trial court abused its discretion in entering the order.[200] After analyzing Texas Rule 196.4 and the comparable federal electronic-discovery rules, the Court established the following procedure for requesting and producing ESI under Texas Rule 196.4:

- The party seeking to discover ESI must make a specific request for that information and specify the form of its production.[201]
- The responding party must then produce any ESI that is "responsive to the request and . . . reasonably available to the responding party in its ordinary course of business."[202]
- If "the responding party cannot—through reasonable efforts—retrieve the data or information requested or produce it in the form requested," it must object on those grounds.[203]
- The parties should make reasonable efforts to resolve the objections without court intervention.[204]
- If the parties are unable to resolve the dispute, either party may request a hearing on the objections.[205] The responding party has the burden of demonstrating that the requested ESI is not reasonably available because of undue burden or cost.[206]
- If the trial court determines the requested ESI is not reasonably available, the court may nevertheless order production upon a showing by the requesting party that the benefits of production outweigh the burdens imposed, subject to the general discovery limitations set forth in the Texas Rules.[207]
- If the benefits are shown to outweigh the burdens of production and the trial court orders production of ESI that is not reasonably available, sensitive information should be protected and the least intrusive means should be employed.[208]

---

199 *In re Weekley Homes, L.P.*, 295 S.W.3d 309, 311–13 (Tex. 2009) (orig. proceeding).

200 *In re Weekley Homes, L.P.*, 295 S.W.3d 309, 322–23 (Tex. 2009) (orig. proceeding).

201 *In re Weekley Homes, L.P.*, 295 S.W.3d 309, 322 (Tex. 2009) (orig. proceeding) (citing Tex. R. Civ. P. 196.4).

202 *In re Weekley Homes, L.P.*, 295 S.W.3d 309, 322 (Tex. 2009) (orig. proceeding) (citing Tex. R. Civ. P. 196.4).

203 *In re Weekley Homes, L.P.*, 295 S.W.3d 309, 322 (Tex. 2009) (orig. proceeding) (citing Tex. R. Civ. P. 196.4).

204 *In re Weekley Homes, L.P.*, 295 S.W.3d 309, 322 (Tex. 2009) (orig. proceeding) (citing Tex. R. Civ. P. 191.2).

205 *In re Weekley Homes, L.P.*, 295 S.W.3d 309, 322 (Tex. 2009) (orig. proceeding) (citing Tex. R. Civ. P. 193.4(a)).

206 *In re Weekley Homes, L.P.*, 295 S.W.3d 309, 322 (Tex. 2009) (orig. proceeding) (citing Tex. R. Civ. P. 192.4(b)).

207 *In re Weekley Homes, L.P.*, 295 S.W.3d 309, 315, 322 (Tex. 2009) (orig. proceeding); Tex. R. Civ. P. 192.4(b).

208 *In re Weekley Homes, L.P.*, 295 S.W.3d 309, 322 (Tex. 2009) (orig. proceeding) (citing Tex. R. Civ. P. 192.6(b)).

The requesting party must also pay the reasonable expenses of any extraordinary steps required to retrieve and produce the ESI.[209]

- Finally, when determining how the sources should be searched and ESI produced, direct access to another party's electronic storage device is discouraged, and the trial court should be extremely cautious to guard against undue intrusion.[210]

In 2017, the Texas Supreme Court reentered the fray of electronic discovery and adopted a "proportionality inquiry" "[w]hen a reasonably usable form [of ESI] is readily available in the ordinary course of business" and the trial court must determine "whether any enhanced burden or expense associated with a requested form [of ESI] is justified when weighed against the proportional needs of the case."[211]

Finally, in 2018, the Texas Supreme Court revisited the procedure for requesting ESI and the standards governing direct access to another party's electronic storage device and, in doing so, reinforced the applicable guidelines that it established nine years earlier in *In re Weekley Homes*.[212] The guidelines are discussed in Chapter 8, sections 8-6:3 and 8-6:7.

---

209 *In re Weekley Homes, L.P.*, 295 S.W.3d 309, 322 (Tex. 2009) (orig. proceeding) (citing Tex. R. Civ. P. 196.4).

210 *In re Weekley Homes, L.P.*, 295 S.W.3d 309, 317, 322 (Tex. 2009) (orig. proceeding). *In re Weekley Homes* involved a request for direct access to hard drives on employees' individual work computers. *In re Weekley Homes, L.P.*, 295 S.W.3d 309, 313 (Tex. 2009) (orig. proceeding). Courts of appeals have relied upon the procedure set forth in *In re Weekley* to analyze whether an order allowing direct access to other types of devices was a proper exercise of the trial court's discretion. *See, e.g. In re Wilcox*, No. 09-20-00271-CV, 2021 Tex. App. LEXIS 2042, at *9–11, 2021 WL 1031141 (Tex. App.—Beaumont Mar. 18, 2021, orig. proceeding) (mem. op.) (personal computer and cell phone); *In re Methodist Primary Care Grp.*, 553 S.W.3d 709, 721 (Tex. App.—Houston [14th Dist.] 2018, orig. proceeding) (data stored on remote servers and accessible via the internet); *In re VERP Inv., LLC*, 457 S.W.3d 255 (Tex. App.—Dallas 2015, orig. proceeding) (defendant's computer hard drive); *In re Clark*, 345 S.W.3d 209 (Tex. App.—Beaumont 2011, orig. proceeding) (per curiam) (all of defendant's personal electronic-storage devices); *In re M*, No. 09-12-00179-CV, 2012 Tex. App. LEXIS 3934, at *6–7, 2012 WL 1808236 (Tex. App.—Beaumont May 17, 2012, orig. proceeding) (mem. op.) (per curiam) (cell phones); *In re Jordan*, 364 S.W.3d 425, 426–27 (Tex. App.—Dallas 2012, orig. proceeding) (plaintiff's personal computer). One such court has noted that a trial court's failure "to observe the electronic-discovery procedures explicated in . . . *In re Weekley Homes* . . . is an abuse of discretion." *In re VERP Inv., LLC*, 457 S.W.3d 255, 260 (Tex. App.—Dallas 2015, orig. proceeding); *accord In re Jordan*, 364 S.W.3d 425, 426–27 (Tex. App.—Dallas 2012, orig. proceeding) ("*In re Weekley Homes* controls here. It binds the parties as well as the trial court. By not observing the procedures elaborated in *Weekley*, the trial court abused its discretion.").

211 *In re State Farm Lloyds*, 520 S.W.3d 595, 607 (Tex. 2017) (orig. proceeding); *see In re State Farm Lloyds*, 520 S.W.3d 595, 608–12 (Tex. 2017) (orig. proceeding) (listing and explaining the factors to balance when engaging in the proportionality inquiry). See Chapter 8, section 8-6:5, for a discussion of the proportionality inquiry with respect to electronic discovery.

212 *In re Shipman*, 540 S.W.3d 562, 566–70 (Tex. 2018) (orig. proceeding) (per curiam).

8-6:2 Parties' Responsibility to Confer

Parties have a responsibility to communicate with one another about the scope of discovery requests for ESI.[213] It is prudent to prepare for e-discovery as soon as practicable in a proceeding. Often this should occur before conferring with the opposing party to identify: the methods of organization; persons who might possess relevant ESI; locations of ESI; and its accessibility. In addition, counsel should be able to explain if the ESI is not reasonably accessible and the extraordinary measures and cost associated with accessing said ESI.

The earlier discussions with the opposing party occur in the discovery process, the better.[214] That is, "*prior to* promulgating requests for [ESI], parties and their attorneys should share relevant information concerning electronic systems and storage methodologies so that agreements regarding protocols may be reached."[215] Certainly, "[o]nce a specific request [for ESI] is made the parties can, and should, communicate as to the particularities of a party's computer storage system and potential methods of retrieval to assess the feasibility of their recovery."[216]

8-6:3 Requests for Electronic Discovery

Requests for production of ESI must be in writing—an oral request "is not a permissible discovery device."[217] Under Texas Rule 196.4, a request to obtain discovery of ESI must satisfy two requirements:[218] (1) the request must specifically describe the

---

213 *E.g., In re State Farm Lloyds*, 520 S.W.3d 595, 606 (Tex. 2017) (orig. proceeding); *In re Weekley Homes, L.P.*, 295 S.W.3d 309, 322 (Tex. 2009) (orig. proceeding).

214 The federal discovery rules expressly address early communications about ESI. *See* Fed. R. Civ. P. 16(b)(3)(B)(iii) (permitting the parties to include, within the initial scheduling order, provisions regarding the disclosure, discovery or preservation of ESI), Fed. R. Civ. P. 26(f)(3)(C) (requiring the parties, following their initial Federal Rule 26 conference, to submit a discovery plan that includes, among other things, "any issues about disclosure, discovery, or preservation of [ESI], including the form or forms in which it should be produced"). Although the Texas discovery rules do not contain similar conference requirements, the Texas Supreme Court encourages "early discussions between the parties or early discovery directed toward learning about an opposing party's electronic storage systems and procedures." *In re Weekley Homes, L.P.*, 295 S.W.3d 309, 314 n.6 (Tex. 2009) (orig. proceeding).

215 *In re Weekley Homes, L.P.*, 295 S.W.3d 309, 321 (Tex. 2009) (orig. proceeding) (emphasis added).

216 *In re Weekley Homes, L.P.*, 295 S.W.3d 309, 314 (Tex. 2009) (orig. proceeding); *see also In re State Farm Lloyds*, 520 S.W.3d 595, 606 (Tex. 2017) (orig. proceeding) ("Meeting and conferring to resolve e-discovery disputes without court intervention is essential because discovery of electronic data involves case-specific considerations and each side possesses unique access to information concerning reasonable and viable production methods, resources (technological or monetary, for instance), and needs."); *In re Waste Mgmt. of Tex., Inc.*, 392 S.W.3d 861, 874 (Tex. App.—Texarkana 2013, orig. proceeding) ("Communication between the parties is essential, and, if a party feels a request is too ambiguous, that party should contact the opposing side.").

217 *See In re M*, No. 09-12-00179-CV, 2012 Tex. App. LEXIS 3934, at *4, 2012 WL 1808236 (Tex. App.—Beaumont May 17, 2012, orig. proceeding) (mem. op.) (per curiam).

218 Tex. R. Civ. P. 196.4. *But see* Tex. R. Civ. P. 196.4 cmt. 3 to 1999 change (adding a third requirement—not set forth in the text of the Rule—that the requesting party specify "any extraordinary steps for retrieval and translation").

ESI sought;[219] and (2) the request must specify the form in which the requesting party wants the ESI produced.[220] "The purpose of [Texas] Rule 196.4's specificity requirement is to ensure that requests for [ESI] are clearly understood and disputes

[219] Tex. R. Civ. P. 196.4; *see In re Weekley Homes, L.P.*, 295 S.W.3d 309, 315 (Tex. 2009) (orig. proceeding) ("[P]arties seeking production of deleted emails should specifically request them."); *In re Methodist Primary Care Grp.*, 553 S.W.3d 709, 717 (Tex. App.—Houston [14th Dist.] 2018, orig. proceeding) (concluding that a request that defined "documents" as "all other electronic information which shall be produced in their native format" sufficiently requested the production of electronic data); *MRT, Inc. v. Vounckx*, 299 S.W.3d 500, 506, 508–09 (Tex. App.—Dallas 2009, no pet.) (concluding that, because the requests for certain "documents"—which was defined to include "any computer-generated, computer-stored, or electronically-stored matter"—did not request the production of or refer specifically to backup tapes, the responding party was not required to address backup tapes in its responses or objections); *In re Pinnacle Eng'g, Inc.*, 405 S.W.3d 835, 842 (Tex. App.—Houston [1st Dist.] 2013, orig. proceeding) (production requests for computer hard drives from certain individuals' laptops, desktops, Dell notebooks, and tablets, as well as the network servers used for electronic data by those individuals, "did not inform relators of the exact nature of the information sought and do not meet the requirements of [Texas R]ule 196.4"); *In re Jordan*, 364 S.W.3d 425, 426 (Tex. App.—Dallas 2012, orig. proceeding) (production requests merely asking for computer hard drives are insufficient under Texas Rule 196.4); *In re Harris*, 315 S.W.3d 685, 700–02 (Tex. App.—Houston [1st Dist.] 2010, orig. proceeding) (conditionally granting mandamus relief because the trial court ordered the production of "hard drives, external hard drives, jump drives, and other such repositories of electronic communications" where the discovery request was limited to "emails and other electronic communications in their native format").

[220] Tex. R. Civ. P. 196.4; *see, e.g., In re State Farm Lloyds*, 520 S.W.3d 595, 599 (Tex. 2017) (orig. proceeding) ("The requesting party must specify the desired form of production[.]"); *In re Methodist Primary Care Grp.*, 553 S.W.3d 709, 715-16 (Tex. App.—Houston [14th Dist.] 2018, orig. proceeding) (concluding that a request for "electronic documents" in their "native format" was sufficient to indicate that manner in which the ESI is to be produced).

The Texas discovery rules do not contain a default form for producing ESI. *In re Waste Mgmt. of Tex., Inc.*, 392 S.W.3d 861, 874 (Tex. App.—Texarkana 2013, orig. proceeding) (noting that the Texas Rules "do not contain a default form" for electronic discovery). Under the Federal discovery rules, the default is "a form or forms in which it is ordinarily maintained or in a reasonably useable form or forms." Fed. R. Civ. P. 34(b)(2)(E)(ii); *In re State Farm Lloyds*, 520 S.W.3d 595, 612 (Tex. 2017) (orig. proceeding) (Federal "Rule 34's plain language does not permit either party to unilaterally dictate the form of production for ESI. The default form is 'a form or forms in which [ESI] is ordinarily maintained or in a reasonably usable form or forms,' and the trial court retains discretion to order discovery in a format that is appropriate to the circumstances."). Because Texas state courts "look to the federal rules of guidance" on electronic-discovery issues, the Texarkana Court of Appeals has held that a request for ESI to be "produced in a 'reasonable manner' is the functional equivalent of the Federal 'reasonably useable form or forms'" and, thus, sufficient. *In re Waste Mgmt. of Tex., Inc.*, 392 S.W.3d 861, 874 (Tex. App.—Texarkana 2013, orig. proceeding) (quoting *In re Weekley Homes, L.P.*, 295 S.W.3d 309, 317 (Tex. 2009) (orig. proceeding)). Although the Texas Supreme Court has aligned some Texas electronic-discovery standards with Federal electronic-discovery standards, it has not addressed whether a requesting party satisfies Texas Rule 196.4's requirement to specify the form in which it wants ESI produced by requesting that ESI be produced in "a reasonable manner." To avoid the risk of noncompliance with Texas Rule 196.4's form-specification requirement, more specificity is advised.

avoided."[221] With that purpose in mind, the Texas Supreme Court has held that a failure to adhere to the specificity requirement will not be fatal to a request for ESI if the request is "'clearly understood'" before trial-court intervention and, as a result, the responding party is not prejudiced by the "'failure to follow the [R]ule.'"[222] Thus, for example, it may suffice for the requesting party to specify the ESI sought in a motion to compel.[223] The better practice, however, is to comply with Texas Rule 196.4's specificity requirement when possible, to reduce the odds of a dispute.

Among the ESI that may be requested are deleted documents, including emails and backup tapes or records.[224] It is also permissible to request metadata, which the Texas Supreme Court has defined as "information describing the history, tracking, or management of an electronic file."[225] Courts across the United States disagree about

---

221 *In re Weekley Homes, L.P.*, 295 S.W.3d 309, 314 (Tex. 2009) (orig. proceeding); *accord In re Shipman*, 540 S.W.3d 562, 566 (Tex. 2018) (orig. proceeding) (per curiam); *MRT, Inc. v. Vounckx*, 299 S.W.3d 500, 508 (Tex. App.—Dallas 2009, no pet.); *In re Pinnacle Eng'g, Inc.*, 405 S.W.3d 835, 841–42 (Tex. App.—Houston [1st Dist.] 2013, orig. proceeding).

222 *In re Shipman*, 540 S.W.3d 562, 566–67 (Tex. 2018) (orig. proceeding) (per curiam) ("Jamie's discovery requests do not explicitly seek direct access to Shipman's computer. Rather, Jamie seeks access to Shipman's computer through a motion to compel as a remedy for perceived inadequate production, not as a discovery request in itself. The function of [Texas] Rule 196.4's specificity requirement is to ensure electronic-information requests are 'clearly understood and disputes avoided.' Jamie's request to directly access Shipman's computer is, in her view, a response to Shipman's failure to comply with her 'clearly understood' requests for electronically stored information. She properly sought that remedy through her second motion to compel; she did not need to separately lodge a [Texas] Rule 196.4–specific discovery request for direct access to Shipman's computer." (citation omitted) (quoting *In re Weekley Homes, L.P.*, 295 S.W.3d 309, 314–15 (Tex. 2009) (orig. proceeding))); *In re Weekley Homes, L.P.*, 295 S.W.3d 309, 314–15 (Tex. 2009) (orig. proceeding) ("[E]ven though it was not stated in . . . [the] written request that deleted emails were included within its scope, that [the requesting party] thought they were and was seeking [deleted emails] became abundantly clear in the course of discovery and before the hearing on the motion to compel; . . . [thus, the responding party] was not prejudiced by [the] failure to follow the rule and the trial court did not abuse its discretion by ordering production of the deleted emails."); *see also In re Clark*, 345 S.W.3d 209, 212 (Tex. App.—Beaumont 2011, orig. proceeding) (per curiam) (explaining that a "request is reasonably specific if the responding party understands the scope of the request before the trial court intervenes").

223 *See In re Shipman*, 540 S.W.3d 562, 567 (Tex. 2018) (orig. proceeding) (per curiam) ("Regardless of the specificity of Jamie's initial requests, she argued in her second motion to compel that 'Shipman should be required to produce all paper and electronic records he can locate using diligent efforts, and to make his computer[s] available for forensic examination.' If Jamie's discovery requests did not technically meet [Texas] Rule 196.4's specificity requirement, Shipman cannot argue Jamie's intent was not 'clearly understood.'"). See also authorities cited in note 219.

224 *See In re Weekley Homes, L.P.*, 295 S.W.3d 309, 314 (Tex. 2009) (orig. proceeding) ("[E]mail communications constitute 'electronic data,' and their characterization as such does not change when they are deleted from a party's inbox."); *In re CI Host, Inc.*, 92 S.W.3d 514, 516–17 (Tex. 2002) (orig. proceeding) (finding that a request for the production of computer backup tapes was appropriate under Texas Rule 192.3(b) and approving the trial court's order requiring production of the backup tapes).

225 *In re Weekley Homes, L.P.*, 295 S.W.3d 309, 320 n.9 (Tex. 2009) (orig. proceeding) (citing Fed. R. Civ. P. 26(f), Advisory Committee Notes to 2006 Amend.); *In re Waste Mgmt. of Tex., Inc.*, 392 S.W.3d 861, 865 n.2 (Tex. App.—Texarkana 2013, orig. proceeding) (same); *see In*

whether and when metadata associated with electronic documents falls within discovery's scope.[226] As discussed in Chapter 8, section 8-6:5, metadata's discoverability is determined on a case-by-case basis in Texas courts. Practitioners should always check the local rules and the applicable court's or judge's specific requirements (such as standing orders) for additional guidance.

8-6:4 Responding to Requests for Electronic Discovery

In response to production requests for ESI, a party must produce the ESI in the form specifically requested unless the party timely objects or asserts a privilege in compliance with the Texas Rules.[227] As explained in Chapter 8, section 8-4:3.1, in responding

---

re State Farm Lloyds, 520 S.W.3d 595, 601 (Tex. 2017) (orig. proceeding) ("Metadata, 'colloquially known as "data about data," encompasses the structural information of a file that contains data about it as opposed to describing its actual substantive content. Often hidden and embedded within the original file, metadata does not normally appear on a printed page.'" (quoting *U.S. ex rel. Carter v. Bridgepoint Educ., Inc.*, 305 F.R.D. 225, 228 (S.D. Cal. 2015))).

[226] *Compare Aguilar v. Immig. & Customs Enf't Div.*, 255 F.R.D. 350, 357 (S.D.N.Y. 2008) ("There is a clear pattern of case law concerning motions to compel the production of metadata. Courts generally have ordered the production of metadata when it is sought in the initial document request and the producing party has not yet produced the documents in any form. On the other hand, if metadata is not sought in the initial document request, and particularly if the producing party has produced documents in another form, courts tend to deny later requests, often concluding that the metadata is not relevant.") (citations omitted), *Williams v. Sprint/United Mgmt. Co.*, 230 F.R.D. 640, 656 (D. Kan. 2005) (stating that when a Court "orders a party to produce an electronic document in the form in which it is regularly maintained, i.e., in its native format or as an active file, that production must include all metadata unless that party timely objects to production of the metadata, the parties agree that the metadata should not be produced, or the producing party requests a protective order"), *Romero v. Allstate Ins. Co.*, 271 F.R.D. 96, 108 (E.D. Pa. 2010) (ordering production of documents "produced in native format with their associated metadata"), *Wyeth v. Impax Labs., Inc.*, 248 F.R.D. 169, 171 (D. Del. 2006) (noting a "general presumption against the production of metadata"), *and Ky. Speedway, LLC v. NASCAR, Inc.*, No. 05-138-WOB, 2006 U.S. Dist. LEXIS 92028, at *24, 2006 WL 5097354 (E.D. Ky. Dec. 18, 2006) (concluding that "[i]n most cases and for most documents, metadata does not provide relevant information"), *with In re Waste Mgmt. of Tex., Inc.* 392 S.W.3d 861, 876 (Tex. App.—Texarkana 2013, orig. proceeding) (upholding trial court's discovery order requiring production of metadata because $5,500 cost associated with such production was not "unduly burdensome"), *Holick v. Burkhart*, No. 16-1188-JTM-KGG, 2018 U.S. Dist. LEXIS 4844, at *10–12, 2018 WL 372440 (D. Kan. Jan. 11, 2018) (granting motion to compel metadata regarding plaintiff's claimed attorney's fees in light of the "death of information" regarding the plaintiff's fees claim), *In re Payment Card Interchange Fee, & Merch. Disc. Antitrust. Litig.*, No. MD 05-1720 (JG) (JO), 2007 U.S. Dist. LEXIS 2650, at *14–18, 2007 WL 121426 (E.D.N.Y. Jan. 12, 2007) (holding that documents stripped of metadata do not comply with Federal Rule 34(b)), *Williams v. Sprint/United Mgmt. Co.*, 230 F.R.D. 640, 652 (D. Kan. 2005) (noting that the removal of metadata "ordinarily requires an affirmative act by the producing party that alters the electronic document"), *and Wyeth v. Impax Labs., Inc.*, 248 F.R.D. 169, 171 (D. Del. 2006) ("Removal of metadata from an electronic document usually requires an affirmative alteration of that document, through scrubbing or converting the file from its native format to an image file, for example.").

[227] *See* Tex. R. Civ. P. 196.4 "(If the responding party cannot—through reasonable efforts—retrieve the data or information requested or produce it in the form requested, the

to a request for ESI, a party does not have to create electronic documents that never existed.[228] Rather, as explained in this Chapter, when a specific request for ESI has been served, Texas Rule 196.4 "requires a responding party to either produce [ESI] that is reasonably available to [it] in its ordinary course of business, or object on the grounds that the information cannot through reasonable efforts be retrieved or produced in the form requested."[229]

"Because parties' electronic systems, electronic storage, and retrieval capabilities will vary," Texas courts must assess whether requested ESI is "reasonably available in the ordinary course of business" on a case-by-case basis.[230] To do so, the trial court may order additional discovery, such as "requiring the responding party to sample or inspect the sources potentially containing information identified as not reasonably

---

responding party must state an objection complying with these rules."); Tex. R. Civ. P. 193 (addressing objections and assertions of privilege); *In re CI Host, Inc.*, 92 S.W.3d 514, 516 (Tex. 2002) (orig. proceeding) ("Without addressing the merits of CI Host's ECPA objection, we conclude that the trial court did not abuse its discretion in ordering the [backup] tapes produced because CI Host did not meet its burden to support its objection under our [Texas Rules] governing discovery. To object to a discovery request, the responding party must make a timely objection in writing and 'state specifically the legal or factual basis for the objection and the extent to which the party is refusing to comply with the request.' . . . Any party making an objection or asserting a privilege must present any evidence necessary to support the objection or privilege." (quoting Tex. R. Civ. P. 193.2(a))).

228 *In re Family Dollar Stores of Tex., LLC*, No. 09-11-00432-CV, 2011 Tex. App. LEXIS 8782, at *4–5, 2011 WL 5299578 (Tex. App.—Beaumont Nov. 3, 2011, orig. proceeding) (mem. op.) (per curiam) ("We conclude that requiring a party to reduce raw data from an electronic database to a paper report or to a list in an electronic form requires [the responding party] to make a list that does not currently exist" and, thus, an order compelling such production "is broader than the scope of discovery permitted by" the Texas Rules.).

229 Tex. R. Civ. P. 196.4; *see In re Weekley Homes, L.P.*, 295 S.W.3d 309, 315 (Tex. 2009) (orig. proceeding); *In re State Farm Lloyds*, 520 S.W.3d 595, 606 (Tex. 2017) (orig. proceeding).

230 *In re Weekley Homes, L.P.*, 295 S.W.3d 309, 315 (Tex. 2009) (orig. proceeding); *see In re State Farm Lloyds*, 520 S.W.3d 595, 606 (Tex. 2017) (orig. proceeding) (providing that "discovery of electronic data involves case-specific considerations"). There is little Texas law construing Texas Rule 196.4's requirement that a party produce ESI that is "reasonably available in the ordinary course of business." Federal cases construing the term "reasonably accessible" consider whether the ESI "is kept in an *accessible* or *inaccessible* format (a distinction that corresponds closely to the expense of production)." *Zubulake v. UBS Warburg LLC*, 217 F.R.D. 309, 318 (S.D.N.Y. 2003). In *Zubulake*, the court held that "[a]ctive, online data," "near-line data," and "offline storage/archives" are "typically . . . accessible," but "backup tapes" and "erased, fragmented or damaged data" are typically "inaccessible." *Zubulake v. UBS Warburg LLC*, 217 F.R.D. 309, 318–20 (S.D.N.Y. 2003); *see Best Buy Stores, L.P. v. Developers Diversified Realty Corp.*, 247 F.R.D. 567, 569–70 (D. Minn. 2007) (finding that ESI "no longer in a searchable format" and needing database restoration was "not at present reasonably accessible"); *Canon U.S.A., Inc. v. S.A.M., Inc.*, No. 07-01201 SECTION: "S", 2008 U.S. Dist. LEXIS 47712, at *7–8, 2008 WL 2522087 (E.D. La. June 20, 2008) ("Machine-readable data, such as active, online, near-line, or offline data in storage or archives are accessible, however, backup tapes and erased, fragmented, or damaged data is not accessible.").

available."[231] Depositions of witnesses knowledgeable about the responding party's information systems may also be permitted.[232]

8-6:5 Proportionality Inquiry and Case-by-Case Balancing Test

Although Texas Rule 196.4 requires the requesting party to specify the form in which it wants responsive ESI produced,[233] the Rule does not permit that party to determine unilaterally the form of production.[234] Rather, as the Texas Supreme Court stressed in *In re State Farm Lloyds*,[235] a party's entitlement to metadata and other forms of ESI ultimately turns on whether the discovery sought is proportional to the needs of the case.[236]

If a responding party timely objects that ESI "cannot be retrieved in the form requested through 'reasonable efforts' and asserts that the information is readily 'obtainable from some other source that is more convenient, less burdensome, or less expensive,' the trial court is obliged to consider whether production in the form requested should be denied in favor of a 'reasonably usable' alternative form."[237] If a reasonably usable alternative "form is readily available [to the responding party] in the ordinary course of business, the trial court must assess whether any enhanced burden or expense associated with a requested form is justified when weighed against the proportional needs of the case."[238] This fact-specific "proportionality inquiry requires case-by-case balancing[.]"[239]

In assessing proportionality, a trial court must consider the following factors: (1) the likely benefit of producing ESI in the requested form,[240] (2) the needs of the

---

231 *In re Weekley Homes, L.P.*, 295 S.W.3d 309, 315 (Tex. 2009) (orig. proceeding); *accord* Fed. R. Civ. P. 26(b)(2)(B), Advisory Committee Notes to the 2006 Amend.

232 *In re Weekley Homes, L.P.*, 295 S.W.3d 309, 315 (Tex. 2009) (orig. proceeding); Tex. R. Civ. P. 195.1; *cf. O'Gara v. Equifax Info. Servs. LLC,* No. 1:16-cv-01237-TWP-MPB, 2018 U.S. Dist. LEXIS 10361, at *12–14 (S.D. Ind. Jan. 23, 2018) (compelling discovery of documents sufficient to identify responding party's electronic-storage systems).

233 *In re State Farm Lloyds*, 520 S.W.3d 595, 599 (Tex. 2017) (orig. proceeding).

234 *In re State Farm Lloyds*, 520 S.W.3d 595, 607 (Tex. 2017) (orig. proceeding).

235 *In re State Farm Lloyds*, 520 S.W.3d 595, 614–15 (Tex. 2017) (orig. proceeding).

236 *See In re State Farm Lloyds*, 520 S.W.3d 595, 607 (Tex. 2017) (orig. proceeding) ("Ultimately, the court's responsibility, using all the information provided by the parties, is to consider the proportionality factors in reaching a case-specific determination of the appropriate scope of discovery. The same applies with regard to electronic-discovery practices under the Texas Rules of Civil Procedure.") (footnote omitted) (internal quotation marks omitted).

237 *In re State Farm Lloyds*, 520 S.W.3d 595, 607 (Tex. 2017) (orig. proceeding).

238 *In re State Farm Lloyds*, 520 S.W.3d 595, 607 (Tex. 2017) (orig. proceeding) (quoting Tex. R. Civ. P. 192.4(a)).

239 *In re State Farm Lloyds*, 520 S.W.3d 595, 607 (Tex. 2017) (orig. proceeding) (quoting Tex. R. Civ. P. 192.4(a)).

240 *In re State Farm Lloyds*, 520 S.W.3d 595, 608 (Tex. 2017) (orig. proceeding) ("If the benefits of the requested form are negligible, nonexistent, or merely speculative, any enhanced efforts or expense attending the requested form of production is undue and sufficient to deny the requested discovery. In such cases, quantifying or estimating time and expenses would not be critical, as it may be when benefits clearly exist. At the opposite end of the spectrum, a particularized need for the proposed discovery will weigh heavily in favor of

case,[241] (3) the amount in controversy,[242] (4) the parties' resources,[243] (5) the importance of the issues at stake in the litigation,[244] (6) the importance of the proposed discovery in resolving the litigation,[245] and (7) "[a]ny other articulable factor bearing on proportionality[.]"[246] The Texas Supreme Court explained each factor in *In re State Farm Lloyds*.[247] It addressed metadata in relation to second factor, providing the following guidance:

> Relevance of metadata and the relative significance to the case must be determined on a case-by-case basis. But metadata's relevance must be obvious or at least linked, more or less concretely, to a claim or defense. Hypothetical needs, surmise, and suspicion should be afforded no weight. As a general proposition, metadata may be necessary to the litigation when the who, what, where, when, and why ESI was generated is an actual issue in the case, not merely a helpful or theoretical issue.[248]

In sum, whether metadata or any other form of ESI is discoverable varies with the circumstances of each case pending in Texas state court. As aforementioned, this case-specific approach to assessing discoverability of ESI is based on, and consistent with, federal discovery procedures relating to ESI.[249]

---

allowing discovery as requested but, depending on the force of other prudential concerns, may warrant cost-shifting for any 'extraordinary steps' required. Courts should consider cumulative effects rather than viewing benefits and burdens in a vacuum. . . ."); *see also In re Waste Mgmt. of Tex., Inc.*, 392 S.W.3d 861, 875–76 (Tex. App.—Texarkana 2013, orig. proceeding) (holding that the additional cost of $5,500 to produce metadata to comply with a court order was not "unduly burdensome").

241 *In re State Farm Lloyds*, 520 S.W.3d 595, 608–09 (Tex. 2017) (orig. proceeding).

242 *In re State Farm Lloyds*, 520 S.W.3d 595, 609 (Tex. 2017) (orig. proceeding).

243 *In re State Farm Lloyds*, 520 S.W.3d 595, 610 (Tex. 2017) (orig. proceeding).

244 *In re State Farm Lloyds*, 520 S.W.3d 595, 610–11 (Tex. 2017) (orig. proceeding).

245 *In re State Farm Lloyds*, 520 S.W.3d 595, 611 (Tex. 2017) (orig. proceeding).

246 *In re State Farm Lloyds*, 520 S.W.3d 595, 611–12 (Tex. 2017) (orig. proceeding).

247 *See In re State Farm Lloyds*, 520 S.W.3d 595, 608–12 (Tex. 2017) (orig. proceeding).

248 *In re State Farm Lloyds*, 520 S.W.3d 595, 609 (Tex. 2017) (orig. proceeding); *see also In re State Farm Lloyds*, 520 S.W.3d 595, 605 (Tex. 2017) (orig. proceeding) ("[W]hile metadata may generally be discoverable if relevant and unprivileged, that does not mean production in a metadata-friendly format is necessarily required. Indeed, as a federal district court recently observed, 'a weak presumption against the production of metadata has taken hold,' which may be due to 'metadata's status as "the new black," with parties increasingly seeking its production in every case, regardless of size or complexity.'" (quoting *U.S. ex rel. Carter v. Bridgepoint Educ., Inc.*, 305 F.R.D. 225, 246 (S.D. Cal. 2015))).

249 *See In re State Farm Lloyds*, 520 S.W.3d 595, 611–12 (Tex. 2017) (orig. proceeding) ("Our application of proportionality principles in this context aligns electronic-discovery practice under the Texas Rules of Civil Procedure with electronic-discovery practice under the Federal Rules of Civil Procedure."). Despite the Texas Supreme Court's alignment of Texas's electronic-discovery procedure with its federal counterpart, practitioners who turn to federal law for guidance on electronic-discovery issues should be mindful that the federal courts' treatment of certain electronic-discovery issues has been inconsistent. One common point of disagreement involves the scope of the requirements imposed by Federal Rule 34(b)(2)(E)(i) and (ii), that is, whether ESI produced as it is kept in the usual course of business pursuant to Federal Rule 34(b)(2)(E)(ii) must also comply with the organizational requirement imposed by Federal Rule 34(b)(2)(E)(i). *See, e.g., McKinney/Pearl Rest.*

8-6:6 Objections and Hearing on Requests for Production of ESI

The party responding to a request for ESI has a duty to object only to the production of ESI that is specifically requested.[250] If the party has produced all responsive ESI in its possession, custody, and control, the party does not need to object under Texas Rule 196.4.[251] If an objection is made, "either party may request a hearing at which the responding party must present evidence to support the objection."[252]

The responding party bears the burden of proving that requested ESI is not reasonably available.[253] As discussed in Chapter 8, section 8-5:6, conclusory allegations of undue burden are insufficient. Rather, "a party resisting discovery of [ESI]

Partners, L.P. v. Metro. Life Ins. Co., 322 F.R.D. 235, 249 (N.D. Tex. 2016) ("Courts are split on whether both [Federal] Rule 34(b)(2)(E)(i) and [Federal] Rule 34(b)(2)(E)(ii) apply to ESI productions or whether an ESI production must comply with only [Federal] Rule 34(b)(2)(E)(ii)."). Given the unambiguous organization standard set forth in Texas Rule 196.3(c), the absence of any analog to Federal Rule 34(b)(2)(E)(ii) in the Texas Rules, and the Texas Supreme Court's focus on the form rather than the organization of electronic-discovery productions in *In re State Farm Lloyds*, federal cases on this issue should not affect Texas practice.

250 *MRT Inc. v. Vounckx*, 299 S.W.3d 500, 508–09 (Tex. App.—Dallas 2009, no pet.) ("Because appellant did not initially specifically request production of the backup tapes or documents that resided only on IMEC's backup tapes, we conclude IMEC had no duty to object in its responses that the backup tapes or the documents contained on them were not reasonably available.").

251 *In re Shipman*, 540 S.W.3d 562, 567 (Tex. 2018) (orig. proceeding) (per curiam) ("Insisting her request was sufficiently specific, Jamie argues we should decline to consider Shipman's arguments because he failed to object to her request as required under [Texas] Rule 196.4. She points us to Shipman's response to her second requests for production, in which Shipman objects to some requests and agrees to others, but never takes the position that the information requested is reasonably unavailable to him under [Texas] Rule 196.4. Shipman responds simply that because no specific [Texas] Rule 196.4 request was made, no [Texas] Rule 196.4 objection was required. Neither Jamie's argument nor Shipman's response correctly contemplates the relationship of [Texas] Rule 196.4 to this case. [Texas] Rule 196.4 requires the producing party to produce 'data that is responsive to the request and is reasonably available to the responding party in its ordinary course of business.' Shipman's position is that all responsive documents in his possession have been produced. He does not claim to hold back anything on the basis that it is not reasonably available to him in the course of his business. In this case, Shipman could not lodge a [Texas] Rule 196.4 objection without contradicting his position that he had produced all responsive documents in his possession." (citations omitted) (quoting Tex. R. Civ. P. 196.4)).

252 *In re State Farm Lloyds*, 520 S.W.3d 595, 615 (Tex. 2017) (orig. proceeding); *In re Weekley Homes, L.P.*, 295 S.W.3d 309, 315 (Tex. 2009) (orig. proceeding); Tex. R. Civ. P. 193.4(a); *see also In re Harris*, 315 S.W.3d 685, 701–02 (Tex. App.—Houston [1st Dist.] 2010, orig. proceeding) ("We conclude that the trial court abused its discretion . . . by compelling production of overly broad discovery without addressing Harris's objections and without a motion to compel discovery from Harris before it[.]").

253 *In re Weekley Homes, L.P.*, 295 S.W.3d 309, 315, 322 (Tex. 2009) (orig. proceeding); *In re Waste Mgmt. of Tex., Inc.* 392 S.W.3d 861, 873 (Tex. App.—Texarkana 2013, orig. proceeding); *cf. Allstate Ins. Co. v. Papanek*, No. 3:15-CV-240, 2018 U.S. Dist. LEXIS 2253, at *12–13 (S.D. Ohio Jan. 5, 2018) (granting motion to compel production of ESI because respondent failed to present any "actual evidence" that the information requested imposed and undue burden or cost).

must produce some evidence supporting its objection."[254] To gather such evidence, focused discovery may be required, such as "sampling of the sources, to learn more about what burdens and costs are involved in assessing the information, what the information consists of, and how valuable it is for the litigation in light of information that can be obtained by exhausting other opportunities for discovery."[255] If the responding party fails to meet its burden of proof on the objection, a trial court may order production subject to the general limitations on discovery imposed by Texas Rule 192.4.[256]

Even if the responding party satisfies its burden of proving that requested ESI is not reasonably available, the trial court may nevertheless order targeted production upon a showing that "any enhanced burden or expense associated with [the] requested form is justified when weighed against the proportional needs of the case."[257] Under those circumstances, however, the trial court "must also order that the requesting party pay the reasonable expenses of any extraordinary steps required to retrieve and produce the information."[258]

When assessing proportionality complaints, a trial court should consider Federal Rule 26(b)(1) and cases construing it because "[t]he factors expressly identified [in Federal Rule 26(b)(1)] as limitations on the scope of discovery accord with the proportionality analysis that [the Texas Supreme Court has] explicated under [the Texas] discovery rules, keeping [Texas] procedures in line with their federal counterparts."[259] In its decision in *In re State Farm Lloyds*, the Supreme Court addressed "[r]ecent federal cases provid[ing] helpful examples of proportionality analyses in e-discovery cases," pointing out that: "Ultimately, the [federal] 'court's responsibility, using all the information provided by the parties, is to consider [the proportionality] factors in reaching a case-specific determination of the appropriate scope of discovery.'"[260] The Court then concluded that "[t]he same applies with regard to electronic-discovery practices under the Texas Rules of Civil Procedure."[261]

8-6:7 Access to Electronic-Storage Devices

Any "[i]ntrusive discovery measures"—including orders granting "direct access to an opponent's electronic[-]storage device—require, at a minimum, that the benefits of

---

[254] *In re Waste Mgmt. of Tex., Inc.*, 392 S.W.3d 861, 875 (Tex. App.—Texarkana 2013, orig. proceeding).

[255] *In re Weekley Homes, L.P.*, 295 S.W.3d 309, 315–16 (Tex. 2009) (orig. proceeding) (quoting Fed. R. Civ. P. 26(b)(2)(B), Advisory Committee Notes to the 2006 Amend.).

[256] *E.g., In re Weekley Homes, L.P.*, 295 S.W.3d 309, 315 (Tex. 2009) (orig. proceeding).

[257] *In re State Farm Lloyds*, 520 S.W.3d 595, 607 (Tex. 2017) (orig. proceeding); *see In re Wilcox*, No. 09-20-00271-CV, 2021 Tex. App. LEXIS 2042, at *9–11, 2021 WL 1031141 (Tex. App.—Beaumont Mar. 18, 2021, orig. proceeding) (mem. op.) ("There must be proportionality between the devices and media covered by the order and the documents sought by the requesting party.").

[258] Tex. R. Civ. P. 196.4; *In re State Farm Lloyds*, 520 S.W.3d 595, 608 (Tex. 2017) (orig. proceeding); *In re Weekley Homes, L.P.*, 295 S.W.3d 309, 316 (Tex. 2009) (orig. proceeding).

[259] *In re State Farm Lloyds*, 520 S.W.3d 595, 613 (Tex. 2017) (orig. proceeding).

[260] *In re State Farm Lloyds*, 520 S.W.3d 595, 615 (Tex. 2017) (orig. proceeding) (quoting Fed. R. Civ. P. 26, Advisory Committee Notes to the 2015 Amend.).

[261] *In re State Farm Lloyds*, 520 S.W.3d 595, 615 (Tex. 2017) (orig. proceeding).

the discovery measure outweigh the burden imposed upon the discovered party."[262] Direct access to a responding party's electronic-storage device "is particularly intrusive and should be generally discouraged, just as permitting open access to a party's file cabinets for general perusal would be."[263] The Texas Supreme Court's decisions in *In re Shipman*[264] and *In re Weekley Homes*[265] set forth when a party's request to take possession of, and examine, another party's electronic-storage device can be granted.[266]

To obtain access to an electronic-storage device, the requesting party must make a threshold showing "that the responding party has somehow defaulted in its obligation to search its records and produce the requested data."[267] This showing cannot

---

[262] *In re Weekley Homes, L.P.*, 295 S.W.3d 309, 322 (Tex. 2009) (orig. proceeding), *quoted in In re Shipman*, 540 S.W.3d 562, 565 (Tex. 2018) (orig. proceeding) (per curiam); *accord In re Wilcox*, No. 09-20-00271-CV, 2021 Tex. App. LEXIS 2042, at *9, 2021 WL 1031141 (Tex. App.—Beaumont Mar. 18, 2021, orig. proceeding) (mem. op.).

[263] *In re Weekley Homes, L.P.*, 295 S.W.3d 309, 317 (Tex. 2009) (orig. proceeding), *quoted in In re Shipman*, 540 S.W.3d 562, 566 (Tex. 2018) (orig. proceeding) (per curiam); *accord In re Pinnacle Eng'g, Inc.*, 405 S.W.3d 835, 846 (Tex. App.—Houston [1st Dist.] 2013, orig. proceeding).

[264] *In re Shipman*, 540 S.W.3d 562 (Tex. 2018) (orig. proceeding) (per curiam).

[265] *In re Weekley Homes, L.P.*, 295 S.W.3d 309 (Tex. 2009) (orig. proceeding).

[266] *See In re Weekley Homes, L.P.*, 295 S.W.3d 309, 317–19 (Tex. 2009) (orig. proceeding) (adopting the "basic principles regarding direct access to a party's electronic storage device" established under federal law); *accord In re Shipman*, 540 S.W.3d 562, 565, 567–70 (Tex. 2018) (orig. proceeding) (per curiam) (applying the direct-access standards established in *In re Weekley Homes*); *accord In re VERP Inv., LLC*, 457 S.W.3d 255, 261 (Tex. App.—Dallas 2015, orig. proceeding) (explaining that *In re Weekley Homes* imposes "evidentiary requirements . . . on a party requesting direct access to an opponent's electronic device"); *In re Master Flo Valve Inc.*, 485 S.W.3d 207, 219–21 (Tex. App.—Houston [14th Dist.] 2016, orig. proceeding) (citing *In re Weekley* to deny motion to compel certain keyword searches on responding party's email and electronic filing systems).

[267] *In re Weekley Homes, L.P.*, 295 S.W.3d 309, 317 (Tex. 2009) (orig. proceeding); *accord In re Shipman*, 540 S.W.3d 562, 567 (Tex. 2018) (orig. proceeding) (per curiam); *accord In re Wilcox*, No. 09-20-00271-CV, 2021 Tex. App. LEXIS 2042, at *9, 2021 WL 1031141 (Tex. App.—Beaumont Mar. 18, 2021, orig. proceeding) (mem. op.); *In re Methodist Primary Care Grp.*, 553 S.W.3d 709, 718 (Tex. App.—Houston [14th Dist.] 2018, orig. proceeding); *In re VERP Inv., LLC*, 457 S.W.3d 255, 262 (Tex. App.—Dallas 2015, orig. proceeding); *In re Pinnacle Eng'g, Inc.*, 405 S.W.3d 835, 843–44 (Tex. App.—Houston [1st Dist.] 2013, orig. proceeding) (holding that the trial court abused its discretion in compelling the responding parties to turn over their computer and network server hard drives without requiring the requesting party to demonstrate that they defaulted on their discovery obligations or that their production was otherwise inadequate); *cf. Scotts Co. v. Liberty Mut. Ins. Co.*, No. Civ. A. 2:06-CV-899, 2007 U.S. Dist. LEXIS 43005, at *5, 2007 WL 1723509 (S.D. Ohio June 12, 2007) ("Plaintiff in this case requests intrusive examination of its opponent's computer systems on the mere suspicion, based solely on the nature of the claims asserted, that defendant may be withholding discoverable information. Plaintiff's speculation is, in the view of this Court, entirely insufficient."); *Diepenhorst v. City of Battle Creek*, No. 1:05-CV-734, 2006 U.S. Dist. LEXIS 48551, at *10, 2006 WL 1851243 (W.D. Mich. June 30, 2006) (mem. op.) ("In the absence of a strong showing that the responding party has somehow defaulted in this obligation, the court should not resort to extreme, expensive, or extraordinary means to guarantee compliance."); *Powers v. Thomas M. Cooley Law Sch.*, No. 5:05-CV-117, 2006 U.S. Dist. LEXIS 67706, at *14, 2006 WL 2711512 (W.D. Mich. Sept. 21, 2006) (mem. op.) (same).

be made through "mere skepticism or bare allegations that the responding party has failed to comply with its discovery duties."[268] Thus, for example, the requesting party must show "that the responding party's production has been inadequate and that a search of the opponent's electronic-storage device could recover deleted relevant materials."[269] An allegation that a responding party failed to search for relevant deleted information, without evidence that an electronic search would likely reveal deleted emails or that they could be recovered, is insufficient to permit direct access.[270] In this regard, "[t]he Texas Supreme Court has specifically rejected as insufficient . . . conclusory statements made by requesting counsel that certain emails 'must exist,' and [has] held that such statements do not justify" a trial court's order requiring production of hard drives for direct access.[271] The Texas Supreme Court also has rejected as insufficient unsubstantiated assertions about a responding party's technical ineptitude as well as the notion that a responding party's "equivocation about the existence of discrete documents . . . [will] transform general skepticism into discovery default" that justifies direct access to an electronic-storage device.[272] Direct access is more

---

[268] *In re Weekley Homes, L.P.*, 295 S.W.3d 309, 318 (Tex. 2009) (orig. proceeding); *quoted in In re Shipman*, 540 S.W.3d 562, 567 (Tex. 2018) (orig. proceeding) (per curiam).

[269] *In re Weekley Homes, L.P.*, 295 S.W.3d 309, 317 (Tex. 2009) (orig. proceeding); *In re VERP Inv., LLC*, 457 S.W.3d 255, 262 (Tex. App.—Dallas 2015, orig. proceeding); *accord In re Methodist Primary Care Grp.*, 553 S.W.3d 709, 718 (Tex. App.—Houston [14th Dist.] 2018, orig. proceeding) ("Specifically, the requesting party should show that there is a reasonable likelihood that a search of the computers will reveal the information that the requesting party seeks."); *In re Pinnacle Eng'g, Inc.*, 405 S.W.3d 835, 844 (Tex. App.—Houston [1st Dist.] 2013, orig. proceeding) ("Houde presented no evidence that relator's production has been inadequate or a search of relators' computers and network server hard drives could recover relevant materials."); *In re Stern*, 321 S.W.3d 828, 845 (Tex. App.—Houston [1st Dist.] 2010, orig. proceeding) ("There was thus no showing that a search of Stern's computer hard drive could recover deleted relevant materials.").

[270] *In re Weekley Homes, L.P.*, 295 S.W.3d 309, 320 (Tex. 2009) (orig. proceeding) ("The missing step is a demonstration that the particularities of Weekley's electronic information storage methodology will allow retrieval of emails that have been deleted or overwritten, and what that retrieval will entail."); *In re Methodist Primary Care Grp.*, 553 S.W.3d 709, 718 (Tex. App.—Houston [14th Dist.] 2018, orig. proceeding) ("A court may not rely on 'mere skepticism or bare allegations that the responding party has failed to comply with its discovery duties.'" (quoting *In re Weekley Homes, L.P.*, 295 S.W.3d 309, 317–18))); *In re Pinnacle Eng'g, Inc.*, 405 S.W.3d 835, 844–45 (Tex. App.—Houston [1st Dist.] 2013, orig. proceeding) ("The requesting party must demonstrate that data retrieval is feasible. . . . The trial court did not require Houde to demonstrate that relators' electronic information storage methodology would allow the retrieval of these documents, including the deleted version of Houde's resume, or what the retrieval will entail as required by *In re Weekley Homes* to justify the appointment of a forensic expert to examine the hard drives."); *see also In re Clark*, 345 S.W.3d 209, 212 (Tex. App.—Beaumont 2011, orig. proceeding) (per curiam) (considering affidavit testimony from a forensic expert that "a forensic analysis of Clark's computer will produce relevant information that has been requested but has not been produced").

[271] *In re Pinnacle Eng'g, Inc.*, 405 S.W.3d 835, 844 (Tex. App.—Houston [1st Dist.] 2013, orig. proceeding) (citing *In re Weekley Homes, L.P.*, 295 S.W.3d 309, 317–18, 320 (Tex. 2009) (orig. proceeding)).

[272] *In re Shipman*, 540 S.W.3d 562, 569 (Tex. 2018) (orig. proceeding) (per curiam).

likely to be granted "when there is some direct relationship between the electronic storage device and the claim itself."[273]

When these threshold requirements are met, the trial court still "should not permit the requesting party itself to access the opponent's storage device; rather, only a qualified expert should be afforded such access."[274] The responding party need not challenge the expert's qualifications; rather, the requesting party must establish that its expert is qualified to perform the forensic examination of the electronic devices.[275] An expert will be afforded access "only when there is some indication that retrieval of the data sought is feasible."[276]

An expert, however, will not be given "carte blanche authorization to sort through the responding party's electronic[-]storage device."[277] When a court order for direct

---

[273] *In re Weekley Homes, L.P.*, 295 S.W.3d 309, 319 (Tex. 2009) (orig. proceeding); *In re Wilcox*, No. 09-20-00271-CV, 2021 Tex. App. LEXIS 2042, at *9–11, 2021 WL 1031141(Tex. App.—Beaumont Mar. 18, 2021, orig. proceeding) (mem. op.) (conditionally granting mandamus relief when, in a business dispute, a trial court ordered the defendant's personal home computer, personal cell phone, and personal account and storage information be turned over to a third party for examination when the court could have required that the defendant to run "specific searches and produce responsive data narrowly tailored to the parties' dispute"); *In re Stern*, 321 S.W.3d 828, 845 (Tex. App.—Houston [1st Dist.] 2010, orig. proceeding) (conditionally granting mandamus relief because "there was no showing of a direct relationship between the ordered search of Stern's hard drive and the establishment of the trial court's jurisdiction over Stern").

[274] *In re Weekley Homes, L.P.*, 295 S.W.3d 309, 318 (Tex. 2009) (orig. proceeding); *In re Pinnacle Eng'g, Inc.*, 405 S.W.3d 835, 845 (Tex. App.—Houston [1st Dist.] 2013, orig. proceeding).

[275] *In re VERP Inv., LLC*, 457 S.W.3d 255, 263 (Tex. App.—Dallas 2015, orig. proceeding); *see In re Weekley Homes, L.P.*, 295 S.W.3d 309, 321 (Tex. 2009) (orig. proceeding) (finding that the trial court abused its discretion by ordering forensic examination of hard drives without any evidence that the experts are familiar with the particularities of the hard drives, that they are qualified to search those hard drives, and that the proposed methodology for searching those hard drives is reasonably likely to yield the information sought); *In re Pinnacle Eng'g, Inc.*, 405 S.W.3d 835, 845 (Tex. App.—Houston [1st Dist.] 2013, orig. proceeding) ("Houde presented nothing in his motion to show that his expert is qualified to perform the searches on the specific storage devices at issue or the search methodology would likely retrieve the documents. . . . Houde [had to] demonstrate that his expert is familiar with the particularities of relators' computer and network server hard drive, he is qualified to search those hard drives, and the expert's proposed search methodology is reasonably likely to yield the information he seeks."); *In re Jordan*, 364 S.W.3d 425, 426–27 (Tex. App.—Dallas 2012, orig. proceeding) (finding an abuse of discretion in allowing direct access to the plaintiff's personal computer where the defendant failed to demonstrate the particular characteristics of the personal computer, the familiarity of its experts with those characteristics, the search methodology or how the proposed search methodology would yield the information sought, or its experts' credentials).

[276] *In re Weekley Homes, L.P.*, 295 S.W.3d 309, 318 (Tex. 2009) (orig. proceeding); *In re VERP Inv., LLC*, 457 S.W.3d 255, 263 (Tex. App.—Dallas 2015, orig. proceeding); *see, e.g., In re Stern*, 321 S.W.3d 828, 846 (Tex. App.—Houston [1st Dist.] 2010, orig. proceeding) (finding that the trial court "clearly erred" by ordering the production of a hard drive without any showing that retrieval of emails was feasible).

[277] *In re Pinnacle Eng'g, Inc.*, 405 S.W.3d 835, 846 (Tex. App.—Houston [1st Dist.] 2013, orig. proceeding); *accord In re Stern*, 321 S.W.3d 828, 846 (Tex. App.—Houston [1st Dist.] 2010, orig. proceeding) ("Granting a special master carte blanch authorization to sort through Stern's computer hard drive clearly violated the longstanding prohibition against impermissible 'fishing expeditions'.").

access to a party's electronic-storage device is appropriate, the trial court must order "the least intrusive means of retrieval" and otherwise address privilege, privacy, and confidentiality concerns.[278] Courts in Texas and elsewhere also have held that certain protocols are necessary and appropriate for allowing such access, including limitations on what may be searched.[279] For example, the Waco Court of Appeals held the following protocol was not "overbroad" and was "appropriately tailored . . . to prohibit the unauthorized disclosure of privileged or confidential information":

> First, the party seeking discovery selects a forensic expert to make a mirror image of the computer hard drives at issue. This expert is required to perform the analysis subject to the terms of a protective order, generally prohibiting the expert from disclosing confidential or otherwise privileged information other than under the terms of the discovery order.
>
> After creating the mirror images and analyzing them for relevant documents or partial documents, courts typically require the expert to compile the documents or partial documents obtained and provide copies to the party opposing discovery. That party is then to review the documents, produce those responsive to the discovery request, and create a privilege log for those withheld. Finally, the trial court will conduct an in-camera review should any disputes arise regarding the entries in the privilege log.[280]

---

278 *In re Weekley Homes, L.P.*, 295 S.W.3d 309, 316, 318 (Tex. 2009) (orig. proceeding); *accord In re Pinnacle Eng'g, Inc.*, 405 S.W.3d 835, 846 (Tex. App.—Houston [1st Dist.] 2013, orig. proceeding) (holding that the trial court abused its discretion when electronic-discovery order did not provide "any mechanism through which Relators can withhold from discovery any documents or information that is privileged or confidential"); *In re M*, No. 09-12-00179-CV, 2012 Tex. App. LEXIS 3934, at *6–7 (Tex. App.—Beaumont May 17, 2012, orig. proceeding) (mem. op.) (per curiam) ("Because the trial court ordered intrusive discovery of the cellular phones for use in future hearings without first having the parties comply with [Texas] Rule 196 and without providing an adequate mechanism for the assertion of objections and privileges concerning data that had not been published in the previous hearing, we hold that the trial court abused its discretion."); *In re Clark*, 345 S.W.3d 209, 213 (Tex. App.—Beaumont 2011, orig. proceeding) (per curiam) ("[T]he trial court must provide a mechanism through which Clark can withhold from discovery any documents or information that is privileged or confidential and provide instead a privilege log subject to in camera review by the trial court.").

279 *E.g., In re Honza*, 242 S.W.3d 578, 581–83 (Tex. App.—Waco 2008, orig. proceeding); *Antioch Co. v. Scrapbook Borders, Inc.*, 210 F.R.D. 645, 653–54 (D. Minn. 2002) (setting forth protocol for expert direct access to computer equipment); *Simon Prop. Grp. L.P. v. MySimon, Inc.*, 194 F.R.D. 639, 641–42 (S.D. Ind. 2000) (same); *Row Entm't, Inc. v. William Morris Agency, Inc.*, 205 F.R.D. 421, 432–33 (S.D.N.Y. 2002) (same); *see also In re Pinnacle Eng'g, Inc.*, 405 S.W.3d 835, 846–47 (Tex. App.—Houston [1st Dist.] 2013, orig. proceeding) (holding that the trial court abused its discretion in compelling the responding parties to turn over their computer and network server hard drives without providing search parameters limiting access by the forensic-computer expert).

280 *In re Honza*, 242 S.W.3d 578, 582 (Tex. App.—Waco 2008, orig. proceeding). *But see In re Weekley Homes, L.P.*, 295 S.W.3d 309, 320–21 (Tex. 2009) (orig. proceeding) (acknowledging the similarities between the order entered in *Honza* and the order at issue in *Weekley*, but distinguishing the facts of the two cases because, in *Honza*: (1) the requesting party sought metadata associated with two specific documents that had already been produced in

Texas courts generally have rejected the appointment of special masters to oversee the imaging and production of ESI.[281] If such an approach is taken, the court must comply with the requirements of Texas Rule 171 regarding the appointment of special masters.[282]

8-6:8 Availability of Mandamus

A party may seek mandamus relief to address an electronic-discovery order that fails to comply with Texas Rule 196.4's electronic-discovery procedures, is overbroad, or fails to protect from disclosure either confidential or privileged information.[283]

8-7 Request or Motion for Entry on Property

Few "reported decisions interpret [Texas] Rule 196.7."[284] However, a few main principles "have emerged from those decisions."[285] First, Texas Rule 196.7 does not allow for

---

electronic form, (2) a direct relationship between the hard drives sought and the plaintiff's claims existed, and (3) the forensic expert testified extensively about his experience and qualifications); *In re VERP Inv., LLC*, 457 S.W.3d 255, 262 n.4 (Tex. App.—Dallas 2015, orig. proceeding) (distinguishing the order entered in *Honza* from the order at issue because the *Honza* order was (1) based on extensive testimony about the expert's experience and qualifications, (2) was extremely narrow, allowing a search for only two documents, and (3) provided that responsive documents be delivered to the responding party before production).

[281] *In re Stern*, 321 S.W.3d 828, 843–46 (Tex. App.—Houston [1st Dist.] 2010, orig. proceeding) (considering a discovery order requiring a party to turn ESI over to a court appointed special master); *In re Harris*, 315 S.W.3d 685, 703–06 (Tex. App.—Houston [1st Dist.] 2010, orig. proceeding) (same).

[282] *See In re Stern*, 321 S.W.3d 828, 845 (Tex. App.—Houston [1st Dist.] 2010, orig. proceeding) ("[T]he failure to follow the requirements of [Texas] Rule 171 in appointing a special master is an abuse of discretion."); *In re Harris*, 315 S.W.3d 685, 705–06 (Tex. App.—Houston [1st Dist.] 2010, orig. proceeding) (holding that the appointment of a forensic expert as a special master did not meet the "exceptional case/good cause criterion of [Texas] Rule 171").

[283] *E.g., In re Shipman*, 540 S.W.3d 562, 565–66 (Tex. 2018) (orig. proceeding) (per curiam); *In re Weekley Homes, L.P.*, 295 S.W.3d 309, 322–23 (Tex. 2009) (orig. proceeding); *In re Wilcox*, No. 09-20-00271-CV, 2021 Tex. App. LEXIS 2042, at *8–11, 2021 WL 1031141(Tex. App.—Beaumont Mar. 18, 2021, orig. proceeding) (mem. op.); *In re Methodist Primary Care Grp.*, 553 S.W.3d 709, 714 (Tex. App.—Houston [14th Dist.] 2018, orig. proceeding); *In re Pinnacle Eng'g, Inc.*, 405 S.W.3d 835, 847 (Tex. App.—Houston [1st Dist.] 2013, orig. proceeding); *see In re M*, No. 09-12-00179-CV, 2012 Tex. App. LEXIS 3934, at *6–7 (Tex. App.—Beaumont May 17, 2012, orig. proceeding) (mem. op.) (per curiam) ("Because the trial court ordered intrusive discovery of the cellular phones for use in future hearings without first having the parties comply with [Texas] Rule 196 and without providing an adequate mechanism for the assertion of objections and privileges concerning data that had not been published in the previous hearing, we hold that the trial court abused its discretion.").

[284] *In re Plains Pipeline, L.P.*, 08-19-00224-CV, 2020 Tex. App. LEXIS 8546, at *16, 2020 WL 6375332 (Tex. App.—El Paso Oct. 30, 2020, orig. proceeding); *see e.g. In re Sun City Gun Exch., Inc.*, 545 S.W.3d 1, 7 (Tex. App.—El Paso 2017, orig. proceeding); *In re Goodyear Tire & Rubber Co.*, 437 S.W.3d 923, 928 (Tex. App.—Dallas 2014, orig. proceeding); *In re Kimberly-Clark Corp.*, 228 S.W.3d 480, 486 (Tex. App.—Dallas 2007, orig. proceeding) (following cases because of a dearth of on-point Texas-specific decisions).

[285] *In re Plains Pipeline, L.P.*, 08-19-00224-CV, 2020 Tex. App. LEXIS 8546, at *16, 2020 WL 6375332 (Tex. App.—El Paso Oct. 30, 2020, orig. proceeding).

blanket discovery on threadbare requests when confronted with an objection.[286] Said requests mandate a heightened review "[b]ecause discovery involving entry onto the property of another involves unique burdens and risks[.]"[287] Second, Texas Rule 196.7 is subject to general discovery principals.[288] In other words, the request must be relevant,[289] the discovery sought cannot be obtainable from a more convenient, less burdensome, or less expensive source,[290] and the burden of the proposed discovery must not outweigh its likely benefits.[291]

Texas Rule 196.7 authorizes the entry "on designated land or other property" of both parties and nonparties "to inspect, measure, survey, photograph, test, or sample the property or any designated object or operation thereon[.]" "[M]ost cases involving on-site inspections concern a specific object on the premises, which is the subject matter of the action, e.g., a particular machine in a personal injury case or a patent infringement case."[292] Courts, under Texas Rule 196.7 and the comparable Federal Rule, Rule 34(a)(2),[293] have allowed entry on an oil and gas lease,[294] a coal mine,[295] a

---

286 *In re Plains Pipeline, L.P.*, 08-19-00224-CV, 2020 Tex. App. LEXIS 8546, at *16, 2020 WL 6375332 (Tex. App.—El Paso Oct. 30, 2020, orig. proceeding); *In re Kimberley-Clark Corp.*, 228 S.W.3d 480, 487 (Tex. App.—Dallas 2007, orig. proceeding).

287 *In re Plains Pipeline, L.P.*, 08-19-00224-CV, 2020 Tex. App. LEXIS 8546, at *16, 2020 WL 6375332 (Tex. App.—El Paso Oct. 30, 2020, orig. proceeding) (concluding that cases recognize the unique burdens and risks inherent to entry onto land, e.g., confusion and disruption of defendant's business and employees); *see also, e.g.*, *In re Goodyear Tire & Rubber Co.*, 437 S.W.3d 923, 928 (Tex. App. —Dallas 2014, orig. proceeding); *In re Kimberly-Clark Corp.*, 228 S.W.3d 480, 486 (Tex. App. —Dallas 2007, orig. proceeding) (same).

288 *In re Plains Pipeline, L.P.*, 08-19-00224-CV, 2020 Tex. App. LEXIS 8546, at *16, 2020 WL 6375332 (Tex. App.—El Paso Oct. 30, 2020, orig. proceeding); *In re Kimberley-Clark Corp.*, 228 S.W.3d 480, 486–87 (Tex. App.—Dallas 2007, orig. proceeding).

289 *In re Plains Pipeline, L.P.*, 08-19-00224-CV, 2020 Tex. App. LEXIS 8546, at *16, 2020 WL 6375332 (Tex. App.—El Paso Oct. 30, 2020, orig. proceeding); *In re Kimberley-Clark Corp.*, 228 S.W.3d 480, 487 (Tex. App.—Dallas 2007, orig. proceeding).

290 *In re Plains Pipeline, L.P.*, 08-19-00224-CV, 2020 Tex. App. LEXIS 8546, at *16, 2020 WL 6375332 (Tex. App.—El Paso Oct. 30, 2020, orig. proceeding); *In re Kimberley-Clark Corp.*, 228 S.W.3d 480, 487 (Tex. App.—Dallas 2007, orig. proceeding).

291 *In re Plains Pipeline, L.P.*, 08-19-00224-CV, 2020 Tex. App. LEXIS 8546, at *16, 2020 WL 6375332 (Tex. App.—El Paso Oct. 30, 2020, orig. proceeding (quoting *In re Sun City Gun Exch., Inc.*, 545 S.W.3d 1, 7 (Tex. App.—El Paso 2017, orig. proceeding)). See Chapter 8, section 8-7:2.

292 *In re Kimberley-Clark Corp.*, 228 S.W.3d 480, 486 (Tex. App.—Dallas 2007, orig. proceeding).

293 Federal Rule 34(a)(2) allows entry on a party's land or other property. Fed. R. Civ. P. 34(a)(2) ("A party may serve on any other party a request within the scope of [Federal] Rule 26(b) . . . to permit entry onto designated land or other property possessed or controlled by the responding party, so that the requesting party may inspect, measure, survey, photograph, test, or sample the property or any designated object or operation on it."). Federal Rule 45 allows entry on a nonparty's land or other property. Fed. R. Civ. P. 45 (a)(1)(A)(iii) ("A subpoena may command each person to whom it is directed to do the following at a specified time and place: . . . permit the inspection of premises[.]").

294 *In re Kimberley-Clark Corp.*, 228 S.W.3d 480, 486 (Tex. App.—Dallas 2007, orig. proceeding).

295 *E.g.*, *Clay v. Consol Pa. Coal Co.*, No. 5:12CV92, 2013 U.S. Dist. LEXIS 102896, *8–9 (N.D.W. Va. July 23, 2013).

manufacturing facility,[296] a business office,[297] a shopping center,[298] a store,[299] a school,[300] a prison or jail,[301] a distillery,[302] and a mental-health facility.[303]

8-7:1 The Request and Motion or Notice

To obtain entry on the land or other property of a party, the requesting party must serve a written request on all the parties to the action.[304] If, however, a nonparty owns the land or other property, the requesting party instead must serve "a motion and notice of hearing on all parties and the nonparty"[305] and must obtain a court order allowing entry.[306]

The nonparty notice can be served by one of the methods permitted by Texas Rule 21a.[307] "If the identity or address of the nonparty is unknown and cannot be obtained through reasonable diligence, the court must permit service by means other than those specified in [Texas] Rule 21a that are reasonably calculated to give the nonparty notice of the motion and hearing."[308] As with other written-discovery requests, the request or motion and notice must be served no later than 30 days (and in some cases 31 or 33 days) before the discovery period ends.[309]

---

296 *E.g., Cuno Inc. v. Pall Corp.*, 116 F.R.D. 279, 280–81 (E.D.N.Y. 1987); *Eirhart v. Libbey-Owens-Ford Co.*, 93 F.R.D. 370, 371–72 (N.D. Ill. 1981).

297 *E.g., Welzel v. Bernstein*, 233 F.R.D. 185, 186–87 (D.D.C. 2005).

298 *E.g., McConnell v. Canadian Pac. Realty Co.*, 280 F.R.D. 188, 193–96 (M.D. Pa. 2011) (in an Americans with Disability Act action, allowing inspection of barriers to access of a shopping mall).

299 *Wilson v. Wal-Mart Stores, Inc.*, No. 2:15-cv-1791-RCJ-VCF, 2016 U.S. Dist. LEXIS 15640, at *5–11, 2016 WL 526225 (D. Nev. Feb. 9, 2016) (allowing inspection of a Wal-Mart store in a slip-and-fall action).

300 *E.g., Keith H. v. Long Beach Unified School Dist.*, 228 F.R.D. 652, 658–59 (C. D. Cal. 2005); *City of Kingsport v. SCM Corp.*, 352 F. Supp. 287, 288 (E.D. Tenn. 1972) (allowing entry to remove roof panel for testing).

301 *E.g., Soler v. Cnty. of San Diego*, No. 14cv2470-MMA (RBB), 2016 U.S. Dist. LEXIS 82614, at *10–12, 2016 WL 3460255, (S.D. Cal. June 24, 2016) (county jail); *U.S. v. Erie Cnty.*, No. 09-CV-849S, 2010 U.S. Dist. LEXIS 25646, at *7–9, 2010 WL 986505 (W.D.N.Y. Mar. 17, 2010) (same); *Coleman v. Schwarzenegger*, Nos. CIV S-90-0520 LKK JFM P, C01-1351 TEH, 2007 U.S. Dist. LEXIS 99928, at *24–25, 2007 WL 3231706 (E.D. Cal. Oct. 30, 2007) (state prisons).

302 *Hofmann v. Fifth Generation, Inc.*, No. 14-cv-02569-JM-JLB, 2015 U.S. Dist. LEXIS 159515, at *8–11, 2015 WL 7582425 (S. D. Cal. Nov. 25, 2015).

303 *E.g., N.Y. State Ass'n for Retarded Children Inc. v. Carey*, 706 F.2d 956, 960–61 (2d Cir. 1983) (mental-health facility); *N.O. v. Callahan*, 110 F.R.D. 637, 640 (D. Mass. 1986) (same).

304 Tex. R. Civ. P. 196.7(a)(1).

305 Tex. R. Civ. P. 196.7(a)(2).

306 Tex. R. Civ. P. 196.7(d); *see In re Berry*, 578 S.W.3d 173, 179 (Tex. App.—Corpus Christi 2019, orig. proceeding) ("A party may compel discovery from a non-party—that is, a person who is not a party or subject to a party's control—only by obtaining a court order under [Texas] Rule[] 196.7. . . ."); *In re Total Petrochemicals & Ref. USA, Inc.*, 595 S.W.3d 904, 909 (Tex. App.—Houston [14th Dist.] 2020, orig. proceeding) (same).

307 *See* Tex. R. Civ. P. 196.7(d) (implication).

308 Tex. R. Civ. P. 196.7(d).

309 Tex. R. Civ. P. 196.7(a); *In re Swepi L.P.*, 103 S.W.3d 578, 590 (Tex. App.—San Antonio, 2003, orig. proceeding) ("To enter upon the land of a nonparty, the movant must, no later than 30 days before the end of the discovery period, serve a motion and notice of hearing on all

Texas Rule 196.7(b) sets forth the contents of the request for entry on a party's property and the order for entry on a nonparty's property.[310] Both "must state the time, place, manner, conditions, and scope of the inspection, and must specifically describe any desired means, manner, and procedure for testing or sampling, and the person or persons by whom the inspection, testing, or sampling is to be made."[311] A request or notice that lacks such specificity is objectionable and an order that lacks it is improper and can be challenged in a mandamus proceeding.[312]

A request to a party, like other written discovery served on parties, is not filed with the trial court.[313] The parties, however, are required by Texas Rule 191.4(d) to retain the request during the action's pendency and any appellate proceedings begun within six months after the judgment is signed.[314] The nonparty notice and motion, however, must be filed with the trial court by the requesting party.[315]

8-7:2 The Scope of a Request for Entry on a Party's Property

The scope of a request for entry on a party's property is subject to the general scope of discovery under Texas Rule 192.3(a) (i.e., the requested inspection, measurement, survey, photographing, testing, or sampling must be relevant to action's subject matter or reasonably calculated to lead to the discovery of admissible evidence).[316] Accordingly, the results of the inspection, measurement, survey, photographing, test-

---

parties and the nonparty owner."). If the request or notice and motion is served by mail, it must be served at least thirty-three days before the discovery period's end. *See* Tex. R. Civ. P. 21a(c). If it is served by fax after 5:00 p.m. local time of the recipient, the request or notice and motion must be served at least thirty-one days before the discovery period ends. *See* Tex. R. Civ. P. 21a(b)(2).

310 Tex. R. Civ. P. 196.7(b).

311 Tex. R. Civ. P. 196.7(b).

312 *In re Fuljenz's Mktg. Corp.*, No. 09-06-324 CV, 2006 Tex. App. LEXIS 9188, at *8, 2006 WL 3026821 (Tex. App.— Beaumont Oct. 26, 2006, orig. proceeding) (mem. op.) (per curiam) ("The record indicates that neither the June 6, 2006, nor the June 12, 2006, letter from Charnock's trial counsel to counsel for UCB mentioned anything about videotaping UCB's business offices or witnessing the business operations, nor do the letters indicate 'the scope of the inspection' or describe with any specificity what particular scenes are to be photographed, videotaped, or witnessed with regard to UCB's business operations. Obviously, since no detailed description of what scenes and/or items are to be photographed, videotaped, and/or witnessed by Charnock's trial counsel was provided, no threshold showing of relevance of any of this to the subject matter of the pending action has been made."); *see also In re Goodyear Tire & Rubber Co.*, 437 S.W.3d 923, 928 (Tex. App.—Dallas 2014orig. proceeding) ("Texas Rule of Civil Procedure 196.7 governs discovery that involves entering onto the land or property of another party to inspect, measure, survey, photograph, test, or sample the property or any designated object or operation. [Texas] Rule 196.7 'does not permit blanket discovery on a skeletal request when confronted with an objection.'" (quoting *In re Kimberly-Clark Corp.*, 228 S.W.3d 480, 487 (Tex. App.—Dallas 2007, orig. proceeding))).

313 Tex. R. Civ. P. 191.4(a)(2).

314 Tex. R. Civ. P. 191.4(d).

315 Tex. R. Civ. P. 191.4(b)(1), (2).

316 *In re Plains Pipeline, L.P.*, 08-19-00224-CV, 2020 Tex. App. LEXIS 8546, at *16, 2020 WL 6375332 (Tex. App.—El Paso Oct. 30, 2020, orig. proceeding); *In re Kimberley-Clark Corp.*,

ing, or sampling need not be admissible at trial to warrant the discovery. Thus, for example, the fact that some time has elapsed since an accident's occurrence does not necessarily preclude an inspection and photographing of the accident scene because the admissibility of any resulting photographs, measurements or tests can be determined at trial.[317]

Nonetheless, courts have "recognize[d] the unique burdens and risks inherent to entry onto land, e.g., confusion and disruption of defendant's business and employees."[318] Accordingly, "mere relevance is not sufficient to justify a request for entry upon the property of another[and] the trial court should conduct a 'greater inquiry into the necessity for the inspection, testing, or sampling."[319] And requests for entry

---

228 S.W.3d 480, 487 (Tex. App.—Dallas 2007, orig. proceeding). See also Chapter 4, section 4-3 (discussing written discovery's scope).

317 *Cf. Mulligan v. E. S.S. Lines, Inc.*, 6 F.R.D. 601, 606 (S.D.N.Y. 1946) (ordering a vessel's inspection two years after the plaintiff's injury occurred); *Farr v. Del., L. & W.R.R.*, 7 F.R.D. 494, 495 (S.D.N.Y. 1944) (ordering inspection of premises and equipment three years after the accident occurred).

318 *In re Plains Pipeline, L.P.*, 08-19-00224-CV, 2020 Tex. App. LEXIS 8546, at *16, 2020 WL 6375332 (Tex. App.—El Paso Oct. 30, 2020, orig. proceeding) (noting that cases recognize the unique burdens and risks inherent to entry onto land, e.g., confusion and disruption of defendant's business and employees); *In re Kimberley-Clark Corp.*, 228 S.W.3d 480, 486 (Tex. App.—Dallas 2007, orig. proceeding) ("Federal cases recognize the unique burdens and risks inherent to entry onto land, e.g., confusion and disruption of defendant's business and employees. In the context of a discovery request for entry onto land, the court must balance the degree to which the proposed inspection will aid in the search for truth against the burdens and dangers created by the inspection.") (citations omitted); *In re Plains Pipeline, L.P.*, 08-19-00224-CV, 2020 Tex. App. LEXIS 8546, at *16, 2020 WL 6375332 (Tex. App.—El Paso Oct. 30, 2020, orig. proceeding) (noting that cases recognize the unique burdens and risks inherent to entry onto land, e.g., confusion and disruption of defendant's business and employees); *In re Goodyear Tire & Rubber Co.*, 437 S.W.3d 923, 928 (Tex. App.—Dallas 2014, orig. proceeding) (same); *cf. Soler v. Cnty. of San Diego*, No. 14cv2470-MMA (RBB), 2016 U.S. Dist. LEXIS 82614, at *10–12, 2016 WL 3460255 (S.D. Cal. June 24, 2016) ("Since entry upon a party's premises may entail greater burdens and risks than mere production of documents, a greater inquiry into the necessity for inspection would seem warranted." (quoting *Keith H. v. Long Beach Unified Sch. Dist.*, 228 F.R.D. 652, 658–59 (C. D. Cal. 2005))).

319 *In re Plains Pipeline, L.P.*, 08-19-00224-CV, 2020 Tex. App. LEXIS 8546, at *16, 2020 WL 6375332 (Tex. App.—El Paso Oct. 30, 2020, orig. proceeding) (quoting *In re Goodyear Tire & Rubber Co.*, 437 S.W.3d 923, 928 (Tex. App.—Dallas 2014, orig. proceeding)); *In re Goodyear Tire & Rubber Co.*, 437 S.W.3d 923, 928 (Tex. App.—Dallas 2014, orig. proceeding) (quoting *In re Kimberley-Clark Corp.*, 228 S.W.3d 480, 486 (Tex. App.—Dallas 2007, orig. proceeding)); *accord In re Sun City Gun Exch., Inc.*, 545 S.W.3d 1, 7 (Tex. App.—El Paso 2017, orig. proceeding) ("Because discovery involving entry onto the property of another involves unique burdens and risks, the trial court is required to conduct a greater inquiry into the necessity for the inspection, testing, or sampling. In conducting this inquiry, the trial court must balance the degree to which the proposed inspection will aid in the search for truth against the burdens and dangers created by the inspection.") (citations omitted); *In re Goodyear Tire & Rubber Co.*, No. 04-16-00590-CV, 2017 Tex. App. LEXIS 3676, at *8–9, 2017 WL 1787735 (Tex. App.—San Antonio Apr. 26, 2017, orig. proceeding) (mem. op.) ("A party seeking entry onto property bears the burden of showing more than 'mere relevance.' 'Discovery involving entry onto the property of another involves unique burdens and risks including, among other things, confusion and disruption of the defendant's

on land or other property, more so than other discovery devices, are subject to both proportionality objections and Texas Rule 192.4, which limits a party's ability to obtain discovery that is "unreasonably cumulative or duplicative, or can be obtained from some other source that is more convenient, less burdensome, or less expensive" or whose burden "likely outweighs its likely benefit."[320] "However, the burden is on the responding party to satisfy the court that the [inspection, measurement, survey, photographing,] testing [, or sampling] 'should not be had.'"[321]

---

business and employees.'" (quoting *In re Goodyear Tire & Rubber Co.*, 437 S.W.3d 923, 928 (Tex. App.—Dallas 2014, orig. proceeding))); *cf. Belcher v. Bassett Furniture Indus., Inc.*, 588 F.2d 904, 908 (4th Cir. 1978) ("Since entry upon a party's premises may entail greater burdens and risks than mere production of documents, a greater inquiry into the necessity for inspection would seem warranted. We therefore reject the plaintiffs' contention that the inspection in this case must necessarily be governed by the general relevancy standard of [Federal R]ule 26(b)."); *Dusa Pharm., Inc. v. Queen's Univ.*, 232 F.R.D. 153, 154 (D. Mass. 2005) ("In this case, the Court will deny plaintiffs' motion to compel entry and inspection of defendant's premises and operations. Plaintiffs seek a highly intrusive form of discovery. While the source and quality of NECP's ALA solution may be relevant to claims in this case, any benefit from the inspection sought by plaintiffs is outweighed by the burdens that such inspection will impose.").

320 Tex. R. Civ. P. 192.4(a).

321 *In re Kimberley-Clark Corp.*, 228 S.W.3d 480, 486 (Tex. App.—Dallas 2007, orig. proceeding) (quoting 8A Charles A. Wright, Arthur R. Miller, & Richard L. Marcus, *Federal Practice and Procedure* § 2214 (2d ed. 1994)); *In re Plains Pipeline, L.P.*, 08-19-00224-CV, 2020 Tex. App. LEXIS 8546, at *16, 2020 WL 6375332 (Tex. App.—El Paso Oct. 30, 2020, orig. proceeding) (in a dispute between the parties regarding who controlled the water rights related to an oil and gas lease holding that the trial court did abuse its discretion by allowing a groundwater company to drill seven test holes). *Compare, e.g., In re Swepi L.P.*, 103 S.W.3d 578, 590 (Tex. App.—San Antonio, 2003, orig. proceeding) (holding that the trial court abused its discretion in denying entry onto a nonparty's lease to test gas well because the testing was the only way of obtaining the information sought), *with, e.g., In re Goodyear Tire & Rubber Co.*, No. 04-16-00590-CV, 2017 Tex. App. LEXIS 3676, at *1, 2017 WL 1787735 (Tex. App.—San Antonio Apr. 26, 2017, orig. proceeding) (mem. op.) (holding that the trial court, in a products-liability action, involving an allegedly defective tire erred in allowing the plaintiff access to a Goodyear facility to observe and record tire manufacturing machines in operation), *In re Michelin N. Am., Inc.*, No. 14-14-00578-CV, 2015 Tex. App. LEXIS 12026, at *16–17, 2015 WL 7456101 (Tex. App.—Houston [14th Dist.] Nov. 24, 2015, orig. proceeding) (mem. op.) (same), *In re Goodyear Tire & Rubber Co.*, 437 S.W.3d 923, 928–30 (Tex. App.—Dallas 2014, orig. proceeding) (same), *In re Kimberley-Clark Corp.*, 228 S.W.3d 480, 486, 489 (Tex. App.—Dallas 2007, orig. proceeding) (holding that the trial court's order allowing Phase II environmental testing of a building to help establish fraud by nondisclosure was an abuse of discretion because the plaintiff had "not demonstrated why other means of discovery would not yield evidence directly relevant to the fraud by nondisclosure claim without imposing the burdens Kimberly-Clark argues will be visited on it"), *and Amis v. Ashworth*, 802 S.W.2d 374, 376 (Tex. App.—Tyler 1990, orig. proceeding) (holding that that the trial court abused its discretion in allowing the plaintiff to enter the defendant's property to make a video "to portray his opponent's version of the occurrence in its most favorable light") (footnote omitted); *cf. Belcher v. Bassett Furniture Indus., Inc.*, 588 F.2d 904, 908 (4th Cir. 1978) ("We see no reason why the plaintiffs should not engage in normal methods of deposing witnesses prior to requesting the sweeping relief they seek here. Although the Federal Rules do not prescribe an order of preference for discovery techniques, one method cannot arbitrarily be demanded over another simply because it is less burdensome to the moving party. Depositions do much to identify the items of discovery and to establish

The right to enter the property of a party under a Texas Rule 196.7 generally does not include the right to interview employees or other agents of the party in control of the property or equipment on it,[322] observe the responding party's inspections, measurements, surveys, photographing, tests, or sampling,[323] or require the responding party to conduct measurements, tests, or sampling for the requesting party.[324] When appropriate, consultants and experts of the requesting party needed to adequately perform the inspection and related acts should be allowed entry on the responding party's property.[325]

---

the rights of the parties under [Federal R]ule 34. The information concerning job desirability, if that is to be the subject of the expert's inspection, can be obtained, as we have already observed, far more easily and reliably in the judicial atmosphere surrounding deposition than in the inspection atmosphere anticipated by the order. And if the testimony taken by depositions should prove unsatisfactory or if they could be profitably illuminated by testimony gleaned from a visual inspection, it would be time enough to consider an order for a simple inspection of the plants.") (footnotes omitted); *Dusa Pharm., Inc. v. Queen's Univ.*, 232 F.R.D. 153, 154 (D. Mass. 2005) ("While the source and quality of [the defendant's] solution may be relevant to the claims in this case, any benefit from the inspection sought by plaintiffs is outweighed by the burdens the inspection will impose."); *Johnson vs. Mundy Indus. Contractors, Inc.*, No. 7:01-CV-99-BO(3), 2002 U.S. Dist. LEXIS 19346, at *7, 2002 WL 31464984 (E.D.N.C. Mar. 15, 2002) (denying inspection of the facilities where the alleged sexual harassment occurred because "Plaintiff's request is justified by little more than, 'it could help.'").

[322] *Cf. Belcher v. Bassett Furniture Indus., Inc.*, 588 F.2d 904, 908 (4th Cir. 1978) (holding that interrogations during an inspection are inappropriate because they lack the traditional safeguards of a deposition such as swearing an oath, a written record, and cross-examination); *U.S. v. Territory of the V.I.*, 280 F.R.D. 232, 235–36 (D.V.I. 2012) (holding that [Federal] Rule 34(a)(2) did not entitle a party to interview the opposing party's staff during a premise's inspection); *Schofield v. U.S. Steel Corp.*, No. 2:04-CV-520-PRC, 2005 U.S. Dist. LEXIS 30478, at *8, 2005 WL 8170022 (N.D. Ind. Nov. 7, 2005) ("The Defendant's final proposed condition forbids representatives of the Plaintiff from discussing the 'lines' with the Defendant's employees during the Portage inspection or additional plant inspections. While the party requesting the inspection usually determines the 'reasonable time, place and manner' of the inspection, the Court finds that such a condition on the inspection is reasonable."). *But see N.Y. State Ass'n for Retarded Children, Inc. v. Carey*, 706 F.2d 956, 960–61 (2d Cir. 1983) (allowing interviews).

[323] *Cf. Teer v. Law Eng'g & Env't Servs, Inc.*, 176 F.R.D. 206, 207 (E.D.N.C. 1997) ("Defendant seeks, under authority of [Federal] Rule 34, to observe Plaintiffs' experts as they conduct tests and take steps to reduce or eliminate the alleged chemical contamination on the subject property. The things they seek to observe may well be protected from discovery by the attorney work product rule; however, it is not necessary for the court to decide this. It is quite sufficient to note that Defendants have not cited one case from any court that ever has permitted such a thing.").

[324] *Cf. Sladen v. Girltown, Inc.*, 425 F.2d 24, 25 (7th Cir. 1970) (holding that it was improper to order the plaintiff to conduct flammability tests on garments that were allegedly manufactured by defendant and that had caught fire and burned the plaintiff); *Sperberg v. Firestone Tire & Rubber Co.*, 61 F.R.D. 80, 83 (N.D. Ohio 1973) (denying a motion requesting an order compelling the defendants to conduct test on tires and to permit the plaintiff's entry onto defendant's property to observe the testing).

[325] *In re Kimberley-Clark Corp.*, 228 S.W.3d 480, 486, 489 (Tex. App.—Dallas 2007, orig. proceeding) (allowing the defendant's expert's to perform a directional survey and bottom-pressure test of a nonparty's gas well); *cf. N.Y. State Ass'n for Retarded Children Inc. v. Carey*, 706 F.2d 956, 960 (2d Cir. 1983) (allowing access to an institution by the plaintiffs'

As is the case with the document inspections, a trial court can set conditions governing the entry and any related acts to safeguard against unnecessary disruptions of the responding party's operations and to protect against unwarranted disclosures of confidential or propriety information.[326] A court also can order the requesting party to pay compensation if any damage occurs during the inspection or testing.[327]

8-7:3 The Scope of an Order for Entry on a Nonparty's Property

"An order for entry on a nonparty's property may issue only for good cause shown and only if the land, property, or object thereon as to which discovery is sought is relevant to the subject matter of the action."[328] Thus, discovery's scope for entry on a nonparty's property is not as broad as for entry on a party's land or other property. This is because entry on a nonparty's land or other property, unlike a party's land or

---

counsel, consultants, and experts); *Eirhart v. Libbey-Owens-Ford Co.*, 93 F.R.D. 370, 372 (N.D. Ill. 1981) (allowing a plant inspection by the plaintiffs and their attorneys and consultants).

326 *Cf. N.Y. State Ass'n for Retarded Children Inc. v. Carey*, 706 F.2d 956, 960 (2d Cir. 1983) (ordering the plaintiffs' representatives to minimize disruptions of operation of the mental-health facility and limiting the number of observers to four); *Soler v. Cnty. of San Diego*, No. 14cv2470-MMA (RBB), 2016 U.S. Dist. LEXIS 82614, at *10–12, 2016 WL 3460255 (S.D. Cal. June 24, 2016) (allowing the plaintiff to take still photographs of relevant areas of the county jail, but prohibiting him from videotaping them because "[t]he burden and disruption of a video and audio inspection and recording outweigh the benefits to the Plaintiff. There are approximately 900 inmates housed at San Diego Central Jail; protecting the privacy of inmates and jail staff is a concern. Furthermore, there are legitimate safety and security considerations raised by Defendants. The watch commander stated that '[i]n [his] experience, when the inmates see any video camera they begin 'acting up' and make additional noise and commotion. . . .' For the safety of the visitors and to protect the privacy of inmates and jail staff, 'booking areas of the jail would have to be shut down and cleared.' Taking still photographs is less disruptive than making audio and video recordings.") (citations omitted); *Wilson v. Wal-Mart Stores, Inc.*, No. 2:15-cv-1791-RCJ-VCF, 2016 U.S. Dist. LEXIS 15640, at *5–11, 2016 WL 526225 (D. Nev. Feb. 9, 2016) (limiting the plaintiff's videotaped inspection in a slip-and-fall action to the aisle of the store where she sustained her injury); *Keith H. v. Long Beach Unified Sch. Dist.*, 228 F.R.D. 652, 658–59 (C. D. Cal. 2005) (ordering that the plaintiff's videotaped inspection of a school take place on a non-school day, when no students were present, and that the videotape not identify any students); *McConnell v. Canadian Pac. Realty Co.*, 280 F.R.D. 188, 193–96 (M.D. Pa. 2011) (in an Americans with Disability Act action, allowing inspection only of barriers to access of a shopping mall); *N.O. v. Callahan*, 110 F.R.D. 637, 640–41 (D. Mass. 1986) (ordering the parties to negotiate a procedure and protective order to safeguard privacy while photographing patients at mental-health facility).

327 *Cf. Martin v. Reynolds Metals Corp.*, 297 F.2d 49, 57 (9th Cir. 1961) (order permitting inspection of, and taking urine samples from, cattle required compensation for any damage done).

328 Tex. R. Civ. P. 196.7(d); *In re Plains Pipeline, L.P.*, 618 S.W.3d 780, 793 (Tex. App.—El Paso 2020, orig. proceeding) (noting that when an inspection order is sought against a non party, Texas Rule 196.7 imposes an additional requirement that an order for entry onto non party property may issue only for good cause shown); *In re Swepi L.P.*, 103 S.W.3d 578, 583 (Tex. App.—San Antonio, 2003, orig. proceeding) ("An order for entry onto the property of a nonparty may only issue upon good cause shown and only if the discovery is relevant to the cause of action.").

property, cannot be ordered if it might only "lead to the discovery of admissible evidence." "Good cause" for entry on a nonparty's land or other property is shown when the requesting party "establishes (1) the discovery sought is relevant and material, that is, the information will in some way aid the movant in the preparation or defense of the case; and (2) the substantial equivalent of the material cannot be obtained through other means."[329]

The right to enter land or other property of a nonparty under a Texas Rule 196.7 generally does not include the right to interview employees or other agents of the nonparty in control of the property or equipment on it,[330] observe the responding party's inspections, measurements, surveys, photographing, tests, or sampling,[331] or require the nonparty to conduct measurements, tests, or sampling for the requesting party.[332] When appropriate, the consultants and experts of the requesting party needed to adequately perform the inspection and related acts should be allowed entry on the nonparty's land or other property.[333]

As is the case with the nonparty document inspections, a trial court can set conditions governing the entry and any related acts to safeguard against unnecessary disruptions of the nonparty's operations and to protect against unwarranted disclosures of confidential or propriety information.[334] A court also can order the requesting party to pay compensation if any damage occurs during the inspection or testing.[335]

8-7:4 Response to a Request or Motion and Notice

Texas Rule 196.7(c) governs a party's response to a request for entry on its property. It does not apply to a motion and notice to a nonparty because a response to a motion, unless dictated by the trial court's local rules, can be in any form.

A party's response, like responses to other written-discovery requests, must be served on all the other parties[336] and be made within thirty days after the request's service unless the time is extended due to the manner of service, by the parties' agreement, or by court order,[337] "except that a defendant served with a request before the defendant's answer is due need not respond until 50 days after service of the request."[338] The response, like other written-discovery responses, must include any objections or privilege assertions.[339] It also must state one of the following alternatives: "(A) entry or other requested action will be permitted as requested; (B) entry or other requested action will take place at a specified time and place, if the responding party is objecting to the time and place of production; or (C) entry or other requested

---

[329] *In re Swepi L.P.*, 103 S.W.3d 578, 584 (Tex. App.—San Antonio, 2003, orig. proceeding).

[330] See cases cited in note 322.

[331] See cases cited in note 323.

[332] See cases cited in note 324.

[333] See cases cited in note 325.

[334] See cases cited in note 326.

[335] See cases cited in note 327.

[336] Tex. R. Civ. P. 191.5.

[337] Tex. R. Civ. P. 196.7(c)(1). Three days are added to the response date if the request is served by mail. Tex. R. Civ. P. 21a(c). One day is added if it is received by fax after 5:00 p.m. local time of the recipient. Tex. R. Civ. P. 21a(b)(2).

[338] Tex. R. Civ. P. 196.7(c)(1).

[339] Tex. R. Civ. P. 196.7(c)(2).

action cannot be permitted for reasons stated in the response."[340] These are similar to the statements required in the response to production requests.[341]

The response to a request for entry on a party's property, like other written-discovery responses, is not filed with the trial court.[342] The parties, however, are required by Texas Rule 191.4(d) to retain the response during the action's pendency and any appellate proceedings begun within six months after the judgment is signed.[343]

---

[340] Tex. R. Civ. P. 196.7(c)(2)(A)–(C).

[341] *Compare* Tex. R. Civ. P. 196.2(b). See also Chapter 8, section 8-4:1 (discussing responses to production requests).

[342] Tex. R. Civ. P. 191.4(a)(2).

[343] Tex. R. Civ. P. 191.4(d).

CHAPTER 9

Interrogatories—Texas Rule 197

9-1 Text of Rule 197

RULE 197. INTERROGATORIES TO PARTIES

197.1. Interrogatories

A party may serve on another party—no later than 30 days before the end of the discovery period—written interrogatories to inquire about any matter within the scope of discovery except matters covered by Rule 195. An interrogatory may inquire whether a party makes a specific legal or factual contention and may ask the responding party to state the legal theories and to describe in general the factual bases for the party's claims or defenses, but interrogatories may not be used to require the responding party to marshal all of its available proof or the proof the party intends to offer at trial.

197.2. Response to Interrogatories

(a) **Time for response.** The responding party must serve a written response on the requesting party within 30 days after service of the interrogatories.

(b) **Content of response.** A response must include the party's answers to the interrogatories and may include objections and assertions of privilege as required under these rules.

(c) **Option to produce records.** If the answer to an interrogatory may be derived or ascertained from public records, from the responding party's business records, or from a compilation, abstract or summary of the responding party's business records, and the burden of deriving or ascertaining the answer is substantially the same for the requesting party as for the responding party, the responding party may answer the interrogatory by specifying and, if applicable, producing the records or compilation, abstract or summary of the records. The records from which the answer may be derived or ascertained must be specified in sufficient detail to permit the requesting party to locate and identify them as readily as can the responding party. If the responding party has specified business records, the responding party must state a reasonable time and place for examination of the documents. The responding party must produce the documents at the time and place stated, unless otherwise agreed by the parties or ordered by the court, and must provide the requesting party a reasonable opportunity to inspect them.

(d) **Verification required; exceptions.** A responding party—not an agent or attorney as otherwise permitted by Rule 14—must sign the answers under oath except that:

(1) when answers are based on information obtained from other persons, the party may so state, and

(2) a party need not sign answers to interrogatories about persons with knowledge of relevant facts, trial witnesses, and legal contentions.

197.3. Use

Answers to interrogatories may be used only against the responding party. An answer to an interrogatory inquiring about matters described in Rule 194.2(b)(3) and (b)(4) that has been amended or supplemented is not admissible and may not be used for impeachment.

Comments

Comments to 1999 change:

1. Interrogatories about specific legal or factual assertions—such as, whether a party claims a breach of implied warranty, or when a party contends that limitations began to run—are proper, but interrogatories that ask a party to state all legal and factual assertions are improper. As with requests for disclosure, interrogatories may be used to ascertain basic legal and factual claims and defenses but may not be used to force a party to marshal evidence. Use of the answers to such interrogatories is limited, just as the use of similar disclosures under Rule 194.6 is.

2. Rule 191's requirement that a party's attorney sign all discovery responses and objections applies to interrogatory responses and objections. In addition, the responding party must sign some interrogatory answers under oath, as specified by the rule. Answers in amended and supplemental responses must be signed by the party under oath only if the original answers were required to be signed under oath. The failure to sign or verify answers is only a formal defect that does not otherwise impair the answers unless the party refuses to sign or verify the answers after the defect is pointed out.

9-1:1 2021 Amendments to the Texas Rules of Civil Procedure

The 2021 amendments to the Texas discovery rules generally prohibit a party from serving "discovery on another party until after the other party's initial disclosures are due."[1] Accordingly, as part of the 2021 amendments, the Texas Supreme Court struck the part of former Texas Rule of Civil Procedure 197.2(a) providing that "a defendant served with interrogatories before the defendant's answer is due need not respond until 50 days after service of the interrogatories."[2] In addition, cross references to Texas Rule 194 were updated to reflect changes to that Rule. Otherwise, the 2021 amendments did not modify Texas Rule 197.

---

[1] Tex. R. Civ. P 192.2(a) ("Unless otherwise agreed to by the parties or ordered by the court, a party cannot serve discovery on another party until after the other party's initial disclosures are due.").

[2] Former Tex. R. Civ. P. 197.2(a)

9-2 Interrogatories in General

Texas Rule 197 governs interrogatories—written questions propounded by one party to another.[3] Like other written-discovery requests, interrogatories must be served no later than 30 days (and in some cases 31 or 33 days) before the discovery period ends[4] but—in cases filed on or after January 1, 2021—not until after the responding party's initial disclosures are due.[5]

Interrogatories may inquire about any discoverable matter other than matters covered by Texas Rule 195, which relates to testifying experts.[6] They are a relatively

---

[3] Tex. R. Civ. P. 197.1 ("A party may serve on another party . . . written interrogatories."). The other Texas discovery rules relating to interrogatories are Rules 190–93, 195, and 215. Tex. R. Civ. P. 190-93, 195, 215.

Interrogatories cannot be served on nonparties. Tex. R. Civ. P. 197.1 ("A party may serve on another *party* . . . written interrogatories[.]") (emphasis added); *cf. Obinyan v. Prime Therapeutics LLC*, 3:18-CV-0933-D, 2021 U.S. Dist. LEXIS 7168, at *2, 2021 WL 135983 (N.D. Tex. Jan. 14, 2021) ("As stated above, interrogatories directed to nonparties are not permitted under [Federal] Rule 33."); *Univ. of Tex. v. Vratil*, 96 F.3d 1337, 1340 (10th Cir. 1996) ("Under Fed. R. Civ. P. 33(a), interrogatories may only be directed to a party to an action."); *Jackson v. Boise Locomotive*, No. H-08-2545, 2009 U.S. Dist. LEXIS 64832, at *20–21, 2009 WL 2252246 (S.D. Tex. July, 28, 2009) ("Under Federal Rule of Civil Procedure 33, 'courts have uniformly denied litigants' attempts to use interrogatories to obtain information from nonparties.'" (quoting *Ackah v. Greenville Cnty. Sch. Dist.*, No. 6:07-2796-HFF-WMC, 2008 U.S. Dist. LEXIS 29227, at *1–2 (D.S.C. Apr. 9, 2008))). This prohibition extends to dismissed parties as well. *Cf. Carp v. Marcus*, 498 N.Y.S.2d 174 (N.Y. App. 1986). However, interrogatories can be served on parties whose interests are not adverse. *Cf. Ferrara v. U.S.*, No. 90 Civ. 0972 (DNE), 1992 U.S. Dist. LEXIS 601, at *3, 1992 WL 18836 (S.D.N.Y. Jan. 23, 1992) ("The [Federal] Rule does not limit discovery only to parties that have a hostile stance toward each other in the litigation."); *Andrulonis v. U.S.*, 96 F.R.D. 43, 45 (N.D.N.Y. 1982) ("[N]o degree of adversity between the parties is required . . . to serve interrogatories.").

[4] Tex. R. Civ. P. 197.1 ("A party may serve on another party—no later than 30 days before the end of the discovery period—written interrogatories to inquire about any matter within the scope of discovery except matters covered by Rule 195."). If the interrogatories are by served mail, they must be served at least thirty-three days before the discovery period ends. *See* Tex. R. Civ. P. 21a(c). If they are served by fax after 5:00 p.m. local time of the recipient, the interrogatories must be served at least thirty-one days before the discovery period ends. *See* Tex. R. Civ. P. 21a(b)(2).

[5] Tex. R. Civ. P. 192.2(a) ("Unless otherwise agreed to by the parties or ordered by the court, a party cannot serve discovery on another party until after the other party's initial disclosures are due."). Cases filed before January 1, 2021 are governed by the pre-2021 version of the discovery rules, which allow interrogatories to be served at any time during the discovery period, including before the defendant's answer is due. *See, e.g.,* Former Tex. R. Civ. P. 197.2 ("The responding party must serve a written response on the requesting party within 30 days after service of the interrogatories, except that a defendant served with interrogatories before the defendant's answer is due need not respond until 50 days after service of the interrogatories.").

[6] Tex. R. Civ. P. 195.1 ("A party may obtain information concerning testifying expert witnesses only through disclosure under this rule and through depositions and reports as permitted by this rule."); *In re Nat'l Lloyds Ins. Co.*, 532 S.W.3d 794, 814 (Tex. 2017) (orig. proceeding) ("[Texas] Rule 195 does not provide for interrogatories or requests for production[.]") (footnote omitted). Interrogatories, however, can be used to obtain information about discoverable consulting-expert witnesses. Tex. R. Civ. P. 195 cmt.

inexpensive method of discovery and, when properly worded, can be an effective way to obtain facts, narrow the issues, and obtain information to make proper use of other permissible forms of discovery.[7]

Interrogatories, like all other written discovery, must be signed by either the party's attorney or a pro se party.[8] If they are not properly signed, they "must be stricken unless [they are] signed promptly after the omission is called to the attention of the [requesting] party[.]"[9] Moreover, a responding party need not answer an interrogatory set that is not signed.[10]

Like other written-discovery devices, interrogatories are not filed,[11] but must be served on all parties to the action.[12] However, interrogatories, like other discovery materials, may be filed pursuant to a court order, in support of or in opposition to a motion or for other use in a court proceeding, and a person may file discovery materials necessary for a proceeding in an appellate court.[13] In addition, the serving party "must retain the original or exact copy of [the interrogatories or interrogatory responses] during the pendency of the case and any related appellate proceedings begun within six months after judgment is signed, unless otherwise provided by the trial court."[14]

---

1 to 1999 change. In addition, because an interrogatory can be used to ascertain trial witnesses, a request for the identification of all experts anticipated to testify at trial is proper. Tex. R. Civ. P. 197.2(d)(2); *see Alvarado v. Farah Mfg. Co., Inc.*, 830 S.W.2d 911, 915 (Tex. 1992) ("A party is entitled to prepare for trial assured that a witness will not be called because opposing counsel has not identified him or her in response to a proper interrogatory."); *OIC Holdings, LLC v. Gleason*, 05-18-00029-CV, 2019 Tex. App. LEXIS 3863, at *22, 2019 WL 2098616 (Tex. App.—Dallas May 14, 2019, no pet.) (mem. op.) (same). See also Chapters 7, sections 7-4 and 7-5 (discussing discovery concerning testifying and consulting experts).

[7] *See, e.g., In re W. Dairy Transp.*, L.L.C., 574 S.W.3d 537, 550 (Tex. App.—El Paso 2019, no pet. orig. proceeding) ("[T]he ultimate purpose of discovery is to seek the truth, so that disputes may be decided by what the facts reveal, not by what facts are concealed."); *cf. Richard v. Dignean*, 332 F.R.D. 450, 459 (W.D.N.Y. 2019) ("There are many purposes for interrogatories but the general aims are to expeditiously narrow the scope of litigation, reduce the element of surprise, serve as admissions for trial, and in a significant matter avoid unnecessary discovery and minimize the expense."); *U.S. v. Quebe*, 321 F.R.D. 303 (S.D. Ohio 2017) ("Interrogatories serve not only as a discovery device but as a means of producing admissible evidence; there is no better example of an admission of a party opponent, which is admissible because it is not hearsay, than an answer to an interrogatory.").

[8] Tex. R. Civ. P. 191.3(a) (providing that interrogatories and the responses to them must be signed "(1) by an attorney, if the party is represented by an attorney, and must show the attorney's State Bar of Texas identification number, address, telephone number, and fax number, if any; or (2) by the party, if the party is not represented by an attorney, and must show the party's address, telephone number, and fax number, if any.").

[9] Tex. R. Civ. P. 191.3(d).

[10] Tex. R. Civ. P. 191.3(d) ("A party is not required to take any action with respect to a request or notice that is not signed.").

[11] Tex. R. Civ. P. 191.4(a)(1)–(2).

[12] Tex. R. Civ. P. 191.5.

[13] Tex. R. Civ. P. 191.4(c)(1)–(3).

[14] Tex. R. Civ. P. 191.4(d).

9-3 Interrogatory Types

There are two basic interrogatory types: identification and contention interrogatories.[15] Identification interrogatories call for factual information, such as the identity of documents, tangible things, persons with knowledge of relevant facts, or communications.[16]

---

[15] Robert K. Wise, *Ending Evasive Responses to Written Discovery: A Guide for Properly Responding (and Objecting) to Interrogatories and Document Requests Under the Texas Discovery Rules*, 65 Baylor L. Rev. 510, 512 (2013); *cf. Buckner v. Montgomery Cnty. Jobs & Fam. Servs. Div.*, No. 3:11-cv-320, 2012 U.S. Dist. LEXIS 43251, at *3, 2012 WL 786948 (S.D. Ohio Mar. 29, 2012) ("There are basically two types of interrogatories: identification interrogatories and contention interrogatories."); *Buckner v. Montgomery Cty. Jobs & Family Servs. Div.*, No. 3:11-cv-320, 2012 U.S. Dist. LEXIS 43251, at *3, 2012 WL 78694 (S.D. Ohio Mar. 29, 2012) ("There are basically two types of interrogatories: identification interrogatories and contention interrogatories. 'Contention' interrogatories are interrogatories that seek to clarify the basis for or scope of an adversary's legal claim. Identification interrogatories request the responding party to identify relevant documents and tangible objects or the identity of individuals having knowledge of facts relating to the suit.") (citation omitted); *Reittinger v. Verizon Commc'ns, Inc.*, No. 1:05-CV-1487 (FJS/RFT), 2006 U.S. Dist. LEXIS 83293, at *18, 2006 WL 3327676 (N.D.N.Y. Nov. 15, 2006) (same); *Citibank (S.D.), N.A. v. Savage (In re Savage)*, 303 B.R. 766, 773–74 (Bankr. D. Md. 2003) (same); *see Harvey v. Circle*, 4:19-CV-902-NAB, 2020 U.S. Dist. LEXIS 138809, at *11, 2020 WL 4472999 (E.D. Mo. Aug. 4, 2020) ("The term 'contention interrogatories' refers to several types of questions. They may ask another party to indicate what it contends, to state all the facts on which it bases its contentions, to state all the evidence on which it bases its contentions, or to explain how the law applies to the facts. *They are distinct from interrogatories that request identification of witnesses or documents that bear on the allegations.*" (quoting *In re Grand Casinos, Inc.*, 168 F.R.D. 615, 618 (D. Minn. 1998))); *Dalmatia Imp. Grp., Inc. v. FoodMatch, Inc.*, No. 16-2767, 2016 U.S. Dist. LEXIS 136743, at *3–4, 2016 WL 5721161 (E.D. Pa. Oct. 3, 2016) ("Contention interrogatories can be characterized as: 'any question that asks another party to indicate what it contends . . . [a question asking] another party whether it makes some specified contention[,] . . . [a question asking] an opposing party to state all facts on which it bases some specified contention[,] . . . [a question asking] the responding party to take a position, and then to explain and defend that position, with respect to how the law applies to facts[, or] . . . [a question asking] parties to spell out the legal basis for, or theory behind, some specified contention.' Interrogatories that seek the identification of documents or of witnesses are not contention interrogatories." (quoting *In re Auto. Refinishing Paint Antitrust Litig.*, No. 1426, 2006 U.S. Dist. LEXIS 34129, at *12, 2006 WL 1479819 (E.D. Pa. May 26, 2006))); *Black Hills Molding, Inc. v. Brandom Holdings, LLC*, 295 F.R.D. 403, 413 (D.S.D. 2013) ("A contention interrogatory should not be conflated with a fact-based interrogatory. A fact-based interrogatory seeks to identify witnesses and documents bearing on the allegations."); *Shqeirat v. U.S. Airways Grp., Inc.*, No. 07-1513 (ADM/AJB), 2008 U.S. Dist. LEXIS 108338, at *12, 2009 WL 4232018 (D. Minn. Sept. 9, 2008) ("The term 'contention interrogatories' may encompass several types of questions. For example: 'They may ask another party to indicate what it contends, to state all the facts on which it bases it contentions, or to explain how the law applies to the facts. They are distinct from interrogatories that request identification of witnesses or documents that bear on the allegations.'" (quoting *In re Grand Casinos, Inc. Sec. Litig.*, 181 F.R.D. 615, 618 (D. Minn. 1998))).

[16] See authorities cited in note 15.

The Texas discovery rules expressly permit contention interrogatories.[17] Texas Rule 197.1 defines a contention interrogatory as one "inquir[ing] whether a party makes a specific legal or factual contention" or "ask[ing] the responding party to state the legal theories and to describe in general the factual bases for the party's claims or defenses[.]"[18] Such interrogatories may, for example, ask a party to (1) state what it contends or whether it is making a particular factual or legal contention, (2) explain the facts underlying an allegation, claim, or defense, (3) assert a position or explain a position with regard to how the law applies to the facts, or (4) articulate the legal or

---

[17] Tex. R. Civ. P. 197.1 ("An interrogatory may inquire whether a party makes a specific legal or factual contention and may ask the responding party to state the legal theories and to describe in general the factual bases for the party's claims or defenses . . . ."); *In re Sting Soccer Grp., LP*, No. 05-17-00317-CV, 2017 Tex. App. LEXIS 11197, at *13, 2017 WL 5897454 (Tex. App.—Dallas Nov. 30, 2017, orig. proceeding) (mem. op.) ("[Texas] Rule 197.1 permits a party to serve contention interrogatories to 'inquire whether a party makes a specific legal or factual contention and may ask the responding party to state the legal theories and to describe in general the factual bases for the party's claims or defenses . . . .'" (quoting Tex. R. Civ. P. 197.1)); *Sheffield Dev. Co. v. Carter & Burgess, Inc.*, No. 02-00204-CV, 2012 Tex. App. LEXIS 10599, at *16, 2012 WL 6632500 (Tex. App.—Fort Worth 2012, pet. dism'd) (mem. op.) ("Contention discovery is permitted by the rules of civil procedure."); *see* Tex. R. Civ. P. 192.3(j) ("A party may obtain discovery of any other party's legal contentions and the factual bases for those contentions.").

[18] Tex. R. Civ. P. 197.1. Federal Rule 33(a)(2) defines a contention interrogatory as one "asking for an opinion or contention that relates to fact or the application of law to fact[.]" Fed R. Civ. P. 33(a)(2). As one federal court has explained:

> [T]he phrase "contention interrogatory" is used imprecisely to refer to many different kinds of questions. Some people would classify as a contention interrogatory any question that asks another party to indicate *what* it contends. Some people would define contention interrogatories as embracing only questions that ask another party *whether* it makes some specified contention. Interrogatories of this kind typically would begin with the phrase "Do you contend that . . . ." Another kind of question that some people put in the category of "contention interrogatory" asks an opposing party to state all the *facts* on which it *bases* some specified contention. Yet another form of this category of interrogatory asks an opponent to state all the *evidence* on which it *bases* some specified contention. Some contention interrogatories ask the responding party to take a position, and then explain or defend that position, with respect to *how the law applies to facts.* A variation on this theme involves interrogatories that ask parties to spell out the *legal basis* for, or theory behind, some specified contention.

In re Convergent Techs. Sec. Litig., 108 F.R.D. 328, 332 (N.D. Cal. 1985); *accord Firefighters' Ret. Sys. v. Citco Grp. Ltd.*, No. 13-373-SDD-EWD, 2017 U.S. Dist. LEXIS 101747, at *27–28, 2017 WL 2825925 (M.D. La. June 30, 2017); *Sprint Commc'ns Co. L.P. v. Crow Creek Sioux Tribal Ct.*, 316 F.R.D. 254, 272 (D.S.D. 2016); *Sigman v. CSX Corp.*, No. 3:15-cv-13328, 2016 U.S. Dist. LEXIS 178563, at *64–66, 2016 WL 7444947 (S.D. W. Va. Dec. 27, 2016); *Koninklijke Philips N.V. v. Zoll LifeCor Corp.*, No. 2:12-cv-1369, 2014 U.S. Dist. LEXIS 131078, at *33, 2014 WL 4660338 (W.D. Pa. Aug. 22, 2014); *Gilmore v. City of Minneapolis*, No. 13-1019 (JRT/FLN), 2014 U.S. Dist. LEXIS 132543, at *12–13, 2014 WL 4722488 (D. Minn. Sept. 22, 2014); *SEC v. Berry*, No. C07-04431 RMW (HRL), 2011 U.S. Dist. LEXIS 64437, at *4 n.1, 2011 WL 2441706 (N.D. Cal. June 15, 2011); *Gregg v. Local 305 IBEW*, No. 1:08-CV-160, 2009 U.S. Dist. LEXIS 40761, at *15, 2009 WL 1325103 (N.D. Ind. May 13, 2009); *see Ziemack v. Centel Corp.*, No. 92 C 3551, 1995 U.S. Dist. LEXIS 18192, at *5, 1995 WL 729295 (N.D. Ill. Dec. 7, 1995) ("Basically, contention interrogatories require the answering party to commit to a position and give factual specifics supporting its claim.").

theoretical reason for a contention or allegation.[19] In other words, contention interrogatories require parties to put meat on the relatively barebones information required by Texas notice pleading.[20]

Although Texas Rule 197 expressly permits contention interrogatories,[21] it makes clear that such interrogatories cannot be used "to require the responding party to marshal all of its available proof or the proof it intends to offer at trial."[22] What constitutes

---

[19] Robert K. Wise, *Ending Evasive Responses to Written Discovery: A Guide for Properly Responding (and Objecting) to Interrogatories and Document Requests Under the Texas Discovery Rules*, 65 Baylor L. Rev. 510, 515–16 (2103); *cf. In re Convergent Techs. Sec. Litig.*, 108 F.R.D. 328, 332 (N.D. Cal. 1985).

[20] *See State Farm Fire & Cas. Co. v. Moura*, 979 S.W.2d 616, 618 (Tex. 1998) ("Interrogatories serve to flesh out the facts of the case and prevent trial by ambush."); *cf. Mach. Sols., Inc. v. Doosan Infracore Am. Corp.*, 323 F.R.D. 522, 528 (D.S.C. 2018) ("[I]nterrogatories which seek opinions or contentions that call for the application of law to facts are proper, and an interrogatory may properly inquire into a party's contentions in the case."); *Rivera v. Guevara*, 319 F. Supp. 3d 1004, 1057 (N.D. Ill. 2018) ("An interrogatory response or expert report can put the defendant on notice of a plaintiff's theory; indeed, that is often the point of contention interrogatories."); *Sprint Commc'ns. Co. L.P. v. Crow Creek Sioux Tribal Ct.*, 316 F.R.D. 254, 272 (D. Kan. 2016) ("When properly used, contention interrogatories can be helpful 'in that they may narrow and define the issues for trial and enable the propounding party to determine the proof required to rebut the responding party's claim or defense.'" (quoting *Moses v. Halstead*, 236 F.R.D. 667, 674 (D. Kan. 2006))); *Sigman v. CSX Corp.*, No. 3:15-cv-13328, 2016 U.S. Dist. LEXIS 178563, at *64–66, 2016 WL 7444947 (S.D.W. Va. Dec. 27, 2016) (same); *Summy-Long v. Pa. State Univ.*, No. 1:06-cv-1117, 2015 U.S. Dist. LEXIS 138247, at *9–10, 2015 WL 5924505 (M.D. Pa. Oct. 9, 2015) ("It is well established that [contention] 'interrogatories will serve to clarify the issues and narrow the scope of the dispute.' [Contention] interrogatories 'serve an important purpose in helping to discover facts supporting the theories of the parties.'" (quoting *In re Domestic Drywall Antitrust Litig.*, 300 F.R.D. 228, 230 (E.D. Pa. 2014), and *Woods v. DeAngelo Marine Exhaust, Inc.*, 692 F.3d 1272, 1280 (Fed. Cir. 2012))); *Barnes v. D.C.*, 270 F.R.D. 21, 24 (D.D.C. 2010) ("This type of request 'can be most useful in narrowing and sharpening the issues, which is a major purpose of discovery.'" (quoting Fed. R. Civ. P. 33, Advisory Committee's Note to 1970 Amend.)); *Bell v. Woodward Governor Co.*, No. 03 C 50190, 2005 U.S. Dist. LEXIS 27051, at *9, 2005 WL 8179365 (N.D. Ill. Sept. 8, 2005) ("Answers to [contention] interrogatories are useful because they, amongst other things, aid the propounding party in 'pinning down' *a party's position* and determining the proof required to rebut the *party's position*.") (emphasis added).

[21] Tex. R. Civ. P. 197.1 ("An interrogatory may inquire whether a party makes a specific legal or factual contention" or "ask the responding party to state the legal theories and to describe in general the factual bases for the party's claims or defenses. . . ."); Tex. R. Civ. P. cmt. 1 to 1999 change ("Interrogatories about specific legal or factual assertions—such as whether a party claims a breach of implied warranty, or when a party contends that limitations began to run—are proper[.]").

[22] Tex. R. Civ. P. 197.1; *see* Tex. R. Civ. P. 194.2 cmt. 2 to 1999 change (stating that contention interrogatories "are not properly used to require a party to marshal evidence or brief legal issues"); 197 cmt. 1 to 1999 change ("[I]nterrogatories that ask a party to state all legal and factual assertions are improper. . . . [I]nterrogatories may be used to ascertain basic legal and factual claims and defenses, but may not be used to force a party to marshal evidence."); *In re Sting Soccer Grp., LP*, No. 05-17-00317-CV, 2017 Tex. App. LEXIS 11197, at *13, 2017 WL 5897454 (Tex. App.—Dallas Nov. 30, 2017, orig. proceeding) (mem. op.) ("The party may not use interrogatories to require the responding party to marshal all of its available proof or the proof the party intends to offer at trial."); *In re Ochoa*,

evidence marshalling is not clearly explained by Texas Rule 197 or by Texas Rule 194, which similarly provides that "the responding party need not marshal all evidence that may be offered at trial" in providing the initial disclosure required under Texas Rule 194.2(b)(3)—or, for cases filed before January 1, 2021, in responding to a Texas Rule 194.2(c) request for disclosure—of "the legal theories and, in general, the factual bases of the responding party's claims or defenses[.]"[23] Rather, Comment 2 to the 1999 change to Texas Rule 197 merely explains that "interrogatories that ask a party to state all factual and legal assertions are improper."[24] Because undefined words in procedural rules are given their ordinary meaning,[25] "marshalling" as used in Texas Rule 197.1 and the other discovery rules should be given it ordinary meaning—"[a]rranging all of a party's evidence in the order that it will be presented at trial."[26]

An interrogatory asking the responding party to state "all" facts or "every" or "each" fact concerning a cause of action or defense appears to be improper.[27] In contrast,

---

No. 12-04-00163-CV, 2004 Tex. App. LEXIS 4866, at *4, 2004 WL 1192444 (Tex. App.—Tyler May 28, 2004, orig. proceeding) (mem. op.) ("A party's legal contentions and factual bases for them are discoverable. . . . However, [disclosures and interrogatories cannot] be used to require a party to marshal all of its available proof.").

[23] Tex. R. Civ. P. 194.2(b)(3); Former Tex. R. Civ. P. 194.2(c); *accord* Tex. R. Civ. P. 194 cmt. 2 to 1999 change.

[24] Tex. R. Civ. P. 197 cmt. 2 to 1999 change.

[25] *E.g.*, ***In re Tex. Educ. Agency***, 619 S.W.3d 679, 687 (Tex. 2021) ("We apply the plain meaning of statutory language unless (1) the Legislature has prescribed definitions, (2) the words have acquired a technical or particular meaning, (3) a contrary intention is apparent from the context, or (4) a plain-meaning construction leads to nonsensical or absurd results.") (footnote omitted) (citation omitted); ***In re Silver***, 540 S.W.3d 530, 534 (Tex. 2018) (orig. proceeding) ("[W]hen determining a rule's meaning we typically rely on the ordinary meaning of the words used, unless the text or relevant definitions indicate a different meaning. When determining the ordinary meaning of a word, we frequently consult dictionaries.") (citation omitted); ***In re Bridgestone Americas Tire Operations, LLC***, 459 S.W.3d 565, 569 (Tex. 2015) (orig. proceeding) ("When we analyze Texas's procedural rules, we apply the same rules of construction that govern the interpretation of statutes. That is, we look first to the rule's language and construe it according to its plain meaning.") (citation omitted); *Assignees of Best Buy v. Combs*, 395 S.W.3d 847, 864 (Tex. App.—Austin 2013, pet. denied) ("When construing rules of civil procedure, we apply the same rules of construction that we use when interpreting statutes. If the rule's language is unambiguous, we must interpret it according to its plain meaning, giving meaning to the language consistent with other provisions in the rule. We typically give undefined terms in a statute their ordinary meaning[.]") (citations omitted).

[26] ***Sheffield Dev. Co. v. Carter & Burgess, Inc.***, No. 02-00204-CV, 2012 Tex. App. LEXIS 10599, at *16, 2012 WL 6632500 (Tex. App.—Fort Worth 2012, pet. dism'd) (mem. op.) (quoting ***Marshaling, Black's Law Dictionary*** 1063 (9th ed. 2009)), ***cited with approval in In re Sting Soccer Grp., LP***, No. 05-17-00317-CV, 2017 Tex. App. LEXIS 11197, at *13, 2017 WL 5897454 (Tex. App.—Dallas Nov. 30, 2017, orig. proceeding) (mem. op.).

[27] *Cf.* ***In re Keurig Green Mountain Single-Serve Coffee Antitrust Litig.***, CV14MD2542VSBSLC, 2020 U.S. Dist. LEXIS 199859, at *25–26, 2020 WL 6290584 (S.D.N.Y. Oct. 27, 2020) ("'Courts generally resist efforts to use contention interrogatories as a vehicle to obtain every fact and every piece of evidence a party may wish to offer concerning a given issue at trial.' A contention interrogatory is proper where it asks the party to 'explain the factual bases for [that party's] contentions by providing the material facts upon which they will rely, but not a detailed and exhaustive listing of all the evidence that will be offered.' A contention interrogatory is improper where it 'would merely "produce . . . a mass of data that contains,

incidental, secondary, and perhaps irrelevant and trivial details.'" (quoting *Linde v. Arab Bank, PLC*, No. 04 Civ. 2799 (VVP), 2012 U.S. Dist. LEXIS 39518, at *7–8, 2012 WL 957970 (E.D.N.Y. Mar. 21, 2012), and *Morel v. Reed*, No. 11 Civ. 1808 (DLI) (LB), 2013 U.S. Dist. LEXIS 195585, at *4, 2013 WL 12129656 (E.D.N.Y. Oct. 2, 2013))); *Tellis v. LeBlanc*, 18-CV-0541, 2019 U.S. Dist. LEXIS 107317, at *4, 2019 WL 2622421 (W.D. La. June 26, 2019) ("But courts have held that 'blockbuster' interrogatories, which require a party to state every fact supporting all of its allegations, as well as identify each person with knowledge of each fact and all documents supporting each count, are impermissible." (quoting *HCB Fin. Corp. v. Kennedy*, 2016 U.S. Dist. LEXIS 199885, at *4, 2016 WL 6216179 (S.D. Miss. 2016))); *Flynn v. FCA US LLC*, 3:15-CV-855-SMY-RJD, 2019 U.S. Dist. LEXIS 66363, at *17, 2019 WL 1746266 (S.D. Ill. Apr. 18, 2019) ("[C[ourts have determined that a party need not respond to contention interrogatories that would be an unduly burdensome task requiring a party to 'produce veritable narratives of their entire case.'" (quoting *Gregg v. Local 305 IBEW*, 2009 U.S. Dist. LEXIS 40761, at *16, 2009 WL 1325103, (N.D. Ind. May 13, 2009))); *Mach. Sols., Inc. v. Doosan Infracore Am. Corp.*, 323 F.R.D. 522, 528 (D.S.C. 2018) ("'[C]ontention interrogatories' are overly broad and unduly burdensome on their face if they seek 'all facts' supporting a claim or defense, such that the answering party is required to provide a narrative account of its case."); *Luken v. Christensen Grp. Inc.*, No. C16-5214 RBL, 2017 U.S. Dist. LEXIS 189131, at *4, 2017 WL 5483782 (W.D. Wash. Nov. 15, 2017) ("Numerous federal courts, including this one, have held that contention interrogatories which 'systematically track all of the allegations in an opposing party's pleadings, and that ask for "each and every fact" and application of law to fact that supports the party's allegations are an abuse of the discovery process because they are overly broad and unduly burdensome.'" (quoting *Lucero v. Valdez*, 240 F.R.D. 591, 594 (D.N.M. 2007))); *Hicks v. Arya*, No. 2:16-cv-2465 MCE KJN P, 2017 U.S. Dist. LEXIS 135401, at *3, 2017 WL 3614301 (E.D. Cal. Aug. 23, 2017) ("[P] laintiff is not required to present his entire case in discovery responses. 'Each and every fact' interrogatories pose problems for a responding party and a reviewing court. Parties are not tasked with laying out every jot and tittle of their evidentiary case in response to interrogatories."); *Romero v. Macy's, Inc.*, No. 15cv815-GPC-MDD, 2016 U.S. Dist. LEXIS 123439, at *8, 2016 WL 4729580 (S.D. Cal. Sept. 12, 2016) ("Defendant does have a point, however, regarding the requirement that it state 'all' facts and identify 'all' documents supporting its contention. 'Courts will generally find [contention interrogatories] overly broad and unduly burdensome on their face to the extent they ask for "every fact" [or "all facts"] which support identified allegations or defenses. Interrogatories may, however, properly ask for the principal or material facts which support an allegation or defense.'" (quoting *Hernandez v. Best Buy Co.*, No. 13cv2587-JM(KSC), 2014 U.S. Dist. LEXIS 152117, at *16–17, 2014 WL 5454505 (S.D. Cal. Oct. 24, 2014), and *Hiskett v. Wal-Mart Stores, Inc.*, 180 F.R.D. 403, 404–05 (D. Kan. 1998)))); *Megdal Assocs., LLC v. La-Z-Boy, Inc.*, No. 14-81476-CIV-ZLOCH, 2016 U.S. Dist. LEXIS 187487, at *17–18, 2016 WL 4503337 (S.D. Fla. Feb. 1, 2016) ("[C]ommentators have often suggested that contention interrogatories—like the one here—are 'unduly broad if they ask in an undifferentiated way for "all" facts or witnesses that support an opposing party's case.' Indeed, courts in other districts have found that interrogatories that 'indiscriminately sweep an entire pleading' impermissibly 'require the responding party to provide in essence a running narrative or description of the entire case. . . .' Still more cast these 'blockbuster' interrogatories as 'an abuse of the discovery process because they are overly broad and unduly burdensome.' The courts that have rejected these sorts of interrogatories have reasoned that 'requir[ing] answers for them would likely cause delay and unreasonable expense of time energy, and perhaps money.' The Court agrees with th[is] reasoning . . . and notes that such broad interrogatories are not consistent with Rule 1 of the Federal Rules of Civil Procedure. For, 'if the [Federal] Rules' drafters intended to authorize interrogatories with an impact as wide as the entire case, they could more realistically and easily have adopted a simple rule to require every pleading to be accompanied by a statement of all facts supporting every allegation and the identification of every knowledgeable person and supporting document. They did not do so.'" (citations an interrogatory asking for the "general bases" or the "material" or "principal" facts concerning such a matter should be proper.[28] Therefore, it stands to reason that an interrogatory asking a plaintiff to "state, in general, the facts supporting its breach of contract claim" or a defendant to "state the principal [or material] facts supporting its estoppel defense" does not require evidence marshalling and is proper.[29]

Moreover, an interrogatory asking the responding party to identify "all documents concerning or relating to" or "all persons with knowledge about" a matter or subject is an identification, rather than a contention, interrogatory that does not require evidence marshalling and generally is appropriate if it is not otherwise unduly burdensome, overbroad, or disproportionate to the case's needs.[30]

---

omitted) (quoting 8B Wright, Miller, & Kane, *Federal Practice and Procedure* § 2167 (3d ed. 2015), *Hilt v. SFC, Inc.*, 170 F.R.D. 182, 188 (D. Kan. 1997), and *Lucero v. Valdez*, 240 F.R.D. 591, 594 (D.N.M. 2007))); *U.S. v. La.*, No. 11-470-JWD-RLB, 2015 U.S. Dist. LEXIS 168039, at *13–14, 2015 WL 9165910 (M.D. La. Dec. 16, 2015) ("To begin, while [Federal] Rule 33 itself allows for the use of contention interrogatories, a contention interrogatory may be overly broad where it seeks 'each and every' single fact upon which a party bases its case. An interrogatory may reasonably ask for the material or principal facts which support a contention. [Federal] Rule 33 contemplates that a responding party may not object merely because a contention interrogatory requires the application of opinion to fact. To require 'each and every' fact or application of law to fact, however, 'would too often require a laborious, time-consuming analysis. . . . The burden to answer then outweighs the benefit to be gained.'" (citation omitted) (quoting *IBP, Inc. v. Mercantile Bank of Topeka*, 179 F.R.D. 316, 321 (D. Kan. 1998))); *K.R.S. v. Bedford Cnty. Sch. Dist.*, No. 4:13-cv-00147-HCA, 2014 U.S. Dist. LEXIS 187432, at *8, 2014 WL 11513167 (S.D. Iowa Dec. 15, 2014) ("In some cases, contention interrogatories may be viewed by courts as overly broad and unduly burdensome on their face by asking for 'each and every fact' or 'all facts' which support a claim or defense. . . . Courts emphasize that '[c]ontention interrogatories should not require a party to provide the equivalent of a narrative account of the case.' When faced with contention interrogatories with overly broad language, courts typically direct that an answer still be provided but narrow the scope of the needed response to the 'material' or 'principal' facts supporting a specific claim or defense." (citations omitted) (quoting *Lucero v. Valdez*, 240 F.R.D. 591, 595 (D.N.M. 2007))); *Lubrication Techs., Inc. v. Lee's Oil Serv., LLC*, No. 11-2226 (DSD/LIB), 2012 U.S. Dist. LEXIS 69440, at *28, 2012 WL 1633259 (D. Minn. Apr. 10, 2012) ("'The parties' interrogatories may properly ask for the principal or material facts which support an allegation or defense, and may seek the identities of knowledgeable persons and supporting documents for the principal or material facts supporting an allegation or defense.'" (quoting *Turner v. Moen Steel Erection Co.*, No. 8:06CV227, 2006 U.S. Dist. LEXIS 72874, at *12–13, 2006 WL 3392206 (D. Neb. Oct. 5, 2006))); *Ritchie Risk-Linked Strategies Trading (Ir.), Ltd. v. Coventry First LLC*, 273 F.R.D. 367, 369 (S.D.N.Y. 2010) ("[W]hile contention interrogatories are a perfectly acceptable form of discovery, Defendants' requests, insofar as they seek every fact, every piece of evidence, every witness, and every application of law to fact . . . are overly broad and unduly burdensome.") (citations omitted).

[28] See cases cited in note 27.

[29] See cases cited in note 27.

[30] *See* Tex. R. Civ. P. 194.2(b)(5) (requiring disclosure of "the name . . . of persons having knowledge or relevant facts, and a brief statement of each identified person's connection with the case"); Former Tex. R. Civ. P. 194.2(e) (allowing a party to request the disclosure of "the name . . . of persons having knowledge or relevant facts, and a brief statement of each identified person's connection with the case"); Robert K. Wise, *Ending Evasive Responses to Written Discovery: A Guide for Properly Responding (and Objecting) to Interrogatories and Document Requests Under the Texas Discovery Rules*, 65 Baylor L. Rev. 510, 519 (2013); *cf.*

Further, the mere fact that an interrogatory uses the word "all," "every," or "each" does not necessarily mean that it requires evidence marshalling.[31] This principle is illustrated by *Sheffield Development Co. v. Carter & Burgess, Inc.*[32] In that case, a homebuilder sued a residential subdivision developer for post-construction damage to houses that it built on subdivision lots, claiming that the damage was due to the lots' improper leveling and drainage.[33] The developer then joined the engineering firm that provided the engineering and surveying services for the lots' grading as a third-party defendant and sought contribution from it.[34] During discovery, the engineering firm served the following interrogatory on the developer:

> Please identify/specify each and every lot in the Development which you contend deviated from or failed to conform to the approved grading and drainage plans. For each such lot, please identify and specify:
>
> (a) the specific nature of the alleged deviation or non-conformity;

Harvey v. Circle, 4:19-CV-902-NAB, 2020 U.S. Dist. LEXIS 138809, at *12, 2020 WL 4472999 (E.D. Mo. Aug. 4, 2020) ("'[C]ontention interrogatories are overly broad and unduly burdensome on their face if they seek "all facts" supporting a claim or defense, such that the answering party is required to provide a narrative account of its case.' 'Thus, . . . interrogatories may "properly ask for the 'principal or material' facts which support an allegation or defense." In addition, interrogatories may seek the identities of knowledgeable persons and supporting documents for the 'principal' or 'material' facts supporting an allegation or defense.'" (quoting *Moses v. Halstead*, 236 F.R.D. 667, 674 (D. Kan. 2006))); *Dalmatia Imp. Grp., Inc. v. FoodMatch, Inc.*, No. 16-2767, 2016 U.S. Dist. LEXIS 136743, at *4, 2016 WL 5721161 (E.D. Pa. Oct. 3, 2016) ("Interrogatories that seek the identification of documents or of witnesses are not contention interrogatories."); *EEOC v. Sterling Jewelers Inc.*, No. 08-CV-00706(A)(M), 2012 U.S. Dist. LEXIS 67220, at *24, 2012 WL 1680811 (W.D.N.Y. May 14, 2012) (same); *High Point SARL v. Sprint Nextel Corp.*, CIV.A. 09-2269-CM, 2011 U.S. Dist. LEXIS 103118, at *59, 2011 WL 4036424, at *19 (D. Kan. Sept. 12, 2011) ("Not all interrogatories that use the 'each and every' language, however, are objectionable. An interrogatory that asks for a party to identify 'each and every element of the design' that the party contends is defective has been found sufficiently narrow so as to not be unduly burdensome or overly broad on its face."); *Lucero v. Valdez*, 240 F.R.D. 591, 594 (D.N.M. 2007) ("Contention interrogatories are distinct from interrogatories that request identification of witnesses or documents that support a party's contentions."); *U.S. ex rel. Hunt v. Merck-Medco Managed Care, LLC*, No. 00-CV-737, 2005 U.S. Dist. LEXIS 17014, at *8, 2005 WL 1971885 (E.D. Pa. Aug. 15, 2005) (same); *In re Grand Casinos, Inc.*, 181 F.R.D. 615, 618–19 (D. Minn. 1998) ("Moreover, the 'non-contentious' nature of the Interrogatory [requesting witness identification] is confirmed by the fact that it is largely duplicative of the disclosure obligations of [Federal] Rule 26(a)(1)(A) . . ., which require a party to initially disclose the identity of 'each individual likely to have discoverable information relevant to disputed facts alleged with particularity in the pleadings[.]"). See also cases cited in note 15.

The fact that such an interrogatory does not require evidence marshalling does not mean that it is not unduly burdensome overbroad, or disproportionate to the case's needs. Depending on the question asked, it may be so. See cases cited in notes 27.

31 See cases cited in note 39.

32 *Sheffield Dev. Co. v. Carter & Burgess, Inc.*, No. 02-00204-CV, 2012 Tex. App. LEXIS 10599, 2012 WL 6632500 (Tex. App.—Fort Worth 2012, pet. dism'd) (mem. op.).

33 *Sheffield Dev. Co. v. Carter & Burgess, Inc.*, No. 02-00204-CV, 2012 Tex. App. LEXIS 10599, at *1–2, 2012 WL 6632500 (Tex. App.—Fort Worth 2012, pet. dism'd) (mem. op.).

34 *Sheffield Dev. Co. v. Carter & Burgess, Inc.*, No. 02-00204-CV, 2012 Tex. App. LEXIS 10599, at *1–2, 2012 WL 6632500 (Tex. App.—Fort Worth 2012, pet. dism'd) (mem. op.).

(b) the date(s) on which the alleged deviation or non-conformity existed;

(c) the person(s) and/or event(s) which you contend caused or contributed to the alleged deviation or non-conformity;

(d) the date the alleged deviation or non-conformity was discovered and by whom; and

(e) any and all steps taken to correct or remedy the alleged deviation or non-conformity.[35]

The developer objected to the interrogatory because, among other things, it required evidence marshalling.[36] The trial court disagreed and "barred [the developer] from offering evidence of defects or errors by [the engineering firm] pertaining to grading or drainage . . . until it more fully answered the interrogatory [and further] ordered that [the engineering firm] did not need to produce any witnesses for deposition or respond to any discovery requests regarding [the developer's] claims until the question was answered[.]"[37]

In the appeal from the engineering firm's summary judgment, the developer argued that the trial court's discovery order was improper because the interrogatory was objectionable.[38] The Fort Worth Court of Appeals, in rejecting the argument, held that the interrogatory did not require evidence marshalling because it did not require the developer to "'arrang[e] all of [its] evidence in the order that it will be presented at trial.' . . . Instead, it sought the facts underlying [the developer's] claims against [the engineering firm], which 'is the very purpose of discovery.'"[39]

---

[35] *Sheffield Dev. Co. v. Carter & Burgess, Inc.*, No. 02-00204-CV, 2012 Tex. App. LEXIS 10599, at *4, 2012 WL 6632500 (Tex. App.—Fort Worth 2012, pet. dism'd) (mem. op.).

[36] *Sheffield Dev. Co. v. Carter & Burgess, Inc.*, No. 02-00204-CV, 2012 Tex. App. LEXIS 10599, at *5, 2012 WL 6632500 (Tex. App.—Fort Worth 2012, pet. dism'd) (mem. op.).

[37] *Sheffield Dev. Co. v. Carter & Burgess, Inc.*, No. 02-00204-CV, 2012 Tex. App. LEXIS 10599, at *10–11, 2012 WL 6632500 (Tex. App.—Fort Worth 2012, pet. dism'd) (mem. op.).

[38] *Sheffield Dev. Co. v. Carter & Burgess, Inc.*, No. 02-00204-CV, 2012 Tex. App. LEXIS 10599, at *13–14, 16, 2012 WL 6632500 (Tex. App.—Fort Worth 2012, pet. dism'd) (mem. op.).

[39] *Sheffield Dev. Co. v. Carter & Burgess, Inc.*, No. 02-00204-CV, 2012 Tex. App. LEXIS 10599, at *17, 2012 WL 6632500 (Tex. App.—Fort Worth 2012, pet. dism'd) (mem. op.) (quoting *Marshalling, Black's Law Dictionary* 1063 (9th ed. 2009), and *In re Swepi L.P.*, 103 S.W.3d 578, 590 (Tex. App.—San Antonio 2003, orig. proceeding)); *accord In re Sting Soccer Grp., LP*, No. 05-17-00317-CV, 2017 Tex. App. LEXIS 11197, at *13–14, 2017 WL 5897454 (Tex. App.—Dallas Nov. 30, 2017, orig. proceeding) (mem. op.) ("The party may not use interrogatories to require the responding party to marshal all of its available proof or the proof the party intends to offer at trial. . . . Relators' interrogatories asked Vola to identify facts of which Vola is specifically aware that Vola contends establishes, demonstrates or proves specific allegations made by Vola in its pleadings. Such requests fall within the parameters of [Texas] Rule 197.1 and do not require a marshaling of evidence.") (citation omitted); *In re Swepi L.P.*, 103 S.W.3d 578, 590 (Tex. App.—San Antonio, 2003, orig. proceeding) ("Casas complains the interrogatories require plaintiffs to marshal all their proof or all the proof they intend to present at trial. We disagree with this interpretation of the questions. The interrogatories seek the facts underlying the plaintiffs' claims. This is the very purpose of discovery. Casas cannot avoid providing facts by assuming Shell is asking for more than the rules allow."); *Nealy v. Southlawn Palms Apartments*, 196 S.W.3d 386, 394–95 (Tex. App.—Houston [1st Dist.] 2006, no pet.) (finding an interrogatory requesting a landlord to identify each undesirable tenant behavior and how it breached the lease was a proper contention

Accordingly, interrogatories like the interrogatory at issue in *Sheffield Development* that, for example, ask a plaintiff to state each misrepresentation or omission underlying its fraud or DTPA claim, each fiduciary breach underlying its breach of fiduciary claim, each trade secret or item of confidential information stolen or misappropriated, each breach of a lease provision in a wrongful eviction action, each discriminatory action, or each construction defect do *not* require evidence marshalling.[40]

The difficulty is that there is a large middle ground between these types of interrogatories and ones that ask a party to state "all" or "every" fact supporting a cause of action or defense.[41] Accordingly, what constitutes evidence marshalling often must be decided on an interrogatory-by-interrogatory basis.[42] In doing so, a court should use a pragmatic, common-sense approach that weighs the interrogatory's scope, the burden and expense involved in responding to it, the action's complexity, and whether the information can be more readily obtained through depositions or another discovery form (i.e., by engaging in a proportionality analysis).[43]

---

interrogatory); Robert K. Wise, *Ending Evasive Responses to Written Discovery: A Guide for Properly Responding (and Objecting) to Interrogatories and Document Requests Under the Texas Discovery Rules*, 65 Baylor L. Rev. 510, 519 (2103) (discussing what constitutes evidence marshalling); *cf. High Point SARL v. Sprint Nextel Corp.*, CIV.A. 09-2269-CM, 2011 U.S. Dist. LEXIS 103118, at *59, 2011 WL 4036424, at *19 (D. Kan. Sept. 12, 2011) ("Not all interrogatories that use the 'each and every' language, however, are objectionable. An interrogatory that asks for a party to identify 'each and every element of the design' that the party contends is defective has been found sufficiently narrow so as to not be unduly burdensome or overly broad on its face." (quoting *Cardenas v. Dorel Juvenile Grp., Inc.*, 231 F.R.D. 616, 619 (D. Kan. 2005))); *Roberts v. Heim*, 130 F.R.D. 424, 427 (N.D. Cal. 1989) ("It is not difficult to discern a significant difference between an interrogatory which, for example, asks a plaintiff to 'state all facts upon which you base your contention that defendant is liable in this action' and an interrogatory which asks a plaintiff to 'state all facts upon which you base your contention that defendant was in attendance at the meeting of January 10, 1989.' The latter is a reasonable interrogatory, and the former is not. The difficulty is that there is a substantial middle ground between these extremes and, therefore, each interrogatory has to be judged in terms of its scope and in terms of the overall context of the case at the time it is asked.").

40 See cases cited in note 39.

41 Robert K. Wise, *Ending Evasive Responses to Written Discovery: A Guide for Properly Responding (and Objecting) to Interrogatories and Document Requests Under the Texas Discovery Rules*, 65 Baylor L. Rev. 510, 519 (2103) (discussing what constitutes evidence marshalling).

42 Robert K. Wise, *Ending Evasive Responses to Written Discovery: A Guide for Properly Responding (and Objecting) to Interrogatories and Document Requests Under the Texas Discovery Rules*, 65 Baylor L. Rev. 510, 519 (2103) (discussing what constitutes evidence marshalling).

43 *See, e.g., In re State Farm Lloyds*, 520 S.W.3d 595, 599 (Tex. 2017) (orig. proceeding) ("[A]ll discovery is subject to the proportionality overlay embedded in our discovery rules . . . .") (footnote omitted) (citation omitted); *Cf. Estate of Swayzer v. Clarke*, 16-CV-1703, 2019 U.S. Dist. LEXIS 74769, at *7, 2019 WL 1980349 (E.D. Wis. May 3, 2019) ("In assessing whether to require a party to answer contention interrogatories, the court should be guided by '[t]he twin aims of efficiency and fairness' and consider whether the 'answers will meaningfully contribute to issue clarification, narrow the scope of the dispute, or provide for early settlement.'" (quoting *BASF Catalysts LLC v. Aristo, Inc.*, No. 2:07-cv-222, 2009 U.S. Dist. LEXIS 4780, at *5, 2009 WL 187808 (N.D. Ind. Jan. 23, 2009))); *Roberts v. Heim*, 130 F.R.D. 424, 427 (N.D. Cal. 1989) (explaining that, in determining whether an interrogatory that ask a party to "state all facts on which an allegation or a denial is based"

Although a court may defer answers to contention interrogatories until after other designated discovery has been completed,[44] there is no reason why a court cannot

is objectionable or violated a discovery guideline, the interrogatory must, "be judged in terms of its scope and in terms of the overall context of the case at the time it is asked").

[44] Tex. R. Civ. P. 192.6(b)(4) (allowing a court to enter a protective order specifying when certain discovery can be undertaken); ***In re Alford Chevrolet-Geo***, 997 S.W.2d 173, 182 (Tex. 1999) (orig. proceeding) ("[I]t is within the trial court's discretion to schedule discovery and decide whether and how much discovery is warranted[.]"); ***Ramon v. Teacher Ret. Sys.***, No. 01-09-00684-CV, 2010 Tex. App. LEXIS 2316, at *17, 2010 WL 1241293 (Tex. App.—Houston [1st Dist.] Apr. 1, 2010, pet. denied) (mem. op.) ("A trial court has broad discretion to schedule and define the scope of discovery."); ***In re CNA Lloyds***, No. 13-07-386-CV, 2007 Tex. App. LEXIS 7790, at *3, 2007 WL 2812147 (Tex. App.—Corpus Christi Sept. 24, 2007, orig. proceeding) (mem. op.) (same).

Federal Rule 33(a), unlike Texas Rule 197.1, specifically allows a trial court to "order" that contention interrogatories "need not be answered until designated discovery is complete, or until a pretrial conference, or some other time." ***Compare*** Fed. R. Civ. P. 33(a), ***with*** Tex. R. Civ. P. 197.1. Accordingly, federal courts often hold that contention interrogatories are most appropriate after the parties have had the opportunity to take substantial discovery. ***Compare, e.g., Smash Tech., LLC v. Smash Sols., LLC***, 335 F.R.D. 438, 448 (D. Utah 2020) ("Although a contention interrogatory must be answered, the nature of such interrogatories warrants special treatment. [Federal] Rule 33 provides that 'the court may order that the [contention] interrogatory need not be answered until designated discovery is complete . . . or some other time. Under this provision, many courts defer the obligation to respond to the contention interrogatory until near the end of the discovery period unless the proponent carries its burden of demonstrating why they are necessary earlier on.") (citation omitted); ***Sigman v. CSX Corp.***, No. 3:15-cv-13328, 2016 U.S. Dist. LEXIS 178563, at *64, 2016 WL 7444947 (S.D.W. Va. Dec. 27, 2016) ("[M]ost courts agree that '[d]ue to the nature of contention interrogatories, they are more appropriately used after a substantial amount of discovery has been conducted—typically at the end of the discovery period.'" (quoting ***Capacchione v. Charlotte-Mecklenburg Bd. of Educ.***, 182 F.R.D. 486, 489 (W.D.N.C. 1998))), ***Wide Voice, LLC v. Sprint Commc'ns Co.***, No. 2:15-cv-1604-GMN-VCF, 2016 U.S. Dist. LEXIS 66667, at *4, 2016 WL 11507772 (D. Nev. May 19, 2016) ("While 'there is no outright prohibition on propounding contention interrogatories early on in litigation,' courts disfavor early contention interrogatories." (quoting ***Cardoza v. Bloomin' Brands, Inc.***, No. 2:13-cv-1820-JAD-NJK, 2015 U.S. Dist. LEXIS 82015, at *4, 2015 WL 3875916 (D. Nev. June 22, 2015))), ***Harvey v. Circle***, No. 4:19-CV-902-NAB, 2020 U.S. Dist. LEXIS 138809, at *12, 2020 WL 4472999 (E.D. Mo. Aug. 4, 2020) ("[C]ontention interrogatories need not be answered until discovery is complete or nearly complete in accordance with Fed. R. Civ. P. 33(a)(2).") (citation omitted), ***U.S. ex rel. Scott v. Humana Inc.***, No. 3:18-CV-61-JRW-CHL, 2019 U.S. Dist. LEXIS 223906, at *4, 2019 WL 7406784 (W.D. Ky. Dec. 19, 2019) ("[A] court may postpone a response to contention interrogatories until discovery is closer to completion."), ***Hill-Rom Servs. Inc. v. Tellisense Med., LLC***, No. 117CV04725TWPMJD, 2019 U.S. Dist. LEXIS 234049, at *8, 2019 WL 10888459 (S.D. Ind. Nov. 18, 2019) ("Federal Rule of Civil Procedure 33(a)(2) . . . provides that the court may order that a contention interrogatory need not be answered until designated discovery is complete, or until a pretrial conference or some other time."), ***Burnett & Morand P'ship v. Estate of Youngs***, No. 3:10–cv–3–RLY–WGH, 2011 U.S. Dist. LEXIS 36916, at *10, 2011 WL 1237950 (S.D. Ind. Apr. 4, 2011) ("There must be an initial answer and response [to contention interrogatories] in good faith and as complete as possible. . . . Resolution of disputes cannot occur in an orderly manner if there are no preliminary answers to help guide the parties in identification of the facts and documents which support a theory, or if helpful responses are not served, until the very last day discovery can be completed."), ***SEC v. Berry***, No. C07-04431 RMW (HRL), 2011 require answers to contention interrogatories early in the action. Such a requirement is consistent with Texas Rule 192.2, which provides that "the permissible forms of discovery . . . may be taken in any order or sequence," and, more importantly, with Section 10.001 of the Texas Civil Practice and Remedies Code, which requires a party to have some "evidentiary support" for its claims or defenses.[45] Thus, the responding party can answer a contention interrogatory served early in the action with the infor-

---

U.S. Dist. LEXIS 64437, at *6, 2011 WL 2441706 (N.D. Cal. June 15, 2011) ("'[C]ourts tend to deny contention interrogatories filed before substantial discovery has taken place, but grant them if discovery is almost complete.'" (quoting *In re eBay Seller Antitrust Litig.*, No. C 07-1882 JF (RS), 2008 U.S. Dist. LEXIS 102815, at *4, 2008 WL 5212170 (N.D. Cal. Dec. 11, 2008))), *Helmert v. Butterball, LLC*, No. 4:08CV00342 JLH, 2010 U.S. Dist. LEXIS 121902, at *4, 2010 WL 4537096 (E.D. Ark. Nov. 3, 2010) ("[A] number of district courts, including several in this circuit, have determined that contention interrogatories need not be answered until discovery is complete or nearing completion."), *and Cornell Research Found., Inc. v. Hewlett Packard Co.*, 223 F.R.D. 55, 67 (N.D.N.Y. 2003) ("[C]ontention interrogatories are often reserved for use at the end of discovery in order to crystallize the issues to be presented to the court[.]"), *with, e.g., Firetrace USA, LLC v. Jesclard*, No. CV-07-2001-PHX-ROS, 2009 U.S. Dist. LEXIS 2972, at *7–8, 2009 WL 73671 (D. Ariz. Jan. 9, 2009) ("Although the Court does have the authority to defer Defendants' response to Plaintiffs' second interrogatory, Defendants have not convincingly argued that the Court should exercise its discretion in this way."), *and Strauss v. Credit Lyonnais, S.A.*, 242 F.R.D. 199, 235 (E.D.N.Y. 2007) ("Requiring plaintiffs in this case to answer subparts (ii) and (iii) at this early stage in discovery would not be futile or burdensome because the interrogatories track the allegations in the complaint, upon which plaintiffs presumably have sufficient facts to plead."). *See also Firefighters' Ret. Sys. v. Citco Grp. Ltd.*, No. 13-373-SDD-EWD, 2017 U.S. Dist. LEXIS 101747, at *29–31, 2017 WL 2825925 (M.D. La. June 29, 2017) ("It is within the court's discretion to determine the appropriate time for responding to a contention interrogatory. Some courts considering this issue have required a party to answer contention interrogatories tracking the language of their complaint early in the discovery process. Others 'tend to deny contention interrogatories filed before substantial discovery has taken place, but grant them if discovery is almost complete.'" (citations omitted) (quoting *In re eBay Seller Antitrust Litig.*, 2008 U.S. Dist. LEXIS 102815, at *4, 2008 WL 5212170(N.D. Cal. Dec. 11, 2008))).

Federal courts, however, have held that identification interrogatories generally should be answered whenever they are served. *Cf. Kolker v. VNUS Med. Techs., Inc.*, No. C 10-0900 SBA (PSG), 2011 U.S. Dist. LEXIS 122810, at *19–20, 2011 WL 5057094 (N.D. Cal. Oct. 24, 2011) ("Along the lines of [Federal] Rule 26's initial disclosures, courts generally approve of such 'identification interrogatories,' whether early or late in a case.").

45 Tex. Civ. Prac. & Rem. Code § 10.001(3); *cf. Green Crush, LLC v. Paradise Splash I, Inc.*, No. SACV1701856CJCJDEX, 2019 U.S. Dist. LEXIS 230749, at *6, 2019 WL 8640653 (C.D. Cal. Apr. 8, 2019) ("Requiring an answer to straightforward factual contention interrogatories is consistent with [Federal] Rule 11, which requires the plaintiff to have some factual basis for the allegations in its complaint."); *Firetrace USA, LLC v. Jesclard*, No. CV-07-2001-PHX-ROS, 2009 U.S. Dist. LEXIS 2972, at *6, 2009 WL 73671 (D. Ariz. Jan. 9, 2009) ("Defendants, who asserted affirmative defenses in their Answer, must have contemplated a [Federal] Rule 11 basis in law or fact when they asserted these defenses and should be required to reveal this [Federal] Rule 11 basis, as well as other presently-known facts on the matter, when responding to Plaintiffs' contention interrogatories, regardless of how much discovery has transpired."); *U.S. ex rel. O'Connell v. Chapman Univ.*, 245 F.R.D. 646, 649 (C.D. Cal. 2007) ("Requiring a party to answer contention interrogatories is 'consistent with Rule 11 of the Federal Rules of Civil Procedure, [which requires that] plaintiffs must have some factual basis for the allegations in their complaint[.]'" (quoting *Cooperman v. One Bancorp (In re One Bancorp Sec. Litig.)*, 134 F.R.D. 4, 8 (D. Me. 1991))).

mation presently available and seasonably amend or supplement its answer as more information becomes available through discovery.[46] In this regard, the responding party is not prejudiced by having to respond to contention interrogatories early in the action because, under Texas Rule 197.3, "an answer to an interrogatory inquiring about [the opposing party's contentions or damages] that has been amended or supplemented may not be used for impeachment."[47]

Contrary to the belief of many practitioners, contention interrogatories that ask for the factual bases for an allegation, claim, or defense do not seek information protected by the work-product privilege even if the facts were learned by the party or its attorney during witness interviews or the investigation during, or in anticipation of, the litigation.[48] In fact, Texas Rule 192.5(c)(1) makes this clear by providing that "information discoverable under [Texas] Rule 192.3 concerning . . . contentions" is not work-product protected from discovery "[e]ven if made or prepared in anticipation of litigation or for trial[.]"[49] In the same vein, the work-product privilege does not apply to interrogatories asking a party to identify persons with knowledge about, or

---

Well-tailored contention interrogatories are particularly appropriate early in an action when a true "notice pleading" is involved because they help the requesting party learn the responding party's theories. This, in turn, allows the requesting party to narrow discovery's scope and seek information relevant to the claim or defense, thereby saving valuable time and resources.

[46] *Cf. Burnett & Morand P'ship v. Estate of Youngs*, No. 3:10-cv-3-RLY-WGH, 2011 U.S. Dist. LEXIS 36916, at *10, 2011 WL 1237950 (S.D. Ind. Apr. 4, 2011) ("There must be an initial answer and response [to contention interrogatories] in good faith and as complete as possible. . . . Resolution of disputes cannot occur in an orderly manner if there are no preliminary answers to help guide the parties in identification of the facts and documents which support a theory, or if helpful responses are not served, until the very last day discovery can be completed."); *Firetrace USA, LLC v. Jesclard*, No. CV-07-2001-PHX-ROS, 2009 U.S. Dist. LEXIS 2972, at *7 (D. Ariz. Jan. 9, 2009); *Cornell Research Found., Inc. v. Hewlett Packard Co.*, 223 F.R.D. 55, 67 (N.D.N.Y. 2003); *Cable & Comput. Tech. v. Lockheed Saunders, Inc.*, 175 F.R.D. 646, 651 (C.D. Cal. 1997); *Cooperman v. One Bancorp (In re One Bancorp Sec. Litig.)*, 134 F.R.D. 4, 8 (D. Me. 1991).

[47] Tex. R. Civ. P. 197.3.

[48] *See* Tex. R. Civ. P. 192.5(c)(1).

[49] *See* Tex. R. Civ. P. 192.5(c)(1); *accord* Tex. R. Civ. P. 194.2(b)(3) (requiring disclosure of legal theories and factual bases of responding party's claims or defenses); Former Tex. R. Civ. P. 194.2(c) (providing that a party may request disclosure of legal theories and factual bases of responding party's claims or defenses), 197.1 (providing that an interrogatory may ask a responding party to state legal theories and to describe in general the factual bases for its claims or defenses); *In re Sting Soccer Grp., LP*, No. 05-17-00317-CV, 2017 Tex. App. LEXIS 11197, at *14, 2017 WL 5897454 (Tex. App.—Dallas Nov. 30, 2017, orig. proceeding) (mem. op.) ("[D]iscovery requests seeking a party's legal or factual contentions are excepted from the work product doctrine and cannot be protected from discovery even if they otherwise fit the definition of work product."); *In re Ochoa*, No. 12-04-00163-CV, 2004 Tex. App. LEXIS 4866, at *4, 2004 WL 1192444 (Tex. App.—Tyler May 28, 2004, orig. proceeding) (mem. op.) ("A party's legal contentions and the factual bases for those contentions are discoverable. Even if made or prepared in anticipation of litigation or for trial, information discoverable under [Texas] Rule 192.3 concerning a party's contentions is not work product protected from discovery.") (citation omitted); *Owens v. Wallace*, 821 S.W.2d 746, 748 (Tex. App.—Tyler 1992, orig. proceeding) ("'It is also not ground for objection that an interrogatory propounded pursuant to [former Texas] Rule 168 involves an opinion or contention that relates to fact or the application of law to fact.' The six interrogatories at

documents concerning, an allegation, claim, defense, or particular facts, irrespective of how the party or its attorney learned about the persons or documents.[50] However,

---

issue fall squarely within that provision. The plaintiffs' work product objections to interrogatories numbers 3, 5, 7, 8, 9, and 10, were without merit.") (citations omitted).

Federal courts have consistently held that the work-product and attorney-client privileges do *not* apply to contention interrogatories. *E.g., MCC Controls v. Hal Hays Constr.*, No. 191655ABKKX, 2020 U.S. Dist. LEXIS 190705, at *9, 2020 WL 6034321 (C.D. Cal. July 23, 2020) ("Primex's interrogatories do not seek to discover the contents of any attorney-client communications; they ask simply for the facts supporting HHC's defenses. Hence, HHC's attorney-client privilege objections are OVERRULED."); *Mountain Valley Pipeline, LLC v. 6.5 Acres of Land Owned by Sizemore Inc. of Virginia*, No. 7:18CV610, 2019 U.S. Dist. LEXIS 231435, at *5, 2019 WL 8918904 (W.D. Va. Apr. 5, 2019) ("Courts do not, as a general matter, allow a party to use the work-product doctrine to avoid answering contention interrogatories."); *Bank of Am., N.A. v. Barnes Hill, LLC*, No. 16-11583-DJC, 2018 U.S. Dist. LEXIS 233146, at *4–5, 2018 WL 10247150 (D. Mass. July 26, 2018) ("[T]he work product doctrine is not a valid objection to a contention interrogatory. In answering contention interrogatories the party is only giving the factual specifics which the party contends support a claim, and this in no way impinges on the attorney's impressions or analysis as to how the attorney will endeavor to apply the law to the facts. If this elementary principle were not applicable, contention interrogatories would not exist.") (citation omitted); *Avila v. Mohave Cnty.*, No. 3:14-cv-8124-HRH, 2015 U.S. Dist. LEXIS 148956, at *20, 2015 WL 6660187 (D. Ariz. Nov. 2, 2015) ("Defendants' contention that providing the factual basis for their affirmative defenses might intrude upon the attorney-client privilege or work-product doctrine is unavailing. Courts have repeatedly rejected this ground for refusing to answer such interrogatories."); *Zamperla, Inc. v. I.E. Park SRL*, No. 6:13-cv-1807-Orl-37KRS, 2015 U.S. Dist. LEXIS 183900, at *5, 2015 WL 12836001 (M.D. Fla. Sept. 22, 2015) ("[T]he advisory notes to [Federal] Rule 33 make clear, '[a]s to requests for opinions or contentions that call for the application of law to fact, they can be most useful in narrowing and sharpening the issues, which is a major purpose of discovery.' Accordingly, courts have consistently declined to find that contention interrogatories encroach on an attorney's work product or upon the attorney-client privilege." (quoting Fed. R. Civ. P. 33, Advisory Note to 1970 Amend.)); *Hernandez v. Best Buy Co.*, No. 13cv2587-JM(KSC), 2014 U.S. Dist. LEXIS 152117, at *17–18, 2014 WL 5454505 (S.D. Cal. Oct. 24, 2014) ("'Contention interrogatories' that ask a party what it contends or to state all the [principal or material] facts upon which it bases a contention are perfectly legitimate.' Contrary to defendant's argument, answering contention interrogatories does not 'encroach[] upon an attorney's work product.' '[I]n answering contention interrogatories the party is only giving the factual specifics which the party contends supports a claim, and this in no way impinges on the attorney's impressions or analysis as to how the attorney will endeavor to apply the law to the facts.[.]'" (quoting *Hiskett v. Wal-Mart Stores, Inc.*, 180 F.R.D. 403, 404–05 (D. Kan. 1998), and *King v. E.F. Hutton & Co., Inc.*, 117 F.R.D. 2, 5 (D.D.C. 1987))); *Gilmore v. City of Minneapolis*, No. 13-1019 (JRT/FLN), 2014 U.S. Dist. LEXIS 132543, at *13, 2014 WL 4722488 (D. Minn. Sept. 22, 2014) (same); *In re Rail Freight Surcharge Antitrust Litig.*, 281 F.R.D. 1, 4 (D.D.C. 2011) (same); *Okla. v. Tyson Foods, Inc.*, 262 F.R.D. 617, 630, 630 n.15 (N.D. Okla. 2009) (same).

50 *See* Tex. R. Civ. P. 192.3(b)-(c), 192.5(c)(3); *cf. Courtland Co., Inc. v. Union Carbide Corp.*, No. 2:19-CV-00894, 2021 U.S. Dist. LEXIS 33596, at *4, 2021 WL 707158 (S.D.W. Va. Feb. 23, 2021) ("Plaintiff is advised that it cannot employ the work product doctrine to withhold the identities of any potential witnesses with discoverable information."); *Bell v. Pension Comm.*, LLC, 330 F.R.D. 517, 523 (S.D. Ind. 2018) ("[I]nformation that is merely factual may not be withheld under the umbrella of work product but must be available, if not through the production of otherwise protectable documents, then through interrogatories or depositions."); *U.S. v. Talmage*, No. 1:16-cv-19-DN-PMW, 2017 U.S. Dist. LEXIS 88251, at *29,

contention interrogatories asking the responding party to identify the legal *authorities* supporting their causes of action or defenses are improper because such information is protected by work-product privilege.[51]

2017 WL 2483797 (D. Utah June 8, 2017) ("Plaintiffs' argument that identifying specific documents responsive to the interrogatories violates the work product doctrine when they had already been produced as part of an earlier production is less persuasive in a complex commercial case. In today's electronic age, a complex commercial case can easily involve a production of several hundred thousand, if not millions, of pages of documents. Upholding such a rigid rule would encourage parties to overproduce documents in order to make it more difficult for the receiving party to locate the documents that are truly relevant. Such conduct unnecessarily drives up both the cost and duration of litigation." (quoting *Lance v. Ginsburg*, 32 F.R.D. 51, 52 (E.D. Pa. 1962))); *Slavkov v. Fast Water Heater Partners I, LP*, No. 14-cv-04324-JST, 2015 U.S. Dist. LEXIS 148369, at *2–4, 2015 WL 6648170 (N.D. Cal. Oct. 30, 2015) ("First, Defendants object that identification of the facts and documents they intend to rely on is protected by the attorney work product privilege. . . . In fact, 'as a general proposition, without some special showing, the work product doctrine cannot be used as a shield to deflect contention questions,' particularly where the interrogatory seeks only the identification of documents or knowledgeable witnesses. The Court overrules this objection." (citations omitted) (quoting *In re Convergent Techs. Sec. Litig.*, 108 F.R.D. 328, 335 n.20 (N.D. Cal. 1985))); *Pouncil v. Branch L. Firm*, 277 F.R.D. 642, 649 (D. Kan. 2011) ("The interrogatories ask for Defendants' contentions with respect to the factual issues of [the case]. . . . The interrogatories also request that Defendants identify the facts and documents supporting their contentions. Defendants, who have the burden of supporting their work product objection, have not shown that answering these interrogatories would reveal the mental impressions, conclusions, opinions, or legal theories of their counsel."); *Kolker v. VNUS Med. Techs., Inc.*, No. C 10-0900 SBA (PSG), 2011 U.S. Dist. LEXIS 122810, at *20–21, 2011 WL 5057094 (N.D. Cal. Oct. 24, 2011) ("The court agrees with Covidien that Kolker cannot claim a privilege over the identity or description of witnesses or documents that may be used to support Kolker's allegations. Covidien has not requested a summary or even identification of 'interviews, statements, memoranda, correspondence, briefs, mental impressions,' or other aspects of an attorney's work product subject to the protections of the work product doctrine. Kolker argues that the identity of '[t]he exact witness by whom a relevant fact may be proven at the trial' is protected work product. In *McNamara v. Erschen*, [8 F.R.D. 427, 429 (D. Del. 1948),] however, the court distinguished between an interrogatory 'seeking only the identity of persons known to the plaintiff in connection with those allegations of the complaint' and 'the subsequent mental determination of what precise witnesses are best available to prove a relevant fact,' especially when such identity is requested at an early stage of the litigation.") (footnote omitted); *Smith v. Café Asia*, 256 F.R.D. 247, 255 (D.D.C. 2009) ("This Court has stated that an interrogatory which requests the identification of documents relating to facts may be served on a party."); *Unites States v. Exxon Corp.*, 87 F.R.D. 624, 638 (D.D.C. 1980) ("For example, Interrogatory 42 asks the DOE to identify documents directing FEA personnel that a lease-by-lease BPCL was permissible for unitized property. Exxon argues that, even if the underlying documents constitute work product materials, the DOE cannot claim work product in refusing to at least identify these documents. The mere identification of documents fails to violate the work product privilege.").

[51] *See Ferruccio v. Davis*, No. 5:19-CV-346-BO, 2020 U.S. Dist. LEXIS 212300, at *7, 2020 WL 6706354 (E.D.N.C. Nov. 13, 2020) ("Plaintiff is asking that Defendants tell her what legal authorities support their arguments. Defendants are not required to do Plaintiff's legal research for her."); *U.S. ex rel. Scott v. Humana Inc.*, No. 3:18-CV-61-JRW-CHL, 2019 U.S. Dist. LEXIS 223906, at *19, 2019 WL 7406784 (W.D. Ky. Dec. 19, 2019) ("The Court finds that opposing counsel's legal research implicates the mental impressions of an attorney thus it may not be inquired into under [Federal] Rule 26(b)(1)."); *Gilmore v. City of Minneapolis*, Civil No. 0:13-CV-1019-JRT-FLN, 2014 U.S. Dist. LEXIS 132543, at *14–15, 2014 WL

9-4 Number of Interrogatories

The discovery-control plan applicable to the case, rather than Texas Rule 197, governs the number of interrogatories permitted.[52] In Level 1 and Level 2 actions, fifteen interrogatories and twenty-five interrogatories, including "discrete subpart[s,]" other than those seeking to identify or authenticate documents, are permitted, respectively.[53] Unless the Level 3 discovery-control plan expressly provides for more interrogatories, the number of interrogatories in a Level 3 action will be the number that was permitted before the action was moved to Level 3.[54] Thus, if the plaintiff initially pleaded the action into Level 1 and the court later enters a Level 3 discovery-control plan that does not address the number of interrogatories, the 15-interrogatory limit of Texas Rule 190.2(b)(3) will control. Similarly, if the action was a Level 2 one before the Level 3 discovery-control plan's entry, and the plan does not address the number of interrogatories, the 25-interrogatory limit of Texas Rule 190.3(b)(3) will control.

4722488 (D. Minn. Sept. 22, 2014) ("The Court concludes that the Magistrate Judge erred in requiring Defendants to 'specify the statutes or other legal authority supporting their position' and produce 'relevant legal authorities' in response to Gilmore's interrogatories because requiring a party to produce relevant legal authorities goes beyond the permissible scope of a contention interrogatory and constitutes protected work product. Gilmore has not cited, and the Court has not found, a single case requiring a party to provide citations to all relevant legal authority in response to contention interrogatories which ask for the basis of a party's claim. Instead, courts have routinely concluded that interrogatories which seek purely legal information are not permissible." (citing *Kendrick v. Sullivan*, 125 F.R.D. 1, 4 (D.D.C. 1989), and *McCrink v. Peoples Benefit Life Ins. Co.*, No. 04-1068, 2004 U.S. Dist. LEXIS 23990, at *4, 2004 WL 2743420 (E.D. Pa. Nov. 29))).

52 Tex. R. Civ. P. 190 cmt. 1 to 1999 change. Texas Rule 190 provides for three levels of discovery: Levels 1, 2, and 3. Tex. R. Civ. P. 190.2–190.4. See Chapter 2, section 2-3 (discussing the three discovery levels).

53 Tex. R. Civ. P. 190.2(b)(3), 190.3(b)(3).

54 Tex. R. Civ. P. 190.4(b) ("The discovery limitations of [Texas] Rule 190.2, if applicable, or otherwise of [Texas] Rule 190.3 apply unless specifically changed in the [Level 3] discovery control plan ordered by the court."); *Brescia v. Slack & Davis, L.L.P.*, No. 03-08-00042-CV, 2010 Tex. App. LEXIS 9204, at *10, 2010 WL 4670322 (Tex. App.—Austin Nov. 19, 2010, pet. denied) (mem. op.) ("[E]ven under a Level 3 scheduling order, Level 2 deadlines continue to apply "unless specifically changed in the discovery control plan ordered by the court." (quoting Tex. R. Civ. P. 190.4(b))); *Allen v. United of Omaha Life Ins. Co.*, 236 S.W.3d 315, 327 (Tex. App.—Fort Worth 2007, pet. denied) ("The rule addressing level 3 discovery control plans states that '[t]he court must, on a party's motion, . . . order that discovery be conducted in accordance with a discovery control plan tailored to the circumstances of the specific suit.' While the rule states that the court 'must' enter a level 3 scheduling order on a party's motion, it does not require that the order provide deadlines different from those under a level 2 case; even under a level 3 scheduling order, the level 2 deadlines continue to apply 'unless specifically changed in the discovery control plan ordered by the court.' That decision is left to the trial court's discretion: 'The discovery control plan ordered by the court . . . may change any limitation on the time for . . . discovery set forth in these rules.'" (citations omitted) (quoting Tex. R. Civ. P. 190.4(a), (b))); *see Estate of Grogan*, 595 S.W.3d 807, 824 (Tex. App.—Texarkana 2020, no pet.) (Texas "Rule 190.4 does not automatically set deadlines different from Level II deadlines, because they remain under Level III 'unless specifically changed in the discovery control plan ordered by the court.'" (quoting *Border States Elec. Supply of Tex., Inc. v. Coast to Coast Elec., LLC*, No. 13-13-00118-CV, 2014 Tex. App. LEXIS 5681, at *31, 2014 WL 3953961 (Tex. App.—Corpus Christi May 29, 2014, pet. denied) (mem. op.), and *Allen v. United of Omaha Life Ins. Co.*, 236 S.W.3d 315, 327 (Tex. App.—Fort Worth 2007, pet. denied))).

As pointed out above, under Texas Rules 190.2 and 190.3 and most Level 3 discovery-control plans, the limit on the number of interrogatories includes "[e]ach discrete subpart," but excludes interrogatories "asking a party only to identify or authenticate specific documents."[55] Accordingly, each discrete subpart of an interrogatory is considered a separate interrogatory. Comment 3 to the 1999 Change to the Rule explains that a "discrete subpart" "is, in general, one that calls for information that is not logically or factually related to the primary interrogatory."[56]

---

[55] Tex. R. Civ. P. 190.2(b)(3), 190.3(b)(3).

[56] Tex. R. Civ. P. 190 cmt. 3 to 1999 change; *accord In re Sting Soccer Grp., LP*, No. 05-17-00317-CV, 2017 Tex. App. LEXIS 11197, at *16, 2017 WL 5897454 (Tex. App.—Dallas Nov. 30, 2017, orig. proceeding) (mem. op.) ("A discrete subpart calls for information that is not logically or factually related to the primary interrogatory."). The concept of "discrete subparts" is derived from Federal Rule 33(a), which limits parties to "25 written interrogatories, including all discrete subparts." Tex. R. Civ. P. 190 cmt. 1 to 1999 change (citing Fed. R. Civ. P. 33, Advisory Committee's Note to 1993 Amend.).

Neither Federal Rule 33 nor its Advisory Committee's Note defines "discrete subpart." Rather, the note provides a single illustration of a non-discrete subpart: "a question asking about communications of a particular type should be treated as a single interrogatory even though it requests that the times, place, persons present, and contents be stated separately for each communication." Fed. R. Civ. P. 33, Advisory Committee's Note to 1993 Amend. Accordingly, federal courts use a variety of tests in determining whether interrogatory subparts are discrete. *Moser v. Navistar Int'l Corp.*, No. 4:17-CV-00598, 2018 U.S. Dist. LEXIS 127007 2018 WL 3614012 (E.D. Tex. July 27, 2018) (applying the "related question approach," under which "subparts that are logically or factually subsumed within and necessarily related to the primary question should not be treated as separate interrogatories."); *Erfindergemeinschaft UroPep GbR v. Eli Lilly & Co.*, 315 F.R.D. 191, 195–96 (E.D. Tex. May 13, 2016) ("The courts and treatise writers have used different verbal formulations in an effort to fashion a test for whether particular interrogatories contain 'discrete subparts.' One test that has occasionally been used is the 'discrete bits of information' test. Another test asks whether a subpart of an interrogatory 'introduces a line of inquiry that is separate and distinct from the inquiry made by the portion of the interrogatory that precedes it.' One leading treatise states that 'it would appear that an interrogatory containing subparts directed at eliciting details concerning a common theme should be considered a single question.' That 'common theme' standard can be useful and has been invoked by some courts. . . . [M]ost courts have followed what is sometimes referred to as the 'related question' approach. In an effort to give some specificity to the inquiry, the test applied under the 'related question' approach is generally stated as follows: subparts that are logically or factually subsumed within and necessarily related to the primary question should not be treated as separate interrogatories. Another way that approach has been articulated is to say that 'where the first question can be answered fully and completely without answering the second question, then the second question is totally independent of the first and not factually subsumed within [it].'" (quoting 8B Charles Alan Wright, Arthur R. Miller & Richard L. Marcus, *Federal Practice and Procedure* § 2168.1, at 39–40 (2010), and *FTC v. Think All Publ'g, L.L.C.*, No. 4:07-cv-011, 2008 U.S. Dist. LEXIS 18557, at *4–5, 2008 WL 687455 (E.D. Tex. Mar. 10, 2008))); *Mezu v. Morgan State Univ.*, 269 F.R.D. 565, 572–73 (D. Md. 2010) ("[A]n interrogatory containing subparts directed at eliciting details concerning the common theme should be considered a single question," but "an interrogatory with subparts inquiring into discrete areas is more likely to be counted as more than one for purposes of limitation." (quoting 8A Charles A. Wright, Arthur R. Miller & Richard L. Marcus, *Federal Practice and Procedure* § 2168, at 261 (2d ed. 1994))); *Dimitrijevic v. TV & C GP Holding Inc.*, No. H-04-3457, 2005 U.S. Dist. LEXIS 41399, 2005 WL 8164073 (S.D. Tex. Aug. 24, 2005) (employing the "full and complete answer test," under which a court asks if "the first

Although no Texas decision discusses what constitutes a "discrete subpart,"[57] many decisions of federal courts have done so in construing the federal rule on which the Texas rule is based: Federal Rule 33(a)(1). Federal courts uniformly have held that a "discrete subpart" is not determined by whether the inquiry is a sub-numbered or sub-lettered part of an interrogatory.[58] If such numbering or lettering were required, a party could easily circumvent the limit by eliminating numbering or lettering. In other words, unnumbered or unlettered "subparts" can be counted as "discrete subparts"[59]

---

question can be answered fully and completely without answering the second question."); *Kendall v. GES Exposition Servs. Inc.*, 174 F.R.D. 684, 685 (D. Nev. 1997) ("Probably the best test of whether subsequent questions, within a single interrogatory, are subsumed and related, is to examine whether the first question is primary and subsequent questions are secondary to the primary question. Or, can the subsequent question stand alone? Is it independent of the first question? Genuine subparts should not be counted as separate interrogatories. However, discrete or separate questions should be counted as separate interrogatories, notwithstanding [that] they are joined by a conjunctive word and may be related.").

[57] In *In re Sting Soccer Grp., LP*, No. 05-17-00317-CV, 2017 Tex. App. LEXIS 11197, at *16–17, 2017 WL 5897454 (Tex. App.—Dallas Nov. 30, 2017, orig. proceeding) (mem. op.), and *In re Swepi L.P.*, 103 S.W.3d 578, 589 (Tex. App.—San Antonio 2003, orig. proceeding), the courts, after parroting the definition in Comment 3 to Texas Rule 190.3, concluded without explanation that the interrogatories at issue did not contain discrete subparts. In *Estate of Flarity*, No. 09-19-00089-CV, [LEXIS], 2020 WL 5552140 (Tex. App.—Beaumont Sept. 17, 2020, pet. denied), the court, after referencing pertinent content in Texas Rule 190.3, concluded without explanation that the interrogatories in question "required that each [responding party] provide [the requesting party] with more than the twenty-five answers in violation of [Texas] Rule 190.3(3)."

[58] *In re Anderson News*, LLC, 615 B.R. 45, 59 (Bankr. D. Del. 2020) ("When determining whether subparts constitute separate interrogatories, the Court neither considers whether the subparts are joined by a conjunctive word nor relies on the formalism of numerical labeling."); *Engage Healthcare Commc'ns, LLC v. Intellisphere, LLC*, No. 12-cv-00787(FLW)(LHG), 2017 U.S. Dist. LEXIS 83068, at *8–12, 2017 WL 2371834 (D.N.J. Feb. 10, 2017) ("[I]t is now well settled that the question whether an interrogatory contains more than one 'discrete separate subject' does not turn on whether the interrogatory has separately enumerated subparts. The subparts can be explicit or implicit; the number of subparts does not turn on the formalism of labeling." (quoting *Erfindergemeinschaft UroPep GbR v. Eli Lilly & Co.*, 315 F.R.D. 191, 195 (E.D. Tex. May 13, 2016))); *Ott v. Mortg. Inv'rs Corp.*, No. 3:14-CV-00645-ST, 2015 U.S. Dist. LEXIS 19050, at *3, 2015 WL 691643 (D. Or. Feb. 17, 2015) ("[O]nce a subpart of an interrogatory introduces a line of inquiry that is separate and distinct from the inquiry made by the portion of the interrogatory that precedes it, the subpart must be considered a separate interrogatory no matter how it is designated.") (citation omitted); *Hasan v. Johnson*, No. 1:08-cv-00381-GSA-PC, 2012 U.S. Dist. LEXIS 21578, at *12–13, 2012 WL 569370 (E.D. Cal. Feb. 21, 2012) (same).

[59] *Cf. Sampson v. Schenck*, No. 8:07CV155, 2010 U.S. Dist. LEXIS 82486, at *14, 2010 WL 2737050 (D. Neb. July 9, 2010) ("'Not numbering the subparts of interrogatories does not change the fact that, if the interrogatories require discrete pieces of information, those interrogatories are to be counted as if the subparts were specifically itemized.'" (quoting *Prochaska & Assoc. v. Merrill Lynch, Pierce, Fenner & Smith, Inc.*, 155 F.R.D. 189, 191 (D. Neb. 1993))); *Semsroth v. City of Wichita*, No. 06-2376-KHV-DJW, 2008 U.S. Dist. LEXIS 35380, at *4–5, 2008 WL 1924945 (D. Kan. Apr. 28, 2008) ("'Extensive use of subparts, whether explicit or implicit, could defeat the purposes of the numerical limit contained in [Federal] Rule 33(a), or in a scheduling order, by rendering it meaningless unless each subpart counts as a separate interrogatory.'" (quoting *Williams v. Bd. of Cnty. Comm'rs*, 192 F.R.D. 698, 701 (D. Kan. 2000))); *Safeco of Am. v. Rawstron*, 181 F.R.D. 441, 445 (C.D.

and, conversely, sub-numbered or sub-lettered parts of an interrogatory may not be "discrete subparts."[60]

The best test of whether questions within a single interrogatory are "logically or factually related" is as follows:

> [W]hether the first question is primary and subsequent questions are secondary to the primary question; or whether the subsequent question could stand alone and is independent of the first question? In other words, "if the first question can be answered fully and completely without answering the second question, then the second question is totally independent of the first and not factually subsumed within and necessarily related to the primary question."[61]

Stating the rule, however, is easier than applying it.[62] In this regard, the determination of what constitutes a discrete subpart must be decided on an interrogatory-by-interrogatory basis. As one court explained:

> It is important to acknowledge at the outset that the issue of "discreteness" cannot reliably be captured by a verbal formula, and that ultimately the issue turns on a case-by-case assessment of the degree to which the subpart is logically

---

Cal. 1998) ("One question that is easily answered is whether subparts must be separately numbered or lettered to count as multiple interrogatories. The better view is that they need not be, or any party could easily circumvent the rule simply by eliminating the separate numbering or lettering of the subparts.").

The opposite is also true—a party serving interrogatories need not identify each "discrete" subpart. *Cf. Parks, LLC v. Tyson Foods, Inc.*, No. 5:15-cv-00946, 2015 U.S. Dist. LEXIS 112861, at *14 n.3, 2015 WL 5042918 (E.D. Pa. Aug. 25, 2015) ("Plaintiff also objects to six of the eight interrogatories because they 'fail[] to identify subparts and thus do[] not comply with Fed. R. Civ. P. Rule 26 making it more difficult to comply with Fed. R. Civ. P. Rule 26.' But [Federal] Rule 26 contains no such requirement, and neither does [Federal] Rule 33, which is the only discovery rule to discuss subparts of interrogatories. [Federal] Rule 33(a)(1) provides that a 'discrete subpart' of an interrogatory counts separately toward the twenty-five interrogatory limit imposed by the Rule, but the Rule does not require an interrogatory that contains multiple parts to separately identify each part.").

60 See cases cited in notes 58 and 59.

61 *Estate of Manship v. U.S.*, 232 F.R.D. 552, 555 (M.D. La. 2005) (footnote omitted) (citation omitted) (quoting *Krawczyk v. City of Dall.*, No. 3:03-CV-0584-D, 2004 U.S. Dist. LEXIS 30011, at *7, 2004 WL 614842 (N.D. Tex. Feb. 27, 2004))); *accord Progressive Paloverde Ins. Co. v. Estate of Jenkins*, No. 19-12840, 2020 U.S. Dist. LEXIS 107127, 2020 WL 3128837 (E.D. La. June 12, 2020); *Sprint Commc'ns, Inc. v. Calabrese*, No. 18-60788-CIV, 2019 U.S. Dist. LEXIS 142977, 2019 WL 9598506 (S.D. Fla. Aug. 20, 2019); *Moser v. Navistar Int'l Corp.*, 4:17-CV-00598, 2018 U.S. Dist. LEXIS 127007, at *17, 2018 WL 3614012 (E.D. Tex. July 27, 2018); *Pulchalski v. Franklin Cnty.*, No. 15-CV-1365, 2017 U.S. Dist. LEXIS 1151, at *9, 2017 WL 57143 (M.D. Pa. Jan. 5, 2017); *Erfindergemeinschaft UroPep GbR v. Eli Lilly & Co.*, 315 F.R.D. 191, 194 (E.D. Tex. May 13, 2016); *Nguyen v. Lowe's Home Ctrs., LLC*, No. 15CV1085 H NLS, 2015 U.S. Dist. LEXIS 188923, at *9–10, 2015 WL 12672153 (S.D. Cal. Nov. 19, 2015); *Mezu v. Morgan State Univ.*, 269 F.R.D. 565, 572–73 (D. Md. 2010); *Kendall v. GES Exposition Servs., Inc.*, 174 F.R.D. 684, 685–86 (D. Nev. 1997).

62 Counting interrogatories requires a pragmatic approach that is reminiscent of Supreme Court Justice Stewart's memorable definition of obscenity (i.e., most courts know a discrete subpart when they see it). *See Jacobellis v. Ohio*, 378 U.S. 184, 197 (1964) ("I know [obscenity] when I see it.").

> related to the primary question in the interrogatory, as opposed to being separate and distinct. That approach acknowledges that the issue of "discreteness" often cannot be resolved by resort to a crisp verbal formula; it recognizes the reality that "discreteness" is a matter of degree and that deciding whether a subpart of an interrogatory is sufficiently "discrete" to be regarded as a separate interrogatory will frequently depend on the particular circumstances of each case and may not always be answerable with complete confidence.[63]

In doing so, a court should "utilize a common sense, rather than overly technical, approach to construing subparts of interrogatories."[64] Nonetheless, a few hard and fast rules regarding what constitutes a discrete subpart exist.

For example, an interrogatory asking for the factual bases for the denial of *each* request for admission in a set of requests for admission containing multiple requests generally should be counted as one interrogatory for each denied request.[65] This is

---

[63] *Erfindergemeinschaft UroPep GbR v. Eli Lilly & Co.*, 315 F.R.D. 191, 197 (E.D. Tex. May 13, 2016) (citations omitted).

[64] *Cf. Danielle Gamino v. KPC Healthcare Holdings, Inc., et al.*, No. 520CV01126SBSHKX, 2021 U.S. Dist. LEXIS 85706, at *11, 2021 WL 1731673 (C.D. Cal. Apr. 14, 2021) ("Whether contention interrogatories are appropriate is appropriately addressed on a case-by-case and interrogatory-by-interrogatory basis."); *Monster Energy Co. v. Vital Pharm., Inc.*, No. 518CV01882JGBSHKX, 2020 U.S. Dist. LEXIS 215890, 2020 WL 6653583 (C.D. Cal. Jan. 2, 2020) (same); *Synopsys, Inc. v. ATopTech, Inc*, 319 F.R.D. 293, 295 (N.D. Cal. Nov. 16, 2016) ("[T]he task of counting interrogatories requires a case-specific assessment."); *Erfindergemeinschaft UroPep GbR v. Eli Lilly & Co.*, 315 F.R.D. 191, 197 (E.D. Tex. May 13, 2016) ("It is important to acknowledge at the outset that the issue of 'discreteness' cannot reliably be captured by a verbal formula, and that ultimately the issue turns on a case-by-case assessment of the degree to which the subpart is logically related to the primary question in the interrogatory, as opposed to being separate and distinct."); *accord Synopsys, Inc. v. Atoptech, Inc.*, 319 F.R.D. 293, 295 (N.D. Cal. 2016); *see Superior Sales W., Inc. v. Gonzalez*, 335 F.R.D. 98, 104 (W.D. Tex. 2020) ("The test cannot reliably be captured by a verbal formula, and depends upon a case-by-case assessment.") (citation omitted); *Diversified Lenders, LLC v. Amazon Logistics, Inc.*, No. C16-1232RSL, 2017 U.S. Dist. LEXIS 95069, at *2–3, 2017 WL 11562026 (W.D. Wash. June 20, 2017) ("Courts have formulated various tests for determining when subparts are actually a separate interrogatory. . . . 'Since many of these formulations are difficult to apply or perhaps even conflicting, some courts have taken a "pragmatic approach," looking to see if an interrogatory threatens the purpose of [Federal] Rule 33 by combining into one interrogatory several lines of inquiry that should be kept separate.'" (quoting *Paananen v. Cellco P'ship*, No. C08-1042 RSM, 2009 U.S. Dist. LEXIS 98997, at *6, 2009 WL 3327227 (W.D. Wash. Oct. 8, 2009))); *Engage Healthcare Commc'ns, LLC v. Intellisphere, LLC*, No. 12-cv-00787(FLW)(LHG), 2017 U.S. Dist. LEXIS 83068, at *10–12, 2017 WL 2371834 (D.N.J. Feb. 10, 2017) (same).

[65] *Cf. Superior Sales W., Inc. v. Gonzalez*, 335 F.R.D. 98, 104 (W.D. Tex. May 27, 2020) ("Despite the fact-bound nature of this inquiry, in the context of interrogatories that seek additional information regarding a party's denials of requests for admission, there is a robust consensus that each request for admission constitutes a discrete subpart and a separate interrogatory."); *In re Dealer Mgmt. Sys. Antitrust Litig.*, No. 18 C 864, 2018 U.S. Dist. LEXIS 197042, at *30, 2018 WL 6048262 (N.D. Ill. Nov. 19, 2018) ("This interrogatory asks Authenticom to explain the factual basis that supports each denial of a request for admission, identify all documents and information that supports the denial, and identify all persons with knowledge of facts supporting its response. The Court agrees with Authenticom that the use of a single interrogatory for this purpose circumvents the limit on the number of interrogatories

because each request for admission usually deals with a separate or discrete topic.[66] In the same vein, an interrogatory seeking the factual bases for multiple affirmative defenses or the denials of the allegations of multiple paragraphs of a pleading typically is counted as a separate interrogatory for each defense or paragraph.[67] Further,

---

permitted by [Federal] Rule 33 and effectively turns each request for admission into a separate interrogatory."); *Certain Interested Underwriters v. Am. Realty Advisors*, No. 5:16-cv-940, 2018 U.S. Dist. LEXIS 168628, 2018 WL 4765157 (E.D.N.C. Sep. 30, 2018) (same); *Byard v. City & Cnty. of S. F.*, No. 16-cv-00691-WHA (DMR), 2017 U.S. Dist. LEXIS 37313, at *8, 2017 WL 988497 (N.D. Cal. Mar. 15, 2017) ("As to the interrogatory, the court finds that it contains a separately countable subpart for each admitted RFA under [Federal] Rule 33."); *McClellan v. Kern Cnty. Sheriff's Office*, No. 1:10-cv-0386-LJO-MJS (PC), 2015 U.S. Dist. LEXIS 98524, at *17–18, 2015 WL 4598871 (E.D. Cal. July 27, 2015) (same); *Saliga v. Chemtura Corp.*, No. 3:12cv832(RNC), 2013 U.S. Dist. LEXIS 164812, at *10–11, 2013 WL 6247219 (D. Conn. Nov. 26, 2013) (same and citing cases); *Bourdganis v. N. Tr. Bank*, No. 08-CV-11282, 2008 U.S. Dist. LEXIS 82089, at *6 n.2, 2008 WL 4615653 (E.D. Mich. Oct. 16, 2008) (same); *Mitchell Co. v. Campus*, No. CA 07-0177-KD-C, 2008 U.S. Dist. LEXIS 47505, at *55–56, 2008 WL 2468564 (S.D. Ala. June 16, 2008) (same); *Estate of Manship v. U.S.*, 232 F.R.D. 552, 557 (M.D. La. 2005) (same).

66 *See Estate of Manship v. U.S.*, 232 F.R.D. 552, 557 (M.D. La. 2005). This may not always be the case: "[A]n interrogatory seeking the basis for the denial of several requests for admission may be viewed as a single interrogatory where each area of the requests for admission concerns the same subject area." *Estate of Manship v. U.S.*, 232 F.R.D. 552, 557 (M.D. La. 2005).

67 *Cf. Solaria Corp. v. GCL Sys. Integration Tech. Co.*, No. 20CV07778BLFVKD, 2021 U.S. Dist. LEXIS 97114, at *5, 2021 WL 2022246 (N.D. Cal. May 21, 2021) ("Interrogatory No. 2 asks GCL to describe the bases for, and to identify documents relating to, each of its defenses to Solaria's breach of contract claim. GCL asserts eight 'affirmative defenses' in its answer, but several of these appear to be place holders or asserted pro forma. GCL may also have other defenses that are not 'affirmative defenses' but are nevertheless encompassed by Interrogatory No. 2. To the extent a defense relies on a distinct legal theory and distinct set of facts, it is appropriate to treat each such defense as a separate subject. Accordingly, for each distinct defense GCL intends to assert, Interrogatory No. 2 will count as a separate interrogatory—i.e. if GCL asserts eight defenses, this interrogatory counts as eight interrogatories."); *MCC Controls v. Hal Hays Constr.*, No. 191655ABKKX, 2020 U.S. Dist. LEXIS 190705, 2020 WL 6034321 (C.D. Cal. July 23, 2020) (same); *Am. Airlines, Inc. v. Delta Air Lines, Inc.*, No. 4:19-CV-01053-O, 2020 U.S. Dist. LEXIS 247687, at *12, 2020 WL 8115870 (N.D. Tex. July 14, 2020) ("The Court agrees with Delta that 'when a party serves an interrogatory that requires a responding party to explain why it denied certain allegations—say, 46 of them—the requesting party served 46 interrogatories, not one, as each discrete subpart constitutes a separate interrogatory.'"); *Vega v. Honeywell Int'l, Inc.*, No. 19-CV-00663-W-BGS, 2020 U.S. Dist. LEXIS 77065, 2020 WL 2098199 (S.D. Cal. May 1, 2020) (finding a single interrogatory requesting the basis for each affirmative defenses should be treated as separate interrogatories); *Alexander v. 1328 Uptown, Inc.*, No. 18-cv-1544, 2019 U.S. Dist. LEXIS 173315, at *43, 2019 WL 4929931 (D. Minn. Oct. 7, 2019) ("Serving a single interrogatory seeking 'all facts upon which [the defendants] base such denial' for over fifty denials amounts to over fifty interrogatories."); *Hansen v. Savage Arms Co.*, No. 17-CV-3002-LTS, 2017 U.S. Dist. LEXIS 204937, at *21, 2017 WL 6376342 (N.D. Iowa Dec. 13, 2017) ("Because the nature of the information requested is necessarily different with request to each of the twenty affirmative defenses, the Court finds that each subsection of Interrogatory Number Three may be considered a separate question."); *Nguyen v. Lowe's Home Ctrs., LLC*, No. 15CV1085 H NLS, 2015 U.S. Dist. LEXIS 188923, at *10–11, 2015 WL 12672153 (S.D. Cal. Nov. 19, 2015) ("[T]he Court finds Interrogatory No. 14 contains at least nine discrete subparts—one subpart for Defendant's general denial plus eight subparts for the additional affirmative defenses.") (citation omitted); *Brutscher v. Geico Gen. Ins. Co.*, No. C14-1094RSL, 2015 U.S.

"[q]uestions which address separate subjects count as numerous interrogatories. (E.g., 'Were you ever discharged from any employment for incompetency, or did you ever sue a former employer for any reason?')."[68] Also, an interrogatory asking for information as well as the identity of persons with knowledge about the information often is held to constitute two interrogatories.[69]

Dist. LEXIS 180703, at *3, 2015 WL 11921417 (W.D. Wash. Mar. 4, 2015) ("[A]n inquiry requesting the same information regarding disparate claims, defenses, or events counts as multiple interrogatories."); *Procongps, Inc. v. Skypatrol, LLC*, No. C 11-3975 SI, 2013 U.S. Dist. LEXIS 47133, at *4 (N.D. Cal. Apr. 1, 2013) ("Courts in the Northern and Eastern Districts of California have concluded that a single interrogatory asking the bases of multiple affirmative defenses should count as separate interrogatories. This Court agrees with those decisions because each affirmative defense may be factually different."); *Williams v. Serra Chevrolet Auto., LLC*, No. 12-11756, 2013 U.S. Dist. LEXIS 140345, at *3–4, 2013 WL 5447878 (E.D. Mich. Sept. 30, 2013) ("Interrogatory no. 12 asks for detailed information concerning sixteen separate paragraphs of the complaint. The Court finds that Interrogatory no. 12 contains discrete subparts and must be counted as multiple interrogatories.").

68 *Lopez v. Flores*, No.: 1:08-cv-01975-LJO-JLT (PC), 2013 U.S. Dist. LEXIS 76237, at *3, 2013 WL 2385240 (E.D. Cal. May 30, 2013) (citation omitted) (quoting *Singleton v. Hedgepath*, No. 1:08-CV-00095-AWI, 2011 U.S. Dist. LEXIS 71496, at *19, 2011 WL 1806515 (E.D. Cal. May 10, 2011)); *see Pangborn v. Los Angeles County Deputy Sheriffs Lieutenant Baudino*, No. 15-6812 AB(JC), 2018 U.S. Dist. LEXIS 226176, 2018 WL 6265055 (C.D. Cal. Sept. 27, 2018) (holding that a single interrogatory that asks about the defendants conduct with regard to five other defendants should be treated as five interrogatories rather than one); *12W RPO, LLC v. Victaulic Co.*, No. 3:15-CV-01411, 2017 U.S. Dist. LEXIS 229031, at *6, 2017 WL 7312757 (D. Or. Feb. 28, 2017) ("Subparts (a)–(k) each reflect a different negligence claim asserted by Plaintiffs. While the primary question and underlying theory for all claims and interrogatories is negligence, I find that negligence here is not a 'common theme,' as each claim relies on different facts. I find the individual subparts present 'independent line[s] of inquiry' because each is sufficiently independent and each seeks different facts. For example, it should be clear that the factual basis for a negligence claim based on Victaulic's failure to properly design components (Interrogatory No. 11(a)) and the factual basis for a negligence claim based on Victaulic's failure to issue a public recall (Interrogatory No. 11(j)) seek much different information.") (citation omitted); *Pulchalski v. Franklin Cnty.*, No. 15-CV-1365, 2017 U.S. Dist. LEXIS 1151, at *10–11, 2017 WL 57143 (M.D. Pa. Jan. 5, 2017) ("[W]e find that the interrogatories propounded by the plaintiff exceed the 25 interrogatory limit set by [Federal] Rule 33(a)(1). In particular, we note that a number of these interrogatories are framed in multiple sub-parts asking a series of discrete inquiries about multiple events, spanning several years. Other interrogatories pose a series of discrete and specific questions regarding Pulchaski's past pay, projected future earnings, commissions, bonuses and retirement benefits. Still other interrogatories pose multiple sub-part inquiries into what are potentially a host of hiring, consultant and independent contractor decisions made at the prison in the months preceding and following Pulchaski's termination. Furthermore, other interrogatories are framed in multiple subparts and seek numerous discrete categories of information concerning prison staff disciplinary actions ranging over a 5 year period.").

69 *Compare, e.g., MCC Controls v. Hal Hays Constr.*, No. 191655ABKKX, 2020 U.S. Dist. LEXIS 190705, at *10, 2020 WL 6034321 (C.D. Cal. July 23, 2020) ("Interrogatories Nos. 8, 11, and 14 seek both documents and communications and are, therefore, compound."), *Nguyen v. Lowe's Home Ctrs., LLC*, No. 15CV1085 H NLS, 2015 U.S. Dist. LEXIS 188923, at *11–12, 2015 WL 12672153 (S.D. Cal. Nov. 19, 2015) ("[M]any courts have concluded an interrogatory that asks a party to identify facts, documents, and witnesses should count these items as discrete separate interrogatories."), *Walech v. Target Corp.*, No. C11-254 RAJ, 2012 U.S. Dist. LEXIS 44119, at *12, 2012 WL 1068068 (W.D. Wash. Mar. 28, 2012) ("[T]hese are two separate inquiries: (1) state the relevant facts for a particular contention, and (2) identify

In contrast, an interrogatory asking for the details about communications or allegedly false or fraudulent representations are counted as one interrogatory "even though it requests that the times, places, persons present, and contents be stated separately for each communication" or representation.[70] Similarly, an interrogatory

---

the evidence (either documents or witnesses) that support the facts stated."), *Imbody v. C & R. Plating Corp.*, No. 1:08-CV-00218, 2010 U.S. Dist. LEXIS 12682, at *11, 2010 WL 3184392 (N.D. Ind. Feb. 12, 2010) ("This interrogatory propounds two separate interrogatories—[one] inquiring about the physical requirements of the job, and the remaining subpart requesting the names of co-workers."), *Superior Commc'ns v. Earhugger*, 257 F.R.D. 215, 218 (C.D. Cal. 2009) (collecting cases and holding that a contention interrogatory that asked the alleged infringer to identify all facts that supported or undermined "the allegation in the answer," all persons with knowledge of those facts, and all documents and things that related to those facts "ha[d] at least three discrete subparts: facts, persons, and documents."), *U.S. ex rel. Pogue v. Diabetes Treatment Ctrs. of Am., Inc.*, 235 F.R.D. 521, 527 (D.D.C. 2006) (noting that an interrogatory that seeks "all facts supporting Relator's contention. . . .; asks Relator to identify each person who knew[;] . . . [and] requests that Relator identify all documents that support the contention" is "more accurately counted as three separate interrogatories"), *and Dimitrijevic v. TV&C GP Holding Inc.*, CV H-04-3457, 2005 U.S. Dist. LEXIS 41399, at *12–13, 2005 WL 8164073 (S.D. Tex. Aug. 24, 2005) ("A summary review of the 13 numbered questions and 122 separately lettered subparts plainly reveals that Dimitrijevic has exceeded the permissible limit. For example, Interrogatory No. 1 contains at least seven different questions; the primary question deals with 'all reasons supporting a case for reduction in force at the warehouse,' while each of the subparts (except for subpart f) seeks specified information which may or may not have supported a reduction in force. . . . The primary question could certainly be fully answered without disclosing the information sought by these subparts. Likewise, Interrogatory No. 8 contains 17 discrete subparts, asking not only about the general selection process for warehouse foreman, but also details on the selection of six named individuals. Even assuming the other numbered interrogatories contained no discrete subparts (which is not the case), Dimitrijevic's interrogatories exceed the maximum permitted by [Federal] Rule 33(a).") (citation omitted), *with, e.g., Engage Healthcare Commc'ns, LLC v. Intellisphere, LLC*, No. 12-cv-00787(FLW)(LHG), 2017 U.S. Dist. LEXIS 83068, at *20–24, 2017 WL 2371834 (D.N.J. Feb. 10, 2017) (noting that "[c]ourts have been divided in determining whether an interrogatory seeking facts, documents and people with knowledge constitutes one interrogatory or three discrete subparts" and holding that, in a complex case, subparts asking for facts, persons with knowledge, and documents were one interrogatory), *and Synopsys, Inc. v. Atoptech, Inc.*, 319 F.R.D. 293, 294–99 (N.D. Cal. 2016) (noting that "[t]here is a split among courts as to whether an interrogatory asking for facts, documents, and witnesses contains three discrete subparts, or should be counted as one interrogatory" and holding to the extent the subparts to a contention interrogatory ask for facts, documents, and persons relating to one subject or contention, the court will count it as one interrogatory).

As is evident from the above-cited cases, federal courts are divided on the question of whether interrogatories seeking facts and documents constitute one or two interrogatories. Under the Texas discovery rules, they arguably constitute one interrogatory because Texas Rules 190.2 and 190.3 provide that interrogatories asking a party "only to identify or authenticate specific documents" do not count against an interrogatory limit. Tex. R. Civ. P. 190.2(b)(3), 190.3(b)(3). Nonetheless, an interrogatory asking the responding party to identify "all documents concerning" an allegation, contention, or defense can be unduly burdensome in an action in which large numbers of documents are involved.

[70] *Cf.* Fed. R. Civ. P. 33, Advisory Committee's Note to 1993 Amend.; *see Bolding v. Banner Bank*, No. C17-0601RSL, 2021 U.S. Dist. LEXIS 56720, at *3, 2021 WL 1080742 (W.D. Wash. Mar. 19, 2021) ("Thus, the only interrogatory at issue here is Interrogatory No. 14

which seeks the identity of: all members of management of Defendant who communicated with [opt-in plaintiff] about her compensation, how she would be paid, her entitlement to overtime, whether or not she was required to seek pre-approval to work overtime, and/or recording hours worked and describe: a. The date he/she communicated this information to [opt-in plaintiff]; b. The subject matter and substance of what he/she communicated to [opt-in plaintiff]; and c. Whether there were any follow-up communications regarding the subject matter or substance communicated to [opt-in plaintiff]. If so, identify the date of the follow-up communication, the person who made the follow-up communication, and the substance of the follow-up communication. Defendant maintains that this interrogatory contains five discrete subparts. The Court disagrees. Plaintiffs are seeking information regarding all communications with each opt-in plaintiff regarding certain topics, including the participants, dates, and content of the communications. Although plaintiffs list five topics in the body of the interrogatory, the first three are part and parcel of 'compensation.' Thus, Interrogatory No. 14 contains three discrete subparts seeking information regarding what the opt-in plaintiffs were told regarding compensation, pre-approval for overtime hours, and recording of hours worked."); *Ott v. Mortg. Investors Corp. of Ohio, Inc.*, No. 3:14-cv-00645-ST, 2015 U.S. Dist. LEXIS 19050, at *5, 7–8, 2015 WL 691643 (D. Or. Feb. 17, 2015) ("Interrogatory No. 3 is a single interrogatory. It asks MIC to provide information regarding the allegedly unlawful calls at issue in this lawsuit. The subparts seek to clarify the scope of the information plaintiffs seek regarding the calls, namely the telephone number, date of the call, identity of the person being called, the person(s) responsible for making the calls, the manner in which the calls were placed (preview, manual, or autodialed), the campaign each call was made for, and the 'status' of the call, specifically whether it was answered by a person rather than a voicemail or answering machine. The primary question of describing or identifying the calls cannot be answered unless this information is provided. Thus, this interrogatory counts as one. . . . The remaining interrogatory in dispute is Interrogatory No. 14 which asks MIC to identify each 'opt-in' outbound calling campaign, including the name, dates, numbers of outbound calls made, sources of telephone numbers called, and whether and how the numbers were scrubbed, and the identity of files produced by MIC that contain those numbers and related information. Because MIC cannot completely respond to this central request without providing all of the enumerated information, this request should count as a single interrogatory."); *Rowell v. NCO Fin. Sys.*, No. 13-2514-CM, 2014 U.S. Dist. LEXIS 70095, at *8, 10–11, 2014 WL 2154422 (D. Kan. May 22, 2014) ("Plaintiff asserts that Interrogatory No. 3 should count as five interrogatories. Defendant responds that the common theme of Interrogatory No. 3 is the identification of plaintiff's communications with defendant and the details relating to those communications—who, what, when, and where. The court agrees. The common theme of this question is communications between plaintiff and defendant. Subparts seeking 'who, what, when, where, and how' information logically and factually subsumed within the primary question are not counted as separate interrogatories. The subparts of this question delineate details that should be included in response to the primary question and are consistent with the common theme. Thus, this question constitutes one interrogatory. . . . Plaintiff argues [I]nterrogatory [No. 6] should count as twenty interrogatories because it asks for the same information as Interrogatory No. 3, but does so with respect to four parties. As the court previously determined, Interrogatory No. 3 counts as one interrogatory, not five. Under plaintiff's reasoning, even if the court agreed that communications with four different lenders concerning the same loan should count as four separate themes, this interrogatory would count as four interrogatories at a maximum-one for each possible lender named. However, the court disagrees with plaintiff's assertion. The court finds that this question should be counted as one interrogatory because it asks for details supporting a common theme: to identify communications with lenders regarding plaintiff's federal consolidation loan. Once again, the subparts delineate details that should be included in a response to the primary question. Therefore, this question also constitutes asking about (1) persons with knowledge about a claim, defense, allegation, or fact and the subject area of their knowledge, or (2) other lawsuits, including the identity of each cause of action asserted, the parties, the court in which it was filed, the date it was filed, and its outcome, are one interrogatory.[71] Further, an interrogatory asking the responding party to identify each negligent act or omission, contract breach,

---

a single interrogatory."); *Estate of Manship v. U.S.*, 232 F.R.D. 552, 555 (M.D. La. 2005) (holding that interrogatory subparts seeking the substance of communications, their dates and places, and all persons participating in them constituted a single interrogatory); *Theobles v. Indus. Maint. Co.*, 247 F.R.D. 483, 485 (D.V.I. 2006) (noting that an interrogatory asking the responding party "to state whether a particular product was tested and then . . . when the tests occurred, who performed them, how . . . they were conducted and the result" constituted a single interrogatory (quoting *Banks v. Office of Senate Sergeant-At-Arms*, 222 F.R.D. 7, 10 (D.D.C. 2004))).

[71] *Cf. Dawson v. HITCO Carbon Coponsites, Inc*, No. 167337PSGFFMX, 2018 U.S. Dist. LEXIS 217505, at *8, 2018 WL 3815032 (C.D. Cal. June 22, 2018) ("The fact that the interrogatories request information as to a number of individuals does not equate to subparts."); *Walech v. Target Corp.*, No. C11-254 RAJ, 2012 U.S. Dist. LEXIS 44119, at *15–16, 2012 WL 1068068 (W.D. Wash. Mar. 28, 2012) ("[I]dentifying parties, nature of case, agency or court, etc. are logically subsumed within and necessarily relate to the primary question of identifying lawsuits."); *Calderon v. Reederei Claus-Peter Offen GmbH & Co.*, No. 07-61022-CIV-COHN/SELTZER, 2008 U.S. Dist. LEXIS 76323, at *5, 2008 WL 4194810 (S.D. Fla. Sept. 11, 2008) (noting that questions about prior lawsuits "have been deemed to be not discrete and, hence, constitute one interrogatory"); *Powell v. Home Depot USA, Inc.*, No. 07-80435-Civ-Hurley/Hopkins, 2008 U.S. Dist. LEXIS 49144, at *8–9, 2008 WL 2473748 (S.D. Fla. June 16, 2008) (stating that an interrogatory requesting the names, addresses, and telephone numbers of persons with knowledge concerning the facts or claims, as well as the subject matter of the knowledge, "should be treated as a single interrogatory"); *Forum Architects LLC v. Candela*, No. 1:07CV190-SPM/AK, 2008 U.S. Dist. LEXIS 4705, at *4, 2008 WL 217119 (N.D. Fla. Jan. 23, 2008) ("No. 2 is also a standard question about persons with knowledge and the subject matters of their knowledge. This is considered one item of the initial disclosure requirement of [Federal] Rule 26(a) (1) (A) and will be considered one question here as well."); *Cardenas v. Dorel Juvenile Grp., Inc.*, 231 F.R.D. 616, 619–20 (D. Kan. 2005) (overruling an objection that an interrogatory seeking information about "each and every element of the design" which plaintiff contended was defective was actually multiple interrogatories that exceed the limit of allowable interrogatories); *see Perez v. Aircom Mgmt. Corp.*, No. 12-60322-CIV-WILLIAMS/SELTZER, 2012 U.S. Dist. LEXIS 136140, at *3, 2012 WL 6811079 (S.D. Fla. Sept. 24, 2012) ("By way of example, the following types of interrogatories have been deemed to be not discrete and, hence, constitute one interrogatory: (1) questions about persons with knowledge and the subject area of their knowledge; (2) questions about prior lawsuits, the nature of the cause of action, the parties, the court in which the lawsuit was filed, and the dates filed; (3) questions about witness statements, by and to whom made, when made, and the substance and context of the statements; (4) questions about persons with documentary evidence in their possession, custody, and control, what documents they have, the location of the documents, and when the documents were prepared; (5) questions about expert witnesses, their addresses, qualifications, subject matter of their testimony, and grounds for their opinions; (6) questions about damages, when the damages occurred, to whom expenses were paid; and ([7]) questions about lost income, benefits, or earning capacity, the nature of each loss, and how the loss was computed."); *Semsroth v. City of Wichita*, No. 06-2376-KHV-DJW, 2008 U.S. Dist. LEXIS 35380, at *17–18, 2008 WL 1924945 (D. Kan. Apr. 28, 2008) (stating that instructions requiring multiple facts of information in order to identify people,

fraudulent representation, fiduciary breach, and the like underlying a claim is a single interrogatory even though the answer may reveal multiple acts, breaches, representations, or omissions.[72]

---

documents, or events did not "automatically convert a single question into multiple interrogatories").

[72] For example, in *Cardenas v. Dorel Juvenile Grp., Inc.*, 231 F.R.D. 616 (D. Kan. 2005), an interrogatory asked the plaintiffs:

> If you contend that the Child Restraint System was defectively designed, state with particularity each and every element of the design which you contend was defective, how such design was defective and the manner in which the injuries were caused, contributed to and/or permitted to occur as the result of each alleged design defect.

Cardenas v. Dorel Juvenile Grp., Inc., 231 F.R.D. 616, 619–20 (D. Kan. 2005). The plaintiffs refused to answer it, claiming that it comprised more than 40 separate interrogatories, exceeding the number allotted to the parties. *Cardenas v. Dorel Juvenile Grp., Inc.*, 231 F.R.D. 616, 619–20 (D. Kan. 2005). Although the court recognized that the interrogatory spanned multiple alleged design defects, the court ultimately disagreed with the plaintiffs and held that the question constituted a single interrogatory surrounding a common theme:

> While this interrogatory could be construed as having three discrete subparts (i.e., (1) identify the element of each alleged design defect, (2) state how such element of design was defective, and (3) identify the manner in which each defect caused any alleged injuries), the fact that it seeks this information about multiple alleged design defects does not turn it into multiple interrogatories. This interrogatory does not contain multiple subparts that discuss various, unrelated topics.

Cardenas v. Dorel Juvenile Grp., Inc., 231 F.R.D. 616, 619–20 (D. Kan. 2005); *see also Bolding v. Banner Bank*, No. C17-0601RSL, 2021 U.S. Dist. LEXIS 56720, at *5, 2021 WL 1080742, at *2 (W.D. Wash. Mar. 19, 2021) ("With regards to Interrogatory No. 1, which defendant maintains contains eleven discrete subparts, the interrogatory seeks information regarding the actions defendant took, if any, to ensure that each opt-in plaintiff was compensated for all hours worked. The list of eleven specific activities does not convert the interrogatory into eleven separate interrogatories. The inquiry can be rewritten as, 'Describe any and all efforts defendant made to ensure that opt-in plaintiffs received compensation for all hours worked, including the identity of all individuals involved, such as:' (a)—(k). Interrogatory No. 1 is properly characterized as a single interrogatory."); *MCC Controls v. Hal Hays Constr.*, No. 191655ABKKX,2020 U.S. Dist. LEXIS 190705, at *10, 2020 WL 6034321 (C.D. Cal. July 23, 2020) ("Interrogatories Nos. 4, 5, 6, 7, 9, 10, 13, and 15-17 seek all facts regarding specific contentions and are, therefore, not compound."); *Perez v. KDE Equine, LLC*, No. 3:15-CV-00562-CRS, 2017 U.S. Dist. LEXIS 570, at *8–9, 2017 WL 56616 (W.D. Ky. Jan. 4, 2017) (holding, in a FLSA action, that two numbered interrogatories did "not create hundreds of separate interrogatories simply by asking for information concerning numerous employees"); *Fleming v. Parnell*, No. C13-5062 BHS, 2014 U.S. Dist. LEXIS 250, at *4–5, 2014 WL 25621 (W.D. Wash. Jan. 2, 2014) ("Although, as Plaintiffs' observe, Defendants seek information about many invoices, accounts receivable statements and photographs, the Court finds that the subparts of each interrogatory at issue are logically and factually subsumed in the central question posed in each interrogatory at issue and are highly relevant to the core issues in this document-intensive case. For example, the invoice information Defendants ask for in interrogatory number 4 is specific to ramp systems, sections, landings or stairs, and ramp-related goods and services, which is highly relevant to central issues in this case and discoverable information that is part of a single question or common theme (invoices related to or potentially related to ramps systems or similar items or services that may implicate the use of the Fredrickson drawings at the heart of the case and Defendants' counterclaims). The Court views the information sought in interrogatories 11 and 13 similarly."); *Dawson v. New Life Cmty. Servs., Inc.*, No.: 5:13-cv-0881-PSG, 2013 U.S. Dist. LEXIS 174234, at *4–5, 2013 WL 6512052 (N.D. Cal. Dec. 12, 2013) (holding that an interrogatory that "requests the name, title, and role of 'each employee, agent, officer or director of New Life Community Service, Inc. who made any material decision regarding plaintiff Cynthia Dawson's admission, recovery, medical treatment or condition, conduct, reasonable accommodation request, discharge or removal at any time since January 1, 2012'" does not contain discrete subparts because "all the purported 'subparts' are related to the overarching question of who made decisions regarding Dawson's status at New Life"); *Mt. Hamilton Partners, LLC v. Google Inc.*, Nos. CV 12-01698, CV 12-01700, 2013 U.S. Dist. LEXIS 104556, at *4–5 (N.D. Cal. July 25, 2013) ("A review of Google's interrogatories 1-4 reveals that each interrogatory begins with a primary theme and follows with subparts that are logically related to that primary theme. Interrogatory no. 1, for example, requests detailed information related to the broader theme of the conception and reduction to practice of each asserted claim of the patent-in-suit, and in subparts, requests information about the persons, dates, and documents in relation to the general theme. Interrogatory no. 2, similarly, requests information about the broad theme of MHP's knowledge of prior art to the patent-in-suit, and its subparts request detailed information about persons, dates, and circumstances related to knowledge of prior art. Interrogatories no. 3 and no. 4, similarly, proceed with a general theme followed by related, detailed subparts. An interrogatory with subparts necessarily related to the primary question—as Google's are here— count only as one interrogatory for purposes of [Federal] Rule 33."); *Faglie v. Meritage Homes of Tex., LLC*, No. 3:12-cv-966-D (BF), 2013 U.S. Dist. LEXIS 55046, at *5, 2013 WL 1608727 (N.D. Tex. Apr. 15, 2013) ("Here, Defendant's first interrogatory, which asked Plaintiffs to '[i]dentify each defect or damage at the Property for which [Plaintiffs] have asserted a claim,' constitutes a single interrogatory. The interrogatory is not converted into multiple interrogatories because Plaintiffs' answer identifies multiple defects. The same is true for the other eight of Defendant's interrogatories.") (citation omitted).

Not all "identification" questions necessarily relate to a common theme. For example, an interrogatory asking for the identity of executives who have been disciplined but not terminated for five different types of actions counts as five distinct interrogatories. *Swackhammer v. Sprint Corp. PCS*, 225 F.R.D. 658, 663–65 (D. Kan. 2004); *accord Precision of N. Hampton, Inc. v. Tricomponent Prods. Corp.*, No. C12-2020, 2012 U.S. Dist. LEXIS 176908, at *8, 2012 WL 6520139 (N.D. Iowa Dec. 13, 2012) ("The Court concludes that TriComponent's request for the names and dates of employment for 18 separate positions does, in fact, contain 18 'discrete subparts' and, therefore, constitutes 18 interrogatories. That is, naming the officers and directors of Precision, including their dates of service—as requested in Interrogatory Number 1(A)—may stand alone and is independent of the names of the plant manager and his or her dates of employment—as requested in Interrogatory Number 1(B).").

The following cases provide examples of interrogatories with and without discrete subparts: *Solaria Corp. v. GCL Sys. Integration Tech. Co., Ltd.*, No. 20CV07778BLFVKD, 2021 U.S. Dist. LEXIS 97114, at *4–7 2021 WL 2022246 (N.D. Cal. May 21, 2021); *Bolding v. Banner Bank*, No. C17-0601RSL, 2021 U.S. Dist. LEXIS 56720, at *3–6, 2021 WL 1080742 (W.D. Wash. Mar. 19, 2021); *Brown-Thomas v. Hynie*, No. 1:18-CV-02191-JMC, 2021 WL 651014 (D.S.C. Feb. 19, 2021); *Nance-Bush v. Lone Star Coll. Sys. Dist.*, 337 F.R.D. 135, 137 (S.D. Tex. Jan. 6, 2021); *Superior Sales W., Inc. v. Gonzalez*, 335 F.R.D. 98, 105 (W.D. Tex. May 27, 2020); *In re Anderson News, LLC*, 615 B.R. 45, 60 (Bankr. D. Del. 2020); Athwal *v. Nijjer*, No. C17-00740RSL, 2018 U.S. Dist. LEXIS 35645, at *6–8, 2018 WL 1156233 (W.D. Wash. Mar. 5, 2018); *Avent v. State Farm Fire & Cas. Co.*, No. 5:16-CV-278-BO, 2017 U.S. Dist. LEXIS 95873, at *14–15, 2017 WL 4171971 (E.D.N.C. June 20, 2017); *B&D Nutritional*

Unlike the number of interrogatories, which almost always is limited, there is no limit on the number of sets of interrogatories that can be served if the total number of interrogatories in the sets does not exceed the limitation of Texas Rule 190.2 or 190.3 or the Level 3 discovery-control plan.[73]

9-5 Interrogatory Responses

9-5:1 In General

A party must respond to interrogatories within thirty days after their service[74] unless the time is extended due to the manner of service, by the parties' agreement, or by court order.[75] The response to each interrogatory must be in writing,[76] must be

---

Ingredients, Inc. v. Unique Bio Ingredients, LLC, No. 16-62364-CIV-COHN/SELTZER, 2017 U.S. Dist. LEXIS 73808, at *4, 2017 WL 8751744 (S.D. Fla. May 15, 2017); *Engage Healthcare Commc'ns, LLC v. Intellisphere, LLC*, No. 12-cv-00787(FLW)(LHG), 2017 U.S. Dist. LEXIS 83068, at *8–12, 2017 WL 2371834 (D.N.J. Feb. 10, 2017); *Synopsys, Inc. v. Atoptech, Inc.*, 319 F.R.D. 293, 294–99 (N.D. Cal. Nov. 16, 2016); *Am. Auto. Ins. Co. v. Omega Flex, Inc.*, No. 6:16-cv-1033-Orl-TBS, 2016 U.S. Dist. LEXIS 171277, at *3–9, 2016 WL 7188894 (M.D. Fla. Dec. 12, 2016); *EEOC v. State of Mex.*, No. 15-879 KG/KK, 2016 U.S. Dist. LEXIS 139049, at *11–15, 2016 WL 9777238 (D.N.M. Sept. 30, 2016); *Gagnon v. Fla. 595 Travel Ctr. Corp.*, No. 15-62380-CIV-COHN/SELTZER, 2016 U.S. Dist. LEXIS 112214, at *2–7 (S.D. Fla. Aug. 23, 2016); *Asarco LLC v. Union Pac. R.R.*, No. 2:12-cv-00283-EJL-REB, 2016 U.S. Dist. LEXIS 58262, at *30–32, 2016 WL 1755241 (D. Idaho May 2, 2016); *Commodores Entm't Corp. v. Thomas McClary & Fifth Ave. Entm't, LLC*, No. 6:14-cv-1335-Orl-37GJK, 2015 U.S. Dist. LEXIS 187779, at *11–14, 2015 WL 12843874 (M.D. Fla. Nov. 6, 2015); *EEOC v. BMW Mfg. Co.*, No. 7:13-cv-01583-HMH-JDA, 2015 U.S. Dist. LEXIS 155627, at *5–6, 2015 WL 7180285 (D.S.C. May 26, 2015); *In re Lithium Ion Batteries Antitrust Litig.*, No. 13-md-02420-YGR (DMR), 2015 U.S. Dist. LEXIS 111275, at *51–57, 2015 WL 4999762 (N.D. Cal. Aug. 21, 2015); *Warren v. Bastyr Univ.*, No. 2:11-cv-01800-RSL, 2013 U.S. Dist. LEXIS 50408, at *5–12, 2013 WL 1412419 (W.D. Wash. Apr. 8, 2013); *Shell v. Am. Fam. Rights Assoc.*, No. 09-cv-00309-MSK-KMT, 2012 U.S. Dist. LEXIS 123520, at *4–10, 2012 WL 13005966 (D. Colo. Aug. 30, 2012); *U.S. v. La.*, No. 11-470-JJB-DLD, 2012 U.S. Dist. LEXIS 121193, at *11–15, 2012 WL 3726754 (M.D. La. Aug. 27, 2012); *Porto Venezia Condo. Ass'n, v. WB Fort Lauderdale, LLC*, No.11-60665-CIV-DIMITROULEAS/Snow, 2012 U.S. Dist. LEXIS 186962, at *15–17, 2012 WL 7635868 (S.D. Fla. Aug. 13, 2012); *Walech v. Target Corp.*, No. C11-254 RAJ, 2012 U.S. Dist. LEXIS 44119, at *11–17, 2012 WL 1068068 (W.D. Wash. Mar. 28, 2012); *Hasan v. Johnson*, No. 1:08-cv-00381-GSA-PC, 2012 U.S. Dist. LEXIS 21578, at *11–15, 2012 WL 569370 (E.D. Cal. Feb. 21, 2012); *High Point Sarl v. Sprint Nextel Corp.*, No. 09-2269-CM-DJW, 2011 U.S. Dist. LEXIS 103118, at *13–33, 2011 WL 4036424 (D. Kan. Sept. 12, 2011); *Mitchell Co. v. Campus*, No. CA 07-0177-KD-C, 2008 U.S. Dist. LEXIS 47505, at *42–56, 2008 WL 2468564 (S.D. Ala. June 16, 2008); *In re Ullico Inc. Litig.*, No. 03-01556 (RJL/AK), 2006 U.S. Dist. LEXIS 97578, at *9–17, 2006 WL 2398742 (D.D.C. July 18, 2006).

[73] *See* Tex. R. Civ. P. 190.2(b)(3), 190.3(b)(3).

[74] Tex. R. Civ. P. 197.2(a).

[75] *See* Tex. R. Civ. P. 193.1 ("A party must respond to written discovery within the time provided by court order or these rules."). Three days are added to the response date if the production request is served by mail. Tex. R. Civ. P. 21a(c). One day is added if it is received by fax after 5:00 p.m. local time of the recipient. Tex. R. Civ. P. 21a(b)(2).

[76] Tex. R. Civ. P. 197.2(a). Oral information is not a substitute for written answers. *See, e.g.*, *Sharp v. Broadway Nat'l Bank*, 784 S.W.2d 669, 671 (Tex. 1990) (holding that oral identification of witnesses was insufficient).

preceded by the interrogatory,[77] must include the party's answer if the interrogatory is not objected to in its entirety,[78] and may include objections and privilege assertions as allowed by Texas Rule 193.[79] Answers to interrogatories may be used only against the responding party at trial or a hearing.[80]

---

[77] Tex. R. Civ. P. 193.1 ("The responding party's answers, objections, and other responses must be preceded by the request to which they apply.").

[78] *See* Tex. R. Civ. P. 193.2(b) ("A party must comply with as much of the request to which the party has made no objection unless it is unreasonable under the circumstances to do so before obtaining a ruling on the objection.").

[79] Tex. R. Civ. P. 193.2(b). Objections and privilege assertions in general are discussed in Chapter 5, sections 5-3 and 5-4, respectively.

[80] Tex. R. Civ. P. 197.3; *see Yates v. Fisher*, 988 S.W.2d 730, 731 (Tex. 1998) (per curiam) ("The court of appeals acted contrary to [former Texas] Rule 168(2) and erroneously used Fisher's interrogatory answers in Fisher's favor by relying on them to defeat Yates's motion for summary judgment."), *overruled on other grounds, Agar Corp., Inc. v. Electro Circuits Int'l*, LLC, 580 S.W.3d 136, 143 & n. 4 (Tex. 2019); *RHI Tech Servs. LLC v. Owens*, 11-17-00234-CV, 2019 Tex. App. LEXIS 7521, at *8 n.1, 2019 WL 3955879 (Tex. App.—Eastland Aug. 22, 2019, no pet.) (mem. op.) ("A party may not resort to its own answers to interrogatories to establish the existence of a genuine issue of material fact in response to a motion for summary judgment."); *Gilmore v. Rotan*, 11-16-00253-CV, 2018 Tex. App. LEXIS 7705, at *8, 2018 WL 4496232, (Tex. App.—Eastland Sept. 20, 2018, no pet.) (mem. op.) (same); *Armstrong-Cody v. Kinder Morgan Prod. Co.*, No. 11-13-00073-CV, 2015 Tex. App. LEXIS 549, at *4–5, 2015 WL 302002 (Tex. App.—Eastland Jan. 22, 2015, no pet.) (mem. op.) ("In her responses to [one defendant's summary judgment] motion, [the plaintiff] attached [another defendant's] . . . answers to interrogatories . . . . However, we cannot consider [the other defendant's] answers to interrogatories because answers to interrogatories can only be used against the party who answered."); *Vodicka v. Lahr*, No. 03-10-00126-CV, 2012 Tex. App. LEXIS 4557, at *29 n.10, 2012 WL 2075713 (Tex. App.—Austin June 6, 2012, no pet.) (mem. op.) (same); *Buck v. Blum*, 130 S.W.3d 285, 290 (Tex. App.—Houston [14th Dist.] 2004, no pet.) ("[A] party's answers to interrogatories can only be used against that party and not against another party, including a codefendant."). Nor can a party rely on its own interrogatory answers as evidence. *E-Learning LLC v. AT&T Corp.*, 517 S.W.3d 849, 857 (Tex. App.—San Antonio Mar. 1, 2017, no pet.) (mem. op.) ("Answers to interrogatories may not be used as self-serving statements for the party making them. A party may not resort to his own answers to interrogatories to establish the existence of a genuine issue of material fact. 'Answers to interrogatories may be used only against the responding party.'" (quoting Tex. R. Civ. P. 197.3)); *Sauls v. Munir Bata, LLC*, Nos. 02-14-00208-CV, 02-14-00214-CV, 2015 Tex. App. LEXIS 5950, at *41 n.19, 2015 WL 3905671 (Tex. App.—Fort Worth June 11, 2015, no pet.) (mem. op.) ("Sauls attempted to rely on his interrogatory answers to raise a genuine issue of material fact in the trial court on his quantum-meruit counterclaim. But Sauls may not use his own interrogatory answers in his favor to defeat MB and Colony Asset's summary-judgment motion."); *Maxwell v. Willis*, 316 S.W.3d 680, 685–86 (Tex. App.—Eastland 2010, no pet.) (same); *Zarzosa v. Flynn*, 266 S.W.3d 614, 619 (Tex. App.—El Paso 2008, no pet.) (holding that a party's interrogatory answers did not raise a fact issue in response to a summary judgment motion even though the opposing party put them into evidence); *Garcia v. Nat'l Eligibility Express, Inc.*, 4 S.W.3d 887, 890–91 (Tex. App.—Houston [1st Dist.] 1999, no pet.) (holding that a party's own interrogatory answers are incompetent summary judgment evidence); *cf. Gilmer v. Macy's Retail Holdings*, No. 06-3020 (JBS), 2009 U.S. Dist. LEXIS 4937, at *31–32 (D.N.J. Jan. 20, 2009) ("More fundamentally, a litigant 'may not introduce statements from its own answers to interrogatories or requests for admission as

Interrogatory responses, like all other written-discovery responses, must be signed by either the party's attorney or a pro se party.[81] If the responses are not properly signed, they "must be stricken unless it is signed promptly after the omission is called to the attention of the [requesting or responding] party[.]"[82]

Like other written-discovery responses, interrogatory answers are not filed[83] but must be served on all parties to the action.[84] In addition, the parties "must retain the original or exact copy of [the answers] during the pendency of the case and any related appellate proceedings begun within six months after judgment is signed, unless otherwise provided by the trial court."[85]

The responding party should answer each interrogatory separately and completely.[86] This means that an interrogatory answer must include sufficient detail to respond fully to the question.[87] If the responding party cannot answer the interrogatory because it lacks the information to do so, it should not simply refuse to answer.[88] Rather, the responding party should respond in such a way that apprises the requesting party that the information is unavailable and set forth its effort to find

---

evidence because such answers typically constitute hearsay when used in this manner." (quoting *Gross v. Burggraf* Constr., 53 F.3d 1531, 1541–42 (10th Cir. 1995))). However, in a multi-party case, any party may use the responding party's interrogatories against the responding party, thereby obviating the need for redundant interrogatories. *Ticor Title Ins. Co. v. Lacy*, 803 S.W.2d 265, 266 (Tex. 1991).

81 Tex. R. Civ. P. 191.3(a) (Interrogatories and the responses to them must be signed "(1) by an attorney, if the party is represented by an attorney, and must show the attorney's State Bar of Texas identification number, address, telephone number, and fax number, if any; or (2) by the party, if the party is not represented by an attorney, and must show the party's address, telephone number, and fax number, if any.").

82 Tex. R. Civ. P. 191.3(d).

83 Tex. R. Civ. P. 191.4(a)(1)–(2).

84 Tex. R. Civ. P. 191.5.

85 Tex. R. Civ. P. 191.4(d).

86 Tex. R. Civ. P. 193.2(b); *see* Tex. R. Civ. P. 193.1 ("When responding to written discovery, a party must make a complete response based on all information reasonably available to the responding party or its attorney at the time the response is made."); *Orkin Exterminating Co. v. Williamson*, 785 S.W.2d 905, 910 (Tex. App.—Austin 1990, writ denied) (holding, under former Texas Rule 168, that "interrogatories must be answered separately and fully"); *cf. Richard v. Dignean*, 332 F.R.D. 450, 459 (W.D.N.Y. 2019) ("[T]he responding party must provide the best answer they can based upon current information in their possession.") (citation omitted); *Stevens v. Federated Mut. Ins. Co.*, No. 5:05-CV-149, 2006 U.S. Dist. LEXIS 51001, at *10, 2006 WL 2079503 (N.D.W. Va. July 25, 2006) (noting that a party must answer each interrogatory "fully").

87 Tex. R. Civ. P. 193.1.

88 *Cf. IMA N. Am., Inc., v. Marlyn Nutraceuticals, Inc.*, No. CV-06-0344-PHX-LOA, 2007 U.S. Dist. LEXIS 61269, at *8–9, 2007 WL 2391099 (D. Ariz. Aug. 17, 2007) ("If a party is unable to supply the requested information, the party may not simply refuse to answer, but must state under oath that he is unable to provide the information and set forth the efforts he used to obtain the information." (quoting *Stevens v. Federated Mut. Ins. Co.*, No. 5:05-CV-149, 2006 U.S. Dist. LEXIS 51001, at *10, 2006 WL 2079503 (N.D.W. Va. July 25, 2006))); *EEOC v. Kovacevich "5" Farms*, No. 1:06-cv-0165-OWW-TAG, 2007 U.S. Dist. LEXIS 43672, at *6–7, 2007 WL 1599772 (E.D. Cal. June 1, 2007) (same); *Frontier-Kemper Constructors, Inc. v. Elk Run Coal Co.*, 246 F.R.D. 522, 529 (S.D.W. Va. 2007) (same); *Hansel v. Shell Oil Corp.*, 169 F.R.D. 303, 305 (E.D. Pa. 1996) (same).

the information.[89] Moreover, "a promise to provide the requested information in the future is not a sufficient response to an interrogatory."[90]

Additionally, because each interrogatory must be answered separately and fully, it generally is improper to incorporate outside material by reference.[91] Nonetheless, the

---

89 *Cf. U.S. ex rel. Martino-Fleming v. S. Bay Mental Health Ctr., Inc.*, 332 F.R.D. 1, 7 (D. Mass. 2019) ("If a party cannot provide the requested information, it must state under oath that it is unable to provide the information and set forth the efforts used to obtain the information."); *Rega v. Beard*, No. 08-156, 2010 U.S. Dist. LEXIS 57668, at *4–6, 2010 WL 2404420 (W.D. Pa. June 10, 2010) (same); *EEOC v. Kovacevich "5" Farms*, No. 1:06-cv-0165-OWW-TAG, 2007 U.S. Dist. LEXIS 43672, at *6–7, 2007 WL 1599772 (E.D. Cal. June 1, 2007) (same); *Frontier-Kemper Constructors, Inc. v. Elk Run Coal Co.*, 246 F.R.D. 522, 529 (S.D. W. Va. 2007) (same); *Hansel v. Shell Oil Corp.*, 169 F.R.D. 303, 305–06 (E.D. Pa. 1996) (same).

90 *Innovative Piledriving Prods., LLC v. Unisto Oy*, No. 1:04-CV-453, 2005 U.S. Dist. LEXIS 23652, at *4, 2005 WL 8169578 (N.D. Ind. Oct. 14, 2005); *accord Oleson v. Kmart Corp.*, 175 F.R.D. 560, 564 (D. Kan. 1997).

91 *Cf. Advantage Indus. Sys., LLC v. Aleris Rolled Products, Inc.*, No. 418CV00113JHM-HBB, 2020 U.S. Dist. LEXIS 136305, at *16, 2020 WL 4432415 (W.D. Ky. July 31, 2020) ("[P]roviding general references to pleadings filed in this and a related state court action does not comply with AIS's duty under [Federal] Rule 33(b)(3) to provide fulsome answers to each interrogatory."); *V5 Techs. v. Switch, Ltd.*, 334 F.R.D. 297, 305 (D. Nev. 2019) ("An interrogatory response is improper if it merely references information contained in declarations, pleadings, or other discovery responses."); *Copeland v. City of Lawton*, No. CIV-18-558-PRW, 2019 U.S. Dist. LEXIS 147375, at *3, 2019 WL 4131089 (W.D. Okla. Aug. 29, 2019) ("Plaintiff's references to the Complaint, as well as Interrogatory Nos. 1-12, to answer Interrogatory Nos. 13-19, are improper. Answers to interrogatories should be complete in and of themselves, and should not refer to pleadings, depositions, or other documents.") (citation omitted); *Firefighters' Ret. Sys. v. Citco Grp. Ltd.*, No. 13-373-SDD-EWD, 2017 U.S. Dist. LEXIS 101747, at *21–22, 2017 WL 2825925 (M.D. La. June 29, 2017) ("Fed. R. Civ. P. 33(b)(3) provides that '[e]ach interrogatory must, to the extent it is not objected to, be answered separately and fully in writing[.]' The undersigned has previously held that interrogatory responses that referred generally to a deposition transcript do not meet this standard. Courts interpreting [Federal] Rule 33 have found that 'it is "technically improper and unresponsive for an interrogatory to refer to outside material, such as pleadings, depositions, or other interrogatories."' Plaintiffs' interrogatory responses that refer to the Trustees' Reports do not comply with [Federal] Rule 33." (citations omitted) (quoting *Kleppinger v. Tex. Dep't of Transp.*, No. 5:10-cv-124, 2013 U.S. Dist. LEXIS 197897, at *7–8, 2013 WL 12138545 (S.D. Tex. Jan. 3, 2013))); *In re Wilmington Tr. Sec. Litig.*, No. 10-990-SLR-SRF (Consolidated Securities Class Action), 2017 U.S. Dist. LEXIS 87045, at *7, 2017 WL 2467059 (D. Del. June 6, 2017) ("First, Defendants allege that Plaintiffs' responses to the Interrogatories are deficient because the responses include cross-references to the complaint and witness deposition testimony instead of separate sworn answers. . . . As a matter of law, courts have held that cross-referencing the complaint is impermissible under [Federal] Rule 33's requirement that each interrogatory be answered separately."); *Tadlock v. Arctic Cat Sales, Inc.*, No. 15-766-JJB-EWD, 2017 U.S. Dist. LEXIS 38429, at *14–16, 2017 WL 1032516 (M.D. La. Mar. 17, 2017) ("The Court finds that Plaintiff's supplemental responses, which refer generally to Plaintiff's September 20, 2016 deposition transcript, a report by Thomas Shelton, and further suggest that the information can be obtained by deposing Shelton, are insufficient under Federal Rule of Civil Procedure 33. At least two courts in this circuit have held that responses to interrogatories that refer to deposition testimony do not satisfy the requirements of [Federal Rule] 33."); *French v. Wachovia Bank NA*, No. 06-CV-869, 2010 U.S. Dist. LEXIS 82222, at *4, 2010 WL 2643385 (E.D. Wis. June 29, 2010) ("Referring to a multiple page expert report does not constitute a proper response

propriety of such incorporation by reference is evaluated on an interrogatory-by-interrogatory basis, and it may be acceptable for an interrogatory answer to refer to other interrogatories or discovery if the referral is clear and precise and the other discovery fully answers the interrogatory.[92] It is, however, never proper to merely incorporate by reference the allegations in the responding party's pleadings even if the pleadings are verified.[93] This is because interrogatory answers are admissible in support of a summary judgment motion and as affirmative or impeachment evidence at trial, whereas

---

to an interrogatory. It is not the defendant's duty to sift through an expert report in an attempt to glean the information sought in the interrogatory."); *Gipson v. Sw. Bell Tel. Co.*, No. 08-2017-EFM-DJW, 2009 U.S. Dist. LEXIS 25457, at *19–20, 2009 WL 790203 (D. Kan. Mar. 24, 2009) ("As a general rule, a responding party may not answer an interrogatory by simply referring the requesting party to other documents."); *Equal Rights Ctr. v. Post Props., Inc.*, 246 F.R.D. 29, 35 (D.D.C. 2007) ("[I]t is technically improper and unresponsive for an answer to an interrogatory to refer to outside material, such as pleadings, depositions, or other interrogatories."); *Pac. Lumber Co. v. Nat'l Union Fire Ins. Co.*, No. C 02-4799 SBA (JL), 2005 U.S. Dist. LEXIS 1773, at *14–15, 2005 WL 318811 (N.D. Cal. Jan 5, 2005) ("Responding to an interrogatory with a reference to another interrogatory or to a document or pleading is improper. 'It is well established that an answer to an interrogatory must be responsive to the question. It should be complete in itself and should not refer to the pleadings, or to depositions or other documents, or to other interrogatories, at least when such references make it impossible to determine whether an adequate answer has been given without an elaborate comparison of answers.'" (quoting *Smith v. Logansport Cmty. Sch. Corp.*, 139 F.R.D. 637, 650 (N.D. Ind. 1991))).

92 *Cf. V5 Techs. v. Switch, Ltd.*, 334 F.R.D. 297, 305 (D. Nev. 2019) ("The sufficiency of an interrogatory response must be analyzed on a case-by-case basis in light of the particular question being asked."); *Walls v. Paulson*, 250 F.R.D. 48, 52 (D.D.C. 2008) ("While not 'strictly proper,' there is authority that one may answer one interrogatory by referring to another interrogatory. Such determinations must be made on a case-by-case basis[.]") (citations omitted).

93 *Cf. Hawn v. Shoreline Towers Phase I Condo. Ass'n*, No. 3:07cv97/RV/EMT, 2007 U.S. Dist. LEXIS 58032, at *6–7, 2007 WL 2298009 (N.D. Fla. Aug. 9, 2007) ("[I]t is insufficient to answer an interrogatory by merely referencing allegations of a pleading. Plaintiff's verbatim copying of paragraphs contained in the complaint is no more effective an answer to question two than his bare citation to the complaint.") (citations omitted); *Davidson v. Goord*, 215 F.R.D. 73, 77 (W.D.N.Y. 2003) ("Nor it is permissible to refuse to provide answers to interrogatories . . . or documents in response to a request . . . on the ground that information sought can be gleaned from the requested party's pleading. . . . As answers to interrogatories . . . must be in a form suitable for use at trial, it is insufficient to answer by merely referencing allegations of a pleading."); *DiPietro v. Jefferson Bank*, 144 F.R.D. 279, 282 (E.D. Pa. 1992) ("[T]he fact that plaintiff's complaint is sworn does not make it any more acceptable to answer an interrogatory solely by referencing paragraphs of that sworn complaint."); *Stabilus v. Haynsworth, Baldwin, Johnson & Greaves, P.A.*, 144 F.R.D. 258, 263–64 (E.D. Pa. 1992) ("As defendant argues, merely restating the general allegations of the complaint is not a proper answer to an interrogatory. However, plaintiff does not even restate the allegations in the complaint. Rather, plaintiff's response is to 'See plaintiff's Complaint.' Plaintiff cannot avoid answering interrogatories by referring the defendant to the complaint, no matter how detailed. Thus it is improper to answer an interrogatory merely by repeating the allegations of the complaint."); *King v. E.F. Hutton & Co.*, 117 F.R.D. 2, 6 (D.D.C. 1987) ("Nor is it an adequate response to say that the information is reflected in the complaint, no matter how detailed. . . ."). See also cases cited in note 91.

pleadings cannot be used by the pleader to establish facts in support of its claim or defense as they are merely statements of the drafting attorney.[94]

Under Texas Rule 193.1, a party answering an interrogatory "must make a complete response, based on all information reasonably available to the responding party or its attorney at the time the response is made."[95] The obvious purpose of this requirement is to require parties to provide complete interrogatory answers as early in the action as possible.

As discussed in Chapter 5, section 5-2:1, nothing in Texas Rule 193 or 197 or the other discovery rules explains when "information" is "reasonably available." As also pointed out therein, what material is reasonably available depends in large measure on the responding party's obligation of reasonable inquiry (i.e., how extensive a search the responding party must make to respond to the discovery request) and whether the information is within the responding party's possession, custody, or control. This, of course, depends on the facts of each action.

9-5:2 Option to Produce Business Records

When an interrogatory answer can be derived or ascertained from public records, the responding party's business records, or from a compilation, abstract, or summary of the responding party's business records, the responding party, under Texas Rule 197.2(c), may, instead of answering the interrogatory, specify the records from which the answer may be derived, giving sufficient detail to permit the requesting party to identify the records and then, if the records are the responding party's business records or a compilation, abstract, or summary of them, afford the requesting party a reasonable opportunity to examine the records, compilation, abstract, or summary.[96] However, there are a number of prerequisites to the Rule's invocation.

First, the option is limited to the types of records specified in Texas Rule 197.2(c)—"public records, . . . the responding party's business records, or . . . a compilation, abstract, or summary of the responding party's business records."[97] Thus, for example, the responding party cannot properly refer the requesting party to its own records or another party's records;[98] to pleadings, deposition transcripts, interrogatory

---

94 *Cf. King v. E.F. Hutton & Co.*, 117 F.R.D. 2, 6 (D.D.C. 1987) ("Answers to interrogatories may be relied upon by the opposing party in connection with a motion for summary judgment, can be used as affirmative evidence at trial, and certainly can be used for cross-examination and impeachment. Assertions in the complaint cannot be so used since they are merely the statements of counsel.") (footnote omitted).

95 Tex. R. Civ. P. 193.1.

96 Tex. R. Civ. P. 197.2(c). Although Texas Rule 197.2(c) is based on Federal Rule 33(d), it is broader than the Federal Rule because the Federal Rule does not allow for a reference to public records. Rather, the Federal Rule is limited to the responding party's "business records (including electronically stored information)." Fed. R. Civ. P. 33(d).

97 Tex. R. Civ. P. 197.2(c).

98 *Cf. Poshard v. Madison Cnty.*, No. 319CV00324SMYGCS, 2020 WL 5645303 (S.D. Ill. Sept. 22, 2020) ("Defendant's mere reference to documents produced by other defendants is clearly insufficient to satisfy the requirements of [Federal Rule 33(d)]."); *McSwiggin v. Omni Limousine*, No. 2:14-cv-02172-JCM-NJK, 2016 U.S. Dist. LEXIS 30865, at *18, 2016 WL 1030053 (D. Nev. Mar. 10, 2016) ("Plaintiffs cannot answer Defendant's interrogatories by referring Defendant to Defendant's own business records. Rather, as the responding

answers, affidavits, or exhibits;[99] to documents submitted by the responding party to

---

party, Plaintiffs' permissible use of [Federal] Rule 33(d) is limited to their own business records, if any."); *U.S. ex rel. Landis v. Tailwind Sports Corp.*, 317 F.R.D. 592, 595 (D.D.C. 2016) ("[C]ourts and commentators have long agreed that Rule 33(d) applies 'only where the answers to the interrogatories may be found in the business records of the party upon whom the interrogatories have been served.'" (quoting *McSwiggin v. Omni Limousine*, No. 2:14-cv-02172-JCM-NJK, 2016 U.S. Dist. LEXIS 30865, at *18, 2016 WL 1030053 (D. Nev. Mar. 10, 2016))); *Covad Commc'ns Co. v. Revonet, Inc.*, 258 F.R.D. 17, 20 (D.D.C. 2009) ("Covad is not answering the interrogatories by producing its own records and directing Revonet to search for the answer in them. It is referring Revonet to Revonet's internal files. This approach is not sanctioned by the Federal Rules of Civil Procedure. They only permit the responding party to answer an interrogatory by producing records from which the answer responsive to the interrogatory may be derived, provided the burden of ascertaining the answer is the same for both parties. Obviously, if Covad's approach was correct, propounding an interrogatory and getting an answer would become a perfect circle. If the responding party were permitted to say that the answer to the interrogatory is to be found in the producing party's records then the process of getting the information responsive to the inquiry would not move forward an inch.") (citations omitted); *Hawn v. Shoreline Towers Phase I Condo. Ass'n*, No. 3:07cv97/RV/EMT, 2007 U.S. Dist. LEXIS 58032, at *7, 2007 WL 2298009 (N.D. Fla. Aug. 9, 2007) (same); *see In re Savitt/Adler Litig.*, 176 F.R.D. 44, 49 (N.D.N.Y. 1997) (holding that Federal Rule 33(d)'s invocation was improper because "the records to which plaintiffs refer in their responses are not their business records as required for use of [Federal] Rule 33(d)").

99 *Cf. V5 Techs. v. Switch, Ltd.*, 334 F.R.D. 297, 305 (D. Nev. 2019) ("An interrogatory response is improper if it merely references information contained in declarations, pleadings, or other discovery responses. Similarly, an interrogatory response may not simply refer to the litigation record in an underlying action.") (citations omitted); *Chinn v. Elmwood Franklin Sch.*, No. 15-CV-00938-FPG-JJM, 2018 U.S. Dist. LEXIS 188307, at *13, 2018 WL 6738326 (W.D.N.Y. Nov. 1, 2018), report and recommendation adopted, No. 15-CV-938-FPG, 2018 WL 6266193 (W.D.N.Y. Nov. 29, 2018) ("Plaintiff answered virtually every one of those interrogatories by stating that she 'can't respond to this overbroad request at this time. However, please see audiotapes submitted as part of Elmwood Franklin's first discovery demand dated April 13, 2018.' These responses are patently improper: 'answering interrogatories simply by directing the proponent to rummage through other discovery materials falls short of the obligations imposed by Rule 33.'" (citing *MuleroAbreu v. P.R. Police Dep't*, 675 F.3d 88, 93 (1st Cir. 2012))); *Creative Touch Interiors, Inc. v. Nicholson*, No. 6:14-cv-2043-Orl-40TBS, 2015 U.S. Dist. LEXIS 139110, at *9–11, 2015 WL 5952986 (M.D. Fla. Oct. 13, 2015) ("Plaintiff responded to this interrogatory by referring Defendants to paragraphs 92–96 of the complaint and the transcript of the preliminary injunction hearing held on December 23, 2014. [Federal] Rule 33(d) gives a party responding to interrogatories the option of producing business records. . . . Plaintiff's response does not comply with [Federal] Rule 33(d). The complaint and transcript of the preliminary injunction hearing are not business records, and Plaintiff does not argue that the other documents it produced are business records."); *SEC v. Elfindepan*, 206 F.R.D. 574, 577–78 (M.D.N.C. 2002) ("Next, the documents plaintiff intends to use are not business records as required by [Federal] Rule 33(d). Pleadings, depositions, exhibits, and affidavits . . . are not [Federal] Rule 33(d) business records.") (footnote omitted); *Melius v. Nat'l Indian Gaming Comm'n*, No. 98-2210 (TFH/JMF), 2000 U.S. Dist. LEXIS 22747, at *4 n.2, 2000 WL 1174994 (D.D.C. July 21, 2000) ("Plaintiff cannot seriously protest that [Federal Rule] 33(d) . . . permits him to answer the interrogatory the way he did. The assertion that pleadings, depositions, or exhibits are 'business records' under this rule has been rejected by every court to consider it."); *In re Savitt/Adler Litig.*, 176 F.R.D. 44, 49–50 (N.D.N.Y. 1997) ("The records referred to by plaintiffs include depositions, answers to interrogatories by other parties and documents

a federal or state agency;[100] or to a private nonparty's documents.[101] Further, when the responding party is a natural person, it cannot refer the requesting party to his or her personal records unless they, in fact, are business records.[102]

Second, even though Texas Rule 197.2(c) says that the interrogatory answer need only indicate that the information "may" be found in the specified records, by invoking it, the responding party necessarily is representing that the information needed to fully answer the interrogatory is in the designated records.[103]

---

produced by defendants during discovery. None of these documents constitute business records of plaintiffs and, therefore, references to those documents and materials by plaintiffs in response to interrogatories was improper."); *Cont'l Ill. Nat'l Bank & Tr. Co. v. Caton*, 136 F.R.D. 682, 687 (D. Kan. 1991) (Federal Rule 33(d) "does not mention deposition transcripts, documents or writings that were generated or discovered, respectively, during the course of prior discovery in the same case.")

100 *Cf. Hoffman v. United Telecomms., Inc.*, 117 F.R.D. 436, 438 (D. Kan. 1987) (holding that documents submitted to the EEOC by defendants in connection with the EEOC's investigation of discrimination claims remain the submitter's business records and do not become the EEOC's business records).

101 *Cf. FTC v. AMG Servs.*, No. 2:12-cv-536-GMN-VCF, 2015 U.S. Dist. LEXIS 114550, at *14, 2015 WL 5097526 (D. Nev. Aug. 28, 2015) ("Here, Defendants listed thousands of pages of documents that were produced by third party banks when answering the Commission's interrogatory. This abused [Federal] Rule 33."); *E. & J. Gallo Winery v. Cantine Rallo, S. p. A.*, No. 1:04cv5153 OWW DLB, 2006 U.S. Dist. LEXIS 84048, at *7, 2006 WL 3251830 (E.D. Cal. Nov. 8, 2006) ("[M]any of the documents do not qualify as 'business records of the party upon whom the interrogatory has been served' as they appear to be third party business records."); *Bradley v. Val-Mejias*, No: 00-2395-GTV, 2001 U.S. Dist. LEXIS 25278, at *6–7, 2001 WL 1249339 (D. Kan. Oct. 9, 2001) ("While Fed. R. Civ. P. 33(d) allows a party to answer an interrogatory by producing business records in certain circumstances, that rule applies only to the business records 'of the party upon whom the interrogatory has been served.' The business records option does not apply here, because the medical records are the business records of various non-party hospitals and not those of Plaintiff." (quoting Fed. R. Civ. P. 33(d))); *Jobin v. Bank of Boulder (In re M & L Bus. Mach. Co.)*, 167 B.R. 631, 634 n.3 (Bankr. D. Colo. 1994) ("The records referred to, at least those of the Bank or prepared by third party experts, are not M & L's business records. Therefore, [Former Federal] Rule 33(c), which the Trustee has repeatedly invoked, is not applicable.").

102 *Cf. Gipson v. Sw. Bell Tel. Co.*, No. 08-2017-EFM-DJW, 2009 U.S. Dist. LEXIS 25457, at *20 n.40, 2009 WL 790203 (D. Kan. Mar. 24, 2009) ("Plaintiffs are individuals who would not possess 'business' records within the meaning of [Federal] Rule 33(d). . . . If the answering party is not engaged in a business, it would appear unlikely that it would have 'business records.'") (citation omitted), *overruled on other grounds*, No. 08-2017-EFM-DJW, 2009 U.S. Dist. LEXIS 109083, 2009 WL 4157948 (D. Kan. Nov. 23, 2009).

103 *Cf. Advantage Indus. Sys., LLC v. Aleris Rolled Prods., Inc.*, No. 418CV00113JHMHBB, 2020 U.S. Dist. LEXIS 136305, at *25, 2020 WL 4432415 (W.D. Ky. July 31, 2020) ("The Court concludes AIS's production of 131 documents does not comport with [Federal] Rule 33(d). Specifically, AIS failed to certify that the answer may be found in the referenced records and specify the subparts to Interrogatory Nos. 3 and 11 that these records answer and where in the records the answer can be found."); *Int'l Aero. Grp. Corp. v. Evans Meridians, Ltd.*, No. 16-24997-Civ-KING/TORRES, 2017 U.S. Dist. LEXIS 71304, at *7–9, 2017 WL 1927957 (S.D. Fla. May 10, 2017) ("The producing party must satisfy a number of factors in order to meet its justification burden. First, it must show that a review of the documents will actually reveal answers to the interrogatories." (quoting *SEC v. Elfindepan, S.A.*, 206 F.R.D. 574, 576 (M.D.N.C. 2002))); *U.S. v. Maverick Mktg.*, LLC, 427 F. Supp. 3d 1386, 1399–400 (CIT, 2020) ("Vague references to documents do not suffice; rather, the responding party 'adequately

Not every type of interrogatory can be answered by a review of public records or the responding party's business records. For example, an interrogatory asking a party to identify specific documents relating to a subject, contention, claim, defense, or the recollections of parties or their employees generally cannot be answered by a

---

and precisely specif[y] for each interrogatory, the actual documents where information will be found.'"); *Smith v. TFI Family Servs. Inc.*, No. 17-02235-JWB-GEB, 2019 U.S. Dist. LEXIS 9074, at *8–9, 2019 WL 266234 (D. Kan. Jan. 18, 2019) ("[R]esponding parties cannot, under the guise of [Federal] Rule 33(d), generally refer to a mass of records. Responding parties must specifically identify in their interrogatory answers which documents contain the responsive information. Otherwise, the interrogatories must be answered without referring to records.") (citations omitted); *Circuit Check, Inc. v. QxQ Inc.*, No. 12-C-1211, 2013 U.S. Dist. LEXIS 165612, at *11–12, 2013 WL 6153234 (E.D. Wis. Nov. 20, 2013) ("I am satisfied that [Federal] Rule 33(d) was not designed to be so broad as to encompass a situation in which an inquiring party must resort to speculation to determine whether its opponent's business records actually reveal damages or not. The Rule, which provides an exception to the normal process of answering interrogatories, requires the answer to be manifest in the records such that the answer to the interrogatory 'may be determined.' Here, it is apparent that additional steps would be required to make the connection between the files QxQ would provide and the identity of customers who were using accused products. Thus, it is not clear that the answer to the interrogatory may be determined from the records themselves. Moreover, it is similarly doubtful that it would be just as easy for Circuit Check to perform the review as it would be for QxQ. Accordingly, I conclude that QxQ's reliance on Federal Rule 33(d) is not appropriate under these circumstances." (quoting Fed. R. Civ. P. 33(d))); *Sabel v. Mead Johnson & Co.*, 110 F.R.D. 553, 555 (D. Mass. 1986) ("[T]he party invoking the option provided by [former Federal] Rule 33(c) may not do so if all which can be said is that the answer 'might' be found in the records; the party invoking the option must be able to represent that the party will be able to secure the information which is sought by the interrogatory in the records."); *see In re Lithium Ion Batteries Antitrust Litig.*, No. 13-md-02420-YGR (DMR), 2015 U.S. Dist. LEXIS 111275, at *57–58, 2015 WL 4999762 (N.D. Cal. Aug. 21, 2015) ("LG Chem's arguments are unpersuasive. Its assertion that Plaintiffs can obtain the missing information through deposition is a concession that the documents themselves do not contain all of the responsive material. That alone is fatal to LG Chem's [Federal] Rule 33(d) argument, since reference to the identified documents is admittedly insufficient. It is LG Chem's burden to show that the documents contain complete answers to the interrogatory. While some pertinent information may be found in the documents, this is not enough: Plaintiffs are entitled to a complete response."); *Toyo Tire & Rubber Co. v. Atturo Tire Corp.*, No: 14 C 206, 2015 U.S. Dist. LEXIS 22026, at *8–9 (N.D. Ill. Feb. 24, 2015) ("And we are unable to identify a federal case within the Seventh Circuit that directly addresses whether a party responding to interrogatories by reference to documents in a foreign language is obligated to translate the documents at its own expense. Other districts, however, have held that where a party makes the decision to produce documents in lieu of responding to an interrogatory, the burden generally falls on the party answering the interrogatory. [Federal] Rule 33(d) provides that a party answering the interrogatory may specify records to be reviewed, but must do so 'in sufficient detail to enable the interrogating party to locate and identify them as readily as the responding party could.' Courts have found that by answering through untranslated foreign documents, the interrogatory response 'runs afoul of [Federal] Rule 33(d).' Toyo has provided no reason why it cannot extract the necessary information from the documents it has referenced to provide an English language answer to Atturo's interrogatories." (quoting *Nature's Plus Nordic A/S v. Natural Organics, Inc.*, 274 F.R.D. 437, 441 (E.D.N.Y. 2011))).

reference to such records.[104] Similarly, contention interrogatories generally cannot be answered by a review of public records or the responding party's business records because a search of such records is unlikely to reveal the party's contentions or the facts supporting them.[105]

Third, based on federal courts' uniform construction of Federal Rule 33(d), it is reasonable to conclude that Texas Rule 197.2(c) should be used only when answering the interrogatory would impose a burden or expense on the responding party.[106] The burden, however, need not be so great as to warrant a protective

---

[104] *Cf. Budget Rent-A-Car of Mo., Inc. v. Hertz Corp.*, 55 F.R.D. 354, 358 (W.D. Mo. Mar. 24, 1972) ("Since interrogatory numbered 29 basically seeks to elicit such specificity in identifying certain documents rather than a compilation of information, this is clearly not a situation in which [former Federal] Rule 33(c) may properly be used.").

[105] *Cf. Int'l Aero. Grp. Corp. v. Evans Meridians, Ltd.*, No. 16-24997-Civ-KING/TORRES, 2017 U.S. Dist. LEXIS 71304, at *7–9, 2017 WL 1927957 (S.D. Fla. May 10, 2017) ("Reliance on [Federal] Rule 33(d) is appropriate when the interrogatory requests objective facts that are obvious from the specified documents, but is generally inappropriate when the interrogatory asks a party to state its contentions or to state facts supporting its allegations." (quoting *Morock v. Chautauqua Airlines, Inc.*, No. 8:07-cv-210-T-17-MAP, 2007 U.S. Dist. LEXIS 88532, at *4, 2007 WL 4247767 (M.D. Fla. Dec. 3, 2007))); *U.S. ex rel. Landis v. Tailwind Sports Corp.*, 317 F.R.D. 592, 594 (D.D.C. 2016) ("Courts have consistently held that [Federal Rule 33(d)] cannot be used with respect to contention interrogatories, like those at issue here. This is because documents normally reveal evidence, not a party's contentions or statement of facts which a party contends supports the complaint. This is especially true here, given that items produced by the government account for most of the documents itemized in 'Attachment A.' Of course, Armstrong's present legal contentions will not be found in the opposing party's records.") (citations omitted); *Colony Ins. Co. v. 9400 Abercom, LLC*, No. 4:11-cv-255, 2012 U.S. Dist. LEXIS 131839, at *15, 2012 WL 3985088 (S.D. Ga. Sept. 12, 2012) ("[R]esponding parties normally may not utilize [Federal] Rule 33(d) in answering contention interrogatories because documents reveal evidence, not the facts or contentions a party alleges support its assertions."); *Hypertherm, Inc. v. Am. Torch Tip Co.*, No. 05-cv-373-JD, 2008 U.S. Dist. LEXIS 108269, at *7–8, 2008 WL 5423837 (D.N.H. Dec. 29, 2008) ("On the other hand, contention interrogatories that ask for 'each and every' or all documents . . . that support a claim may be overly broad and unduly burdensome."); *United Oil Co. v. Parts Assocs., Inc.*, 227 F.R.D. 404, 419 (D. Md. 2005) ("'[D]efendants are entitled to know the factual content of plaintiff's claims with a reasonable degree of precision[,]'" which cannot be done by a search of documents.); *SEC v. Elfindepan*, 206 F.R.D. 574, 577 (M.D.N.C. 2002) ("[Federal] Rule 33(d) was intended to be used in the situation where an interrogatory makes broad inquires and numerous documents must be consulted to ascertain facts, such as identities, quantities, data, action, tests, results, etc. . . . [T]he interrogatories were a mixture of contention interrogatories and requests for statements of fact. These types of interrogatories do not lend themselves to answer by use of [Federal] Rule 33(d).") (citation omitted); *In re Savitt/Adler Litig.*, 176 F.R.D. 44, 49 (N.D.N.Y. 1997) ("Each of the interrogatories at issue directs a plaintiff to 'state the facts' supporting various allegations. Given the particular allegations, . . . the resort to [Federal] Rule 33(d) in response to these interrogatories was inappropriate.").

[106] *Cf. U.S. ex rel. Dougherty v. Guild Mortg. Co.*, No. 16CV2909-JAH(BLM), 2020 U.S. Dist. LEXIS 115126, at *14, 2020 WL 3542391 (S.D. Cal. June 30, 2020) ("For both of its responses to Defendant's interrogatories, the Government suggests that, pursuant to [Federal] Rule 33(d), Defendant should look at the loan files and figure out what it did wrong. This is an improper use of [Federal]Rule 33(d). If a party wishes to rely on [Federal] Rule 33(d), the burden of deriving or ascertaining the answer must be substantially the same for the party serving the interrogatory as for the party served and the party responding must

order's entry. Also, there is no burden or expense if the responding party would have to answer the interrogatory to properly prosecute its claims or defend against the action.[107]

Fourth, as expressly required by Texas Rule 197.2(c), the burden of compiling the information must be "substantially the same" for the requesting and responding parties.[108] This requires, at the minimum, that the interrogatory's answer can be obtained only from the pertinent records—if the interrogatory can be answered in another way, the other way should be used.[109] For example, if the responding party has already

---

specify in sufficient detail where the answers can be found. Merely directing Defendant to hundreds of loan records and citing to the general HUD underwriting and origination requirements does not suffice to alert Defendant to what the Government's allegations are or what evidence it has to support its claims.") (citations omitted); *Hege v. Aegon USA, LLC*, No. 8:10-cv-01578-GRA, 2011 U.S. Dist. LEXIS 31772, at *10–11, 2011 WL 1119871 (D.S.C. Mar. 25, 2011) ("[T]he burden on the respondent must be significant; information that can readily be found by simple reference to documents is insufficient."); *Anderson v. Wade*, No. 94–111, 1997 U.S. Dist. LEXIS 24079, at *40 (E.D. Ky. Aug. 13, 1997) ("An interrogated party may rely on [Federal Rule] 33(d) only if there is some burden involved in compiling or extracting the requested information, above and beyond the simple task of referring to the records in order to obtain the information necessary to answer the interrogatory."); *Am. Hoist & Derrick Co. v. Manitowoc Co.*, No. 86 C 9383, 1990 U.S. Dist. LEXIS 18569, at *79 n.31 (N.D. Ill. Dec. 14, 1990) ("The rule does not relieve the party of all obligation to answer, especially where only limited information is sought and the interrogated party can easily answer the interrogatories with reference to its own records."); *Sabel v. Mead Johnson & Co.*, 110 F.R.D. 553, 556 (D. Mass. 1986) ("The next prerequisite for invoking the [former Federal] Rule 33(c) option is that there be a burden on the interrogated party if it were required to answer the interrogatory. This prerequisite, although not explicitly contained in the rule, is implicit in its provisions."); *Clean Burn Fuels v. Purdue Bioenergy, LLC*, Bankr. No. 11–09046, Adversary No. 11–80562, 2012 Bankr. LEXIS 4732, at *15, 2012 WL 4792907 (Bankr. M.D.N.C. Oct. 9, 2012) ("[T]he interrogated party can rely on former [Federal] Rule 33(d) only upon a showing that it would be burdensome to compile or extract the information beyond what is necessary to sufficiently refer to the records.").

[107] *Cf. L.H. v. Schwarzenegger*, No. S-06-2042 LKK GGH, 2007 U.S. Dist. LEXIS 73752, at *9–10, 2007 WL 2781132 (E.D. Cal. Sept. 21, 2007) ("[I]f the responding party would necessarily have to gather the requested information to prepare its own case, objections that it is too difficult to obtain the information for the requesting party are not honored."); *Flour Mills of Am., Inc. v. Pace*, 75 F.R.D. 676, 680 (E.D. Okla. 1977) (same).

[108] Tex. R. Civ. P. 197.2(c); *see Daiflon, Inc. v. Allied Chem. Corp.*, 534 F.2d 221, 226–27 (10th Cir. 1976) (discussing whether the burden is substantially the same for the parties); *Taylor v. HD & Associates*, LLC, CV 19-10635, 2020 U.S. Dist. LEXIS 213478, at *7–8, 2020 WL 6708383 (E.D. La. Nov. 16, 2020) (same); *U.S. ex rel. Martino-Fleming v. S. Bay Mental Health Ctr., Inc.*, 332 F.R.D. 1, 8–9 (D. Mass. 2019) (same); *Huawei Techs. Co., Ltd. v. Huang*, 4:17-CV-00893, 2018 U.S. Dist. LEXIS 136929, at *10, 2018 WL 3862061, at *4 (E.D. Tex. Aug. 14, 2018) (same); *P.R. Aqueduct & Sewer Auth. v. Clow Corp.*, 108 F.R.D. 304, 307 (D.P.R. 1985) (same); *Pulsecard, Inc. v. Discover Card Servs., Inc.*, 168 F.R.D. 295, 304–05 (D. Kans. 1996) (same). In *Oppenheimer Fund, Inc. v. Sanders*, 437 U.S. 340, 357 (1978), the U.S. Supreme Court framed the test as "where the burden of deriving the answer would not be 'substantially the same,' and the task could be performed more efficiently by the responding party, the discovery rules normally require the responding party to derive the answer itself."

[109] *Cf. Daiflon, Inc. v. Allied Chem. Corp.*, 534 F.2d 221, 226 (10th Cir. 1976) ("[I]f an answer is readily available in a more convenient form, [former Federal] Rule 33(c) should not be used to avoid giving the ready information to a serving party."); *Kates v. Packer*,

culled the requested information as part of its trial preparation or for other purposes, the burden is not substantially equal.[110]

Although the burden need not be equal, the mere fact that the responding party is more familiar with its records often is insufficient to tip the balance.[111] Instead, other

---

No. 3:13-cv-01525, 2017 U.S. Dist. LEXIS 113516, at *4, 2017 WL 3118774 (N.D. Pa. July 21, 2017) (same); *Advanced Visual Image Design, LLC v. Exist, Inc.*, No. EDCV 14-2525-JGB (KKx), 2015 U.S. Dist. LEXIS 102798, at *13, 2015 WL 4652762 (C.D. Cal. Aug. 5, 2015) (same); *Sadofsky v. Fiesta Prods., LLC*, 252 F.R.D. 143, 148 (E.D.N.Y. 2008) ("A responding party creates an unequal burden for the receiving party when it has the answer to an interrogatory in the form of a compilation but responds to the interrogatory by producing and identifying business records, such that the receiving party must then compile the records to obtain the answer to the interrogatory. Some interrogatories call for a simple answer and any response other than a written answer creates an unequal burden between the parties."); *Convermat Corp. v. St. Paul Fire & Marine Ins. Co.*, No. CV 06-1045 (JFB) (AKT), 2007 U.S. Dist. LEXIS 69102, at *17–18, 2007 WL 2743696 (E.D.N.Y. Sept. 18, 2007) ("The language of the [Federal] Rule 33(d) requires the burden among the producing and reviewing parties to be equal and that there be a sufficiently detailed specification so that the interrogating party is able to locate and identify the responsive documents. Interrogatory Nos. 4 and 5 call for straightforward information which is relevant to the issues in this action. The argument that Plaintiff will be able to obtain a description as to each individual's involvement solely from reviewing the referenced business records is unavailing. I further find that this interrogatory can be responded to more readily and easily by written answer rather than referring to documents."); *Compagnie Francaise d'Assurance Pour le Commerce Exterieur v. Phillips Petroleum Co.*, 105 F.R.D. 16, 44 (S.D.N.Y. 1984) (stating that Federal Rule 33(d) "is not an available alternative if an interrogatory can be responded to more readily and conveniently by written answer"); *ITT Life Ins. Co. v. Thomas Nastoff, Inc.*, 108 F.R.D. 664, 666 (N.D. Ind. 1985) (same); *Petroleum Ins. Agency, Inc. v. Hartford Accident & Indem. Co.*, 111 F.R.D. 318, 321 (D. Mass. 1983) (same).

110 *Cf. In re Sulfuric Acid Antitrust Litig.*, 231 F.R.D. 351, 366 (N.D. Ill. 2005) ("Added to that familiarity is the familiarity of defense counsel, who have already undertaken at least one review of the documents. Consequently, the defense will be more easily able to locate the answers in the documents than would plaintiffs."); *SEC v. Elfindepan*, 206 F.R.D. 574, 577 (M.D.N.C. 2002) (holding that the plaintiff did not meet the threshold for using [Federal] Rule 33(d) because it already culled the documents for answers to some or all of the interrogatories, meaning it was not equally or less burdensome for defendants to obtain the information); *Petroleum Ins. Agency, Inc. v. Hartford Accident & Indem. Co.*, 111 F.R.D. 318, 322 (D. Mass. 1983) ("[T]he fact is that as of this time, the defendants have done considerable work to gather the information requested by interrogatories # 25(d) and (e), and, it therefore follows that it is not equally burdensome for the parties to search the records to come up with the answers, since the defendants have already done so.").

111 *Cf. Sadofsky v. Fiesta Prods., LLC*, 252 F.R.D. 143, 148 (E.D.N.Y. 2008) ("'[O]ne party's familiarity with the documents does not necessarily create a disparity in the ease of discovery that would preclude resort to [former Federal] Rule 33(c).'" (quoting *Compagnie Francaise d'Assurance Pour le Commerce Exterieur v. Phillips Petroleum Co.*, 105 F.R.D. 16, 44 (S.D.N.Y. 1984))); *Hege v. Aegon USA, LLC*, No. 8:10-cv-01578-GRA, 2011 U.S. Dist. LEXIS 31772, at *8, 2011 WL 1119871 (D.S.C. Mar. 25, 2011) ("'[A Federal] Rule 33(d) response is inappropriate where the interrogatory calls for 'the exercise of particular knowledge and judgment on the part of the responding party.' In that case, the respondent must fully answer the interrogatory by traditional means." (citation omitted) (quoting *United Oil Co. v. Parts Assocs., Inc.*, 227 F.R.D. 404, 419 (D. Md. 2005))); *Sabel v. Mead Johnson & Co.*, 110 F.R.D. 553, 556 (D. Mass. 1986) ("While an interrogated party will always be more familiar with its own records than the interrogating party, familiarity with the records cannot be

factors must be balanced with the responding party's familiarity with the records, such as the expense of reviewing them and their nature.[112] Familiarity, however, may be the deciding factor with respect to certain records, such as documents that are difficult to read, handwritten notes, or the responding party's financial records.[113] If the burden is substantially the same for the parties, the fact that the requesting party's burden is a heavy one does not prevent the responding party from exercising its option to refer to the records rather than compiling the answer.[114]

---

the sole test. The inquiry is whether the relative burdens are ***substantially*** the same, not whether they are precisely equal.").

[112] *See State Farm Mut. Auto. Ins. Co. v. Engelke*, 824 S.W.2d 747, 752 (Tex. App.—Houston [1st Dist.] 1992, orig. proceeding) ("Clearly, the plain terms of [former Texas R]ule 168 require a balancing analysis of the relative burden imposed upon the party seeking and the party responding to discovery by the assertion that the information sought is a matter of public record."); *cf. Goodrich Corp. v. Emhart Indus., Inc.*, No. EDCV 04-00079-VAP (SSx), 2005 U.S. Dist. LEXIS 25158, at *10–11 (C.D. Cal. Oct. 12, 2005) ("In determining the relative burdens to the parties, the court must balance the costs of research, the nature of the business records, and the familiarity of the interrogated party with its own documents."); *P.R. Aqueduct & Sewer Auth. v. Clow Corp.*, 108 F.R.D. 304, 307 (D.P.R. 1985) (same).

[113] *Cf. Al Barnett & Son, Inc. v. Outboard Marine Corp.*, 611 F.2d 32, 35 (3d Cir. 1979) ("Many of the records were handwritten, and apparently difficult to read. The district further observed that each party served with interrogatories was more familiar with his bookkeeping methods and records than the defendant."); *C&N Corp. v. Kane*, No. 12-C-0257, 2013 U.S. Dist. LEXIS 2097, at *12–13, 2013 WL 74366 (E.D. Wis. Jan. 7, 2013) ("[M]aking records available for inspection may be a permissible response to an interrogatory or a request for production. However, given that defendants have repeatedly stated that their business records are in disarray and require searches equivalent to finding 'a needle in a haystack,' it is doubtful that ascertaining an answer will be substantially the same for both parties. Parties may not simply dump disorganized documents on their opponents in an effort to evade their discovery obligations."); *RSI Corp. v. IBM Corp.*, No. 5:08-cv-3414 RMW, 2012 U.S. Dist. LEXIS 105986, at *5, 2012 WL 3095439 (N.D. Cal. July 30, 2012) ("IBM emphasizes that it 'has distinct legal entities operating in more than 170 countries,' each with its 'own accounting systems and entries,' supporting RSI's contention that deciphering IBM's records is 'feasible only for one familiar with the records.'"); *Hege v. Aegon USA, LLC*, No. 8:10-cv-01578-GRA, 2011 U.S. Dist. LEXIS 31772, at *12, 2011 WL 1119871 (D.S.C. Mar. 25, 2011) ("Given the complexity of the calculations, the judgment involved in claims processing, and Mr. Byrne's demonstrated familiarity with the calculation process, this Court cannot conclude that the burden is substantially the same for both parties.").

[114] *Cf. HTC Corp. v. Tech. Props. Ltd.*, No. C08-00882 JF (HRL), 2011 U.S. Dist. LEXIS 4531, at *16–18, 2011 WL 97787 (N.D. Cal. Jan. 12, 2011) (requiring the requesting party to review 1.8 million documents); *P.R. Aqueduct*, 108 F.R.D. at 309 ("The mere fact that an interrogated party has to screen 30,000 documents . . . does not, without more, trigger [former Federal] Rule 33(c)."); *Mid-Am. Facilities, Inc. v. Argonaut Ins. Co.*, 78 F.R.D. 497, 498 (E.D. Wis. 1978) (holding that, because the burden of obtaining the information was substantially the same for the parties, the fact that it might take the requesting party thirty days to obtain the information was immaterial).

If the court decides that the burden is not substantially the same for the parties and that Texas Rule 197.2(c)'s option is unavailable to the responding party, it may still refrain from ordering the interrogatory answered under Texas Rule 192.4 or 192.6, if the interrogatory is unreasonably cumulative or duplicative, is disproportionate to the case's needs, or the burden or expense of answering the interrogatory outweighs the likely benefit. *See* Tex. R. Civ. P. 192.4, 192.6(b).

Fifth, the responding party must specify the records "in sufficient detail to permit the requesting party to locate and identify them as readily as can the responding party."[115] At the minimum, the responding party must specify, by location, the category or type of record from which the interrogatory answer can be derived or ascertained.[116]

---

[115] Tex. R. Civ. P. 197.2(c); *cf. ATD Combustors, LLC v. Ameritube*, LLC, 618CV00077ADAJCM, 2019 U.S. Dist. LEXIS 74558, at *4–5, 2019 WL 1921615 (W.D. Tex. Jan. 23, 2019) (holding a that an interrogatory answer that failed to direct the other party to specific emails was insufficient); *Moser v. Navistar Int'l Corp.*, 4:17-CV-00598, 2018 WL 3614012 (E.D. Tex. July 27, 2018) ("[Federal] Rule 33(d) provides that when a party serves an interrogatory 'to another party which can be answered by examination of the responding party's business records, and the burden of deriving the answer would be the same for both parties, it is sufficient to answer the interrogatory by specifying the business records from which the answer may be derived or ascertained.' When this happens, 'the responding party must specify the documents from which the answer may be derived in "sufficient detail to [enable] the interrogating party to locate and to identify" them' as the responding party could.") (citation omitted); *Lopez v. Don Herring Ltd.*, 327 F.R.D. 567, 575 (N.D. Tex. 2018) ("Federal Rule of Civil Procedure 34(b) provides that a request for production or inspection 'must describe with reasonable particularity each item or category of items to be inspected' or produced."); *Vailes v. Rapides Par. Sch. Bd.*, No. CV 15-429, 2016 WL 744559, at *4 (W.D. La. Feb. 22, 2016) ("The goal is that the description be sufficient to apprise a man of ordinary intelligence which documents are required."); *Haughton v. D.C.*, 315 F.R.D. 424, 429 (D.D.C. 2014), objections overruled, 161 F. Supp. 3d 100 (D.D.C. 2014) ("Defendant provided Plaintiff with over 1,000 pages of documents in many of its responses. Although the documents were divided into three separate files and Bates-Stamped, there was not an index sufficient to help Plaintiff recover the necessary information with reasonable effort."); *Hager v. Graham*, 267 F.R.D. 486, 493 (N.D. W. Va. 2010) ("'The test for reasonable particularity is whether the request places the party upon "reasonable notice of what is called for and what is not."' . . . 'Therefore, the party requesting the production of documents must provide "sufficient information to enable [the party to whom the request is directed] to identify responsive documents."').

[116] *Cf. ATD Combustors, LLC v. Ameritube*, LLC, 618CV00077ADAJCM, 2019 U.S. Dist. LEXIS 74558, at *4, 2019 WL 1921615 (W.D. Tex. Jan. 23, 2019) ("While [Federal] Rule 33 allows [Defendant] to direct to business records that answer the interrogatory, [Federal] Rule 33(d)(1) requires [Defendant] to specify 'in sufficient detail' the responsive documents so [Plaintiff] can locate and identify them as readily as [Defendant] could."); *English v. Wash. Metro. Area Transit Auth.*, 323 F.R.D. 1, 19 (D.D.C. 2017) ("[Federal] Rule 33 requires a complete response, and a generic reference to prior productions lacking any citation to specific documents does not meet that requirement."); *Int'l Aero. Grp. Corp. v. Evans Meridians, Ltd.*, No. 16-24997-Civ-KING/TORRES, 2017 U.S. Dist. LEXIS 71304, at *8–9, 2017 WL 1927957 (S.D. Fla. May 10, 2017) ("The producing party must satisfy a number of factors in order to meet its justification burden. . . . Second, the producing party must precisely specify for each interrogatory 'the actual documents where [the] information will be found.'" (quoting *SEC v. Elfindepan, S.A.*, 206 F.R.D. 574, 576 (M.D.N.C. 2002))); *U.S. v. Kellogg Brown & Root Servs., Inc.*, 284 F.R.D. 22, 30 (D.D.C. 2012) (noting that Federal Rule 33(d) requires a party to "specify [] the records that must be reviewed, in sufficient detail to enable the interrogating party to locate and identify them as readily as the responding party could"); *Dunkin' Donuts, Inc. v. N.A.S.T., Inc.*, 428 F. Supp. 2d 761, 770 (N.D. Ill. 2005) ("Any party that seeks to pursue that [Federal] Rule 33(d) option has the duty to specify 'by category and location, the records from which answers to interrogatories can be derived.'"); *In re G-I Holdings Inc.*, 218 F.R.D. 428, 438 (D.N.J. 2003) ("[T]he responding party has a 'duty to specify, by category and location' the records from which he knows the

Directing the requesting party to a mass of undifferentiated or unspecified records is insufficient.[117]

---

answers to the interrogatories can be found."); *Walt Disney Co. v. DeFabiis*, 168 F.R.D. 281, 284 (C.D. Cal. 1996) (same).

[117] *Finley Oilwell Serv., Inc. v. Retamco Operating, Inc.*, 248 S.W.3d 314, 321 (Tex. App.—San Antonio 2007, pet. denied) (holding that responding to an interrogatory with boxes of documents and a paper instructing the requesting party to look in specific boxes filled with documents for information related to the interrogatory did not comply with Texas Rule 197.2(c)); *cf. Dickey v. Apache Indus. Servs., Inc.*, CV 18-572-SDD-RLB, 2019 U.S. Dist. LEXIS 153075, at *11–13, 2019 WL 4261117 (M.D. La. Sept. 9, 2019) (finding that interrogatory answers referencing voluminous disorganized documents that the party previously been produced was insufficient); *Quintel Tech. Ltd. v. Huawei Techs. USA, Inc.*, No. 4:15-CV-307-AM-CMC, 2017 U.S. Dist. LEXIS 186655, at *20, 2017 WL 3712346 (E.D. Tex. June 29, 2017) ("A plaintiff may not simply refer a defendant to a mass of records but must specifically identify which documents contain the requested *information* in its answer to the interrogatory. If the party cannot comply with these requirements, it must otherwise answer the interrogatory fully and completely.") (citation omitted); *Boyette Bros. Produce, LLC v. Arvila, LLC*, No. No. 5:16-CV-00140-BR, 2017 U.S. Dist. LEXIS 91668, at *5 (E.D.N.C. June 14, 2017) ("[Federal Rule 33(d)] prohibits the responding party from '[d]irecting the opposing party to an undifferentiated mass of records[.]'" (quoting *Am. Rockwool, Inc. v. Owens-Corning Fiberglas Corp.*, 109 F.R.D. 263, 266 (E.D.N.C. 1985))); *Harrison v. Carrington Mortg., Servs. LLC*, No. 3:16-CV-00014, 2017 U.S. Dist. LEXIS 65125, at *6 (W.D. Va. Apr. 28, 2017) (same); *KeyBank Nat. Ass'n v. Perkins Rowe Assocs.*, LLC, No. 09-497, 2011 U.S. Dist. LEXIS 19635, at *12 n. 12, 2011 WL 765925 (M.D. La. Feb. 25, 2011) ("[Federal] Rule 33(d)(1) requires that answers using the business records option must specify the records to be reviewed in enough detail so that the interrogating party can locate and identify them as easily as the responding party. Thus, it is improper to direct the interrogating party to a mass of business records or offer to make all of the party's business records available."); *Mancini v. Ins. Corp.*, No. 07cv1750-L(NLS), 2009 U.S. Dist. LEXIS 51321, at *7, 2009 WL 1765295 (S.D. Cal. June 18, 2009) ("[R]eferring to a wide universe of documents does not specify the records in sufficient detail."); *Dibbs v. Franklin Mint*, No. C06-604RSM, 2007 U.S. Dist. LEXIS 98903, at *5, 2007 WL 4327876 (W.D. Wash. Dec. 10, 2007) (holding that a reference to the responding party's entire document production does not specify records in sufficient detail); *Cambridge Elecs. Corp. v. MGA Elecs., Inc.*, 227 F.R.D. 313, 322–23 (C.D. Cal. 2004) (holding that a responding party's failure to identify where in its records answers could be found made its answer insufficient under Federal Rule 33(d)); *see Toshiba Am. Med. Sys. v. Cent. Park Imaging, Ltd.*, No. A-15-CV-013 RP, 2015 U.S. Dist. LEXIS 150569, at *3–4, 2015 WL 6813395 (W.D. Tex. Nov. 5, 2015) ("In Interrogatories Nos. 21, 22 and 23, Toshiba asked Central Park to identify the misrepresentations Toshiba made to Central Park about the leased equipment or Toshiba's performance under the Lease Agreement and Master Lease Agreement. After the motion to compel was filed, Central Park supplemented its response to state that the information could be found in two documents—Toshiba's 47-page Quotation/Order for the MRI equipment and 9-page MRI Application Schedule, both of which Central Park had produced in prior responses. Toshiba argues that this answer is insufficient because it fails to identify which portions of these documents include alleged misrepresentations. While [Federal] Rule 33(d) provides that a party may produce business records in place of a narrative answer to an interrogatory, when it does so it must 'specify[] the records . . . in sufficient detail to enable the interrogating party to locate and identify them as readily as the responding party could.' Pointing to 56 pages of documents without identifying the allegedly false statements fails to comply with this duty."); *Parks, LLC v. Tyson Foods, Inc.*, No. 5:15-cv-00946, 2015 U.S. Dist. LEXIS 112861, at *13, 2015 WL 5042918 (E.D. Pa. Aug. 25, 2015) ("While [Federal] Rule 33(d) provides the option to respond to an interrogatory by reference to business records containing

Finally, if the responding party's business records or a compilation, abstract, or summary of them are specified, the responding party must state a reasonable time and place for examining the records in its response, produce the records at the stated time and place, unless another time and place is agreed to or ordered, and provide the requesting party a reasonable opportunity to review the records.[118]

Although no Texas case has articulated a standard for evaluating a Texas Rule 197.2(c) response, federal courts have followed a two-step analytical framework. "First, the moving party must make a prima facie showing that a [Federal] Rule 33(d) response is an inadequate means to answering the interrogatories, 'whether because the information is not fully contained in the documents, is too difficult to extract, or other such reasons.' If the moving party makes this showing, the burden then shifts to the producing party to justify responding under [Federal] Rule 33(d) instead of directly answering the interrogatories."[119]

The mere fact that Texas Rule 197.2(c)'s option is available to the responding party does not mean that the party should avail itself of it.[120] The responding party may decide not to exercise the option because the pertinent records contain other information that it does not want to disclose to the requesting party or because different conclusions can be drawn from the records and it wants to set forth its own conclusion in the interrogatory answer.[121]

9-5:3 Objections

Texas Rule 193.2 sets forth the obligations and procedures for objecting to written-discovery requests, such as interrogatories.[122] The general principles relating to objections are discussed in Chapter 5, section 5-3. Proper and improper interrogatory objections are discussed below.

---

the information sought, the Rule requires more than a promise to produce certain unspecified records at some future time. A party relying on the procedure in [Federal] Rule 33(d) must specify the responsive records in sufficient detail within thirty days after being served with the interrogatory.", (citations omitted).

118 Tex. R. Civ. P. 197.2(c).

119 *In re Lithium Ion Batteries Antitrust Litig.*, No. 13-md-02420-YGR (DMR), 2015 U.S. Dist. LEXIS 111275, at *55, 2015 WL 4999762 (N.D. Cal. Aug. 21, 2015); *accord Wonderland Switzerland AG v. Britax Child Safety, Inc.*, No. 0:19-CV-02475-JMC, 2020 U.S. Dist. LEXIS 201819, at *14–15, 2020 WL 6365382 (D.S.C. Oct. 29, 2020); *Hands on Chiropractic PL v. Progressive Select Ins. Co.*, No. 618CV192ORL37DCI, 2018 U.S. Dist. LEXIS 223752, at *21, 2018 WL 6983622 (M.D. Fla. Nov. 20, 2018); *Int'l Aero. Grp. Corp. v. Evans Meridians, Ltd.*, No. 16-24997-Civ-KING/TORRES, 2017 U.S. Dist. LEXIS 71304, at *7–8, 2017 WL 1927957 (S.D. Fla. May 10, 2017); *Colony Ins. Co. v. 9400 Abercorn, LLC*, No. 4:11-cv-255, 2012 U.S. Dist. LEXIS 131839, at *15, 2012 WL 3985088 (S.D. Ga. Sept. 12, 2012); *SEC v. Elfindepan*, 206 F.R.D. 574, 576 (M.D.N.C. 2002).

120 *Cf. Gipson v. Sw. Bell Tel. Co.*, No. 08-2017-EFM-DJW, 2009 U.S. Dist. LEXIS 25457, at *20, 2009 WL 790203 (D. Kan. Mar. 24, 2009) ("An answering party may, however, produce its business records in accordance with [Federal] Rule 33 in lieu of providing a written response, but only if it makes an 'affirmative election' to do so.").

121 Robert K. Wise, *Ending Evasive Responses to Written Discovery: A Guide for Properly Responding (and Objecting) to Interrogatories and Document Requests Under the Texas Discovery Rules*, 65 Baylor L. Rev. 510, 539 (2013).

122 Tex. R. Civ. P. 193.2.

9-5:3.1 General, Subject-to, and Boilerplate Objections

As discussed in Chapter 5, sections 5-3:2 and 5-3:3, respectively, "general" and "subject-to" objections to interrogatories[123] generally are improper and boilerplate objections to them always are improper.[124]

9-5:3.2 Proportionality

As discussed in Chapter 5, section 5-3:4, a lack of "proportionality" can be asserted as an objection to an interrogatory set in its entirety or to an individual interrogatory.[125]

9-5:3.3 Privilege

Privilege is not a proper objection to an interrogatory. Texas Rule 193.2(f) provides "[a] party should *not* object to a request for written discovery on the grounds that it calls for production of material or information that is privileged but should instead comply with [Texas] Rule 193.3."[126] Privilege assertions under that Rule are discussed

---

[123] "General" objections occur when the responding party includes a section at the beginning of its response entitled "general objections," which contains every imaginable objection, such as overbreadth, undue burden, relevance, vagueness, ambiguity, harassment, cumulativeness, duplicativeness, and privilege, which are then incorporated by reference "to the extent" they apply in each response to the individual production request to the pertinent discovery request. See Chapter 5, section 5-3:2 (discussing "general" objections). "Subject-to" objections occur when the responding party sets forth in the response to each individual production request a litany of prophylactic, boilerplate objections, such as those set forth above, and then, "subject to and without waiving" the objections, says nonprivileged responsive documents will be produced. See Chapter 5, section 5-3:2 (discussing "subject-to" objections).

[124] A boilerplate objection is an objection that "merely states the legal grounds for the objection without (1) specifying how the discovery request is deficient and (2) specifying how the objecting party would be harmed if it were forced to respond to the request. For example, a boilerplate objection might state that a discovery request is irrelevant or overly broad without taking the next step to explain why. These objections are taglines, completely devoid of any individualized factual analysis." ***Liguria Foods, Inc. v. Griffith Labs., Inc.***, 320 F.R.D. 168, 170 n.1 (N.D. Iowa 2017) (quoting Matthew L. Jarvey, *Boilerplate Discovery Objections: How They Are Used, Why They Are Wrong, and What We Can Do About Them*, 61 Drake L. Rev. 913, 914–16 (2013)). They often constitute "general" and "subject-to" objections. See Chapter 5, section 5-3:3 (discussing boilerplate objections).

[125] The proportionality factors are: (1) the likely benefit of the requested discovery; (2) the needs of the case; (3) the amount in controversy; (4) the parties' resources; (5) the importance of the issues at stake in the litigation; (6) the importance of the proposed discovery in resolving the litigation; and (7) any other articulable factor bearing on proportionality. ***In re State Farm Lloyds***, 520 S.W.3d 595, 607–12 (Tex. 2017). See also Chapter 5, section 5-3:4 (discussing proportionality).

[126] Tex. R. Civ. P. 193.2(f) (emphasis added); *see, e.g.*, ***In re WHC, LLC***, 570 S.W.3d 349, 353 (Tex. App.—El Paso 2018, orig. proceeding) (citing Texas Rule 193.2(f) for the proposition that "a party should not object to a written request for discovery on the grounds that it calls for production of privileged materials or information but should instead comply with [Texas] Rule 193.3"); ***In re Park Cities Bank***, 409 S.W.3d 859, 870 (Tex. App.—Tyler 2013, orig. proceeding) ("No objection needs to be made to preserve a privilege, and the rules set no time limit for asserting a privilege."); ***In re Graco Children's Prods., Inc.***, 173 S.W.3d 600, 605 (Tex. App.—Corpus Christi 2005, orig. proceeding) ("[N]o objection needs to be made

in Chapter 5, section 5-4. The attorney-client and work-product privileges generally are not proper objections to contention interrogatories, and the work-product privilege does not apply to interrogatories asking a party to identify persons with knowledge, trial witnesses, or documents concerning an allegation, claim, defense, or particular facts, irrespective of how the party or its attorney learned about the persons or documents.[127]

An interrogatory asking the responding party to identify the persons who assisted in preparing the interrogatory answers generally does not invade the attorney-client or work-product privileges.[128]

9-5:3.4 Scope Objections: Relevance and Not Reasonably Calculated to Lead to the Discovery of Admissible Evidence

If an interrogatory seeks information that neither is relevant to the action's subject matter nor reasonably calculated to lead to the discovery of admissible evidence, the responding party should object on those grounds. Discovery's scope (i.e., information that is relevant or reasonably calculated to lead to the discovery of admissible evidence) is discussed in Chapter 4, section 4-3.

9-5:3.5 Overbreadth

Texas courts often use the term "overly broad" or "overbroad" in describing objectionable interrogatories.[129] An interrogatory suffers from this malady when it

---

to preserve a privilege."); *In re Christus Health Se. Tex.*, 167 S.W.3d 596, 599 (Tex. App.—Beaumont 2005, orig. proceeding) (same); *In re Anderson*, 163 S.W.3d 136, 140 (Tex. App.—San Antonio 2005, orig. proceeding) (same); *In re Shipmon*, 68 S.W.3d 815, 822 (Tex. App.—Amarillo 2001, orig. proceeding) (same); *In re Monsanto Co.*, 998 S.W.2d 917, 924 (Tex. App.—Waco 1999, orig. proceeding) (same).

[127] See notes 49–51 and accompanying text.

[128] *Myers v. Anthem Life Ins. Co.*, 316 F.R.D. 186, 197–98 (W.D. Ky. 2016) (An interrogatory asking a responding to "[i]dentify each person making and assisting with Defendant's Interrogatory answers" "is permissible under Rule 33 of the Federal Rules of Civil Procedure."); *Omega Eng'g, Inc. v. Omega, S.A.*, No. CIV. 398CV2464AVC, 2001 U.S. Dist. LEXIS 2016, at *10–11, 2001 WL 173765 (D. Conn. Feb. 6, 2001) ("Interrogatories Nos. 7 and 8 represent the most standard of discovery requests in that they simply seek: 1) the names of individuals who participated in the preparation of the interrogatory answers, and 2) the identity of any document used for that same purpose."); *EEOC v. Sterling Jewelers, Inc.*, No. 08-CV-00706(A)(M), 2010 U.S. Dist. LEXIS 71429, at *14, 2010 WL 2803017 (W.D.N.Y. July 15, 2010) (holding that a party is "entitled to the identity of the individuals that assisted in preparation of the interrogatory responses"). *But see Strauss v. Credit Lyonnais, S.A.*, 242 F.R.D. 199, 232 (E.D.N.Y. 2007) ("Credit Lyonnais's motion to compel a response to Interrogatory No. 5 is denied because it seeks information regarding individuals who assisted plaintiffs' counsel with the preparation of their interrogatory responses, which is protected work product.").

[129] *E.g., In re Graco Children's Prods., Inc.*, 210 S.W.3d 598, 600–01 (Tex. 2006) (orig. proceeding) (per curiam); *In re CSX Corp.*, 124 S.W.3d 149, 152–53 (Tex. 2003) (orig. proceeding) (per curiam); *In re Alford Chevrolet-Geo*, 997 S.W.2d 173, 180 n.1 (Tex. 1999) (orig. proceeding); *Texaco, Inc. v. Sanderson*, 898 S.W.2d 813, 815 (Tex. 1995) (orig. proceeding) (per curiam); *In re Sun Coast Res., Inc.*, 562 S.W.3d 138 (Tex. App.—Houston [14th Dist.] 2018, orig. proceeding) ("A central consideration in examining overbreadth is "whether the request could

encompasses time periods, activities, locations, or products that are not relevant to the action's subject matter.[130] For example:

- In an action in which the plaintiff was abducted from the parking lot of one of the defendant's stores and then assaulted, interrogatories requesting information about all criminal activities at the store for seven years and similar crimes at all the defendant's stores nationwide for ten years were overbroad.[131]
- A discovery order was overbroad because it required the defendant to provide reimbursements rates with private insurers, Medicare, and Medicaid for services not received by the plaintiff.[132]

---

have been more narrowly tailored to avoid including tenuous information and still obtain the necessary, pertinent information."). An overbreadth objection generally is a surrogate for an objection that the interrogatory seeks information that is neither relevant nor reasonably calculated to lead to the discovery of admissible evidence. *See, e.g., In re Graco Children's Prods., Inc.*, 210 S.W.3d 598, 600 (Tex. 2006) (per curiam) (orig. proceeding).

130 *E.g., In re CSX Corp.*, 124 S.W.3d 149, 152–53 (Tex. 2003) (orig. proceeding) ("Discovery orders requiring document production from an unreasonably long period of time or from distant or unrelated locations are impermissibly overbroad."); *In re Alford Chevrolet-Geo*, 997 S.W.2d 173, 180 n.1 (Tex. 1999) (orig. proceeding) ("We have identified as overbroad requests those encompassing time periods, products, or activities beyond those at issue in the case—in other words, matters of questionable relevancy to the case at hand."); *In re UPS Ground Freight, Inc.*, 12-19-00412-CV, 2020 Tex. App. LEXIS 1746, at *10–11, 2020 WL 975357, (Tex. App.—Tyler Feb. 28, 2020, orig. proceeding) (mem. op.) ("Here, the passage of time results in a sliding scale of relevance where information provided by previous employees becomes too attenuated from [Defendant's] situation to be of use. The likelihood that employees and test results from eleven years prior to the accident that is the focus of this litigation would shed any light on this case is too small to justify discovery. [Plaintiff's] request could be more narrowly tailored to include only relevant matters pertinent to a more appropriate time period."); *In re BNSF Ry.*, No. 09-07-538 CV, 2008 Tex. App. LEXIS 634, at *4, 2007 WL 4822488 (Tex. App.—Beaumont Jan. 31, 2008, orig. proceeding) (mem. op.) ("A discovery request that is unlimited as to time, place or subject matter is overbroad as a matter of law.").

131 *K Mart Corp. v. Sanderson*, 937 S.W.2d 429, 431 (Tex. 1996) (orig. proceeding) (per curiam); *see In re Pioneer Nat. Res. USA, Inc.*, 05-20-00536-CV, 2020 Tex. App. LEXIS 7098, at *8–9, 2020 WL 5107284 (Tex. App.—Dallas Aug. 31, 2020, orig. proceeding) (mem. op.) (concluding that the trial court's discovery order "requiring relator to investigate all communications [Defendant] might have had during the course of his employment in an attempt to identify potentially responsive communications place[d] a burden on relator that is far out of proportion to any benefit with respect to the disposition of the case on its merits"); *In re EOG Res., Inc.*, No. 10-10-00455-CV, 2011 Tex. App. LEXIS 969, at *2, 4–5, 2011 WL 455280 (Tex. App—Waco Feb 9, 2011, orig. proceeding) (mem. op.) (holding that discovery requests seeking information and documents about policies for the use and installation of all trailers in any geographic region where the defendant did business for a period of ten years was overly broad because it was not limited in geographic scope and to the same type of trailer that the plaintiff was in when it shifted during a storm and injured him); *In re Steadfast Ins. Co.*, No. 01-09-00235-CV, 2009 Tex. App. LEXIS 3556, at *3–4, *9–11, 2009 WL 1424634 (Tex. App.—Houston [14th Dist.] May 18, 2009, orig. proceeding) (mem. op.) (holding that an interrogatory asking the defendant-insurance company to "[i]dentify each insurance claim in which you have been alleged to have acted in bad faith or in breach of an insurance policy with respect to a claim against an employee, borrowed servant, consultant or subcontractor for your insured" was improper in a suit against the insurer for breach of contract and the duty of good faith and fair dealing).

132 *In re Mem'l Hermann Health Sys.*, 607 S.W.3d 913, 920 (Tex. App.—Houston [14th Dist.] 2020, orig. proceeding).

- Interrogatories requesting the identity of safety, medical, and industrial hygiene personnel from 1970 to the present were overbroad in an action in which the plaintiff was only employed by the defendant's predecessor from 1972 to 1977.[133]
- A discovery order compelling an electric utility to answer an interrogatory regarding all lawsuits involving its electrical poles, power lines, guy wires, or anchors for the five years preceding the accident was overbroad because it was not limited to accidents like the one at issue, which involved an allegedly rotten utility pole.[134]
- In an individual employment-discrimination action, an order requiring the defendant to produce information about all the defendant's Texas offices was overbroad.[135]
- In an action involving a malfunctioning automatic door at a grocery store, the trial court did not abuse its discretion in limiting interrogatories to the door involved in the accident, rather than all the doors in defendant's stores for a ten-year period.[136]
- In a multiple-car fatality case, the trial court abused its discretion in compelling the production of information about all drivers under the defendant's control in a particular facility for an eleven-year period.[137]

---

[133] *In re CSX Corp.*, 124 S.W.3d 149, 153 (Tex. 2003) (orig. proceeding) (per curiam) (holding that the plaintiff was entitled to discovery of "industry custom," but only for the period when he worked for the defendant's predecessor).

[134] *In re Oncor*, 313 S.W.3d 910, 910 (Tex. App.—Dallas 2010, orig. proceeding).

[135] *In re Greyhound Lines, Inc.*, 138 S.W.3d 19, 22 (Tex. App.—San Antonio 2004, orig. proceeding) ("We agree that Ramirez has not alleged a company-wide policy of discrimination, therefore, ideally her discovery should be limited to the San Antonio terminal and to employees that are similarly situated. The time period need not be limited to the period she was employed.").

[136] *Fethkenher v. Kroger Co.*, 139 S.W.3d 24, 30 (Tex. App.—Fort Worth 2004, no pet.); *see In re Daimler Trucks N. Am. LLC*, No. 09-20-00145-CV, 2020 Tex. App. LEXIS 9638, at *8 (Tex. App.—Beaumont Dec. 10, 2020, orig. proceeding) (per curiam) (mem. op.) (after noting that "[i]n a product liability case, evidence of other incidents involving a product may be relevant if the incidents occurred under reasonably similar conditions[,]" "conclud[ing] that the scope of the discovery ordered by the trial court . . . is overbroad because it requires production of documents from cases that did not involve a Columbia truck with one of the four defects identified in the Doirons' petition. . . . Only documents relating to the Columbia truck and with a common alleged defect are discoverable by the Doirons."); *In re Allstate Ins. Co.*, 551 S.W.3d 798, 801 (Tex. App.—San Antonio 2018, orig. proceeding) (finding that an interrogatory asking an insurer to identify each insured within a five-mile radius for which the insurance company paid claims was overbroad).

[137] *In re UPS Ground Freight, Inc.*, 12-19-00412-CV, 2020 Tex. App. LEXIS 1746, at *10–11, 2020 WL 975357, (Tex. App.—Tyler Feb. 28, 2020, orig. proceeding) (mem. op.) ("Here, the passage of time results in a sliding scale of relevance where information provided by previous employees becomes too attenuated from [Defendant's] situation to be of use. The likelihood that employees and test results from eleven years prior to the accident that is the focus of this litigation would shed any light on this case is too small to justify discovery. [Plaintiff's] request could be more narrowly tailored to include only relevant matters pertinent to a more appropriate time period.").

- In an action claiming that the defendant-insurer undervalued the plaintiff-homeowner's insurance claim for storm damage, the trial court abused its discretion in compelling the production of information related to insurance claims filed by other residents in the area in connection with other storms that damaged their houses that were assessed by the same adjusting firm that assessed the plaintiff's home's damage because the discovery was overly broad and irrelevant.[138]

The volume of responsive information does not necessarily make an interrogatory overbroad.[139] But an interrogatory that is reasonably limited to activities, locations, or products may be overbroad if it not limited to a reasonable time.[140]

A central consideration in determining overbreadth is whether the interrogatory could have been more narrowly tailored.[141] However, a reasonably tailored interrogatory is not overbroad merely because it may require some information of

---

[138] *In re Nat'l Lloyds Ins. Co.*, 449 S.W.3d 486, 489 (Tex. 2014) (orig. proceeding) (per curiam) ("[W]e fail to see how [the defendant-insurer's] overpayment, underpayment, or proper payment of the claims of unrelated third parties is probative of its conduct with respect to [the plaintiff's undervaluation claims at issue in this case."); *accord In re GMAC Direct Ins. Co.*, No. 09-10-00493-CV, 2010 Tex. App. LEXIS 10336, at *3–6, 2010 WL 5550672 (Tex. App.—Beaumont Dec. 30, 2010, orig. proceeding) (mem. op.) (holding, in the context of the plaintiffs' tort and contract claims in connection with the adjustment of their homeowner's insurance claim, that requests for information about damage to other properties that were not tailored to include the information "actually used in adjusting the [plaintiffs'] claim" were overly broad and amount to a fishing expedition).

[139] *In re K & L Auto Crushers, LLC*, 627 S.W.3d 239, 252 (Tex. 2021) (orig. proceeding) ("[D]iscovery requests and orders are overbroad if they are not properly 'tailored with regard to time, place, or subject matter. . . .'" (citing *In re Nat'l Lloyds Ins. Co.*, 507 S.W.3d 219, 226 (Tex. 2016) (per curiam))); *In reAlford Chevrolet-Geo*, 997 S.W.2d 173, 180 n.1 (Tex. 1999) (orig. proceeding) ("[I]t is clear that the sheer volume of a discovery request does not in itself render the request irrelevant or overbroad as a matter of law."); *In re Waste Mgmt. of Tex., Inc.*, 392 S.W.3d 861, 872 (Tex. App.—Texarkana 2013, orig. proceeding) (mem. op.) (same); *In re Am. Home Assurance Co.*, 88 S.W.3d 370, 374 (Tex. App.—Texarkana 2002, orig. proceeding) (same); *In re Whiteley*, 79 S.W.3d 729, 734 (Tex. App.—Corpus Christi 2002, orig. proceeding) (same). The volume of information or material, however, may make the discovery request disproportionate to the case's needs, unduly burdensome, or unnecessarily expensive. See Chapter 5, section 5-3:4 (discussing proportionality), and Chapter 8, section 8-5:6 (discussing undue-burden objections to production requests).

[140] *See, e.g., In re Valvoline Co.*, No. 01-10-00208-CV, 2010 Tex. App. LEXIS 3696, at *16, 2010 WL 2025825 (Tex. App.—Houston [1st Dist.] May 14, 2010, orig. proceeding) (mem. op.).

[141] *E.g., In re K & L Auto Crushers, LLC*, 627 S.W.3d 239, 253 (Tex. 2021) (orig. proceeding); *In re Allstate Cnty. Mut. Ins. Co.*, 227 S.W.3d 667, 669 (Tex. 2007) (orig. proceeding) (per curiam); *In re CSX Corp.*, 124 S.W.3d 149, 153 (Tex. 2003) (orig. proceeding) (per curiam); *In re Am. Optical Corp.*, 988 S.W.2d 711, 713 (Tex. 1998) (orig. proceeding) (per curiam); *In re Fed. Corp.*, No. 13-16-00219-CV, 2016 Tex. App. LEXIS 11816, at *5 (Tex. App.—Corpus Christi Nov. 1, 2016, orig. proceeding) (mem. op.); *In re Nat'l Lloyds Ins. Co.*, No. 13-15-00390-CV, 2015 Tex. App. LEXIS 11299, *15–16 n.3, 2015 WL 6759153 (Tex. App.—Corpus Christi Nov. 3, 2015, orig. proceeding) (mem. op.); *In re Halliburton Energy Servs., Inc.*, No. 01-11-00358-CV, 2011 Tex. App. LEXIS 7974, at *9, 2011 WL 4612726 (Tex. App.—Houston [1st Dist.] Oct. 4, 2011, orig. proceeding) (mem. op.); *In re Hernandez*, No. 14-11-00408-CV, 2011 Tex. App. LEXIS 7981, at *10, 2011 WL 4600706 (Tex. App.—Houston [14th Dist.] Oct. 6, 2011, orig. proceeding) (mem. op.); *In re Waste Mgmt. of Tex., Inc.*, No. 13-11-00197-CV, 2011 Tex. App. LEXIS 7192, at *23, 2011 WL 3855745 (Tex. App.—Corpus Christi Aug. 31, 2011, orig. proceeding) (mem. op.).

doubtful relevance, and the parties have some latitude in fashioning proper interrogatories.[142]

The responding party is not required to show that responding to an overbroad interrogatory is burdensome because such discovery requests are improper whether they are burdensome or not.[143] Oftentimes no evidence is needed to establish overbreadth.[144]

9-5:3.6 Undue Burden or Unnecessary Expense

The mere fact that answering an interrogatory may be burdensome or expensive is an insufficient basis for objecting to the interrogatory.[145] It is only when answering the

---

142 *E.g., In re Nat'l Lloyds Ins. Co.*, 449 S.W.3d 486, 488 (Tex. 2014) (orig. proceeding) (per curiam) ("A request 'is not overbroad merely because [it] may call for some information of doubtful relevance' so long as it is 'reasonably tailored to include only matters relevant to the case.'" (quoting *Texaco, Inc. v. Sanderson*, 898 S.W.2d 813, 815 (Tex. 1995) (orig. proceeding) (per curiam))); *In re Am. Optical Corp.*, 988 S.W.2d 711, 713 (Tex. 1998) (orig. proceeding) (per curiam) (same); *In re Allstate Ins. Co.*, 551 S.W.3d 798, 800 (Tex. App.—San Antonio 2018, orig. proceeding) ("Significantly, whether a request for discovery is overbroad is distinct from whether it is burdensome or harassing. We have held that [o]verbroad requests for irrelevant information are improper whether they are burdensome or not.") (citation omitted); *In re Fed. Corp.*, No. 13-16-00219-CV, 2016 Tex. App. LEXIS 11816, at *5 (Tex. App.—Corpus Christi Nov. 1, 2016, orig. proceeding) (mem. op.) (same); *In re MHCB (USA) Leasing & Fin. Corp.*, No. 01-06-00075-CV, 2006 Tex. App. LEXIS 3515, at *23, 2006 WL 1098922 (Tex. App.—Houston [1st Dist.] Apr. 27, 2006, orig. proceeding) (mem. op.) (same).

143 *E.g., In re Nat'l Lloyds Ins. Co.*, 449 S.W.3d 486, 488 (Tex. 2014) (orig. proceeding) (per curiam) ("Significantly, whether a request for discovery is overbroad is distinct from whether it is burdensome or harassing. We have held that '[o]verbroad requests for irrelevant information are improper whether they are burdensome or not.'" (quoting *In re Allstate Cnty. Mut. Ins. Co.*, 227 S.W.3d 667, 669–70 (Tex. 2007) (orig. proceeding) (per curiam))); *In re Allstate Ins. Co.*, 551 S.W.3d 798, 800 (Tex. App.—San Antonio 2018, orig. proceeding) (same); *In re Waste Mgmt. of Tex., Inc.*, 392 S.W.3d 861, 871 (Tex. App.—Texarkana 2013, orig. proceeding) (same); *In re Waste Mgmt. of Tex., Inc.*, No. 13-11-00197-CV, 2011 Tex. App. LEXIS 7192, at *23, 2011 WL 3855745 (Tex. App.—Corpus Christi Aug. 31, 2011, orig. proceeding) (mem. op.) ("Overbroad requests for irrelevant information are improper whether they are burdensome or not, so evidence is not necessary to support an objection if the discovery requests themselves demonstrate overbreadth as a matter of law.").

144 *In re Allstate Cnty. Mut. Ins. Co.*, 227 S.W.3d 667, 670 (Tex. 2007) (orig. proceeding) (per curiam) ("Overbroad requests for irrelevant information are improper whether they are burdensome or not, so the defendants were not required to detail what they might encompass."); *In re Union Pac. Res. Co.*, 22 S.W.3d 338, 341 (Tex. 1999) (orig. proceeding) ("[I]t is not clear what evidence could have been produced on the [overbroad] issue."); *In re Wal-Mart Stores, Inc.*, 545 S.W.3d 626, 634–35 (Tex. App.—El Paso 2016, orig. proceeding [mand. denied]) ("Wal-Mart's overbreadth and irrelevance objections can be resolved by examining the language of the discovery requests. We conclude that Wal-Mart was not required to present evidence in support of its overbreadth and relevance objections to these three discovery requests.").

145 Tex. R. Civ. P. 192.6(b) (providing for a protective order "to protect the movant from undue burden, unnecessary expense"); *In re K & L Auto Crushers, LLC*, 627 S.W.3d 239, 253 (Tex. 2021) (orig. proceeding) ("The providers made no effort to establish the burdens they would bear to respond to the substantially narrowed requests K & L Auto made at the

interrogatory is unduly burdensome or unnecessarily expensive that the interrogatory is objectionable.[146]

"Undue burden" or "unnecessary expense" is shorthand for the standard in Texas Rule 192.4, which is that a trial court "should" limit discovery if "the discovery sought is obtainable from some other source that is more convenient, less burdensome, or less expensive"[147] or "the burden or expense of the proposed discovery outweighs

---

hearing on its motion for reconsideration. And although a responding party is not required to affirmatively address each modification a requesting party makes to its discovery requests, the providers' original objections and affidavits failed to provide more than conclusory estimates of the time, effort, and expenses they would incur in responding specifically to the original requests; they simply noted that responding would be burdensome and expensive, particularly because their electronic records software was not configured for searching. Thus, those objections were likewise too conclusory to establish that the narrowed requests were unduly burdensome.") (citations omitted); *In re State Farm Lloyds*, 02-20-00163-CV, 2020 Tex. App. LEXIS 7207, at *17–18, 2020 WL 5242414 (Tex. App.—Fort Worth Sept. 3, 2020, orig. proceeding) (mem. op.) ("State Farm put on uncontroverted evidence that it would take at least 706 hours to review the subject files at a cost of $26,298.50. And pursuant to their original petition, the [plaintiffs] were seeking damages 'in an amount greater than $100,000 but no more than $200,000.' Given the negligible relevance of the sought discovery . . ., coupled with the uncontroverted evidence of the great time and expense State Farm would expend in obtaining the sought discovery, and given the amount in controversy in the case, the trial court clearly abused its discretion by ordering production of the engineering reports."); *In re State Farm Lloyds*, 519 S.W.3d 647, 657 (Tex. App.—Corpus Christi 2015, orig. proceeding) (mem. op.) ("We first note that a party's failure to comply with a discovery request is not excused because the request is burdensome; it is only an 'undue burden' that warrants nonproduction."); *In re Waste Mgmt. of Tex., Inc.*, 392 S.W.3d 861, 871 (Tex. App.—Texarkana 2013, orig. proceeding) (same); *Forward v. Hous. Auth.*, 864 S.W.2d 167, 169 (Tex. App.—Tyler 1993, no writ) (same); *In re Energas Co.*, 63 S.W.3d 50, 55 (Tex. App.—Amarillo 2001, orig. proceeding) (same); *cf. McGuire v. Cooper*, No. 8:16CV04, 2016 U.S. Dist. LEXIS 180361, at *6, 2016 WL 7496112 (D. Neb. Dec. 30, 2016) ("[G]enerally '[a]ll discovery requests are a burden on the party who must respond thereto. Unless the task of producing or answering is unusual, undue or extraordinary, the general rule requires the entity answering or producing the documents to bear that burden.'" (quoting *Cont'l Ill. Nat'l Bank & Tr. Co. v. Caton*, 136 F.R.D. 682, 684–85 (D. Kan. 1991))); *Maples v. Safeway, Inc.*, No. 5:14-CV-05082-JLV, 2016 U.S. Dist. LEXIS 112135, at *13 (D.S.D. Aug. 23, 2016) (same).

146 See authorities cited in note 145.

147 Tex. R. Civ. P. 194.2(a); *accord In re Weekly Homes, L.P.*, 295 S.W.3d 309, 317 (Tex. 2009) (orig. proceeding) ("[B]oth the federal rule and ours require trial courts to weigh the benefits of production against the burden when the requested information is not reasonably available in the ordinary course of business."); *In re Waste Mgmt. of Tex., Inc.*, No. 13-11-00197-CV, 2011 Tex. App. LEXIS 7192, at *33, 2011 WL 3855745 (Tex. App.—Corpus Christi Aug. 31, 2011, orig. proceeding) (mem. op.) ("Under the rules of civil procedure, discovery should be limited if it. . . . is obtainable from some other source that is more convenient, less burdensome or expensive."); *In re Harris*, 315 S.W.3d 685, 696 (Tex. App.—Houston [1st Dist.] 2010, orig. proceeding) ("[T]he discovery rules explicitly encourage trial courts to limit discovery when the burden or expense of the proposed discovery outweighs its likely benefit, taking into account the needs of the case, the amount in controversy, the parties' resources, the importance of the issues at stake in the litigation, and the importance of the proposed discovery in resolving the issues." (quoting *In re Alford Chevrolet-Geo*, 997 S.W.2d 173, 181 (Tex. 1999) (orig. proceeding))).

its likely benefit, taking into account the needs of the case, the amount in controversy, the parties' resources, the importance of the issues at stake in the litigation, and the importance of the proposed discovery in resolving them."[148] In other words, the determination of whether an interrogatory is unduly burdensome or unnecessarily expensive is not solely dependent on the inconvenience or expense of gathering the responsive information. To the contrary, the inconvenience and expense must be weighed against the other factors set forth in Texas Rule 192.4.[149]

Although the responding party has the burden of pleading and proving undue burden or unnecessary expense, very rarely does a responding party attempt to describe the nature of the undue burden or why the answering of the interrogatory is unnecessarily expensive. To prove undue burden or unnecessary expense, the responding party must do more than make a conclusory assertion that answering the interrogatory would be unduly burdensome or unnecessarily expensive.[150] Rather, it must adduce evidence establishing the undue burden or unnecessary expense or that the information is obtainable from a more convenient source or in a less burdensome or expensive manner.[151] Although most practitioners tend to equate undue burden and

---

148 Tex. R. Civ. P. 192.4(b); *accord In re Weekly Homes, L.P.*, 295 S.W.3d 309, 317 (Tex. 2009) (orig. proceeding); *In re State Farm Lloyds*, 02-20-00163-CV, 2020 Tex. App. LEXIS 7207, at *17–18, 2020 WL 5242414 (Tex. App.—Fort Worth Sept. 3, 2020, orig. proceeding) (mem. op.); *In re Harris*, 315 S.W.3d 685, 696 (Tex. App.—Houston [1st Dist.] 2010, orig. proceeding).

149 Tex. R. Civ. P. 192.4(a)–(b).

150 *In re K & L Auto Crushers, LLC*, 627 S.W.3d 239, 251-52 (Tex. 2021) (orig. proceeding); *In re Alfred Chevrolet-Geo*, 997 S.W.2d 173, 181 (Tex. 1999) (orig. proceeding); *In re Sting Soccer Grp., LP*, No. 05-17-00317-CV, 2017 Tex. App. LEXIS 11197, at *19–20, 2017 WL 5897454 (Tex. App.—Dallas Nov. 30, 2017, orig. proceeding) (mem. op.).

151 *In re K & L Auto Crushers, LLC*, 627 S.W.3d 239, 253 (Tex. 2021) (orig. proceeding) ("The providers made no effort to establish the burdens they would bear to respond to the substantially narrowed requests K & L Auto made at the hearing on its motion for reconsideration. And although a responding party is not required to affirmatively address each modification a requesting party makes to its discovery requests, the providers' original objections and affidavits failed to provide more than conclusory estimates of the time, effort, and expenses they would incur in responding specifically to the original requests; they simply noted that responding would be burdensome and expensive, particularly because their electronic records software was not configured for searching. Thus, those objections were likewise too conclusory to establish that the narrowed requests were unduly burdensome.") (citations omitted); *In re Alfred Chevrolet-Geo*, 997 S.W.2d 173, 181 (Tex. 1999) (orig. proceeding) ("A party resisting discovery . . . cannot simply make conclusory allegations that the requested discovery is unduly burdensome or unnecessarily harassing. The party must produce some evidence supporting its request for a protective order."); *In re Marshall*, 04-20-00450-CV, 2021 Tex. App. LEXIS 593, at *8, 2021 WL 260242 (Tex. App.—San Antonio Jan. 27, 2021, orig. proceeding) (same); *In re Liberty Cnty. Mut. Ins. Co.*, 606 S.W.3d 866, 874 (Tex. App.—Houston [14th Dist.] 2020, orig. proceeding) ("This record does not reflect that Liberty produced any evidence that Forrest could obtain the information from other sources that would be more convenient, less burdensome, or less expensive than having its corporate representative deposed. Thus, Liberty's conclusory allegations are not sufficient to support its position that taking the deposition of its corporate representative would be unduly burdensome.") (citation omitted); *In re United Fire Lloyds*, 578 S.W.3d 572, 581 (Tex. App.—Tyler 2019, orig. proceeding, no pet.) (mem. op.) ("Absent evidence demonstrating that the requested discovery is unduly burdensome or harassing, Respondent could not make an informed judgment on whether to limit discovery or place the cost for complying with the discovery."); *In re Sting Soccer Grp., LP*, No. 05-17-00317-CV, 2017 Tex. App. LEXIS

unnecessary expense with the number of hours of search time, the number of boxes of documents or emails that must be reviewed, or the number of employees who must be interviewed to answer an interrogatory, burden also includes the difficulty of the search process, including the interference with ongoing business activities and the number of diverse geographic locations and personnel that must be contacted, the commercial sensitivity of the information or documents, privacy issues, and personal embarrassment.[152]

An undue burden or unnecessary expense objection is improper if the burden or expense is the result of the party's "own 'conscious, discretionary decisions.'"[153] Thus, for example, a responding party cannot rely on problems retrieving the information caused by the haphazard manner in which it maintains its records.[154] An undue burden or unnecessary expense objection also is improper if the responding party would have

---

11197, at *19–20, 2017 WL 5897454 (Tex. App.—Dallas Nov. 30, 2017, orig. proceeding) (mem. op.) ("Vola's objections that the requests for production are overbroad, burdensome, and an improper fishing expedition should not have been sustained by the trial court because Vola presented no evidence to support those objections. Here, Vola presented no arguments or evidence to support these objections. Because the trial court below was neither presented with arguments nor actual evidence to support these objections before ruling to limit discovery, the trial court abused its discretion in sustaining these objections.") (citation omitted); *In re Master Flo Valve Inc.*, 485 S.W.3d 207, 217 n.2 (Tex. App.—Houston [14th Dist.] Jan. 26, 2016, orig. proceeding) ("A party resisting discovery cannot simply make conclusory allegations that the requested discovery is unduly burdensome. 'The party must produce some evidence supporting its request for a protective order.' Any party who seeks to exclude matters from discovery on grounds that the requested information is unduly burdensome or costly has the affirmative duty to prove the work necessary to comply with discovery." (citation omitted) (quoting *In re Alford Chevrolet-Geo*, 997 S.W.2d 173, 181 (Tex. 1999) (orig. proceeding))); *In re Gen. Elec. Railcar Servs. Corp.*, No. 09-03-530 CV, 2004 Tex. App. LEXIS 630, at *5–6, 2003 WL 23189458 (Tex. App.—Beaumont Jan. 22, 2004, orig. proceeding) (mem. op.) (same).

152 Robert K. Wise, *Ending Evasive Responses to Written Discovery: A Guide for Properly Responding (and Objecting) to Interrogatories and Document Requests Under the Texas Discovery Rules*, 65 Baylor L. Rev. 510, 590 (2013).

153 *In re Waste Mgmt. of Tex., Inc.*, 392 S.W.3d 861, 875 (Tex. App.—Texarkana 2013, orig. proceeding) (quoting *ISK Biotech Corp. v. Lindsay*, 933 S.W.2d 565, 569 (Tex. App.—Houston [1st Dist.] 1996, orig. proceeding)); *accord In re HEB Grocery Co.*, No. 13-10-00533-CV, 2010 Tex. App. LEXIS 9014, at *5, 2010 WL 4523765 (Tex. App.—Corpus Christi Nov. 8, 2010, orig. proceeding) (mem. op.).

154 *In re Waste Mgmt. of Tex., Inc.*, 392 S.W.3d 861, 875 (Tex. App.—Texarkana 2013, orig. proceeding) ("A discovery request will not result in an undue burden when the burdensomeness of responding to it is the result of the responding party's own 'conscious, discretionary decisions.'" (quoting *ISK Biotech Corp. v. Lindsay*, 933 S.W.2d 565, 569 (Tex. App.—Houston [1st Dist.] 1996, orig. proceeding))); *cf. Fagan v. D.C.*, 136 F.R.D. 5, 7 (D.D.C. 1991) (overruling the responding party's undue burden objection to interrogatories because the burden was due to the inefficiency of its filing system); *see In re Luna*, No. 13-16-00467-CV, 2016 Tex. App. LEXIS 12011, at *23 (Tex. App.—Corpus Christi Nov. 7, 2016, orig. proceeding) (mem. op.) ("We further note that many of the costs that State Farm estimates for the proposed deposition are the result of State Farm's own internal policies or procedures, and a discovery request will not result in an undue burden when the burdensomeness of responding to it is the result of the responding party's own 'conscious, discretionary decisions.'" (quoting *ISK Biotech Corp. v. Lindsay*, 933 S.W.2d 565, 569 (Tex. App.—Houston [1st Dist.] 1996, no writ))).

to gather the requested information in the preparation of its own case.[155] Accordingly, such an objection to a contention interrogatory seeking the "general bases" or the "material" or "principal" facts of the responding party's allegation, claim, or defense generally should be overruled.[156]

9-5:3.7 Vagueness, Ambiguity, or Lack of Specificity

An objection that an interrogatory is ambiguous or vague is proper.[157] An interrogatory is vague or ambiguous when its wording is such that it is uncertain what information is sought.[158] However, the fact that a word or phrase in an interrogatory is undefined does not necessarily make it vague or ambiguous. Rather, a responding party should use common sense when interpreting words and phrases in interrogatories, giving them their ordinary meanings, giving them their specialized meaning used in the industry at issue, defining them as the opposing party has defined or used them in its pleadings, or providing its own definition of the term or phrase.[159]

---

155 *Cf. Bell v. Woodward Governor Co.*, No. 03 C 50190, 2005 U.S. Dist. LEXIS 4451, at *7, 2005 WL 289963 (N.D. Ill. Feb. 7, 2005) ("[W]hen the responding party will need to research the same information requested to prepare their own case, courts are more inclined to require parties to compile information for the other side.").

156 *Cf. Labrier v. State Farm Fire & Cas. Co.*, 314 F.R.D. 637, 642 (W.D. Mo. 2016) (compelling discovery because the defendant "would need to gather information anyway, which is further reason for [it] being required to incur this expense."); *Asberry v. Cate*, No. 2: 11-cv-2462 KJM KJN P, 2014 U.S. Dist. LEXIS 46334, at *8, 2014 WL 1286191 (E.D. Cal. Mar. 31, 2014) ("[I]f the responding party would necessarily have to gather the requested information to prepare its own case, objections that it is too difficult to obtain the information for the requesting party are not honored."); *In re Folding Carton Antitrust Litig.*, 83 F.R.D. 256, 259 (N.D. Ill. 1979) (overruling an undue burden objection because the interrogatories related to the bases for the responding party's statute-of-limitations defense and, therefore, was information that the party would gather in preparation of its own case); *Flour Mills of Am., Inc., v. Pace*, 75 F.R.D. 676, 680–81 (E.D. Okla. 1977) ("An interrogatory will not be held objectionable as calling for research if it relates to details alleged in the pleading . . . or if the interrogated party would gather the information in the preparation of its own case.").

As discussed above, contention interrogatories asking the responding party to state "all" facts or "every" or "each" fact concerning an allegation, claim, or defense generally require improper evidence marshalling. See note 27 and accompanying text.

157 *Cf. City of Seattle v. Prof'l Basketball Club, LLC*, No. CO7-1620MJP, 2008 U.S. Dist. LEXIS 108533, at *8, 2008 WL 539809 (W.D. Wash. Feb. 25, 2008).

158 *Black's Law Dictionary* (11th ed. 2019) (defining "ambiguity" and "ambiguous" as "[a]n uncertainty of meaning or intention" and "vague" as "imprecise . . . [and] uncertain"); *Ambiguous, Merriam-Webster Online Dictionary*, https://www.merriam-webster.com/dictionary/ambiguous, (last visited July 19, 2021) (defining "ambiguous" as "doubtful or uncertain" or "capable of being understood in two or more possible senses or ways"); *Vague, Merriam-Webster Online Dictionary*, https://www.merriam-webster.com/dictionary/vague, (last visited July 19, 2021) (defining "vague" as "not clearly expressed" "stated in indefinite term" or "not having precise meaning").

159 *In re Swepi L.P.*, 103 S.W.3d 578, 590 (Tex. App.—San Antonio, 2003, orig. proceeding) ("[S]ometimes the lack of a definition can render an interrogatory objectionably vague, that is not the case here . . . . The terms Shell has used to describe these claims are easily defined in the context of the lawsuit."); *see* Tex. R. Civ. P. 193.2(c) ("A party may object to written discovery only if a good faith factual and legal basis for the objection exists at the

One of the ultimate ironies is that most vague and ambiguous objections are Delphic because they fail to explain why the interrogatory suffers from the alleged malady. Thus, the objections leave both the requesting party and the court guessing as to why the interrogatory is unclear. Of course, such a bald objection does not meet Texas Rule 193.2(a)'s specificity requirement for objections.

To properly object to an interrogatory in its entirety as vague or ambiguous, the responding party should explain why it is vague or ambiguous. For example, it should not only identify the words or phrases in the interrogatory that are vague or ambiguous, but also should explain why they are such (i.e., why they are reasonably susceptible of more than one meaning and why the responding party cannot use the word's or phrase's ordinary or other meaning in responding to the interrogatory).[160]

---

time the objection is made."); *cf. Lopez v. Don Herring Ltd.*, 327 F.R.D. 567, 580 (N.D. Tex. 2018) ("A party objecting to discovery as vague or ambiguous has the burden to show such vagueness or ambiguity; that [a] party objecting on these grounds must explain the specific and particular way in which a request is vague; that [t]he responding party should exercise reason and common sense to attribute ordinary definitions to terms and phrases utilized in interrogatories and, [i]f necessary to clarify its answers, . . . may include any reasonable definition of the term or phrase at issue; and that, [i]f a party believes that the request is vague, that party [should] attempt to obtain clarification [by conferring with the requesting party] prior to objecting on this ground." (quoting *Heller v. City of Dall.*, 303 F.R.D. 466, 491–92 (N.D. Tex. 2014))); ***Samsung Elecs. Am., Inc. v. Chung***, 321 F.R.D. 250, 289 (N.D. Tex. 2017) (same); ***Cenea v. Stasiuk***, No. 15cv1265-AJB-BGS, 2016 U.S. Dist. LEXIS 122475, at *4, 2016 WL 4720370 (S.D. Cal. Sept. 9, 2016) ("Other than the mere assertion, Plaintiff offers no analysis of why she views Interrogatory No. 8 as too vague and ambiguous to respond. The party objecting to discovery as vague or ambiguous has the burden to show such vagueness or ambiguity by demonstrating that 'more tools beyond mere reason and common sense are necessary to attribute ordinary definitions to terms and phrases.'" (quoting *Thomas v. Cate*, 715 F. Supp. 2d 1012, 1030 (E.D. Cal. 2010))); *Vlasich v. Fishback*, No. 1:05-cv-016150-LJO-GSA-PC, 2009 U.S. Dist. LEXIS 43098, at *12–13, 2009 WL 1309727 (E.D. Cal. May 11, 2009) ("These phrases are not so overbroad, vague, and ambiguous that defendant could not, in good faith, frame an intelligent reply using wording clarifying what defendant believes is meant."); ***Heartland Surgical Specialty Hosp., LLC v. Midwest Div., Inc.***, No. 05-2164-MLB-DWB, 2007 U.S. Dist. LEXIS 16816, at *33, *41–42, 2007 WL 756631 (D. Kan. Mar. 8, 2007) ("The words objected to as vague and ambiguous ('knowledge and information') have an understandable meaning in the common, everyday usage of the words.").

160 *Cf. Heller v. City of Dall.*, 303 F.R.D. 466, 488 (N.D. Tex. 2014) ("[F]or example, if part or all of an interrogatory is allegedly vague and ambiguous, the responding party, to comply with the Federal Rules, must, if possible, explain its understanding of the allegedly vague and ambiguous terms or phrases and explicitly state that its answer is based on that understanding. If an entire interrogatory or document request is truly so vague and ambiguous that the responding party cannot understand its meaning and what information it seeks, the party should stand on its objection and provide no answer at all or promise no production of responsive documents on the ground that the responding party simply cannot do so based on the discovery request's wording. But making an objection to a request as vague and ambiguous, without more, and then fully answering the interrogatory or promising production of all documents responsive to the request 'subject to' the vagueness and ambiguity objection betrays that the objection was made reflexively and without a factual basis.") (citations omitted). See also cases cited in note 159.

9-5:3.8 Unreasonably Cumulative or Duplicative

As pointed out in Chapter 8, section 8-5:8, cumulative discovery refers to discovery that tends to prove the same point, whereas duplicative discovery refers to discovery that duplicates or is substantively identical to earlier discovery. A court generally will not limit discovery merely because it is somewhat cumulative or duplicative.[161] Rather, the discovery must be unreasonably so,[162] and can be unreasonably cumulative or duplicative of the same or a different type of discovery. For example, an interrogatory not only can be duplicative of other interrogatories, but also can be unreasonably duplicative of deposition testimony, requests for admission, or production requests.[163]

---

161 *See* Tex. R. Civ. P. 192.4(a) (allowing a court to limit "***unreasonably*** cumulative or duplicative discovery") (emphasis added).

162 Tex. R. Civ. P. 192.4; *cf.* ***Uniram Tech., Inc. v. Monolithic Sys. Tech., Inc.***, No. C 04-1268 VRW (MEJ), 2007 U.S. Dist. LEXIS 24869, at *6, 2007 WL 915225 (N.D. Cal. Mar. 23, 2007) ("[T]he question here is not whether topic 1 is duplicative of the June 2006 deposition, but whether topic 1 is ***unreasonably*** duplicative."); ***Van Wagenen v. Consol. Rail Corp.***, 170 F.R.D. 86, 87 (N.D.N.Y. 1997) (holding that requests seeking the admission of the truth of various sentences taken from a document, the authenticity of which had already been admitted, were unreasonably duplicative and cumulative); ***Aramburu v. Boeing Co.***, 885 F. Supp. 1434, 1444 (D. Kan. 1995) (holding that when information already provided by the defendant-employer should have been enough for the plaintiff-employee to make a preliminary determination as to whether the employer treated the employee's ethnic group differently, employee could not compel employer to cull information from 1,700 personnel files, even though files might contain some relevant information).

163 *Cf.* ***SEC v. Berry***, No. C07-04431 RMW (HRL), 2011 U.S. Dist. LEXIS 39907, at *9–11, 2011 WL 1296043 (N.D. Cal. Apr. 1, 2011) (holding that interrogatories were not unreasonably cumulative or duplicative of defendant's deposition testimony); ***Sloan v. Oakland Police Dep't***, No. C-00-4117 CW (JCS), 2006 U.S. Dist. LEXIS 25100, at *14 n.2, 2006 WL 753013 (N.D. Cal. Mar. 23, 2006) (noting that, should defendants bring a motion to compel responses to interrogatories served before plaintiff's deposition, such a motion will only be granted if the additional interrogatory responses sought are not unreasonably duplicative of information already obtained, through deposition or otherwise); ***Pulsecard, Inc. v. Discover Card Servs., Inc.***, 168 F.R.D. 295, 306 (D. Kan. 1996) ("That litigants may engage in successive forms of discovery 'is not a license to engage in repetitious, redundant and tautological inquiries.'" (quoting ***Richlin v. Sigma Design W. Ltd.***, 88 F.R.D. 634, 640 (E.D. Cal. 1980))).

Nonetheless, disclosures, production requests, "written interrogatories and requests for admission are not adequate substitutes for conducting a deposition." ***Barnett v. Norman***, No. 1:05-cv-01022-SKOPC, 2010 U.S. Dist. LEXIS 92077, at *2, 2010 WL 3220122 (E.D. Cal. Aug. 10, 2010). As one federal court aptly noted:

> Written interrogatories are rarely, if ever, an adequate substitute for a deposition. . . . Only by examining a witness live can a lawyer use the skills of his trade to plumb the depths of a witness' recollection, using to advantage not only what a witness may have admitted in answering interrogatories, but also any new tidbits that usually come out in the course of answering carefully framed and pin-pointed deposition questions. Written interrogatories are not designed for that purpose; pointed questions at deposition are the only effective way to discover facts bottled up in a witness' recollection, particularly when the witness is . . . hostile.

To establish that an interrogatory is unreasonably cumulative or duplicative, the responding party must specifically identify the other discovery to which the interrogatory is unreasonably cumulative or duplicative.[164]

9-5:3.9 Expert Opinion

As discussed in Chapter 7, section 7-4, a party cannot use interrogatories to obtain information about or from a testifying expert. Accordingly, an objection that an interrogatory improperly seeks information about or from a testifying expert is a proper objection. In fact, it is the only proper "expert-opinion" objection with respect to testifying experts.

Despite this fact, many practitioners faced with contention interrogatories attempt to avoid answering them because doing so requires an "expert opinion" (i.e., to answer the interrogatories, the responding party must consult with its experts before its expert designations are due). This expert-opinion objection is nonsense

---

Barnett v. Norman, No. 1:05-cv-01022-SKOPC, 2010 U.S. Dist. LEXIS 92077, at *2–3, 2010 WL 3220122 (E.D. Cal. Aug. 10, 2010) (quoting *Shoen v. Shoen*, 5 F.3d 1289, 1297 (9th Cir. 1993)); *accord U.S. v. Educ. Mgmt. LLC*, No. 2:07-cv-00461, 2014 U.S. Dist. LEXIS 50519, at *22 (W.D. Pa. Feb. 24, 2014) ("[T]hat Defendants have already propounded questions through their interrogatories that may be similar to those to be asked at the deposition should not prevent the deposition from proceeding in this case inasmuch as Defendants assert that the information contained in Plaintiffs' responses arguably necessitates a certain amount of clarification. A party should not be prevented from questioning a live . . . witness in a [Federal Rule 30(b)(6)] deposition setting just because the topics proposed are similar to those contained in documents provided or interrogatory questions answered. . . . When information has already been provided in other forms, a witness may still be useful to testify as to the interpretation of papers, and 'any underlying factual qualifiers of those documents.'" (quoting *Dongguk Univ. v. Yale Univ.*, 270 F.R.D. 70, 74 (D. Conn. 2010))); *Barnett v. Norman*, No. 1:05-cv-01022-SKO PC, 2010 U.S. Dist. LEXIS 92077, at *2, 2010 WL 3220122 (E.D. Cal. Aug. 10, 2010) ("[W]ritten interrogatories and requests for admission are not adequate substitutes for conducting a deposition."); *N.J. v. Spring Corp.*, No. 03-20710JWL, 2010 U.S. Dist. LEXIS 14890, at *9–10, 2010 WL 610671 (D. Kan. Feb. 19, 2010) (same); *Great Am. Ins. Co. of N.Y. v. Vegas Constr. Co.*, 251 F.R.D. 534, 541 (D. Nev. 2008) ("Producing documents and responding to written discovery is not a substitute for providing a thoroughly educated [Federal] Rule 30(b)(6) deponent. As the cases cited in this order make clear, the two forms of discovery are not equivalent, and depositions provide a more complete means to obtain information and are, therefore, favored.") (citation omitted); *see Reynolds v. Jamison*, 488 F.3d 756, 769–70 (7th Cir. 2007) ("Affidavits, responses to interrogatories, and other written statements are typically drafted by lawyers and by their nature are self-serving. Even something like a police report, prepared after the fact to document what the police officer observed, what he knew, and why he did what he did, is often written with a calculating eye to litigation and to the author's potential liability. There is no reason to believe that such written statements invariably tell the complete and unvarnished truth, and that is why the parties are entitled to take depositions.") (citation omitted).

164 *Cf. Wye Oak Tech., Inc. v. Republic of Iraq*, No. 1:10-cv-01182-RCL, 2018 U.S. Dist. LEXIS 159096, at *3 (D.D.C. 2018) ("By simply objecting to Wye Oak's request without referring to the specific documents that were previously produced, defendants have not met their burden of demonstrating that Wye Oak's request is in fact 'unreasonably cumulative or duplicative.'"); *Alexander v. FBI*, 194 F.R.D. 299, 302 (D.D.C. 2000) (same).

because contention interrogatories do not seek "expert discovery." Rather, they merely seek the factual bases for claims, defenses, or allegations in the responding party's pleadings.

For example, in *Wagner v. St. Paul Fire & Marine Insurance Co.*, the plaintiffs sued their insurer for bad faith.[165] In response to an interrogatory asking them whether they claimed that the attorneys hired by their insurer to represent them engaged in wrongful conduct and, if so, to state each wrongful act, the plaintiffs objected because "the interrogatory impermissibly asks for an expert opinion."[166] The court, in overruling the objection, reasoned:

> [P]arties may use interrogatories to "ask questions regarding evidence on which an opposing party bases some specific contention; a position taken by a party and an explanation or defense for that position with respect to how the law applies to the facts; and the legal basis for, or theory behind, some specific contention."
>
> This interrogatory merely asks Plaintiffs to state whether they allege wrongful litigation conduct by defense attorneys and if so the facts upon which they base that argument. It does not ask for an expert opinion.[167]

In addition, courts consistently and repeatedly have held that an interrogatory is ***not*** transformed into "expert discovery" merely because a complete answer requires the responding party to consult with its designated testifying experts to answer it fully. As explained by one federal court in rejecting an expert-opinion objection on this basis:

---

[165] *Wagner v. St. Paul Fire & Marine Ins. Co.*, 238 F.R.D. 418, 420 (N.D.W. Va. 2006).

[166] *Wagner v. St. Paul Fire & Marine Ins. Co.*, 238 F.R.D. 418, 428 (N.D.W. Va. 2006).

[167] *Wagner v. St. Paul Fire & Marine Ins. Co.*, 238 F.R.D. 418, 428 (N.D.W. Va. 2006) (citation omitted) (quoting *Am. Civil Liberties Union v. Gonzalez*, 237 F.R.D. 120, 123 (E.D. Pa. 2006)); *accord Feinberg v. T. Rowe Price Group, Inc.*, No. 17-CV-00427-JKB, 2019 U.S. Dist. LEXIS 207668, at *14–15, 2019 WL 6497959 (D. Md. Dec. 3, 2019) *McKinney/Pearl Rest., L.P. v. Metro. Life Ins. Co.*, 322 F.R.D. 235, 254 (N.D. Tex. 2016); *Geer v. Cox*, No. 01-2583-JAR, 2003 U.S. Dist. LEXIS 9230, at *10–11, 2003 WL 21254731 (D. Kan. May 21, 2003); *Cook v. Rockwell Int'l Corp.*, 161 F.R.D. 103, 105 (D. Colo. 1995) (same); *see Dennis v. U.S.*, No. 3:16-cv-3148-G-BN, 2017 U.S. Dist. LEXIS 174856, at *24–25, 2017 WL 4778708 (N.D. Tex. Oct. 23, 2017) (rejecting an expert-objection objection to a Federal Rule 30(b)(6) deposition notice); *AMTRAK v. Cimarron Crossing Feeders, LLC*, No. 16-cv-1094-JTM-TJJ, 2017 U.S. Dist. LEXIS 60822, at *8–10, 2017 WL 1408226 (D. Kan. Apr. 20, 2017) (rejecting an expert-opinion objection because "Railroad Plaintiffs must answer the Requests with the knowledge and information they presently possess, or can obtain after reasonable inquiry (independent of their experts)"); *Baugh v. Bayer Corp.*, No. 4:11-cv-525-RBH, 2012 U.S. Dist. LEXIS 131867, at *7 (D.S.C. Sept. 17, 2012) (overruling the defendants' objection to requests for admissions and directing defendants to supplement their response even though the defendants had to consult with their expert to do so); *Drutis v. Rand McNally & Co.*, 236 F.R.D. 325, 329–31 (D. Ky. 2006) (same); *House v. Giant of Md., LLC*, 232 F.R.D. 257, 262 (E.D. Va. 2005) ("Defendants' answers reflect folklore within the bar which holds that requests for admission need not be answered if the subject matter of the request . . . 'addresses a subject for expert testimony[.]' . . . As the authorities set forth in this Opinion demonstrate, the folklore is wrong.").

[A] party cannot avoid discovery—whether by an interrogatory, a [Federal] Rule 36 request, or Federal Rule of Civil Procedure 30(b)(6) deposition testimony—of its own views on a factual matter in dispute (or perhaps, in fact, not in dispute) simply because its view on that matter may be informed by consulting with its retained experts. As other courts have observed, "[e]ven if complete answers to discovery requests may require the answering party to consult with experts, such considerations do not transform permissible factual discovery into 'expert discovery.'"[168]

---

[168] *McKinney/Pearl Rest., L.P. v. Metro. Life Ins. Co.*, 322 F.R.D. 235, 254 (N.D. Tex. 2016 (quoting *Geer v. Cox*, No. 01-2583-JAR, 2003 U.S. Dist. LEXIS 9230, at *10–11 (D. Kan. May 21, 2003)). *But see Emerson v. Lab. Corp. of Am.*, Civ. A. No. 1:11-CV-01709-RWS, 2012 U.S. Dist. LEXIS 60636, at *5–9, 2012 WL 1564683 (N.D. Ga. May 1, 2012) (sustaining objections to requests for admission because the requests for admission could only be answered by an expert).

In *In re Young*, 410 S.W.3d 542 (Tex. App.—Beaumont 2013, no pet.), the State, in a civil-commitment action against an allegedly violent sexual predator, moved for a protective order with respect to certain requests for admission because they "[would be] best answered by the psychological and/or psychiatric experts who have been designated by Petitioner in this case, which Respondent will have the opportunity to do at the time of the expert's deposition" and apparently because they also sought information protected by the work-product privilege. *In re Young*, 410 S.W.3d 542, 549. (Tex. App.—Beaumont 2013, no pet.).

The Beaumont Court of Appeals, without either quoting or describing in any detail the specific requests at issue, held that the trial court did not abuse its discretion in granting the protective order:

> With respect to these thirty-six requests, Young suggested in the trial court that "[o]ne party cannot limit the method or methods by which the other party chooses to conduct discovery." However, the reasonable inquiry required of a party in formulating responses to requests for admissions [sic] does not require that the attorneys ask its designated experts for the information that may be needed to answer requests for admission. Instead, discovery from experts is permitted "only through a request for disclosure under [Texas] Rule 194 and through depositions and reports as permitted by this rule."
>
> Based on the arguments that Young presented to the trial court, the trial court could reasonably conclude that Young improperly used [the] requests . . . in an effort to conduct discovery against the State's designated experts. We conclude the trial court did not abuse its discretion by granting the State's motion with respect to [the] requests[.]

In re Young, 410 S.W.3d 542, 549 (Tex. App.—Beaumont 2013, no pet.) (citations omitted).

Although *In re Young* can be read as supporting the proposition that an expert-opinion objection is proper in Texas, the opinion does not quote or clearly describe the requests for admission at issue. Thus, it is unclear whether the requests sought information specifically about the State's experts (e.g., their identities, the subject matters about which they would testify, or their mental impressions or conclusions) or simply sought admissions about matters that required some expert input. Moreover, the defendant in *In re Young*, in response to the motion for protective order, did not make the arguments set forth in this section or cite any of the case law set forth above. *In re Young*, 410 S.W.3d 542, 549 (Tex. App.—Beaumont 2013, no pet.). Accordingly, *In re Young* should be limited to cases in which the requests for admission seek information specifically about the responding party's experts.

Just as importantly, a responding party's failure to answer an interrogatory on the basis that it requires an "expert opinion" violates Texas Rule 193.1, which requires a party, "[w]hen responding to written discovery," to "make a complete response, based on *all information reasonably available to the responding party or the attorney at the time the response is made*."[169] This means that a party should answer the interrogatory with the discoverable information that is currently available to the party and its attorney and supplement its answer after its testifying experts are designated. For example, in *Forbes v. City of Jackson*, the plaintiff sued, among others, TASER International, Inc., claiming that a design defect in the TASER used on her son by the police caused his death.[170] The court, in rejecting an expert-opinion objection, held:

> The primary basis for Plaintiff's objections to the discovery is that the interrogatories pose questions regarding the alleged design defect which Plaintiff is unable to answer as a lay person; she must depend on her experts for the responses. And, as discussed, Plaintiff does not yet have her expert reports. Plaintiff requests that she not be compelled to respond to the discovery until such time as the expert reports are completed.
>
> It must be assumed that Plaintiff and her attorney have discussed the factual basis for why they believe TASER is liable for Rafael Forbes's death. It may be that Plaintiff's understanding of the technical aspects of any defect is rudimentary; however, her responses may reflect that lack of understanding. It is customary that counsel investigates the claim prior to filing the Complaint, discusses the claims with potential experts, and explains and discusses the factual basis for liability to Plaintiff. These are the facts which should be disclosed to Defendant at this stage of the litigation, to be supplemented as more expert information is obtained.
>
> For these reasons, Plaintiff shall be compelled to fully respond to the outstanding discovery; she should supplement her answers as more information is obtained.[171]

In the rare case in which an interrogatory cannot truly be answered at all without a testifying expert's input and the answer is due before the responding party is required to designate its testifying experts, the responding party, rather than objecting to the interrogatory, should either reach an agreement with the requesting party to defer the answer until a reasonable time after the responding party's expert designations are due or move for an extension of time to respond to the request.[172]

---

[169] Tex. R. Civ. P. 193.1 (emphasis added).

[170] *Forbes v. City of Jackson*, No. 3:09CV423-HTW-LRA, 2010 U.S. Dist. LEXIS 58868, at *5–6, 2010 WL 1980421 (S.D. Miss. May 14, 2010).

[171] *Forbes v. City of Jackson*, No. 3:09CV423-HTW-LRA, 2010 U.S. Dist. LEXIS 58868, at *5–6, 2010 WL 1980421 (S.D. Miss. May 14, 2010); *accord In re Urethane Antitrust Litig.*, No. 04-MD-1616-JWL, 2009 U.S. Dist. LEXIS 60496, at *28, 2009 WL 2058759 (D. Kan. July 15, 2009); *Geer v. Cox*, No. 01-2583-JAR, 2003 U.S. Dist. LEXIS 9230, at *10–11, 2003 WL 21254731 (D. Kan. May 21, 2003); *Flying J Inc. v. TA Operating Corp.*, No. 1:06-CV-30 TC, 2007 U.S. Dist. LEXIS 32518, at *15–17, 2007 WL 1302756 (D. Utah May 2, 2007); *EEOC v. Kovacevich "5" Farms*, No. 1:06-cv-0165-OWW-TAG, 2007 U.S. Dist. LEXIS 43672, at *30 (E.D. Cal. June 1, 2007).

[172] *Cf. Baugh v. Bayer Corp.*, No. 4-11-cv-525-RBH, 2012 U.S. Dist. LEXIS 131867, at *9 n.3, 2012 WL 4069582 (D.S.C. Sept. 17, 2012) (deferring the answer date for requests for admission until after the responding party's expert designation date).

9-5:3.10 Marshalling Evidence

As discussed in Chapter 9, section 9-3, Texas Rule 197.1 provides that interrogatories may not be used to require the responding party to marshal its available proof.[173] For example, a marshalling objection is proper to an interrogatory that asks for "all" facts or "each" or "every" fact concerning a cause of action or defense.[174] It is improper with

---

[173] See notes 22–43 and accompanying text. Federal court often hold that so-called "blockbuster" interrogatories that require the responding party to state every fact supporting all of its allegations as well as the identity of each person with knowledge and each document concerning about each fact are improper. *E.g., Heuskin v. D&E Transp., LLC*, No. 19-957 MV/GBW, 2020 U.S. Dist. LEXIS 51644, at *5–6, 2020 WL 1450575 (D.N.M. Mar. 25, 2020) ("However, 'blockbuster' narrative interrogatories, which 'require the responding party to provide the equivalent of a narrative of its entire case together with identification of virtually all supporting evidence for each and every fact,' are disfavored."); *HCB Fin. Corp. v. Kennedy*, No. 1:10CV559-HSO-JCG, 2016 U.S. Dist. LEXIS 199885, at *4–5, 2016 WL 6216179, (S.D. Miss. Mar. 28, 2016) (same); *EEOC v. BNSF Ry.*, No. 12–02634–JWL–KGG, 2014 U.S. Dist. LEXIS 78432, at *4, 2014 WL 2589182 (D. Kan. June 10, 2014) ("These 'blockbuster' interrogatories require the responding party to provide the equivalent of a narrative of its entire case together with identification of virtually all supporting evidence for each and every fact. Indiscriminate use of blockbuster interrogatories, such as these, do not comport with the just, speedy, and inexpensive determination of the action.") (citation omitted); *Nieman v. Hale*, No. 3:12-cv-2433-L-BN, 2013 U.S. Dist. LEXIS 180397, at *29–32, 2013 WL 6814789 (N.D. Tex. Dec. 26, 2013) (denying motion to compel response to "blockbuster" interrogatory); *Brassell v. Turner*, No. 3:05-cv-476-TSL-JCS, 2006 U.S. Dist. LEXIS 49810, 2006 WL 1806465 (S.D. Miss. June 29, 2006) (finding interrogatories overly broad an unduly burdensome where they sought an open-ended narrative that was not tailored in any way); *Grynberg v. Total S.A.*, No. 3-cv-01280-WYD-BNB, 2006 U.S. Dist. LEXIS 28854, at *16–18, 2006 WL 1186836 (D. Colo. May 3, 2006) (denying motion to compel answer to "blockbuster" interrogatory); *Hilt v. SFC, Inc.*, 170 F.R.D. 182, 186–87 (D. Kan. 1997) (finding interrogatories that required the party to identify all facts supporting its position, all witnesses with knowledge of those facts, and all documents supporting the position unduly burdensome).

[174] See notes 22–43 and accompanying text. Federal court often hold that so-called "blockbuster" interrogatories that require the responding party to state every fact supporting all of its allegations as well as the identity of each person with knowledge and each document concerning about each fact are improper. *E.g., Heuskin v. D&E Transp., LLC*, No. 19-957 MV/GBW, 2020 U.S. Dist. LEXIS 51644, at *5–6, 2020 WL 1450575 (D.N.M. Mar. 25, 2020) ("However, 'blockbuster' narrative interrogatories, which 'require the responding party to provide the equivalent of a narrative of its entire case together with identification of virtually all supporting evidence for each and every fact,' are disfavored."); *HCB Fin. Corp. v. Kennedy*, No. 1:10CV559-HSO-JCG, 2016 U.S. Dist. LEXIS 199885, at *4–5, 2016 WL 6216179 (S.D. Miss. Mar. 28, 2016) (same); *EEOC v. BNSF Ry.*, No. 12–02634–JWL–KGG, 2014 U.S. Dist. LEXIS 78432, at *4, 2014 WL 2589182 (D. Kan. June 10, 2014) ("These 'blockbuster' interrogatories require the responding party to provide the equivalent of a narrative of its entire case together with identification of virtually all supporting evidence for each and every fact. Indiscriminate use of blockbuster interrogatories, such as these, do not comport with the just, speedy, and inexpensive determination of the action.") (citations omitted); *Nieman v. Hale*, No. 3:12-cv-2433-L-BN, 2013 U.S. Dist. LEXIS 180397, 2013 WL 6814789 (N.D. Tex. Dec. 26, 2013) (denying motion to compel response to "blockbuster" interrogatory); *Brassell v. Turner*, No. 3:05-cv-476-TSL-JCS, 2006 U.S. Dist. LEXIS 49810, 2006 WL 1806465 (S.D. Miss. June 29, 2006) (finding interrogatories overly broad an unduly burdensome where they sought an open-ended narrative that was not tailored in any way); *Grynberg v. Total S.A.*, No. 3-cv-01280-WYD-BNB, 2006 U.S. Dist. LEXIS 28854, 2006 WL 1186836

respect to an interrogatory asking for (1) the "general," "principal," or "material" facts concerning such matters, (2) the identity of persons with knowledge about a claim, defense, or allegation, (3) the identity of documents concerning a claim, defense, or allegation, or (4) the identification of each contractual provision breached, each negligent act or omission, each fraudulent misrepresentation or omission, and the like.[175]

9-5:3.11 Supernumerary Objections

The number of permitted interrogatories in an action is expressly limited by Texas Rules 190.2(b)(3) and 190.3(b)(3) in Level 1 and 2 actions, respectively, and likely will be limited by a Level 3 discovery-control plan.[176] Nonetheless, a responding party faced with too many interrogatories cannot refuse to answer the entire interrogatory set. Instead, it should answer the first twenty-five interrogatories (or other number of interrogatories for which the discovery-control order provides) and interpose a supernumerary objection to the rest.[177] Of course, either answering a supernumerary

---

(D. Colo. May 3, 2006) (denying motion to compel answer to "blockbuster" interrogatory); *Hilt v. SFC, Inc.*, 170 F.R.D. 182, 186–87 (D. Kan. 1997) (finding interrogatories that required the party to identify all facts supporting its position, all witnesses with knowledge of those facts, and all documents supporting the position unduly burdensome).

175 See notes 22–43 and accompanying text.

176 Tex. R. Civ. P. 190.2(b)(3), 190.3(b)(3), 190.4(b).

177 *See* Tex. R. Civ. P. 192.6(a), 193.2(a) ("A person should not move for protection when an objection to written discovery . . . is appropriate."); ***Childs v. Argenbright***, 927 S.W.2d 647, 652 (Tex. App.—Tyler 1996, no writ) (holding that, under former Texas Rule 168, which allowed no more than thirty interrogatory answers, the responding party should answer the first thirty questions); ***Owens v. Wallace***, 821 S.W.2d 746, 749 (Tex. App.—Tyler 1992, orig. proceeding) (same); ***cf. Osucha v. Alden State Bank***, No. 17CV1026V, 2019 U.S. Dist. LEXIS 214744, at *8–9, 2019 WL 6783289 (W.D.N.Y. Dec. 12, 2019) ("The party asked to respond to Interrogatories need not answer more than 25 posed and can choose merely to answer the first 25 (including distinct subparts that would total 25)."); ***Mondragon v. Scott Farms, Inc.***, 329 F.R.D. 533, 541 (E.D.N.C. 2019), objections overruled, No. 5:17-CV-00356-FL, 2019 U.S. Dist. LEXIS 19896, 2019 WL 489117 (E.D.N.C. Feb. 7, 2019) ("When a party is confronted with what it believes to be an excessive number of interrogatories, the appropriate course of action is to either move for a protective order before answering any interrogatories or 'answer up to the numerical limit and object to the remainder without answering.'"); ***EEOC v. State of Mex.***, No. 15-879 KG/KK, 2016 U.S. Dist. LEXIS 139049, at *8–9, 2016 WL 9777238 (D.N.M. Sept. 30, 2016) ("In future, should a party to this matter believe that a supernumerary objection is warranted, that party is instructed to 'either seek a protective order and not answer the requests at issue[,] or answer up to the numerical limit and object to the remaining requests without answering.' This procedure will prevent the objecting party from randomly (or strategically) choosing which interrogatories to answer, but, absent a motion for protective order, will also allow the party serving discovery to receive responses to some portion of its requests." (quoting *Lowery v. Cnty. of Riley*, No. 04-3101-JTM-DWB, 2009 U.S. Dist. LEXIS 19957, at *11, 2009 WL 648928 (D. Kan. Mar. 12, 2009))); ***Avila v. Mohave Cnty.***, No. 3:14-CV-8124-HRH, 2015 U.S. Dist. LEXIS 148956, at *26, 2015 WL 6660187 (D. Ariz. Nov. 2, 2015) (citing cases and holding that the proper method for challenging a party's excessive interrogatories is to answer the requests chronologically until the allotted number is exhausted); ***Rowell v. NCO Fin. Sys.***, No. 13-2514-CM, 2014 U.S. Dist. LEXIS 70095, at *11–12 (D. Kan. May 22, 2014) ("Plaintiff did not follow the court's procedure for a party making a supernumerary objection. When such a situation arises, the objecting party is to either seek a protective order and not answer the requests at issue or answer up to the

interrogatory or failing to object to it as supernumerary interrogatory it waives the supernumerary objection.[178]

---

numerical limit and object to the remaining requests without answering. Instead, plaintiff chose to selectively apply this objection out of order and respond to some requests subject to that objection, but not others. This is improper. '[T]he responding party is not entitled to randomly select which of the . . . interrogatories it will answer.'" (quoting *Lowery v. Cnty. of Riley*, No. 04-3101, 2009 U.S. Dist. LEXIS 19957, at *11, 2009 WL 648928 (D. Kan. Mar. 12, 2009))); *Serigne v. Preveau*, No. 11-3160 SECTION: "R" (4), 2013 U.S. Dist. LEXIS 60004, at *6–8 n. 3, 2013 WL 1789520 (E.D. La. Apr. 26, 2013) ("Where analysis of 'subparts' yields more than 25 interrogatories, courts have found that a party to whom excessive interrogatories had been propounded had an obligation to respond to the 'first' 25 Interrogatories which constitute discrete questions, and strike the rest."); *Gautier v. Plains Bros. Pipeline, LP*, No. 12-1064c/w12-1186 SECTION: "L" (4), 2013 U.S. Dist. LEXIS 59349, at *6 n.3, 2013 WL 1787559 (E.D. La. Apr. 25, 2013) (same); *Paananen v. Celloc P'ship*, No. C08-1042 RSM, 2009 U.S. Dist. LEXIS 98997, at *12, 2009 WL 3327227 (W.D. Wash. Oct. 8, 2009) ("[T]he best rule, and the one this Court applies here, is that a responding party must answer the first 25 interrogatories.").

The reason why courts do not allow the responding party to choose which requests to respond to is because "[s]uch a rule would allow the responding party to 'selectively respond to the interrogatories and thereby strategically omit the most prejudicial information.'" *Paananen v. Celloc P'ship*, No. C08-1042 RSM, 2009 U.S. Dist. LEXIS 98997, at *11, 2009 WL 3327227 (W.D. Wash. Oct. 8, 2009) (quoting *Herdlein Techs. Inc. v. Century Contractors, Inc.*, 147 F.R.D. 103, 104 (W.D.N.C. 1993))).

178 *Childs v. Argenbright*, 927 S.W.2d 647, 652 (Tex. App.—Tyler 1996, no writ) (holding that a supernumerary objection was waived when the responding party interposed substantive objections to the excessive interrogatories); *cf. Mondragon v. Scott Farms, Inc.*, 329 F.R.D. 533, 541–42 (E.D.N.C., 2019) ("Scott has selectively answered interrogatories beyond what it contends is the 25-interrogatory limit. By doing so, it has waived any objection that it had to the number of interrogatories that Plaintiffs served on it. Thus, the motion to compel shall be granted and, to the extent Scott did not respond to certain interrogatories on the basis of this objection, it shall do so."); *Engage Healthcare Commc'ns, LLC v. Intellisphere, LLC*, No. 12-cv-00787(FLW)(LHG), 2017 U.S. Dist. LEXIS 83068, at *24–25 (D.N.J. Feb. 10, 2017) ("Here, Plaintiffs have answered and/or objected to the April 2013 Interrogatories, which number 18. In response to the October 2013 Interrogatories, which number 10, Plaintiffs did not object on the grounds that they, together with the April 2013 Interrogatories, exceeded the 25-interrogatory limit, and thus waived that objection."); *Cmty. Voice Line, LLC v. Great Lakes Commc'n Corp.*, No. C12-4048-MWB, 2013 U.S. Dist. LEXIS 112415, at *22–23, 2013 WL 4048495 (N.D. Iowa Aug. 1, 2013) ("CVL's response to Interrogatory Number 24 did not include an objection based on the number of interrogatories GLCC had served. As such, that objection has been waived."); *Porto Venezia Condo. Ass'n, v. WB Fort Lauderdale, LLC*, No.11-60665-CIV-DIMITROULEAS/Snow, 2012 U.S. Dist. LEXIS 186962, at *13–14 (S.D. Fla. Aug. 13, 2012) ("As an initial matter, the Court notes that although the Porto Venezia objects to each of the interrogatories on the same basis, it then proceeds to answer them. While this practice is an increasingly common approach to responding to discovery, courts in this District and elsewhere have held the practice in disfavor. Therefore, the Court need not consider Porto Venezio's repeated objection with regard to the total number of interrogatories WB has propounded in this case.") (citation omitted) (footnote omitted); *Paananen v. Celloc P'ship*, No. C08-1042 RSM, 2009 U.S. Dist. LEXIS 98997, at *12, 2009 WL 3327227 (W.D. Wash. Oct. 8, 2009) ("If [the responding party] answers more, the numerosity objection is waived as to those interrogatories that were answered."); *Capacchione v. Charlotte-Mecklenburg Schs.*, 182 F.R.D. 486, 492 (W.D.N.C. 1998) ("Yet, CMS, by responding to Interrogatories 21–25 without moving for a protective order, waived any

Just as the responding party is not allowed to pick and choose which supernumerary interrogatories to answer, the requesting party cannot circumvent its violation by voluntarily withdrawing selected supernumerary interrogatories. The operative word in Texas Rule 190 is "serve" and every interrogatory served counts against the numerical limit.[179] So do interrogatories to which objections have been interposed, and a requesting party cannot withdraw them.[180]

Finally, when the responding party believes that too many interrogatories have been asked, the better rule is that it need not interpose its substantive objections to the supernumerary interrogatories unless and until the supernumerary objections are resolved adversely to it. Otherwise, the responding party would have to answer and object, which is contrary to the very purpose of the supernumerary objections in the first instance.[181]

9-5:3.12 The Requested Information or Material Is in the Requesting Party's or a Nonparty's Possession

Oftentimes a responding party will object to an interrogatory because the information already is in the requesting party's possession or is equally available from a

---

objection on grounds of the 20-interrogatory limit. As stated by this Court: 'The responding party must object *(to the Court)* to the number of interrogatories before responding in order to rely on this rule.'" (quoting *Herdlein Techs. Inc. v. Century Contractors, Inc.*, 147 F.R.D. 103, 104 (W.D.N.C. 1993))).

179 *Cf. Walker v. Lakewood Condo. Owners Ass'n*, 186 F.R.D. 584, 586 (C.D. Cal. 1999) ("Contrary to FHF's argument, neither [Federal] Rule 33(a) nor Local Rule 8.2.1, expressly or implicitly, state that only interrogatories that are served and answered count against the numerical limit. Indeed, the use of the term 'serve' in both [Federal] Rule 33(a) and Local Rule 8.2.1 is absolute and unqualified. Nor do either of these rules state or reasonably suggest that interrogatories disintegrate and vanish as if they were never served when timely objections, but not answers, are made pursuant to [Federal] Rule 33(b). Moreover, FHF's suggested interpretation also conflicts with [Federal] Rule 33(b)'s express terms authorizing a party served with interrogatories to respond with either objections or answers. FHF's argument is also flawed because it ignores that, in the context of [Federal] Rule 33(a), Local Rule 8.2.1, and the Rules pertaining to discovery, the term 'serve' is more than just an active verb; it is a term of art.") (citation omitted); *see McClellan v. Kern Cnty. Sheriff's Office*, No. 1:10-cv-0386-LJO-MJS (PC), 2015 U.S. Dist. LEXIS 131685, at *2, 2015 WL 5732077 (E.D. Cal. Sept. 29, 2015) ("Fed. R. Civ. P. 33(a)(1) limits to 25 the number of interrogatories one party may serve on another. An interrogatory need not be answered, but merely served and properly objected to, in order to count against the numerical limit.").

180 *Cf. Walker v. Lakewood Condo. Owners Ass'n*, 186 F.R.D. 584, 586–88 (C.D. Cal. 1999) (construing Federal Rule 33(a)(1)).

181 *Cf. Peach v. City of Kewanee*, No. 05-4012, 2006 U.S. Dist. LEXIS 77379, at *6 (C.D. Ill. Oct. 23, 2006) ("In order to give meaningful teeth to the numeric limitation imposed by the Rule, this second line of cases defers the obligation to respond and object until [the supernumerary] objection is resolved. This second line of cases makes sense."); *Herdlein Techs. Inc. v. Century Contractors, Inc.*, 147 F.R.D. 103, 104 (W.D.N.C. 1993) ("The responding party must object *(to the Court)* to the number of interrogatories before responding in order to rely on this rule.") (emphasis added). See also cases cited in notes 177–78.

nonparty or a public source.[182] Such an objection is almost always improper because the requesting party is entitled to ascertain what information the responding party knows to determine whether it is the information that the requesting party knows.[183]

9-5:3.13 Fishing Expedition

Although more commonly used with respect to production requests, responding parties at times object to interrogatories because they constitute a "fishing expedition."[184]

---

[182] If an interrogatory can be answered from public records, a responding party, in appropriate circumstances under Texas Rule 197.2(c) can refer the requesting party to the specific records from which the answer can be obtained. See Chapter 9, section 9-5:2 (discussing Texas Rule 197.2(c)'s option to produce records). This is much different than objecting to the interrogatory because its answer can be ascertained from unidentified public records.

[183] *See In re Ochoa*, No. 12-04-00163-CV, 2004 Tex. App. LEXIS 4866, at *5, 2004 WL 1192444 (Tex. App.—Tyler May 28, 2004, orig. proceeding) (mem. op.) (Plaintiffs contend that they do not have to answer contention interrogatories because "[defendants] have equal access to their medical records and should be able to determine for themselves any prior or pre-existing injuries. The rules contain no such limit on the use of contention interrogatories. . . ."); *cf. Copeland v. City of Lawton Oklahoma*, No. 18-558-PRW, 2019 U.S. Dist. LEXIS 147375, at *4–5, 2019 WL 4131089 (W.D. Okla. Aug. 29, 2019) ("But Plaintiff's burden is to answer interrogatories in a 'responsive, full, complete and unevasive' manner. Plaintiff focuses on his contention that the requested information is equally as available to Defendant in other documents, but this is an interrogatory, not a request for production. In answering an interrogatory, a 'party cannot limit his answers to matters within his own knowledge and ignore information immediately available to him or under his control.' The amount of Plaintiff's own medical bills, and how those medical bills were paid, is information that is immediately available to him." (quoting *Miller v. Doctor's Gen. Hosp.*, 76 F.R.D. 136, 140 (W.D. Okla. 1977))); *U.S. ex rel. Brown v. Celgene Corp.*, No. CV 10-3165 GHK (SS), 2015 U.S. Dist. LEXIS 189371, at *13, 2015 WL 12731923 (C.D. Cal. July 24, 2015) ("'It is not a valid objection to state the requested information is already in the requesting party's control.'" (quoting *Wagner v. St. Paul Fire & Marine Ins. Co.*, 238 F.R.D. 418, 427 (N.D. W.Va. 2006))); *Pangborn v. L. A. Cty. Deputy Sheriffs Lieutenant Baudino*, CV 15-6812 AB(JC), 2018 U.S. Dist. LEXIS 226176, at *13, 2018 WL 6265055, (C.D. Cal. Sept. 27, 2018) ("To the extent defendants object that discovery requests in issue call for the production of information equally available to plaintiff, such objections are overruled. Multiple courts have unambiguously stated that this exact objection is insufficient to resist a discovery request."); *Nat'l Acad. of Recording Arts & Sciences, Inc. v. On Point Events, LP*, 256 F.R.D. 678, 682 (C.D. Cal. 2009) ("First, to the extent defendant objects that certain requests, such as Interrogatory no. 13, seek information equally available to plaintiff, courts have unambiguously stated that this exact objection is insufficient to resist a discovery request.") (citations omitted); *Kenneth v. Nationwide Mut. Fire Ins. Co.*, No. 03-CV-521F (Consent), 2007 U.S. Dist. LEXIS 83973, at *51, 2007 WL 3533887 (W.D.N.Y. Nov. 13, 2007) ("A requested party may not refuse to respond to the requesting party's discovery request on the ground that the requested information is in the possession of the requesting party.").

The exceptions to this rule are when the responding party establishes that answering the interrogatory would be disproportionate to the case's needs, unduly burdensome or expensive, or that obtaining the information or material from a nonparty or public source is more convenient or less burdensome or expensive.

[184] *E.g., In re Nat'l Lloyds Ins. Co.*, 449 S.W.3d 486, 489 (Tex. 2014) ("Scouring claim files in hopes of finding similarly situated claimants whose claims were evaluated differently from [Plaintiff's] is at best an 'impermissible fishing expedition.' Without more, the

As explained in Chapter 8, section 8-5:13, such an objection is nothing more than a colorful and wholly imprecise way of objecting to the discovery request's scope (i.e., it either seeks irrelevant information or documents or seeks information or documents not reasonably calculated to lead to the discovery of admissible evidence). As such, it really is not a proper objection.

9-5:3.14 The Responding Party's Failure to Provide Discovery

As explained in Chapter 8, section 8-5:14, it is improper to refuse to respond to any type of written discovery request because the requesting party has withheld discovery. Courts strongly disfavor "tit for tat" discovery practices.[185]

---

information sought does not appear reasonably calculated to lead to the discovery of evidence that has a tendency 'to make the existence of any fact that is of consequence to the determination of the action more probable or less probable.'") (citation omitted); *In re Marshall*, 617 S.W.3d 670, 674 (Tex. App.—San Antonio 2021, orig. proceeding) ("Discovery, even of potentially relevant or admissible evidence, may not be used as a costly fishing expedition."); *In re Muller*, 612 S.W.3d 701, 706 (Tex. App.—Amarillo 2020, orig. proceeding) ("Additionally, discovery may not be used as a fishing expedition or to impose unreasonable discovery expenses on the opposing party."); *In re Sun Coast Res., Inc.*, 562 S.W.3d 138, 147 (Tex. App.—Houston [14th Dist.] 2018, orig. proceeding) ("Requests not so reasonably tailored as to time, place, or subject matter are overbroad as a matter of law."); *In re Steadfast Ins. Co.*, No. 01-09-00235-CV, 2009 Tex. App. LEXIS 3556, at *3–4, 10–11, 2009 WL 1424634 (Tex. App.—Houston [1st Dist.] May 18, 2009, orig. proceeding) (mem. op.) ("Because request for production 28 and interrogatory 8 are overbroad and not narrowly tailored, they constitute an impermissible fishing expedition.").

185 *Cf.* Fed. R. Civ. P. 26(d)(2) ("[M]ethods of discovery may be used in any sequence; and . . . discovery by one party does not require any other party to delay its discovery."); *Nat'l Acad. of Recording Arts & Scis., Inc. v. On Point Events, LP*, 256 F.R.D. 678, 681 (C.D. Cal. 2009) ("As an initial matter, defendant extensively discusses in the joint stipulation plaintiff's failure to provide discovery to defendant. However, the motions before the Court are brought by plaintiff, not defendant, and discovery is not conducted on a 'tit-for-tat' basis."); *Acushnet Co. v. Birdie Golf Ball Co., Inc.*, 166 F.R.D. 42, 43 (S.D.Fla.1996) ("As is not uncommon, Defendants seek to emulate the perceived faults of their adversaries. The federal rules, however, contain no provision authorizing a litigant to behave only as well as his opponent. Instead, they require the utmost good faith of attorneys at all times. Defendants' counsel should not seek this Court's approval of a 'tit for tat' approach to litigation. Instead, let him lead by example, fulfill his obligations, and let the Court determine whether his opponent has failed to do so.") (citation omitted) (footnote omitted); *Lumbermens Mut. Casualty Ins. Co. v. Maffei,* No. 3:03-cv-262 JWS, 2006 U.S. Dist. LEXIS 67754, at *14 n.21, 2006 WL 2709835 (D. Alaska 2006) ("The court does not consider 'tit-for-tat' objections to discovery to be legitimate objections. If the opposing party is recalcitrant in responding to discovery requests, the rules provide a mechanism for compelling responses and/or imposing sanctions. The rules do not authorize one party to withhold discoverable material in retaliation for the opposing party's withholding of discoverable material.").

9-5:3.15 Harassment

Although a "harassment" objection is clearly a proper one,[186] as with harassment objections to production requests, it is difficult to envision a situation in which such an objection is a proper one to an interrogatory.[187]

9-5:3.16 Invasion of Protected Rights

An interrogatory that improperly invades a party's personal, constitutional, or property rights is objectionable.[188]

---

186 *E.g.*, Tex. R. Civ. P. 191.3(c)(3) (by signing a written-discovery request, the attorney certifies that the discovery was not sought for the purpose of harassment), 192.6(b) (allowing a party to ask for protection from harassing discovery), 215.3 (providing that harassing discovery is a ground for sanctions); *Alexson, Inc. v. McIlhany*, 798 S.W.2d 550, 553 (Tex. 1990) (orig. proceeding) (The scope of discovery is also "limited by the legitimate interest of the opposing party to avoid overbroad requests, harassment or the disclosure of privileged information."); *Jampole v. Tourchy*, 673 S.W.2d 569, 573 (Tex. 1984) (orig. proceeding) (same), *disapproved of on other grounds by Walker v. Parker*, 827 S.W.2d 833, 842 (Tex. 1992) (orig. proceeding); *In re John Crane, Inc.*, No. 01-03-00698-CV, 2003 Tex. App. LEXIS 9684, at *5, 2003 WL 22682613 (Tex. App.—Houston [1st Dist.] Nov. 13, 2003, orig. proceeding) (mem. op.) ("A party resisting discovery, however, cannot simply make conclusory allegations that the requested discovery is unduly burdensome or unnecessarily harassing."); *In re State Farm Lloyds*, No. 04-98-00018, 1998 Tex. App. LEXIS 2072, at *11, 1998 WL 161260 (Tex. App.—San Antonio Apr. 8, 1998, orig. proceeding) (not designated for publication) ("The right to broad discovery is limited by the opposing party's right to be free from harassment and the burden of overly broad requests.").

187 See Chapter 8, section 8-5:15 (discussing harassment objections to production requests).

188 Tex. R. Civ. P. 192.6(b) (authorizing protection from a discovery request that invades a "personal, constitutional, or property right."); *see In re Baylor Univ.*, 01-20-00439-CV, 2020 Tex. App. LEXIS 9200, at *13, 2020 WL 6878411 (Tex. App.—Houston [1st Dist.] Nov. 24, 2020, orig. proceeding) ("[T]he person noticed for deposition has the right to protection 'from undue burden, unnecessary expense, harassment or annoyance, or invasion of personal, constitutional, or property rights.'"); *In re Hamilton*, 13-20-00254-CV, 2020 Tex. App. LEXIS 7378, at *8, 2020 WL 5494503, (Tex. App.—Corpus Christi Sept. 10, 2020, orig. proceeding) (same); *In re Cook*, 05-19-01283-CV, 2020 Tex. App. LEXIS 3999, at *7, 2020 WL 2552881 (Tex. App.—Dallas May 20, 2020, orig. proceeding) (mem. op.) (same); *In re H.E.B. Grocery Co.*, No. 13-14-00023-CV, 2014 Tex. App. LEXIS 1777, at *18–20, 2014 WL 700749 (Tex. App.—Corpus Christi Feb. 18, 2014, orig. proceeding) (mem. op.) ("As a general rule, the party who seeks to limit discovery by asserting a privilege has the burden of producing evidence to support its assertions. . . . This rule applies when a party asserts privacy rights as a ground for limiting discovery. A party asserting that privacy rights protect information from disclosure must present evidence showing 'a particular, articulated and demonstrable injury.'" (quoting *In re Crestcare Nursing & Rehab. Ctr.*, 222 S.W.3d 68, 73 (Tex. App.—Tyler 2006, orig. proceeding))); *In re Does 1-10*, 242 S.W.3d 805, 812 (Tex. App.—Texarkana 2007, orig. proceeding) ("One of the reasons to ask [for a protective order] is to protect the movant from 'invasion of personal, constitutional, or property rights.'" (quoting Tex. R. Civ. P. 192.6(b))); *cf. Soto v. City of Concord*, 162 F.R.D. 603, 616 (N.D. Cal. 1995) ("Federal Courts ordinarily recognize a constitutionally based right of privacy that can be raised in response to discovery requests.").

9-5:3.17 A Claim's or Defense's Invalidity

A responding party cannot properly object to an interrogatory because the cause of action or defense to which it relates is invalid unless the cause of action or defense has been dismissed pursuant to special exception, a dismissal motion, or summary judgment.[189] The only exception to this rule concerns exemplary-damages claims.

Under Chapter 41 of the Texas Civil Practice and Remedies Code, net-worth discovery is prohibited unless the court enters a "written order" finding that "the claimant has demonstrated a substantial likelihood of success on the merits of a claim for exemplary damages."[190] A party served with an interrogatory seeking information about its net worth before the requisite finding is made should object to the interrogatory as "premature" because the prerequisite for net-worth discovery has not been established.

9-5:3.18 Confidentiality

As with production requests, an objection to an interrogatory because it seeks "confidential" or "proprietary" information generally is improper.[191] Rather, the proper way for a responding party to deal with its contractual and other "confidentiality" obligations is to disclose any allegedly confidential information pursuant to a protective order's terms.[192]

---

[189] *Lunsford v. Morris*, 746 S.W.2d 471, 473 (Tex. 1988) (orig. proceeding) (holding that discovery is based on matters relevant to the claims pleaded and a party need not prove a claim before being entitled to discovery on it), ***disapproved of on other grounds by Walker v. Parker***, 827 S.W.2d 833, 842 (Tex. 1992) (orig. proceeding); ***In re Citizens Supporting Metro Sols., Inc.***, No. 14-07-00190-CV, 2007 Tex. App. LEXIS 8550, at *8 (Tex. App.—Houston [14th Dist.] Oct. 18, 2007, orig. proceeding) (mem. op.) (holding that "the scope of discovery is measured by the live pleadings regarding the pending claims" and, "as here, where the trial court [has] not ruled on the merits of any of the claims, then the scope of discovery in the mandamus proceeding will be based on the pleadings"); ***In re Rogers***, 200 S.W.3d 318, 324 (Tex. App.—Dallas 2006, orig. proceeding) (holding that, when a petition was "broadly pleaded" and had not been challenged or narrowed through special exceptions or any other pleading vehicle, the responding party "cannot attempt to limit the scope of discovery through objection").

[190] Tex. Civ. Prac. & Rem. Code § 41.0115(a). Discovery about a party's net worth for exemplary-damages purposes is discussed in Chapter 4, section 4-3:4.

[191] See Chapter 8, section 8-5:18 (discussing confidentiality objections to production requests).

[192] ***E.g., In re Cont'l Ins. Co.***, 994 S.W.2d 423, 425 (Tex. App.—Waco 1999) ("Individuals cannot protect relevant information from discovery by confidentiality provisions in contracts, even settlement agreement. The private agreement between two individuals does ***not*** override the discovery rules. The rules of civil procedure specifically allow for a method to produce relevant information to the opposing party in litigation while at the same time keep the information confidential.") (emphasis added), ***mandamus granted on other grounds sub nom., In re Union Pac. Res. Co.***, 22 S.W.3d 338, 341 (Tex. 1999); ***cf. Benney v. Midwest Health, Inc.***, No. 17-2548-HLT-KGG, 2018 U.S. Dist. LEXIS 196331, at *14–15, 2018 WL 6042591 (D. Kan. Nov. 19, 2018) ("It is well settled that confidentiality does not act as a bar to discovery and is not grounds to withhold documents or information from discovery. 'A concern for protecting confidentiality does not equate to privilege.' While a confidentiality objection may be appropriate when a party seeks a protective order limiting the parties' use or disclosure of confidential information, it is generally not a valid objection to withholding discovery altogether." (quoting *High Point SARL v. Spring Nextel Corp.*, No. 09-2269-CM-DJW,

9-5:3.19 Compound or Calls for a Legal Conclusion

Oftentimes an objection is interposed to an interrogatory because it allegedly is compound or calls for a legal conclusion. The former objection is always without merit and the latter often is without merit. The fact that an interrogatory is "compound" does not make it objectionable. To the contrary, the Texas discovery rules contemplate that interrogatories may cover more than one topic.[193]

Similarly, a legal-conclusion objection often is without merit because Texas Rule 197.1 specifically permits a party to ask its opponent if it makes a "specific legal . . . contention" and to apply law to fact.[194] As pointed out by one federal court in construing the comparable federal interrogatory rule: "Federal Rule of Civil Procedure 33 draws a distinction between questions of fact or of the application of law to fact on one hand and pure questions of law on the other. Courts police this implied distinction by 'permitting interrogatories involving law and fact' but declining to require response to those 'asking solely about questions of law.'"[195]

2011 U.S. Dist. LEXIS 101700, 2011 WL 4008009 (D. Kan. Sept. 9, 2011))); *EEOC v. Thorman & Wright Corp.*, 243 F.R.D. 426, 430 (D. Kan. 2007) ("[A]s this Court previously has held, 'a concern for protecting confidentiality does not equate to privilege.' With that said, a party may request the court enter a protective order pursuant to [Federal Rule] 26(c) as a means to protect such confidential information." (footnote omitted) (quoting *DIRECTV, Inc. v. Puccinelli*, 224 F.R.D. 677, 682 (D. Kan. 2004))). See also Chapter 8, section 8-5:18 (discussing confidentiality objections to production requests). A nonparty owner of confidential information has the right to seek protection from its disclosure. Tex. R. Civ. P. 192.6(a) ("[A]ny other person affected by the discovery request[] may move . . . for an order protecting that person from the discovery sought.").

193 *See* Tex. R. Civ. P. 190.2(b)(3), 190.3(b)(3) (providing that each discrete subpart of an interrogatory counts as a separate interrogatory); *cf. Silva v. McKenna*, No. C11-5629 RBL/KLS, 2012 U.S. Dist. LEXIS 63973, at *9, 2012 WL 1596971 (W.D. Wash. May 7, 2012) ("The interrogatories are compound. . . . However, Plaintiff is correct that the compound nature of these interrogatories would not absolve Defendants from answering them. Even if each interrogatory is counted as two or three, the number would simply count toward Plaintiff's limit of twenty-five interrogatories under [Federal Rule 33].") (citations omitted); *Kelly v. FedEx Ground Package Sys., Inc.*, No. 3:10-cv-01265, 2011 U.S. Dist. LEXIS 45180, at *21, 2011 WL 1584764 (S.D. W. Va. Apr. 26, 2011) ("[B]eing 'compound' does not make [an interrogatory] objectionable"); *Jordan v. Chapnick*, No. 1:07-cv-202-OWW-MJS (PC), 2010 U.S. Dist. LEXIS 84634, at *4–5, 2010 WL 2899057 (E.D. Cal. July 15, 2010) ("The Court agrees that the interrogatories are compound. . . . However, the compound nature of these interrogatories does not absolve Plaintiff from answering them. Even if each interrogatory is counted as two . . . [,] Defendant is still within [Federal] Rule 33's limit of no more than twenty-five interrogatories.") (citations omitted); *see Kates v. Packer*, No. 3:13-cv-01525, 2017 U.S. Dist. LEXIS 113516, at *7–8, 2017 WL 3118774 (M.D. Pa. July 21, 2017) ("The defendants object that this interrogatory poses a compound question, but the mere fact that an interrogatory addresses multiple topics does not render it unduly burdensome."). See Chapter 9, section 9-4 (discussing numbers of interrogatories).

194 Tex. R. Civ. P. 197.1.

195 *Perez v. KDE Equine, LLC*, No. 3:15-CV-00562-CRS, 2017 U.S. Dist. LEXIS 570, at *19, 2017 WL 56616 (W.D. Ky. Jan. 4, 2017) (quoting *Everest Nat'l Ins. Co. v. Santa Cruz Cnty. Bank*, No. 15-cv-02085-BLF, 2016 U.S. Dist. LEXIS 149975, at *10, 2016 WL 6311876 (N.D. Cal. Oct. 28, 2016)); *accord In re Ohio Execution Protocol Litig.*, No. 2:11-CV-1016, 2018 U.S. Dist. LEXIS 200371, 2018 WL 6177169 (S.D. Ohio Nov. 27, 2018) ("A court must distinguish between interrogatories which properly seek to identify the legal theory of a claim

9-5:3.20 Assumes Facts Not in Evidence

On occasion, a responding party will object to an interrogatory because it purportedly "assumes facts not in evidence" or "calls for speculation." These objections generally are improper because (1) they are trial objections, (2) a responding party has a duty of reasonable inquiry in responding to interrogatories, (3) an opposing party is entitled to discovery regarding "any matter that is not privileged and is relevant to the subject matter of the pending action" or that "appears reasonably calculated to lead to the discovery of relevant evidence."[196] In other words, the objection is contrary to the purpose of discovery, which is to learn facts.

---

or defense or to narrow the focus of the case and improper interrogatories which relate to pure questions of law."); *AngioScore, Inc. v. TriReme Med., Inc.*, No. 12-cv-03393-YGR (JSC), 2014 U.S. Dist. LEXIS 173700, at *25–26, 2014 WL 7188779 (N.D. Cal. Dec. 16, 2014) ("Federal Rule of Civil Procedure 33(a)(2) provides that 'an interrogatory is not objectionable merely because it asks for an opinion or contention that relates to fact or the application of law to fact.' However, 'interrogatories directed to issues of "pure law"—i.e., abstract legal issues not dependent on the facts of the case' are not permitted.") (citations omitted); *Gov't Benefits Analysts, Inc. v. Gradient Ins. Brokerage, Inc.*, No. 10-2558-KHV-DJW, 2012 U.S. Dist. LEXIS 113223, at *14–15, 2012 WL 3292850 (D. Kan. Aug. 13, 2012) ("The Court begins by overruling Defendants' objection to Interrogatory No. 13 as calling for legal conclusions. [Federal Rule] 33(a)(2) clearly states that '[a]n interrogatory is not objectionable merely because it asks for an opinion or contention that relates to fact or the application of law to fact.' To the extent that it calls for application of law to the facts of this case, Plaintiffs' Interrogatory No. 13 is within the bounds of [Federal] Rule 33."); *Hunt v. Fields*, No. CIV S-09-3525 FCD GGH P, 2011 U.S. Dist. LEXIS 76418, at *16–17, 2011 WL 2709250 (E.D. Cal. July 8, 2011) ("Defendant objected to these interrogatories on the grounds that they are vague, ambiguous, compound, presume as true facts that have not been established as true, call for a legal conclusion, and are not reasonably calculated to lead to the discovery of admissible evidence. These objections are waived and overruled. An interrogatory is not objectionable merely because it asks for an opinion or contention that relates to fact or the application of law to fact[.]" (quoting Fed. R. Civ. P. 33(a)(2))).

196 *See* Tex. R. Civ. P. 192.3(a); *cf. Sutton v. Mgmt. & Training Corp.*, No. 1:13-cv-1344 - AWI-JLT, 2015 U.S. Dist. LEXIS 11399, at *15–16, 2015 WL 402024 (E.D. Cal. 2015) ("As an initial matter, the objection that an interrogatory 'assumes facts not in evidence' is not proper in the course of discovery."); *Vickers v. JP Morgan Chase N.A.*, No. SA-12-CA-31-XR, 2013 U.S. Dist. LEXIS 208157, at *26–27 (W.D. Tex. 2013) ("JPMC's objections, 'assumes facts not in evidence, and assumes that such recording is required,' do not appear to be sufficient to avoid providing a further response, as the purpose of discovery is to learn facts.") (footnote omitted); *Richards v. Convergys Corp.*, Nos. 2:05-CV-00790-DAK, 2:05-CV-00812 DAK, 2006 U.S. Dist. LEXIS 63567, at *4–5 (D. Utah Sept. 5, 2006) (rejecting speculation and assumes-facts-not-in-evidence objections to an interrogatory because the responding party "has a duty to make a reasonable inquiry for information in its possession"); *McGrath v. Cosco, Inc.*, No. 98-cv-1502, 1999 U.S. Dist. LEXIS 5893, at *3, 1999 WL 269920 (E.D. Pa. Apr. 21, 1999) ("That an interrogatory assumes facts not in evidence is not a valid objection in the context of discovery."); *see also Sprint Communs. Co. L.P. v. Charter Communs.*, No. 20-cv-2161-JWB-TJJ, 2021 U.S. Dist. LEXIS 66408, at *8, 2021 WL 1265135 (D. Kan. Apr. 6, 2021) ("Individual Defendants also object to this RFP as assuming facts not in evidence 'regarding the purported "loss" or "deletion" of information.' The Court overrules this objection as an improper objection to Sprint's discovery request." (footnotes omitted)); *Two Rivers Pipeline & Constr. Co. v. Cimarex Energy Co.*, No. PE:19-CV-00049-DC-DF, 2020 U.S. Dist. LEXIS 206472, at *13–14, 2020 WL 6379302 (W.D. Tex. Sept. 14, 2020) ("Two Rivers objects to Cimarex's RFP Nos. 36–38, 40–46, and 51 as assuming facts not in evidence.

9-6 Signature and Verification

The party's attorney or a pro se party must sign the interrogatory response.[197] In addition, the responding party must sign most interrogatory answers under oath.[198] The verification must be unqualified and cannot be made "to the best of [the party's] knowledge."[199] There are two exceptions to the rule requiring an unqualified verification. *First*, the responding party may qualify its verification by stating that an answer was "based on information obtained from other persons."[200] This conforms to the reality of how entities often gather responsive information. *Second*, "a party need not sign answers to interrogatories about persons with knowledge of relevant facts, trial witnesses, and legal contentions"[201] because such matters generally are determined by the party's attorney's investigation or involve issues of strategy that are not within the responding party's personal knowledge.

Amended or supplemental interrogatory answers must be signed by the party under oath only if the original answers were required to be signed under oath.[202] As

---

Cimarex asserts that federal courts have rejected this objection. As noted by the Western District of Texas, '[a]ssuming facts not in evidence may be the basis for an objection during trial or some other evidentiary hearing. This, however, is discovery.'" (quoting *Vickers v. JP Morgan Chase N.A.*, SA-12-CA-31-XR, 2013 U.S. Dist. LEXIS 208157, at *26 & n.99, 2013 WL 12134153 (W.D. Tex. Feb. 22, 2013))); *Baker v. Cty. of Missaukee*, No. 1:09-cv-1059, 2013 U.S. Dist. LEXIS 154072, at *19, 2013 WL 5786899 (W.D. Mich. Oct. 28, 2013) ("Plaintiff is correct that defendant's objection to request [for admission] 8 on the ground that it 'assumes facts not in evidence' is meritless. This trial objection has no place in discovery practice and is overruled."); *Michilin Prosperity Co. v. Fellowes Mfg. Co.*, No. 04-1025 (RWR/JMF), 2006 U.S. Dist. LEXIS 32064, at *3, 2006 WL 1441575 (D.D.C. May 23, 2006) (rejecting a speculation objection to requests for admission because "to the extent that the requests may call for factual speculation, Michilin should have stated that it was unable to admit or deny and then explained why it could not truthfully admit or deny the request").

197 Tex. R. Civ. P. 191.3(a), 197 cmt 2 to 1999 change.

198 *Double Diamond-Del., Inc. v. Alfonso*, 487 S.W.3d 265, 272 (Tex. App.—Corpus Christi 2016, no pet.) ("Texas Rule of Civil Procedure 197.2(d) requires that an individual responding to interrogatories must sign the answers under oath."). Because interrogatories must be answered by the party on whom they are served and generally answered under oath, emails from the responding party's attorney purporting to answer the interrogatories are insufficient. *See, e.g., Villarreal v. El Chile, Inc.*, 266 F.R.D. 207, 211 (N.D. Ill. 2010). Oral responses also are insufficient. *See, e.g., Sharp v. Broadway Nat'l Bank*, 784 S.W.2d 669, 671 (Tex. 1990). The party's attorney need not verify the interrogatory answers. Tex. R. Civ. P. 197.2(d).

199 *See Ebeling v. Gawlik*, 487 S.W.2d 187, 189 (Tex. App.—Houston [1st Dist.] 1972, no writ) (construing former Texas Rule 168); *see also Kramer v. Lewisville Mem'l Hosp.*, 858 S.W.2d 397, 407 (Tex. 1993) ("The supplemental answers were verified based on mere 'knowledge and belief,' while [former] Texas Rule of Civil Procedure 168(5) requires *original* answers to interrogatories to be verified under oath. We have held similar requirements not to be satisfied by verification upon 'information and belief.'") (citation omitted).

200 Tex. R. Civ. P. 197.2(d); *see In re Swepi L.P.*, 103 S.W.3d 578, 590 (Tex. App.—San Antonio 2003, orig. proceeding) ("The discovery rules specifically allow a party to state when facts in his or her answer are derived from some other source, such as an expert or another witness.").

201 Tex. R. Civ. P. 197.2(d).

202 Tex. R. Civ. P. 197 cmt. 2 to 1999 change; *accord Warriner v. Warriner*, 394 S.W.3d 240, 250 (Tex. App.—El Paso 2012, no pet.).

a practical matter, a responding party seldom should have to deal with verification issues in connection with supplemental or amended interrogatory answers. Formal supplementation or amendment is required only with respect to the identification of persons with knowledge of relevant facts and trial witnesses.[203] Parties normally will seek the identity of persons with knowledge of relevant facts and experts by means of Texas Rule 194 disclosures,[204] which need not be verified.[205] Also, a responding party need not verify interrogatory answers regarding persons with knowledge of relevant facts or trial witnesses.[206] If any other discovery requires supplementation or amendment, the responding party's attorney simply can write a letter to the requesting party's attorney providing the additional or corrected information, thereby relieving the responding party from the obligation of formal supplementation or amendment, including verification.

"The failure to sign or verify answers is only a formal defect that does not otherwise impair the answers unless the party refuses to sign or verify the answers after the defect is pointed out."[207]

---

[203] Tex. R. Civ. P. 193.5(a)(1).

[204] See Chapter 6, sections 6-3:3.5 and 6-3:3.14 (respectively discussing disclosures of persons having knowledge of relevant facts and testifying experts).

[205] Tex. R. Civ. P. 194.2(b)(5).

[206] Tex. R. 197.2(d)(2).

[207] Tex. R. Civ. P. 197 cmt. 2 to 1999 change.

CHAPTER 10

Requests for Admission—Texas Rule 198

10-1 Text of Rule 198

RULE 198. REQUESTS FOR ADMISSIONS

198.1. Request for Admissions

A party may serve on another party—no later than 30 days before the end of the discovery period—written requests that the other party admit the truth of any matter within the scope of discovery, including statements of opinion or of fact or of the application of law to fact, or the genuineness of any documents served with the request or otherwise made available for inspection and copying. Each matter for which an admission is requested must be stated separately.

198.2. Response to Requests for Admissions

(a) **Time for response.** The responding party must serve a written response on the requesting party within 30 days after service of the request.

(b) **Content of response.** Unless the responding party states an objection or asserts a privilege, the responding party must specifically admit or deny the request or explain in detail the reasons that the responding party cannot admit or deny the request. A response must fairly meet the substance of the request. The responding party may qualify an answer, or deny a request in part, only when good faith requires. Lack of information or knowledge is not a proper response unless the responding party states that a reasonable inquiry was made but that the information known or easily obtainable is insufficient to enable the responding party to admit or deny. An assertion that the request presents an issue for trial is not a proper response.

(c) **Effect of failure to respond.** If a response is not timely served, the request is considered admitted without the necessity of a court order.

198.3. Effect of Admissions; Withdrawal or Amendment

Any admission made by a party under this rule may be used solely in the pending action and not in any other proceeding. A matter admitted under this rule is conclusively established as to the party making the admission unless the court permits the party to withdraw or amend the admission. The court may permit the party to withdraw or amend the admission if:

(a) the party shows good cause for the withdrawal or amendment; and

(b) the court finds that the parties relying upon the responses and deemed admissions will not be unduly prejudiced and that the presentation of the merits of the action will be subserved by permitting the party to amend or withdraw the admission.

10-1:1 2021 Amendment of Texas Rule 198

The 2021 amendments to the Texas Rules of Civil Procedure made one minor change to Rule 198 regarding requests for admission. Because Texas Rule 192.2, as amended effective January 1, 2021, generally "prohibits a party from serving discovery on another party until after the other party's initial disclosures are due,"[1] Rule 198.2(a), regarding the "time for response" to a request for admission was amended to conform with this change. That is, the portion of the Rule providing that a defendant served with a request for admission before its answer has fifty days to respond to the request was deleted.[2]

10-2 Requests for Admission in General

Texas Rule 198 provides for requests for admission[3]—a written request propounded by one party to another asking the other to admit or deny the truth of a specific matter

---

[1] Tex. R. Civ. P. 192.2(a).

[2] Before its amendment, Texas Rule 198.2(a) provided: "The responding party must serve a written response on the requesting party within 30 days after service of the request, except that a defendant served with a request before the defendant's answer is due need not respond until 50 days after service of the request."

[3] Requests for admission are perhaps the least used of the major discovery devices: disclosures, production requests, interrogatories, requests for admission, and depositions. *E.g.*, 8B Charles Alan Wright, *et. al.*, *Federal Practice and Procedure* § 2252 (3d ed. 2021) ("[Federal] Rule 36 has not been resorted to as much as some of the other discovery rules. . . ."); Robert K. Wise & Katherine Hendler Fayne, *A Guide to Properly Using and Responding to Requests for Admission Under the Texas Discovery Rules*, 45 St. Mary's L.J. 655, 657–58 (2014) ("Requests for admission are effective, but misunderstood and are perhaps the least used of the major discovery devices: disclosure requests, production requests, interrogatories, requests for admission, and depositions."). Despite their potential to eliminate unnecessary proof at trial, streamline discovery and motion practice, and reduce pretrial and trial expenses, they are used much less frequently than other discovery devices because of a perceived inability to obtain substantive concessions through their use. Robert K. Wise & Katherine Hendler Fayne, *A Guide to Properly Using and Responding to Requests for Admission Under the Texas Discovery Rules*, 45 St. Mary's L.J. 655, 658 (2014).

Among the many misconceptions about requests for admission is the proper plural form of "request for admission." Among the variations used are: requests for admission, request for admissions, and requests for admissions. *E.g., N.J. v. Del.*, 552 U.S. 597, 612–13 (2008) (request for admissions); *Société Nationale Industrielle Aérospatiale v. U.S. Dist. Ct. for S.D. Iowa*, 482 U.S. 522, 526, 544 n.29, 546 (1987) (requests for admission and requests for admissions); *Marino v. King*, 355 S.W.3d 629, 632, 633 (Tex. 2011) (per curiam) (requests for admission and requests for admissions); *El Apple I, Ltd. v. Olivas*, 370 S.W.3d 757, 765 (Tex. 2012) (request for admissions); Tex. R. Civ. P. 198.1 (request for admissions); Tex.

"within the scope of discovery, including statements of opinion or of fact or of the application of law to fact, or the genuineness of any documents served with the request or otherwise made available for inspection and copying."[4] Like other written-discovery requests, requests for admission must be served no later than thirty days (and in some cases thirty-one or thirty-three days) before the discovery period ends.[5]

Although Texas Rule 198 is included in the division of the Texas Rules regarding discovery, requests for admission are different from other discovery devices. Unlike depositions, disclosures, interrogatories, and production requests, whose primary

---

R. Civ. P. 198.2 (requests for admissions). The first—requests for admission—is the proper plural form of the discovery device. ***Webster's Third New International Dictionary of the English Language Unabridged*** 25a (Phillip Babcock Gove, *et al.* eds., 3d ed. 2002) ("Three-word compounds consisting of an initial noun plus prepositional phrase hyphened or open customarily pluralize the initial noun: . . . coat of mail coats of mail[.]"); Bryan A. Garner, *A Dictionary of Modern Legal Usage* 684–85 (3d ed. 2009) (discussing proper plural form of a compound noun such as "requests for admission").

4 Tex. R. Civ. P. 198.1. Like other written-discovery devices, requests for admission can only be served on a party. Tex. R. Civ. P. 198.1 ("A party may serve on another party . . . written requests that the other party admit the truth of any matter within the scope of discovery[.]"); *accord In re N.L.W.*, 534 S.W.3d 102, 111 (Tex. Civ. App.—Texarkana 2017, no pet.) ("A party is allowed, under the Texas Rules of Civil Procedure, to serve requests for admissions on another party."); *Lynd v. Bass Pro Outdoor World, Inc.*, No. 05-12-00968-CV, 2014 Tex. App. LEXIS 2801, at *29, 2014 WL 1010120 (Tex. App.—Dallas Mar. 12, 2014, pet. denied) (mem. op.) ("A party may request admissions only from other parties."); *In re Estate of Ayala*, 986 S.W.2d 724, 726 (Tex. App.—Corpus Christi 1999, no pet.) ("The Texas Rules of Civil Procedure limit the use of requests for admissions [sic] and interrogatories to parties only.").

In addition to Texas Rule 198, Texas Rules 190, 191, 192, 193, 195, and 215 relate to requests for admission.

5 Tex. R. Civ. P. 198.1. If the requests are served by mail, they must be served at least thirty-three days before the discovery period's end. Tex. R. Civ. P. 21a(c). If they are served by fax after 5:00 p.m. local time of the recipient, the requests must be served at least thirty-one days before the discovery period ends. Tex. R. Civ. P. 21a(b)(2); *see Paskauskiene v. Tex. Workforce Comm'n*, No. 02-12-00358-CV, 2013 Tex. App. LEXIS 9900, at *2–3, 2013 WL 4017472 (Tex. App.—Fort Worth Aug. 8, 2013, pet. denied) (mem. op.) ("Paskauskiene served the requests on TWC's counsel by facsimile on February 7, 2012 at 5:35 p.m. TWC's counsel mailed responses to the requests on March 9, 2012. [Texas] Rule 198.2 provides that '[t]he responding party must serve a written response [to requests for admissions] on the requesting party within 30 days after service of the request.' If a response is not timely served, the request is considered admitted without the necessity of a court order. Documents served after 5:00 p.m. of the local time of the recipient are deemed served the following day. Thus, Paskauskiene's requests were deemed served February 8, 2012, and TWC's responses were due March 9, 2012. The record contains a certificate of service showing that TWC's counsel mailed the responses to Paskauskiene by first class mail on March 9, 2012. Because proper service by mail is complete upon mailing and because Paskauskiene received the responses on March 11, 2012, within three days of mailing, TWC's responses were timely and thus not admitted.") (citations omitted).

Because Texas Rule 21a does not address when service by email is complete, it presumably is complete upon sending unless opposing counsel does not receive the email. *Cf.* Fed. R. Civ. P. 5(b)(2)(E) (noting that electronic service "is complete upon filing or sending, but is not effective if the filer or sender learns that it did not reach the person to be served[.]")

purpose is to discover facts or to obtain information and documents, requests for admission were *not* designed for these purposes. As recently explained by the Texas Supreme Court:

> "Requests for admission are a tool, not a trapdoor." They primarily serve "to simplify trials by eliminating matters about which there is no real controversy, but which may be difficult or expensive to prove." When used "as intended," requests for admissions are useful in "addressing uncontroverted matters or evidentiary ones like the authenticity or admissibility of documents."[6]

Because requests for admission were not designed to obtain facts or information, they should not be used for those purposes. For example, they are not "intended to be used as a demand upon a plaintiff or defendant to admit that he had no cause of action or ground of defense[,]"[7] and the Texas Supreme Court has shown great antipathy to requests for admission that asks a party to admit disputed ultimate facts.[8] Requests for admissions also should not be used to circumvent rules or discovery-control plans limiting the number of interrogatories.[9]

---

[6] *Medina v. Zuniga*, 593 S.W.3d 238, 244 (Tex. 2019) (quoting *U.S. Fid. & Guar. Co. v. Goudeau*, 272 S.W.3d 603, 610 (Tex. 2008), *Sanders v. Harder*, 227 S.W.2d 206, 208 (Tex. 1950), and *Wheeler v. Green*, 157 S.W.3d 439, 443 (Tex. 2005) (per curiam)); *accord Marino v. Kerry*, 355 S.W.3d 629, 630 (Tex. 2011) (per curiam); *Stelly v. Papania*, 927 S.W.2d 620, 622 (Tex. 1996).

[7] *Medina v. Zuniga*, 593 S.W.3d 238, 244 (Tex. 2019) (quoting *Sanders v. Harder*, 227 S.W.2d 206, 208 (Tex. 1950)); *Marino v. Kerry*, 355 S.W.3d 629, 630 (Tex. 2011) (per curiam) ("King's requests here, however, asked essentially that Marino admit to the validity of his claims and concede her defenses—matters King knew to be in dispute. Requests for admission were never intended for this purpose."); *Stelly v. Papania*, 927 S.W.2d 620, 622 (Tex. 1996) (Former Texas Rule 169 "was never intended to be used as a demand upon a plaintiff or defendant to admit that he had no cause of action or ground of defense." (quoting *Sanders v. Hader*, 227 S.W.2d 206, 208 (Tex. 1950))).

[8] *E.g.*, *Medina v. Zuniga*, 593 S.W.3d 238, 245 (Tex. 2019); *Marino v. Kerry*, 355 S.W.3d 629, 630 (Tex. 2011) (per curiam); *Stelly v. Papania*, 927 S.W.2d 620, 622 (Tex. 1996) (discussing former Texas Rule 169). Recently, the Texas Supreme Court, after noting that "[o]ur rules do not, strictly speaking, prohibit merits-preclusive requests for admissions," pointed out that "[j]ust as a defendant may answer the claims against him with a general denial, he may also deny a merits-preclusive request for admission for which the other party bears the burden of proof . . . [e]specally at the outset of discovery." *Medina v. Zuniga*, 593 S.W.3d 238, 245 (Tex. 2019).

[9] *Cf. Misco, Inc. v. U.S. Steel Corp.*, 784 F.2d 198, 206 (6th Cir. 1986) ("Misco's filing of 2,028 'requests for admissions [sic]' was both an abuse of the discovery process and an improper attempt to circumvent the local district court rule which limited the number of interrogatories."); *Martin Marietta Materials, Inc. v. Bedford Reinforced Plastics, Inc.*, No. 3:2003-57, 2007 U.S. Dist. LEXIS 32228, at *9, 2007 WL 1300772 (W.D. Pa. May 2, 2007) (ordering the plaintiff to respond to certain requests for admission because they were "not an attempt by Bedford to put forth interrogatories in the disguise of a request for admission without being subject to the limits in Federal Rule of Civil Procedure 33"); *Whitaker v. Belts Concepts of Am., Inc. (In re Olympia Holding Corp.)*, 189 B.R. 846, 853 (Bankr. M.D. Fla. 1995) ("Requests for admissions [sic] and interrogatories are not interchangeable procedures. . . . Utilizing interrogatories disguised as requests for admissions [sic] in an attempt to circumvent a local rule limiting the number of interrogatories is an abuse of the discovery process.") (citation omitted); *Phillips Petroleum Co. v. N. Petroleum Co.*, No. 84 C 2028, 1986

10-2:1 Form of Requests for Admissions

Requests for admission, like other written-discovery requests, must be in writing.[10] A typical request begins with the statement: "Admit that ________" or "Admit the truth of the following statement: ______________."

"Each matter for which an admission is requested must be stated separately."[11] Thus, for example, a request for admission cannot ask the responding party to admit every allegation in a pleading.[12] Requests for admission should be drafted so that they are simple and concise and can be answered readily by the responding party with a simple admit, deny, or statement that, after reasonable inquiry, the information known or easily obtainable is insufficient to enable the responding party to admit or deny the request.[13]

U.S. Dist. LEXIS 19750, at *1, 1986 WL 11004 (N.D. Ill. Sept. 29, 1986) ("The court agrees with the magistrate that Phillips' service on [the defendant] . . . of 2068 separate requests for admission appears to be an attempt to circumvent the limit of Local Rule 9(g) on the number of interrogatories.").

[10] Tex. R. Civ. P. 198.1.

[11] Tex. R. Civ. P. 198.1; *see Hendler v. N. Shore Boat Works, Inc.*, No. 13-03-00273-CV, 2004 Tex. App. LEXIS 6617, at *3, 2004 WL 1632653 (Tex. App.—Corpus Christi July 22, 2004, no pet.) (mem. op.) (Texas Rule 198.1 "does not specify the precise form admissions shall take, other than that each matter for which an admission is requested should be stated separately."); *cf. Kajeet, Inc. v. Qustodio, LLC*, No. SA CV 18-1519-JAK (PLAx), 2019 U.S. Dist. LEXIS 227979, at *10, 2019 WL 8060078 (C.D. Cal. Oct. 22, 2019) ("RFAs are required to be simple and direct, and should be limited to singular relevant facts."); *Downey v. Trenary*, No. C17-1024-JCC-MAT, 2018 U.S. Dist. LEXIS 62003, at *4 (W.D. Wash. 2018) ("Because the purpose of requests for admission is to narrow the issues of the case, 'the requesting party bears the burden of setting forth its requests simply, directly, not vaguely or ambiguously, and in such a manner that they can be answered with a simple admit or deny without an explanation, and in certain instances, permit a qualification or explanation for purposes of clarification. . . . To facilitate clear and succinct responses, the facts stated within the request must be singularly, specifically, and carefully detailed.'" (quoting *Henry v. Champlain Enters., Inc.*, 212 F.R.D. 73, 77 (N.D.N.Y. 2003))); *U.S. ex. rel. Englund v. L.A. Cty.*, 235 F.R.D. 675, 684 (E.D. Cal. 2006) ("Requests for admissions [sic] may not contain compound, conjunctive, or disjunctive (e.g., 'and/or') statements."); *Herrera v. Scully*, 143 F.R.D. 545, 549 (S.D.N.Y. 1992) ("[E]ach request for admissions [sic] must be direct, simple and 'limited to singular relevant facts,' so that 'it can be admitted or denied without explanation.'" (citations omitted) (quoting *U.S. v. Consol. Edison Co.*, No. CV-88-0049 (RJD), 1988 U. S. Dist. LEXIS 14547, at *5, 1988 WL 138275 (E.D.N.Y. Dec. 15, 1998)), and 8B Charles Alan Wright & Arthur R. Miller, *Federal Practice and Procedure*, § 2258 (1970))).

[12] *E.g., Birdo v. Hammers*, 842 S.W.2d 700, 701 (Tex. App.—Tyler 1992, writ denied) (holding that a request for admission asking the defendant to admit that "each allegation made in the Amended Original Petition filed in this case is true" was improper).

[13] *Cf. Vickers v. Thompson*, No. 1:15-cv-00129-SAB (PC), 2017 U.S. Dist. LEXIS 141079, at *9 (E.D. Cal. Aug. 31, 2017) ("Because admissions are designed to limit factual issues in a case, 'the requesting party bears the burden of setting forth its requests simply, directly, not vaguely or ambiguously, and in such a manner that they can be answered with a simple admit or deny without an explanation, and in certain instances, permit a qualification or explanation for purposes of clarification. . . .'" (quoting *Jones v. McGuire*, No. 2:08-CV-2607 MCE CKD, 2012 U.S. Dist. LEXIS 87040, at *18—19, 2012 WL 2376290 (E.D. Cal. June 22, 2012))); *Uber Promotions, Inc. v. Uber Techs., Inc.*, No. 1:15cv206-MW/GRJ, 2016 U.S. Dist. LEXIS 188280, at *4 (N.D. Fla. May 26, 2016) (same); *Sparton Corp. v. U.S.*, 77 Fed. Cl. 10, 18–19 (Ct. Cl. 2007) ("[F]ederal courts have long required that requests for

Ordinarily the facts to be admitted should be set forth in the request for admission.[14] Accordingly, except when the request relates to establishing the authenticity or admissibility of a document, incorporation by reference usually is not permitted.[15] This limitation, however, is flexible, and incorporation by reference may be permitted depending on the request's complexity. For example, if the request asks a single, straightforward question about an attached document or one readily available to the responding party, the request likely will be found to be proper.[16]

---

admission be simple, direct, and concise so that they can be admitted or denied with little or no explanation or qualification," and noting the long required practice that each matter seeking a response "be *separately* set forth in a request for admission."); *Martin Marietta Materials, Inc. v. Bedford Reinforced Plastics, Inc.*, No. 3:2003-57, 2007 U.S. Dist. LEXIS 32228, at *6, 2007 WL 1300772 (W.D. Pa. May 2, 2007) (mem. op.) ("Requests for admission should be phrased in such a manner that the responding party need only respond with 'yes' or 'no,' 'denied' or 'admitted' or otherwise claim a privilege with minimal explanation."); *T. Rowe Price Small-Cap Fund, Inc. v. Oppenheimer & Co.*, 174 F.R.D. 38, 46 (S.D.N.Y. 1997) (noting that requests for admission must "be simple and concise and state facts singly so that they can easily and coherently be admitted or denied").

14 *Cf. Layne Christensen Co. v. Purolite Co.*, No. CIV.A 09-2381-JWL-GLR, 2011 U.S. Dist. LEXIS 6737, at *29 (D. Kan. Jan. 25, 2011) (discussing cases).

15 *Cf. Layne Christensen Co. v. Purolite Co.*, No. CIV.A 09-2381-JWL-GLR, 2011 U.S. Dist. LEXIS 6737, at *29–30 (D. Kan. Jan. 25, 2011) (discussing cases); *Vergara v. City of Waukegan*, No 04 C 6586, 2007 U.S. Dist. LEXIS 82562, at *5, 2007 WL 3334501 (N.D. Ill. Nov. 6, 2007) ("The Court agrees requests that require reliance on documentation of facts outside the requests themselves are generally considered improper. Usually facts admitted in an answer to a request for admission should be ascertainable by examination of the request and only a certain amount of incorporation by reference, in exceptional circumstances, is allowed.") (footnote omitted); *Martin Marietta Materials, Inc. v. Bedford Reinforced Plastics, Inc.*, No. 3:2003-57, 2007 U.S. Dist. LEXIS 32228, at *7, 2007 WL 1300772 (W.D. Pa. May 2, 2007) (mem. op.) ("The Court finds that . . . the . . . requests . . . shall be subject to a protective order as . . . [they] . . . do not comply with [Federal] Rule 36 because of their form which references outside matters that must be reviewed prior to answering each request."); *U.S. v. Watchmakers of Switz. Info. Ctr., Inc.*, 25 F.R.D. 197, 200 (S.D.N.Y. 1959) (noting that objections to requests for admission because they incorporate by reference other documents are generally improper because "the facts admitted in an answer to a request for admissions [sic] should be ascertainable merely by examination of the request and of the answer").

Another criticism of the practice of incorporating documents by reference in a request for admission is that it generates needless confusion and "unjustly casts upon the [responding parties] the burden of determining at their peril what portions of the incorporated material contain relevant matters of fact which must either be admitted or denied." *Layne Christensen Co. v. Purolite Co.*, No. CIV.A 09-2381-JWL-GLR, 2011 U.S. Dist. LEXIS 6737, at *29 (D. Kan. Jan. 25, 2011) (quoting *SEC v. Micro-Moisture Controls, Inc.*, 21 F.R.D. 164, 166 (S.D.N.Y. 1957)); *accord U.S. v. Consol. Edison Co.*, No. CV-88-0049 (RJD), 1988 U.S. Dist. LEXIS 14547, at *5, 1988 WL 138275 (E.D. N.Y. Dec. 15, 1998).

16 *Compare Layne Christensen Co. v. Purolite Co.*, No. CIV.A 09-2381-JWL-GLR, 2011 U.S. Dist. LEXIS 6737, at *29–33 (D. Kan. Jan. 25, 2011) (ordering the plaintiffs to answer a few requests for admission regarding the subject matter of other patents and an article written by one of the plaintiffs), *and U.S. v. Gwinn*, Civ. A. No. 5:06-00267, 2008 U.S. Dist. LEXIS 27974, at *29–30, 2008 WL 906486 (S.D.W. Va. Mar. 31, 2008) (ordering the defendant to respond to requests for admission related to medical records incorporated by reference because they were not voluminous and because the requests were not ambiguous), *with Martin Marietta Materials, Inc. v. Bedford Reinforced Plastics, Inc.*, No. 3:2003-57, 2007 U.S. Dist. LEXIS 32228, at 7, 2007 WL 1300772 (W.D. Pa. May 2, 2007) ("The majority of

Requests for admission may contain definitions and instructions, including an instruction (or warning) that "a failure to timely respond to the requests shall result in each matter being admitted by you and not subject to further dispute." Nonetheless, no definitions, instructions, or warning are required. For example, in *Hendler v. North Shore Boat Works, Inc.*,[17] the plaintiff argued that the trial court improperly granted the defendant summary judgment based on deemed admissions because the requests did not have instructions or warn him about the consequences of not timely answering them.[18] In affirming the judgment, the Corpus Christi Court of Appeals held, among other things, that no instructions or warning were needed because Texas Rule 198.1 "does not specify the precise form the [requests for] admission should take, other than that each matter for which an admission is requested should be stated separately."[19]

Like other written-discovery devices, requests for admission are not filed,[20] but must be served on all parties to the action.[21] In addition, the parties "must retain the original or exact copy of [the requests] during the pendency of the case and any related appellate proceedings begun within six months after judgment is signed, unless otherwise provided by the trial court."[22]

Bedford's requests seek to have Martin admit or deny that a reference 'teaches and/or describes' specific claims of the patents-in-suit in light of this Court's claim construction. This goes beyond the permissible parameters of a request for admission. . . . Not only does this drafting of requests require Martin to reference at least two documents outside of a request to answer it, but the requests of such a character number over five hundred. [Such] requests . . . shall be subject to a protective order as these requests do not comply with [Federal] Rule 36 because of their form which references outside matters that must be reviewed prior to answering each request.") (footnote omitted), *SEC v. Micro-Moisture Controls, Inc.*, 21 F.R.D. 164, 166 (S.D.N.Y. 1957) (holding that a request for admission that referenced multi-page affidavits and stock-purchase transactions was improper), *and Sparton Corp. v. U.S.*, 77 Fed. Cl. 10, 19 (Fed. Cl. 2007) ("The Court agrees with Defendant that Plaintiff's requests for admission are much too complicated to answer with a simple admit or deny. Plaintiff incorporates by reference its voluminous Pretrial Submission and asks Defendant to admit to large sections of the document. Because the referenced sections of the document contain numerous different facts, Defendant cannot possibly be expected to respond with a simple admit or deny, without explanation or qualification.").

17 *Hendler v. N. Shore Boat Works, Inc.*, No. 13-03-00273-CV, 2004 Tex. App. LEXIS 6617, 2004 WL 1632653 (Tex. App.—Corpus Christi July 22, 2004, no pet.) (mem. op.).

18 *Hendler v. N. Shore Boat Works, Inc.*, No. 13-03-00273-CV, 2004 Tex. App. LEXIS 6617, at *2, 2004 WL 1632653 (Tex. App.—Corpus Christi July 22, 2004, no pet.) (mem. op.).

19 *Hendler v. N. Shore Boat Works, Inc.*, No. 13-03-00273-CV, 2004 Tex. App. LEXIS 6617, at *3, 2004 WL 1632653 (Tex. App.—Corpus Christi July 22, 2004, no pet.) (mem. op.). Some courts "have concluded that the inclusion of [such a warning] strengthens the case for deemed admissions in connection with a motion to amend or withdraw the requests [where] the litigants are *pro se*." *Abdul-Waali v. Restart, Inc.*, No. 10-0567-CV-W-JTM, 2011 U.S. Dist. LEXIS 132582, at *5, 2011 WL 5599257 (W.D. Mo. Nov. 17, 2011); *accord Jones-Bey v. Chief*, No. 3:16-cv-723-DJH, 2020 U.S. Dist. LEXIS 91006, at *9, 2020 WL 2736436 (W.D. Ky. May 26, 2020); *U.S. v. One Sony Wega 42" Plasma TV*, No. 06-2843, 2008 U.S. Dist. LEXIS 20192, at *7 n.1 (W.D. Tenn. Mar. 7, 2008).

20 Tex. R. Civ. P. 191.4(a)(1)–(2).

21 Tex. R. Civ. P. 191.5.

22 Tex. R. Civ. P. 191.4(d).

10-2:2 Scope of Requests for Admission

Requests for admission may inquire about any discoverable matter other than matters covered by Texas Rule 195, which relates to testifying experts.[23] Thus, they are an inexpensive method of discovery and, when properly worded, can be an effective way to narrow the issues, to establish undisputed facts, and to authenticate documents and establish the evidentiary foundation for their admissibility.

10-2:2.1 Statements of Fact or Opinion or the Application of Law to Fact

By Texas Rule 198.1's express language, requests can properly seek admissions about (1) "statements of opinion[,]" (2) statements of . . . fact[,]" or (3) the "application of law to fact."[24] Although requests for admission applying law to fact are permissible, requests regarding pure questions or conclusions of law are not.[25] However, because

---

[23] Tex. R. Civ. P. 195.1 ("A party may obtain information concerning testifying expert witnesses only through disclosure under this rule and through depositions and reports as permitted by this rule."), 198.1 ("A party may serve on another party . . . written requests that the other party admit the truth of any matter within the scope of discovery, statements of opinion or of fact or of the application of law to fact, or the genuineness of any documents served with the request or otherwise made available for inspection and copying."); *In re Nat'l Lloyds Ins. Co.*, 532 S.W.3d 794, 814 (Tex. 2017) (orig. proceeding) (Texas "Rule 195 addresses the *methods* for obtaining such information, limiting testifying-expert discovery to that acquired through disclosures, expert reports, and oral depositions of expert witnesses." (footnote omitted) (quoting *In re Ford Motor Co.*, 427 S.W.3d 396, 397 (Tex. 2014) (orig. proceeding) (per curiam))); *In re Young*, 410 S.W.3d 542, 549 (Tex. App.—Beaumont 2013, no pet.) (holding that requests for admission cannot be used to obtain information about testifying experts). See also Chapter 6, section 6-3:3.14, and Chapter 7, section 7-4 (discussing discovery concerning testifying experts).

Requests for admission, however, in theory, can be used to obtain information about discoverable consulting expert witnesses. Tex. R. Civ. P. 195 cmt. 1 to 1999 change ("This rule does not limit the permissible methods of discovery concerning consulting experts whose mental impressions or opinions have been reviewed by a testifying expert."). See also Chapter 7, section 7-5 (discussing discovery concerning consulting experts).

[24] Tex. R. Civ. P. 198.1. Examples of these are as follows:

Statement of fact: "Defendant is a lawyer practicing in Dallas, Texas," "John Smith was Defendant's Chief Executive Officer when the contract at issue was signed," and "ABC Corporation is a Texas corporation."

Statement of opinion: "Plaintiff believes that its employee, Smith, can enter into contracts on its behalf" and "Defendant electric utility believes that the wires on its transmissions poles must comply with applicable provisions of the National Electric Safety Code."

Application of law to fact: "Smith acted as Plaintiff's agent in negotiating the contract at issue with Defendant," "Defendant was negligent when she ran the red light," and "After Defendant former employee left Plaintiff's employ, he violated his covenant not to compete by soliciting business from ABC Corporation for his new business."

[25] *Garcha v. Chatha*, No. 05-17-00084-CV, 2018 Tex. App. LEXIS 2622, at *10, 2018 WL 1755391 (Tex. App.—Dallas Apr. 12, 2018, no pet.) (mem. op.) ("A request for admission asking a party to admit or deny a purely legal issue is improper, and a deemed admission involving a purely legal issue is of no substantive, evidentiary effect."); *In re Sting Soccer Grp., LP*, No. 05-17-00317-CV, 2017 Tex. App. LEXIS 11197, at *22, 2017 WL 5897454 (Tex. App.—Dallas Nov. 30, 2017, orig. proceeding) (mem. op.) ("Parties may not be compelled to answer legal

Texas Rule 197.1 specifically permits a party to ask another party if it is making a "specific legal or factual contention,"[26] it is proper to ask a party about its legal contentions or the factual bases for them. Accordingly, the requesting party properly can request the responding party to admit that it is, or is not, asserting a particular cause of action or affirmative defense or to admit that its cause of action or defense is, or is not, based on specified facts.

Admissions of law are not binding on the court and have no legal effect or evidentiary value.[27] The distinction between a request for an admission of law and one for the

---

conclusions, and such conclusions do not bind the court. An admission of a purely legal issue is of no effect."); *Maswoswe v. Nelson*, 327 S.W.3d 889, 896–97 (Tex. App.—Beaumont 2010, no pet.) (same); *Elliot v. Newsome*, No. 01-07-00692-CV, 2009 Tex. App. LEXIS 569, at *4–6, 2009 WL 214551 (Tex. App.—Houston [1st Dist.] Jan. 20, 2009, no pet.) (mem. op.) ("Unambiguous contracts are enforced as written. The meaning of an unambiguous contract is a question of law. Here the contract says builder must pay the commission. The deemed admissions that purport to interpret the agreement in a different way cannot be given effect because they are contrary to the express terms of the agreement."); *Cedyco Corp. v. Whitehead*, 253 S.W.3d 877, 881 (Tex. App.—Beaumont 2008, pet. denied) ("The deemed admissions Numbers 8 and 9 . . . are purely questions of law and, therefore, are improper summary judgment evidence."); *Boulet v. State*, 189 S.W.3d 833, 838 (Tex. App.—Houston [1st Dist.] 2006, no pet.) ("The rule regarding requests for admission does not contemplate or authorize admissions to questions involving points of law. Furthermore this court has previously held that requests for admission merely constituting admissions of law are not binding on the court and a party is not precluded from proving a fact necessary to a cause or defense.") (citation omitted); *Neal v. Wis. Hard Chrome, Inc.*, 173 S.W.3d 891, 894 (Tex. App.—Texarkana 2005, no pet.) ("Answers merely constituting admissions of law are not binding on the court.").

26 Tex. R. Civ. P. 197.1; *see* Tex. R. Civ. P. 192.3(j) ("A party may obtain discovery of any other party's legal contentions and the factual bases for those contentions.").

27 *E.g., In re Sting Soccer Grp., LP*, No. 05-17-00317-CV, 2017 Tex. App. LEXIS 11197, at *22, 2017 WL 5897454 (Tex. App.—Dallas Nov. 30, 2017, orig. proceeding) (mem. op.) ("An admission of a purely legal issue is of no effect."); *Williams v. Am. First Lloyds Ins.*, No. 02-12-00318-CV, 2013 Tex. App. LEXIS 7293, at *8–9, 2013 WL 2631141 (Tex. App.—Fort Worth June 13, 2013, pet. denied) (mem. op.) ("While answers constituting admissions of law are not binding on a court, requests for admission may properly ask a party to apply the law to a set of facts. Answers to these types of requests are competent summary judgment evidence.") (citations omitted); *Stephenson v. Perata*, No. 2-08-375-CV, 2009 Tex. App. LEXIS 3172, at *4, 2009 WL 1270907 (Tex. App.—Fort Worth May 7, 2009, no pet.) (mem. op.) ("Admissions of law are not binding on a court."); *Luke v. Unifund CCR Partners*, No. 2-06-444-CV, 2007 Tex. App. LEXIS 7096, at *5, 2007 WL 2460327 (Tex. App.—Fort Worth Aug. 3, 2007, no pet.) (mem. op.) ("While answers constituting admissions of law are not binding on a court, a request for admission may properly ask a court to apply law to a set of facts. Answers to these types of requests are proper summary judgment evidence.").

Requests for admission based on the application of law to hypothetical facts are improper. *Cf. Hopfinger v. City of Nashville*, No. 3:18-CV-1523-NJR, 2020 U.S. Dist. LEXIS 42006, at *6–7, 2018 WL 6171780 (S.D. Ill. Nov. 26, 2020) ("Hopfinger is asking Defendants to admit conclusions based upon assumptions and what-if scenarios (e.g., Hopfinger's final 2017 earnings had she worked 2,080 hours, her years of service at age 62, her total pension if she lived to be 83, and the percent of her final earnings she would be entitled to for 36 years of service). While the Court agrees that these requests are related to the facts of the case, they are presented as impermissible hypothetical questions."); *Buchanan v. Chi. Transit Auth.*, No. 16-cv-4577, 2016 U.S. Dist. LEXIS 168983, at *14, 2016 WL 116591 (N.D. Ill. Dec. 7, 2016) ("Since requests to admit 'must be connected to the facts of the case, courts application of law to fact often is not obvious.[28] One way to determine if the request asks

---

do not permit "hypothetical" questions within requests for admission.'" (quoting *Morley v. Square, Inc.*, Nos. 4:14cv172, 4:10cv2243 SNLJ CONSOLIDATED, 2016 U.S. Dist. LEXIS 318, at *11, 2016 WL 28990 (E.D. Mo. Jan. 4, 2016))); *Parsons v. Best Buy Stores, L.P.*, No. 3:09CV771, 2010 U.S. Dist. LEXIS 49274, at *4–5, 2010 WL 2243980 (S.D.W. Va. May 19, 2010) (same); *Friedman v. Godiva Chocolatier, Inc.*, No. 09cv977-L (BLM), 2010 U.S. Dist. LEXIS 108862, at *4, 2010 WL 4009660 (S.D. Cal. Oct. 13, 2010) (same).

[28] *Cf. Oliva v. Cox Communs. Las Vegas, Inc.*, No. 2:18-cv-01718-RFB-NJK, 2018 U.S. Dist. 199461, at *7, 2018 WL 6171780 (D. Nev. Nov. 26, 2018) ("[T]he distinction between the application of law to fact and a legal conclusion is not always easy to draw." (quoting *Benson Tower Condo. Owners Ass'n v. Victaulic Co.*, 105 F. Supp. 3d 1184, 1196 (D. Or. 2015))); *U.S. ex rel. Bibby v. Mortg. Inv'rs Corp.*, 323 F.R.D. 424, 428 (N.D. Ga. 2017) (same); *Perez v. KDE Equine, LLC*, No. 3:15-CV-00562-CRS, 2017 U.S. Dist. LEXIS 570, at *25 (W.D. Ky. Jan. 4, 2017) (same); *In re NCAA Student-Athlete Name & Likeness Licensing Litig.*, No. 09-cv-01967 CW (NC), 2012 U.S. Dist. LEXIS 143486, at *12, 2012 WL 4743121 (N.D. Cal. Oct. 3, 2012) (same). *Compare, e.g.*, *District of Columbia ex rel. Z-Modular, LLC v. MCN Build, Inc.*, No. 18-cv-2947 (RJL/GMH), 2020 U.S. Dist. LEXIS 124719, at *7 (D.D.C. July 15, 2020) ("Courts have held that, although an RFA that seeks a pure legal conclusion may be improper, 'where the question of the meaning of the document is at issue in the case, a request directed to another party seeking admission or denial of a document's meaning or intent by that party as stated in the request relates to a statement [of] fact, and [is] authorized by [Federal] Rule 36.' That is true '[e]ven if the meaning of a document or the intent of the parties as to a contractual provision is the issue ultimately to be decided.'" (quoting *Sigmund v. Starwood Urban Retail VI, LLC*, 236 F.R.D. 43, 46 (D.D.C. 2006))), *Whole Woman's Health All. v. Hill*, No. 1:18-cv-01904-SEB-MJD, 2020 U.S. Dist. LEXIS 35880, at *9, 2020 WL 1028040 (S.D. Ind. Mar. 20, 2020) ("Nos. 1-5 do not require Defendants to, for example, interpret a statute, but instead ask them simply to apply the law to the facts and state whether or not certain situations would require a license by Defendant Indiana Department of Health."), *Gurzi v. Penn Credit Corp.*, No. 6:19-cv-823-Orl-31EJK, 2019 U.S. Dist. LEXIS 229559, at *5 (M.D. Fla. Dec. 30, 2019) (holding that a request for admission asking the defendant that it "used an 'automatic dialing system' within the meaning of the TCPA" did not ask for a legal conclusion); *Taylor v. Cty. of Calaveras*, No. 1:18-cv-00760-BAM, 2019 U.S. Dist. LEXIS 206485, at *15 (E.D. Cal. Nov. 26, 2019) (explaining that a request for admission asking "whether the Deputy Defendants had probable cause to arrest Plaintiff Michael Scott Taylor for a violation of California Penal Code § 246.3" did not seek a legal conclusion because it was "tied to the specific facts of the case and involves a legal determination that is typically within the knowledge of a trained police officer"), *U.S. ex rel. Bibby v. Mortg. Inv'rs Corp.*, 323 F.R.D. 424, 428 (N.D. Ga. 2017) ("[E]xamples of permissible requests seeking the application of law to fact include: a request to admit that a corporation was a citizen of a particular state under 28 U.S.C. § 1332, a request to admit that 'Defendant used an "automatic dialing system" within the meaning of the TCPA,' a request that 'relate[d] to the interpretation of a contract at issue in [the] case,' a request to admit 'that no state law required an identified Defendant to contract with [plaintiff],' [and] a request to admit generally to a party's obligations as a matter of law under the contract at issue in the case[.]") (citations omitted), *Embotteladora Electropura S.A. de C.V. v. Accutek Packaging Equip. Co.*, No. 16-cv-0724-GPC (DHB), 2017 U.S. Dist. LEXIS 66148, at *11, 2017 WL 1550048 (S.D. Cal. May 1, 2017) ("Defendant's Request for Admission No. 20 validly sought admission of an application of law and fact by requesting Plaintiff admit that this instant dispute is governed by the substantive law of the State of California."), *AngioScore, Inc. v. TriReme Med., Inc.*, No. 12-cv-03393-YGR (JSC), 2014 U.S. Dist. LEXIS 173700, at *30–31, 2014 WL 7188779 (N.D. Cal. Dec. 12 2014) ("A request for admission calls for a legal conclusion when it purports to require a party to admit, for example, that a statute or regulation imposes a particular obligation. In contrast, a request which asks how a particular source of a legal obligation

applies to a given set of facts is permissible.") (citation omitted), *Brown v. Montoya*, No. CIV 10-0081 JB/ACT, 2013 U.S. Dist. LEXIS 35625, at *72, 2013 WL 1010390 (D.N.M. Mar. 8, 2013) ("The Plaintiffs' requests whether an individual Defendant's duty or authority includes implementing certain tasks or policies at issue in the case, like the RFAs asking if the Defendant is in charge with ensuring his or her department's compliance with law, are not asking a pure question of law without regard to the facts."), *Seropian v. Wachovia Bank, N.A.*, No. 10-80397-CIV-MARRA/JOHNSON, 2011 U.S. Dist. LEXIS 168934, at *10–11 (S.D. Fla. 2011) ("Request Nos. 37, 38, and 39 ask Wachovia to admit that it was obligated to comply with Florida Statutes Section 709.08 when dealing with Caruso's durable powers of attorney and Bleyer's CDs. Request No. 40 asks Wachovia to admit that the CDs were 'Pay-On-Death Accounts' within the meaning of Florida Statutes Section 655.82. Wachovia objects to these requests on the basis that they call for legal conclusions. . . . [T]he Court holds that Plaintiffs' requests do not call for naked conclusions of law. Instead, the requests merely ask for Wachovia's opinion on the application of law to the particular facts of this case."), *Stark-Romero v. Nat'l R.R. Passenger Co.*, 275 F.R.D. 551, 557 (D.N.M. 2011) (holding that a request for admission that the New Mexico Department of Transportation was responsible for administering the federal grade-crossing improvement program involved an application of law to fact), *Heartland Surgical Specialty Hosp., LLC v. Midwest Div., Inc.*, No. 05-2164-MLB-DWB, 2007 U.S. Dist. LEXIS 80182, at *17–18, 2007 WL 3171768 (D. Kan. Oct. 29, 2007) ("Here, the requests identified by Heartland appear to require no more than the application of law to the facts of the case. HCA Midwest requests 7, 10 and 11 merely seek to establish HCA Midwest's succession to contracts and whether Heartland meets certain requirements under federal laws, which are inquiries more of a factual than legal nature. Saint Luke's requests ask Heartland to admit that no state law required an identified Defendant to contract with Heartland and therefore directly relate to the facts of the case. Requests for admissions seeking the application of law to the facts of the case are proper under [Federal] Rule 36."), *Miller v. Holzmann*, 240 F.R.D. 1, 5 (D. D.C. 2006) (overruling a legal conclusion objection to requests for admission that asked whether a party's interest in a joint venture was assigned on a particular date and whether a joint venture was created to complete certain projects), *Sigmund v. Starwood Urban Retail* VI, LLC, 236 F.R.D. 43, 46 (D.D.C. 2006) (observing that "[a] request for admission that relates to the interpretation of a contract at issue in a case involves the application of law to the unique facts of that case and, therefore, would be permissible under the amended [Federal] Rule 36"), *In re A.I.T-A.*, No. 02-13-00164-CV, 2013 Tex. App. LEXIS 13757, at *16 n.15, 2013 WL 5967029 (Tex. App—Fort Worth Nov. 7, 2013, no pet) (mem. op.) ("While answers constituting admissions of law are not binding on a court, a request for admission may properly ask a party to apply the law to a set of facts. The parents cite no authority for their contention that whether termination is in a child's best interest is legal issue.") (citations omitted), *Duong v. Bank One, N.A.*, 169 S.W.3d 246, 251–52 (Tex. App.—Fort Worth 2005, no pet.) ("[R]equest number 6 asked appellants if Dao had authority to 'supply information determining the names or addresses of payees of instruments to be issued in [Duong's] name.' Although the language of the request tracks the language used in the statute, the inquiry itself is factual: the request asks whether or not the facts of the case fit the definition of one of the types of responsibility set forth in the statute."), *Hoffman v. Tex. Commerce Bank*, 846 S.W.2d 336, 339 (Tex. App.—Houston [14th Dist.] 1992, writ denied) (holding that requests for admission that the testator was of sound mind and not under undue influence were proper applications of law to fact); *Laycox v. Jaroma*, 709 S.W.2d 2, 4 (Tex. App.—Corpus Christi 1986, writ ref'd n.r.e.) (holding that a Jones Act defendant's requests for admission that the ship at issue was seaworthy and that the ship's owner, operator, and captain were not negligent were applications of law to fact), *and* Advisory Committee Note to Fed. R. Civ. P. 36, 1970 Amend.) (providing as an example of proper request for admission: "an admission that an employee acted in the scope of his employment"), *with, e.g., Transamerica Life Ins. Co. v. Bell*, No. 1:19-CV-1552-MHC, 2020 U.S. Dist. LEXIS 63808, at *5 (N.D. Ga. Feb. 3, 2020) (explaining that the following requests for admission called for legal conclusions:

for the application of law to fact is to review the pertinent Texas pattern jury charge on

---

(1) "Admit that you are barred from recovering any insurance proceeds in this action by O.C.G.A. § 53-1-5[,]" (2) "Admit that the death of Ms. Lisa Samuel constitutes a 'felonious killing; as contemplated by O.C.G.A. § 53-1-5[,]" and (3) "Admit that your Rockdale County conviction in *The State of Georgia v. LeTron Bell* is conclusive proof that you are barred from recovery by O.C.G.A § 53-1-5."), *U.S. v. Lain*, No. 17-cv-113-J, 2019 U.S. Dist. LEXIS 189717, at *7, 2019 WL 2051961 (D. Wyo. January 18, 2019) ("Mr. Lain requested Plaintiff to legally interpret various federal tax codes without indicating how such interpretations apply to his defenses or Plaintiff's assertions against him. For example, in Request for Admission No. 61, Mr. Lain states, 'Admit that, IRC § 7804(c) refers to assessments against IRS Officers and Employees who embezzle or otherwise fail to properly handle and account for money received in connection with the Internal revenue Laws [sic].' Mr. Lain does not indicate how an interpretation regarding the application of 26 U.S.C. § 7804 has any bearing on the facts of the case. Because a number of Mr. Lain's requests for admission relate to legal conclusions that appear to be unmoored from any relevant factual matters, Plaintiff properly objected to such requests."), *Davi v. Roberts*, No. 16-CV-5060 (RRM) (PK), 2018 U.S. Dist. LEXIS 166717, at *3, 2018 WL 4636805 (E.D.N.Y. Sept. 26, 2018) ("Although Davi is correct that [Federal] Rule 36 does allow requests to be made relating to 'the application of law to fact,' the question of whether speech addresses a matter of public concern is a question of law."), *Landberg v. Universal Trailer Corp. Horse/Livestock Grp.*, No. 1:06-CV-2971-BBM, 2008 U.S. Dist. LEXIS 129783, at *14–15 (N.D. Ga. Mar. 14, 2008) (holding that the following requests for admission called for legal conclusions: admit that Enkei "did not breach any duty to Universal," "cause or contribute to the accident at issue in this case," "was not negligent in its manufacture of the trailer wheels at issue in this case," and "was not negligent in its design of the trailer wheels at issue in this case"), *Miller v. Holzmann*, 240 F.R.D. 1, 5 (D.D.C. 2006) ("A request may be said to call for a legal conclusion when it purports to require a party to admit, for example, that a statute or regulation imposes a particular obligation."), *Disability Rights Council v. Wash. Metro. Area Transit Auth.*, 234 F.R.D. 1, 3 (D.D.C. 2006) ("In Request No. 1, WMATA asks plaintiffs to 'admit that in Maryland, D.C. and Virginia, any otherwise qualified voter who is a qualified person with a disability is entitled to vote by absentee ballot.' Plaintiffs objected to this request on the ground that it seeks a purely legal conclusion. The court agrees. There is nothing in this request that applies law to fact, let alone to the facts of this case. Moreover, plaintiffs have no special knowledge that would enable them to answer the request with any more certainty than WMATA or the court through judicial notice. Therefore, plaintiffs' objection was appropriate. In Request No. 18, WMATA asks plaintiffs to 'admit that consistent with the regulations, Metroaccess patrons must meet their rides at a designated pick-up spot, which is outdoors.' This request seeks a purely legal opinion about what is required by the FTA regulations. Specifically, it asks whether the regulations require that Metroaccess patrons meet the Metroaccess vehicle at a designated outdoor pick-up spot. Plaintiffs' objection was appropriate."), *U.S. ex rel. Bibby v. Mortg. Inv'rs Corp.*, 323 F.R.D. 424, 428 (N.D. Ga. 2017) ("Examples of requests held to seek conclusions of pure law are: 'generally-worded legal conclusions, without tying those conclusions to any facts presented,' (e.g., 'that it is unlawful to discriminate against someone on the basis of a disability[,]' requests to admit that provisions of statutes either do or do not apply to the case, [(*e.g.*, 'Admit that the FTA has not adopted any regulations nor published any guidance requiring drivers to compensate for traffic and accidents on their route' and 'admit that the Fair Labor Standards Act and the Florida Minimum Wage Act apply to its business and to Plaintiff's work at the time she was employed by the Defendant[,)'] and 'requests to admit that a party is or is not compliant with federal regulations'") (citations omitted), *San Diego Unified Port Dist. v. Nat'l Union Fire Ins. Co.*, No. 15cv1401-BEN-MDD, 2017 U.S. Dist. LEXIS 143389, at *8–9, 2017 WL 3877731 (S.D. Cal. Sept. 5, 2017) (holding that a request for admission asking the plaintiff to admit "that the California Regional Water Quality Control Board has the authority under the law to issue Cleanup and Abatement Orders in order to impose liability

the issue. If it is one that the jury would decide, it clearly is not a pure question of law.

Because requests for admission can ask questions regarding the application of law to fact, they, in theory, can seek admissions about the ultimate factual issue(s) in the action, such as whether the responding party breached the contract at issue, misappropriated the trade secrets or confidential information at issue, violated the covenant not to compete at issue, or was negligent.[29] Generally, however, there is little to be

---

against persons that it determines to be responsible for the discharge of pollutants" "poses a legal question"), *McDonald v. Equifax Inc.*, No. 3:15-CV-3212-B, 2017 U.S. Dist. LEXIS 30815, at *18, 2017 WL 879224 (N.D. Tex. Mar. 6, 2017) (holding that admissions that the plaintiff's "causes of action for negligence and negligence per se are preempted by the Fair Credit Reporting Act" "appear to be" conclusions of law, not fact), *Tobkin v. Fla. Bar*, 509 B.R. 731, 734 (S.D. Fl. 2014) (holding that a request for admission that the Florida Bar Association was not a governmental "entity" called for a conclusion of law), *Playboy Enter.,Tulip Computs. Int'l, B.V. v. Dell Comput. Corp.*, 210 F.R.D. 100, 108 (D. Del. 2002) (holding that a request for admission that a patent was valid called for a legal conclusion), *Playboy Enter., Inc. v. Welles*, 60 F. Supp. 2d 1050, 1057 (S.D. Cal. 1999) (holding, in a trademark-infringement, trademark-dilution, and unfair-competition case, that a request for admission asking the defendant to admit that she was a public figure under the case law "required the defendant to make an improper conclusion of law"), *U.S. v. Block 44, Lots 3, 6, Plus W. 80 Feet of Lots 2 and 5*, 177 F.R.D. 695 (M.D. Fla. 1997) (holding that a request for admission that the plaintiff had the burden of proof was an improper question of law), *Golden Valley Microwave Foods, Inc. v. Weaver Popcorn Co.*, 130 F.R.D. 92, 96 (N.D. Ind. 1990) (holding that a request for admission that certain patent claims were invalid was an improper question of law), *Currie v. U.S.*, 111 F.R.D. 56, 59 (M.D.N.C. 1986) (holding that a request for admission that the defendant owed a legal duty to the plaintiff was an improper question of law), *Morris v. Marshall Cty. Bd. of Educ.*, 560 F. Supp. 43, 45–46 (N.D.W. Va. 1983) (holding that a request for admission that the removal of the action to federal court was proper was an improper question of law), *Elliot v. Newsome*, No. 01-07-00692-CV, 2009 Tex. App. LEXIS 569, at *4–6, 2009 WL 214551 (Tex. App.—Houston [1st Dist.] Jan. 20, 2009, no pet.) (mem. op.) (holding that requests for admission regarding an unambiguous contract's interpretation were improper questions of law), *Fort Bend Cent. Appraisal Dist. v. Narserus*, 844 S.W.2d 857, 858–59 (Tex. App.—Texarkana 1992, writ denied) (holding that a request for admission that a tax-appraisal result was a clerical error was a question of law), *and Neal v. Wis. Hard Chrome, Inc.*, 173 S.W.3d 891, 894 (Tex. App.—Texarkana 2005, no pet.) (holding that that a request for admission that the plaintiff was an employee of the defendant was an improper question of law).

[29] *See* Tex. R. Civ. P. 198.1 (providing that a request for admission can ask another party to "admit the truth of any matter within the scope of discovery, including statements of opinion or of fact or of the application of law to fact"), 198.2(b) ("An assertion that the request presents an issue for trial is not a proper response."); *cf. Casey v. Albertson's Inc.*, 362 F.3d 1254, 1256 (9th Cir. 2004) (enforcing deemed admissions that the defendant did not discriminate against the plaintiff on the basis of gender, her marital status, or her pregnancy); *999 Corp. v. C.I.T. Corp.*, 776 F.2d 866, 868–69 (9th Cir. 1985) (enforcing an admission that there was "an agreement" even though its existence was an ultimate issue in the case); *Pittman v. Wakefield & Assocs., Inc.*, No. 16-cv-02695-RBJ-KMT, 2017 U.S. Dist. LEXIS 192506, at *6, 2017 WL 5593287 (D. Colo. Nov. 21, 2017) ("Rule 36 of the Federal Rules of Civil Procedure 'allows litigants to request admissions to a broad range of matters, including ultimate facts, as well as applications of law to fact.'" (quoting *In re Carney*, 258 F.3d 415, 419 (5th Cir. 2001))); *Hart v. Dow Chem.*, No. 95C1811, 1997 U.S. Dist. LEXIS 15685, at *22, 1997 WL 627645, (N.D. Ill. Oct. 17, 1997) ("There is nothing improper about a request simply because it goes to an ultimate fact that may be dispositive of the case[.]"); *Cerghino v. Boeing Co.*, 873 F. Supp. 398, 401

gained from asking such requests because they invariably will be denied.[30]

In reality, requests for admission are most effectively used to confirm incidental but important facts in the action, such as the parties' relationship (e.g., employer-employee, independent contractor, agent-principal, manufacturer-distributor); the identity of a property's owner, lessor, or lessee; whether a relevant contract was entered into; the validity of signatures on a contract or other documents; whether a required demand or notice has been made or whether it was timely; whether a relevant meeting or conversation occurred at all or on a specific date or at a particular place; or a meeting's or conversation's participants or subject matter. Requests for admission also can ask for admissions about facts bearing on the court's jurisdiction.[31]

(D. Or. 1994) (enforcing an admission that contamination was not caused by the defendant even though determining causation in contamination cases "is often impossible").

[30] *See, e.g.*, *In re Hodge*, No. 12-02000314-CV, 2002 Tex. App. LEXIS 8776, at *11, 2002 WL 31769635 (Tex. App.—Tyler Dec. 11, 2002, orig. proceeding) (not designated for publication) ("The requests in the case at hand comprise the factual basis for Fitts and Gill's claims in the underlying proceeding. Hodge contests his liability on these claims as evidenced by his general denial. Consequently, Hodge was entitled to deny the requests, thereby identifying each as a disputed issue.") (citation omitted); *cf. Paramount Fin. Commc'ns, Inc. v. Broadridge Inv'r Cmty. Sols., Inc.*, No. 15-405, 2017 U.S. Dist. LEXIS 16802, at *3, 2017 WL 495784 (E.D. Pa. Feb. 7, 2017) ("Where, as here, issues in dispute are requested to be admitted, a denial is a perfectly reasonable response."); *Coleman v. So. Bank (In re Sportsman Link)*, Adv. No. 09-1058, 2011 Bank. LEXIS 5344, at *11, 2011 WL 7268049, (Bankr. S.D.N.Y. Sept. 28, 2011) ("Defendant's Requests for Admission sought to secure an admission from Trustee regarding the ultimate issue of insolvency. Where a request for admission asks the responding party to concede the ultimate issue of its case, rather than merely an undisputed fact or assertion, the Court finds that the responding party is within its rights to refuse to admit such a request.").

Although requests for admission regarding ultimate factual issues technically are proper under Texas Rule 198, the Texas Supreme Court has expressed great antipathy to such requests: "[A]s we have held for almost 70 years, they were 'never intended to be used as a demand upon a plaintiff or defendant to admit that he had no cause of action or ground of defense.'" *Medina v. Zuniga*, 593 S.W.3d 238, 244 (Tex. 2019) (quoting *Sanders v. Harder*, 227 S.W.2d 206, 208 (Tex. 1950)); *accord Marino v. King*, 355 S.W.3d 629, 632 (Tex. 2011) (per curiam); *Stelly v. Papania*, 927 S.W.2d 620, 622 (Tex. 1996) (per curiam). Accordingly, Texas courts almost always will allow a responding party to withdraw deemed merits-preclusive admissions under Texas Rule 198.3. See Chapter 10, section 10-7 (discussing the withdrawal or amendment of merits-preclusive admissions).

[31] *Motor Car Classics, LLC v. Abbott*, 316 S.W.3d 223, 231–33 (Tex. App.—Texarkana 2010, no pet.) (holding that deemed admissions established minimum contacts for personal jurisdiction); *Sw. Aviation Specialties, L.L.C. v. Wilmington Air Ventures IV, Inc.*, No. 02-08-062-CV, 2008 Tex. App. LEXIS 8707, at *13–14, 2008 WL 4938334 (Tex. App—Fort Worth Nov. 20, 2008, pet. denied) (mem. op.) (same); *cf. Fields v. Household Bank*, 280 F. Supp. 2d 530, 532 (N.D. Miss. 2003) (holding that a request for admission asking the plaintiff to admit that its claim exceeded the jurisdictional limit was proper in connection with the determination of whether diversity jurisdiction existed); *Oroco Marine, Inc. v. Nat'l Marine Serv., Inc.*, 71 F.R.D. 220, 221–22 (S.D. Tex. 1976) ("On March 18, 1976, the third party plaintiff submitted a written request for admissions [sic] of fact by the third party defendant which would establish that the corporate litigants to the third party action are of diverse citizenship as defined in 28 U.S.C. § 1332(c). Because a period in excess of 30 days has elapsed since service of the request without reply from the third party defendant, these jurisdictional

10-2:2.2 Mirror-Image (or Converse) Requests for Admission

A requesting party often will pair a request for admission with its opposite. For example, one request might ask the responding party to admit that "Smith was your employee when the accident occurred," whereas another request might ask it to admit the converse, "Smith was not your employee when the accident occurred." Although there is nothing inherently improper about such "mirror-image" or "converse" requests,[32] mirror-image admissions, which result if the responding party fails to respond to the requests[33] or admits both requests, are useless because they create a fact issue. As explained by the Houston (Fourteenth) Court of Appeals in *CEBI Metal Sanayi Ve Ticaret A.S. v. Garcia*:

> Summary judgment is appropriate only if no fact questions exist after resolving all doubts in the nonmovant's favor. Normally, admissions (whether admitted or deemed) serve this purpose, as they conclusively establish the facts stated therein. But because each of Garcia's requests was paired with its opposite, they conclusively established every proposition ***and its opposite as well***. When all were deemed admitted, they *created* fact questions rather than resolving them.
>
> Garcia cannot avoid this conflict by relying on half of his requests. We cannot pick and choose among controverted facts in a summary judgment record, and these admissions became part of that record when they were filed. Nor could Garcia have arranged for half the requests to be deemed admitted and the other half quietly ignored, as deeming occurs automatically without either motion or order.[34]

Until the Texas Supreme Court determines the effect of deemed mirror-image requests for admission, a prudent party served with such requests should not rely on the foregoing reasoning and simply fail to respond to the requests.

---

facts are deemed admitted. Therefore, the Court finds that jurisdiction based on diversity of citizenship exists over the third party action.") (citation omitted).

32 *Cf. Layne Christensen Co. v. Purolite Co.*, No. CIV.A 09-2381-JWL-GLR, 2011 U.S. Dist. LEXIS 6737, at *23 (D. Kan. Jan. 25, 2011) ("The Court finds nothing per se objectionable about 'converse' requests for admission that ask a party to admit one set of facts and then to admit the negative. . . . A party may admit one request and deny the other, moreover, or respond that it has insufficient information to admit or deny either request."); *Interland, Inc. v. Bunting*, No. 1:04-CV-444-ODE, 2005 U.S. Dist. LEXIS 36112, at *31, 2005 WL 2414990 (N.D. Ga. Mar. 31, 2005) (suggesting that mirror-image requests are proper).

33 Tex. R. Civ. P. 198.2(c) ("If a response is not timely served, the request is considered admitted without the necessity of a court order."). See also Chapter 10, sections 10-5 and 10-5:9 (discussing deemed admissions).

34 *CEBI Metal Sanayi Ve Ticaret A.S. v. Garcia*, 108 S.W.3d 464, 466–67 (Tex. App.—Houston [14th Dist.] 2003, no pet.); *accord Carter v. Perry*, No. 02-14-00185-CV, 2015 Tex. App. LEXIS 7133, at *15, 2015 WL 4297586 (Tex. App.—Fort Worth July 9, 2015, no pet.) (mem. op.); *Triple R. Auto Sales v. Fort Worth Transp. Auth.*, No. 2-08-173-CV, 2009 Tex. App. LEXIS 437, at *2–5, 2009 WL 161039 (Tex. App.—Fort Worth Jan. 22, 2009, no pet.) (mem. op.); *Luke v. Unifund CCR Partners*, No. 2-06-444-CV, 2007 Tex. App. LEXIS 7096, at *13–15, 2007 WL 2460327 (Tex. App.—Fort Worth Aug. 3, 2007, no pet.) (mem. op.). *But see Manafort Bros. v. State*, No. PC-2016-4542, 2018 R.I. Super. LEXIS 42, at *12–14 (R.I. Super. Ct. 2018) (granting summary judgment based on deemed mirror-image admissions because the responding party cannot use the converse admissions as summary judgment evidence).

10-2:2.3 Genuineness of Documents

Requests for admission can expedite the trial process by establishing evidentiary foundations for documents that would otherwise consume considerable trial time.[35] It is not, however, enough to ask the responding party to admit that a document is genuine (i.e., authentic);[36] rather, the requesting party also should ensure that all foundational questions needed for the document's admission into evidence are included in the requests. For example, if the party intends to establish that documents are "business records" under Texas Rule of Evidence 803(6), the requests for admission should establish not only the document's genuineness or authenticity, but also each of the hearsay exception's elements. Moreover, requests for admission properly can ask the responding party to admit the genuineness or authenticity, or establish the foundation for the admission, of documents belonging to an opposing party or a nonparty.[37]

---

[35] Tex. R. Civ. P. 198.1 (providing that requests for admission may inquire about "the genuineness of any documents").

[36] "In the English language authenticity and genuineness mean the same thing." *Caruso v. Coleman Co.*, No. 93-CV-6733, 1995 U.S. Dist. LEXIS 7934, at *21, 1995 WL 347003 (E.D. Pa. June 7, 1995); *see Sanchez Y Martin, S.A. de C.V. v. Dos Amigos, Inc.*, No. 17CV1943 LAB (JMA), 2018 U.S. Dist. LEXIS 101719, at *7, 2018 WL 3020192 (S.D. Cal. June 15, 2018) ("A document is genuine or authentic when it is what it claims to be."); *Inventio AG v. ThyssenKrupp Ams. Corp.*, No 08-874-RGA, 2013 U.S. Dist. LEXIS 116680, at *3 (D. Del. July 29, 2013) (same); *Black's Law Dictionary* at 151 (9th ed. 2009) (defining "authenticate" as "[t]o prove the genuineness of [a thing]" and "authentication" as, among other things, as "the act of proving something (as a document) is true or genuine, esp. so that it may be admitted into evidence").

To be admissible into evidence, a document not only must be relevant, it must also be "authentic." To authenticate evidence means to identify it by a competent witness's testimony (or otherwise as permitted by rules of evidence) to be what the proponent claims it is. Tex. R. Evid. 901(a) ("[A]uthentication . . . as a condition precedent to admissibility of evidence . . . requires the proponent to make a threshold showing that is satisfied by evidence sufficient to support a finding that the matter in question is what its proponent claims."); *see Tienda v. State*, 358 S.W.3d 633, 638 (Tex. Crim. App. 2012) ("Evidence has no relevance if it is not authentically what its proponent claims it to be. Rule 901(a) of the Rules of Evidence defines authentication as a 'condition precedent' to admissibility of evidence that requires the proponent to make a threshold showing that would be 'sufficient to support a finding that the matter in question is what its proponent claims.'") (footnote omitted).

"An admission as to the genuineness of a document is made subject to all pertinent objections to admissibility that could be made at trial." *Inventio AG v. ThyssenKrupp Ams. Corp.*, No 08-874-RGA, 2013 U.S. Dist. LEXIS 116680, at *3–4 (D. Del. July 29, 2013); *accord Caruso v. Coleman Co.*, No. 93-CV-6733, 1995 U.S. Dist. LEXIS 7934, at *24, 1995 WL 347003 (E.D. Pa. June 7, 1995).

[37] *Cf. Iron Workers Local No. 60 Annuity Pension Fund v. Solvay Iron Works, Inc.*, No. 5:15-CV-0054 (BKS/DEP), 2017 U.S. Dist. LEXIS 61394, at *9–10, 2017 WL 1458772 (N.D.N.Y. Apr. 24, 2017) ("The fact that they are being asked to admit the authenticity of documents they did not author does not necessarily provide a basis for refusing to admit authenticity because '[Federal] Rule 36 requires the responding party to make a reasonable inquiry, a reasonable effort, to secure information that is readily obtainable from persons and documents within the responding party's relative control to state fully those efforts.'" (quoting *Henry v. Champlain Enters., Inc.*, 212 F.R.D. 73, 78 (N.D.N.Y. 2003))); *Inventio AG v. ThyssenKrupp Ams. Corp.*, No 08-874-RGA, 2013 U.S. Dist. LEXIS 116680, at *9–12 (D. Del. July 29, 2013) (holding that "[t]here is nothing in [Federal] Rule 36 that suggests a

Under Texas Rule 198.1, the relevant document can be "served with the request or otherwise made available for inspection and copying."[38] In other words, the Rule does not require that the referenced document be attached to the requests for admission as an exhibit.[39] Rather, if the document has already been identified in the action (e.g., as an exhibit to a pleading or deposition transcript) or has been produced by the parties in discovery, it need not be attached to the set of requests for admission as long as the reference to it is clear. For example, a request asking the responding party to admit that the "Lease attached as Exhibit A to Plaintiff's Original Petition [or marked as Exhibit 1 to John Smith's deposition or produced by Plaintiff with the Bates Nos. 1-10] is a true and correct copy of the parties' lease" is proper.

The self-authentication provisions of Texas Rules 176.6(c) and 193.7 for documents produced respectively by nonparties and parties in response to Texas Rule 205 and 196 production requests[40] reduce somewhat the need to use admissions to establish

---

responding party does not have to respond to a request for admission simply because it did not create the documents" and ordering the plaintiff to admit or deny the authenticity of documents of its former agents); *Pasternak v. Kim*, No. 10-cv-5045 (LTS) (JLC), 2011 U.S. Dist. LEXIS 113998, *16, 2011 WL 4552389 (S.D.N.Y., Sept. 28, 2011) ("Kim has not cited to any authority for the proposition that a party need not respond to RFAs that certain documents are authentic because the party did not produce them. That is not surprising. RFAs are intended to narrow issues for trial, and if parties were constrained to use RFAs to authenticate only documents that had been produced by an opponent, the intent behind the Rule would be largely defeated."); *Heartland Surgical Specialty Hosp., LLC v. Midwest Div., Inc.*, No. 05-2164-MLB-DWB, 2007 U.S. Dist. LEXIS 80182, at *19, 2007 WL 3171768 (D. Kan. Oct. 29, 2007) (overruling objections to requests for admission because they required the plaintiff to admit the authenticity of documents produced by the defendants); *Doe v. Mercy Health Corp.*, No. 92-6712, 1993 U.S. Dist. LEXIS 13347, at *33 (E.D. Pa. Sept. 15, 1993) (Federal "Rule 36(a) is not limited in scope only to documents produced or authored by a party. . . ."); *In re Gulf Oil/Cities Serv. Tender Offer Litig.*, Nos. 87 Civ. 5253 (MBM), 87 CIV 8982 (MBM),1990 U.S. Dist. LEXIS 5009, at *8–13, 1990 WL 657537 (S.D.N.Y. May 2, 1990) (ordering the plaintiff to respond to requests for admission whose answers required it to review documents of a nonparty because the plaintiff and nonparty had parallel interests and had been closely cooperating in discovery in two related cases); *Berry v. Federated Mut. Ins. Co.*, 110 F.R.D. 441, 443 (N.D. Ind. 1986) (denying protection from requests for admission seeking to establish the authenticity of 244 exhibits because the trial would be document intensive and Federal Rule 36 was an appropriate tool for establishing the genuineness and authenticity of documents before trial).

Whether the responding party can authenticate the documents of the requesting party or a nonparty depends on the extent of the responding party's obligation to make a reasonable inquiry and the timing of the request. *Cf. Inventio AG v. ThyssenKrupp Ams. Corp.*, No. 08-874-RGA, 2013 U.S. Dist. LEXIS 116680, at *9–10 (D. Del. July 29, 2013); *In re Gulf Oil/ Cities Serv. Tender Offer Litig.*, Nos. 87 Civ. 5253 (MBM), 87 CIV 8982 (MBM), 1990 U.S. Dist. LEXIS 5009, at *8–13, 1990 WL 657537 (S.D.N.Y. May 2, 1990). If the requests are served early in discovery, the responding party can move the trial court to defer answers to the requests until sufficient discovery has been taken. The "reasonable inquiry" obligation is discussed in Chapter 5, section 5-3:1.

[38] Tex. R. Civ. P. 198.1.

[39] Tex. R. Civ. P. 198.1.

[40] Texas Rule 193.7 provides, in full:

> A party's production of a document in response to written discovery authenticates the document for use against that party in any pretrial proceeding or at trial unless—within ten days or a longer or shorter time ordered by the court, after the producing

the genuineness of documents. Because the self-authentication provisions only apply to the party producing the documents, in a multi-party action, requests for admission are still useful to anticipate, and perhaps to avoid, objections by parties who have not produced the documents.

10-3 Types of Admissions

There are two types of admissions: "express" and "deemed." An express admission is one in which the responding party expressly admits the request, in whole or in part, in its answer. A "deemed" admission occurs when the responding party fails to timely respond to the request[41] or when a trial court, in ruling on a motion regarding the sufficiency of a response to a request for admission, deems the request admitted because the response does not comply with Texas Rule 198's requirements.[42]

10-4 Number of Requests for Admission

The action's discovery-control plan, rather than Texas Rule 198, governs the number of requests for admission.[43] In Level 1 actions, each party is limited to fifteen requests for admission, including "discrete subpart[s]."[44] In contrast, the Texas discovery rules do not limit either the number of requests for admission or the number of sets of requests for admission in Level 2 and 3 actions.[45]

> party has actual notice that the document will be used—the party objects to the authenticity of the document, or any part of it, stating the specific basis for objection. An objection must be either on the record or in writing and must have a good faith factual and legal basis. An objection made to the authenticity of only part of a document does not affect the authenticity of the remainder. If objection is made, the party attempting to use the document should be given a reasonable opportunity to establish its authenticity.

Tex. R. Civ. P. 193.7. Texas Rule 176.6(c) provides that "[a] nonparty's production of a document authenticates the document for use against the nonparty to the same extent as a party's production of a document is authenticated for use against the party under [Texas] Rule 193.7." Tex. R. Civ. P. 176.6(c).

41 See Chapter 10, sections 10-2 and 10-5:9 (discussing deemed admissions).

42 See Chapter 10, section 10-8 (discussing motions to test the sufficiency of responses to requests for admission).

43 Tex. R. Civ. P. 190 (providing for three discovery levels: Levels 1, 2, and 3). See Chapter 2, section 2-3 (discussing the three discovery levels).

44 Tex. R. Civ. P. 190.2(b)(5). Texas Rule 190.2(b)(5)'s "discrete subpart" provision appears to conflict with the requirement in Texas Rule 198.1 that "[e]ach matter for which an admission is requested must be stated separately." The rules can be reconciled by interpreting the former as giving the responding party the option of answering a compound request and counting it as multiple requests against the 15-request limit rather than objecting to it. See Chapter 10, section 10-5:8.11 (discussing compound objections to requests for admission).

There is no limitation on the number of sets for requests for admission in a Level 1 action so long as the total number of requests does not exceed fifteen. *See* Tex. R. Civ. P. 190.2(b)(5).

45 Tex. R. Civ. P. 190.3–190.4. A Level 3 discovery-control order can limit the number of requests for admission. Tex. R. Civ. P. 190.4(b)(3) (allowing the court to place "appropriate limits on the amount of discovery").

As pointed out above, under Texas Rule 190.1, the limit on the number of requests for admission in a Level 1 action includes "[e]ach discrete subpart."[46] Although nothing in Texas Rule 190 or its comments explains what constitutes a discrete subpart for a request for admission, Comment 3 to Texas Rule 190 explains what constitutes a discrete subpart for an interrogatory: "While not susceptible of precise definition, a 'discrete subpart' is, in general, one that calls for information that is not logically or factually related to the primary interrogatory." The test should be same as that with respect to interrogatories.[47]

---

[46] Tex. R. Civ. P. 190.2(b)(5).

[47] See Chapter 9, section 9-4 (discussing what constitutes a discrete interrogatory subpart). In *Gamevice, Inc. v. Nintendo Co.*, No. 18-cv-01942-RS (TSH), 2019 U.S. Dist. LEXIS 143917 (N.D. Cal. Aug. 23, 2019), a federal magistrate judge decided whether a defendant's requests for admission violated the district judge's order limiting the parties to forty-five such requests. In doing so, the magistrate judge provided an excellent explanation of what constitutes a discrete subpart in the context of requests for admission:

> Some of the RFAs are more complicated, even though they follow the same structure. Gamevice highlights RFA 5 as an example. It asks Gamevice to "[a]dmit that the keytop of each of the 'shoulder buttons' and 'trigger buttons' on the GV157, GV157A, GV167, GV169, and GV189 rotates about a point provided at a position at an end of the keytop further from the horizontal center of the device." It asks Gamevice to admit that five of its devices have this feature in common.
>
> Gamevice's first objection to these RFAs is that they are compound and violate Judge Seeborg's order that each side is limited to 45 RFAs (other than for authentication purposes). Gamevice's theory is that if you ask someone to admit something about multiple things, then you've asked a number of RFAs equal to the number of things. For example, if you ask someone to admit that his computers are password-protected, and he owns five computers, that would be five RFAs. Or if you ask Toyota to admit that every car it sold last year had four wheels, you've asked 9.6 million RFAs.
>
> The Court disagrees. Asking whether a group of things all have the same characteristic is a question about similarity. It's true that the question requires an answer as to each thing, but the essence of the question is whether there is a point of commonality among the things. This is a good use of RFAs, which are designed to remove issues from contention if they are not really in dispute. For example, RFA 18 asks Gamevice to "[a]dmit that each of GV140, GV141, GV150, GV156, GV157, GV160, GV161, have not been certified under Apple's MFi program." Presumably, Gamevice knows which of its devices have been certified under Apple's MFi program, and in one swoop this RFA seeks to determine if certification is a contested issue in this lawsuit. A response to this RFA just tells Nintendo whether or not there is a fight about that point. All of these RFAs have this quality that an admission would simply remove issues from dispute.
>
> These RFAs are consistent with [Federal] Rule 36, which states that "when good faith requires that a party qualify an answer or deny only a part of a matter, the answer must specify the part admitted and qualify or deny the rest." This rule contemplates that the "matter" that is the subject of the RFA may have "part[s]" to it, which is inconsistent with Gamevice's argument that an RFA can only ask one specific question about one specific item. As the Ninth Circuit has explained, responding parties "should admit to the fullest extent possible, and explain in detail *why other portions* of a request may not be admitted."
>
> There are some cases stating that RFAs should not ask compound questions. Further, where the Court has set a limit on RFAs, as is the case here, that limit must be enforced.

Although the Texas discovery rules do not limit the number of requests for admission in Level 2 and 3 actions, Texas Rules 192.4 and 192.6 allow a court to limit their number when (1) the requests are "unreasonably cumulative or duplicative" of other discovery requests,[48] harassing, annoying, or invasive of personal, constitutional, or property rights,[49] (2) the information "sought is obtainable from some other source that is more convenient, less burdensome, or less expensive,"[50] or (3) "the burden or expense of the proposed discovery outweighs its likely benefit, taking into account the needs of the case, the amount in controversy, the parties' resources, the importance of the issues at stake in the litigation, and the importance of the proposed discovery in resolving the issues" (i.e., they are disproportionate to the action's needs).[51] Whether a party has served too many requests for admission depends on the action's complexity.[52]

> Here, Nintendo's RFAs do not flout Judge Seeborg's limit on their number. Each RFA asks for an admission on a narrow, specific subject. The fact that they seek admissions as to multiple products does not render them compound. A litigant can ask an opponent to "admit the eggs you sold me were rotten," and that's one RFA, not a dozen. The RFAs do not group unrelated subjects together or ask for multiple pieces of information in a way that would suggest an attempt to get around the limit of 45.

Gamevice, Inc. v. Nintendo Co., No. 18-cv-01942-RS (TSH), 2019 U.S. Dist. LEXIS 143917, at *3–6 (N.D. Cal. Aug. 23, 2019) (citations omitted) (quoting Fed. R. Civ. P. 36(a)(4) and *Marchland v. Mercy Med. Ctr.*, 22 F.3d 933, 938 (9th Cir. 1994)).

[48] Tex. R. Civ. P. 192.4(a).

[49] Tex. R. Civ. P. 192.6(b).

[50] Tex. R. Civ. P. 192.4(a).

[51] Tex. R. Civ. P. 192.4(b); *see* Tex. R. Civ. P. 192.6(b) (allowing a protective order to protect "the movant from undue burden, unnecessary expense, harassment, annoyance, or invasion of personal, constitutional, or property rights").

[52] *Cf. Roland Corp. v. inMusicBrands, Inc.*, No. 17-CV-22405, 2019 U.S. Dist. LEXIS 163031, at *4 (S.D. Fla. Sept. 24, 2019) ("The volume of requests for admission is not, in a vacuum, sufficient grounds for a protective order."); *McKinney/Pearl Rest., L.P. v. Metro. Life Ins. Co.*, 322 F.R.D. 235, 254 (N.D. Tex. 2016) ("As to Defendants' first ground for seeking a protective order, the Court does not believe that there is any particular absolute number of [Federal] Rule 36 requests that will be excessive across every case."); *Murphy v. Gospel for ASIA, Inc.*, No. 5:17-CV-5035, 2017 U.S. Dist. LEXIS 193854, at *6, 2017 WL 5593783 (W.D. Ark. Nov. 21, 2017) (same); *Asarco LLC v. Union Pac. R.R.*, No. 2:12-cv-00283-EJL-REB, 2016 U.S. Dist. LEXIS 58262, at *39–40 (D. Idaho May 2, 2016) (same); *Hardy v. Bartmess*, No. 1:09CV00041 DPM/HDY, 2011 U.S. Dist. LEXIS 162811, at *3, 2011 WL 13195971 (E.D. Ark. 2011) (Federal Rule 36 "does not specify a maximum number of requests for admissions that a party may present to an opposing party; rather, the relevant case law appears to provide that the number simply be reasonable, given the complexity of the litigation."); *BP Amoco Chem. Co. v. Flint Hills Res., LLC*, No. 05C5661, 2008 U.S. Dist. LEXIS 85966, at *4–5, 2008 WL 4542738 (N.D. Ill. June 11, 2008) ("No presumptive limit has ever been set on the number of requests a party can propound. However, lines have been drawn on a case-by-case basis, depending on the factual complexity of the case and whether or not the propounding party is truly seeking admissions or seeking to circumvent the Federal Rules regarding discovery.") (citation omitted); *see Murphy v. Gospel for ASIA, Inc.*, No. 5:17-CV-5035, 2017 U.S. Dist. LEXIS 193854, at *4–7, 2017 WL 5593783 (W.D. Ark. Nov. 21, 2017) (noting that the determining factor with respect to whether a party has served too many requests for admission is the action's complexity).

In other words, the issue is determined on a case-by-case basis.[53]

Because requests for admission's purpose is "to simplify trials by eliminating matters about which there is no real controversy, but which may be difficult or expensive to prove[,]" *Medina v. Zuniga*, 593 S.W.3d 238, 244 (Tex. 2019) (quoting *Sanders v. Harder*, 227 S.W.2d 206, 208 (Tex. 1950)), rather than to discover facts and information, *cf. Erie Ins. Prop. & Cas. Co. v. Johnson*, 272 F.R.D. 177, 183 (S.D. W. Va. 2010), a court, in evaluating whether a party has served too many requests, besides considering the action's complexity, should review the requests to determine if they improperly seek admissions about obviously disputed matters or if they are interrogatories in disguise because they are seeking substantive discovery.

[53] *Compare, e.g., Miller v. White*, No. CV 14-7543-GW (KK), 2019 U.S. Dist. LEXIS 230759, at *10–12 (C.D. Cal. Nov. 8, 2019) ("Defendants appear to primarily rely on the fact that Plaintiff's requests are numerically excessive to support their argument the requests are overly burdensome and harassing. Although the Court notes the large number of Requests for Admission, this fact alone is not dispositive. The Motion for Protective Order contains no declarations or specific facts showing how responding to Plaintiff's Requests for Admission would be unduly burdensome or otherwise deserving of a protective order. The number of requests appears to be primarily due to the specificity of each request. Defendants have failed to demonstrate any particular burden or expense associated with responding to the Requests for Admission. Hence, the Requests for Admission do not appear to be disproportionate to the needs of the case.") (citation omitted), *Roland Corp. v. inMusicBrands, Inc.*, No. 17-CV-22405, 2019 U.S. Dist. LEXIS 163031, at *4 (S.D. Fla. Sept. 24, Fla. 2019) (ruling that 511 requests for admission was not excessive given the that the case was "fairly complex as Plaintiff has filed multiple patent infringement claims against Defendant, which requires the evaluation of several of Defendant's products and over 100 asserted claims belonging to 8 different patents"), *U.S. ex rel. Ferris v. Afognak Native Corp.*, No. 3:15-cv-0150-HRH, 2018 U.S. Dist. LEXIS 93634, at *5–6, 2018 WL 2656152 (D. Alaska June 4, 2018) (holding that 537 requests for admission were not excessive "given the nature of this case"), *Murphy v. Gospel for ASIA, Inc.*, No. 5:17-CV-5035, 2017 U.S. Dist. LEXIS 193854, at *4–7 (D. Kan. Nov. 21, 2017) (denying a protective order even though the plaintiff served 1000 requests for admission because "[t]his proposed class action lawsuit involves a large charitable organization and many international partners. As such, this is not a simple case involving two parties and a limited amount of discoverable material."), *McKinney/Pearl Rest., L.P. v. Metro. Life Ins. Co.*, 322 F.R.D. 235, 254–55 (N.D. Tex. 2016) (ordering the defendants to answer 564 requests for admission because they were "proportional" to the action's needs), *Davis v. Harding*, No. 12-cv-559-wmc, 2013 U.S. Dist. LEXIS 120740, at *1, 2013 WL 4509491 (W.D. Wis. Aug. 26, 2013) (denying a motion to quash 826 requests for admission because, as the "plaintiff points out that with 18 defendants in the case, it works out to about 46 requests per defendant, which is not an exceedingly large number"), *Hardy v. Bartmess*, No. 1:09CV00041 DPM/HDY, 2011 U.S. Dist. LEXIS 162811, at *3–4, 2011 WL 13195971 (E.D. Ark. Apr. 1, 2011) (holding that 248 requests for admission was not excessive), *Layne Christensen Co. v. Purolite Co.*, No. CIV.A 09-2381-JWL-GLR, 2011 U.S. Dist. LEXIS 6737, at *13–20 (D. Kan. Jan. 25, 2011) (ruling that 277 requests for admission served on one defendant and another 329 requests served on the other defendant were not excessive given the number of claims and counterclaims in the action), *Gen. Elec. Co. v. Prince*, No. 06 Civ. 0050 (SAS) (MHD), 2007 U.S. Dist. LEXIS 6029, at *4–6, 2007 WL 86940 (S.D.N.Y. Jan. 10, 2007) (denying a protective order for 573 requests for admission), *Escobedo v. Ram Shirdi, Inc.*, No. 10C6598, 2011 U.S. Dist. LEXIS 27124, at *5–6 (N.D. Ill. Mar. 16, 2011) (ruling that 145 requests for admission were neither excessive nor burdensome), *Heartland Surgical Specialty Hosp., LLC v. Midwest Div., Inc.*, No. 05-2164-MLB-DWB, 2007 U.S. Dist. LEXIS 80182, at *11–12, 2007 WL 3171768 (D. Kan. Oct. 29, 2007) (ruling that 1,351 requests for admission served by

multiple defendants, including 751 by a single defendant, were not excessive given that the case involved eighteen defendants, multiple conspiracy allegations, and $121 million in alleged damages), ***and Sequa Corp. v. Gelmin***, No. 91 Civ. 8675 (CSH), 1993 U.S. Dist. LEXIS 12417, at *1–2, 1993 WL 350029 (S.D.N.Y. Sept. 7, 1993) (denying a protective order for a party served with 1441 requests for admission), ***with, e.g., Misco, Inc. v. U.S. Steel Corp.***, 784 F.2d 198, 206 (6th Cir. 1986) ("Misco's filing of 2,028 'requests for admissions [sic]' was both an abuse of the discovery process and an improper attempt to circumvent the local district court rule which limited the number of interrogatories."), ***Entsminger v. Aranas***, No. 3:16-cv-00555-MMD-WGC, 2020 U.S. Dist. LEXIS 16580, at *5–6 (D. Nev. Jan. 31, 2020) (concluding that "71 requests for admissions [sic] seem totally disproportionate to the claims asserted against Dr. Johns, who is named only in Count III (among eight counts)"), ***Kamdem-Ouaffo v. Balchem Corp.***, No. 17 Civ. 2810 (KMK) (PED), 2020 U.S. Dist. LEXIS 15648, at *3 (S.D.N.Y. Jan. 29, 2020) (holding that 737 requests for admission are "not 'proportional to the needs of [this] case,' and that a protective order is warranted to protect defendants from 'oppression, or undue burden[.]'" (quoting Fed. R. Civ. P. 26(b)(1), (c)(1))), ***Tamas v. Family Video Movie Club, Inc.***, 301 F.R.D. 346, 347–48 (N.D. Ill. 2014) ("[T]he Court finds that the 29,440 requests—or the 14,720 requests after Defendant's offer to reduce the requests to 230 per discovery opt-in Plaintiff—and the associated interrogatories are unduly burdensome on the responding Plaintiffs and their counsel."), ***FTC v. Forensic Case Mgmt. Servs.***, No. CV 11-07484 RGK (SSx), 2012 U.S. Dist. LEXIS 201068, at *8, 2012 WL 13134719 (C.D. Cal. 2012) ("The Court finds that 1002 requests for admission represent a failure by the requesting party to exercise good judgment in crafting its discovery. The sheer number of requests for admission is clearly abusive, regardless of the issues in dispute."), ***Fleming v. Escort, Inc.***, No. CV 09-105-S-BLW, 2011 U.S. Dist. LEXIS 14254, at *6–7, 2011 WL 573599 (D. Idaho Feb. 13, 2011) (ruling that 216 requests for admission were "excessive" because they were redundant of deposition testimony), ***Murray v. U.S. Dep't of Treasury***, No. 08-cv-15147, 2010 U.S. Dist. LEXIS 90512, at *4, 2010 WL 3464914 (E.D. Mich. Sept. 1, 2010) ("The Court finds that 182 requests for admission is oppressive and unduly burdensome. There are only two named Defendants in this action and one Plaintiff and the issues, while notably important, are fairly succinct."), ***Taylor v. Great Lakes Waste Servs.***, No. 06-CV-12312-DT, 2007 U.S. Dist. LEXIS 97966, at *5–6, 2007 WL 422036 (E.D. Mich. Feb. 2, 2007) (holding that 297 requests for admission were unduly burdensome in an "uncomplicated" employment-discrimination case), ***Robinson v. Morgan Stanley***, No. 06 C 5158, 2009 U.S. Dist. LEXIS 93971, at *6, 2009 WL 3233909 (N.D. Ill. 2009) ("Courts routinely disallow requests for admission that run into the hundreds on the grounds that they are abusive, unreasonable, and oppressive."), ***Gannon v. U.S.***, No. 03-6626, 2006 U.S. Dist. LEXIS 74308, at *3–4, 2006 WL 2927639 (E.D. Pa. Oct. 6, 2006) (ruling that 1,407 requests for admission were "grossly excessive" and "abusive, burdensome, and oppressive"), ***Joseph L. v. Conn. Dep't of Children & Families***, 225 F.R.D. 400, 403 (D. Conn. 2005) (ruling that 163 requests for admissions, with each having up to ten subparts, were excessive and abusive), ***Leonard v. Univ. of Del.***, No. 96-360 MMS, 1997 U.S. Dist. LEXIS 4196, at *25–26, 1997 WL 158280 (D. Del. Mar. 20, 1997) (holding that 800-plus requests for admission were oppressive in an action alleging wrongful termination and breach of a settlement agreement and that an "objective attorney would be hard-pressed to quibble with the conclusion that a reasonable inquiry would reveal the requests are unreasonable and unduly burdensome"), ***and Wigler v. Elec. Data Sys. Corp.***, 108 F.R.D. 204, 205–06 (D. Md. 1985) ("Where a case is particularly complex, a large number of requests for admission may be justifiable. In contrast, the case ***sub judice*** is relatively straightforward. This litigation involves a single plaintiff and two affiliated corporate defendants, posing issues which are customary in employment discrimination actions.") (citations omitted).

10-5 Responses to Requests for Admission

A party must respond to a request for admission in writing within thirty days after its service[54] unless the time is extended due to the manner of service, by the parties' agreement, or by court order.[55] Each response must be preceded by the request[56] and may include objections and assertions of privilege as allowed by Texas Rule 193.[57] Unlike interrogatory answers, the response to a request for admission need not be verified, but rather only signed by the responding party's attorney or a pro se party.[58] If the response is not properly signed, it "must be stricken unless it is signed promptly after the omission is called to the attention of the [responding] party[.]"[59]

Like other written-discovery responses, responses to requests for admission are not filed,[60] but must be served on all parties to the action.[61] In addition, responding parties "must retain the original or exact copy of [the responses] during the pendency of the case and any related appellate proceedings begun within six months after judgment is signed, unless otherwise provided by the trial court."[62]

A responding party has a variety of responses to a request for admission: (1) admit the entire request; (2) deny the entire request; (3) admit the request in part and deny the request in part; (4) state that, despite a reasonable inquiry, the information known or easily obtainable is insufficient to enable an admission or denial; (5) move for a

---

54 Tex. R. Civ. P. 198.2(a); *accord Marino v. Kerry*, 355 S.W.3d 629, 630 (Tex. 2011) (per curiam) ("Generally, a party responding to requests for admission must serve a written response on the requesting party within 30 days after service. The response time may be extended by agreement or court order."); *Ramirez v. Noble Energy, Inc.*, 521 S.W.3d 851, 856 (Tex. App.—Houston [1st Dist.] 2017, no pet.) ("The responding party must serve a written response within thirty days after service of the request.").

55 *See* Tex. R. Civ. P. 193.1 ("A party must respond to written discovery in writing within the time provided by court order or these rules."). Three days are added to the response date if the requests for admission are served by mail. Tex. R. Civ. P. 21a(c). One day is added if they are served by fax after 5:00 p.m. local time of the responding party. Tex. R. Civ. P. 21a(b)(2).

56 Tex. R. Civ. P. 193.1 ("The responding party's answers, objections, and other responses must be preceded by the request to which they apply.").

57 *See* Tex. R. Civ. P. 193.2–193.3. Privilege assertions to requests for admission are discussed in Chapter 10, section 10-5:7.

58 Tex. R. Civ. P. 191.3(a); *accord Pinal v. Carnevale*, 964 S.W.2d 311, 313–14 (Tex. App.—Corpus Christi 1998, no pet.) (holding that responses to requests for admission do not have to be verified).

A failure to sign the responses may result in the requests being deemed admitted. *In re Estate of Herring*, 970 S.W.2d 583, 588–89 (Tex. App.—Corpus Christi 1998, pet. denied) ("For, under [former Texas] Rule 169, the requests are deemed admitted automatically unless the responding party timely complies with the specific requirements of [former Texas] Rule 169(1), including the signature of his answer. Rather than being a mere formality, the signature on a response to a request for admissions [sic] is some indication that the responding party has adopted and stands behind the answers he has provided in the same manner and with the same general consequences as the prior requirement for verification of the answers.") (citation omitted).

59 Tex. R. Civ. P. 191.3(d).

60 Tex. R. Civ. P. 191.4(a)(1)–(2).

61 Tex. R. Civ. P. 191.5.

62 Tex. R. Civ. P. 191.4(d).

protective order; (6) move for (or request) an extension of time to respond; (7) assert a privilege; (8) object; or (9) do nothing.[63] Each response is discussed in the following sections of this chapter.

Admissions can only be used against the admitting party.[64]

10-5:1 Admissions

The responding party can answer a request for admission by admitting it. To do so, it need only respond, "Admitted." No further elaboration is required.[65] If the party, in "good faith," cannot admit without some explanation or qualification, it can admit with a qualification, an explanation, or a denial of part of the request.[66] As explained by one federal court:

---

[63] *Cf. Braun v. Palantine*, No. 18 C 4850, 2020 U.S. Dist. LEXIS 66932, at *2–3 (N.D. Ill. 2020) ("[Federal] Rule 36 only provides five possible responses: (1) admit; (2) deny; (3) partial admissions and denials; (4) lack of knowledge or information to admit or deny; and (5) objection to the request."); *Montes v. Pinnacle Propane, LLC*, No. 16-cv-0126 JCH/SMV, 2016 U.S. Dist. LEXIS 144369, at *7 (D.N.M. Oct. 18, 2016) ("As discussed above, a party served with a request for admission has a number of options. He or she can admit the matter at issue, deny the matter, object to the request, move for a protective order, do nothing, or state the reasons why he or she cannot respond."); *Nat'l Semiconductor Corp. v. Ramtron Int'l Corp.*, 265 F. Supp. 2d 71, 73 (D.D.C. 2003) (same).

[64] *U.S. Fid. & Guar. Co. v. Goudeau*, 272 S.W.3d 603, 608 (Tex. 2008) ("[Texas] Rule 198 expressly provides that a response to a request for admission can only be used against 'the party making the admission.'" (quoting Tex. R. Civ. P. 198.3)); *Clanton v. Interstate Telecomms., Inc.*, No. 13-19-00107-CV, 2020 Tex. App. LEXIS 3155, at *8, 2020 WL 1887759 (Tex. App.—Corpus Christi Apr. 16, 2020) (mem. op.) (same); *U.S. Fid. & Guar. Co. v. Goudeau*, 272 S.W.3d 603, 608 (Tex. 2008) (same); *Allen v. Allen*, 280 S.W.3d 366, 376 (Tex. App.—Amarillo 2008, pet. denied) (same); *Davis v. Coastal States Petrochemical Co.*, 405 S.W.2d 854, 855 (Tex. Civ. App.—Houston 1966, no writ) (same); *cf. Becerra v. Asher*, 105 F.3d 1042, 1048 (5th Cir. 1997) ("Deemed admissions by a party opponent cannot be used against a co-party."); *Fiberglass, Inc. v. Techni-Glass Indus., Inc.*, 811 F.2d 565, 566–67 (11th Cir. 1987) (same); *In re Leonetti*, 28 Bankr. 1003, 1009 (E.D. Pa.1983) (same), *aff'd mem. sub nom. Earl Realty, Inc. v. Leonetti*, 725 F.2d 667 (3d Cir. 1983). Thus, when a person appears in a case in two capacities, an admission is only binding on the person in the capacity in which the admission was made. *U.S. Fid. & Guar. Co. v. Goudeau*, 272 S.W.3d 603, 608–09 (Tex. 2008) (applying rule to insurers) (citing with approval *Krasa v. Derrico*, 193 S.W.2d 891, 893 (Tex. Civ. App.—San Antonio 1946, no writ), which held deemed admissions could support judgment against Krasa individually, but not against her as executor of her husband's estate, as the requests were not directed to her in that capacity).

[65] *Cf. U.S. v. Lain*, No. 17-cv-113-J, 2019 U.S. Dist. LEXIS 189717, at *7–8, 2019 WL 2051961 (D. Wyo. Jan. 18, 2019) ("With respect to the requests for admission Plaintiff answered, the Court finds Plaintiff properly answered such requests pursuant to [Federal] Rule 36. Although Plaintiff responded with either 'Admit' or 'Deny' without further explanation, such responses are sufficient."); *Cont'l Cas. Co. v. Brummel*, 112 F.R.D. 77, 81 n.2 (D. Colo. 1986) ("Defendant's answers to the questions either admit, deny or qualify the denial which is in compliance with the rule. Therefore, the answers are sufficient.") (footnote omitted).

The admission's use at trial still is subject to pertinent objections, such as hearsay, relevance, or that it involves an impermissible admission of law. See cases cited in notes 170–74, 192, 195.

[66] Tex. R. Civ. P. 198.2(b) ("The responding party may qualify an answer, or deny a request in part only when *good faith* requires.") (emphasis added); *accord In re Sting Soccer Grp., LP*,

There will be times, however, when the answer cannot be a succinct yes or no, and a qualification of the response is indeed necessary. Under these circumstances, the answering party is obligated to specify so much of its answer as true and qualify or deny the remainder of the request. "Generally, qualification is permitted if the statement, although containing some truth, . . . standing alone out of context of the whole truth . . . convey[s] unwarranted unfair references." These qualifications are to provide clarity and lucidity to the genuineness of the issue and not to obfuscate, frustrate, or compound the references.[67]

For example, a qualification is appropriate if the request uses a vague or ambiguous term[68] or "if the request is sweeping, multi-part, involves sharply contested issues, or

---

No. 05-17-00317-CV, 2017 Tex. App. LEXIS 11197, at *22, 2017 WL 5897454 (Tex. App.—Dallas Nov. 30, 2017, orig. proceeding) (mem. op.).

[67] *Henry v. Champlain Enters., Inc.*, 212 F.R.D. 73, 77–78 (N.D.N.Y. 2003) (citations omitted) (quoting *Diederich v. Dep't of Army*, 132 F.R.D. 614, 619 (S.D.N.Y. 1990)); *accord Sanchez Y Martin, S.A. de C.V. v. Dos Amigos, Inc.*, No. 17CV1943 LAB (JMA), 2018 U.S. Dist. LEXIS 101719, at *9, (S.D. Cal. June 14, 2018); *SEC v. Stifel, Nicolaus & Co.*, No. 11-C-0755, 2016 U.S. Dist. LEXIS 113012, at *4, 2016 WL 4471859 (E.D. Wis. 2016); *Tequila Centinela S.A. de C.V. v. Bacardi & Co.*, 242 F.R.D. 1, 14 (D.D.C. 2007).

[68] *E.g., Kovari v. Brevard Extraditions, LLC*, No. 5:18cv0070, 2020 U.S. Dist. LEXIS 87340, at *11–12, 2020 WL 2549702 (W.D. Va. May 18, 2020) ("[T]he court finds Kovari's request for admission 18 to be vague in scope and therefore sustains Brevard's objections to its unqualified admission. In it, Kovari asks Brevard to admit that it 'did not measure or evaluate Plaintiff's blood pressure during his September 2016 transport.' Brevard responded by objecting to the use of the term 'evaluate,' admitting that they did not take Kovari's blood pressure and denying 'that they did not evaluate his condition during his September transport.' The term 'evaluate' can encompass many definitions, and the court agrees with Brevard that a qualification in its response to this request is necessary."); *Eclipse Grp. LLP v. Target Corp.*, No. 15cv1411-JLS (BLM), 2017 U.S. Dist. LEXIS 96748, at *10–11, 2017 WL 2692883 (S.D. Cal. June 21, 2017) ("Plaintiff has responded to the RFAs with reasonable qualifications because the RFAs are unclear since they can be interpreted to seek admission that only Aquawood hired/selected Eclipse or that Aquawood was one of the entities that hired/selected Eclipse."); *Lewis v. Michaels Stores, Inc.*, No. 3:05-cv-1323-J-33HTS, 2007 U.S. Dist. LEXIS 50506, at *3–4, 2007 WL 2021833 (M.D. Fla. July 12, 2007) ("Yet, some circumstances call for a qualified response. Here, Defendant's use of the word *found*, while in one sense conveying merely that Plaintiff was encountered or located, could be interpreted as suggesting Mr. Lewis was hiding in the break room when discovered. Thus, it would be permissible for Plaintiff to qualify his response in order to dispel any impression he admits to the latter, such as by clarifying 'that Plaintiff . . . was[, prior to clocking out,] in the break room awaiting further instructions from Mr. Zimmerman, per the custom and practice in the store he worked in.'") (citations omitted); *Harris v. Oil Reclaiming Co.*, 190 F.R.D. 674, 676–77 (D. Kan. 1999) (holding, in an action alleging that the defendant's actions made him individually liable for a partnership's obligations, that a response to a request asking the defendant "to admit that a certain document is a list of checks 'that you signed as Bill E. Harrison,'" that the checks were signed "'in his capacity' as an agent or officer of Inc.," was an appropriate good faith qualification of the answer to "fairly meet the substance of the requested admission" and that a response to another request seeking an admission that "certain phone calls were 'made on behalf of' Ltd. and that the calls were made not as an agent of Ltd., but 'in his capacity as an agent of' Inc. [wa]s also a good faith qualification to 'fairly meet the substance of the requested admission.'" (quoting Fed. R. Civ. P. 36(a))); *Audiotext Commc'ns Network, Inc. v. US Telecom, Inc.*, No. 94-2395-GTV, 1995 U.S. Dist. LEXIS 15395, at *8, 1995 WL 625744 (D. Kan. Oct. 5, 1995) ("A compound request (seeking

goes to the heart of a defendant's liability."[69] The responding party must make certain that its qualified admission "fairly meet[s] the substance of the request"[70] because, under Texas Rules 215.1(c) and 215.4(a), an evasive or incomplete answer can be treated as a failure to answer and a court, in connection with a motion to determine the sufficiency of an answer, can deem the request admitted.[71]

Because the response must "fairly meet the [request's] substance,"[72] it cannot incorporate by reference other discovery responses, deposition testimony, or the responding party's business records.[73] Moreover, a party cannot admit a request "on

---

admission of multiple facts) or an ambiguous one should be answered as far as possible with appropriate qualification or explanation, rather than objected to entirely.").

69 *Wiwa v. Royal Dutch Petroleum Co.*, No. 01CIV1909, 2009 U.S. Dist. LEXIS 45621, at *17. 2009 WL 1457142 (S.D.N.Y. May 26, 2009).

70 Tex. R. Civ. P. 198.2(b) ("A response must fairly meet the substance of the request."); *see, e.g.*, *Aprile Horse Transp., Inc. v. Prestige Delivery Sys.*, No. 5:13-CV-15-GNS-LLK, 2015 U.S. Dist. LEXIS 86379, at *16–18, 2015 WL 4068457 (W.D. Ky. July 22, 2015) ("As to request 19, the Stacks requested that Prestige admit a document is a 'true and accurate copy' of a vehicle registration. Prestige responded that it the document 'appears to be the same document' possessed by Prestige. But this response does not admit or deny the request made. Prestige must respond as to the document's true and accurate nature, not that it possesses an identical copy, which may be neither true nor accurate. . . . As to request 36, the Stacks requested Prestige admit that attached documents were 'true and accurate copies' of documents Prestige keeps in the ordinary course of its business and previously provided in another lawsuit. Prestige responded that the 'documents appear to be accurate' but that it cannot admit to the method used to obtain the documents because another attorney represents it in that matter. The information to determine the accuracy of the records is available to Prestige. Based on its response, it must possess similar records because these 'appear accurate.' The rules require Prestige to compare the documents. To avoid the comparison and not admit or deny the genuineness of the documents subverts the purpose of the rule. Moreover, Prestige may contact its state-court counsel, even if he or she does not appear in the instant matter. Prestige did not make any allegation that it lacked the knowledge to admit or deny this request or that it would not have the information available to it upon a reasonable inquiry.").

71 Tex. R. Civ. P. 215.4(a) ("If the court determines that an answer does not comply with the requirements of [Texas] Rule 198, it may order either that the matter is admitted or that an amended answer be served."); *Kovari v. Brevard Extraditions, LLC*, No. 5:18cv0070, 2020 U.S. Dist. LEXIS 87340, at *11, 2020 WL 2549702 (W.D. Va. May 18, 2020) ("The court finds no grounds for clear error in the Magistrate Judge's decision to deem requests 15, 17, and 21 admitted without qualification. [Federal] Rule 36 provisions for qualified answers, when 'good faith *requires* that a party qualify an answer,' which is not the case here. No qualification is required in this case where there is no factual dispute about whether Kovari was provided medical care (RFA 15), whether any medical professionals were contacted (RFA 17), and whether any doctors or nurses were contacted (RFA 21). Magistrate Judge Hoppe found these requests did not necessarily imply that Kovari asked for medical care, therefore finding Brevard's qualifications unresponsive and unjustified."). Sufficiency challenges to responses to requests for admission are discussed in Chapter 10, section 10-8.

72 Tex. R. Civ. P. 198.2(b).

73 *Cf. City of Rome v. Hotels.com L.P*, No. 4:05-CV-0249-HLM, 2012 U.S. Dist. LEXIS 198573, at *32, 2012 WL 13020827 (N.D. Ga. May 8, 2012) ("It is improper for the responding party to answer a request for admission by referring to previously produced discovery materials."); *In re Heritage Bond Litig.*, 220 F.R.D. 624, 626–27 (C.D. Cal. 2004) ("Here, defendant responded to requests for admissions [sic] nos. 2, 3, 4, 6 and 9 by (creatively) citing [Federal] Rule 33(d) and stating its answers are to be found in 'previously produced business

information and belief."[74] If such a response is challenged, the court should strike the qualification and (1) generally order the responding party to properly respond to the request by either admitting or denying the request or stating that it cannot admit or deny it after reasonable inquiry, or (2) on the rare occasion, strike the response and deem the request admitted.[75]

10-5:2 Denials

The responding party can answer a request for admission by denying it. To do so, it need only respond, "Denied." No further elaboration is required.[76]

---

records' or 'business records previously produced.' This is improper. Unfortunately for defendant, [Federal] Rule 33(d) is responsive only to interrogatories. . . . Further, by referring to 'previously produced business records,' defendant is inferentially admitting that had it conducted a reasonable inquiry, it would have found the information to respond to the requests for admissions [sic]; however, it chose not to do so. Since defendant has inferentially admitted it could have obtained the information to respond to these requests for admissions [sic], and it chose not to do so, the Court would have had no difficulty deeming requests for admissions [sic] nos. 2, 3, 4, 6 and 9 admitted—even if defendant's responses had been timely.") (citations omitted).

74 *McIntire v. Sawicki*, 353 S.W.2d 952, 953 (Tex. Civ. App.—Eastland 1962, writ ref'd n.r.e.) ("A reply to a request for admission made on information and belief, or to the best of the knowledge and belief of the affiant, is not sufficient under [former Texas] Rule 169[.]"), *superseded on other grounds* by amendment of former Tex. R. Civ. P. 169; *Taylor v. Owen*, 290 S.W.2d 771, 776 (Tex. Civ. App.—San Antonio 1956, writ ref'd n.r.e.) (same), *superseded on other grounds* by amendment of former Tex. R. Civ. P. 169; *cf. In re K-Dur Antitrust Litig.*, No. 01-1652 (JAG), 2007 U.S. Dist. LEXIS 96066, at *40, 2007 WL 5302308 (D.N.J. Jan. 2, 2007) (holding that such a qualification is improper because it violates the reasonable inquiry requirement); *Interland, Inc. v. Bunting*, No. 1:04-CV-444-ODE, 2005 U.S. Dist. LEXIS 36112, at *36, 2005 WL 2414990 (N.D. Ga. Mar. 31, 2005) ("In response to several requests Bunting responded, '[a]dmitted (or denied), based on "information and belief."' Interland claims the latter phrase is an invalid qualification. This Court agrees.").

75 *Cf. In re K-Dur Antitrust Litig.*, No. 01-1652 (JAG), 2007 U.S. Dist. LEXIS 96066, at *40, 2007 WL 5302308 (D.N.J. Jan. 2, 2007) (deeming admitted requests for admission that were admitted on information and belief); *Interland, Inc. v. Bunting*, No. 1:04-CV-444-ODE, 2005 U.S. Dist. LEXIS 36112, at *36, 2005 WL 2414990 (N.D. Ga. Mar. 31, 2005) (same). See also Chapter 10, section 10-8 (discussing motions to test the sufficiency of responses to requests for admission).

76 *Cf. United Coal Cos. v. Powell Constr. Co.*, 839 F.2d 958, 967 (3d Cir. 1988) ("[T]he use of only the word 'denied' is often sufficient under the rule."); *District of Columbia ex rel. Z-Modular, LLC v. MCN Build, Inc.*, No. 18-cv-2947 (RJL/GMH), 2020 U.S. Dist. LEXIS 124719, at *10–11 (D.D.C. July 15, 2020) ("Plaintiff's attempt to litigate the accuracy of Defendant's responses to these RFAs is not appropriate at this time. '[A] motion to determine the sufficiency of a response is "not to be used as an attempt to litigate the accuracy of a response." A response can be sufficient, even if it is not ultimately determined to have been accurate.' Here, Plaintiff has a sufficient response: a clear denial. The accuracy of that response can, if appropriate, be litigated at a later time in connection with a motion pursuant to [Federal] Rule 37(c)." (quoting *Wiwa v. Royal Dutch Petroleum Co.*, Nos. 96 Civ. 8386 (KMW) (HBP), 01 Civ. 1909 (KMW)(HBP), 2009 U.S. Dist. LEXIS 45621, at *19, 2009 WL 1457142 (S.D.N.Y. May 26, 2009), and 7 *Moore's Federal Practice* §36.12[3] (3d ed. 2009))); *Superior Sales W., Inc. v. Gonzalez*, No. EP-19-CV-329-KC, 335 F.R.D. 98, 102-03 (W.D. Tex. 2020) ("District courts across the country, as well as preeminent treatises on federal civil procedure, agree that '[Federal] Rule 36 does not authorize the court to make determinations

As with admissions, the responding party can explain or qualify its denial or deny the request in part when "good faith requires"[77] so long as the qualified or partial denial "fairly meet[s] the substance of the request[.]"[78] Accordingly, "[w]hen the

---

on the accuracy of responses before trial.' Stated differently, '[i]f a responding party files a response that contains the proper detail, . . . the propounding party may not challenge the denial on the ground that it is unsupported by the evidence.' Here, none of Gonzalez's denials are insufficient simply because other evidence—however extensive or unassailable it may be—appears to show that those denials are mendacious. Gonzalez's denials are clear and specific; they are neither equivocal nor evasive. Therefore, Gonzalez's denials are adequate under [Federal] Rule 36. . . ." (quoting ***In re TFT-LCD (Flat Panel) Antitrust Litig.***, No. M 07-1827 SI, 2011 U.S. Dist. LEXIS 90730, at *61, 2011 WL 3566419 (N.D. Cal. Aug. 12, 2011), and ***Duncan v. Nunez***, No. 1:17-CV-1623-P, 2019 U.S. Dist. LEXIS 194262, at *4, 2019 WL 5862001 (W.D. La. Nov. 7, 2019))); ***Braun v. Palantine***, No. 18 C 4850, 2020 U.S. Dist. LEXIS 66932, at *3 (N.D. Ill. Apr. 6, 2020) ("Defendants have responded with 'Deny' and that is all the rule requires. If Plaintiff later determines that these facts should have been admitted, he may move for sanctions" under Federal Rule 37(c)(2), which provides that if a "party fails to admit what is requested under Rule 36 and if the requesting party later proves a document to be genuine or the matter true, the requesting party may move that the party who failed to admit pay the reasonable expenses, including attorney's fees, incurred in making that proof."); ***U.S. v. Lain***, No. 17-cv-113-J, 2019 U.S. Dist. LEXIS 189717, at *7–8, 2019 WL 2051961 (D. Wyo. Jan. 18, 2019) ("With respect to the requests for admission Plaintiff answered, the Court finds Plaintiff properly answered such requests pursuant to [Federal] Rule 36. Although Plaintiff responded with either 'Admit' or 'Deny' without further explanation, such responses are sufficient. [Federal] Rule 36 states, 'A denial must fairly respond to the substance of the matter[.]' Courts have interpreted this provision as allowing the responding party to merely deny a request for admission." (quoting Fed. R. Civ. P. 36(a)(4))); ***Wu v. Seoul Garden, Inc.***, No. 1:16-CV-03613 (ARR) (ST), 2018 U.S. Dist. LEXIS 9820, at *27–28 (E.D.N.Y. Jan. 22, 2018) ("Plaintiffs asserted that every denial to a RFA must be supported with 'detailed reasons for each denial.' To put it simply, Plaintiffs were wrong. Parties need not state the specific factual basis of a denial, as RFAs are not 'a discovery procedure at all. . . . [and a] party desiring to learn what the facts actually are should use other discovery devices.' Plaintiffs, by insisting upon specific factual bases for denials, were attempting to improperly 'avoid the limits on the number of interrogatories authorized under Rule 33(a)(1).'" (citations omitted) (quoting ***Baker v. Cty. of Missaukee***, 2013 U.S. Dist. LEXIS 154072, at *11 n.2 (W.D. Mich. Oct. 28, 2013))); ***N.U. v. Wal-Mart Stores, Inc.***, No. 15-4885-KHV, 2017 U.S. Dist. LEXIS 53074, at *4, 2017 WL 1250804 (D. Kan. Apr. 5, 2017) ("The plain language of the rule does not require a party denying in full a request to admit to explain its denial. '[T]he use of only the word "denied" is often sufficient under the rule.' Typically, a party qualifies or explains its answer only when it is denying part of the request and admitting or objecting to the remainder." (footnotes omitted) (quoting ***Caruso v. Coleman Co.***, No. 93-CV-6733, 1995 U.S. Dist. LEXIS 7934, at *7 (E.D. Pa. June 7, 1995))).

[77] Tex. R. Civ. P. 198.2(b).

[78] Tex. R. Civ. P. 198.2(b); ***accord In re Sting Soccer Grp., LP***, No. 05-17-00317-CV, 2017 Tex. App. LEXIS 11197, at *22, 2017 WL 5897454 (Tex. App.—Dallas Nov. 30, 2017, orig. proceeding) (mem. op.); *cf.* ***Thalheim v. Eberheim***, 124 F.R.D. 34, 38 (D. Conn. 1988) ("Defendant's response to Request No. 16 admits that the Stardust Too was ***moored*** in Greenwich Cove on September 28, 1985. Defendant's cute pre-motion response to Request No. 17, however, denies that the boat was afloat. Since it is entirely possible for a boat to sink while it is moored, defendant's inappropriate response left plaintiff no alternative but to file the pending motion. After the plaintiff incurred the expense associated with his motion—to say nothing of the costs associated with plaintiff's repeated attempts since November of 1987 to obtain forthright answers—the defendant filed an 'Amended Response' which finally

purpose and significance of a request are reasonably clear, courts do not permit denials based on an overly-technical reading of the request."[79] As with admissions, the responding party cannot deny a request "on information and belief."[80]

The fact that the responding party previously has denied the substance of a request for admission in a pleading or in response to other discovery, such as in a disclosure, an interrogatory answer, or deposition testimony, does not constitute a denial of a request for admission.[81]

10-5:3 Admitting or Denying in Part

When good faith requires, the responding party may admit part and deny part of a request for admission.[82] In fact, under Texas Rule 198.2, the responding party must

---

admits 'that the boat was moored and afloat.' Obviously, this should have been admitted in defendant's initial pre-motion response. Defendant's pre-motion response was not in good faith.").

79 *U.S. ex. rel. Englund v. L.A. Cty.*, 235 F.R.D. 675, 684 (E.D. Cal. 2006); *accord Holmgren v. State Farm Mut. Auto. Ins. Co.*, 976 F.2d 573, 580 (9th Cir. 1992) ("[E]pistemological doubts speak highly of [party's] philosophical sophistication, but poorly of its respect for [Federal] Rule 36(a)."); *Tequila Centinela, S.A. de C.V. v. Bacardi & Co.*, 242 F.R.D. 1, 14 (D.D.C. 2007) ("While it is permissible under [Federal Rule 36] to qualify answers which are only partly correct, hair-splitting disingenuous distinctions are inappropriate."); *Caruso v. Coleman Co.*, No. 93-CV-6733, 1995 U.S. Dist. LEXIS 7934, at *9–10, 1995 WL 347003 (E.D. Pa. June 7, 1995) ("Both RFAs No. 37 and No. 39 contained typographical errors and were specifically denied by defendant because of those errors. . . . Such responses by defendant are clearly deficient under [Federal] Rule 36.").

80 *McIntire v. Sawicki,* 353 S.W.2d 952, 953 (Tex. Civ. App.—Eastland 1962, writ ref'd n.r.e.) ("A reply to a request for admissions made on information and belief, or to the best of the knowledge and belief of the affiant, is not sufficient under [former Texas] Rule 169[.]"), *superseded on other grounds* by amendment of former Tex. R. Civ. P. 169; *Taylor v. Owen,* 290 S.W.2d 771, 776 (Tex. Civ. App.—San Antonio 1956, writ ref'd n.r.e.), *superseded on other grounds* by amendment of former Tex. R. Civ. P. 169; *cf. In re K-Dur Antitrust Litig.,* No. 01-1652 (JAG), 2007 U.S. Dist. LEXIS 96066, at *40, 2007 WL 5302308 (D.N.J. Jan. 2, 2007) (holding that such a qualification is improper because it violates the reasonable inquiry requirement and deeming admitted requests that were admitted on information and belief); *Interland, Inc. v. Bunting,* No. 1:04-CV-444-ODE, 2005 U.S. Dist. LEXIS 36112, at *36, 2005 WL 2414990 (N.D. Ga. Mar. 31, 2005) ("In response to several requests Bunting responded, '[a]dmitted (or denied), based on "information and belief." Interland claims the latter phrase is an invalid qualification. This Court agrees.'"). See also Chapter 10, section 10-8 (discussing motions to test the sufficiency of responses to requests for admission) and cases cited in notes 74–75.

81 *See, e.g., Lee v. Unifund CCR Partners,* No. 03-07-00286-CV, 2008 Tex. App. LEXIS 6226, at *5, 2008 WL 3539938 (Tex. App.—Austin Aug. 15, 2008, no pet.) (mem. op.) (holding that a general denial or a verified denial are not objections or responses to requests for admission).

82 Tex. R. Civ. P. 198.2(b); *cf.* Tex. R. Civ. P. 198.2(b); *cf. Aprile Horse Transp., Inc. v. Prestige Delivery Sys.*, No. 5:13-CV-15-GNS-LLK, 2015 U.S. Dist. LEXIS 86379, at *15–16, 2015 WL 4068457 (W.D. Ky. 2015) ("As to request 2, the Stacks requested Prestige admit that its Department of Transportation number was painted on the vehicle involved in the accident. Prestige stated that it '[a]dmits so much' of the request 'that there was a placard on the outside of the van.' The Stacks did not request an admission that a placard was on the outside of the van. Prestige must respond to the request posed. Moreover, the language used

admit those portions of the request that it knows are true, while denying the remaining matters.[83] Nonetheless, when a request "contains interdependent, compound issues, a party may deny the entire statement if it is premised upon a fact which is denied."[84]

10-5:4 Lack of Information

In many instances, the responding party will not know whether the matter it has been asked to admit is true. Texas Rule 198.2(b) deals with this situation, providing, in full:

> Unless the responding party states an objection or asserts a privilege, the responding party must specifically admit or deny the request *or explain in detail the reasons that the responding party cannot admit or deny the request.* A response must fairly meet the substance of the request. The responding party may qualify an answer, or deny a request in part, only when good faith requires. *Lack of information or knowledge is not a proper response unless the responding party states that a reasonable inquiry was made but that the information known or easily obtainable is insufficient to enable the responding party to admit or deny.* An assertion that the request presents an issue for trial is not a proper response.[85]

Tension exists between the Rule's first and fourth sentences. The first suggests that the answer must describe in detail what efforts have been made to answer the request, whereas the fourth sentence suggests that such detail is unnecessary and that the answer need only track the sentence's language.

---

by Prestige indicated a partial denial. The partial denial does not comport with [Federal] Rule 36, which requires a denial to 'fairly respond to the substance of the matter.' Moreover, a partial denial must 'specify the part admitted and qualify or deny the rest.' Prestige must respond to the request's substance: that the number 512674 was painted on the vehicle on February 10, 2011, and that the number 512674 is a USDOT number assigned to Prestige."); *Sayler v. Gilbert*, No. 2:08-cv-516, 2009 U.S. Dist. LEXIS 98141, at *7, 2009 WL 3259455 (S.D. Ohio Oct. 8, 2009) ("Defendants are entitled to admit in part or deny in part the request 'but the answer must specify the part admitted and qualify or deny the rest.'"); *Martin v. El Paso Natural Gas Co.*, No. EP-79-CA-23, 1981 U.S. Dist. LEXIS 17053, at *4, 1981 WL 2348 (W.D. Tex. Oct. 19, 1981) ("Rule 36(a), F.R.Civ.P., allows a party to object to a request for admission, or to deny part of it, if he acts in good faith.").

[83] Tex. R. Civ. P. 198.2(b).

[84] *Harris v. Oil Reclaiming Co.*, 190 F.R.D. 674, 678 (D. Kan. 1999), *quoted with approval in Helget v. City of Hays*, 300 F.R.D. 496, 499 (D. Kan. 2014); *accord Diederich v. Dep't of Army*, 132 F.R.D. 614, 621 (S.D.N.Y. 1990); *Audiotext Commc'ns Network, Inc. v. US Telecom, Inc.*, No. 94-2395-GTV, 1995 U.S. Dist. LEXIS 15395, at *5–6, 1995 WL 625744 (D. Kan. Oct. 5, 1995); *Diederich v. Dep't of Army*, 132 F.R.D. 614, 621 (S.D.N.Y. 1990). Examples of this type of request are: "Admit that your president, John Smith, signed the lease at issue" or "Admit that your driver, John Doe, drove the truck that ran the light and crashed into Plaintiff." If any of the facts in the requests are untrue, the responding party can deny the request in its entirety. Nonetheless, a better response would be to admit those portions of the request that are true and deny the rest (e.g., "Defendant admits that John Smith is its president, but denies that he signed the lease at issue" or "Defendant admits that John Doe was the driver of the truck that collided with Plaintiff, but denies that he ran the light or otherwise was negligent.").

[85] Tex. R. Civ. P. 198.2(b) (emphasis added).

No Texas court has recognized the conflict, much less decided how to resolve it. Federal courts, however, have split on the issue in interpreting Federal Rule 36(a)(4)'s similar language.[86] Although some courts have held that the responding party must detail its inquiry,[87] most courts have held that a simple statement that the party has made a reasonable inquiry and lacks adequate information to admit or to deny the request is sufficient.[88]

The latter construction not only is the majority one, but it also is the better one. As explained by one federal court:

> One common situation is where the respondent lacks adequate knowledge to answer. The third sentence [of Federal Rule 36(a)(4), which is substantially the same as the fourth sentence of Texas Rule 198.2(b),] tells the respondent what he or she must do to answer "in detail." In other words, the sentence sets forth what "in detail" means for the common situation when the answering party lacks information or knowledge. There may be other situations where a respondent cannot admit or deny; in such a situation, the respondent must use the more general directions in the first sentence. If the Court were to interpret [Federal R]ule 36(a)(4) as requiring a person who lacked knowledge to make the statements in the third sentence and describe in detail the inquiry, there would be little need to even have the third sentence—rendering it effectively surplusage, a disfavored result. "In detail" would require at least setting forth what the third sentence requires. The Court is reluctant to give [Federal R]ule 36(a)(4) a construction that gives the third sentence little, if any, effect. Further, the plain language of the first sentence of [Federal R]ule 36(a)(4) does not state that the answer must describe "in detail" the inquiry made; the first sentence states that the respondent must "state in detail why the answering party cannot truthfully admit or deny it"—not what the answering party has done. To add the requirement that the answering party must describe in detail what the party has

---

86 Federal Rule 36(a)(4) provides, in full:

> If a matter is not admitted, the answer must specifically deny it or state *in detail why the answering party cannot truthfully admit or deny it.* A denial must fairly respond to the substance of the matter; and when good faith requires that a party qualify an answer or deny only a part of a matter, the answer must specify the part admitted and qualify or deny the rest. *The answering party may assert lack of knowledge or information as a reason for failing to admit or deny only if the party states that it has made reasonable inquiry and that the information it knows or can readily obtain is insufficient to enable it to admit or deny.*

Fed. R. Civ. P. 36(a)(4) (emphasis added).

87 *E.g.,* Jacobs v. Sullivan, No. 1:05-cv-01625-LJO-GSA-PC, 2012 U.S. Dist. LEXIS 102161, at *24–26, 66, 78, 2012 WL 2995648 (E.D. Cal. July 20, 2012); *A. Farber & Partners., Inc. v. Garber*, 237 F.R.D. 250, 254 (C.D. Cal. 2006); *Henry v. Champlain Enters, Inc.*, 212 F.R.D. 73, 78 (N.D.N.Y. 2003).

88 *E.g., Asea, Inc. v. S. Pac. Transp. Co.*, 669 F.2d 1242, 1245–46 (9th Cir. 1981); *Casun Invest, A.G. v. Ponder*, No. 2:16-cv-02925-JCM-GWF, 2017 U.S. Dist. LEXIS 144668, at *19–20, 2017 WL 3925417 (D. Nev. Sept. 6, 2017); *SEC v. Goldstone*, 300 F.R.D. 505, 524 (D.N.M 2014); *Wildearth Guardians v. Pub. Serv. Co.*, No. 09-cv-01862-ZLW-MEH, 2010 U.S. Dist. LEXIS 138972, at *9, 2010 WL 5464313 (D. Colo. Dec. 29, 2010); *Tequila Centinela S.A. v. Bacardi & Co.*, 242 F.R.D. 1, 15 (D.D.C. 2007); *Interland, Inc. v. Bunting*, No. 1:04-CV-444-ODE, 2005 U.S. Dist. LEXIS 36112, at *34, 2005 WL 2414990 (N.D. Ga. Mar. 31, 2005).

> done to reasonably inquire is to write into the rule language that is not there. The Court is reluctant to read into the rule a requirement that the drafters did not write, and which Congress and the Supreme Court of the United States did not approve.
>
> There is also a policy rationale for not reading the "in detail" requirement into the subject that the third sentence covers. [Federal] Rule 36 deals with requests for admissions [sic] and not with interrogatories. To require the answering party to describe in detail the efforts it has made to inquire would be to turn the request for admissions [sic] into an open-ended interrogatory. Moreover, an in-detail description of the inquiry does not advance the discovery ball much; such an answer still does not produce an admission or denial. The detail is not much use for discovery. The detail is more useful for after trial to determine whether [Federal R]ule 37(a)(5) expenses should be awarded for failure to admit, but requiring that information now pushes to an early part of the case a lot of work and squabbles that may never need to be addressed if the case settles or the issue proves to be irrelevant down the road. . . . The third sentence is made under [Federal R]ule 11, which is probably the best end to request-for-admission disputes; to read a requirement that the answering party describe in detail the reasonable inquiry only promotes satellite litigation with little benefit.[89]

Accordingly, when a responding party, having made a reasonable inquiry, lacks the information needed to admit or deny a request for admission, its answer need not detail the inquiry, but merely can track Texas Rule 198.2(b)'s fourth sentence (i.e., the responding party can state that "after reasonable inquiry, the information known or easily obtainable is insufficient to enable an admission or denial").[90] However, if the requesting party challenges the response's sufficiency under Texas Rule 215.4, the responding party bears the burden of proving that it made a reasonable inquiry and that the information known or easily obtainable was insufficient to allow it to admit or deny the request. As explained by the San Antonio Court of Appeals:

---

[89] *Stark-Romero v. Nat'l R.R. Passenger Co.*, 275 F.R.D. 551, 556–57 (D.N.M. 2011) (citations omitted); *accord SEC v. Goldstone*, 300 F.R.D. 505, 524 (D.N.M 2014); *Radian Asset Assur., Inc. v. College of Christian Bros.*, No. Civ. 09-0885 JB/DJS, 2010 U.S. Dist. LEXIS 127396, at *47–58, 2019 WL 5173571 (D.N.M. Nov. 11, 2010).

[90] Although no Texas case has expressly considered the issue, several cases suggest that a response that tracks Texas Rule 198.2(b)'s fourth sentence is sufficient. *See, e.g., Larrison v. Catalina Design*, No. 02-10-00167-CV, 2011 Tex. App. LEXIS 1196, at *12, 2011 WL 582730 (Tex. App.—Fort Worth Feb. 17, 2011, no pet.) (mem. op.) ("A response to a request for admission based on lack of information or knowledge is insufficient 'unless the responding party states that a reasonable inquiry was made but that the information known or easily obtainable is insufficient to enable the responding party to admit or deny.' Larrison's response does not state that a reasonable inquiry was made, as required by the rules of civil procedure. The trial court was correct in ruling that the answer was insufficient." (quoting Tex. R. Civ. P. 198.2(b))); *CherCo Props., Inc. v. Law, Snakard & Gambill, P.C.*, 985 S.W.2d 262, 267 (Tex. App.—Fort Worth 1999, no pet.) ("[A] party may not give lack of information or knowledge as a reason for failure to admit or deny unless it states that it has made reasonable inquiry into the facts and still has inadequate information to admit or deny the request for admission.") (citation omitted).

The crux of the State's argument is that the trial court had no authority to deem the admissions because its refusal to either admit or deny tracked the language in the rules. We disagree. The State's responses were an attempt to avoid the operation of [former Texas Rule] 169 and [Texas Rule] 215.

[Former Texas] Rule 169 requires that where a party has insufficient information to admit or deny, he must state that he has made reasonable inquiry to discover the information. The State argues that simply reciting the language in the statute is enough. However, [former Texas] Rule 169 also requires that parties['] responses to requests for admissions [sic] must be made in good faith. It seems implicit in the rule that one must actually make a reasonable inquiry and that as a result of that reasonable inquiry the party answering the request still did not have sufficient knowledge to either admit or deny. The State's answer that it had made a reasonable inquiry and that it had insufficient knowledge to ascertain whether the $10,057 dollars seized from Carrillo was derived from the distribution of a controlled substance is not adequate. The State presented no evidence to support its claim that it had made a reasonable inquiry prior to answering the requests for admissions.[91]

---

[91] *State v. Carrillo*, 885 S.W.2d 212, 215 (Tex. App.— San Antonio 1994, no pet.); *see CherCo Props., Inc. v. Law, Snakard & Gambill, P.C.*, 985 S.W.2d 262, 267–68 (Tex. App.—Fort Worth 1999, no writ) ("CherCo had an affirmative duty to make a reasonable inquiry into the facts—including questioning Ralph Ayers, [its sole shareholder,] if necessary—before answering the requests.") (citation omitted); *U.S. Fire Ins. Co. v. Maness*, 775 S.W.2d 748, 749–51 (Tex. App.—Houston [1st Dist.] 1989, writ ref'd) (holding that the defendant's lack-of-information response was improper because it "sought to avoid the duty to make reasonable inquiry by simply saying, in effect, 'we deny these requests, even though we have no factual basis to deny them.' [Former Texas] Rule 169's requirement to make a reasonable inquiry should not be so easily defeated. . . . A party may not guarantee its ignorance by foregoing reasonable inquiry into relevant facts and then refuse to admit the facts due to insufficient information."); *Trevino v. Cent. Freight Lines, Inc.*, 613 S.W.2d 356, 360 (Tex. Civ. App.—Waco 1981, no writ) ("[I]f defendant did not have personal knowledge of the matters in question, he should have ascertained their accuracy if that could have been done without cost or considerable burden."); *cf. Asea, Inc. v. S. Pac. Transp. Co.*, 669 F.2d 1242, 1247 (9th Cir. 1981) ("We hold, therefore, that a response which fails to admit or deny a proper request for admission does not comply with the requirements of [Federal] Rule 36(a) if the answering party has not, in fact, made 'reasonable inquiry,' or if information 'readily obtainable' is sufficient to enable him to admit or deny the matter."); *U.S. ex. rel. Englund v. L.A. Cty.*, 235 F.R.D. 675, 685 (E.D. Cal. 2006) ("The responding party's simple statement that he or she has made a 'reasonable' inquiry and is unable to admit or deny the request because insufficient information is available may not suffice as an answer to the request for admission. Moreover, the fact that the party has not done so may be asserted as a basis for challenging the response."); *Harris v. Oil Reclaiming Co.*, 190 F.R.D. 674, 679 (D. Kan. 1999) ("Intonation of the words of . . . [Federal] Rule [36(a)(4)] that the party has made a 'reasonable inquiry' is not determinative [of] whether the answer is sufficient. The party must in some way show that he has, in fact, made a 'reasonable inquiry' and that information 'readily available' to him is insufficient to enable him to admit or deny the statement.").

A lack-of-information response is inadequate if the responding party, when challenged, fails to prove that there, in fact, was insufficient information to admit or deny the request or that it failed to make a reasonable inquiry.[92]

---

[92] *Compare, e.g., T. Rowe Price Small-Cap Fund, Inc. v. Oppenheimer & Co.*, 174 F.R.D. 38, 44 (S.D.N.Y. 1997) (holding that the defendant was not required to subpoena FDIC records needed to admit or deny requests for admission because such a requirement would "far exceed" the reasonable inquiry provision of Federal Rule 36), ***Kendrick v. Sullivan***, No. 83-3175 (CRR), 1992 U.S. Dist. LEXIS 6715, at *9, 1992 WL 119125 (D.D.C. May 5, 1992) ("The Court finds that the review of the documentary evidence in plaintiffs' possession was sufficient to constitute a reasonable inquiry. Therefore their claim that they had inadequate information to respond was proper. Although they are unable to contradict various factual assertions, the information they seek is in the hands of the defendant or adverse third parties. . . . The plaintiffs have exhaustively reviewed the information under their control. This effort constitutes compliance with the rule."), ***Morreale v. Willcox & Gibbs DN, Inc.***, No. 89 Civ. 5531 (MJL), 1991 U.S. Dist. LEXIS 7741, at *1–2, 1991 WL 107441 (S.D.N.Y. June 6, 1991) ("Schwarz'[s] suggestion that defendants had an obligation to take the additional action of interviewing former employees of Peat Marwick, a third party, is unprecedented, and indeed there is some authority to the contrary."), ***and Gaynier v. Ginsberg***, 715 S.W.2d 749, 758–59 (Tex. App.—Dallas 1986, writ ref'd n.r.e.) ("As to the requests that Gaynier admit that certain records were those of Dr. Harrington, deceased, Gaynier replied that she did not have sufficient knowledge to answer those requests. Dr. Harrington was deceased and, after reasonable inquiry, Gaynier stated that she had no knowledge of whether those particular documents were prepared and maintained by Dr. Harrington and whether they related to her. A party is not required to admit or deny facts of which he has no personal knowledge and has no reasonable means of obtaining such knowledge."), ***with, e.g., Whole Woman's Health All. v. Hill***, No. 1:18-cv-01904-SEB-MJD, 2020 U.S. Dist. LEXIS 35880, at *13–14, 2020 WL 1028040 (S.D. Ind. Mar. 2, 2020) ("As to RFA Nos. 10-12, Defendants further contend that they are not required to make inquiries of third parties in response to these requests, asserting that '[i]t is true that Defendants regulate these hospitals through the licensure and inspection process, but these private hospitals are not involved in this litigation, are not co-defendants or even parties, and are not working closely with Defendants concerning this case. Absent any such relationship, Defendants are not required to chase down non-party discovery for Plaintiffs.' A 'reasonable inquiry is limited to review and inquiry of those persons and documents that are within the responding party's control.' However, under certain circumstances, parties may be required to inquire of third parties to properly respond to requests for admissions. RFA Nos. 10-12 do not require Defendants to 'chase down non-party discovery;' rather, RFA Nos. 10-12 simply requests Defendants, including Defendant the Health Department, to admit whether the referenced private hospitals—which Defendants regulate, inspect, and license—provide such services. Since Defendants have access to these facilities and to the documents necessary to respond to the requests without unreasonable expense or effort, such a third-party inquiry is appropriate." (citations omitted) (quoting *Hanley v. Como Inn, Inc.*, 2003 U.S. Dist. LEXIS 7130, at *5, 2003 WL 1989607 (N.D. Ill. Apr. 28, 2003))), ***Hernandez v. Ditech Fin. LLC***, No. CV 17-04294-GW (JEMx), 2018 U.S. Dist. LEXIS 225093, at *6–7, 2018 WL 5928133 (C.D. Cal. Oct. 5, 2018) ("SFS, for example, objects to the inclusion of 'agencies,' 'bureaus' and 'assignors' in the definition of YOU (SFS). It then answers Deny 'on behalf of itself alone' to Request Nos. 4-27. These definitional limitations are not consistent with the authorities above. . . . Agencies, bureaus and assignors are persons or entities acting on behalf of SFS or within its 'relative control' and/or readily available to it. Assignors usually involve a relationship that might yield information on inquiry. Also, SFS speaks of entities acting on its behalf but then limits its answer to 'on behalf of itself alone.' SFS is ORDERED to reconsider its responses and to revise its answers to Request Nos. 4-27 to state, 'Based on a reasonable effort to secure information from documents reasonably available to it

As discussed in Chapter 5, section 5-3:1, nothing in Texas Rules 193 or 198 explains when "information" is "reasonably available." As also pointed out in that Chapter, what material is reasonably available depends in large measure on the responding party's obligation of reasonable inquiry (i.e., how extensive a search the responding party must make to respond to the discovery request) and whether the information is within the responding party's control. This, of course, depends on the facts of each action.

10-5:5 Motion for Protective Order

In appropriate situations, the responding party, rather than responding to a set of requests for admission, can move for a protective order pursuant to Texas Rule 192.6 if the requests subject the answering party to "undue burden, unnecessary expense, harassment, annoyance, or invasion of personal, constitutional, or property rights."[93] Such a motion is proper when the requests are (1) so voluminous that responding to them will be unduly burdensome or unnecessarily expensive, (2) unreasonably cumulative or duplicative of other discovery, or (3) disproportionate to the case's needs.[94] When assessing these factors, the court must balance the legitimate needs of the requesting party with the burden or expense on the responding party considering the factors in Texas Rule 192.4.[95]

10-5:6 Move for (or Request) an Extension of Time to Respond

If the responding party cannot in good faith respond to requests for admission within the time allowed by Texas Rule 198.2—for example, if the request relates to a matter

---

and from persons and entities reasonably available to it, acting on its behalf and/or within SFS' relative control, [DENY] or [ADMIT].'"), *Erie Ins. Prop. & Cas. Co. v. Johnson*, 272 F.R.D. 177, 184 (S.D. W. Va. 2010) (holding that a "reasonable inquiry" requires an insurer to ask its insured about the information needed to answer a request for admission), *Adkins Energy, LLC v. Farmland Mut. Ins. Co.*, No. 044 C 5048250492, 2009 U.S. Dist. LEXIS 38099, at *17–18, 2009 WL 1259344 (N.D. Ill. May 6, 2009) (holding that the plaintiff's lack-of-information response to a request asking it to admit the name of its former law firm was "improper because . . . [t]he information sought may be attainable through reasonable inquiry"), *Fireman's Fund Ins. Co. v. Commer. Standard Ins. Co.*, 490 S.W.2d 818, 825 (Tex. 1972) (Former Texas Rule 169 "extend[s] to matters of fact within the knowledge of or readily ascertainable by the litigant of whom the request is made. In the spirit of cooperation required by this Rule, [defendants] should have ascertained the accuracy of [the deposition transcript attached to the requests for admission] if [it] could have been done without cost or considerable burden."), *overruled on other grounds, Ethyl Corp. v. Daniel Constr. Co.*, 725 S.W.2d 705 (Tex. 1987), *and CherCo Props., Inc. v. Law, Snakard & Gambill, P.C.*, 985 S.W.2d 262, 267–68 (Tex. App.—Fort Worth 1999, no pet.) (holding that a "reasonable inquiry" required the plaintiff corporation to ask its sole shareholder for information needed to answer requests for admission).

93 Tex. R. Civ. P. 192.6. The filing of the motion will prevent the requests from being deemed admitted even if the responding party never obtains a ruling on it. *Reynolds v. Murphy*, 188 S.W.3d 252, 261 (Tex. App.—Fort Worth 2006, pet. denied), *cert. denied*, 549 U.S. 1281, (2007).

94 Tex. R. Civ. P. 192.4(a).

95 See Chapter 4, section 4-5 (discussing protective orders), and Chapter 5, section 5-3:4 (discussing proportionality).

requiring additional or expert discovery—the responding party should move for an extension of time to respond. The motion should be made well in advance of the response period's expiration. The trial court has authority to lengthen the time for response.[96] Moreover, the parties can agree to extend the time to respond pursuant to an enforceable agreement under Texas Rule 11.[97]

After the time to respond expires, it is too late to move the court for an extension of time to respond to requests for admission because, as discussed in Chapter 10, section 10-5:9, below, the requests are automatically deemed admitted the day after the answers are due.

10-5:7 Privilege Assertions and Objections

As discussed in Chapter 5, section 5-4, privilege generally is not a proper objection to requests for admission. Nonetheless, if a request for admission seeks privileged information, it is proper to respond to it by stating that it cannot be admitted or denied because to do so would result in the disclosure of privileged information and then identifying the applicable privilege(s). For example, if a request asks a party to admit that certain documents will, or will not, be offered as evidence, it is appropriate to state that the request cannot be admitted or denied because it seeks protected work product.[98]

The Fifth Amendment privilege against self-incrimination ordinarily is available in civil litigation due to the fear that information elicited in a civil proceeding can be used in a criminal prosecution.[99] Because, however, Texas Rule 198.3 expressly provides

---

[96] Tex. R. Civ. P. 191.1 ("Except where specifically prohibited, the procedures and limitations set forth in the rules pertaining to discovery may be modified in any suit by the agreement of the parties or by court order for good cause. An agreement of the parties is enforceable if it complies with [Texas] Rule 11. . . ."); *Marino v. Kerry*, 355 S.W.3d 629, 633 (Tex. 2011) (per curiam) ("Generally, a party responding to requests for admissions [sic] must serve a written response on the requesting party within 30 days after service. The response time may be extended by agreement or court order.").

[97] Tex. R. Civ. P. 191.1 (noting that the parties can modify discovery procedures and limitations by agreement and that "[a]n agreement of the parties is enforceable if it complies with [Texas] Rule 11"); *accord Marino v. Kerry*, 355 S.W.3d 629, 633 (Tex. 2011) (per curiam).

[98] *Cf. U.S. v. 260 Tonawanda Trail*, 95 F.3d 422, 428 n.10 (6th Cir. 1996) ("Although courts most commonly apply the work product privilege to documents and things, the Supreme Court in [*Hickman v. Taylor*, 329 U.S. 495, 91 L. Ed. 451, 67 S. Ct. 385 (1947),] made clear that disclosure of the opinions or mental processes of counsel may occur when nontangible work product is sought through depositions, interrogatories, and requests for admissions [sic]."); *Stevens v. U.S.*, No. 03-81110-CIV-HURLEY, 2011 U.S. Dist. LEXIS 161641, at *4 (S.D. Fla. July 25, 2011) ("[A] request for admission exceeds the scope of [Federal] Rule 36 where it seeks to compel discovery protected under the work product privilege. For example, a request for admission which seeks to uncover an opponent's evidentiary plans for trial is improper."); *Howell v. Maytag*, 168 F.R.D. 502, 504 (M.D. Pa. 1996) (same).

[99] *E.g., Tex. Dep't of Pub. Safety Officers Ass'n v. Denton*, 897 S.W.2d 757, 760 (Tex. 1995) ("Denton had the right to assert his Fifth Amendment privilege to avoid civil discovery if he reasonably feared the answers would tend to incriminate him."); *In re Marriage of Cone*, No. 10-14-00179-CV, 2016 Tex. App. LEXIS 4445, at *9, 2016 WL 1722821 (Tex. App.—Waco Apr. 28, 2016, no pet.) (mem. op.) (same); *Alief Indep. Sch. Dist. v. Perry*, 440 S.W.3d 228, 242–43 (Tex. App.—Houston [14th Dist.] 2013, pet. denied) (same); *In re Lowe*, 151 S.W.3d 739, 745 (Tex. App.—Beaumont 2004, pet. denied) (same).

that an admission cannot be used in another proceeding, a question exists regarding whether the Fifth Amendment privilege applies to requests for admission. Although no Texas case has directly considered the issue,[100] the privilege should apply to requests for admission because Texas Rule 198.3 neither provides immunity from criminal prosecution nor provides the responding party with adequate protection if a criminal proceeding involving the same facts is pending or possible.[101] For example,

---

[100] A few Texas cases, however, can be read as suggesting that the privilege does not apply to requests for admission. *E.g., In re Ferguson*, 445 S.W.3d 270, 277 (Tex. App.—Houston [1st Dist.] Mar. 12, 2013, orig. proceeding) (discussing cases and holding that "[f]rom the record before us, it cannot be determined whether Ferguson established to the trial court how her answers may tend to incriminate her in the criminal proceedings despite the provision in [Texas Rule] 198.3 that her answers could 'not be used against [her] in any other proceeding.'"); *In re Speer*, 965 S.W.2d 41, 46 (Tex. App.—Fort Worth 2008, orig. proceeding) (*dictum*); *Katin v. City of Lubbock*, 655 S.W.2d 360, 363 (Tex. App.—Amarillo 1983, writ ref'd n.r.e.) (rejecting an Fifth Amendment privilege assertion because the action was a civil injunctive one seeking only civil, and not criminal, penalties). *But see In re Marriage of Mize*, 558 S.W.3d 187, 194 (Tex. App.—Texarkana 2018, no pet.) ("The [Fifth Amendment] privilege may be invoked 'during the discovery process to avoid answering questions at a deposition, responding to interrogatories or requests for admissions, or to produce documents.'" (quoting *In re Ferguson*, 445 S.W.3d 270, 276 (Tex. App.—Houston [1st Dist.] Mar. 12, 2013, orig. proceeding))). Federal courts and most other state courts, however, have held that the Fifth Amendment privilege applies to requests for admission. *E.g., Davis-Lynch v. Moreno*, 667 F.3d 539, 547 (5th Cir. 2012) ("[A] party may invoke the Fifth Amendment privilege during the discovery process to avoid answering questions at a deposition, responding to interrogatories or requests for admissions [sic], or to produce documents."), *quoted with approval in Evans v. Capps*, No. 7:15-CV-252-BO, 2018 U.S. Dist. LEXIS 167930, at *14 (E.D.N.C. 2018), *Longoria v. Cty. of Dall.*, No. 3:14-cv-3111-L, 2015 U.S. Dist. LEXIS 79514, at *9, 2016 WL 6893625 (N.D. Tex. 2015), and *In re Marriage of Mize*, 558 S.W.3d 187, 194 (Tex. App.—Texarkana 2018, no pet.); *McCauley v. Sierra Cty. Bd.*, No. 16-1046 MV/GBW, 2017 U.S. Dist. LEXIS 125099, at *20, 2017 WL 3412084 (D.N.M. 2017) (sustaining an objection to a request for admission on Fifth Amendment grounds); *Gordon v. FDIC*, 427 F.2d 578, 581 (D.C. Cir. 1970) (recognizing that the privilege applied because admissions could be used by a criminal prosecutor "as a confirmation that facilitates preparation of the criminal case, or perhaps as a lead to other evidence, which is part of the protection of the constitutional privilege"); *Weinstein v. Univ. of Conn.*, No. 3:11CV1906 (WWE), 2014 U.S. Dist. LEXIS 107104, at *11, 2014 WL 3849971 (D. Conn. Aug. 5, 2014) ("Objections [to a request for admission] may properly be based on privilege, vagueness, Fifth Amendment protection, and that the request goes beyond the scope of discovery."); *Helena Chem. Co. v. Skinner*, No. 4:11CV00691 SWW, 2012 U.S. Dist. LEXIS 125736, at *5, 2012 WL 3860604 (E.D. Ark. Sept. 5, 2012) (upholding a Fifth Amendment objection to requests for admission); *State v. Ott*, 808 P.2d 305, 310–12 (Ariz. Ct. App. 1990) ("[T]he better rule is that a civil litigant may invoke the privilege against self-incrimination to justify his refusal to respond to requests for admission."); *First Fed. Savs. & Loan Ass'n v. Schamanek*, 684 P.2d 1257, 1262 (Utah 1984) ("Full and complete protection of that right can be afforded only if a party may decline to answer by interposing an objection to requests for admissions [sic]."); *Zakia v. Zakia*, 104 Va. Cir. 168, 171–72 (Va. Cir. Ct. 2020) (allowing the defendant to invoke his Fifth Amendment privilege against self-incrimination in response to a request for admission).

[101] *Cf. FDIC v. Logsdon*, 18 F.R.D. 57, 58 (W.D. Ky. 1955) ("Neither this Rule nor any other statute, however, guarantees this defendant absolute immunity from federal criminal prosecution. Consequently to require the defendant in this case to give self-incriminating testimony would be a violation of his constitutional rights."); *First Fed. Sav. & Loan Ass'n v.*

an admission not only can be used by a criminal prosecutor "as a confirmation that facilitates preparation of the criminal case, [but also] as a lead to other evidence, which is part of the protection of the constitutional privilege."[102]

No compelling reason, however, exits for treating a timely, properly asserted Fifth Amendment privilege to a request for admission any differently than an assertion to a deposition question or an interrogatory. Thus, the requesting party can have the requests read into evidence, followed immediately by the responding party's Fifth Amendment assertion and an explanation of the adverse legal inference that can be drawn from the assertion.[103]

10-5:8 Objections

Texas Rule 193.2 sets forth the obligations and procedures for objecting to written-discovery requests, such as requests for admission.[104] The general principles relating to objections are discussed in Chapter 5, section 5-3. Proper and improper objections to requests for admission are discussed in the following sections of this chapter.

10-5:8.1 General, Subject-to, and Boilerplate Objections

As discussed in Chapter 5, sections 5-3:2 and 5-3:3, respectively, "general" and "subject-to" objections to requests for admission[105] generally are improper and boilerplate objections to them always are improper.[106]

Schamanek, 684 P.2d 1257, 1262 (Utah 1984) ("In our view, the interests that the privilege against self-incrimination were designed to safeguard cannot be adequately protected by compelling a person to trade that right for the attenuated protection of [Utah] Rule 36(b).").

102 *Gordon v. FDIC*, 427 F.2d 578, 581 (D.C. Cir. 1970); *accord State v. Ott*, 808 P.2d 305, 311 (Ariz. Ct. App. 1990) ("Significantly, the rule does not address the use of the fruits of the admission or protect against an admission that may furnish one tiny link in the chain of evidence establishing criminal liability. . . . Because [Arizona R]ule 36 does not protect against derivative use of information obtained through admissions, its protection is not coextensive with the scope of the privilege against self-incrimination.").

103 *E.g., Wilson v. Misko*, 508 N.W.2d 238, 253 (Neb. 1993); *Kramer v. Levitt*, 558 A.2d 760, 766–67 (Md. Ct. Spec. App. 1989).

104 Tex. R. Civ. P. 193.2.

105 "General objections" typically are set forth in a section at the beginning of a discovery response entitled "general objections" that includes every imaginable objection, such as overbreadth, undue burden, relevance, vagueness, ambiguity, harassment, cumulativeness, duplicativeness, and privilege, and are asserted by reference "to the extent they apply" in the response to each request for admission. "Subject-to" objections are a litany of prophylactic, boilerplate objections, such as those set forth above, in the response to each request for admission and then, "subject to and without waiving" the objections, the response purports to admit or deny, in whole or part, the request. See Chapter 5, section 5-3:2 (discussing "general" and "subject-to" objections).

106 *Liguria Foods, Inc. v. Griffith Labs., Inc.*, 320 F.R.D. 168, 170 n.1 (N.D. Iowa Mar. 13, 2017) (A boilerplate objection is an objection that "merely states the legal grounds for the objection without (1) specifying how the discovery request is deficient and (2) specifying how the objecting party would be harmed if it were forced to respond to the request. For example, a boilerplate objection might state that a discovery request is irrelevant or overly broad without taking the next step to explain why. These objections are taglines, completely devoid of any individualized factual analysis." (quoting Matthew L. Jarvey, *Boilerplate Discovery*

10-5:8.2 Proportionality

As discussed in Chapter 5, section 5-3:4, want of "proportionality" can be asserted as an objection to a set of requests for admission.[107]

10-5:8.3 Scope Objections: Relevance and Not Reasonably Calculated to Lead to the Discovery of Admissible Evidence

If a request for admission seeks an admission about a matter that neither is relevant to the action's subject matter nor reasonably calculated to lead to the discovery of admissible evidence, the responding party should object on those grounds.[108] Discovery's scope (i.e., information that is relevant or reasonably calculated to lead to the discovery of admissible evidence) is discussed in Chapter 4, section 4-3.

10-5:8.4 Overbreadth

Overbreadth is a proper objection to a request for admission.[109] A request for admission suffers from this malady when it encompasses time periods, activities, locations,

---

Objections: How They Are Used, Why They Are Wrong, and What We Can Do About Them, 61 Drake L. Rev. 913, 914–16 (2013))). "General" and "subject-to" objections typically are boilerplate ones. See Chapter 5, section 5-3:3 (discussing boilerplate objections).

107 *In re State Farm Lloyds,* 520 S.W.3d 595, 599 (Tex. 2017) (orig. proceeding) ("[A]ll discovery is subject to the proportionality overlay embedded in our discovery rules and inherent in the reasonableness standard to which our electronic-discovery rule is tethered."). The proportionality factors are: (1) the likely benefit of the requested discovery; (2) the needs of the case; (3) the amount in controversy; (4) the parties' resources; (5) the importance of the issues at stake in the litigation; (6) the importance of the proposed discovery in resolving the litigation; and (7) any other articulable factor bearing on proportionality. *In re State Farm Lloyds,* 520 S.W.3d 595, 607–12 (Tex. 2017) (orig. proceeding). See also Chapter 5, section 5-3:4 (discussing proportionality).

108 *In re Young,* 410 S.W.3d 542, 551 (Tex. App.—Beaumont 2013, no pet.) (affirming the trial court's ruling that requests for admission were improper because they did not seek admissions regarding relevant matters); *cf. Faynik v. Magical Cruise Co.,* No. 6:17-cv-1282-Orl-37TBS, 2018 U.S. Dist. LEXIS 224244, at *23, 2018 WL 7360669 (M.D. Fla. Sept. 4, 2018) ("Defendant objected to all of these requests as harassing, irrelevant and not reasonably calculated to lead to the discovery of admissible evidence, contending that Plaintiff has not alleged or testified to any type of design defect as causing or contributing in any way to her alleged slip and fall. While the Court does not find the requests to be harassing, it agrees that they are not relevant. Plaintiff claims she slipped or tripped on a foreign liquid or object. Matters relating to the construction of the vessel are not shown to be relevant to that issue."); *Foley v. Orange Cty.,* No. 6:12-cv-269-Orl-37KRS, 2013 U.S. Dist. LEXIS 81163, at *34, 2013 WL 2477231 (M.D. Fla. 2013) ("Requests for admission are limited to information that is otherwise discoverable. Therefore, objections that requests must be relevant are proper."); *Bridgewater v. Sweeny,* No. 2:11-cv-1216-CMK-P, 2012 U.S. Dist. LEXIS 157188, at *7–10, 2012 WL 5387968 (E.D. Cal. Nov. 1, 2012) (sustaining relevance objections to requests for admission); *Jacobs v. Sullivan,* No. 1:05-cv-01625-LJO-GSA-PC, 2012 U.S. Dist. LEXIS 102161102171, at *45, 66, 75, 78, 2012 WL 2995648 (E.D. Cal. July 23, 2012) (same); *McCormick v. Allmond,* 773 N.W.2d 409, 414–15 (Neb. 2009) (same).

109 *Cf. Illes v. Beavan,* No. 1:12-CV-0395, 2013 U.S. Dist. LEXIS 20826, at *11, 2013 WL 522075 (M.D. Pa. Feb. 11, 2013) (sustaining an overbreadth objection to a request for admission);

or products that are not relevant to the action's subject matter.[110] It also suffers from the malady when it seeks sweeping admissions regarding liability or damages that are not tied to any facts. For example, a request asking a plaintiff to "admit that [it] no longer wish[es] to pursue [its] cause of action[,]"[111] admit "that [it] ha[s] not been injured in any manner as a direct result of the alleged acts of [the defendant] as set forth in . . . Plaintiff's Original Petition[,]"[112] "[a]dmit or deny that each allegation made in the Amended Original Petition filed in this case is true[,]"[113] or admit "[a]s a proximate result of your breaching the contract made the basis of this suit, the Plaintiffs have suffered consequential damages in an amount not less than 10 million dollars"[114] are so sweeping and nonspecific that they are overbroad.[115] A central consideration in determining overbreadth is whether the request could have been more narrowly tailored.[116]

10-5:8.5 Undue Burden or Expense

An undue burden or expense objection to a request for admission generally is improper[117] because (1) a proper request for admission should relate to a single, discrete matter,[118] and (2) the responding party is only required to make a "reasonable inquiry" into "information known or easily obtainable."[119] Thus, rather than interposing such

---

Hageman v. Accenture, LLP, No. 10-1759 (RHR/TNL), 2012 U.S. Dist. LEXIS 6192, at *4–5 (D. Minn. Jan. 18, 2012) (same).

110 *In re K & L Auto Crushers, LLC*, 627 S.W.3d 239, 251 (Tex. 2021) (orig. proceeding) ("In essence, an overbroad discovery request is one that seeks irrelevant information.").

111 *Powell v. City of McKinney*, 711 S.W.2d 69, 70 (Tex. App.—Dallas 1986, writ ref'd n.r.e.).).

112 *In re Estate of Herring*, 970 S.W.2d 583, 589 (Tex. App.—Corpus Christi 1998, pet. denied).

113 *Birdo v. Hammers*, 842 S.W.2d 700, 701 (Tex. App.—Tyler 1992, writ denied).

114 *Lucas v. Clark*, 347 S.W.3d 800, 802-03 (Tex. App.—Austin 2011, pet. denied).

115 *Lucas v. Clark*, 347 S.W.3d 800, 804 (Tex. App.—Austin 2011, pet. denied); *In re Estate of Herring*, 970 S.W.2d 583, 589 (Tex. App.—Corpus Christi 1998, pet. denied); *Birdo v. Hammers*, 842 S.W.2d 700, 701 (Tex. App.—Tyler 1992, writ denied); *Powell v. City of McKinney*, 711 S.W.2d 69, 71 (Tex. App.—Dallas 1986,writ ref'd n.r.e.).

116 *E.g., In re Allstate Cty. Mut. Ins. Co.*, 227 S.W.3d 667, 669 (Tex. 2007) (orig. proceeding) (per curiam); *In re CSX Corp.*, 124 S.W.3d 149, 153 (Tex. 2003) (orig. proceeding) (per curiam); *In re Am. Optical Corp.*, 988 S.W.2d 711, 713 (Tex. 1998) (orig. proceeding) (per curiam); *In re Fed. Corp.*, No. 13-16-00219-CV, 2016 Tex. App. LEXIS 11816, at *5, 2016 WL 6519110 (Tex. App.—Corpus Christi Nov. 1, 2016, orig. proceeding) (mem. op.); *In re Nat'l Lloyds Ins. Co.*, No. 13-15-00390-CV, 2015 Tex. App. LEXIS 11299, *15 n.3, 2015 WL 6759153 (Tex. App.—Corpus Christi Nov. 3, 2015, orig. proceeding) (mem. op.); *In re Halliburton Energy Servs., Inc.*, No. 01-11-00358-CV, 2011 Tex. App. LEXIS 7974, at *9, 2011 WL 4612726 (Tex. App.—Houston [1st Dist.] Oct. 4, 2011, orig. proceeding) (mem. op.); *In re Hernandez*, No. 14-11-00408-CV, 2011 Tex. App. LEXIS 7981, at *10, 2011 WL 4600706 (Tex. App.—Houston [14th Dist.] Oct. 6, 2011, orig. proceeding) (mem. op.); *In re Waste Mgmt. of Tex., Inc.*, No. 13-11-00197-CV, 2011 Tex. App. LEXIS 7192, at *23, 2011 WL 3855745 (Tex. App.—Corpus Christi Aug. 31, 2011, orig. proceeding) (mem. op.).

117 *Cf. Interland, Inc. v. Bunting*, No. 1:04-CV-444-ODE, 2005 U.S. Dist. LEXIS 36112, at *28, 2005 WL 2414990 (N.D. Ga. Mar. 31, 2005) ("Objections that claim the requests are burdensome . . . are not proper."); *Henry v. Champlain Enters., Inc.*, 212 F.R.D. 73, 78 n.2 (N.D.N.Y. 2003) (same); *Diederich v. Dep't of Army*, 132 F.R.D. 614, 617 (S.D.N.Y. 1990) (same).

118 *See* Tex. R. Civ. P. 198.1 ("Each matter for which an admission is requested must be stated separately.").

119 Tex. R. Civ. P. 198.2(b).

an objection, the responding party, if an answer to the request really would impose an undue burden or expense, can properly answer that, after reasonable inquiry, the information known or easily obtainable is insufficient to enable the responding party to admit or deny the request.[120] If, however, responding to a *set* of requests for admission would be unduly burdensome or expensive because, for example, it contains an excessive number of requests or is unreasonably cumulative or duplicative of other discovery, the responding party either can object to the set of requests for admission on proportionality grounds or move for protection under Texas Rule 192.6.

10-5:8.6 Vagueness and Ambiguity

An objection that a request for admission is vague or ambiguous is proper.[121] A request for admission is vague or ambiguous when its wording is such that it is uncertain what information is sought.[122]

To properly object to a request in its entirety as vague or ambiguous, the responding party should explain why it is vague or ambiguous.[123] Not only should the responding

---

120 See Chapter 10, section 10-5:4 (discussing lack-of-information responses to requests for admission).

121 *Cf. Bowers v. Mortg. Elec. Registration Sys.*, No. 10-4141-JTM-DJW, 2012 U.S. Dist. LEXIS 93864, at *9, 2012 WL 2798801 (D. Kan. July 9, 2012) ("Here, the Court agrees with Defendant MERS that the Request's use of the vague and ambiguous phrase "fix problems" makes the request too speculative to be admitted or denied."); *Erie Ins. Prop. & Cas. Co. v. Johnson*, 272 F.R.D. 177, 185 (S.D. W. Va. 2010) (finding that the word "insurer" was ambiguous); *Vlasich v. Fishback*, No. 1:05-cv-01615-LJO-GSA-PC, 2009 U.S. Dist. LEXIS 43098, at *11, 14, 15, 2009 WL 1309727 (E.D. Cal. May 11, 2009) (sustaining vagueness and ambiguity objections); *Cunningham v. Standard Fire Ins. Co.*, No. 07-cv-02538, 2008 U.S. Dist. LEXIS 52518, at *7 (D. Colo. May 29, 2008) (same).

122 *Black's Law Dictionary* 93, 1689 (11th ed. 2019) (defining "ambiguity" and "ambiguous" as "[a]n uncertainty of meaning or intention" and "vague" as "imprecise . . . [and] uncertain"); *Merriam-Webster.com Dictionary*, https://www.merriam-webster.com/dictionary/ambiguous (last visited July 21, 2021) (defining "ambiguous" as "doubtful or uncertain or "capable of being understood in two or more possible senses or ways"); *Merriam-Webster.com Dictionary*, https://www.merriam-webster.com/dictionary/vague (last visited July 21, 2021) (defining "vague" as "not clearly expressed: stated in indefinite term" or "not having precise meaning").

123 *Cf. Whole Woman's Health All. v. Hill*, No. 1:18-cv-01904-SEB-MJD, 2020 U.S. Dist. LEXIS 35880, at *9, 2020 WL 1028040 (S.D. Ind. Mar. 20, 2020) ("Instead of a semantic quibble on the wording, Defendants should have also applied their commonsense interpretation of the phrase 'such as'—comparing a similar expert report like Dr. Stroud's—and identified this interpretation in their response."); *Kajeet, Inc. v. Qustodio, LLC*, No. SA CV 18-1519-JAK (PLAx), 2019 U.S. Dist. LEXIS 227979, at *10, 2019 WL 8060078 (C.D. Cal. Oct. 22, 2019) ("When the meaning of a particular term in a request is somewhat inexact, the responding party should supply its own definition and admit or deny, or qualify its admission or denial to make it accurate and responsive."); *State Auto. Mut. Ins. Co. v. Freehold Mgmt.*, No. 3:16-cv-2255-L, 2018 U.S. Dist. LEXIS 123283, at *31–32, 2018 WL 3548866 (N.D. Tex. July 24, 2018) ("The Court has previously explained that a 'party objecting to discovery as vague or ambiguous has the burden to show such vagueness or ambiguity'; that '[a] party objecting on these grounds must explain the specific and particular way in which a request is vague'; that '[t]he responding party should exercise reason and common sense to attribute ordinary definitions to terms and phrases utilized in [requests for admission]' and, '[i]f necessary to clarify its answers, . . . may include any reasonable definition of the

party identify the words or phrases in the request that are vague or ambiguous, but it also should explain why they are vague or ambiguous (i.e., why they are reasonably susceptible of more than one meaning and why the responding party cannot use the word's or phrase's ordinary or other meaning in responding to the request).

The mere fact that a word or phrase in a request for admission is undefined or unclear does not necessarily make the entire request objectionable. Rather, the responding party should use common sense when interpreting words and phrases used in the request, giving them their ordinary meanings, giving them their specialized meaning used in the industry at issue, defining them as the opposing party has defined or used them in its pleadings or discovery responses, or providing its own definition of the term or phrase.[124]

---

term or phrase at issue'; and that, '[i]f a party believes that the request is vague, that party [should] attempt to obtain clarification [by conferring with the requesting party] prior to objecting on this ground.'" (quoting *Heller v. City of Dall.*, 303 F.R.D. 466, 488 (N.D. Tex. 2014))); *AMTRAK v. Cimarron Crossing Feeders, LLC*, No. 16-cv-1094-JTM-TJJ, 2017 U.S. Dist. LEXIS 60822, at *13, 2017 WL 1408226 (D. Kan. Apr. 20, 2017) ("A party objecting to a discovery request as vague or ambiguous has the burden to show such vagueness or ambiguity."); *In re K-Dur Antitrust Litig.*, No. 01-1652 (JAG), 2007 U.S. Dist. LEXIS 96066, at *104–05, 2007 WL 5302308 (D.N.J. Jan. 2, 2007) ("An objection that does not quantify the nature of the vagueness or ambiguity is worthless. With respect to Request Nos. 54 and 119, it is not clear what about the respective Requests is 'vague' or 'ambiguous' and Schering makes no attempt to articulate the same. Absent this specificity, this objection, as stated, is improper.") (citation omitted).

[124] *Cf. Perez v. KDE Equine, LLC*, No. 3:15-CV-00562-CRS, 2017 U.S. Dist. LEXIS 570, at *27–28, 2017 WL 56616 (W.D. Ky. Jan. 4, 2017) ("Defendants' objection to the Secretary's failure to define the term 'typically' is similarly meritless. When a party is in doubt about the meaning of a discovery request, the responding party should give it a 'reasonable interpretation,' which may be specified in the response. Defendants should ascribe a reasonable interpretation to the term 'typically' in more specifically denying this request." (quoting *Connectus LLC v. Ampush Media, Inc.*, No. 8:15-cv-2778-T-33-JSS, 2016 U.S. Dist. LEXIS 165010, at *13–14, 2016 WL 6996147 (M.D. Fl. Nov. 30, 2016))); *Keycorp v. Holland*, No. 3:16-CV-1948-D, 2016 U.S. Dist. LEXIS 147926, at *41, 2016 WL 6277813 (N.D. Tex. Oct. 26, 2016) (overruling respondent's vagueness objections where they did not "reflect that she made an effort to attribute ordinary definitions to the terms and phrases utilized, to include any reasonable definition of the term or phrase at issue to clarify her answers, or attempted to obtain clarification prior to objecting on this ground"); *Heller v. City of Dall.*, 303 F.R.D. 466, 491–92 (N.D. Tex. 2014) ("The responding party 'should exercise reason and common sense to attribute ordinary definitions to terms and phrases utilized in [requests for admission]. If necessary to clarify its answers, the responding party may include any reasonable definition of the term or phrase at issue.' Further, '[i]f a party believes that the request is vague, that party [should] attempt to obtain clarification prior to objecting on this ground.'" (quoting *McCoo v. Denny's Inc.*, 192 F.R.D. 675, 694 (D. Kan. 2000), and *Consumer Elecs. Ass'n v. Compras & Buys Magazine, Inc.*, No. 08-21085-CIV-UNGARO/SIMONTON, 2008 U.S. Dist. LEXIS 80465, at *5–6, 2008 WL 4327253 (S.D. Fla. Sept. 18, 2008))); *Johnson v. Mission Support*, No. 2:08-CV-0877-DN-EJF, 2013 U.S. Dist. LEXIS 11314, at *18, 2013 WL 318707 (D. Utah Jan. 28, 2013) ("The phrases 'policies and procedures' and 'the contract' are not so ambiguous, at this late stage in the litigation, so as to prevent a response. Federal Rule of Civil Procedure 36 requires the responding party to admit, qualify, or deny as necessary to provide a fair response to the substance of the request. Mission Support can qualify its response by providing its own definitions of 'policies and procedures' and 'contract' and respond as completely as it can."); *Clean Earth of Md., Inc. v. Total Safety,*

10-5:8.7 Unreasonably Cumulative or Duplicative

An objection that a request for admission is unreasonably duplicative or cumulative of another request or other discovery, such as a disclosure, an interrogatory answer, or deposition testimony, is proper.[125] To establish that a request for admission is

---

Inc., No. 2:10-cv-119, 2011 U.S. Dist. LEXIS 118146, at *11, 2011 WL 4832381 (N.D.W. Va. Oct. 12, 2011) ("Defendant objected to the requests on an equally unfounded objection to the word 'processing.' Defendant in this case has produced documents referencing processing functions and Plaintiff has also produced many documents making similar references to 'processing.' To now claim that Defendant has no idea what the word 'processing' means makes little sense."); *Ice Corp. v. Hamilton Sundstrand Inc.*, No. 05-4135-JAR, 2007 U.S. Dist. LEXIS 32078, at *12, 2007 WL 1297120 (D. Kan. Apr. 30, 2007) (overruling vague and ambiguous objections to requests for admission because the responding party could easily have used reason and common sense to interpret the phrases used in the requests); *A. Farber & Partners, Inc. v. Garber*, 237 F.R.D. 250, 255 n.4 (C.D. Cal. 2006) ("At oral argument, plaintiff noted that defendant . . . had set forth his own definition of a phrase set forth in the request (and other requests), and then admitted the request; thus, plaintiff argued, the motion was not moot as to request no. 123 (and others). However, since plaintiff had not defined the phrase in the request, the Court finds defendant . . . could properly give it a common and reasonable meaning and then respond to the request."); *U.S. ex. rel. Englund v. L.A. Cty.*, 235 F.R.D. 675, 685 (E.D. Cal. 2006) ("It is not ground for objection that the request is 'ambiguous' unless so ambiguous that the responding party cannot, in good faith, frame an intelligent reply. Parties should 'admit to the fullest extent possible, and explain in detail why other portions of a request may not be admitted.' Failure to do so may result in sanctions." (quoting *Marchand v. Mercy Med. Ctr.*, 22 F.3d 933, 938 (9th Cir. 1994))); *Audiotext Commc'ns Network, Inc. v. US Telecom, Inc.*, No. 94-2395-GTV, 1995 U.S. Dist. LEXIS 15395, at *16, 1995 WL 625744 (D. Kan. Oct. 5, 1995) ("Plaintiffs quibble about the meaning of certain undefined phrases and other alleged ambiguity. If necessary plaintiffs can admit or deny requests which contain undefined phrases by defining the phrase themselves.").

125 *Cf. Bruno v. City of Schenectady*, No. 1:12-CV-0285 (GTS/DJS), 2018 U.S. Dist. LEXIS 211770, at *6–7 & n.3, 2018 WL 211770 (N.D.N.Y. 2018) (explaining that requests for admission "as to the accuracy of sentences in a document that has already been admitted as authentic" or "as to whether or not a particular witness testified to certain information at a deposition" are unreasonably duplicative and cumulative); *K.C.R. v. Cty. of L.A.*, No. CV 13-3806 PSG (SSx), 2014 U.S. Dist. LEXIS 98276, at *14–15, 2014 WL 3433772 (C.D. Cal. July 14, 2014) (same); *Vergara v. City of Waukegan*, No. 04 C 6586, 2007 U.S. Dist. LEXIS 82562, at *8–9, 2007 WL 3334501 (N.D. Ill. Nov. 6, 2007) (finding a request for admission unreasonably duplicative of deposition testimony); *see also Fleming v. Escort, Inc.*, No. CV 09-105-S-BLW, 2011 U.S. Dist. LEXIS 14254, at *6–7, 2011 WL 573599 (D. Idaho Feb. 13, 2011) (ruling that 216 requests for admission were "excessive" because they were redundant of deposition testimony).

It should be noted, however, that "written interrogatories and requests for admission are not adequate substitutes for conducting a deposition." *Barnett v. Norman*, No. 1:05-cv-01022-SKO PCSKOPC, 2010 U.S. Dist. LEXIS 92077, at *2–3, 2010 WL 3220122 (E.D. Cal. Aug. 10, 2010); *accord N.J. v. Spring Corp.*, No. 03-2071-JWL20710JWL, 2010 U.S. Dist. LEXIS 14890, at *9–10, 2010 WL 610671 (D. Kan. Feb. 19, 2010). Moreover, requests for admission and interrogatories generally are not duplicative or cumulative of production requests. *Cf. Becker v. Dahl*, No. CIV S-10-0519 FCD EFB P, 2011 U.S. Dist. LEXIS 5724, at *4, 2011 WL 121697 (E.D. Cal. Jan. 1312, 2011) ("Plaintiff's objection on the ground that these requests are duplicative lacks merit. As defendants note, a request for production of documents seeks documents, while an interrogatory is a question seeking a written unreasonably cumulative or duplicative, the responding party should specifically identify the other discovery to which the objected-to request is unreasonably cumulative or duplicative and explain why it is so.[126]

10-5:8.8 Assumes Facts Not in Evidence

On occasion, a responding party will object to a request for admission because it purportedly "assumes facts not in evidence" or "calls for speculation." These objections generally are improper because (1) they are trial objections, (2) a responding party has a duty of reasonable inquiry in responding to interrogatories, (3) an opposing party is entitled to discovery regarding "any matter that is not privileged and is relevant to the subject matter of the pending action" or that "appears reasonably calculated to lead to the discovery of relevant evidence."[127] In other words, the objection is contrary to the purpose of discovery, which is to learn facts.

---

response. While the nature of the information sought may in some respect be 'duplicative,' the responses sought take different forms, and defendants are entitled to use both vehicles for conducting discovery.").

126 *Cf. Wye Oak Tech., Inc. v. Republic of Iraq*, No. 1:10-cv-01182-RCL, 2018 U.S. Dist. LEXIS 159096, *3 (D.D.C. Sept. 18, 2018) ("By simply objecting to Wye Oak's request without referring to the specific documents that were previously produced, defendants have not met their burden of demonstrating that Wye Oak's request is in fact 'unreasonably cumulative or duplicative.'"); *Alexander v. FBI*, 194 F.R.D. 299, 302 (D.D.C. 2000) (rejecting unreasonably cumulative and duplicative objection because the responding party failed to identify the duplicative discovery).

127 *Cf. Baker v. Cty. of Missaukee*, No. 1:09-cv-1059, 2013 U.S. Dist. LEXIS 154072, at *19, 2013 WL 5786899 (W.D. Mich. Oct. 28, 2013) ("Plaintiff is correct that defendant's objection to request [for admission] 8 on the ground that it 'assumes facts not in evidence' is meritless. This trial objection has no place in discovery practice and is overruled."); *Martinez v. Allison*, No. 1:11-cv-00293-LJO-DLB PC, 2013 U.S. Dist. LEXIS 67956, at *13, 2013 WL 1982678 (E.D. Cal. May 13, 2013) (holding that an objection to request for admission because it "assumes facts not in evidence" is improper); *see also Sprint Communs. Co. L.P. v. Charter Communs.*, No. 20-cv-2161-JWB-TJJ, 2021 U.S. Dist. LEXIS 66408, at *8, 2021 WL 1265135 (D. Kan. Apr. 6, 2021) ("Individual Defendants also object to this RFP as assuming facts not in evidence 'regarding the purported "loss" or "deletion" of information.' The Court overrules this objection as an improper objection to Sprint's discovery request.") (footnotes omitted); *Two Rivers Pipeline & Constr. Co. v. Cimarex Energy Co.*, No. PE:19-CV-00049-DC-DF, 2020 U.S. Dist. LEXIS 206472, at *13–14, 2020 WL 6379302 (W.D. Tex. Sept. 14, 2020) ("Two Rivers objects to Cimarex's RFP Nos. 36–38, 40–46, and 51 as assuming facts not in evidence. Cimarex asserts that federal courts have rejected this objection. As noted by the Western District of Texas, '[a]ssuming facts not in evidence may be the basis for an objection during trial or some other evidentiary hearing. This however, is discovery.'" (quoting *Vickers v. JP Morgan Chase N.A.*, SA-12-CA-31-XR, 2013 U.S. Dist. LEXIS 208157, at *26 & n.99, 2013 WL 12134153 (W.D. Tex. Feb. 22, 2013))); *Sutton v. Mgmt. & Training Corp.*, No. 1:13-cv-1344 - AWI-JLT, 2015 U.S. Dist. LEXIS 11399, at *15–16, 2015 WL 402024 (E.D. Cal. 2015) ("As an initial matter, the objection that an interrogatory 'assumes facts not in evidence' is not proper in the course of discovery."); *Vickers v. JP Morgan Chase N.A.*, No. SA-12-CA-31-XR, 2013 U.S. Dist. LEXIS 208157, at *26–27 (W.D. Tex. 2013) ("JPMC's objections [to an interrogatory], 'assumes facts not in evidence, and assumes that such recording is required,' do not appear to be sufficient to avoid providing a further response, as the purpose of discovery is to learn facts.") (footnote omitted); *Richards v. Convergys Corp.*, Nos. 2:05-CV-00790-DAK, 2:05-CV-00812 DAK, 2006 U.S. Dist. LEXIS 63567, at *4–5 (D. Utah Sept. 5, 2006) (rejecting speculation and assumes-facts-not-in-evidence objections to

10-5:8.9 Expert Opinion

An objection that a request for admission improperly seeks "expert opinion" is proper only if the request specifically seeks an admission about the identity of the responding party's testifying expert, the subject matter on which the expert will testify, the expert's mental impressions or opinions, the identity of the expert's reviewed and relied upon documents, and other matters specifically relating to the expert's mental impressions or opinions or reviewed or relied upon documents.[128] In fact, it is the only proper expert-opinion objection with respect to testifying experts.[129]

Despite this fact, many practitioners will attempt to avoid answering requests for admission because doing so requires an "expert opinion" (i.e., to answer the request, the responding party must consult with its testifying experts). Most courts have rejected such an objection.[130]

---

an interrogatory because the responding "has a duty to make a reasonable inquiry for information in its possession"); *McGrath v. Cosco, Inc.*, No. 98-cv-1502, 1999 U.S. Dist. LEXIS 5893, at *3, 1999 WL 269920 (E.D. Pa. Apr. 21, 1999) ("That an interrogatory assumes facts not in evidence is not a valid objection in the context of discovery.") *Michilin Prosperity Co. v. Fellowes Mfg. Co.*, No. 04-1025 (RWR/JMF), 2006 U.S. Dist. LEXIS 32064, at *3, 2006 WL 1441575 (D.D.C. May 23, 2006) (rejecting a speculation objection to requests for admission because "to the extent that the requests may call for factual speculation, Michilin should have stated that it was unable to admit or deny and then explained why it could not truthfully admit or deny the request").

128 *In re Nat'l Lloyds Ins. Co.*, 532 S.W.3d 794, 814 (Tex. 2017) (orig. proceeding) (Texas "Rule 195 addresses the *methods* for obtaining such information, limiting testifying-expert discovery to that acquired through disclosures, expert reports, and oral depositions of expert witnesses." (footnote omitted) (quoting *In re Ford Motor Co.*, 427 S.W.3d 396, 397 (Tex. 2014) (orig. proceeding) (per curiam))); *In re Young*, 410 S.W.3d 542, 549 (Tex. App.—Beaumont 2013, no pet.) (holding that requests for admission cannot be used to obtain information about testifying experts). See also Chapter 6, section 6-3:3.14, and Chapter 7, section 7-4 (discussing discovery from testifying experts).

129 "Information concerning purely consulting experts, of course, is not discoverable." Tex. R. Civ. P. 195 cmt. 1 to 1999 change. See also Chapter 7, section 7-5 (discussing discovery from consulting experts).

130 *Cf. AMTRAK v. Cimarron Crossing Feeders, LLC*, No. 16-cv-1094-JTM-TJJ, 2017 U.S. Dist. LEXIS 60822, at *8–10, 2017 WL 1408226 (D. Kan. Apr. 20, 2017) (rejecting expert-opinion objection because "Railroad Plaintiffs must answer the Requests with the knowledge and information they presently possess, or can obtain after reasonable inquiry (independent of their experts)"); *McKinney/Pearl Rest., L.P. v. Metro. Life Ins. Co.*, 322 F.R.D. 235, 253–54 (N.D. Tex. 2016) (same); *Baugh v. Bayer Corp.*, No. 4-11-cv-525-RBH, 2012 U.S. Dist. LEXIS 131867, at *6–8, 2012 WL 4069582 (D.S.C. Sept. 17, 2012) (same); *House v. Giant of Md., LLC*, 232 F.R.D. 257, 262 (E.D. Va. 2005) (noting that the defendants' "answers reflect folklore within the bar which holds that requests for admission need not be answered if the subject matter of the request . . . 'addresses a subject for expert testimony'"); *Drutis v. Rand McNally & Co.*, 236 F.R.D. 325, 330–31 (E.D. Ky. 2006) (overruling the plaintiffs' objection to request for admission and directing them to supplement their responses even though they had to consult with their expert to do so); *Heartland Surgical Specialty Hosp., LLC v. Midwest Div., Inc.*, No. 05-2164-MLB-DWB, 2007 U.S. Dist. LEXIS 80182, at *18–19, 2007 WL 3171768 (D. Kan. Oct. 29, 2007) ("Heartland objects to Saint Luke's requests 531–42 on the basis that the requests seek to elicit expert testimony in advance of the expert disclosure deadline. It is insufficient, however, for a responding party to refuse to respond to a request for admission or simply state that its expert will provide the requested information

As explained by one federal court:

Federal Rule of Civil Procedure 26 does impose some limits on discovery of another party's testifying expert's opinions, through expert reports under Federal Rule 26(a)(2) and depositions under Federal Rule 26(b)(4)(A).

But those rules limit discovery targeted directly to or about an expert or the expert's knowledge or opinions. [Federal] Rule 36 requests [for admission], like those here, are properly directed to a party's position on a fact or the application of law to fact or the party's opinion about a fact or the application of law to fact—and can address ultimate facts that may present a genuine issue for trial. The party's position on a factual question may well be informed by consultation

---

in accordance with the expert disclosure deadlines; notwithstanding any expert disclosure deadlines, the responding party is required to respond with whatever discoverable information it presently has."). *But see Emerson v. Lab. Corp. of Am.*, No. 1:11-CV-01709-RWS, 2012 U.S. Dist. LEXIS 60636, at *9–10 (N.D. Ga. May 1, 2012) (sustaining objections to requests for admission because the requests for admission could only be answered by an expert).

In *In re Young*, 410 S.W.3d 542-49 (Tex. App.—Beaumont 2013, no pet.), the State, in a civil-commitment action against an allegedly violent sexual predator, moved for a protective order with respect to certain requests for admission because they would be "best answered by the psychological and/or psychiatric experts who [were] designated by Petitioner in this case, which Respondent [would] have the opportunity to [question] at the time of the expert's deposition" and apparently because they also sought information protected by the work-product privilege.

The Beaumont Court of Appeals, without either quoting or describing in any detail the specific requests at issue, held that the trial court did not abuse its discretion in granting the protective order:

> With respect to these thirty-sex requests, Young suggested in the trial court that "[o]ne party cannot limit the method or methods by which the other party chooses to conduct discovery." However, the reasonable inquiry required of a party in formulating responses to requests for admissions [sic] does not require that the attorneys ask its designated experts for the information that may be needed to answer requests for admission. Instead, discovery from experts is permitted "only through a request for disclosure under [Texas] Rule 194 and through depositions and reports as permitted by this rule."
>
> Based on the arguments that Young presented to the trial court, the trial court could reasonably conclude that Young improperly used [the] requests . . . in an effort to conduct discovery against the State's designated experts. We conclude the trial court did not abuse its discretion by granting the State's motion with respect to [the] requests. . . .

In re Young, 410 S.W.3d 542, 549 (Tex. App.—Beaumont 2013, no pet.) (citations omitted).

Although *In re Young* can be read as supporting the proposition that an expert-opinion objection is proper in Texas, the opinion does not quote or clearly describe the requests for admission at issue. Thus, it is unclear whether the requests sought information specifically about the State's experts (e.g., their identities, the subject matters about which they would testify, or their mental impressions or conclusions) or simply sought admissions about matters that required some expert input. Moreover, the defendant in *In re Young*, in response to the motion for protective order, did not make the arguments set forth in this section or cite any of the case law set forth above. *In re Young*, 410 S.W.3d 542, 549 (Tex. App.—Beaumont 2013, no pet.). Accordingly, *In re Young* should be limited to cases in which the requests for admission seek information specifically about the responding party's experts.

> with a retained expert. But an expert's knowledge or opinions, on the one hand, and a party's position on a fact or the application of law to fact or opinion about either, on the other, are separate objects of discovery. [Federal] Rule 26(b)(4) addresses discovery of the former, and [Federal] Rule 36 requests address the latter. And, further highlighting this conceptual difference, an expert's opinion or position on a fact and a party's position or opinion as to the same factual question may not be the same—for lack of a better phrase—as a factual matter. Indeed, a party's position and its expert's view or opinion on the same matter do not always line up at all—a sometimes vexing phenomenon to which many experienced trial lawyers can attest.
>
> [Federal] Rule 26 no more prohibits a party from asking another party for an admission on an ultimate fact as to which an expert witness may testify or on which a non-testifying expert may consult with the answering party than it prohibits a contention interrogatory to a party directed to the same matter. In short, a party cannot avoid discovery—whether by an interrogatory, a [Federal] Rule 36 request, or Federal Rule of Civil Procedure 30(b)(6) deposition testimony—of its own views on a factual matter in dispute (or perhaps, in fact, not in dispute) simply because its view on that matter may be informed by consulting with its retained experts. As other courts have observed, "[e]ven if complete answers to discovery requests may require the answering party to consult with experts, such considerations do not transform permissible factual discovery into 'expert discovery.'"[131]

The correctness of this holding is supported by Texas Rule 193.1, which requires a responding party, in responding to written discovery, to make "a complete response, based on all information reasonably available to the responding party or its attorney at the time the response is made."[132] Of course, information in the possession of a party's testifying expert is reasonably available to that party and that party's attorney after the expert's designation.

If a proper response to a request for admission truly requires a testifying expert's input and the answer date is before the responding party is required to designate such experts, the appropriate action is to reach an agreement with the requesting party to defer the answer until a reasonable time after the responding party's expert designations are due, move for an extension of time to respond to the request, or respond to the request by stating that the responding party cannot admit or deny the request because, after reasonable inquiry was made, the information known or easily obtainable is insufficient to enable the responding party to admit or deny it and then amend the response after the party's testifying experts are designated.[133]

---

131 *McKinney/Pearl Rest., L.P. v. Metro. Life Ins. Co.*, 322 F.R.D. 235, 253–54 (N.D. Tex. 2016) (citation omitted) (quoting *Geer v. Cox*, No. 01-2583-JAR, 2003 U.S. Dist. LEXIS 9230, at *10–11, 2003 WL 21245731 (D. Kan. May 21, 2003)).

132 Tex. R. Civ. P. 193.1.

133 *E.g., Baugh v. Bayer Corp.*, No. 4-11-cv-525-RBH, 2012 U.S. Dist. LEXIS 131867, at *9 n.3, 2012 WL 4069582 (D.S.C. Sept. 17, 2012) (deferring answer date for requests for admission until after the responding party's expert designation date).

10-5:8.10 Mirror-Image or Converse Requests

As pointed out in Chapter 10, section 10-2:2.2, the fact that two requests for admission are the mirror-image or converse of each other does not make the requests objectionable. Nonetheless, as also pointed out in Chapter 10, section 10-2:2.2, such requests for admission have limited utility if the responding party either fails to answer them or expressly admits both requests because mirror-image admissions merely create a fact issue with respect to the request's subject matter.

10-5:8.11 Compound Requests

Because Texas Rule 198.1 requires that "[e]ach matter for which an admission is requested must be stated separately," an objection that a request for admission is compound is proper.[134] A compound request for admission is one that asks the

---

[134] *Cf. King v. Biter*, No. 1:15-cv-00414-LJO-SAB (PC), 2018 U.S. Dist. LEXIS 3874, at *11, 2018 WL 339052 (E.D. Cal. Jan. 9, 2018) ("Defendant's objection as compound is proper as each request seeks admission of multiple facts regarding the submission or processing of inmate appeal."); *Bridgewater v. Sweeny*, No. 2:11-cv-1216-CMK-P, 2012 U.S. Dist. LEXIS 157188, at *6–7, 2012 WL 5387968 (E.D. Cal. Nov. 1, 2012) (sustaining compound objection to requests for admission); *James v. Maguire Corr. Facility*, No. C10-1795-SI (pr), 2012 U.S. Dist. LEXIS 128534, at *10, 2012 WL 3939343 (N.D. Cal. Sept. 10, 2012) ("Moreover, requests for admissions [sic] should not contain 'compound, conjunctive, or disjunctive . . . statements.'" (quoting *U.S. ex. rel. Englund v. L.A. Cty.*, 235 F.R.D. 675, 684 (E.D. Cal. 2006))); *Bovarie v. Schwarzenegger*, No. 08cv1661 LAB (NLS), 2011 U.S. Dist. LEXIS 17006, at *19, 2011 WL 719206 (S.D. Cal. Feb. 22, 2011) (sustaining compound objection to a request for admission); *McCormick v. Allmond*, 773 N.W.2d 409, 414–15 (Neb. 2009) ("A request for admission should necessitate only a simple response—not one where the entire request must be dissected into separate, unrelated parts and answered as such. Because McCormick's requests were compound and unnecessarily complicated, we conclude that '[t]here was other good reason for the failure to admit'[.]"). *But see Alexander v. 1328 Uptown, Inc.*, No. 18-cv-1544 (ECT/ECW), 2019 U.S. Dist. LEXIS 173315, at *55–56, 61, 2019 WL 4929931 (D. Minn. 2019) (overruling compound objections to requests for admission asking the defendants to "[10.] [a]dmit that the [Fortney Companies, Inc./Fortney Hospitality Group, Inc.] created and/or approved all official policies and procedures that Bar Louie and Bar Louie employees were to follow at all times relevant to the complaint in this matter[,]" "[13.] [a]dmit that Eric Fortney, Marc Fortney and/or Ronald Fortney were involved in the incorporation of (Fortney Companies, Inc./Fortney Hospitality Group, Inc.)", and "[14. [a]dmit that Eric Fortney, Marc Fortney and/or Ronald Fortney were involved in the incorporation of 1328 Uptown, Inc." because "while [they] contain the term 'and/or' or are otherwise compound, the Court concludes that at least some of the requests are capable of separation into distinct components. For example, . . . Request for Admission Nos. 13 and 14 may be answered as to Eric Fortney, Marc Fortney, and Ronald Fortney. Request for Admission No. 10 may be answered with respect to both 'created' and 'approved.'"); *In re Inc.*, No. 1:10-CV-51, 2018 U.S. Dist. LEXIS 239160, at *138 (E.D. Tex. June 8, 2018) ("Specifically regarding AET's Requests for Admissions Nos. 48, 49, 52, and 53, the compound nature of these requests do not excuse Kirby's obligation to respond to them."); *Eclipse Grp., LLP v. Target Corp.*, No. 15cv1411-JLS (BLM), 2017 U.S. Dist. LEXIS 77574, at *23–24 (S.D. Cal. May 19, 2017) (denying motion to compel as to one request for admission because it was compound, but ordering the defendants to respond to two other compound requests for admission because they were "not misleading, confusing, or ambiguous given the facts of this case"); *Akins v. State Farm Mut. Auto. Ins. Co.*, No. 10-CV-12755, 2011 U.S. Dist. LEXIS 82806, at *5, 2011 WL 3204839 (E.D. Mich. July 28, 2011) ("To the extent the request covers

responding party to admit multiple discrete facts and often uses the words "and," "or," or "and/or."[135] The mere fact, however, that the request contains interdependent facts does not make it compound. For example, a request asking a party to admit that "Smith, as defendant's president, had authority to sign the contract" is not compound even though it involves two facts: Smith was the defendant's president, and he had authority to sign the contract.[136]

Although a compound objection is proper, to avoid a motion testing the response's sufficiency, a responding party may be better served by answering the request if each part can be readily admitted or denied and, in a Level 1 action, by counting the request as one request for each discrete subpart.[137]

10-5:8.12 Genuine Issue for Trial or the Requesting Party Has the Burden of Proof

Objections to requests for admission because they relate to a matter in dispute, raise a genuine issue for trial, or relate to a matter on which the requesting party has the

---

more than one topic, Defendant still has an obligation to admit any portion that it can and deny the remainder."); *Plascencia v. BNC Mort., Inc. (In re Plascencia)*, No. 08-56305-ASW, 2012 Bankr. LEXIS 2855, at *36–37, 2012 WL 2161412 (Bankr. N.D. Cal. June 12, 2012) ("However, to the extent that the requests are compound, the requests are easily broken down into component parts, and 'should be denied or admitted in sequence with appropriate designation or qualification.'" (quoting *Tequila Centinela, S.A. de C.V. v. Bacardi & Co.*, 247 F.R.D. 198, 203 (D.D.C. 2008))); *Audiotext Commc'ns Network, Inc. v. US Telecom., Inc.*, No. 94-2395-GTV, 1995 U.S. Dist. LEXIS 15395, at *8, 1995 WL 625744 (D. Kan. Oct. 5, 1995) ("A compound request (seeking admission of multiple facts) or an ambiguous one should be answered as far as possible with appropriate qualification or explanation, rather than objected to entirely.").

Texas Rule 198.1's "separate matter" requirement arguably conflicts with language in Texas Rule 190.2(b)(5), which limits the number of requests for admission in a Level 1 action to fifteen, plus "[e]ach discrete subpart." The latter rule should not be read as negating compound objections to requests for admission, but rather merely as giving the responding party the option of answering a compound request and counting it as multiple requests against the fifteen-request limit.

135 For example, a request for admission asking the responding party to admit that it is a Texas corporation and has its principal place of business in Dallas, Texas, is compound because it requests an admission of two discrete topics: the locations of the responding party's state of incorporation and its principal place of business.

136 If one of the facts is wrong, the responding party can deny the request or, even better, deny the wrong one and admit the other (e.g., "Defendant denies that Smith was its president, but admits that, as its vice president, he had authority to sign the contract."). *Cf. Alexander v. 1328 Uptown, Inc.*, No. 18-cv-1544 (ECT/ECW), 2019 U.S. Dist. LEXIS 173315, at *61–62, 2019 WL 4929931 (D. Minn. 2019) ("Where it is evident that multiple, interdependent issues are contained in one request, defendant may deny the entire statement if one fact, on which the remainder of the request is premised, is denied; plaintiff drafts complex requests at his peril. Compound requests that are capable of separation into distinct components and that follow a logical or chronological order, however, should be denied or admitted in sequence with appropriate designation or qualification by defendant in its response." (quoting *Diederich v. Dep't of the Army*, 132 F.R.D. 614, 621 (S.D.N.Y. 1990))); *Harris v. Oil Reclaiming Co.*, 190 F.R.D. 674, 678 (D. Kan. 1999) (same).

137 Tex. R. Civ. P. 190.2(b)(5) (providing for a maximum of fifteen requests for admission, including discrete subparts, in a Level 1 action).

burden of proof are all improper.[138] Rather than objecting on these grounds, the responding party should deny the request if the matter really is in dispute.

10-5:8.13 The Matter Is Within the Requesting Party's Knowledge, Is Equally Available to the Parties, or Is Unknown to the Responding Party

A request for admission is not objectionable merely because the requesting party already knows the information sought by it or because the information is equally available to the parties. As explained by one federal court: "An objection based on a claim that a party already has all of the relevant information at their disposal is never a proper objection to a request for admission."[139] This is because the "purpose of [the] rule pertaining to requests for admissions [sic] is to expedite trial by removing essentially undisputed issues, thereby avoiding time, trouble and expense which otherwise would be required to prove issues."[140]

Similarly, a response that the responding party lacks personal knowledge is improper if the information is obtainable on reasonable inquiry.[141]

10-5:8.14 Supernumerary Objections

The Texas discovery rules limit the number of requests for admission only in Level 1 actions.[142] Thus, there is no express limit on the number of requests for admission

---

138 Tex. R. Civ. P. 198.2(b) ("An assertion that the request presents an issue for trial is not a proper response."); *cf. CUMIS Ins. Soc'y, Inc. v. Clark*, 318 F. Supp. 3d 199, 215 (D.D.C. 2018) (noting that "[a] party must not object solely on the ground that the request presents a genuine issue for trial." (quoting Fed. R. Civ. P. 36(a)(5))); *Layne Christensen Co. v. Purolite Co.*, No. CIV.A 09-2381-JWL-GLR, 2011 U.S. Dist. LEXIS 6737, at *26–27, 2011 WL 381611 (D. Kan. Jan. 25, 2011) (same); *Guinan v. A.I. duPont Hosp.*, No. 88-228, 2008 U.S. Dist. LEXIS 27798, at *5, 2008 WL 938874 (E.D. Pa. Apr. 7, 2008) (same); *House v. Giant of Md., LLC*, 232 F.R.D. 257, 260-62261 (E.D. Va. 2005) (same).

139 *In re K-Dur Antitrust Litig.*, No. 01-1652 (JAG), 2007 U.S. Dist. LEXIS 96066, at *49, 2007 WL 5302308 (D.N.J. Jan. 2, 2007); *accord HHCS Pharm., Inc. v. Express Scripts, Inc.*, No. 4:16-CV-1169 (CEJ), 2017 U.S. Dist. LEXIS 12938, at *9, 2017 WL 411367 (E.D. Mo. Jan. 31, 2017); *Longoria v. Cty. of Dall.*, No. 3:14-cv-3111-L, 2016 U.S. Dist. LEXIS 161675, at *20–21, 2016 WL 6893625 (N.D. Tex. Nov. 22, 2016); *Interland, Inc. v. Bunting*, No. 1:04-CV-444-ODE, 2005 U.S. Dist. LEXIS 36112, at *28, 2005 WL 2414990 (N.D. Ga. Mar. 31, 2005); *House v. Giant of Md.*, LLC, 232 F.R.D. 257, 261 (E.D. Va. 2005); *Henry v. Champlain Enters., Inc.*, 212 F.R.D. 73, 78 n.2 (N.D.N.Y. 2003); *Kutner Buick, Inc. v. Crum & Foster Corp.*, No. 95-CV-1268, 1995 U.S. Dist. LEXIS 12524, at *9, 1995 WL 508175 (E.D. Pa. Aug. 24, 1995).

140 *Diederich v. Dep't of Army*, 132 F.R.D. 614, 616 (S.D.N.Y. 1990) (quoting *Burns v. Phillips*, 50 F.R.D. 187, 188 (N.D. Ga. 1970)); *accord Miller v. White*, No. CV 14-7543-GW (KK), 2019 U.S. Dist. LEXIS 230759, at *11–12 (C.D. Cal. 2019); *Longoria v. Cty. of Dall.*, No. 3:14-cv-3111-L, 2016 U.S. Dist. LEXIS 161675, at *20–21, 2016 WL 6893625 (N.D. Tex. Nov. 22, 2016); *Concerned Citizens v. Belle Haven Club*, 223 F.R.D. 39, 445 (D. Conn. 2004).

141 *Herrara v. Scully*, 143 F.R.D. 545, 548 (S.D.N.Y. 1992). See also Chapter 5, section 5-2:1 (discussing a responding party's reasonable inquiry requirement).

142 Tex. R. Civ. P. 190.2(b)(5) (providing for a maximum of fifteen requests for admission, including discrete subparts, in a Level 1 action).

in Level 2 and 3 actions.[143] A responding party in a Level 2 or 3 action faced with an excessive number of requests for admission, however, is not without remedy. If it believes that the requesting party is abusing discovery by serving too many requests for admission, the responding party can move for a protective order that either limits the number of requests or orders that it need not respond to requests already served.[144] In ruling on such a motion, the court is to be guided by the proportionality considerations in Texas Rule 192.4.[145]

A responding party in a Level 1 action or a Level 3 action, whose discovery-control plan limits the number of requests for admission, that is faced with too many requests for admission, however, is in a much different and better position. But it cannot simply refuse to answer the entire set of requests for admission—it should answer the first fifteen (or the number set forth in the discovery-control plan) and interpose a supernumerary objection to the rest.[146] Of course, answering a supernumerary request waives the objection.[147]

Just as the responding party is not allowed to pick and choose which supernumerary requests for admission to answer, the requesting party cannot circumvent its violation by voluntarily withdrawing selected supernumerary requests. The operative word in Texas Rule 190.2(b)(5) is "serve" and every request served counts against the numerical limit.[148] So do requests to which objections have been interposed, and a requesting party cannot withdraw them.[149]

10-5:8.15 The "Document Speaks for Itself"

Requests for admission often ask the responding party to admit that contracts, statutes, or regulations impose a particular obligation, to admit that contractual provisions, statutes, regulations, or documents have a particular meaning, or to admit the accuracy of quoted or textual material from a contract, statute, regulation, or document. Rather than admitting or denying such requests, responding parties often object to them because "the document[, statute, or regulation] speaks for itself." This is not a proper objection. As explained by one federal court:

> [A]s a statement of a document's text is a matter of fact, a request calling upon a party to admit or deny that such quoted material is the actual text of an identified document, relevant to the case, may not be ignored on the ground that the request seeks an interpretation of the text or that the document in question "speaks for itself." Documents do not speak, rather, they represent factual information from which legal consequences may follow. The existence of a

---

143 Tex. R. Civ. P. 190.3-190.4. A Level 3 discovery-control plan can limit the number of requests for admission. Tex. R. Civ. P. 190.4(b)(3).

144 Tex. R. Civ. P. 192.6(b).

145 See Chapter 4, section 4-5 (discussing protective orders).

146 *See* Tex. R. Civ. P. 193.2 ("A party must comply with as much of the request to which the party has made no objection unless it is unreasonable under the circumstances to do so before obtaining a ruling on the objection."). See also Chapter 9, section 9-5:3.11 (discussing supernumerary objections to interrogatories).

147 See Chapter 9, section 9-5:3.11 (discussing supernumerary objections to interrogatories).

148 See Chapter 9, section 9-5:3.11 (discussing supernumerary objections to interrogatories).

149 See Chapter 9, section 9-5:3.11 (discussing supernumerary objections to interrogatories).

referenced document and whether it contains a particular provision may well present factual issues of importance to the case. Thus, just as a [Federal] Rule 36 request may seek to remove the issue of a document's "genuineness" or authenticity, whether a particular document contains textual material as described in a request equally seeks to eliminate an unnecessary issue of fact for trial. It is therefore permissible to request that a party admit or deny a [Federal] Rule 36 request as to the accuracy of quoted textual material from a particular document relevant to the case.

[Also,] it is generally held that questions of contractual meaning or intent are questions of fact at trial. A statement of a party's understanding of the meaning or intent of a document is therefore a statement of fact, and where the question of the meaning of the document is at issue in the case, a request directed to another party seeking an admission or denial of a document's meaning or intent by that party as stated in the request relates to a statement fact, and is authorized by [Federal] Rule 36. Nor are such requests objectionable because the request may call for an admission as to an interpretation of a contractual provision which could otherwise require a judicial determination. "[Federal] Rule 36 would cover an admission by [a party] as to what its obligations were as a matter of law, because the text of the [Federal] Rule specifically authorizes requests for admissions of propositions of law as applied to fact." Moreover, the fact that an admission, provided in response to a request, may prove decisive to the case is no ground for refusal to respond.

Even if the meaning of a document or the intent of the parties as to a contractual provision is the issue ultimately to be decided, such questions do not raise a valid objection to a request to admit a party's understanding of a document's meaning or the intent of the parties as otherwise a party that does not intend to dispute such matters could refuse to answer thus requiring needless proof. Such a result is contrary to the purpose of [Federal] Rule 36 which is "to eliminate from controversy matters that will not be disputed." Conversely, if both sides agree as to the meaning and intent of particular contractual provisions, there will be no issue as to their meaning on summary judgment or at trial and the purpose of [Federal] Rule 36 will have been served. In this case, if Defendants do not admit to a proffered interpretation, Plaintiff will be on notice as to which provisions remain at issue thereby facilitating the orderly preparation of the case for submission to the court and furthering the purposes of [Federal] Rule 36.

Moreover, in this case, the Requests at issue do not relate to material which, like a line of lyrical poetry, may be subject to multiple interpretations. Rather, they are directed to business agreements, involving the parties to the instant litigation, using standard acquisition clauses applied to the particulars of the transactions, and routine business correspondence. As such, the range of interpretative possibilities is fairly limited thus constituting straightforward requests within the purview of [Federal] Rule 36.[150]

---

[150] *Booth Oil Site Admin. Grp. v. Safety-Kleen Corp.*, 194 F.R.D. 76, 80–81 (W.D.N.Y. 2000) (quoting *Langer v. Monarch Life Ins. Co.*, 966 F.2d 786, 805 (3d Cir. 1992)); *accord Aleris Rolled Prods.*, No. 4:18-CV-00113-JHM-HBB, 2020 U.S. Dist. LEXIS 136305, at *51, 2020 WL 4432415 (W.D. Ky. July 31, 2020); *District of Columbia ex rel. Z-Modular, LLC v. MCN Build, Inc.*, No. 18-cv-2947 (RJL/GMH), 2020 U.S. Dist. LEXIS 124719, at *6 (D.D.C. July 15,

In response to such a request for admission, the responding party should either admit or deny it or interpose one of the form or substantive objections discussed in this chapter. For example, if the request for admission asks the party to interpret a statute, rule, regulation, or an unambiguous contractual provision, an objection on the ground that the request seeks a legal conclusion is proper because the interpretation of such items is a question of law for the court.[151]

Many federal courts have held that requests for admission that do no more than ask a party to admit that a document, statute, rule, or regulation contains a quoted sentence or that a deponent testified in a certain way are improper.[152]

2020); *Light of the World Gospel Ministries v. Walthill*, No. 8:18CV312, 2020 U.S. Dist. LEXIS 110335, at *16, 2020 WL 3447641 (D. Neb. June 24, 2020); *Whole Woman's Health All. v. Hill*, No. 1:18-cv-01904-SEB-MJD, 2020 U.S. Dist. LEXIS 35880, at *19 n.4, 2020 WL 1028040 (S.D. Ind. Mar. 2, 2020); *U.S. ex rel. VT Milcom, Inc. v. PAT USA, Inc.*, No. 5:16-cv-00007, 2017 U.S. Dist. LEXIS 109574, at *6–7 (W.D. Va. July 14, 2017); *Iron Workers Local No. 60 Annuity Pension Fund v. Solvay Iron Works, Inc.*, No. 5:15-CV-0054 (BKS/DEP), 2017 U.S. Dist. LEXIS 61394, at *10–11, 2017 WL 1458772 (N.D.N.Y. Apr. 24, 2017); *Lewis v. Michaels Stores, Inc.*, No. 3:05-cv-1323-J-33HTS, 2007 U.S. Dist. LEXIS 50506, at *7 n.1, 2007 WL 2021833 (M.D. Fla. July 12, 2007); *House v. Giant of Md., LLC*, 232 F.R.D. 257, 261 (E.D. Va. 2005).

151 *Elliot v. Newsome*, No. 01-07-00692-CV, 2009 Tex. App. LEXIS 569, at *4–6, 2009 WL 214551 (Tex. App.—Houston [1st Dist.] Jan. 20, 2009, no pet.) (mem. op.) (reversing summary judgment based on deemed admissions that purported to interpret an unambiguous contract "contrary to the express terms of the agreement"); *see Entergy Gulf States, Inc. v. Summers*, 282 S.W.3d 433, 437 (Tex. 2009) ("The meaning of a statute is a legal question. . . ."); *Coker v. Coker*, 650 S.W.2d 391, 393 (Tex. 1983) ("If the written instrument is so worded that it can be given a certain or definite legal meaning or interpretation, then it is not ambiguous and the court will construe the contract as a matter of law.").

152 *Bruno v. City of Schenectady*, No. 1:12-CV-0285 (GTS/DJS), 2018 U.S. Dist. LEXIS 211770, at *6–7, 2018 WL 6599403 (N.D.N.Y. Dec. 17, 2018) ("Nor does the Court dispute that in a proper case, particularly one where the wording of a legal contract is at issue, a party may properly identify terms in the writing and seek an admission as to those. The present case, however, does not present this type of issue, and is much more akin to the case of *Van Wagenen v. CONRAIL.*, 170 F.R.D. 86, 87 (N.D.N.Y. 1997), wherein Magistrate Judge Homer held that requests for admission as to the accuracy of sentences in a document that has already been admitted as authentic, are requests that are 'unreasonably duplicative and cumulative within the meaning of [Federal] Rule 26(b)(2)(i).'") (footnote omitted); *Rios v. Tilton*, No. 2:07-cv-0790 WBS KJN P, 2010 U.S. Dist. LEXIS 108377, at *23–24, 2010 WL 3784703 (E.D. Cal. Sept. 24, 2010) (holding that requests for admission asking a party to admit the "authenticity of quoted portions" of a California Code and Department Operations Manual were "impermissible in scope and unduly burdensome"); *Caruso v. Coleman Co.*, No. 93-CV-6733, 1995 U.S. Dist. LEXIS 7934, at *9–10, 1995 WL 347003 (E.D. Pa. June 7, 1995) ("A request for admission as to whether or not a particular witness testified to certain information at a deposition is duplicative of the deposition itself."); *Workman v. Chinchinian*, 807 F. Supp. 634, 647–48 (E.D. Wash. 1992) ("Since the defendants have admitted that the letter is true and accurate, the only purpose served by the admission would be to bolster the effect of the letter in attacking Dr. Kempson's credibility. This was not the intent of the drafters of the rule.").

10-5:8.16 The Responding Party's Failure to Provide Discovery

It is improper to refuse to respond to requests for admission because the requesting party has withheld discovery.[153]

10-5:8.17 Harassment

Although a "harassment" objection is clearly a proper one,[154] it is difficult to envision a situation in which such an objection is a proper one to a request for admission. First, the definition of harassment does not readily lend itself to requests for admissions. "Harassment" is defined as "[w]ords, conduct, or action (usu[sually] repeated or persistent) that, being directed at a specific person, annoys, alarms, or causes substantial emotional distress in that person and serves no legitimate purpose."[155] Thus, what constitutes harassment is generally subjective because what annoys or alarms one person may not annoy or alarm another.[156] Second, a request that seeks an admission about a matter or document that is relevant or reasonably calculated to lead to the discovery of admissible evidence generally cannot be harassing.[157] Conversely, a request for admission that is interposed solely for "harassment" purposes clearly cannot seek the discovery of information that is either relevant or reasonably calculated to lead to the discovery of admissible evidence.

---

[153] *Cf. Covad Commc'ns Co. v. Revonet, Inc.*, 258 F.R.D. 17, 23–24 (D.D.C. 2009); *Estate of Broccolino v. McKesson Corp.*, No. WDQ-05-0438, 2006 U.S. Dist. LEXIS 97220, at *5, 2006 WL 5217766 (D. Md. Feb. 23, 2006); *Jayne H. Lee, Inc. v. Flagstaff Indus. Corp.*, 173 F.R.D. 651, 657 (D. Md. 1997); *Mahoney v. Kempton*, 142 F.R.D. 32, 33 (D. Mass. 1992).

[154] *E.g.*, Tex. R. Civ. P. 191.3(c)(3) (by signing written-discovery requests, the attorney certifies that the discovery was not sought for the purpose of harassment); Tex. R. Civ. P., 192.6(b) (allowing party to ask for protection from harassing discovery), 215.3 (providing that harassing discovery is a ground for sanctions); *Alexson, Inc. v. McIlhany*, 798 S.W.2d 550, 553 (Tex. 1990) (orig. proceeding) (The scope of discovery is "limited by the legitimate interests of the opposing party to avoid overly broad requests, harassment, or the disclosure of privileged information."); *Jampole v. Tourchy*, 673 S.W.2d 569, 573 (Tex. 1984) (orig. proceeding) (same), *disapproved of on other grounds by Walker v. Parker*, 827 S.W.2d 833, 842 (Tex. 1992) (orig. proceeding); *In re John Crane, Inc.*, No. 01-03-00698-CV, 2003 Tex. App. LEXIS 9684, at *5, 2003 WL 22682613 (Tex. App.—Houston [1st Dist.] Nov. 13, 2003, orig. proceeding) (mem. op.) ("A party resisting discovery, however, cannot simply make conclusory allegations that the requested discovery is unduly burdensome or unnecessarily harassing."); *In re State Farm Lloyds*, No. 04-98-00018, 1998 Tex. App. LEXIS 2072, at *11, 1998 WL 161260 (Tex. App.—San Antonio Apr. 8, 1998, orig. proceeding) (mem. op.) ("The right to broad discovery is limited by the opposing party's right to be free from harassment and the burden of overly broad requests.").

[155] *Black's Law Dictionary* 784 (11th ed. 2019); *accord Merriam-Webster.com Dictionary*, https://www.merriam-webster.com/dictionary/harass (last visited July 28, 2021) (defining "harass" as "to annoy persistently").

[156] See Chapter 8, section 8-5:15 (discussing harassment objections to Texas Rule 196 production requests).

[157] *ISK Biotech Corp. v. Lindsay*, 933 S.W.2d 565, 568 (Tex. App.—Houston [1st Dist.] 1996, orig. proceeding) ("[W]e have already concluded, however, that these discovery requests were reasonably calculated to lead to the discovery of admissible evidence; a request that meets that criterion is manifestly not . . . 'sought *solely* for the purposes of harassment.'").

10-5:8.18 Invasion of Protected Rights

A request for admission that improperly invades a party's personal, constitutional, or property rights is objectionable.[158]

10-5:8.19 A Claim's or Defense's Invalidity

A responding party cannot properly object to a request for admission because the cause of action or defense to which it relates is invalid unless the cause of action or defense has been dismissed pursuant to a dismissal motion, special exception, or summary judgment motion.[159] The only exception to this rule concerns exemplary-damages claims.

Under Chapter 41 of the Texas Civil Practice and Remedies Code, net-worth discovery is prohibited unless the court enters a "written order" finding that "the claimant has demonstrated a substantial likelihood of success on the merits of a claim for exemplary damages."[160] A party served with requests for admission seeking admissions about its net worth before the requisite finding is made should object to the request as "premature" because the prerequisite for net-worth discovery has not been established.

10-5:8.20 Confidentiality

An objection to a request for admission because it seeks "confidential" or "proprietary" information generally is improper. Rather, the proper way for a responding party to deal with its contractual and other "confidentiality" obligations is to answer the request pursuant to a protective order's terms.[161]

---

158 Tex. R. Civ. P. 192.6(b) (authorizing protection from a discovery request that invades a "personal, constitutional, or property right"); *see In re Does 1–10*, 242 S.W.3d 805, 812 (Tex. App.—Texarkana 2007, orig. proceeding) ("One of the reasons to ask [for a protective order] is to protect the movant from 'invasion of personal, constitutional, or property rights.'" (quoting Tex. R. Civ. P. 192.6(b))); *cf. Soto v. City of Concord*, 162 F.R.D. 603, 616 (N.D. Cal. 1995) ("Federal Courts ordinarily recognize a constitutionally-based right of privacy that can be raised in response to discovery requests.").

159 *Lunsford v. Morris*, 746 S.W.2d 471, 473 (Tex. 1988) (orig. proceeding) (holding that discovery is based on matters relevant to the claims pleaded and a party need not prove a claim before being entitled to discovery on it); *In re Citizens Supporting Metro Sols., Inc.*, No. 14-07-00190-CV, 2007 Tex. App. LEXIS 8550, at *8–9, 2007 WL 4277850 (Tex. App.—Houston [14th Dist.] Oct. 18, 2007, orig. proceeding) (mem. op.) (holding that "[t]he scope of discovery is measured by the live pleadings regarding the pending claims."); *In re Rogers*, 200 S.W.3d 318, 324 (Tex. App.—Dallas 2006, orig. proceeding) (holding that, when a petition was "broadly pleaded" and had "not been challenged or narrowed through special exceptions or any other pleading vehicle[,]" the responding party could not "attempt to limit the scope of the pleading through discovery objections.").

160 Tex. Civ. Prac. & Rem. Code § 41.0115(a); See Chapter 4, section 4-3:4 (discussing about net worth for exemplary-damages purposes).

161 See Chapter 8, section 8-5:18 (discussing confidentiality objections to Texas Rule 196 production requests).

10-5:8.21 Calls for a Legal Conclusion or the Application of Law to Fact

As discussed in Chapter 10, section 10-2:2.1, a request asking for the admission of a pure question of law is improper, whereas one asking for an admission of law applied to fact is proper. Accordingly, an objection that the request seeks a legal conclusion is proper, whereas an objection that a request seeks the application of law to fact is improper.

Because Texas Rule 197.1 specifically permits a party to ask its opponent if it is making a "specific legal . . . contention,"[162] it is proper to ask the party to admit whether it is making such a contention and whether specific facts underlie it.[163]

10-5:8.22 Hearsay

Hearsay is not a proper objection to a request for admission.[164] However, the fact that a request involving hearsay is admitted does not mean that it is admissible.[165]

10-5:8.23 Improper Incorporation of, or Reference to, Documents

As discussed in Chapter 10, section 10-2:1, an objection that that a request for admission incorporates or references a document generally is a proper objection unless the

---

[162] Tex. R. Civ. P. 197.1; *see* Tex. R. Civ. P. 192.3(j) ("A party may obtain discovery of any other party's legal contentions and the factual bases for those contentions.").

[163] *In re Young*, 410 S.W.3d 542, 548 (Tex. App.—Beaumont 2013, no pet.) ("[T]he rules of procedure specifically allow a party to request disclosure of legal theories and factual bases of the opposing party's claims. We conclude the twelve requests at issue do not require the State's attorneys to disclose their mental impressions, opinions, conclusions, or legal theories about Young's case." (citing Tex. R. Civ. P. 194.2(c)).

[164] *Cf. Booth Oil Site Admin. Grp. v. Safety-Kleen Corp.*, 194 F.R.D. 76, 81 (W.D.N.Y. 2000) ("That a requested admission may involve hearsay is not disqualifying as statements of facts" because hearsay objections are waivable.).

[165] *Cf. Walsh v. McCain Foods, Ltd.*, 81 F.3d 722, 726–27 (7th Cir. 1996) ("It is only when the admission is offered against the party who made it that it comes within the exception to the hearsay rule for admissions of a party opponent. 'Admissions obtained under [Federal] Rule 36 may be offered in evidence at the trial of the action, but they are subject to all pertinent objections to admissibility that may be interposed at the trial.'" (quoting Charles Alan Wright et al., *Federal Practice and Procedure* § 2264, at 571–72 (2d ed.1994))); *see Tex. Workforce Comm'n v. Antonini & Assocs.*, No. 01-96-01459-CV, 1998 Tex. App. LEXIS 4865, at *4 (Tex. App.—Houston [1st Dist.] Aug. 6, 1998, no pet.) (not designated for publication) ("Generally, admissions are not effective against a co-party. The rationale for this rule is that the admissions are hearsay to co-parties."); *Tex. Supply Ctr., Inc. v. Doan Corp.*, 641 S.W.2d 335, 338 (Tex. App.—Dallas 1982, writ ref'd n.r.e.) ("As against a co-defendant, such admissions are hearsay and are admissible, if at all, only as extra-judicial admissions where there is a 'joint interest or privity in design' between the defendants."); *Mnyufo v. Bd. of Educ.*, No. 03 C 8717, 2007 U.S. Dist. LEXIS 31589, at *5–6, 2007 WL 1308523 (N.D. Ill. Apr. 27, 2007) ("Admissions of a party-opponent are not hearsay, and thus may be considered in ruling on a motion for summary judgment. But co-defendant Taylor is not the District 227 defendants' party opponent. Her admissions are hearsay and defendants make no argument that they fall within any exception to the hearsay rule.") (citation omitted). See also cases cited in notes 172–73, 177, 192.

request is seeking an admission regarding (1) the genuineness or authenticity of a document, or (2) the foundational elements needed for a document's admission into evidence.

10-5:9 Do Nothing

Unlike Texas Rules 194, 196, and 197, which respectively relate to disclosures, production requests, and interrogatories, Texas Rule 198 is self-executing—requests for admission are automatically deemed admitted without the need for a court order on the day after they are due if no response is served.[166] Thus, a party, rather than expressly admitting a request, can choose not to respond at all and the request will automatically be admitted without the necessity of a motion or court order.

As discussed in more detail in Chapter 10, section 10-6:4, unless the trial court allows the admissions to be withdrawn or amended, matters admitted generally are conclusively established for all purposes, including summary judgment and trial.[167] The exception to this rule is that admissions, like other evidence, are subject to pertinent objections at trial or in connection with a summary judgment motion and may be excluded if the admission's matter is inadmissible or constitutes an admission of law.[168]

10-6 Use and Effect of Admissions

10-6:1 Persons Bound by Admissions

An admission is binding only on the party making it.[169] Thus, the requesting party is not bound by an admission merely because it served the request. Rather, the requesting party may disregard an admission even if it offers other admissions from the same set into evidence or introduces evidence consistent with the admission.[170]

---

166 Tex. R. Civ. P. 198.2(c) ("If a response is not timely served, the request is considered admitted without the necessity of a court order."); *accord Medina v. Zuniga*, 593 S.W.3d 238, 244–47 (Tex. 2019); *Marino v. Kerry*, 355 S.W.3d 629, 630 (Tex. 2011) (per curiam); *Ralls v. Funk*, 592 S.W.3d 178, 182 (Tex. App.—Tyler 2019, pet. denied) (same); *In re N.L.W.*, 534 S.W.3d 102, 111 (Tex. Civ. App.—Texarkana 2017, no pet.); *In re T.L.R.*, No. 14-14-00812-CV, 2015 Tex. App. LEXIS 3242, at *7, 2015 WL 1544796 (Tex. App.—Houston [14th Dist.] Apr. 2, 2015, no pet.) (mem. op.).

167 *See* Tex. R. Civ. P. 198.3 ("A matter admitted under this rule is conclusively established as to the party making the admission unless the court permits the party to withdraw or amend the admission."). An admission regarding a legal conclusion, however, has no effect. See Chapter 10, section 10-2:2-1

168 See cases cited in notes 172–73, 177, 192.

169 *Bleeker v. Villarreal*, 941 S.W.2d 163, 168 (Tex. App.—Corpus Christi 1996, writ dism'd by agr.) ("[M]atters admitted in response to requests for admissions [sic] are conclusively established only against the party making the admission."); *Cartwright v. MBank Corpus Christi, N.A.*, 865 S.W.2d 546, 551 (Tex. App.—Dallas 1993, writ denied) (same); *see Thalman v. Martin*, 635 S.W.2d 411, 414 (Tex. 1982) (holding that a grantor's admission was binding on the decedent's heirs, but not on his grantee).

170 *Cf. Brook Vill. N. Assocs. v. Gen. Elec. Co.*, 686 F.2d 66, 75 (1st Cir. 1982) (holding that a trial court could not properly force the requesting party to elect between relying on admissions and introducing evidence relevant to them and, because the testimony indicated

Nor is an admission generally binding on other opposing parties, third parties, or co-parties.[171] As to a non-admitting party, the admission is hearsay evidence to which a hearsay objection should be made, if the admission is offered as evidence against the party.[172]

There are two exceptions to this rule. The first is when the admission falls within one of the hearsay exceptions to Texas Rule of Evidence 801(e)(2). That is, when the statement:

[1] is one the party manifested that it adopted or believed to be true;

[2] was made by a person whom the party authorized to make a statement on the subject; . . .

---

that damages were greater than the amount established by the admission, "the admission should be viewed as setting the minimum amount of damages").

If the requesting party introduces evidence that directly contradicts the admission, it waives its right to rely on the admission's conclusiveness. *E.g.*, *Marshall v. Vise*, 767 S.W.2d 699, 700 (Tex. 1989) ("An admission once admitted, deemed or otherwise, is a judicial admission, and a party may not then introduce testimony to controvert it. We have held, however, that a party relying upon an opponent's pleadings as judicial admissions of fact must protect the record by objecting to the introduction of controverting evidence and to the submission of any issue bearing on the facts admitted. In the present case, Vise failed to object to the controverting testimony on the ground that he was relying upon Marshall's deemed admissions. In fact, Vise actually elicited much of the contradictory evidence. Vise has waived, therefore, his right to rely upon those admissions which were controverted by testimony admitted at trial without objection."); *Wertz v. Mass Mut. Life Ins. Co.*, 898 S.W.2d 414, 422 (Tex. App.—Amarillo 1995, no writ) (same). See also cases cited in notes 197–98.

171 *Fiebig v. Fiebig*, No. 14-12-01166-CV, 2012 Tex. App. LEXIS 10966, at *8, 2012 WL 9390623 (Tex. App.—Houston [14th Dist.] Oct. 22, 2012, no pet.) (mem. op.) ("[M]atters admitted by one defendant are not conclusively established as to another defendant."); *Allen v. Allen*, 280 S.W.3d 366, 376 (Tex. App.—Amarillo 2008, pet. denied) ("In a suit against multiple defendants, evidence in the form of responses to requests for admissions made by one defendant is not admissible against other defendants."); *Hartman v. Trio Transp., Inc.*, 937 S.W.2d 575, 578 (Tex. App.—Texarkana 1996, writ denied) (same); *USX Corp. v. Salinas*, 818 S.W.2d 473, 479 (Tex. App.—San Antonio 1991, writ denied) (same); *Tex. Supply Ctr., Inc. v. Daon Corp.*, 641 S.W2d 335, 337–38 (Tex. App.—Dallas 1982, writ ref'd n.r.e.) (same); *cf. Becerra v. Asher*, 105 F.3d 1042, 1048 (5th Cir. 1997) ("Deemed admissions by a party opponent cannot be used against a co-party."); *Riberglass, Inc. v. Techni-Glass Indus., Inc.*, 811 F.2d 565, 566 (11th Cir. 1987) ("Clearly, the deemed admissions of his codefendants cannot bind Morris where he actually responded to plaintiff's requests in a timely and legally sufficient manner."); *Allen v. Destiny's Child*, No. 06 C 660606C6606, 2009 U.S. Dist. LEXIS 63001, at *8, 2009 WL 2178676 (N.D. Ill. July 21, 2009) ("This court joins in holding that a plaintiff cannot use one defendant's deemed admissions as evidence against a codefendant.").

172 *Tex. Workforce Comm'n v. Antonini & Assocs.*, No. 01-96-01459-CV, 1998 Tex. App. LEXIS 4865, at *4 (Tex. App.—Houston [1st Dist.] Aug. 6, 1998, no pet.) (not designated for publication) ("Generally, admissions are not effective against a co-party. The rationale for this rule is that the admissions are hearsay to co-parties."); *Hartman v. Trio Transp., Inc.*, 937 S.W.2d 575 578 (Tex. App.—Texarkana 1996, writ denied) (same); *Tex. Supply Ctr., Inc. v. Doan Corp.*, 641 S.W.2d 335, 338 (Tex. App.—Dallas 1982, writ ref'd n.r.e.) ("As against a co-defendant, such admissions are hearsay and are admissible, if at all, only as extra-judicial admissions where there is a 'joint interest or privity in design' between the defendants.").

[3] was made by the party's agent or employee on a matter within the scope of that relationship and while it existed; or

[4] was made by the party's coconspirator during and in furtherance of the conspiracy.[173]

The second exception is when there is privity or a joint interest between the admitting party and the other party.[174]

10-6:2 Who Can Use Admissions

Any party to an action, even those joined after the admissions were made, can use an admission against the admitting party.[175] However, when a party appears in two capacities, an admission by the party in one capacity cannot be used against the party in the other.[176]

---

173 Tex. R. Evid. 801(e)(2)(B)–(E); *see Mnyufo v. Bd. of Educ.*, No. 03 C 87173C8717, 2007 U.S. Dist. LEXIS 31589, at *5–6, 2007 WL 1308523 (N.D. Ill. Apr. 27, 2007) ("Admissions of a party-opponent are not hearsay, and thus may be considered in ruling on a motion for summary judgment. But co-defendant Taylor is not the District 227 defendants' party opponent. Her admissions are hearsay and defendants make no argument that they fall within any exception to the hearsay rule.") (citation omitted); ***Hartman v. Trio Transp., Inc.***, 937 S.W.2d 575, 578–79 (Tex. App.—Texarkana 1996, writ denied) (holding that deemed admissions by a truck driver were not binding on the driver's *former* employer).

174 *Tex. Workforce Comm'n v. Antonini & Assocs.*, No. 01-96-01459-CV, 1998 Tex. App. LEXIS 4865, at *4 (Tex. App.—Houston [1st Dist.] Aug. 6, 1998, no pet.) (not designated for publication) ("[A]dmissions are binding on co-parties where there is privity or a joint interest between them."); *Gen. Fin. Servs. Inc. v. Practice Place, Inc.*, 897 S.W.2d 516, 521 (Tex. App.—Fort Worth 1995, no writ) ("Admissions are equally binding on co-parties where there is privity or a joint interest between them, they are represented by the same counsel and assert the same rights and defenses."); *see Thalman v. Martin*, 635 S.W.2d 411, 414 (Tex. 1982) (holding that a grantor's admissions were binding on his heirs); *cf. Diamond State Ins. Co. v. Deardorff*, No. 1:10-cv-00004 A WI JLT, 2011 U.S. Dist. LEXIS 60834, at *11–12, 2011 WL 2414391 (E.D. Cal. Jun 8, 2011) ("Plaintiffs, as subrogees, 'stand in the shoes of their insureds and are bound by certain admissions of their insureds. Because the Plaintiffs are bound by certain admissions, any arguments by the Plaintiffs that are contrary to . . . admissions [made] by their insureds are proscribed.'") (citation omitted).

175 *Jolet v. Garcia*, No. 05-97-0146-CV, 2000 Tex. App. LEXIS 1680, at *11, 2000 WL 276906 (Tex. App.—Dallas Mar. 15, 2000, pet. denied) (not designated for publication) ("Admissions may be used by all parties to an action, including parties joined after the admissions were made."); *Grimes v. Jalco, Inc.*, 630 S.W.2d 282, 284 (Tex. App.—Houston [1st Dist.] 1991, writ ref'd n.r.e.) (same), ***overruled on other grounds, Medina v. Herrara***, 927 S.W.2d 597 (Tex. 1996).

176 *U.S. Fid. Guar. Co. v. Gourdeau*, 272 S.W.3d 603, 608–09 (Tex. 2008) (holding that an admission by an insurer in its capacity as an intervenor could not be used against the insurer in its capacity as a defendant because the admissions were served on the insurer in its capacity as an intervenor); *Wasserberg v. RES-TX One, LLC*, No. 14-13-00674-CV, 2014 Tex. App. LEXIS 13085, at *17–18, 2014 WL 6922545 (Tex. App.—Houston [14th Dist.] Dec. 9, 2014, pet. denied) (mem. op.) ("Second, Wasserberg contends that deemed admissions 1-3 were insufficient evidence to support the summary judgment. Those requests sought admissions from Wasserberg regarding Waterhill's breach by failure to pay. Wasserberg argues that because he was not sued in his capacities as a limited partner of Waterhill and an officer of its corporate general partner, these admissions do not determine the conduct of Waterhill. Instead, Wasserberg contends, the admissions bind him only in the individual

A party cannot use its own admission at trial or for summary judgment. Only when the admission is offered against the responding party does it come within the hearsay exception for a party-opponent's admissions.[177]

10-6:3 Limitations on Use of Requests for Admission Against the State of Texas

Sections 41.003 and 402.004 of the Texas Government Code provide that, in any action to which the State is a party, an admission by the attorney general, a district attorney or a county attorney does not prejudice the rights of the State.[178] However, as a general rule, the State of Texas is bound by the same rules as any other litigant and must respond to discovery requests.[179] Thus, if the State fails to timely object to the requests for admissions on the statutory bar, it waives any protection it provides.[180]

---

capacity in which he was sued. This distinction does not defeat the summary judgment. Although admissions are effective against a party only in the capacity in which they are served, they are still conclusively established against the party in that capacity. Thus, these admissions can support a judgment against Wasserberg individually.") (citation omitted); *Krasa v. Derrico*, 193 S.W.2d 891, 892–93 (Tex. Civ. App.—San Antonio 1946, no writ) (holding that an admission by a widow individually could not be used against her in her capacity as the executor of her husband's estate because the requests were served on her individually).

177 *Schulz v. State Farm Mut. Auto. Ins.*, 930 S.W.2d 872, 876 (Tex. App.—Houston [1st Dist.] 1996, no writ) (holding that "[a]nswers to interrogatories and discovery responses may only be used against the party who answered them" and that a party's "reliance upon . . . the answers she provided to discovery . . . did not provide competent summary judgment evidence"); *Sympson v. Mor-Win Prods.*, 501 S.W.2d 362, 364 (Tex. Civ. App.—Fort Worth 1973, no writ) ("[S]elf-serving answers to the adversary's requests for admissions [sic] can be used only against him."); *cf. Walsh v. McCain Foods, Inc.*, 81 F.3d 722, 726 (7th Cir. 1996) ("It is only when the admission is offered against the party who made it that it comes within the exception to the hearsay rule for admissions of a party opponent." (quoting 8A Charles Alan Wright et al., *Federal Practice and Procedure* § 2264, at 571–72 (2d ed., 1994))); *Gilmer v. Macy's Retail Hldgs.*, No. 06-3020 (JBS), 2009 U.S. Dist. LEXIS 4937, at *31–32, 2009 WL 140518 (D.N.J. Jan. 20, 2009) ("More fundamentally, a litigant 'may not introduce statements from its own answers to interrogatories or requests for admission as evidence because such answers typically constitute hearsay when used in this manner.'" (quoting *Gross v. Burggraf Constr.*, 53 F.3d 1531, 1541–42 (10th Cir. 1995))); *In re Air Crash at Charlotte, N.C.*, 982 F. Supp. 1060, 1067–68 (D.S.C. 1996) ("Because the admission was apparently obtained by USAir under circumstances that suggest a cooperative arrangement, USAir should not be allowed to use the admission as that of a 'party opponent' simply because the parties were not truly adverse.").

178 Tex. Gov't Code §§ 41.003, 402.004.

179 *In re Young*, 410 S.W.3d 542, 547 (Tex. App.—Beaumont 2013, no pet.) ("As a general rule, the State litigates as any other party in Texas courts[.] 'When the [S]tate becomes a litigant in the courts[,] it must observe and is bound by the same rules of procedure that bind all other litigants, except where special provision is made to the contrary.'" (quoting *Tex. Dep't of Corr. v. Herring*, 513 S.W.2d 6, 7 (Tex. 1974))); *Carrasco v. Tex. Transp. Instit.*, 908 S.W.2d 575, 578 (Tex. App.—Waco 1995, no writ) ("The Texas Supreme Court has made clear that, when the state becomes a litigant in the courts, it is bound by the same rules of procedure that bind all other litigants, except where special provision is made to the contrary.").

180 *In re Gore*, 251 S.W.3d 696, 700–01 (Tex. App.—San Antonio 2007, orig. proceeding) ("The State, just as other civil litigants, must timely plead and prove its entitlement to protection from discovery. Failure to do so can result in waiver of any objection or claimed privilege.")

Moreover, to the extent the request for admission merely clarifies or elicits facts and does not prejudice the State, Sections 41.003 and 402.004 do not apply, and the State must respond to the request.[181] If, however, the request for admission calls for a response that will prejudice the State, the attorney general (or a district or county attorney) has a valid objection based on those statutes.[182]

10-6:4 Effect of Admissions and Denials

A matter admitted in accordance with Texas Rule 198, whether expressed or deemed, is conclusively established in the pending action unless the court on motion permits withdrawal or amendment of the admission or it is a legal conclusion.[183] An admission made in response to a request for admission is comparable to an admission in a pleading or a stipulation, as opposed to evidentiary admissions of a party for use at trial.[184] A matter admitted does not require further proof, and, as long as the admission stands, the admitting party will not be allowed to introduce directly contradicting evidence, whether in the form of live testimony at trial or summary judgment affidavits, over the requesting party's objection.[185]

(citations omitted); *Carrasco v. Tex. Transp. Instit.*, 908 SW.2d 575, 579 (Tex. App.—Waco 1995, no writ) ("Because the attorney general did not object to the requests for admissions [sic] under section 402.004 in accordance with [former Texas] Rule 169, TTI waived any objection it may have had to the requests, and all facts contained in TTI's admissions are conclusively established.").

181 *Lowe v. Texas Tech Univ.*, 540 S.W.2d 297, 300–01 (Tex. 1976).

182 *Lowe v. Texas Tech Univ.*, 540 S.W.2d 297, 301 (Tex. 1976).

183 Tex. R. Civ. P. 198.3 ("A matter admitted under this rule is conclusively established as to the party making the admission unless the court permits the party to withdraw or amend the admission."); *accord GJ Partners, Ltd. v. Cima Contractors, LLC*, No. 05-18-01412-CV, 2020 Tex. App. LEXIS 665, at *13–14, 2020 WL 400180 (Tex. App.—Dallas Jan. 23, 2020, no pet.) (mem. op.); *Ralls v. Funk*, 592 S.W.3d 178, 182–83 (Tex. App.—Tyler 2019, pet. denied); *In re N.L.W.*, 534 S.W.3d 102, 111 (Tex. Civ. App.—Texarkana 2017, no pet.); *Ramirez v. Noble Energy, Inc.*, 521 S.W.3d 851, 856, 858–59 (Tex. App.—Houston [1st Dist.] 2017, no pet.); *In re T.L.R.*, No. 14-14-00812-CV, 2015 Tex. App. LEXIS 3242, at *7–8, 2015 WL 1544796 (Tex. App.—Houston [14th Dist.] Apr. 2, 2015, no pet.) (mem. op.); *In re Bunn*, No. 09-12-00349-CV, 2013 Tex. App. LEXIS 13502, at *5, 2013 WL 5874460 (Tex. App.—Beaumont Oct. 31, 2013, no pet.) (mem. op.); *Cleveland v. Taylor*, 397 S.W.3d 683, 695 (Tex. App.—Houston [1st Dist.] 2012, pet. denied); *Boulet v. State*, 189 S.W.3d 833, 836 (Tex. App.—Houston [1st Dist.] 2006, no pet.).

184 *Marshall v. Vise*, 767 S.W.2d 699, 700 (Tex. 1989) ("An admission once admitted, deemed or otherwise, is a judicial admission, and a party may not then introduce testimony to controvert it."); *In re N.L.W.*, 534 S.W.3d 102, 111 (Tex. Civ. App.—Texarkana 2017, no pet.) (same); *Lucas v. Clark*, 347 S.W.3d 800, 803 (Tex. App.—Amarillo 2011, no pet.); *USAA Cty. Mut. Ins. Co. v. Cool*, 241 S.W.3d 93, 102 (Tex. App.—Houston [1st Dist.] 2007, no pet.) (same).

185 *Odela Grp., LLC v. Double-R Walnut Mgmt. L.L.C.*, No. 05-16-00206-CV, 2017 Tex. App. LEXIS 3224, at *15, 2017 WL 1360209 (Tex. App.—Dallas Apr. 12, 2017, no pet.) (mem. op.) ("These admissions were conclusively established as true, and Jones may not contradict them."); *Stephenson v. Perata*, No. 2-08-375-CV, 2009 Tex. App. LEXIS 3172, at *3–4, 2009 WL 1270907 (Tex. App.—Fort Worth May 7, 2009, no pet) (mem. op.) ("Admissions, once made or deemed by the court, may not be contradicted by any evidence, whether in the form of live testimony or summary judgment affidavits."); *USAA Cty. Mut. Ins. Co. v. Cool*, 241 S.W.3d 93, 102 (Tex. App.—Houston [1st Dist.] 2007, no pet.) (same); *Luke v. Unifund*

An ambiguous admission, however, is not conclusive of anything. For example, in *Sedillo v. Valtierra*,[186] the San Antonio Court of Appeals reversed a summary judgment because the use of the term "and/or" in a request for admission asking the plaintiff to admit that the defendant's "negligence and/or negligence per se was not a proximate cause of the accident in question," made the admission ambiguous.

> The term "and/or" is "used to imply that either or both of the things mentioned may be affected or involved." We agree that the use of the term "and/or" raises a genuine issue of material fact regarding whether the deemed admission addresses both negligence claims or only one of the negligence claims.[187]

Before admissions can be used, they must be filed with the trial court.[188] Also, if the party is relying on deemed admissions, it also must show that they were properly served.[189]

CCR Partners, No. 2-06-444-CV, 2007 Tex. App. LEXIS 7096, at *6, 2007 WL 2460327 (Tex. App.—Fort Worth Aug. 31, 2007, no pet.) (mem. op.) (same).

[186] *Sedillo v. Valtierra*, 115 S.W.3d 52 (Tex. App.—San Antonio 2003, pet. denied).

[187] *Sedillo v. Valtierra*, 115 S.W.3d 52, 53 (Tex. App.—San Antonio 2003, pet. denied) (quoting *Webster's College Dictionary* 49 (2d ed. 1999)); *cf. Driscoll v. Dennis*, 513 F. App'x 702, 705 (10th Cir. 2013) ("[B]ecause these requests for admissions [sic] were compound and ambiguous, we 'regard the admission as limited in practical effect.' Under these circumstances, we cannot conclude that the district court was required to treat the admissions as conclusively establishing Mrs. Driscoll's ownership." (citation omitted) (quoting *Dixon v. Kirkpatrick*, 553 F.3d 1294, 1303 (10th Cir. 2009))); *Rolscreen Co. v. Pella Prods. of St. Louis, Inc.*, 64 F.3d 1202, 1210 (8th Cir. 1995) ("The conclusive effect envisioned by [Federal Rule 36] may not be appropriate where requests for admissions [sic] or the responses to them are subject to more than one interpretation.").

[188] Tex. R. Civ. P. 191.4(c).

[189] *Ordonez v. Solorio*, 480 S.W.3d 56, 62 (Tex. App.—El Paso 2015, no pet.) ("Service on an attorney before that attorney becomes the party's attorney of record is not valid service under [Texas] Rule 21a, and a request for admissions so served is neither properly served under [Texas] Rule 198.1 nor deemed admitted under [Texas] Rule 198.2(c)."); *Holmes v. Graham Mortg. Corp.*, 449 S.W.3d 257, 261–62 (Tex. App.—Dallas 2014, pet. denied) (holding that the trial court did not err in refusing to consider allegedly deemed admissions in connection with the defendant's summary judgment motion because the requests for admission were not properly served on the defendant); *Approximately $14,980.00 v. State*, 261 S.W.3d 182, 186 (Tex. App.—Houston [14th Dist.] 2008, no pet.) ("A party's duty to respond is dependent upon receipt of the requests. Where service is not perfected, the receiving party cannot be made to suffer the consequences of not answering or untimely answering.") (citation omitted); *Payton v. Ashton*, 29 S.W.3d 896, 898 (Tex. App.—Amarillo 2000, no pet.) (affirming the trial court's refusal to consider alleged deemed admissions because the requests were not properly served on the defendant); *City of Hous. v. Rener*, 896 S.W.2d 317, 319–20 (Tex. App.—Houston [1st Dist.] 1995, writ denied) (reversing a summary judgment based on deemed admissions because the requests were left with a building security guard who was not the defendant's attorney's representative and who never delivered them to the attorney); *Withem v. Underwood*, No. 05-94-01310-CV, 1997 Tex. App. LEXIS 5978, at *6–7, 1997 WL 717041 (Tex. App.—Dallas Nov. 19, 1997, no writ) (not designated for publication) ("Before unanswered requests are automatically deemed admitted, proper service must be shown. In a summary judgment context, the burden is on the movant seeking to rely on deemed admissions as evidence to establish proper service conclusively. In essence, proper service becomes an element of the movant's proof that must be established before the movant is entitled to summary judgment based on deemed

Unlike other discovery, such as disclosures, interrogatories, and deposition testimony, which must be admitted into evidence to have probative value or to be considered as evidence in support of a judgment, admissions do *not* have to be introduced as evidence to be before a trial or appellate court.[190] Nonetheless, admissions should be introduced into evidence to avoid confusion.[191] Before an admission can be admitted into evidence or otherwise used at trial or in connection with a summary judgment motion, it is subject to all pertinent objections to its use.[192] And, if the trier of fact finds facts contrary to an admission, the admission controls.[193]

Admissions, both express and deemed, are competent summary judgment evidence, and they can establish that there is no genuine issue of material fact, thereby justifying a summary judgment's entry.[194] A trial court has no discretion to ignore

---

admissions."); *Sosa v. Williams*, 936 S.W.2d 708, 710 (Tex. App.—Waco 1996, writ denied) (same); *White v. Tricontinental Leasing Corp.*, 760 S.W.2d 23, 24–25 (Tex. App.—Dallas 1988, no writ) (holding that a request for admission served on an attorney when he was not an attorney of record was not properly deemed admitted under former Texas Rule 169).

[190] *Clark v. Porter*, No. 04-08-0052-CV, 2009 Tex. App. LEXIS 6680, at *6, 2009 WL 2618359 (Tex. App.—San Antonio Aug. 26, 2009, pet. denied) (mem. op.) ("Deemed admissions filed with the trial court clerk and part of the record at the time of trial need not be introduced in evidence to be properly before the court."); *Red Ball Motor Freight, Inc. v. Dean*, 549 S.W.2d 41, 43 (Tex. Civ. App.—Tyler 1977, writ dism'd) (same); *Richards v. Boettcher*, 518 S.W.2d 286, 288 (Tex. Civ. App.—Texarkana 1974, writ ref'd n.r.e.) (same).

[191] Ordinarily, this is done in the requesting party's case in chief. Alternatively, if the trial court reads factual stipulations to the jury before receiving evidence, the requesting party can ask the court to include key admissions. Because many studies indicate that the first information heard by jurors has the greatest impact and because jurors consider communications from the court with great respect and creditability, Larry S. Kaplan, *Complex Federal Litigation* § 17.25 (1993), using this methodology may give the admission more credibility and importance in the jurors' minds.

[192] *Cf. Palmetto State Med. Ctr., Inc. v. Op. Lifeline*, 117 F.3d 142, 146 (4th Cir. 1997) (holding that admissions were properly excluded by the trial court because they were hearsay as to a non-admitting party); *Walsh v. McCain Foods, Inc.*, 81 F.3d 722, 727 (7th Cir. 1996) ("Admissions obtained under [Federal] Rule 36 may be offered in evidence at the trial of the action, but they are subject to all pertinent objections to admissibility that may be interposed at the trial." (quoting Charles Alan Wright, *et al.*, *Federal Practice and Procedure* § 2264, at 571–72 (2d ed.1994))); *Simien v. Chem. Waste Mgmt., Inc.*, 30 F. Supp. 2d 939, 942 n.3 (W.D. La. 1998) (same); *see Sedillo v. Valtierra*, 115 S.W.3d 52, 53 (Tex. App.—San Antonio 2003, pet. denied) (reversing summary judgment because it was based on admissions of law).

[193] *E.g.*, *Luna v. Runyon*, No. 03-06-00615-CV, 2008 Tex. App. LEXIS 4979, at *7 (Tex. App.—Austin July 3, 2008) (mem. op.) ("Unless the party who failed to respond to a request for admissions obtains a court order setting aside the deemed admissions—which Luna did not attempt to do here —they constitute judicial admissions that bind the party and render inadmissible contrary trial or summary-judgment evidence."); *Beutel v. City of Dall. Cty. Flood Control*, 916 S.W.2d 685, 695 (Tex. App.—Waco 1996, writ denied) ("An admission, once admitted, deemed or otherwise, is a judicial admission, and a party may not then introduce testimony to controvert it. Accordingly, when findings by the trier of fact contradict properly admitted judicial admissions, the judicial admissions must be accepted as superior.") (citation omitted).

[194] *E.g.*, *In re N.L.W.*, 534 S.W.3d 102, 115 (Tex. Civ. App.—Texarkana 2017, no pet.) ("Admissions of fact on file at the time of a summary judgment hearing are proper summary judgment proof and will, therefore, support a motion for summary judgment." (quoting *Cedyco Corp. v. Whitehead*, 253 S.W.3d 877, 880 (Tex. App.—Beaumont 2008, pet. denied))); *Odela*

admissions, express or deemed, in ruling on a summary judgment motion unless the admission is a legal conclusion or otherwise inadmissible.[195] As pointed out above, they cannot be contradicted by other summary judgment evidence.[196]

A party, however, can waive its right to rely on an admission's conclusiveness. Waiver occurs when either the party relying on the admission or the admitting party without objection introduces evidence directly contradicting the admitted matter.[197]

Grp., LLC v. Double-R Walnut Mgmt. L.L.C., No. 05-16-00206-CV, 2017 Tex. App. LEXIS 3224, at *13, 2017 WL 1360209 (Tex. App.—Dallas Apr. 12, 2017, no pet.) (mem. op.) (same); *Maswoswe v. Nelson*, 327 S.W.3d 889, 897 (Tex. App.—Beaumont 2010, no pet.) (same); *Acevedo v. Comm'n For Law. Discipline*, 131 S.W.3d 99, 105 (Tex. App.—San Antonio 2004, pet. denied) (same).

[195] *Rowlands v. Unifund CCR*, No. 14-05-01122-CV, 2007 Tex. App. LEXIS 23322336, at *10, 2007 WL 1395101 (Tex. App.—Houston [14th Dist.], Mar. 27, 2007, no pet.) (mem. op.) ("The trial court did not err in considering the deemed admissions in ruling on Unifund's motion for summary judgment. Indeed, the trial court had no discretion to ignore the deemed admissions."); *Hendler v. N. Shore Boat Works, Inc.*, No. 13-03-00273-CV, 2004 Tex. App. LEXIS 6617, at *7, 2004 WL 1632653 (Tex. App.—Corpus Christi July 22, 2004) (mem. op.) (same); *Pathfinders Personnel Serv., Inc. v. Worsham*, 619 S.W.2d 475, 476 (Tex. Civ. App.—Houston [14th Dist.] 1981, no writ) (same); *cf. REC Marine Logistics, LLC v. Richard*, No. 19-11149, 2020 U.S. Dist. LEXIS 114911, at *10 n.39 (E.D. La. July 1, 2020) ("[T]he Court will not consider as admitted any pure legal conclusions set forth in Richard's requests for admissions. Although Richard argues that REC Marine admitted that it was 'negligent in causing the injuries sustained by Richard,' and Gulf Offshore admitted that the Dustin Danos 'was unseaworthy at the time of [the] incident,' the findings of negligence and unseaworthiness are legal conclusions that the Court declines to consider admitted pursuant to [Federal] Rule 36 to establish the absence of genuine issues of material fact."); *B.S. v. York Cty.*, No. 1:17-CV-01789, 2020 U.S. Dist. LEXIS 165006, at *8 n.3 (M.D. Pa. Sept. 20, 2020) ("[T]he request for admission is ambiguous with respect to the date on which B.S. admitted that R.S. returned him to the Stough/Witmer residence. Given this ambiguity, coupled with the standard of review on a motion for summary judgment, the court declines to treat B.S.'s admission as conclusively establishing that R.S. returned him to the Stough/Witmer residence on November 16, 2012.") (citation omitted).

[196] *In re Gore*, 251 S.W.3d 696, 700–01 (Tex. App.—San Antonio 2007, orig. proceeding) ("The State, just as other civil litigants, must timely plead and prove its entitlement to protection from discovery. Failure to do so can result in waiver of any objection or claimed privilege.") (citation omitted); *Carrasco v. Tex. Transp. Instit.*, 908 SW.2d 575, 579 (Tex. App.—Waco 1995, no writ) ("Because the attorney general did not object to the requests for admissions [sic] under section 402.004 in accordance with [former Texas] Rule 169, TTI waived any objection it may have had to the requests, and all facts contained in TTI's admissions are conclusively established."). See also cases cited in note 180.

[197] *E.g., Marshall v. Vise*, 767 S.W.2d 699, 700 (Tex. 1989) ("We hold that a party waives the right to rely upon an opponent's deemed admissions unless objection is made to the introduction of evidence contrary those admissions."); *In re Estate of Campos*, No. 04-19-00350-CV, 2020 Tex. App. LEXIS 3122, at *18–19, 2020 WL 1866460 (Tex. App.—San Antonio Apr. 15, 2020, no pet.) (mem. op.) ("[A] party may waive the conclusive effect of deemed admissions by failing to object to the presentation of controverting evidence. This is true even in summary judgment proceedings. Here, Campos does not contend that he objected to Tavitas's summary judgment evidence based on the conclusive nature of the deemed admissions, and we have found no such objection in the record. Because Campos did not object to Tavitas's summary judgment evidence, he waived the conclusive effect of the deemed admissions.") (citations omitted); *In re T.L.R.*, No. 14-14-00812-CV, 2015 Tex. App. LEXIS 3242, at *10, 2015 WL 1544796 (Tex. App.—Houston [14th Dist.] Apr. 2, 2015, no pet.) (mem. op.)

Evidence that merely explains the admission or is consistent with it will not result in waiver.[198]

A denial or other refusal to admit a fact in response to a request for admission is not evidence and, therefore, is inadmissible. As explained by the San Antonio Court of Appeals: "When an answering party denies or refuses to make an admission of fact, such refusal is nothing more than a refusal to admit a fact. It is not evidence of any fact except the fact of refusal. Admitting such denial into evidence is error."[199] In other words, a "denial of a request for admission does not 'admit the opposite of the

("[W]hen unanswered admissions are deemed against a party, the party relying on the admissions must protect the record by objecting to controverting evidence on the facts at issue; otherwise, the admissions are waived. The Mother testified at trial and her testimony supported the elements of the Department's case. The Mother acknowledged her long history of drug use, her positive drug tests during the pendency of this case, and her criminal history, among other matters as more fully set out below. No objections were lodged to the Mother's testimony about matters that were not disclosed in discovery.") (citations omitted); *Fiebig v. Fiebig*, No. 14-12-01166-CV, 2012 Tex. App. LEXIS 10966, at *8, 2012 WL 9390623 (Tex. App.—Houston [14th Dist.] Oct. 22, 2012, no pet.) (mem. op.) (holding that a party moving for summary judgment waived his reliance on deemed admissions by failing to object to a summary judgment affidavit controverting matters established by the admissions); *USAA Cty. Mut. Ins. Co. v. Cook*, 241 S.W.3d 93, 102 (Tex. App.—Houston [1st Dist.] 2007, no pet.) (holding that the failure to object to testimony about the cause of the damage to the insured's car waived the insurer's right to rely upon any admissions which were controverted by testimony admitted at trial without objection); *Duff v. Spearman*, 322 S.W.3d 869, 884 (Tex. App.—Beaumont 2010, pet. denied) (same).

198 *E.g., RTC v. Thurlow*, 820 S.W.2d 51, 53 (Tex. App.—San Antonio 1991, no writ) ("[T]he evidence elicited merely attempted to clarify the deemed admissions by including the accrued interest to date of the trial. Accordingly, we find that the appellant did not waive its right to rely upon the appellee's deemed admissions."); *Collision Ctr. Paint & Body, Inc. v. Campbell*, 773 S.W.2d 354, 356 (Tex. App.—Dallas 1989, no writ) ("A party waives the right to rely upon an opponent's deemed admissions unless objection is made to the introduction of evidence contrary to those admissions."); *Willowbrook Foods, Inc. v. Grinnell Corp.*, 147 S.W.3d 492, 503 (Tex. App.—San Antonio 2004, pet. denied) ("However, an objection is required only when the offered evidence clearly contradicts the admissions.").

199 *Am. Commc'ns Telecomms., Inc., v. Comerica Nat'l Bank*, 691 S.W.2d 44, 48 (Tex. App.—San Antonio 1985, writ ref'd n.r.e.); *accord Mack Boring & Parts Co. v. Novis Marine, Ltd.*, No. 06-2692 (HAA), 2008 U.S. Dist. LEXIS 71239, at *12–13, 2008 WL 4371769 (D.N.J. Sept. 18, 2008) (applying Texas law); *Hynds v. Foster*, No. 01-15-01034-CV, 2017 Tex. App. LEXIS 1686, at *19–22, 2017 WL 769909 (Tex. App.—Houston [1st Dist.] Feb. 28, 2017, no pet.) (mem. op.); *Nguyen v. Citibank N.A.*, 403 S.W.3d 927, 932 (Tex. App.—Houston [14th Dist.] 2013, pet. denied); *Hill v. Trinci*, No. 14-10-00862-CV, 2012 Tex. App. LEXIS 5934, at *15, 2012 WL 3016855 (Tex. App.—Houston [14th Dist.] July 24, 2012, no pet.); *Luke v. Unifund CCR Partners*, No. 02-06-444-CV, 2007 Tex. App. LEXIS 7096, at *6, 2007 WL 2460327 (Tex. App.—Fort Worth Aug. 31, 2007, no pet.) (mem. op.); *cf. Langer v. Monarch Life Ins. Co.*, 966 F.2d 786, 805 (3rd Cir. 1992) ("[A] denial of a [Federal] Rule 36 request for admission simply leaves the denied proposition in dispute for trial."); *Stockdale v. Stockdale*, No. 4:08-CV-1773, 2009 U.S. Dist. LEXIS 121346, at *5, 2009 WL 5217001 (E.D. Mo. Dec. 30, 2009) ("Further, a party cannot read into evidence the other party's denial or refusal to admit a fact, as a denial or refusal to answer is not evidence of any fact."); *Sarachek v. Jaffe* (*In re Agriprocessors, Inc.*), Adv. No. 10-09170, 2013 Bankr. LEXIS 1279, at *18–19, 2013 WL 1332428 (Bankr. N.D. Iowa Mar. 28, 2013) ("Unlike admissions, denials of requests for admissions [sic] do not have *conclusive* effect. Rather than establishing a conclusive proposition, a denial creates a factual dispute.") (citation omitted).

proposition offered for admission, but rather is simply to establish that the matter is in dispute.'"[200]

10-6:5 Use of Admissions or Denials in Other Proceedings

Under Texas Rule 198.3, "[a]ny admission made by a party under this rule may be used solely in the pending action and not in any other proceeding."[201] This rule prevents the use of an admission in other civil or criminal actions as well as in administrative proceedings or arbitrations.[202] Thus, one way for a party to avoid the effect of damning admissions in an action is to dismiss it and re-file another action, if the limitations period has not run.[203]

Texas Rule 198.3 also should prevent the use of a judgment based solely on deemed admissions for collateral estoppel purposes in another proceeding because the "actually-litigated" requirement of such an estoppel is not met by a deemed admission.[204]

---

[200] *Barker v. Dollar Gen.*, 778 F. Supp. 2d 1267, 1269–70 (M.D. Ala. 2011) (quoting *Harmon v. Wal-Mart Stores, Inc.*, No. 3:08-cv-309, 2009 U.S. Dist. LEXIS 21040, at *10, 2009 WL 707403 (M.D. Ala. Mar. 16, 2009)); *accord Schoeps v. MOMA*, 594 F. Supp. 2d 461, 465 (S.D.N.Y. 2009).

[201] Tex. R. Civ. P. 198.3.

[202] *See Crowson v. Wakeman*, No. 05-93-01552-CV, 1996 Tex. App. LEXIS 2158, at *12–13, 1996 WL 283277 (Tex. App.—Dallas May 26, 1996, no writ) (not designated for publication) ("We conclude that because the application to probate the will and will contest was a separate proceeding, the deemed admissions could not be used against Crowson in the heirship proceeding."); *Osteen v. Glynn Dodson, Inc.*, 875 S.W.2d 429, 431 (Tex. App.—Waco 1994, writ denied) ("[W]e hold that the admissions deemed in the prior suit were not available to Dodson for use in the second suit under [former Texas] Rule 169."); *see John H. Carney & Assocs. v. Ahmad*, No. 07-15-00252-CV, 2016 Tex. App. LEXIS 989, at *8–9, 2016 WL 368527 (Tex. App.—Amarillo Jan. 28, 2016) (mem. op.) (holding that admission made in a case before severance cannot be used in the severed action); *cf. Kohler v. Leslie, Hindeman, Inc.*, 80 F.3d 1181, 1185 (7th Cir. 1996) ("But a statement made in one lawsuit cannot be a judicial admission in another."); *ConnectU, LLC v. Zuckerberg*, 240 F.R.D. 34, 36 (D. Mass. 2006) (holding that a qualified admission in a state-court action could not be used in a later federal-court action), *rev'd on other grounds*, 522 F.3d 82 (1st Cir. 2008); *Maxwell v. Ark.*, 41 S.W.3d 402, 408 (Ark. Ct. App. 2001) (holding that a criminal defendant's admission in a civil action could not be used against him in a criminal prosecution).

[203] *See, e.g., Osteen v. Glynn Dodson, Inc.*, 875 S.W.2d 429, 431 (Tex. App.—Waco 1994, writ denied) (holding that the plaintiff was entitled to a nonsuit to avoid a summary judgment based on deemed admissions).

[204] *Cf. In re Cassidy*, 892 F.2d 637, 640 (7th Cir.) ("[T]he judgment of the tax court on that factual issue, which is based solely on the admissions, cannot be a bar in this later proceeding.") (footnote omitted), *cert. denied*, 498 U.S. 812 (1990); *Shaban v. Hertz Corp.*, No. H-19-0987, 2020 U.S. Dist. LEXIS 88957, at *7–8 (S.D. Tex. May 19, 2020) ("The Texas Rules of Civil Procedure provide that requests for admissions are deemed admitted if not timely responded to. But those rules also limit such admissions to use 'solely in the pending action and not in any other proceeding.' This prohibits the application of collateral estoppel to matters deemed admitted under [Texas] Rule 198.2. Federal courts have refused to apply collateral estoppel to deemed admissions under Federal Rule of Civil Procedure 36(b), which has a similar prohibition against the use of discovery admissions in other proceedings. A prior court's determination of an issue cannot satisfy the 'fully and fairly litigated' requirement for collateral estoppel if it is based on admissions and may not be used in subsequent proceedings." (citations omitted) (quoting Tex. R. Civ. P. 198.3)); *Thomas v. Pickens (In re Pickens)*, No. 16-4063, 2017 Bankr. LEXIS 312, at *15 (Bank. N.D. Tex. Feb. 3, 2017)

However, some questions remain. *First*, can the responding party's admission be used to impeach its testimony in another proceeding? Although no case has considered this question, read literally, Texas Rule 198.3's prohibition on an admission's use in other proceedings prevents this.

Second, can a denial, as opposed to an admission, be used in another proceeding, for example, to show that the admitting party's current position or testimony is inconsistent with that in an earlier proceeding? Even though Texas Rule 198.3 only provides that "[a]ny admission made by a party" cannot be used "in any other proceeding[,]" the answer is "no" because, under Texas law, admission denials are neither evidence nor admissible.

This principle is illustrated by *Mack Boring & Parts Co. v. Novis Marine, Ltd.*[205] In that case, Mack Boring, a boat-parts manufacturer, sued Novis in a New Jersey federal district court for amounts due and owing for parts—Yanmar saildrives—sold to Novis.[206] Novis counterclaimed, alleging that Mack Boring had breached the parties' contract and express and implied warranties because the saildrives were defective.[207]

While the action was pending, one of Novis's customers sued Novis in a Texas state court, claiming that the boat and Yanmar saildrive Novis sold him were defective. During discovery in that action, Novis denied requests for admission regarding: "(i) whether the Yanmar saildrives it purchased from Mack Boring (and subsequently sold to [the customer]) were defective; (ii) whether Mack Boring breached an express warranty; (iii) whether Mack Boring breached the implied warranty of merchantability; and (iv) whether Mack Boring breached the implied warranty of fitness for a particular purpose."[208]

Mack Boring moved for summary judgment in its federal action, arguing, among other things, that Novis's admission denials in the Texas state court proceeding judicially estopped it from asserting its counterclaims.[209] The United States District Court for the District of New Jersey relying on the fact that, under Texas law, admission denials are neither evidence nor admissible, rejected the argument:

(same); *Hildebrand v. Kugler (In re Kugler)*, 170 B.R. 291, 301, 301 n.14 (Bankr. E.D. Va. 1994) (holding that where issues are deemed admitted due to a party's failure to respond to requests for admission, the "actually litigated . . . element of collateral estoppel is unsatisfied"); *Cozzone v. Ingui*, No. 06-1541, 2006 U.S. Dist. LEXIS 80752, at *7–8 (E.D. Pa. Oct. 25, 2006) ("The Bankruptcy Court correctly held that Appellee's state court admissions were inadmissible under both Fed. R. Civ. P. 36 and Pa. R. Civ. P. 4014. . . . The meaning of the rules is clear; admissions shall not be used in a proceeding beyond the action for which they are offered. It necessarily follows that a verdict or judicial finding predicated exclusively on those admissions is likewise inadmissible.").

205 *Mack Boring & Parts Co. v. Novis Marine, Ltd.*, No. 06-2692 (HAA), 2008 U.S. Dist. LEXIS 71239, 2008 WL 4371769 (D.N.J. Sept. 18, 2008).

206 *Mack Boring & Parts Co. v. Novis Marine, Ltd.*, No. 06-2692 (HAA), 2008 U.S. Dist. LEXIS 71239, at *2, 2008 WL 4371769 (D.N.J. Sept. 18, 2008).

207 *Mack Boring & Parts Co. v. Novis Marine, Ltd.*, No. 06-2692 (HAA), 2008 U.S. Dist. LEXIS 71239, at *3, 2008 WL 4371769 (D.N.J. Sept. 18, 2008).

208 *Mack Boring & Parts Co. v. Novis Marine, Ltd.*, No. 06-2692 (HAA), 2008 U.S. Dist. LEXIS 71239, at *4, 2008 WL 4371769 (D.N.J. Sept. 18, 2008).

209 *Mack Boring & Parts Co. v. Novis Marine, Ltd.*, No. 06-2692 (HAA), 2008 U.S. Dist. LEXIS 71239, at *4, 2008 WL 4371769 (D.N.J. Sept. 18, 2008).

> Applying the first part of the estoppel test, the January 25, 2008 admission responses might seem clearly inconsistent with Novis's present counterclaims.... At first blush, it would seem the inconsistency requirement [of judicial estoppel] has been met.
>
> Yet when considered in the context of Texas civil procedure, Novis's statements of denial do not contradict its present counterclaims as a matter of law. Mack Boring contends that Novis's admission responses satisfy the judicial adoption requirement because Texas courts automatically adopt [Texas] Rule 198 admissions by operation of law. Although Plaintiff is correct that a [Texas] Rule 198 admission is conclusive and binding on the presiding Texas court, a denial of a request for admission does not have the same legal effect. In *Newman v. Utica Nat'l Ins. Co. of Texas*, a Texas appeals court held that "when an answering party denies or refuses to make an admission of fact, such refusal is nothing more than a refusal to admit a fact. It is not evidence of any fact except the fact of refusal." 868 S.W.2d 5, 8 (Tex. App. 1993). Because admission denials "[are] not legal and competent evidence," *Newman*, 868 S.W.2d at 8, it cannot be gainsaid that Novis truly contradicted itself in denying the requests, nor that a court or agency accepted Novis's answers. Rather, Novis merely put the Texas plaintiff to his proof, and any sanctions for bad faith false admissions answers, if necessary, will lie in the Texas court.
>
> Because Defendant has not made clearly inconsistent statements in separate proceedings and, in any event, no court or agency has adopted the challenged statements, the judicial estoppel inquiry must end. The Court will deny summary judgment on the basis of judicial estoppel.[210]

10-7 Withdrawal, Supplementation, or Amendment of Responses to Requests for Admission

According to Texas Rule 193.5, a responding party is under a duty to amend or supplement a written-discovery response if it learns that it "was incomplete or incorrect when made, or, although complete and correct when made, is no longer complete and correct[.]"[211] This obligation seemingly is inconsistent with Texas Rule 198.3, which requires court permission to withdraw or amend an admission:

> A matter admitted under this rule is conclusively established as to the party making the admission unless the court permits the party to withdraw or amend the admission. The court may permit the party to withdraw or amend the admission if:
>
> (a) the party shows good cause for the withdrawal or amendment; and
>
> (b) the court finds that the parties relying upon the responses and deemed admissions will not be unduly prejudiced and that the presentation of the

---

[210] *Mack Boring & Parts Co. v. Novis Marine, Ltd.*, No. 06-2692 (HAA), 2008 U.S. Dist. LEXIS 71239, at *11–13, 2008 WL 4371769 (D.N.J. Sept. 18, 2008).

[211] Tex. R. Civ. P. 193.5(a). See also Chapter 5, section 5-6 (discussing supplementation and amendment of written-discovery responses).

merits of the action will be subserved by permitting the party to amend or withdraw the admission.[212]

Although Texas Rule 198.3's specific limitation controls Texas Rule 193.5's general rule, the two rules can be reconciled by interpreting them so that a responding party has a duty to promptly seek to file a motion to amend a response to a request for admission when Texas Rule 193.5 imposes such a duty, but it may not do so unilaterally and must satisfy the court that Texas Rule 198.3's requirements are met.

Because Texas Rule 198.3 only applies to admissions, there is no problem applying Texas Rule 193.5's requirement to a denial or an inability to admit or deny. Accordingly, if the responding party obtains new information creating a duty to amend or supplement with respect to such a response, it must do so reasonably promptly after it discovers the need for the amendment or supplement and need not obtain leave of court before doing so.[213]

Texas Rule 198.3 sets forth three requirements for the withdrawal or amendment of an admission: (1) good cause for the withdrawal or amendment, (2) no undue prejudice to the requesting party from the withdrawal or amendment, and (3) the presentation of the action's merits will be subserved by the withdrawal or amendment.[214] The responding party has the burden of proof on all three elements.[215] Moreover, the test applies to both express and deemed admissions.[216]

---

[212] Tex. R. Civ. P. 198.3.

[213] Tex. R. Civ. P. 193.5.

[214] *City of Saginaw v. Cruz*, No. 05-19-01141-CV, 2020 Tex. App. LEXIS 6984, at *17, 2020 WL 5054802 (Tex. App.—Dallas Aug. 27, 2020, no pet.) (mem. op.) (citing the three requirements); *GJ Partners, Ltd. v. Cima Contractors, LLC*, No. 05-18-01412-CV, 2020 Tex. App. LEXIS 665, at *14, 2020 WL 400180 (Tex. App.—Dallas Jan. 23, 2020, no pet.) (mem. op.) ("A court may permit a party to withdraw or amend an admission if the party shows good cause, and the court finds that the parties relying on the admission will not be unduly prejudiced and the presentation of the merits will be subserved by permitting withdrawal or amendment."); *Ralls v. Funk*, 592 S.W.3d 178, 182 (Tex. App.—Tyler 2019, pet. denied) (same); *S. Tex. Innovations, LLC v. Rise Residential Constr.*, LP, No. 02-18-00021-CV, 2018 Tex. App. LEXIS 10908, at *7–8, 2018 WL 6844135 (Tex. App.—Fort Worth Dec. 31, 2018) (mem. op.) (same); *In re TT Fountains of Tomball, Ltd.*, No. 01-15-00817-CV, 2016 Tex. App. LEXIS 7781, at *16, 2016 WL 3965117 (Tex. App.—Houston [1st Dist.] July 21, 2016, orig. proceeding) (mem. op.) (same).

[215] *In re Sewell*, 472 S.W.3d 449, 455 (Tex. App.—Texarkana 2015, orig. proceeding) ("The burden of proof on all *three requirements* [of Texas Rule 198.3] is on the party seeking withdrawal." (quoting *Morgan v. Timmers Chevrolet, Inc.*, 1 S.W.3d 803, 807 (Tex. App.—Houston [1st Dist.] 1999, pet. denied))), *overruled on other grounds, In re Bayview Loan Servicing, LLC*, 532 S.W.3d 510, 512 n.3 (Tex. App.—Texarkana 2017, orig. proceeding); *Time Warner, Inc. v. Gonzalez*, 441 S.W.3d 661, 666 (Tex. App.—San Antonio 2014, pet. denied) ("Ordinarily, the burden of showing good cause and no undue prejudice lies with the party seeking withdrawal of deemed admissions."); *Luna v. State*, No. 03-96-0055-CV, 1997 Tex. App. LEXIS 3150, at *6–7 (Tex. App.—Amarillo June 19, 1997, no writ) (per curiam) (not designated for publication) (same); *Tinney v. Team Bank*, 819 S.W.2d 560, 562 (Tex. App.—Fort Worth 1991, writ denied) (same); *see Ralls v. Funk*, 592 S.W.3d 178, 182 (Tex. App.—Tyler 2019, pet. denied) ("The party seeking withdrawal of the deemed admissions has the burden to establish good cause.").

[216] *Stelly v. Papania*, 927 S.W.2d 620, 622 (Tex. 1996) (applying the test to express admissions and finding "instructive" cases applying Texas Rule 198.3 to deemed admissions);

"A trial court has broad discretion to permit or deny the withdrawal of deemed admissions."[217] Accordingly, on appeal, its ruling is reviewed for an abuse of discretion.[218] A trial court, however, cannot order the withdrawal or amendment of deemed admissions on its own motion.[219] Moreover, a responding party may not seek withdrawal of deemed admissions after judgment in a motion for new trial, if the party realized its mistake before judgment and, therefore, had other avenues for relief available.[220]

Wal-Mart Stores, Inc. v. Deggs, 968 S.W.2d 354, 356–57 (Tex. 1998) (per curiam) (applying the test to deemed admissions); *Duong v. Bank One, N.A.*, 169189 S.W.3d 246, 252 (Tex. App.—Fort Worth 2005, no pet.) (applying the test to express admissions); *Boulet v. State*, 189 S.W.3d 833, 836 (Tex. App.—Houston [1st Dist.] 2006, no pet.) (applying the test to deemed admissions).

217 *Stelly v. Papania*, 927 S.W.2d 620, 622 (Tex. 1996); *accord Wheeler v. Green*, 157 S.W.3d 439, 443 (Tex. 2005) (per curiam); *City of Saginaw v. Cruz*, No. 05-19-01141-CV, 2020 Tex. App. LEXIS 6984, at *8, 2020 WL 5054802 (Tex. App.—Dallas Aug. 27, 2020, no pet.) (mem. op.); *In re Cagle*, 585 S.W.3d 618, 623 (Tex. App.—Houston [14th Dist.] 2019, orig. proceeding); *In re TT Fountains of Tomball, Ltd.*, No. 01-15-00817-CV, 2016 Tex. App. LEXIS 7781, at *7, 2016 WL 3965117 (Tex. App.—Houston [1st Dist.] July 21, 2016, orig. proceeding) (mem. op.); *Tommy Gio, Inc. v. Dunlop*, 348 S.W.3d 503, 508 (Tex. App.—Dallas 2011, pet. denied).

218 *Stelly v. Papania*, 927 S.W.2d 620, 622 (Tex. 1996); *Tommy Gio, Inc. v. Dunlop*, 348 S.W.3d 503, 509 (Tex. App.—Dallas 2011, pet. denied); *Arango v. Davila*, No. 13-09-00470-CV, 2011 Tex. App. LEXIS 3806, at *8, 2011 WL 1900189 (Tex. App.—Corpus Christi May 19, 2011, pet. denied) (mem. op.), *overruled on other grounds, Haygood v. De Escabedo*, 356 S.W.3d 390, 399 & n.63 (Tex. 2011).

219 *See Standard Fire Ins. Co. v. Magan*, 745 S.W.2d 310, 312 (Tex. 1987) ("[B]ecause Standard never requested the trial court to withdraw or amend the admission, the admitted facts were conclusively established.").

220 *Unifund CCR Partners v. Weaver*, 262 S.W.3d 796, 798 (Tex. 2008) (holding that, because a summary judgment motion put the appellant on notice of the deficiency of his response to requests for admission, he knew about his mistake before judgment but failed to respond, thereby waiving his right to challenge deemed admissions); *Hewitt v. Roberts*, No. 13-11-00449-CV, 2013 Tex. App. LEXIS 873, at *15 (Tex. App.—Corpus Christi Jan. 31, 2013, no pet.) (mem. op.) ("Hewitt, by his own admission, knew of his 'mistake' in early January 2011, well before the February 18 hearing, and could have responded to the Roberts' motion, or sought leave to file late responses, but because he did not, he waived his right to raise the issue thereafter."); *Cleveland v. Taylor*, 397 S.W.3d 683, 695 (Tex. App.—Houston [1st Dist.] 2012, pet. denied) ("The notice of deemed admissions, two motions for summary judgment, trial exhibit list, and discussion on the record in the presence of two of the Cleveland parties and their attorney demonstrate that the Cleveland parties had notice of their mistake before the trial court rendered judgment and that they had other avenues of relief available, but that they failed to take action until after the trial court's judgment. Thus, we conclude that the Cleveland parties waived their right to challenge the deemed admissions.").

If, however, the responding party first realizes that it needed to move to withdraw its deemed admission after judgment was entered, it may raise the issue for the first time in a motion for new trial. *Wheeler v. Green*, 157 S.W.3d 439, 442 (Tex. 2005) (per curiam) ("Nothing in this record suggests that before summary judgment was granted, Sandra realized that her responses were late [or] that she needed to move to withdraw deemed admissions. . . . Accordingly, we hold she was entitled to raise them in her motion for new trial.").

10-7:1 Good Cause

"[G]ood cause is established by showing the failure [to timely respond or the mistaken answer] was an accident or mistake, not intentional or the result of conscious indifference."[221] As one court explained:

> In deciding whether a failure to timely answer was the result of an accident or mistake, the controlling issue is the absence of purposefulness or bad faith failure to answer which reflects conscious indifference. Consequently, even a slight excuse will suffice, especially when the delay or prejudice will not result against the opposing party. An accident or mistake upon the part of counsel may constitute negligence . . . but it will not necessarily constitute conscious indifference.[222]

The following have been found to constitute good cause for the withdrawal or amendment of deemed admissions: (1) a mistake in calculating the time to serve the

---

[221] *Wheeler v. Green*, 157 S.W.3d 439, 442 (Tex. 2005) (per curiam); *accord Stelly v. Papania*, 927 S.W.2d 620, 622 (Tex. 1996); *City of Saginaw v. Cruz*, No. 05-19-01141-CV, 2020 Tex. App. LEXIS 6984, at *17, 2020 WL 5054802 (Tex. App.—Dallas Aug. 27, 2020, no pet.) (mem. op.); *Ralls v. Funk*, 592 S.W.3d 178, 183 (Tex. App.—Tyler 2019, pet. denied); *In re Cagle*, 585 S.W.3d 618, 623 (Tex. App.—Houston [14th Dist.] 2019, orig. proceeding); *In re TT Fountains of Tomball, Ltd.*, No. 01-15-00817-CV, 2016 Tex. App. LEXIS 7781, at *16–17, 2016 WL 3965117 (Tex. App.—Houston [1st Dist.] July 21, 2016, orig. proceeding) (mem. op.); *Swanson v. State*, No. 03-16-00729-CV, 2017 Tex. LEXIS 3934, at *7, 2017 WL 1832492 (Tex. Austin May 2, 2017, no pet.) (mem. op.); *Tommy Gio, Inc. v. Dunlop*, 348 S.W.3d 503, 510 (Tex. App.—Dallas 2011, pet. denied). This is essentially the same standard applied to a defaulting party's conduct in ruling on an equitable motion for new trial. *Cudd v. Hydroelectric Trans., Inc.*, 867 S.W.2d 101, 104 (Tex. App.—Corpus Christi 1993, no writ); *Esperaza v. Diaz*, 802 S.W.2d 772, 776 (Tex. App.—Houston [14th Dist.] 1990, no writ).

[222] *N. River Ins. Co. v. Greene*, 824 S.W.2d 697, 700 (Tex. App.—El Paso 1992, writ denied) (citations omitted); *see Ralls v. Funk*, 592 S.W.3d 178, 183 (Tex. App.—Tyler 2019, pet. denied) ("Simple bad judgment does not rise to the level of bad faith or callous disregard for the rules. Bad faith is the conscious doing of a wrong for dishonest, discriminatory, or malicious purpose. A determination of bad faith or callous disregard can be made when a party is mindful of pending deadlines and nonetheless either consciously or flagrantly fails to comply with the rules."); *Swanson v. State*, No. 03-16-00729-CV, 2017 Tex. App. LEXIS 3934, at *7–8, 2017 WL 1832492 (Tex. App.—Austin May 2, 2017, no pet.) (mem. op.) (same); *Boulet v. State*, 189 S.W.3d 833, 836 (Tex. App.—Houston [1st Dist.] 2006, no pet.) ("Even a slight excuse will suffice, especially when delay or prejudice to the opposing party will not result."); *Matelski v. Matelski*, 840 S.W.2d 124, 128 (Tex. App.—Fort Worth 1992, no writ) (same); *Ramirez v. Noble Energy, Inc.*, 521 S.W.3d 851, 856 (Tex. App.—Houston [1st Dist.] 2017, no pet.) ("Courts have held that a showing of a clerical error is sufficient to establish good cause, even if the party is negligent, as long as the party's negligence does not rise to the level of conscious indifference.").

response;[223] (2) an inadvertent failure to docket the response date;[224] (3) an inadvertent failure to serve responses after they were timely prepared;[225] (4) an inadvertent failure to respond because the client was ill and the attorney was out-of-state;[226] (5) a party's inadvertent failure to respond to requests for admission served on multiple parties represented by the same attorney;[227] and (6) an inadvertent failure to respond because of a substitution of counsel.[228]

Neither a busy schedule nor reliance on an oral agreement to extend the time to respond, however, constitutes good cause for the withdrawal of a deemed admission.[229] Moreover, good cause does not exist when the responding party does not act promptly to move to withdraw or amend the admission after it discovers the need to do so.[230]

---

223 *Wheeler v. Green*, 157 S.W.3d 439, 442 (Tex. 2005) (per curiam); *In re Seizure of Gambling Proceeds*, 388 S.W.3d 874, 879–80 (Tex. App.—Houston [14th Dist.] 2012, no pet.); *Boulet v. State*, 189 S.W.3d 833, 837 (Tex. App.—Houston [1st Dist.] 2006, no pet.); *TNT Bestway Transp., Inc. v. Whitworth*, No. 05-96-01900-CV, 1999 Tex. App. LEXIS 4311, at *13, 1999 WL 374158 (Tex. App.—Dallas June 10, 1999, pet. denied) (not designated for publication).

224 *Brewer v. Harris*, No. 01-01-00151-CV, 2001 Tex. App. LEXIS 7708, at *7, 2001 WL 1442124 (Tex. App.—Houston [1st Dist.] Nov. 15, 2001, no pet.) (not designated for publication); *N. River Ins. Co. v. Greene*, 824 S.W.2d 697, 698–701 (Tex. App.—El Paso 1992, writ denied).

225 *Ramsey v. Criswell*, 850 S.W.2d 258, 259 (Tex. App.—Texarkana 1993, no writ).

226 *Emp'rs Ins. v. Halton*, 792 S.W.2d 462, 466–67 (Tex. App.—Dallas 1990, writ denied).

227 *Watson v. Dall. Indep. Sch. Dist.*, 135 S.W.3d 208, 216215 (Tex. App.—Waco 2004, no pet.); *Credit-Car Ctrs., Inc. v. Chambers*, 969 S.W.2d 459, 461–63 (Tex. App.—El Paso 1998, no pet.).

228 *Taylor Made Homes, Inc. v. Gianotti*, No. 04-00-00818-CV, 2001 Tex. App. LEXIS 7786, at *7–8, 2001 WL 1479257 (Tex. App.—San Antonio Nov. 21, 2001, no pet.) (not designated for publication).

229 *London Mkt. Co. v. Schattman*, 811 S.W.2d 550, 552 (Tex. 1991) (oral agreement); *Gordon v. Brunig*, No. 02-09-040-CV, 2010 Tex. App. LEXIS 3774, at *12–13, 2010 WL 1999313 (Tex. App.—Fort Worth May 20, 2010, pet. denied) (mem. op.) (busy schedule); *Eshmen v. Centennial Sav. Bank*, 757 S.W.2d 392, 396 (Tex. App.—Dallas 1988, writ denied) (same); *Hoffman v. Tex. Commerce Bank Nat'l Ass'n*, 846 S.W.2d 336, 339–40 (Tex. App.—Houston [14th Dist.] 1992, writ denied) (oral agreement); *see Hoose v. Vanderbilt Mortg. & Fin., Inc.*, No. 03-08-00573-CV, 2009 Tex. App. LEXIS 3136, at *7, 2009 WL 1256646 (Tex. App.—Austin May 8, 2009, pet. denied) (mem. op.) (holding that a failure to timely respond to requests for admission because of the responding party's "medical condition, which required her to avoid the stress of court proceedings" did not constitute good cause).

230 *E.g.*, *City of Saginaw v. Cruz*, No. 05-19-01141-CV, 2020 Tex. App. LEXIS 6984, at *19, 2020 WL 5054802 (Tex. App.—Dallas Aug. 27, 2020, no pet.) (mem. op.) (holding that a failure to act promptly negates good cause); *Qui Phuoc Ho v. MacArthur Ranch, LLC*, No. 05-14-00741-CV, 2015 Tex. App. LEXIS 9175, at *22–23, 2015 WL 5093273 (Tex. App.—Dallas Aug. 28, 2015, pet. denied) (mem. op.) (holding that good cause was not established because the moving party had been aware of the deemed admission for thirteen months); *Hewitt v. Roberts*, No. 13-11-0044-CV, 2013 Tex. App. LEXIS 873, at *15, 2013 WL 39894013 (Tex. App.—Corpus Christi Jan. 31, 2013, no pet.) (mem. op.) (holding that there was no good cause because the responding party "by his own admission, knew of his 'mistake' in early January 2011, well before the February 18 hearing, and could have responded to the Roberts' motion, or sought leave to file late responses," but did not); *Darr v. Humble Auto.*, 20 S.W.3d 802, 808 (Tex. App.—Houston [14th Dist.] 2000, no pet.) (holding that the responding party's failure to move to withdraw deemed admissions until three months after a summary judgment motion's service was not good cause).

10-7:2 Undue Prejudice

"Undue prejudice depends on whether withdrawing an admission or filing a late response will delay trial or significantly hamper the opposing party's ability to prepare for it."[231] As explained by one federal court: "The prejudice contemplated by [Federal Rule 36] is not simply that the party who obtained the admission will now have to convince the factfinder of the truth; rather, it relates to the difficulty a party may face in proving its case, for example by the unavailability of key witnesses in light of the delay."[232]

Accordingly, the mere fact that the requesting party will have to prove the matters previously admitted or even that it will incur significant expense in conducting the additional discovery needed to replace the withdrawn or amended admission does not constitute prejudice.[233] Similarly, the requesting party's reliance on an admission in moving for summary judgment generally does not constitute undue prejudice.[234]

---

231 *Marino v. Kerry*, 355 S.W.3d 629, 633 (Tex. 2011) (per curiam) (quoting *Wheeler v. Green*, 157 S.W.3d 439, 443 (Tex. 2005)); *accord In re Cagle*, 585 S.W.3d 618, 624 (Tex. App.—Houston [14th Dist.] 2019, orig. proceeding); *S. Tex. Innovations, LLC v. Rise Residential Constr., LP*, No. 02-18-00021-CV, 2018 Tex. App. LEXIS 10908, at *12, 2018 WL 6844135 (Tex. App.—Fort Worth Dec. 31, 2018, pet. denied) (mem. op.); *In re TT Fountains of Tomball, Ltd.*, No. 01-15-00817-CV, 2016 Tex. App. LEXIS 7781, at *17, 2016 WL 3965117 (Tex. App.—Houston [1st Dist.] July 21, 2016, orig. proceeding) (mem. op.); *see Wal-Mart Stores, Inc. v. Deggs*, 968 S.W.2d 354, 357 (Tex. 1998) (per curiam) (holding that there was no undue prejudice because the responding party had been deposed); *Rodriguez v. Kapilivsky*, No. 13-11-00976-CV, 2012 Tex. App. LEXIS 10370370, at *7, 2012 WL 7849308 (Tex. App.—Corpus Christi Dec. 1312, 2012, no pet.) (mem. op.) (holding that there was no undue prejudice because the action had not yet been set for trial); *Cudd v. Hydroelectrstatic Trans., Inc.*, 867 S.W.2d 101, 105 (Tex. App.—Corpus Christi 1993, no writ) (holding that there was no undue prejudice because the deemed admissions' withdrawal would not delay the trial); *Esperaza v. Diaz*, 802 S.W.2d 772, 776 (Tex. App.—Houston [14th Dist.] 1990, no writ) (holding there was no undue prejudice when the defendants filed their late responses to requests for admission six months before the trial date).

232 *Sonosha v. Cabrera*, 255 F.3d 1035, 1039 (9th Cir. 2001); *accord Siewertsen v. Worthington Indus.*, 783 F. App'x 563, 569 (6th Cir. 2019); *Le v. Cheesecake Factory Rests., Inc.*, No. 06-20006, 2007 U.S. App. LEXIS 5232, at *9, 2007 WL 715260 (5th Cir. 2007); *FDIC v. Prusia*, 18 F.3d 637, 640 (8th Cir. 1994); *In re Cagle*, 585 S.W.3d 618, 624 (Tex. App.—Houston [14th Dist.] 2019, orig. proceeding) ("The mere fact that a trial on the merits is necessary does not constitute undue prejudice." (quoting *City of Hous. v. Riner*, 896 S.W.2d 317, 320 (Tex. App.—Houston [1st Dist.] 1995, writ denied))); *Boulet v. State*, 189 S.W.3d 833, 837–38 (Tex. App.—Houston [1st Dist.] 2006, no pet.) (same).

233 See cases cited in notes 231–32.

234 *Cf. Conlon v. U.S.*, 474 F.3d 616, 624 (9th Cir. 2007) ("We agree with the other courts that have addressed the issue and conclude that reliance on a deemed admission in preparing a summary judgment motion does not constitute prejudice. Although the United States relied on the deemed admissions in choosing not to engage in any other discovery, we are reluctant to conclude that a lack of discovery, without more, constitutes prejudice. The district court could have reopened the discovery period and prejudice must relate to the difficulty a party may face in proving its case at trial.") (citation omitted); *FDIC v. Prusia*, 18 F.3d 637, 640 (8th Cir. 1994) (same); *see Watson v. Dall. Indep. Sch. Dist.*, 135 S.W.3d 208, 218 (Tex. App.—Waco 2004, no pet.) (finding no prejudice even though the plaintiff relied on deemed admissions in moving for summary judgment because there was ample time to conduct discovery before the trial date); *TNT Bestway Transp., Inc. v. Whitworth*,

A requesting party, however, cannot "lie behind the log" and create undue prejudice. Thus, for example, if responses to requests for admissions were served late, but while there was adequate time to conduct discovery, the requesting party cannot simply decline to take discovery and then claim that it relied on the deemed admission and has been unduly prejudiced.[235] Nonetheless, where the moving party waits

---

No. 05-96-01900-CV, 1999 Tex. App. LEXIS 4311, at *15, 1999 WL 374158 (Tex. App.—Dallas June 10, 1999, pet. denied) (not designated for publication) (same).

[235] *Marino v. Kerry*, 355 S.W.3d 629, 633–34 (Tex. 2011) (per curiam) (holding that there was no undue prejudice when the defendant's responses were two days late and the plaintiff immediately moved for summary judgment based on deemed admissions); *Wheeler v. Green*, 157 S.W.3d 439, 443 (Tex. 2005) (per curiam) ("As Sandra's proof attached to her motion for new trial showed, Darrin's attorney received her responses two days late but six months *before* the summary judgment motion was heard. The lower courts could not have concluded on this record that Darrin would suffer any undue prejudice if the admissions were withdrawn."); *In re TT Fountains of Tomball, Ltd.*, No. 01-15-00817-CV, 2016 Tex. App. LEXIS 7781, at *37–41, 2016 WL 3965117 (Tex. App.—Houston [1st Dist.] July 21, 2016, orig. proceeding) (mem. op.) (holding that there was no undue prejudice because the defendants' motion to withdraw was filed when "nearly five months remained until trial, giving [the plaintiff] ample time to conduct additional discovery and retain expert witnesses without the necessity of delaying trial[,]" and because the defendants made clear that they contested liability. Accordingly, the plaintiff's "decision not to pursue additional discovery . . . or to retain an expert witness . . . was made at her own risk."); *Swanson v. State*, No. 03-16-00729-CV, 2017 Tex. App. LEXIS 3934, at *13–14, 2017 WL 1832492 (Tex. App.—Austin May 2, 2017, no pet.) (mem. op.) ("[T]here is nothing in the record to support a determination that the State was unduly prejudiced by the delay in filing the response. As discussed earlier, Swanson sent his response to the State just a few days after the deadline and before the State filed its motion for summary judgment, and the State received the response more than a month before the scheduled trial date."); *In re Seizure of Gambling Proceeds*, 388 S.W.3d 874, 880 (Tex. App.—Houston [14th Dist.] 2012, no pet.) ("[I]n the present case, assuming Worldwide's responses were late by five days, they were filed more than *one year before* the submission of the State's motion for summary judgment; no undue prejudice would have been suffered by the State if the deemed admissions were withdrawn."); *Wells v. Best Ins. Servs., Inc.*, No. 13-09-00236-CV, 2010 Tex. App. LEXIS 8652, at *12–13, 2010 WL 4264792 (Tex. App.—Corpus Christi Oct. 28, 2010, no pet.) (mem. op.) (holding that there was no undue prejudice because, among other reasons, "the first trial setting in this case was set for sixty days after Wells's responses to the requests for admissions [sic] were finally filed. This was ample time for Best to continue discovery and request additional time from the trial court."); *In re Kellogg-Brown & Root, Inc.*, 45 S.W.3d 772, 776 (Tex. App.—Tyler 2001, orig. proceeding) ("Concerning prejudice to the opposing party, we note that the responses to the requests for admission were delivered eight weeks prior to trial. In light of the time Fambrough had to assess the responses and to take any appropriate action, we hold that she would not be unduly prejudiced by the amendment of the deemed admissions."); *Hourani v. Winn*, No. 14-92-0331-CV, 1992 Tex. App. LEXIS 2991, at *4–5, 1992 WL 347787 (Tex. App.—Houston [14th Dist.] Nov. 25, 1992, writ denied) (not designated for publication) ("We reject the appellee's argument that he relied on the deemed admissions while preparing for trial. The argument suggests that the appellee knew the answers were one day late, yet failed to inform the appellant by a motion to compel, a motion for sanctions, or a motion for summary judgment. Instead, the appellee waited until trial, and used [former Texas] Rule 169 to avoid a decision on the merits. As many courts have stated, [former Texas] Rule 169 should be used to simplify trials by eliminating uncontested matters. [Former Texas] Rule 169 was not designed as a trap for the unwary and should not be used to prevent a litigant from presenting his case.") (citations omitted).

until shortly before trial to file its withdrawal motion, undue prejudice likely will be found.[236]

10-7:3 Merits Would Be "Subserved"

The withdrawal of an admission "subserves" the presentation of the action's merits when upholding the admission would practically or effectively eliminate presentation of the action's merits.[237]

---

[236] *Time Warner, Inc. v. Gonzalez*, 441 S.W.3d 661, 668–69 (Tex. App.—San Antonio 2014, pet. denied) ("[U]ndue prejudice has generally been found in those instances in which a party waited until the day of trial or after to request the withdrawal of deemed admissions. In those instances, the party relies on the deemed admissions in deciding not to take depositions or otherwise develop evidence to support the deemed facts. If the trial court allows the deemed admissions to be withdrawn, the party relying on them would need additional time to develop the evidence, and the delay in trial would cause undue prejudice. Likewise, undue prejudice results because that party is denied an opportunity to develop necessary evidence, hampering its ability to prepare for trial." (quoting *Watson v. Dall. Indep. Sch. Dist.*, 135 S.W.3d 208, 215 (Tex. App.—Dallas 2004))), *overruled on other grounds*, *Univ. of Tex. Med. Branch v. Barrett* 159 S.W.3d 631, 632–33 (Tex. 2005) (per curium); *Morgan v. Timmers Chevrolet, Inc.*, 1 S.W.3d 803, 807 (Tex. App.—Houston [1st Dist.] 1999, pet. denied) ("Timmers Chevrolet's waiting more than two years, until after the trial began, to try to withdraw deemed admissions upon which the Morgans had relied in preparing their case, caused undue prejudice to the Morgans."); *Reyes v. Int'l Metals Supply Co.*, 666 S.W.2d 622, 625 (Tex. App.—Houston [1st Dist.] 1984, no writ.) (holding that the defendant suffered undue prejudice where the plaintiff requested withdrawal of deemed admissions after the trial was underway because the defendant "had no reason to be prepared to offer proof" of the facts deemed admitted); *see City of Saginaw v. Cruz*, No. 05-19-01141-CV, 2020 Tex. App. LEXIS 6984, at *19, 2020 WL 5054802 (Tex. App.—Dallas Aug. 27, 2020, no pet.) (mem. op.) (holding that there was undue prejudice because the City waited until six days before a hearing on its plea to the jurisdiction to move to withdraw its admissions relevant to the plea and offered no explanation for the delay); *cf. Clement Grp., LLC v. ETD Servs., LLC*, No. 4:16-CV-00773, 2018 U.S. Dist. LEXIS 6994, at *23 (E.D. Tex. Jan. 17, 2018) ("Clement on two occasions notified Defendants that the responses to admissions were late and Defendants did not respond to these notices. Defendants waited until August 9, 2017, over four months after they missed their deadline, less than two weeks before the discovery deadline, and the morning of Davis's deposition, to inform Clement of their intent to withdraw and amend their responses. ETD and Davis waited even longer until filing their motion, waiting until October 10, 2017, over six months after they missed their deadline, less than four months before the final pretrial conference, and after the close of the discovery period to ask the Court to withdraw their admissions. At this stage, Clement made tactical decisions in its case based on these admissions and would now be prejudiced if the admissions were withdrawn.") (citation omitted); *Brach Banking & Trust Co. v. Deutz-Allis Corp.*, 120 F.R.D. 655, 658–59 (E.D.N.C. 1988) (holding that courts may consider "the diligence of the party seeking withdrawal and the adequacy of time remaining for additional discovery before trial").

[237] *See Wheeler v. Green*, 157 S.W.3d 439, 443 n.2 (Tex. 2005) (per curiam) (holding that the "subserve" requirement is met if the action will be "decided on deemed (but perhaps untrue) facts"); *S. Tex. Innovations, LLC v. Rise Residential Constr., LP*, No. 02-18-00021-CV, 2018 Tex. App. LEXIS 10908, at *17–18, 2018 WL 6844135 (Tex. App.—Fort Worth Dec. 31, 2018, pet. denied) (mem. op.) (holding that the "subserve" requirement was met "[b]ecause this case was decided on deemed admissions [and] the merits were not litigated"); *Rodriguez v. Kapilivsky*, No. 13-11-00976-CV, 2012 Tex. App. LEXIS 10370370, at *8,

10-7:4 Withdrawal of Merits-Preclusive Deemed Admissions

Although Texas Rule 198.3 does not distinguish between merits-preclusive and non-merits-preclusive deemed admissions,[238] Texas courts do so. Because Texas Rule 198.2(c) automatically deems a request admitted if the responding party fails to respond timely,[239] the Rule essentially imposes an automatic sanction.[240] Accordingly,

---

2012 WL 7849308 (Tex. App.—Corpus Christi Dec. 1312, 2012, no pet.) (mem. op.) (holding that the "subserve" requirement was met because upholding the deemed admissions would result in summary judgment); *Wells v. Best Ins. Servs., Inc.*, No. 13-09-00236-CV, 2010 Tex. App. LEXIS 8652, at *12–13, 2010 WL 4264792 (Tex. App.—Corpus Christi Oct. 28, 2010, no pet.) (mem. op.) (same); *In re Kellogg-Brown & Root, Inc.*, 45 S.W.3d 772, 777 (Tex. App.—Tyler 2001, orig. proceeding) (holding that the "subserve" requirement was met because upholding the deemed admissions would have "eliminated [the defendant's] ability to present any viable defense at trial and acted as a death penalty sanction."); *cf. Colon v. U.S.*, 474 F.3d 616, 622 (9th Cir. 2007) (holding that the "subserved" requirement was met because upholding deemed admissions eliminated the need for a presentation on the merits); *Dynasty Apparel Indus., Inc. v. Rentz*, 206 F.R.D. 596, 602 (S.D. Ohio 2001); *Baker v. Potter*, 212 F.R.D. 8, 13 (D.D.C. 2002) ("Courts in this district have interpreted this prong as satisfied if the admission effectively would bar the party from presenting its case on its merits.").

The Texas Supreme Court has explained that the "subserve" and "no-undue-prejudice" requirements "are different sides of the same coin, as presentation of the merits will suffer (1) if the requesting party *cannot* prepare for trial, and also (2) if the requestor *can* prepare but the case is decided on deemed (but perhaps untrue) facts anyway." *Wheeler v. Green*, 157 S.W.3d 439, 443 n.2 (Tex. 2005) (per curiam).

238 A merits-preclusive admission is one that conclusively establishes an ultimate factual issue in the case, such as an admission that a defendant was negligent, committed fraud, or breached the contract at issue. *See, e.g.*, *Medina v. Zuniga*, 593 S.W.3d 238, 244 (Tex. 2019) (explaining that a merits-preclusive admission is "one in which the requestor essentially seeks an admission of liability"); *Ralls v. Funk*, 592 S.W.3d 178, 184 (Tex. App.—Tyler 2019, pet. denied) ("We agree that deemed admission number two is merits preclusive. This request did not seek to discover information. It relieved Funk of the burden to prove an ultimate issue of fact necessary to establish his case, that he performed as required by the consultant agreement."); *S. Tex. Innovations, LLC v. Rise Residential Constr., LP*, No. 02-18-00021-CV, 2018 Tex. App. LEXIS 10908, at *12, 2018 WL 6844135 (Tex. App.—Fort Worth Dec. 31, 2018, pet. denied) (mem. op.) ("STI's deemed admissions conclusively established the ultimate legal and factual issues in this case. Because Rise, GCRE, and LCAR moved for summary judgment based solely on the deemed admissions, the trial court's summary judgment against STI was based only on those admissions and so they had a merits-preclusive effect."); *Time Warner, Inc. v. Gonzalez*, 441 S.W.3d 661, 666 (Tex. App.—San Antonio 2014, pet. denied) (holding that requests for admissions had merits-preclusive effect when it was "clear that the trial court's decision to render judgment in favor of Gonzalez was based solely on the deemed admissions conclusively establishing the ultimate legal issues in the case").

239 Tex. R. Civ. P. 198.2(c).

240 *Medina v. Zuniga*, 593 S.W.3d 238, 244 (Tex. 2019); *Pickaree-Champagne v. Metro. Transit Auth.*, No. 01-16-00138-CV, 2017 Tex. App. LEXIS 5451, at *5–6, 2017 WL 2590290 (Tex. App.—Houston [1st Dist.] June 14, 2017, no pet.) (mem. op.); *Swanson v. State*, No. 03-16-00729-CV, 2017 Tex. App. LEXIS 3934, at *7, 2017 WL 1832492 (Tex. App.—Austin May 2, 2017, no pet.) (mem. op.); *In re Am. Gunite Mgmt. Co.*, No. 02-11-00349-CV, 2011 Tex. App. LEXIS 7913, at *2–3, 2011 WL 4550159 (Tex. App.—Fort Worth Oct. 3, 2011, orig. proceeding) (mem. op.).

the Texas Supreme Court consistently has held that when deemed admissions are merits-preclusive, they are subject to the long-standing due-process principles applicable to other judicially-imposed, death-penalty sanctions and must be set aside "absent flagrant bad faith or callous disregard for the rules," provided the requesting party is not unduly prejudiced by the withdrawal.[241] As recently explained by the Court:

> When a deemed admission arises from a merits-preclusive request—one in which the requestor essentially seeks an admission of liability—the deemed admission can amount to a death-penalty sanction. But we have recognized that due process limits the application of this rule. In short, "there are constitutional limitations upon the power of courts, even in aid of their own valid processes, to dismiss an action without affording a party the opportunity for a hearing on the merits of his cause."
>
> "When requests for admissions are used as intended—addressing uncontroverted matters or evidentiary ones like the authenticity or admissibility of documents—deeming admissions by default is unlikely to compromise presentation of the merits." But a deemed admission that precludes a defendant from contesting the validity of the plaintiff's claims or that forces him to concede his defenses, wields a result more severe than our rules intend or that due process will tolerate. Our cases on this point are not constitutional holdings per se, but rather reflect judicially created prophylactic measures designed to ensure that our rules of civil procedure—rules this Court promulgated—are not applied in a way that risks violating due process.[242]

Although a party moving to withdraw a deemed admission generally has the burden of showing good cause, when the request for admission is a merits-preclusive one, the party opposing the admission's withdrawal has the burden to show that the

---

[241] *Marino v. Kerry*, 355 S.W.3d 629, 633–34 (Tex. 2011) (per curiam); *accord Medina v. Zuniga*, 593 S.W.3d 238, 244–45 (Tex. 2019); *Wheeler v. Green*, 157 S.W.3d 439, 443 (Tex. 2005) (per curiam); *Ralls v. Funk*, 592 S.W.3d 178, 182–83 (Tex. App.—Tyler 2019, pet. denied); *In re TT Fountains of Tomball, Ltd.*, No. 01-15-00817-CV, 2016 Tex. App. LEXIS 7781, at *17, 2016 WL 3965117 (Tex. App.—Houston [1st Dist.] July 21, 2016, orig. proceeding) (mem. op.); *Ramirez v. Noble Energy, Inc.*, 521 S.W.3d 851, 857 (Tex. App.—Houston [1st Dist.] 2017, no pet.); *Swanson v. State*, No. 03-16-00729-CV, 2017 Tex. App. LEXIS 3934, at *9, 2017 WL 1832492 (Tex. App.—Austin May 2, 2017, no pet.) (mem. op.); *Arrow Automatic Fire Prot., Inc. v. Wesleyan Corp.*, No. 11-14-00295-CV, 2017 Tex. App. LEXIS 1826, at *5 (Tex. App.—Eastland Mar. 3, 2017, no pet.) (mem. op.).

[242] *Medina v. Zuniga*, 593 S.W.3d 238, 244–45 (Tex. 2019) (citations omitted) (quoting *Societe Internationale Pour Participations Industrielles et Commerciales, S.A. v. Rogers*, 357 U.S. 197, 209 (1958), and *Wheeler v. Green*, 157 S.W.3d 439, 443 (Tex. 2005) (per curiam)); *accord Ralls v. Funk*, 592 S.W.3d 178, 182–83 (Tex. App.—Tyler 2019, pet. denied); *Ramirez v. Noble Energy, Inc.*, 521 S.W.3d 851, 857 (Tex. App.—Houston [1st Dist.] 2017, no pet.); *Swanson v. State*, No. 03-16-00729-CV, 2017 Tex. App. LEXIS 3934, at *9, 2017 WL 1832492 (Tex. App.—Austin May 2, 2017, no pet.) (mem. op.); *Arrow Automatic Fire Prot., Inc. v. Wesleyan Corp.*, No. 11-14-00295-CV, 2017 Tex. App. LEXIS 1826, at *5 (Tex. App.—Eastland Mar. 3, 2017, no pet.) (mem. op.); *In re TT Fountains of Tomball, Ltd.*, No. 01-15-00817-CV, 2016 Tex. App. LEXIS 7781, at *17, 2016 WL 3965117 (Tex. App.—Houston [1st Dist.] July 21, 2016, orig. proceeding) (mem. op.).

party seeking the withdrawal acted with bad faith or callous disregard of the rules.[243] "Bad faith is the conscious doing of a wrong for dishonest, discriminatory, or malicious purpose. A determination of bad faith or callous disregard can be made when a party is mindful of pending deadlines and nonetheless either consciously or flagrantly fails to comply with the rules."[244]

---

243 *Ralls v. Funk*, 592 S.W.3d 178, 183 (Tex. App.—Tyler 2019, pet. denied) ("Ordinarily, the burden of showing good cause lies with the party seeking withdrawal of deemed admissions. But when the requests for admission are merits preclusive, the party opposing the withdrawal of the admissions has the burden to show that the party seeking the withdrawal acted with bad faith or callous disregard of the rules."); *Sadeghian v. Wright*, No. 06-18-00062-CV, 2019 Tex. App. LEXIS 354, at *9, 2019 WL 255741 (Tex. App.—Texarkana Jan. 18, 2019, no pet.) (same); *S. Tex. Innovations, LLC v. Rise Residential Constr., LP*, No. 02-18-00021-CV, 2018 Tex. App. LEXIS 10908, at *12, 2018 WL 6844135 (Tex. App.—Fort Worth Dec. 31, 2018, pet. denied) (mem. op.) (same) *In re Sewell*, 472 S.W.3d 449, 456 (Tex. App.—Texarkana 2015, orig. proceeding) (same), *overruled on other grounds, In re Bayview Loan Servicing, LLC*, 532 S.W.3d 510, 512 n.3 (Tex. App.—Texarkana 2017, orig. proceeding); *Yacoub v. SureTec Ins. Co.*, No. 14-13-00274-CV, 2015 Tex. App. LEXIS 4285, at *7–8 (Tex. App.—Houston [14th Dist.] Apr. 28, 2015, no pet.) (mem. op.) (same); *Time Warner, Inc. v. Gonzalez*, 441 S.W.3d 661, 666 (Tex. App.—San Antonio 2014, pet. denied) (same).

244 *Ralls v. Funk*, 592 S.W.3d 178, 183 (Tex. App.—Tyler 2019, pet. denied) ("Simple bad judgment does not rise to the level of bad faith or callous disregard for the rules. Bad faith is the conscious doing of a wrong for dishonest, discriminatory, or malicious purpose. A determination of bad faith or callous disregard can be made when a party is mindful of pending deadlines and nonetheless either consciously or flagrantly fails to comply with the rules.") (citations omitted); *Ramirez v. Noble Energy, Inc.*, 521 S.W.3d 851, 860 (Tex. App.—Houston [1st Dist.] 2017, no pet.) ("'[A] lack of care, simple bad judgment, or a mistaken belief that no discovery had been served does not rise to the level of bad faith or callous disregard for the rules.' This Court stated, 'Rather, a determination of bad faith or callous disregard for the rules has been reserved for cases in which the evidence shows that a party is mindful of pending deadlines and nonetheless either consciously or flagrantly fails to comply with the rules.'" (quoting *In re TT-Fountains of Tomball, Ltd.*, No. 01-15-00817-CV, 2016 Tex. App. LEXIS 7781, at *35, 2016 WL 3965117 (Tex. App.—Houston [1st Dist.] July 21, 2016, orig. proceeding) (mem. op.))). *Compare, e.g.*, *Sadeghian v. Wright*, No. 06-18-00062-CV, 2019 Tex. App. LEXIS 354, at *9, 2019 WL 255741 (Tex. App.—Texarkana Jan. 18, 2019, no pet.) (mem. op.) (holding that the trial court did not abuse its discretion in finding callous disregard because "Sadeghian was properly served through counsel, the Wrights informed Stephens that he had missed the deadline to respond, and Stephens still failed to respond. Although Sadeghian claimed he was unaware of the requests for admissions and Stephens was unresponsive to telephone calls, the Wrights asserted that those representations were false since Stephens was working on a different case for Sadgehian and was responsive to their email scheduling the hearing. While Sadeghian attempted to distance himself from Stephens' acts and omissions, an attorney's callous disregard for the rules can support the denial of a motion to withdraw deemed admissions. Moreover, Sadeghian was duly served with the requests for disclosure, but had failed to respond to those as well. Sadeghian hired new counsel, who could have, but failed to, ask permission to file late responses to the requests for admissions. No explanation was offered by Sadeghian's new counsel as to the reason for their omissions. The Wrights also demonstrated that Sadeghian was aware of his responsibility to answer discovery since he was a named party in many other cases, but had a pattern of unwillingness to do so. They also showed that Sadeghian had previously been determined to exhibit bad faith in litigation.") (citation omitted), *In re Adams*, No. 05-15-00536-CV, 2015 Tex. App. LEXIS 4733, at *1, 2015 WL 2195091 (Tex. App.—Dallas May 8, 2015, orig. proceeding) (mem. op.) (holding that the "trial court could

"Undue prejudice depends on whether withdrawing an admission or filing a late response will delay trial or significantly hamper the opposing party's ability to prepare for it."[245]

---

have reasonably concluded that relator's repeated failure to respond in a timely fashion to the requests for admission was intentional or the result of conscious indifference" after relator had twice failed to respond timely to requests), *Soto v. Gen. Foam & Plastics Corp.*, 458 S.W.3d 78, 83 (Tex. App.—El Paso 2014, no pet.) (holding that the evidence showed that the defendant acted with bad faith and callous disregard of the rules sufficient to support decision that deemed admissions should not be withdrawn because he had refused his attorney's requests to respond to discovery and had refused to respond even when faced with sanctions by the trial court), ***Bernstein v. Adams***, No. 01-12-00703-CV, 2013 Tex. App. LEXIS 11093, at *10–11, 2013 WL 4680396 (Tex. App.—Houston [1st Dist.] Aug. 29, 2013, no pet.) (mem. op.) (affirming summary judgment based on deemed admissions when the defendants never at any point attempted to respond to requests for admissions or summary-judgment motion and knowingly failed to appear at hearing, which indicated "conscious[] indifferen[ce] to the deadlines and consequences [they] imposed"), ***with, e.g.***, ***Ralls v. Funk***, 592 S.W.3d 178, 184–85 (Tex. App.—Tyler 2019, pet. denied) ("Ralls answered three weeks late and never produced documents. Although requests and responses were sent within the court's scheduling order deadline, there was no written agreement between the parties to extend the deadline for responses to Funk's requests for admissions, or a court order of abatement. Ralls's excuse, based on an untethered assertion, invites skepticism. His failure to confirm the due date was imprudent. However, there is nothing in the record to show Ralls consciously missed the deadline for dishonest, discriminatory, or malicious purposes."), ***In re TT Fountains of Tomball, Ltd.***, No. 01-15-00817-CV, 2016 Tex. App. LEXIS 7781, at *33–36, 2016 WL 3965117 (Tex. App.—Houston [1st Dist.] July 21, 2016) (holding that there was no conscious disregard because the "Relators asserted they did not respond because they did not know that they had been served with discovery"), ***Rodriguez v. Kapilivsky***, No. 13-11-00796-CV, 2012 Tex. App. LEXIS 10370, at *7, 2012 WL 7849308, at *2 (Tex. App.—Corpus Christi Dec. 13, 2012, no pet) (mem. op.) (concluding that no evidence was presented that the plaintiff's tardy response to requests for admission was intentional or the result of conscious indifference, bad faith, or a callous disregard for the rules because the plaintiff's attorney swore that he had misfiled the requests for admission, failed to calendar them, and first learned about them when he received motion for summary judgment relying on the deemed admissions), and ***In re Reagan***, No. 09-07-00113-CV, 2007 Tex. App. LEXIS 2783, at *1, 3, 2007 WL 1087148 (Tex. App.—Beaumont Apr. 12, 2007, orig. proceeding) (mem. op.) (granting mandamus relief and holding that the defendant was entitled to withdraw deemed admission because his attorney swore that "each time she examined the petition, she failed to notice the requests for admissions were there").

245 *Wheeler v. Green*, 157 S.W.3d 439, 443 (Tex. 2005) (per curiam); ***accord S. Tex. Innovations, LLC v. Rise Residential Constr., LP***, No. 02-18-00021-CV, 2018 Tex. App. LEXIS 10908, at *8, 2018 WL 6844135 (Tex. App.—Fort Worth Dec. 31, 2018, pet. denied) (mem. op.); ***accord Ralls v. Funk***, 592 S.W.3d 178, 182–83 (Tex. App.—Tyler 2019, pet. denied); ***see In re Sewell***, 472 S.W.3d 449, 458–59 (Tex. App.—Texarkana 2015, orig. proceeding) (concluding that there was no undue prejudice because the requesting party knew that the deemed admissions' substance was contested as the movant had been deposed before the requests for admission were served and his deposition testimony contradicted the substance of the requests for admissions and as the requesting party failed to apprise the movant's new attorney that requests for admission had never been answered), ***overruled on other grounds***, ***In re Bayview Loan Servicing, LLC***, 532 S.W.3d 510, 512 n.3 (Tex. App.—Texarkana 2017, orig. proceeding); ***Time Warner, Inc. v. Gonzalez***, 441 S.W.3d 661, 668–69 (Tex. App.—San Antonio 2014, pet. denied) (holding that there was no undue prejudice when the requesting party knew before trial that the movant contested the substance of the merits-preclusive

Finally, in the case of merits-preclusive admissions, the presentation of the merits is not served because "the case [will be] decided on deemed (but perhaps untrue) facts[.]"[246]

A trial court's failure to allow the withdrawal of merits-preclusive admissions is reviewable by mandamus.[247]

Not only must a trial court allow a party to withdraw a merits-preclusive admission (absent flagrant bad faith or callous disregard for the rules and a lack of prejudice to the non-responding party) but the court also generally cannot properly impose sanctions against the responding party under Texas Rule 215.4, the admit-or-pay rule,[248] for denying such requests even if it, contrary to its admissions, later admits liability.[249]

---

admissions); *In re A.A.*, No. 01-13-00542-CV, 2013 Tex. App. LEXIS 14997, at *38–39 (Tex. App.—Houston [1st Dist.] Dec. 12, 2013, pet. denied) (mem. op.) (same).

[246] *S. Tex. Innovations, LLC v. Rise Residential Constr., LP*, No. 02-18-00021-CV, 2018 Tex. App. LEXIS 10908, at *18, 2018 WL 6844135 (Tex. App.—Fort Worth Dec. 31, 2018, pet. denied) (mem. op.) ("Because this case was decided on deemed admissions, the merits were not litigated, and thus withdrawing the admissions will allow the merits to be presented."); *Arrow Automatic Fire Prot., Inc. v. Wesleyan Corp.*, No. 11-14-00295-CV, 2017 Tex. App. LEXIS 1826, at *9 (Tex. App.—Eastland Mar. 3, 2017, no pet.) (mem. op.) ("[P]resentation of the merits is not served when 'the case is decided on deemed (but perhaps untrue) facts.'" (quoting *Wheeler v. Green*, 157 S.W.3d 439, 443 n. 2 (Tex. 2005) (per curiam))); *Time Warner, Inc. v. Gonzalez*, 441 S.W.3d 661, 669 (Tex. App.—San Antonio 2014, pet. denied) (same).

[247] *In re Cagle*, 585 S.W.3d 618, 624 (Tex. App.—Houston [14th Dist.] 2019, orig. proceeding) (conditionally granting mandamus relief because the trial court improperly refused to allow the withdrawal of deemed merits-preclusive admissions); *In re Sewell*, 472 S.W.3d 449, 456 (Tex. App.—Texarkana 2015, orig. proceeding) ("B]ecause non-merit-preclusive requests do not involve due process considerations, a trial court's order relating to discovery, which is 'merely incidental to the normal trial process,' may be corrected on appeal, and mandamus is not available." (quoting *In re Rozelle*, 229 S.W.3d 757, 761 (Tex. App.—San Antonio 2007, orig. proceeding))), *overruled on other grounds, In re Bayview Loan Servicing, LLC*, 532 S.W.3d 510, 512 n.3 (Tex. App.—Texarkana 2017, orig. proceeding); *In re Rozelle*, 229 S.W.3d 757, 761 (Tex. App.—San Antonio 2007, orig. proceeding) (holding that an order denying the withdrawal of merits-preclusive admissions is reviewable by mandamus).

[248] Rule 215.4(b) provides:

> If a party fails to admit the genuineness of any document or the truth of any matter as requested under Rule 198 and if the party requesting the admissions thereafter proves the genuineness of the document or the truth of the matter, he may apply to the court for an order requiring the other party to pay him the reasonable expenses incurred in making that proof, including reasonable attorney fees. The court shall make the order unless it finds that (1) the request was held objectionable pursuant to Rule 193, or (2) the admission sought was of no substantial importance, or (3) the party failing to admit had a reasonable ground to believe that he might prevail on the matter, or (4) there was other good reason for the failure to admit.

Tex. R. Civ. P. 215.4(b). Sanctions under Rule 215.4 are discussed in Chapter 10, section 10-9.

[249] *Medina v. Zuniga*, 593 S.W.3d 238, 245–47 (Tex. 2019). See also Chapter 10, section 10-9 (discussing sanctions under Texas Rule 215.4, the admit-or-pay rule).

10-7:5 Use of Withdrawn or Amended Admissions

The general rule regarding a withdrawn pleading is that it is no longer a conclusive judicial admission,[250] but rather is admissible in evidence as an evidentiary admission with the party free to explain why it was withdrawn.[251] No Texas case has focused on this question as it applies to a withdrawn or amended admission. Nonetheless, an express admission, later withdrawn or amended, should be treated in the same fashion as a pleading,[252] but a withdrawn deemed admission should be inadmissible.[253]

10-8 Testing the Sufficiency of Answers, Objections, and Privilege Assertions to Requests for Admission

Under Texas Rule 215.4, a requesting party "may move to determine the sufficiency of the answer or objection" to a request for admission.[254] It can challenge a qualified admission or denial, an admission or denial that does not "fairly meet the substance of the request,"[255] a statement of inability to admit or deny, an objection, or a privilege

---

[250] *Sosa v. Cent. Power & Light*, 909 S.W.2d 893, 895 (Tex. 1995) (per curiam) (noting that "[c]ontrary to statements in live pleadings, [statements] contained in superseded pleadings are not conclusive and indisputable judicial admissions"); *Nguyen v. Nguyen*, 355 S.W.3d 82, 92 (Tex. App.—Houston [1st Dist.] 2011, pet. denied) (same); *Quick v. Plastic Sols. of Tex., Inc.*, 270 S.W.3d 173, 188 (Tex. App.—El Paso 2008, no pet.) (same).

[251] *Bay Area Healthcare Grp., Ltd. v. McShane*, 239 S.W.3d 231, 235 (Tex. 2007) (per curiam) (holding that superseded pleadings are admissible in evidence as an admission of a party opponent); *Nguyen v. Nguyen*, 355 S.W.3d 82, 92 (Tex. App.—Houston [1st Dist.] 2011, pet. denied) (same); *Quick v. Plastic Sols. of Tex., Inc.*, 270 S.W.3d 173, 185188 (Tex. App.—El Paso 2008, no pet.) (same).

[252] *Cf. Tuomey Reg'l Med. Ctr., Inc. v. McIntosh*, 432 S.E.2d 485, 487 (S.C. 1993) ("Once an answer to a Request for Admissions [sic] is amended under [South Carolina] Rule 36, both the initial answers and the amended answer may be published to the jury. The jury may consider the initial answer as evidence, while the party who such answers 'is free to explain why it was made and [amended].'" (quoting Charles Alan Wright, *et al.*, *Federal Practice and Procedure: Civil* § 2264m at 745 (1970))).

[253] *Cf. Collins Entm't, Inc. v. White*, 611 S.E.2d 262, 268 (S.C. 2005) ("We find where an admission is made solely by the failure to make a timely response, such admission being later withdrawn, the party is not allowed to publish the admission to the jury. The party may publish the late-filed response, but may not assert before the jury that the requests were previously admitted. Accordingly, we conclude the trial court properly refused to allow Appellants to publish to the jury the fact that Collins admitted the requests by failing to make a timely response.").

[254] Tex. R. Civ. P. 215.4(a); *accord, e.g.*, *In re Commitment of Williams*, 539 S.W.3d 429, 443 (Tex. App.—Houston [1st Dist.] 2017, no pet.); *Pickaree-Champagne v. Metro. Transit Auth.*, No. 01-16-00138-CV, 2017 Tex. App. LEXIS 5451, at *10 n.1, 2017 WL 2590290 (Tex. App.—Houston [1st Dist.] June 14, 2017, no pet.) (mem. op.); *Guerrero-McDonald v. Nassour*, 516 S.W.3d 198, 213 (Tex. App.—Eastland 2017, no pet.); *Bell v. Nichols*, No. 10-13-00151-CV, 2014 Tex. App. LEXIS 4523, at *8–9, 2014 WL 1681985 (Tex. App.—Waco Apr. 24, 2014, no pet.) (mem. op.); *Thomas v. Select Portfolio Servicing, Inc.*, 293 S.W.3d 316, 320 (Tex. App.—Beaumont 2009, no pet.); *In re RLS Legal Sols. L.L.C.*, 156 S.W.3d 160, 165 (Tex. App.—Beaumont 2005, orig. proceeding), *mand. conditionally granted on other grounds*, 221 S.W.3d 629 (Tex. 2007) (per curiam); *In re Hodge*, No. 12-02-00314-CV, 2002 Tex. App. LEXIS 8776, at *8, 2002 WL 31769635 (Tex. App.—Tyler Dec. 11, 2002, orig. proceeding) (not designated for publication).

[255] Tex. R. Civ. P. 198.2(b).

assertion.[256] This does not mean, however, that the requesting party can litigate the accuracy of a request's unqualified denial.

Neither Texas Rule 198 nor Texas Rule 215.4 authorizes a trial court to determine the accuracy of denials before trial.[257] Accordingly, a trial court cannot order that a request be admitted because the responding party's denial is unsupported by evidence or even because it was made in bad faith.[258] An incorrect or even a bad-faith denial

---

[256] The requesting party's motion technically is not a motion to compel and should be styled "Motion to Test Sufficiency of Responses [and/or] Objections to Requests for Admission."

[257] *In re Hodge*, No. 12-02-0031402000314-CV, 2002 Tex. App. LEXIS 8776, at *11, 2002 WL 31769635 (Tex. App.—Tyler Dec. 11, 2002, orig. proceeding) (not designated for publication) ("[Plaintiffs] cite no case law, and we are not aware of any, supporting their contention that, as here, a party may file a motion to deem admissions requesting that a trial court determine whether such a denial has merit. Therefore, we conclude that such action by the trial court is not permitted by the rules of procedure or interpretation of the case law."); *cf. District of Columbia ex rel. Z-Modular, LLC v. MCN Build, Inc.*, No. 18-cv-2947 (RJL/GMH), 2020 U.S. Dist. LEXIS 124719, at *10–11 (D.D.C. July 15, 2020) ("Plaintiff's attempt to litigate the accuracy of Defendant's responses to these RFAs is not appropriate at this time. '[A] motion to determine the sufficiency of a response is "not to be used as an attempt to litigate the accuracy of a response." A response can be sufficient, even if it is not ultimately determined to have been accurate.'" (quoting *Wiwa v. Royal Dutch Petroleum Co.*, Nos. 96 Civ. 8386 (KMW) (HBP), 01 Civ. 1909 (KMW) (HBP), 2009 U.S. Dist. LEXIS 45621, at *19, 2009 WL 1457142 (S.D.N.Y. May 26, 2009))); *Lodestar Anstalt v. Route 66 Junkyard Brewery LLC*, No. CV 17-0062 JCH/WPL, 2017 U.S. Dist. LEXIS 115625, at *5–6 (D.N.M. July 25, 2017) ("It is well-established that a party may not request, under [Federal] Rule 36, that the court determine pretrial the accuracy of a denial of a request for admission, and that [Federal] Rule 37(c)(2) provides, in a post-judgment motion for sanctions, the sole avenue to assess the substantive accuracy of a denial of a request for admission."); *Brown v. Mohr*, No. 2:13-cv-0006, 2017 U.S. Dist. LEXIS 102082, at *7–8, 2017 WL 2832631 (S.D. Ohio June 30, 2017) (same); *Fatihah v. Neal*, No. CIV-16-058-JHP, 2017 U.S. Dist. LEXIS 91452, at *5–6, 2017 WL 2559992 (E.D. Okla. May 22, 2017) (same).

[258] *Cf. Superior Sales W., Inc. v. Gonzalez*, No. EP-19-CV-329-KC, 335 F.R.D. 98, 102–03 (W.D. Tex. 2020) ("District courts across the country, as well as preeminent treatises on federal civil procedure, agree that '[Federal] Rule 36 does not authorize the court to make determinations on the accuracy of responses before trial.' Stated differently, '[i]f a responding party files a response that contains the proper detail, . . . the propounding party may not challenge the denial on the ground that it is unsupported by the evidence.' Here, none of Gonzalez's denials are insufficient simply because other evidence—however extensive or unassailable it may be—appears to show that those denials are mendacious. Gonzalez's denials are clear and specific; they are neither equivocal nor evasive. Therefore, Gonzalez's denials are adequate under [Federal] Rule 36. . . ." (quoting *In re TFT-LCD (Flat Panel) Antitrust Litig.*, No. M 07-1827 SI, 2011 U.S. Dist. LEXIS 90730, at *61, 2011 WL 3566419 (N.D. Cal. Aug. 12, 2011), and *Duncan v. Nunez*, No. 1:17-CV-1623-P, 2019 U.S. Dist. LEXIS 194262, at *4, 2019 WL 5862001 (W.D. La. Nov. 7, 2019))); *Wu v. Seoul Garden, Inc.*, No. 1:16-CV-03613 (ARR) (ST), 2018 U.S. Dist. LEXIS 9820, at *27–28 (E.D.N.Y. Jan. 22, 2018) ("Plaintiffs asserted that every denial to a RFA must be supported with 'detailed reasons for each denial.' To put it simply, Plaintiffs were wrong. Parties need not state the specific factual basis of a denial, as RFAs are not 'a discovery procedure at all. . . . [and a] party desiring to learn what the facts actually are should use other discovery devices.' Plaintiffs, by insisting upon specific factual bases for denials, were attempting to improperly 'avoid the limits on the number of interrogatories authorized under Rule 33(a)(1).'" (citations omitted) (quoting *Baker v. Cty. of Missaukee*, 2013 U.S. Dist. LEXIS 154072, at *11 n.2 (W.D. Mich. Oct. 28, 2013))); *Interland, Inc. v. Bunting*, No. 1:04-CV-444-ODE, 2005 U.S. Dist. LEXIS 36112, at *31, 2005

does *not* constitute an insufficient response for purposes of Texas Rule 215.4(a).[259] Rather, the requesting party's sole recourse is to prove the denial's incorrectness at trial and then move for expenses under Texas Rule 215.4(b).[260]

The requesting party has the burden of challenging the sufficiency of an answer, an objection, or a privilege assertion to a request for admission in the first instance.[261] If no challenge to the answer, objection, or privilege assertion is made or if no ruling on a motion to test its sufficiency is obtained from the trial court, the requesting party waives any complaint about the answer, objection, or privilege assertion.[262]

When an answer, objection, or privilege assertion is challenged, the responding party has the burden to (1) establish the answer's sufficiency, including whether it made reasonable inquiry and whether the information known or easily obtainable was insufficient to enable an admission or denial, or (2) the objection's or privilege

---

WL 2414990 (N.D. Ga. Mar. 31, 2005) ("Most of Interland's requests for admission were mirror image requests. . . . Bunting denied both requests. While Interland claims defendant's responses were improper, [Federal] Rule 36 only requires an admission, denial, or objection. Defendant has complied. The accuracy of its responses will be determined at trial. The implicit meaning of [Federal] Rule 37 . . . is that issue obviously subject to dispute should be resolved at trial, not in a discovery motion. Those responses where Defendant simply admitted or denied a request are sufficient as they are completely within the purview of [Federal] Rule 36." (citations omitted) (quoting *Perez v. Miami-Dade Cty.*, 297 F.3d 1255, 1269 (11th Cir. 2002))); *Foretich v. Chung*, 151 F.R.D. 3, 5 (D.D.C. 1993) (holding that an answer to a request for admission is insufficient if it is not specific or the explanation for the refusal to admit or to deny is improper, and not because a denial may be contrary to the evidence); *see Lodestar Anstalt v. Route 66 Junkyard Brewery LLC*, No. CV 17-0062 JCH/WPL, 2017 U.S. Dist. LEXIS 115625, at *5–6, (D.N.M. July 25, 2017) ("It is well-established that a party may not request, under [Federal] Rule 36, that the court determine pretrial the accuracy of a denial of a request for admission, and that [Federal] Rule 37(c)(2) provides, in a post-judgment motion for sanctions, the sole avenue to assess the substantive accuracy of a denial of a request for admission."); *Brown v. Mohr*, No. 2:13-cv-0006, 2017 U.S. Dist. LEXIS 102082, at *7–8, 2017 WL 2832631 (S.D. Ohio June 30, 2017) (same); *Fatihah v. Neal*, No. CIV-16-058-JHP, 2017 U.S. Dist. LEXIS 91452, at *5–6, 2017 WL 2559992 (E.D. Okla. May 22, 2017) (same); *In re Hodge*, No. 12-02-00314-CV, 2002 Tex. App. LEXIS 8776, at *11, 2002 WL 31769635 (Tex. App.—Tyler Dec. 11, 2002, orig. proceeding) (not designated for publication) ("[Plaintiffs] cite no case law, and we are not aware of any, supporting their contention that, as here, a party may file a motion to deem admissions requesting that a trial court determine whether such a denial has merit. Therefore, we conclude that such action by the trial court is not permitted by the rules of procedure or the interpretative case law."). See also cases cited in notes 76, 257.

259 See cases cited in notes 76, 257–58.

260 See Chapter 10, section 10-9 (discussing expenses for failure to admit under Texas Rule 215.4(b)).

261 *In re RLS Legal Sols., L.L.C.*, 156 S.W.3d 160, 165–66 (Tex. App.—Beaumont 2005, orig. proceeding) ("The party who has requested admissions may move to determine the sufficiency of an answer or objection."), ***mand. conditionally granted on other grounds***, 221 S.W.3d 629 (Tex. 2007) (per curiam); *State v. Carillo*, 885 S.W.2d 212, 216 (Tex. App.—San Antonio 1994, no writ) (same); *Taylor v. Taylor*, 747 S.W.2d 940, 945 (Tex. App.—Amarillo 1988, writ denied) (same).

262 See Chapter 5, section 5-5 (discussing hearings and rulings on objections and privilege assertions).

assertion's propriety.[263] Unless the trial court finds that the objection or privilege assertion was justified, it must order the responding party to answer the request for admission.[264] In contrast, on finding that an answer was insufficient because it was evasive, incomplete, or otherwise did not comply with Texas Rule 198's requirements, the trial court can either deem the request admitted or order that an answer be served.[265] The first time a response to a request for admission is found to be insufficient, a court generally should order the responding party to serve a supplemental answer to the request, rather than deeming it admitted.[266] Nevertheless, a trial court may deem the

---

[263] See Chapter 5, section 5-5 (discussing hearings and rulings on objections and privilege assertions).

[264] Tex. R. Civ. P. 215.4(a) ("Unless the court determines that an objection is justified, it shall order that an answer be served."); *see Bell v. Nichols*, No. 10-13-00151-CV, 2014 Tex. App. LEXIS 4523, at *9, 2014 WL 1681985 (Tex. App.—Waco Apr. 24, 2014, no pet.) (mem. op.) ("As Bell argues, [Texas] Rule 215 does not authorize a trial court to deem a matter admitted because of an improper objection; in that situation, the trial court is to 'order that an answer be served.'"). If a privilege assertion is overruled, the responding party, in its new response to the request, can interpose appropriate objections to the request if they were not interposed initially.

[265] Tex. R. Civ. P. 215.4(a) ("If the court determines that an answer does not comply with the requirements of [Texas] Rule 198, it may order either that the matter is admitted or that an amended answer be served."); *see Guerrero-McDonald v. Nassour*, 516 S.W.3d 198, 214 (Tex. App.—Eastland 2017, no pet.) ("[W]e conclude that the trial court did not abuse its direction in deeming the request for admission to be admitted because of Guerrero–McDonald's evasive and incomplete answer."); *In re RLS Legal Sols., L.L.C.*, 156 S.W.3d 160, 165–66 (Tex. App.—Beaumont 2005, orig. proceeding) (holding that a trial court can deem requests for admission admitted in ruling on a motion to test the sufficiency of answers), *mand. conditionally granted on other grounds*, 221 S.W.3d 629 (Tex. 2007) (per curiam); *In re Hodge*, No. 12-02-0031402000314-CV, 2002 Tex. App. LEXIS 8776, at *8, 2002 WL 31769635 (Tex. App.—Tyler Dec. 11, 2002, orig. proceeding) (not designated for publication) ("If the court determines that the answer does not comply with the requirements of [Texas] Rule 198, it may order either that the matter is admitted or that an amended answer be served."); *State v. Carillo*, 885 S.W.2d 212, 216 (Tex. App.—San Antonio 1994, no writ) ("Pursuant to [Texas] Rule 215(4), an evasive or incomplete answer may be treated by the trial court as a deemed admission. The party propounding the request may challenge the sufficiency of the answers, and if the court finds the answer insufficient under [former Texas] Rule 169, the court may deem the matter admitted.") (citation omitted); *Taylor v. Taylor*, 747 S.W.2d 940, 945 (Tex. App.—Amarillo 1988, writ denied) (holding that, once the trial court found that the answers did not comply with former Texas Rule 169, "the court was authorized, if not required, by the rules to deem the matters admitted").

[266] *Cf. Asea, Inc. v. S. Pac. Transp. Co.*, 669 F.2d 1242, 1247 (9th Cir. 1981) ("Although the [trial] court should ordinarily first order an amended answer, and deem the matter admitted only if a sufficient answer is not timely filed, this determination, like most involved in the oversight of discovery, is left to the sound discretion of the [trial] judge. The general power of the [trial] court to control the discovery process allows for the severe sanction of ordering a matter admitted when it has been demonstrated that a party has intentionally disregarded the obligations imposed by [Federal] Rule 36(a).") (citation omitted); *CX Reinsurance Co. v. Johnson*, No. RWT-15-3132, 2018 U.S. Dist. LEXIS 11209, at *7, 2018 WL 10075929 (D. Md. Jan. 24, 2018) ("Ordinarily, a district court should first order an amended answer, and deem the matter admitted only if a sufficient answer is not timely filed." (quoting *Louis v. Martinez*, No. 5:08-CV-151, 2011 U.S. Dist. LEXIS 51744, at *6, 2011 WL 1832808 (N.D.W. Va. May 13, 2011))); *Iron Workers Local No. 60 Annuity Pension Fund v. Solvay Iron Works, Inc.*, No. 5:15-CV-0054 (BKS/DEP), 2017 U.S. Dist. LEXIS 61394, at *15, 2017 WL 1458772

request admitted if it finds the responding party was acting in bad faith or where the evidence clearly indicates that the request should have been admitted.[267] Moreover, it clearly is appropriate to deem a request for admission admitted if the responding party fails to properly respond after being ordered to do so.[268]

The losing party in connection with a motion to test the sufficiency of an answer, objection, or privilege assertion to a request for admission can be required to pay

---

(N.D.N.Y. Apr. 24, 2017) ("[I]t is clear that certain of the responses of the Maestri defendants to plaintiffs' RFAs are improper. There are several potential consequences associated with this finding. First, the matters may be deemed admitted. Such a result, however, is generally disfavored other than as a last resort in light of its obvious severity. The court could also direct that an amended answer be served after defendants have made a reasonable inquiry.") (citations omitted); *Essex Builders Grp., Inc. v. Amerisure Ins. Co.*, 230 F.R.D. 682, 687–88 (M.D. Fla. 2005) ("The sanction of deeming a response an admission, however, is a severe one. Rather, the courts generally order an amended answer or order the responding party to make a reasonable inquiry."); *JZ Buckingham Invs., LLC v. U.S.*, 77 Fed. Cl. 37, 45 (Fed. Cl. 2007) (discussing cases and noting that, "[m]ore typically, when the responding party's answer to requests for admission is deemed to be noncompliant with [Federal] Rule 36, federal courts order the responding party to serve a supplemental answer."); *see Shadburne v. Bullitt Cty.*, No. 3:17CV-00130-DJH, 2017 U.S. Dist. LEXIS 205450, at *23–24, 2017 WL 6391483 (W.D. Ky. Dec. 14, 2017) ("Because Defendants here neither admitted nor denied the request and instead relied on the unacceptable 'speaks for itself' objection, the Court finds the appropriate remedy is to have Defendants amend their answer to Request for Admission No. 3.").

Given Texas courts' antipathy to merits-preclusive requests for admission, see Chapter 10, section 10-6:4, a motion to test the sufficiency of such a request is certain to fail.

267 *Cf. Asea, Inc. v. S. Pac. Transp. Co.*, 669 F.2d 1242, 1247 (9th Cir. 1981) (concluding that the trial court could properly deem requests admitted if the evidence revealed that the responding party had knowledge sufficient to admit them and had failed to make reasonable inquiry, but remanding for a factual determination on these issues); *CX Reinsurance Co. Ltd. v. Johnson*, No. RWT-15-3132, 2018 U.S. Dist. LEXIS 11209, at *7, 2018 WL 10075929 (D. Md. Jan. 24, 2018) ["(I)t is often appropriate to order the matter admitted where a party responds to a [Federal] Rule 36 request in bad faith or does so evasively." (quoting *Ball-Rice v. Bd. of Educ.*, No. PJM-11-1398, 2013 U.S. Dist. LEXIS 73719, at *4–5, 2013 WL 2299725 (D. Md. May 24, 2013))); *JZ Buckingham Invs., LLC v. U.S.*, 77 Fed. Cl. 37, 45 (Fed. ClCl. 2007) ("Nevertheless, where a federal court finds a lack of good faith on the part of the responding party, it may deem the matter admitted. Typically, courts have ordered matters admitted either when the evidence shows that it should have been admitted or when the court finds the responding party's conduct in answering the requests for admission to be reprehensible.") (citations omitted); *Uniden Am. Corp. v. Ericsson Inc.*, 181 F.R.D. 302, 304–05 (M.D.N.C. 1998) (deeming request admitted when deposition testimony confirmed the document's authenticity); *Caruso v. Coleman Co.*, No. 93-CV-6733, 1995 U.S. Dist. LEXIS 7934, at *8, 1995 WL 347003 (E.D. Pa. June 7, 1995) (deeming matter admitted when qualified answer implied that admission was appropriate).

268 *Cf. Guerrero-McDonald v. Nassour*, 516 S.W.3d 198, 214 (Tex. App.—Eastland 2017, no pet.) (holding that trial court did not abuse its discretion in deeming requests for admission admitted because the responding party "did not amend her response when these objections were overruled"); *cf. A. Farber & Partners, Inc. v. Garber*, 237 F.R.D. 250, 256–58 (C.D. Cal. 2006) (deeming requests admitted when the responding party gave evasive answers after the court had sanctioned it for failing to make a reasonable inquiry); *Cochrane v. IRS*, 107 T.C. 18, 26 (T.C. 1996) (deeming requests admitted when responses were evasive, incomplete and not in good faith despite prior court order).

the other party's expenses, including reasonable attorneys' fees under Texas Rule 215.1(d).[269]

10-9 Expenses for Failure to Admit: The "Admit-or-Pay" Rule

A requesting party may invoke the "admit-or-pay" rule of Texas Rule 215.4(b) for an unjustified refusal to admit a request for admission. That is, a responding party who fails to admit a matter or the genuineness or authenticity of a document can be ordered to pay the requesting party's reasonable expenses, including attorneys' fees, incurred in proving the matter or document's authenticity. Texas Rule 215.4(b) provides, in full:

> If a party fails to admit the genuineness of any document or the truth of any matter as requested under [Texas] Rule 198 and if the party requesting the admissions thereafter proves the genuineness of the document or the truth of the matter, he may apply to the court for an order requiring the other party to pay him the reasonable expenses incurred in making that proof, including reasonable attorney fees. The court shall make the order unless it finds that (1) the request was held objectionable pursuant to [Texas] Rule 193, or (2) the admission sought was of no substantial importance, or (3) the party failing to admit had a reasonable ground to believe that he might prevail on the matter, or (4) there was other good reason for the failure to admit.[270]

The obvious purpose of the "admit-or-pay" rule is to increase the parties' incentive to respond properly and in good faith to appropriate requests for admission because they can eliminate unnecessary proof at trial, streamline discovery and motion practice, and reduce pretrial expenses.[271] Texas Rule 215.4(b), however, does not apply if

---

[269] Tex. R. Civ. P. 215.4(a) ("The provisions of [Texas] Rule 215.1(d) apply to the award of expenses incurred in relation to the motion.").

[270] Tex. R. Civ. P. 215.4(b). Texas Rule 215.4 does not "establish an independent cause of action for damages; rather, [it] provide[s] a basis for a trial court to impose sanctions or attorney's fees upon motion or the court's own initiative." *Skyline Commer., Inc. v. ISC Acquisition Corp.*, No. 05-17-00028-CV, 2018 Tex. App. LEXIS 6764, at *25, 2018 WL 4039863 (Tex. App.—Dallas Aug. 23, 2018, pet. denied).

There are very few Texas cases applying Texas Rule 215.4(b). The Rule, however, is virtually identical to Federal Rule 37(c)(2), which provides:

> If a party fails to admit what is requested under [Federal] Rule 36 and if the requesting party later proves a document to be genuine or the matter true, the requesting party may move that the party who failed to admit pay the reasonable expenses, including attorney's fees, incurred in making that proof. The court must so order unless:
>
> (A) the request was held objectionable under [Federal] Rule 36(a);
>
> (B) the admission sought was of no substantial importance;
>
> (C) the party failing to admit had a reasonable ground to believe that it might prevail on the matter; or
>
> (D) there was other good reason for the failure to admit.

Fed. R. Civ. P. 37(c)(2).

[271] *See Marchand v. Mercy Med. Ctr.*, 22 F.3d 933, 936 (9th Cir. 1994) ("Enforcement encourages attorneys and parties to identify undisputed issues early to avoid unnecessary costs. Failure to identify those issues wastes the resources of parties and courts."). For example,

the responding party fails to respond to a request for admission because such a failure results in the ***automatic sanction*** of the request being deemed admitted.[272]

The Texas Supreme Court has made clear that [Texas] Rule 215.4 generally does not apply to merits-preclusive requests for admission. As explained by the Court in *Medina v. Zuniga*, a case in which a trial court awarded expenses under the Rule when the defendant, after denying merits-preclusive requests for admissions in a negligence case arising out of an automobile accident, conceded liability for ordinary negligence at trial while contesting liability for gross negligence:[273]

> The same due-process concerns that arise in the deemed-admission context also come up when a trial court sanctions a party under Rule 215.4 for denying merits-preclusive requests for admissions. The sanction here—requiring Medina to pay Zuniga's reasonable expenses and attorney's fees—is admittedly lighter than a merits-preclusive deemed admission. Medina was, after all, allowed to defend the lawsuit as he wanted, including his concession of ordinary negligence at trial. But he should have been able to do so without the prospect of Rule 215.4 sanctions waiting in the wings.
>
> It is axiomatic that the plaintiff bears the burden to prove the defendant's negligence. It cannot follow that the defendant who puts the plaintiff to her burden should later face sanctions for not admitting what he was entitled to deny. Our rules do not, strictly speaking, prohibit merits-preclusive requests for admissions. But due process nevertheless limits the extent to which sanctions can attach to denials of those requests. Simply put, merits-preclusive requests for admissions that carry the threat of sanctions risk putting the responding party to an impossible choice: give up your case now or face sanctions later. Worse, the responding party typically will be put to this election long before any significant discovery has occurred, leaving him unable to make an informed decision on whether to concede or contest liability.
>
> That is not how our system works. Just as a defendant may answer the claims against him with a general denial, he may also deny a merits-preclusive request for admission for which the other party bears the burden of proof. The very nature of the request provides the respondent "good reason" for failing to admit. Likewise, absent present knowledge that he will later concede he acted negligently, a defendant acting in good faith when responding to requests for admissions may maintain that his conduct was consistent with the ordinary standard of care. This is especially true at the outset of discovery. In this case, Medina decided at trial to concede negligence he had thus far denied. He was entitled to base this decision on how various aspects of the case had turned out—discovery,

---

federal courts award expenses under Federal Rule 37(c)(2) when a party's denials were made without a reasonable inquiry into the requests' truth. *E.g.*, *Sun River Energy, Inc. v. Nelson*, 800 F.3d 1219, 1224–25 (3d Cir. 2015); *Yoder & Frey Auctioneers, Inc. v. EquipmentFacts, LLC*, 774 F.3d 1065, 1076 (6th Cir. 2014); *BNSF Ry. v. Gilster-Mary Lee Corp.*, No. 15-cv-250-JPG-SCW, 2017 U.S. Dist. LEXIS 28988, at *2–5 (S.D. Ill. Mar. 1, 2017); *Block v. Meharry Med. Coll.*, No. 3:15-cv-0204, 2016 U.S. Dist. LEXIS 141728, *6–7 (M.D. Tenn. Sept. 30, 2016).

[272] Tex. R. Civ. P. 198.2(c).

[273] *Medina v. Zuniga*, 593 S.W.3d 238, 241, 243 (Tex. 2019).

pre-trial rulings, jury selection, etc. And he was entitled to do so without fear he would be unduly punished for defending himself at the case's outset.[274]

Expenses under Texas Rule 215.4(b) may be awarded only if the requesting party proves the genuineness of the document or the truth of the matter asked about in the request for admission.[275] Because the Rule uses the word "shall," an expense award is mandatory unless the court finds one of the Rule's four exceptions apply.[276]

---

[274] *Medina v. Zuniga*, 593 S.W.3d 238, 245–46 (Tex. 2019) (citations omitted). In *Peralta v. Durkham*, 133 S.W.3d 339, 341–42 (Tex. App.—Dallas 2004, no pet.), the Dallas Court of Appeals affirmed an award of expenses under Texas Rule 215.4 when the defendant, after denying merits-preclusive requests for admission, admitted liability shortly before trial. Its holding is inconsistent with *Medina* and has been overruled by implication.

[275] Tex. R. Civ. P. 215.4(b) ("If a party fails to admit the genuineness of any document or the truth of any matter as requested under [Texas] Rule 198 *and if the party requesting the admissions thereafter proves the genuineness of a document or the truth of the matter*, he may apply to the court for an order requiring the other party to pay him the reasonable expenses incurred in making that proof, including reasonable attorney fees.") (emphasis added); *cf. AKH Co. v. Universal Underwriters Ins. Co.*, No. 13-2003-JAR-KGG, 2017 U.S. Dist. LEXIS 187801, at *21, 2017 WL 5465240 (D. Kan. Nov. 14, 2017) ("Pursuant to Fed-.R.Civ.P. 37(c)(2), when a party fails to properly admit a [Federal] Rule 36 RFA and the requesting party later proves the matter to be true, the Court must order the failing party to pay reasonable expenses, including attorney's fees, incurred in making that proof unless there was good reason for the failure to admit."); *Reynolds v. Univ. of Pa.*, No. 06-1237, 2010 U.S. Dist. LEXIS 113206, at *6 (E.D. Pa. Oct. 25, 2010) ("To qualify for [Federal] Rule 37(c)(2) costs and fees, the requesting party must later prove the matter true."); *Joseph v. Fratar*, 197 F.R.D. 20, 22 (D. Mass. 2000) (same); *Bd. of Dirs., Water's Edge v. Anden Grp.*, 136 F.R.D. 100, 105 (E.D. Va. 1991) ("As previously noted, [Federal] Rule 37(c) applies only when the requesting party 'proves the. . . . truth of the matter.'" (quoting Fed. R. Civ. P. 37(c))); *see Marchand v. Mercy Med. Ctr.*, 22 F.3d 933, 937–38 (9th Cir. 1994) (holding that the defendant was not liable for expenses for failing to admit that he removed a device from the plaintiff's spine because he was only asked to admit that the device had been removed); *Apex Oil Co. v. Belcher Co.*, 855 F.2d 1009, 1017 (2d Cir. 1988) ("We do not believe that sanctions can be imposed on a party or an attorney solely on the basis of composite paraphrasing of several requests for admission.").

[276] Tex. R. Civ. P. 215.4(b); *accord In re Commitment of Williams*, 539 S.W.3d 429, 444 n.3 (Tex. App.—Houston [1st Dist.] 2017, no pet.) ("The trial court shall make the order unless it finds (1) the request was held objectionable under Rule 193, (2) the admission sought was of no substantial importance, (3) the responding party had a reasonable ground to believe he might prevail on the matter, or (4) there was other good reason for the failure to admit."); *Peralta v. Durkham*, 133 S.W.3d 339, 341 (Tex. App.—Dallas 2004, no pet.) (holding that an expense award "must" be made unless one of the exceptions applies); *cf. McCarthy v. Ameritech Publ'g, Inc.*, 763 F.3d 488, 492 (6th Cir. 2014) ("When a litigant expends resources to prove a fact that an opposing party refused to admit, [Federal] Rule 37(c)(2) directs (and does not just permit) the court to award monetary sanctions equal to 'the reasonable expenses, including attorney's fees, incurred in making that proof.'"); *U.S. v. Pecore*, 664 F.3d 1125, 1136 (7th Cir. 2011) ("Federal Rule of Civil Procedure 37(c)(2) provides that a district court must impose reasonable expenses including attorney's fees on a party that fails to properly admit the genuineness of a document pursuant to a [Federal] Rule 36 request for admission."); *Hicklin Eng'g, L.C. v. Bartell*, 439 F.3d 346, 351 (7th Cir. 2006) ("[Federal] Rule 37(c) directs (and does not just permit) a district court to award attorneys' fees and other costs to the party put to such proof by refusal to admit."), *aff'd*,

The first exception—the request was held objectionable under Texas Rule 193—is self-evident. No adverse consequences can stem from an objection or privilege assertion to a request for admission that was either sustained by the trial court or not challenged by the requesting party.[277] The responding party, however, cannot defend against an award of expenses on the basis that had it objected, the objection would have been sustained.[278]

The second exception—the admission sought was of no substantial importance—also is self-evident. A matter is of "substantial importance" when it is material to the action's resolution.[279] Of course, this determination depends upon the action's facts. For example, if the requesting party was required by the controlling law to prove the matter to prevail on its claim or defense, the request relates to a matter of substantial importance.[280] Conversely, if the matter was not essential to the

---

439 F.3d 346 (7th Cir. 2006); *Marchand v. Mercy Med. Ctr.*, 22 F.3d 933, 936 (9th Cir. 1994) (same).

[277] Although federal courts applying Federal Rule 37(c)(2) are split on the issue, *see Russo v. Baxter Healthcare Corp.*, 51 F. Supp. 2d 70, 78 (D.R.I. 1997) (discussing cases), Texas law is clear that a requesting party's failure to challenge an objection or privilege assertion waives its right to the discovery. See Chapter 5, section 5-5 (discussing hearings and rulings on objections and privilege assertions). Accordingly, a party who fails to challenge an objection or privilege assertion to a request for admission cannot later seek expenses under Texas Rule 215.4(b) because the responding party failed to admit the request.

[278] *Cf. U.S. v. Smith*, 303 F.R.D. 630, 638–39 (S.D. Ala. 2014) ("While there is no question but that Smith admitted Request for Admission 18 in part, as reflected above, it is equally clear that Smith denied the request for admission in part as well; therefore, his partial admission argument cannot save him from the government's [Federal] Rule 37(c)(2) motion. Moreover, Smith did not *object* to this request for admission; instead, he merely qualified his admission and, therefore, exception (A) [to Federal Rule 37(c)(2)] is inapplicable.").

[279] *Cf. McCarthy v. Ameritech Publ'g, Inc.*, 763 F.3d 488, 492 (6th Cir. 2014) ("A fact is of substantial importance when it is 'material to the disposition of the case,' meaning that it tends to prove or disprove one of the disputed elements of the claim. The importance of the disputed fact is assessed at the time the request for admission is made, not at the end of the case. An otherwise important fact does not become unimportant simply because the requesting party subsequently loses the claim on some other basis." (citations omitted) (quoting *SEC v. Happ*, 392 F.3d 12, 34 (1st Cir. 2004))); *Berry v. Office of the Fayette Cty. Sheriff*, No. 5: 14-356-DCR, 2015 U.S. Dist. LEXIS 82352, at *5, 2015 WL 3916126 (E.D. Ky. June 25, 2015) (same); *Reynolds v. Univ. of Pa.*, No. 06-1237, 2010 U.S. Dist. LEXIS 113206, at *6 (E.D. Pa. Oct. 25, 2010) (same).

[280] *Cf. Leonard v. Stemtech Int'l, Inc.*, 834 F.3d 376, 402 (3d Cir. 2016) ("Leonard sought the admission of facts concerning Stemtech's control over its distributors' websites, which was a crucial component of Leonard's vicarious and contributory infringement claims. Because this issue was central to Leonard's secondary infringement claims, Stemtech had no factual basis for denying the request, and Leonard incurred expenses to prove these facts during Tashjian's deposition, the District Court did not abuse its discretion in awarding sanctions to Leonard."); *McCarthy v. Ameritech Publ'g, Inc.*, 763 F.3d 488, 492 (6th Cir. 2014) ("API contends that McCarthy's August 2008 eligibility for post-retirement healthcare benefits was of no substantial importance to the causes of action alleged in her original complaint. That argument plainly lacks merit. If McCarthy was eligible for post-retirement healthcare benefits in August 2008, API's representations to the contrary were false and misleading. Those misleading representations allegedly led McCarthy to forgo retirement in August 2008 and instead opt into the Employment Opportunity Pool—a decision, it turns out, that led her to work for nine months with no added benefit. The representations therefore go to the

requesting party's success, it was not of substantial importance.[281] A matter concerning a party's or a key witness's credibility is one of substantial importance.[282]

---

heart of her unjust-enrichment claim, which alleged that 'AT&T has been unjustly enriched as a result of its improper and unlawful conduct in the approximate amount of $31,547.49, which constitutes the value of McCarthy's services for the 1,443 hours she worked from August 15, 2008 until May 7, 2009.'"); *Longoria v. Cty. of Dall.*, No. 3:14-cv-3111-L, 2016 U.S. Dist. LEXIS 161675, at *19–20, 2016 WL 6893625 (N.D. Tex. Nov. 22, 2016) (holding, in a civil rights action alleging that the plaintiff was assaulted by a guard while incarnated in the county jail, that a request for admission that the plaintiff had a sexual encounter with the guard was of substantial importance).

281 *Cf. Wash. State Dep't of Transp. v. Nat. Gas Co.*, 59 F.3d 793, 806 (8th Cir. 1995) (holding that a request that the plaintiff admit that pollutants posed an immediate risk was of no substantial importance because the plaintiff was not required to make such a showing); *Haiping Su v. NASA*, No. 5:09-cv-02838-EJD, 2016 U.S. Dist. LEXIS 122604, at *12–14, 2016 WL 4719274 (N.D. Cal. Sept. 9, 2016) ("In two of the identified requests, Plaintiff's Requests for Admissions [sic] Nos. 16 and 17, Plaintiff asked the United States to admit that a statement asserting that Plaintiff had taken money from a foreign government or characterizing him as a security risk 'contains personal information of an extremely private nature.' Subject to a number of objections, . . . the United States denied both requests. After trial, the Court found that Dolci had made both of these statements and that they constituted serious invasions of Plaintiff's privacy rights. Plaintiff contends that the United States' failure to admit these legal conclusions subjects the United States to sanctions. . . . [W]hether the information was of an extremely private nature was 'of no substantial importance' to the case . . . [because i]n deciding Plaintiff's privacy claims, the Court considered whether he had a legally protectable interest in the investigatory determination that he was a security risk. However, whether the information disclosed was of an extremely private nature did not figure into the Court's analysis. The Court therefore finds that these requested admissions were immaterial to the disposition of the case, and that the failure to admit them does not merit a sanction."); *Vantage Trailers, Inc. v. Beall Corp.*, No. H-06-3008, 2008 U.S. Dist. LEXIS 68402, at *6, 2008 WL 4093691 (S.D. Tex. Aug. 28, 2008) ("[O]ther [requests], though false, are not directly relevant to the controlling issue and, hence, are not sanctionable under [Federal] Rule 37(c)(2)."); *Howard Opera House Assocs. v. Urban Outfitters, Inc.*, No. 2:99-CV-140, 2002 U.S. Dist. LEXIS 26258, at *12 n.4 (D. Vt. Apr. 17, 2002) ("The fact that the requests to admit . . . did not involve matters that were the bases for summary judgment also means that these requests to admit were not of substantial importance. . . ."); *Read-Rite Corp. v. Burlington Air Express, Ltd.*, 183 F.R.D. 545, 547 (N.D. Cal. 1998) ("Since these requests [for admission] were based on the 'entire shipment' theory of liability and Judge Wilken found that that theory did not apply, these requested admissions were not substantially important to the litigation."), *aff'd*, 186 F.3d 1190 (9th Cir. 1999); *see Mane v. Tri-City Healthcare Dist.*, No. 05cv397-WQH (CAB), 2007 U.S. Dist. LEXIS 102633, at *9–11 (S.D. Cal. Mar. 21, 2007) (holding that wrongful admission denials were of no substantial import because the requests were denied after one of the plaintiffs was deposed and summary judgment was granted in defendant's favor based on that plaintiff's deposition testimony. Accordingly, "had Plaintiffs admitted request Nos. 12 and 15 when they were served [after the deposition], the [defendant] would have gained nothing that it did not already have.").

282 *See SEC v. Happ*, 392 F.3d 12, 34–35 (1st Cir. 2004) (holding that the requested matter was of substantial importance because it would allow the defendant to challenge the SEC's key witness's credibility); *Reynolds v. Univ. of Pa.*, No. 06-1237, 2010 U.S. Dist. LEXIS 113206, at *6 (E.D. Pa. Oct. 25, 2010) (ruling that a requested matter was of substantial importance because an admission would have "negatively impacted [the plaintiff's] credibility").

The third exception—the responding party had a reasonable ground to believe it might prevail on the matter—is the one most commonly invoked. The test is not whether the responding party prevailed, but whether it had a reasonable belief that it might prevail.[283] This exception preserves both the party's right to its day in court and the "American rule" that each party bears its own attorneys' fees.

As the word "reasonably" suggests, the test is objective, and a court should reject a responding party's attempt to invoke the exception if there was too little evidence to permit a rational fact finder to resolve the matter in the responding party's favor. The exception has been invoked successfully in actions involving substantially conflicting evidence,[284] complicated legal or factual issues,[285] and cases in which the parties' *credible* experts

[283] *Cf. U.S. v. Pecore*, 664 F.3d 1125, 1137 (7th Cir. 2011); *Marchand v. Mercy Med. Ctr.*, 22 F.2d 933, 937–38 (9th Cir. 1994); *Wash. State Dep't of Transp. v. Natural Gas Co.*, 59 F.3d 793, 806 (8th Cir. 1995).

[284] *E.g., Shipley v. Holt Tex., Ltd.*, No. 2-09-122-CV, 2010 Tex. App. LEXIS 3773, at *24–25, 2010 WL 1999016 (Tex. App.—Fort Worth May 20, 2010, no pet.) (mem. op.) (affirming the denial of expenses because "[t]he jury could have believed that Sam jumped from the cab of his 930G Caterpillar or from its top ladder step and that, therefore, no other design 'would have prevented or significantly reduced the risk of the injury in question.' Accordingly, Appellees possessed a reasonable ground to believe that they might prevail on the issue of whether a safer alternative design existed in these circumstances, and in fact, they may have prevailed on that issue since the jury answered 'no' to Question One."); *Duggan v. Northpark Cent. Vefii, L.P.*, No. 05-98-00099-CV, 2001 Tex. App. LEXIS 5909, at *12, 2001 WL 985144 (Tex. App.—Dallas Aug. 29, 2001, no pet.) (not designated for publication) (affirming the denial of expenses "[b]ecause the trial judge could have concluded Duggan had a reasonable ground to believe that he might prevail on the matter"); *cf. ARB Inc. v. E-Sys., Inc.*, 663 F.2d 189, 200 (D.C. Cir. 1980) (holding that the losing party's failure to admit certain matters in a contract dispute "fell squarely" in the reasonable ground exception); *Ohio Cas. Ins. Co. v. Twin City Fire Ins. Co.*, No. 14-CV-858 (NGG) (PK), 2020 U.S. Dist. LEXIS 50962, at *9–11, 2020 WL 3656394 (E.D.N.Y. Mar. 23, 2020) (holding that a responding party need not accept "the uncontradicted deposition testimony or declarations of hostile or interested witnesses as true" and need not admit a request where it has contradictory evidence); *Haiping Su v. NASA*, No. 5:09-cv-02838-EJD, 2016 U.S. Dist. LEXIS 122604, at *12, 2016 WL 4719274 (N.D. Cal. Sept. 9, 2016) ("The Court finds that the United States 'had a reasonable ground to believe that it might prevail on the matter.' Throughout this case, Dolci denied that he had told anyone other than Plaintiff's supervisors that Plaintiff was a security risk or that Plaintiff had trouble answering a question in a polygraph examination. In the end, the Court concluded otherwise after hearing contradictory testimony from a number of other witnesses. However, '[t]he issue is not whether [the party failing to admit] prevailed at trial 'but whether [it] acted reasonably in believing that it might prevail.' In light of Dolci's consistent testimony, the United States acted reasonably in considering the facts disputed and in refusing to admit them." (citations omitted) (quoting Fed. R. Civ. P. 37(c)(2)(C) and *Wash. State Dep't of Transp. v. Wash. Nat. Gas Co.* 59 F.3d 793, 806 (9th Cir. 2005))); *Escriba v. Foster Poultry Farms*, No. 1:09-CV-1878 OWW MJS, 2011 U.S. Dist. LEXIS 112883, at *6, 2011 WL 4591096 (E.D. Cal. Sept. 30, 2011) (holding that the reasonable-ground exception applied because the discrimination "case boiled down to a 'he said, she said' credibility issue").

[285] *Compare, e.g., Wash. State Dep't of Transp. v. Wash. Nat. Gas Co.*, 59 F.3d 793, 806 (8th Cir. 1995) (affirming a denial of expenses in action involving environmental matters subject to complex regulations), *Ohio Cas. Ins. Co. v. Twin City Fire Ins. Co.*, No. 14-CV-858 (NGG) (PK), 2020 U.S. Dist. LEXIS 50962, at *6, 12–13, 2020 WL 3656394 (E.D.N.Y. Mar. 23, 2020) (explaining that "[a] party has 'reasonable ground' under [Federal] Rule 37(c)(2)(C) to

disagreed.[286] It also applies when summary judgment or a directed verdict on the

believe it might prevail at trial where the admission requested involves a difficult factual question . . . " and concluding that whether an insurance company had "actual opportunity to settle" a claim "is a complex issue of fact and law"), *Bd. of Dirs., Water's Edge v. Anden Grp.*, 136 F.R.D. 100, 107 (E.D. Va. 1991) ("[T]he admission sought here, namely that the FRT plywood used at Water's Edge was defectively manufactured and that such defect had caused the failure of the roofs at Water's Edge, involved numerous complex technical facts and legal conclusions."), *Baird v. Consol. City of Indianapolis*, 830 F. Supp. 1183, 1189–90 (S.D. Ind. 1993) (denying expenses when the requests involved sophisticated statistical analyses regarding information not readily available), *Dyer v. U.S.*, 633 F. Supp. 750, 753 (D. Or. 1985) ("[T]he issue of the time it takes for wake turbulence from a helicopter to dissipate is a difficult factual question. The Court finds that the government had reasonable ground to believe that it might prevail on the matter."), *aff'd on other grounds*, 832 F.2d 1062 (9th Cir. 1987), *and U.S. v. Article of Drug*, 428 F. Supp. 278, 281 (E.D. Tenn. 1976) (finding the reasonable-ground exception applied because the issue of "whether such articles of drug were 'new animal drugs' involved complex issues of both fact and law"), *with, e.g., Foster Poultry Farms, Inc. v. SunTrust Bank*, 377 F. App'x 665, 672 (9th Cir. 2010) (affirming an award of expenses because the defendant conceded a key issue at trial and as such it could not have reasonably believed that it would prevail at trial), *Marchand v. Mercy Med. Ctr.*, 22 F.R.D. 933, 937 (9th Cir. 1994) (affirming expense award because the responding party's subsequent admission at trial directly contradicted his earlier admission denial), *Chem. Eng'g Corp. v. Essef Indus., Inc.*, 795 F.2d 1565, 1575 (Fed. Cir. 1986) (holding the reasonable ground exception inapplicable because the responding party was in possession of "test results" and other pertinent information that required it to admit the request), *Reynolds v. Univ. of Pa.*, No. 06-1237, 2010 U.S. Dist. LEXIS 113206, at *9–10 (E.D. Pa. Oct. 25, 2010) ("Penn requested that Reynolds admit the truth of six straightforward and readily ascertainable facts. Penn supplemented its request with a press release from Adobe announcing May 2003 as the release date for the 6.0 software. Penn did not submit complex requests pertaining to facts crucial to Reynolds's success and on which reasonable minds could disagree. Based on the type of facts requested and the supplemental documents provided by Penn, Reynolds could not have reasonably believed he could prove Adobe 6.0 was publicly released at any time other than May 2003."), *and Diamond State Ins. Co. v. Deardorff*, No. 1:10-cv-00004 A WI JLT, 2011 U.S. Dist. LEXIS 60834, at *13–14, 2011 WL 2414391 (E.D. Cal. Jun 8, 2011) (finding the reasonable-ground exception inapplicable because the defendant insurer failed to inquire of its insured and such inquiry would have established that the admission denial was wrong).

[286] *Howard Opera House Assocs. v. Urban Outfitters, Inc.*, No. 2:99-CV-140, 2002 U.S. Dist. LEXIS 26258, at *5 (D. Vt. Apr. 17, 2002) ("UO had reasonable grounds to believe that it might prevail on the nuisance claim at trial. . . . It also knew that in May 1999 the expert commissioned by Howard Opera House Associates . . . found, after requesting UO to play its music at the maximum level it desired, that the music did not alter background decibel levels in OCG's space. The report also noted that the distracting low frequency impulse noise produced by the music could be reduced through various methods. These methods included soundproofing that might be considered to be structural improvements and the responsibility of the landlord under the lease."); *Rebman v. Perry*, No. CV-04-5064-EFS, 2007 U.S. Dist. LEXIS 35054, at *4–5, 2007 WL 1430210 (E.D. Wash. May 14, 2007) ("In this case, the Defendants did in fact have reasonable ground to believe they might prevail. There was contradiction between the experts as to whether there was a tibial plateau fracture or a knee dislocation, and the consequence that may have had on the popliteal artery. The experts testifying for the defense testified there was no dislocation, which led them to believe there was no popliteal artery injury. The fact that this was different from the diagnosis of Plaintiffs' experts, and that the jury found Plaintiffs' experts to be persuasive, does not make Defendants' reliance on the testimony unreasonable."); *Mane v. Tri-City*

matter has been denied.[287] And, the Texas Supreme Court has made clear that a party has the right to deny merits-preclusive requests for admission without fear that sanctions under Texas Rule 215.4 will be imposed later.[288]

Healthcare Dist., No. 05cv397-WQH (CAB), 2007 U.S. Dist. LEXIS 102633, at *12 (S.D. Cal. Mar. 21, 2007) (holding that the losing plaintiff had a reasonable ground to believe that she might prevail, in part, on the basis of her expert's report); *Scheufler v. Gen. Host Corp.*, 915 F. Supp. 236, 239 (D. Kan. 1995) ("The requests dealing with whether salt pollution prevented the plaintiffs from irrigating appear simple at first look, but embrace a number of complicated technical issues, including the depth of the aquifer at a given location, the amount of water necessary for irrigation of crops, the level of pollution, the location of the irrigation well, the distance from which an irrigation well draws water, the concentration of salt which renders water unusable, and the movement and rate of recharge of the aquifer. Each of these matters was the subject of a great deal of conflicting expert testimony."), *aff'd*, 126 F.3d 1261 (10th Cir. 1997); *see Diamond State Ins. Co. v. Deardorff*, No. 1:10-cv-00004 A WI JLT, 2011 U.S. Dist. LEXIS 60834, at *16–18, *26–27, 2011 WL 2414391 (E.D. Cal. Jun 8, 2011) (applying the reasonable-ground exception because the admission denials were based on a police report).

The mere fact, however, that the responding party's admission denial was supported by expert testimony does not always mean that the requesting party satisfies the reasonable-ground exception. For example, in *Marchand v. Mercy Med. Ctr.*, 22 F.3d 933, 937 (9th Cir. 1994), the court held that, notwithstanding expert testimony supporting the defendant's admission denials, the trial court did not abuse its discretion in awarding sanctions under Federal Rule 37(c)(2) because the defendant "had ample evidence to discredit the expert testimony, as well as that of [the defendant] Farris. Critical to both were the trial statements of Farris that he removed the cervical collar supporting Marchand's neck due to respiratory distress, and that he cleared Marchand's cervical spine as being within normal limits based on the x-rays and consultation with radiologist Dr. Walker. Scant trial testimony or evidence corroborated either assertion." *Accord Foster Poultry Farms, Inc. v. SunTrust Bank*, 377 F. App'x 665, 672–73 (9th Cir. 2010) ("SunTrust had apparently relied on its lawyer to structure the monetization so as to make SunTrust a holder. However, such reliance at the time of the August 2002 transaction does not excuse SunTrust's independent duty as of the time of its January 2005 response to the RFA to try to determine the truth of the matter, and to establish whether its reliance on its former counsel's legal advice about its holder status was reasonable. There is no 'per se rule that reliance on an expert opinion provides a reasonable ground for a party to believe he would prevail at trial.' SunTrust could have determined, during the intervening years, that its former lawyer lacked a reasonable basis for his legal opinion, and that in fact, it was not the holder of the notes. It failed to do so, and Foster had to prove those facts at the September 2007 trial. [Federal] Rule 37(c)(2) requires the award of expenses incurred in developing that proof." (quoting *Marchand v. Mercy Med. Ctr.*, 22 F.2d 933, 937 (9th Cir. 1994))).

287 *E.g., Fabick, Inc. v. JFTCO, Inc.*, No. 16-cv-172-wmc, 2019 U.S. Dist. LEXIS 47828, at *28–29, 2019 WL 1320298 (W.D. Wis. 2019) (holding that the defendant had a reasonable belief that it might prevail because, among other reasons, the court previously denied plaintiffs' motions for summary judgment on the issue to which the denied requests for admission related); *Howard Opera House Assocs. v. Urban Outfitters, Inc.*, No. 2:99-CV-140, 2002 U.S. Dist. LEXIS 26258, at *5–7 (D. Vt. Apr. 17, 2002) (same); *Scheufler v. Scheufler v. Gen. Host Corp.*, 915 F. Supp. 236, 239 (D. Kan. 1995) (holding that the defendant had a reasonable belief that it might prevail because, among other reasons, "[t]he court denied plaintiffs' motions for summary judgment and directed verdict because there was sufficient evidence supporting the defendant's contentions to create a jury question.").

288 See discussion at notes 273–74.

The final exception—there was other good reason for the failure to admit—is undefined and left to the trial court's discretion. Perhaps the best example is when the responding party did not have, and could not have obtained through reasonable inquiry, sufficient information to admit the request for admission.[289] Such a party would not fall under the third exception because it would not know if it could prevail and thus could not have had a reasonable belief that it might prevail. Because such an "inability-to-admit-or-deny" response is expressly permitted by Texas Rule 198.2(b), it would be anomalous if a responding party were found liable for the requesting party's expenses if it so answered and the requesting party never challenged the answer's sufficiency.[290]

The good-reason exception also applies where the request was improper because it related to a pure question of law or otherwise is improper on its face.[291]

Although federal courts uniformly hold that a motion for expenses for failure to admit a request for admission is premature if it is made *before* the trial's completion or a summary judgment,[292] it is unclear whether this is the rule in Texas. The lack of

---

[289] *Cf. Ohio Cas. Ins. Co. v. Twin City Fire Ins. Co.*, No. 14-CV-858 (NGG) (PK), 2020 U.S. Dist. LEXIS 50962, at *20–21, 2020 WL 3656394 (E.D.N.Y. Mar. 23, 2020) (holding that expenses are not appropriate when the responding failed to admit requests for admission after "reasonable inquiry"); *Dove v. McOmber (In re Dove)*, No. 13-11778, A.P. No. 14-1155, 2016 Bankr. LEXIS 2856, at *2–3 (N.D. Cal. Aug. 5, 2016) ("[T]he duty of inquiry in answering a request for admission is 'limited to obtaining information from persons and entities over which the party has actual control.' The responding party is not required to admit the truth of facts which are exclusively within the knowledge of the requesting party. McOmber had no way of knowing if Dove's allegations of emotional distress were true, so he is not liable for Dove's expenses in proving them." (citations omitted) (quoting *U.S. ex rel. Englund v. L.A. Cty.*, 235 F.R.D. 675, 685 (E.D. Cal. 2006))); *Dallas v. Aetna Life Ins. Co.*, 100 F.R.D. 765, 767 (N.D. Ga. 1984) ("This [exception] applies to situations where the party does not have, or cannot get through reasonable inquiry the information on whether the matter contained in the request is true or not."); *see Nat. Gas Pipeline of Am. v. Pool*, 30 S.W.3d 639, 652 (Tex. App.—Amarillo 2000) (reversing an award of expenses against the defendants who failed to admit a request because of lack of information because "[w]e do not believe that the requests for admission imposed on [the defendants] the burden to incur cost by performing a title search outside of their own records to determine if the ownership percentages set forth in the requests for admission were currently accurate"), *rev'd on other grounds*, 120 S.W.3d 317 (Tex. 2002).

[290] *Cf. Martin v. Mabus*, 734 F. Supp. 1216, 1224 (S.D. Miss. 1990).

[291] *Cf. Sponer v. Wells Fargo Bank N.A.*, No. 3:17-cv-02035-HZ, 2020 U.S. Dist. LEXIS 75307, at *11–12 (D. Or. Apr. 28, 2020) (refusing to award expenses under Federal Rule 37(c) because the request was an improper one as it sought the admission of a legal conclusion); *Ohio Cas. Ins. Co. v. Twin City Fire Ins. Co.*, No. 14-CV-858 (NGG) (PK), 2020 U.S. Dist. LEXIS 50962, at *6, 2020 WL 3656394 (E.D.N.Y. Mar. 23, 2020) (same); *Phillips v. Gilman (In re Gilman)*, Nos. CC-18-1066-TaLS, CC-18-1100-TaLS, 2019 Bankr. LEXIS 2089, at *35–36 (B.A.P. 9th Cir. July 12, 2019) (same).

[292] *Cf. N.U. v. Wal-Mart Stores, Inc.*, No. 15-4885-KHV, 2017 U.S. Dist. LEXIS 53074, at *6, 2017 WL 1250804 (D. Kan. Apr. 5, 2017) ("The majority of courts addressing this issue have held that motions under [Federal] Rule 37(c)(2) must be made after the matter is proven at trial.") (footnote omitted); *Montes v. Pinnacle Propane, LLC*, No. 16-cv-0126 JCH/SMV, 2016 U.S. Dist. LEXIS 144369, at *7 (D.N.M. Oct. 18, 2016) (same); *Affiliated FM Ins. Co. v. LTK Consulting Servs., Inc.*, No. C06-1750JLR, 2012 U.S. Dist. LEXIS 60894, at *23, 2012 WL 1533887 (W.D. Wash. May 1, 2012) (same); *Point Blank Sols., Inc. v. Toyobo Am., Inc.*, No

clarity stems from the Texas Supreme Court's decision in *Meyer v. Cathey*.[293]

In that case, the plaintiff, during his pretrial deposition and in answers to requests for admission, maintained that a resume previously given to the defendant was accurate.[294] Thereafter, the defendant deposed several individuals whose testimony contradicted the resume's assertions.[295] At trial, the plaintiff admitted not only that his resume contained many inaccuracies, but also that he lied when questioned about them during his deposition. Several weeks after the trial court rendered its final judgment, the defendant moved for sanctions under Texas Rule 215.3, which provides for sanctions for discovery abuse, and Texas Rule 215.4(b).[296] The trial court granted the motion and awarded $25,978.73 as sanctions.[297]

On appeal, the Texas Supreme Court, without distinguishing between the two rules, held that the trial court abused its discretion in awarding the sanctions.

> Under our decision *Remington Arms Co. [v. Caldwell*, 850 S.W.2d 167, 170 (Tex. 1993) (per curiam),] waiver bars a trial court from awarding post trial sanctions based on pretrial conduct of which a party "was aware" before trial; lack of "conclusive evidence" is not an excuse. Here, the [plaintiff] was clearly aware of [the defendant's] discovery misconduct before trial: he obtained pretrial deposition testimony that directly contradicted [the defendant's] deposition testimony

---

09-61166-CIV-SEITZ-GOODMAN, 2011 U.S. Dist. LEXIS 25046, at *8–15 (S.D. Fla. Feb. 24, 2011) (same) (discussing cases); *Keithley v. Home Store.com, Inc.*, No. C-03-04447 SI (EDL), 2008 U.S. Dist. LEXIS 120252, at *2–5, 2008 WL 2024977 (N.D. Cal. May 8, 2008) (same); *Morrison v. Indianapolis Fire Dep't*, No. 1:06-cv-24-SEB-JBG, 2007 U.S. Dist. LEXIS 56135, at *52–53, 2007 WL 2237624 (S.D. Ind. July 31, 2007) (same) (discussing cases).

Federal courts have granted Federal Rule 37(c)(2) expenses after summary judgment. *Jennings v. Moreland*, No. 2:08-cv-01305 LKK CKD P, 2013 U.S. Dist. LEXIS 51891, at *6–7, 2013 WL 1500712 (E.D. Cal. Apr. 10, 2013) ("[I]f a party later proves at trial or on summary judgment that certain matters improperly not admitted are true, the party may seek recourse in the form of reasonable expenses incurred in making that proof."); *Howard Opera House Assocs. v. Urban Outfitters, Inc.*, No. 2:99-CV-140, 2002 U.S. DIST. LEXIS 26258, at *9–10 (D. Vt. Apr. 17, 2002) ("Courts have granted attorneys' fees and expenses under [Federal] Rule 37(c) after summary judgment when the factual issue involved in the request was in effect not in dispute, that is that the 'matter' denied was known to be true by the respondent at the time of the response."); *Joseph v. Fratar*, 197 F.R.D. 20, 23 (D. Mass. 2000) (holding that Federal Rule 37(c) expenses can be awarded after summary judgment, but refusing to award them because they were not established by the judgment); *Guzik v. Albright*, No. 16cv2257 (JPO) (DF), 2019 U.S. Dist. LEXIS 49468, at *9 (S.D.N.Y. Feb. 8, 2019) ("While [Federal] Rule 37(c)(2) was initially 'intended to provide posttrial relief' to a party for its expenses in 'making the necessary proof at trial,' courts in this Circuit have—although rarely—considered motions for costs-of-proof sanctions, brought under [Federal] Rule 37(c)(2), upon a party's successful offering of proof on a motion for summary judgment." (quoting Advisory Committee Notes to Fed. R. Civ. P. 37, 1970 Amend.)).

[293] *Meyer v. Cathey*, 167 S.W.3d 327 (Tex. 1993) (per curiam).

[294] *Meyer v. Cathey*, 167 S.W.3d 327, 332 (Tex. 1993) (per curiam).

[295] *Meyer v. Cathey*, 167 S.W.3d 327, 332 (Tex. 1993) (per curiam).

[296] *Meyer v. Cathey*, 167 S.W.3d 327, 332 (Tex. 1993) (per curiam).

[297] *Meyer v. Cathey*, 167 S.W.3d 327, 332 (Tex. 1993) (per curiam).

and other discovery responses. Accordingly, by not objecting prior to trial, [the plaintiff] waived his sanctions claim.[298]

Significantly, the Court in *Meyer* failed to consider Texas Rule 215.4(b)'s language or the adverse effect of its holding on trial practice and Texas Rule 215.4(b)'s language. For example, the plain language of the Rule suggests that an expense award is appropriate only *after* a trial is held or a summary judgment is granted.[299]

Moreover, a trial court cannot always conclusively determine during an action's pretrial stage whether a refusal to admit falls within the "no substantial importance" exception to the otherwise mandatory expense award.[300] For example, in both *Howard Opera House Associates v. Urban Outfitters, Inc.*[301] and *Read-Rite Corporation v.*

---

[298] *Meyer v. Cathey*, 167 S.W.3d 327, 333 (Tex. 1993) (per curiam). One case following *Meyer* has held that a pretrial failure to challenge improper admission denials waived Texas Rule 215.4(b) expenses. In *McGowen v. Lewis*, No. 01-07-01095-CV, 2010 Tex. App. LEXIS 3204, 2010 WL 1729331 (Tex. App.—Houston [1st Dist.] Apr. 29, 2010, no pet.) (mem. op.), the court held that, when the defendant, having denied a request for admission that his negligence proximately caused the automobile collision at issue, stipulated to liability before trial, the plaintiff waived Texas Rule 215.4(b) expenses by moving for them after trial.

> The discovery conduct upon which Lewis based his sanctions motion occurred two years before trial. McGowen stipulated to liability for the collision before trial. Lewis first moved for sanctions only after trial. This is not a circumstance in which pretrial discovery abuse was not revealed until after the trial had begun, or even after trial. Under *Meyer* and *Remington Arms*, Lewis waived his right to seek sanctions based on pretrial discovery. We hold that the trial court abused its discretion by granting Lewis's motion for sanctions. . . .

McGowen v. Lewis, No. 01-07-01095-CV, 2010 Tex. App. LEXIS 3204, at *9, 2010 WL 1729331 (Tex. App.—Houston [1st Dist.] Apr. 29, 2010, no pet.) (mem. op.). *See also Zuniga v. Medina*, No. 04-14-00360-CV, 2017 Tex. App. LEXIS 4692, at *10–11 (Tex. App.—San Antonio May 24, 2017) (mem. op.) (distinguishing *Meyer* because "the record does not establish that Zuniga 'was clearly aware of [Medina's] discovery misconduct (i.e., improperly denying requests for admission] before trial,' we hold she did not waive her sanctions claim by filing her motion after the trial concluded"), *rev'd on other grounds*, 593 S.W.3d 238 (Tex. 2019).

In *Medina v. Zuniga*, 593 S.W.3d 238, 247 n.2 (Tex. 2019), the Texas Supreme Court declined to decide the issue because it held that the "responses to [the merits-preclusive] requests for admissions [at issue] were not sanctionable as a matter of law[.]"

[299] Tex. R. Civ. P. 215.4(b) ("[I]f the party requesting the admissions *thereafter proves* the genuineness of the document or the truth of the matter, he may apply to the court for an order requiring the other party to pay him the reasonable expenses incurred in making that proof[.]") (emphasis added). In fact, the 1970 Advisory Committee Notes to Federal Rule 37, the rule on which Texas Rule 215.4(b) is based, points out: "Federal Rule 37(c) is intended to provide *post-trial relief* in the form of a requirement that the party improperly refusing the admission pay the expenses of the other side in making the necessary proof at trial." Advisory Committee Notes to the Fed. R. Civ. P. 37, 1970 Amend. (emphasis added).

[300] *Cf. Affiliated FM Ins. Co. v. LTK Consulting Servs., Inc.*, No. C06-1750JLR, 2012 U.S. Dist. LEXIS 60894, at *23–25, 2012 WL 1533887 (W.D. Wash. May 1, 2012) (construing Federal Rule 38(c)(2)); *Keithley v. Home Store.com, Inc.*, No. C-03-04447 SI (EDL), 2008 U.S. Dist. LEXIS 120252, at *6–8, 2008 WL 2024977 (N.D. Cal. May 8, 2008) (same).

[301] *Howard Opera House Assocs. v. Urban Outfitters, Inc.*, No. 2:99-CV-140, 2002 U.S. Dist. LEXIS 26258 (D. Vt. Apr. 17, 2002).

Burlington Air Express, Ltd.,[302] the courts denied expenses under Federal Rule 37(c)(2), reasoning that the requests for admission were not of substantial importance because they were irrelevant to the grounds on which summary judgment was granted.[303]

Finally, *Meyer* effectively requires parties whose requests for admission were denied to try their action through discovery motions. As noted by one federal court, in holding that a pretrial motion for expenses for an improper refusal to admit was premature:

> There are, of course, significant, obvious, and practical disadvantages to disposing of this case piecemeal through discovery practice, not the least of which is that I would necessarily have to conduct an inefficient fact-finding exercise and resolve factual disputes ahead of trial. This procedural alternative would be extremely counterproductive and inefficient and is understandably contrary to the clear weight of authority. . . . The Federal Rules also clearly differentiate between pre-trial or discovery motions and fact-finding proceedings.[304]

In sum, *Meyer* was wrongly decided as it relates to Texas Rule 215.4(b) and should be limited to its facts, that is, where the responding party abused the discovery process in general and not when it improperly failed to make an admission. Accordingly, a requesting party seeking expenses under the Rule should file a motion for them after a summary judgment or trial, but before the trial court loses its plenary power.[305]

---

302 *Read-Rite Corp. v. Burlington Air Express, Ltd.*, 183 F.R.D. 545 (N.D. Cal. 1998), *aff'd*, 186 F.3d 1190 (9th Cir. 1999), *aff'd*, 186 F.3d 1190 (9th Cir. 1999).

303 *Howard Opera House Assocs. v. Urban Outfitters, Inc.*, No. 2:99-CV-140, 2002 U.S. Dist. LEXIS 26258, at *12 n.4 (D. Vt. Apr. 17, 2002) ("The fact that the requests to admit . . . did not involve matters that were the bases for summary judgment also means that these requests to admit were not of substantial import[.]"); *Read-Rite Corp. v. Burlington Air Express, Ltd.*, 183 F.R.D. 545, 547 (N.D. Cal. 1998) ("Since these requests [for admission] were based on the 'entire shipment' theory of liability and Judge Wilken found that that theory did not apply, these requested admissions were not substantially important to the litigation."), *aff'd*, 186 F.3d 1190 (9th Cir. 1999).

304 *Point Blank Sols., Inc. v. Toyobo Am., Inc.*, No 09-61166-CIV-SEITZ-GOODMAN, 2011 U.S. Dist. LEXIS 25046, at *14–15, 2011 WL 742657 (S.D. Fla. Feb. 24, 2011), *followed by Schmalz, Inc. v. Better Vacuum Cups, Inc.*, No. 16-10040, 2017 U.S. Dist. LEXIS 154260, at *4–7 (E.D. Mich. July 14, 2017).

305 *See In re Bennett*, 960 S.W.2d 35, 38 (Tex. 1997) (per curiam) ("It is only after plenary jurisdiction has expired that a trial court may not sanction counsel for pre-judgment conduct.") (citation omitted); *Scott & White Mem'l Hosp. v. Schexnider*, 940 S.W.2d 594, 596 (Tex. 1996) ("[A] trial court's plenary power to act in a case does not expire until 30 days after the court has signed the judgment. A trial court's power to decide a motion for sanctions pertaining to matters occurring before judgment is no different than its power to decide any other motion during its plenary jurisdiction. Thus, the time during which the trial court has authority to impose sanctions on such a motion is limited to when it retains plenary jurisdiction[.]").

The only expenses that can be assessed under Texas Rule 215.4(b) are those that could have been avoided by the admission before and during trial.[306] They can be the

---

306 *Ohio Cas. Ins. Co. v. Twin City Fire Ins. Co.*, No. 14-CV-858 (NGG) (PK), 2020 U.S. Dist. LEXIS 50962, at *6, 2020 WL 3656394 (E.D.N.Y. Mar. 23, 2020) ("Only expenses that could have been avoided by an admission are recoverable pursuant to [Federal] Rule 37(c)(2)."); *Haiping Su v. NASA*, No. 5:09-cv-02838-EJD, 2016 U.S. Dist. LEXIS 122604, at *9, 2016 WL 4719274 (N.D. Cal. Sept. 9, 2016) ("The reasonable expenses recoverable under [Federal] Rule 37(c)(2) are those 'expenses that flowed directly from the improper answers to the [denied] requests.' 'In determining the magnitude of the expenses that the failure to admit caused the propounding party to suffer, courts must look for a sufficient causal nexus between the expenses claimed, and the failure to admit.' 'The expenses that may be assessed are only those that could have been avoided by the admission, and do not include expenses incurred prior to the filing of the answers to the requests for admission.'" (quoting *Marchand v. Mercy Med. Ctr.*, 22 F.3d 933, 939 (9th Cir. 1994), 7 *Moore's Federal Practice* § 37.73 (3d ed. 1997), and 8B Wright, Miller & Marcus, *Federal Practice & Procedure* § 2290 (3d ed. 2010))); *Diamond State Ins. Co. v. Deardorff*, No. 1:10-cv-00004 A WI JLT, 2011 U.S. Dist. LEXIS 60834, at *32–33, 2011 WL 2414391 (E.D. Cal. Jun 8, 2011) (awarding deposition and associated travel costs, but refusing to award expenses for a summary judgment motion because it would have had to have been filed even if the requests had been admitted. Accordingly, "they were not *caused* by the failure to admit[.]") (emphasis added); *Afcan v. U.S.*, No. 3:07-cv-00258 JWS, 2011 U.S. Dist. LEXIS 52267, at *5–6, 2011 WL 1869353 (D. Alaska, May 13, 2011) ("The task really is to separate the amount of work done to prove recklessness, which would also have been done to prove the standard of care from the amount of work done to prove recklessness only. The former is compensable, but the latter would not be compensable.") (footnote omitted); *JD Factors, LLC v. FreightCo, LLC*, No. 1:09-CV-95, 2010 U.S. DIST. LEXIS 114352, at *11–12, 2010 WL 4316881 (N.D. Ind. Oct. 25, 2010) ("In determining the amount of fees that should be awarded under [Federal] Rule 37(c)(2), a court looks 'for a sufficient causal nexus between the expenses claimed, and the failure to admit.' That is, a party is 'only entitled to those expenses incurred in obtaining and proffering the evidence necessary to prove those facts which they would not have had to prove if the [other party] had admitted the . . . requests for admission.'" (quoting *Hicklin Eng'g, L.C. v. R.J. Bartell*, No. 00-C-1516, 2005 U.S. Dist. LEXIS 41445, at *3–4, 2005 WL 3805914 (E.D. Wis. Mar. 31, 2005), *aff'd*, 439 F.3d 346 (7th Cir. 2006))); *Hillside Prods., Inc. v. Cty. of Macomb*, No. 06-11566, 2009 U.S. Dist. LEXIS 87898, at *6, 2009 WL 3059147 (E.D. Mich. Sept. 24, 2009) ("[Federal] Rule 37(c)(2) awards are inappropriate where the denied admission is proven with evidence that the requesting party would have offered regardless of the denial."); *Hicklin Eng'g, L.C. v. R.J. Bartell*, No. 00-C-1516, 2005 U.S. Dist. LEXIS 41445, at *8–9, 2005 WL 3805914 (E.D. Wis. Mar. 31, 2005) ("[F]ees related to drafting the subpoenas for Duane Schultz, serving the subpoenas, as well as correspondence, research and conferences relating to the subpoenas are not recoverable. The defendants would have incurred those costs and fees regardless of the plaintiffs' responses to the requests to admit. Amounts requested for working on a motion to compel Mr. Schultz to appear for the deposition and conferences on this issue have been excluded since these costs, likewise, would have been incurred in any event."), *aff'd*, 439 F.3d 346 (7th Cir. 2006); *Read-Rite Corp. v. Burlington Air Express, Ltd.*, 183 F.R.D. 545, 547–48 (N.D. Cal. 1998) (holding that expenses were not recoverable because the plaintiff intended to take the depositions before the answers to the requests for admission were served), *aff'd*, 186 F.3d 1190 (9th Cir. 1999); *Lawrence v. Nw. Nat'l Life Ins. Co.*, 716 F. Supp. 883, 886 (D. Md. 1989) ("Even if Lawrence had made the requested admissions, the depositions of the doctors still should have been taken. . . . Therefore, NWNL suffered no damage from the failure to admit."); *see Leonard v. Stemtech Int'l, Inc.*, 834 F.3d 376, 402 (3d Cir. 2016) ("Leonard sought the admission of facts concerning Stemtech's control over its distributors' websites, which was a crucial

costs of the additional discovery, motions, or experts.[307] In determining the expenses' amount, a trial court should look for a causal connection between the claimed expenses and the failure to admit.[308] If the failure to admit did not cause the requesting party to incur additional expense (for example, because it would have been required to introduce the same evidence, use the same experts, or take the same discovery to properly present its claims or defenses), no award is justified.[309] Similarly, expenses incurred before the denial's service are not recoverable.[310]

Texas Rule 215.4(b) contains limitations that do not exist with respect to most discovery sanctions provisions. First, the requesting party is *not* entitled to recover attorneys' fees and expenses incurred in moving for the expenses because Texas Rule 215.4(b) is expressly limited to expenses "incurred in making that proof."[311] Second, only the responding party, and *not* its attorney, can be ordered to pay expenses because the Rule expressly provides that the requesting party "may apply to the court

---

component of Leonard's vicarious and contributory infringement claims. Because this issue was central to Leonard's secondary infringement claims, Stemtech had no factual basis for denying the request, and Leonard incurred expenses to prove these facts during Tashjian's deposition, the District Court did not abuse its discretion in awarding sanctions to Leonard.").

[307] *E.g., Diamond State Ins. Co. v. Deardorff*, No. 1:10-cv-00004 A WI JLT, 2011 U.S. Dist. LEXIS 60834, at *32–33, 2011 WL 2414391 (E.D. Cal. Jun 8, 2011) (awarding deposition and associated travel costs); *House v. Giant of Md., LLC*, 232 F.R.D. 257, 261 (E.D. Va. 2005) (awarding expert costs).

[308] See cases cited in note 306.

[309] *Berry v. Office of the Fayette Cty. Sheriff*, No. 5: 14-356-DCR, 2015 U.S. Dist. LEXIS 82352, at *7, 2015 WL 3916126 (E.D. Ky. June 25, 2015) ("[A]n award under [Federal] Rule 37(c)(2) compensates for only 'reasonable expenses incurred' while refuting the answering party's denial. Accordingly, sanctions are inappropriate where the denied admission is proven with evidence that the requesting party would have offered regardless of the denial. Here, the defendant incurred no expense in refuting the plaintiffs' denial of overtime pay for football games because the defendant would have relied on the same documents to defend against the plaintiffs' other claims, regardless of the denial. The defendant concedes that the 'cost to collect these records is the same regardless of whether the Plaintiff admitted to receiving overtime payment for security details.' Thus, an award compensating the defendant for those expenses is not appropriate under the facts presented." (citations omitted) (quoting Fed. R. Civ. P. 37(c)(2))). See also cases cited in note 306.

[310] *Cf. Hicklin Eng'g, L.C. v. R.J. Bartell*, No. 00-C-1516, 2005 U.S. Dist. LEXIS 41445, at *8–9, 2005 WL 3805914 (E.D. Wis. Mar. 31, 2005) ("Attorneys' fees for work performed before the plaintiff submitted its response to the requests for admissions [sic] are not included in the fees to be awarded since these expenses were incurred before any conduct occurred which fell within the scope of [Federal] Rule 37."), *aff'd*, 439 F.3d 346 (7th Cir. 2006).

[311] Tex. R. Civ. P. 215.4(b); *cf. House v. Giant of Md., LLC*, 232 F.R.D. 257, 261 (E.D. Va. 2005) (construing Federal Rule 37(c)(2)'s similar language).

for an order requiring the *other party* to pay the reasonable expenses[.]"[312] An expense award is reviewed for an abuse of discretion.[313]

---

312 *E.g.*, Tex. R. Civ. P. 215.4(b) (emphasis added); *cf. Maynard v. Nygren*, 332 F.3d 462, 470 (7th Cir. 2003) (construing Federal Rule 37(c)(2)'s similar language); *Apex Oil Co. v. Belcher Co.*, 855 F.2d 1009, 1013–14 (2d Cir. 1982) (same).

A court that concludes that the party's attorney is culpable for his or her client's improper refusal to make an admission must look to other sources of authority to impose sanctions against the attorney, such as Texas Rules 13 and 215.3, which respectively authorize sanctions for a violation of the certification requirement and discovery abuse.

313 *E.g.*, *Medina v. Zuniga*, 593 S.W.3d 238, 244 (Tex. 2019); *Perez v. Perez*, No. 13-11-00169-CV, 2013 Tex. App. LEXIS 962, at *40, 2013 WL 398932 (Tex. App.—Corpus Christi Jan. 31, 2012, no pet.) (mem. op.); *Duggan v. Northpark Cent. Vefii, L.P.*, No. 05-98-00099-CV, 2001 Tex. App. LEXIS 5909, at *12, 2001 WL 985144 (Tex. App.—Dallas Aug. 29, 2001, no pet.) (not designated for publication); *Natural Gas Pipeline of Am. v. Pool*, 30 S.W.3d 639, 652 (Tex. App.—Amarillo 2000), *rev'd on other grounds*, 120 S.W.3d 317 (Tex. 2002).

CHAPTER 11

Depositions—Texas Rules 199–203

11-1 Depositions in General

A deposition records sworn testimony taken outside the courtroom that is certified in conformity with the Texas Rules of Civil Procedure so that it is the equivalent to testimony given in the courtroom under oath. As a discovery device, depositions allow the questioning of witnesses before trial by oral questions asked by a party's attorney[1] or by written questions asked by a deposition officer (i.e., the person recording the deposition, usually a court reporter).[2]

Depositions are central to civil litigation and perhaps the single most important discovery device.[3] As one federal court somewhat cynically noted:

> Depositions are the factual battleground where the vast majority of litigation actually takes place. It may safely be said that [Federal] Rule 30 has spawned a veritable cottage industry. The significance of depositions has grown geometrically over the years to the point where their pervasiveness now dwarfs both

---

1 *See* Tex. R. Civ. P. 199; *cf. In re Amezaga*, 195 B.R. 221, 227 (Bankr. D.P.R. 1996) (explaining that "a deposition is a 'question-and-answer conversation' between the witness and the deposing attorney to garner facts in relation to that and the witness' actions and experiences" (quoting *Hall v. Clifton Precision*, 150 F.R.D. 525, 528 (E.D. Pa. 1993))). Oral depositions are discussed in Chapter 11, section 11-2.

2 *See* Tex. R. Civ. P. 200. Depositions upon written questions are discussed in Chapter 11, section 11-3.

3 *Luangisa v. Interface Operations*, No. 2:11-cv-00951-RCJ-CWH, 2011 U.S. Dist. LEXIS 139700, at *17, 2011 WL 6029880 (D. Nev. Dec. 5, 2011) ("Statistics show that fewer and fewer civil cases proceed all the way to trial. As a result, '[d]epositions are the factual battleground where the vast majority of litigation actually takes place.'" (quoting *Hall v. Clifton Precision*, 150 F.R.D. 525, 531 (E.D. Pa. 1993))); *GMAC Bank v. HTFC Corp.*, 248 F.R.D. 182, 185 (E.D. Pa. 2008) ("More than 98% of all civil cases filed in the federal courts result in disposition by way of settlement or pretrial adjudication. Very often, these results turn on evidence obtained during depositions. Thus, depositions play an extremely important role in the American system of justice."); *Hall v. Clifton Precision*, 150 F.R.D. 525, 531 n.12 (E.D. Pa. 1993) ("The reality is that what is learned at depositions becomes the factual basis upon which most cases are disposed of—not by trial, but by settlement.").

the time spent and the facts learned at the actual trial—assuming there is a trial, which there usually is not.[4]

After an action is commenced, depositions are used for a wide variety of purposes, including basic fact discovery, preserving the testimony of witnesses who might be unavailable for trial, and establishing facts needed for settlement or pretrial motions (e.g., summary judgment motions).[5] Depositions also may be taken before suit is commenced to perpetuate the testimony of a person or to investigate a potential claim or suit.[6] At trial, depositions generally are used as the testimony of unavailable witnesses and to cross-examine live witnesses and impeach their trial testimony to the extent it differs from their earlier deposition testimony.[7]

The most common type of deposition is the oral deposition, consisting of questions by the attorney for one party, answers by the deponent, and objections and

---

4 *Hall v. Clifton Precision*, 150 F.R.D. 525, 531 (E.D. Pa. 1993) (footnote omitted); *accord In re Fetzima*, No. 2:17-cv-10230 (ES) (SCM), 2020 U.S. Dist. LEXIS 198891, at *4, 2020 WL 6268684 (D.N.J. Oct. 23, 2020); *Slabisak v. Univ. of Tex. Health Sci. Ctr.*, No. 4:17-CV-597, 2018 U.S. Dist. LEXIS 171636, at *5, 2018 WL 4842690 (E.D. Tex. Oct. 4, 2018); *see Soliz v. State*, 97 S.W.3d 137, 144 n.33 (Tex. Crim. App. 2003) ("The stakes at a deposition can be high—or at least perceived to be high by the litigants and their counsel. When evaluating the strength of their client's case, litigators often accord great weight to witnesses' and attorneys' performances during depositions. Thus, if an attorney's client performs well while the opponent performs poorly, the attorney may attach a higher settlement value to the case. Moreover, deposition transcripts are often an important trial resource, sometimes substituting for live witnesses, and at other times serving as fodder for cross-examination and impeachment. Depositions are a dress rehearsal—and due to high settlement rates are often a substitute—for trial. Therefore, attorneys tend to attach more importance to depositions than to most 'paper discovery.'" (quoting A. Darby Dickerson, *Deposition Dilemmas: Vexatious Scheduling and Errata Sheets*, 12 Geo. J. Legal Ethics 1, 3–4 (1998))).

5 *Soliz v. State*, 97 S.W.3d 137, 144 (Tex. Crim. App. 2003) ("Depositions are widely used in civil lawsuits. They are used to reveal the strengths and weaknesses of a case. They are used as evidence in motions for summary judgment. They serve as evidence at trial without the necessity of showing that a witness is unable to testify. They can, under certain circumstances, be used in other lawsuits.") (footnotes omitted); *cf. In re Fetzima*, No. 2:17-cv-10230 (ES) (SCM), 2020 U.S. Dist. LEXIS 198891, at *3–4, 2020 WL 6268684 (D.N.J. Oct. 23, 2020) ("The underlying purpose of a deposition is to find out what a witness saw, heard, or did—what the witness thinks. A deposition is meant to be a question-and-answer conversation between the deposing lawyer and the witness." (quoting *Hall v. Clifton Precision*, 150 F.R.D. 525, 531 (E.D. Pa. 1993))); *Kleppinger v. Tex. Dept. of Transp.*, 283 F.R.D. 330, 335 (S.D. Tex. 2012) ("[W]hile one purpose of a deposition is for basic discovery, it is also utilized for the preservation of information, for the establishment of facts crucial to settlement or rulings on pretrial motions, and for potential impeachment purposes if a witness's testimony deviates at trial.").

6 Tex. R. Civ. P. 202 ("A person may petition the court for an order authorizing the taking of a deposition on oral examination or written questions either: (a) to perpetuate or obtain the person's own testimony or that of any other person for use in an anticipated suit; or (b) to investigate a potential claim or suit."). Depositions to perpetuate testimony or investigate a claim or suit are discussed in Chapter 11, section 11-5.

7 *Soliz v. State*, 97 S.W.3d 137, 145 (Tex. Crim. App. 2003) ("[Depositions] serve as evidence at trial without the necessity of showing that a witness is unable to testify.").

cross-examination by the other parties' attorneys.[8] Depositions generally can be taken without leave of court, although a deposition to perpetuate testimony or to investigate a potential claim or suit requires a court order.[9] Once an action is commenced, the party noticing the deposition generally is not required to establish that the deponent has information about which the deponent can testify at trial.[10] Indeed, one of discovery's important purposes is to ascertain who has such information. Of course, if the noticing party is proceeding in bad faith, the proper response is to move for protection under Texas Rule 192.6.[11]

Texas Rules relevant to depositions are Rules 176 (subpoenas),[12] 190 (deposition time limits),[13] 199 (oral depositions generally),[14] 200 (depositions upon written question),[15] 201 (depositions in foreign jurisdictions for use in Texas proceedings and depositions in Texas for use in foreign proceedings),[16] 202 (depositions before suit or to investigate claims),[17] 203 (signing, certification, and use of oral and written depositions),[18] 205 (discovery from nonparties),[19] and 215 (abuse of discovery and sanctions).[20]

11-1:1 Who Can Be Deposed

11-1:1.1 Introduction

The testimony of "any person or entity" may be taken by oral examination or on written questions.[21] This includes any natural person; any entity, irrespective of its

---

8 Oral depositions are governed by Texas Rule199, which is discussed in Chapter 11, section 11-2.

9 Tex. R. Civ. P. 202. See Chapter 11, section 11-5 (discussing presuit depositions).

10 The principal exception to this rule is an "apex deposition." See Chapter 11, section 11-1:1.4.

11 Tex. R. Civ. P. 192.6(b)(1) ("To protect the movant from undue burden, unnecessary expense, harassment, annoyance, or invasion of personal, constitutional, or property rights, the court may make any order in the interest of justice and may—among other things—order that: (1) the requested discovery not be sought in whole or in part[.]"). See also Chapter 4, section 4-5 (discussing protective orders).

12 See Chapter 13, section 13-4.

13 See Chapter 2, section 2-3.

14 See Chapter 11, section 11-2.

15 See Chapter 11, section 11-3.

16 See Chapter 11, section 11-4.

17 See Chapter 11, section 11-5.

18 See Chapter 11, section 11-6.

19 See Chapter 13.

20 See Chapter 14.

21 Tex. R. Civ. P. 199.1(a) ("A party may take the testimony of any person or entity by deposition on oral examination before any officer authorized by law to take depositions."), 200.1(a) ("A party may take the testimony of any person or entity by deposition on written questions before any person authorized by law to take depositions on written questions."); *see* Tex. R. Civ. P. 176.6(b) ("If a subpoena commanding testimony is directed to a corporation, partnership, association, governmental agency, or other organization, and the matters on which examination is requested are described with reasonable particularity, the organization must designate one or more persons to testify on its behalf as to matters known or reasonably available to the organization."); *Crown Cent. Petroleum Corp. v. Garcia*, 904 S.W.2d 125, 127 (Tex. 1995) (orig. proceeding) (noting that parties are generally permitted

nature (e.g., corporation, partnership, limited partnership, limited liability company, or association), as well as the entity's officers, directors, employees, and agents; public officials; and any governmental entity, subdivision, body, or agency as well as its directors, officers, employees, and agents. This is made clear by Texas Rule 199.2(b)(1), which expressly provides that a deponent can be "either an individual or a public or private corporation, partnership, association, governmental agency, or other organization."[22] A party can even take his, her, or its own deposition.

Importantly, Texas Rules 199 and 200 draw no distinction between depositions of parties and nonparties.[23] In contrast, interrogatories and requests for admission only can be addressed to parties.[24] Document requests pursuant to Texas Rule 196 also are limited to parties,[25] but the substantial equivalent of a Texas Rule 196 production request can be obtained from a nonparty by serving a notice and subpoena pursuant to Texas Rules 205 and 176, respectively,[26] or, if the nonparty is to be deposed, by including a document request in the deposition notice and subpoena, which requires the nonparty witness to bring the requested documents to the deposition.[27]

11-1:1.2 Attorneys

The fact that the proposed deponent is an attorney or even the attorney for the opposing party in the action is not an *absolute* bar to deposing the attorney,[28] although the

---

to take the deposition of "any person" (quoting former Tex. R. Civ. P. 200))); *In re West*, 346 S.W.3d 612, 615, (Tex. App.—El Paso 2009, orig. proceeding) (same).

22 Tex. R. Civ. P. 199.2(b)(1). This is confirmed by the facts that "person," as defined by Section 311.005 of the Texas Government Code "includes corporation, organization, government or governmental subdivision or agency, business trust, estate, trust, partnership, association, and any other legal entity" and that the "[t]he Code Construction Act applies to the Texas Rules of Civil Procedure[.]" *Simulis, L.L.C. v. G.E. Capital Corp.*, 276 S.W.3d 109, 113–14 (Tex. App.—Houston [1st Dist.] 2008, no pet.) (quoting *In re Walkup*, 122 S.W.3d 215, 217 (Tex. App.—Houston [1st Dist.] 2003, orig. proceeding)).

23 *In re Miscavige*, 436 S.W.3d 430, 437 (Tex. App.—Austin 2014, orig. proceeding) ("[T]he Texas Rules of Civil Procedure do not distinguish between depositions of named parties and depositions of other individuals."); *see In re Perry*, No. 13-18-00676-CV, 2019 Tex. App. LEXIS 3176, at *9, 2019 WL 1723509 (Tex. App.—Corpus Christi Apr. 18, 2019, orig. proceeding) ("The rules of civil procedure permit a party to take the deposition of 'any person or entity.'" (quoting Tex. R. Civ. P. 200.1(a))).

24 Tex. R. Civ. P.197.1 (interrogatories), 198.1 (requests for admission).

25 Tex. R. Civ. P. 196.1(a).

26 Tex. R. Civ. P. 176.2(b), 205.1(c), 205.3. See also Chapter 13 (discussing nonparty discovery).

27 Tex. R. Civ. P. 176.2, 205.1(a)-(b), 205.2. See also Chapter 13 (discussing nonparty discovery).

28 This is made clear by Texas Rules 199.1(a) and 200.1(a), which provide that "any person" can be deposed. *Accord In re Perry*, No. 13-18-00676-CV, 2019 Tex. App. LEXIS 3176, at *9, 2019 WL 1723509 (Tex. App.—Corpus Christi Apr. 18, 2019, orig. proceeding) ("The rules of civil procedure permit a party to take the deposition of 'any person or entity.'" (quoting Tex. R. Civ. P. 200.1(a))); *cf. State Nat'l Ins. Co. v. Khatri*, No C 13-00433 LB, 2014 U.S. Dist. LEXIS 64549, at *17, 2014 WL 1877618 (N.D. Cal. May 9, 2014) ("Assuming a party seeks relevant information, that party may depose 'any person' under [Federal] Rule 30(a)(1), and there is no express prohibition against deposing an attorney of record in a case."); *Busey v. Richland Sch. Dist.*, No. 13-CV-5022-TOR, 2014 U.S. Dist. LEXIS 50579, at *4, 2014

attorney-client and work-product privileges may provide bases for the attorney to refuse to answer some or all of the questions asked during the deposition. Nonetheless, noticing the deposition of opposing counsel is viewed with disfavor. As noted by one Texas court:

> Generally, an attorney of record in litigation is an advocate, not a fact witness, in the litigation process. As with compelling production of opposing counsel's litigation file, ***compelling a deposition of the opposing party's attorney of record concerning the subject matter of the litigation is inappropriate under most circumstances***. Calling opposing counsel of record as a witness seriously disrupts the counsel's functioning as an advocate and may create a false impression that the advocate was improperly involved in the underlying issues in the litigation.[29]

Federal courts similarly limit depositions of opposing counsel. One line of federal cases, based on *Shelton v. American Motors Corp.*, allows the deposition of opposing counsel only when "the party seeking to take the deposition has shown that (1) no other means exist to obtain the information than to depose opposing counsel; (2) the information sought is relevant and nonprivileged; and (3) the information is crucial to the preparation of the case."[30] Other federal courts, as exemplified by *In re Subpoena*

WL 1404580 (E.D. Wash. Apr. 10, 2014) (same); *Am. Cas. Co. v. Krieger*, 160 F.R.D. 582, 585 (S.D. Cal. 1995) (same).

[29] *In re Baytown Nissan Inc.*, 451 S.W.3d 140, 149–150 (Tex. App.—Houston [1st Dist.] 2014, orig. proceeding) (emphasis added) (quoting *In re Baptist Hosps.*, 172 S.W.3d 136, 145 (Tex. App.—Beaumont 2005, orig. proceeding)); *accord In re Burroughs*, 203 S.W.3d 858, 860 (Tex. App.—Beaumont 2006, orig. proceeding); *In re Baytown Nissan Inc.*, 451 S.W.3d 140, 149–150 (Tex. App.—Houston [1st Dist.] 2014, orig. proceeding); *In re SouthPak Container Corp.*, 418 S.W.3d 360, 364 (Tex. App.—Dallas 2013, orig. proceeding); *In re Exxon Corp.*, 208 S.W.3d 70, 76 (Tex. App.—Beaumont 2006, orig. proceeding).

[30] *Shelton v. Am. Motors Corp.*, 805 F.2d 1323, 1327 (8th Cir. 1986) (citation omitted); *accord Nationwide Mut. Ins. Co. v. Home Ins. Co.*, 278 F.3d 621, 628–29 (6th Cir. 2002); *Thiessea v. Gen. Elec. Capital Corp.*, 255 F.3d 1221, 1237 (10th Cir. 2001); *Therot v. Parish of Jefferson*, 185 F.3d 477, 491 (5th Cir. 1999), *cert. denied*, 529 U.S. 1129 (2000); *Broyles v. Convergent Outsourcing, Inc.*, No. C16-775-RAJ, 2017 U.S. Dist. LEXIS 79151, at *3, 2017 WL 2256773 (W.D. Wash. May 23, 2017) ("The 'leading case on attorney depositions' is *Shelton v. Am. Motors Corp.*, 805 F.2d 1323 (8th Cir. 1986)." (quoting *FMC Techs., Inc. v. Edwards*, No. C05-946-JCC, 2007 U.S. Dist. LEXIS 18328, at *7–8, 2007 WL 836709 (W.D. Wash. Mar. 15, 2007))); *see Dewey v. Bechthold*, No. 18-CV-1739-JPS, 2019 U.S. Dist. LEXIS 183381, at *16–18, 2019 WL 5429373 (E.D. Wis. Oct. 23, 2019) ("The law on attorney depositions in the Seventh Circuit is currently unsettled. Although there is no question that attorneys may be deposed, there are some limits to this practice so as to prevent abuse by opposing parties. Many district courts in this circuit apply a flexible version of the test set forth by the Eighth Circuit in *Shelton v. American Motors Corporation*[, 805 F.2d 1323 (8th Cir. 1986)] . . . . Other courts in this circuit, however, have either criticized or roundly rejected *Shelton* as being too narrow or, simply, wrongly decided. . . . Without a clear directive from the Seventh Circuit, the Court will consider the factors set forth in *Shelton* as instructive to its analysis, but will not apply them as rigorous criteria."); *U.S. v. All Assets Held in Account No. 80020796*, No. 13-1832 (JDB), 2019 U.S. Dist. LEXIS 805, at *12–13 n.4, 2019 WL 95605 (D.D.C. Jan. 3, 2019) ("The D.C. Circuit has not addressed whether the Shelton test applies to depositions of opposing trial counsel" but noting that "[t]he *Shelton* test has been adopted by some judges on this court, however."); *Adria MM Prods. v. Worldwide Entm't Grp., Inc.*, No. 17-21603-CIV-MORENO, 2017 U.S. Dist. LEXIS 196868, at *3 (S.D. Fla. Nov. 30, 2017)

to Friedman, have adopted a "flexible" approach to such depositions that takes into consideration all relevant facts and circumstances in determining whether the deposition would entail an inappropriate burden or hardship, including the need to depose the attorney, the attorney's role in connection with the matter on which discovery is sought, the extent of discovery already conducted, and the risk of encountering issues relating to the attorney-client and work-product privileges.[31]

Although the few Texas courts that have considered the propriety of deposing opposing counsel have not adopted either test used by federal courts or set forth an alternative one,[32] as noted above, they hold that depositions of opposing counsel generally are "inappropriate" and disfavored.[33] It is clear, however, that opposing counsel can be deposed when the attorney's advice is used by the client as a defense or the attorney is a fact witness with unique knowledge, an actor (e.g., a defrauder), or the creator of relevant non-privileged records.[34] In such circumstances, the deposition should be limited to those matters and not address the attorneys' role in the action or any investigation of the incident at issue that would be work product.[35]

("The circuit courts are split on whether to apply the *Shelton* test or the 'flexible approach' test in determining whether to allow the deposition of a party's attorney. The Eleventh Circuit has not expressly ruled on the issue. But, courts in the Southern District of Florida have generally held that to allow the deposition of a party's attorney, the movant must show that: (1) the deposition is the only practical means of obtaining the information; (2) the information sought will not invade the realm of the attorney's work product or interfere with the attorney-client privilege; (3) the information sought is relevant and crucial to the preparation of the case; and (4) the movant's needs outweigh the dangers of deposing a party's attorney.").

[31] *In re Subpoena to Friedman*, 350 F.3d 65, 72 (2d Cir. 2003); *accord Wilson v. O'Brien*, No. 07 C 3994, 2010 U.S. Dist. LEXIS 33721, at *7–8, 2010 WL 1418401 (N.D. Ill. Apr. 6, 2010); *Younger Mfg. Co. v. Kaenon, Inc.*, 247 F.R.D. 586, 588 (C.D. Cal. 2007).

[32] *E.g., In re Baytown Nissan Inc.*, 451 S.W.3d 140, 149–50 (Tex. App.—Houston [1st Dist.] 2014, orig. proceeding) (holding that the trial court abused its discretion in denying a protective order precluding the plaintiff from deposing the defendant's attorney about a witness interview); *In re Exxon Corp.*, 208 S.W.3d 70, 77 (Tex. App.—Beaumont 2006, orig. proceeding) (holding that the trial court abused its discretion in not granting a protective order precluding the deposition of the defendant's general counsel regarding the defendant's document production); *In re Burroughs*, 203 S.W.3d 858, 860 (Tex. App.—Beaumont 2006, orig. proceeding) (holding that the trial court abused its discretion in compelling opposing counsel's deposition); *In re Baptist Hosps.*, 172 S.W.3d 136, 146 (Tex. App.—Beaumont 2005, orig. proceeding) (holding that the trial court abused its discretion in not quashing a deposition notice for the opposing counsel's deposition because he was not a fact witness).

[33] See cases cited in note 30.

[34] *In re SouthPak Container Corp.*, 418 S.W.3d 360, 364 (Tex. App.—Dallas 2013, orig. proceeding) (holding that a defense attorney could be deposed about matters learned while he was the defendants' corporate secretary); *cf. Niagara Mohawk Power Corp. v. Stone & Webster Eng'g Corp.*, 125 F.R.D. 578, 593 n.4 (N.D.N.Y 1989) ("There are instances where the deposition of an attorney is clearly appropriate. This is usually where the attorney is a fact witness or an actor, the creator of non-privileged records, or the attorney's advice is used by the client as a defense."); *N.F.A. Corp. v. Riverview Narrow Fabrics, Inc.*, 117 F.R.D. 83, 85 n.2 (M.D.N.C. 1987) (same).

[35] *See In re SouthPak Container Corp.*, 418 S.W.3d 360, 364 (Tex. App.—Dallas 2013, orig. proceeding) (holding that an order compelling defense counsel to testify was overbroad because it was not limited to matters learned by the attorney as the defendants' corporate secretary). Of course, if an attorney is a fact witness in litigation, the attorney may not

The rule disfavoring depositions of opposing counsel is not limited to trial counsel. It also applies to any attorney involved the action's preparation for trial. "[C]ourts have found that 'the critical factor in determining whether the *Shelton* test applies is not the status of the lawyer as trial counsel, but the extent of the lawyer's involvement in the pending litigation[,]'"[36] with the goal being to protect the opposing party's trial strategy, work product, and attorney-client communications. The heightened protection does not apply, however, in other circumstances, such as when the attorney sought to be deposed is not trial counsel or assisting in the litigation, but rather, for example, represented the party in another unrelated, but relevant, action, was involved in the negotiation of the contract at issue, or provided relevant business advice to the party.[37]

---

ethically be able to represent his or her client in that litigation. *See* Tex. Disciplinary Rules Prof'l Conduct R. 3.08, *reprinted in* Tex. Gov't Code tit. 2, subtit. G. app. A. (Tex. State Bar R. art. x, 9) (generally prohibiting a lawyer from "accept[ing] or continu[ing] employment as an advocate before a tribunal in a contemplated or pending adjudicatory proceeding if the lawyer knows or believes that [she] is or may be a witness necessary to establish an essential fact on behalf of [her] client"); *Anderson Producing v. Koch Oil Co.*, 929 S.W.2d 416, 418 (Tex. 1996) ("Subject to certain exceptions, Texas Disciplinary Rule of Professional Conduct 3.08 prohibits an attorney from representing a party in an adjudicatory proceeding if the attorney knows or believes that he or she may be a witness at trial.").

[36] *Nat'l W. Life Ins. Co. v. W. Nat'l Life Ins. Co.*, No. 09-cv-711, 2010 U.S. Dist. LEXIS 132024, at *10, 2010 WL 5174366 (W.D. Tex. Dec. 13, 2010) (quoting *Murphy v. Adelphia Recovery Tr.*, No. 3:09-mc-105, 2009 U.S. Dist. LEXIS 122027, at *3, 2009 WL 4755368 (N.D. Tex. Nov. 3, 2009))); *accord Thiessen v. Gen. Elec. Capital Corp.*, 267 F.3d 1095, 1112 (10th Cir. 2001) (applying the rule to an in-house attorney involved in presuit investigation), *cert. denied*, 536 U.S. 934 (2002); *Massillon Mgmt., LLC v. Americold Realty Tr.*, No. 5:08CV0799, 2009 U.S. Dist. LEXIS 22415, at *16–17, 2009 WL 614831 (N.D. Ohio Jan. 21, 2009) (applying the rule to a party's general counsel who was involved in presuit and trial strategy); *Malcolm D. Smithson & Christine B. Smithson Trs. v. Amerada Hess Corp.*, No.CIV-06-624 JB, 2007 U.S. Dist. LEXIS 97729, at *24, 2007 WL 5685112 (D.N.M. Dec. 19, 2007) (applying the rule to in-house counsel assisting in the lawsuit); *In re Boxer Prop. Mgmt. Corp.*, No. 14-00579-CV, 2009 Tex. App. LEXIS 7279, at *17–18, 2009 WL 4250123 (Tex. App.—Houston [14th Dist.] Sept. 3, 2009, orig. proceeding) (mem. op.) (applying the rule to in-house attorneys); *In re Exxon Corp.*, 208 S.W.3d 70, 76 (Tex. App.—Beaumont 2006, orig. proceeding) (applying the rule to defendant's general counsel).

[37] *E.g., In re SouthPak Container Corp.*, 418 S.W.3d 360, 364 (Tex. App.—Dallas 2013, orig. proceeding) (allowing the plaintiff to depose defense counsel regarding matters he learned as defendants' corporate secretary); *cf. Pamida, Inc. v. E.S. Originals, Inc.*, 281 F.3d 726, 730, 731 (8th Cir. 2002) ("But *Shelton* was not intended to provide heightened protection to attorneys who represented a client in a completed case and then also happened to represent that same client in a pending case where the information known only by the attorneys regarding the prior concluded case was crucial. In such circumstances, the protection *Shelton* provides to opposing counsel only applies because opposing counsel is counsel in the instant case and not because opposing counsel had represented the client in the concluded case."); *Insogna v. Hetero Labs Ltd.*, No. 3:19-cv-1589-LAB-AHG, 2020 U.S. Dist. LEXIS 3189, at *7, 2020 WL 85487 (S.D. Cal. 2020) ("Courts have declined to apply *Shelton* when the proposed deponent is not trial or litigation counsel in the underlying case."); *Andre v. Ricoh USA, Inc.*, No. 19-mc-80266-VKD, 2019 U.S. Dist. LEXIS 212899, at *6, 2019 WL 6699958 (N.D. Cal. Dec. 9, 2019) ("[T]he *Shelton* analysis applies only where the discovery sought concerns matters relating to counsel's representation of a litigant in the current litigation. It does not apply to discovery of facts known to counsel as a percipient witness relating to matters that preceded the litigation."); *Allen v. TV One, LLC*, No. DKC 15-1960, 2016 U.S. Dist. LEXIS 169641, at *5 n.3, 2016 WL 7157420 (D. Md. Dec. 8, 2016) ("Plaintiff seeks

In such circumstances, whether the attorney should be deposed and any limitations on the deposition are governed by the general rules regarding protective orders.[38]

11-1:1.3 Lack of Knowledge

Often, prospective deponents will seek to quash a deposition notice or subpoena on the basis that the deponent lacks any relevant knowledge. If the deposition is not an "apex" one,[39] a claimed lack of knowledge generally is an insufficient basis for a protective order because "the general rule is that a claimed lack of knowledge does not provide sufficient grounds for a protective order; the other side is allowed to test this claim by deposing the witness."[40] If, however, the deponent or non-noticing party

---

to depose, as a fact witness, Defendant's former in-house counsel, who left Defendant's employ more than a year before Plaintiff filed her EEOC claim or this lawsuit. Ms. Wishart is not opposing counsel in this case, and her deposition could not lead to the disclosure of Defendant's litigation strategy. The *Shelton* test is inapplicable."); *In re Allergan, Inc. Sec. Litig.*, No. 14-cv-02004-DOC (KES), 2016 U.S. Dist. LEXIS 186537, at *9, 2016 WL 5922717 (C.D. Cal. Sept. 23, 2016) ("The three part test from *Shelton* does not apply if a party seeks discovery from opposing counsel regarding a previously concluded case. Here, Pershing generally seeks discovery from BLB&G regarding a prior, concluded case. As a result, *Shelton*'s three part test is inapposite.") (citation omitted); *Anserphone of New Orleans, Inc. v. Protocol Commc'ns, Inc.*, No. Civ. A. 01-3740 section "A" (1), 2002 U.S. Dist. LEXIS 16876, at *5, 2002 WL 31016572 (E.D. La. Sept. 10, 2002) (holding that *Shelton* did not apply to the deposition of a transactional lawyer who negotiated the agreement at issue); *Mass. Mut. Life Ins. Co. v. Cerf*, 177 F.R.D. 472, 479 (N.D. Cal. 1998) ("In this case, however, such concerns do not require the issuance of a protective order because Ms. Pfeiffer did not represent Cerf in this action."); *Rowe v. Liberty Mut. Grp., Inc.*, No. 11-cv-366-JL, 2013 U.S. Dist. LEXIS 99065, at *20–21, 2013 WL 3762662 (D.N.H. July 16, 2013) ("Liberty Mutual also invokes the rule that '[t]aking depositions of opposing trial counsel is generally disfavored and discouraged.' That rule is irrelevant here. Neither of the deponents are 'trial counsel' in this action (Buckley is not an attorney at all) and, while some courts have treated 'supervising in-house counsel' for the litigation as 'trial counsel' for purposes of this rule, Attorney Brown, so far as the court is aware, has no involvement in managing this litigation for Liberty Mutual.").

38 *See* Tex. R. Civ. P. 192.6(b) ("To protect the movant from undue burden, unnecessary expense, harassment, annoyance, or invasion of personal, constitutional, or property rights, the court may make any order in the interest of justice and may—among other things—order that: (1) the requested discovery not be sought in whole or in part; (2) the extent or subject matter of discovery be limited; (3) the discovery not be undertaken at the time or place specified; [or] (4) the discovery be undertaken only by such method or upon such terms and conditions or at the time and place directed by the court[.]"). See also Chapter 4, section 4-5 (discussing protective orders).

39 See Chapter 11, section 11-1:1.4 (discussing apex depositions).

40 *Cf. Amherst Leasing Corp. v. Emhart Corp.*, 65 F.R.D. 121, 122 (D. Conn. 1974) (footnote omitted); *accord Valvetech, Inc. v. Aerojet Rocketdyne, Inc.*, No. 17-CV-6788-FPG-MJP, 2020 U.S. Dist. LEXIS 191825, at *14–15, 2020 WL 6120348 (W.D.N.Y. Oct. 16, 2020) ("(A) professed lack of knowledge typically does not constitute good cause and is insufficient to warrant [issuing a protective order for] a deposition." (quoting *Kamps, v. Fried, Frank, Harris, Shriver & Jacobson, L.L.P.*, No 9-CV-10392(RMB)(KNF), 2010 U.S. Dist. LEXIS 132749, at *8, 2010 WL 5158183 (S.D.N.Y. Dec. 9, 2010))); *City of Huntington v. AmerisourceBergen Drug Corp.*, No. 3:17-01362, 2020 U.S. Dist. LEXIS 113010, at *14, 2020 WL 3520314 (S.D. W. Va. 2020) (noting "the long-standing rule that '[a] witness ordinarily cannot escape examination by denying knowledge of any relevant facts, since the party seeking to take the

believes that the noticing party is proceeding in bad faith, the proper response is to move for protection under Texas Rule 192.6.[41]

In the same vein, the mere prospect that the witness may be asked questions that would be objectionable on privilege grounds is not a basis for failure to attend a deposition; instead, the deponent must appear and object to specific questions seeking privileged information on the basis of privilege.[42] Of course, if the witness is a consulting

---

deposition is entitled to test the witness's lack of knowledge.'" (quoting *In re C. R. Bard, Inc.*, MDL No. 2187, 2014 U.S. Dist. LEXIS 89147, at *459 (S.D. W. Va. 2014))); *Mir v. Kirchmeyer*, No. 12cv2340-GPC (DHB), 2016 U.S. Dist. LEXIS 84751, at *6–7, 2016 WL 3548536 (S.D. Cal. June 29, 2016) ("[T]he fact that Kirchmeyer claims she has insufficient information about a potential topic of inquiry is insufficient to excuse her from appearing for deposition."); *Libertarian Party v. Husted*, 302 F.R.D. 472, 479 (S.D. Ohio 2014) ("[I]n ordinary circumstances, [it] does [not] matter that the proposed witness is a busy person or professes lack of knowledge of the matters at issue, as the party seeking the discovery is entitled to test the asserted lack of knowledge." (quoting *Naftchi v. N.Y. Univ. Med. Ctr.*, 172 F.R.D. 130, 132 (S.D.N.Y. 1997))); *Balfour Beatty Rail, Inc. v. Vaccarello*, No. 3:06-cv-551-J-20MCR, 2007 U.S. Dist. LEXIS 19525, at *8, 2007 WL 842765 (M.D. Fla. Mar. 20, 2007) ("The reason why alleged lack of knowledge is not a sufficient ground to prevent a deposition is obvious. The very purpose of the deposition discovery is to test the extent of the deponent's knowledge and claims of ignorance.").

Because a deponent is not required to have personal knowledge of relevant facts, a claimed lack of personal knowledge is insufficient to prevent a deposition. *See* Tex. R. Civ. P. 192.3(c) ("A person has knowledge of relevant facts when the person has or may have knowledge of any discoverable matter. ***The person need not have admissible information or personal knowledge of the facts.***") (emphasis added); *In re Garrison Prop. & Cas. Ins. Co.*, No. 12-20-00190-CV, 2020 Tex. App. LEXIS 8409, at *15, 2020 WL 6164982 (Tex. App.—Tyler Oct. 21, 2020, orig. proceeding) (mem. op.) ("[Texas] Rule 199.1(a) permits the deposition of any person or entity without any limitation that the proposed deponent have personal knowledge of the facts."); *In re Luna*, No. 13-16-00467-CV, 2016 Tex. App. LEXIS 12011, at *22, 2016 WL 6576879 (Tex. App.—Corpus Christi Nov. 7, 2016, orig. proceeding) (mem. op.) (same); *In re Jinsun LLC*, No. 14-15005680CV, 2015 Tex. App. LEXIS 9011, at *11–12, 2015 WL 5092176 (Tex. App.—Houston [14th Dist.] Aug. 27, 2015, orig. proceeding) (mem. op.) ("Jinsun was not required to show that Dolcefino had 'personal knowledge of any facts relevant to the disputed issues in this case.' The trial court abused its discretion by quashing Dolcefino's deposition on the ground of lack of personal knowledge."); *In re Team Transp., Inc.*, 996 S.W.2d 256, 259 (Tex. App.—Houston [14th Dist.] 1999, orig. proceeding) ("A person with knowledge of relevant facts need not have personal knowledge of the facts.").

41 *See* Tex. R. Civ. P. 192.6(b)(1) ("To protect the movant from undue burden, unnecessary expense, harassment, annoyance, or invasion of personal, constitutional, or property rights, the court may make any order in the interest of justice and may—among other things—order that . . . the requested discovery not be sought in whole or in part[.]"). See also Chapter 4, section 4-5 (discussing protective orders).

42 *See In re Nichol*, 602 S.W.3d 595, 601 (Tex. App.—El Paso 2019, orig. proceeding) ("The [Fifth Amendment] privilege does not permit a party or witness in a civil case to refuse to submit to a deposition or take the witness stand; rather, the witness must assert the privilege on a question-by-question basis. At that point, the trial judge must make a ruling as to whether the assertion of privilege is proper.") (citation omitted); *Finkelstein v. West*, No. 01-89-01214-CV, 1990 Tex. App. LEXIS 358, at *5, 1990 WL 15566 (Tex. App.—Houston [1st Dist.] Feb. 21, 1990, no writ) ("The possibility that a deponent will assert a privilege against answering a specific deposition question does not justify the quashing of a depo-

expert whose mental impressions and opinions have *not* been reviewed by a testifying expert, the deposition is improper and a motion for a protective order or to quash the deposition notice is proper.[43]

11-1:1.4 Apex Depositions

In *Crown Central Petroleum Corp. v. Garcia*,[44] the Texas Supreme Court established the "apex doctrine." The doctrine applies, and potentially allows an organization's high-level officials[45] to avoid being deposed, when the deposition is noticed solely

---

sition notice."); *cf. Papst Licensing GmbH & Co. KG v. Apple, Inc.*, No. 6:15-cv-1095, 2017 U.S. Dist. LEXIS 51274, at *16–17, 2017 WL 1233047 (N.D. Ill. Apr. 4, 2017) ("'The claim of privilege must be made and sustained on a question-by-question or document-by-document basis; a blanket claim of privilege is unacceptable.' As such, one cannot simply make a blanket claim of privilege at a deposition, let alone make one in advance and avoid testifying entirely. The proper course is to assert the privilege in response to a specific question or questions during the deposition." (quoting *U.S. v. Lawless*, 709 F.2d 485, 487 (7th Cir. 1983))); *In re Chevron Corp.*, 736 F. Supp. 2d 773, 783–84 (S.D.N.Y. 2010) ("The extraordinary nature of Berlinger's claim that he and his associates cannot be subjected to deposition, even to test largely conclusory and certainly overbroad claims of privilege, is evident by comparing this position to that of one claiming attorney-client privilege, a privilege which, unlike the journalist privilege, is absolute in the sense that it is not overcome even by a compelling showing of need. Where a party seeks disclosure from a witness who may have relevant information concerning allegedly privileged attorney-client communications, the fact that the witness may be asked questions that call for information as to privileged communications does not protect a witness from being deposed or called to testify at a trial or before a grand jury. Rather, the witness must appear and give testimony. When a question seeking disclosure of allegedly privileged material is posed, however, the holder of the alleged privilege may object and delay disclosure until a court rules on the objection. When an objection is made, however, the party seeking disclosure nevertheless is entitled to discover the dates and places of and the identities of the participants in the communications, the identities of others who were present and to whom the communications were disclosed, and the general subject matter (but not the content) of the communications. This permits the party seeking disclosure and, if need be, the court to know which communications are at issue, something about their general nature, whether they in fact were confidential, and whether any privilege has been waived by disclosure of the contents of the communications to persons other than the attorney and client. Once such a record is developed, the court rules on the objection."); *Elkins v. D.C.*, 250 F.R.D. 20, 27 (D.D.C. 2008) ("[T]he District cannot claim privilege pre-emptively, before any deposition question has been propounded."); *see SEC v. Kramer*, 778 F. Supp. 2d 1320, 1328 (M.D. Fla. 2011) ("Permitting the Commission in this instance to assert a blanket claim of privilege in response to a [Federal] Rule 30(b)(6) notice creates an unworkable circumstance in which a defendant loses a primary means of discovery without a meaningful review of his opponent's claim of privilege.").

43 Tex. R. Civ. P. 192.3(c) (defining discovery's scope as to testifying and consulting experts). See Chapter 7 (discussing expert discovery).

44 *Crown Cent. Petroleum Corp. v. Garcia*, 904 S.W.2d 125, 127 (Tex. 1995) (orig. proceeding).

45 *Crown Cent. Petroleum Corp. v. Garcia*, 904 S.W.2d 125, 128 (Tex. 1995) (orig. proceeding) (holding that the apex doctrine potentially applies "[w]hen a party seeks to depose a corporate president or other high level corporate official"); *In re Alcatel USA, Inc.*, 11 S.W.3d 173, 175 (Tex. 2000) (orig. proceeding) (same); *In re Baylor Univ.*, No. 01-20-00439-CV, 2020 Tex. App. LEXIS 9200, at *14, 2020 WL 6878411 (Tex. App.—Houston [1st Dist.] Nov. 24, 2020, orig. proceeding) (mem. op.) ("An apex deposition is the deposition of a corporate officer at the apex of the corporate hierarchy." (quoting *AMR Corp. v. Enlow*, 926 S.W.2d

because of the official's position in the organization.[46] If, however, the official is named as a party because the official, for example, participated in or committed the underlying tort, is a party to the contract at issue, or is an owner of the condemned land or damaged property at issue, the doctrine is inapplicable.[47] Nor does it apply when the official "has unique or superior knowledge of discoverable information."[48] This occurs when the official "is 'the only person with personal knowledge of the information sought[,]' 'arguably possesses relevant knowledge greater in quality or quantity than other available sources,'"[49] or has first-hand knowledge of the facts (e.g., as an eyewitness to the incident at issue or one of the principal negotiators of the contract at issue).[50] As explained by the Austin Court of Appeals:

640, 642 (Tex. App.—Fort Worth 1996, orig. proceeding))); *In re Sam Hous. Elec. Coop., Inc.*, No. 09-19-00285-CV, 2019 Tex. App. LEXIS 8845, at *8, 2019 WL 4865199 (Tex. App.—Beaumont Oct. 3, 2019, orig. proceeding) (per curiam) (mem. op.) (same).

46 *In re Miscavige*, 436 S.W.3d 430, 437 (Tex. App.—Austin 2014, orig. proceeding) ("The apex-deposition rule becomes a potential issue only when an executive's corporate position bears some relationship to the underlying information the deposing party seeks."); *In re Titus Cnty.*, 412 S.W.3d 28, 35, (Tex. App.—Texarkana 2013, orig. proceeding) ("[T]he doctrine applies 'only when the deponent has been noticed for deposition because of his corporate position.'" (quoting *Simon v. Bridewell*, 950 S.W.2d 439, 442 (Tex. App.—Waco 1997, orig. proceeding) (per curiam))).

The doctrine is applicable to governmental organizations. *E.g., Barnes v. Sulak*, No. 03-01-00159-CV, 2002 Tex. App. LEXIS 5727, at *13–15, 2002 WL 1804912 (Tex. App.—Austin Aug. 8, 2002, pet. denied) (mem. op.) (applying the apex doctrine to a noticed deposition of a county judge).

47 *E.g., In re Miscavige*, 436 S.W.3d 430, 438 (Tex. App.—Austin 2014, orig. proceeding) ("If a high-level executive is named as a defendant based on some dispute that is unrelated to his status as an executive, then the plaintiff has a right to obtain the executive's deposition just as he or she would any other party."); *In re Titus Cnty.*, 412 S.W.3d 28, 35 (Tex. App.—Texarkana 2013, orig. proceeding) (concluding that the apex doctrine did not apply in a condemnation case because the official was the landowner).

48 *In re Alcatel USA, Inc.*, 11 S.W.3d 173, 175 (Tex. 2000) (orig. proceeding); *accord Crown Cent. Petroleum Corp. v. Garcia*, 904 S.W.2d 125, 128 (Tex. 1995) (orig. proceeding); *In re Sam Hous. Elec. Coop., Inc.*, No. 09-19-00285-CV, 2019 Tex. App. LEXIS 8845, at *8, 2019 WL 4865199 (Tex. App.—Beaumont Oct. 3, 2019, orig. proceeding) (per curiam) (mem. op.); *In re Taylor*, 401 S.W.3d 69, 73–74 (Tex. App.—Houston [14th Dist.] 2009, orig. proceeding).

49 *In re TMX Fin. of Tex., Inc.*, 472 S.W. 3d 864, 872 (Tex. App.—Houston [1st Dist.] 2015, orig. proceeding) (quoting *In re Alcatel USA Inc.*, 11 S.W.3d 173, 170 (Tex. 2000) (orig. proceeding)).

50 *In re TMX Fin. of Tex.*, Inc., 472 S.W. 3d 864, 879 (Tex. App.—Houston [1st Dist.] 2015, orig. proceeding) (The apex doctrine "does not, for instance, protect corporate officials who have 'first-hand knowledge of certain facts.' Here, LoanStar presented evidence that Bielss was actively involved in TMX's marketing efforts and operations in Texas, regularly holding conference calls concerning marketing and performance goals with regional and district managers and occasionally visiting individual stores in Texas to inquire about marketing practices. Bielss was the one who informed McDonald, Vice President of Operations for Texas, that LoanStar had made allegations of improper conduct against TMX. We conclude that LoanStar has shown that Bielss arguably has 'unique or superior personal knowledge of discoverable information.'" (quoting *Boales v. Brighton Builders, Inc.*, 29 S.W.3d 159, 168 (Tex. App.—Houston [14th Dist.] 2000, pet. denied), and *Crown Cent. Petroleum Corp. v. Garcia*, 904 S.W.2d 125, 128 (Tex. 1995) (orig. proceeding))); *Boales v. Brighton Builders, Inc.*, 29 S.W.3d 159, 168 (Tex. App.—Houston [14th Dist.] 2000, pet. denied) ("First, we note that the 'apex' doctrine does not apply. Appellants do not seek to depose Krugh merely

> For example, if a party sought to depose the CEO of General Motors based on some alleged design flaw in a vehicle, then the deposition relates to her status as CEO, and the apex-deposition rule would be implicated. However, if a plaintiff sought to depose the same CEO because she witnessed a car accident, then her status as CEO would be irrelevant to the deposition, and the plaintiff would be entitled to take the CEO's deposition as if she were any other eyewitness.[51]

It, however, is unclear whether the apex doctrine applies when the high-level official is named as a defendant solely because he is an official of the organization.[52]

To prevent an apex deposition, the organization or high-level official must file a motion for a protective order or to quash the deposition notice, accompanied by an affidavit from the official denying any unique or superior knowledge of relevant facts.[53] The trial court then must "first determine whether the party seeking the deposition arguably has shown that the official has ***any unique or superior personal knowledge of***

---

because of his corporate position. Rather they seek to depose him because they allege he has first-hand knowledge of certain facts, that is, the advice he gave to a Perry Homes vice president during contract negotiations between Perry Homes and Wimpey and to Perry Homes' sales representatives during training sessions regarding buyer disclosure and the DTPA.").

[51] *In re Miscavige*, 436 S.W.3d 430, 437 (Tex. App.—Austin 2014, orig. proceeding); *accord Simon v. Bridewell*, 950 S.W.2d 439, 442 (Tex. App.—Waco 1997, orig. proceeding) (per curiam) ("A corporate officer is not exempt from deposition by the 'apex' doctrine merely because he is a corporate official. Rather, the doctrine may be invoked only when the deponent has been noticed for deposition because of his corporate position. For example, if the president of a Fortune 500 corporation personally witnesses a fatal car accident, he cannot avoid a deposition sought in connection with a resulting wrongful death action because of his 'apex' status.").

[52] *Compare In re Miscavige*, 436 S.W.3d 430, 438 (Tex. App.—Austin 2014, orig. proceeding) ("If an executive is sued based on an alleged tort, contract dispute, or other theory of liability that does not arise from actions he took in his capacity as an executive, then the executive is subject to deposition just as any other individual would be. Conversely, we conclude that if an apex executive is named as a defendant based on his capacity as an executive, then the apex doctrine is implicated and the *Crown Central* standard should be applied to a request for his deposition."), ***and In re TMX Fin. of Tex. Inc.***, 472 S.W. 3d 864, 873–76 (Tex. App.—Houston [1st Dist.] 2015, orig. proceeding) (following *Miscavige*), ***with In re Titus Cnty.***, 412 S.W.3d 28, 35 (Tex. App.—Texarkana 2013, orig. proceeding) (holding that the apex doctrine does not apply when a high-level office is named as a defendant), ***and Simon v. Bridewell***, 950 S.W.2d 439, 443 (Tex. App.—Waco 1997, orig. proceeding) (per curiam) (same).

[53] ***In re Alcatel USA, Inc.***, 11 S.W.3d 173, 175–76 (Tex. 2000) (orig. proceeding); ***Crown Cent. Petroleum Corp. v. Garcia***, 904 S.W.2d 125, 128 (Tex. 1995) (orig. proceeding); ***In re Baylor Univ.***, No. 01-20-00439-CV, 2020 Tex. App. LEXIS 9200, at *14, 2020 WL 6878411 (Tex. App.—Houston [1st Dist.] Nov. 24, 2020, orig. proceeding) (mem. op.); ***In re Sam Hous. Elec. Coop., Inc.***, No. 09-19-00285-CV, 2019 Tex. App. LEXIS 8845, at *8, 2019 WL 4865199 (Tex. App.—Beaumont Oct. 3, 2019, orig. proceeding) (per curiam) (mem. op.); ***In re Sw. Key Programs Inc.***, No. 13-19-00409-CV, 2019 Tex. App. LEXIS 8360, at *3, 2019 WL 4458799 (Tex. App.—Corpus Christi Sep. 17, 2019, orig. proceeding); ***In re SemGroup Corp.***, No. 04-16-00230-CV, 2016 Tex. App. LEXIS 5741, at *5, 2016 WL 3085875 (Tex. App.—San Antonio June 1, 2016, orig. proceeding) (mem. op.); ***In re TMX Fin. of Tex., Inc.***, 472 S.W. 3d 864, 872 (Tex. App.—Houston [1st Dist.] Aug. 20, 2015, orig. proceeding); ***In re Taylor***, 401 S.W.3d 69, 74 (Tex. App.—Houston [14th Dist.] 2009, orig. proceeding).

discoverable information."[54] A mere showing that the official has some knowledge of discoverable information or that the official knows about the complained-of activity is insufficient to warrant the apex deposition. As explained by the Texas Supreme Court:

> This evidence arguably shows that Kang may have discoverable information. But the first *Crown Central* guideline requires more; it requires that the person to be deposed arguably have "unique or superior personal knowledge of discoverable information." This requirement is not satisfied by merely showing that a high-level executive has some knowledge of discoverable information. If "some knowledge" were enough, the apex deposition guidelines would be meaningless; they would be virtually indistinguishable from the scope of general discovery. Although *Crown Central* did not elaborate on what character of knowledge makes it unique or superior, there must be some showing beyond mere relevance, such as evidence that a high-level executive is the only person with personal knowledge of the information sought or that the executive arguably possesses relevant knowledge greater in quality or quantity than other available sources.[55]

---

54 *Crown Cent. Petroleum Corp. v. Garcia*, 904 S.W.2d 125, 128 (Tex. 1995) (orig. proceeding) (emphasis added); *accord In re Daisy Mfg. Co.*, 17 S.W.3d 654, 656 (Tex. 2000) (orig. proceeding) (per curiam); *In re Alcatel USA, Inc.*, 11 S.W.3d 173, 175–76 (Tex. 2000); *In re Baylor Univ.*, No. 01-20-00439-CV, 2020 Tex. App. LEXIS 9200, at *15, 2020 WL 6878411 (Tex. App.—Houston [1st Dist.] Nov. 24, 2020) (mem. op.); *In re Sam Hous. Elec. Coop., Inc.*, No. 09-19-00285-CV, 2019 Tex. App. LEXIS 8845, at *8–9, 2019 WL 4865199 (Tex. App.—Beaumont Oct. 3, 2019, orig. proceeding) (per curiam) (mem. op.); *In re Sw. Key Programs Inc.*, No. 13-19-00409-CV, 2019 Tex. App. LEXIS 8360, at *3, 2019 WL 4458799 (Tex. App.—Corpus Christi Sep. 17, 2019, orig. proceeding); *In re Newport Classic Homes, L.P.*, No. 04-18-00126-CV, 2018 Tex. App. LEXIS 8231, at *11, 2018 WL 4903065 (Tex. App.—San Antonio Oct. 10, 2018, orig. proceeding) (mem. op.).

55 *In re Alcatel USA, Inc.*, 11 S.W.3d 173, 179 (Tex. 2000) (orig. proceeding); *accord In re Sam Hous. Elec. Coop., Inc.*, No. 09-19-00285-CV, 2019 Tex. App. LEXIS 8845, at *9–11, 2019 WL 4865199 (Tex. App.—Beaumont Oct. 3, 2019, orig. proceeding) (per curiam) (mem. op.) (holding that the plaintiff in a wrongful-death case asserting that the defendant electric cooperative negligently caused the decedent's death by cutting off electricity to his house without proper notice failed to establish that the cooperative's directors "possessed unique or superior personal knowledge" because the subject matter of the depositions was not "reasonably calculated to lead to the discovery of admissible evidence" and because the directors uncontroverted affidavits denied any personal knowledge about the circumstances of the decedent's death and that they were involved in the cooperative's day-to-day activities); *In re Baylor Univ.*, No. 01-20-00439-CV, 2020 Tex. App. LEXIS 9200, at *19–22 & n.4, 2020 WL 6878411 (Tex. App.—Houston [1st Dist.] Nov. 24, 2020) (mem. op.) (holding in a personal-injury suit arising out an sexual assault in college housing that (1) the college president did not have unique and superior knowledge because she was hired long after the alleged assault occurred and the mere fact that she made public statements about the campus' current safety and lessons learned from prior incidents was insufficient, and (2) rejecting an argument that "merely showing that [other] witness[es] cannot answer questions about an apex official's subjective intent [in making general statements regarding an incident does not] satisfies the deposition-seeking party's burden to demonstrate that the apex official has unique and superior knowledge [because i]f we agreed with [the plaintiff's] argument, the apex guidelines would be eviscerated for any apex official who has ever made a public statement"); *In re Newport Classic Homes, L.P.*, No. 04-18-00126-CV, 2018 Tex. App. LEXIS 8231, at *17–19, 2018 WL 4903065 (Tex. App.—San Antonio Oct. 10,

If the party seeking the deposition establishes the official has unique or superior personal knowledge, the motion must be denied and the apex deposition allowed.[56]

2018, orig. proceeding) (mem. op.) (holding in a personal-injury action by a subcontractor's employee against, among other others, a general contractor that the trial court abused its discretion in compelling the deposition of the general contractor's CEO, President, and owner, even though the executive "might possess some knowledge relevant to [the] suit," because (1) the evidence "fail[ed] to establish [the executive] is the only person with personal knowledge of subcontracts, change orders, or how the work is or is not progressing on the project—or that his knowledge of these matters is 'greater in quality or quantity than other available sources,'" (2) the evidence "amounted to nothing more than the simple, obvious recognition that the highest-ranking corporate officer of any corporation has the ultimate responsibility for all corporate decisions and falls far short of the [*Crown Central*] standard", and (3) even though the executive visited the project site regularly, "there [was] no evidence to support any assertion that [he] was at the worksite on the day [the plaintiff] was injured" (quoting *AMR Corp. v. Enlow*, 926 S.W.2d 640, 644 (Tex. App.—Fort Worth 1996, orig. proceeding))); *In re SemGroup Corp.*, No. 04-16-00230-CV, 2016 Tex. App. LEXIS 5741, at *6–8, 2016 WL 3085875 (Tex. App.—San Antonio June 1, 2016, orig. proceeding) (mem. op.) (holding that the plaintiffs in a wrongful-death case in which their decedent was killed in a traffic accident allegedly caused by the defendant's truck driver cellphone's use failed to establish that the defendant's Chief Executive Officer had superior knowledge merely because he "appointed a team to develop a corporate mobile device policy and offered input during the development of the policy" or because he was familiar with "discussions by industry safety experts regarding the value of a total ban on the use of mobile devices by drivers"); *In re Miscavige*, 436 S.W.3d 430, 436 (Tex. App.—Austin 2014, orig. proceeding) ("Although *Alcatel* was decided under the *Crown Central* standard, it extended the apex-deposition doctrine by establishing that allegations and evidence indicating that an apex executive must have known about the complained-of corporate activity is insufficient, in and of itself, to support taking an apex deposition."); *In re TMX Fin. of Tex. Inc.*, 472 S.W. 3d 864, 873–75 (Tex. App.—Houston [1st Dist.] 2015, orig. proceeding) (holding that the mere fact that the official was the sole member, manager, and employee of one of three related defendant-limited liability companies was insufficient to warrant taking the official's deposition); *In re Cont'l Airlines, Inc.*, 305 S.W.3d 849, 858 (Tex. App.—Houston [14th Dist.] 2010, orig. proceeding) (holding that the mere fact that an airline's Chief Executive Officer and Chairman gave a statement and answered questions at a press conference following an accident and sent a letter to the passengers expressing his concern about it was insufficient because "the information he gave at the press conference was provided to him by other Continental employees [and] he did not discuss with the deadheading pilots what occurred before, during, and after the accident; he has not received information about the cause of the accident in the executive briefs"); *AMR Corp. v. Enlow*, 926 S.W.2d 640, 644 (Tex. App.—Fort Worth 1996, orig. proceeding) (holding that testimony by the corporation's President, Chief Executive Officer, and Chairman that he had ultimate authority over any policy because he had "about all the authority he needs on most issues in business" amounted to "nothing more than the simple, obvious recognition that the highest-ranking corporate officer of any corporation has the ultimate responsibility for all corporate decisions and falls far short of the [*Crown Central*] standard").

[56] *In re Alcatel USA, Inc.*, 11 S.W.3d 173, 176 (Tex. 2000) (orig. proceeding) ("Under *Crown Central*, if the party seeking the deposition has 'arguably shown that the official has any unique or superior personal knowledge of discoverable information,' the trial court should deny the motion for protection and the party seeking discovery should be entitled to take the apex depositions."); *see In re Blue Creek Real Props., LLC*, No. 13-18-00308-CV, 2018 Tex. App. LEXIS 5809, at *3–4, 2018 WL 3583645 (Tex. App.—Corpus Christi July 26, 2018, orig. proceeding) (mem. op.) (holding that the trial court did not abuse its discretion in ordering the deposition of the CEO and Chairman of a third-party defendant in "a multi-

If, however, the party seeking the deposition does not make this showing, the trial court must "'first require the party seeking that deposition to attempt to obtain the discovery through less intrusive methods.'"[57] "Less intrusive methods" depend on "the circumstances of the case, but can include depositions of lower-level employees, the deposition of the corporation itself, and interrogatories and requests for production of documents directed to the corporation."[58]

"The discovering party may thereafter depose the apex official if, after making a 'good faith effort to obtain the discovery through less intrusive methods,' the party shows that (1) there is a reasonable indication that the official's deposition is calculated to lead to the discovery of admissible evidence, and (2) the less-intrusive methods are unsatisfactory, insufficient or inadequate."[59] However, "[m]erely completing some less-intrusive discovery does not trigger an automatic right to depose the apex official."[60] Even if the showing is met, as with any deposition, the trial court retains discretion to restrict the apex deposition's duration, scope, and location under Texas Rule 192.6, which governs protective orders.[61]

---

party suit over the construction of a grass turf runway" on a ranch because the executive "ha[d] unique and superior personal knowledge of discoverable information related to the construction project at issue pertaining to, inter alia, the timeline for completion and various design decisions pertaining to the project, including the style and size for the hangar, the number of airplanes to be stored there, the size and construction materials for the ramp, the runway width and length, the installation of an irrigation system, and the site layout and because the mandamus record contains flatly conflicting statements by various witnesses regarding [executive's] knowledge of the project").

57 *In re Daisy Mfg. Co.*, 17 S.W.3d 654, 656 (Tex. 2000) (orig. proceeding) (per curiam) (quoting *Crown Cent. Petroleum Corp. v. Garcia*, 904 S.W.2d 125, 128 (Tex. 1995) (orig. proceeding)); *accord In re Baylor Univ.*, No. 01-20-00439-CV, 2020 Tex. App. LEXIS 9200, at *16, 2020 WL 6878411 (Tex. App.—Houston [1st Dist.] Nov. 24, 2020, orig. proceeding) (mem. op.); *In re Newport Classic Homes, L.P.*, No. 04-18-00126-CV, 2018 Tex. App. LEXIS 8231, at *11, 20–21, 2018 WL 4903065 (Tex. App.—San Antonio Oct. 10, 2018, orig. proceeding) (mem. op.); *In re SemGroup Corp.*, No. 04-16-00230-CV, 2016 Tex. App. LEXIS 5741, at *6, 2016 WL 3085875 (Tex. App.—San Antonio June 1, 2016, orig. proceeding) (mem. op.).

58 *In re TMX Fin. of Tex. Inc.*, 472 S.W. 3d 864, 873 (Tex. App.—Houston [1st Dist.] 2015, orig. proceeding); *accord Crown Cent. Petroleum Corp. v. Garcia*, 904 S.W.2d 125, 128 (Tex. 1995) (orig. proceeding); *In re Baylor Univ.*, No. 01-20-00439-CV, 2020 Tex. App. LEXIS 9200, at *14, 2020 WL 6878411 (Tex. App.—Houston [1st Dist.] Nov. 24, 2020, orig. proceeding) (mem. op.).

59 *In re Daisy Mfg. Co.*, 17 S.W.3d 654, 657 (Tex. 2000) (orig. proceeding) (per curiam) (quoting *Crown Cent. Petroleum Corp. v. Garcia*, 904 S.W.2d 125, 128 (Tex. 1995) (orig. proceeding)); *accord In re Alcatel USA, Inc.*, 11 S.W.3d 173, 176 (Tex. 2000) (orig. proceeding); *In re Newport Classic Homes, L.P.*, No. 04-18-00126-CV, 2018 Tex. App. LEXIS 8231, at *11, 20–22, 2018 WL 4903065 (Tex. App.—San Antonio Oct. 10, 2018, orig. proceeding) (mem. op.); *In re TMX Fin. of Tex. Inc.*, 472 S.W. 3d 864, 872 (Tex. App.—Houston [1st Dist.] Aug. 20, 2015, orig. proceeding).

60 *In re Daisy Mfg. Co.*, 17 S.W.3d 654, 657–58 (Tex. 2000) (orig. proceeding) (per curiam); *accord In re TMX Fin. of Tex. Inc.*, 472 S.W. 3d 864, 872 (Tex. App.—Houston [1st Dist.] 2015, orig. proceeding); *In re Cont'l Airlines, Inc.*, 305 S.W.3d 849, 859 (Tex. App.—Houston [14th Dist.] 2010, orig. proceeding).

61 *Crown Cent. Petroleum Corp. v. Garcia*, 904 S.W.2d 125, 128 (Tex. 1995) (orig. proceeding) ("As with any deponent, the trial court retains discretion to restrict the duration, scope and location of the deposition."); Tex. R. Civ. P. 192.6(b)(4) (allowing the trial court to issue a protective order that a deposition be taken only "upon such terms and conditions or at the

"With regard to apex depositions, the [Texas S]upreme [C]ourt has specifically held that a party may seek mandamus relief to determine whether the trial court correctly ordered an apex deposition."[62]

11-1:1.5 Depositions of Organizations (i.e., Representative Depositions)

Under Texas Rules 199.2, 200.1, and 202.1, a party—both during discovery in an action or in a presuit deposition to perpetuate testimony or investigate a claim or suit under Texas Rule 202—can depose an organization itself instead of merely its officers, directors, employees, or agents. Texas Rule 199.2(b)(1) sets forth the procedure for doing so:

> The [deposition] notice must state the name of the witness, which may be either an individual or a public or private corporation, partnership, association, governmental agency, or other organization. If an organization is named as the witness, the notice must describe with reasonable particularity the matters on which examination is requested. In response, the organization named in the notice must—a reasonable time before the deposition—designate one or more individuals to testify on its behalf and set forth, for each individual designated, the matters on which the individual will testify. Each individual designated must testify as to matters that are known or reasonably available to the organization. This subdivision does not preclude taking a deposition by any other procedure authorized by these rules.[63]

---

time and place directed by the court"). See Chapter 4, section 4-5 (discussing protective orders).

[62] *In re Newport Classic Homes, L.P.,* No. 04-18-00126-CV, 2018 Tex. App. LEXIS 8231, at *5, 2018 WL 4903065 (Tex. App.—San Antonio Oct. 10, 2018, orig. proceeding) (mem. op.) (citing *In re Alcatel USA, Inc.*, 11 S.W.3d 173, 175 (Tex. 2000) (orig. proceeding)); *accord In re Baylor Univ.*, No. 01-20-00439-CV, 2020 Tex. App. LEXIS 9200, at *13, 2020 WL 6878411 (Tex. App.—Houston [1st Dist.] Nov. 24, 2020, orig. proceeding) (mem. op.); *In re Sam Hous. Elec. Coop., Inc.*, No. 09-19-00285-CV, 2019 Tex. App. LEXIS 8845, at *8, 2019 WL 4865199 (Tex. App.—Beaumont Oct. 3, 2019, orig. proceeding) (per curiam) (mem. op.); *In re Blue Creek Real Props., LLC,* No. 13-18-00308-CV, 2018 Tex. App. LEXIS 5809, at *3–4, 2018 WL 3583645 (Tex. App.—Corpus Christi July 26, 2018, orig. proceeding) (mem. op.).

[63] Tex. R. Civ. P. 199.2(b)(1). Texas Rule 201.1, governing depositions upon written question, adopts the procedure of Texas Rule 199.2(b)(1): "The [deposition] notice must comply with [Texas] Rule 199.1(b)[.]" Tex. R. Civ. P. 201.1. So does Texas Rule 202.5, which governs presuit depositions. *See* Tex. R. Civ. P. 202.5 (noting that "depositions authorized by this rule are governed by the rules applicable to depositions of nonparties in a pending suit," which in turn allow for representative depositions). Texas Rule 176.6(b), which relates to subpoenas, similarly provides: "If a subpoena commanding testimony is directed to a corporation, partnership, association, governmental agency, or other organization, and the matters on which examination is requested are described with reasonable particularity, the organization must designate one or more persons to testify on its behalf as to matters known or reasonably available to the organization." Tex. R. Civ. P. 176.6(b).

Texas Rule 199.2(b)(1) is based on Federal Rule 30(b)(6),[64] which was adopted to balance the needs of parties seeking discovery from an organization and the organization itself. Both Rules protect the party seeking discovery from the organization by preventing "bandying" by organizational witnesses, each of whom denies knowledge of relevant information or facts known by, or reasonably available to, the organization.[65] At the same time, the Rules protect the organization from multiple depositions of its officers and employees by parties taking "shots in the dark" trying to identify

[64] *See In re Fina Oil & Chem. Co.*, No. 13-98-640-CV, 1999 Tex. App. LEXIS 1751, at *14–15, 1999 WL 33589153 (Tex. App.—Corpus Christi Mar. 11, 1999, orig. proceeding) (not designated for publication) (noting that former Texas "Rule 201(4) is patterned after Federal Rule of Civil Procedure 30(b)(6)" and following federal cases interpreting the Federal Rule); *Hosp. Corp. of Am. v. Farrar*, 733 S.W.2d 393, 394–95 (Tex. App.—Fort Worth 1987, orig. proceeding) (equating former Texas Rule 201(4) to Federal Rule 30(b)(6) and following federal cases interpreting the Federal Rule).

Federal Rule 30(b)(6) provides:

> In its notice or subpoena, a party may name as the deponent a public or private corporation, a partnership, an association, a governmental agency, or other entity and must describe with reasonable particularity the matters for examination. The named organization must then designate one or more officers, directors, or managing agents, or designate other persons who consent to testify on its behalf; and it may set out the matters on which each person designated will testify. A subpoena must advise a nonparty organization of its duty to make this designation. The persons designated must testify about information known or reasonably available to the organization. This paragraph (6) does not preclude a deposition by any other procedure allowed by these rules.

There is one significant difference between Texas Rule 199.2(b)(1) and Federal Rule 30(b)(6): the Texas Rule requires the organization to designate the matters on which each representative will testify, *see* Tex. R. Civ. P. 199.2(b)(1) (providing that the organization "*must* . . . set forth, for each individual designated, the matters on which the individual will testify") (emphasis added), whereas the Federal Rule does not, *see* Fed. R. Civ. P. 30(b)(6) (providing that the organization "*may* set out the matters on which each person designated will testify") (emphasis added).

[65] Fed. R. Civ. P. 30, Advisory Committee Note to 1970 Amend. ("[Federal Rule 30(b)(6)] will curb the 'bandying' by which officers or managing agents of a corporation are deposed in turn but each disclaims knowledge of facts that are clearly known to persons in the organization and thereby to it."); *see Brazos River Auth. v. GE Ionics, Inc.*, 469 F.3d 416, 432–33 (5th Cir. 2006) ("[Federal] Rule 30(b)(6) is designed 'to avoid the possibility that several officers and managing agents might be deposed in turn, with each disclaiming personal knowledge of facts that are clearly known to persons within the organization and thus to the organization itself.'" (footnote omitted) (quoting 8A Charles A. Wright, Arthur R. Miller & Richard L. Marcus, *Federal Practice and Procedure* § 2103, at 33 (2d ed. 1994))); *Russo v. Aerojet Rocketdyne, Inc.*, No. MDL 875, 2020 U.S. Dist. LEXIS 140208, at *42, 2020 WL 4530703 (E.D. Pa. Aug. 6, 2020) ("The Third Circuit has noted that the purpose of [Federal] Rule 30(b)(6) is to 'curb the "bandying by which officers or managing agents of a corporation are deposed in turn but each disclaims knowledge" of relevant facts.'" (quoting *Black Horse Lane Assoc., L.P. v. Dow Chem. Corp.*, 228 F.3d 275, 304 (3d Cir. 2000))); *N. Ala. Fabricating Co. v. Bedeschi Mid-W. Conveyor Co.*, No. 16-cv-2740-DDC-TJJ, 2018 U.S. Dist. LEXIS 756, at *16–17, 2018 WL 276772 (D. Kan. Jan. 3, 2018) (same); *Murphy v. Kmart Corp.*, 255 F.R.D. 497, 504 (D.S.D. 2009) (same).

the ones who have relevant information.[66] They also give the organization control over the person to be deposed.[67]

A representative deposition can be taken of both party and nonparty organizations.[68] If the organization designates more than one individual to testify on its behalf, each individual is considered a separate witness for purposes of the six-hour, per-deposition time limit of Texas Rule 199.5(c).[69]

Unlike the typical deposition, a representative deposition is akin to answering interrogatories. In fact, the 1970 Advisory Committee Notes to the 1970 amendments to Federal Rule 30(b), in reference to the burden on an organization to prepare its witness, recognized this fact: "This burden is not essentially different from that of answering interrogatories under Federal Rule of Civil Procedure 33."[70] Thus, as discussed below, as with interrogatories, the representative deposition notice must "describe with reasonable particularity the matters on which examination is requested."[71] Based on this advanced notice, the organization's designated witnesses are required to gather the information needed to fully answer questions about the matters on which they have been designated to testify, with the goal of setting forth the full breadth of the organization's knowledge about them.[72] This is similar to the process of answering interrogatories and generally, as is common with answering interrogatories, requires counsel's assistance to ensure accuracy and completeness and to avoid the inadvertent disclosure of privileged information.

11-1:1.5a The Representative Deposition Notice

Under Texas Rules 199.2 and 200.1, the party seeking an organization's deposition must serve a deposition notice naming the organization as the deponent.[73] The notice

[66] *E.g.*, Fed. R. Civ. P. 30, Advisory Committee Note to 1970 Amend. (Federal Rule 30(b)(6) "should also assist organizations which find that an unnecessarily large number of their officers and agents are being deposed by a party uncertain of who in the organization has knowledge."); *see Murphy v. Kmart Corp.*, 255 F.R.D. 497, 504 (D.S.D. 2009) (Federal Rule 30(b) "protects the organization by eliminating unnecessary and unproductive depositions of employees who have no knowledge of the topics at issue"); *U.S. v. Taylor*, 166 F.R.D. 356, 360 (M.D.N.C. 1996), *aff'd*, 166 F.R.D. 367 (M.D.N.C. 1996) (Federal Rule 30(b)(6) "was added in 1970 . . . to assist corporations which found an unnecessarily large number of their officers and agents were being deposed.").

[67] *E.g., QBE Ins. Corp. v. Jorda Enters.*, 277 F.R.D. 676, 687 (S.D. Fla. 2012) ("The rule gives the corporation being deposed more control by allowing it to designate and prepare a witness to testify on the corporation's behalf."); *U.S v. Taylor*, 166 F.R.D. 356, 360 (M.D.N.C. 1996), *aff'd*, 166 F.R.D. 367 (M.D.N.C. 1996) (same).

[68] *See* Tex. R. Civ. P. 176.6(b), 199.1(a), 199.2(b), 200.1(a), 200.1(b), 202.5.

[69] Tex. R. Civ. P. 199 cmt. 2 to 1999 change ("For purposes of [Texas] Rule 199.5, each person designated by an organization under [Texas] Rule 199.2(b)(1) is a separate witness.").

[70] Fed. R. Civ. P. 30, Advisory Committee Note to 1970 Amend.

[71] Tex. R. Civ. P. 199.2(b)(1); *see also* Tex. R. Civ. P. 176.6(a) (requiring the same for a subpoena for a nonparty organization's deposition), 200.1(b) (incorporating Texas Rule 199.2(b)(1)'s requirement for depositions upon written questions). The particularity requirement for a representative deposition is discussed in Chapter 11, section 11-1:1.5c.

[72] See notes 114–22 and accompanying text (discussing the organization's duty of reasonable inquiry in connection with a representative deposition).

[73] Tex. R. Civ. P. 199.2(b)(1) ("The notice must state the name of the witness, which may be either an individual or a public or private corporation, partnership, association,

alone is sufficient to trigger a duty to respond by the party organization, whereas a nonparty organization must be served with the notice and a subpoena.[74] The representative deposition notice, unlike one for an individual's deposition, "must describe with reasonable particularity the matters on which examination is requested."[75] Nothing in the Texas discovery rules, however, permits a party to serve a trial subpoena requiring an organization to designate representatives to testify about topics specified in the subpoena.[76]

The following questions arise regarding representative deposition notices. *First*, can the noticing party require the organization to designate specific officers, directors, or employees to testify on its behalf or, alternatively, require the organization to

---

governmental agency, or other organization."), 200.1(b) ("The notice must comply with [Texas] Rule[] . . . 199.2(b)[.]").

74 Tex. R. Civ. P. 199.3 ("A party may compel the witness to attend the oral deposition by serving the witness with a subpoena under [Texas] Rule 176. If the witness is a party or is retained by, employed by, or otherwise subject to the control of a party, however, service of the notice of oral deposition upon the party's attorney has the same effect as a subpoena served on the witness."), 200.2 ("A party may compel the witness to attend the deposition on written questions by serving the witness with a subpoena under [Texas] Rule 176. If the witness is a party or is retained by, employed by, or otherwise subject to the control of a party, however, service of the notice of oral deposition upon the party's attorney has the same effect as a subpoena served on the witness."), 205.1 ("A party may compel discovery from a nonparty—that is, a person who is not a party or subject to a party's control—only by obtaining a court order under [Texas] Rules 196.7, 202, or 204, or by serving a subpoena compelling: (a) an oral deposition; (b) a deposition on written questions; (c) a request for production of documents or tangible things, pursuant to [Texas] Rule 199.2(b)(5) or [Texas] Rule 200.1(b), served with a notice of deposition on oral examination or written questions; and (d) a request for production of documents and tangible things under this Rule.").

75 Tex. R. Civ. P. 199.2(b)(1); *accord* Tex. R. Civ. P. 176.6(b) ("If a subpoena commanding testimony is directed to a corporation, partnership, association, governmental agency, or other organization, and the matters on which examination is requested are described with reasonable particularity, the organization must designate one or more persons to testify on its behalf as to matters known or reasonably available to the organization."), 200.1(b) ("The notice must comply with [Texas] Rule[] . . . 199.2(b) . . . ."); *cf. Alexander v. FBI*, 186 F.R.D. 137, 139 (D.D.C. 1998) ("[B]efore defendant EOP even needed to designate a witness under the notice of deposition, plaintiffs must have 'described with reasonable particularity the matters on which examination is requested.'" (quoting Federal Rule 30(b)(6))).

76 *In re FedEx Ground Package Sys.*, No. 14-19-00861-CV, 2020 Tex. App. LEXIS 4188, at *13–14, 2020 WL 2832683 (Tex. App.—Houston [14th Dist.] May 28, 2020, orig. proceeding) (mem. op.) ("FedEx contends that there is no authority under which the trial court could compel FedEx to produce an unnamed corporate representative to testify at trial about a list of 25 topics. . . . We may look to federal authority for guidance when the state law mirrors the federal law. In interpreting [Federal] Rule 30(b)(6), federal courts hold that [Federal] Rule 30(b)(6) does not allow a party to subpoena a corporate representative to compel testimony at trial. Following the federal courts' interpretation of [Federal] Rule 30(b)(6), we conclude that [Texas] Rule 199.2(b)(1) similarly does not provide for trial subpoenas with designated topics." (footnote omitted) (citing *Hill v. Homeward Residential, Inc.*, 799 F.3d 544, 553 (6th Cir. 2015), *Dopson-Troutt v. Novartis Pharms. Corp.*, 295 F.R.D. 536, 539–40 (M.D. Fla. 2013), *MC Asset Recovery, LLC v. Castex Energy, Inc.*, No. 4:07-CV-076-Y, 2013 U.S. Dist. LEXIS 197278, at *2–3, 2013 WL 12171724 (N.D. Tex. Jan. 7, 2013), and *Hill v. Nat'l R.R. Passenger Corp.*, No. 88-5277, 1989 U.S. Dist. LEXIS 9011, at 81, 1989 WL 87621 (E.D. La. July 28, 1989))).

designate an individual with the most knowledge or with personal knowledge about the matters identified in the notice? *Second*, what constitutes "reasonable particularity?" *Third*, is the noticing party, during the deposition, limited to asking questions only about the subject matters in the deposition notice or those matters for which the representative has been designated to testify? *Fourth*, what is the proper way to object to a deposition notice that, for example, is not reasonably particular or purports to require the organization to produce a specific officer or employee to testify on its behalf? The answers to these questions are discussed below.

11-1:1.5b The Organization Is Not Required to Produce a Specific Individual as Its Representative or an Individual with the Most Knowledge About the Notice's Subject Matters or Even One with Personal Knowledge About Them

Representative deposition notices often attempt to designate the specific officer, director, or employee who the noticing party wants to depose on the organization's behalf. For example, the notice might state: "Pursuant to Texas Rule of Civil Procedure 199.2(b)(1), Plaintiff will depose John Smith, Defendant's Chief Financial Officer, on the following subjects as Defendant X Corporation's representative." Other times, the notice will ask the organization to produce a representative with "the most knowledge" about its subject matters or one with "personal knowledge" about them. Such notices are improper.

As is clear from Texas Rule 199.2(b)(1)'s language, the organization has the sole right to designate the individual(s) who will testify on its behalf: "the *organization* . . . *must* . . . designate one or more individuals to testify on its behalf[.]"[77] For example, in *Cleveland v. Palmby*, a federal district court rejected a motion to compel the defendant corporation to produce a specific employee as its representative, reasoning that:

> [Federal Rule 30(b)(6)] provides that a party who is unable to name the specific employee or agent of an organization that he wishes to depose, can simply name the organization as the deponent and describe with reasonable particularity the matters on which examination is requested. It is then the duty of the organization to name one or more persons who consent to testify on its behalf and these persons must testify as to matters known or reasonably available to the organization. This Rule does not provide that a party can specifically name an employee of an organization and then require the organization to designate such employee as a witness to testify on behalf of the organization.[78]

---

[77] Tex. R. Civ. P. 199.2(b)(1) (emphasis added).

[78] *Cleveland v. Palmby*, 75 F.R.D. 654, 657 (W.D. Okla. 1977); *accord Wood v. Paccar, Inc.*, No. 19-cv-1010-LRR, 2020 U.S. Dist. LEXIS 28116, at *30, 2020 WL 831142 (N.D. Iowa Feb. 19, 2020) ("[Federal] Rule 30(b)(6) does not give the party who issues the notice the right to pick the designee."); *McIntyre v. BF Capital Holding, LLC*, No. 3:14cv33(RNC), 2016 U.S. Dist. LEXIS 127873, at *4, 2016 WL 5219445 (D. Conn. Sept. 20, 2016) ("The Petrucci defendants[] ask the court to order MAB to designate Cottrell as its corporate designee and produce him for a [Federal] Rule 30(b)(6) deposition. That request ignores an important facet of [Federal] Rule 30(b)(6): the noticed organization is empowered with the right—and obligation—to designate the person(s) to testify on its behalf. There is no procedural vehicle for the Petrucci defendants to choose MAB's corporate designee. Nor does the court have authority to enter an order requiring MAB to designate and produce Cottrell as its

In the same vein, a deposition notice requiring the organization to designate an individual with personal knowledge of the notice's subject matters is improper.[79]

30(b)(6) witness."); *Wultz v. Bank of China Ltd.*, 298 F.R.D. 91, 99 (S.D.N.Y. 2014) ("[T]here is no binding authority permitting the court to compel a corporation deponent to designate a specific person to be its [Federal] Rule 30(b)(6) witness."); *Thornton v. UL Enters., LLC*, No. Civ. 09-287E, 2011 U.S. Dist. LEXIS 41149, at *3–4, 2011 WL 1459725 (W.D. Pa. Apr. 14, 2011) (holding defective, under Federal Rule 30(b)(6), an "Amended Notice of Deposition of Steve Larson" stating that "NOTICE is hereby given that the deposition upon oral examination of Steve Larson, has been rescheduled and will be taken, pursuant to Fed.R.Civ.P. 30" because "[t]he Notice does not designate whether Mr. Larson is to testify in his individual capacity and/or on behalf of STNA"); *Wultz v. Bank of China Ltd.*, 298 F.R.D. 91, 99 (S.D.N.Y. 2014) ("Of course the court cannot compel Hapoalim to designate a *specific* person. But a court *can* compel Hapoalim to select a designee and educate her in accordance with its duty under [Federal] Rule 30(b)(6)."); *Booker v. Mass. Dep't of Pub. Health*, 246 F.R.D. 387, 389 (D. Mass. 2007) ("Plaintiff may not impose his belief on Defendants as to whom to designate as a 30(b)(6) witness."); *Operative Plasterers' & Cement Masons' Int'l Ass'n v. Benjamin*, 144 F.R.D. 87, 89–90 (N.D. Ind. 1992) (holding defective, under Federal Rule 30(b)(6), a deposition notice identifying the proposed deponents as "Mr. Beam," "Vince Panepinto," "Dominic Martell[,]" and "Mr. Martinez" and stating that the depositions were being taken pursuant to "Federal Rules of Civil Procedure 26, 30(b)(6) and 32(a)(2)"); *Fraser Yachts Fla., Inc. v. Milne*, No. 05-21168-Civ-JORDAN/TORRES, 2007 U.S. Dist. LEXIS 27546, at *6, 2007 WL 1113251 (S.D. Fla. Apr. 13, 2007) ("When a party notices a [Federal] Rule 30(b)(6) deposition, however, it leaves to the corporation's discretion who it chooses to be its representative."); *Sears v. Am. Entm't Grp.*, No 94 C 0165, 1995 U.S. Dist. LEXIS 1754, at *1, 1995 WL 66411 (N.D. Ill. Feb. 10, 1995) ("In their motion for protective order, defendants initially argue that the Notice of Deposition is defective. This argument is well taken. The Notice does not identify whether the deposition is being taken pursuant to Federal Rule of Civil Procedure 30(b)(1) or 30(b)(6). Since plaintiff has designated the deponents, the Notice cannot be made pursuant to [Federal] Rule 30(b)(6)."); *GTE Prods. Corp. v. Gee*, 115 F.R.D. 67, 68–69 (D. Mass. 1987) (holding defective, under Federal Rule 30(b)(6), deposition notices stating that the defendants "'will take the deposition upon oral examination of [the plaintiff] GTE Products Corporation, by [a named person] on [a given date]'").

[79] *In re Luna*, No. 13-16-00467-CV, 2016 Tex. App. LEXIS 12011, at *21–22, 2016 WL 6576879 (Tex. App.—Corpus Christi Nov. 7, 2016, no pet.) (mem. op.) ("Fundamentally, State Farm asserts that its corporate representative will not have personal knowledge of the facts at issue in this lawsuit.... [Texas] Rule 199.1(a) permits the deposition 'of any person or entity' without any limitation that the proposed deponent have personal knowledge of the facts." (quoting Tex. R. Civ. P. 199.1(a))); *cf. PPM Fin., Inc. v. Norandal USA, Inc.*, 392 F.3d 889, 894–95 (7th Cir. Ill. 2004) ("[A]s Jackson correctly points out, Krupinski was designated as a witness under Fed. R. Civ. P. 30(b)(6), which authorized him to testify not only to matters within his personal knowledge but also to 'matters known or reasonably available to the organization.' Thus, Krupinski was free to testify to matters outside his personal knowledge as long as they were within the corporate rubric.") (citation omitted); *JAM Indus. USA, LLC v. Gibson Brands, Inc.*, No. 19 MC 508-LTS, 2020 U.S. Dist. LEXIS 124293, at *11 (S.D.N.Y. July 15, 2020) ("A witness designated pursuant to [Federal] Rule 30(b)(6) need not have personal knowledge of the events at issue but, rather, must testify about information known or reasonably available to the organization."); *Richardson v. Fiat Chrysler Auto. (FCA) US, LLC*, No. 7:19-CV-15 (HL), 2020 U.S. Dist. LEXIS 20076, at *5, 2020 WL 592329 (M.D. Ga. Feb. 6, 2020) ("[Federal] Rule 30(b)(6) deponents do not need personal knowledge of the events because their testimony 'represents the collective knowledge of the corporation, not of the specific individual deponents.'" (quoting *QBE Ins. Corp. v. Jorda Enters., Inc.*, 277 F.R.D. 676, 688 (S.D. Fla. 2012))); *Entrust Datacard Corp. v. Zeiser GmbH*, No. 3:17-cv-110-

Because the organization does not have to designate a representative with personal knowledge, it follows that it also does not have to designate the "most knowledgeable" person. As explained by a federal court:

> [Federal] Rule 30(b)(6) does not expressly or implicitly require the corporation or entity to produce the "person most knowledgeable" for the corporate deposition. Nevertheless, many lawyers issue notices and subpoenas which purport to require the producing party to provide "the most knowledgeable" witness. Not only does the rule not provide for this type of discovery demand, but the request is also fundamentally inconsistent with the purpose and dynamics of the rule. As noted, the witness/designee need not have *any* personal knowledge, so the "*most* knowledgeable" designation is illogical. Moreover, a corporation may have good grounds not to produce the "most knowledgeable" witness for a 30(b)(6) deposition. For example, that witness might be comparatively inarticulate, he might have a criminal conviction, she might be out of town for an extended trip, he might not be photogenic (for a videotaped deposition), she might prefer to avoid the entire process, or the corporation might want to save the witness for trial. From a practical perspective, it might be difficult to determine which witness is the "most" knowledgeable on any given topic. And permitting a requesting party to insist on the production of the most knowledgeable witness could lead to time-wasting disputes over the comparative level of the witness's knowledge. For example, if the rule authorized a demand for the most knowledgeable witness, then the requesting party could presumably obtain sanctions if the witness produced had the *second* most amount of knowledge. This result is impractical, inefficient and problematic, but it would be required by a procedure authorizing a demand for the "most" knowledgeable witness. But the rule says no such thing.[80]

J-39MCR, 2019 U.S. Dist. LEXIS 223891, at *11 (M.D. Fla. 2019) ("A [Federal] Rule 30(b)(6) witness does not need to possess personal knowledge of the subject matter designated. 'The mere fact that an organization no longer employs a person with knowledge on the specified topics does not relieve the organization of the duty to prepare and produce an appropriate designee.'" (citation omitted) (quoting *QBE Ins. Corp. v. Jorda Enters., Inc.*, 277 F.R.D. 676, 689 (S.D. Fla. 2012))); *Elan Microelectronics Corp. v. Pixcir Microelectronics Co.*, No. 2:10-cv-00014-GMN-PAL, 2013 U.S. Dist. LEXIS 114164, at *14, 2013 WL 4101813 (D. Nev. Aug. 7, 2013) (same).

[80] *QBE Ins. Corp. v. Jorda Enters.*, 277 F.R.D. 676, 688–89 (S.D. Fla. 2012); *accord In re Family Dollar Stores of Tex., LLC*, No. 04-14-00656-CV, 2015 Tex. App. LEXIS 4325, at *7, 2015 WL 1938662 (Tex. App—San Antonio Apr. 29, 2015, orig. proceeding) (mem. op.) ("The corporation is entitled to present one or more witnesses to meet this obligation with respect to the topics specified in the corporate representative deposition notice. There is no obligation to present the 'most knowledgeable' person, or an individual with personal knowledge of the specified topics, but only a person reasonably prepared to address the subject matters designated in the notice.") (citation omitted); *JAM Indus. USA, LLC v. Gibson Brands, Inc.*, No. 19 MC 508-LTS, 2020 U.S. Dist. LEXIS 124293, at *11 (S.D.N.Y. July 15, 2020) ("A witness designated pursuant to [Federal] Rule 30(b)(6) need not have personal knowledge of the events at issue but, rather, must testify about information known or reasonably available to the organization."); *González-Berrios v. Mennonite Gen. Hosp., Inc.*, No. 18-1146 (RAM), 2019 U.S. Dist. LEXIS 171104, at *17 (D.P.R. 2019) ("While under Fed. R. Civ. P. 30(b)(6) deposition representatives need not have personal knowledge of the matters as to which they will testify, they must be duly prepared to testify as to matters in the notice

11-1:1.5c Reasonable Particularity

"Reasonable particularity" with respect to the "matters" on which the organization is to be examined, like "reasonable particularity" with respect to a Texas Rule 196 production request, is not susceptible to a precise definition.[81] Rather, it depends on whether a reasonable person would understand about what matters the notice

---

with the 'information known or reasonably available to the organization' and their answers are binding on the organization. Moreover, 'it is settled law that a party need not produce the organizational representative with the greatest knowledge about a subject; instead, it need only produce a person with knowledge whose testimony will be binding on the party.'" (quoting *Mitsui & Co. (U.S.A), Inc. v. Puerto Rico Water Res. Auth., Inc.*, 93 F.R.D. 62, 67 (D.P.R. 1981), and *Rodriguez v. Pataki*, 293 F. Supp. 2d 305, 311 (S.D.N.Y. 2003))); *Estate of Betty Goldberg v. Goss-Jewett Co., Inc.*, No. ED CV 14-01872 DSF (AFMx), 2016 U.S. Dist. LEXIS 190674, at *11, 2016 WL 7471427 (Cal. Feb. 19, 2016) ("Applicants are incorrect when they refer to the obligation under [Federal] Rule 30(b)(6) as requiring designation of the 'person most knowledgeable.'"); *Eid v. KLM*, No. 14CV9066-PKC-FM, 2015 U.S. Dist. LEXIS 136409, at *5–6, 2015 WL 5772951 (S.D.N.Y. Oct. 2, 2015) ("[I]t was not improper for the Defendants to fail to produce Abelmoneim. '[I]t is settled law that a party need not produce the organizational representative with the greatest knowledge about a subject; instead, it need only produce a person with knowledge whose testimony will be binding on the party.' Here, the Defendants met that burden." (quoting *Rodriguez v. Pataki*, 293 F. Supp. 2d 305, 311 (S.D.N.Y. 2003))); *Aldridge v. Lake Cnty. Sheriff's Office*, No. 11 C 3041, 2012 U.S. Dist. LEXIS 102514, at *10, 2012 WL 3023340 (N.D. Ill. July 24, 2012) ("While the 'most knowledgeable person' about the chain of custody may, ultimately, have been Ms. Robin's colleague because he took the plastic coyote into evidence and released it, the most knowledgeable person is not required under [Federal] Rule 30(b)(6)."); *Towers Condo. Ass'n v. Pac. Ins. Co.*, No. 10-24310-CIV-GRAHAM/GOODMAN, 2011 U.S. Dist. LEXIS 138953, at *24–25, 2011 WL 6190160 (S.D. Fla. Dec. 2, 2011) ("Pacific frames the issue as one of Kendall's failure to provide the person with *the* most knowledge concerning the relevant issues, but this is not what [Federal] Rule 30(b)(6) requires. Under the Rule, the deponent selected to be the designee does not even need to have personal knowledge of the subject matter of the testimony so long as he can *become* knowledgeable of information that is generally known to the organization through reasonable preparation. Because [Federal] Rule 30(b)(6) imposes an obligation *on the organization* to select an individual to testify, the party seeking discovery is not entitled to insist on a specific person as the corporate representative and it likewise cannot demand the testimony of a designee the with the 'most' knowledge of a given matter.").

Because Texas Rule 199.2(b)(1) requires the organization to identify each of its representatives and the topics on which they will testify "a reasonable time before the deposition," practitioners often respond to the designation by amending the deposition notice to state, for example, that "Defendant will take the deposition of John Doe, as the corporate representative of Plaintiff X Corporation, on the following topics." Such an amended notice generally is objectionable because the organization can change its representative even after his or her designation as long as the organization gives reasonable notice of the change before the deposition date.

[81] No Texas cases, and only a few federal cases, discuss the "reasonable particularity" requirement for a representative deposition notice. Cases discussing the "reasonable-particularity" requirement for production requests, however, should be instructive. See Chapter 8, section 8-2 (discussing the requirement that production requests describe the items to be produced or inspected with "reasonable particularity").

is requesting examination.[82] This, in turn, depends on the facts of the particular case.

Two common types of subject-matter designations, however, are never "reasonably particular." The first is a subject matter that uses the word "including" or the phrase, "including, but not limited to." As explained by the court in *Innomed Labs, LLC v. Alza Corp.*: "Innomed's subpoena requests a person to be deposed about the documents 'including but not limited to' the areas specified. This language turns the subpoena into an overbroad notice, in contradiction to the 'reasonable particularity' required by [Federal] Rule 30(b)(6)."[83]

The second is an omnibus subject matter calling for all information supporting all of the opposing parties' allegations, claims, or defenses. As explained by one federal court: "While the notice does call for the designation of a witness to testify as to any statement of fact set forth in the amended complaint to which defendant has denied, such a request does not provide with reasonable particularity the matters on which examination is requested. Plaintiff should have specifically listed all subject matters for which a 30(b)(6) designation is sought."[84]

---

[82] *Cf. Koninklijke Philips N.V. v. Zoll LifeCor Corp.*, No. 2:12-cv-1369, 2014 U.S. Dist. LEXIS 131078, at *12, 2014 WL 4660338 (W.D. Pa. Aug. 22, 2014), ("[W]hen determining whether a [Federal] Rule 30(b)(6) deposition notice satisfies the 'reasonable particularity' standard, it is appropriate to bear in mind that a producing party potentially faces sanctions for failing to adequately prepare a corporate representative to testify on its behalf. Practically speaking, that means that the producing party must be able to reasonably identify the metes and bounds of the listed topics."), *quoted with approval in Fifth Third Bank v. Westwood Zamias Ltd. P'ship*, No. 3:18-cv-143, 2019 U.S. Dist. LEXIS 59512, at *4–5, 2019 WL 1383713 (W.D. Pa. 2019), *adopted in relevant part by* No. 12-1369, 2014 U.S. Dist. LEXIS 129756, 2014 WL 4660539 (W.D. Pa. Sept. 17, 2014); *see Hager v. Graham*, 267 F.R.D. 486, 493 (N.D. W. Va. 2010) (discussing Federal Rule 34 and holding that "'[t]he test for reasonable particularity is whether the request places the party upon 'reasonable notice of what is called for and what is not. Therefore, the party requesting the production of documents must provide 'sufficient information to enable [the party to whom the request is directed] to identify responsive documents.' This test, however, is a matter of degree depending on the circumstances of the case." (quoting *Kidwiler v. Progressive Paloverde Ins. Co.*, 192 F.R.D. 193, 202 (N.D.W. Va. 2000))).

[83] *Innomed Labs, LLC v. Alza Corp.*, 211 F.R.D. 237, 240 (S.D.N.Y. 2002); *accord Dotson v. Experian Info. Sols., Inc.*, No. CIV-17-575-D, 2019 U.S. Dist. LEXIS 17392, at *9, 2019 WL 440588 (W.D. Okla. Feb. 4, 2019); *UPS Co. v. DNJ Logistic Grp., Inc.*, No. 3:16-CV-00609-GNS, 2018 U.S. Dist. LEXIS 112961, at *34 (W.D. Ky. Apr. 16, 2018); *Anaheim Gardens v. U.S.*, 125 Fed. Cl. 88, 108 (2016); *Health Grades, Inc. v. MDx Med., Inc.*, No. 11-cv-00520-PAB-BNB, 2013 U.S. Dist. LEXIS 59271, at *11, 2013 WL 1777575 (D. Colo. Apr. 25, 2013); *Fed. Ins. Co. v. Delta Mech. Contractors*, LLC, No. 11-048ML, 2013 U.S. Dist. LEXIS 47582, at *12–13, 2013 WL 1343528 (D.R.I. Apr. 2, 2013); *Tri-State Hosp. Supply Corp. v. U.S.*, 226 F.R.D. 118, 125 (D.D.C. 2005); *Reed v. Bennett*, 193 F.R.D. 689, 692 (D. Kan. 2000); *Anaheim Gardens v. U.S.*, 125 Fed. Cl. 88, 108–09 (2016).

[84] *Skladzien v. St. Francis Reg'l Med. Ctr.*, No. 95-1518-MLB, 1996 U.S. Dist. LEXIS 20621, at *2, 1996 WL 807353 (D. Kan. Dec. 18, 1996).

11-1:1.5d The Noticing Party Generally Can Question an Organization's Representative About Matters for Which the Representative Was Not Designated and About Matters Outside the Deposition Notice's Scope

A question arising from Texas Rule 199.2(b)(1)'s reasonable-particularity requirement for representative deposition notices is whether the organization's representative, at the deposition, can decline to answer questions about matters either for which the representative has not been designated or which are outside the deposition notice's scope. No Texas case has considered the question, and federal courts are divided on the issue.

One federal court, reasoning that Federal Rule 30(b)(6) implicitly restricts the scope of examination by requiring the noticing party to describe "with reasonable particularity the matters for examination," has held: "[I]f a party opts to employ the procedures of [Federal] Rule 30(b)(6) . . . to depose the representative of a corporation, that party must confine the examination to the matters stated 'with reasonable particularity' which are contained in the Notice of Deposition."[85] Every other federal court that has considered the question, however, has held the opposite. As explained by the leading federal case on the issue:

> [Federal] Rule 30(b)(6) should not be read to confer some special privilege on a corporate deponent responding to this type of notice. Clearly, Plaintiff could simply re-notice a deponent under the regular notice provisions and ask him the same questions that were objected to. However, Plaintiff should not be forced to jump through that extra hoop absent some compelling reason. Rather, the Rule is best read as follows:
>
> (1) [Federal] Rule 30(b)(6) obligates the responding corporation to provide a witness who can answer questions regarding the subject matter listed in the notice.
>
> (2) If the designated deponent cannot answer those questions, then the corporation has failed to comply with its [Federal] Rule 30(b)(6) obligations and may be subject to sanctions, etc. The corporation has an affirmative duty to produce a representative who can answer questions that are both within the scope of the matters described in the notice and are "known or reasonably available" to the corporation. [Federal] Rule 30(b)(6) delineates this affirmative duty.
>
> (3) If the examining party asks questions outside the scope of the matters described in the notice, the general deposition rules govern (i.e. Fed.R.Civ.P. 26(b)(1)), so that relevant questions may be asked and no special protection is conferred on a deponent by virtue of the fact that the deposition was noticed under 30(b)(6).

---

[85] *Paperilli v. Prudential Life Ins. Co.*, 108 F.R.D. 727, 730 (D. Mass. 1985). The court in *Paperilli* also ruled that the organization's attorney must seek a protective order rather than simply instructing the witness not to answer matters outside the notice's scope. *Paperilli v. Prudential Life Ins. Co.*,108 F.R.D. 727, 730 (D. Mass. 1985).

(4) However, if the deponent does not know the answer to questions outside the scope of the matters described in the notice, then that is the examining party's problem.

This interpretation does not render the "describe with reasonable particularity" language "superfluous"; rather, it imposes an obligation on a corporation to provide someone who can indeed answer the particular questions presaged by the notice. [Federal] Rule 30(b)(6) does not limit what can be asked at deposition.

Since there is no specific limitation of what can be asked at deposition, the general deposition standards govern. The reason for adopting [Federal] Rule 30(b)(6) was not to provide greater notice or protections to corporate deponents, but rather to have the right person present at deposition. The Rule is not one of limitation but rather of specification within the broad parameters of the discovery rules. This is made clear by both the Advisory Committee's statement that 30(b)(6) "should be viewed as an added facility for discovery . . ." and the Rule's final sentence: "This subdivision (b)(6) does not preclude taking a deposition by any other procedure authorized in these rules." This Court sees no harm in allowing all relevant questions to be asked at a [Federal] Rule 30(b)(6) deposition or any incentive for an examining party to somehow abuse this process.

In sum, this Court concludes that [Federal] Rule 30(b)(6) cannot be used to limit what is asked of a designated witness at a deposition. Rather, the Rule simply defines a corporation's obligations regarding whom they are obligated to produce for such a deposition and what that witness is obligated to be able to answer.[86]

---

[86] *King v. Pratt & Whitney*, 161 F.R.D. 475, 476 (S.D. Fla. 1995); *accord Essmaker v. Smith's Food & Drug Ctrs., Inc.*, No. 1:18-cv-496-BLW, 2019 U.S. Dist. LEXIS 190383, at *5–6, 2019 WL 5685201 (D. Idaho Nov. 1, 2019) ("This Court has held that the examining party may ask questions outside the scope of the [Federal] Rule 30(b)(6) notice. 'Limiting the scope of a 30(b)(6) deposition to what is noticed in the deposition subpoena frustrates the objectives of [Federal] Rule 26(b)(1) whenever a deposing party seeks information relevant to the subject matter of the pending litigation that was not specified.' . . . Thus, Essmaker's questioning of Ellison that exceeded the scope of the [Federal] Rule 30(b)(6) notice was not improper and did not trigger any right in the defendant to instruct the witness not to answer. Counsel's demand that Essmaker re-notice Ellison's deposition for another time to question her in her individual capacity would be 'artificial and wasteful of both the parties' resources and the witness's time.' '[I]f the witness is capable of testifying on behalf of the designated entity, the witness is also capable of testifying as an individual, at the same deposition.'" (quoting *Detoy v. City and Cnty. of S.F.*, 196 F.R.D. 362, 367 (N.D. Cal. July 19, 2000))); *Robinson v. Chefs' Warehouse*, No. 3:15-cv-05421-RS (KAW), 2017 U.S. Dist. LEXIS 167406, at *3, 2017 WL 4509142 (N.D. Cal. Oct. 10, 2017) ("However, the 'reasonable particularity' requirement of [Federal] Rule 30(b)(6) cannot be used to limit what is asked of the designated witness at a deposition." (quoting *UniRAM Tech., Inc. v. Monolithic Sys. Tech., Inc.*, No. C 04-1268 VRW (MEJ), 2007 U.S. Dist. LEXIS 24869, at *6, 2007 WL 915225 (N.D. Cal. Mar. 23, 2007))); *Green v. Wing Enters., Inc.*, No. 1:14-CV-01913-RDB, 2015 U.S. Dist. LEXIS 13654, at *23, 2015 WL 506194 (D. Md. Feb. 15, 2015) ("It has however been established that a 'deponent's answers to questions outside the scope of the notice will not bind the organization.' In this regard, the proper course to take when a deponent is asked a question outside the scope of the notice is to 'object that the question [is] outside the scope of the 30(b)(6) notice, and state on the records that the answer would not bind the [organization].'" (quoting *EEOC. v. Freeman*, 288 F.R.D. 92, 99 (D. Md. 2012))); *First Fin.*

The majority view is the better one. Accordingly, if the organization's representative is asked questions about subject matters on which the representative has not been designated or that are outside the scope of those in the deposition notice or subpoena, instead of instructing the representative not to answer such questions, the organization's counsel should object to the questions as beyond the representative's designation or the notice's scope, noting that the witness is not testifying regarding such matters on the organization's behalf in answering them.[87] In fact, federal courts

---

Bank, N.A. v. Bauknecht, No. 12-cv-1509, 2014 U.S. Dist. LEXIS 31394, at *9–10, 2014 WL 949640 (C.D. Ill. Mar. 11, 2014) ("[A]ll district courts that have addressed the issue [since *King*] have followed suit, concluding that any relevant questions can be asked during a 30(b)(6) deposition, not just on matters listed in the notice of deposition."); *Am. Gen. Life Ins. Co. v. Billard*, No. C10-1012, 2010 U.S. Dist. LEXIS 114961, at *11–12, 2010 WL 4367052 (N.D. Iowa Oct. 28, 2010) (same) (collecting cases).

[87] *Cf. Essmaker v. Smith's Food & Drug Ctrs., Inc.*, No. 1:18-cv-496-BLW, 2019 U.S. Dist. LEXIS 190383, at *6–7, 2019 WL 5685201 (D. Idaho Nov. 1, 2019) ("Counsel may note on the record that answers to questions beyond the scope of the [Federal] Rule 30(b)(6) designation are not intended as the answers of the designating party and do not bind the designating party." (quoting *Detoy v. City & Cnty. of S.F.*, 196 F.R.D. 362, 367 (N.D. Cal. July 19, 2000))); *A&R Body Specialty & Collision Works, Inc. v. Progressive Cas. Ins. Co.*, No. 3:07CV929 (WWE), 2013 U.S. Dist. LEXIS 167800, at *6, 2013 WL 6212159 (D. Conn. Nov. 26, 2013) ("Courts in the Second Circuit, and others, have recognized a party's right to object during a 30(b)(6) deposition where matters fall outside the scope of the 30(b)(6) notice. Indeed, '[a]n objection at the time of examination [. . .] must be noted on the record, but the examination still proceeds; the testimony is taken subject to any objection.'" (citation omitted) (quoting Fed. R. Civ. P. 30(c)(2))); *Merger Corp. U.S. v. Alfang Designs, Inc.*, No. CV 2010 3647 (CBA0 (MDG.), 2012 U.S. Dist. LEXIS 113819, at *13–14, 2012 WL 3536987 (E.D.N.Y. Aug. 1213, 2012) (noting that a party "is permitted to object to a question as beyond the scope of the [Federal Rule 30 (b)(6)] notice in order to preserve for the record that the deponent is answering such a question in an individual, not corporate capacity"); *EEOC v. Caesars Entm't, Inc*, 237 F.R.D. 428, 433 (D. Nev. 2006) ("[C]ounsel 'may note on the record that answers to questions beyond the scope of the [Federal] Rule 30(b)(6) designation are not intended as the answers of the designating party and do not bind the designating party.'" (quoting *Detoy v. City & Cnty. of S.F.*, 196 F.R.D. 362, 367 (N.D. Cal. 2000))).

Texas Rule 199.5(f) allows "[a]n attorney [to] instruct a witness not to answer a question . . . if necessary to . . . protect a witness from abuse or one for which an answer would be misleading." Tex. R. Civ. P. 199.5(f). Although it can be argued that asking an organization's representative questions about matters beyond the scope of his or her designation or the deposition notice's subject matters is "misleading," Comment 4 to [Texas] Rule 199 suggests that an instruction not to answer is appropriate only when an objection is "inadequate." Clearly, an objection that a question is beyond the scope of the representative's designation or the deposition notice's subject matters is adequate, and the organization's attorney generally should not instruct the representative not to answer such questions. If, however, the questioning attorney is trying to create a misleading record or acting in bad faith by, for example, turning the deposition into the representative's personal deposition, the best solution is to terminate the deposition and move for a protective order under Texas Rule 192.6. *Cf. Peshlakai v. Ruiz*, No. CIV 13-0752 JB/ACT, 2014 U.S. Dist. LEXIS 14278, at *80–81, 2014 WL 459650 (D.N.M. Jan. 9, 2014) ("In the unusual case where the questioning party abuses the [Federal R]ule 30(b)(6) device—for example, where the questioning party notices the deposition as a [Federal R]ule 30(b)(6) deposition about a few discrete topics, but begins to conduct what is, in substance, a fact-witness deposition—the corporation is free to move to terminate or limit the deposition under [Federal R]ule 30(d)(3) 'on have held that answers to questions exceeding the scope of a representative deposition notice's subject matters do not "bind" the organization, but rather merely are the answers of the representative in the representative's individual capacity.[88] And, "'[p]rior to trial, counsel may request from the trial judge jury instructions that such answers were merely the answers or opinions of individual fact witnesses, not admissions of the party.'"[89] Finally, as noted above, if the representative does not know the answer to questions outside the subject matters for which he or she has been designated or outside of the deposition notice's scope, that "'is the examining party's problem.'"[90]

11-1:1.5e Objecting to a Representative Deposition Notice

Unlike Texas Rules 196.2(b), 197.2(b), 198.2(b), and 176.6(d), which respectively govern responses to production requests, interrogatories, requests for admission, and subpoenas requesting the production of documents and tangible things, there is no provision in Texas Rules 199.2(b)(1) or 176.6(b) allowing an organization to object to a representative deposition notice or subpoena. Accordingly, if the organization believes that the notice's or subpoena's subject matters are not reasonably particular or are otherwise objectionable (e.g., they are overbroad) or that the documents suffer from another malady, such as requiring the organization to designate a specific

---

the ground that it is being conducted in bad faith or in a manner that unreasonably annoys, embarrasses, or oppresses the deponent or party,' that is, the corporation or its designee.") (citation omitted).

[88] *E.g., McKinney/Pearl Rest. Partners, L.P. v. Metro. Life Ins. Co.*, 241 F. Supp. 3d 737, 752 (N.D. Tex. 2017) ("Plaintiff is correct that 'questions and answers exceeding the scope of the 30(b)(6) notice will not bind the corporation.'" (quoting *U.S. ex rel. Fisher v. Ocwen Loan Servicing, LLC*, Nos. 4:12-CV-543, 4:12-CV-461, 2016 U.S. Dist. LEXIS 67779, at *26, 2016 WL 2997120 (E.D. Tex. May 24, 2016))); *FTC v. Vantage Point Servs., LLC*, No. 15-CV-6S(Sr), 2016 U.S. Dist. LEXIS 79890, at *6, 2016 WL 3397717 (W.D.N.Y. June 20, 2016) ("'The proper scope of the questioning of a [Federal] Rule 30(b)(6) witness is not defined by the notice of deposition, but by Rule 26(b)(1) of the Federal Rules of Civil Procedure, unless a court otherwise directs.' As a result, a 30(b)(6) witness may provide individual testimony about additional relevant topics, with the caveat that unless the witness is also an officer or managing agent of the firm, that testimony should not normally be considered to be offered on behalf of the corporation." (quoting *Crawford v. Franklin Credit Mgmt. Corp.*, 261 F.R.D. 34, 39 (S.D.N.Y. 2009))); *EEOC v. Freeman*, 288 F.R.D. 92, 99 (D. Md. 2012) ("The deponent's answers to questions outside the scope of the notice will not bind the organization, and the organization cannot be penalized if the deponent does not know the answer."); *Falchenberg v. N.Y. State Dep't of Educ.*, 642 F. Supp. 2d 156, 164 (S.D.N.Y. 2008) ("Questions and answers exceeding the scope of the 30(b)(6) notice will not bind the corporation, but are merely treated as the answers of the individual deponent."), *aff'd on other grounds*, 338 Fed. Appx. 11 (2d Cir. 2009).

[89] *Essmaker v. Smith's Food & Drug Ctrs., Inc.*, No. 1:18-cv-496-BLW, 2019 U.S. Dist. LEXIS 190383, at *7, 2019 WL 5685201 (D. Idaho Nov. 1, 2019) (quoting *Detoy v. City & Cnty. of S.F.*, 196 F.R.D. 362, 367 (N.D. Cal. July 19, 2000)); *accord EEOC v. Caesars Entm't, Inc.*, 237 F.R.D. 428, 433 (D. Nev. 2006).

[90] *Chrimar Sys. v. Cisco Sys.*, 312 F.R.D. 560, 563 (N.D. Cal. 2016) (quoting *Detoy v. City & Cnty. of S.F.*, 196 F.R.D. 362, 367 (N.D. Cal. 2000)); *accord Falchenberg v. N.Y. State Dep't of Educ.*, 642 F. Supp. 2d 156, 164 (S.D.N.Y. 2008), *aff'd on other grounds*, 338 Fed. Appx. 11 (2d Cir. 2009); *EEOC v. Caesars Entm't, Inc.*, 237 F.R.D. 428, 433 (D. Nev. 2006); *King v. Pratt & Whitney*, 161 F.R.D. 475, 476 (S.D. Fla. 1995).

person as its representative or a representative with personal or the most knowledge about the notice's or subpoena's subject matters, the organization should either file a motion for protective order or move to quash the notice or subpoena before the deposition.[91] The organization "cannot simply 'decide on its own to ignore the notice,' or 'file objections and then state that it will only produce general answers to the topics in accordance with its objections unless given more specific direction by the party seeking the deposition.'"[92] And, because the movant always has the burden to establish that a protective order should be granted,[93] "once the deposition notice is served, 'the [organization] bears the burden of demonstrating to the court that the notice is objectionable or insufficient.'"[94]

---

[91] *See* Tex. R. Civ. P. 192.6(a) ("A person from whom discovery is sought, and any other person affected by the discovery request, may move within the time permitted for response to the discovery request for an order protecting that person from the discovery sought."); *cf. Shuthima Pongsai v. Am. Express Co.*, No. 8:19-cv-01628-DOC (JDEx), 2020 U.S. Dist. LEXIS 113168, at *6 (C.D. Cal. June 29, 2020) ("The 'proper procedure to object to a [Federal] Rule 30(b)(6) deposition notice is not to serve objections on the opposing party, but to move for a protective order.' 'Put simply and clearly, absent agreement, a party who for one reason or another does not wish to comply with a notice of deposition must seek a protective order.'" (quoting *Rutherford v. Evans Hotels, LLC*, No. 18cv435-JLS(MSB), 2018 U.S. Dist. LEXIS 202663, at *6, 2018 WL 6246516 (S.D. Cal. Nov. 29, 2018), and *N. Eng. Carpenters Health Benefits Fund v. First DataBank, Inc.*, 242 F.R.D. 164, 165–66 (D. Mass. 2007))); *Graham v. Dhar*, No. 1:18-00274, 2019 U.S. Dist. LEXIS 218293, at *10–11, 2019 WL 6999688 (S.D. W. Va. 2019) ("BRMC was required to file a protective order, rather than filing objections, when it declined to designate a representative to answer Notice Topics 11 and 12. Federal Rule 37(d)(2) is clear on this matter, as is the law of this district."); *EEOC v. M&T Bank*, No. ELH-16-3180, 2018 U.S. Dist. LEXIS 4219, at *5–6 (D. Md. Jan. 9, 2018) ("Importantly, '[t]he proper procedure to object to a [Federal] Rule 30(b)(6) deposition notice is not to serve objections on the opposing party, but to move for a protective order. Once the deposition notice is served, the corporation bears the burden of demonstrating to the court that the notice is objectionable or insufficient.' Finally, '[i]f the corporation makes no such showing, [it] must produce a witness prepared to testify to the subject matter described in the notice . . . [it] cannot make its objections and then provide a witness that will testify only within the scope of its objections.'" (quoting *Beach Mart, Inc. v. L&L Wings, Inc.*, 302 F.R.D. 396, 406 (E.D.N.C. 2014))); *Fort Worth Emps. Ret. Fund v. J.P. Morgan Chase & Co.*, No. 09 Civ. 3701 (JPO) (JCF), 2013 U.S. Dist. LEXIS 173006, at *7–8, 2013 WL 6439069 (S.D.N.Y. Dec. 9, 2013) ("The weight of the authority holds that a party believing it has received a flawed 30(b)(6) notice may not merely rest upon its objections, but must move for a protective order. . . . This principle applies not only to objections that go to the notice in its entirety, but also to those that define the scope of the 30(b)(6) deposition.") (citations omitted); *Robinson v. Quicken Loans, Inc.*, No. 3:12-cv-00981, 2013 U.S. Dist. LEXIS 59127, at *9, 2013 WL 1776100 (S.D.W. Va. Apr. 25, 2013) (same).

[92] *Robinson v. Quicken Loans, Inc.*, No. 3:12-cv-00981, 2013 U.S. Dist. LEXIS 59127, at *10, 2013 WL 1776100 (S.D.W. Va. Apr. 25, 2013) (quoting *N. Eng. Carpenters Health Benefits Fund v. First DataBank, Inc.*, 242 F.R.D. 164, 166 (D. Mass. 2007), and *Espy v. Mformation Techs., Inc.*, No. 08-2211-EFM-DWB, 2010 U.S. Dist. LEXIS 36594, at *7, 2010 WL 1488555 (D. Kan. Apr. 13, 2010)).

[93] See Chapter 4, section 4-5 (discussing protective orders).

[94] *Cf. Beach Mart, Inc. v. L&L Wings, Inc.*, 302 F.R.D. 396, 406 (E.D.N.C. 2014) (quoting *Robinson v. Quicken Loans, Inc.*, No. 3:12-cv-00981, 2013 U.S. Dist. LEXIS 59127, at *10, 2013 WL 1776100 (S.D.W. Va. Apr. 25, 2013)); *accord Westheimer Regency I, L.P. v. Great Lakes Reinsurance (UK) Se*, No. 5:18-CV-14-OLG, 2018 U.S. Dist. LEXIS 228908, at *3, 2018 WL 7198643 (W.D. Tex. Aug. 20, 2018).

An interesting question is whether an organization may obtain protection from a representative notice that seeks the bases for the organization's contentions and claims or defenses, so-called "contention-representative" topics. A few Texas cases, without any analysis, hold that such topics are appropriate.[95] Federal courts, however, are divided on the question[96] with some federal courts treating such topics favorably[97]

---

[95] *E.g.*, ***Braden v. Downey***, 811 S.W.2d 922, 925 (Tex. 1991) (orig. proceeding); ***In re Allstate Fire & Cas. Ins. Co.***, 617 S.W.3d 635 (Tex. App.—Houston [14th Dist.] 2021, no pet.); ***In re Liberty County Mut. Ins. Co.***, 606 S.W.3d 866, 875 (Tex. App.—Houston [14th Dist.] 2020, orig. proceeding); ***In re Luna***, No. 13-16-00467-CV, 2016 Tex. App. LEXIS 12011, at *23, 2016 WL 6576879 (Tex. App.—Corpus Christi Nov. 7, 2016, orig. proceeding) (mem. op.); ***In re Garcia***, No. 04-07-00173-CV, 2007 Tex. App. LEXIS 3926, at *6, 2007 WL 1481897 (Tex. App.—San Antonio May 23, 2007, orig. proceeding) (per curiam) (mem. op.) None of these cases, however, considered the question of whether contention discovery is better suited for interrogatories and, if so, in what circumstances.

For example, in ***Braden v. Downey***, 811 S.W.2d 922 (Tex. 1991) (orig. proceeding), after the relator refused to answer contention deposition questions on the ground that his contentions were properly discoverable only by interrogatories, the real party served contention interrogatories. ***Braden v. Downey***, 811 S.W.2d 922, 925 (Tex. 1991) (orig. proceeding). After, the relator objected to the interrogatories because they were duplicative of questions asked at his deposition, ***Braden v. Downey***, 811 S.W.2d 922, 925 (Tex. 1991) (orig. proceeding), the trial court entered an order compelling the relator to answer the interrogatories, the relator sought mandamus relief. ***Braden v. Downey***, 811 S.W.2d 922, 926 (Tex. 1991) (orig. proceeding). In denying relief, the Supreme Court held that "[w]hile we do not agree that inquiry may not be made into a party's contentions during a deposition, having taken that position through his counsel, Braden foreclosed any subsequent objection to interrogatories on the ground that they requested information provided in the deposition."). ***Braden v. Downey***, 811 S.W.2d 922, 927 (Tex. 1991) (orig. proceeding).

In the other cases, which all arose in the context of an insured seeking to depose his/her insurer in a lawsuit for related to uninsured-motorist coverage, the courts held that the insured could take the insurer's representative deposition on topics related to the insurer's defenses and/or the insured's damages without considering whether interrogatories were a more suitable means of discovery regarding the insurer's defenses and damage assertions. ***In re Allstate Fire & Cas. Ins. Co.***, 617 S.W.3d 635 (Tex. App.—Houston [14th Dist.] 2021, no pet.); ***In re Liberty County Mut. Ins. Co.***, 606 S.W.3d 866, 875 (Tex. App.—Houston [14th Dist.] 2020, orig. proceeding); ***In re Luna***, No. 13-16-00467-CV, 2016 Tex. App. LEXIS 12011, at *23, 2016 WL 6576879 (Tex. App.—Corpus Christi Nov. 7, 2016, orig. proceeding) (mem. op.); ***In re Garcia***, No. 04-07-00173-CV, 2007 Tex. App. LEXIS 3926, at *6, 2007 WL 1481897 (Tex. App.—San Antonio May 23, 2007, orig. proceeding) (per curiam) (mem. op.).

[96] *E.g.*, ***Landry v. Swire Oilfield Servs., L.L.C.***, No. CIV 16-0621 JB/LF, 2018 U.S. Dist. LEXIS 885, at *56, 2018 WL 279749 (D.N.M. Jan. 3, 2018) ("Courts have split whether to allow parties to use 30(b)(6) depositions to explore facts underlying legal claims and theories."); ***Milwaukee Elec. Tool Corp. v. Chevron N. Am., Inc.***, No. 14-CV-1289-JPS, 2015 U.S. Dist. LEXIS 92546, at *9–10, 2015 WL 4393896 (E.D. Wis. July 16, 2015) ("Courts have split whether to allow parties to use 30(b)(6) depositions to explore facts underlying legal claims and theories."); ***Clauss Constr. v. UChicago Argonne LLC***, No. 13-cv-05479, 2015 U.S. Dist. LEXIS 4131, at *14, 2015 WL 191138 (N.D. Ill. Jan. 13, 2015) ("There is a difference of opinion among courts as to whether a [Federal] Rule 30(b)(6) topic that asks an entity to designate a witness to testify about facts underlying legal claims or defenses is appropriate.").

[97] *E.g.*, ***White v. City of Cleveland***, 417 F. Supp. 3d 896, 910 (N.D. Ohio 2019) ("[N]umerous courts have held that a party may use a [Federal] Rule 30(b)(6) deposition to inquire into the factual bases for another party's claims or defenses."); ***Landry v. Swire Oilfield Servs., L.L.C.***, 323 F.R.D. 360, 384–85 (D.N.M. 2018) ("Courts have split whether to allow parties to

and others taking a more restrictive view because they believe either that interrogatories are better suited to explore the factual bases for an opponent's claims or that it is unreasonable to expect a witness,[98] even an educated one, to be prepared to testify

---

use 30(b)(6) depositions to explore facts underlying legal claims and theories. Th[is] Court has held that the better rule is to allow parties to craft [Federal R]ule 30(b)(6) inquires similar to contention interrogatories, because this rule will ultimately lead to fewer disputes about what subject matter is permitted in 30(b)(6) depositions and advances the policy underlying the rule's favoring disclosure of information. If the Court limits [Federal R]ule 30(b)(6) depositions . . ., courts would have to referee endless disputes about what is permitted and what is not. Moreover, [Federal R]ule 30(b)(6)'s plain language does not limit the deposition in that way.") (citations omitted); *Pipeline Prods. v. Madison Cos., LLC*, No. 15-4890-KHV, 2018 U.S. Dist. LEXIS 116654, at *3–4 (D. Kan. 2018) ("Courts have split on the issue of whether to allow parties to use [Federal] Rule 30(b)(6) depositions to explore facts underlying legal claims and theories. The court believes that the better rule is to allow parties to craft [Federal] Rule 30(b)(6) inquires similar to contention interrogatories, because this rule will ultimately lead to fewer disputes about what subject matter is permitted in 30(b)(6) depositions and advances the policy underlying the rule's favoring disclosure of information. If the court limits [Federal] Rule 30(b)(6) depositions the way that defendants suggest, courts would have to referee endless disputes about what is permitted and what is not. Moreover, [Federal] Rule 30(b)(6)'s plain language does not limit the deposition as defendants state. [Federal] Rule 26(b)(1) states that '[u]nless otherwise limited by court order, the scope of discovery is as follows: Parties may obtain discovery regarding any nonprivileged matter that is relevant to any party's claim or defense.' [Federal] Rule 30(b)(6) is not 'otherwise limited,' but unlimited. Furthermore, the Federal Rules do not require parties to conduct discovery in a particular sequence: 'Unless, on motion, the court orders otherwise for the parties' and witnesses' convenience and in the interests of justice[,] . . . methods of discovery may be used in any sequence. . . .'" (citations omitted) (quoting Fed. R. Civ. P. 26(d)(2)(A))).

[98] *E.g., CX Reinsurance Co. v. B&R Mgmt., Inc.*, No. ELH-15-3364, 2018 U.S. Dist. LEXIS 56386, at *8–11 (D. Md. Apr. 3, 2018) (after recognizing that "federal courts 'have split whether to allow parties to use [Federal Rule] 30(b)(6) depositions to explore facts underlying legal claims and theories'", ruling that the plaintiff could not take one about the factual bases for the defendant's affirmative defenses because they were more suitably explored through interrogatories); *Wilson v. Lakner*, 228 F.R.D. 524, 529 n.8 (D. Md. 2005) (recognizing that, whereas facts of a "relevant incident" fall within Federal Rule 30(b)(6)'s scope, "the contentions, i.e. theories and legal positions, of an organizational party may be more suitably explored by way of interrogatories and the Court may properly order . . . that contentions only be inquired into in this fashion"); *Proa v. NRT Mid-Atlantic, Inc.*, No. AMD-05-2157, 2008 U.S. Dist. LEXIS 129572, at *45–46, 2008 WL 11363286, (D. Md. June 20, 2008) (striking "topics dealing with affirmative defenses" from a party's [Federal Rule] 30(b)(6) deposition notice because, among other reasons: (1) the information was discoverable by other, less burdensome, means [e.g., interrogatories]; and (2) the plaintiff failed to show "substantial need to obtain [the] information through a [Federal] Rule 30(b)(6) deposition"); *see Gauen v. Bd. of Educ. Highland Cmty. Unit Sch. Dist. No. 5*, No. 3:16 CV 207 DRH/RJD, 2017 U.S. Dist. LEXIS 12503, at *4–6 (S.D. Ill. Jan. 17, 2017) ("The Court recognizes that the topics as written may encompass legal strategy and are fairly construable as a substitute for contention interrogatories. To the extent Plaintiff seeks the equivalent of contention interrogatories, the Court agrees with courts who have held that 'contention interrogatories are a better discovery vehicle for that kind of information than a [Federal] Rule 30(b)(6) deposition.' However, the topics could also be construed as merely setting forth the fact allegations as topics for deposition. Upon review of the pleadings, the cited complaint allegations are fact allegations, and the affirmative defense includes fact allegations, stating, 'Specifically, it is the District's practice to determine and establish administrator salaries

about all facts underlying a given claim.[99]

As noted by one federal court, "[t]he issue usually comes down to whether contention interrogatories are a better discovery vehicle for that kind of information than a [Federal] Rule 30(b)(6) deposition."[100] This, in turn, depends on the action's complexity, the scope and complexity of the deposition notice's subject matters, and the accessibility of the information sought through the deposition. For example, if the action relates to events that occurred long ago or actions by a predecessor organization that has not existed for a long period of time, interrogatories may be the better discovery vehicle.

Three facts, however, favor a representative deposition in the "ordinary" action under the Texas discovery rules. First, nothing in Texas Rule 199.2(b)(1) limits the

---

based upon, among other things, a candidate's prior administrative experience and seniority in the position.' Accordingly, Defendant's request for a protective order is granted in part and denied in part. Plaintiff may depose the corporate representative regarding the substance of the factual allegations set forth in the pleadings but cannot merely ask the corporate representative what facts support Defendant's pleadings. Stated otherwise, Plaintiff should refrain from framing questions as contention interrogatories. For instance, Plaintiff may ask questions about Defendant's methodology in establishing administrative salaries but should not ask for a recitation of the factual bases for asserting the First Affirmative Defense or denying related allegations in the complaint." (quoting *Clauss Constr. v. UChicago Argonne LLC*, No. 13-cv-05479, 2015 U.S. Dist. LEXIS 4131, at *814, 2015 WL 191138 (N.D. Ill. 2015))).

[99] *E.g., Lenox Maclaren Surgical Corp. v. Medtronic, Inc.*, No. 10-cv-02139-MSK-NYW, 2015 U.S. Dist. LEXIS 75813, at *15, 2015 WL 3746673 (D. Colo. June 11, 2015) ("While a party may use a [Federal] Rule 30(b)(6) deposition to elicit an opposing party's contentions and the facts it may rely on to support them, proper use of a corporate deposition is not unbounded. For instance, the use of "contention' 30(b)(6) topics—as opposed to contention interrogatories or requests for admission—may heighten the risks of inadvertent waiver of attorney-client privilege and/or waiver of attorney work-product doctrine protection. Moreover, the need to properly educate a corporate representative to extemporaneously and yet competently and reasonably comprehensively detail the entity's positions and all grounds of support as to wide swaths of the litigation can pose a heightened risk of undue burden—particularly in complex cases."); *Castillon v. Corr. Corp. of Am.*, 2014 U.S. Dist. LEXIS 124509, at *4–5, 2014 WL 4365317 (D. Idaho Sept. 2, 2014) ("Topic 9 of Plaintiff's 30(b)(6) deposition notice requires the deponent to testify regarding the 'facts or data CCA contends mitigates the need for a substantial punitive damage verdict in this case.' CCA contends that this topic is not described with reasonable particularity as required by [Federal] Rule 30(b)(6). The Court agrees. Requiring Defendant to prepare a deponent to testify as to all such matters is overbroad and unduly burdensome. 'Even under the present-day liberal discovery rules, [a party] is not required to have counsel marshal all of its factual proof and prepare a witness to be able to testify on a given defense or counterclaim.'" (citations omitted) (quoting *In re Indep. Serv./Organizs. Antitrust Litig*, 168 F.R.D. 651, 654 (D. Kan. 1996))).

[100] *Clauss Constr. v. UChicago Argonne LLC*, No. 13-cv-05479, 2015 U.S. Dist. LEXIS 4131, at *14, 2015 WL 191138 (N.D. Ill. Jan. 13, 2015); *see Bank of Am., N.A. v. SFR Invs. Pool 1 LLC*, No. 2:15-cv-01042-APG-GWF, 2016 U.S. Dist. LEXIS 63534, at *11–12, 2016 WL 2843802 (D. Nev. May 12, 2016) (holding that the issue is one of proportionality under Federal Rule 26(b)(1)); *Canal Barge Co. v. Commonwealth Edison Co.*, No 98 C 0589, 2001 U.S. Dist. LEXIS 10097, at *6, 2001 WL 817853 (N.D. Ill. July 18, 2001) ("Whether a [Federal] Rule 30(b)(6) deposition or a [former Federal] Rule 33(c) contention interrogatory is more appropriate will be a case by case factual determination.").

scope of such depositions.[101] Second, the Texas discovery rules do not require parties to conduct discovery in a particular sequence, but rather expressly provide that "[t]he permissible forms of discovery may be . . . taken in any order."[102] Finally, and perhaps most importantly, depositions are the discovery device that generally provides the most complete and comprehensive information.[103]

11-1:1.6 The Organization's Obligations

The organization, once noticed or subpoenaed, has a myriad of obligations. Initially, it *must* designate one or more individuals to testify on its behalf.[104] More than one individual *must* be designated if more than one is needed to testify fully about the notice's subject matters.[105] Texas Rule 199.2(b)(1), unlike Federal Rule 30(b)(6), requires

---

[101] *Cf.* Tex. R. Civ. P. 194 cmt. 2 to 1999 change ("[Texas] Rule 194.2(c) and (d) permit a party further inquiry into another's legal theories and factual claims than is often provided in notice pleadings. So-called 'contention interrogatories' are used for the same purpose. Such interrogatories are not properly used to require a party to marshal evidence or brief legal issues."), 197.1 ("[Contention i]nterrogatories may not be used to require the responding party to marshal all of its available proof or the proof the party intends to offer at trial."), 197 cmt. 1 to 1999 change ("[I]nterrogatories that ask a party to state all legal and factual assertions are improper. As with requests for disclosure, interrogatories may be used to ascertain basic legal and factual claims and defenses but may not be used to force a party to marshal evidence.").

[102] Tex. R. Civ. P. 192.2.

[103] *Elan Microelectronics Corp. v. Pixcir Microelectronics Co.*, No. 2:10-cv-00014-GMN-PAL, 2013 U.S. Dist. LEXIS 114164, at *17, 2013 WL 4101813 (D. Nev. Aug. 7, 2013) ("Because of its nature, the deposition process provides a means to obtain more complete information and is, therefore, favored." (quoting *Marker v. Union Fid. Life Ins. Co.*, 125 F.R.D. 121, 126 (M.D.N.C.1989))); *Buehrle v. City of O'Fallon,* No. 4:10CV00509, 2011 U.S. Dist. LEXIS 11972, at *7, 2011 WL 529922 (E.D. Mo. Feb. 8, 2011) (same); *Kleppinger v. Tex. Dep't. of Transp.*, 283 F.R.D. 330, 335 (S.D. Tex. 2012) ("While the Court recognizes that in many instances interrogatories and depositions can be utilized to obtain the same information in a lawsuit, these two methods of discovery are not necessarily equivalent. That is, the use of interrogatories may have disadvantages. For example, interrogatories do not provide subjective information, such as the demeanor of the responding party. Further, interrogatories can be ineffective in obtaining complex or possibly confusing information. Moreover, depositions have more flexibility than interrogatories because they permit an attorney to ask follow-up questions based on answers to previous questions or repeat questions if a deponent is being evasive.") (citations omitted).

[104] Tex. R. Civ. P. 199.2(b)(1).

[105] *In re Fina Oil & Chem. Co.*, No. 13-98-640-CV, 1999 Tex. App. LEXIS 1751, at *14–15, 1999 WL 33589153 (Tex. App.—Corpus Christi Mar. 11, 1999, orig. proceeding) (not designated for publication) ("[Former Texas] Rule 201(4) is patterned after Federal Rule of Civil Procedure 30(b)(6), which has been consistently construed to require that a corporation 'must not only produce such number of persons as will satisfy the request, but more importantly, prepare them so that they may give complete, knowledgeable, and binding answers on behalf of the corporation.' At least one Texas court has implicitly adopted this construction of [former Texas] Rule 201(4) as well, by noting with disfavor the fact that a defendant had designated a witness who could not or would not provide responsive information despite 'exhaustive notice of the matters upon which' the witness would be questioned." (quoting *Marker v. Union Fid. Life Ins. Co.*, 125 F.R.D. 121, 126 (M.D.N.C. 1989), and *Allstate Tex. Lloyds v. Johnson*, 784 S.W.2d 100, 103 (Tex. App.—Waco 1989, orig. proceeding))); *cf. Ecclesiastes 9:10-11-12, Inc. v. LMC Holding Co.*, 497 F.3d 1135, 1146 (10th Cir. 2007) ("The law is

the organization to designate, "a reasonable time before the deposition[,]" both each individual who will testify on its behalf and "the matters on which the individual will testify."[106] This requirement helps the noticing party prepare for the deposition and also allows it to object to the designation if it believes the person designated by the organization is an inadequate representative.

The representative, however, need not be an officer or employee of the organization. Often an organization responding to a Texas Rule 199.2(b)(1) notice is hard-pressed to locate present officers or employees who have knowledge about distant events. If the organization is willing to designate a former employee as its deponent (and if the former employee accepts the role), the use of a former employee or any *other* person (e.g., a retained expert or the organization's attorney) as a designee is fully permissible.[107] This is made clear by Texas Rule 199.2(b)(1), which does not require the representative to have any present or past affiliation with the organization and which merely requires the organization to designate "one or more individuals to testify on its behalf[.]"[108]

The organization also can change its representatives, as well as the subject matters about which they have been designated to testify, after their designation as long as notice of the change is given a "reasonable time" before each affected deposition begins. What constitutes a "reasonable time" will depend on the facts of the case, such as the number and complexity of the subject matters and the amount of time the notice was served before the deposition date.

As discussed above, there is no requirement that the representative have personal knowledge about the subject matters on which the representative has been designated to testify, much less the most knowledge about it.[109] Thus, the representative need not have participated in the transaction or events about which inquiry will be made.

---

well-settled that corporations have an 'affirmative duty' to make available as many persons as necessary to give 'complete, knowledgeable, and binding answers' on the corporation's behalf." (quoting *Reilly v. Natwest Mkts. Grp. Inc.*, 181 F.3d 253, 268 (2d Cir. 1999))); *SEC v. Goldstone*, 301 F.R.D. 593, 646–47 (D.N.M. 2014) (same); *Myrdal v. State*, 248 F.R.D. 315, 317 (D.D.C. 2008) ("[A] deponent is under a duty to designate more than one deponent if it is necessary to do so in order to respond to the relevant areas of inquiry that are specified with reasonable particularity by the plaintiff." (quoting *Alexander v. F.B.I.*, 186 F.R.D. 137, 141 (D.D.C. 1998))); *see* Tex. R. Civ. P. 199.2(b)(1) (providing that an "organization . . . must . . . designate *one or more* individuals to testify on its behalf") (emphasis added).

106 Tex. R. Civ. P. 199.2(b)(1).

107 *Cf. Canyon Furniture Co. v. Sanchez*, No. SA-18-cv-00753-OLG, 2018 U.S. Dist. LEXIS 224455, at *41–42, 2018 WL 6265041 (W.D. Tex. Nov. 8, 2018) ("If appropriate, a corporation may designate a non-employee as its corporate representative for the purposes of a [Federal] Rule 30(b)(6) deposition, including a former employee or agent."); *Beauperthuy v. 24 Hour Fitness U.S., Inc.*, No. 06-715 SC, 2009 U.S. Dist. LEXIS 104906, at *14–17 n.5, 2009 WL 3809815 (N.D. Cal. Nov. 10, 2009) ("[T]he text of [Federal] Rule 30(b)(6) leaves no doubt that a former employee can and should be designated as a [Federal] Rule 30(b)(6) deponent, if the former employee is the most knowledgeable individual and as long as the former employee consents. An organization may designate any 'persons who consent to testify on its behalf.'" (citations omitted) (quoting Fed. R. Civ. P. 30(b)(6))).

108 See notes 80 and accompanying text.

109 See notes 80–82 and accompanying text.

Implicit in Texas Rule 199.2(b)(1)'s requirement that the organization designate individuals to testify on its behalf about the deposition notice's subject matters is the obligation to prepare the representative to testify about each matter about which the representative has been designated to testify.[110] This obligation extends not only to "matters known or reasonably available to the organization[,]"[111] but also to the organization's subjective beliefs and opinions.[112]

---

[110] *See In re Fina Oil & Chem. Co.*, No. 13-98-640-CV, 1999 Tex. App. LEXIS 1751, at *14–15, 1999 WL 33589153 (Tex. App.—Corpus Christi Mar. 11, 1999, orig. proceeding) (not designated for publication) ("[Former Texas] Rule 201(4) is patterned after Federal Rule of Civil Procedure 30(b)(6), which has been consistently construed to require that a corporation 'must not only produce such number of persons as will satisfy the request, but more importantly, prepare them so that they may give complete, knowledgeable, and binding answers on behalf of the corporation.' At least one Texas court has implicitly adopted this construction of [former Texas] Rule 201(4) as well, by noting with disfavor the fact that a defendant had designated a witness who could not or would not provide responsive information despite 'exhaustive notice of the matters upon which' the witness would be questioned." (quoting *Marker v. Union Fid. Life Ins. Co.*, 125 F.R.D. 121, 126 (M.D.N.C. 1989), and *Allstate Tex. Lloyds v. Johnson*, 784 S.W.2d 100, 103 (Tex. App.—Waco 1989, orig. proceeding))); *cf. Brazos River Auth. v. GE Ionics, Inc.*, 469 F.3d 416, 433 (5th Cir. 2006) ("[T]he deponent 'must make a conscientious good-faith endeavor to designate the persons having knowledge of the matters sought by [the party noticing the deposition] and to prepare those persons in order that they can answer fully, completely, unevasively, the questions posed . . . as to the relevant subject matters.'" (quoting *Bank of N.Y. v. Meridien BIAO Bank Tanzania Ltd.*, 171 F.R.D. 135, 151 (S.D.N.Y. 1997))); *Maronda Homes, Inc. v. Progressive Express Ins. Co.*, No. 6:14-cv-1287-Orl-31TBS, 2015 U.S. Dist. LEXIS 60603, at *6, 2015 WL 2169234 (M.D. Fla. May 8, 2015) ("The corporation has an implicit duty to prepare its designees so that they are able to 'testify about information known or reasonably available to the organization.'" (quoting Fed. R. Civ. P. 30(b)(6))); *Payless ShoeSource Worldwide, Inc. v. Target Corp.*, No. 05-0423-JAR, 2008 U.S. Dist. LEXIS 28878, at *31, 2008 WL 973118 (D. Kan. Apr. 8, 2008) ("Yet, 'because [Federal] Rule 30(b)(6) explicitly requires a company to have persons testify on its behalf as to all matters reasonably available to it, this Court has held that the rule 'implicitly requires persons to review all matters known or reasonably available to [the corporation] in preparation for the 30(b)(6) deposition.'" (quoting *Raytheon Aircraft Co. v. U.S.*, No. 05-2328-JWL, 2007 U.S. Dist. LEXIS 66156, at *11, 2007 WL 2668725 (D. Kan. Sept. 6, 2007))); *see Poole ex rel. Elliott v. Textron, Inc.*, 192 F.R.D. 494, 504 (D. Md. 2000) ("A party cannot take a laissez faire approach to the inquiry. That is, producing a designee and seeing what he has to say or what he can cover.").

[111] Tex. R. Civ. P. 199.2(b)(1).

[112] *Lindsey v. O'Neill*, 689 S.W.2d 400, 402 (Tex. 1985) (orig. proceeding) (holding that a trial court erred in striking twenty-one subject matters from the deposition notice for a defendant corporation because "[former Texas] Rule 200 makes no distinction between deposition notices directed toward corporations based upon whether the deposition is to pertain to purely factual matters or matters calling for expert opinion"); *see In re Luna*, No. 13-16-00467-CV, 2016 Tex. App. LEXIS 12011, at *21–22, 2016 WL 6576879 (Tex. App.—Corpus Christi Nov. 7, 2016, no pet.) (mem. op.) ("Fundamentally, State Farm asserts that its corporate representative will not have personal knowledge of the facts at issue in this lawsuit. . . . [Texas] Rule 199.1(a) permits the deposition 'of any person or entity' without any limitation that the proposed deponent have personal knowledge of the facts." (quoting Tex. R. Civ. P. 199.1(a))); *cf. Brazos River Auth. v. GE Ionics, Inc.*, 469 F.3d 416, 433 (5th Cir. 2006) ("When a corporation produces an employee pursuant to a [Federal R]ule 30(b)(6) notice, it represents that the employee has the authority to speak on behalf of the corporation with respect to the areas within the notice of deposition. This extends not only to facts, but also to subjective beliefs

Because the organization is required to designate individuals to testify about "matters that are known or reasonably available to the organization," the organization, in preparing its Texas Rule 199.2(b)(1) representatives, has an obligation of "reasonable inquiry" similar to its obligation of reasonable inquiry in making required disclosures and answering interrogatories and requests for admission.[113] Thus, the two key factors are whether the information is "reasonably available" to the organization and whether it is in the organization's control.[114] This generally requires the organi-

---

and opinions.") (footnote omitted); *Critchlow v. Sterling Jewelers, Inc.*, No. 8:18-cv-96-T-30JSS, 2018 U.S. Dist. LEXIS 222933, at *4 (M.D. Fla. Nov. 13, 2018) ("Not only must the designee testify about facts within the corporation's collective knowledge, including the results of an investigation initiated for the purpose of complying with the 30(b)(6) notice, but the designee must also testify about the corporation's position, beliefs and opinions." (quoting *QBE Ins. Corp. v. Jorda Enters., Inc.*, 277 F.R.D. 676, 689 (S.D. Fla. 2012))); *Difiore v. CSL Behring, U.S., LLC*, No. 13-5027, 2015 U.S. Dist. LEXIS 121107, at *2–3, 2015 WL 5316479 (E.D. Pa. Sept. 11, 2015) (same); *Johnson v. Samsung Elecs. Am.*, No. 10-1146; 10-1549 SECTION: "K" (4), 2011 U.S. Dist. LEXIS 77016, at *17–18, 2011 WL 2847696 (E.D. La. July 14, 2011) ("[F] urther, contrary to the Defendants' assertions, corporations are capable of having an opinion. A [Federal] Rule 30(b)(6) designee does not give his personal opinions, but presents the corporation's 'position' on the topic."); *Cooley v. Lincoln Elec. Co.*, 693 F. Supp. 2d 767, 791 (N.D. Ohio 2010) (["F]urther, a corporate designee may testify about not only a corporation's knowledge but also its subjective beliefs.") (footnote omitted).

[113] *Cf. Wilson v. Lakner*, 228 F.R.D. 524, 528–29 (D. Md. 2005) (equating the obligation to that in answering interrogatories); *Twentieth Century Fox Film Corp. v. Marvel Enters.*, No. 01 Civ. 3016 (AGS)(HBP), 2002 U.S. Dist. LEXIS 14682, at *13, 2002 WL 1835439 (S.D.N.Y. Aug. 6, 2002) ("I conclude that the same principle that is applied to interrogatories and document requests should also be applied to determine the scope of a party's obligation in responding to a [Federal] Rule 30(b)(6) notice of deposition. There is no logical reason why the sources researched by a party in responding to a discovery request should be dependent on the particular discovery vehicle used; in all cases, the responding party should be obligated to produce the information under its control."); *Calzaturficio S.C.A.R.P.A., s.p.a. v. Fabiano Shoe Co.*, 201 F.R.D. 33, 38–39 (D. Mass. 2001) (equating the obligation to that in producing documents); *see also Russo v. Aerojet Rocketdyne, Inc.*, No. MDL 875, 2020 U.S. Dist. LEXIS 140208, at *40, 2020 WL 4530703 (E.D. Pa. 2020) ("[I]t is well-established that 'the corporation must prepare its designee to be able to give binding answers on its behalf... [and] perform a reasonable inquiry for information that is noticed and reasonably available to it." (quoting *State Farm Mut. Auto. Ins. Co. v. New Horizont*, Inc., 250 F.R.D. 203, 216 (E.D. Pa. 2008))); *QBE Ins. Corp. v. Jorda Enters., Inc.*, 277 F.R.D. 676, 689 (S.D. Fla. 2012) (same). See also Chapter 5, section 5-2:1 (discussing the duty of reasonable inquiry with respect to disclosures, interrogatories, and requests for admission).

[114] *Cf. JZ Buckingham Invests., LLC v. U.S.*, 77 Fed. Cl. 37, 47 (Ct. Cl. 2007) (discussing responses to requests for admission and holding that "initially a reasonable inquiry is limited to inquiry of documents and persons 'readily available' and within the responding party's control"); *Duncan v. Nunez*, 2019 U.S. Dist. LEXIS 194260, at *6 (W.D. La. 2019) (same); *Twentieth Century Fox Film Corp. v. Marvel Enters.*, No. 01 Civ. 3016 (AGS) (HBP), 2002 U.S. Dist. LEXIS 14682, at *10, 2002 WL 1835439 (S.D.N.Y. Aug. 6, 2002) ("A corporation responding to interrogatories must provide not only the information contained in its own files and possessed by its own employees, it must also provide all information under its control. 'A party served with interrogatories is obliged to respond by furnishing such information *as is available to the party*. [Defendant] therefore is obliged to respond to the interrogatories not only by providing the information it has, but also the information within its control or otherwise obtainable by it.'" (quoting *In re Auction Houses Antitrust Litig.*, 196 F.R.D. 444, 445 (S.D.N.Y. 2000))); *see also Costa v. Kerzner*

zation to (1) gather and review documents within its possession, custody, or control and documents within the possession of reasonably accessible nonparties under the organization's control; (2) interview (a) current directors, officers, employees, or agents who likely may have relevant information, (b) reasonably accessible nonparties within its control (e.g., directors, officers, employees, and agents of subsidiaries and affiliates under its control) or with an identity of interest, (c) reasonably accessible non-adverse parties with an identity of interest (e.g., a cooperating co-defendant or co-plaintiff), and (d) reasonably accessible and cooperative former directors, officers, and employees; (3) review written-discovery responses in the action; and (4) review relevant witness statements, interview summaries, and deposition transcripts and exhibits.[115] If the organization necessarily would have to obtain the information

---

Int'l Resorts, Inc., 277 F.R.D. 468, 470 (S.D. Fla. 2011) ("Furthermore, as with [Federal] Rule 34, a party must provide information in response to a [Federal] Rule 33 interrogatory if such information is under its control."); *Goodrich Corp. v. Emhart Indus.*, No. EDCV 04-00759-VAP (SSx), 2005 U.S. Dist. LEXIS 17190, at *8, 2005 WL 6440828 (C.D. Cal. June 10, 2005) ("A corporation responding to interrogatories must provide not only the information contained in its own files and possessed by its own employees, but also all information under its control."); *T. Rowe Price Small-Cap Fund, Inc. v. Oppenheimer & Co.*, 174 F.R.D. 38, 43 (S.D.N.Y. 1997) ("Generally, a 'reasonable inquiry' is limited to review and inquiry of those persons and documents that are within the responding party's control."); *U.S. v. Taylor*, 166 F.R.D. 356, 363–64 (M.D.N.C. 1996) (holding that the "reasonable inquiry" requirement obligated the responding party to check its own files for documents sent by or to the responding party to determine their authenticity). See also Chapter 5, section 5-2:1 (discussing the duty of reasonable inquiry with respect to disclosures, interrogatories, and requests for admission).

115 *Cf. Brazos River Auth. v. GE Ionics, Inc.*, 469 F.3d 416, 433 (5th Cir. 2006) ("The deponent must prepare the designee to the extent matters are reasonably available, whether from documents, past employees, or other sources."); *Loboa v. Women's Health All., P.A.*, No. 5:18-CV-00329-FL, 2020 U.S. Dist. LEXIS 31395, at *15, 2020 WL 889739 (E.D.N.C. Feb. 24, 2020) (same); *Duncan v. Nunez*, No. 1:17-CV-1623-P, 2019 U.S. Dist. LEXIS 194260, at *6, 2019 WL 5861997 (W.D. La. No. 17, 2019) ("'A reasonable inquiry includes both (1) an investigation of officers, administrators, agents and employees who conceivably and realistically may have information that may lead to a necessary and appropriate response, and (2) a review of relevant documents and regulations.'" (quoting *Dickie Brennan & Co., Inc. v. Lexington Ins. Co.*, 09-CV-3866, 2010 WL 11538525, at *5 (E.D. La. Feb. 10, 2010))); *Preferred Carolinas Realty, Inc. v. Am. Home Realty Network, Inc.*, No. 1:13CV181, 2014 U.S. Dist. LEXIS 41893, at *18–19, 2014 WL 1320133 (M.D.N.C. Mar. 28, 2014) ("[Federal] Rule 30(b)(6) 'requires a good faith effort . . . to find out the relevant facts—to collect information, review documents, and interview employees with personal knowledge.'" (quoting *Dorsey v. TGT Consulting, LLC*, 888 F. Supp. 2d 670, 685 (D. Md. 2012))); *Aldridge v. Lake Cnty. Sheriff's Office*, No. 11 C 3041, 2012 U.S. Dist. LEXIS 102514, at *5, 2012 WL 3023340 (N.D. Ill. July 24, 2012) ("A corporation . . . has an obligation to prepare an individual by having him or her review available materials or talk to others with knowledge."); *QBE Ins. Corp. v. Jorda Enters.*, 277 F.R.D. 676, 689 (S.D. Fla. 2012) (holding that an organization "must prepare its designees by having them review available materials, such as fact witness deposition testimony, exhibits to depositions, documents produced in discovery, materials in former employees' files and, if necessary, interviews of former employees or others with knowledge"); *Great Am. Ins. Co. v. Vegas Constr. Co.*, 251 F.R.D. 534, 539 (D. Nev. 2008) (noting that the organization "must prepare deponents by having them review prior fact witness deposition testimony as well as documents and deposition exhibits" (quoting *U.S v. Taylor*, 166 F.R.D. 356, 361 (M.D.N.C. 1996), *aff'd*, 166 F.R.D. 367 (M.D.N.C. 1996))); *Wilson v. Lakner*, 228 F.R.D. 524, 528–29 (D. Md. 2005) (holding that a corporation is required

to prepare for trial, it should obtain the information in connection with the deposition if it is reasonably and readily available.[116]

As should be obvious from the foregoing, the duty of reasonable inquiry even applies to information lost from the personal knowledge of the organization's current officers and employees due to time's passage. In such a case the organization either must locate a former officer or employee who is willing to testify about such information or prepare a current one (i.e., create a witness).[117] Texas Rule 199.2(b)(1)'s obligation, however, neither is infinite nor requires perfection. It also does not require the organization to conduct discovery for the other side. Thus, the organization does not have to depose uncooperative former officers, directors, or employees or nonparties or subpoena their documents.[118] In other words, if the organization "'genuinely cannot

---

"to collect information [within its control], review documents [within its control], and interview employees with personal knowledge just as a corporate party is expected to do in answering interrogatories"); *Calzaturficio S.C.A.R.P.A., s.p.a. v. Fabiano Shoe Co.*, 201 F.R.D. 33, 39 (D. Mass. 2001) ("I find that the Fabiano sons, in preparing to be deposed as 30(b)(6) representatives of the company, had the obligation to review all documents that were in their control, including the tax returns and related documents that were in the physical possession of Fabiano's accountant.").

The question of whether an organization must provide information within the knowledge of its subsidiaries and affiliates is discussed in note 122 and its accompanying text.

[116] *Cf. Procaps S.A. v. Patheon Inc.*, No. 12-24356-CIV-GOODMAN, 2015 U.S. Dist. LEXIS 47104, at *6–7 (S.D. Fla. Apr. 10, 2015) ("Significantly, an 'interrogatory will not be held objectionable as calling for research if the interrogated party would gather the information in the preparation of its own case.'" (quoting 8B Charles A. Wright, Arthur R. Miller & Richard L. Marcus, *Federal Practice And Procedure* § 2174 (3d ed. 2014))); *Dixie v. Virga*, No. 2:12-cv-2626-MCE-DAD, 2015 U.S. Dist. LEXIS 11429, at *27, 2015 WL 412298 (E.D. Cal. Jan. 29, 2015) ("[I]f the responding party would necessarily have to gather the requested information to prepare its own case, objections that it is too difficult to obtain the information for the requesting party are not honored." (quoting *L.H. v. Schwarzenegger*, No. 2:06-cv-2042-LKK-GGH, 2007 U.S. Dist. LEXIS 73752, at *9–10, 2007 WL 2781132 (E.D. Cal. Sept. 21, 2007))); *In re Gulf Oil/Cities Serv. Tender Offer Litig.*, Nos. 87 Civ. 5253 (MBM), 87 CIV 8982 (MBM),1990 U.S. Dist. LEXIS 5009, at *8–9, 1990 WL 657537 (S.D.N.Y. May 2, 1990) ("[P]laintiffs will obviously be required to obtain this information as part of their trial preparation if they are to meet Gulf's assertion at trial that Cities misrepresented its oil reserves during the tender offer period. It necessarily follows that it would not be unreasonable to require plaintiffs to obtain such data at this stage in order to serve the purpose embodied in [Federal] Rule 36 of narrowing the scope of contested issues and proof at trial."); *Flour Mills, Inc. v. Pace*, 75 F.R.D. 676, 680 (D. Okla. 1977) ("An interrogatory will not be held objectionable as calling for research if it relates to details alleged in the pleading of the interrogated party, about which it presumably has information, or if the interrogated party would gather the information in the preparation of its own case.").

[117] *Cf. Coryn Grp. II, LLC v. O.C. Seacrets, Inc.*, 265 F.R.D. 235, 238 (D. Md. 2010) ("Indeed, the corporation 'is expected to create a witness or witnesses with responsive knowledge,' and in doing so must make a good faith effort to 'find out the relevant facts—to collect information, review documents, and interview employees with personal knowledge.'" (quoting *Wilson v. Lakner*, 228 F.R.D. 524, 528 (D. Md. 2005))).

[118] *Cf. QBE Ins. Corp. v. Jorda Enters.*, 277 F.R.D. 676, 691 (S.D. Fla. 2012) ("A corporation cannot be faulted for not interviewing individuals who refuse to speak with it."); *Costa v. Cnty. of Burlington*, 254 F.R.D. 187, 191 (D.N.J. 2008) ("Some of plaintiffs' complaints are illustrative of their unreasonable expectations. Certainly, defendant cannot be faulted for failing to interview former employees who are deployed in Iraq. Defendant also cannot be

provide an appropriate designee because it does not have the information, cannot reasonably obtain it from other sources and still lacks sufficient knowledge after reviewing all available information,' its obligations under the Rule cease."[119]

---

faulted for not interviewing officers who refused to speak with it.") (citations omitted); *Wilson v. Lakner*, 228 F.R.D. 524, 529 (D. Md. 2005) ("Wilson is not obliged to depose a string of hospital employees, none of whom is able to speak for the hospital as to how the incident or incidents in question occurred[.]"); *see also U.S. ex. rel. Englund v. L.A. Cnty.*, 235 F.R.D. 675, 685 (E.D. Cal. 2006) ("'Reasonable inquiry' is limited to persons and documents within the responding party's control (e.g., its employees, partners, corporate affiliates, etc.). It does not require the responding party to interview or subpoena records from independent third parties in order to admit or deny a request for admission."); *Haggie v. Coldwell Banker Real Estate Corp.*, No. 4:404CV111-M-A, 2007 U.S. Dist. LEXIS 35666, at *14–16, 2007 WL 1452495 (N.D. Miss. May 15, 2007) ("Under [Federal] Rule 36, a defendant's duty to make a 'reasonable inquiry' should not require the defendant to make judgments or put itself in the shoes of another unrelated defendant. In other words, a real estate company is not required to expend time, energy, and money to inquire as to the veracity of a request for admission regarding information that the bank, its employees, a mortgage lender, its employees, or an appraiser may have had or what those individuals may have thought or done in the course of closing a loan for the sale of a specific property. Instead, the court concludes that the defendant, Coldwell Banker, is responsible for responding only to requests for admission that relate directly to its corporate entity, its agents or employees and their acts, omissions, or impressions and not those of third parties or individuals or information outside its control. This does not mean that the defendant should not make every effort to respond to requests for admission completely and truthfully, but simply that the defendant is not under a duty to conclusively establish facts that it or its agents, partners, employees, corporate affiliates, etc., are without knowledge or evidence to determine."); *T. Rowe Price Small-Cap Fund, Inc. v. Oppenheimer & Co.*, 174 F.R.D. 38, 44 (S.D.N.Y. 1997) ("[I]t far exceeds the reasonable inquiry provision of [Federal] Rule 36 to require defendant to subpoena FDIC documents in Chicago, perhaps litigating the subpoena, travel to Chicago to review large volumes of documents and incur whatever additional expenses may be involved in their production. Thus, to the extent various admissions called for admissions as to matters at the Bank of which Oppenheimer had no knowledge, as to which there may have been relevant information in the FDIC documents, it was appropriate to respond that it has made reasonable inquiry and it was unable to admit or deny the requests."); *Diederich v. Dep't of Army*, 132 F.R.D. 614, 620 (S.D.N.Y. 1990) ("The requirement of 'reasonable inquiry' does not generally extend to third parties. . . ."); *Morreale v. Willcox & Gibbs DN, Inc.*, No. 89 Civ. 5531 (MJL)(NRB), 1991 U.S. Dist. LEXIS 7741, at *1–2, 1991 WL 107441 (S.D.N.Y. June 6, 1991) ("Schwarz'[s] suggestion that defendants had an obligation to take the additional action of interviewing former employees of Peat Marwick, a third party, is unprecedented, and indeed there is some authority to the contrary.").

119 *Aldridge v. Lake Cnty. Sheriff's Office*, No. 11 C 3041, 2012 U.S. Dist. LEXIS 102514, at *5, 2012 WL 3023340 (N.D. Ill. July 24, 2012) (quoting *QBE Ins. Corp. v. Jorda Enters.*, 277 F.R.D. 676, 690 (S.D. Fla. 2012)); *accord Suomen Colorize Oy v. Verizon Servs. Corp.*, No. 12-7154-CJB, 2013 U.S. Dist. LEXIS 150992, at *5–6, 2013 WL 5675516 (D. Del. Oct. 15, 2013) ("Although a [Federal] Rule 30(b)(6) deponent must be properly prepared pursuant to the Rule's dictates, he 'need not have perfect responses to each question, nor a clairvoyant ability to predict every single question that may be posed[.]' And where information is not reasonably available to the corporation, a [Federal] Rule 30(b)(6) witness need not answer the question." (citations omitted) (quoting *Estrada v. Wass*, No. 3:10-CV-1560, 2012 U.S. Dist. LEXIS 52817, at *7, 2012 WL 1268533 (M.D. Pa. Apr. 16, 2012))); *In re JDS Uniphase Corp. Sec. Litig.*, No. C-02-1486 CW (EDL), 2007 U.S. Dist. LEXIS 8523, at *12–13, 2007 WL 219857 (N.D. Cal. Jan. 29, 2007) ("While a corporation is not relieved from preparing its [Federal] Rule 30(b)(6) designee to the extent matters are reasonably available, even

The organization's obligations also must be measured by the scope and nature of the deposition notice's subject matters. If the matters are very broad, it is unrealistic to expect the representative(s) to be able to answer every conceivable question about them. As explained by one federal court:

> Faced by such an overly broad list of topics, the entity may seek, but is not obliged to obtain, a protective order. Federal's decision not to move for a protective order to narrow the scope of the list, but instead to produce a witness like Mr. Lopes, who knew a lot about many of the topics and something about virtually all of them, is certainly permissible. In effect, by choosing to list many broad topics, Delta, as the propounder of the notice, made a strategic decision to avoid the risk that a topic would come up outside the scope of the [Federal] Rule 30(b)(6) notice, while accepting the risk that it is simply impractical to expect [Federal] Rule 30(b)(6) witnesses to know the intimate details of everything.[120]

In the same vein, if it will be difficult to access information about the subject matters because, for example, they relate to events that occurred long ago or actions by a predecessor organization that has not existed for a long period of time, it is unrealistic to expect the organization to produce a witness that has in-depth knowledge about the subject matters.[121]

---

when it no longer employs individuals who remember earlier events, it need not make extreme efforts to obtain all information possibly relevant to the requests."); *Calzaturficio S.C.A.R.P.A., s.p.a. v. Fabiano Shoe Co.*, 201 F.R.D. 33, 38 (D. Mass. 2001) ("Certainly, the obligation imposed by [Federal] Rule 30(b)(6) is not infinite. If the Fabiano sons reviewed the available documentation and still would not have been able to give complete answers on behalf of Fabiano with respect to operating losses or other issues, and there were no other available witnesses who could do so, then Fabiano's 'obligations under [Federal] Rule 30(b)(6) cease, since the rule requires testimony only as to 'matters known or reasonably available to the organization.'" (quoting *Dravo Corp. v. Liberty Mut. Ins. Co.*, 164 F.R.D. 70, 75 (D. Neb., 1995), and Fed. R. Civ. P. 30(b)(6))).

[120] *Fed. Ins. Co. v. Delta Mech. Contrs., LLC*, No. 11-048ML, 2013 U.S. Dist. LEXIS 47582, at *13–14, 2013 WL 1343528 (D.R.I. Apr. 2, 2013) (citations omitted); *see Fresquez v. BNSF Ry.*, No. 1:17-cv-00844-WYD-SKC, 2018 U.S. Dist. LEXIS 221499, at *15–16 (D. Colo. Sept. 17, 2018) ("The fact that the designee cannot answer every question posed at the deposition does not mean that the organization failed to satisfy its obligation to prepare the witness. In determining whether a corporate deponent has met its [Federal] Rule 30(b)(6) obligations, courts have examined the degree and type of effort made by the organization to prepare a witness in light of the deposition topics, and whether the organization acted 'in good faith.' Courts have made clear that 'there is no obligation to produce witnesses who know every single fact, only those that are relevant and material to the incident or incidents that underlie the suit.'" (citations omitted) (quoting *Costa v. Cnty. of Burlington*, 254 F.R.D. 187, 190 (D.N.J. 2008), and *Wilson v. Lakner*, 228 F.R.D. 524, 528–29 n. 7 (D. Md. 2005))).

[121] *Cf. Janki Bai Sahu v. Union Carbide Corp.*, 528 F. App'x 96, 104 (2d Cir. 2013) (affirming district court's denial of a request for certain representative depositions as unduly burdensome because the depositions would have required the defendant to "prepare witnesses to respond to questions regarding events that took place between fifteen and thirty-five years ago. Not only would this be difficult and costly, but the benefit to the Plaintiffs would likely be extremely low: no witness can be expected to provide accurate and detailed accounts of events so far in the past"); *Russo v. Aerojet Rocketdyne, Inc.*, No. MDL 875, 2020 U.S. Dist. LEXIS 140208, at *42–44, 2020 WL 4530703 (E.D. Pa. Aug. 6, 2020) ("The determination whether information is 'known or reasonably available to a corporation requires a fact-spe-

An interesting question is whether information is considered "reasonably available" to an organization if it is in the possession of a related entity. Although the answer depends on the facts of each case, the general rule is that the organization must produce a representative to testify about such information if the other entity is within its "control," as the term is used in connection with the production of documents under Texas Rule 196.[122]

---

cific analysis.' . . . The purpose of the [Federal Rule 30(b)(6)] would not be served by requiring additional [Federal] Rule 30(b)(6) deposition testimony under the circumstances of this case. The information sought by plaintiffs is not in Curtiss-Wright's possession or control. This is not a situation where defendant has failed to provide the witness who possesses the information sought, or who has simply failed to review relevant information that is reasonably available to her. Furthermore, the court notes that the materials plaintiffs seek pertain to Curtiss-Wright's legacy airplane and engine products that were last manufactured in the 1960s or 1970s and were donated due to their historical value in 1969 and 2002. Curtiss-Wright has represented that it does not employ any individual with direct knowledge of the topics set forth in the Notices of Deposition, that many of the former employees with such knowledge are deceased, that Curtiss-Wright has no ability to identify or contact any such living former employees, and that all documents that may contain relevant information were either disposed of in the ordinary course of business many years ago, or donated. The corporation's present lack of knowledge with respect to the aviation products can be attributed, in large part, to the passage of time." (citations omitted) (quoting *Sanofi-Aventis v. Sandoz, Inc.*, 272 F.R.D. 391, 393–94 (D.N.J. 2011))); *Kimberly-Clark Worldwide, Inc. v. First Quality Baby Prods., LLC*, No. 09-c-0916, 2011 U.S. Dist. LEXIS 99027, at *6–8, 2011 WL 3880787 (E.D. Wis. Aug. 31, 2011) ("Notably, [Federal] Rule 37 does not contemplate sanctions when a party no longer has information simply because of the passage of time and the fading of memories. The projects relevant here occurred approximately twenty years ago. Ms. Boudry's deposition responses indicate she made a good faith effort to obtain answers but could not in the face of time and memory constraints. Despite First Quality's claims, Ms. Boudry did not need to review every single document created by K-C twenty years ago in connection with these studies; it is enough that she reviewed several documents relating to each pertinent study, including research notes and written reports. In light of the time that has passed, First Quality's demand that K-C contact every former employee listed on the distribution list for the projects in question is not supportable. As Ms. Boudry's testimony suggests, the specific information First Quality is seeking simply seems to exist no longer. I am satisfied that Ms. Boudry's inability to give more specific information in response to particular questions pertaining to the Libra and EZ-On projects is the result of the lengthy passage of time. Plaintiff is free to challenge the credibility of the witness at trial, but I find no violation of [Federal] Rule 30(b)(6)[.]") (citations omitted); *Walden v. City of Chi.*, No. 04 C 47, 2007 U.S. Dist. LEXIS 7400, at *8–9, 2007 WL 328883 (N.D. Ill. Feb. 1, 2007) (holding that "due to the passage of time and the fact that the pertinent records no longer exist . . . it is not appropriate or just to sanction the [defendant] pursuant to [Federal] Rule 37 for its inability to produce a [Federal] Rule 30(b)(6) witness"); *In re JDS Uniphase*, No. C-02-1486 CW (EDL), 2007 U.S. Dist. LEXIS 8523, at *15–16, 2007 WL 219857 (N.D. Cal. Jan. 29, 2007) (denying a motion to compel, noting that since seven years had passed since the events occurred, the Federal Rule 30(b)(6) designee testified on "matters [that] were reasonably available . . . and, not surprisingly, was unable to answer questions about matters which were not reasonably available"); *Barron v. Caterpillar. Inc.*, 168 F.R.D. 175, 177 (E.D. Pa. 1999) (noting that "parties should anticipate the unavailability of certain information" from events transpiring years ago).

[122] As discussed in Chapter 8, section 8-4:3.1, federal courts frequently require a party responding to a Federal Rule 34 production request to produce documents in the possession of its parent or affiliates even though those entities are not literally under the responding party's

Because an organization is required to produce a witness who can testify about the deposition notice's matters and because "artificial entities," such as corporations, limited liability companies, and partnerships, have no Fifth Amendment privilege,[123] the organization cannot properly designate a representative who will assert the Fifth Amendment privilege against self-incrimination.[124]

---

control. Applying the same rational, federal courts also frequently hold information in the possession of a parent or affiliates is reasonably available to a Federal Rule 30(b)(6) deponent even though the parent or affiliates are not under the deponent's literal control. As explained by one federal court:

> [C]ourts have rejected an approach which limits the "reasonably available" requirement to only information possessed by entities over which the corporate deponent has direct legal control. Instead, courts have frequently used the "control" standard of [Federal] Rule 34(a) as a guideline to determine whether information of corporate affiliates is "reasonably available" to the deponent. The majority view appears to be that information is within a deponent's "control" and thus "reasonably available" for purposes of [Federal] Rule 30(b)(6) when the deponent "either can secure [information] from the related entity to meet its business needs or acted with it in the transaction that gave rise to the suit."

Int'l Bhd. of Teamsters, Airline Div. v. Frontier Airlines, Inc., No. 11-cv-02007-MSK-KLM, 2013 U.S. Dist. LEXIS 22986, at *16, 2013 WL 627149 (D. Colo. Feb. 19, 2013) (quoting *Sanofi-Aventis v. Sandoz, Inc.*, 272 F.R.D. 391, 394 (D.N.J. 2011)).

It is doubtful that this is the case under Texas Rule 199.2(b)(1) because the Texas discovery rules define "possession, custody, or control" in terms of a "right to possession," Tex. R. Civ. P. 192.7, whereas many federal courts equate the term to the party's "practical ability" to obtain the requested materials, which is more expansive. See Chapter 8, section 8-4:3.1.

123 *See In re Nat. Gas Consulting & Measurement, LLC,* No. 07-18-00309-CV, 2018 Tex. App. LEXIS 8320, at *2–8 (Tex. App.—Amarillo Oct. 10, 2018, orig. proceeding) (mem. op.) ("[A] a corporation, like other 'artificial entities' has no right under the Fifth Amendment of the United States Constitution to avoid incriminating itself."); *In re Russo*, 550 S.W.3d 782, 788 (Tex. App.—Houston [14th Dist.] 2018, orig. proceeding) (same); *cf. In re Twelve Grand Jury Subpoenas*, 908 F.3d 525 (9th Cir. 2018) (holding that "small, closely held collective entities, including one-person corporations or LLCs" have no Fifth Amendment privilege); *U.S. v. Bhimani*, No. 3:17-324, 2020 U.S. Dist. LEXIS 182839, at *24, 2020 WL 5878413 (M.D. Pa. Oct. 2, 2020) ("The law is well settled that a corporate defendant may not assert the Fifth Amendment privilege against self-incrimination. Further, '[i]t is well understood that an individual may not assert a Fifth Amendment privilege on behalf of a "collective entity"—i.e., "an[y] organization which is recognized as an independent entity apart from its individual members," such as a corporation or partnership.'" (quoting *In re Grand Jury Proceedings*, 961 F.3d 138, 971 F.3d 40, 56 (2d Cir. 2020))); *Constr. Indus. Laborers Pension Fund v. Wellington Concrete, LLC,* No. 4:15-CV-804 CAS, 2018 U.S. Dist. LEXIS 95005, at *7, 2018 WL 2717909 (E.D. Mo. June 6, 2018) ("A corporation, such as a limited liability company, cannot claim the privilege against self-incrimination"); *SEC v. A Chi. Convention Ctr., LLC,* No. 13 C 982, 2013 U.S. Dist. LEXIS 109395, at *5, 2013 WL 4010585 (N.D. Ill. Aug. 5, 2013) ("It is undisputed that a collective entity, such as a partnership or corporation, may not assert the Fifth Amendment privilege.").

124 *Cf. Louis Vuitton Malletier S.A. v. LY USA, Inc.*, 676 F.3d 83, 92 n.5, 102 (2d Cir. 2012) (noting that "a corporation may not refuse to submit to a [Federal] Rule 30(b0(6) deposition . . . on the grounds that such acts may tend to incriminate it," rather it must designate representatives to act as its witness); *Rightchoice Managed Care, Inc. v. Hosp. Partners, Inc.*, No. 5:18-cv-06037-DGK, 2020 U.S. Dist. LEXIS 175978, at *18, 2020 WL 5733207 (W.D. Mo. Sept. 24, 2020) ("It is 'settled that a corporation has no Fifth Amendment privilege.' After being

In preparing the representative for deposition, counsel must be aware of the fact that the organization may be compelled to produce or disclose the documents reviewed by the organization's representative in preparing for the deposition. That is, a Texas trial court might follow the lead of some federal courts and reject an objection that counsel's selection of the documents constitutes attorney-work product or that the documents are otherwise privileged.[125]

---

served notice of a [Federal] Rule 30(b)(6) deposition, a corporate entity must designate one or more representatives who will not invoke the Fifth Amendment. A corporate entity may not simply refuse to designate a corporate representative who will not invoke the Fifth Amendment. To hold otherwise 'would effectively permit the corporation to assert on its own behalf the personal privilege of its individual agents.' Legal entities that refuse to designate non-invoking corporate representatives may be sanctioned under [Federal] Rule 37." (quoting *Braswell v. U.S.*, 487 U.S. 99, 105 (1988), and *U.S. v. Kordel*, 397 U.S. 1, 8 (1970))); *In re Anthracite Coal Antitrust Litig.*, 82 F.R.D. 364, 369–70 (M.D. Pa. 1979) (imposing sanctions on the defendant corporations because the only persons with corporate knowledge to attend Federal Rule 30(b)(6) depositions invoked their individual Fifth Amendment privileges); *Chi. Title Ins. Co. v. Sinikovic*, No. 11 C 2504, 2015 U.S. Dist. LEXIS 114785, at *12–13, 2015 WL 5116829 (N.D. Ill. Aug. 28, 2015) ("Typically, '[a] witness who asserts his Fifth Amendment rights cannot be compelled to serve as a [Federal] Rule 30(b)(6) deponent' and the corporation can be compelled to answer the questions through an agent who will not invoke the privilege.' But where, as here, the parties stipulated that the corporate deponent was one who invoked his Fifth Amendment privilege and M&M has not proffered another witness, a negative inference can be drawn against M&M despite the fact that it has no Fifth Amendment privilege of its own to assert." (quoting *Bank of Am., N.A. v. First Mut. Bancorp*, Nos. 09 C 5108, 09 C 5109, 2010 U.S. Dist. LEXIS 58519, at *13, 2010 WL 2364916 (N.D. Ill. June 14, 2010))); *SEC v. A Chi. Convention Ctr., LLC*, No. 13 C 982, 2013 U.S. Dist. LEXIS 109395, at *5–6, 2013 WL 4010585 (N.D. Ill. Aug. 5, 2013) ("[A] corporation cannot avoid responding to a discovery request merely by stating that the officer or employee with personal knowledge asserts his Fifth Amendment rights. Rather, if a discovery request served on a corporate entity implicates the Fifth Amendment rights of a corporate officer—as here—the corporate entity has an obligation 'to appoint an agent who could, without fear of self-incrimination, furnish such requested information as was available to the corporation.'" (quoting *U.S. v. Kordel*, 397 U.S. 1, 8 (1970))); *Worthington Pump Corp. v. Hoffert Mar., Inc.*, No. A 79-3531, 1982 U.S. Dist. LEXIS 17968, at *6–7, 1982 WL 308871 (D.N.J. Feb. 19, 1982) ("Normally when a corporate official acting as such invokes his fifth amendment privilege, the corporation is required to designate another agent who is capable of furnishing the information without incriminating himself.").

Notwithstanding this rule, a trial court cannot property order the representative of an organization to waive his personal Fifth Amendment privilege. *E.g.*, *In re Nat. Gas Consulting & Measurement, LLC*, No. 07-18-00309-CV, 2018 Tex. App. LEXIS 8320, at *5 (Tex. App.—Amarillo Oct. 10, 2018, orig. proceeding) (mem. op.) ("The trial court may compel a corporate representative to appear for deposition and testify on behalf of the corporation. So too may it order the custodian of corporate books and records to produce same despite the chance that doing so incriminates both the custodian and the corporation. But, the trial court may not compel the representative designated to testify on behalf of the 'artificial entity' to provide oral testimony that would incriminate himself.").

125 Many federal courts have held that an attorney's compilation or selection of relevant documents for use in discovery constitutes protected work product. *E.g.*, *Sporck v. Peil*, 759 F.2d 312, 316–18 (3d Cir. 1985) (the leading case). *But see Chase v. Nova Se. Univ., Inc.*, No. 11-61290-CIV, 2012 U.S. Dist. LEXIS 7858, at *5–6, 2012 WL 204173 (S.D. Jan. 24, Fla. 2012) (requiring "the party raising a 'selection based opinion work product' objection to 'come forward with some evidence that disclosure of the requested documents creates

11-1:1.6a Because the Representative's Testimony Is Not a Judicial Admission, It Can Be Corrected, Contradicted, Amended, or Supplemented

What happens when an organization later realizes that its representative's testimony on a matter was wrong or incomplete? Although courts agree that the testimony of an organization "binds" the organization in the sense that it is an admission by the organization,[126] the testimony is not tantamount to a judicial admission that precludes

---

a real, non-speculative danger of revealing counsel's thoughts'" (quoting *In re Trasylol*, 2009 U.S. Dist. LEXIS 46488, at 864–65, 2009 WL 936597, at *4 (S.D. Fla. Apr. 7, 2009))). They, however, often also hold that the documents used to prepare a witness for a Federal Rule 30(b)(6) deposition are discoverable under Federal Rule of Evidence 612, which gives a trial court discretion to order the production of documents used to refresh a witness's recollection before testifying at trial or a deposition, *e.g., Baxter Int'l, Inc. v. Becton, Dickinson & Co.*, No. 17 C 7576, 2019 U.S. Dist. LEXIS 203234, at *34–35, 2019 WL 6258490 (N.D. Ill. Nov. 22, 2019) ("'Parties have a heightened need to discover documents used to prepare witnesses designated under [Federal Rule] 30(b)(6),' as 'the substance of their testimony may be based on sources beyond personal knowledge.' This need is particularly heightened when a corporation uses privileged documents to prepare its witness; prohibiting the cross-examining party from seeing those documents because of attorney-client privilege would encourage 'parties to use privileged documents to prepare witnesses as a means of limiting the preparation of the cross-examiner.'" (quoting *Adidas Am., Inc. v. TRB Acquisitions Ltd. Liab. Co.*, 324 F.R.D. 389, 397–98 (D. Or. 2017))); *Hsingching Hsu v. Puma Biotechnology, Inc.*, No. 8:15-cv-00865-AG (SHK), 2018 U.S. Dist. LEXIS 103353, at *36–38, 2018 WL 3078589 (C.D. Cal. June 20, 2018) (ordering the production of the documents reviewed by the representative in preparation for a Federal Rule 30(b)(6) deposition); *Coryn Grp. II, LLC v. O.C. Seacrets, Inc.*, 265 F.R.D. 235, 245 (D. Md. 2010) ("Where a 30(b)(6) deponent has no personal (or independent) knowledge of a topic, factual documents prepared for him to allow him to discharge his obligations under [Federal] Rule 30(b)(6) must necessarily be produced [under Federal Rule of Evidence 612]. How would it serve the pursuit of truth to shield such information, where the very same information would be available through other discovery devices? Denial of access would only cloud, rather than clarify, corporate knowledge."); *see Tellis v. LeBlanc*, No. 18-cv-541, 2020 U.S. Dist. LEXIS 176785, at *11, 2020 WL 5732628 (W.D. La. Sept. 24, 2020) ("[C]ounsel must be careful when educating a [Federal] Rule 30(b)(6) witness, who lacks personal knowledge, with documents protected by the attorney-client privilege or work product doctrine. Rigorous cross-examination may force production of these otherwise protected documents."); *Corcoran v. CVS Health*, No. 15-cv-03504-YGR (JSC), 2016 U.S. Dist. LEXIS 170897, at *14 (N.D. Cal. 2016) ("A [Federal] Rule 30(b)(6) witness who must collect information, review documents, or interview other employees cannot claim that his own information-gathering process is protected by the work-product doctrine even if counsel participates in the process."). See also notes 288–297 and accompanying text (discussing the applicability of Texas Rule of Evidence 612 to depositions).

126 *Cf. BBK Tobacco & Foods LLP v. Skunk Inc.*, No. CV-18-02332-PHX-JAT, 2020 U.S. Dist. LEXIS 87734, at *3–4 (D. Ariz. May 19, 2020) ("[T]he answers of a duly noticed 30(b)(6) deponent are binding on the company."); *Engage Healthcare Commc'ns, LLC v. Intellisphere, LLC*, No. 12-cv-00787(FLW)(LHG), 2017 U.S. Dist. LEXIS 214562, at *4, 2017 WL 9481037 (D.N.J. Oct. 30, 2017) ("In stark contrast to an individual's deposition, which is based upon the deponent's individual knowledge, a [Federal] Rule 30(b)(6) designee's testimony is binding on the organizational entity[.]"); *Lifetime Prods. v. Russell Brands, LLC*, No. 1:12-cv-00026-DN-EJF, 2015 U.S. Dist. LEXIS 182647, at *4, 2015 WL 12744294 (D. Utah Dec. 29, 2015) ("The testimony by the 30(b)(6) witness, even if duplicative of

contradiction, correction, amendment, or supplementation. Rather, the organization is "bound" by its representative's testimony only in the same sense as any other witness is bound. That is, the organization has committed to a position at a particular point in time, which may be contradicted, corrected, amended, or supplemented at trial or in later discovery responses. As explained by one federal court:

> Viskase argues that Grace is bound by its [Federal] Rule 30(b)(6) deposition testimony as a matter of law. On this basis, Viskase moves to preclude Grace from introducing any evidence that is contrary to statements made in its [Federal] Rule 30(b)(6) depositions.
>
> Once again, Viskase misconstrues the law. It is true that a corporation is "bound" by its [Federal] Rule 30(b)(6) testimony, in the same sense that any individual deposed under [Federal] Rule 30(b)(1) would be "bound" by his or her testimony. All this means is that the witness has committed to a position at a particular point in time. It does not mean that the witness has made a judicial admission that formally and finally decides an issue. Deposition testimony is simply evidence, nothing more. Evidence may be explained or contradicted. Judicial admissions, on the other hand, may not be contradicted. Viskase ignores the differences between evidentiary testimony and judicial admissions.
>
> If a Grace trial witness makes a statement that contradicts a position previously taken in a [Federal] Rule 30(b)(6) deposition, then Viskase may impeach that witness with the prior inconsistent statement.[127]

---

discovery already provided, has particular significance because it definitively binds the corporation."); *Difiore v. CSL Behring, U.S., LLC*, No. 13-5027, 2015 U.S. Dist. LEXIS 121107, at *2, 2015 WL 5316479 (E.D. Pa. Sept. 11, 2015) ("A corporation is 'bound' by a 30(b)(6) deponent's testimony concerning factual matters."); *Schall v. Suzuki Motor of Am., Inc.*, No. 4:14CV-00074-JHM, 2017 U.S. Dist. LEXIS 147953, at *10, 2017 WL 4050319 (W.D. Ky. Sept. 13, 2017) (same); *Marriott v. Cnty. of Montgomery*, 426 F. Supp. 2d 1, 8 n.8 (N.D.N.Y 2006) ("However, as a [Federal] Rule 30(b)(6) witness, Pecora's testimony is binding upon defendants."); *Twentieth Century Fox Film Corp. v. Marvel Enters.*, No. 01 Civ. 3016 (AGS) (HBP), 2002 U.S. Dist. LEXIS 14682, at *6, 2002 WL 1835439 (S.D.N.Y. Aug. 6, 2002) ("A 30(b)(6) witness testifies as a representative of the entity, his answers bind the entity[.]" (quoting *Sabre v. First Dominion Capital, LLC*, No. 01 Civ. 2145 (BSJ) (HBP), 2001 U.S. Dist. LEXIS 20637, at *2, 2001 WL 1590544 (S.D.N.Y. Dec. 12, 2001))); *Sanders v. Circle K Corp.*, 137 F.R.D. 292, 294 (D. Ariz. 1991) ("The purpose behind [Federal] Rule 30(b)(6) is to create testimony that will bind the corporation.").

127 *W. R. Grace & Co. v. Viskase Corp.*, No. 90-5383, 1991 U.S. Dist. LEXIS 14651, at *5–7, 1991 WL 211647 (N.D. Ill. Oct. 11, 1991); *accord Hanna v. Giant Eagle, Inc.*, 777 F. App'x 41, 42 (3d Cir. 2019); *Snapp v. United Transp. Union*, 889 F.3d 1088, 1103–04 (9th Cir. 2018); *Vehicle Mkt. Research, Inc. v. Mitchell Int'l, Inc.*, 839 F.3d 1251, 1260 (10th Cir. 2016); *S. Wine & Spirits of Am., Inc. v. Div. of Alcohol & Tobacco Control*, 731 F.3d 799, 811 (8th Cir. 2013); *A.I. Credit Corp. v. Legion Ins. Co.*, 265 F.3d 630, 637 (7th Cir. 2001); *AmTrust N. Am., Inc v. KF&B, Inc.*, No. 17-cv-5340 (LJL), 2020 U.S. Dist. LEXIS 170464, at *2–4, 2020 WL 5578675 (S.D.N.Y. Sept. 16, 2020); *Foremost Farms USA v. Diamond V. Mills, Inc.*, No. 16-cv-551-jdp, 2018 U.S. Dist. LEXIS 21488, at *18–19, 2018 WL 813518 (W.D. Wis. Feb. 9, 2018); *U.S. ex rel. Landis v. Tailwind Sports Corp.*, No. 10-cv-976 (CRC), 2017 U.S. Dist. LEXIS 195559, at *9, 2017 WL 5897381 (D.D.C. Nov. 28, 2017).

Although some federal courts construing Federal Rule 30(b)(6) have held that, absent an evidentiary showing that the information was not reasonably available to the organization when its representative was deposed, the organization cannot introduce evidence contrary to the testimony of its representative,[128] nothing in the language of Texas Rule 199.2(b)(1) or any other Texas discovery rule,[129] the Advisory Committee Notes to Federal Rule 30(b)(6) on which the Texas Rule is based,[130] or evidentiary

---

[128] *E.g., Cont'l Cas. Co. v. First Fin. Emps. Leasing, Inc.*, 716 F. Supp. 2d 1176, 1190 (M.D. Fla. 2010) ("[S]ome courts have stated generally that when the [Federal] Rule 30(b)(6) representative claims ignorance of a subject during the deposition, the organization is precluded from later introducing evidence on that subject unless the evidence was previously unavailable."); ***Wilson v. Lakner***, 228 F.R.D. 524, 529–30 (D. Md. 2005) ("[D]epending on the nature and extent of the obfuscation, the testimony given by the non-responsive deponent (e.g. 'I don't know') may be deemed 'binding on the corporation' so as to prohibit it from offering contrary evidence at trial."); ***Rainey v. Am. Forest & Paper Ass'n***, 26 F. Supp. 2d 82, 94 (D.D.C. 1998) ("Unless it can prove that the information was not known or was inaccessible, a corporation cannot later proffer new or different allegations that could have been made at the time of the 30(b)(6) deposition."); *see* ***BBK Tobacco & Foods LLP v. Skunk Inc.***, No. CV-18-02332-PHX-JAT, 2020 U.S. Dist. LEXIS 87734, at *3–4 (D. Ariz. May 19, 2020) ("[T]he answers of a duly noticed 30(b)(6) deponent are binding on the company. Thus, hypothetically, if the duly noticed 30(b)(6) deponent was asked, 'Do you make balloons?' and answered 'I don't know'—'I don't know' is the binding answer on the company. Thus, the hypothetical company would likely not be permitted on summary judgment or at trial to offer evidence that contradicts or supplements the company's final, binding answer from the 30(b)(6) deposition that it does not know if it produces balloons.").

[129] *See* Tex. R. Civ. P. 199.2(b)(1).

[130] For example, unlike written discovery, generally there is no obligation to supplement deposition testimony even if it is wrong or incomplete. Tex. R. Civ. P. 193 cmt. 5 to 1999 change (Texas Rule 193.5 "imposes no duty to supplement or amend deposition testimony. The only duty to supplement deposition testimony is provided in [Texas] Rule 195.6[, relating to testifying experts]."); *see* ***Titus Cnty. Hosp. Dist. v. Lucas***, 988 S.W.2d 740, 740 (Tex. 1998) (per curiam) (holding that, under former Texas Rule 166b(6), "[a] general duty to supplement deposition testimony (as opposed to a narrow duty for certain expert testimony, for example) would impose too great a burden on litigants. We therefore disapprove the court of appeals' holding that deposition testimony must be supplemented.") (citation omitted).

Nonetheless, a party cannot disregard its Texas Rule 199.2(b)(1) representative's testimony with impunity. For example, the "sham-affidavit" rule, which allows a court to disregard a party's summary judgment affidavit that conflicts with the party's deposition testimony if the party does not provide a sufficient explanation for the conflict, ***Lujan v. Navistar, Inc.***, 555 S.W.3d 79, 82, 85–86 (Tex. 2018), is applicable to affidavits that contradict a representative's deposition testimony. *Cf.* ***MKB Constructors v. Am. Zurich Ins. Co.***, 49 F. Supp. 3d 814, 828–29 (W.D. Wash. 2014) ("[I]in an apparent attempt to create an issue of fact with respect to this issue, Mr. Jensen submits a declaration that contradicts his prior [Federal] Rule 30(b)(6) deposition testimony. In the Ninth Circuit, the 'sham affidavit rule' prevents a party from creating an issue of material fact by introducing an affidavit that contradicts prior deposition testimony. The court has little difficulty in finding that Mr. Jensen's statement that 'MKB has never been paid "the withheld contract payment" from LYSD' is clearly and unambiguously inconsistent with his prior deposition testimony that 'MKB was paid—in the arbitration proceedings— . . . the contract balance by [LYSD]' Nowhere in his declaration does Mr. Jensen reference or try to explain his prior inconsistent deposition testimony or try to harmonize the two statements. The court, therefore, finds that Mr. Jensen's subsequent inconsistent declaration creates nothing more than a sham issue of fact. Thus, the court may rely on the Mr. Jensen's deposition testimony in granting summary principles supports this conclusion.[131] Rather, to effectively "bind" an organization, the noticing party should (1) file a motion to compel answers or a new deposition if the organization's representative claimed ignorance about a matter, had limited knowledge about it, or was evasive, or (2) serve an interrogatory or request for admission regarding the matter, the answers to which should preclude the organization from introducing contrary evidence.[132]

11-1:1.6b Duplicative Depositions—Deposing an Organization's Representative Individually After the Organization's Deposition or Vice Versa *and Taking More Than One Representative Deposition*

In the context of representative depositions, several questions arise regarding the propriety of duplicative depositions. *First,* can an organization properly object to a Texas Rule 199.2(b)(1) deposition merely because the person who will be its representative has already been deposed in his or her individual capacity? *Second,* if an individual is deposed in a representative capacity, can the individual properly object to later being deposed in his or her individual capacity? *Third,* can a party take more than one representative deposition?

Relevant to the first two questions is the last sentence of Texas Rule 199.2(b)(1), which provides that "[t]his subdivision does not preclude taking deposition by any other procedure authorized by these rules." Federal courts, based on the identical language of Federal Rule 30(b)(6), recognize that generally "there is no prohibition on deposing a witness as a corporate representative and then in an individual capacity"[133] and that "a second deposition is not improper in the converse factual situation

---

judgment on this issue.") (citations omitted); *Hyde v. Stanley Tools,* 107 F. Supp. 2d 992, 993 (E.D. La. 2000) (striking a summary judgement affidavit that "directly contradict[ed]" the party's [Federal] Rule 30(b)(6) deposition when the party did not provide a "reasonable explanation" for the inconsistency), *aff'd,* 31 Fed. Appx. 151 (5th Cir. 2001) (per curiam); *State Farm Mut. Auto. Ins. Co. v. New Horizont,* 250 F.R.D. 203 (E.D. Pa. 2008) (same); *Tex. Tech. Inst., Inc. v. Silicon Valley, Inc.,* No. H-04-3349, 2006 U.S. Dist. LEXIS 6257, at *21–22, 2006 WL 237027 (S.D. Tex. Jan. 31, 2006) (same).

[131] There is no evidence rule precluding a witness from testifying differently at trial than during his or her deposition. *But see* cases cited in note 127.

[132] Tex. R. Civ. P. 193.6(a) ("A party who fails to make, amend, or supplement a discovery response in a timely manner may not introduce in evidence the material or information that was not timely disclosed, . . . unless the court finds that: (1) there was good cause for the failure to timely make, amend, or supplement the discovery response; or (2) the failure to timely make, amend, or supplement the discovery response will not unfairly surprise or unfairly prejudice the other parties."), 198.3 ("The court may permit the party to withdraw or amend the admission if: (a) the party shows good cause for the withdrawal or amendment; and (b) the court finds that the parties relying upon the responses and deemed admissions will not be unduly prejudiced and that the presentation of the merits of the action will be subserved by permitting the party to amend or withdraw the admission."). Texas Rules 193.6 and 198.3 respectively are discussed in Chapters 5, section 5-7 and 10, section 7.

[133] *Sw. Bell Tel., L.P. v. UTEX Commc'ns, Corp.,* No. A-07-CV-435 RP, 2009 U.S. Dist. LEXIS 131706, at *10, 2009 WL 8541000 (W.D. Tex. Sept. 30, 2009) (citing cases), *cited with approval in Aids Healthcare Found., Inc. v. City of Baton Rouge,* No. 17-229-BAJ-RLB, 2018 U.S. Dist. LEXIS 108211, at *4–5 (M.D. La. 2018); *accord Quarrie v. Wells,* No. 17-350 MV/GBW, 2020 U.S. Dist. LEXIS 162867, at *19–20, 2020 WL 5329886 (D.N.M. Sept. 4, 2020) ("[W]hile the

in which a deposition was first taken of a witness in an individual capacity and then a second deposition was sought of a witness in a representative capacity"[134] Nonetheless as cautioned by one federal court:

Court acknowledges Defendant NMT's frustration regarding Plaintiff's refusal to depose Mr. Wells and Ms. Liebrock on the 30(b)(6) topics during their previously scheduled depositions, Plaintiff is correct that he has the right to depose them separately as individuals and corporate representatives."); *Young v. Physician Office Partners, Inc.*, No. 18-cv-2481-KHV-TJJ, 2019 U.S. Dist. LEXIS 148646, at *5 (D. Kan. Aug. 30, 2019) ("[C]ourts have consistently held that the fact that a company's employee was deposed under [Federal] Rule 30(b)(1) does not insulate the company from producing the same—or another—individual as a corporate representative to give a [Federal] Rule 30(b)(6) deposition. Indeed, [Federal] Rule 30(b)(6) itself contemplates both individual and corporate depositions, stating '[t]his paragraph (6) does not preclude a deposition by any other procedure allowed by these rules.'" (citing *In re Motor Fuel Temperature Sales Practices Litig.*, No. 07-MD-1840-KHV, 2009 U.S. Dist. LEXIS 118705, at *41, 2009 WL 5064441 (D. Kan. Dec. 16, 2009))); *Sunflower Redevelopment, LLC v. Ill. Union Ins. Co.*, No. 4:15-CV-00577-DGK, 2017 U.S. Dist. LEXIS 185830, at *3, 2017 WL 9360848 (W.D. Mo. Nov. 9, 2017) (["O]nce a party names an entity and describes the matter for examination in its notice for deposition, the entity 'must' designate a person to testify on its behalf and 'may' identify the matters the person designated will testify. The same person may be deposed as a fact witness and a corporate representative in separate depositions."); *Sprint Commc'ns Co., L.P. v. Comcast Cable Commc'ns, LLC*, Nos. 11-2684-JWL, 11-2685-JWL, 11-2686-JWL, 2015 U.S. Dist. LEXIS 76845, at *32, 2015 WL 3742929 (D. Kan. June 15, 2015) ("[C]ourts have consistently held that the fact that a company's employee was deposed under [Federal] Rule 30(b)(1) does not insulate the company from producing the same—or another—individual as a corporate representative to give a [Federal] Rule 30(b)(6) deposition on the same topic. Indeed, [Federal] Rule 30(b)(6) itself contemplates both individual and corporate depositions, stating '[t]his paragraph (6) does not preclude a deposition by any other procedure allowed by these rules.'") (footnote omitted); *Purdue Pharma L.P. v. Ranbaxy Inc.*, No. 3:12-MC-1 (CAR), 2012 U.S. Dist. LEXIS 55858, at *8 & n.2, *9, 2012 WL 1414308 (M.D. Ga. Apr. 20, 2012) (allowing a deposition of an organization's representative in his individual capacity); *Ferguson v. Bell Helicopter Textron Inc.*, No. 1:09cv635-MHT (WO), 2011 U.S. Dist. LEXIS 99081, at *4, 2011 WL 13365084 (M.D. Ala. Sept. 2, 2011) (same); *Provide Commerce, Inc. v. Preferred Commerce, Inc.*, No. 07-80185 Civ, 2008 U.S. Dist. LEXIS 9563, at *8–9, 2008 WL 360588 (S.D. Fla. Feb. 8, 2008) ("Although [the corporate president's] testimony may be similar under the law, a corporate entity is distinct from the individuals who control or manage the corporation. Although the limitations on multiple depositions of the same person apply to [Federal] Rule 30(b)(6) motions, this Court did not find any case law that barred a second deposition of an individual who was first deposed in his individual capacity and then called to testify a second time on behalf of the corporation. [The president] has only testified as an individual and not on behalf of the corporation."); *Sabre v. First Dominion Cap., L.L.C.*, No. 01 Civ. 2145 (BSJ) (HBP), 2001 U.S. Dist. LEXIS 20637, at *4, 2001 WL 1590544 (S.D.N.Y. Dec. 12, 2001) ("I conclude that the 30(b)(6) deposition of a witness is a separate deposition from the deposition of that same person as an individual witness and is presumptively subject to a separate, independent seven-hour time limit.").

[134] *Sw. Bell Tel., L.P. v. UTEX Commc'ns Corp.*, No. A-07-CV-435 RP, 2009 U.S. Dist. LEXIS 131706, at *10, 2009 WL 8541000 (W.D. Tex. Sept. 30, 2009) (citing cases); *accord Brown v. Norfolk S. Ry.*, No. 3:18-CV-205-TRM-DCP, 2020 U.S. Dist. LEXIS 8509, at *15–16, 2020 WL 265280 (E.D. Tenn. Jan. 17, 2020) ("Defendant argues that Plaintiff has already had an opportunity to explore the categories of inquiry at great length, given the number of employees who have already testified about regulatory compliance. It is well established, however, 'A [Federal] Rule 30(b)(6) witness differs from a "mere corporate employee" because, unlike an individual witness, the testimony of a [Federal] Rule 30(b)(6) witness

represents the knowledge of the corporation and testimony under the rule binds the corporation.' Therefore, 'prior deposition testimony from individual fact witnesses does not relieve a corporation from designating a corporate spokesperson in response to a [Federal] Rule 30(b)(6) notice of deposition.'" (quoting *Edwards v. Scripps Media, Inc.*, 331 F.R.D. 116, 121 (E.D. Mich. 2019))); *White v. City of Cleveland*, 417 F. Supp. 3d 896, 909 (N.D. Ohio 2019) ("Multiple courts have rejected the 'argument that prior deposition testimony from individual fact witnesses relieves a corporation from designating a corporate spokesperson in response to a [Federal] Rule 30(b)(6) notice of deposition.' Consequently, neither the City's production of documents nor the fact that other witnesses have testified regarding the investigation of the home invasion excuse the City from providing a representative or representatives to testify." (citations omitted) (quoting *Smith v. Gen. Mills, Inc.*, No. C2 04-705, 2006 U.S. Dist. LEXIS 19093, at *15, 2006 WL 7276959 (S.D. Ohio Apr. 13, 2006))); *Difiore v. CSL Behring, U.S., LLC*, No. No. 13-5027, 2015 U.S. Dist. LEXIS 121107, at *3–4, 2015 WL 5316479 (E.D. Pa. Sept. 11, 2015) (rejecting a company's objection to certain subject matters in a representative deposition notice because its employees had already testified about them, reasoning that "[m]any other courts have not found the purported redundancy of deposing both individual fact witnesses and a corporate designee on similar topics to be an obstacle to a 30(b)(6) deposition"); *Matrix Grp., LLC v. Innerlight Holdings, Inc.*, No. 2:11-cv-00987, 2015 U.S. Dist. LEXIS 3304, at *3, 2015 WL 153822 (D. Utah Jan. 12, 2015) ("While the court recognizes that the scope of Defendants' prior depositions were broad, 'courts have consistently held that the fact that a company's employee was deposed under [Federal] Rule 30(b)(1) does not insulate the company from producing the same—or another—individual as a corporate representative to give a 30(b)(6) deposition.'" (quoting *In re Motor Fuel Temperature Sales Practices Litig.*, No. 07-MD-1840-KHV, 2009 U.S. Dist. LEXIS 118705, at *38–39, 2009 WL 5064441 (D. Kan. Dec. 16, 2009))); *Centrix Fin. Liquidating Tr. v. Nat'l Union Fire Ins. Co.*, No. 4:12-MC-624-JAR, 2013 U.S. Dist. LEXIS 88843, at *11–12, 2013 WL 3225802 (E.D. Mo. June 25, 2013) ("[P]rior deposition testimony from individual fact witnesses does not relieve a corporation from designating a corporate spokesperson in response to a [Federal] Rule 30(b)(6) notice of deposition, even when the same witness will testify in an individual and a corporate capacity.").

In the same vein, a party cannot avoid a representative deposition on the basis of that its written discovery responses are sufficient to respond to the notice's topics. *Cf. CRST Expedited, Inc. v. Swift Transp. Co. Ariz., LLC*, No. 17-CV-25-CJW-KEM, 2019 U.S. Dist. LEXIS 113717, at *15–17, 2019 WL 2714508 (N.D. Iowa Mar. 6, 2019) (rejecting argument that written discovery is a substitute for a Federal Rule 30(b) (deposition); *Tolston v. Charles Drew Health Ctr., Inc.*, No. 8:16CV176, 2017 U.S. Dist. LEXIS 101716, at *14–15, 2017 WL 2838134 (D. Neb. 2017) ("'Producing documents and responding to written discovery is not a substitute for providing a thoroughly educated [Federal] Rule 30(b)(6) deponent.' A [Federal] Rule 30(b)(6) deposition serves a unique function—it is the 'sworn corporate admission that is binding on the corporation.' Written discovery and other individual depositions do not excuse Defendant from its obligations under [Federal] Rule 30(b)(6)." (citations omitted) (quoting *Murphy v. Kmart Corp.*, 255 F.R.D. 497, 507 (D.S.D. 2009), and *In re Vitamins Antitrust Litig.*, 216 F.R.D. 168, 174 (D. D.C. 2003))); *CitiMortgage, Inc. v. Chi. Bancorp, Inc.*, No. 4:12-CV-00246 CDP, 2013 U.S. Dist. LEXIS 107131, at *2, 2013 WL 3946116 (E.D. Mo. July 31, 2013) ("A named entity may not take the position that its documents, responses to interrogatories, or other written discovery already produced is sufficient. . . . Written discovery is not a substitute for a [Federal] Rule 30(b)(6) deposition, and a corporation cannot choose to submit answers to a party's [Federal] Rule 30(b)(6) deposition questions at some later date in a form it prefers."); *Buehrle v. City of O'Fallon*, No. 4:10CV00509 AGF, 2011 U.S. Dist. LEXIS 11972, at *7, 2011 WL 529922 (E.D. Mo. Feb. 8, 2011) ("Discovery by means of a [Federal] Rule 30(b)(6) deposition differs from discovery obtained through other means, e.g. interrogatories and requests for production. A [Federal] Rule 30(b)(6) deposition allows the requesting party to obtain 'more complete information and is, therefore favored.' . . . 'Producing documents and responding to written

This is not to say, however, that the inquiring party has carte blanche to depose an individual for seven hours as an individual and seven hours as a 30(b)(6) witness. In the case of many closely-held corporations, the knowledge of an individual concerning a particular subject also constitutes the total knowledge of the entity. In such a situation, the witness could simply adopt the testimony he or she provided in a former capacity, thereby obviating the need for a second deposition. In addition, if the questioning at any deposition becomes repetitive or is otherwise being conducted in an oppressive manner, the aggrieved party can always make application for a protective order.[135]

---

discovery is not a substitute for providing a thoroughly educated [Federal] Rule 30(b)(6) deponent.'" (citations omitted) (quoting *Great Am. Ins. Co. v. Vegas Constr. Co.*, 251 F.R.D. 534, 539, 541 (D. Nev. 2008))).

[135] *Sabre v. First Dominion Cap., L.L.C.*, No. 01 Civ. 2145 (BSJ)(HBP), 2001 U.S. Dist. LEXIS 20637, at *3–4, 2001 WL 1590544 (S.D.N.Y. Dec. 10, 2001); *accord Bank of Am., N.A. v. New Eng. Quality Serv.*, No. 5:16-cv-83, 2017 U.S. Dist. LEXIS 108703, at *9–10, 2017 WL 2955760 (D. Vt. July 10, 2017) ("Here, four BOA witnesses already have been deposed individually. It is not clear whether their testimony represents the knowledge of BOA on the issues that they discussed. If it does, then BOA may elect to deem their testimony to constitute [Federal] Rule 30(b)(6) testimony. On any issues listed in the Subpoena but not answered by a deponent whose testimony that BOA is willing to deem [Federal] Rule 30(b)(6) testimony, BOA must designate and prepare Ms. Grzeskowiak or other suitable witnesses to supply [Federal] Rule 30(b)(6) testimony. At the same time, the court rejects Defendants' request that BOA designate 'individuals in positions of higher authority than Mr. McDermott and Ms. Grzeskowiak' as BOA's [Federal] Rule 30(b)(6) witnesses.") (citations omitted); *Redmond v. San Jose Police Dep't*, No. 14-cv-02345-BLF (SVK), 2017 U.S. Dist. LEXIS 53339, at *3 (N.D. Cal. Apr. 6, 2017) ("An entity may also satisfy its [Federal] Rule 30(b)(6) obligation by offering to be bound by prior deposition testimony regarding a noticed [Federal] Rule 30(b)(6) topic."); *Difiore v. CSL Behring, U.S., LLC*, No. 13-5027, 2015 U.S. Dist. LEXIS 121107, at *3–4, 2015 WL 5316479 (E.D. Pa. Sept. 11, 2015) (suggesting that an organization can avoid a representative deposition by adopting its employees' deposition testimony and agreeing to be bound by it: "In one instance where a court did limit 30(b)(6) depositions on this ground, the corporation had explicitly agreed to be bound by the testimony of an employee previously deposed in his individual capacity. The reasoning of that case is persuasive, but it is easily distinguishable from the present case in which CSL frequently notes that the Plaintiff 'will likely argue' it is bound to its employees' testimony, without agreeing to be so bound. Therefore, I am persuaded that Defendant should still be required to prepare a 30(b)(6) deponent regarding these topics, as they have not agreed to accept their employees' prior testimony as their own."); *Rizzo v. C.R. Bard, Inc. (In re C. R. Bard, Inc.)*, No. MDL No. 2187, 2013 U.S. Dist. LEXIS 57003, at *11–12 (S.D. W. Va. 2013) ("[I]n lieu of designating a corporate witness to address topics that were already the subject of extensive testimony, Bard may designate the testimony that it is willing to adopt as its corporate position. However, to the extent that the witnesses did not provide testimony reflecting Bard's corporate knowledge and opinions, or did not supply complete testimony, Plaintiffs shall be permitted to proceed with [Federal] Rule 30(b)(6) depositions."); *EEOC v. Boeing Co.*, No. CV 05-03034-PHX-FJM, 2007 U.S. Dist. LEXIS 29107, at *4, 2007 WL 1146446 (D. Ariz. Apr. 18, 2007) ("A corporation may also satisfy its [Federal] Rule 30(b)(6) obligation by offering to be bound by prior deposition testimony regarding a noticed [Federal] Rule 30(b)(6) topic."); *A.I.A. Holdings, S.A v. Lehman Bros., Inc.*, No. 97 Civ. 4978, 2002 U.S. Dist. LEXIS 9218, at *18, 2002 WL 1041356 (S.D.N.Y May 20, 2002) ("Since a 30(b)(6) witness is obligated to provide the entity's knowledge, the mere fact that the principal of a corporation has been deposed is not an automatic substitute for a 30(b)(6) deposition. However, common sense teaches that in the case of relatively small, closely-held entities, like [the plaintiff

corporation], there may be no difference between the knowledge of the entity and the knowledge of its principals. . . . A 30(b)(6) deposition may not be justified where, assuming the witness is properly prepared, the entity establishes that the witness's testimony as a 30(b)(6) witness would be identical to his testimony as an individual and the 30(b)(6) is limited, or substantially limited, to topics covered in the deposition taken in the witness's individual capacity. In such a situation, there appears to be no obstacle to the entity's complying with its obligations under [Federal] Rule 30(b)(6) by adopting the witness's testimony in his individual capacity."); *see also Bison Advisors, LLC v. Kessler*, No. 14-3121(DSD/SER), 2015 U.S. Dist. LEXIS 96740, at *4–5, 2015 WL 4509158 (D. Minn. July 24, 2015) ("'The testimony elicited at the [Federal] Rule 30(b)(6) deposition represents the knowledge of the corporation, not of the individual deponents.' As a result, an individual deposed under [Federal] Rule 30(b)(1) but also designated as a corporate representative under [Federal] Rule 30(b)(6) is often required to appear for a separate seven-hour deposition on behalf of the corporation. In contrast, a separate deposition of a closely held corporation may not be appropriate where the testimony of the corporate representative would be identical to the testimony given in his or her individual capacity." (citations omitted) (quoting *A.I.A. Holdings, S.A. v. Lehman Bros., Inc.*, No. 97 Civ. 4978 (LMM)(HBP), 2002 U.S. Dist. LEXIS 9218, at *13, 2002 WL 1041356 (S.D.N.Y. May 20, 2002))); *Sw. Bell Tel., L.P. v. UTEX Commc'ns Corp.*, No. A-07-CV-435 RP, 2009 U.S. Dist. LEXIS 131706, at *10–11, 2009 WL 8541000 (W.D. Tex. Sept. 30, 2009) ("[T]he undersigned is mindful of the possibility raised by UTEX that a second deposition of Feldman could easily be used to cover topics fully addressed in his first deposition. Accordingly, counsel for AT&T is cautioned to restrict questioning of Feldman appropriately so as to minimize duplication and reduce the burden placed on Feldman as a deponent required to undergo a second deposition."); *Williams v. Sprint/United Mgmt. Co.*, No. 03-2200-JWL-DJW, 2006 U.S. Dist. LEXIS 4937, at *4–5, 2006 WL 334643 (D. Kan. Feb. 8, 2006) ("This does not mean, however, that Plaintiffs can ask Mr. St. Angelo questions that they previously asked during his [Federal] Rule 30(b)(6) deposition in that such questions would be unreasonably duplicative and thus subject to the limitation of [Federal] Rule 26(b)(2)."). *But see Sprint Commc'ns Co., L.P. v. Comcast Cable Commc'ns, LLC*, Nos. 11-2684-JWL, 11-2685-JWL, 11-2686-JWL, 2015 U.S. Dist. LEXIS 76845, at *32–34, 2015 WL 3742929 (D. Kan. June 15, 2015) ("Sprint argues that because it has offered to designate the individual testimony of Messrs. Patterson and Elfman as Sprint's corporate testimony on Topics 33, 34, and 36, it would be unduly burdensome to submit to a separate [Federal] Rule 30(b)(6) deposition. This court rejected a similar argument [in *In re Motor Fuel Temperature Sales Practices Litig.*, No. 07-MD-1840-KHV, 2009 U.S. Dist. LEXIS 118705, at *41, 2009 WL 5064441 (D. Kan. Dec. 16, 2009)] because . . . 'the fact that [the two witnesses] addressed the noticed topics when testifying in their individual capacities is of no consequence.' As discussed above, when a person testifies in his individual capacity under [Federal] Rule 30(b)(1), he speaks on behalf of himself, not his company. Plaintiffs are entitled to learn [defendant's] official corporate position—based on the institutional knowledge of the corporation—on the noticed topics.") (footnotes omitted); *Ironshore Indem., Inc. v. Banyon 1030–32, LLC*, No. 12-CV-61678-COOKE/Turnoff, 2014 U.S. Dist. LEXIS 188122, at *12–14, 2014 WL 11531915 (S.D. Fla. Feb. 28, 2014) ("After considering the arguments of the parties and the applicable law, the undersigned finds that the Insurance Companies are entitled to have the Non-Debtor Banyon Entities produce a [Federal] Rule 30(b)(6) representative for deposition, whether or not the prior individual testimony is adopted as corporate testimony at such a deposition. Moreover, whether the representative would be someone involved in the Banyon Entities or someone hired to fulfill the role, the result would be the same. However, neither Levin nor Preve can be compelled to serve as a corporate representative.") (citations omitted); *ICE Corp. v. Hamilton Sundstrand Corp.*, No. 05-4135, 2007 U.S. Dist. LEXIS 42965, at *13–14, 2007 WL 1732369 (D. Kan. June 11, 2007) ("In contrast, the reverse has occurred in the instant case. Here, defendants first deposed plaintiff's witnesses in their individual capacities and now seek to depose plaintiff's 30(b)(6) witnesses. Thus, a caution against duplicative questioning is not

Regarding whether there is any limitation on the number of representative depositions, generally absent the opposing party's agreement, leave of court is required for a second such deposition.[136] Thus, an entity served with a second representative deposition notice should file a motion to quash or for a protective order if it believes a second deposition is unwarranted. In ruling on the motion the trial court should be guided by the factors set forth in Texas Rule 192.4—whether the second deposition would be unnecessarily cumulative or duplicative, whether the information sought by the deposition is obtainable from some other source that is more convenient, less burdensome, or less expensive, and whether the burden of a second deposition outweighs its potential benefit.[137] In other words, the court should only grant the motion if the party seeking the deposition shows a legitimate need or good cause for it because, for example, new information has come to light regarding the topics of the earlier deposition, new parties have been added to the case, new causes of action or allegations have been made in pleadings, or additional, significant documents have been produced.[138]

11-1:1.6c Remedies for an Organization's Failure to Designate a Witness or to Properly Prepare Its Representative

If the organization fails to designate a witness to testify on its behalf, if its witness is unprepared to testify, or if the witness fails to appear for deposition or fails to answer a question at the deposition, the noticing party "may move for an order compelling a designation, an appearance, an answer or answers . . . or apply to the court in which the action is pending for the imposition of any sanction authorized by [Texas] Rule 215.2(b) without the necessity of first having obtained a court order compelling such discovery."[139] In addition to such a discovery order, the noticing party, if it prevails on its motion to compel, is entitled to recover "the reasonable expenses

---

warranted because such a caution would prevent defendants from effectively using 30(b)(6) depositions as they were designed, i.e. to prevent sandbagging.").

136 *Cf. Ameristar Jet Charter, Inc. v. Signal Composites, Inc.*, 244 F.3d 189, 192 (1st Cir. 2001) ("Because this second [Federal] Rule 30(b)(6) subpoena was issued to GEAE without leave of the court, it was invalid."); *Spies v. El Dorado Cnty.*, No. 2:16-cv-02232-WBS-GGH, 2018 U.S. Dist. LEXIS 123827, at *4–5 (E.D. Cal. July 24, 2018) (same); *Apple Inc. v. Mobile Star LLC*, No. C17-1120 RAJ, 2017 U.S. Dist. LEXIS 123504, at *2–3 (W.D. Wash. 2017) (same); *State Farm Mut. Auto. Ins. Co. v. New Horizont, Inc.*, 254 F.R.D. 227, 234 (E.D. Pa. 2008) (same). See also Chapter 11, section 11-2:10 (discussing second depositions of witnesses already deposed).

137 Tex. R. Civ. P. 192.4.

138 See Chapter 11, section 11-2:10 (discussing second depositions of witnesses already deposed).

139 Tex. R. Civ. P. 215.1(b). See Chapter 14, section 14-2 (discussing motions for sanctions and motions to compel discovery). Many federal courts have held that presenting an unprepared representative is a failure to appear under Federal Rule 37(d). As explained by the United States Court of Appeals for the Third Circuit:

> In reality if a [Federal] Rule 30(b)(6) witness is unable to give useful information he is no more present for the deposition than would be a deponent who physically appears for the deposition but sleeps through it. Indeed, we believe that the purpose behind [Federal] Rule 30(b)(6) undoubtedly is frustrated in the situation in which a corporate party produces a witness who is unable and/or unwilling to provide the necessary factual information on the entity's behalf. . . . Thus, we hold that when a witness is designated by a corporate party to speak on its behalf pursuant to

incurred in obtaining the order, including attorney fees, unless the court finds that the opposition to the motion was substantially justified or that other circumstances make an award of expenses unjust."[140]

Because merits-preclusive sanctions are generally disfavored in Texas absent flagrant and callous disregard for the discovery rules and prejudice to the noticing party,[141] an organization that initially fails to present a witness to testify on its behalf or presents an improperly prepared one should be ordered to produce such a witness and pay the noticing party's expenses, including attorneys' fees, incurred either in connection with the prior deposition or the new one.

11-1:2 Depositions' Scope

A deposition's scope is governed by Texas Rule 192.3, the rule governing discovery's scope.[142] Under that Rule, depositions can be used to inquire about "any matter that is not privileged and that is relevant to the subject matter of the pending action, whether it relates to the claim or defense of the party taking the deposition or the claim or defense of another party. It is not a ground for objection that the information sought will be inadmissible at trial if the information sought appears reasonably calculated

---

> [Federal] Rule 30(b)(6), "producing an unprepared witness is tantamount to a failure to appear' that is sanctionable under [Federal] Rule 37(d)."

Black Horse Lane Assoc., L.P. v. Dow Chem. Corp., 228 F.3d 275, 304 (3d. Cir. 2000); *accord Resolution Tr. Corp. v. S. Union Co.*, 985 F.2d 196, 197 (5th Cir. 1993); *Brown v. City of Atlanta*, No. 1:16-CV-008-CAP, 2018 U.S. Dist. LEXIS 6222, at *30, 2018 WL 386308 (N.D. Ga. Jan. 9, 2018); *Maronda Homes, Inc. v. Progressive Express Ins. Co.*, No: 6:14-cv-1287-Orl-31TBS, 2015 U.S. Dist. LEXIS 60603, at *5–7, 2015 WL 2169234 (M.D. Fla. May 8, 2015); *Pioneer Drive, LLC v. Nissan Diesel Am., Inc.*, 262 F.R.D. 552, 559–60 (D. Mont. 2009).

Texas Rule 215.2(b) provides in relevant part:

> [T]he court in which the action is pending may, after notice and hearing, make such orders in regard to the failure as are just, and among others the following:
>
> (1) an order disallowing any further discovery of any kind or of a particular kind by the disobedient party;
>
> (2) an order charging all or any portion of the expenses of discovery or taxable court costs or both against the disobedient party or the attorney advising him;
>
> (3) an order that the matters regarding which the order was made or any other designated facts shall be taken to be established for the purposes of the action in accordance with the claim of the party obtaining the order;
>
> (4) an order refusing to allow the disobedient party to support or oppose designated claims or defenses, or prohibiting him from introducing designated matters in evidence;
>
> (5) an order striking out pleadings or parts thereof, or staying further proceedings until the order is obeyed, or dismissing with or without prejudice the action or proceedings or any part thereof, or rendering a judgment by default against the disobedient party; . . . .

Tex. R. Civ. P. 215.2(b).

[140] Tex. R. Civ. P. 215.1(d).

[141] See Chapter 14, section 14-3:2 (discussing death-penalty sanctions).

[142] See Chapter 4, section 4-3 (discussing discovery's scope).

to lead to the discovery of admissible evidence."[143] Both the opposing party and the deponent, however, have the right to protection "from undue burden, unnecessary expense, harassment or annoyance, or invasion of personal, constitutional, or property rights."[144] And a trial court, on its own motion or in response to a motion to quash or for protection, can "make any order in the interest of justice and may—among other things—order that" the deposition not be taken, be limited in whole or in part, be taken at a certain time or place, or be taken by a specified method (e.g., in person, by telephone, or by video conference) and on specified terms and conditions, or that any deposition transcript or other recording be sealed or otherwise protected, subject to Texas Rule 76a.[145]

---

[143] Tex. R. Civ. P. 192.3(a); *see Crown Cent. Petroleum Corp. v. Garcia*, 904 S.W.2d 125, 127 (Tex. 1995) (orig. proceeding) (discussing depositions and noting that "[i]t is undisputed that a party is entitled to discovery that is relevant to the subject matter of the claim, and which appears reasonably calculated to lead to the discovery of admissible evidence" (quoting *Monsanto Co. v. May*, 889 S.W.2d 274, 276 (Tex. 1994) (orig. proceeding) (Gonzalez, J., dissenting))); *In re West*, 346 S.W.3d 612, 615 (Tex. App.—El Paso 2009, orig. proceeding) (same).

[144] *Crown Cent. Petroleum Corp. v. Garcia*, 904 S.W.2d 125, 127 (Tex. 1995) (orig. proceeding); *accord In re Perry*, No. 13-18-00676-CV, 2019 Tex. App. LEXIS 3176, at *9, 2019 WL 1723509 (Tex. App.—Corpus Christi Apr. 18, 2019, orig. proceeding) (mem. op.) ("Generally speaking, a party to a suit has the right to depose the opposing party. However, the person noticed for deposition also has the right to protection 'from undue burden, unnecessary expense, harassment, annoyance, or invasion of personal, constitutional, or property rights.'" (quoting Tex. R. Civ. P. 192.6)); *In re Titus Cnty.*, 412 S.W.3d 28, 33 (Tex. App.—Texarkana 2013, orig. proceeding) ("A party commanded to appear at a deposition or any other person affected by the subpoena may move for a protective order under Texas Rule of Civil Procedure 192.6(b) . . . . To protect the movant, the court may make any order in the interest of justice, including an order that the discovery not be undertaken at the time or place specified."); *In re Grass*, 153 S.W.3d 659, 662–63 (Tex. App.—Tyler 2004, orig. proceeding) (same); *see In re Liberty Cnty. Mut. Ins. Co.*, 557 S.W.3d 851, 854–55 (Tex. App.—Houston [14th Dist.] 2018, orig. proceeding) (holding that the trial court abused its discretion in requiring an insurance company to produce a representative in an uninsured-motorist case to testify about irrelevant matters and matters about which the company had obtained knowledge solely through discovery in the lawsuit); *In re Baptist Hosps.*, 172 S.W.3d 136, 145–46 (Tex. App.—Beaumont 2005, orig. proceeding) ("Although the discovery rules provide access to material information, the rules also provide effective means of limiting discovery to preserve litigation as a viable dispute resolution mechanism. [Texas] Rule 192.4 authorizes the court to limit discovery methods permitted by the rules if the discovery is obtainable from some other source that is more convenient, less burdensome, or less expensive, or if the burden or expense of the proposed discovery outweighs its likely benefit.").

[145] Tex. R. Civ. P. 192.6(b); *accord In re Univar USA Inc.*, 311 S.W.3d 186, 189 (Tex. App.—Beaumont 2010, orig. proceeding) (holding that the trial court abused its discretion in not granting a protective order limiting the topics and production requests in the plaintiff's representative deposition notice); *In re West*, 346 S.W.3d 612, 616–17 (Tex. App.—El Paso 2009, orig. proceeding) ("In light of the evidence presented, we find that it was reasonable for the trial judge to require that the deposition of CPA Henderson be tailored so as to protect Real Party's privileged matters and to limit the deposition to matters relevant to the case. We also find that in light of Relator's refusal to agree to a limited scope of discovery, it was reasonable for the judge to grant the Motion for Protective Order and to Quash the Notice of Deposition."); *In re Boxer Prop. Mgmt. Corp.*, No. 14-00579-CV, 2009 Tex. App. LEXIS

Generally the discovery rules governing depositions can be modified by the parties' agreement or by court order for good cause shown.[146] Thus, for example, the parties can agree to enlarge or shorten the time allowed for a deposition and to change the manner in which a deposition is conducted notwithstanding Texas Rule 199.5's limitations.[147] Such an agreement "is enforceable if it complies with [Texas] Rule 11 or, as it affects an oral deposition, if it is made a part of the record of the deposition."[148] Under that Rule, an agreement is enforceable if it is "in writing, signed, and filed as part of the record, or if it is made in open court and entered in the record."[149] Although attorneys may choose to follow the deposition procedures set out in the discovery rules, agreements modifying them are commonplace and encouraged:

> [W]herever possible, a trial court should give effect to agreements between the parties. Discovery agreements serve an important role in efficient trial management, permitting the parties to settle their disputes without resort to judicial supervision. The Rules of Civil Procedure encourage parties to reach discovery agreements. When the parties conclude an agreement, the court should not lightly ignore their bargain.
>
> A court should be particularly reluctant to set aside a [Texas] Rule 191.1 agreement after one party has acted in reliance on the agreed procedure and performed its obligations under the agreement.[150]

11-1:3 Expert Depositions

Depositions of experts are governed by Texas Rule 195 and are discussed in detail in Chapter 7.

7279, at *17–18, 2009 WL 4250123 (Tex. App.—Houston [14th Dist.] Sept. 3, 2009, orig. proceeding) (mem. op.) (holding that the trial court abused its discretion in not quashing the deposition notice for the corporate defendant's in-house attorney).

146 *In re Does*, 337 S.W.3d 862, 865 (Tex. 2011) (orig. proceeding) (per curiam) ("It is true that '[e]xcept where specifically prohibited, the procedures and limitations set forth in the rules pertaining to discovery may be modified in any suit by agreement of the parties[.]'" (quoting Tex. R. Civ. P. 191.1)); *In re BP Prods. N. Am., Inc.*, 244 S.W.3d 840, 845 (Tex. 2008) ("[Texas] Rule 191.1 provides that 'except where specifically prohibited' the parties may modify the 'rules pertaining to discovery' by agreement." (quoting Tex. R. Civ. P. 191.1)). See Chapter 3, section 3-2 (discussing modifications of discovery rules by agreement or court order).

147 Tex. R. Civ. P. 191 cmt. 1 to 1999 change.

148 Tex. R. Civ. P. 191.1; *accord In re BP Prods. N. Am., Inc.*, 244 S.W.3d 840, 845–46 (Tex. 2008) ("A [Texas Rule 191.1] agreement is enforceable when it complies with the terms of [Texas] Rule 11, or as it affects an oral deposition, if made a part of the record of the deposition."). See Chapter 3, section 3-2:1 (discussing modifications of discovery rules by agreement).

149 Tex. R. Civ. P. 11.

150 *In re BP Prods. N. Am., Inc.*, 244 S.W.3d 840, 846 (Tex. 2008). See Chapter 3, section 3-2:1 (discussing modifications of discovery rules by agreement).

11-2 Oral Depositions—Texas Rule 199

TEXT OF RULE 199

RULE 199. DEPOSITIONS UPON ORAL EXAMINATION

199.1. Oral Examination; Alternative Methods of Conducting or Recording

(a) **Generally.** A party may take the testimony of any person or entity by deposition on oral examination before any officer authorized by law to take depositions. The testimony, objections, and any other statements during the deposition must be recorded at the time they are given or made.

(b) **Depositions by telephone or other remote electronic means.** A party may take an oral deposition by telephone or other remote electronic means if the party gives reasonable prior written notice of intent to do so. For the purposes of these rules, an oral deposition taken by telephone or other remote electronic means is considered as having been taken in the district and at the place where the witness is located when answering the questions.

(c) **Nonstenographic recording.** Any party may cause a deposition upon oral examination to be recorded by other than stenographic means, including videotape recording. The party requesting the nonstenographic recording will be responsible for obtaining a person authorized by law to administer the oath and for assuring that the recording will be intelligible, accurate, and trustworthy. At least five days prior to the deposition, the party must serve on the witness and all parties a notice, either in the notice of deposition or separately, that the deposition will be recorded by other than stenographic means. This notice must state the method of nonstenographic recording to be used and whether the deposition will also be recorded stenographically. Any other party may then serve written notice designating another method of recording in addition to the method specified, at the expense of such other party unless the court orders otherwise.

199.2. Procedure for Noticing Oral Deposition

(a) **Time to notice deposition.** A notice of intent to take an oral deposition must be served on the witness and all parties a reasonable time before the deposition is taken. An oral deposition may be taken outside the discovery period only by agreement of the parties or with leave of court.

(b) **Content of notice**

(1) **Identity of witness; organizations.** The notice must state the name of the witness, which may be either an individual or a public or private corporation, partnership, association, governmental agency, or other organization. If an organization is named as the witness, the notice must describe with reasonable particularity the matters on which examination is requested. In response, the organization named in the notice must—a reasonable time before the deposition—designate one or more individuals to testify on its behalf and set forth, for each individual designated, the matters on which the individual will testify. Each individual designated must testify as to matters that are known or reasonably available to the organization. This subdivision does not preclude taking a deposition by any other procedure authorized by these rules.

(2) **Time and place.** The notice must state a reasonable time and place for the oral deposition. The place may be in:

(A) the county of the witness's residence;

(B) the county where the witness is employed or regularly transacts business in person;

(C) the county of suit, if the witness is a party or a person designated by a party under Rule 199.2(b)(1);

(D) the county where the witness was served with the subpoena, or within 150 miles of the place of service, if the witness is not a resident of Texas or is a transient person; or

(E) subject to the foregoing, at any other convenient place directed by the court in which the cause is pending.

(3) **Alternative means of conducting and recording.** The notice must state whether the deposition is to be taken by telephone or other remote electronic means and identify the means. If the deposition is to be recorded by nonstenographic means, the notice may include the notice required by Rule 199.1(c).

(4) **Additional attendees.** The notice may include the notice concerning additional attendees required by Rule 199.5(a)(3).

(5) **Request for production of documents.** A notice may include a request that the witness produce at the deposition documents or tangible things within the scope of discovery and within the witness's possession, custody, or control. If the witness is a nonparty, the request must comply with Rule 205 and the designation of materials required to be identified in the subpoena must be attached to, or included in, the notice. The nonparty's response to the request is governed by Rules 176 and 205. When the witness is a party or subject to the control of a party, document requests under this subdivision are governed by Rules 193 and 196.

199.3. Compelling Witness to Attend

A party may compel the witness to attend the oral deposition by serving the witness with a subpoena under Rule 176. If the witness is a party or is retained by, employed by, or otherwise subject to the control of a party, however, service of the notice of oral deposition upon the party's attorney has the same effect as a subpoena served on the witness.

199.4. Objections to Time and Place of Oral Deposition

A party or witness may object to the time and place designated for an oral deposition by motion for protective order or by motion to quash the notice of deposition. If the motion is filed by the third business day after service of the notice of deposition, an objection to the time and place of a deposition stays the oral deposition until the motion can be determined.

199.5. Examination, Objection, and Conduct During Oral Depositions

(a) Attendance

(1) **Witness.** The witness must remain in attendance from day to day until the deposition is begun and completed.

(2) **Attendance by party.** A party may attend an oral deposition in person, even if the deposition is taken by telephone or other remote electronic means. If a deposition is taken by telephone or other remote electronic means, the party noticing the deposition must make arrangements for all persons to attend by the same means. If the party noticing the deposition appears in person, any other party may appear by telephone or other remote electronic means if that party makes the necessary arrangements with the deposition officer and the party noticing the deposition.

(3) **Other attendees.** If any party intends to have in attendance any persons other than the witness, parties, spouses of parties, counsel, employees of counsel, and the officer taking the oral deposition, that party must give reasonable notice to all parties, either in the notice of deposition or separately, of the identity of the other persons.

(b) Oath; examination. Every person whose deposition is taken by oral examination must first be placed under oath. The parties may examine and cross-examine the witness. Any party, in lieu of participating in the examination, may serve written questions in a sealed envelope on the party noticing the oral deposition, who must deliver them to the deposition officer, who must open the envelope and propound them to the witness.

(c) Time limitation. No side may examine or cross-examine an individual witness for more than six hours. Breaks during depositions do not count against this limitation.

(d) Conduct during the oral deposition; conferences. The oral deposition must be conducted in the same manner as if the testimony were being obtained in court during trial. Counsel should cooperate with and be courteous to each other and to the witness. The witness should not be evasive and should not unduly delay the examination. Private conferences between the witness and the witness's attorney during the actual taking of the deposition are improper except for the purpose of determining whether a privilege should be asserted. Private conferences may be held, however, during agreed recesses and adjournments. If the lawyers and witnesses do not comply with this rule, the court may allow in evidence at trial statements, objections, discussions, and other occurrences during the oral deposition that reflect upon the credibility of the witness or the testimony.

(e) Objections. Objections to questions during the oral deposition are limited to "Objection, leading" and "Objection, form." Objections to testimony during the oral deposition are limited to "Objection, nonresponsive." These objections are waived if not stated as phrased during the oral deposition. All other objections need not be made or recorded during the oral deposition to be later raised with the court. The objecting party must give a clear and concise explanation of an objection if requested by the party taking the oral deposition, or the objection is waived. Argumentative or suggestive objections or explanations waive objection and may be grounds for terminating the oral deposition or assessing costs or other sanctions. The officer taking the oral deposition will not rule on objections but must record them for ruling by the court. The officer taking the oral deposition must not fail to record testimony because an objection has been made.

(f) Instructions not to answer. An attorney may instruct a witness not to answer a question during an oral deposition only if necessary to preserve a privilege, comply with a court order or these rules, protect a witness from an abusive question or one for which any answer would be misleading, or secure a ruling pursuant to paragraph (g). The attorney instructing the witness not to answer must give a concise, nonargumentative, nonsuggestive explanation of the grounds for the instruction if requested by the party who asked the question.

(g) Suspending the deposition. If the time limitations for the deposition have expired or the deposition is being conducted or defended in violation of these rules, a party or witness may suspend the oral deposition for the time necessary to obtain a ruling.

(h) Good faith required. An attorney must not ask a question at an oral deposition solely to harass or mislead the witness, for any other improper purpose, or without a good faith legal basis at the time. An attorney must not object to a question at an oral deposition, instruct the witness not to answer a question, or suspend the deposition unless there is a good faith factual and legal basis for doing so at the time.

199.6. Hearing on Objections

Any party may, at any reasonable time, request a hearing on an objection or privilege asserted by an instruction not to answer or suspension of the deposition; provided the failure of a party to obtain a ruling prior to trial does not waive any objection or privilege. The party seeking to avoid discovery must present any evidence necessary to support the objection or privilege either by testimony at the hearing or by affidavits served on opposing parties at least seven days before the hearing. If the court determines that an in camera review of some or all of the requested discovery is necessary to rule, answers to the deposition questions may be made in camera, to be transcribed and sealed in the event the privilege is sustained, or made in an affidavit produced to the court in a sealed wrapper.

Comments to 1999 change:

1. Rule 199.2(b)(5) incorporates the procedures and limitations applicable to requests for production or inspection under Rule 196, including the 30-day deadline for responses, as well as the procedures and duties imposed by Rule 193.

2. For purposes of Rule 199.5(c), each person designated by an organization under Rule 199.2(b)(1) is a separate witness.

3. The requirement of Rule 199.5(d) that depositions be conducted in the same manner as if the testimony were being obtained in court is a limit on the conduct of the lawyers and witnesses in the deposition, not on the scope of the interrogation permitted by Rule 192.

4. An objection to the form of a question includes objections that the question calls for speculation, calls for a narrative answer, is vague, is confusing, or is ambiguous. Ordinarily, a witness must answer a question at a deposition subject to the objection. An objection may therefore be inadequate if a question incorporates such unfair assumptions or is worded so that any answer would necessarily be misleading. A witness should not be required to answer whether he has yet ceased conduct he denies ever doing, subject to an objection to form (i.e., that the question is confusing or assumes facts not in evidence) because any answer would necessarily be misleading

on account of the way in which the question is put. The witness may be instructed not to answer. Abusive questions include questions that inquire into matters clearly beyond the scope of discovery or that are argumentative, repetitious, or harassing.

Comment to 2021 change: Rule 199.1(b) is amended in response to changes to section 154.105 of the Texas Government Code governing the administration of oaths by court reporter

11-2:1 2021 Amendments to the Texas Rules of Civil Procedure

The 2021 amendments to the Texas Rules of Civil Procedure did not modify Texas Rule 199 regarding oral depositions in any respect.

11-2:2 Oral Depositions in General

Oral depositions are the most common type of depositions. They are preferred over other discovery methods because they allow the attorney to question the witness face-to-face, to judge the witness's demeanor, and to gather information that has not been unduly filtered by opposing counsel.[151] Moreover, because of the question-and-answer format, an attorney can readily follow up if the witness gives an unexpected or incomplete answer or if the attorney realizes that his or her question was inartful.

An oral deposition generally consists of questions by the attorney for one party, answers by the deponent, and objections and cross-examination by the other parties' attorneys, which "are recorded at the time they are given or made."[152] The deposition is recorded stenographically by a court reporter or by a mechanical recording device (e.g., a tape recorder or videotape) operated by a notary public, the party, its attorney, or its attorney's employee.[153]

Texas Rule 199 governs oral depositions, allows a party to "take the testimony of any person or entity by oral examination,"[154] and sets forth the procedures for obtain-

---

[151] *Kleppinger v. Tex. Dep't. of Transp.*, 283 F.R.D. 330, 335 (S.D. Tex. 2012) ("While the Court recognizes that in many instances interrogatories and depositions can be utilized to obtain the same information in a lawsuit, these two methods of discovery are not necessarily equivalent. That is, the use of interrogatories may have disadvantages. For example, interrogatories do not provide subjective information, such as the demeanor of the responding party. Further, interrogatories can be ineffective in obtaining complex or possibly confusing information. Moreover, depositions have more flexibility than interrogatories because they permit an attorney to ask follow-up questions based on answers to previous questions or repeat questions if a deponent is being evasive.") (citations omitted); *see Elan Microelectronics Corp. v. Pixcir Microelectronics Co.*, No. 2:10-cv-00014-GMN-PAL, 2013 U.S. Dist. LEXIS 114164, at *17, 2013 WL 4101813 (D. Nev. Aug. 7, 2013) ("Because of its nature, the deposition process provides a means to obtain more complete information and is, therefore, favored." (quoting *Marker v. Union Fid. Life Ins. Co.*, 125 F.R.D. 121, 126 (M.D.N.C.1989))); *Buehrle v. City of O'Fallon*, No. 4:10CV00509, 2011 U.S. Dist. LEXIS 11972, at *7, 2011 WL 529922 (E.D. Mo. Feb. 8, 2011) (same).

[152] Tex. R. Civ. P. 199.1(a).

[153] See Chapter 11, section 11-2:6 (discussing the recording of an oral deposition).

[154] Tex. R. Civ. P. 199.1(a); *cf. In re Amezaga*, 195 B.R. 221, 227 (Bankr. D.P.R. 1996) (explaining that "a deposition is a 'question-and-answer conversation' between the witness and the attorneys used to gather facts about the case and the witness's actions and experiences").

ing, conducting, and recording such depositions. To take an oral deposition, a party must serve a deposition notice on the witness and all other parties that complies with Texas Rule 199.2,[155] compel the witness to comply with the notice as provided in Texas Rule 199.3,[156] and arrange for taking and recording the deposition in compliance with Texas Rules 199.1(b) and (c).[157]

11-2:3 The Deposition Notice

Texas Rule 199.2 sets forth the requirements for, and contents of, the oral-deposition notice.

11-2:3.1 Time for Serving the Deposition Notice

The oral-deposition notice must be served a "reasonable time" before the deposition date.[158] What constitutes a reasonable time depends on the circumstances,[159] including the deposition's location, the time needed to prepare for the deposition, the existence of exigent circumstances (e.g., a newly discovered witness shortly before discovery's close or a witness located in a distant locale in which the parties are currently taking depositions), and whether the notice includes a production request as well as the production request's scope.[160]

---

155 See Chapter 11, section 11-2:3 (discussing deposition notices).

156 See Chapter 11, section 11-2:4 (discussing compelling attendance at the deposition).

157 See Chapter 11, section 11-2:6 (discussing the recording of the deposition).

158 Tex. R. Civ. P. 199.2(a); *accord In re Berrenberg*, 605 S.W.3d 922, 926 (Tex. App.— El Paso 2020, orig. proceeding) ("A notice for an oral deposition must state a reasonable time and place for the deposition." (citing Tex. R. Civ. P. 199.2(b)(2))); *Onwuteaka v. Comm'n for Lawyer Discipline*, No. 14-07-00595-CV, 2009 Tex. App. LEXIS 1694, at *26–27, 2009 WL 620253 (Tex. App.—Houston [14th Dist.] Mar. 12, 2009, pet. denied) (mem. op.) ("The discovery rules require that 'a notice of intent to take an oral deposition . . . be served on the witness and all parties a *reasonable time* before the deposition is taken.'" (emphasis added) (quoting Tex. R. Civ. P. 199.2(a)).

159 *Hycarbex, Inc. v. Anglo-Suisse, Inc.*, 927 S.W.2d 103, 111 (Tex. App.—Houston [14th Dist.] 1996, no writ) ("[Former] Rule 200 of the Texas Rules of Civil Procedure requires a party to give reasonable notice of a deposition. Whether notice is reasonable depends on the circumstances of each case.") (citation omitted); *Bloyed v. Gen. Motors Corp.*, 881 S.W.2d 422, 437 (Tex. App.—Texarkana 1994 writ granted) (same), *aff'd*, 916 S.W.2d 949 (Tex. 1996); *cf. Cropper v. Wal-Mart Stores*, No. 2:19-cv-00629-JCM-NJK, 2020 U.S. Dist. LEXIS 84381, at *1–2 (D. Nev. May 13, 2020) ("What constitutes 'reasonable' notice is determined based on the circumstances of each case, taking into account factors such as the need for preparation before the deposition."); *Engage Healthcare Commc'ns, LLC v. Intellisphere, LLC*, No. 12-cv-00787(FLW)(LHG), 2017 U.S. Dist. LEXIS 214569, at *7, 2017 WL 9481235 (D.N.J. Nov. 1, 2017) ("[W]hat constitutes reasonable notice often turns on the particular circumstances of the case."); *Peterson v. Union Pac. R.R.*, No. 06-CV-3084, 2007 U.S. Dist. LEXIS 62134, at *5–6, 2007 WL 2701268 (C.D. Ill. Aug. 23, 2007) ("The analysis in determining the reasonableness of notice is necessarily case-specific and fact-intensive.").

160 *Cf. Ballard Marine Constr., Inc. v. EHW Constructors*, No. 3:16-cv-05633-RBL, 2019 U.S. Dist. LEXIS 57773, at *4–5, 2019 WL 1436878 (W.D. Wash. Apr. 1, 2019) ("'What constitutes reasonable notice depends on the circumstances of each case.' 'Commonly, courts find that notice of at least five days is sufficient for a party's deposition.' However, what constitutes reasonable notice may vary depending on the complexity of the case and number of depositions requested." (quoting *Gamboa v. King Cnty.*, No. C06-1034RSM, 2008 U.S. Dist. LEXIS

Whereas courts generally hold that one or two days' notice is unreasonable,[161] a

---

122279, at *2, 2008 WL 509324 (W.D. Wash. Feb. 22, 2008))); *Paul v. WinCo Holdings, Inc.*, 249 F.R.D. 643, 656 (D. Idaho 2008) ("Although [Federal] Rule 30(b)(1) requires that reasonable notice of depositions be given, the court must determine what is reasonable based on the circumstances of a particular case. Courts should consider 'the time between the notice and the deposition, with an eye towards preparation and travel.' The opposing party, however, has no basis to complain where it has concealed the identities of the witnesses until late in the game." (citation omitted) (quoting *In re Sulfuric Acid Antitrust Litig.*, 231 F.R.D. 320, 327 (N.D. Ill. 2005))); *Peterson v. Union Pac. R.R.*, No. 06-CV-3084, 2007 U.S. Dist. LEXIS 62134, at *6, 2007 WL 2701268 (C.D. Ill. Aug. 23, 2007) ("A fact to be considered is the time between the notice and the deposition, with an eye toward preparation and travel."); *In re Sulfuric Acid Antitrust Litig.*, 231 F.R.D. 320, 327 (N.D. Ill. 2005) (same); *see Lucas v. Breg, Inc.*, No. 3:15-CV-00258-BAS-NLS, 2015 U.S. Dist. LEXIS 164534, at *7–8, 2015 WL 8328696 (S.D. Cal. Dec. 8, 2015) ("Courts have found approximately ten days' notice generally is considered reasonable notice, although the particular circumstances of a case may shorten or lengthen the amount of notice that is considered reasonable. Under the circumstances presented here, this Court concludes that Plaintiffs did not provide reasonable notice. Breg received the notices only seven days before the scheduled date, for multiple deponents in multiple cities and states, and further with documents designated for production. Moreover, given that this is case involves multiple parties with a number of lawyers, it is unlikely that schedules of the deponents and the lawyers would be able to accommodate the late-noticed depositions. Indeed, Plaintiffs were aware that depositions were being held within the week leading up to the date they noticed the three depositions at issue, leaving little if any time at all for Defendants to prepare and arrange for appearances at the depositions.") (citations omitted).

161 *See Onwuteaka v. Comm'n for Law. Discipline*, No. 14-07-00595-CV, 2009 Tex. App. LEXIS 1694, at *26–27, 2009 WL 620253 (Tex. App.—Houston [14th Dist.] Mar. 12, 2009, pet. denied) (mem. op.) (holding one day's notice was unreasonable); *Bloyed v. Gen. Motors Corp.*, 881 S.W.2d 422, 437 (Tex. App.—Texarkana 1994) (same), *aff'd on other grounds*, 916 S.W.2d 949 (Tex. 1996); *Hogan v. Beckel*, 783 S.W.2d, 307–08 (Tex. App.—San Antonio 1989, writ denied) (same); *cf. Meeks v. Nunez*, No. 13cv973-GPC(BGS), 2016 U.S. Dist. LEXIS 66292, at *4–5, 2016 WL 2931097 (S.D. Cal. 2016) (finding two days' notice was unreasonable); *Carr-Lambert v. Grant Cnty. Bd. of Educ.*, No. 2:09CV61, 2010 U.S. Dist. LEXIS 163689, at *9–10 (N.D.W. Va. Dec. 9, 2010) (citing cases and holding "one business day, especially when another deposition was scheduled for the same day, to be clearly unreasonable"); *Gamboa v. King Cnty.*, No. C06-1034RSM, 2008 U.S. Dist. LEXIS 122279, at *2–4, 2008 WL 509324 (W.D. Wash. Feb. 22, 2008) (holding one day's notice of a deposition was unreasonable); *C&F Packing Co. v. Doskocil Cos.*, 126 F.R.D. 662, 679 (N.D. Ill. 1989) (same); *Bogan v. Kreski*, 546 So. 2d 1132, 1133 (Fla. Dist. Ct. App. 1989) (same); *Lloyd v. Cessna Aircraft Co.*, 430 F. Supp. 25, 26 (E.D. Tenn. 1976) (holding two days' notice was unreasonable). *But see Bleeker v. Standard Fire Ins. Co.*, 130 F. Supp. 2d 726, 737–38 (E.D.N.C. 2000) (holding one day's notice was reasonable because about three weeks before the notice was served, the plaintiff sent the defendants a letter requesting potential deposition dates of a [Federal] Rule 30(b)(6) witness and stating the categories about which testimony would be taken); *Nat. Organics, Inc. v. Proteins Plus, Inc.*, 724 F. Supp. 50, 52 (E.D.N.Y. 1989) ("Although the defendant received only one-days' notice, the parties were on an expedited discovery schedule, the need for her deposition was sudden and unexpected, and her deposition was brief and taken by phone. We find that the defendant received notice 'reasonable under all the circumstances.'" (quoting *Radio Corp. of Am. v. Rauland Corp.*, 21 F.R.D. 113, 115 (N.D. Ill. 1957))); *Radio Corp. of Am. v. Rayland Corp.*, 21 F.R.D. 113, 115 (D. Ill. 1957) (holding one day's notice was sufficient because "counsel were all in Oslo for the taking of the foreign depositions, and it was apparently understood that Zenith was to proceed with its depositions at the time").

week's notice generally is found sufficient.[162] Scheduling numerous depositions on

[162] *See Hycarbex, Inc. v. Anglo-Suisse, Inc.*, 927 S.W.2d 103, 111–12 (Tex. App.—Houston [14th Dist.] 1996, no writ) (holding four days' notice was unreasonable); *Gutierrez v. Walsh*, 748 S.W.2d 27, 28, (Tex. App.—Corpus Christi 1988, no writ) ("The appellants concede that they received eight days [sic] notice for the first deposition and six days [sic] notice for the second deposition. The trial court could have found that such notice was reasonable."). *But see Bohmfalk v. Linwood*, 742 S.W.2d 518, 520 (Tex. App.—Dallas 1987, no writ) ("Inasmuch as the deposition was being taken several weeks prior to trial, four days advance notice was, perhaps, somewhat scant. However, it was not unreasonable per se."). *Compare, e.g., FAA. v. Landy*, 705 F.2d 624, 635 (2d Cir. 1983) ("The court may take judicial notice of frequent flights from New York to Tampa, as well as availability of procedural remedies, in concluding that [four days' notice of a deposition] was reasonable."), *Ballard Marine Constr., Inc. v. EHW Constructors*, No. 3:16-cv-05633-RBL, 2019 U.S. Dist. LEXIS 57773, at *4–5, 2019 WL 1436878 (W.D. Wash. Apr. 1, 2019) (noting that "[c]ommonly, courts find that notice of at least five days is sufficient for a party's deposition" and holding that "[a]lthough Ballard's deposition notice came late in the litigation, 'the "eleventh hour" of a discovery period is still within the discovery period, and there is no basis for denying a discovery request simply because it is served toward the end of the designated period. Notice of eight calendar days and five business days minimally satisfied [Federal] Rule 30's reasonableness requirement. The topics proposed for the deposition were expansive, but not so expansive as to make preparation impossible." (quoting *Gamboa v. King Cnty.*, No. C06-1034RSM, 2008 U.S. Dist. LEXIS 122279, at *2, 2008 WL 509324 (W.D. Wash. Feb. 22, 2008), and *Doe v. Trump*, 329 F.R.D. 262, 274 (W.D. Wash. 2018))), *Kirst v. Ottosen Propeller & Accessories Inc.*, No. 3:16-cv-00188-TMB, 2017 U.S. Dist. LEXIS 225133, at *4, 2017 WL 11454434 (D. Alaska Oct. 24, 2017) (citing cases and holding that, "while unadvisedly short," a deposition notice "sent on a Monday, setting deposition for the coming Thursday" was reasonable under the circumstances), *Millennium Labs., Inc. v. Allied World Assurance Co. (U.S.), Inc.*, No. 12cv2280-H(KSC), 2014 U.S. Dist. LEXIS 8158, at *5 n.1, 2014 WL 197744 (S.D. Cal. Jan. 15, 2014) ("Given the continuances granted to date and the January 31, 2014 fact discovery deadline, this Court construes reasonable notice to be 5 business days."), *Guzman v. Bridgepoint Educ., Inc.*, No.11-0069-WQH(WVG), 2014 U.S. Dist. LEXIS 58806, at *4–5, 2014 WL 1670094 (S.D. Cal. Apr. 28, 2014) ("Courts construe 'reasonable notice' to be five days, if the deposition notice does not require production of documents at the deposition. . . . Here, Plaintiff's Deposition Notice was served on March 19, 2014 for a deposition to be taken on March 28, 2014. The time between March 19, 2014 and March 28, 2014 is nine days. Therefore, Plaintiff's Deposition Notice, to the extent it did not request production of documents at the deposition, was timely and reasonable."), *Charm Floral v. Wald Imps., Ltd.*, No. C10-1550-RSM, 2012 U.S. Dist. LEXIS 16007, at *5–7, 2012 WL 424491 (W.D. Wash. Feb. 9, 2012) ("[M]ore than one week's notice generally is considered reasonable. Less than one week generally is not considered reasonable. Notice of a week or more is not, however, required in all circumstances.") (citations omitted), *Zone Sports Ctr., LLC v. Nat'l Sur. Corp.*, No. 1:11-cv-00845-LJO-BAM, 2012 U.S. Dist. LEXIS 30208, at *3, 2012 WL 13034350 (E.D. Cal. Mar. 7, 2012) ("Commonly, courts find that notice of at least five business days' notice is required to constitute reasonable notice."), *Leamon v. KBR, Inc.*, No. H-10-253, 2011 U.S. Dist. LEXIS 167527, at *4 (S.D. Tex. Dec. 11, 2011) (finding seven days' notice reasonable), *Davidson v. Dean*, 204 F.R.D. 251, 256 (S.D.N.Y. 2001) (holding eight days' notice was "not unreasonable as a matter of law"); *In re Stratosphere Corp. Sec. Litig.*, 183 F.R.D. 684, 687 (D. Nev. 1999) (holding five days' notice was unreasonable); *Pearl v. Keystone Consol. Indus., Inc.*, 884 F.2d 1047, 1052 (7th Cir. Ill. 1989) (holding six days' notice was reasonable), *Jones v. U.S.*, 720 F. Supp. 355, 366 (S.D.N.Y. 1989) (holding eight days' notice was reasonable), *with, e.g., Kolon Indus., Inc. v. E.I. DuPont de Nemours & Co.*, 748 F.3d 160, 173 (4th Cir.) (holding five days' notice was unreasonable, particularly when the local rule required eleven days' notice), *cert. denied*, 547 U.S. 987 (2014), *Cropper v.*

the same day in different cities or in a very short period of time often will be found to be unreasonable.[163]

11-2:3.2 The Notice's Content

Texas Rule 199.2(b) requires the oral deposition notice to state: (1) the deponent's name,[164] (2) the deposition's time and place,[165] (3) the method by which the testimony will be recorded,[166] (4) the names of any "additional attendees" (i.e., persons other than the witness, the parties, the parties' spouses, attorneys, and attorneys' employees, and the deposition officer—i.e., the person recording the deposition, usually a

---

Wal-Mart Stores, No. 2:19-cv-00629-JCM-NJK, 2020 U.S. Dist. LEXIS 84381, at *1–2 (D. Nev. May 13, 2020) (suggesting that five business days' notice "for testimony from an appropriate corporate representative on 28 topics" is unreasonable "given the preparation necessary for such a corporate deposition"), *Fernandez v. Penske Truck Leasing Co.*, No. 2:12-CV-295 JCM (GWF), 2013 U.S. Dist. LEXIS 77603, at *6, 2013 WL 438669 (D. Nev. Feb. 1, 2013) (holding eleven days' notice was unreasonable because "[a]fter nearly a year of pendency, Plaintiff delayed until two weeks before the close of discovery to notice the subject depositions, without explanation, and the depositions were also noticed during the Christmas holiday"), *U.S. v. Philip Morris Inc.*, 312 F. Supp. 2d 27, 36–37 (D.D.C. 2004) (holding three days' notice was unreasonable); *U.S. v. Philip Morris Inc.*, 312 F. Supp. 2d 27, 36–37 (D.D.C. 2004) (holding three business days' notice unreasonable, "especially to busy litigators who need to prepare to testify about events occurring six to nine years previously"); *Peterson v. Union Pac. R.R.*, No. 06-CV-3084, 2007 U.S. Dist. LEXIS 62134, at *5–6, 2007 WL 2701268 (C.D. Ill. Aug. 23, 2007) (holding four days' notice was unreasonable); *and Vardon Golf Co., Inc. v. Supreme Golf Sales, Inc.*, No. 89-CV-2654, 1989 U.S. Dist. LEXIS 13183, at *3–4, 1989 WL 153335 (N.D. Ill., Nov. 2, 1989) (finding four days' notice was unreasonable), *and Nielsen v. Nielsen,* 141 P.2d 415, 416 (Colo. 1943) (holding three days' notice was unreasonable).

[163] *Cf. Havadjias v. Vanguard Ins. Co.*, No. 93-56693, 1995 U.S. App. LEXIS 2694, at *7, 1995 WL 41396 (9th Cir. Feb. 1, 1995) (affirming the imposition of sanctions on pro se litigants who, among other things, sent notices scheduling forty depositions at the same time); *Mims v. Cent. Mfrs. Mut. Ins. Co.*, 178 F.2d 56, 59 (5th Cir. 1949) ("We are unwilling to give countenance to the propositions that the notices given as set forth above calling, as they did, for the taking of depositions of numerous witnesses on the same date, in scattered localities across the continent, were in any sense reasonable."); *Harry A. v. Duncan*, 223 F.R.D. 536, 538–39 (D. Mont. 2004) (holding that noticing eighty-five depositions during a two-week period was unreasonable); *Triple Crown Am. v. Biosynth AG*, No.96-7476, 1998 U.S. Dist. LEXIS 6117, at *13 n.6, 1998 WL 227886 (E.D. Pa. Apr. 29, 1998) ("The scheduling of five depositions at the same hour on the same day, as plaintiff initially did, is unreasonable[.]"); *Imperial Chems. Indus., PLC v. Barr Labs, Inc.*, 126 F.R.D. 467, 472–73 (S.D.N.Y. 1989) (imposing sanctions in a patent case against an attorney who served deposition notices for the deposition of six expert witnesses from around the world on a single day, in a single place).

[164] Tex. R. Civ. P. 199.2(b)(1) (requiring a deposition notice to "state the name of the witness, which may be either an individual or a public or private corporation, partnership, association, governmental agency, or other organization"). If the deponent is a nonparty, the notice should also contain the nonparty's address so that the person issuing the subpoena knows where to serve it.

[165] Tex. R. Civ. P. 199.2(b)(2) (requiring the deposition notice to "state a reasonable time and place for the oral deposition").

[166] Tex. R. Civ. P. 199.2(b)(3) (requiring the deposition notice to "state whether the deposition is to be taken by telephone or other remote electronic means and identify the means").

court reporter),[167] and (5) the documents to be produced at the deposition.[168] Unless the witness is an organization, the notice need not describe the matters on which examination is requested.[169] A non-noticing party that also intends to examine the witness is not required to serve its own deposition notice.[170]

The deposition notice must be signed either by the party's attorney or a pro se party[171] and "must show the attorney's State Bar of Texas identification number, address, telephone number, and fax number, if any"[172] or the pro se party's "address, telephone number, and fax number, if any."[173] If the notice is not signed, it must be stricken unless signed promptly after the omission is called to the attention of the party serving the notice.[174] The deposition notice also must be served on the witness and the other parties and must contain a certificate of service stating it was properly served on them.[175] If it is not served on the other parties, the deposition cannot be used at trial or at a hearing if the other parties did not have a reasonable time to redepose the witness.[176] The notice can be served "in person, by mail, by commercial

---

167 Tex. R. Civ. P. 199.2(b)(4) (providing that the deposition notice "may include the notice concerning additional attendees required by [Texas] Rule 199.5(a)(3)").

168 Tex. R. Civ. P. 199.2(b)(5) (providing that the deposition notice "may include a request that the witness produce at the deposition documents or tangible things within the scope of discovery and within the witness's possession, custody, or control").

169 Tex. R. Civ. P. 199.2(b); *cf. United Phosphorus, Ltd. v. Midland Fumigant, Inc.*, 164 F.R.D. 245, 248 (D. Kan. 1995) ("[U]nder [Federal] Rule 30 there is no requirement that the notice to take depositions include an identification of the subject matters upon which the witness is to be deposed, as is required when the notice identifies a corporation as a deponent."). Depositions of organizations are discussed in Chapter 11, section 11-1:1.5.

170 *Cf. Smith v. Wilson*, No. CV 17-00119-H-DLC-JTJ, 2019 U.S. Dist. LEXIS 190315, at *12, 2019 WL 5685338 (D. Mont. Oct. 8, 2019) ("There is no formal requirement for a party seeking to cross-examine a deponent to serve a separate notice of deposition. 'In a multi-party lawsuit, one party may notice the deposition and other parties may attend and cross-examine the deponent without also having to notice the deposition.'" (quoting *FCC v. Mizuho Medy Co.*, 257 F.R.D. 679, 681–82 (S.D. Cal. 2009))).

171 Tex. R. Civ. P. 191.3(a).

172 Tex. R. Civ. P. 191.3(a)(1).

173 Tex. R. Civ. P. 191.3(a)(2).

174 Tex. R. Civ. P. 191.3(d) ("If a . . . notice . . . is not signed, it must be stricken unless it is signed promptly after the omission is called to the attention of the party making the request, notice, response, or objection. A party is not required to take any action with respect to a . . . notice that is not signed.").

175 Tex. R. Civ. P. 21(a), (d), 199.2(a); *see Onyung v. Onyung*, No. 01–10–00519–CV, 2013 Tex. App. LEXIS 9190, at *54, 2013 WL 3875548 (Tex. App.—Houston [1st Dist.] July 25, 2013, pet. denied) (mem. op.) ("The Rules of Civil Procedure provide that a 'notice of intent to take an oral deposition must be served on the witness and all parties a reasonable time before the deposition is taken.'" (quoting Tex. R. Civ. P. 199.2(a))).

176 In *Onyung v. Onyung*, No. 01-10-00519-CV, 2013 Tex. App. LEXIS 9190, 2013 WL 3875548 (Tex. App.—Houston [1st Dist.] July 25, 2013, pet. denied) (mem. op.), the court of appeals held that the trial court did not abuse its discretion in allowing the plaintiff to use a deposition even though one of the defendants did not receive notice of it because the defendant had a reasonable time to re-depose the witness before trial. *Onyung v. Onyung*, No. 01-10-00519-CV, 2013 Tex. App. LEXIS 9190, at *56–58, 2013 WL 3875548 (Tex. App.—Houston [1st Dist.] July 25, 2013, pet. denied) (mem. op.). In doing so, it analogized to Texas Rule 203.6(b), which provides that "'[a] deposition is admissible against a party joined after the deposition was taken if . . . that party has had a reasonable opportunity to redepose the

delivery service, by fax, by email, or by such other manner as the court in its discretion may direct"[177] unless the notice is filed electronically (i.e., a notice for a nonparty's deposition), in which case it "must be served electronically through the electronic filing manager if the email address of the party or attorney to be served is on file with the electronic filing manager."[178] The deposition notice should be filed with the trial court *only* if it is served on a nonparty.[179] A notice that is served only on parties should not be filed,[180] but the noticing party must retain a copy of it during the action's pendency and any related appellate proceedings begun within six months after judgment is signed, unless otherwise provided by the trial court.[181]

11-2:3.2a The Deposition's Time and Place

The time and place for an oral deposition must be "reasonable."[182] Although there is no requirement under Texas Rule 199 that the parties confer about the oral deposition's time and place, local court rules may require this, as does the Texas Lawyer's Creed.[183] Whether the time for a deposition is reasonable depends on the circumstances.[184] Ordinarily the designation of any time during normal business hours is reasonable. At least one court has held that it is unreasonable to schedule a deposition on a Sunday.[185]

---

witness and has failed to do so.'" *Onyung v. Onyung*, No. 01-10-00519-CV, 2013 Tex. App. LEXIS 9190, at *56–58 (Tex. App.—Houston [1st Dist.] July 25, 2013, pet. denied) (mem. op.) (quoting Tex. R. Civ. P. 203.6(b)); *see also Shenandoah Assocs. v. J & K Props., Inc.*, 741 S.W.2d 470, 492 (Tex. App.—Dallas 1987, writ denied) ("When other parties are not given notice of the deposition, an 'ex parte' deposition is not admissible."); *In re Baum*, 606 F.2d 592, 593 n.1 (5th Cir. 1979) ("Depositions taken without proper notice may be found to be inadmissible.").

177 Tex. R. Civ. P. 21a(a)(2).

178 Tex. R. Civ. P. 21a(a)(1).

179 Tex. R. Civ. P. 191.4(a)(1) ("The following discovery materials must not be filed: . . . deposition notices[] and subpoenas required to be served only on parties[.]"), 191.4(b)(1) ("The following discovery matters must be filed: . . . deposition notices[] and subpoenas required to be served on nonparties[.]").

180 Tex. R. Civ. P. 191.4(a)(1) ("The following discovery matters must not be filed: . . . deposition notices[] and subpoenas required to be served only on parties[.]").

181 Tex. R. Civ. P. 191.4(d) ("Any person required to serve discovery materials not required to be filed must retain the original or exact copy of the materials during the pendency of the case and any related appellate proceedings begun within six months after judgment is signed, unless otherwise provided by the trial court.").

182 Tex. R. Civ. P. 199.2(b)(2); *accord In re Grass*, 153 S.W.3d 659, 662 (Tex. App.—Tyler 2004, orig. proceeding) ("A notice for an oral deposition must state a reasonable time and place for the deposition.").

183 *Tex. Law. Creed-A Mandate for Professionalism*, Art. III.14 (1989) ("I will not arbitrarily schedule a deposition . . . until a good faith effort has been made to schedule it by agreement.").

184 *Cf. Union Cent. Life Ins. Co. v. Burger*, 27 F. Supp. 556, 557 (S.D.N.Y. 1939) (ordering that the deposition of a sixteen-year-old should be taken when he was not "busy at school").

185 *Cf. Shenker v. U.S.*, 25 F.R.D. 96, 97–98 (E.D.N.Y. 1960); *see HP Tuners, LCC v. Sykes-Bonnett*, No. C17-5760 BHS, 2019 U.S. Dist. LEXIS 232997, at *3–4, 2019 WL 9828399 (W.D. Wash. Apr. 11, 2019) (granting a protective order because the defendant declined to reschedule a deposition noticed for "a religious holiday that Plaintiff's counsel observes").

Oral depositions, like written discovery, must be completed within the discovery period absent an agreement by the parties or leave of court.[186] Accordingly, if the parties agree and the trial court does not order otherwise, depositions can continue until the trial date. Any such agreement should either be stated on the deposition's record or in a Texas Rule 11 agreement.[187]

Texas Rule 199.2(b)(2) specifies the following places where a deposition can be taken: "(A) the county of the witness's residence; (B) the county where the witness is employed or regularly transacts business in person; (C) the county of suit, if the witness is a party or a person designated by a party under [Texas] Rule 199.2(b)(1); (D) the county where the witness was served with the subpoena, or within 150 miles of the place of service, if the witness is not a resident of Texas or is a transient person; or (E) subject to the foregoing, at any other convenient place directed by the court in which the cause is pending."[188] Thus, even if one of the places in subdivisions (A)–(D) of Texas Rule 199.2(b)(2) applies, a trial court, under subdivision (E) of Texas Rule 199.2(b)(2), can order a witness to be deposed at any location that is convenient.[189]

---

[186] Tex. R. Civ. P. 199.2(a) ("An oral deposition may be taken outside the discovery period only by agreement of the parties or with leave of court."); *see* Tex. R. Civ. P. 190.2(b)(1) and 190.3(b)(1) (respectively providing that "all discovery" in Level 1 and 2 actions "must be completed during the discovery period"), 190.4(b)(2) (requiring Level 3 discovery-control plans to include "a discovery period during which either all discovery must be conducted or all discovery requests must be sent").

[187] See Tex. R. Civ. P. 191.1.

[188] Tex. R. Civ. P. 199.2(b)(2); *see In re Family Dollar Stores of Tex., LLC*, No. 04-14-00656-CV, 2015 Tex. App. LEXIS 4325, at *6 (Tex. App.—San Antonio Apr. 29, 2015, orig. proceeding) (mem. op.) ("Generally, oral depositions may be requested in the county of the witness's residence or employment, the county where the witness is served with the subpoena, or another convenient place as directed by the court."); *In re Alamex, NV*, No. 01-12-00037-CV, 2012 Tex. App. LEXIS 3509, at *3–5, 2012 WL 1564323 (Tex. App.—Houston [1st Dist.] May 3, 2012, orig. proceeding) (mem. op.) ("By rule, depositions may be set in the county of the witness's residence; the county where the witness is employed or regularly transacts business in person; the county of suit, if the witness is a party or a person designated by a party under [Texas R]ule 199.2(b)(1); the county where the witness was served with the subpoena, or within 150 miles of the place of service, if the witness is not a resident of Texas or is a transient person; or, subject to the foregoing, at any other convenient place directed by the court in which the cause is pending."); *In re Grass*, 153 S.W.3d 659, 662 (Tex. App.—Tyler 2004, orig. proceeding) (same).

[189] *See In re Turner*, 243 S.W.3d 843, 846 (Tex. App.—Eastland 2008, orig. proceeding) ("When a deposition takes place outside one of the counties specifically identified by [Texas] Rule 199.2(b)(2), it must be at a convenient place."); *In re Rogers*, 43 S.W.3d 20, 29 (Tex. App.—Amarillo 2001, orig. proceeding) ("Suit was filed and pending in Potter County. At the hearing of November 13th, it was represented to the trial judge that Ancona was no longer employed by King's Manor, and that she had moved to Brownsville. Otherwise, no evidence was presented or representation made to the trial judge as to the residence or place of employment or place of business of the witnesses. Nor does the record support a conclusion that Dallas was a reasonable place or otherwise convenient for any of the witnesses. The record of the hearing, therefore, does not support the ordering of Rogers and witnesses Ancona, Vessel and Bunch to appear for deposing in Dallas, Texas."); *Boone v. Fisher*, No. 13-96-001-CV, 1999 Tex. App. LEXIS 612, at *37–38, 1999 WL 33896852 (Tex. App.—Corpus Christi Jan. 28, 1999, pet. denied) (not designated for publication) ("The record reveals the trial court gave no consideration to the reasonableness or the

"'Convenience' is determined from the perspective of the witness."[190] Absent agreement, under Texas Rule 199.2(b)(2), most witnesses will be deposed in the county of the witness's residence, the county where the witness is employed, or any convenient place determined by court where the action is pending provided that it is within subpoena range.[191] A witness who is party or a Texas Rule 199.2(b)(1) representative also can be deposed in the county of suit.[192] The deposition of a witness who is neither a Texas resident nor a party's Texas Rule 199.2(b)(1) representative generally must be taken where the witness lives.[193]

---

convenience of the place of the deposition of the witnesses. This constitutes an abuse of discretion on the part of the court contrary to [former Texas R]ule 201(5).").

[190] *In re Grass*, 153 S.W.3d 659, 662 (Tex. App.—Tyler 2004, orig. proceeding); *accord In re Alamex, NV*, No. 01-12-00037-CV, 2012 Tex. App. LEXIS 3509, at *3, 2012 WL 1564323 (Tex. App.—Houston [1st Dist.] May 3, 2012) (mem. op.); *In re W. Star Trucks US, Inc.*, 112 S.W.3d 756, 765 (Tex. App.—Eastland 2003, orig. proceeding).

[191] *See* Tex. R. Civ. P. 199.2(b)(2)(A), (B), (E); *In re Prince*, No. 14-06-00895-CV, 2006 Tex. App. LEXIS 10558, at *11, 2006 WL 3589484 (Tex. App.—Houston [14th Dist.] Dec. 12, 2006, orig. proceeding) (mem. op.) ("[T]he Texas rules treat non-party witnesses differently from witnesses subject to a party's control. [Texas] Rules 176.3 and 199.3 provide that only parties or witnesses who are 'retained by, employed by, or otherwise subject to the control of a party' may be compelled to attend a deposition at any of the reasonable locations provided in [Texas] Rule 199.2(b)(2), specifically including 'any . . . convenient place directed by the court.' Other persons, by contrast, 'may not be required by subpoena to appear or produce documents or other things in a county that is more than 150 miles from where the person resides or is served.'" (citations omitted) (quoting Tex. R. Civ. P. 176.3(a)). Under Texas Rule 191.1, the parties and witness can agree to take the deposition anywhere. *See* Tex. R. Civ. P. 191.1.

[192] Tex. R. Civ. P. 199.2(b)(2)(C); *see In re Berrenberg*, 605 S.W.3d 922, 927 (Tex. App.— El Paso 2020, orig. proceeding) (holding that, although the trial court had discretion to quash a scheduled deposition based on concerns about the effect of the COVID-19 pandemic, the trial court did not have discretion to order that the party's deposition be taken in a different county without sufficient evidence of undue hardship or unnecessary expense); *In re Family Dollar Stores of Tex., LLC*, No. 04-14-00656-CV, 2015 Tex. App. LEXIS 4325, at *6 (Tex. App.—San Antonio Apr. 29, 2015, orig. proceeding) (mem. op.) ("When a party notices the deposition of a corporation, and the organization designates an individual to testify as a corporate representative on its behalf, the rule allows the deposition to be conducted in the county in which the suit is pending."); *In re Bannum, Inc.*, No. 03-09-00512-CV, 2009 Tex. App. LEXIS 10088, at *1–2, 2009 WL 8599250 (Tex. App.—Austin Oct. 30, 2009, pet. dismissed) (mem. op.) ("If the individual is a party or if the party is an organization and designates a person to act as its representative in a deposition, the rules allow the witness to be deposed in the county of suit."); *Davis v. Ruffino*, 881 S.W.2d 186, 187 (Tex. App.—Houston [1st Dist.] 1994, orig. proceeding) ("When the deponent is a party to the suit, the deposition may be taken in the following counties: where the deponent resides, where the deponent is employed, where the deponent regularly conducts business in person, at such other convenient place as may be directed by the court, or in the county of suit.").

[193] *Wal-Mart Stores Inc. v. Street*, 754 S.W.2d 153, 155 (Tex. 1988) (per curiam) (holding that the Chairman of the Board of the defendant corporation had to be deposed in Bentonville, Arkansas, where he lived and worked); *In re FedEx Ground Package Sys.*, No. 14-19-00861-CV, 2020 Tex. App. LEXIS 4188, at *12–13, 2020 WL 283268 (Tex. App.—Houston [14th Dist.] May 28, 2020, orig. proceeding) (mem. op.) (holding that the trial court abused its discretion in not quashing a notice for the deposition of the defendant's employee in the county of suit because the employee lived in Pennsylvania); *In re Wells Fargo Bank, N.A.*, No. 03-10-00469-CV, 2010 Tex. App. LEXIS 6817, at *3–6, 2010 WL 3271159 (Tex.

11-2:3.2b Alternative Methods of Conducting or Recording the Deposition

Under Texas Rule 199.1, a party can take an oral deposition by telephone or other remote electronic means (e.g., videoconference)[194] and can record the deposition nonstenographically (e.g., by tape recorder or videotape).[195] If the deposition is to be taken by telephone or other remote electronic means, the deposition notice must so state and identify the means by which the deposition will be taken.[196]

If the deposition is to be recorded nonstenographically, a party, at least five days before the deposition date, must serve a written notice on the witness and all other parties: (1) stating the deposition will be recorded nonstenographically, (2) identifying the nonstenographic method that will be used (e.g., tape recorder or videotape), and (3) stating whether the deposition also will be recorded stenographically.[197] This notice can be included in the original deposition notice or in a separate writing served on the witness and the other parties.[198]

After a party gives notice of its intent to record the deposition nonstenographically, any other party can serve a written notice designating that the deposition will be recorded stenographically or by another means *at its expense*.[199] There, however, is no requirement that a nonstenographically recorded deposition also be recorded stenographically. Thus, for example, unless one party decides to pay for a court reporter or the trial court, under Texas Rule 203.6(a), orders the deposition be transcribed

---

App.—Austin Aug. 16, 2010, orig. proceeding) (mem. op.) (holding the defendant bank's employee, who lived and worked in De Moines, Iowa, had to be deposed there because "[i]t is not alleged that he received service within 150 miles of Travis County, Texas, or was a transient, or that Travis County, Texas was convenient for him. Grissom is not a party and he has not been designated as a corporate representative by Wells Fargo under [Texas R]ule 199.2(b)(1)"); ***In re Bannum, Inc.***, No. 03-09-00512-CV, 2009 Tex. App. LEXIS 10088, at *1–5, 2009 WL 8599250 (Tex. App.—Austin Oct. 30, 2009, orig. proceeding) (mem. op.) (holding the president of the defendant corporation, who was not the corporation's Texas Rule 199.2(b)(1) representative and who did not live or work in Texas, had to be deposed in Florida, where he lived); ***Butan Valley, N.V. v. Smith***, 921 S.W.2d 822, 829 (Tex. App.—Houston [14th Dist.] 1996, no writ) (holding that a corporate director, who was not the corporation's Texas Rule 199.2(b)(1) representative, had to be deposed in Saudi Arabia, where he lived).

The Austin Court of Appeals has held that a trial court has no authority to order a witness, who does not live or work in Texas, to appear for a deposition in Texas even as a sanction. ***In re Bannum, Inc.***, No. 03-09-00512-CV, 2009 Tex. App. LEXIS 10088, at *4, 2009 WL 8599250 (Tex. App.—Austin Oct. 30, 2009, orig. proceeding) (mem. op.).

[194] Tex. R. Civ. P. 199.1(b).

[195] Tex. R. Civ. P. 199.1(c).

[196] Tex. R. Civ. P. 199.2(b)(3).

[197] Tex. R. Civ. P. 199.1(c) ("At least five days prior to the deposition, the party must serve on the witness and all parties a notice, either in the notice of deposition or separately, that the deposition will be recorded by other than stenographic means. This notice must state the method of nonstenographic recording to be used and whether the deposition will also be recorded stenographically.").

[198] Tex. R. Civ. P. 199.2(b)(3) ("If the deposition is to be recorded by nonstenographic means, the notice may include the notice required by [Texas] Rule 199.1(c).").

[199] Tex. R. Civ. P. 199.1(c).

for trial,[200] a tape-recorded or videotaped deposition need not also be recorded stenographically.[201]

11-2:3.2c Additional Attendees

Texas Rule 199.5(a) governs who may attend an oral deposition. If a party "intends to have in attendance any persons other than the witness, parties, spouses of parties, counsel, employees of counsel, and the officer taking the oral deposition," the party must give "reasonable notice" to all parties of the other persons' identities.[202] Thus, for example, a party is required to give notice that an expert witness will attend a deposition, unless the expert is the noticing party's attorney's employee rather than an independent contractor.[203] Once such notice is given, the other parties can challenge the notice's adequacy or the person's attendance by moving for a protective order.[204]

The notice can be in the original deposition notice or a separate written document served on the witness and the other parties.[205] Any party can designate additional attendees. Texas Rule 199.5's purpose is to permit other parties to know in advance if an "additional attendee" will be at the deposition so they can seek a protective order if they have an objection to his or her attendance at the deposition. Once proper notice is given that an "additional attendee" will be present at the deposition, the "additional attendee" can attend the deposition unless the objecting party obtains a protective order preventing his or her attendance.[206]

An interesting question and, one not directly addressed by either the Texas discovery rules or Texas courts, is the standard a trial court is to apply in determining whether an "additional attendee" should be allowed to attend the deposition. Under

---

200 Texas Rule 203.6(a) provides, in relevant part: "A nonstenographic recording of an oral deposition, or a written transcription of all or part of such a recording, may be used to the same extent as a deposition taken by stenographic means. However, the court, for good cause shown, may require that the party seeking to use a nonstenographic recording or written transcription first obtain a complete transcript of the deposition recording from a certified court reporter." Tex. R. Civ. P. 203.6(a).

201 Tex. R. Civ. P. 199.1(c).

202 Tex. R. Civ. P. 199.5(a)(3); *see State Farm Lloyds v. Bold Roofing Co.*, No. 05-97-01908-CV, 2000 Tex. App. LEXIS 1602, at *7, 2000 WL 257772 (Tex. App.—Dallas Mar. 9, 2000, no pet.) (not designated for publication) (applying former Texas Rule 200(2)(a) and holding that "[t]he rules of civil procedure mandate that a party give notice if someone other than a party, counsel, spouse, deposition officer, or spouse of a party is going to attend"); *Burrhus v. M&S Supply*, 933 S.W.2d 635, 641 (Tex. App.—San Antonio 1996, no writ) (same and construing former Texas Rule 200(2)(a)).

203 *Burrhus v. M&S Supply*, 933 S.W.2d 635, 641 (Tex. App.—San Antonio 1996, no writ) (construing former Texas Rule 200(2)(a)).

204 *Burrhus v. M&S Supply*, 933 S.W.2d 635, 641 (Tex. App.—San Antonio 1996, no writ) (construing former Texas Rule 200(2)(a)).

205 Tex. R. Civ. P. 199.5(a)(3); *see Burrhus v. M&S Supply*, 933 S.W.2d 635, 641 (Tex. App.—San Antonio 1996, no writ) (construing former Texas Rule 200(2)(a)).

206 *Burrhus v. M&S Supply*, 933 S.W.2d 635, 641 (Tex. App.—San Antonio 1996, no writ) (construing former Texas Rule 200(2)(a) and holding that "[t]he history of the rule makes clear . . . that the drafters of the rule intended that once proper notice was given, the non-exempted person named in the notice could attend the deposition unless the objecting party obtained a protective order precluding the non-exempted person's attendance").

Texas Rule 192.6(b)(4), a court "[t]o protect the movant from . . . harassment, annoyance, or invasion of personal, constitutional, or property rights, . . . may make any order in the interest of justice and may—among other things—order that the discovery be undertaken only . . . upon such terms and conditions . . . directed by the court[.]" Texas Rule 199.5(d) provides that "[t]he oral deposition must be conducted in the same manner as if the testimony were being obtained in court during trial." Texas Rule 267 and Texas Rule of Evidence 614, in turn, govern the sequestration of witnesses at trial.[207] Thus, the question becomes whether the propriety of an additional person's attendance is governed by the protective-order rule, Texas Rule 192.6(b)(4), or the witness-sequestration rules, Texas Rule 267 and Texas Rule of Evidence 614.

Federal decisions are of limited help on this issue.[208] Before 1993, Federal Rule 30(c), similar to Texas Rule 199.5(d), provided that "examination and cross-examination of witnesses may proceed as permitted at the trial under the provisions of the Federal Rules of Evidence."[209] Federal courts were split, however, regarding whether this language meant that the federal witness-sequestration rule, Federal Rule of Evidence

---

[207] *Drilex Sys. v. Flores*, 1 S.W.3d 112, 116–17 (Tex. 1999) ("These rules provide that, at the request of any party, the witnesses on both sides shall be removed from the courtroom to some place where they cannot hear the testimony delivered by any other witness in the cause. Certain classes of prospective witnesses, however, are exempt from exclusion from the courtroom, including: (1) a party who is a natural person or his or her spouse; (2) an officer or employee of a party that is not a natural person and who is designated as its representative by its attorney; or (3) a person whose presence is shown by a party to be essential to the presentation of the cause."); *accord* Tex. R. Civ. P. 267(b) ("This rule does not authorize exclusion of (1) a party who is a natural person or the spouse of such natural person, or (2) an officer or employee of a party that is not a natural person and who is designated as its representative by its attorney, or (3) a person whose presence is shown by a party to be essential to the presentation of the cause."); Tex. R. Evid. 614 ("But this rule does not authorize excluding: (a) a party who is a natural person and, in civil cases, that person's spouse; (b) after being designated as the party's representative by its attorney . . . in a civil case, an officer or employee of a party that is not a natural person; . . . [or] (c) a person whose presence a party shows to be essential to presenting the party's claim or defense[.]").

[208] One Texas case, in *dictum*, suggests that Texas Rule 199.5(d)'s requirement that an oral deposition be conducted in the same manner as if the testimony were being obtained in court during trial incorporates the witness-sequestration rule of Texas Rule 267 and Texas Rule of Evidence 614. *In re Bell Helicopter Textron, Inc.*, 87 S.W.3d 139, 150–51 (Tex. App.—Fort Worth 2002, no pet.).

[209] In 1993, Federal Rule 30(c) was amended to make clear that Federal Rule 26(c)(1) regarding protective orders governs the determination. Federal Rule 30(c)(1) presently provides, in relevant part, that "examination and cross-examination of witnesses [at oral depositions] may proceed as permitted at the trial under the provisions of the Federal Rules of Evidence except Rules 103 and 615." The Advisory Committee Note to the 1993 Amendment to Federal Rule 30 explained the reason for the amendment as follows:

> [T]he revision addresses a recurring problem as to whether other potential deponents can attend a deposition. Courts have disagreed, some holding that witnesses should be excluded through invocation of Rule 615 of the [federal] evidence rules, and others holding that witnesses may attend unless excluded by an order under [Federal] Rule 26(c)(5). The revision provides that other witnesses are not automatically excluded from a deposition simply by the request of a party. Exclusion, however, can be ordered under [Federal] Rule 26(c)(5) when appropriate; and, if exclusion is ordered, consideration should be given as to whether the excluded witnesses

615,[210] applied in determining who could attend a deposition or whether the determination was to made under former Federal Rule 26(c)(5),[211] the discovery rule regarding protective orders, which provided that "[t]he court may, for good cause, issue an order to protect a party or person from annoyance, embarrassment, oppression, or undue burden or expense, including one or more of the following: . . . designating the persons who may be present while the discovery is conducted[.]"[212]

Because witness sequestration is a longstanding practice,[213] because the Texas Supreme Court opted not to adopt the 1993 amendments to Federal Rule 30(c) when making extensive amendments to the Texas discovery rules in 1999, and because

---

> likewise should be precluded from reading, or being otherwise informed about, the testimony given in the earlier depositions.

Fed. R. Civ. P. 30, Advisory Committee Note to 1993 Amend.

210 Federal Rule of Evidence 615 provides:

> At a party's request, the court must order witnesses excluded so that they cannot hear other witnesses' testimony. Or the court may do so on its own. But this rule does not authorize excluding:
>
> (a) a party who is a natural person;
>
> (b) an officer or employee of a party that is not a natural person, after being designated as the party's representative by its attorney;
>
> (c) a person whose presence a party shows to be essential to presenting the party's claim or defense; or
>
> (d) a person authorized by statute to be present.

Fed. R. Evid. 615.

211 Federal Rule 25(c)(5) is now Federal Rule 26(c)(1)(E).

212 *Compare, e.g., Adams v. Shell Oil Co.*, 136 F.R.D. 615, 617 & n.1 (E.D. La. 1991) (applying the witness-sequestration rule), *Lumpkin v. Bi-Lo, Inc.*, 117 F.R.D. 451, 453 (M.D. Ga. 1987) (same), *Naismith v. Prof'l Golfers Ass'n*, 85 F.R.D. 552, 568 (N.D. Ga. 1979) (same), *Williams v. Elec. Control Sys., Inc.*, 68 F.R.D. 703, 703–04 (E.D. Tenn. 1975) (same), *and Marks v. Powell (In re Marks)*, 135 B.R. 344, 345 (Bankr. E.D. Ark. 1991) (same), *with, e.g., In re Shell Oil Refinery*, 136 F.R.D. 615, 617 (E.D. La. 1991) (applying the good-cause requirement of former Federal Rule 26(c)(5)), *and BCI Commc'n Sys., Inc. v. Bell Atlanticom Sys., Inc.*, 112 F.R.D. 154, 157–59 (N.D. Ala. 1986) (same). State courts are similarly divided. *Compare, e.g., Stortz ex rel. Stortz v. Seier*, 835 S.W.2d 540, 542 (Mo. Ct. App. 1992) (applying the witness-sequestration rule), *with, e.g., Hamon Contractors, Inc. v. Dist. Ct.*, 877 P.2d 884, 887 (Colo. 1994) (en banc) (holding that the witness-sequestration rule does not apply to depositions), *and Pettit v. Dolese Bros.*, 943 P.2d 161, 165 (Okla. Civ. App. 1997) (same).

213 The practice of separating witnesses to prevent collusive testimony can be traced to biblical times. *Braswell v. Wainwright*, 330 F. Supp. 281, 283 n.1 (S.D. Fla. 1971) ("The historical origin of 'The Rule' may not be clearly known. But Daniel's effective use of the practice in the trial of Susanna suggests the genesis of this practice." (citing *Daniel* 13:51–59 (New American)); *Bishop v. State*, 194 S.W. 389, 389 (Tex. Crim. App. 1917) ("The story of Susanna is familiar. Her accusers testified in the presence of each other to her guilt. She was about to be condemned when Daniel interposed, saying: 'Put these two aside, one far from the other, and I will examine them.' His examination disclosed such discrepancies in their testimony as resulted in the release of Susanna and the condemnation of her accusers."). Witness sequestration was subsequently integrated into the English common law even before the emergence of jury trials, and the courts in most states embraced the practice when the common law was adopted as the prevailing legal system in this country. *See Drilex Sys., Inc. v. Flores*, 1 S.W.3d 112, 116 (Tex. 1999) ("English courts incorporated sequestration

there is no persuasive policy argument for limiting the witness-sequestration rule's application during discovery, the witness-sequestration rules—Texas Rule 267 and Texas Rule of Evidence 614—generally should inform the decision regarding whether an "additional attendee" should be allowed to attend a deposition. Thus, for example, an expert witness generally should be allowed to attend the depositions of the opposing party's experts,[214] but a fact witness should not be allowed to attend the depositions of other fact witnesses unless the witness also is an organization's representative for the deposition.

Even though Texas Rule 267 and Texas Rule of Evidence 614 are applicable to oral depositions, a trial court nonetheless has discretion to exclude anyone—even a party or an organization's representative—from a deposition because Texas Rule 192.6(b)(4), which governs protective orders, provides that a trial court "[t]o protect the movant from . . . harassment [or] annoyance . . . may make any order in the interest of justice and may—*among other things*—order that . . . the discovery be undertaken only . . . upon such terms and conditions, . . . directed by the court[.]"[215] A protective order excluding a party or an organization's representative from a deposition, however, should be granted only in exceptional circumstances. As explained by one federal court:

> However, due to the heightened interests of parties in the proceedings, "factors that might justify exclusion of non-parties from a deposition might not be sufficient to exclude parties." Hence, the principle has become well-established that a judge may exclude a party from a deposition only with a finding of

---

long ago, and the practice came to the United States as part of our inheritance of the common law.").

214 *See Drilex Sys. v. Flores*, 1 S.W.3d 112, 118–19 (Tex. 1999) ("Drilex is correct that this exception is often relied on to allow expert witnesses to be exempt from the [Texas] Rule. But nothing in [Texas Rule of Evidence] 614 or [Texas Rule] 267 suggests that *all* expert witnesses qualify for exemption. Although an expert witness may *typically* be found exempt under the essential presence exception, experts are not *automatically* exempt. Instead, [those Rules] vest in trial judges broad discretion to determine whether a witness is essential."); *accord U.S. v. Seschillie*, 310 F.3d 1208, 1213 (9th Cir. 2002). Federal courts generally allow experts to attend depositions of the opposing party's experts. *Lisanti v. Lubetkin (In re Lisanti Foods, Inc.)*, 329 B.R. 491, 512 (Bankr. D.N.J. 2005) ("The Court sees no reason to bar one party's expert witness from the deposition of the other party's expert. It is common for experts to assist attorneys in connection with deposition testimony of opposing experts."); *Lumpkin v. Bi-Lo, Inc.*, 117 F.R.D. 451, 453 n.1 (M.D. Ga. 1987) ("Because experts come within one of the exceptions to sequestration, this court is in complete agreement that experts can be excluded from depositions only upon a showing of good cause."); *Skidmore v. Nw. Eng'g Co.*, 90 F.R.D. 75, 76–77 (S.D. Fla. 1981) (allowing the plaintiff's expert to attend the depositions of the defendants' employees); *Williams v. Elec. Control Sys., Inc.*, 68 F.R.D. 703, 703 (E.D. Tenn. 1975) (allowing an expert to attend the deposition of the opposing party's expert).

215 Tex. R. Civ. P. 192.6(b)(4) (emphasis added). Federal courts have excluded parties or their designated representatives from depositions under Federal Rule 26(c)(1)(E), which, unlike Texas Rule 192.6, specifically permits a court to enter a protective order "designating the persons who may be present while the discovery is conducted[.]" *E.g., Stanek v. St. Charles Comm. Unit Sch. Dist. #303*, No. 13 C 3106, 2020 U.S. Dist. LEXIS 47528, at *18 (N.D. Ill. Mar. 19, 2020) ("Federal Rule of Civil Procedure 26(c)(1)(E) allows a court to decide 'the persons who may be present while the discovery is conducted' including those who may attend a party's deposition."); *Esebag v. Whaley*, No. CV 18-0844 R (RAO), 2019 U.S. Dist. LEXIS 228027, at *6–7, 2019 WL 8013118 (C.D. Cal. Sept. 9, 2019) (same).

"extraordinary circumstances." In making this determination, the court must engage in a detailed analysis of the circumstances, parties and issues involved, and require a specific showing of good cause by the movant.[216]

For example, exclusion of a party or an organization's representative may be appropriate under the following circumstances: (1) when there is a significant and real risk that the party or representative will ridicule, harass, or intimidate the deponent;[217]

---

[216] *Nyazie v. Kennedy*, No. 97-0120, 1998 U.S. Dist. LEXIS 10050, at *8, 1998 WL 398250 (E.D. Pa. June 18, 1998) (quoting *Hines v. Wilkinson*, 163 F.R.D. 262, 266 (S.D. Ohio 1995), and 8 Charles Alan Wright & Arthur Miller, *Federal Practice and Procedure* § 2041, at 536 (1994)); *accord Galella v. Onassis*, 487 F.2d 986, 997 (2d Cir. 1973) (holding that, although a trial court has the power to exclude a party from a deposition, "such an exclusion should be ordered rarely indeed"); *Stanek v. St. Charles Comm. Unit Sch. Dist. #303*, No. 13 C 3106, 2020 U.S. Dist. LEXIS 47528, at *18–19 (N.D. Ill. Mar. 19, 2020) ("Because plaintiffs have sued the individual teachers and thereby made them parties to this lawsuit, their right to attend Matthew's deposition 'has a constitutional dimension and is therefore entitled to special protection.' Consequently, although a court can prohibit a party from attending a deposition, '[t]he case law is clear that such power should be used rarely and only in extraordinary circumstances.' To provide good cause to exclude the teachers from his deposition, Matthew must make a 'specific showing of harm' to him that may occur if they are present." (quoting *Lee v. Denver Sheriff's Dep't*, 181 F.R.D. 651, 653 (D. Colo. 1998))); *Esebag v. Whaley*, No. CV 18-0844 R (RAO), 2019 U.S. Dist. LEXIS 228027, 2019 WL 8013118, at *7–8 (C.D. Cal. Sept. 9, 2019) ("Parties generally are entitled to be present at depositions absent 'extraordinary circumstances.' A court has the power to exclude a party from a deposition, but 'such an exclusion should be ordered rarely.' Courts appear to be split on whether there is any sort of constitutional right for a party to attend a deposition. The party moving for exclusion of another party must make a 'specific showing of harm' that is 'more than ordinary garden variety or boilerplate good cause facts which will exist in most civil litigation.' The relevant inquiry is whether the presence of the party would inhibit the deponent's ability to testify. The good cause analysis is highly fact specific." (citations omitted) (quoting *Brodzik v. Contractors Steel, Inc.*, No. 2:13-cv-438-JD-PRC, 2015 U.S. Dist. LEXIS 121237, 2015 WL 13818692 (N.D. Ind. Aug. 21, 2015), *Galella v. Onassis*, 487 F.2d 986, 997 (2d. Cir. 1973), and *Jones v. Circle K Stores, Inc.*, 185 F.R.D. 223, 224 (M.D.N.C. 1999))); *Shelton v. Bledsoe*, No. 3:11-0368, 2017 U.S. Dist. LEXIS 40678, at *8–9, 2017 WL 1062443 (M.D. Pa. Mar. 21, 2017) ("Absent a court order to the contrary, parties may attend depositions, and 'due to the heightened interests of parties in the proceedings, factors that might justify exclusion of non-parties from a deposition might not be sufficient to exclude parties because of the parties' more substantial interests in being present'. For this reason, courts generally are loath to exclude parties from depositions in the absence of 'compelling or exceptional circumstances.'" (citations omitted) (quoting *Dade v. Willis*, No. 95-6869, 1998 U.S. Dist. LEXIS 5941, at *4, 1998 WL 260270 (E.D. Pa. Apr. 20, 1998), and *BCI Commc'n Sys., Inc. v. Bell Atlanticom Sys., Inc.*, 112 F.R.D. 154, 160 (N.D. Ala. 1986))).

[217] *Cf. Galella v. Onassis*, 487 F.2d 986, 997 (2d Cir. 1973) (holding that the trial court properly barred the plaintiff paparazzi photographer from the deposition of the defendant and former First Lady Jacqueline Kennedy Onassis in a suit for damages allegedly resulting from the plaintiff's manhandling by the defendant's security staff because of the plaintiff's history of harassing the defendant); *Stanek v. St. Charles Comm. Unit Sch. Dist. #303*, No. 13 C 3106, 2020 U.S. Dist. LEXIS 47528, at *19–21 (N.D. Ill. Mar. 19, 2020) ("'[P]rotective orders excluding parties from depositions have been granted where there is evidence of potential harm to a deponent's mental health if a party is present at the deposition, or where there was physical contact or multiple threatening encounters between the deponent and the party.' In this case, Matthew does not claim—let alone offer any evidence—that the

(2) to protect privacy concerns or trade secrets;[218] and (3) very rarely, to prevent the

---

teachers' presence at his deposition will threaten his health. Instead, he asserts that their presence will have an intimidating effect on his testimony, and this falls far short of meeting his burden to show that they should be excluded from his deposition. It is not enough that the teachers' presence might make him 'uncomfortable' or cause him to have general concerns about his safety and security because they allegedly violated his rights many years ago. Matthew 'brought this suit against [the teachers]. [H]e will eventually need to face [them] to successfully prosecute h[is] case.' . . . Matthew does not differentiate between the teachers' presence at his deposition and their presence at trial and 'there is no evidence that the particular characteristics of a deposition would uniquely cause any more harm than trial proceedings.' Furthermore, the cases that Matthew relies upon are factually distinguishable because they concern the issue of whether non-parties (such as former supervisors or corporate representatives) should be excluded from a party's deposition. It is well-settled that '[f]actors that might justify exclusion of non-parties from a deposition might not be sufficient to exclude parties because of the parties' more substantial interest in being present." (citations omitted) (quoting *Esebag v. Whaley*, No. CV 18-0844 R (RAO), 2019 U.S. Dist. LEXIS 228027, at *8, 2019 WL 8013118, at *8 (C.D. Cal. Sept. 9, 2019), *Valentine v. Nielsen*, No. 16cv2357-W(KSC), 2018 U.S. Dist. LEXIS 39285, at *22, 2018 WL 2018 1281797 (S.D. Cal. 2018), and *Sincavage v. Schott N. Am.*, No. 3:18-CV-01231, 2019 U.S. Dist. LEXIS 206771, at *3–4, 2019 WL 6280314 (M.D. Pa. 2019))); *Esebag v. Whaley*, No. CV 18-0844 R (RAO), 2019 U.S. Dist. LEXIS 228027, at *8–9, 2019 WL 8013118 (C.D. Cal. Sept. 9, 2019) (same, discussing cases, and holding that a party's single threatening email to a nonparty witness was insufficient to exclude the party from the witness's deposition); *Laul v. Los Alamos Nat'l Labs.*, No. 16-1017 JAP/KBM, 2017 U.S. Dist. LEXIS 182634, at *3–4, 2017 WL 5129002 (D.N.M. Nov. 3, 2017) (excluding the plaintiff from a witness's deposition because the plaintiff had previously threatened and intimidated her); *Wesselmann v. Tyson Foods, Inc.*, No. 15-CV-4247-LTS, 2016 U.S. Dist. LEXIS 163495, at *6, 2016 WL 6986683 (N.D. Iowa Nov. 28, 2016) (excluding the plaintiff in a wrongful termination case from the deposition of defendant's employee because "[g]ood cause can include preventing the intimidation of a witness at a deposition" and the plaintiff was terminated for allegedly assaulting that employee); *Monroe v. Sisters of St. Francis Health Servs., Inc.*, No. 2:09 cv 411, 2010 U.S. Dist. LEXIS 124488, at *8–9, 2010 WL 4876743 (N.D. Ind. Nov. 23, 2010) (excluding the plaintiff's supervisors from attending the plaintiff's deposition because the plaintiff had a history of depression and the supervisors' presence could have an intimidating effect on his testimony and negatively impact his health); *Tolbert-Smith v. Bodman*, 253 F.R.D. 2, 5 (D.D.C. 2008) (excluding the plaintiff's former supervisors, who were designated as the defendant corporation's representatives, from the plaintiff's deposition in a discrimination action "[b]ecause plaintiff's doctor has expressed his concern that going forward with this deposition in the presence of plaintiff's former supervisors is very likely to result in severe and possibly catastrophic harm to the plaintiff"); *Adams v. Shell Oil Co.* (*In re Shell Oil Refinery*), 136 F.R.D. 615, 617 (E.D. La. 1991) (excluding corporate representatives from a deposition because of their intimidating influence on the deponent's testimony); *see also David v. Signal Int'l, LLC*, No. 08-1220 SECTION "E", 2014 U.S. Dist. LEXIS 83109, at *23, 2014 WL 2581319 (E.D. La. May 14, 2014) ("Courts, for example, have found good cause to restrict who may be present when the deponent is likely to be intimidated by a prospective attendee or where the privacy interests of a party or deponent would be compromised. On the other hand, courts have declined to order sequestration based on a conclusory allegation or inchoate fear that witnesses who attend each other's depositions will tailor their testimony to conform.") (citations omitted).

[218] *Cf. Monroe v. Sisters of St. Francis Health Servs., Inc.*, No. 2:09 cv 411, 2010 U.S. Dist. LEXIS 124488, at *4, 2010 WL 4876743 (N.D. Ind. Nov. 23, 2010) ("Other instances of good cause have included separating witnesses, [and] protecting trade secrets[.]" (citing *Marshwood Co. v. Jamie Mills, Inc.*, 10 F.R.D. 386 (N.D. Ohio 1950))).

possibility of a party's testimony being shaped or influenced by the deponent's testimony.[219]

A different question may exist, however, when an organization selects a series of representatives, each of whom is a fact witness, to attend the depositions of other fact witnesses or wants two or more representatives present at a deposition. In such cases, a court properly can limit the organization to a single representative.[220] Nonetheless,

---

219 *Compare, e.g.*, *In re Terra Int'l, Inc.*, 134 F.3d 302, 306 (5th Cir. 1988) (holding that conclusory allegations that witnesses would be inclined to protect each other through senses of "camaraderie" was insufficient to establish good cause for exclusion), *S; Picard v. City of Woonsocket*, No. 09-318 S, 2011 U.S. Dist. LEXIS 94430, at *11–12, 2011 WL 3740673 (D.R.I. Aug. 23, 2011) (same), *Nyazie v. Kennedy*, No. 97-0120, 1998 U.S. Dist. LEXIS 10050, at *9–11, 1998 WL 398250 (E.D. Pa. June 18, 1998) ("Repeatedly, courts have declined to order sequestration based on a broad and conclusory allegation that, should the witnesses be allowed to attend each other's depositions, they will tailor their testimony to conform to one another. . . . Unlike the above cases, no such extraordinary factors exist in this matter. . . . What remains, then, is the exact argument rejected in numerous other cases—an inchoate fear of influence of one party's deposition testimony on another's. The simple fact that the plaintiffs are family members speaking on a matter in which they have a stake does not create good cause sufficient to override their interest in being present at every deposition. Consequently, the request for sequestration must be denied."), *and BCI Commc'n Sys., Inc. v. Bell Atlanticom Sys., Inc.*, 112 F.R.D. 154, 155, 160 (N.D. Ala. 1986) (holding that the defendant's allegations regarding the need to preclude the plaintiff's witnesses, some of whom were its employees, "from hearing or being exposed to deponents' testimony" did not constitute "anything more than ordinary garden variety or boilerplate 'good cause' facts which will exist in most civil litigation"), *with, e.g.*, *Smith v. Ramsey*, No. 2:13-cv-00326, 2016 U.S. Dist. LEXIS 70434, at *6–9, 2016 WL 3059375 (E.D. Pa. May 31, 2016) (excluding defendant police officers from attending each other's depositions in civil rights action in which the plaintiff alleged the police officers beat him during and after his arrest); *Monroe v. Sisters of St. Francis Health Servs., Inc.*, No. 2:09 cv 411, 2010 U.S. Dist. LEXIS 124488, at *4, 2010 WL 4876743 (N.D. Ind. Nov. 23, 2010) ("Other instances of good cause have included separating witnesses to prevent the possibility of one witness shaping the testimony of another[.]"), *Dade v. Willis*, No. 95-6869, 1998 U.S. Dist. LEXIS 5941, at *9, 1998 WL 260270 (E.D. Pa. Apr. 20, 1998) (excluding defendant police officers from each other's depositions in a police brutality case because, "should the defendants be allowed to attend each other's deposition, plaintiff's 'day in court' will be deprived of its full effectiveness"), *and Clark v. Levine (In re Levine)*, 101 B.R. 260, 261–63 (Bankr. D. Colo. 1989) (ordering sequestration of certain defendants from the depositions of other defendants because "[w]hen allegations of fraud and conspiracy to commit fraud are joined, it can be persuasively argued that during discovery the need to test the observation, recollection and communication of each deponent independently should outweigh that party's right to be present for deposition").

220 *Cf. Adams v. Shell Oil Co. (In re Shell Oil Refinery)*, 136 F.R.D. 615, 617 (E.D. La. 1991) ("Thus, by designating multiple corporate representatives who are also fact witnesses, Shell would in effect avoid the sequestration of witnesses rule. That would give Shell an unfair advantage over the plaintiffs."); *Lumpkin v. Bi-Lo, Inc.*, 117 F.R.D. 451, 453–54 (M.D. Ga. 1987) ("Defendant further argues that even if [Federal Rule of Evidence] 615 applies to depositions, both Mr. Carithers and Mr. Barnes should be allowed to attend Plaintiff's deposition under the second exception to [Federal Rule of Evidence] 615 which allows a corporate representative to be present at trial. The court recognizes that although the language of the exception is in the singular, it is not clear from the rule or its legislative history whether more than one representative may be designated. While a district judge may exercise wide discretion in allowing more than one corporate representative to be present,

because depositions, unlike the typical trial (which lasts at most a week or two), often take place over many months or years and in multiple locations, an organization generally need not designate the same representative for each deposition[221] and a deponent generally should not be precluded from discussing the action with other witnesses or reading transcripts of depositions already taken.[222]

The final issue regarding "additional attendees" at depositions is the appropriate sanction for a violation of Texas Rule 199.5(a)(3)'s notice requirement. In *State Farm Lloyds v. Bold Roofing Co.*,[223] the Dallas Court of Appeals explained:

> Assuming there was a violation, neither [former Texas] Rule 200(2)(a) nor [Texas] Rule 215 specify a sanction or a range of sanctions available for a violation of the notice requirement. However, the overarching principle governing sanctions is that "[a] permissible sanction should . . . be no more severe than required to satisfy legitimate purposes." These legitimate purposes "are threefold: (1) to secure compliance with discovery rules; (2) to deter other litigants from similar misconduct; and (3) to punish violators." Sanctions that by their severity, prevent a decision on the merits of a case cannot be justified absent a party's flagrant bad faith or counsel's callous disregard for the responsibilities of discovery under the rules. Given these general rules, an appropriate sanction

---

the court finds that the instant case is not one that would warrant the attendance of both Mr. Carithers and Mr. Barnes at Plaintiff's deposition. Accordingly, counsel for Defendant may be accompanied by only one corporate representative at the deposition.") (citations omitted); *Lowy Dev. Corp. v. Super. Ct.*, 235 Cal. Rptr. 401, 404 (Cal. Ct. App. 1987) (allowing only one corporate representative to attend depositions).

221 *Cf. Breneman v. Kennecott Corp.*, 799 F.2d 470, 474 (9th Cir. 1986) ("Clearly, if a corporation may designate two representatives to remain in court during the trial, there is no violation of [Federal Rule of Evidence] 615 if, as here, a corporation designates a different single representative for the discovery and trial phases of a case.").

222 *Cf. In re Terra Int'l, Inc.*, 134 F.3d 302, 305–07 (5th Cir. 1998) (holding that the trial court abused its discretion in ordering "(1) when preparing witnesses for their depositions, attorneys may not refer 'directly or indirectly by innuendo, to what other witnesses say about the facts;' [or] (2) attorneys and officers of any party may not reveal prior deposition testimony to any witness prior to that witness's deposition"); *Jones v. Circle K Stores, Inc.*, 185 F.R.D. 223, 223, 224–25 (M.D.N.C. 1999) (denying protective order prohibiting the defendants from reading, discussing, or otherwise being informed about questions asked or testimony given in earlier depositions until their own deposition has been taken); *Solar Turbines, Inc. v. U.S.*, 14 Cl. Ct. 551, 552–53 (Cl. Ct. 1988) (denying a protective order precluding deponents from speaking to other witnesses or reviewing deposition transcripts); *Lumpkin v. Bi-Lo, Inc.*, 117 F.R.D. 451, 452–54 (M.D. Ga. 1987) (denying a protective order precluding deponents from speaking to other witnesses or reviewing deposition transcripts); *BCI Commc'n Sys., Inc. v. Bell Atlanticom Sys., Inc.*, 112 F.R.D. 154, 155, 160 (N.D. Ala. 1986) (denying a protective order forbidding "disclosure by a plaintiff of deposition testimony to any person who is expected to be deposed in this case in the future or who is expected to testify at trial or both"). *But see* Fed. R. Civ. P. 26, Advisory Committee Note to 1993 Amend. (noting that when exclusion is ordered under Federal Rule 26(c)(5) "consideration should be given as to whether the excluded witnesses likewise should be precluded from reading, or being otherwise informed about, the testimony given in the earlier depositions").

223 *State Farm Lloyds v. Bold Roofing Co.*, No. 05-97-01908-CV, 2000 Tex. App. LEXIS 1602, at *7–8, 2000 WL 257772 (Tex. App.—Dallas Mar. 9, 2000, no pet.) (not designated for publication).

for a violation of [former Texas] Rule 200(2)(a)'s notice requirement can vary and may include excluding the testimony of the non-exempted and unnoticed witness in extreme cases evidencing bad faith or callous disregard. However, a court is not required to exclude the testimony as a sanction for the alleged violation of [former Texas] Rule 200(2)(a).[224]

11-2:3.2d Document Requests

Under Texas Rule 199.2(b)(5), a deposition notice can "include a request that the witness produce at the deposition documents or tangible things within the scope of discovery and within the witness's possession, custody, or control."[225] If the witness is a party or subject to a party's control, the production request is governed by the rules governing production requests on parties—Texas Rules 193 and 196.[226] Thus, the thirty-day time period for responding to production requests provided by Texas Rule 196.2(a) applies to production requests in a deposition notice to a party or a person subject to a party's control,[227] and the party or person must respond to the request

---

224 *State Farm Lloyds v. Bold Roofing Co.*, No. 05-97-01908-CV, 2000 Tex. App. LEXIS 1602, at *7–8, 2000 WL 257772 (Tex. App.—Dallas Mar. 9, 2000, no pet.) (not designated for publication) (citations omitted) (applying former Texas Rule 200(2)(a)) (quoting *Chrysler Corp. v. Blackmon*, 841 S.W.2d 844, 849 (Tex. 1992)); *accord Burrhus v. M&S Supply*, 933 S.W.2d 635, 641 (Tex. App.—San Antonio 1996, no writ) (construing former Texas Rule 200(2)(a)). In *State Farm*, an individual, Hooper, attended a deposition as the plaintiff's representative. The plaintiff later admitted that Hooper was not its employee and designated another person as its trial representative. As a sanction for violating former Texas Rule 200(2)(a), the trial court ordered the plaintiff to designate Hooper as its trial representative. On appeal, the Dallas Court of Appeals held that this was an "appropriate sanction." *State Farm Lloyds v. Bold Roofing Co.*, No. 05-97-01908-CV, 2000 Tex. App. LEXIS 1602, at *8, 2000 WL 257772 (Tex. App.—Dallas Mar. 9, 2000, no pet.) (not designated for publication); *see Burrhus v. M&S Supply, Inc.*, 933 S.W.2d 635, 642–43 (Tex. App.—San Antonio 1996, writ ref'd n.r.e.) (holding that a trial court did not abuse its discretion in denying a motion to strike the testimony of an expert witness who attended other depositions without notice to the opposing party).

225 *Accord City of Dall. v. City of Corsicana*, Nos. 10-14-00090-CV, 10-14-00171-CV, 2015 Tex. App. LEXIS 8753, at *16, 2015 WL 4985935 (Tex. App.—Waco Aug. 20, 2015, orig. proceeding) (mem. op.) ("[Texas] Rules 199 and 200 plainly allow for the production of documents with an oral deposition or a deposition on written questions. Accordingly, the trial court's order is not an abuse of discretion to the extent that it allows Navarro to obtain documents in an oral deposition under [Texas R]ule 199 or a deposition on written questions under [Texas R]ule 200.") (citations omitted), *rev'd on other grounds*, 501 S.W.3d 71 (Tex. 2016) (orig. proceeding) (per curiam). See notes 239–48 and accompanying text (discussing when a witness is subject to a party's "control").

226 *See In re Yamin*, No. 14-20-00280-CV, 2020 Tex. App. LEXIS 6676, at *9, 2020 WL 4873021 (Tex. App.—Houston [14th Dist.] Aug. 20, 2020, orig. proceeding) (mem. op.) ("[A] request for documents from a nonparty is governed by [Texas] Rule 176, and a request from a witness subject to the control of a party is governed by [Texas] Rules 193 and 196."). See also Chapter 5, section 5-2, and Chapter 8, section 8-4 (respectively discussing responses to written-discovery requests generally and responses to Texas Rule 196 production requests specifically).

227 If the deposition is rescheduled by agreement, another thirty days' notice is required *only* if the noticing party serves an amended or supplemental deposition notice requesting *additional* documents.

(as required by Texas Rule 196.2) without the need for a subpoena.[228] If less than thirty-days' notice is provided, however, the party or person need not respond to the production request or produce the requested documents at or before the deposition, but rather must respond thereafter within the thirty-day period provided by Texas Rule 196.2.[229] Absent objection to the time and place of production, however, the party or person should produce its documents at the time and place requested by the notice's production request, which usually will be at the deposition.[230]

If the witness is not a party or subject to a party's control, the production request and response are governed by Texas Rules 205 and 176—the rules respectively relating to discovery from nonparties and subpoenas.[231] Under these Rules, a witness who is not a party or subject to a party's control must be served with both a deposition notice and a subpoena.[232] Because Texas Rules 176 and 205 neither have set a deadline

---

[228] *In re Markowitz*, No. 10-10-00116-CV, 2010 Tex. App. LEXIS 5327, at *8–9, 2010 WL 2683067 (Tex. App.—Waco July 7, 2010, orig. proceeding) (mem. op.) (holding that a production request in a deposition notice requires a party to produce the requested documents).

[229] *Cf. Edwards v. Scripps Media, Inc.*, 331 F.R.D. 116, 124 (E.D. Mich. 2019) ("[Federal] Rule 30(b)(2) allows a deposition notice to include a request for production of documents, but refers to Federal Rule of Civil Procedure 34, thus triggering [Federal] Rule 34's procedural requirements."); *Olmstead v. Fentress Cnty.*, No. 2:16-cv-00046, 2018 U.S. Dist. LEXIS 201404, at *9, 2018 WL 6198428 (M.D. Tenn. Nov. 28, 2018) ("[Federal] Rule 45 cannot be used to circumvent Rule 34 or other discovery rules. . . . Olmstead's subpoena would also contravene [Federal] Rule 34's instruction that a party have thirty days to respond to a document request. . . . Courts have quashed inter-party subpoenas that would reduce the period of compliance in less than the thirty-day period provided by [Federal] Rule 34(b)(2)(A)) (citations omitted); *Schultz v. Olympic Med. Ctr.*, No. C07-5377FDB, 2008 U.S. Dist. LEXIS 80848, at *7, 2008 WL 3977523 (W.D. Wash. Aug. 22, 2008) ("It is well settled that Fed. R. Civ. P. 30(b)(2) provides that any deposition notice which is served on a party deponent and which requests documents to be produced at the deposition must comply with the thirty-day notice requirement set forth in Fed. R. Civ. P. 34. [Federal] Rule 30(b)(2) provides that a 'notice to a party deponent may be accompanied by a request under [Federal] Rule 34 to produce documents and tangible things at the deposition.' [Federal] Rule 34 grants respondents thirty days to file a written response after service of requests for production. A party may not unilaterally shorten that response period by noticing a deposition and requesting document production at that deposition. The deposition notice for Dr. Ferrell did not allow Defendants the requisite thirty days to respond to the request for production of documents. Such procedural infirmity, however, did not, in and of itself, defeat the discovery. Due to the infirmity, Defendants simply had no duty to produce documents at Dr. Ferrell's deposition. Defendants did, however, have the obligation to respond with the responsive documents and/or written objections by the end of the thirty-day period. Defendants served and filed its written objections to the requested production within that time frame, on August 18, 2008.").

[230] Tex. R. Civ. P. 196.3(a) ("Subject to any objections stated in the response, the responding party must produce the requested documents . . . at either the time and place requested or the time and place stated in the response, unless otherwise agreed by the parties or ordered by the court[.]").

[231] *See In re Yamin*, No. 14-20-00280-CV, 2020 Tex. App. LEXIS 6676, at *9, 2020 WL 4873021 (Tex. App.—Houston [14th Dist.] Aug. 20, 2020, orig. proceeding) (mem. op.) ("[A] request for documents from a nonparty is governed by [Texas] Rule 176, and a request from a witness subject to the control of a party is governed by [Texas] Rules 193 and 196.").

[232] Tex. R. Civ. P. 176.2 ("A subpoena must command the person to whom it is directed to do either or both of the following: (a) attend and give testimony at a deposition . . .; [and]

for responses to production requests nor incorporate Texas Rule 196's deadline, Texas Rule 196.2(a)'s thirty-day deadline does *not* apply to production requests in a deposition notice for a witness who is not a party or under a party's control. Rather, such a production request must be served a "reasonable time" before the deposition,[233] "but no later than 30 days before the end of [the] applicable discovery period"[234] absent the parties' agreement or court order.[235] What is a "reasonable time" depends on the facts of each case.[236]

The subpoena recipient may serve written objections or move for a protective order from objectionable document requests *before* the time specified for compliance

---

(b) produce and permit inspection and copying of documents or tangible things in the possession, custody, or control of that person."), 205.3(a) ("A party may compel production of documents and tangible things from a nonparty by serving—a reasonable time before the response is due but no later than 30 days before the end of any applicable discovery period—the notice required in [Texas] Rule 205.2 and a subpoena compelling production or inspection of documents or tangible things.").

[233] Tex. R. Civ. P. 199.2(a). Of course, factors to be considered in determining what constitutes a "reasonable time" include the scope of any production request. See Chapter 11, section 11-2:3.1 (discussing the time for serving a deposition notice).

[234] Tex. R. Civ. P. 205.3(a).

[235] Tex. R. Civ. P. 191.1. See Chapter 3, section 3-3 (discussing modifications of discovery rules by agreement or court order).

[236] *Cf. Stern v. Shelley*, No. 3:09-CV-00082-JTC-RGV, 2009 U.S. Dist. LEXIS 130148, at *32, 2009 WL 9156145 (N.D. Ga. Aug. 31, 2009) ("Federal Rule of Civil Procedure 45(c)(3), however, does not set a minimum amount of time required to be considered a 'reasonable time to comply' with a subpoena, and 'generally, courts make the determination of reasonableness on a case-by-case basis, considering the factors at work in the given case.'" (quoting *Parrot, Inc. v. Nicestuff Distrib. Int'l, Inc.*, No. 06-61231, 2009 U.S. Dist. LEXIS 8528, at *10–11, 2009 WL 197979 (S.D. Fla. Jan. 26, 2009))).

Under Federal Rule 45, a court is required to quash a subpoena when it "fails to allow a reasonable time to comply." Fed. R. Civ. P. 45(d)(3)(A)(i). The rule does not define a "reasonable time." Federal courts nonetheless often find that fourteen days from the date of service is presumptively reasonable because the deadline for objecting to subpoenas under Federal Rule 45(d)(2)(B) is not more than fourteen days after its service. *E.g., Jones v. Singing River Health Sys.*, No. 1:14CV447-LG-RHW, 2016 U.S. Dist. LEXIS 63469, at *18–19 (S.D. Miss. May 3, 2016) ("[Federal] Rule 45 does not specify the number of days prior to a hearing that a subpoena must be served; the rule merely provides that a subpoena should be quashed if it fails to permit a reasonable amount of time for compliance. However, courts often assume that a minimum of fourteen days is required, because the deadline for objecting to subpoenas is fourteen days after service."); Verisign, Inc. v. XYZ.com, LLC, No. 15-mc-175-RGA-MPT, 2015 U.S. Dist. LEXIS 162772, at *7, 2015 WL 7960976 (D. Del. Dec. 4, 2015) (same); *In re Rule 45 Subpoena Issued to Cablevision Sys. Corp. Regarding IP Address 69.120.35.31*, No. 08-347 ARR MDG, 2010 U.S. Dist. LEXIS 40653, at *17–18, 2010 WL 2219343 (E.D.N.Y. Feb. 5, 2010) (same), *report and recommendation adopted in part*, No. 08MC347 ARR MDG, 2010 U.S. Dist. LEXIS 71061, 2010 WL 1686811 (E.D.N.Y. Apr. 26, 2010).

The Texas Rules of Civil Procedure do not have a similar deadline for objecting or moving for protection with respect to subpoenas. Rather Texas Rules 176.6(d) and (e) allow the person subpoenaed to object to production requests or move for protection with respect to a deposition or production request "before the time specified for compliance" and further provide that the "person need not comply with the part of a subpoena" to which objection was made or protection was sought. Tex. R. Civ. P. 176.6(d), (e).

in the subpoena, and the recipient need not comply with any objected-to requests until ordered to do so by the trial court.[237]

The mere fact that documents are marked as exhibits during the deposition does not make them admissible. Rather, the party who wants to use them at a hearing, for summary judgment purposes, or at trial must establish their admissibility either at the deposition or otherwise (e.g., by requests for admission or interrogatories).[238]

11-2:4 Compelling Attendance at the Deposition

Under Texas Rule 199.3, "[i]f the witness is a party or is retained by, employed by, or otherwise subject to the control of a party," the deposition notice's proper service "has the same effect as a subpoena served on the witness."[239] All other witnesses must also

---

[237] *In re Stagner*, No. 01-18-00758-CV, 2020 Tex. App. LEXIS 630, at *9, 2020 WL 370565 (Tex. App.—Houston [1st Dist.] Jan. 23, 2020, orig. proceeding) (mem. op.) ("A subpoena recipient may serve written objections or move for a protective order from objectionable subpoena requests, and the recipient need not comply with such objectionable requests until ordered to do so by the trial court."); Tex. R. Civ. P. 176.6(d) ("A person commanded to produce and permit inspection or copying of designated documents and things may serve on the party requesting issuance of the subpoena—before the time specified for compliance—written objections to producing any or all of the designated materials. A person need not comply with the part of a subpoena to which objection is made as provided in this paragraph unless ordered to do so by the court. The party requesting the subpoena may move for such an order at any time after an objection is made."); Tex. R. Civ. P. 176.6(e) ("A person commanded to appear at a deposition, hearing, or trial, or to produce and permit inspection and copying of designated documents and things, and any other person affected by the subpoena, may move for a protective order under [Texas] Rule 192.6(b) before the time specified for compliance—either in the court in which the action is pending or in a district court in the county where the subpoena was served. . . . A person need not comply with the part of a subpoena from which protection is sought under this paragraph unless ordered to do so by the court. The party requesting the subpoena may seek such an order at any time after the motion for protection is filed.").

[238] *See James v. Hudgins*, 876 S.W.2d 418, 422 (Tex. App.—El Paso 1994, writ denied) ("At the deposition, the attorney for Appellees questioned Dr. Levin as to what he brought to the deposition in response to each of these twelve requests. All of the documents identified by Dr. Levin and brought to the deposition were marked as deposition exhibits and attached to the deposition transcript, but Dr. Levin was not questioned about the content or substance of any of the documents. The attorney for Appellant made no attempt during the deposition to establish the admissibility into evidence at trial of any of these documents.").

[239] Tex. R. Civ. P. 199.3; *see In re Millwork*, 631 S.W.3d 706, 711 (Tex. 2021) (Texas "Rule 199.3 does not permit the trial court to compel a party to produce a witness when the party does not retain, employ, or control the witness at the time production is requested or required."); *In re Saddles Blazin, LLC*, No. 09-20-00209-CV, 2021 Tex. App. LEXIS 853, at *2, 2021 WL 377247 (Tex. App.—Beaumont Feb. 4, 2021, orig. proceeding) (per curiam) (mem. op.) ("A party may compel a witness to attend an oral deposition by serving the witness with a subpoena. If the witness is retained by, employed by, or otherwise subject to the control of a party, however, service of the notice of oral deposition upon the party's attorney has the same effect as a subpoena served on the witness.") (citation omitted); *In re Markowitz*, No. 10-10-00116-CV, 2010 Tex. App. LEXIS 5327, at *7, 2010 WL 2683067 (Tex. App.—Waco July 7, 2010, orig. proceeding) (mem. op.) ("We first note that, because Markowitz is a party to the suit, Brazos was not required to serve him with a subpoena in order to compel his attendance at the deposition."); *In re Reaud*, 286 S.W.3d 574, 578 (Tex.

be served with a subpoena under Texas Rule 176.[240]

One obvious question is: when is a witness "otherwise subject to the control of a party" within Texas Rule 199.3's meaning? Although nothing in Rule 199.3 or any other Texas discovery rule defines "control," the Texas Supreme Court recently considered the question in *In re Millwork*:[241]

> To dispense with the subpoena requirement for nonparty witnesses, [Texas] Rule 199.3 requires the existence of a specified relationship—retention or employment—and, failing either of those, the witness must be subject to the party's "control." Affording these terms their plain and commonly understood meaning, a deposition notice served on a party cannot, as [Texas] Rule 199.3 contemplates, "ha[ve] the same effect as a subpoena served on the witness" unless the party has the present power or authority to direct the witness to appear as noticed.
>
> Commonly understood, a witness "employed by" a party is one "who works in the service of [the party] under an express or implied contract of hire, under which the [party] has the right to control the details of work performance." Similarly, to "retain" a witness means "to hold . . . under [the party's] control[.]" Both of the specifically enumerated relationships contemplate the type of control that derives from an existing relationship, and as used in [Texas] Rule 199.3, the more general category of witnesses subject to a party's "control" connotes the same.
>
> "Control" over someone is "[t]he direct or indirect power to govern the management . . . of [the] person . . .; the power or authority to manage, direct, or oversee[.]" [Texas] Rule 199.3's use of the modifier "otherwise" invokes the ejusdem generis canon of construction, which limits the scope of the catchall language to

---

App.—Beaumont 2009, orig. proceeding) (per curiam) ("[U]nder the Texas Rules of Civil Procedure, a party may be compelled to present a nonparty witness who is subject to its control."). Texas Rule 205.1, which governs nonparty discovery, defines a nonparty as "a person who is not a party or subject to a party's control[.]" Tex. R. Civ. P. 205.1.

A trial court court's order improperly compelling a witness to appear at a deposition is subject to review by mandamus. *In re Millwork*, 631 S.W.3d 706, 714 (Tex. 2021). Mandamus relief is proper, however, only there is no evidence of employment, retention, or control. *In re Millwork*, 631 S.W.3d 706, 714, (Tex. 2021); *In re Saddles Blazin, LLC*, No. 09-20-00209-CV, 2021 Tex. App. LEXIS 853, at *4-5, 2021 WL 377247 (Tex. App.—Beaumont Feb. 4, 2021, orig. proceeding) (per curiam) (mem. op.); *In re Total Petrochemicals & Ref. USA, Inc.*, 595 S.W.3d 904, 905-07 (Tex. App.—Houston [14th Dist.] 2020, no pet.).

240 Tex. R. Civ. P. 199.3; *see In re Millwork*, 631 S.W.3d 706, 711 (Tex. 2021) (Texas "Rule 199.3 does not permit the trial court to compel a party to produce a witness when the party does not retain, employ, or control the witness at the time production is requested or required."); *In re Saddles Blazin, LLC*, No. 09-20-00209-CV, 2021 Tex. App. LEXIS 853, at *2, 4-5, 2021 WL 377247 (Tex. App.—Beaumont Feb. 4, 2021, orig. proceeding) (per curiam) (mem. op.) ("A party may compel a witness to attend an oral deposition by serving the witness with a subpoena. If the witness is retained by, employed by, or otherwise subject to the control of a party, however, service of the notice of oral deposition upon the party's attorney has the same effect as a subpoena served on the witness. To compel the oral deposition of a non-party, a party must serve a subpoena on the deponent.") (citations omitted).

241 *In re Millwork*, 631 S.W.3d 706 (Tex. 2021).

> the same class or category as the specific items that precede its use. In a similar fashion, the noscitur a sociis canon of construction provides that words must be construed in context to comport with the surrounding text. Applying these interpretive doctrines to [Texas] Rule 199.3, a witness would not be "otherwise subject to the control of" a party absent an existing relationship that imbues a party with a right of control commensurate with the type of control that could be exercised when a witness is "employed by" or "retained by" the party. Presently retained or employed witnesses, for example, can presumably be coerced to appear by the party's threat of adverse employment action. But just as the ability to exert coercive force—to control—does not predate a witness's retention, employment, or other similar relationship, so too it does not survive their cessation.[242]

Texas courts have held that the following persons are not under a party's employment, retention, or control: a former employee; a director of a corporation; and a former manager or member of a limited liability company.[243]

---

[242] *In re Millwork*, 631 S.W.3d 706, 712–13, (Tex. 2021) (citations omitted) (quoting *Employee*, *Retain*, and *Control*, *Black's Law Dictionary* (11th ed. 2019)); *accord In re Reaud*, 286 S.W.3d 574, 580 (Tex. App.—Beaumont 2009, orig. proceeding) (per curiam) ("The term, 'otherwise controlled,' is not defined by the procedural rules. In this instance we think the doctrine of ejusdem generis applies to restrict the potentially broad meaning of 'otherwise controlled' as used in [Texas] Rules 199.3 and 205.1. Ejusdem generis means that "'when words of a general nature are used in connection with the designation of particular objects or classes of persons or things, the meaning of the general words will be restricted to the particular designation.'" In other words, ejusdem generis limits the undefined, general term "otherwise controlled" as used in [Texas] Rules 199.3 and 205.1 to include only control of the same kind, class, or nature as the types of control parties would have over employees or retained experts. A related rule of construction, noscitur a sociis ("a word is known by the company it keeps"), compels the same conclusion. While the current rules contain language that allow them to reach beyond retained experts and employees, it is now clear that these two rules do not extend to nonparties over whom the party does not have the type of control as it has over an employee or a retained expert." (citations omitted) (quoting *State v. Fid. & Deposit Co.*, 223 S.W.3d 309, 312 (Tex. 2007))), *followed by In re Saddles Blazin, LLC*, No. 09-20-00209-CV, 2021 Tex. App. LEXIS 853, at *2-3, 4-5, 2021 WL 377247 (Tex. App.—Beaumont Feb. 4, 2021, orig. proceeding) (per curiam) (mem. op.).

[243] *In re Millwork*, 631 S.W.3d 706, 712–13 (Tex. 2021) (former employee); *In re Saddles Blazin, LLC*, No. 09-20-00209-CV, 2021 Tex. App. LEXIS 853, at *2-4, 4-5, 2021 WL 377247 (Tex. App.—Beaumont Feb. 4, 2021, orig. proceeding) (per curiam) (mem. op.) (a former manager of a limited liability company or a passive member of a such a company "[a]bsent some evidence that [the company's] governing documents granted the limited liability company the power to adversely affect [the member's] status or compensation as a member if he refused to attend the deposition"); *In re Reaud*, 286 S.W.3d at 579, 581–82 (Tex. App.—Beaumont 2009, orig. proceeding) (per curiam) (a director of a corporation absent evidence that the director "was subject to termination, discipline, or a reduction in his fees as a director based upon his refusal to attend the deposition under the circumstances of a notice without an accompanying subpoena").

The Beaumont court of appeals in *In re Reaud* distinguished *Wal-Mart Stores Inc. v. Street*, 754 S.W.2d 153, 154–55 (Tex. 1988) (orig. proceeding) (per curiam), in which the Texas Supreme Court held that Wal-Mart had "control" over the Chairman of its Board of Directors, as follows:

The determination of employment, retention, or control is made at the time the deposition notice is served.[244] The noticing party bears the burden of establishing employment, retention, or control.[245] When employment, retention, or control is in

---

> In *Street*, Wal-Mart sought relief through a writ of mandamus from a trial court's order that required Sam Walton, the chairman of Wal-Mart's board of directors, to give a deposition. At that time, Rule 201(3) of the Rules of Civil Procedure provided that notice could be directed to "'an agent or employee who is subject to the control of a party.'" Without discussing the record pertinent to the issue of Wal-Mart's control over Walton, the Texas Supreme Court stated that "[o]n the present record we find no clear abuse of discretion in Judge Street's decisions that Walton is an agent of the corporation subject to its control."
>
> Without knowing the state of the record before the *Street* Court concerning the proof surrounding Wal-Mart's control over Walton, we cannot determine whether the case stands for the proposition asserted by the Bank that a director, by virtue of his position, is subject to the corporation's control. For example, we do not know whether the record contained Wal-Mart's corporate bylaws or articles of incorporation, Arkansas statutes relevant to the rules on corporate structure, or Arkansas statutes relevant to the duties of Arkansas directors, or whether the testimony of witnesses explained how the rules of corporate governance in Wal-Mart's case made Walton subject to Wal-Mart's control. In any event, we can glean from the sparse discussion about the record in *Street* that Walton had more of a connection to Wal-Mart than the connection shown to exist between Reaud and Huntsman. Unlike the record here, in *Street* the record showed that Walton was the president of Wal-Mart when the underlying accident occurred, but that he was not an employee when the notice was served, that Walton was Wal-Mart's Board Chairman when the notice was issued, and that he was a major shareholder. Here, there is no evidence that Reaud was ever an officer of Huntsman or its board chairman, nor is there evidence that Reaud is a major shareholder in terms of the total shares issued by the corporation.
>
> Most importantly, *Street* was decided under procedural rules that were repealed as of January 1, 1999, and the former rule considered in *Street* contained specific language requiring a party to produce an *agent* under its control.

In re Reaud, 286 S.W.3d 574, 581 (Tex. App.—Beaumont 2009, orig. proceeding) (per curiam) (citations omitted) (quoting former Texas Rule 201(3) and *Wal-Mart Stores Inc. v. Street*, 754 S.W.2d 153, 154–55 (Tex. 1988) (orig. proceeding) (per curiam)).

244 *In re Millwork*, 631 S.W.3d 706, 713 (Tex. 2021) ("While courts have not expressly addressed the temporal limitation inherent in [Texas] Rule 199.3's plain language, courts applying the rule have focused on evidence of the party's present ability to control the witness. Further, in construing [Texas] Rule 199.3's similarly worded predecessor, we referred to the relevant time period as 'when notice was served[.]' In accordance with well-established interpretive principles, we conclude that [Texas] Rule 199.3 does not authorize courts to compel a party to produce a witness when retention, employment, and control are lacking at the time production is sought." (citations omitted) (quoting *Wal-Mart Stores, Inc. v. Street*, 754 S.W.2d 153, 154 (Tex. 1988) (quoting former Tex. R. Civ. P. 201(3))).

245 *See In re Millwork*, 631 S.W.3d 706, 713–14 (Tex. 2021) (reversing the trial court's order compelling the defendant to produce a witness without a subpoena because there was no evidence that the witness was retained by, employed by, or otherwise under the control of the defendant when the deposition notice was served); *cf. In re Summersett*, 438 S.W.3d 74, 81 (Tex. App.—Corpus Christ 2013, orig. proceeding) ("The party seeking production has the burden of proving that the relator has constructive possession or the right to obtain possession of the requested documents."); *In re U-Haul Int'l Inc.*, 87 S.W.3d 653, 656 (Tex. App.—San Antonio 2002, orig. proceeding) (same); *Norman v. Young*, 422 F.2d 470, 472–73

doubt, the best practice is to subpoena the witness to avoid a costly dispute regarding whether the witness is required to appear for deposition without a subpoena.

Once properly compelled to appear at a deposition, the witness "must remain in attendance from day to day until the deposition is begun and completed."[246] This requirement does not supersede the six-hour time limitation per side on depositions under Texas Rule 199.5(c), but merely requires that the witness attend the deposition until it is completed, or each side exhausts its six hours.[247]

As discussed in Chapter 11, section 11-2:3.2d, if the deposition notice contains a production request, the notice is sufficient to compel the documents' production if the witness is a party, or is employed by, retained by, or otherwise subject to the control of a party. Otherwise, the noticing party must serve a subpoena under Texas Rule 176.2(b) on the witness to compel the documents' production.

11-2:5 Taking, Attending, and Participating in Oral Depositions

There are three ways in which a party can participate in an oral deposition: (1) in person, (2) by telephone or other electronic means, or (3) by providing written questions to the deposition officer (i.e., the person recording the deposition, usually a court reporter). Each is discussed below.

11-2:5.1 In Person

Texas Rule 199.5(a)(2) provides that "[a] party may attend an oral deposition in person, even if the deposition is taken by telephone or other remote electronic means." Thus, even if the noticing party does not attend a deposition taken by telephone or other remote means in person, the other parties can do so.

As discussed in Chapter 11, section 11-2:3.2c, pursuant to Texas Rule 193.6, a trial court, in the exercise of its discretion, can exclude any person from attending a deposition, even a party or an organization's representative. However, as also discussed in that section, a party's or organization's representative should be excluded only in extraordinary circumstances.

11-2:5.2 By Telephone or Other Remote Electronic Means

Texas Rule 199.1 allows depositions to be taken by telephone and or other modern electronic communication technology (i.e., "other remote electronic means"), such as telephone or Internet video conferencing, such as Zoom. To take a deposition by such means, the noticing party only needs to give "reasonable prior written notice."[248]

(10th Cir. 1970) (same). See also Chapter 8, section 8-4:3.1 (discussing the meaning of "control" as used in Texas Rule 196.3 relating to production requests).

[246] Tex. R. Civ. P. 199.5(a)(1); *accord* Tex. R. Civ. P. 176.6(a) ("A person commanded to appear and give testimony must remain at the place of deposition . . . from day to day until discharged by the court or by the party summoning the witness.").

[247] Tex. R. Civ. P. 199.5(a)(1)(c), Most practitioners include in their deposition notices a statement that the deposition will "continue day-to-day until completed." This is unnecessary.

[248] Tex. R. Civ. P. 199.1(b).

A deposition taken by telephone or other remote electronic means "is considered as having been taken in the district and at the place where the witness is located when answering the questions."[249] The shorthand reporter recording the deposition need not be with the witness or the attorney taking the deposition.[250]

---

[249] Tex. R. Civ. P. 199.1(b). This is significant because a motion to compel or for protective order regarding the deposition of a nonparty must be filed in an appropriate court where the deposition was, or is to be, taken. Tex. R. Civ. P. 215.1(a) ("On matters relating to a deposition, an application for an order to a party may be made to the court in which the action is pending, or to any district court in the district where the deposition is being taken. An application for an order to a deponent ***who is not a party shall*** be made to the court in the district where the deposition is being taken.") (emphasis added); ***Latham v. Thornton***, 806 S.W.2d 347, 349 (Tex. App.—Fort Worth 1991, orig. proceeding) (same for a motion for protective order); ***see In re Prince***, No. 14-06-00895-CV, 2006 Tex. App. LEXIS 10558, at *7–8, 2006 WL 3589484 (Tex. App.—Houston [14th Dist.] Dec. 12, 2006, orig. proceeding) (mem. op.) ("If a non-party deponent fails to appear for or answer questions during a deposition, a party may apply for an order compelling discovery in the court of the district where the deposition is proceeding.").

[250] Tex. Gov't Code § 154.105(b)-(c). Section 154.105 of the Texas Government Code provides in pertinent part:

> (b) A shorthand reporter may administer oaths to witnesses:
>
> (1) anywhere in this state;
>
> (2) in a jurisdiction outside this state if:
>
> (A) the reporter is at the same location as the witness; and
>
> (B) the witness is or may be a witness in a case filed in this state; and
>
> (3) at any location authorized in a reciprocity agreement between this state and another jurisdiction under Section 152.202(b).
>
> (c) Notwithstanding Subsection (b), a shorthand reporter may administer an oath as provided under this subsection to a person who is or may be a witness in a case filed in this state without being at the same location as the witness:
>
> (1) if the reporter is physically located in this state at the time the oath is administered; or
>
> (2) as authorized in a reciprocity agreement between this state and another jurisdiction under Section 152.202(b) if:
>
> (A) the witness is at a location in the other jurisdiction; and
>
> (B) the reporter is at a location in the same jurisdiction as the witness.
>
> (d) The identity of a witness who is not in the physical presence of a shorthand reporter may be proven by:
>
> (1) a statement under oath on the record by a party to the case stating that the party has actual knowledge of the witness's identity;
>
> (2) a statement on the record by an attorney for a party to the case, or an attorney for the witness, verifying the witness's identity;
>
> (3) a statement on the record by a notary who is in the presence of the witness verifying the witness's identity; or
>
> (4) the witness's presentation for inspection by the court reporter of an official document issued by this state, another state, a federal agency, or another jurisdiction that verifies the witness's identity.
>
> (e) A shorthand reporter to which this section applies shall state on the record and certify in each transcript of the deposition the physical location of:

If a deposition is noticed to be taken by telephone or other remote electronic means, the noticing party "must make arrangements for all persons to attend by the same means."[251] However, those other persons need *not* attend the deposition by that means. Rather, they can attend in person even if the noticing party is not physically present.[252] In the same vein, non-noticing parties can attend a deposition to be taken in person either by telephone or by other remote electronic means. The non-noticing parties do *not* have to give notice of their intent to attend by such means, but they are responsible for "mak[ing] the necessary arrangements with the deposition officer and the party noticing the deposition."[253]

11-2:5.3 By Written Questions

Texas Rule 199.5(b) contains a seldom used practice—it allows a party to furnish written questions to be asked by the deposition officer (i.e., the person recording the deposition, usually a court reporter) at the oral deposition: "Any party, in lieu of participating in the examination, may serve written questions in a sealed envelope on the party noticing the oral deposition, who must deliver them to the deposition officer, who must open the envelope and propound them to the witness."[254]

11-2:6 Recording the Deposition

Under Texas Rule 199.1(a), "[t]he testimony, objections, and any other statements during the deposition must be recorded at the time they are given or made." This clause makes clear that anything said during the deposition, and not merely questions, answers, objections, and instructions not to answer, must be recorded. Of course, the parties can agree to go "off the record" at any time during the deposition.[255]

An oral deposition must be taken "before any officer authorized by law" to take one.[256] Generally, the only such officer is a certified shorthand reporter. Section 154.101(f) of the Texas Government Code provides that, with limited exceptions, "all depositions conducted in this state must be recorded by a certified shorthand reporter." When the statute requires the use of such a reporter, the deposition must be by stenographic transcription.[257]

There are two exceptions to Section 154.101(f)'s requirement that an oral deposition be taken before, and recorded stenographically by, a certified shorthand reporter. First, other persons may record oral depositions stenographically when a certified

---

(1) the witness; and

(2) the reporter.

Tex. Gov't Code § 154.105(b)–(e).

[251] Tex. R. Civ. P. 199.5(a)(2).

[252] Tex. R. Civ. P. 199.5(a)(2).

[253] Tex. R. Civ. P. 199.5(a)(2).

[254] Tex. R. Civ. P. 199.5(b).

[255] *See* Tex. R. Civ. P. 191.1.

[256] Tex. R. Civ. P. 199.1(a).

[257] Tex. Att'y Gen. Op. No. 93-110 (1993) (suggesting that only tape recording an oral deposition violates former Section 52.021(f) of the Texas Government Code, which is now Section 154.101(f)); Tex. Att'y Gen. Op. No. JM-110 (1983) (stating that oral deposition generally must be recorded by a certified shorthand reporter).

shorthand reporter is unavailable and the parties comply with the procedures in Section 154.112 of the Texas Government Code.[258] Second, and more importantly, Section 154.101(f)'s requirements do not apply to "(1) a party to the litigation involved, (2) the attorney of the party, or (3) a full-time employee of a party or a party's attorney."[259] Accordingly, such persons may record an oral deposition without the presence of certified shorthand reporter by a means other than stenographic recording, such as tape or video recording.[260] In addition, any person may record an oral deposition nonstenographically as long as a certified court reporter simultaneously records it stenographically.[261]

The procedure for recording oral depositions nonstenographically is set forth in Texas Rule 199.1(c) as follows:

> Any party may cause a deposition upon oral examination to be recorded by other than stenographic means, including videotape recording. The party requesting the nonstenographic recording will be responsible for obtaining a person authorized by law to administer the oath [e.g., a notary public] and for assuring that the recording will be intelligible, accurate, and trustworthy.[262]

The written notice of nonstenographic recording can be included in the deposition notice required by Texas Rule 199.2(b) or in a separate written notice (e.g., a letter). It must be given "[a]t least five days prior to the deposition" and "must state the method of nonstenographic recording to be used and whether the deposition will also be recorded stenographically."[263] After the notice is served, "[a]ny other party

---

[258] Tex. Gov't Code §§ 154.101, 154.112. Section 154.101 references Section 154.112, which provides:

> (a) A noncertified shorthand reporter may be employed until a certified shorthand reporter is available.
>
> (b) A noncertified shorthand reporter may report an oral deposition only if:
>
> (1) the noncertified shorthand reporter delivers an affidavit to the parties or to their counsel present at the deposition stating that a certified shorthand reporter is not available; or
>
> (2) the parties or their counsel stipulate on the record at the beginning of the deposition that a certified shorthand reporter is not available.
>
> (c) This section does not apply to a deposition taken outside this state for use in this state.

Tex. Gov't Code § 154.112.

[259] Tex. Gov't Code § 154.114; *see* Tex. Att'y Gen. Op. No. GA-0928 (2012) (analyzing former Texas Government Code Sections 52.021(f) and 52.033, which are now Sections 154.101(f) and 154.114 respectively, and concluding: "Construing [Texas] Rule . . . 199.1 in harmony with Government Code sections 52.021 and 52.033, (1) a party to litigation, (2) the attorney of the party, or, (3) a full-time employee of a party or a party's attorney may record a deposition solely by non-stenographic means without violating Government Code section 52.021(f).").

[260] *See Burr v. Shannon*, 593 S.W.2d 677, 678 (Tex. 1980) (construing former Tex. Rev. Civ. Stat. art. 2324b, § 15, the predecessor of Tex. Gov't Code § 154.114).

[261] Tex. Att'y Gen. Op. No. DM-339 (1995).

[262] Tex. R. Civ. P. 199.1(c).

[263] Tex. R. Civ. P. 199.1(c).

may then serve written notice designating another method of recording in addition to the method specified, at the expense of such other party unless the court orders otherwise."[264] Thus, if the noticing party designates stenographic recording of the deposition, any other party may arrange for and serve a notice designating a non-stenographic recording method.[265]

Under Texas Rule 203.6(a): "A nonstenographic recording of an oral deposition, or a written transcription of all or part of such a recording, may be used to the same extent as a deposition taken by stenographic means. However, the court, for good cause shown, may require that the party seeking to use a nonstenographic recording or written transcription first obtain a complete transcript of the deposition recording from a certified court reporter."

11-2:7 Objections to the Time, Place, or Other Arrangements for a Deposition

Objections to the time or place of a deposition set forth in a deposition notice are governed by Texas Rule 199.4, which provides, in relevant part: "A party or witness may object to the time and place designated for an oral deposition by motion for protective order or by motion to quash the notice of deposition." Such a motion, if filed by the third business day after the notice's service, ***automatically*** stays the deposition until the court rules on the motion.[266] If a non-noticing party or witness fails to so object, the deposition is not stayed unless the party or witness obtains a court order staying it before deposition date.[267] Although Texas Rule 199.4 does not specifically require the movant to state a reasonable time and place for the deposition, Texas Rule 192.6(a) requires such a statement in a motion for protective order,[268] but apparently not in a motion to quash.

---

264 Tex. R. Civ. P. 199.1(c).

265 Tex. R. Civ. P. 199.1(c).

266 Tex. R. Civ. P. 199.4 ("If the motion is filed by the third business day after service of the notice of deposition, an objection to the time and place of a deposition stays the oral deposition until the motion can be determined."); *see Min Rong Zheng v. Bridgestone Firestone N. Am. Tire, L.L.C.*, 284 S.W.3d 890, 894 (Tex. App.—Eastland 2009, no pet.) ("On March 23, plaintiffs' counsel filed a motion to quash, asserting that the date conflicted with his schedule. Because plaintiffs' counsel failed to file the motion to quash within three business days after service of the notice of depositions, the depositions were not automatically stayed.").

The federal discovery rules do not have a comparable provision. However, Federal Rule 32(a)(5)(A) provides: "A deposition must not be used against a party who, having received less than 14 days' notice of the deposition, promptly moved for a protective order under [Federal] Rule 26(c)(1)(B) requesting that it not be taken or be taken at a different time or place—and this motion was still pending when the deposition was taken."

267 *Min Rong Zheng v. Bridgestone Firestone N. Am. Tire, L.L.C.*, 284 S.W.3d 890, 894 (Tex. App.—Eastland 2009, no pet.) ("Because plaintiffs' counsel failed to file the motion to quash within three business days after service of the notice of depositions, the depositions were not automatically stayed.").

268 Texas Rule 192.6(a) provides, in relevant part: "If a person seeks protection regarding the time or place of discovery, the person must state a reasonable time and place for discovery with which the person will comply." *Accord Grass v. Golden*, 153 S.W.3d 659, 662 (Tex. App.—Tyler 2004, orig. proceeding) ("A party commanded to appear at a deposition or any other person affected by the subpoena may move for a protective order under Texas Rule of Civil Procedure 192.6(b). A movant seeking protection regarding the time or place of

Texas Rule 199.4 applies only to objections regarding the deposition's time and place. Other objections to a deposition notice or subpoena besides objections to its production request (e.g., failure to give "reasonable notice" of the oral deposition, notice of an apex deposition, failure to designate subject matters in a representative deposition notice under Texas Rule 199.2(b)(1) with particularity, an objection to "additional attendees") also must be made by protective order or motion to quash before the deposition.[269] Although it is clear that a *nonparty* who files a motion for protective order or to quash a subpoena under Texas Rule 176.6(e) need not comply with "the part of the subpoena from which protection is sought . . . unless ordered to do so by the court [,]"[270] this does not appear to be true for a party or a person retained by, employed by, or subject to the control of a party. This is because nothing in the rule governing protective orders, Texas Rule 192.6, or the rule governing oral depositions, Texas Rule 199, contains language comparable to that in Texas Rule 176.6(e). To the contrary, as discussed above, Texas Rule 199 suggests the opposite because *only* a motion for protective order or to quash regarding the time and place designated for an

---

discovery must state a reasonable time and place for discovery with which it will comply.") (citation omitted).

[269] Tex. R. Civ. P. 192.6(a) ("A person from whom discovery is sought, and any other person affected by the discovery request, *may move within the time permitted for response to the discovery request* for an order protecting that person from the discovery sought.") (emphasis added), 176.6(d) ("A person commanded to produce and permit inspection or copying of designated documents and things may serve on the party requesting issuance of the subpoena—before the time specified for compliance—written objections to producing any or all of the designated materials. A person need not comply with the part of a subpoena to which objection is made as provided in this paragraph unless ordered to do so by the court. The party requesting the subpoena may move for such an order at any time after an objection is made."); *see Siegel v. Smith*, 836 S.W.2d 193, 194 (Tex. App.—San Antonio 1992, writ denied) ("If the opposing party considers the notice inadequate or has a scheduling conflict, he has a duty to protest to opposing counsel and to the court as soon as possible."); *Bohmfalk v. Linwood*, 742 S.W.2d 518, 520 (Tex. App.—Dallas 1987, no writ) ("Upon receipt of the notice, Holder, if he had a scheduling conflict or if he simply considered the notice inadequate, had a duty to protest both to opposing counsel and to the court as soon as possible. He had to make his protest before the deposition was ever taken; failing that, he was burdened to show that it was not feasible for him to do so. To allow the respondent to a deposition notice to save his objection until a later day would be most disruptive to the smooth functioning of the law.").

An exception to this rule relates to production requests. If the deposition notice or subpoena contains one, the party or nonparty can file objections to it. Tex. R. Civ. P. 199.2(b)(5) (incorporating Texas Rule 196's procedures with respect to production requests for deposition notices served on a party or a person subject to a party's control), 200.1(b) ("The notice [for a deposition upon written questions] also may include a request for production of documents as permitted by [Texas] Rule 199.2(b)(5), the provisions of which will govern the request, service, and response."), 176.6(d) ("A person commanded to produce and permit inspection or copying of designated documents and things may serve on the party requesting issuance of the subpoena—before the time specified for compliance—written objections to producing any or all of the designated materials. A person need not comply with the part of a subpoena to which objection is made as provided in this paragraph unless ordered to do so by the court. The party requesting the subpoena may move for such an order at any time after an objection is made.").

[270] If the nonparty moves for protection or to quash the subpoena, the party seeking deposition should secure a ruling on the motion as quickly as possible.

oral deposition filed by the third business day after the notice's or subpoena's service "automatically" stays the deposition until the motion is decided.[271] Nonetheless, some local court rules automatically stay a deposition if a motion to quash or for protective order is filed.[272] Accordingly, in the absence of a local rule automatically staying the deposition, if the witness is a party or a person retained by, controlled by, or subject to the control of a party and the protective order or motion to quash relates to something other than the deposition's time and place or relates to those matters but is not filed within three business days of the notice's service and there is insufficient time to secure a ruling on the motion before the deposition date, the witness should not simply fail to appear for the deposition.[273] Rather, he or she should attempt to reach

---

[271] Tex. R. Civ. P. 199.4. Texas Rule 192.6(a) regarding protective orders generally provides that "[a] person must comply with a request to the extent protection is not sought unless it is unreasonable under the circumstances to do so before obtaining a ruling on the motion." Because the Rule uses the term "request," and not notice, it does ***not*** appear to apply to deposition notices.

[272] For example, the Rule 2.12 of the Local Rules for the Dallas County District Courts provides:

> 2.12. EFFECT OF MOTION TO QUASH DEPOSITION
>
> a. For purposes of this Rule, the date of delivery of a notice of deposition or motion to quash a notice of deposition is the date of actual delivery to counsel or a party, unless received after 5:00 p.m. in which case the date of delivery is deemed to be the next day on which the courthouse is open. Delivery by mail is presumed to be the third business day following mailing.
>
> b. The filing of a motion to quash a deposition with the district clerk and service on opposing counsel or parties in accordance with Local Rule 2.05, if done no later than the third day the courthouse is open after delivery of the notice of deposition, is effective to stay the deposition subject to determination of the motion to quash. The filing of a motion to quash does not otherwise stay a deposition.
>
> c. The parties may, by Rule 11 agreement, agree to proceed with a partial deposition while still reserving part or all of the objections made in the motion to quash.

Dall. Cnty. Dist. Cts. Loc. R. 2.12.

[273] Federal courts uniformly hold that a witness must comply with a deposition notice or subpoena unless a court order excuses compliance with it. *E.g., Barnes v. Madison*, 79 Fed. App'x. 691, 707 (5th Cir. 2003) ("[T]he mere act of filing a motion for a protective order does not relieve a party of the duty to appear; the party is obliged to appear until some order of the court excuses attendance."); *Pioche Mines Consol., Inc. v. Dolman*, 333 F.2d 257, 269 (9th Cir. 1964) ("[Federal] Rule 30(b) places the burden on the proposed deponent to get an order, not just to make a motion. And if there is not time to have his motion heard, the least that he can be expected to do is to get an order postponing the time of the deposition until his motion can be heard. He might also appear and seek to adjourn the deposition until an order can be obtained. But unless he has obtained a court order that postpones or dispenses with his duty to appear, that duty remains."); *Choice Hotels Int'l, Inc. v. Special Spaces, Inc.*, No. 2013-MC-0023, 2020 U.S. Dist. LEXIS 97507, at *16–19, 2020 WL 3001044 (D.V.I. June 3, 2020) (sanctioning defendants who failed to appear for their depositions despite their appeal of the magistrate's order denying their motion for protective to the district court because they did not obtain a stay of the order pending a ruling on the appeal and because a "motion for a protective order [does not] have the effect of staying the depositions"); *Batt v. Kimberly-Clark Corp.*, 438 F. Supp. 2d 1315, 1318 (N.D. Okla. 2006) (holding that the mere filing motion for protective order is insufficient to stay a deposition and that "Defendant was required to take some action to stay the deposition until the parties, with or without the Court's assistance, could resolve the dispute. This could have been done

an agreement with the noticing party postponing the deposition until the motion for protection or to quash is decided, file an emergency or accelerated motion to stay the deposition until the motion is decided, or, at least, appear at the deposition and immediately adjourn it until such motion is decided.[274]

11-2:8 The Deposition's Conduct

11-2:8.1 Time Limitations

Oral depositions are subject to two different time limits: one limiting the total number of hours for all such depositions and another limiting the time of each such deposition. The first limitation—the total number of hours for oral depositions—depends on the action's discovery Level.[275] The second limitation—the amount of time for each deposition—is governed by Texas Rule 199.5(c), which provides that "[n]o *side* may examine or cross-examine an individual witness for more than six hours."[276]

Texas Rule 199 and its comments, however, do not define "side." The term is discussed extensively in Texas Rule 190, which addresses the total number of deposition hours, and its concept of "side" should apply to Texas Rule 199.5(c).

Texas Rule 190.3(b)(2) defines "side" as "all the litigants with generally common interests in the litigation." Comment 6 to [Texas] Rule 190 elaborates:

> The concept of "side" in [Texas] Rule 190.3(b)(2) borrows from [Texas] Rule 233, which governs the allocation of peremptory strikes, and from Fed. R. Civ. P. 30(a)(2). In most cases there are only two sides—plaintiffs and defendants. In complex cases, however, there may be more than two sides, such as when defendants have sued third parties not named by plaintiffs, or when defendants have sued each other. As an example, if P1 and P2 sue D1, D2, and D3, and D1 sues D2 and D3, Ps would together be entitled to depose Ds and others permitted by the rule (*i.e.*, Ds' experts and persons subject to Ds' control) for 50 hours, and Ds would together be entitled to depose Ps and others for 50 hours. D1 would also be entitled to depose D2 and D3 and others for 50 hours on matters in controversy among them, and D2 and D3 would together be entitled to depose D1 and others for 50 hours.

---

even without a formal motion. Local Rule 37.2 provides a simple mechanism to invoke the Court's aid. Even only hours before the May 23 deposition, Defendant could have enlisted the Court's assistance by telephone, but did not do so. Thus, under the law, Defendant is in the wrong."); *Goodwin v. City of Boston*, 118 F.R.D. 297, 298 (D. Mass. 1988) ("The filing of a motion to quash or a motion for protective order does not automatically operate to stay a deposition or other discovery. When it appears that a Court is not going to be able to decide a motion to quash or a motion for protective order before the date set for a deposition, counsel for the movant should contact counsel for the party noticing the deposition and attempt to reach an agreement staying the deposition until after the Court acts on the motion to quash and/or the motion for a protective order. If agreement cannot be reached, it is incumbent on counsel for the movant to file a motion to stay the deposition until the Court acts on the motion to quash and/or for a protective order and to alert the clerk to the need for immediate action on the motion to stay.").

[274] See cases cited in note 277.

[275] See Chapter 2, section 2-3 (discussing discovery-control plans).

[276] Tex. R. Civ. P. 199.5(c) (emphasis added).

Texas Rule 190's explanation of "side" should enable the parties and trial court to apply Texas Rule 199.5 in most cases because, as pointed out by Comment 6 to Texas Rule 199, most actions only involve two parties. Moreover, even in multiparty actions in which the concept of "side" becomes murky, the situation should be ameliorated by the fact that most complex actions should be governed by a Level 3 discovery-control plan, which should include deposition-time limits tailored to the action's needs and facts.

Texas Rule 199.5(c)'s six-hour time limit applies to the questioning of an "individual witness" and does not include "breaks."[277] A "break" refers to any stoppage of the deposition, such as when the participants go "off the record" or when a party or the deponent leaves the deposition, whether by agreement or not. The time credited to a side should include ordinary pauses by the questioner or the witness, but not off-the-record discussions or protracted lapses, such as when a witness is reviewing a lengthy document. For purposes of Texas Rule 199.5(c), "each person designated by an organization under [Texas] Rule 199.2(b)(1) is a separate witness."[278]

The deposition officer (i.e., the person recording the deposition, usually a court reporter) is the timekeeper for purposes of keeping track of the amount of time used by each side. When the deposition officer certifies and delivers the deposition transcript or nonstenographic recording, the certificate must indicate the amount of time used by each party at the deposition.[279]

11-2:8.2 Attorneys' and Witnesses' Conduct

Texas Rules 199.5(d)–(h) govern the conduct of witnesses and attorneys during oral depositions. The deposition, according to Texas Rule 199.5(d), must be conducted "in the same manner as if the testimony were being obtained in court during trial."[280] This means that, after the witness is placed under oath,[281] the parties examine and cross-examine the witness as if the witness were testifying in court at trial.[282] An objection to a question and instructions not to answer must be made as permitted by Texas Rules 199.5(e) and (f).[283]

---

[277] Tex. R. Civ. P. 199.5(c) ("Breaks during depositions do not count against this limitation.").

[278] Tex. R. Civ. P. 199 cmt. 2 to 1999 change.

[279] Tex. R. Civ. P. 203.2(e) ("The deposition officer must file with the court, serve on all parties, and attach as part of the deposition transcript or nonstenographic recording of an oral deposition a certificate duly sworn by the officer stating . . . the amount of time used by each party at the deposition[.]").

[280] Tex. R. Civ. P. 199.5(d).

[281] Tex. R. Civ. P. 199.5(b) ("Every person whose deposition is taken by oral examination must first be placed under oath.").

[282] *See* Tex. R. Civ. P. 199.5(b) ("The parties may examine and cross-examine the witness."). Comment 3 to the 1999 change to Texas Rule 199 provides that "[t]he requirement that the deposition be conducted in the same manner as if the testimony were being obtained in court is a limit on the conduct of the lawyers and witnesses in the deposition, not on the scope of the interrogation permitted." Rather, the parties can inquire about any matter relevant to the action's subject matter even though the information sought might not be admissible in evidence at trial as long as the information sought appears reasonably calculated to lead to the discovery of admissible evidence. Tex. R. Civ. P. 192.3(a).

[283] See Chapters 11, sections 11-2:8.3 and 11-2:8.4 (discussing objections and instructions not to answer, respectively). Several federal courts have held that, if the deponent is represented

Because oral depositions must be conducted "in the same manner as if the testimony were being obtained in court during trial," Texas Rule of Evidence 612 should apply to them. That Rule recognizes the right of an adverse party to obtain writings used to refresh the witness's memory both *during* and *before* the deposition. It, however, "distinguishes between those writings used to refresh a witness's testimony *while* testifying and those used to refresh *before* testifying. If a witness uses the writing while testifying, the adverse party must be given access to it, but if the writing is used before the witness testifies, the court has the discretion to order the writing disclosed to the adverse party."[284]

---

by an attorney, only the attorney can object to a question or decide which questions should not be answered. *Van Stelton v. Van Stelton*, No. C11-4045-MWB, 2013 U.S. Dist. LEXIS 145999, at *46–48, 2013 WL 5574566 (N.D. Iowa Oct. 9, 2013) ("For reasons that should be obvious, a represented deponent may not interpose his or her own objections and decide which questions to answer.") (footnote omitted); *GMAC Bank v. HTFC Corp.*, 248 F.R.D. 182, 191 (E.D. Pa. 2008) (same).

[284] *Goode v. Shoukfeh*, 943 S.W.2d 441, 449 (Tex. 1997) (construing former Tex. R. Civ. Evid. 612); *accord In re H.L.B.*, No. 01-12-01082-CV, 2013 Tex. App. LEXIS 9004, at *23, 2013 WL 3866651 (Tex. App.—Houston [1st Dist.] July 23, 2013, no pet.) (mem. op.) ("If a witness uses a writing to refresh her memory, an adverse party 'is entitled to have the writing produced at the hearing, to inspect it, to cross-examine the witness thereon, and to introduce in evidence those portions which relate to the testimony of the witness.' In civil cases where the witness refreshes their memory before testifying, the trial court has discretion to allow an adverse party to review the writing if it is 'necessary in the interests of justice.'" (citations omitted) (quoting Tex. R. Evid. 612)); *Denison v. Grisham*, 716 S.W.2d 121, 122–24 (Tex. App.—Dallas 1986, orig. proceeding) (holding, under former Texas Rule of Evidence 611, that the plaintiffs had to produce notes that they referenced during their deposition testimony).

Texas Rule of Evidence 612 provides, in relevant part:

(a) *Scope.* This rule gives an adverse party certain options when a witness uses a writing to refresh memory:

(1) while testifying;

(2) before testifying, in civil cases, if the court decides that justice requires the party to have those options; or

(3) before testifying, in criminal cases.

(b) *Adverse Party's Options; Deleting Unrelated Matter.* An adverse party is entitled to have the writing produced at the hearing, to inspect it, to cross-examine the witness about it, and to introduce in evidence any portion that relates to the witness's testimony. If the producing party claims that the writing includes unrelated matter, the court must examine the writing in camera, delete any unrelated portion, and order that the rest be delivered to the adverse party. Any portion deleted over objection must be preserved for the record.

. . . .

Tex. R. Evid. 612. The Rule is very similar to the Federal Rule, which provides, in relevant part:

(a) Scope. This rule gives an adverse party certain options when a witness uses a writing to refresh memory:

(1) while testifying; or

(2) before testifying, if the court decides that justice requires the party to have those options.

There, however, is scant Texas authority regarding the applicability of Texas Rule of Evidence 612 to depositions.[285] Federal courts applying the almost identical federal procedural and evidence rules—Federal Rule 30(c) and Federal Rule of Evidence 612—generally hold that the evidence rule applies to depositions.[286] This also should be the case in Texas state courts.[287]

Thus, if the deponent uses a document, even one within the work-product, attorney-client, or other privilege, while testifying *during* the deposition to refresh his or her recollection, the privilege is waived and the document *must* be produced to the adverse party.[288] If, however, the deponent reviews documents *before* the deposition

---

(b) Adverse Party's Options; Deleting Unrelated Matter. Unless 18 U.S.C. § 3500 provides otherwise in a criminal case, an adverse party is entitled to have the writing produced at the hearing, to inspect it, to cross-examine the witness about it, and to introduce in evidence any portion that relates to the witness's testimony. If the producing party claims that the writing includes unrelated matter, the court must examine the writing in camera, delete any unrelated portion, and order that the rest be delivered to the adverse party. Any portion deleted over objection must be preserved for the record.

Fed. R. Evid. 612.

285 Only four Texas cases even tangentially consider Texas Rule of Evidence 612's application to a deposition: *In re McIntyre*, No. 03-12-00134-CV, 2012 Tex. App. LEXIS 7524, at *13–14, 2012 WL 3793159 (Tex. App.—Austin Aug. 31, 2012, orig. proceeding) (mem. op.), *In re Chevron Phillips Chem. Co. LP*, No. 09-06-470 CV, 2006 Tex. App. LEXIS 9186, at *1–3, 2006 WL 3028054 (Tex. App.—Beaumont Oct. 25, 2006) (mem. op.), *In re Brown*, No. 03-97-00609-CV, 1998 Tex. App. LEXIS 2609, at *9–10, 1998 WL 207793 (Tex. App.—Austin Apr. 30, 1998, orig. proceeding) (not designated for publication), and *Denison v. Grisham*, 716 S.W.2d 121, 122–24 (Tex. App.—Dallas 1986, orig. proceeding). These cases are discussed in notes 294–96 and their accompanying text.

286 *Spork v. Peil*, 759 F.2d 312, 317 (3d Cir. 1985) ("[Federal] Rule 612] is applicable to depositions and deposition testimony by operation of Federal Rule of Civil Procedure 30(c)."); *N. Ga. Elec. Mbrshp. Corp. v. Nat'l Union Fire Ins. Co.*, No. 4:17-CV-0065-HLM, 2018 U.S. Dist. LEXIS 224825, at *17 (N.D. Ga. Oct. 22, 2018) (same); *Adidas Am., Inc. v. TRB Acquisitions LLC*, No. 3:15-cv-2113-SI, 2017 U.S. Dist. LEXIS 193445, at *5, 2017 WL 5630038 (D. Or. Nov. 22, 2017) (same); *Reed v. Advocate Health Care*, No. 06 C 3337, 2008 U.S. Dist. LEXIS 3561, at *6, 2008 WL 162760 (N.D. Ill. Jan. 17, 2008) (mem. op.) ("The vast majority of cases that have considered the issue have concluded that [Federal Rule of Evidence] 612 is applicable to depositions by virtue of language contained in Federal Rule of Civil Procedure 30(c)." (quoting 28 Charles Alan Wright & Victor James Gold, *Federal Practice and Procedure* § 6183 (1993))).

287 *Tex. Dep't of Pub. Safety v. Caruana*, 363 S.W.3d 558, 566 n.1 (Tex. 2012) ("When the federal and Texas Rules of evidence are similar, we look to federal case law and the Federal Advisory Committee Notes when interpreting the Texas Rules.").

288 *Denison v. Grisham*, 716 S.W.2d 121, 122–24 (Tex. App.—Dallas 1986, orig. proceeding) (holding, that, under former Texas Rule of Evidence 611, the plaintiffs had to produce notes that they referenced during their deposition testimony); *cf. Heron Interact, Inc. v. Guidelines, Inc.*, 244 F.R.D. 75, 77 (D. Mass. 2007) ("Defendants also assert that Chacho specifically referred to at least two of the documents during the course of the deposition, *i.e.*, his annotated copies of the Covenant Not to Compete and the Asset Purchase Agreement. The court agrees. Those documents, accordingly, must be produced pursuant to [Federal Rule of Evidence] 612(1)."); *Sperling v. City of Kennesaw Police Dep't*, 202 F.R.D. 325, 329 (N.D. Ga. 2001) (holding that the plaintiff's use of a document during her deposition to refresh her memory waived work-product protection as to the document and entitled the defendant

to refresh his or her recollection, the documents are not *automatically* producible. Rather, a trial court has discretion to order them produced.[289]

---

to its production under Federal Rule of Evidence 612); *see Goode v. Shoukfeh*, 943 S.W.2d 441, 449 (Tex. 1997) ("We hold that an *Edmonson* movant has the right to examine the voir dire notes of the opponent's attorney when the attorney relies upon these notes while giving sworn or unsworn testimony in the *Edmonson* hearing.").

[289] *See* Tex. R. Evid. 612; *Goode v. Shoukfeh*, 943 S.W.2d 441, 449 (Tex. 1997) (construing former Tex. R. Civ. Evid. 612); *cf. Sporck v. Peil*, 759 F.2d 312, 318–19 (3d Cir. 1985) ("Proper application of [Federal Rule of Evidence] 612 should never implicate an attorney's selection, in preparation for a witness' deposition, of a group of documents that he believes critical to a case. Instead, identification of such documents under [Federal Rule of Evidence] 612 should only result from opposing counsel's own selection of relevant areas of questioning, and from the witness' subsequent admission that his answers to those specific areas of questioning were informed by documents he had reviewed. In such a case, deposing counsel would discover the documents through his own wit, and not through the wit of his adversary."); *Scalia v. Jani-King of Okla., Inc.*, No. CIV-16-1133-G, 2020 U.S. Dist. LEXIS 59479, at *13–15 (W.D. Okla. Apr. 2, 2020) ("[M]ost courts now reject the proposition that 'the protection afforded by a privilege . . . always is waived with respect to a writing whenever that writing is used to refresh memory.' Instead, more frequently the courts apply 'a test that balances the interests promoted by recognizing [Federal] Rule 612 rights in the adverse party against the burden those rights impose on . . . privilege protections.' The factors applied in these decisions that tend to weigh in favor of the adverse party include 'the inability of the adverse party to obtain access to the matters revealed by the writing' through other means and 'heavy reliance' on the document by the witness. Factors that tend to weigh in favor of retaining privilege protections include 'the use of a writing to refresh memory before rather than during testimony' and an indication that the request is made as part of a fishing expedition." (quoting 28 Victor Gold, *Federal Practice and Procedure (Wright & Miller): Evidence* § 6189 (2d ed. Supp. 2019))); *Adidas Am., Inc. v. TRB Acquisitions LLC*, No. 3:15-cv-2113-SI, 2017 U.S. Dist. LEXIS 193445, at *15, *19–20, 2017 WL 5630038 (D. Or. Nov. 22, 2017) (pointing out that (1) "[s]ome courts . . . have applied an 'automatic' waiver under [Federal Rule of Evidence] 612, regardless of whether a deposition witness is a percipient witness or a corporate representative designated under [Federal Rule] 30(b)(6)," (2) "many courts exercise discretion by applying a case-by-case balancing test," [and] (3) "[l]eading treatises also note that courts are divided between the balancing test and an automatic waiver rule, but generally support the balancing test" because it "is most consistent with the text of [Federal Rule of Evidence] 612, which supports mandatory waiver under the circumstances of [Federal Rule of Evidence] 612(a)(1), but only discretionary waiver under the circumstances of [Federal Rule of Evidence] 612(a)(2)" (footnote omitted) (citations omitted)).

Often a deposition notice will request that the witness bring to the deposition all the documents reviewed by the witness in preparation for it. Such a request is objectionable for two reasons. First, to obtain the documents, the adverse party must establish that the documents were used by the deponent to refresh the witness's memory for the purpose of testifying at the deposition. *See Mata v. State*, No. 10-12-00249-CR, 2013 Tex. App. LEXIS 6939, at *12–13, 2013 WL 2639190 (Tex. App.—Waco June 6, 2013, pet. ref'd) (mem. op.) ("Appellant is only entitled to Wilson's entire file if it was actually used by Wilson to refresh her memory. No one asked Wilson if or when she used the entire file in order to refresh her memory. Since there is no evidence from the record to establish that Wilson did in fact use the entire file to refresh her memory during or before her testimony, the trial court did not err in refusing to admit the file.") (citations omitted); *Love v. State*, No. 01-08-00941-CR, 2009 Tex. App. LEXIS 8952, at *19, 2009 WL 3930900 (Tex. App.—Houston [1st Dist.] 2009, no pet.) (mem. op.) (not designated for publication) (same); *Saldivar v. State*, 980 S.W.2d

The thorniest issue regarding Texas Rule of Evidence Rule 612's applicantion to depositions relates to whether the use of work-product, attorney-client, or other privileged materials to refresh the deponent's recollection in preparation for the deposition waives the privilege. Four Texas cases reveal division on the issue.

Two cases, one in *dictum*, suggest, without any analysis, that Texas Rule of Evidence 612 applies to depositions and that privilege may be waived by using privileged documents to refresh a deponent's recollection before the deposition.[290] The other two

---

475, 497 (Tex. App.—Houston [14th Dist.] 1998, pet. ref'd) (same); *cf. Sporck v. Peil*, 759 F.2d 312, 317 (3d Cir. 1985) ("By its very language, [Federal Rule of Evidence] 612 requires that a party meet three conditions before it may obtain documents used by a witness prior to testifying: 1) the witness must use the writing to refresh his memory; 2) the witness must use the writing for the purpose of testifying; and 3) the court must determine that production is necessary in the interests of justice. The first requirement is consistent with the purposes of the rule, for if the witness is not using the document to refresh his memory, that document has no relevance to any attempt to test the credibility and memory of the witness.") (citation omitted); *Africano v. Atrium Med. Corp.*, No. 17 CV 7238, 2019 U.S. Dist. LEXIS 46789, at *5–7, 2019 WL 1294642 (N.D. Ill. Mar. 21, 2019) (denying motion seeking production of documents reviewed by a witness in deposition preparation because "Plaintiff failed to lay a specific enough foundation to demonstrate that [the witness] reviewed a particular document, that she used the document to refresh her recollection, and that the document impacted her testimony. Merely asking whether [the witness] had seen any of the documents discussed at the deposition was not sufficient. Furthermore, and perhaps most importantly here, production is not in the interests of justice because Defendant explains that the documents [the witness] reviewed have already been produced to Plaintiff. Indeed, Plaintiff had access to the documents [the witness] reviewed prior to her deposition. The only objective to be gained by identifying these documents is to learn which documents Defendant considers to be significant in this case. '[W]here documents sought in a motion to compel have already been produced, [Federal Rule 612 should not require an attorney to reveal up front his selection, in preparation for his client's deposition, of a group of documents he believes critical to the case.'" (quoting *Stone Container Corp. v. Arkwright Mut. Ins. Co.*, No. 93 CV 6626, 1995 U.S. Dist. LEXIS 2400, at *11, 1995 WL 88902 (N.D. Ill. Feb. 28, 1995))).

When the action involves thousands of documents, some federal courts have held that the federal work-product doctrine exception applies to documents shown to witnesses in preparation for their depositions. *E.g., In re Joint E. & S. Dist. Asbestos Litig.*, 119 F.R.D. 4, 6 (E.D. & S.D.N.Y. 1988) ("However, even without [Federal Rule of Evidence] 612, the portion of the product book sought should be disclosed to defendants on the basis of defendants' demonstration of substantial need, as set out in [Federal] Rule 26(b)(3). Defendants have no other method of obtaining the identical material, i.e., the material that was shown to the plaintiff. Defendants cannot by other means learn whether the product book was used in a suggestive fashion so as to encourage plaintiff to recognize items he would not otherwise recognize.").

290 *In re Brown*, No. 03-97-00609-CV, 1998 Tex. App. LEXIS 2609, at *9–10, 1998 WL 207793 (Tex. App.—Austin Apr. 30, 1998, orig. proceeding) (not designated for publication); *Denison v. Grisham*, 716 S.W.2d 121, 123 (Tex. App.—Dallas 1986, orig. proceeding) (after explaining that former Texas Rule of Evidence 611(1) "entitles an adverse party to inspect writings used by a witness to refresh his memory while he is testifying[,]" noting in *dictum* that former Texas "Rule [of Evidence] 611(2) allows opposing counsel to inspect documents examined by the witness *before he testifies*, but only if the court first determines this is necessary in the interest of justice").

cases, *In re Chevron Phillips Chemical Co. LP*[291] and *In re McIntyre*,[292] appear to hold that the applicable privilege rule, rather than Texas Rule of Evidence 612, governs the waiver of privilege with respect to a document used to refresh a witness's recollection before deposition. Those cases are devoid of any analysis of Texas Rule 199.5(d) or Texas Rule of Evidence 612 and the policy behind Texas Rule of Evidence 612 and its interplay with the law of privilege. Perhaps more importantly, both are at odds with the literal language of Texas Rule of Evidence 612, which does not except privileged documents from its scope and which expressly applies to documents used to refresh a witness's recollection before the witness testifies. They also are inconsistent with federal decisions, which uniformly hold that using privileged documents to prepare a deponent can waive their privileged status.[293] Given the present state

---

The court in *In re Brown* held that the trial court abused its discretion in ordering asbestos plaintiffs to produce a twenty-page "Memo" prepared by a legal assistant containing a question-and-answer section with descriptions of asbestos-laden products and blanks for plaintiffs to describe their exposure to those products and a section describing the deposition process and instructing the plaintiffs how to prepare, dress, and conduct themselves because there was no evidence that the "Memo" was used to refresh the plaintiffs' recollection. *In re Brown*, No. 03-97-00609-CV, 1998 Tex. App. LEXIS 2609, at *9–10, 1998 WL 207793 (Tex. App.—Austin Apr. 30, 1998, orig. proceeding) (not designated for publication).

[291] *In re Chevron Phillips Chem. Co. LP*, No. 09-06-470 CV, 2006 Tex. App. LEXIS 9186, at *1–3, 2006 WL 3028054 (Tex. App.—Beaumont Oct. 25, 2006 org. proceeding) (mem. op.).

[292] *In re McIntyre*, No. 03-12-00134-CV, 2012 Tex. App. LEXIS 7524, at *13–14, 2012 WL 3793159 (Tex. App.—Austin Aug. 31, 2012, orig. proceeding) (mem. op.).

[293] Although a few federal decisions hold that privileged documents used to prepare a witness for deposition that refresh the witness's recollection automatically are producible, most of the recent federal decisions balance the need for disclosure for effective cross-examination against the protection against disclosure afforded by relevant privilege. *E.g., Scalia v. Jani-King of Okla., Inc.*, No. CIV-16-1133-G, 2020 U.S. Dist. LEXIS 59479, at *13–15 (W.D. Okla. Apr. 2, 2020) ("[M]ost courts now reject the proposition that 'the protection afforded by a privilege . . . always is waived with respect to a writing whenever that writing is used to refresh memory.' Instead, more frequently the courts apply 'a test that balances the interests promoted by recognizing [Federal] Rule 612 rights in the adverse party against the burden those rights impose on . . . privilege protections.' The factors applied in these decisions that tend to weigh in favor of the adverse party include 'the inability of the adverse party to obtain access to the matters revealed by the writing' through other means and 'heavy reliance' on the document by the witness. Factors that tend to weigh in favor of retaining privilege protections include 'the use of a writing to refresh memory before rather than during testimony' and an indication that the request is made as part of a fishing expedition." (quoting 28 Victor Gold, *Federal Practice and Procedure (Wright & Miller): Evidence* § 6189 (2d ed. Supp. 2019))); *Adidas Am., Inc. v. TRB Acquisitions LLC.*, No. 3:15-cv-2113-SI, 2017 U.S. Dist. LEXIS 193445, at *15, *19–21, 2017 WL 5630038 (D. Or. Nov. 22, 2017) (pointing out that (1) "[s]ome courts . . . have applied an 'automatic' waiver under [Federal Rule of Evidence] 612, regardless of whether a deposition witness is a percipient witness or a corporate representative designated under [Federal Rule] 30(b)(6)," (2) "many courts exercise discretion by applying a case-by-case balancing test," [and] (3) "[l]eading treatises also note that courts are divided between the balancing test and an automatic waiver rule, but generally support the balancing test" because it "is most consistent with the text of [Federal Rule of Evidence] 612, which supports mandatory waiver under the circumstances of [Federal Rule of Evidence] 612(a)(1), but only discretionary waiver under the circumstances of [Federal Rule of Evidence] 612(a)(2), and applying the balancing test"); *In re Managed Care Litig.*, 415 F. Supp. 2d 1378, 1381 (S.D. Fla. 2006) ("Although the Defendants point to a few old district court cases finding that use of a privileged document to refresh a witness's

of uncertainty, practitioners should avoid using privileged materials to prepare witnesses for deposition.

During the deposition, "[c]ounsel should cooperate with and be courteous to each other and to the witness[, and t]he witness should not be evasive and should not unduly delay the examination."[294] Not only can a witness who is a party, a party's officer, director, or managing agent, or an organization's representative be sanctioned for inappropriate deposition conduct, but so can the witness's attorney.[295] For example, in

---

recollection results in an automatic waiver of the privilege, this Court agrees with the more recent decisions holding that automatic waiver is inconsistent with both the plain language of [Federal Rule of Evidence] 612 and with the advisory committee notes.").

Unfortunately, the federal cases do not provide a uniform framework for analyzing these competing interests, but rather tailor it to the particular privilege asserted. *E.g., In re Managed Care Litig.*, 415 F. Supp. 2d 1378, 1380–81 (S.D. Fla. 2006); *Mfg. Admin. & Mgmt. Sys. v. ICT Grp., Inc.*, 212 F.R.D. 110, 118 (E.D.N.Y. 2002); *Suss v. MSX Int'l Eng'g Servs., Inc.*, 283 F. Supp. 2d 469 (S.D.N.Y. 2002); *EEOC v. Cont'l Airlines, Inc.*, 395 F. Supp. 2d 738, 744 (N.D. Ill. 2005).

Not only can documents reviewed by a witness in preparation for deposition possibly be obtained under Texas Rule of Evidence 612, but the opposing party may also be able to obtain them under the work-product rule, Texas Rule 192.5(b). As discussed above, see note 289 and accompanying text, an attorney's compilation or selection of relevant documents for use in discovery arguably is work product. If a party or witness claims that the documents reviewed by the witness in preparation for the deposition are protected work product, the question becomes whether the compilation is "core" work product. If it is not, the compilation may be discoverable "upon a showing that the party seeking discovery has a substantial need of the materials in the preparation of the party's case and that the party is unable without undue hardship to obtain the substantial equivalent of material by other means." Tex. R. Civ. P. 192.5(b)(2). See Chapter 4, section 4-4 (discussing the work-product doctrine in Texas).

294 Tex. R. Civ. P. 199.5(d); *cf. State Farm Mut. Auto. Ins. Co. v. Lincow*, 715 F. Supp. 2d 617, 642 (E.D. Pa. 2010) (holding that it was proper to play the portion of a party's expert's videotaped deposition to the jury, where he became upset and unruly, noting: "Defendants had notice that the deposition was being videotaped and could be used at trial. Dr. Lincow had served as an expert witness at several trials and knew the purpose of a deposition. That Dr. Lincow may have come to regret his boorish behavior at the deposition is not grounds for excluding it. In the final analysis, a deposition is a court proceeding and a witness and counsel are responsible for how they behave at depositions.").

295 Under Texas Rules 215.1(b)(2)(B) and (C) and 215.2(b)(2), such a witness or the witness's attorney can be sanctioned (e.g., ordered to pay the expenses of discovery) if the witness fails to answer a question or answers one evasively. In addition, a *party* can be sanctioned under Texas Rule 215.3 for "abusing the discovery process in seeking, making or resisting discovery[.]" See Chapter 14, sections 14-2:4, 14-3:3, 14-3:4, and 14-4 (addressing grounds for discovery sanctions, persons who may be sanctioned, and permissible discovery sanctions).

A number of Texas cases hold that the sanctions provided by Texas Rule 215.2(b) cannot be imposed against a nonparty. *E.g., In re White*, 227 S.W.3d 234, 236–37 (Tex. App.—San Antonio 2007, orig. proceeding) (holding that the trial court abused its discretion in ordering a deponent to pay, as sanctions, the court reporter's fees to continue the deposition); *In re Prince*, No. 14-06-00895-CV, 2006 Tex. App. LEXIS 10558, at *12, 2006 WL 3589484 (Tex. App.—Houston [14th Dist.] Dec. 12, 2006, orig. proceeding) (mem. op.) ("[A] court's power to impose sanctions on non-parties is limited to its contempt power."); *see City of Hous. v. Chambers*, 899 S.W.2d 306, 309 (Tex. App.—Houston [14th Dist.] 1995, orig. proceeding) (holding that the trial court abused its discretion in ordering a nonparty

GMAC Bank v. HTFC, a federal court sanctioned both the witness (the defendant's CEO) and defense counsel. The witness was sanctioned because his deposition conduct was "outrageous"[296]—he was hostile, uncivil, and vulgar and refused to answer many questions or provided intentionally evasive answers.[297] The attorney was sanctioned because his "complicity" was inexcusable—he willfully failed to intervene and control his client.[298]

In addition, "[a]n attorney must not ask a question at an oral deposition solely to harass or mislead the witness, for any other improper purpose, or without a good faith legal basis at the time."[299]

---

deponent, as sanctions, to pay the court reporter's fees to continue the deposition.). In so holding, the courts in *White* and *Prince* relied on the fact that Texas "Rule 215.2(b) only authorizes the trial court to impose sanctions for discovery abuses committed by 'a party or an officer, director, or managing agent of a party or a person designated . . . to testify on behalf of a party.'" *In re White*, 227 S.W.3d 234, 236 (Tex. App.—San Antonio 2007, orig. proceeding); *accord In re Prince*, No. 14-06-00895-CV, 2006 Tex. App. LEXIS 10558, at *12, 2006 WL 3589484 (Tex. App.—Houston [14th Dist.] Dec. 12, 2006, orig. proceeding) (mem. op.) (citing Tex. R. Civ. P 215(b), (c)). Texas Rule 215.1(a), however, provides that if "a party[] or *other deponent* . . . fails to answer a question propounded or submitted upon oral examination or upon written questions . . . the discovering party may . . . apply to the court in which the action is pending for the imposition of any sanction authorized by [Texas] Rule 215(b) without the necessity of first having obtained a court order compelling such discovery.") (emphasis added). This language is inconsistent with Texas Rule 215.2(b). The courts in *White, Prince*, and *Chambers* did not mention this conflict. Thus, it is unclear whether, under Texas Rule 215.2(b)(2), sanctions can be imposed against a nonparty or the nonparty's attorney for failing to answer or evasively answering a deposition question. See Chapter 14, section 14-3:4 (discussing sanctionable discovery conduct).

296 *GMAC Bank v. HTFC*, 248 F.R.D. 182, 198 (E.D. Pa. 2008).

297 *GMAC Bank v. HTFC*, 248 F.R.D. 182, 186 (E.D. Pa. 2008); *accord Marion-Johns v. Agency of Credit Control, Inc.*, No. CIV-17-438-F, 2018 U.S. Dist. LEXIS 229831, at *22–29 (W.D. Okla. May 4, 2018) (sanctioning a nonparty for his abhorrent deposition conduct as well his attorney for not controlling his client); *Carroll v. Allstate Fire & Cas. Ins. Co.*, No. 12-cv-00007-WJM-KLM, 2014 U.S. Dist. LEXIS 28061, at *31–32, 37, 41, 2014 WL 859238 (D. Colo. Mar. 4, 2014) (imposing sanctions against the plaintiff's expert witness for inappropriate deposition behavior consisting of repeated and unnecessary commentary regarding defense counsel's skills and methods and repeated verbal attacks against defense counsel); *Van Stelton v. Van Stelton*, No. C11-4045-MWB, 2013 U.S. Dist. LEXIS 145999, at *45–46, *54–56, 2013 WL 5574566 (N.D. Iowa Oct. 9, 2013) (sanctioning both the defendant and his attorney because, to circumvent proper deposition procedure, they agreed that the defendant, instead of his attorney, would interpose improper objections and refuse to answer questions).

298 *GMAC Bank v. HTFC*, 248 F.R.D. 182, 186, 198 (E.D. Pa. 2008); *accord Marion-Johns v. Agency of Credit Control, Inc.*, No. CIV-17-438-F, 2018 U.S. Dist. LEXIS 229831, at *22–29 (W.D. Okla. May 4, 2018) (sanctioning a nonparty for his abhorrent deposition conduct as well his attorney for not controlling his client); *Van Stelton v. Van Stelton*, No. C11-4045-MWB, 2013 U.S. Dist. LEXIS 145999, at *45–46, *54–56, 2013 WL 5574566 (N.D. Iowa Oct. 9, 2013) (sanctioning both the defendant and his attorney, because to circumvent proper deposition procedure, they agreed that the defendant, instead of his attorney, would interpose improper objections and refuse to answer questions).

299 Tex. R. Civ. P. 199.5(h); *cf. Baines v. City of N.Y.*, No. 10 CV 9545 (JMF) (JLC), 2016 U.S. Dist. LEXIS 69967, at *9 (S.D.N.Y. 2016) ("Pursuant to [Federal] Rule 26(c)(1) or [Federal] Rule 30(d)(3), a deponent may also move for a protective order and/or to limit or terminate a

Texas Rule 199.5(d) governs conferences, providing, in relevant part: "Private conferences between the witness and the witness's attorney during the actual taking of the deposition are improper except for the purpose of determining whether a privilege should be asserted. Private conferences may be held, however, during agreed recesses and adjournments."[300]

---

deposition on the ground that it 'unreasonably annoys, embarrasses, or oppresses the deponent or party.' When seeking to limit or terminate a deposition under [Federal] Rule 30(d)(3), the moving party may demand that the deposition be suspended for the time necessary for the court to rule on the objection. Questions that delve into a deponent's sexual history or other elements of his or her personal life that have no possible relevance to the case may be the subject of a successful [Federal] Rule 30(d)(3) motion."); *Van Stelton v. Van Stelton*, No. 11-CV-4045 (MWB), 2013 U.S. Dist. LEXIS 145999, at *44, 2013 WL 5574566, at *17 (N.D. Iowa Oct. 9, 2013) (noting that "asking a deponent questions about personal or confidential matters, such as his . . . sex life . . . would quickly qualify [for protection] if such matters had no possible relevance to the case' while also cautioning that, because 'it is black-letter law that relevance is not an appropriate basis for . . . a refusal to answer[,] . . . [c]ouching the instruction or refusal in terms of "harassment" [pursuant to [Federal] Rule 30(d)(3)] does not change the analysis when the cry of "harassment" is based solely on an argument that certain topics are not relevant").

The Texas Lawyer's Creed and the Texas Disciplinary Rules of Professional Conduct also prohibit such questioning. For example, the Lawyer's Creed instructs attorneys to treat adverse parties and witnesses with "fairness and due consideration" and to advise clients that they will not pursue conduct that is "intended to harass . . . an opposing party." Tex. Law. Creed Art. II, §§ 6–7. The Disciplinary Rules similarly prohibit an attorney, in the representation of a client, from using "means that have no substantial purpose other than to embarrass, delay, or burden a third person[,]" Tex. Disciplinary R. Prof. Conduct 4.04(a), or "ask[ing] any questions intended to degrade a witness or other person except whether the lawyer reasonably believes that the question will lead to admissible evidence[.]" Tex. Disciplinary R. Prof'l Conduct R. 4.04(c)(4).

The Lawyer's Creed and Disciplinary Rules further prohibit an attorney from making false statements and misrepresentations during a deposition. The former provides that an attorney will not "knowingly misrepresent, mischaracterize, misquote, or miscite facts or authorities to gain an advantage." Tex. Law. Creed Art. IV, § 6. Similarly, the Disciplinary Rules not only prohibits an attorney from making a false statement or misrepresentation during a deposition, Tex. Disciplinary R. Prof'l Conduct R. 4.01, but also generally prohibits an attorney from engaging in dishonest, fraudulent, or deceptive conduct, Tex. Disciplinary R. Prof'l Conduct R. 8.04.

[300] Tex. R. Civ. P. 199.5(d); *cf. Medline Indus. v. Wypetech, LLC*, No. 20 CV 4424, 2020 U.S. Dist. LEXIS 201694, at *8–9, 2020 WL 6343089 (N.D. Ill. Oct. 29, 2020) ("'Once the deposition has begun, the preparation period is over,' and 'the right to counsel is somewhat tempered by the underlying goal of our discovery rules: getting to the truth.' To this end, 'a questioning attorney is entitled to have the witness, and the witness alone, answer questions' during a deposition. Furthermore, courts have uniformly held that an attorney has no right to confer with his or her client while a deposition question is pending for the purpose of helping the client to formulate their answer to the question. 'If the deponent lacks knowledge or understanding, then the deponent should say so, [and] not seek understanding or direction about how to answer the question from his or her attorney.'" (quoting *Hall v. Clifton Precision*, 150 F.R.D. 525, 529 (E.D. Pa. 1993), *Vnuk v. Berwick Hosp. Co.*, No. 3:14-CV-01432, 2016 U.S. Dist. LEXIS 25693, at *7, 2016 WL 907714 (M.D. Pa. Mar. 2, 2016), *Eid v. Greyhound Lines, Inc.*, No. 04 C 3220, 2005 U.S. Dist. LEXIS 61182, at *12, 2005 WL 8178347 (N.D. Ill. July 12, 2005), and *In re Stratosphere Corp. Sec. Litig.*, 182 F.R.D. 614, 621 (D. Nev. 1998))); *LM Ins. Corp. v. ACEO, Inc.*, 275 F.R.D. 490, 491 (N.D. Ill. 2011) ("Instead of allowing the witness to

If an attorney *or* witness violates Texas Rule 199.5(d)'s requirements regarding courteousness, responsiveness, or conferences, "the court may allow in evidence at trial statements, objections, discussions, and other occurrences during the oral deposition that reflect upon the credibility of the witness or the testimony."[301]

11-2:8.3 Objections

Objections are made and recorded during the deposition by the deposition officer (i.e., the person recording the deposition, usually a court reporter) and reserved for ruling by the trial court, not the deposition officer.[302] Texas Rule 199.5(e) sets forth the permissible types of objections, including the *exact* words that *must* be used: "Objections to questions during the oral deposition are limited to 'Objection, leading' and 'Objection, form.' Objections to testimony during the oral deposition are limited to 'Objection, nonresponsive.'"[303] These objections "are *waived* if not stated as phrased during the oral deposition."[304]

An argumentative or suggestive objection waives the objection and may "be grounds for terminating the oral deposition or assessing costs or other sanctions."[305]

---

answer the question, Mr. O'Connor interrupted and informed the examiner that he wanted to confer with his client and immediately left the deposition room with Ms. Finke. No explanation or justification was even attempted by Mr. O'Connor. This was improper. Because a deposition generally proceeds as at trial, Rule 30(c)(1), Federal Rules of Civil Procedure, courts have uniformly held that once a deposition starts, counsel has no right to confer during the deposition, with perhaps one narrow exception, which is not applicable here and which Mr. O'Connor never sought to invoke as the basis for the conference.").

301 Tex. R. Civ. P. 199.5(d); *cf. State Farm Mut. Auto. Ins. Co. v. Lincow*, 715 F. Supp. 2d 617, 642 (E.D. Pa. 2010) (holding that it was proper to play the portion of a party's expert's videotaped deposition to the jury, where he became upset and unruly, noting: "Defendants had notice that the deposition was being videotaped and could be used at trial. Dr. Lincow had served as an expert witness at several trials and knew the purpose of a deposition. That Dr. Lincow may have come to regret his boorish behavior at the deposition is not grounds for excluding it. In the final analysis, a deposition is a court proceeding and a witness and counsel are responsible for how they behave at depositions.").

302 Tex. R. Civ. P. 199.5(e) ("The officer taking the oral deposition will not rule on objections but must record them for ruling by the court. The officer taking the oral deposition must not fail to record testimony because an objection has been made.").

303 Tex. R. Civ. P. 199.5(e). Unlike Texas Rule 199.5(e), which specifically sets forth how a form objection should be made, Federal Rule 32(d)(3)(B)(i) merely provides that "[a]n objection to an error or irregularity at an oral examination is waived if . . . it relates to . . . the form of a question or answer[.]" Accordingly many federal courts require the objecting attorney to state the basis for the form objection in a few words (e.g., "objection, leading," "objection, compound," or "objection, narrative"). *E.g., Otis v. Demarasse*, 399 F. Supp. 3d 759, 765–66 (E.D. Wis. 2019) (citing cases); *Sec. Nat'l Bank v. Abbott Labs.*, 299 F.R.D. 595, 602–03 (N.D. Iowa 2014) (citing cases), *rev'd on other grounds*, 800 F.3d 936 (8th Cir. 2015). But other federal courts require the objecting attorney to state nothing more than an unspecified "form" objection during depositions, as Texas Rule 199.5(c) requires. *Otis v. Demarasse*, 399 F. Supp. 3d 759, 765–66 (E.D. Wis. 2019) (citing cases); *Sec. Nat'l Bank v. Abbott Labs.*, 299 F.R.D. 595, 602–03 (N.D. Iowa 2014) (citing cases), *rev'd on other grounds*, 800 F.3d 936 (8th Cir. 2015).

304 Tex. R. Civ. P. 199.5(e) (emphasis added).

305 Tex. R. Civ. P. 199.5(e); *see In re Harvest Cmtys. of Hous., Inc.*, 88 S.W.3d 343, 346–48 (Tex. App.—San Antonio 2002, orig. proceeding) ("Mennellas' counsel, who was taking the

An attorney, however, need not, and should not, make any objections other than "form," "leading," or "nonresponsive" during the deposition to preserve those objections, and substantive objections (e.g., hearsay, relevance, materiality, the witness's competency)[306] can be raised later with the trial court in connection with a summary judgment motion, at the pretrial conference, or during trial.[307]

A leading question is "one that suggests the desired answer or puts words into the witness's mouth to be echoed back."[308] Such questions "should not be used on direct examination except as necessary to develop the witness's testimony. Ordinarily, the court should allow leading questions (1) on cross-examination and (2) when a party calls a hostile witness, an adverse party, or a witness identified with an adverse party."[309]

"Form" objections for purposes of Texas Rule 199.5(e) include that the question (a) assumes facts in dispute or not in evidence, (b) is argumentative or abusive, (c) misquotes the witness, (d) calls for speculation, (e) is confusing, ambiguous, vague, or unintelligible, (f) is compound, (g) calls for a narrative, (h) has been asked and answered, (i) misstates the record, (j) calls for an opinion from an unqualified witness, (k) lacks a foundation, or (l) exceeds the scope of an organization's representative's designation or the subject matters in the deposition notice for an organization's

---

deposition, was repeatedly interrupted by long, argumentative objections by Hirsch, some of which lasted several pages. These objections were in violation of [Texas] Rule 199.5(e) which limits objections to questions during the oral deposition to 'Objection, leading' and 'Objection, form.' The purpose of the [Texas] Rule was to prevent the kind of obstructive behavior that was exhibited here and to save substantive complaints for a later hearing before the trial court. . . ." (quoting Tex. R. Civ. P. 199.5(e))); *cf. Cerda v. Cillessen & Sons*, No. 19-1111-JWB, 2020 U.S. Dist. LEXIS 139456, at *10–11 (D. Kan. 2020) (ordering the plaintiff's attorney to pay all costs associated with the plaintiff's deposition because he improperly made speaking objections and coached his client); *Deville v. Givaudan Fragrances Corp.*, 419 Fed. App'x 201, 209 (3d Cir. 2011) (affirming a magistrate judge's imposition of sanctions pursuant to Federal Rule 30(d)(2) because the sanctioned attorney "testified on behalf of her witness by way of suggestive speaking objections"); *Craig v. St. Anthony's Med. Ctr.*, 384 Fed. App'x 531, 533 (8th Cir. 2010) (affirming a district judge's award of sanctions pursuant to Federal Rule 30(d)(2) due to "a substantial number of argumentative objections together with suggestive objections and directions to the deponent to refrain from answering questions without asserting a valid justification"); *Howard v. Offshore Liftboats, LLC*, Nos. 13-4811; 13-4811, 13-6407, 2015 U.S. Dist. LEXIS 26629, at *28–30, 2015 WL 965976 (E.D. La. Mar. 4, 2015) (imposing monetary sanctions against an attorney and barring him from participating in further depositions in the action for, among other things, making improper speaking objections).

306 A question exists regarding whether an attorney can instruct his client not to answer a question that seeks irrelevant information or information not calculated to lead the discovery of admissible evidence. See notes 324–26 and accompanying text.

307 Tex. R. Civ. P. 199.5(e) ("All other objections need not be made or recorded during the oral deposition to be later raised with the court.").

308 *Sahualla v. Guseman Constr., LLC*, No. 09-14-00342-CV, 2015 Tex. App. LEXIS 4645, at *4, 2015 WL 2124988 (Tex. App.—Beaumont May 7, 2015, no pet.) (mem. op.); *accord Navarro v. State*, No. 11-14-00216-CR, 2016 Tex. App. LEXIS 8725, at *18–19, 2016 WL 4385900 (Tex. App.—Eastland Aug. 11, 2016, pet. ref'd) (mem. op.); *Mega Child Care v. Texas Dep't of Protective & Regulatory Servs.*, 29 S.W.3d 303, 307 (Tex. App.—Houston [14th Dist.] 2000, no pet.); *GAB Bus. Servs. v. Moore*, 829 S.W.2d 345, 351 (Tex. App.—Texarkana 1992, no writ).

309 Tex. R. Evid. 611(c).

deposition under Texas Rule 199.2(b)(1).[310] Although under Texas Rule 199.5(e), an attorney has the right and duty to object to protect his or her witness from improper

[310] *Ordonez v. M.W. McCurdy & Co.*, 984 S.W.2d 264, 274 (Tex. App.—Houston [1st Dist.] 1998, no writ) (Form objections "usually involve the following objections: '(1) assumes facts in dispute or not in evidence; (2) is argumentative; (3) misquotes a deponent; (4) is leading; (5) calls for speculation; (6) is ambiguous or unintelligible; (7) is compound; (8) is too general; (9) calls for a narrative answer; (10) has been asked and answered.'"); *St. Luke's Episcopal Hosp. v. Garcia*, 928 S.W.2d 307, 309 (Tex. App.— Houston [14th Dist.] 1996, no writ) (same); Tex. R. Civ. P. 199 cmt. 4 to 1999 change ("An objection to the form of a question includes objections that the question calls for speculation, calls for a narrative answer, is vague, is confusing, or is ambiguous."); *cf. Otis v. Demarasse*, 399 F. Supp. 3d 759, 765 (E.D. Wis. 2019) ("'Form' objections is a category that includes objections to leading questions, lack of foundation, assuming facts not in evidence, mischaracterization, vague or misleading questions, lack of personal knowledge, speculative, asked and answered, argumentative, and compound questions."); *Fletcher v. Honeywell Int'l, Inc.*, No. 3:16-cv-302, 2017 U.S. Dist. LEXIS 28325, at *3, 2017 WL 775852 (S.D. Ohio Feb. 28, 2017) ("'Form' objections include a broad category of objections, such as objections that the question is too broad, compound or ambiguous, that it has been asked and answered, that it calls for speculation, is argumentative, assumes facts not in evidence, calls for an opinion from a witness who is not qualified to give one, or is leading under circumstances where leading questions are not permitted."); *Sec. Nat'l Bank v. Abbott Labs.*, 299 F.R.D. 595, 601 (N.D. Iowa 2014) ("'[F]orm' objections refer to a *category* of objections, which includes objections to 'leading questions, lack of foundation, assuming facts not in evidence, mischaracterization or misleading question, non-responsive answer, lack of personal knowledge, testimony by counsel, speculation, asked and answered, argumentative question, and witness' answers that were beyond the scope of the question.'" (quoting *NGM Ins. Co. v. Walker Const. & Dev., LLC*, No. 1:11-CV-146, 2012 U.S. Dist. LEXIS 177161, at *7, 2012 WL 6553272 (E.D. Tenn. Dec. 13, 2012))), *rev'd on other grounds*, 800 F.3d 936 (8th Cir. 2015))); *Abu Dhabi Comm. Bank v. Morgan Stanley & Co.*, No. 08 Civ. 7508 (SAS), 2011 U.S. Dist. LEXIS 116840, at *26–27, 2011 WL 4526141 (S.D.N.Y. Sept. 9, 2011) ("At least one secondary source has identified eleven grounds upon which a party or its counsel may state an objection to the form of a question posed at a deposition. Those grounds are: (1) compound; (2) asked and answered; (3) overbroad/calls for a narrative; (4) calls for speculation; (5) argumentative; (6) vague or unintelligible; (7) assumes facts not in evidence; (8) misstates the record; (9) calls for an opinion from an unqualified witness; (10) leading where not permitted; and (11) lack of foundation."); *Boyd v. Univ. of Md. Med. Sys.*, 173 F.R.D. 143, 147 n. 8 (D. Md. 1997) ("Fed. R. Civ. P. 32(d)(3)(B) requires attorneys to make seasonable objections to the form of questions which are asked, or else they are waived. The most frequent grounds for objecting to the form of a question are: (1) the question is too broad or calls for an excessive narrative answer, (2) the question is compound, (3) the question has been asked and responsively and completely answered, (4) the question calls for conjecture, speculation or judgment of veracity, (5) the question is ambiguous, imprecise, unintelligible or calls for a vague answer, (6) the question is argumentative, abusive or contains improper characterization, (7) the question assumes as true facts in dispute or not in evidence, (8) the question misquotes a witness' earlier testimony, (9) the question calls for an opinion from a witness not qualified to give one, and (10) the question is leading under circumstances where leading questions would not be permitted by Fed. R. Evid. 611(c).") (citation omitted).

As noted in the foregoing authorities, although "leading" is a form objection, under Texas Rule 199.5(e), "leading" is treated as a distinct objection.

The last objection—the question exceeds the scope of an organization's representative's designation or the subject matters in a deposition notice for an organization's deposition under Texas Rule 199.2(b)(1)—is discussed in note 87 and accompanying text.

questions, the attorney must do so as permitted by Texas Rules 199.5(d)–(h). For example, an attorney "properly cannot demand clarification of a question the *attorney* claims not to understand—the witness should be permitted to answer the question posed, or to ask for clarification if he or she does not understand the question."[311] Moreover, attorneys "are strictly prohibited from making any comments . . . which might suggest or limit a witness's answer to an unobjectionable question."[312] Likewise,

---

[311] *Cmty. Ass'n Underwriters of Am. v. Queensboro Flooring Corp.*, No. 3:10-CV-1559, 2014 U.S. Dist. LEXIS 90939, at *22, 2014 WL 3055358 (M.D. Pa. July 3, 2014); *accord Pogue v. Nw. Mut. Life Ins. Co.*, No. 3:14-cv-598-CRS, 2017 U.S. Dist. LEXIS 110990, at *38, 2017 WL 3044763 (W.D. Ky. July 18, 2017) ("If the deponent does not know how to answer a question, he or she may state as much, but it is not appropriate for his or her attorney to push him or her in that direction."); *Lucas v. Breg, Inc.*, No. 3:15-CV-00258-BAS-NLS, 2016 U.S. Dist. LEXIS 64399, at *13, 2016 WL 2996843 (S.D. Cal. May 13, 2016) ("'There is no proper need for the witness's own lawyer to act as an intermediary, interpreting questions, deciding what questions the witness should answer.' If the deponent is confused about a question, 'the witness may ask deposing counsel to clarify the question; securing clarification is not the job of the witness' counsel.'" (quoting *Plaisted v. Geisinger Med. Ctr.*, 210 F.R.D. 527, 534 (M.D. Pa. 2002), and *Cordova v. U.S.*, No. CIV 05-563 JB/LFG, 2006 U.S. Dist. LEXIS 98226, at *5–6, 2006 WL 4109659 (D.N.M. July 31, 2006))); *Sec. Nat'l Bank v. Abbott Labs.*, 299 F.R.D. 595, 605–06 (N.D. Iowa 2014) ("These clarification-inducing objections are improper. Unless a question is truly so vague or ambiguous that the defending lawyer cannot possibly discern its subject matter, the defending lawyer may not suggest to the witness that the lawyer deems the question to be unclear. Lawyers may not object simply because they find a question to be vague, nor may they assume that the witness will not understand the question. The witness—not the lawyer—gets to decide whether he or she understands a particular question[.]"), *rev'd on other grounds*, 800 F.3d 936 (8th Cir. 2015); *Cincinnati Ins. Co. v. Serrano*, No. 11-2075-JAR, 2012 U.S. Dist. LEXIS 1363, at *13, 2012 WL 28071 (D. Kan. Jan. 5, 2012) ("Only the witness knows whether she understands a question, and the witness has a duty to request clarification if needed. This duty is traditionally explained to the witness by the questioner before the deposition. If defending counsel feels that an answer evidences a failure to understand a question, this may be remedied on cross-examination."); *Meyer Corp. U.S. v. Alfay Designs, Inc.*, No. CV 2010 3647 (CBA) (MDG), 2012 U.S. Dist. LEXIS 113819, at *8–9, 2012 WL 3536987 (E.D.N.Y. Aug. 13, 2012) ("'Moreover, 'it is not counsel's place to interrupt if a question is perceived to be potentially unclear to the witness.' Rather '[t]he Federal Rules of Civil Procedure provide two mechanisms to correct or clarify deposition testimony, namely cross-examination and through submission to the witness for review.'" (quoting *Phillips v. Mfrs. Hanover Tr. Co.*, No. 92 Civ. 8527 (KTD), 1994 U.S. Dist. LEXIS 3748, at *6, 1994 WL 116078 (S.D.N.Y. Mar. 29, 1994), and *Cameron Indus., v. Mothers Work, Inc.*, No. 06 Civ. 1999 (BSJ) (HBP), 2007 U.S. Dist. LEXIS 41482, at *12, 2007 WL 1649856 (S.D.N.Y. June 6, 2007))).

[312] *Cmty. Ass'n Underwriters of Am. v. Queensboro Flooring Corp.*, No. 3:10-CV-1559, 2014 U.S. Dist. LEXIS 90939, at *23, 2014 WL 3055358 (M.D. Pa. July 3, 2014) (quoting *Hall v. Clifton Precision*, 150 F.R.D. 525, 531 (E.D. Pa. 1993)); *accord RightCHOICE Managed Care, Inc. v. Hosp. Partners, Inc.*, No. 4:18-cv-06037-DGK, 2019 U.S. Dist. LEXIS 121808, at *11–12, 2019 WL 3291570 (W.D. Mo. July 22, 2019) ("The Court also notes the suggestiveness inherent in telling deponents to answer only 'if they know,' and therefore directs Mr. Minana to cease using this qualification."); *Sec. Nat'l Bank of Sioux City v. Abbott Labs.*, 299 F.R.D. 595, 604 (N.D. Iowa 2014) ("[T]he law clearly prohibits a lawyer from coaching a witness during a deposition."), *rev'd on other grounds*, 800 F.3d 936 (8th Cir. 2015); *Cincinnati Ins. Co. v. Serrano*, No. 11-2075-JAR, 2012 U.S. Dist. LEXIS 1363, at *12, 2012 WL 28071 (D. Kan. Jan. 5, 2012) ("Instructions to a witness that they may answer a question 'if they know' or 'if they understand the question' are raw, unmitigated coaching, and are never appropriate.

attorneys "are not permitted to state on the record their interpretations of questions, since those interpretations are irrelevant and often suggestive of a particularly desired answer."[313]

To prevent the deposing attorney from being "sandbagged" by a form objection, Texas Rule 199.5(e) allows the deposing attorney to request the objecting attorney to explain the objection's basis.[314] When asked for a form objection's basis, the objecting attorney "must give a clear and concise explanation of [the] objection[.]"[315] An argumentative or suggestive explanation waives the objection and "may be grounds for terminating the oral deposition or assessing costs or other sanctions."[316]

After a form objection is made and any requested explanation of it is given, the witness should answer the question.[317] If the answer is offered at trial, the objecting party can then renew the objection and obtain a ruling from the trial court. "An attor-

---

This conduct, if it persists after the deposing attorney requests that it stop, is misconduct and sanctionable. Mr. Schmidt's parenthetical after a question 'If you know the difference between the two' is in the same category."); *Cordova v. U.S.*, No. CIV.05 563 JB/LFG, 2006 U.S. Dist. LEXIS 98226, at *9, 2006 WL 1737225 (D.N.M. July 31, 2006) (imposing sanctions because "it became impossible to know if [a witness's] answers emanated from her own line of reasoning or whether she adopted [the] lawyer's reasoning from listening to his objections"); *Calzaturficio S.C.A.R.P.A. s.p.a. v. Fabiano Shoe Co., Inc.*, 201 F.R.D. 33, 40 (D. Mass. 2001) (stating that an attorney may not "interpret" questions for a deponent, coach him or her as to how to answer, or engage in lengthy speaking objections and colloquies).

Unlike Texas Rule 199, its federal counterpart, Federal Rule 30, expressly requires leave of court for a second deposition of a party or other person. Fed. R. Civ. P. 30(a)(2)(A)(ii) ("A party must obtain leave of court, and the court must grant leave to the extent consistent with [Federal] Rule 26(b)(1) and (2): . . . (A) if the parties have not stipulated to the deposition and: . . . (ii) the deponent has already been deposed in the case. . . .")

313 *Cmty. Ass'n Underwriters of Am. v. Queensboro Flooring Corp.*, No. 3:10-CV-1559, 2014 U.S. Dist. LEXIS 90939, at *23, 2014 WL 3055358 (M.D. Pa. July 3, 2014) (quoting *Hall v. Clifton Precision*, 150 F.R.D. 525, 530 n.10 (E.D. Pa. 1993)); *accord Specht v. Google, Inc.*, 268 F.R.D. 596, 598 (N.D. Ill. 2010) ("Objections that are argumentative or that suggest an answer to a witness are called 'speaking objections' and are improper under [Federal] Rule 30(c)(2)."); *Damaj v. Farmers Ins. Co.*, 164 F.R.D. 559, 560 (N.D. Okla. 1995) ("[T]he purpose of a deposition is to find out what the witness saw, heard and knows, or what the witness thinks, through a question and answer conversation between the deposing lawyer and the witness. Frequent and suggestive objections by opposing counsel can, and oft times do, completely frustrate that objective. Additionally, suggestive objections by counsel can tend to obscure or alter the facts of the case and consequently frustrate the entire civil justice system's attempt to find the truth.") (footnote omitted); *see Deville v. Givaudan Fragrances Corp.*, 419 Fed. App'x 201, 209 (3d Cir. 2011) (affirming sanctions against an attorney who "testified on behalf of her witness by way of suggestive speaking objections").

314 Tex. R. Civ. P. 199.5(e) ("The objecting party must give a clear and concise explanation of an objection if requested by the party taking the oral deposition, or the objection is waived.").

315 Tex. R. Civ. P. 199.5(e).

316 Tex. R. Civ. P. 199.5(e). In *In re Harvest Cmtys. of Hous., Inc.*, 88 S.W.3d 343, 346–48 (Tex. App.—San Antonio 2002, orig. proceeding), the court upheld sanctions imposed under Texas Rule 215.3 against an attorney for discovery abuse involving long, argumentative objections and insulting comments directed at opposing counsel during a deposition.

317 Tex. R. Civ. P. 199 cmt. 4 to 1999 change ("Ordinarily, a witness must answer a question at a deposition subject to the objection.").

ney must not object to a question at an oral deposition . . . unless there is a good faith factual and legal basis for doing so at the time."[318]

11-2:8.4 Instructing a Witness Not to Answer and Suspending a Deposition

Texas Rule 199.5(f) sets forth four instances when an attorney may instruct a witness "not to answer a question during an oral deposition[.]"[319] As with form objections, "[t]he attorney instructing the witness not to answer must give a concise, nonargumentative, nonsuggestive explanation of the grounds for the instruction if requested by the party who asked the question."[320]

The first instance in which an instruction not to answer a question is proper is "to preserve a privilege[.]"[321] Of course, if privilege is asserted as a reason for instructing a witness not to answer, it must be a recognized privilege.[322]

The second instance in which an instruction not to answer a question is proper is to "comply with a court order or these rules[.]"[323] If a court, for example, has ruled in connection with a motion to compel interrogatories or the production of documents that certain information is not discoverable or has granted summary judgment on a claim or defense, an attorney properly can instruct the witness not to answer questions seeking such information or about the claim or defense because such an instruction complies with a court order.

It is unclear, however, whether a question asking about matters beyond discovery's scope under Texas Rule 192.3 (i.e., information that is neither relevant nor reasonably calculated to lead to the discovery of admissible evidence) would "comply with . . . these rules." Arguably, an instruction not to answer a question seeking information that is neither relevant nor reasonably calculated to lead to the discovery of admissible evidence is one that "compl[ies] with . . . these rules." The only Texas case to consider the matter, *In re Lowe's Companies*, however, held, without any analysis, that

---

318 Tex. R. Civ. P. 199.5(h).

319 Tex. R. Civ. P. 199.5(f).

320 Tex. R. Civ. P. 199.5(f).

321 Tex. R. Civ. P. 199.5(f); *see In re Daimler Trucks N. Am. LLC*, 551 S.W.3d 833, 838 (Tex. App.—San Antonio 2018, orig. proceeding) ("An attorney may instruct a witness not to answer a question during an oral deposition if it is necessary to preserve a privilege. A trade secret is privileged and, therefore, can be the basis of an objection during a deposition.") (citation omitted); *In re Lowe's Cos.*, 134 S.W.3d 876, 878 (Tex. App.—Houston [14th Dist.] 2004, orig. proceeding) (holding that objections to deposition questions on the basis of the trade-secret privilege were proper).

322 *Cf. Neuberger Berman Real Estate Income Fund, Inc. v. Lola Brown Tr. No. 1B*, 230 F.R.D. 398, 421 (D. Md. 2005) ("Obviously, if privilege is asserted as a reason to not answer, it must be a recognized privilege."); *Gober v. City of Leesburg*, 197 F.R.D. 519, 520–21 (M.D. Fla. 2000) (holding that the plaintiff's attorney improperly instructed the plaintiff not to disclose his social security number on grounds of "financial privilege" because there is no such privilege).

323 Tex. R. Civ. P. 199.5(f).

"relevance . . . is not a valid ground for instructing a witness not to answer a deposition question."[324]

Even if *In re Lowe's Companies'* holding is correct, it nonetheless is clear that "if counsel's questions go so far beyond the realm of possible relevance [that] the deposition is being conducted in an abusive manner (i.e., in bad faith or in a manner that unreasonably annoys, embarrasses, or oppresses the deponent or party), then it would be permissive to instruct a deponent not to answer," and, if appropriate, to stop the deposition and move for a protective order under Texas Rule 192.6.[325] This is because Texas Rule 199.5(f) specifically allows an instruction not to answer a question to protect a witness from abusive questions and Comment 4 to the 1999 change to Texas Rule 199 points out that "questions that inquire into matters clearly beyond the scope of discovery" are abusive. As one federal court explained:

> Clearly, inquiry into irrelevant topics can constitute bad faith, or unreasonable annoyance, embarrassment or oppression, as described in [Federal] Rule 30(d)(3). For example, asking a deponent questions about personal or confidential matters, such as his or her medical history, sex life or financial condition, would quickly qualify if such matters had no possible relevance to the case.[326]

---

[324] *In re Lowe's Cos.*, 134 S.W.3d 876, 878 (Tex. App.—Houston [14th Dist.] 2004, orig. proceeding) (noting that "relevance is . . . not a valid ground for instructing a witness not to answer a deposition question"); *cf. Conning v. Halpern*, No. 18-cv-12336-ADB, 2020 U.S. Dist. LEXIS 178635, at *8 (D. Mass. Sept. 29, 2020) ("During a deposition, a 'person may instruct a deponent not to answer only when necessary to preserve privilege, to enforce a limitation ordered by the court, or to present a motion under [Federal] Rule 30(d)(3).' Lack of relevance is not referenced in [Federal] Rule 30 as a sufficient justification for instructing a deponent not to answer a question and courts have generally held that it is not." (quoting Fed. R. Civ. P. 30(c)(2))); *Armstrong ex rel. U.S. v. Andover Subacute & Rehab Ctr. Servs. One, Inc.*, No. 12-cv-03319, 2020 U.S. Dist. LEXIS 1569, at *6–7, 2020 WL 57947 (D.N.J. Jan. 6, 2020) ("A relevance objection is not itself proper grounds for instructing a witness not to answer questions in a deposition."); *Law Firm of Omar T. Mohammedi, LLC v. Comput. Assisted Practice Elec. Mgmt. Sols.*, No. 17-cv-04567, 2018 U.S. Dist. LEXIS 177818, at *4, 2018 WL 5016605 (S.D.N.Y. Oct. 16, 2018) (collecting cases).

[325] *Cf. Rangel v. Mascorro*, 274 F.R.D. 585, 591 (S.D. Tex. 2011) ("Because the plain language of [Federal] Rule 30 is rather clear on what types of objections counsel may make and when counsel may instruct a deponent not to answer a question, courts have generally concluded that it is improper to instruct a witness not to answer a question based on a relevancy objection. However, if counsel's questions go so far beyond the realm of possible relevance where the deposition is being conducted in an abusive manner (i.e., in bad faith or in a manner that unreasonably annoys, embarrasses, or oppresses the deponent or party), then it would be permissive to instruct a deponent not to answer and move for a protective order under [Federal] Rule 30(d)(3).") (citations omitted); *accord Coach, Inc. v. Hubert Keller, Inc.*, 911 F. Supp. 2d 1303, 1311 (S.D. Ga. 2012) ("The irrelevancy of a question is not grounds to instruct a witness not to answer the question, unless and until the nature of the questioning makes it obvious that it is necessary to stop the [deposition] and seek relief under [Federal] Rule 30(d)(3) for being conducted in a manner evidencing bad faith, or to embarrass, annoy, or oppress the deponent."); *Quantachrome Corp. v. Micromeritics Instrument Corp.*, 189 F.R.D. 697, 700 (S.D. Fla. Oct. 30, 1999) (same). See also cases cited in note 303.

[326] *Van Stelton v. Van Stelton*, No. C11-4045-MWB, 2013 U.S. Dist. LEXIS 145999, at *44, 2013 WL 12424213 (N.D. Iowa Oct. 9, 2013); *accord Baines v. City of N.Y.*, No. 10 CV 9545 (JMF) (JLC), 2016 U.S. Dist. LEXIS 69967, at *9 (S.D.N.Y. 2016) ("Pursuant to [Federal] Rule 26(c)

As noted above, the third instance in which an instruction not to answer a question is proper is to "protect a witness from an abusive question or one for which any answer would be misleading."[327] Comment 4 to Texas Rule 199 provides the following explanation:

> An objection may therefore be inadequate if a question incorporates such unfair assumptions or is worded so that any answer would necessarily be misleading. A witness should not be required to answer whether he has yet ceased conduct he denies ever doing, subject to an objection to form (i.e., that the question is confusing or assumes facts not in evidence) because any answer would necessarily be misleading on account of the way in which the question is put. The witness may be instructed not to answer. Abusive questions include questions that inquire into matters clearly beyond the scope of discovery or that are argumentative, repetitious, or harassing.[328]

The final instance in which an instruction not to answer is proper is when the attorney suspends the deposition to secure a ruling from the trial court.[329] Texas Rule 199.5(g) allows a party to suspend a deposition "[i]f the time limitations for the deposition have expired or the deposition is being conducted or defended in violation of these rules[.]"[330]

"An attorney must not . . . instruct the witness not to answer a question or suspend the deposition unless there is a good faith factual and legal basis for doing so at the time."[331] When counsel instructs the witness not to answer based on an improper reason, the trial court can order the witness to be re-deposed.[332]

---

(1) or [Federal] Rule 30(d)(3), a deponent may also move for a protective order and/or to limit or terminate a deposition on the ground that it 'unreasonably annoys, embarrasses, or oppresses the deponent or party.' When seeking to limit or terminate a deposition under [Federal] Rule 30(d)(3), the moving party may demand that the deposition be suspended for the time necessary for the court to rule on the objection. Questions that delve into a deponent's sexual history or other elements of his or her personal life that have no possible relevance to the case may be the subject of a successful [Federal] Rule 30(d)(3) motion."). See also cases cited in notes 303.

327 Tex. R. Civ. P. 199.5(f).

328 Tex. R. Civ. P. 199 cmt. 4 to the 1999 change. See also cases cited in notes 329 and 330.

329 Tex. R. Civ. P. 199.5(f).

330 Tex. R. Civ. P. 199.5(g). Texas Rule 215.1(b)(2)(D) similarly provides that, when a deponent fails to answer a question during the deposition, "the proponent of the question may complete or adjourn the examination before he applies for an order." Tex. R. Civ. P. 215.1(b)(2)(D).

331 Tex. R. Civ. P. 199.5(h).

332 Tex. R. Civ. P. 215.1(b)(2)(B), (c) (authorizing the trial court to order "a party or other deponent" to be re-deposed to answer questions that the deponent refused to answer during the deposition); *cf. Medline Indus. v. Wypetech, LLC*, No. 20 CV 4424, 2020 U.S. Dist. LEXIS 201694, at *3–16, 2020 WL 6343089 (N.D. Ill. Oct. 29, 2020) (sanctioning attorney who interposed improper objections and ordering his client to produce a fully prepared representative for a second deposition); *Winters v. Ocean Spray Cranberries, Inc.*, No. 12-12016-RWZ, 2019 U.S. Dist. LEXIS 182211, at *6 (D. Mass. Oct. 22, 2019) ("[P]laintiffs ask the court to grant leave to re-depose Michael Stamatakos or order Ocean Spray to make him available for trial. Because Ocean Spray's numerous and unnecessary objections muddled the first deposition transcript and rendered it virtually unusable at trial, plaintiffs' request is allowed."); *In re Ford Motor*

In sum, Texas Rules 199.5(d)–(g)'s purpose is to ensure that depositions are exactly what they are supposed to be—question-and-answer sessions between the attorney and the witness aimed at uncovering the facts in an action. When a deposition becomes something other than that because of strategic interruptions, instructions not to answer questions, coaching, and statements on the record, it not only becomes unnecessarily long, but it ceases to serve discovery's purpose—to find the truth.[333]

11-2:8.5 Motions to Compel Answers to Deposition Questions

If a witness refuses to answer a question at his or her deposition, any party can file a motion to compel.[334] The burden is on the witness to establish the propriety of the objection, privilege, or instruction not to answer "either by testimony at the hearing or by affidavits served on opposing parties at least seven days before the hearing."[335] The witness, however, need not obtain a ruling on the propriety of the objection, privilege assertion, or instruction because "the failure of a party to obtain a ruling prior to trial does not waive any objection or privilege."[336]

Co. DPS6 Powershift Transmission Prods. Liab. Litig., No. 2:18-cv-1893 AB (FFMx), 2019 U.S. Dist. LEXIS 91557, at *8–18, 2019 WL 3815721 (C.D. Cal. May 13, 2019) (ordering a plaintiff to be re-deposed due to his attorney's improper speaking objections, coaching, and instructions not to answer during his deposition); *Hunter v. GEICO Gen. Ins. Co.*, No. 17-05070, 2018 U.S. Dist. LEXIS 155335, at *45–46, 2018 WL 4352823 (E.D. La. Sept. 12, 2018) (ordering the witness to be deposed "anew" because "of the hundreds of objections lodged . . . in the . . . deposition, many were without legal basis or were otherwise unnecessary or excessive. The frequency and length of the interruptions clearly impeded, delayed, and frustrated a fair examination of the deponent."); *Pilates, Inc. v. Georgetown Bodyworks Deep Muscle Massage Ctrs., Inc.*, 201 F.R.D. 261, 262 (D.D.C. 2000) (ordering the witness to be re-deposed because counsel improperly instructed him not to answer certain questions).

333 As noted by the court in *Hall v. Clifton Precision*, 150 F.R.D. 525, 528 (E.D. Pa. 1993):

> [T]he underlying purpose of a deposition is to find out what a witness saw, heard, or did—what the witness thinks. A deposition is meant to be a question-and-answer conversation between the deposing attorney and the witness. There is no proper need for the witness's own lawyer to act as an intermediary, interpreting questions, deciding which questions the witness should answer, and helping the witness to formulate answers. The witness comes to the deposition to testify, not to indulge in a parody of Charlie McCarthy, with lawyers coaching or bending the witness's words to mold a legally convenient record. It is the witness—not the lawyer—who is the witness. As an advocate, the lawyer is free to frame those facts in a manner favorable to the client, and also to make favorable and creative arguments of law. But the lawyer is not entitled to be creative with the facts. Rather, a lawyer must accept the facts as they develop.

334 Tex. R. Civ. P. 199.6 ("Any party may, at any reasonable time, request a hearing on an objection or privilege asserted by an instruction not to answer or suspension of the deposition. . . ."); 215.1(b)(2)(B) ("[I]f a party, or other deponent, or a person designated to testify on behalf of a party or other deponent fails . . . to answer a question propounded or submitted upon oral examination or upon written questions . . . the discovering party may move for an order compelling an answer."). See also Chapter 14, section 14-2:4 (discussing grounds for motions to compel).

335 Tex. R. Civ. P. 199.6 ("The party seeking to avoid discovery must present any evidence necessary to support the objection or privilege either by testimony at the hearing or by affidavits served on opposing parties at least seven days before the hearing.").

336 Tex. R. Civ. P. 199.6.

11-2:9 Supplementing Oral Deposition Testimony

Unlike with respect to written discovery, there generally is no obligation to supplement deposition testimony even if it is wrong or incomplete. This is made clear by Comment 5 to the 1999 change to Texas Rule 193, which provides that Texas Rule 193.5, regarding supplementation, "imposes no duty to supplement or amend deposition testimony. The only duty to supplement deposition testimony is provided in [Texas] Rule 195.6[, relating to testifying experts]."[337]

11-2:10 Second Depositions of a Witness Already Deposed

A witness faced with a second deposition should file a motion to quash or for a protective order. In ruling on the motion, the trial court should be guided by the factors set forth in Texas Rule 192.4, that is, whether a second deposition would be unnecessarily cumulative or duplicative, whether the information sought by the it is obtainable from some other source that is more convenient, less burdensome, or less expensive, and whether the burden of a second deposition outweighs its potential benefit.[338] In other words, the court should deny the motion unless the party seeking the second deposition shows a legitimate need or good cause for it. As explained by one federal court:

> Typically, if, after a witness is deposed, new information comes to light relating to the subject of that deposition, new parties are added to the case, new allegations are made in pleadings, or new documents are produced, the witness may be re-deposed with respect to these new developments. A re-deposition may also be ordered if the examining party was inhibited from conducting a full examination as a result of obstructive conduct at the first deposition. However, the Court may deny leave to conduct a second deposition of the witness even if relevant documents are produced subsequent to the deposition if the party taking the deposition either failed to request those documents in a timely fashion or chose to conduct the deposition prior to the completion of document discovery.[339]

---

[337] Tex. R. Civ. P. 195.6 cmt. 5 to 1999 change; *accord Titus Cnty. Hosp. Dist. v. Lucas*, 988 S.W.2d 740, 740 (Tex. 1998) (per curiam) (holding that, under former Texas Rule 166b(6), "[a] general duty to supplement deposition testimony (as opposed to a narrow duty for certain expert testimony, for example) would impose too great a burden on litigants. We therefore disapprove the court of appeals' holding that deposition testimony must be supplemented.") (citation omitted); *cf. Pilates, Inc. v. Georgetown Bodyworks*, 201 F.R.D. 261, 262 (D.D.C. 2000) (recognizing that "[t]he Federal Rules of Civil Procedure impose no affirmative duty for deponents to supplement deposition testimony").

[338] Tex. R. Civ. P. 192.4.

[339] *Fresenius Med. Care Holdings, Inc. v. Roxane Labs., Inc.*, No. 2:05-cv-0889, 2007 U.S. Dist. LEXIS 17834, at *5–6, 2007 WL 764302 (S.D. Ohio Mar. 9, 2007) (citations omitted); *accord Retif v. Lloyds*, No. 19-4899, 2020 U.S. Dist. LEXIS 201144, at *3–4 (E.D. La. Apr. 6, 2020) ("Plaintiff argues that courts in this district have denied second depositions when their burden on the plaintiff outweighs the benefit of the deposition and the information can be obtained from other sources. Plaintiff maintains that the information that defendant seeks can be obtained from sources other than him such as his experts. Courts have typically reopened a deposition 'where a witness was inhibited from providing full information at the first deposition' or 'where new information comes to light triggering questions that the discovering party would not have thought to ask at the first deposition.' However, '[w]here the deposition is reopened because of newly discovered information, the questioning of

When a second deposition is permitted, its scope generally should be limited to matters *not* covered in the first deposition.[340]

---

the witness is limited to those questions relating to the newly produced information.' The lack of diligence in obtaining information before the initial or first deposition may result in a court denying leave to conduct a second deposition. A party seeking a court order to extend the duration of the examination must show 'good cause' to justify such an order." (quoting *Briggs v. Phebus*, No. 12-2145, 2014 U.S. Dist. LEXIS 36088, at *9–10, 2014 WL 1117888 (E.D. La. Mar. 19, 2014), *Ganci v. U.S. Limousine Serv., Ltd.*, No. CV 10-3027, 2011 U.S. Dist. LEXIS 106320, at *5, 2011 WL 4407461 (E.D.N.Y. Sept. 21, 2011), and *Kleppinger v. Tex. Dep't of Transp.*, 283 F.R.D. 330, 333 (S.D. Tex. 2012))); *O'Connor v. Cory*, No. 3:16-CV-1731-B, 2018 U.S. Dist. LEXIS 177160, at *6–7, 2018 WL 5016291 (N.D. Tex. Oct. 16, 2018) ("Courts have allowed parties to reopen depositions when 'new information comes to light' that creates the need for further questioning. 'New information' can include the addition of new parties to the case, the addition of new allegations to the pleadings, and the production of new documents.' If a deposition is reopened because of newly discovered information, the court should limit the deposition to questions related to this information. Here, the Court will grant Plaintiffs leave to reopen Defendants' depositions. Defendant Cory's amended answer asserts a new affirmative defense under the Release that could work as an absolute bar to Plaintiffs' claims." (quoting *Kleppinger v. Tex. Dep't of Transp.*, 283 F.R.D. 330, 333 & n.3 (S.D. Tex. 2012))); *Yiping Luan v. Advanced Title Ins. Agency, L.C.*, No. 2:13-cv-00983, 2015 U.S. Dist. LEXIS 106201, at *6–8, 2015 WL 4773075 (D. Utah Aug. 12, 2015) ("Absent a showing of need or good cause, '[c]ourts generally disfavor repeat depositions.' In turn, courts must also 'be careful not to deprive a party of discovery that is reasonably necessary to afford a fair opportunity to develop and prepare the case.' Overall, a court's decision to grant or deny a request for leave to re-depose a witness is guided by [F]ederal [R]ule 26. [Federal] Rule 26 requires the court to limit discovery if: '(i) the discovery sought is unreasonably cumulative or duplicative, or can be obtained from some other source that is more convenient, less burdensome, or less expensive; (ii) the party seeking discovery has had ample opportunity to obtain the information by discovery in the action; or (iii) the burden or expense of the proposed discovery outweighs its likely benefit, considering the needs of the case, the amount in controversy, the parties' resources, the importance of the issues at stake in the litigation, and the importance of the proposed discovery in resolving the issues.'" (quoting *Dixon v. Certainteed Corp.*, 164 F.R.D. 685, 690 (D. Kan. 1996), *Ast v. BNSF* Ry., 2011 U.S. Dist. LEXIS 123838, at*4, 2011 WL 5080256 (D. Kan. Oct. 25, 2011), and Fed. R. Civ. P. 26(b)(2)(C))); *Settles v. Livengood*, No. 4:13-CV-662 (CEJ), 2015 U.S. Dist. LEXIS 57833, at *3–4, 2015 WL 2089222 (E.D. Mo. May 4, 2015) ("Typically, a party may conduct a second deposition of a witness if new information comes to light relating to the subject of that deposition, new parties are added to the case, new allegations are made in pleadings, or new documents are produced. Under these circumstances, the second deposition is limited to the new information. A second deposition may also be ordered if the examining party was inhibited from conducting a full examination as a result of obstructive conduct at the first deposition. None of these circumstances apply in this instance: plaintiff elected not to pose questions to Drs. Johnson and Chen during their depositions out of concern for their demeanor and appearance and may not now impose the expense of second depositions on defendants.") (citations omitted).

[340] *Retif v. Lloyds*, No. 19-4899, 2020 U.S. Dist. LEXIS 201144, at *3–4 (E.D. La. Apr. 6, 2020) (noting that when "a deposition is reopened because of newly discovered information, the questioning of the witness is limited to those questions relating to the newly produced information" (quoting *Ganci v. U.S. Limousine Serv., Ltd.*, No. CV 10-3027, 2011 U.S. Dist. LEXIS 106320, at *5, 2011 WL 4407461 (E.D.N.Y. Sept. 21, 2011))); *O'Connor v. Cory*, No. 3:16-CV-1731-B, 2018 U.S. Dist. LEXIS 177160, at *6–7, 2018 WL 5016291 (N.D. Tex. Oct. 16, 2018) (same); *Yiping Luan v. Advanced Title Ins. Agency, L.C.*, No. 2:13-cv-00983, 2015 U.S. Dist. LEXIS 106201, at *6–9, 2015 WL 4560383 (D. Utah Aug. 12, 2015) (limiting deposition

11-3 Depositions on Written Questions—Texas Rule 200

TEXT OF RULE 200

RULE 200. DEPOSITIONS UPON WRITTEN QUESTIONS

200.1. Procedure for Noticing Deposition Upon Written Questions

(a) **Who may be noticed; when.** A party may take the testimony of any person or entity by deposition on written questions before any person authorized by law to take depositions on written questions. A notice of intent to take the deposition must be served on the witness and all parties at least 20 days before the deposition is taken. A deposition on written questions may be taken outside the discovery period only by agreement of the parties or with leave of court. The party noticing the deposition must also deliver to the deposition officer a copy of the notice and of all written questions to be asked during the deposition.

(b) **Content of notice.** The notice must comply with Rules 199.1(b), 199.2(b), and 199.5(a)(3). If the witness is an organization, the organization must comply with the requirements of that provision. The notice also may include a request for production of documents as permitted by Rule 199.2(b)(5), the provisions of which will govern the request, service, and response.

200.2. Compelling Witness to Attend

A party may compel the witness to attend the deposition on written questions by serving the witness with a subpoena under Rule 176. If the witness is a party or is retained by, employed by, or otherwise subject to the control of a party, however, service of the deposition notice upon the party's attorney has the same effect as a subpoena served on the witness.

200.3. Questions and Objections

(a) **Direct questions.** The direct questions to be propounded to the witness must be attached to the notice.

(b) **Objections and additional questions.** Within ten days after the notice and direct questions are served, any party may object to the direct questions and serve cross-questions on all other parties. Within five days after cross-questions are served, any party may object to the cross-questions and serve redirect questions on all other parties. Within three days after redirect questions are served, any party may object to the redirect questions and serve recross questions on all other parties. Objections to recross questions must be

---

to material produced after the first deposition); *Dash v. Seagate Tech. (US) Holdings, Inc.*, No. CV 13-6329 (LDW) (AKT), 2015 U.S. Dist. LEXIS 91105, at *16–17, 2015 WL 4257329 (E.D.N.Y. July 14, 2015) (same); *Collins v. Int'l Dairy Queen*, 189 F.R.D. 496, 498 (M.D. Ga. 1999) (limiting second depositions to four hours each and limiting inquiry to subjects not previously inquired about as well as alleged facts and developments since the initial depositions); *Judicial Watch, Inc. v. Dep't of Commerce*, 34 F. Supp. 2d 47, 54–55 (D.D.C. 1998) (limiting second depositions to information concerning documents' unlawful destruction or removal); *Dixon v. Certainteed Corp.*, 164 F.R.D. 685, 690 (D. Kan. 1996) (limiting second deposition to inquiry about certain statements made by a witness about which the plaintiff was unaware at first deposition).

served within five days after the earlier of when recross questions are served or the time of the deposition on written questions.

(c) **Objections to form of questions.** Objections to the form of a question are waived unless asserted in accordance with this subdivision.

200.4. Conducting the Deposition Upon Written Questions

The deposition officer must: take the deposition on written questions at the time and place designated; record the testimony of the witness under oath in response to the questions; and prepare, certify, and deliver the deposition transcript in accordance with Rule 203. The deposition officer has authority when necessary to summon and swear an interpreter to facilitate the taking of the deposition.

Comments to 1999 change:

1. The procedures for asserting objections during oral depositions under Rule 199.5(e) do not apply to depositions on written questions.

2. Section 20.001 of the Civil Practice and Remedies Code provides that a deposition on written questions of a witness who is alleged to reside or to be in this state may be taken by a clerk of a district court, a judge or clerk of a county court, or a notary public of this state.

11-3:1 2021 Amendments to the Texas Rules of Civil Procedure

The 2021 amendments to the Texas Rules of Civil Procedure did not modify Texas Rule 200 regarding depositions on written questions in any respect.

11-3:2 In General

Depositions on written questions are an alternative to oral depositions. Although similar to interrogatories because the witness responds to written questions under oath, unlike interrogatories, depositions on written questions are not "written discovery" under Texas Rule 192.7(a).[341] Accordingly, Texas Rules 193 and 197, as well as other discovery rules regarding written discovery, including those relating to supplementation and asserting privilege, do not apply to depositions on written questions. In addition, unlike interrogatories, there is no limit on the number of questions that can be asked in a deposition on written questions. Comment 5 to Texas Rule 190, however, provides that "depositions on written questions cannot be used to circumvent the limits on interrogatories."[342]

Depositions on written questions are an affordable, alternative means of discovery for parties when they need to conduct discovery from a nonparty, but do not want to incur the high cost of an oral deposition. The fundamental difference between an oral deposition under Texas Rule 199 and one on written questions under Texas Rule 200 is that, under Texas Rule 200, the questions are prepared in advance and sent to the

[341] Texas Rule 192.7(a) defines "written discovery" as "required disclosures, requests for production and inspection of documents and tangible things, requests for entry onto property, interrogatories, and requests for admission."

[342] Tex. R. Civ. P. 201 cmt. 5 to 1999 Change.

deposition officer (i.e., the person recording the deposition, usually a court reporter), who asks the questions at the deposition.

Depositions on written questions are used less frequently than oral depositions because there are no follow-up questions and because questions are provided in advance, enabling the witness's attorney to craft answers to them.[343] Accordingly, the procedure is much more cumbersome than oral examination and unsuited for pursuing complicated inquiries or for interrogating a hostile or reluctant witness. Rather, depositions on written question are best suited for securing testimony from a witness with limited relevant information, such as information from a business-records custodian.

As with oral depositions, "any person or entity" can be deposed on written questions.[344]

---

[343] *Cf. In re Porsche Automobil Holding SE*, No. 19-mc-91129-LTS, 2019 U.S. Dist. LEXIS 194103, at *33–37, 2019 WL 5806913 (D. Mass. Nov. 6, 2019) (noting that "[d]epositions on written questions are generally disfavored" and that, such depositions "can be appropriate 'in limited circumstances . . . where the issues to be addressed by the witness are narrow and straightforward[,] and the hardships of taking an oral deposition would be substantial'" (quoting *Mill-Run Tours, Inc. v. Khashoggi*, 124 F.R.D. 547, 549 (S.D.N.Y. 1989))); ***Stanek v. St. Charles Comm. Unit Sch. Dist. # 303***, No. 13 C 3106, 2020 U.S. Dist. LEXIS 47528, at *15–16 (N.D. Ill. Mar. 19, 2020) ("Although a deposition by written questions may be appropriate under 'limited circumstances,' such depositions 'are rarely, if ever, used in modern litigation.' This is so because deposing a witness through written questions is disfavored since it deprives counsel 'the opportunity to [promptly] ask follow-up questions, observe the witness's demeanor, or evaluate his credibility.' The 'limited circumstances' under which depositions by written questions have been considered appropriate include 'where the issues to be addressed by the witness are narrow and straightforward and the hardships of taking an oral deposition would be substantial,' or 'when dealing with neutral or "friendly" witnesses.' On the other hand, such a deposition is 'not suitable for a situation' where 'the witness is hostile and the testimony is likely to be controversial.'" (quoting *Mill-Run Tours, Inc. v. Khashoggi*, 124 F.R.D. 547, 549 (S.D.N.Y. 1989), ***Fid. Int'l Currency Advisor A Fund, LLC v. U.S.***, No. CV 05-40151-FDS, 2007 U.S. Dist. LEXIS 103819, at *11–12, 2007 WL 9412764 (D. Mass. May 23, 2007), ***Jones v. Hollenback***, No. CV F 05 1048 OWW DLB, 2006 U.S. Dist. LEXIS 108164, at *13, 2006 WL 8458647 (E.D.Ca. Feb. 8, 2006), and *P.H. Int'l Trading Co. v. Christia Confezioni S.p.A.*, No. 04 C 903, 2004 U.S. Dist. LEXIS 19191, at *3, 2004 WL 2538299 (N.D. Ill. Sept. 24, 2004))); ***In re N. Eng. Compounding Pharmacy Prods. Liab. Litig.***, No. MDL No. 13-2419-RWZ, 2015 U.S. Dist. LEXIS 197744, at *1–2 (D. Mass. Dec. 18, 2015) ("While generally disfavored, depositions on written questions can be a valuable and efficient tool for discovery when the issues to be addressed by the witness are narrow and straightforward and the hardships of taking an oral deposition would be substantial. Here, the notices of deposition appear to be targeted to the narrow topic of what due diligence was conducted by various NECC customers prior to purchasing MPA from NECC. In addition, the deponents are all non-parties to this litigation. Therefore, under the circumstances, the PSC has failed to show good cause for a protective order.") *Mill-Run Tours, Inc. v. Khashoggi*, 124 F.R.D. 547, 549 (S.D.N.Y. 1989) (explaining that "written questions provide an opportunity for counsel to assist the witness in providing answers so carefully tailored that they are likely to generate additional discovery disputes").

[344] Tex. R. Civ. P. 200.1(a) ("A party may take the testimony of any person or entity by deposition on written questions[.]").

11-3:3 Notice of a Deposition on Written Questions

To take a deposition on written questions, a party must serve "[a] notice of intent to take the deposition . . . on the witness and all parties at least 20 days before the deposition is taken."[345] Because a deposition on written questions, like an oral deposition, must be completed within the discovery period, the party noticing the deposition must complete the deposition within that period absent agreement of the parties or leave of court.[346] Twenty days' notice, however, may be insufficient if the witness is a party or subject to a party's control and the deposition notice contains a production request. In such a case, the noticing party must give at least thirty days' notice because document requests served with such a notice are governed by Texas Rule 196.2(a)'s thirty-day response period.[347]

In addition to serving the deposition notice on the witness and all other parties, the noticing party "must also deliver to the deposition officer a copy of the notice and of all written questions to be asked during the deposition."[348] The deposition officer can be a district court clerk, a county court judge or clerk, a certified shorthand reporter, or a notary public.[349] The deposition's officer's duties in a deposition on written questions

---

345 Tex. R. Civ. P. 200.1(a); *see Ruff v. Ruff*, No. 05-18-00326-CV, 2020 Tex. App. LEXIS 6344, at *34–35 (Tex. App.—Dallas Aug. 11, 2020, pet. denied) (mem. op.) (holding that a subpoena for a deposition on written questions "was technically deficient" because "[t]he subpoena was served on January 5, 2018, setting the deposition and document production for January 17, 2018. Thus, the subpoena did not provide twenty days' notice for the deposition.") (citations omitted).

346 *See* Tex. R. Civ. P. 200.1(a) ("A deposition on written questions may be taken outside the discovery period only by agreement of the parties or with leave of court.").

347 *See* Tex. R. Civ. P. 200.1(a) (incorporating Texas Rule 199.2(b), which, in turn, incorporates Texas Rule 196's procedures for responding to production requests). Under Texas Rule 4, the day the notice is served is not counted. *Accord* Tex. Gov't Code § 311.114(a). Under Texas Rule 21a(b), if the deposition notice is served by (1) mail, service is complete when the notice is mailed, but three days are added to the time to respond to the production request, and the witness has thirty-three days to respond to it, Tex. R. Civ. P. 4, 21a(b)-(c); (2) hand-delivery, service is complete on delivery, and the witness has thirty days to respond to the production request, Tex. R. Civ. P. 4, 21a(b); or (3) fax, service is complete on receipt, however, service completed after 5:00 p.m. local time of the witness is deemed served on the following day, and the witness will have either thirty or thirty-one days to respond to the production request depending when the fax was received, Tex. R. Civ. P. 4, 21a(b). Texas Rule 21a does not address when service by email is complete. In contrast, Federal Rule 5(b)(2)(E) addresses service by "electronic means" and provides that such service is complete "upon . . . sending, but is not effective if the . . . sender learns that it did not reach the person to be served." Fed. R. Civ. P. 5(b)(2)(E). This is a reasonable way to determine when service by email is complete under Texas Rule 21a. Due to uncertainty under the Rule, however, it is prudent to reach an agreement with opposing counsel about when service by electronic means is deemed complete.

348 Tex. R. Civ. P. 200.1(a).

349 Tex. Govt. Code § 154.101(f) Section 154.101(f) of the Texas Government Code provides: "Except as provided by Section 154.112 and by Section 20.001, Civil Practice and Remedies Code, all depositions in this state must be taken by a certified shorthand reporter." Tex. Gov't. Code § 154.011(f). Section 20.011(a) of the Texas Civil Practice and Remedies Code, in turn, provides: "A deposition on written questions of a witness who is alleged to reside or to be in this state may be taken by: (1) a clerk of a district court; (2) a judge or clerk of a county court; or (3) a notary public of this state." Tex. Civ. Prac. & Rem. Code § 20.001(a).

are virtually the same as those in an oral deposition—the officer must swear in the witness, "take the deposition . . .; record the testimony of the witness under oath in response to the questions; and prepare, certify, and deliver the deposition transcript in accordance with [Texas] Rule 203. The deposition officer has authority when necessary to summon and swear an interpreter to facilitate the taking of the deposition."[350]

Texas Rule 200.1(b) incorporates by reference three of Texas Rule 199's provisions regarding the deposition notice's content: (1) Texas Rule 199.1(b), which authorizes oral depositions by telephone or remote electronic means; (2) Texas Rule 199.2(b), which specifies the oral deposition notice's content; and (3) Texas Rule 199.5(a)(3), which governs who may attend an oral deposition. Texas Rule 200.1(b) allows for the deposition of an organization and production requests, providing: "If the witness is an organization, the organization must comply with the requirements of [Texas Rule 199.2(b)(1)]. The notice also may include a request for production of documents as permitted by [Texas] Rule 199.2(b)(5), the provisions of which will govern the request, service, and response."[351] Accordingly, the notice for a deposition on written questions must: (1) state the name of the witness, which can be either an individual or an organization;[352] (2) state a reasonable time and place for the deposition that, absent agreement by the parties or court order, must be within the discovery period and (a) at least twenty days after the notice's service or (b) at least thirty days after the notice's service, if the notice is for a deposition of a witness who is not party or subject to a party's control and includes a production request;[353] (3) state whether the deposition is to be taken by telephone or other remote electronic means and identify the means;[354] (4) identify any documents to be produced at the deposition;[355] (5) describe with reasonable particularity the matters on which examination is requested, if the witness is an organization;[356] and (6) contain all of the written questions to be asked by the noticing party during the deposition.[357]

The deposition notice must be signed either by the party's attorney or a pro se party[358] and "must show the attorney's State Bar of Texas identification number, address, telephone number, and fax number, if any"[359] or the pro se party's "address, telephone number, and fax number, if any."[360] If the notice is not signed, it must be

---

350 Tex. R. Civ. P. 200.4.

351 Tex. R. Civ. P. 200.1(b).

352 Tex. R. Civ. P. 200.1(b) (incorporating by reference Texas Rule 199.2(b)(1)).

353 Tex. R. Civ. P. 200.1(b) (incorporating by reference Texas Rule 199.2(b)(2)); *see In re Yamin*, No. 14-20-00280-CV, 2020 Tex. App. LEXIS 6676, at *9–10, 2020 WL 4873021 (Tex. App.—Houston [14th Dist.] Aug. 20, 2020, orig. proceeding) (mem. op.) (holding that the deadline to object to production requests accompanying a notice for a deposition on written questions to "a nonparty is governed by [Texas] Rule 176" and to "a witness subject to the control of a party is governed by [Texas] Rules 193 and 196").

354 Tex. R. Civ. P. 200.1(b) (incorporating by reference Texas Rule 199.2(b)(3)). This notice also can be given separately in another written notice or can be given by a non-noticing party. Tex. R. Civ. P. 199.1(c).

355 Tex. R. Civ. P. 200.1(b) (incorporating by reference Texas Rule 199.2(b)(5)).

356 *See* Tex. R. Civ. P. 200.1(b) (incorporating by reference Texas Rule 199.2(b)(1)).

357 Tex. R. Civ. P. 200.3(a) ("The direct questions to be propounded to the witness must be attached to the notice.").

358 Tex. R. Civ. P. 191.3(a).

359 Tex. R. Civ. P. 191.3(a)(1).

360 Tex. R. Civ. P. 191.3(a)(2).

stricken unless signed promptly after the omission is called to the attention of the party serving the notice.[361] The deposition notice also must be served on the witness and the other parties and must contain a certificate of service stating it was properly served on them.[362] If it is not served on all parties, the deposition cannot be used at trial or at a hearing if the party on which it was not served did not have a reasonable time to re-depose the witness.[363] The notice can be served on the witness and other parties "in person, by mail, by commercial delivery service, by fax, by email, or by such other manner as the court in its discretion may direct"[364] unless the notice is filed electronically (i.e., a notice for a nonparty's deposition), in which case it "must be served electronically through the electronic filing manager if the email address of the party or attorney to be served is on file with the electronic filing manager."[365] The deposition notice should be filed with the trial court *only* if it is served on a nonparty.[366] A notice that is served only on parties should not be filed,[367] but the party must retain a copy of it during the action's pendency and any related appellate proceedings begun within six months after judgment is signed, unless otherwise provided by the trial court.[368]

---

361 Tex. R. Civ. P. 191.3(d) ("If a request, notice, response, or objection is not signed, it must be stricken unless it is signed promptly after the omission is called to the attention of the party making the request, notice, response, or objection. A party is not required to take any action with respect to a request or notice that is not signed.").

362 Tex. R. Civ. P. 21(a), (d).

363 In *Onyung v. Onyung*, No. 01-10-00519-CV, 2013 Tex. App. LEXIS 9190, 2013 WL 3875548 (Tex. App.—Houston [1st Dist.] July 25, 2013, pet. denied) (mem. op.), the court held that the trial court did not abuse its discretion in allowing the plaintiff to use a deposition even though one of the defendants did not receive notice of it because the defendant had a reasonable time to re-depose the witness. *Onyung v. Onyung*, No. 01-10-00519-CV, 2013 Tex. App. LEXIS 9190, at 56–58, 2013 WL 3875548 (Tex. App.—Houston [1st Dist.] July 25, 2013, pet. denied) (mem. op.). In doing so, it analogized to Texas Rule 203.6(b), which provides that "[a] deposition is admissible against a party joined after the deposition was taken if . . . that party has had a reasonable opportunity to redepose the witness and has failed to do so." *Onyung v. Onyung*, No. 01-10-00519-CV, 2013 Tex. App. LEXIS 9190, at 56–58, 2013 WL 3875548 (Tex. App.—Houston [1st Dist.] July 25, 2013, pet. denied) (mem. op.); *see Shenandoah Assocs. v. J & K Props., Inc.*, 741 S.W.2d 470, 492 (Tex. App.—Dallas 1987, writ denied) ("When other parties are not given notice of the deposition, an 'ex parte' deposition is not admissible."); *cf. In re Baum*, 606 F.2d 592, 593 n.1 (5th Cir. 1979) ("Depositions taken without proper notice may be found to be inadmissible."); *Hoffman v. Lassen Cnty.*, No. 2:15-cv-1382 DB P, 2017 U.S. Dist. LEXIS 81432, at *13, 2017 WL 2311683 (E.D. Cal. May 25, 2017) ("Because plaintiff failed to properly notice the deposition, defendants had no obligation to attend the deposition. However, the court notes that the better course would have been to inform plaintiff of the defective notice.") (citation omitted).

364 Tex. R. Civ. P. 21a(a)(2).

365 Tex. R. Civ. P. 21a(a)(1).

366 Tex. R. Civ. P. 191.4(a)(1) ("The following discovery materials must not be filed: . . . deposition notices[] and subpoenas required to be served on parties[.]"), 191.4(b)(1) ("The following discovery materials must be filed: . . . deposition notices[] and subpoenas required to be served on nonparties[.]").

367 Tex. R. Civ. P. 191.4(a)(1) ("The following discovery materials must not be filed: . . . deposition notices[] and subpoenas required to be served only on parties[.]").

368 Tex. R. Civ. P. 191.4(d) ("Any person required to serve discovery materials not required to be filed must retain the original or exact copy of the materials during the pendency of

The proper location for a deposition on written questions is governed by Texas Rule 199.2(b)(2), which governs an oral deposition's proper location.[369]

11-3:4 Compelling the Witness's Attendance

Texas Rule 200.2 relates to compelling the witness's attendance at the deposition on written questions and is virtually identical to Texas Rule 199.3, which relates to compelling a witness's attendance at an oral deposition. "If the witness is a party or is retained by, employed by, or otherwise subject to the control of a party, . . . service of the deposition notice upon the party's attorney has the same effect as a subpoena served on the witness."[370] If, however, the witness is neither a party nor subject to a party's control, the witness must be served with a notice under Texas Rule 205.2 and a subpoena under Texas Rule 176.[371]

If a production request is contained in the deposition notice and the witness is a party or subject to a party's control, the notice and request are sufficient to compel the production,[372] the response to which will be governed by Texas Rule 196.2(a).[373] Other witnesses must be served with the notice and subpoena under Texas Rules 205.2 and 176.2(a), respectively.

11-3:5 Questions and Objections

As noted above, the direct questions to be asked of the witness must be attached to, and served with, the deposition notice.[374] The procedure by which the parties can ask other questions and interpose objections to other parties' questions is set forth in Texas Rule 200.3(b), as follows:

- Within ten days after the notice and the direct questions are served, "any party may object to the direct questions and serve cross-questions on all other parties."[375]

---

the case and any related appellate proceeding begun within six months after judgment is signed, unless otherwise provided by the trial court.").

369 Tex. R. Civ. P. 200.1(b) (incorporating by reference Texas Rule 199.2(b)). See Chapter 11, section 11-2:3.2a (discussing a deposition's time and place).

370 Tex. R. Civ. P. 200.2.

371 Tex. R. Civ. P. 200.2 ("A party may compel the witness to attend the deposition on written questions by serving the witness with a subpoena under [Texas] Rule 176."); *see* Tex. R. Civ. P. 205.1(b) ("A party may compel discovery from a nonparty . . . by serving a subpoena compelling . . . a deposition on written questions[]"), 205.2 ("A party seeking discovery by subpoena from a nonparty must serve, on the nonparty and all parties, a copy of the form of notice required under the rules governing the applicable form of discovery.").

372 Tex. R. Civ. P. 200.1(b) (incorporating by reference Texas Rule 199.2(b)(5)).

373 *See* Tex. R. Civ. P. 200.1(b) (incorporating by reference Texas Rule 199.2(b), which, in turn, incorporates Texas Rule 196's procedures for responding to production requests).

374 Tex. R. Civ. P. 200.3(a) ("The direct questions to be propounded to the witness must be attached to the notice."); *see* Tex. R. Civ. P. 200.1(a) ("The party noticing the deposition must also deliver to the deposition officer a copy of the notice and of all written questions to be asked during the deposition.").

375 Tex. R. Civ. P. 200.3(b).

- Within five days after the cross-questions are served, "any party may object to the cross-questions and serve redirect questions on all other parties."[376]
- Within three days after the redirect questions are served, "any party may object to the redirect questions and serve recross questions on all other parties."[377]
- Objections to recross questions must be served within five days after the earlier of when recross questions are served or the time of the deposition on written questions.[378]

The objections must be signed and served by the attorney or a pro se party in the same manner as the deposition notice.[379] Although "[t]he party noticing the deposition must also deliver to the deposition officer a copy of the notice and of all written questions[,]"[380] the party asking the questions or objecting to them also should send a copy of its questions or objections to the deposition officer as a matter of prudence.

Comment 1 to the 1999 change to Texas Rule 200 makes clear that "[t]he procedures for asserting objections during oral depositions under [Texas] Rule 199.5(e) do not apply to depositions on written questions."[381] Texas Rule 200.3(c), however, provides that "[o]bjections to the form of a [written] question are waived unless asserted in accordance with this subdivision."[382] Thus, it appears that whereas a party can, but need not, interpose substantive objections to a written question,[383] it should specify the applicable form objection (e.g., leading, compound, calls for a narrative, confusing, ambiguous, vague, unintelligible, argumentative, asked and answered) instead of merely stating "Objection, leading" or "Objection, form" as specified by Texas Rule 199.5(e).[384]

Finally, unlike oral depositions for which there are limits on the total number of hours of the depositions in the action and on the number of hours for a witness's examination, there are no such limitations on depositions on written questions.[385] A party who believes, however, that another party is abusing the discovery process by either asking too many questions in a deposition on written question or

---

[376] Tex. R. Civ. P. 200.3(b).

[377] Tex. R. Civ. P. 200.3(b).

[378] Tex. R. Civ. P. 200.3(b).

[379] Tex. R. Civ. P. 21a(a).

[380] Tex. R. Civ. P. 200.1(a).

[381] Tex. R. Civ. P. 200 cmt. 1 to 1999 change.

[382] Tex. R. Civ. P. 200.3(c).

[383] *St. Luke's Episcopal Hosp. v. Garcia*, 928 S.W.2d 307, 310 (Tex. App.—Houston [14th Dist.] 1996, no writ) ("Because relator has no objection to the form of TMC's written questions, relator claims the provision in [former Texas] Rule 208 regarding timeliness of objections is inapplicable. We agree. In its objections to the deposition notice and subpoena duces tecum, relator's primary objections are substantive objections relating to privilege. We hold that the ten-day limitation in [former Texas] Rule 208 is inapplicable to substantive objections. Therefore, the trial court abused its discretion to the extent the trial court's July 26, 1996 order finds relator's objections untimely pursuant to [former Texas] Rule 208.").

[384] Form objections are discussed in Chapter 11, section 11-2:8.3.

[385] *See generally* Tex. R. Civ. P. 200.

taking too many such depositions can move for a protective order under Texas Rule 192.6.[386]

11-3:6 Supplementing Deposition Testimony upon Written Questions

Unlike written discovery and like oral-deposition testimony, there is no obligation to supplement deposition-on-written-question testimony even if it is wrong or incomplete. This is made clear by Comment 5 to Texas Rule 193, which provides that Texas Rule 193.5, regarding supplementation, "imposes no duty to supplement or amend deposition testimony. The only duty to supplement deposition testimony is provided in [Texas] Rule 195.6[, relating to testifying experts]."[387]

11-4 Depositions in Foreign-Jurisdictions for Use in Texas-Proceedings and Depositions in Texas for Use in Foreign Proceedings—Texas Rule 201

TEXT OF RULE 201

RULE 201. DEPOSITIONS IN FOREIGN JURISDICTIONS FOR USE IN TEXAS PROCEEDINGS; DEPOSITIONS IN TEXAS FOR USE IN FOREIGN PROCEEDINGS

201.1. Depositions in Foreign Jurisdictions for Use in Texas Proceedings

(a) **Generally.** A party may take a deposition on oral examination or written questions of any person or entity located in another state or a foreign country for use in proceedings in this State. The deposition may be taken by:

(1) notice;

(2) letter rogatory, letter of request, or other such device;

(3) agreement of the parties; or

(4) court order.

(b) **By notice.** A party may take the deposition by notice in accordance with these rules as if the deposition were taken in this State, except that the deposition officer may be a person authorized to administer oaths in the place where the deposition is taken.

---

386 An interesting question is whether the parties can attend a deposition on written questions. No case applying Texas Rule 200 or its predecessor has considered the question. The only case applying the comparable Federal Rule held, after examining the history and procedure and purpose of such depositions, that parties have no right to attend them. *Pueblo of Jemez v. U.S.*, No. CIV 12-0800 RB/JHR, 2017 U.S. Dist. LEXIS 209298, at *6–10, 2017 WL 6512230 (D.N.M. Dec. 19, 2017) (applying Federal Rule 31).

387 *Accord Titus Cnty. Hosp. Dist. v. Lucas*, 988 S.W.2d 740, 740 (Tex. 1998) (per curiam) (holding that, under former Texas Rule 166b(6), "[a] general duty to supplement deposition testimony (as opposed to a narrow duty for certain expert testimony, for example) would impose too great a burden on litigants. We therefore disapprove the court of appeals' holding that deposition testimony must be supplemented.") (citation omitted); *cf. Pilates, Inc. v. Georgetown Bodyworks*, 201 F.R.D. 261, 262 (D.D.C. 2000) (recognizing that "[t]he Federal Rules of Civil Procedure impose no affirmative duty for deponents to supplement deposition testimony").

(c) **By letter rogatory.** On motion by a party, the court in which an action is pending must issue a letter rogatory on terms that are just and appropriate, regardless of whether any other manner of obtaining the deposition is impractical or inconvenient. The letter must:

(1) be addressed to the appropriate authority in the jurisdiction in which the deposition is to be taken;

(2) request and authorize that authority to summon the witness before the authority at a time and place stated in the letter for examination on oral or written questions; and

(3) request and authorize that authority to cause the witness's testimony to be reduced to writing and returned, together with any items marked as exhibits, to the party requesting the letter rogatory.

(d) **By letter of request or other such device.** On motion by a party, the court in which an action is pending, or the clerk of that court, must issue a letter of request or other such device in accordance with an applicable treaty or international convention on terms that are just and appropriate. The letter or other device must be issued regardless of whether any other manner of obtaining the deposition is impractical or inconvenient. The letter or other device must:

(1) be in the form prescribed by the treaty or convention under which it is issued, as presented by the movant to the court or clerk; and

(2) must state the time, place, and manner of the examination of the witness.

(e) **Objections to form of letter rogatory, letter of request, or other such device.** In issuing a letter rogatory, letter of request, or other such device, the court must set a time for objecting to the form of the device. A party must make any objection to the form of the device in writing and serve it on all other parties by the time set by the court, or the objection is waived.

(f) **Admissibility of evidence.** Evidence obtained in response to a letter rogatory, letter of request, or other such device is not inadmissible merely because it is not a verbatim transcript, or the testimony was not taken under oath, or for any similar departure from the requirements for depositions taken within this State under these rules.

(g) **Deposition by electronic means.** A deposition in another jurisdiction may be taken by telephone, videoconference, teleconference, or other electronic means under the provisions of Rule 199.

201.2. Depositions in Texas for Use in Proceedings in Foreign Jurisdictions

If a court of record of any other state or foreign jurisdiction issues a mandate, writ, or commission that requires a witness's oral or written deposition testimony in this State, the witness may be compelled to appear and testify in the same manner and by the same process used for taking testimony in a proceeding pending in this State.

Comments to 1999 Change:

1. Rule 201.1 sets forth procedures for obtaining deposition testimony of a witness in another state or foreign jurisdiction for use in Texas court proceedings. It does not, however, address whether any of the procedures listed are, in fact, permitted or recognized by the law of the state or foreign jurisdiction where the witness is located.

A party must first determine what procedures are permitted by the jurisdiction where the witness is located before using this rule.

2. Section 20.001 of the Civil Practice and Remedies Code provides a nonexclusive list of persons who are qualified to take a written deposition in Texas and who may take depositions (oral or written) in another state or outside the United States.

3. Rule 201.2 is based on Section 20.002 of the Civil Practice and Remedies Code.

11-4:1 2021 Amendments to the Texas Rules of Civil Procedure

The 2021 amendments to the Texas Rules of Civil Procedure did not modify Texas Rule 201 regarding depositions in foreign jurisdictions for use in Texas proceeding depositions and deposition in Texas for use in foreign proceedings in any respect.

11-4:2 In General

Texas Rule 201 governs the procedures for obtaining (1) an oral or written deposition in another state or foreign country for use in a Texas court proceeding,[388] and (2) an oral or written deposition in Texas for use in a court proceeding in another state or foreign country.[389]

11-4:3 Depositions in Another State or Foreign Country for Use in a Texas Court Proceeding

Texas Rule 201.1, which governs the procedure for obtaining the deposition of a witness located outside of Texas for use in a Texas court proceeding, is needed because a Texas court cannot issue a subpoena compelling a witness located outside Texas to appear for a deposition in or outside Texas.[390] Under the Rule, a deposition may be taken in another state or foreign country by one of four procedures: "(1) notice; (2) letter rogatory, letter of request, or other such device; (3) agreement of the parties; or (4) court order."[391] As pointed out in Comment 1 to the 1999 change to Texas Rule 201, although Texas "Rule 201.1 sets forth procedures for obtaining deposition testimony of a witness in another state or foreign jurisdiction for use in Texas court proceedings[, i]t does not . . . address whether any of the procedures listed are, in fact, permitted or recognized by the law of the state or foreign jurisdiction where the witness is located. A party must first determine what procedures are permitted by the jurisdiction where the witness is located before using this rule."[392]

---

388 Tex. R. Civ. P. 201.1.

389 Tex. R. Civ. P. 201.2.

390 *In re Bannum, Inc.*, No. 03-09-00512-CV, 2009 Tex. App. LEXIS 10088, at *2–4, 2009 WL 8599250 (Tex. App.—Austin Oct. 30, 2009, orig. proceeding) (mem. op.) (noting that "the rules covering oral depositions do not allow a court to order an out-of-state nonparty to appear").

391 Tex. R. Civ. P. 201.1(a).

392 Tex. R. Civ. P. 201 cmt. 1 to 1999 change.

Moreover, the discovery and evidentiary rules of the state or foreign country, and not the Texas discovery and evidentiary rules, generally will apply to the deposition even if they are inconsistent with Texas's discovery[393] or evidentiary rules.[394]

11-4:3.1 Notice

If permitted by the state or country where the witness is located, a party can take the deposition by notice in the same manner as provided by Texas Rules 199 or 200, "except that the deposition officer may be a person authorized to administer oaths in the place where the deposition is taken."[395] Taking a deposition in another state or a foreign country by notice is problematic for two reasons. First, the service of a notice does not give the noticing party the ability to compel the witness's attendance. Second, in some civil-law countries, the taking of testimony by private attorneys without the involvement of the local judiciary is forbidden.[396]

11-4:3.2 Letter Rogatory

If required or permitted by the law of the state or country where the witness is located, a party can file a motion for a letter rogatory in the Texas court where the action is pending.[397] A letter rogatory is "[a] formal communication in writing, sent by a court in which an action is pending to a court or judge of a foreign country, requesting that the testimony of a witness resident within the jurisdiction of the latter court may be there formally taken under its direction and transmitted to the first court for use in the pending action."[398]

---

393 *See Owens-Corning Fiberglas Corp. v. Martin*, 942 S.W.2d 712, 721 (Tex. App.—Dallas 1997, no writ) ("Matters of remedy and procedure, however, are governed by the law of the forum where the suit is maintained."); Restatement (Second) of Conflict Of Laws § 122 (1971) ("A court usually applies its own local law rules prescribing how litigation shall be conducted even when it applies the local law rules of another state to resolve other issues in the case.").

394 *Cf. Samuelson v. Susen*, 576 F.2d 546, 549 (3d Cir. 1978) (noting that Federal Rule of Evidence 501 requires a district court exercising diversity jurisdiction "to apply the law of privilege which would be applied by the courts of the state in which it sits"); *Palmer v. Fisher*, 228 F.2d 603, 608–09 (7th Cir. 1955) ("Questions of evidence, including privilege, are generally decided by the law of the forum. Since the proceeding to suppress a deposition is an independent action, the law of the forum is the law of Illinois." (citation omitted), *abrogated on other grounds, Carter Prods., Inc. v. Eversharp, Inc.*, 360 F.2d 868 (7th Cir. 1966))); *Wilmington Tr. Co. v. AEP Generating Co.*, No. 2:13-cv-01213, 2015 U.S. Dist. LEXIS 144274, at *6–7, 2015 WL 6438754 (S.D. Ohio Oct. 23, 2015) ("'A federal court, sitting in diversity, must look to the choice-of-law rules of the state in which it sits . . . to resolve conflict-of-law questions' including questions about the applicability of evidentiary privileges." (quoting *AroChem Int'l, Inc. v. Buirkle*, 968 F.2d 266, 269–70 (2d Cir. 1992))); *Wright v. Jeep Corp.*, 547 F. Supp. 871, 875 (E.D. Mich. 1982) ("[B]ecause the defendant seeks to depose the respondent in Michigan, the appropriate law regarding privilege is the law of Michigan.").

395 Tex. R. Civ. P. 201.1(b).

396 Doak Bishop, *International Litigation in Texas: Obtaining Evidence in Foreign Countries*, 19 Hous. L. Rev. 361, 364–65 (1982).

397 Tex. R. Civ. P. 201.1(c).

398 *Ex parte Fierro*, 934 S.W.2d 370, 371 n.1 (Tex. Crim. App. 1996) (quoting *Black's Law Dictionary* 471 (5th ed. 1983)); *accord Union Carbide Corp. v. Martin*, 349 S.W.3d 137, 140 n.2 (Tex. App.—Dallas 2011, no pet.) ("'Letters rogatory' indicates a formal communication

The court "must issue a letter rogatory on terms that are just and appropriate, regardless of whether any other manner of obtaining the deposition is impractical or inconvenient."[399] In addition, the letter rogatory must:

(1) be addressed to the appropriate authority in the jurisdiction in which the deposition is to be taken;

(2) request and authorize that authority to summon the witness before the authority at a time and place stated in the letter for examination on oral or written questions; and

(3) request and authorize that authority to cause the witness's testimony to be reduced to writing and returned, together with any items marked as exhibits, to the party requesting the letter rogatory.[400]

11-4:3.3 Letter of Request or Other Such Device

"On motion by a party, the court in which an action is pending, or the clerk of that court, must issue a letter of request or other such device in accordance with an applicable treaty or international convention on terms that are just and appropriate."[401] The Hague Convention is such a treaty and "sets forth a number of provisions that must be included in a letter of request, including specific information about the lawsuit and the information sought."[402]

The court or its clerk "must" issue the letter or other device "regardless of whether any other manner of obtaining the deposition is impractical or inconvenient. The letter or other device must: (1) be in the form prescribed by the treaty or convention under which it is issued, as presented by the movant to the court or clerk; and (2) must state the time, place, and manner of the examination of the witness."[403]

11-4:3.4 Objections to the Form of the Letter Rogatory, the Letter of Request, or Other Such Device

Under Texas Rule 201.1(e), a court, before issuing a letter rogatory, letter of request, or other such device, "must set a time for objecting to the form of the device. A party must make any objection to the form of the device in writing and serve it on all other parties by the time set by the court, or the objection is waived."[404]

---

from a court in which an action is pending to a foreign court requesting that the testimony of a witness residing in such foreign jurisdiction may be taken under the direction of the court addressed and transmitted to the court making the request." (quoting 26B C.J.S. *Depositions* § 34 (2001))); *cf. Intel Corp. v. Advanced Micro Devices, Inc.*, 542 U.S. 241, 247 n.1 (2004) ("[A] *letter rogatory* is the request by a domestic court to a foreign court to take evidence from a certain witness." (quoting Harry Leroy Jones, *International Judicial Assistance: Procedural Chaos and a Program for Reform*, 62 YALE L.J. 515, 519 (1953))).

399 Tex. R. Civ. P. 201.1(c).

400 Tex. R. Civ. P. 201.1(c).

401 Tex. R. Civ. P. 201.1(d).

402 *In re Urethane Antitrust Litig.*, No. 04-MD-1616-JWL, 2010 U.S. Dist. LEXIS 129536, at *30 n.9, 2010 WL 4963019 (D. Kan. Dec. 1, 2010).

403 Tex. R. Civ. P. 201.1(d).

404 Tex. R. Civ. P. 201.1(e).

11-4:3.5 The Deposition Officer

Section 20.001 of the Texas Civil Practice and Remedies Code provides a nonexclusive list of persons who are qualified to take depositions on oral examination or written questions in another state or a foreign country. If the witness "is alleged to reside or to be outside [Texas], but inside the United States," the deposition "may be taken in another state by: (1) a clerk of a court of record having a seal; (2) a commissioner of deeds appointed under the laws of this state; or (3) any notary public."[405]

If, however, the witness "is alleged to reside or to be outside the United States[,]" the deposition can be taken by: "(1) a minister, commissioner, or charge d'affaires of the United States who is a resident of and is accredited in the country where the deposition is taken; (2) a consul general, consul, vice-consul, commercial agent, vice-commercial agent, deputy consul, or consular agent of the United States who is a resident of the country where the deposition is taken; or (3) any notary public."[406]

If the witness "is alleged to be a member of the United States Armed Forces or of a United States Armed Forces Auxiliary or . . . is alleged to be a civilian employed by or accompanying the armed forces or an auxiliary outside the United States[,]" the deposition "may be taken by a commissioned officer in the United States Armed Forces or United States Armed Forces Auxiliary or by a commissioned officer in the United States Armed Forces Reserve or an auxiliary of it."[407]

11-4:3.6 Method of Taking the Deposition

Under Texas Rule 201.1(g), "[a] deposition in another jurisdiction may be taken by telephone, videoconference, teleconference, or other electronic means under the provisions of [Texas] Rule 199."[408]

11-4:3.7 The Testimony's Admissibility

The "[e]vidence obtained in response to a letter rogatory, letter of request, or other such device is not inadmissible merely because it is not a verbatim transcript, or the testimony was not taken under oath, or for any similar departure from the requirements for depositions taken within [Texas] under [its discovery] rules."[409]

11-4:4 Depositions in Texas for Use in Foreign Proceedings

Section 20.002 of the Texas Civil Practice & Remedies Code governs the manner in which parties to foreign proceedings can obtain a deposition on oral examination or

---

405 Tex. Civ. Prac. & Rem. Code § 20.001(b).

406 Tex. Civ. Prac. & Rem. Code § 20.001(c); *see Kugle v. Daimler Chrysler Corp.*, 88 S.W.3d 355, 363 (Tex. App.—San Antonio 2002, pet. denied) (holding that a trial court properly admitted deposition testimony of Mexican police officers and an ambulance driver in a personal-injury action in which witnesses were sworn in only by a Texas notary public).

407 Tex. Civ. Prac. & Rem. Code § 20.001(d).

408 Tex. R. Civ. P. 201.1(g).

409 Tex. R. Civ. P. 201.1(f).

written questions of a witness in Texas. Texas Rule 201.2 simply restates the statute[410] and provides:

> If a court of record of any other state or foreign jurisdiction issues a mandate, writ, or commission that requires a witness's oral or written deposition testimony in this State, the witness may be compelled to appear and testify in the same manner and by the same process used for taking testimony in a proceeding pending in this State.[411]

Because the statute uses the word "may," a Texas court need not compel the witness to appear.[412] Nonetheless, in *In re Bennett*, the court made clear that, in considering whether to compel the witness to appear, although the trial court should not consider the relevancy of the information sought by the deposition as that is an issue for the court in which the action is pending,[413] it can consider whether a protective order under Texas Rule 192.6 should issue with respect to the deposition.[414]

11-5 Depositions Before Suit or to Investigate Claims

TEXT OF RULE 202

RULE 202. DEPOSITIONS BEFORE SUIT OR TO INVESTIGATE CLAIMS

202.1. Generally

A person may petition the court for an order authorizing the taking of a deposition on oral examination or written questions either:

---

410 Tex. R. Civ. P. 201 cmt. 3 to 1999 change ("[Texas] Rule 201.2 is based on Section 20.002 of the [Texas] Civil Practice and Remedies Code.").

411 *Accord* Tex. Civ. Prac. & Rem. Code 20.002 ("If a court of record in any other state or foreign jurisdiction issues a mandate, writ, or commission that requires a witness's testimony in this state, either to written questions or by oral deposition, the witness may be compelled to appear and testify in the same manner and by the same process used for taking testimony in a proceeding pending in this state.").

412 *In re Seavall*, No. 03-13-00205-CV, 2013 Tex. App. LEXIS 7020, at *3–4, 2013 WL 3013872 (Tex. App.—Austin June 11, 2013, orig. proceeding) (mem. op.) (holding that the trial court abused its discretion in compelling a deposition in connection with an attempt to enforce a long-dormant judgment because Texas "[R]ule 201.2 'authorizes Texas courts to enforce foreign discovery orders' but . . . does not *mandate* that Texas courts do so" (quoting Tex. R. Civ. P. 201.2)).

413 *In re Bennett*, 502 S.W.3d 373, 377–78 (Tex. App.—Houston [14th Dist.] 2016, no pet.) ("In *Ex parte Taylor*, [220 S.W. 74, 75 (Tex. 1920),] the high court concluded that the court with jurisdiction over the underlying case is generally charged with determining the relevancy and materiality of evidence sought by a party seeking a deposition in Texas under letters rogatory, while the Texas court has the obligation to protect the witness's legal rights, including, for example, the witness's right to avoid compelled production of privileged evidence. This overarching principle promotes comity toward other states' courts while vesting Texas trial courts with authority to protect Texas residents subjected to depositions for lawsuits pending in other states.").

414 *In re Bennett*, 502 S.W.3d 373, 381 (Tex. App.—Houston [14th Dist.] 2016, no pet.) ("Because Bennett, Clark, and Lowe did not meet their burden of establishing the depositions would cause undue burden, unnecessary expense, harassment, annoyance, or invasion of personal, constitutional or property rights, the trial court abused its discretion to the extent it restricted their depositions based on [Texas] Rule 192.6(b).").

(a) to perpetuate or obtain the person's own testimony or that of any other person for use in an anticipated suit; or

(b) to investigate a potential claim or suit.

202.2. Petition

The petition must:

(a) be verified;

(b) be filed in a proper court of any county:

  (1) where venue of the anticipated suit may lie, if suit is anticipated; or

  (2) where the witness resides, if no suit is yet anticipated;

(c) be in the name of the petitioner;

(d) state either:

  (1) that the petitioner anticipates the institution of a suit in which the petitioner may be a party; or

  (2) that the petitioner seeks to investigate a potential claim by or against petitioner;

(e) state the subject matter of the anticipated action, if any, and the petitioner's interest therein;

(f) if suit is anticipated, either:

  (1) state the names of the persons petitioner expects to have interests adverse to petitioner's in the anticipated suit, and the addresses and telephone numbers for such persons; or

  (2) state that the names, addresses, and telephone numbers of persons petitioner expects to have interests adverse to petitioner's in the anticipated suit cannot be ascertained through diligent inquiry, and describe those persons;

(g) state the names, addresses and telephone numbers of the persons to be deposed, the substance of the testimony that the petitioner expects to elicit from each, and the petitioner's reasons for desiring to obtain the testimony of each; and

(h) request an order authorizing the petitioner to take the depositions of the persons named in the petition.

202.3. Notice and Service

(a) **Personal service on witnesses and persons named.** At least 15 days before the date of the hearing on the petition, the petitioner must serve the petition and a notice of the hearing—in accordance with Rule 21a—on all persons petitioner seeks to depose and, if suit is anticipated, on all persons petitioner expects to have interests adverse to petitioner's in the anticipated suit.

(b) **Service by publication on persons not named**

  (1) **Manner.** Unnamed persons described in the petition whom the petitioner expects to have interests adverse to petitioner's in the anticipated suit, if any, may be served by publication with the petition and notice of the hearing.

The notice must state the place for the hearing and the time it will be held, which must be more than 14 days after the first publication of the notice. The petition and notice must be published once each week for two consecutive weeks in the newspaper of broadest circulation in the county in which the petition is filed, or if no such newspaper exists, in the newspaper of broadest circulation in the nearest county where a newspaper is published.

(2) **Objection to depositions taken on notice by publication.** Any interested party may move, in the proceeding or by bill of review, to suppress any deposition, in whole or in part, taken on notice by publication, and may also attack or oppose the deposition by any other means available.

(c) **Service in probate cases.** A petition to take a deposition in anticipation of an application for probate of a will, and notice of the hearing on the petition, may be served by posting as prescribed by Section 33(f)(2) of the Probate Code. The notice and petition must be directed to all parties interested in the testator's estate and must comply with the requirements of Section 33(c) of the Probate Code insofar as they may be applicable.

(d) **Modification by order.** As justice or necessity may require, the court may shorten or lengthen the notice periods under this rule and may extend the notice period to permit service on any expected adverse party.

202.4. Order

(a) **Required findings.** The court must order a deposition to be taken if, but only if, it finds that:

(1) allowing the petitioner to take the requested deposition may prevent a failure or delay of justice in an anticipated suit; or

(2) the likely benefit of allowing the petitioner to take the requested deposition to investigate a potential claim outweighs the burden or expense of the procedure.

(b) **Contents.** The order must state whether a deposition will be taken on oral examination or written questions. The order may also state the time and place at which a deposition will be taken. If the order does not state the time and place at which a deposition will be taken, the petitioner must notice the deposition as required by Rules 199 or 200. The order must contain any protections the court finds necessary or appropriate to protect the witness or any person who may be affected by the procedure.

202.5. Manner of Taking and Use

Except as otherwise provided in this rule, depositions authorized by this rule are governed by the rules applicable to depositions of nonparties in a pending suit. The scope of discovery in depositions authorized by this rule is the same as if the anticipated suit or potential claim had been filed. A court may restrict or prohibit the use of a deposition taken under this rule in a subsequent suit to protect a person who was not served with notice of the deposition from any unfair prejudice or to prevent abuse of this rule.

Comments to 1999 change:

1. This rule applies to all discovery before suit covered by former rules governing depositions to perpetuate testimony and bills of discovery.

2. A deposition taken under this rule may be used in a subsequent suit as permitted by the rules of evidence, except that a court may restrict or prohibit its use to prevent taking unfair advantage of a witness or others. The bill of discovery procedure, which Rule 202 incorporates, is equitable in nature, and a court must not permit it to be used inequitably.

11-5:1 2021 Amendments to the Texas Rules of Civil Procedure

The 2021 amendments to the Texas Rules of Civil Procedure did not modify Texas Rule 202 regarding pre-suit depositions in any respect.

11-5:2 In General

Texas Rule 202 allows "a person" to "petition the court for an order authorizing the taking of a deposition" on oral examination or on written questions to (1) perpetuate testimony for use in an anticipated suit, or (2) investigate a potential claim or suit.[415] The testimony to be perpetuated may be that of the petitioner or "any other person."[416] With respect to anticipated suits or claims, a presuit deposition is available whether the petitioner would be a plaintiff or a defendant.[417]

The "persons" who can file the petition or be deposed include any natural person, any entity irrespective of its nature (e.g., corporation, partnership, limited partnership, limited liability company, or association), and any governmental entity, subdivision, body, or agency.[418] A petitioner who lacks standing to bring the claim or suit

---

[415] Tex. R. Civ. P. 201.1; *accord Glassdoor, Inc. v. Andra Grp., LP*, 560 S.W.3d 281, 286 (Tex. App.—Dallas 2017) (Texas "Rule 202 authorizes a person to seek a court order authorizing an oral deposition or a deposition on written questions for two purposes: (i) to perpetuate or obtain a person's testimony for use in an anticipated suit or (ii) to investigate a potential claim or suit."), *pet. dism'd as moot*, 575 S.W.3d 523 (Tex. 2019); ***In re East***, 476 S.W. 3d 61, 65 (Tex. App.—Corpus Christi 2014, orig. proceeding); ***see In re City of Dall.***, 501 S.W.3d 71, 73 (Tex. 2016) (orig. proceeding) (per curiam) ("Rule 202 of the Texas Rules of Civil Procedure allows a court to authorize depositions 'to investigate a potential claim or suit.'" (quoting Tex. R. Civ. P. 202.1(b)).

[416] Tex. R. Civ. P. 202.1(a).

[417] Tex. R. Civ. P. 202.2(d) ("The petition must . . . state . . . the petitioner seeks to investigate a potential claim *by or against* petitioner.") (emphasis added); ***In re Donna Indep. Sch. Dist.***, 299 S.W.3d 456, 460 (Tex. App.—Corpus Christi 2009, orig. proceeding) ("[T]here is no requirement in [Texas] Rule 202 that the person sought to be deposed be a potentially liable defendant in the claim under investigation." (quoting *City of Hous. v. U.S. Filter Wastewater Grp., Inc.*, 190 S.W.3d 242, 245 (Tex. App.—Houston [1st Dist.] 2006, no pet.))); *see Glassdoor, Inc. v. Andra Grp., LP*, 560 S.W.3d 281, 286 (Tex. App.—Dallas 2017) ("The petition must state either that the petitioner anticipates a suit in which the petitioner may be a party or that the petitioner seeks to investigate a potential claim by or against the petitioner."), *pet. dism'd as moot*, 575 S.W.3d 523 (Tex. 2019); ***In re East***, 476 S.W. 3d 61, 65 (Tex. App.—Corpus Christi 2014, orig. proceeding) (same).

[418] This is because "person" as defined by Section 311.005 of the Texas Government Code "includes corporation, organization, government or governmental subdivision or agency, business trust, estate, trust, partnership, association, and any other legal entity[,]" Tex. Govt. Code § 311.005(2), and because the "[t]he Code Construction Act applies to the Texas Rules of Civil Procedure[,]" *Simulis, L.L.C. v. G.E. Cap. Corp.*, 276 S.W.3d 109, 113

being investigated, however, cannot properly seek a presuit deposition under Texas Rule 202.[419] The person to be deposed need not be the potential plaintiff or defendant, but rather can be someone who has evidence relevant to the claim or suit.[420]

"Pre-suit discovery pursuant to [Texas R]ule 202 'is not an end in itself,' but rather 'is in aid of a suit which is anticipated' and 'ancillary to the anticipated suit.'"[421] A petition for a presuit deposition involves no substantive claim or cause of action upon which relief can be granted. Rather, a successful petitioner merely acquires the right to obtain discovery—discovery that may or may not result in a lawsuit.[422]

(Tex. App.—Houston [1st Dist.] 2008, no pet.) (quoting *In re Walkup*, 122 S.W.3d 215, 217 (Tex. App.—Houston [1st Dist.] 2003, orig. proceeding)).

419 *In re Does*, 337 S.W.3d 862, 865 (Tex. 2011) (orig. proceeding) (per curiam) (holding that a trial court abused its discretion in allowing presuit depositions, in part because the petition's allegations "mostly concern possible causes of action by Klein, who is not a party to the proceeding"); *In re Wolfe*, 341 S.W.3d 932, 933 (Tex. 2011) (orig. proceeding) (per curiam) (holding that, because individual citizens cannot maintain a suit to remove public officials without the joinder of an appropriate state official, they likewise cannot obtain presuit discovery about a potential removal action under Texas Rule 202); *In re UBS Fin. Servs.*, No. 14-20-00087-CV, 2020 Tex. App. LEXIS 7972, at *4–6, 2020 WL 5902955 (Tex. App.—Houston [14th Dist.] Oct. 6, 2020, orig. proceeding) (mem. op.) (holding that the trial court lacked subject-matter jurisdiction to grant a Texas Rule 202 petition because the petitioner lacked standing to bring the claim he sought to investigate); *In re Dolcefino Commc'ns, LLC*, No. 01-20-00382-CV, 2020 Tex. App. LEXIS 7362, at *2 (Tex. App.—Houston [1st Dist.] Sep. 10, 2020, orig. proceeding) (mem. op.) (same); *In re Hochheim Prairie Farm Mut. Ins. Ass'n*, 115 S.W.3d 793, 795–96 (Tex. App.—Beaumont 2003, orig. proceeding) (holding that a trial court abused its discretion in allowing an injured plaintiff to take a presuit deposition of the defendant's insurance carrier regarding a *Stowers* claim because such a claim belongs to the insured, not to the injured party); *see In re Jorden*, 249 S.W.3d 416, 418 (Tex. 2008) ("Because [Section 74.351(s) of the Texas Civil Practice & Remedies Code regarding healthcare-liability claims] prohibits all discovery other than three exceptions—and [Texas] Rule 202 depositions are not listed among them—we hold the statute prohibits such depositions until after an expert report is served.").

420 *In re Donna Indep. Sch. Dist.*, 299 S.W.3d 456, 460 (Tex. App.— Corpus Christi 2009, orig. proceeding) ("[T]here is no requirement in [Texas] Rule 202 that the person sought to be deposed be a potentially liable defendant in the claim under investigation." (quoting *City of Hous. v. U.S. Filter Wastewater Grp., Inc.*, 190 S.W.3d 242, 245 (Tex. App.—Houston [1st Dist.] 2006, orig. proceeding))).

421 *City of Dall. v. Dall. Black Fire Fighters Ass'n*, 353 S.W.3d 547, 553 (Tex. App.—Dallas 2011, no pet.) (quoting *In re Wolfe*, 341 S.W.3d 932, 933 (Tex. 2011) (orig. proceeding) (per curiam)); *see Office Emps. Int'l Union Local 277, AFL-CIO v. Sw. Drug Corp.*, 391 S.W.2d 404, 407 (Tex. 1965) (construing former Texas Rule 187).

422 *Combs v. Tex. Civil Rights Project*, 410 S.W.3d 529, 534 (Tex. App.—Austin 2013, no pet.) ("[A] petition under [Texas R]ule 202 is ultimately a petition that asserts no substantive claim or cause of action upon which relief can be granted. A successful [Texas R]ule 202 petitioner simply acquires the right to obtain discovery—discovery that may or may not lead to a claim or cause of action.") (quoted with approval in *In re Baxter*, No. 05-16-01174-CV, 2016 Tex. App. LEXIS 11328, at *4, 2016 WL 6099547 (Tex. App.—Dallas Oct. 19, 2016, orig. proceeding) (mem. op.))).

Texas Rule 202 can be used only to obtain depositions, not other forms of discovery.[423] The Rule governs all presuit discovery that was governed by former Texas Rules 187 and 737, which respectively related to depositions to perpetuate testimony and bills of discovery.[424]

11-5:3 The Petition

Before taking a presuit deposition, the person seeking it must file a petition that complies with Texas Rule 202.2's requirements[425] and request an order authorizing the deposition.[426]

11-5:3.1 The Petition's Contents

The petition's contents are set forth in Texas Rule 202.2. They are different when the petitioner seeks a deposition to investigate a claim than when the petitioner anticipates the institution of a suit in which the petitioner may be a party. A petition to investigate a claim "must:"

1. "be verified"[427]—i.e., "be sworn to on personal knowledge;"[428]

---

[423] *In re Akzo Nobel Chem., Inc.*, 24 S.W.3d 919, 921 (Tex. App.—Beaumont 2000, orig. proceeding) ("The Relators also complain of the order requiring them to make the accident scene available for inspection because it is not authorized by [Texas] Rule 202. Neither by its language nor by implication can we construe [Texas] Rule 202 to authorize a trial court, before suit is filed, to order any form of discovery but deposition."). As discussed below, a production request can be included in a Texas Rule 202 deposition notice.

[424] Tex. R. Civ. P. 202 cmt. 1 to 1999 change ("This rule applies to all discovery before suit covered by former rules governing depositions to perpetuate testimony and bills of discovery.").

[425] Tex. R. Civ. P. 202.1 (providing that "[a] person may petition the court for an order"); *see In re East*, 476 S.W.3d 61, 65 (Tex. App.—Corpus Christi 2014, orig. proceeding) ("Texas Rule of Civil Procedure 202 permits a person to petition the court for authorization to take a deposition before suit is filed."); *In re Contractor's Supplies, Inc.*, No. 12-09-00231-CV, 2009 Tex. App. LEXIS 6396, at *5, 2009 WL 2488374 (Tex. App.—Tyler Aug. 17, 2009, orig. proceeding) (mem. op.) ("The person seeking the deposition must file a verified petition[.]").

[426] Tex. R. Civ. P. 202.2(h) (providing that the petition must "request an order authorizing . . . the depositions"), 202.4 (requiring an order to take a presuit deposition).

[427] Tex. R. Civ. P. 202.2(a); *see In re East*, 476 S.W. 3d 61, 63 n.3 (Tex. App.—Corpus Christi 2014, orig. proceeding) ("Texas Rule of Civil Procedure 202.2 provides that a petition seeking presuit depositions must be verified."); *In re Contractor's Supplies, Inc.*, No. 12-09-00231-CV, 2009 Tex. App. LEXIS 6396, at *5, 2009 WL 2488374 (Tex. App. Tyler Aug. 17, 2009) (mem. op.) ("The person seeking the deposition must file a verified petition[.]").

[428] *In re East*, 476 S.W. 3d 61, 63 n. 3 (Tex. App.—Corpus Christi 2014, orig. proceeding) (providing further that a petition based on the petitioner's "best knowledge and belief" is insufficient and noting, in *dictum*, that "language 'to the best of my knowledge' does not attest to the truthfulness of the facts alleged and is not legally effective as a verification"); *cf. Kerlin v. Arias*, 274 S.W.3d 666, 668 (Tex. 2008) ("[T]he only representation Castillo makes about the truth of her [summary-judgment] affidavit is that '[a]ll statements contained herein are true and correct to the best of my personal knowledge and belief.' To have probative value, an affiant 'must swear that the facts presented in the affidavit reflect his personal knowledge.' An affiant's *belief* about the facts is legally insufficient." (citations omitted) (quoting

2. "be in the name of the petitioner;"[429]
3. state that "the petitioner seeks to investigate a potential claim by or against petitioner;"[430]
4. state "the subject matter of the anticipated action, if any, and the petitioner's interest therein;"[431]
5. "state the names, addresses, and telephone numbers of the persons to be deposed;"[432]
6. state "the substance of the testimony that the petitioner expects to elicit from each" deponent;[433]
7. state "the petitioner's reasons for desiring to obtain the testimony of each" deponent;[434]
8. identify the documents requested, if any;[435] and

In re E.I. DuPont de Nemours & Co., 136 S.W.3d 218, 224 (Tex. 2004) (orig. proceeding))); *Lightfoot v. Weissgarber*, 763 S.W.2d 624, 628 (Tex. App.—San Antonio 1989, writ denied) ("It is a long established rule in Texas that affidavits, in order to constitute summary judgment proof, must be sworn to on personal knowledge and that those sworn to on best knowledge and belief are insufficient.").

[429] Tex. R. Civ. P. 202.2(c).

[430] Tex. R. Civ. P. 202.2(d)(2).

[431] Tex. R. Civ. P. 202.2(e).

[432] Tex. R. Civ. P. 202.2(g); *see City of Dall. v. City of Corsicana*, Nos. 10-14-00090-CV, 10-14-00171-CV, 2015 Tex. App. LEXIS 8753, at *17, 2015 WL 4985935 (Tex. App.—Waco Aug. 20, 2015, orig. proceeding) (mem. op.), *rev'd on other grounds*, 501 S.W.3d 71 (Tex. 2016) (orig. proceeding) (per curiam). A trial court abuses its discretion if it authorizes the deposition of a person not *specifically* named in the petition. *E.g., City of Dall. v. City of Corsicana*, Nos. 10-14-00090-CV, 10-14-00171-CV, 2015 Tex. App. LEXIS 8753, at *17, 2015 WL 4985935 (Tex. App.—Waco Aug. 20, 2015, orig. proceeding) (mem. op.) (holding that the trial court abused its discretion in ordering the "deposition of 'a person or persons whose identities are revealed in the documents to be produced' by the deponent"), *rev'd on other grounds*, 501 S.W.3d 71 (Tex. 2016) (orig. proceeding) (per curiam).

[433] Tex. R. Civ. P. 202.2(g); *accord City of Dall. v. City of Corsicana*, Nos. 10-14-00090-CV, 10-14-00171-CV, 2015 Tex. App. LEXIS 8753, at *17, 2015 WL 4985935 (Tex. App.—Waco Aug. 20, 2015, orig. proceeding) (mem. op.), *rev'd on other grounds*, 501 S.W.3d 71 (Tex. 2016) (orig. proceeding) (per curiam).

[434] Tex. R. Civ. P. 202.2(g); *accord City of Dall. v. City of Corsicana*, Nos. 10-14-00090-CV, 10-14-00171-CV, 2015 Tex. App. LEXIS 8753, at *17, 2015 WL 4985935 (Tex. App.—Waco Aug. 20, 2015, orig. proceeding) (mem. op.), *rev'd on other grounds*, 501 S.W.3d 71 (Tex. 2016) (orig. proceeding) (per curiam).

[435] *In re Perrilloux*, No. 05-19-01584-CV, 2020 Tex. App. LEXIS 3737, at *9–10 (Tex. App.—Dallas May 1, 2020, orig. proceeding) (mem. op.) ("There is nothing in the language of [Texas] Rule 202 that prohibits the petitioner from requesting that documents be produced along with the deposition. [Texas] Rule 202.5 expressly provides that 'depositions authorized by this rule are governed by the rules applicable to depositions of nonparties in a pending suit.' [Texas] Rule 205, which governs discovery of non-parties, permits a party to compel discovery from a non-party by serving a subpoena requesting 'production of documents or tangible things . . . served with a notice of deposition on oral examination or written questions.' Accordingly, the plain language of the rules permits a petition seeking a pre-suit deposition under [Texas] Rule 202 to request the production of documents

9. "request an order authorizing the petitioner to take the depositions of the persons named in the petition."[436]

If, however, the petitioner anticipates the institution of a suit and seeks the deposition to perpetuate or obtain testimony for use in the lawsuit, all of the foregoing requirements apply to the petition except that: (1) instead of stating that "the petitioner seeks to investigate a potential claim by or against petitioner[,]" item 3 above, the petition must state "that the petitioner anticipates the institution of a suit in which the petitioner may be a party;" and (2) the petition must either "state the names of the persons petitioner expects to have interests adverse to the petitioner's in the anticipated suit, and the addresses and telephone numbers for such persons; or . . . state that the names, addresses, and telephone numbers of persons petitioner expects to

---

as well.") (citations omitted); *In re City of Tatum*, 567 S.W.3d 800, 808 (Tex. App.—Tyler 2018, orig. proceeding) (same); *City of Dall. v. City of Corsicana*, Nos. 10-14-00090-CV, 10-14-00171-CV, 2015 Tex. App. LEXIS 8753, at *15–16, 2015 WL 4985935 (Tex. App.—Waco Aug. 20, 2015, orig. proceeding) (mem. op.) ("Under [Texas R]ule 202, documents can be requested in connection with a deposition. [Texas] Rule 202.4(b) provides that if 'the order does not state the time and place at which a deposition will be taken, the petitioner must notice the deposition as required by [Texas] Rules 199 or 200,' and [Texas] Rule 202.5 provides that 'depositions authorized by this rule are governed by the rules applicable to depositions of nonparties in a pending suit.' [Texas] Rules 199 and 200 plainly allow for the production of documents with an oral deposition or a deposition on written questions. Accordingly, the trial court's order is not an abuse of discretion to the extent that it allows Navarro to obtain documents in an oral deposition under [Texas R]ule 199 or a deposition on written questions under [Texas R]ule 200." (citing Tex. R. Civ. P. 199.2(b)(5) (requiring the request for production of documents to comply with Texas Rule 205 if the witness is a nonparty), 200.1(b) (requiring the request for production of documents to comply with Texas Rule 199.2(b)(5), and 205.1(a)–(c)), and 205.2 (setting forth the requirements for the deposition of a nonparty with a production request)), *rev'd on other grounds*, 501 S.W.3d 71 (Tex. 2016) (orig. proceeding) (per curiam); *In re Anand*, No. 01-12-01106-CV, 2013 Tex. App. LEXIS 4157, at *8–9, 2013 WL 1316436 (Tex. App.—Houston [1st Dist.] Apr. 2, 2013, orig. proceeding) (mem. op.) ("With respect to Relators' first contention that the production of documents is not permitted by [Texas] Rule 202, there is nothing in the language of [Texas] Rule 202 that prohibits the petitioner from requesting that documents be produced along with the deposition. Furthermore, [Texas] Rule 202.5 expressly provides that 'depositions authorized by this rule are governed by the rules applicable to depositions of nonparties in a pending suit.' The rule further provides that '[t]he scope of discovery in depositions authorized by this rule is the same as if the anticipated suit or potential claim had been filed.' [Texas] Rule 205, which governs discovery of nonparties, permits a party to compel discovery from a nonparty by serving a subpoena compelling 'a request for production of documents or tangible things . . . served with a notice of deposition on oral examination or written questions.' Therefore, the language of these rules when read together permits a petition seeking a pre-suit deposition under [Texas] Rule 202 to also request the production of documents." (quoting Tex. R. Civ. P. 202.5, 205.1(c))). ***But see In re Pickrell***, No. 10-17-00091-CV, 2017 Tex. App. LEXIS 3457, at *13, 2017 WL 1452851 (Tex. App.—Waco Apr. 19, 2017, orig. proceeding) (mem. op.) (incorrectly holding that that the trial court abused its discretion by ordering the production of documents in connection with a presuit deposition because "[n]either by its language nor by implication can we construe [Texas] Rule 202 to authorize a trial court, before suit is filed, to order any form of discovery but deposition.").

436 Tex. R. Civ. P. 202.2(h).

have interests adverse to petitioner's in the anticipated suit cannot be ascertained through diligent inquiry, and describe those persons."[437]

Although a petition to investigate a potential suit must state "the subject matter of the anticipated action[,]"[438] it need not allege a specific cause of action. As explained by the Austin Court of Appeals:

> [Texas R]ule 202 does not require a petitioner to plead a specific cause of action; instead, it requires only that the petitioner "state the subject matter of the anticipated action, if any, and the petitioner's interest therein[.]" Thus, the pleading requirements of [Texas R]ule 202, on their face, are less stringent than those normally required to demonstrate a trial court's jurisdiction. More importantly, as a practical matter, a party filing a [Texas R]ule 202 petition will often not know enough facts or have enough information to allege facts that, if true, would establish the trial court's jurisdiction. If a party could sufficiently plead these factual allegations without violating [Texas R]ule 13, it is likely that the party could not demonstrate a need for the [Texas R]ule 202 deposition at all.[439]

In fact, one court has held that the defendants' "merits-based defense to the potential lawsuit is not a valid objection to a petition seeking presuit depositions."[440]

---

[437] Tex. R. Civ. P. 202.2(d)(1), (f).

[438] Tex. R. Civ. P. 202.2(e); *see In re Meeker*, 497 S.W.3d 551, 556–57 (Tex. App.—Fort Worth 2016) (holding that the trial court abused its discretion in allowing intervenor to take a Texas Rule 202 presuit deposition because her Texas Rule 202 petition "does not explicitly allege that she has a potential claim or that she anticipates a suit that she will be involved in. Instead, her intervention petition focuses on Alan's potential claim, states that other parties are interested in Alan's [Texas R]ule 202 petition, and discusses a potential will contest brought by 'other parties' based on Lawrence's alleged lack of mental and testamentary capacity. Margaret does not explicitly contend that Lawrence lacked testamentary capacity, that she would be a plaintiff in any such potential suit, or that she has an interest in such a suit. Also, Margaret does not state the substance of testimony that she expects to elicit during the presuit depositions or her reasons for eliciting the testimony. Rather, by seeking to join Alan's petition, she appears to attempt to piggyback on his reasons. We cannot conclude that this attempt satisfies the detailed requirements of [Texas R]ule 202, which relate specifically to the 'person' or 'petitioner' seeking presuit discovery.") (citation omitted).

[439] *Combs v. Tex. Civil Rights Project*, 410 S.W.3d 529, 535–36 (Tex. App.—Austin 2013, pet. denied) (citations omitted) (quoting *City of Hous. v. U. S. Filter Wastewater Grp., Inc.*, 190 S.W.3d 242, 245 n.2 (Tex. App.—Houston [1st Dist.] 2006, no pet.), and Tex. R. Civ. P. 202.2(e))); *accord Akzo of Tobolowsky*, No. 05-19-00073-CV, 2020 Tex. App. LEXIS 8306, at *5–6, 2020 WL 6143676 (Tex. App.—Dallas Oct. 20, 2020, no pet.) (mem. op.); *Estate of Nicholas*, No. 14-19-00716-CV, 2020 Tex. App. LEXIS 2532, at *10–11 (Tex. App.—Houston [14th Dist.] Mar. 26, 2020, pet. denied) (mem. op.); *Rodriguez v. Cantu*, 581 S.W.3d 859, 867 (Tex. App.—Corpus Christi 2019, orig. proceeding); *In re Pickrell*, No. 10-17-00091-CV, 2017 Tex. App. LEXIS 3457, at *6, 2017 WL 1452851 (Tex. App.—Waco Apr. 19, 2017, orig. proceeding) (mem. op.); *Int'l Ass'n of Drilling Contrs. v. Orion Drilling Co.*, 512 S.W.3d 483, 491 (Tex. App.—Houston [1st Dist.] 2016, pet. denied); *In re Emergency Consultants, Inc.*, 292 S.W.3d 78, 79 (Tex. App.—Houston [14th Dist.] 2007, orig. proceeding).

[440] *In re East*, 476 S.W. 3d 61, 67 (Tex. App.—Corpus Christi 2014, orig. proceeding); *see City of Dall. v. City of Corsicana*, Nos. 10-14-00090-CV, 10-14-00171-CV, 2015 Tex. App. LEXIS 8753, at *11–12, 2015 WL 4985935 (Tex. App.—Waco Aug. 20, 2015, orig. proceeding) (mem. op.) ("We also disagree with Dallas's additional argument that we should address its merits-based arguments on why Navarro does not have a valid claim for tortious interference

Texas Rule 202 cannot be used to investigate a claim or suit against a healthcare provider before an expert report is filed.[441] Nor can it be used to obtain otherwise impermissible discovery in an existing action.[442] It also is difficult, if not impossible, to obtain a presuit deposition in connection with a trade-secret misappropriation claim. As explained by the Austin Court of Appeals:

> When the issue of discovery of trade secrets arises in the context of a [Texas R]ule 202 deposition request, it will be difficult—if not impossible—for a [Texas R]ule 202 petitioner relying on the investigatory purpose of [Texas R]ule 202 to meet his or her burden to establish the necessity of the information to adjudicate a claim or defense. This is because, by its very nature, a [Texas R]ule 202 proceeding to investigate claims does not involve the adjudication of any claim or defense. It involves only the investigation of potential claims. The standard for allowing discovery of trade secrets under *Bass*, *Bridgestone/Firestone*, and *Continental General Tire* requires a showing of necessity for the information to adjudicate existing claims or defenses. The trial court must weigh the degree of the requesting party's need for the information against the potential harm to the resisting party from disclosure. Thus, the balance is between the need for confidentiality versus the need to adjudicate existing disputes. The standard is not based on a potential litigant's desire to obtain confidential information merely to evaluate possible or suspected claims. If it were, business entities would have an extraordinary tool to obtain the trade secrets of their competitors whether or not they have a legitimate dispute with the competitor. We do not believe [Texas R]ule 202 was intended to be used this way.[443]

---

against Dallas. As we have noted, [Texas R]ule 202 'does not require a potential litigant to *expressly* state a viable claim before being permitted to take a pre-suit deposition.'" (quoting *In re Denton*, No. 10-08-00255-CV, 2009 Tex. App. LEXIS 1322, at *7, 2009 WL 471524 (Tex. App.—Waco Feb. 25, 2009, orig. proceeding) (mem. op.), *rev'd on other grounds*, 501 S.W.3d 71 (Tex. 2016) (orig. proceeding) (per curiam))). *But see Glassdoor, Inc. v. Andra Grp., L.P.*, 575 S.W.3d 523, 530 (Tex. 2019) (holding that a Texas Rule 202 petition was moot because the statute of limitations had run); *Estate of Tobolowsky*, No. 05-19-00073-CV, 2020 Tex. App. LEXIS 8306, at *5–6, 2020 WL 6143676 (Tex. App.—Dallas Oct. 20, 2020, no pet.) (mem. op.) (same).

441 *In re Jorden*, 249 S.W.3d 416, 418 (Tex. 2008) (orig. proceeding) (Section 74.351(s) of the Texas Civil Practice & Remedies Code "limits discovery in health-care lawsuits until the plaintiff serves an expert report summarizing how each defendant violated standards of care and caused the plaintiff injury. The issue here is whether that statute applies to presuit depositions authorized by Rule 202 of the Texas Rules of Civil Procedure. Because the statute prohibits 'all discovery' other than three exceptions—and [Texas] Rule 202 depositions are not listed among them—we hold the statute prohibits such depositions until after an expert report is served.").

442 *In re Hanover Ins. Co.*, No. 01-13-01066-CV, 2014 Tex. App. LEXIS 13930, at *9–11, 2014 WL 7474203 (Tex. App.— Houston [1st Dist.] Dec. 30, 2014, orig. proceeding) (mem. op.) (holding that Texas Rule 202 cannot be "used as a mechanism for obtaining third-party discovery that a party was unable to obtain in pending litigation under Texas Rule 176").

443 *In re Hewlett Packard*, 212 S.W.3d 356, 363 (Tex. App.—Austin 2006, orig. proceeding); *see In re Prairiesmarts LLC*, 421 S.W.3d 296, 305–06 & n.11 (Tex. App.—Fort Worth 2014, orig. proceeding) (holding that the trial court abused its discretion in allowing presuit discovery of trade secrets, but declining to hold that a Texas Rule 202 "petitioner can never obtain presuit discovery of trade secret information simply because a suit has not been filed" because Texas Rule 202.5 provides that "[t]he scope of discovery in depositions authorized

Texas courts are divided about whether the Texas Citizens Participation Act,[444] applies to a Texas Rule 202 petition.[445]

11-5:3.2 Where the Petition Must Be Filed

Under Texas Rule 202.2(b), the petition must be filed "in a proper court of any county." If suit is anticipated, such court is one "where venue of the anticipated action may lie[.]"[446] Otherwise, it is one "where the witness resides[.]"[447] The respondent can challenge venue,[448] and if such a challenge is made, the trial court must rule on the venue motion before it considers the merits of petition for a presuit deposition.[449] Review of a trial

---

by this rule is the same as if the anticipated suit or potential claim had been filed"); *In re Rockafellow*, No. 07-11-00066-CV, 2011 Tex. App. LEXIS 5495, at *10–14, 2011 WL 2848638 (Tex. App.—Amarillo July 19, 2011, orig. proceeding) (mem. op.) (holding that the trial court abused its discretion in allowing presuit discovery of trade secrets). *But see In re NCH Corp.*, No. 05-17-00360-CV, 2017 Tex. App. LEXIS 3656, at *1, 2017 WL 1536499 (Tex. App.—Dallas Apr. 25, 2017, orig. proceeding) (mem. op.) (denying mandamus relief even though "[r]elator argues that the documents and testimony sought include privileged trade secret materials").

444 Tex. Civ. Prac. & Rem. Code Ann. §§ 27.001–.011.

445 *Compare Hous. Tennis Ass'n v. Thibodeaux*, 602 S.W.3d 712, 718–19 (Tex. App.—Houston [14th Dist.] 2020, no pet.) (holding that the Texas Citizens Participation Act (the TCPA) does not apply to petitions seeking Texas Rule 202 pre-suit depositions because such proceedings are not "legal actions" as defined by the statute), *and Caress v. Fortier*, 576 S.W.3d 778, 781 (Tex. App.—Houston [1st Dist.] 2019, pet. denied) (same), *with In re Elliott*, 504 S.W.3d 455, 464 (Tex. App.—Austin 2016, no pet.) (holding that the TCPA applies to Texas Rule 202 petitions for pre-suit deposition, *and DeAngelis v. Protective Parents Coalition*, 556 S.W.3d 836, 849 (Tex. App.—Fort Worth 2018, no pet.) (same)

446 Tex. R. Civ. P. 202.2(b)(1); *see In re Doe*, 444 S.W.3d 603, 608 (Tex. 2014) (orig. proceeding) ("[A] proper court must be one with venue over an anticipated action, though if none is anticipated, the court must be in the county where the witness resides. Reynolds filed the petition in Harris County, which qualifies as a county 'where venue of the anticipated suit may lie' in light of the verified allegations that Brockman resided there" and because, under Tex. Civ. Prac. & Rem. Code § 15.017, a defamation suit may be filed "in the county in which the plaintiff resided at the time of the accrual of the cause of action[.]"); *In re Akzo Nobel Chem., Inc.*, 24 S.W.3d 919, 920 (Tex. App.—Beaumont 2000, orig. proceeding) ("A petition under [Texas] Rule 202 must be filed where venue of the anticipated suit may lie, if suit is anticipated; or where the witness resides, if no suit is yet anticipated.").

447 Tex. R. Civ. P. 202.2(b)(2); *In re Doe*, 444 S.W.3d 603, 608 (Tex. 2014) (orig. proceeding) ("[A] proper court must be one with venue over an anticipated action, though if none is anticipated, the court must be in the county where the witness resides."); *In re Akzo Nobel Chem., Inc.*, 24 S.W.3d 919, 920 (Tex. App.—Beaumont 2000, orig. proceeding) ("A petition under [Texas] Rule 202 must be filed . . . where the witness resides, if no suit is yet anticipated.").

448 *See In re Velvin Oil Co.*, No. 01-17-00384-CV, 2018 Tex. App. LEXIS 3198, at *10–11, 2018 WL 2107246 (Tex. App.—Houston [1st Dist.] May 8, 2018, orig. proceeding) (mem. op.) (conditionally granting mandamus petition in a case in which the trial court granted a petition for a presuit deposition without considering the respondent's venue motion); see Tex. R. Civ. P. 202.2(b) (providing that the petition for a presuit deposition "must . . . be filed in a proper court of any county: (1) where venue of the anticipated suit may lie, if suit is anticipated; or (2) where the witness resides, if no suit is yet anticipated.").

449 *In re Velvin Oil Co.*, No. 01-17-00384-CV, 2018 Tex. App. LEXIS 3198, at *10–11, 2018 WL 2107246 (Tex. App.—Houston [1st Dist.] May 8, 2018, orig. proceeding) (mem. op.) ("Once

court's failure to consider the venue motion before granting the petition is proper by means of a mandamus proceeding.[450]

In addition, the court must have subject-matter jurisdiction over the suit or claim,[451] the petitioner must have standing to bring the suit or claim,[452] and the "'potential claim

---

Velvin properly filed its motion to transfer venue and requested a hearing, the trial court was required to hear the motion before ruling on the merits of the case. Accordingly, it was an abuse of discretion for the trial court not to determine the motion to transfer before determining the [Texas] Rule 202 Petition.") (citations omitted).

[450] *In re Velvin Oil Co.*, No. 01-17-00384-CV, 2018 Tex. App. LEXIS 3198, at *10–11, 2018 WL 2107246 (Tex. App.—Houston [1st Dist.] May 8, 2018, orig. proceeding) (mem. op.) (conditionally granting mandamus petition in a case in which the trial court granted a petition for a presuit deposition without considering the respondent's venue motion).

[451] *In re City of Dall.*, 501 S.W.3d 71, 73 (Tex. 2016) (orig. proceeding) (per curiam) ("[A] party 'cannot obtain by [Texas] Rule 202 what it would be denied in the anticipated action.' Therefore, 'for a party to properly obtain [Texas] Rule 202 pre-suit discovery, the court *must* have subject-matter jurisdiction over the anticipated action.'" (quoting *In re Wolfe*, 341 S.W.3d 932, 933 (Tex. 2011) (orig. proceeding) (per curiam), and *In re DePinho*, 505 S.W.3d 621, 623 (Tex. 2016) (orig. proceeding) (per curiam))); *In re Doe*, 444 S.W.3d at 608 ("While [Texas] Rule 202 is silent on the subject, we think it implicit, as it has always been, that the court must [have] subject-matter jurisdiction over the anticipated action. The rule cannot be used, for example, to investigate a potential federal antitrust suit or patent suit, which can be brought only in federal court."); *City of Dall. v. Dall. Companion Animal Project (In re City of Dall.)*, No. 05-18-00453-CV, 2018 Tex. App. LEXIS 8787, at *17–18 (Tex. App.—Dallas Oct. 26, 2018, pet. dism'd) (mem. op.) ("A trial court can authorize a [Texas R]ule 202 deposition only if it has personal jurisdiction over the potential defendant, and the [Texas R]ule 202 petitioner has the burden to plead allegations showing personal jurisdiction over the potential defendant. In its amended [Texas R]ule 202 petition, DCAP alleged that it assisted the City by providing services and supplies to DAS, the City questioned DCAP's activities and required it to submit financial information to the City, a reporter with the DMN told DCAP a criminal investigation had been instituted by the City into DCAP's activities, and one or more persons leaked information regarding the investigation to the DMN and to DCAP's donors with the intent to 'smear' DCAP. We conclude these pleaded facts, if true, are sufficient to establish that potential third-party defendants, even if not residents of Texas, may have committed a tort in Texas and are therefore subject to personal jurisdiction in the trial court.") (citations omitted); *Estate of Nicholas*, No. 14-19-00716-CV, 2020 Tex. App. LEXIS 2532, at *10–15 (Tex. App.—Houston [14th Dist.] Mar. 26, 2020, pet. denied) (mem. op.) (holding that the trial court must have subject-matter jurisdiction over the anticipated suit and that a probate court had such jurisdiction because the petitioners sought to investigate their decedent's survival claims).

If the allegations in the Texas Rule 202 petition do not affirmatively demonstrate or negate the court's subject-matter jurisdiction, the petitioner should be given an opportunity to amend its petition. *Vestal v. Pistikopoulos,* Nos. 10-16-00034-CV, 10-16-00035-CV, 2016 Tex. App. LEXIS 7958, at *12, 2016 WL 4045081 (Tex. App.—Waco July 27, 2016, orig. proceeding) (mem. op.) ("[T]he Texas Supreme Court has stated that if allegations made in pleadings do not affirmatively demonstrate or negate the court's jurisdiction, as is the case here, the plaintiff, Pistikopoulos, should be given an opportunity to amend the pleadings. Accordingly, we reverse the trial court's denial of Vestal's plea to the jurisdiction and granting of Pistikopoulos's [Texas] Rule 202 petition and remand to the trial court to allow Pistikopoulos an opportunity to amend his [Texas] Rule 202 petition to avoid immunity or other undiscoverable issues.").

[452] *In re UBS Fin. Servs.*, No. 14-20-00087-CV, 2020 Tex. App. LEXIS 7972, at *4–6, 2020 WL 5902955 (Tex. App.—Houston [14th Dist.] Oct. 6, 2020, orig. proceeding) (mem. op.)

or suit' must be ripe"[453] and not moot.[454] For example, (1) where the claim or suit would be barred by the doctrines of sovereign, governmental, or judicial immunity[455] or by the exhaustion-of-administrative-remedies doctrine (i.e., where an administrative agency has exclusive jurisdiction over the subject matter of the dispute),[456] or

---

(holding that the trial court lacked subject-matter jurisdiction to grant a Texas Rule 202 petition because the petitioner lacked standing to bring the claim he sought to investigate); *In re Dolcefino Commc'ns, LLC,* No. 01-20-00382-CV, 2020 Tex. App. LEXIS 7362, at *2 (Tex. App.—Houston [1st Dist.] Sep. 10, 2020, orig. proceeding) (mem. op.) (same); *City of S.F. v. Exxon Mobil Corp.*, No. 02-18-00106-CV, 2020 Tex. App. LEXIS 5226, at *57 (Tex. App.—Fort Worth June 18, 2020, pet. filed) (mem. op.) (rejecting argument that the trial need only have personal jurisdiction over a potential witness, rather than the potential defendant, in ruling on a petition to take a presuit deposition: "[W]e conclude that the relevant personal-jurisdiction inquiry in a [Texas] Rule 202 proceeding is whether Texas has personal jurisdiction over a potential defendant. If not, a trial court has no discretion to grant a [Texas] Rule 202 petition. Thus, whether Texas has personal jurisdiction over a person or entity that is only a prospective witness is irrelevant."); *ShopStyle, Inc. v. rewardStyle, Inc.*, No. 05-19-00736-CV, 2020 Tex. App. LEXIS 5638, at *15 (Tex. App.—Dallas July 21, 2020, no pet.) (mem. op.) ("To authorize [a presuit] deposition, the court must have subject matter jurisdiction over the anticipated action and personal jurisdiction over the potential defendants. We conclude the trial court abused its discretion in granting rewardStyle's [Texas R]ule 202 petition because the record does not show the court had personal jurisdiction over the potential defendants.") (citations omitted).

453 *In re DePinho*, 505 S.W.3d 621, 624 (Tex. 2016) (orig. proceeding) (per curiam).

454 *Glassdoor, Inc. v. Andra Grp., L.P.*, 575 S.W.3d 523, 530 (Tex. 2019) (holding that the trial court lacked subject-matter jurisdiction over a Texas Rule 202 petition because the claim was moot as it was barred by limitations); *Estate of Tobolowsky,* No. 05-19-00073-CV, 2020 Tex. App. LEXIS 8306, at *5–6, 2020 WL 6143676 (Tex. App.—Dallas Oct. 20, 2020, no pet.) (mem. op.) (same); *In re Overhead Door Garage Door, LLC,* No. 07-18-00015-CV, 2018 Tex. App. LEXIS 1334, at *8, 2018 WL 934814 (Tex. App.—Amarillo Feb. 16, 2018, orig. proceeding) (mem. op.) (holding that a trial court abused its discretion in ordering a presuit deposition because the respondent filed lawsuit in federal court regarding the subject matter of the proposed deposition, thereby making the petition moot); *Tex. Lottery Comm'n v. Willis,* No. 03-10-00330-CV, 2011 Tex. App. LEXIS 5185, at *1–2 (Tex. App.—Austin July 6, 2011, orig. proceeding) (per curiam) (mem. op.) (dismissing the Texas Rule 202 petition as moot because the petitioner "has since filed suit against persons and entities he named in the [Texas R]ule 202 petition").

455 *Cooper v. Reynolds,* No. 02-18-00270-CV, 2019 Tex. App. LEXIS 7659, at *5, 2019 WL 4010220 (Tex. App.—Fort Worth Aug. 26, 2019, no pet.) (mem. op.) (affirming the trial court's dismissal of a petition for a presuit deposition of a magistrate because the magistrate had judicial immunity and because the petitioner failed to allege or prove any exception to any potential party's governmental immunity); *In re Dall. Cnty. Hosp. Dist.*, No. 05-14-00249-CV, 2014 Tex. App. LEXIS 3542, at *8–9, 2014 WL 1407415 (Tex. App.—Dallas Apr. 1, 2014, orig. proceeding) (mem. op.) ("The trial court abused its discretion in concluding that real party was entitled to discovery under [Texas] Rule 202 under the facts of this case because there was no evidence before the trial court that could provide a basis for concluding that real party's potential claim would not be barred by sovereign immunity."); *Combs v. Tex. Civil Rights Project*, 410 S.W.3d 529, 535 (Tex. App.—Austin 2013, pet. denied) ("[W]e conclude that [Texas R]ule 202 depositions may not be used solely to investigate potential claims that are otherwise barred by sovereign immunity.").

456 *In re Bailey-Newell,* No. 01-13-00783-CV, 2014 Tex. App. LEXIS 6663, at *8, 2014 WL 2779420 (Tex. App.—Dallas June 19, 2014, orig. proceeding) (mem. op.) ("Tang's contemplated retaliation claim under the Texas Labor Code would be subject to exhaustion of administrative

(2) where the subject matter of the presuit deposition is within valid arbitration clause,[457] the Texas Rule 202 petition must be denied. This is because "pre-suit discovery 'is not an end within itself'; rather, it 'is in aid of a suit which is anticipated' and 'ancillary to the anticipated suit.' To prevent an end-run around discovery limitations

---

remedies, and Tang cannot circumvent the statutorily required administrative procedures through the use of [Texas] Rule 202."). *But see In re Contractor's Supplies, Inc.*, No. 12-09-00231-CV, 2009 Tex. App. LEXIS 6396, at *9, 2009 WL 2488374 (Tex. App.—Tyler Aug. 17, 2009, orig. proceeding) (mem. op.) (holding the exhaustion-of-administrative-remedies doctrine did not preclude Texas Rule 202 depositions in a worker's compensation case because a Texas Rule 202 petition 'does not request final or even preliminary adjudication of the petitioner's claims' and therefore does not interfere with the exclusive jurisdiction of an administrative agency), *cited with approval* in *In re INVISTA S.a.r.l.*, No. 09-18-00351-CV, 2018 Tex. App. LEXIS 8962, at *8–9 (Tex. App.—Beaumont Nov. 1, 2018, orig. proceeding) (mem. op.).

In *City of Willow Park v. Squaw Creek Downs, L.P.*, 166 S.W.3d 336, 341 (Tex. App.—Fort Worth 2005, no pet.), the court declined to dismiss a Texas Rule 202 petition under the primary-jurisdiction doctrine:

> We reject the application of the primary jurisdiction doctrine in this case for three reasons. First, Squaw Creek's [Texas R]ule 202 petition, which simply asks for permission to take investigative depositions, does not raise a "complex problem" that requires the input of administrative "experts." Second, the [Texas R]ule 202 petition does not require the district court to interpret the "laws, rules, and regulations" of Willow Park, the Commission, or the water code. We find no provision in the water code equivalent to [Texas R]ule 202. The water code does not provide a mechanism for taking investigative depositions. Third, the fact that Squaw Creek seeks presuit discovery under [Texas R]ule 202 rather than final adjudication of its claims militates against application of the primary jurisdiction doctrine. Primary jurisdiction precludes a court from "finally adjudicating a claim until the agency has an opportunity to act on the matter." Squaw Creek does not seek final or even preliminary adjudication of its claims; rather, it seeks only to investigate potential claims. Under these circumstances, primary jurisdiction does not preclude the trial court from allowing Squaw Creek to take investigative depositions.

City of Willow Park v. Squaw Creek Downs, L.P., 166 S.W.3d 336, 341 (Tex. App.—Fort Worth 2005, no pet.) (citations omitted) (quoting *Subaru of Am., Inc. v. David McDavid Nissan, Inc.*, 84 S.W.3d 212, 221 (Tex. 2002)).

457 *In re Amarillo II Enters.*, No. 07-17-00005-CV, 2017 Tex. App. LEXIS 1000, at *5–9, 2017 WL 491938 (Tex. App.—Amarillo Feb. 3, 2017, orig. proceeding) (mem. op.) (holding that a Texas Rule 202 deposition cannot be taken if the potential claim or suit is subject to arbitration); *see Valerus Compression Servs., LP v. Woodcock (In re Valerus Compression Servs., LP)*, Nos. 14-14-00019-CV, 14-14-00042-CV, 2015 Tex. App. LEXIS 4647, at *8, 2015 WL 2169656 (Tex. App.—Houston [14th Dist.] May 7, 2015, orig. proceeding) (mem. op.) ("[A] trial court abuses its discretion when it defers a decision on a motion to compel arbitration until after a [Texas] Rule 202 deposition is conducted."); *In re Bill Heard Chevrolet, Ltd.*, No. 14-05-00744-CV, 2005 Tex. App. LEXIS 8838, at *1, 2005 WL 2787468 (Tex. App.—Houston [14th Dist.] Oct. 27, 2005, orig. proceeding) (mem. op.) (per curiam) (same); *In re MHI P'ship., Ltd.*, 7 S.W.3d 918, 923 (Tex. App.—Houston [1st Dist.] 1999, orig. proceeding) (same). *But see Patton Boggs LLP v. Moseley*, 394 S.W.3d 565, 572 (Tex. App.—Dallas 2011, orig. proceeding) (holding that the trial court has no jurisdiction to compel arbitration in connection with a petition for a presuit deposition).

that would govern the anticipated suit, [Texas] Rule 202 restricts discovery in depositions to 'the same as if the anticipated suit or potential claim had been filed.'"[458]

Moreover, a Texas Rule 202 petition becomes moot if, before the deposition, either the petitioner or respondent file a lawsuit regarding the subject matter of the deposition.[459]

Finally, the court must have personal jurisdiction over the potential defendant (i.e., the potential defendant must have sufficient minimum contacts with Texas for the exercise of such jurisdiction).[460] For that reason, the petition must contain "allegations showing personal jurisdiction over the defendant" even when "the potential defendant's identity is unknown and may even be impossible to ascertain."[461] Due to this requirement, Texas Rule 202 may be an ineffective mechanism for seeking the identity of persons engaging in conduct anonymously.

11-5:3.3 The Petition's Notice and Service

Because Texas Rule 202 requires a court order to take a presuit deposition, there must be a hearing on the petition: "At least 15 days before the date of the hearing on the petition, the petitioner must serve the petition and a notice of the hearing—in accordance with [Texas] Rule 21a—on all persons petitioner seeks to depose[.]"[462]

---

458 *In re Wolfe*, 341 S.W.3d 932, 933 (Tex. 2011) (quoting *Office Emps. Int'l Union Local 277 v. Sw. Drug Corp.*, 391 S.W.2d 404, 406 (Tex. 1965), and Tex. R. Civ. P. 202.5)); *In re Depinho*, 505 S.W.3d 621, 623 (Tex. 2016) (orig. proceeding) (per curiam) (quoting *In re Wolfe*, 341 S.W.3d 932, 933 (Tex. 2011), and holding that a presuit deposition is inappropriate when the trial court would lack subject-matter jurisdiction over the anticipated suit).

459 *In re Overhead Door Garage Door, LLC*, No. 07-18-00015-CV, 2018 Tex. App. LEXIS 1334, at *8, 2018 WL 934814 (Tex. App.—Amarillo Feb. 16, 2018, orig. proceeding) (mem. op.) (holding that a trial court abused its discretion in ordering a presuit deposition because the respondent filed lawsuit in federal court regarding the subject matter of the proposed deposition, thereby making the petition moot); *Tex. Lottery Comm'n v. Willis*, No. 03-10-00330-CV, 2011 Tex. App. LEXIS 5185, at *1–2 (Tex. App.—Austin July 6, 2011, orig. proceeding) (per curiam) (mem. op.) (dismissing the Texas Rule 202 petition as moot because the petitioner "has since filed suit against persons and entities he named in the [Texas R]ule 202 petition").

460 *In re Doe*, 444 S.W.3d 603, 608 (Tex. 2014) (orig. proceeding) (holding that to be a "proper court," the court must have personal jurisdiction over the potential defendant).

461 *In re Doe*, 444 S.W.3d 603, 610 (Tex. 2014) (orig. proceeding); *accord eBay Inc. v. Mary Kay Inc.*, No. 05-14-00782-CV, 2015 Tex. App. LEXIS 6563, at *8, 2015 WL 3898240 (Tex. App.—Dallas June 25, 2015, pet. denied) (mem. op.) ("We reject Mary Kay's contention that the allegations in its petition about the nature of its claims, as well as the fact that Mary Kay is based in Dallas County and eBay is available here, are sufficient to show the court had personal jurisdiction over the potential defendants. Mary Kay's petition does not allege any jurisdictional facts to establish personal jurisdiction over the anonymous eBay sellers. Because Mary Kay did not meet its burden, albeit a heavy one, to plead jurisdictional facts sufficient to establish the trial court had personal jurisdiction over the potential defendants and thus was a proper court, the trial court abused its discretion in granting Mary Kay's [Texas R]ule 202 petition.").

462 Tex. R. Civ. P. 202.3(a); *accord Glassdoor, Inc. v. Andra Grp., LP*, 560 S.W.3d 281, 286 (Tex. App.—Dallas 2017), *pet. dism'd as moot*, 575 S.W.3d 523 (Tex. 2019). If the petition and notice are filed electronically and the email address of the person being served is on file with the electronic filing manager, then the petition and notice "must be served electronically through the electronic filing manager" under Texas Rule 21a(a)(1). In all other

In addition, "if suit is anticipated," the petition and notice of hearing must also be served on "all persons petitioner expects to have interests adverse to petitioner's in the anticipated suit."[463] The petitioner can request a shorter notice period if "justice or necessity" so requires.[464]

If the petitioner does not know the names of the adverse persons, notice may be served by publication.[465] "Any interested party may move, in the proceeding or by bill of review, to suppress any deposition, in whole or in part, taken on notice by publication, and may also attack or oppose the deposition by any other means available."[466]

"A petition to take a deposition in anticipation of an application for probate of a will, and notice of the hearing on the petition, may be served by posting as prescribed by Section 33(f)(2) of the Probate Code [now Sections 51.002 and .003 of the Texas Estates Code]. The notice and petition must be directed to all parties interested in the testator's estate and must comply with the requirements of Section 33(c) of the Probate Code [now Section 51.053 of the Texas Estates Code] insofar as they may be applicable."[467] Posting, however, is not a favored service method because the service

---

circumstances, Texas Rule 21a(a)(2) allows service "in person, by mail, by commercial delivery service, by fax, by email, or by such other manner as the court in its discretion may direct."

[463] Tex. R. Civ. P. 202.3(a).

[464] Tex. R. Civ. P. 202.3(d) ("As justice or necessity may require, the court may shorten or lengthen the notice periods under this Rule and may extend the notice period to permit service on any expected adverse party.").

[465] Tex. R. Civ. P. 202.3(b)(1) governs service by publication and provides:

> Unnamed persons described in the petition whom the petitioner expects to have interests adverse to petitioner's in the anticipated suit, if any, may be served by publication with the petition and notice of the hearing. The notice must state the place for the hearing and the time it will be held, which must be more than 14 days after the first publication of the notice. The petition and notice must be published once each week for two consecutive weeks in the newspaper of broadest circulation in the county in which the petition is filed, or if no such newspaper exists, in the newspaper of broadest circulation in the nearest county where a newspaper is published.

Tex. R. Civ. P. 202.3(b)(1); *see Glassdoor, Inc. v. Andra Grp., LP*, 560 S.W.3d 281, 286 (Tex. App.—Dallas 2017) (Texas Rule 202.3(b)(1) "authorizes service by publication on '[u]named persons described in the petition whom the petitioner expects to have interests adverse to petitioner's in the anticipated suit, if any.'" (quoting Tex. R. Civ. P. 202.3(b)(1)), *pet. dism'd as moot*, 575 S.W.3d 523 (Tex. 2019)).

[466] Tex. R. Civ. P. 202.3(b)(2).

[467] Tex. R. Civ. P. 202.3(c).

Section 51.002 of the Texas Estates Code provides:

> (a) A writ or other process other than a citation or notice must be directed "To any sheriff or constable within the State of Texas."
>
> (b) Notwithstanding Subsection (a), a writ or other process other than a citation or notice may not be held defective because the process is directed to the sheriff or a constable of a named county if the process is properly served within that county by the sheriff or constable.

Tex. Est. Code § 51.002.

Section 51.003 of the Texas Estates Code provides:

> (a) A citation or notice must:

can be attacked on due process grounds. Accordingly, if the witnesses and potential adverse parties are known, they should be served as permitted by Texas Rule 21a.

Texas federal district courts have held that Texas Rule 202 petitions are not removable. A number of them have held that such petitions are not "civil actions" within the meaning of the removal statute, 28 U.S.C. § 1441.[468] And at least one federal district

---

(1) be directed to the person to be cited or notified;

(2) be dated;

(3) state the style and number of the proceeding;

(4) state the court in which the proceeding is pending;

(5) describe generally the nature of the proceeding or matter to which the citation or notice relates;

(6) direct the person being cited or notified to appear by filing a written contest or answer or to perform another required action; and

(7) state when and where the appearance or performance described by Subdivision (6) is required.

(b) A citation or notice issued by the county clerk must be styled "The State of Texas" and be signed by the clerk under the clerk's seal.

(c) A notice required to be given by a personal representative must be in writing and be signed by the representative in the representative's official capacity.

(d) A citation or notice is not required to contain a precept directed to an officer, but may not be held defective because the citation or notice contains a precept directed to an officer authorized to serve the citation or notice.

Tex. Est, Code § 51.003.

Finally, Section 51.053 of the Texas Estates Code provides:

(a) The county clerk shall deliver the original and a copy of a citation or notice required to be posted to the sheriff or a constable of the county in which the proceeding is pending. The sheriff or constable shall post the copy at the door of the county courthouse or the location in or near the courthouse where public notices are customarily posted.

(b) Citation or notice under this section must be posted for at least 10 days before the return day of the service, excluding the date of posting, except as provided by Section 51.102(b). The date of service of citation or notice by posting is the date of posting.

(c) A sheriff or constable who posts a citation or notice under this section shall return the original citation or notice to the county clerk and state the date and location of the posting in a written return on the citation or notice.

(d) The method of service prescribed by this section applies when a personal representative is required or permitted to post a notice. The notice must be:

(1) issued in the name of the representative;

(2) addressed and delivered to, and posted and returned by, the appropriate officer; and

(3) filed with the county clerk.

Tex. Est. Code § 51.053.

[468] *See, e.g.*, *In re Johnson*, No. 3:13-cv-00231, 2013 U.S. Dist. LEXIS 115908, at *4–7, 2013 WL 4459021 (S.D. Tex. Aug. 15, 2013) (mem. op.); *Sawyer v. E.I. du Pont de Nemours & Co.*, No. 06-1420, 2006 U.S. Dist. LEXIS 44026, at *6, 2006 WL 1804614 (S.D. Tex. June 28, 2006) (mem. op.); *Davidson v. S. Farm Bureau Cas. Ins. Co.*, No. H-05-03607, 2006

court has noted that, even if a Texas Rule 202 proceeding is a "civil action," it is not removable because it is not one over "which [the] district courts of the United States have original jurisdiction[.]"[469]

11-5:4 Hearing and Standards for the Order

To authorize a presuit deposition, the trial court *must* make one of two specific findings,[470] depending on whether the petition pertains to a deposition for an anticipated suit or a deposition to investigate a potential claim.

> If the petitioner requests a deposition to obtain testimony for use in an anticipated suit, the trial court must find that allowing the petitioner to take the requested deposition may prevent a failure or delay of justice. If the petitioner requests a deposition to investigate a potential claim, however, the trial court must find that the likely benefit of allowing the petitioner to take the requested deposition to investigate a potential claim outweighs the burden or expense of the procedure.[471]

U.S. Dist. LEXIS 40654, at *5–6, 2006 WL 1716075 (S.D. Tex. June 19, 2006) (mem. op.); *McCrary v. Kan. City S. R.R.*, 121 F. Supp. 2d 566, 569 (E.D. Tex. 2000). ***But see L&S Tri Star Invs., LLC v. Certain Underwriters at Lloyd's***, No. SA-18-CA-1278-OLG (HJB), 2019 U.S. Dist. LEXIS 106101, at *4–6, 2019 WL 2565286 (W.D. Tex. 2019) (holding that defendants properly removed a petition to take a presuit deposition under 9 U.S.C. § 205, which provides that "[w]here the subject matter of an action or proceeding pending in a State court relates to an arbitration agreement . . . falling under the [Convention for the Recognition and Enforcement of Foreign Arbitral Awards], the defendant or the defendants may, at any time before the trial thereof, remove such action or proceeding to the district court of the United States for the district and division embracing the place where the action or proceeding is pending.").

469 *Mayfield-George v. Tex. Rehab. Comm'n*, 197 F.R.D. 280, 283 (N.D. Tex. 2000); ***see In re Enable Commc'n, Inc.***, 256 F.R.D. 527, 531 (N.D. Tex. 2009) (doubting a federal court's ability to manage a Texas Rule 202 petition after removal because the *Erie* doctrine mandates the application of federal procedural law and no federal rule is comparable to Texas Rule 202).

470 Tex. R. Civ. P. 202.4(a) ("The court must order a deposition to be taken if, but only if, it finds that: (1) allowing the petitioner to take the requested deposition may prevent a failure or delay of justice in an anticipated suit; or (2) the likely benefit of allowing the petitioner to take the requested deposition to investigate a potential claim outweighs the burden or expense of the procedure."); ***accord In re Pickrell***, No. 10-17-00091-CV, 2017 Tex. App. LEXIS 3457, at *7, 2017 WL 1452851 (Tex. App.—Waco Apr. 19, 2017, orig. proceeding) (mem. op.); *Glassdoor, Inc. v. Andra Grp., LP*, 560 S.W.3d 281, 286 (Tex. App.—Dallas 2017), *pet. dism'd as moot*, 575 S.W.3d 523 (Tex. 2019).

471 *In re Dall. Cnty., Hosp. Dist.*, No. 05-14-00249-CV, 2014 Tex. App. LEXIS 3542, at *4, 2014 WL 1407415 (Tex. App.—Dallas Apr. 1, 2014, orig. proceeding) (mem. op.) (citation omitted); ***accord In re Noriega***, No. 05-14-00307-CV, 2014 Tex. App. LEXIS 3462, at *4–5, 2014 WL 1415109 (Tex. App.—Dallas Mar. 28, 2014, orig. proceeding) (mem. op.); *Patton Boggs LLP v. Moseley*, 394 S.W.3d 565, 570 (Tex. App. Dallas 2011, orig. proceeding); *In re Denton*, No. 10-08-00255-CV, 2009 Tex. App. LEXIS 1322, at *6–7, 2009 WL 471524 (Tex. App.—Waco Feb. 25, 2009, orig. proceeding) (mem. op.); *In re Legate*, No. 04-10-00874-CV, 2011 Tex. App. LEXIS 8107, at *3–4, 2011 WL 4828192 (Tex. App.—San Antonio Oct. 12, 2011, orig. proceeding) (mem. op.).

The requisite finding must be express and cannot be implied from the record.[472] Accordingly, the mere fact that the prospective deponent does not oppose the order is insufficient.[473]

To make the requisite finding, a hearing on the petition is required at which "the petitioner must present evidence to meet its burden to establish the facts necessary to obtain the deposition."[474] In this regard, neither the verified petition nor the petitioner's

---

[472] *In re Does*, 337 S.W.3d 862, 865 (Tex. 2011) (orig. proceeding) (per curiam) ("Nor can the required findings be implied in support of the trial court's order compelling discovery."); *In re Jorden*, 249 S.W.3d 416, 423 (Tex. 2008) (orig. proceeding) ("[P]resuit depositions are available under [Texas] Rule 202 only if a trial court makes one of the two findings [under Texas R]ule 202.4(a).]"); *In re City of Tatum*, 578 S.W.3d 203, 208 (Tex. App.—Tyler 2019, orig. proceeding) (holding that the findings cannot be implied and that "[a] trial court has no discretion to order presuit discovery without the required findings and abuses its discretion by doing so"); *In re Cauley*, 437 S.W.3d 650, 657 (Tex. App.—Tyler 2014, orig. proceeding) ("Presuit discovery under [Texas] Rule 202 expressly requires that discovery be ordered 'only if' the required findings are made. Thus, we are not permitted to deem the findings implied from support in the record. The trial court has no discretion to order presuit discovery without the required finding and abuses its discretion when it does so." (quoting *In re Does*, 337 S.W.3d 862, 865 (Tex. 2011) (orig. proceeding) (per curiam))); *In re Dall. Cnty. Hosp. Dist.*, No. 05-14-00249-CV, 2014 Tex. App. LEXIS 3542, at *4, 2014 WL 1407415 (Tex. App.—Dallas Apr. 1, 2014) (mem. op.) (same).

[473] *In re Does*, 337 S.W.3d 862, 865 (Tex. 2011) (orig. proceeding) (per curiam) ("PRK argues that compliance with [Texas] Rule 202 was excused because of its agreement with Google. It is true that '[e]xcept where specifically prohibited, the procedures and limitations set forth in the rules pertaining to discovery may be modified in any suit by agreement of the parties. . . .' But PRK and Google were not the only parties to the proceeding. [Texas] Rule 202.3(a) requires that 'all persons petitioner expects to have interests adverse to petitioner's in the anticipated suit' be served with the petition and given notice of hearing. PRK asserted that relators would be defendants in the anticipated lawsuit, and by their motions to quash, relators made an appearance in the proceeding. PRK and Google could not modify the procedures prescribed by [Texas] Rule 202 by an agreement that did not include relators." (citations omitted) (quoting Tex. R. Civ. P. 191.1)); *In re City of Tatum*, 567 S.W.3d 800, 807–08 (Tex. App.—Tyler 2018, orig. proceeding) ("When a petitioner requests a deposition to obtain testimony for use in an anticipated suit, the trial court must find that allowing the petitioner to take the requested deposition may prevent a failure or delay of justice. If a petitioner requests a deposition to investigate a potential claim, the trial court must find that the likely benefit of allowing the petitioner to take the requested deposition to investigate a potential claim outweighs the burden or expense of the procedure. Respondent made neither finding in his order granting Peterson's [Texas] Rule 202 request. Peterson maintains that this failure is excused because the City did not object to the absence of findings. We disagree. The Texas Supreme Court has made clear that [Texas] Rule 202.4 findings cannot be implied from the record. And, under the plain language of [Texas] Rule 202.4, Respondent 'must order a deposition to be taken if, but only if' he makes certain findings before granting relief under either subsection of [Texas] Rule 202.1. Accordingly, these findings are mandatory. Because the requirements of [Texas] Rule 202.4 are mandatory, the City's failure to object in the trial court does not result in waiver." (citations omitted) (quoting Tex. R. Civ. P. 202.4(a))).

[474] *In re INVISTA S.a.r.l.*, No. 09-18-00351-CV, 2018 Tex. App. LEXIS 8962, at *11–12 (Tex. App.—Beaumont Nov. 1, 2018, orig. proceeding) (mem. op.) (quoting *In re East*, 476 S.W.3d 61, 68 (Tex. App.—Corpus Christi 2014, orig. proceeding))); *In re City of Tatum*, 567 S.W.3d 800, 805–06 (Tex. App.—Tyler 2018, orig. proceeding) ("Peterson failed to meet her burden of introducing evidence to support her request for presuit depositions under [Texas]

attorney's arguments constitute evidence.[475] An order granting a presuit deposition is reviewed for an abuse of discretion.[476]

In addition to containing the requisite findings, the order granting a presuit deposition "must state whether a deposition will be taken on oral examination or written questions."[477] It "may also state the time and place at which a deposition will be taken. If the order does not state the time and place at which a deposition will be taken, the petitioner must notice the deposition as required by [Texas] Rules 199 or 200."[478] Because Texas Rule 202.4(b) incorporates the rules regarding oral depositions and depositions on written questions, the order can allow the deposition notice to include a production request.[479]

To protect against any unfairness or undue burden on the deponent, Texas Rule 202.4(b) requires the order to "contain any protections the court finds necessary or appropriate to protect the witness or any person who may be affected by the procedure."[480] Accordingly, the trial court has broad discretion to control the deposition's

---

Rule 202. . . . If Peterson sought presuit depositions for use in an anticipated suit, she was required to show that allowing her to take the requested depositions may prevent a failure or delay of justice in an anticipated suit. If she sought presuit depositions to investigate a potential claim or suit, she was required to show that the likely benefit of allowing her to take the requested depositions to investigate a potential claim outweighs the burden or expense of the procedure. Aside from counsel's arguments at the hearing on Peterson's petition and reliance on the petition itself, Peterson presented no testimony or other competent evidence to support her request. Peterson maintains that she offered her verified petition and met her evidentiary burden. However, pleadings, such as the petition itself, are not generally competent evidence to prove the facts alleged in them, even when sworn or verified. Nor could Respondent take judicial notice of the truth of the allegations in the pleadings.") (citations omitted).

[475] *In re INVISTA S.a.r.l.*, No. 09-18-00351-CV, 2018 Tex. App. LEXIS 8962, at *11–12 (Tex. App.—Beaumont Nov. 1, 2018, orig. proceeding) (mem. op.) ("Sworn, verified pleadings are generally not competent evidence to prove the facts asserted in the pleading."); *In re City of Tatum*, 567 S.W.3d 800, 805–06 (Tex. App.—Tyler 2018, orig. proceeding) (same); *In re Pickrell*, No. 10-17-00091-CV, 2017 Tex. App. LEXIS 3457, at *9–11, 2017 WL 1452851 (Tex. App.—Waco Apr. 19, 2017, orig. proceeding) (mem. op.) (same); *In re Dall. Cnty. Hosp. Dist.*, No. 05-14-00249-CV, 2014 Tex. App. LEXIS 3542, at *5–6, 2014 WL 1407415 (Tex. App.—Dallas Apr. 1, 2014, orig. proceeding) (mem. op.) (holding that neither verified pleadings nor the counsel's argument is competent evidence to provide the basis a Texas Rule 202 presuit deposition); *In re Noriega*, No. 05-14-00307-CV, 2014 Tex. App. LEXIS 3462, at *5–6, 2014 WL 1415109 (Tex. App.—Dallas Mar. 28, 2014, orig. proceeding) (mem. op.) (same); *In re Contractor's Supplies, Inc.*, No. 12-09-00231-CV, 2009 Tex. App. LEXIS 6396, at *15–16, 2009 WL 2488374 (Tex. App.—Tyler Aug. 17, 2009, orig. proceeding) (mem. op.) (same); *In re Rockafellow*, No. 07-11-00066-CV, 2011 Tex. App. LEXIS 5495, at *13, 2011 WL 2848638 (Tex. App.—Amarillo July 19, 2011, orig. proceeding) (mem. op.) (same).

[476] *City of Dall. v. City of Corsicana*, Nos. 10-14-00090-CV, 10-14-00171-CV, 2015 Tex. App. LEXIS 8753, at *14 n.6, 2015 WL 4985935 (Tex. App.—Waco Aug. 20, 2015, orig. proceeding) (mem. op.) ("A [Texas R]ule 202 order authorizing pre-suit depositions is reviewable for abuse of discretion."), *rev'd on other grounds*, 501 S.W.3d 71 (Tex. 2016) (orig. proceeding) (per curiam); *Patton Boggs LLP v. Moseley*, 394 S.W.3d 565, 568–69 (Tex. App.—Dallas 2011, orig. proceeding) (same).

[477] Tex. R. Civ. P. 202.4(b).

[478] Tex. R. Civ. P. 202.4(b).

[479] See cases cited in note 435.

[480] Tex. R. Civ. P. 202.4(b); *accord Combs v. Tex. Civil Rights Project*, 410 S.W.3d 529, 531 (Tex. App.—Austin 2013, pet. denied) ("[T]he trial court's order granting the request must

conduct and scope,[481] and defense counsel should attempt to have the order limit the deposition's scope to the petition's specific allegations.

11-5:5 The Deposition's Taking and Use

Except as otherwise provided in Texas Rule 202, presuit depositions "are governed by the rules applicable to depositions of nonparties in a pending suit."[482] Thus, when the order granting the Texas Rule 202 petition does not specify the deposition's time and place, the witness must be served with both a deposition notice and a subpoena a reasonable time before the deposition is taken, specifying a place permitted by Texas Rule 199.2(b)(2).

To prevent an end-run around discovery limitations that would govern an actual lawsuit, Texas Rule 202.5 provides that the scope of discovery in presuit depositions is "the same as if the anticipated suit or potential claim had been filed."[483] In other words, Texas Rule 192.3 governs the scope of discovery in presuit depositions.

A presuit deposition "may be used in a subsequent suit as permitted by the rules of evidence[.]"[484] Under Texas Rule of Evidence 801(e)(3), a deposition taken in the "same proceeding" is exempt from the hearsay rule irrespective of the witness's availability.[485] Same proceeding includes "a proceeding in a different court, but involving the same subject matter and the same parties or their representatives or successors in interest."[486] In addition to the admissibility standards in Texas Rule of Evidence 801(e)(3), a party's deposition is admissible against the party as a party

---

contain any protections it finds necessary or appropriate to protect the witness or any person who may be affected by the procedure."); *In re Fernandez*, No. 04-99-00841-CV, 1999 Tex. App. LEXIS 9553, at *5, 1999 WL 1327603 (Tex. App.—San Antonio Dec. 30, 1999, orig. proceeding) (not designated for publication) (same); *Valley Baptist Med. Ctr. v. Gonzalez*, 18 S.W.3d 673, 678 (Tex. App.—Corpus Christi 1999) (same), *vacated as moot*, 33 S.W.3d 821 (Tex. 2000).

481 *See In re Fernandez*, No. 04-99-00841-CV, 1999 Tex. App. LEXIS 9553, at *7–8, 1999 WL 1327603 (Tex. App.—San Antonio Dec. 30, 1999, orig. proceeding) (not designated for publication) (holding that the trial court, in ordering a presuit deposition to perpetuate testimony under Texas Rule 202 in connection with an anticipated suit by a frail, ill nursing-home patient against a nursing home for injuries suffered when she was abused or assaulted by the nursing home's staff, did not abuse its discretion in ordering the patient's nursing home's attorneys to consult with the patient's treating physician regarding the conditions under which she could be deposed); *Valley Baptist Med. Ctr. v. Gonzalez*, 18 S.W.3d 673, 676 (Tex. App.—Corpus Christi 1999) (suggesting that, because Texas Rule 202, "essentially is an equitable procedure," a trial court could order a bond to protect the deponent from costs), *vacated as moot*, 33 S.W.3d 821 (Tex. 2000).

482 Tex. R. Civ. P. 202.5.

483 Tex. R. Civ. P. 202.5; *accord In re Wolfe*, 341 S.W.3d 932, 933 (Tex. 2011) (orig. proceeding) (per curiam).

484 Tex. R. Civ. P. 202 cmt. 2 to 1999 change.

485 Tex. R. Evid. 801(e)(3) ("A statement that meets the following conditions is not hearsay: . . . In a civil case, the statement was made in a deposition taken in the same proceeding. 'Same proceeding' is defined in [Texas] Rule of Civil Procedure 203.6(b). The deponent's unavailability as a witness is not a requirement for admissibility.").

486 Tex. R. Civ. P. 203.6(b).

admission[487] and a nonparty's deposition from another proceeding is admissible if it meets the requirements of the hearsay rule's former-testimony exception (i.e., (1) the deponent is unavailable as a witness,[488] and (2) the party against whom the deposition testimony is offered, or a person with a similar interest, had an opportunity and similar motive to develop the testimony by direct, cross, or redirect examination).[489]

Accordingly, if a presuit deposition results in a lawsuit involving the same subject matter and parties to the Texas Rule 202 petition (i.e., the lawsuit is the "same proceeding"), the deposition likely can be used in the lawsuit under Texas Rule of Evidence 801(e)(3) irrespective of whether it is the deposition of a party or a nonparty. Conversely, if the lawsuit is not the "same proceeding" because it involves a different subject matter or parties, the presuit deposition can be used only if the requirements of the former-testimony exception to the hearsay rule are met, against a party as an admission, or to impeach a nonparty's testimony.

Even if the deposition is otherwise admissible, the trial court has discretion "to restrict or prohibit" its use in a later lawsuit "to protect a person who was not served with notice of the deposition from any unfair prejudice or to prevent abuse of [Texas Rule 202]."[490]

---

[487] *Dillee v. Sisters of Charity of the Incarnate Word Health Care Sys.*, 912 S.W.2d 307, 310 n.6 (Tex. App.—Houston [14th Dist.] 1995, no writ) (holding that the deposition of a party from an earlier action was admissible under former Texas Rule of Evidence 801(e)(2) as an admission by a party opponent); *accord* Tex. R. Evid. 801(e)(2) ("A statement that meets the following conditions is not hearsay: . . . The statement is offered against an opposing party and: (A) was made by the party in an individual or representative capacity; (B) is one the party manifested that it adopted or believed to be true; (C) was made by a person whom the party authorized to make a statement on the subject; (D) was made by the party's agent or employee on a matter within the scope of that relationship and while it existed; or (E) was made by the party's coconspirator during and in furtherance of the conspiracy.").

[488] Tex. Evid. R. 804(a) provides:

> A declarant is considered to be unavailable as a witness if the declarant:
>
> (1) is exempted from testifying about the subject matter of the declarant's statement because the court rules that a privilege applies;
>
> (2) refuses to testify about the subject matter despite a court order to do so;
>
> (3) testifies to not remembering the subject matter;
>
> (4) cannot be present or testify at the trial or hearing because of death or a then existing infirmity, physical illness, or mental illness; or
>
> (5) is absent from the trial or hearing and the statement's proponent has not been able, by process or other reasonable means, to procure the declarant's attendance or testimony.
>
> But this subdivision (a) does not apply if the statement's proponent procured or wrongfully caused the declarant's unavailability as a witness in order to prevent the declarant from attending or testifying.

Tex. R. Evid. 804(a).

[489] Tex. R. Evid. 804(b)(1).

[490] Tex. R. Civ. P. 202.5.

11-5:6 Appellate Review

An order under Texas Rule 202 allowing or denying a presuit deposition from a third party against which suit is not contemplated is a final appealable order.[491] Such an order, however, is not a final appealable order by a party against whom suit is

[491] *E.g., In re City of Tatum*, 578 S.W.3d 203, 208 (Tex. App.—Tyler 2019, orig. proceeding) ("'Presuit deposition orders are appealable only if sought from someone against whom suit is not anticipated[.]' Accordingly, an improper order under [Texas] Rule 202 may be set aside by mandamus when sought from an anticipated defendant." (quoting *In re Jorden*, 249 S.W.3d 416, 419 (Tex. 2008) (orig. proceeding))); *City of Dall. v. Russell (In re City of Dall.)*, No. 05-18-00289-CV, 2018 Tex. App. LEXIS 8784, at *4–5 (Tex. App.—Dallas Oct. 26, 2018, no pet.) (mem. op.) ("When a pre-suit deposition is sought from an anticipated defendant such orders have been considered ancillary to the subsequent suit. As a result, those orders are interlocutory, i.e., they are neither final nor appealable. However, a trial court order granting a petition involving a requested pre-suit deposition of a potential or anticipated defendant, i.e., person against whom a suit is contemplated, is subject to mandamus review. The determination of whether an order granting a [Texas R]ule 202 petition is an interlocutory or final order is based on whether the deponent is a potential or anticipated defendant or a third party, not whether the petition was filed under [Texas R]ule 202.1(a) or 202.1(b). Further, 'just as a summary judgment as to one of multiple parties does not make [an] order granting summary judgment appealable because it is only an interlocutory order, [] the denial of [a] Texas R]ule 202 [petition] when a suit or claim is contemplated against one of several deponents is also an interlocutory order and not appealable.'" (citations omitted) (quoting *Watson v. Magnablend, Inc.*, No. 10-12-00145-CV, 2013 Tex. App. LEXIS 4942, at *2, 2013 WL 1697350 (Tex. App.—Waco Apr. 18, 2013, no pet.) (mem. op.))); *City of Dall. v. Dall. Companion Animal Project (In re City of Dall.)*, No. 05-18-00453-CV, 2018 Tex. App. LEXIS 8787, at *8–9 (Tex. App.—Dallas Oct. 26, 2018, pet. dism'd) (mem. op.) ("[T]he supreme court has concluded: 'Presuit deposition orders are appealable only if sought from someone against whom suit is not anticipated; when sought from an anticipated defendant (as here), such orders have been considered ancillary to the subsequent suit, and thus neither final nor appealable.' In determining whether the City is a potential defendant, we look to the substance of DCAP's pleading. In its amended [Texas R]ule 202 petition, DCAP requested the deposition so that it could investigate potential claims against the City and other parties. Further, at the hearing on the amended [Texas R]ule 202 petition, DCAP stated that it believed it might have viable claims against the City. Accordingly, because the City is a potential defendant in a possible subsequent suit, the trial court's order granting the requested deposition is ancillary to that possible suit against the City and is neither final nor appealable." (citations omitted) (quoting *In re Jorden*, 249 S.W.3d 416, 419 (Tex. 2008) (orig. proceeding))); *Sossamon v. Bardin*, No. 11-12-00164-CV, 2012 Tex. App. LEXIS 6818, at *2, 2012 WL 3537817 (Tex. App.—Eastland Aug. 16, 2012, no pet.) (mem. op.) (per curiam) ("A ruling on a [Texas] Rule 202 petition constitutes a final, appealable order only if the petition seeks discovery from a third party against whom a suit is not contemplated, but a [Texas] Rule 202 ruling is interlocutory and does not constitute a final, appealable order if discovery is sought from a person against whom litigation is either pending or contemplated."); *IFS Sec. Grp., Inc. v. Am. Equity Ins.*, 175 S.W.3d 560, 563 (Tex. App.—Dallas 2005, no pet.) (same); *Thomas v. Fitzgerald*, 166 S.W.3d 746, 747 (Tex. App.—Waco 2005, no pet.) (same).

anticipated.[492] Consequently, such a person should challenge the order by filing a mandamus petition, which will be reviewed for an abuse of discretion.[493]

11-6 Signing, Certification, and Use of Oral Depositions—Texas Rule 203

TEXT OF RULE 203

RULE 203. SIGNING, CERTIFICATION AND USE OF ORAL AND WRITTEN DEPOSITIONS

203.1. Signature and Changes

(a) **Deposition transcript to be provided to witness.** The deposition officer must provide the original deposition transcript to the witness for examination and signature. If the witness is represented by an attorney at the deposition, the deposition officer must provide the transcript to the attorney instead of the witness.

(b) **Changes by witness; signature.** The witness may change responses as reflected in the deposition transcript by indicating the desired changes, in writing, on a separate sheet of paper, together with a statement of the reasons for making the changes. No erasures or obliterations of any kind may be made to the original deposition transcript. The witness must then sign the transcript under oath and return it to the deposition officer. If the witness does not return the transcript to the deposition officer within 20 days of the date the transcript was provided to the witness or the witness's attorney, the witness may be deemed to have waived the right to make the changes.

(c) **Exceptions.** The requirements of presentation and signature under this subdivision do not apply:

(1) if the witness and all parties waive the signature requirement;

(2) to depositions on written questions; or

(3) to nonstenographic recordings of oral depositions.

---

492 *In re Hewlett Packard*, 212 S.W.3d 356, 360 (Tex. App.—Austin 2006, orig. proceeding) ("[A]n order pursuant to [Texas R]ule 202 allowing pre-suit discovery incident to a contemplated lawsuit against the party from whom the discovery is sought is not a final, appealable order."); *IFS Sec. Grp., Inc. v. Am. Equity Ins.*, 175 S.W.3d 560, 563 (Tex. App.—Dallas 2005, no pet.) (same); *Thomas v. Fitzgerald*, 166 S.W.3d 747 (Tex. App.—Waco 2005, no pet.) (same).

493 *In re Elliott*, 504 S.W.3d 455, 459–60 (Tex. App.—Austin 2016, orig. proceeding); *In re Baxter*, No. 05-16-01174-CV, 2016 Tex. App. LEXIS 11328, at *3, 2016 WL 6099547 (Tex. App.—Dallas Oct. 19, 2016, orig. proceeding) (mem. op.) ("The trial court order granting the [Texas R]ule 202 petition in this case, involving a requested pre-suit deposition of a person against whom a suit is contemplated, is subject to mandamus review."); *In re Cauley*, 437 S.W.3d 650, 655 (Tex. App.—Tyler 2014, orig. proceeding) ("An order allowing a presuit deposition pursuant to [Texas] Rule 202 is not a final, appealable order. Therefore, there is no adequate remedy by appeal, and mandamus is the proper avenue to challenge the trial court's order granting Efficien's petition for Cauley's presuit deposition. Consequently, our focus in this proceeding is whether Cauley has shown an abuse of discretion by the trial court.") (citations omitted); *In re Prairiesmarts LLC*, 421 S.W.3d 296, 304 (Tex. App.—Fort Worth 2014, orig. proceeding) (same); *In re Hewlett Packard*, 212 S.W.3d 356, 360 (Tex. App.—Austin 2006, orig. proceeding) (same).

203.2. Certification

The deposition officer must file with the court, serve on all parties, and attach as part of the deposition transcript or non-stenographic recording of an oral deposition a certificate duly sworn by the officer stating:

(a) that the witness was duly sworn by the officer and that the transcript or non-stenographic recording of the oral deposition is a true record of the testimony given by the witness;

(b) that the deposition transcript, if any, was submitted to the witness or to the attorney for the witness for examination and signature, the date on which the transcript was submitted, whether the witness returned the transcript, and if so, the date on which it was returned.

(c) that changes, if any, made by the witness are attached to the deposition transcript;

(d) that the deposition officer delivered the deposition transcript or nonstenographic recording of an oral deposition in accordance with Rule 203.3;

(e) the amount of time used by each party at the deposition;

(f) the amount of the deposition officer's charges for preparing the original deposition transcript, which the clerk of the court must tax as costs; and

(g) that a copy of the certificate was served on all parties and the date of service.

203.3. Delivery

(a) **Endorsement; to whom delivered.** The deposition officer must endorse the title of the action and "Deposition of (name of witness)" on the original deposition transcript (or a copy, if the original was not returned) or the original nonstenographic recording of an oral deposition, and must return:

   (1) the transcript to the party who asked the first question appearing in the transcript, or

   (2) the recording to the party who requested it.

(b) **Notice.** The deposition officer must serve notice of delivery on all other parties.

(c) **Inspection and copying; copies.** The party receiving the original deposition transcript or non-stenographic recording must make it available upon reasonable request for inspection and copying by any other party. Any party or the witness is entitled to obtain a copy of the deposition transcript or non-stenographic recording from the deposition officer upon payment of a reasonable fee.

203.4. Exhibits

At the request of a party, the original documents and things produced for inspection during the examination of the witness must be marked for identification by the deposition officer and annexed to the deposition transcript or non-stenographic recording. The person producing the materials may produce copies instead of originals if the party gives all other parties fair opportunity at the deposition to compare the copies with the originals. If the person offers originals rather than copies, the deposition officer must, after the conclusion of the deposition, make copies to be attached to the original deposition transcript or non-stenographic recording, and then return the originals to the person who produced them. The person who produced the originals must preserve them for hearing or trial and make them available for inspection or copying by any other party upon seven days' notice. Copies annexed to the original deposition transcript or nonstenographic recording may be used for all purposes.

203.5. Motion to Suppress

A party may object to any errors and irregularities in the way the testimony is transcribed, signed, delivered, or otherwise dealt with by the deposition officer by filing a motion to suppress all or part of the deposition. If the deposition officer complies with [Texas] Rule 203.3 at least one day before the case is called to trial, with regard to a deposition transcript, or 30 days before the case is called to trial, with regard to a non-stenographic recording, the party must file and serve a motion to suppress before trial commences to preserve the objections.

203.6. Use

(a) **Non-stenographic recording; transcription.** A non-stenographic recording of an oral deposition, or a written transcription of all or part of such a recording, may be used to the same extent as a deposition taken by stenographic means. However, the court, for good cause shown, may require that the party seeking to use a non-stenographic recording or written transcription first obtain a complete transcript of the deposition recording from a certified court reporter. The court reporter's transcription must be made from the original or a certified copy of the deposition recording. The court reporter must, to the extent applicable, comply with the provisions of this rule, except that the court reporter must deliver the original transcript to the attorney requesting the transcript, and the court reporter's certificate must include a statement that the transcript is a true record of the non-stenographic recording. The party to whom the court reporter delivers the original transcript must make the transcript available, upon reasonable request, for inspection and copying by the witness or any party.

(b) **Same proceeding.** All or part of a deposition may be used for any purpose in the same proceeding in which it was taken. If the original is not filed, a certified copy may be used. "Same proceeding" includes a proceeding in a different court but involving the same subject matter and the same parties or their representatives or successors in interest. A deposition is admissible against a party joined after the deposition was taken if:

   (1) the deposition is admissible pursuant to Rule 804(b)(1) of the Rules of Evidence, or

   (2) that party has had a reasonable opportunity to redepose the witness and has failed to do so.

(c) **Different proceeding.** Depositions taken in different proceedings may be used as permitted by the Rules of Evidence.

11-6:1 2021 Amendments to the Texas Rules of Civil Procedure

The 2021 amendments to the Texas Rules of Civil Procedure did not modify Texas Rule 203 regarding signing, certification, and use of oral and written deposition in any respect.

11-6:2 Presentment, Signature, and Changes

Texas Rule 203.1 requires the deposition officer (i.e., the person recording the deposition, such as the court reporter) to provide the original transcript of an oral deposition to the witness for signature.[494] If the witness was represented by any attorney at the deposition, the transcript must be provided to the attorney.[495] The Rule does not apply (1) when the "witness and all parties waive the signature requirement,[496] (2) to depositions on written questions,[497] or (3) to nonstenographic recordings."[498] If the oral deposition was recorded both stenographically and nonstenographically (e.g., videotaped), the witness (or the witness's attorney) is presented only with the transcript for signature and change.

Once the oral-deposition transcript is presented to the witness or the witness's attorney, the witness can make changes to his answers as reflected in the transcript. The changes must be made on a separate sheet of paper (i.e., an "errata sheet") because Texas Rule 203.1(b) prohibits "erasures or obliterations of any kind . . . to the original deposition transcript." The witness must give a reason for *each* change.[499] A court should strike any change for which no reason is given.[500]

---

494 Tex. R. Civ. P. 203.1(a).

495 Tex. R. Civ. P. 203.1(a).

496 Tex. R. Civ. P. 203.1(c)(1).

497 Tex. R. Civ. P. 203.1(c)(2).

498 Tex. R. Civ. P. 203.1(c)(3).

499 Tex. R. Civ. P. 203.1(b); *cf. E.I. du Pont de Nemours & Co. v. Kolon Indus.*, 277 F.R.D. 286, 295 (E.D. Va. 2011) ("But, the mere statement of some reason does not alone satisfy the rule. That is because courts require that each proffered change be accompanied by a specific reason that explains the nature of, and the need to make, the change."); *Holland v. Cedar Creek Min., Inc.*, 198 F.R.D. 651, 653 (S.D.W. Va. 2001) ("The witness is also plainly bound by the Rule to state specific reasons for each change."); *Duff v. Lobdell-Emery Mfg. Co.*, 926 F. Supp. 799, 804 (N.D. Ind. 1996) ("The Rule is not onerous . . . but there must be a reason for every change."); *Lugtig v. Thomas*, 89 F.R.D. 639, 641 (N.D. Ill. 1981) ("[A]fter each change, the deponent must state the specific reason for that particular change.").

500 *Cf. EBC, Inc. v. Clark Bldg. Sys.*, 618 F.3d 253, 266 (3d Cir. 2010) ("Courts have found that the failure to provide a statement of reasons alone suffices to strike a proposed change. We agree with these courts. If the party or deponent proffering changes in the form or substance of a deposition transcript fails to state the reasons for the changes, the reviewing court may appropriately strike the errata sheet.") (footnote omitted) (citations omitted); *Blount v. Stanley Eng'g Fastening*, No. 5:19-CV-00109-JRW-LLK, 2020 U.S. Dist. LEXIS 155013, at *6, 2020 WL 5038522 (W.D. Ky. Aug. 25, 2020) (striking Plaintiff's changes to his deposition testimony because he "failed to provide any reason for them" as required by Federal Rule 30(e)(1).); *Travelers Indem. Co. v. Attorney's Title Ins. Fund, Inc.*, No. 2:13-cv-670-FtM-38CM, 2016 U.S. Dist. LEXIS 29397, at *13–15, 2019 WL 354881 (M.D. Fla. Mar. 7, 2016) ("Courts have found that the failure to provide a statement of reasons alone suffices as grounds to strike an errata sheet. It is not enough for a deponent to provide no reasons at all but to claim that the reasons are 'either explicit or reasonably implied from the circumstances.' As the Court of Appeals for the Ninth Circuit has explained, '[a] statement of reasons explaining corrections is an important component of errata submitted pursuant to [Federal Rule] 30(e), because the statement permits an assessment concerning whether the alterations have a legitimate purpose.' Moreover, '[j]ust as a court may disregard objections to discovery requests first advanced in a response to a motion to compel, a court may strike an errata sheet that fails to state the reasons for each change, even if the party offers reasons for the changes in responding to the motion to strike.'

There are three general types of deposition changes: (1) form ones that correct misspellings, typographical errors, and transcription errors, (2) "fill-in-the-blank" ones that provide additional information that the witness agreed to provide during the deposition, and (3) substantive ones that either wholly change an answer or contradict the original answer (e.g., changing a "no" to a "yes" or *vice versa*). Substantive changes are clearly permitted by Texas Rule 203. This is because nothing in Texas Rule 203.1(b) places any limitation on the type of change that can be made by the witness. Rather, it simply provides that the "witness may change the responses as reflected in the deposition transcript by indicating the desired changes." Nor does the Rule permit the trial court to examine the sufficiency, reasonableness, or legitimacy of the reasons for the changes—even if the given reasons are unconvincing. This means that the witness can change his or her deposition testimony carte blanche, and changes of any nature, no matter how considerable or fundamental, are permitted, even if the changes are wholly inconsistent with, or contradictory to, the original testimony.[501]

Here, it is undisputed that the untimely errata sheet does not include reasons for any of the changes made to Ms. Vesely's testimony. . . . The Court finds that the errata sheet fails to meet [Federal] Rule 30(e)'s procedural requirement in its failure to include any reasons for the changes made. The untimeliness of the errata sheet coupled with its failure to include any reasons for the changes made are sufficient grounds to strike the errata by Ms. Vesey." (quoting *Norelus v. Denny's, Inc.*, 628 F.3d 1270, 1305 (11th Cir. 2010) (Tjoflat, J., dissenting), *Hambleton Bros. Lumber Co. v. Balkin Enters., Inc.*, 397 F.3d 1217, 1224–25 (9th Cir. 2005), and *Maronda Homes, Inc. v. Progressive Express Ins. Co.*, No. 6:14-cv-1287-Orl-31TBS, 2015 U.S. Dist. LEXIS 89227, at *5, 2015 WL 4716108 (M.D. Fla. July 9, 2015))); *Kouassi v. W. Ill. Univ.*, No. 13-cv-1265, 2015 U.S. Dist. LEXIS 64926, at *8–9, 2015 WL 4464544 (C.D. Ill. May 18, 2015) ("The Court, however, will not consider Dr. Kouassi's corrections because he did not offer them in a manner that complies with [Federal] Rule 30(e) . . . . [T]o change deposition testimony in form or substance, deponents must satisfy a number of procedural hurdles. Among them, and one that trips Dr. Kouassi, is the requirement that deponents provide a statement of reasons for necessary changes. General reasons will not suffice; courts require that deponents submit a reason for every change they would like made to a deposition transcript. Here, rather than providing specific reasons for each requested change to the deposition, Plaintiff has made a blanket assertion that the deposition transcript does not accurately reflect the answers that he provided. In certain places of the transcript, where Plaintiff has identified minor transcription errors that do not change the substance of his answers, the Court has little doubt that his requested changes are well-taken. Yet, in these places, Plaintiff fails to state a reason even though the Rule requires that he provide one."); *E.I. du Pont de Nemours & Co. v. Kolon Indus.*, 277 F.R.D. 286, 295 (E.D. Va. 2011) ("The first relevant procedural requirement at issue here is found in [Federal] Rule 30(e)(1)(B) which requires the deponent to 'sign a statement listing the changes and reasons for making them.' It is, of course, clear that, if the deponent does not provide any reasons for a change, then the Rule is violated and that procedural defect alone renders the errata sheet improper.").

501 *Texaco, Inc. v. Pursley*, 527 S.W.2d 236, 242 (Tex. Civ. App.—Eastland 1975, writ ref'd n.r.e.) (holding that a deponent can make substantive changes to his deposition); *see Wohlstein v. Aliezer*, 321 S.W.3d 765, 771–72 (Tex. App.—Houston [14th Dist.] 2010, no pet.) ("[E]ven were we to read that portion of the deposition as some sort of binding admission, Wohlstein clarified that testimony through an errata sheet that accompanied the signature page to his deposition. Noting he had misunderstood counsel's questions, Wohlstein corrected that testimony to read, 'It is my claim.' Therefore, that equivocal testimony, later revised, cannot form the basis for summary judgment.").

Federal Rule 30(e)(1) governs changes to oral-deposition transcripts and provides, in relevant part: "On request by the deponent or a party before the deposition is completed, the deponent must be allowed 30 days after being notified by the officer that the transcript or recording is available in which (A) to review the transcript or recording; and (B) if there are changes in form or substance, to sign a statement listing the changes and the reasons for making them." Fed. R. Civ. P. 30(e)(1). Federal courts are divided about whether the Rule allows the deponent to make substantive changes to the deponent's testimony. *E.g.*, ***Frank v. Costco Wholesale Corp.***, No. CV 18-4532 (DRH) (AKT), 2020 U.S. Dist. LEXIS 225577, at *3–4, 2020 WL 7060142 (E.D.N.Y. Nov. 30, 2020) ("Although the Circuits are split with regard to the scope of permissible changes which may be made to a deposition transcript, the Second Circuit has 'allowed deponents to make any change, in form or substance, to their deposition transcript.' . . . Having reviewed the transcript excerpts and the errata sheet, the Court here finds that witness Fazio did provide a reason for each change, albeit a one-word rationale: 'clarification.' The Court points out that the changes on the errata sheet in certain instances are more than a clarification—they essentially add testimony. However, under the law in this Circuit, this errata sheet is permissible and will not be stricken." (quoting *N. Trade U.S., Inc. v. Guinness Bass Imp. Co.*, No. 3:03-CV-1892, 2006 U.S. Dist. LEXIS 54435, at *5, 2006 WL 2263885 (D. Conn. Aug. 7, 2006))); ***Hernandez v. Rush Enters.***, No. 4:19-cv-638, 2020 U.S. Dist. LEXIS 209860, at *2–4, 2020 WL 6581874 (E.D. Tex. Nov. 10, 2020) ("'The Fifth Circuit has not ruled on the scope of permissible substantive corrections to a deposition under [Federal] Rule 30(e),' and 'federal courts are split over the scope of permissible changes that can be made pursuant to [Federal] Rule 30(e),' 'The majority of federal courts place no limit on the nature of the changes a witness may make to the substance of his testimony.' These courts 'generally rely on the plain meaning of the language in [Federal] Rule 30(e)(1)(B) and the availability of corrective mechanisms to prevent abuses.' But '[a] growing minority of courts takes a more restrictive approach[,] . . . permit[ting] a deponent to correct only typographic and transcription errors.' Courts propounding this view are generally concerned with parties 'generat[ing] from whole cloth a genuine issue of material fact (or eliminat[ing] the same) simply by re-tailoring sworn deposition testimony to his or her satisfaction.'" (citations omitted) (quoting *Minshall v. Hartman Equine Reprod. Ctr., P.A.*, No. 4:15-CV-00764-ALM, 2016 U.S. Dist. LEXIS 159067, at *2–3, 2016 WL 6804863 (E.D. Tex. Nov. 17, 2016), Christopher Macchiaroli & Danielle Tarin, *Rewriting the Record: A Federal Court Split on the Scope of Permissible Changes to A Deposition Transcript*, 3 Fed. Cts. L. Rev. 1, 2 (2009), *Raytheon Co. v. Indigo Sys. Corp.*, No. 4:07-CV-109, 2009 U.S. Dist. LEXIS 12558, at *6–7, 2009 WL 424773 (E.D. Tex. Feb. 18, 2009), *Holden v. Ill. Tool Works, Inc.*, No. CIV.A. H-06-3958, 2007 U.S. Dist. LEXIS 94470, at *8, 2007 WL 4591752 (S.D. Tex. Dec. 27, 2007), and *EBC, Inc. v. Clark Bldg. Sys., Inc.*, 618 F.3d 253, 267–68 (3d Cir. 2010))); ***Walkingstick v. Simmons Bank***, No. 6:19-03184-CV-RK, 2020 U.S. Dist. LEXIS 219468, at *2–3 (W.D. Mo. Nov. 23, 2020) ("'Many courts read this language broadly to allow a deponent to make any changes to the testimony, as long as the alterations satisfy the procedural requirements of the Rule.' However, '[a] minority, but rapidly expanding, number of courts holds the contrary: that [Federal] Rule 30(e) does not allow a deponent to make substantive or contradictory changes to prior sworn testimony.' 'These cases typically allow only corrections of court reporter errors, whether they be in form or substance, or changes that do not contradict earlier testimony.' The Eighth Circuit has not directly addressed this issue. The Court here agrees with the cases holding limitations exist for [Federal] Rule 30(e). As other courts have said, depositions are not take-home exams, and a deponent should not be able to materially alter their testimony after the fact and most likely with the direct assistance of counsel. Such would transform live deposition testimony into another version of written discovery and thwart the purposes of depositions." (quoting *Cham v. McNeilus Truck & Mfg., Inc.*, No. CV 11-2569 (DWF/JJG), 2012 WL 12873768, at *2 (D. Minn. July 9, 2012))); ***Blount v. Stanley Eng'g Fastening***, No. 5:19-CV-00109-JRW-LLK, 2020 U.S. Dist. LEXIS 155013, at *6, 2020 WL 5038522 (W.D. Ky. Aug. 26, 2020) ("A majority of courts in the Sixth Circuit [hold] that errata sheets can only

The witness, however, cannot delete or change the questions asked during the deposition.[502]

If, however, substantive changes make the deposition incomplete or useless without further testimony,[503] the party who took the deposition should be allowed to reopen the deposition to ask questions that are "made necessary by the changed answers, questions about the reasons the changes were made, and questions about where the changes originated, whether with the deponent or with his attorney."[504] In addition, if the witness is a party, a court may be able to order the party to pay the costs, including

---

be used to correct typographic and transcription errors, not to make substantive changes to deposition testimony.").

[502] *Cf. Kocurek v. Frank's Casing Crew & Rental Tools, LLC*, No. 6:16-CV-00543, 2017 U.S. Dist. LEXIS 84190, at *7, 2017 WL 2406987 (W.D. La. May 31, 2017) ("While [Federal] Rule 30(e) permits a deponent to revise her testimony, it does not permit a deponent to delete questions asked during the deposition. In this case, the plaintiffs seek to delete not only Ms. Kocurek's response to the question asked but also the next question and her response to it. This Court finds that the plain language of [Federal] Rule 30(e) does not contemplate the deletion of questions asked during the deposition.").

[503] *Cf. Aldapa v. Fowler Packing Co.*, No. 1:15-cv-00420-DAD-SAB, 2016 U.S. Dist. LEXIS 35522, at *28, 2016 WL 8731316 (E.D. Cal. Mar. 18, 2016) ("[I]t is clear that a deposition may be reopened where the changed answers result in the deposition being incomplete without additional testimony."); *Bay State HMO Mgmt. v. Tingley Sys.*, 152 F. Supp. 2d 95, 120 (D. Mass. 1995) ("The standard to reopen a deposition is whether the changes contained in the errata sheets "make the deposition incomplete or useless without further testimony." (quoting *Sanford v. CBS, Inc.*, 594 F. Supp. 713, 715 (N.D. Ill. 1984))); *Lugtig v. Thomas*, 89 F.R.D. 639, 642 (N.D. Ill. 1981) (same); *see Knoth v. Keith*, No. 5:18-cv-49-DCB-MTP, 2020 U.S. Dist. LEXIS 179972, at *1 n.2 (S.D. Miss. Sept. 30, 2020) ("Courts that have allowed substantive changes under [Federal] Rule 30(e)—including this Court—have employed remedial measures to limit the potential for abuse, including reopening the deposition for limited purposes and requiring the deponent to pay the costs of reopening the deposition."); *Ruiz v. Safeco Ins. Co.*, No. 18-21036-CV, 2019 U.S. Dist. LEXIS 37208, at *9, 2019 WL 11504701 (S.D. Fla. Mar. 8, 2019) ("[T]here are several procedural safeguards in place to protect a party staring down the barrel of an errata sheet. The original testimony may remain part of the record and can be read at trial for impeachment purposes. Or the court may reopen a deposition to allow for further cross examination of the deponent concerning the changes in testimony.") (citation omitted); *Branford v. Wash. Cnty.*, No. 3:17-cv-94-SI, 2018 U.S. Dist. LEXIS 81607, at *6, 2018 WL 2221674 (D. Or. May 15, 2018) ("When the deponent has made extensive or substantial changes to his or her testimony, the court may allow the deposition to be reopened (or a second deposition taken) so that the opposing party may thoroughly explore the reasons for the changes. Indeed, a court may even require the party who changed his or her deposition testimony to pay the expenses of the other side that are incurred in reopening the deposition (or taking a second deposition.") (citation omitted).

[504] *Lugtig v. Thomas*, 89 F.R.D. 639, 642 (N.D. Ill. 1981); *accord Reilly v. TXU Corp.*, 230 F.R.D. 486, 491 (N.D. Tex. 2005) ("[I]n light of the number and significance of Plaintiffs' changes, the Court finds that reopening the deposition is an appropriate remedy. Consistent with the case law on point, the reopening should be limited in scope. Defendants may inquire about the reasons for the changes and the source of the changes, such as whether they came from Plaintiff himself or his counsel. In addition, Defendants may also ask-follow-up questions to the changed responses. Plaintiff, as the party making the 111 changes, will be responsible for costs and attorney's fees."). See also cases cited in note 503.

reasonable attorneys' fees, incurred in connection with the second deposition.[505] Finally, the original answers to the deposition questions remain part of the record and either can be used to impeach the witness at trial or can be read into evidence. This is because nothing in Texas Rule 203.1(b)'s language requires or implies that the original answers are to be stricken when changes are made and because under Texas Rule of Evidence 804, such testimony is an admissible admission by a party-opponent.[506]

---

505 Federal courts almost uniformly require this. *E.g.*, *Walker v. George Koch Sons, Inc.*, No. 2:07cv274 KS-MTP, 2008 U.S. Dist. LEXIS 81919, at *8, 2008 WL 4371372 (S.D. Miss. Sept. 18, 2008) ("These courts that interpret [Federal] Rule 30(e) broadly generally have adopted remedial measures to limit the potential for abuse. Such measures include reopening the deposition for limited purposes, requiring the deponent to pay the costs of reopening his deposition, and ordering that the original and changed answers, as well as the reasons for the changes, remain in the record and may be used during summary judgment and/or at trial."); *Reilly v. TXU Corp.*, 230 F.R.D. 486, 491 (N.D. Tex. 2005) ("Plaintiff, as the party making the 111 changes, will be responsible for costs and attorney's fees."); *Sanford v. CBS, Inc.*, 594 F. Supp. 713, 715 (N.D. Ill. 1984) ("In this case, Jackson has made numerous changes in his deposition, many of them differing significantly from his original testimony. . . . Should plaintiff choose to reopen the deposition, defendants will bear the related costs and attorney's fees."). See also cases cited in notes 503 and 504.

Neither Texas Rule 215, which governs sanctions and discovery abuse, nor any other Texas discovery rule specifically allows a trial court to order a witness, whose substantive changes to a deposition require his or her re-deposition, to pay the cost of the second deposition. *See In re Prince*, No. 14-06-00895-CV, 2006 Tex. App. LEXIS 10558, at *12, 2006 WL 3589484 (Tex. App.—Houston [14th Dist.] Dec. 12, 2006, orig. proceeding) (mem. op.) ("[A] court's power to impose sanctions on non-parties is limited to its contempt power."); *see also In re Berry*, 578 S.W.3d 173, 180 (Tex. App.—Corpus Christi 2019, orig. proceeding) ("[W]e observe that the Texas Rules of Civil Procedure generally treat nonparties differently from parties or those subject to a party's control as may be seen with respect to, e.g., the locations for deposition, sanctions, and compelling discovery. Non-party witnesses stand in a different position before the court than do parties to the litigation, over whom the court has both personal and subject matter jurisdiction.") (citations omitted). Texas Rule 215.3, however, allows a trial to sanction a ***party*** "abusing the discovery process in seeking, making or resisting discovery" by "charging all or any portion of the expenses of discovery or taxable court costs or both against the disobedient party[.]" Tex. R. Civ. P. 215.3. If a party's substantive changes to his or her deposition transcript require a second deposition, there certainly has been a sufficient abuse of the discovery process to allow a trial court to order the party to pay the expenses incurred by the opposing party in connection with the second deposition.

506 *Cf. Podell v. Citicorp Diners Club*, 112 F.3d 98, 103 (2d Cir. N.Y. 1997) ("At the same time, when a party amends his testimony under [Federal] Rule 30(e), 'the original answer to the deposition questions will remain part of the record and can be read at the trial.' 'Nothing in the language of [Federal] Rule 30(e) requires or implies that the original answers are to be stricken when changes are made.' This Court has recognized that because 'any out-of-court statement by a party is an admission,' a deponent's 'original answer should [be] admitted [into evidence]' even when he amends his deposition testimony—with the deponent 'of course . . . free to introduce the amended answer and explain the reasons for the change.'" (quoting *Lugtig v. Thomas*, 89 F.R.D. 639, 641 (N.D. Ill. 1981), and *Usiak v. N.Y. Tank Barge Co.*, 299 F.2d 810 (2d Cir. 1962))); *Branford v. Wash. Cnty.*, No. 3:17-cv-94-SI, 2018 U.S. Dist. LEXIS 81607, at *5–6, 2018 WL 2221674 (D. Or. May 15, 2018) (same); *Ruiz v. Safeco Ins. Co.*, No. 18-21036-CV, 2019 U.S. Dist. LEXIS 37208, at *9 (S.D. Fla. Mar. 8, 2019) ("[T]here are several procedural safeguards in place to protect a party staring down the barrel of an errata sheet. The original testimony may remain part of the record and can be read at trial

The witness must sign the transcript, as well as the errata sheet, and return them to the deposition officer within twenty days after the transcript was provided to the witness or the witness's attorney.[507] Because Texas Rule 203.1(b) provides that a failure to return the transcript within the twenty-day period "may be deemed" a waiver of "the right to make the changes," the trial court has discretion to allow changes to be made after the twenty-day period if the late changes do not prejudice any party to the action.[508] It appears that the party objecting to the change's admissibility has the burden to establish that it was prejudiced by the untimely change.[509]

---

for impeachment purposes.") (footnote omitted); ***Orchestrate HR, Inc. v. Trombetta***, No. 3:13-CV-2110-KS, 2017 U.S. Dist. LEXIS 7984, at *31, 2016 WL 5942223 (N.D. Tex. Jan. 20, 2017) (mem. op.) ("Defendants ask that reference to any timely revised video deposition testimony be excluded. While this Court takes a broad approach in allowing the revising of deposition testimony, as a safeguard, it allows for the original answers to be read at trial. As such, Defendants' Motion In Limine will be denied as to this point.") (citation omitted); ***Maharaj v. Geico Cas. Co.***, 996 F. Supp. 2d 1303, 1312 (S.D. Fla. 2014) (same); ***Foutz v. Town of Vinton***, 211 F.R.D. 293, 295 (W.D. Va. 2002) (same).

One Texas case has held that a trial court has discretion to exclude the original testimony under Texas Rule of Evidence 403 if its probative value is substantially outweighed by the danger of unfair prejudice, confusing the issues, misleading the jury, undue delay, or needlessly presenting cumulative evidence. ***Ramsey v. Cravey***, No. 04-03-00342-CV, 2004 Tex. App. LEXIS 5724, at *3–5, 2004 WL 1453455 (Tex. App.—San Antonio June 30, 2004, pet. denied) (mem. op.). Such exclusion should be the exception rather than the rule.

[507] Tex. R. Civ. P. 203.1(b).

[508] ***Dickerson v. State Farm Lloyd's Inc.***, No. 10-11-00071-CV, 2011 Tex. App. LEXIS 6061, at * 39–41, 2011 WL 3334964 (Tex. App.—Waco Aug. 3, 2011, pet. denied) (mem. op.) ("[E]ven though it is undisputed that appellees did not return the revised deposition transcript to the deposition officer within the twenty-day deadline, it was within the discretion of the trial court to accept the changes or conclude that appellees waived the right to make the tendered changes. . . . Should it believe that a party's changes would inflict harm or prejudice on opposing parties, the trial court has the discretion to conclude that such changes were waived.").

Unlike Texas Rule203.1(b), Federal Rule 30(e) gives a federal trial court no discretion to allow late changes to a deposition transcript. *E.g.*, ***Joan Cravens, Inc. v. Deas Constr. Inc.***, No. 1:15-cv-385-KS-MTP, 2016 U.S. Dist. LEXIS 137645, at *8–9 (S.D. Miss. 2016) ("This Court agrees with other courts which have held that '[t]here are no exceptions provided in [Federal] Rule 30(e) to the thirty-day time frame for making changes to deposition testimony.' A deponent who wishes to utilize the privilege of [Federal] Rule 30(e) must strictly comply with the Rule's requirements." (quoting ***In re Kugel Mesh Hernia Repair Patch Litig.***, No. 07-1842ML, 2010 U.S. Dist. LEXIS 16538, at *13–14, 2008 WL 2420997 (D.R.I. Feb. 23, 2010))); ***Griswold v. Fresenius USA***, 978 F. Supp. 718, 722 (N.D. Ohio 1997) (Federal "Rule 30(e) permits a deponent to amend his deposition only within thirty days after receiving notice that the transcript is available; that date has passed with respect to the deposition at issue. Therefore, Plaintiff's corrections to his October 15, 1996 deposition must be stricken.").

[509] ***Dickerson v. State Farm Lloyd's Inc.***, No. 10-11-00071-CV, 2011 Tex. App. LEXIS 6061, at *42, 2011 WL 3334964 (Tex. App.—Waco Aug. 3, 2011, pet. denied) (mem. op.) ("Based on our reading of [Texas R]ule 203.1, we cannot agree with appellants' insistence that Laura and Miguel were duty-bound to provide an excuse to explain the delay. To endorse appellants' argument would be to add language to [Texas R]ule 203.1(b) which does not exist. We decline to do so.") (citations omitted).

The witness's failure to sign the transcript, however, has no consequence. Under Texas Rule 203.1(b), an unsigned transcript may be certified and used to the same extent as a signed one.[510]

11-6:3 Certification

For all types of depositions, the deposition officer "must file with the court, serve on all parties, and attach as part of the deposition transcript or nonstenographic recording of an oral deposition a certificate duly sworn by the officer"[511] stating:

(a) that the witness was duly sworn by the officer and that the transcript or nonstenographic recording of the oral deposition is a true record of the testimony given by the witness;

(b) that the deposition transcript, if any, was submitted to the witness or to the attorney for the witness for examination and signature, the date on which the transcript was submitted, whether the witness returned the transcript, and if so, the date on which it was returned.

(c) that changes, if any, made by the witness are attached to the deposition transcript;

(d) that the deposition officer delivered the deposition transcript or nonstenographic recording of an oral deposition in accordance with [Texas] Rule 203.3;

(e) the amount of time used by each party at the deposition;

(f) the amount of the deposition officer's charges for preparing the original deposition transcript, which the clerk of the court must tax as costs; and

(g) that a copy of the certificate was served on all parties and the date of service.[512]

Although Texas Rule 203.2 refers to "deposition officer" in the singular, there may be two deposition officers if the deposition was recorded both stenographically and nonstenographically. In such a case, the court reporter and the person recording the deposition nonstenographically (e.g., the videographer) must each certify the

---

[510] Tex. R. Civ. P. 203.2(b); *Marty's Food & Wine, Inc. v. Starbucks Corp.*, No. 05-01-0008-CV, 2002 Tex. App. LEXIS 7672, at *11, 2002 WL 31410923 (Tex. App. Dallas—Oct. 28, 2002, no pet.) (mem. op.) ("Marty's objected that Shapiro had not signed the deposition and that the excerpts should not be allowed because twenty days had not elapsed since the deposition was taken to allow for any corrections by the witness. 'Mere lack of signature will not justify suppression of a deposition, even when timely motion is made, unless the reasons for not signing impugn the verity or reliability of the deposition.' No allegation was made that the deposition was unreliable. Therefore, the trial court did not err in overruling Marty's objection to the use of Shapiro's deposition." (citation omitted) (quoting *Hill v. Rich*, 522 S.W.2d 597, 600 (Tex. Civ. App.—Austin 1975, writ ref'd n.r.e.))); *Klorer v. Block*, 717 S.W.2d 754, 757 (Tex. App.—San Antonio 1986, writ ref'd n.r.e.) ("It is settled law that the absence of the signature alone is not grounds for suppressing a deposition. 'It is not the mere lack of signature which justifies suppression, but reasons which may impugn the verity or reliability of the deposition.'" (quoting *Bell v. Linehan*, 500 S.W.2d 228, 230 (Tex. Civ. App.—Texarkana 1973, writ ref'd n.r.e))).

[511] Tex. R. Civ. P. 203.2.

[512] Tex. R. Civ. P. 203.2.

recording for which he or she is responsible. But the parties can agree to designate one of them as the deposition officer taking the deposition's official record, relieving the other one of the certification requirement.[513]

As noted above, Texas Rule 203.2(f) requires the deposition officer's certificate to state the cost for "preparing the original deposition transcript," which the clerk of the court must tax as costs. Because the Rule does not mention the cost of a deposition's nonstenographic recording, a question exists regarding whether such costs are taxable ones if the deposition is noticed for nonstenographic recording only as permitted by Texas Rule 199.1(c). If a deposition is noticed only for nonstenographic recording, Texas Rule 199.1(c) permits any other party to notice it for another method of recording (e.g., stenographic recording) at that *party's expense* unless otherwise ordered by the court.[514] Because the Rule does not require the original noticing party to pay the cost of the deposition's nonstenographic recording, arguably its cost is a taxable one.

Whether this is the case is unclear because Section 31.007(b) of the Texas Civil Practice and Remedies Code, which defines taxable recoverable costs, does not specifically provide for the recovery of costs for nonstenographic deposition recordings.[515] The majority of the Texas courts of appeals to have considered the issue have held that the costs of nonstenographic deposition recordings (i.e., videotapes) are not recoverable under the statute.[516]

11-6:4 Delivery

"The deposition officer must endorse the title of the action and 'Deposition of (name of witness)' on the original deposition transcript (or a copy, if the original was not

---

[513] Tex. R. Civ. P. 191.1.

[514] Tex. R. Civ. P. 199.1(c).

[515] "[F]ees of the court reporter for the original of stenographic transcripts necessarily obtained for use in the suit" and "such other costs and fees as may be permitted by these Rules and state statutes" are recoverable. Tex. Civ. Prac. & Rem. Code § 37.007(b)(2), (4).

[516] *Compare Lion Copolymer Holdings, LLC v. Lion Polymers, LLC*, No. 01-17-00671-CV, 2019 Tex. App. LEXIS 2222, at *48–49, 2019 WL 1285115 (Tex. App.—Houston [1st Dist.] Mar. 21, 2019) (mem. op.) ("[T]o the extent that the trial court's award includes fees for copies of deposition transcripts, we note that section 31.007(b) [of the Texas Civil Practice and Remedies Code] expressly limits recovery of costs to the fees of the court reporter for the original of stenographic transcripts necessarily obtained for use in the suit" and does not allow for the recovery of nonstenographic recordings), *rev'd on other grounds*, 2020 Tex. LEXIS 1157, 2020 WL 7413725 (Tex. Dec. 18, 2020), *Waste Mgmt. of Tex. v. Tex. Disposal Sys. Landfill*, No. 03-10-00826-CV, 2014 Tex. App. LEXIS 12391, at *12 (Tex. App.—Austin Nov. 14, 2014, no pet.) (mem. op.) ("The costs for video depositions or copies of depositions or transcripts, however, are not recoverable as court costs."), *Gumpert v. ABF Freight Sys., Inc.*, 312 S.W.3d 237, 242 (Tex. App.—Dallas 2010, no pet.) (holding that "because no statute or rule authorizes the recovery of the costs to videotape a deposition or obtain a copy of a deposition transcript," those items are not recoverable costs), *and Shaikh v. Aerovias De Mex.*, 127 S.W.3d 76, 82 (Tex. App.—Houston [1st Dist.] 2003, no pet.) ("[T]he rule providing for the taxing the costs for depositions does not include taxing the cost of copies of depositions. . . . The copies of deposition transcripts, videotapes, and litigation documents listed in Aeromexico's Bill of Costs are not required by law and are part of the expenses of litigation."), *with Crescendo Invs. v. Brice*, 61 S.W.3d 465, 480–81 (Tex. App.—San Antonio 2001, pet. denied) (holding that certified copies of depositions can be taxed as costs).

returned) or the original nonstenographic recording of an oral deposition[.]"[517] The officer must return the oral-deposition transcript to the party "who asked the first question appearing in the transcript."[518] If the deposition was recorded nonstenographically, the officer must return the nonstenographic recording (e.g., the videotape) to the party who requested it.[519] The officer also must serve notice of the delivery on all other parties.[520] The transcript or recording is not filed with the court by the deposition officer.

"The party receiving the original deposition transcript or nonstenographic recording *must* make it available on reasonable request for inspection and copying by any other party."[521] Accordingly, it is not necessary for the parties to pay the court reporter for more than the original deposition transcript, and the parties can agree to split that cost and the cost of making copies of the original. Of course, "[a]ny party or the witness is entitled to obtain a copy of the deposition transcript or nonstenographic recording from the deposition officer on payment of a reasonable fee."[522]

11-6:5 Exhibits

Texas Rule 203.4 governs deposition exhibits. It requires the deposition officer, "at the request of a party" during the deposition, to mark and annex to the deposition transcript or nonstenographic recording any documents and things produced for inspection during the deposition.[523]

The producing witness, under Texas Rule 203.4, can produce copies instead of original documents provided the witness gives "all other parties fair opportunity at the

---

517 Tex. R. Civ. P. 203.3(a).

518 Tex. R. Civ. P. 203.3(a)(1). Charges for a deposition are governed by Section 52.059 of the Texas Government Code. The attorney who takes the deposition, as well as the attorney's law firm, are "jointly and severally liable for a shorthand reporter's charges for: (1) the shorthand reporting of the deposition; (2) transcribing the deposition; and (3) each copy of the deposition transcript requested by the attorney." Tex. Gov't Code § 52.069(a). An attorney "'takes' a deposition if the attorney: (A) obtains the deponent's appearance through an informal request; (B) obtains the deponent's appearance through formal means, including a notice of deposition or subpoena; or (C) asks the first question in the deposition." Tex. Gov't Code § 52.059(d)(2); *see* Tex. R. Civ. P. 203.3(a) (providing that the original deposition transcript is delivered to the attorney "who asked the first question"). An attorney who asks for a copy of the deposition transcript, as well as the attorney's law firm, are "jointly and severally" liable for the reporter's charges for "each copy of the deposition transcript requested by the attorney." Tex. Gov't Code § 52.059(b). If an attorney does not want to be bound by the requirements of Section 52.059, the attorney must so state on the record before the deposition begins and "a determination of the person who will pay for the deposition costs will be made on the record[.]" Tex. Gov't Code § 52.059(c).

In *Cole v. Gwendolyn Parker, Inc.*, No. 05-13-01655-CV, 2015 Tex. App. LEXIS 8162, at *11–14 (Tex. App.—Dallas Aug. 4, 2015, no pet.) (mem. op.), the Dallas Court of Appeals rejected an argument that Section 52.059 applies only to individual court reporters and not to court-reporting firms.

519 Tex. R. Civ. P. 203.3(a)(2).

520 Tex. R. Civ. P. 203.3(b).

521 Tex. R. Civ. P. 203.3(c) (emphasis added).

522 Tex. R. Civ. P. 203.3(c).

523 Tex. R. Civ. P. 203.4.

deposition to compare the copies with the originals." If, however, the witness offers originals rather than copies:

> the deposition officer must, after the conclusion of the deposition, make copies to be attached to the original deposition transcript or nonstenographic recording, and then return the originals to the person who produced them. The person who produced the originals must preserve them for hearing or trial and make them available for inspection or copying by any other party on seven days' notice. Copies annexed to the original deposition transcript or nonstenographic recording may be used for all purposes.[524]

Texas Rule 203.4's requirement that the witness bring the original documents to the deposition is inconsistent with Texas Rules 196.3(b) and 199.2(b)(5)'s requirements for parties and persons subject to a party's control. Texas Rule 196.3(b) provides that "[t]he responding party may produce copies in lieu of originals unless a question is raised as to the authenticity of the original or in the circumstances it would be unfair to produce copies in lieu of originals."[525] Texas Rule 199.2(b)(5), in turn, provides that production requests in a deposition notice for the deposition of a party or a person subject to a party's control are governed by Texas Rule 196. Thus, it is unclear whether Texas Rule 203.4's requirement regarding the production of original documents trumps Texas Rule 196.3(b)'s requirement that original documents need not be produced by parties or persons subject to their control.

If the witness is not a party or subject to a party's control, Texas Rule 203.4's provisions regarding the production of originals would apply because Texas Rule 199.2(b)(5) incorporates the provisions of Texas Rules 176 and 205 with respect to the witness's responses to subpoenas[526] and neither Rule provides that only copies need be produced.

11-6:6 Motions to Suppress

To object to errors or irregularities in how a deposition was prepared, transcribed, signed, certified, sealed, endorsed, or delivered, a party must file a written motion to suppress the deposition and serve it on the other parties.[527] If the deposition was transcribed stenographically and, if it was properly delivered at least one day before trial, the motion must be filed *before* trial.[528] However, if the deposition was recorded

---

[524] Tex. R. Civ. P. 203.4

[525] Tex. R. Civ. P. 196.3(b).

[526] Tex. R. Civ. P. 199.2(b)(5) ("A notice may include a request that the witness produce at the deposition documents or tangible things within the scope of discovery and within the witness's possession, custody, or control. If the witness is a nonparty, the request must comply with [Texas] Rule 205 and the designation of materials required to be identified in the subpoena must be attached to, or included in, the notice. The nonparty's response to the request is governed by [Texas] Rules 176 and 205.").

[527] Tex. R. Civ. P. 203.5. ("A party may object to any errors and irregularities in the manner in which the testimony is transcribed, signed, delivered, or otherwise dealt with by the deposition officer by filing a motion to suppress all or part of the deposition.").

[528] Tex. R. Civ. P. 203.5; *Garza v. Guerrero*, 993 S.W.2d 137, 140 (Tex. App.—San Antonio 1999, no pet.) (construing former Texas Rule 207(3) and explaining: "If a deposition transcript has been on file with the trial court for one day or more before trial, any error in the manner in which the deposition transcript is signed is waived unless a written motion to suppress is

nonstenographically, the motion need be filed before trial *only* if the nonstenographic recording was properly delivered at least thirty days before trial. Otherwise, the motion can be filed during the trial.[529]

11-6:7 Using Depositions

The admissibility of deposition testimony is governed by a combination of Texas Rule 203.6(b) and the hearsay rules in the Texas Rules of Evidence.

11-6:7.1 Depositions Taken in the Same Proceeding

Texas Rule 203.6(b) provides that "[a]ll or part of a deposition may be used for any purpose in the same proceeding in which it was taken."[530] "Same proceeding" includes both the action in which the deposition was taken and "a proceeding in a different court but involving the same subject matter and the same parties or their representatives or successors in interest."[531]

Under Texas Rule of Evidence 801(e)(3), a deposition taken in the same proceeding is exempt from the hearsay rule irrespective of the witness's availability.[532] Thus, such deposition testimony can be used instead of, or in addition to, the witness's live testimony irrespective of whether the witness is available to testify.[533]

Under Texas Rule 191.4, deposition transcripts are not automatically filed by the deposition officer but may be filed for use in court proceedings. Thus, if the custodial attorney files the original deposition transcript or a noncustodial attorney files a certified copy of it, the transcript may be used at trial by any party for any purpose.[534]

Under Texas Rule 203.6(b), "[a] deposition is admissible against a party joined after the deposition was taken if: (1) the deposition is admissible pursuant to Rule 804(b)(1) of the Texas Rules of Evidence, [the former-testimony exception to the hearsay rule,]

---

filed and delivered before the trial commences. Only if the deposition has not been on file for one day prior to trial may the motion to suppress be made orally at the time the deposition is offered into evidence. The deposition in this case was taken on September 5, 1997, and trial commenced September 15, 1997. There is no evidence in the record with regard to the date the deposition was filed with the trial court. The Garzas' attorney states in his objection, however, that the deposition was not on file for more than one day before trial; therefore, we conclude that the Garzas did not waive their objection by failing to file a written motion to suppress. The Garzas' oral motion to suppress was sufficient to preserve error.").

[529] Tex. R. Civ. P. 203.5.

[530] Tex. R. Civ. P. 203.6(b).

[531] Tex. R. Civ. P. 203.6(b).

[532] Tex. R. Evid. 801(e)(3) ("A statement that meets the following conditions is not hearsay: . . . In a civil case, the statement was made in a deposition taken in the same proceeding. 'Same proceeding' is defined in [Texas] Rule of Civil Procedure 203.6(b). The deponent's unavailability as a witness is not a requirement for admissibility.").

[533] The fact that testimony was elicited by the objecting party's attorney does not make it admissible. *E.g.*, *EM Bldg. Contractors Servs., LLC v. Byrd Bldg. Servs., LLC*, No. 05-19-00153-CV, 2020 Tex. App. LEXIS 6342, at *46–47 (Tex. App.—Dallas Aug. 11, 2020, no pet) (mem. op.) ("The fact that this testimony was in response to questions from Byrd's counsel does not render the testimony admissible. We note that no rule precludes a party from objecting to testimony elicited in deposition by the party's own counsel.") (citations omitted).

[534] Tex. R. Civ. P. 203.6(b).

or (2) that party has had a reasonable opportunity to redepose the witness and has failed to do so." The former-testimony exception to the hearsay rule allows a deposition to be used if (1) the declarant is unavailable as a witness, and (2) the party against whom the deposition testimony is offered, or a person with a similar interest, had an opportunity and similar motive to develop the testimony by direct, cross, or redirect examination.[535]

If a party fails to attend a deposition for which the party received proper notice, the deposition can be used against the party for all purposes in the action. Even if the party did not receive proper notice of the deposition, it appears that it can be used against the party if the party had a reasonable time to redepose the witness and failed to do so.[536]

11-6:7.2 Depositions Taken in Another Proceeding

A deposition from another proceeding can be used in an action only if it is admissible under the Texas Rules of Evidence.[537] If the deposition is one of a party to the action, it is admissible as a party admission.[538]

A nonparty's deposition from another proceeding is admissible only if it meets the requirements of the hearsay rule's former-testimony exception, Texas Rule of Evidence 804(b)(1), which requires that the (1) the declarant (i.e., the deponent) is unavailable as a witness,[539] and (2) the party against whom the deposition testimony is

---

[535] Tex. R. Evid. 804(b)(1).

[536] *Onyung v. Onyung*, No. 01-10-00519-CV, 2013 Tex. App. LEXIS 9190, at *56–57 (Tex. App.—Houston [1st Dist.] July 25, 2013, pet. denied) (mem. op.) (applying Texas Rule 203.6(b) by analogy to a situation in which a party did not receive notice of a deposition, but had ample opportunity to redepose the witness, noting that "[a]lthough [Texas] Rule 203.6(b) does not directly apply to this situation because the Yuen law firms were not parties 'joined' after the deposition was taken, the principle undergirding the rule applies nevertheless").

[537] Tex. R. Civ. P. 203.6(c) ("Depositions taken in different proceedings may be used as permitted by the Rules of Evidence.").

[538] *Dillee v. Sisters of Charity of the Incarnate Word Health Care Sys.*, 912 S.W.2d 307, 310 n.6 (Tex. App.—Houston [14th Dist.] 1995, no writ) (holding that the deposition of a party from an earlier action was admissible under former Texas Rule of Civil Evidence 801(e)(2) as an admission by a party opponent); *accord* Tex. R. Evid. 801(e)(2) ("A statement that meets the following conditions is not hearsay: . . . The statement is offered against an opposing party and: (A) was made by the party in an individual or representative capacity; (B) is one the party manifested that it adopted or believed to be true; (C) was made by a person whom the party authorized to make a statement on the subject; (D) was made by the party's agent or employee on a matter within the scope of that relationship and while it existed; or (E) was made by the party's coconspirator during and in furtherance of the conspiracy.").

[539] Tex. Evid. R. 804(a) provides:

> A declarant is considered to be unavailable as a witness if the declarant:
>
> (1) is exempted from testifying about the subject matter of the declarant's statement because the court rules that a privilege applies;
>
> (2) refuses to testify about the subject matter despite a court order to do so;
>
> (3) testifies to not remembering the subject matter;
>
> (4) cannot be present or testify at the trial or hearing because of death or a then-existing infirmity, physical illness, or mental illness; or

offered, or a person with a similar interest, had an opportunity and similar motive to develop the testimony by direct, cross, or redirect examination.[540]

11-6:7.3 Procedure for Using Deposition Testimony

At trial, the party offering deposition testimony either must read the relevant portions of the deposition transcript or play the relevant portion of the videotaped deposition into the record.[541] When using a deposition transcript, generally one attorney, sitting at counsel table, reads the questions, and another, sitting in the witness stand, reads the answers. Unless the parties agreed otherwise, leading, form, and nonresponsiveness objections made during the deposition can be urged during the trial along with any non-form, substantive objections (e.g., relevance, hearsay, materiality, and the witness's competency).[542]

Deposition testimony also can be used in support of or opposition to a summary judgment motion.[543] Deposition excerpts submitted as summary judgment evidence need not be authenticated by an affidavit certifying the truthfulness and correctness of the copied excerpts.[544]

11-6:7.4 Use of Nonstenographic Recordings

"A nonstenographic recording of an oral deposition, or a written transcription of all or part of such a recording, may be used to the same extent as a deposition taken by stenographic means."[545] The trial court, for good cause shown, such as when there is a dispute regarding the nonstenographic recording's or the written transcript's contents, can order the party seeking to use the nonstenographic deposition or written

---

> (5) is absent from the trial or hearing and the statement's proponent has not been able, by process or other reasonable means, to procure the declarant's attendance or testimony.
>
> But this subdivision (a) does not apply if the statement's proponent procured or wrongfully caused the declarant's unavailability as a witness in order to prevent the declarant from attending or testifying.

Tex. R. Evid. 904(a).

540 Tex. R. Evid. 804(b)(1).

541 *See* Tex. R. Civ. P. 203.6(b).

542 *See* Tex. R. Civ. P. 199.5(e). Deposition objections are discussed in Chapters 11, section 11-2:8.3.

543 Tex. R. Civ. P. 166a(d) ("Discovery products not on file with the clerk may be used as summary judgment evidence[.]"); *accord McConathy v. McConathy*, 869 S.W.2d 341, 342 (Tex. 1994).

544 *McConathy v. McConathy*, 869 S.W.2d 341, 342 (Tex. 1994) ("All parties have ready access to depositions taken in a cause, and thus deposition excerpts submitted with a motion for summary judgment may be easily verified as to their accuracy. Authentication is not necessary and is not required under the present rules.") (footnote omitted); *accord City of Fort Worth v. Hart*, No. 10-17-00258-CV, 2019 Tex. App. LEXIS 12, at *4–5 (Tex. App.—Waco Jan. 2, 2019, pet. denied) (mem. op.); *City of Dall. v. Papierski*, No. 05-17-00157-CV, 2017 Tex. App. LEXIS 9267, at *8 (Tex. App.—Dallas Oct. 2, 2017, no pet.) (mem. op.).

545 Tex. R. Civ. P. 203.6(a).

transcription of it to first obtain a complete stenographic recording prepared by a certified shorthand reporter.[546]

If a certified shorthand court reporter is asked to prepare a transcript of the nonstenographic deposition recording, "[t]he court reporter must, to the extent applicable, comply with the provisions of [Texas Rule 203], except that the court reporter must deliver the original transcript to the attorney requesting the transcript, and the court reporter's certificate must include a statement that the transcript is a true record of the nonstenographic recording."[547]

As is the case with the original deposition, "[t]he party to whom the court reporter delivers the original transcript must make the transcript available, upon reasonable request, for inspection and copying by the witness or any party."[548]

---

546 Tex. R. Civ. P. 203.6(a).

547 Tex. R. Civ. P. 203.6(a). Because such a transcript is not "the original deposition transcript," Texas Rule 203.1's signature requirements do not apply. *See* Tex. R. Civ. P. 203.1(c)(3).

548 Tex. R. Civ. P. 203.6(a).

CHAPTER 12

Physical and Mental Examinations—Texas Rule 204

12-1 Text of Rule 204

RULE 204. PHYSICAL AND MENTAL EXAMINATION

204.1. Motion and Order Required

(a) **Motion.** A party may—no later than 30 days before the end of any applicable discovery period—move for an order compelling another party to:

(1) submit to a physical or mental examination by a qualified physician or a mental examination by a qualified psychologist; or

(2) produce for such examination a person in the other party's custody, conservatorship or legal control.

(b) **Service.** The motion and notice of hearing must be served on the person to be examined and all parties.

(c) **Requirements for obtaining order.** The court may issue an order for examination only for good cause shown and only in the following circumstances:

(1) when the mental or physical condition (including the blood group) of a party, or of a person in the custody, conservatorship or under the legal control of a party, is in controversy; or

(2) except as provided in Rule 204.4, an examination by a psychologist may be ordered when the party responding to the motion has designated a psychologist as a testifying expert or has disclosed a psychologist's records for possible use at trial.

(d) **Requirements of order.** The order must be in writing and must specify the time, place, manner, conditions, and scope of the examination and the person or persons by whom it is to be made.

204.2. Report of Examining Physician or Psychologist

(a) **Right to report.** Upon request of the person ordered to be examined, the party causing the examination to be made must deliver to the person a copy of a detailed written report of the examining physician or psychologist setting out the findings, including results of all tests made, diagnoses and conclusions, together with like reports of all earlier examinations of the same condition. After delivery of the report, upon request of the party causing the examination, the party against whom the order is made must produce a like report of any examination made before or after the ordered examination of the same condition, unless the person examined is not a party and the party shows that the party is unable to obtain it. The court on motion may limit delivery of a report on such terms as are just. If a physician or psychologist fails or refuses to make a report the court may exclude the testimony if offered at the trial.

(b) **Agreements; relationship to other rules.** This subdivision applies to examinations made by agreement of the parties, unless the agreement expressly provides otherwise. This subdivision does not preclude discovery of a report of an examining physician or psychologist or the taking of a deposition of the physician or psychologist in accordance with the provisions of any other rule.

204.3. Effect of No Examination

If no examination is sought either by agreement or under this subdivision, the party whose physical or mental condition is in controversy must not comment to the court or jury concerning the party's willingness to submit to an examination, or on the right or failure of any other party to seek an examination.

204.4. Cases Arising Under Titles II or V, Family Code

In cases arising under Family Code Titles II or V, the court may—on its own initiative or on motion of a party—appoint:

(a) one or more psychologists or psychiatrists to make any and all appropriate mental examinations of the children who are the subject of the suit or of any other parties, and may make such appointment irrespective of whether a psychologist or psychiatrist has been designated by any party as a testifying expert;

(b) one or more experts who are qualified in paternity testing to take blood, body fluid, or tissue samples to conduct paternity tests as ordered by the court.

204.5. Definition

For the purpose of this rule, a psychologist is a person licensed or certified by a state or the District of Columbia as a psychologist.

12-1:1 2021 Amendments to the Texas Rules of Civil Procedure

The 2021 amendments to the Texas Rules of Civil Procedure did not modify Texas Rule 204 in any respect.

12-2 Motion and Order Required

12-2:1 Motion to Compel Physical or Mental Examination

12-2:1.1 In General

Texas Rule 204 permits a court to order physical or mental examinations.[1] It only permits the examination of a "another party" or "a person in the other party's custody,

---

[1] Tex. R. Civ. P. 204.1. Because Texas Rule 204 is similar to, and largely based on, Federal Rule 35, cases addressing Federal Rule 35 provide guidance in construing Texas Rule 204. *In re Soc'y of Our Lady of the Most Holy Trinity*, 622 S.W.3d 1, 12-13 (Tex. App.—Corpus Christi 2019, orig. proceeding) (noting that "the Texas Supreme Court held that the federal courts' construction of the analogous federal rule was 'helpful' to an analysis of our Texas rule" and applying federal decisions in construing the rule) (citing *Coates v. Whittington*, 758 S.W.2d 749, 751 (1988) (orig. proceeding))); *see Coates v. Whittington*, 758 S.W.2d 749, 751 (1988) (orig. proceeding) (Former Texas "Rule 167a was derived from [Federal] Rule 35 . . . and largely duplicates the language of the original federal rule. Federal courts' construction of [Federal] Rule 35 is thus helpful to an analysis of [former Texas] Rule 167a.") (citations omitted).

Federal Rule 35 provides:

(a) *Order for an Examination.*

(1) *In General.* The court where the action is pending may order a party whose mental or physical condition—including blood group—is in controversy to submit to a physical or mental examination by a suitably licensed or certified examiner. The court has the same authority to order a party to produce for examination a person who is in its custody or under its legal control.

(2) *Motion and Notice; Contents of the Order. The order:*

(A) may be made only on motion for good cause and on notice to all parties and the person to be examined; and

(B) must specify the time, place, manner, conditions, and scope of the examination, as well as the person or persons who will perform it.

(b) *Examiner's Report.*

(1) *Request by the Party or Person Examined.* The party who moved for the examination must, on request, deliver to the requester a copy of the examiner's report, together with like reports of all earlier examinations of the same condition. The request may be made by the party against whom the examination order was issued or by the person examined.

(2) *Contents.* The examiner's report must be in writing and must set out in detail the examiner's findings, including diagnoses, conclusions, and the results of any tests.

(3) *Request by the Moving Party.* After delivering the reports, the party who moved for the examination may request—and is entitled to receive—from the party against whom the examination order was issued like reports of all earlier or later examinations of the same condition. But those reports need not be delivered by the party with custody or control of the person examined if the party shows that it could not obtain them.

(4) *Waiver of Privilege.* By requesting and obtaining the examiner's report, or by deposing the examiner, the party examined waives any privilege it may have—in that action or any other action involving the same controversy—concerning testimony about all examinations of the same condition.

conservatorship, or legal control."[2] "Another party" is any other party to the case, not merely the opposing party, and includes plaintiffs, defendants, and third-party defendants.[3] It does not include nonparties.[4] The Rule also does not permit a party to move a court to appoint an expert to perform a physical or mental examination of the moving party.[5] Federal courts have held that parents suing on behalf of their child are not within Federal Rule 35's scope.[6] No Texas case has considered this question.

---

(5) *Failure to Deliver a Report.* The court on motion may order—on just terms—that a party deliver the report of an examination. If the report is not provided, the court may exclude the examiner's testimony at trial.

(6) *Scope.* This subdivision (b) applies also to an examination made by the parties' agreement, unless the agreement states otherwise. This subdivision does not preclude obtaining an examiner's report or deposing an examiner under other rules.

Fed. R. Civ. P. 35.

[2] Tex. R. Civ. P. 204.1(a).

[3] *Cf. Schlagenhauf v. Holder*, 379 U.S. 104, 112, 115 ("[Federal] Rule 35 only requires that the person to be examined be a party to the 'action,' not that he be an opposing party vis-a-vis the movant."); *Clark v. Geiger*, 31 F.R.D. 268, 270 (E.D. Pa. 1962) (implying that Federal Rule 35a applies to a third-party defendant).

[4] Tex. R. Civ. P. 204.1(a) (referring to "another party"); *cf. Young v. U.S.*, 311 F.R.D. 117, 121 (D.N.J. 2015) ("The Court is without authority to compel a non-party to submit to an examination under [Federal] Rule 35."); *Cutting v. U.S.*, No. 07-cv-02053-PAB-MEH, 2008 U.S. Dist. LEXIS 100723, at *3–4, 2008 WL 5064267 (D. Colo. Nov. 24, 2008) (same); *Dunford v. Rolly Marine Serv. Co.*, 233 F.R.D. 635, 637 (S.D. Fla. 2005) ("No authority has been provided for the proposition that a [Federal] Rule 35 examination can ever be applied to a non-party witness, even if that witness is an officer of a party."); *Lewis v. Herrman's Excavating, Inc.*, 200 F.R.D. 657, 661 (D. Kan. 2001) ("The Court is unpersuaded that, outside of [Federal] Rule 35, it has any inherent power to order a physical examination of [a non-party witness].").

[5] *Grogan v. Kumar*, 873 F.3d 273, 280–81 (5th Cir. 2017) (holding that Federal Rule 35 does not allow a trial court to order the movant's examination); *Jones v. Cuddy*, No. 13-cv-2942-MSN-tmp, 2019 U.S. Dist. LEXIS 71701, at *2, 2019 WL 1905164 (W.D. Tenn. Apr. 29, 2019) ("[M]any federal courts construing [Federal] Rule 35 have concluded that the rule 'does not vest the court with authority to appoint an expert to examine a party wishing an examination of himself' but applies only where an opposing party moves for the examination." (quoting *Baxter v. Tenn.*, No. 10-2667, 2014 U.S. Dist. LEXIS 76483, at *5–6, 2014 WL 2533812 (W.D. Tenn. June 5, 2014) (quoting *Brown v. U.S.*, 74 F. App'x 611, 614 (7th Cir. 2003))); *Brown v. Wolf*, No. 16-1081, 2019 U.S. Dist. LEXIS 49501, at *2, 2019 WL 1331594 (W.D. Pa. Mar. 25, 2019) (Federal Rule 35 "does not permit a party to seek his own medical examination. . . ." (quoting *Gannaway v. PrimeCare Med., Inc.*, 150 F. Supp. 3d 511, 523 n.4 (E.D. Pa. 2015), *aff'd*, 652 F. App'x 91 (3d Cir. 2016), *cert. denied*, ___ U.S. ___, 138 S. Ct. 162 (2017))).

[6] *Cf. Scharf v. U.S.*, 597 F.2d 1240, 1243 (9th Cir. 1979) ("[T]he court's authority to order a physical examination under [Federal R]ule 35 was limited to [the infant-plaintiff] and . . . it [was] error to order blood tests of [her purported parents]. [The purported father's] status as guardian ad litem does not alter that result.") (citations omitted); *Young v. U.S.*, 311 F.R.D. 117, 121, 123 (D.N.J. 2015) ("[A] party seeking a [Federal] Rule 35 examination must demonstrate that the person to be examined is 'a party' or 'a person who is [either] in [a party's] custody or under [a party's] legal control.' The Court is without authority to compel a non-party to submit to an examination under [Federal] Rule 35. . . . The Court finds [Federal] Rule 35 does not authorize a court to order representatives or natural guardians of minor-plaintiffs to submit to genetic testing. The Court further rejects Defendants' attempt to characterize Ms. Young as a party based on her purported 'financial interest' in

Under Texas Rule 204.1(a), a party must file a motion for an order compelling the examination.[7] Accordingly, a trial court cannot order an examination on its own initiative except in cases arising under Title II or Title V of the Texas Family Code, which are subject to the unique requirements described in Chapter 12, section 12-6. In addition, as discussed in Chapter 12, section 12-4, the parties can agree to a physical or mental examination, thereby bypassing Texas Rule 204.1's motion and order requirements.

12-2:1.2 Timing and Service of Motion

A motion for an order compelling a physical or mental examination must be filed "no later than 30 days before the end of any applicable discovery period[.]"[8] As with other discovery types, the deadline for such motions can be modified "by the agreement of the parties or by court order for good cause."[9] Read literally, Texas Rule 204.1(a)

---

the litigation. Ms. Young's purported interest in obtaining a monetary judgment for her child does not render her within the scope of [Federal] Rule 35." (citations omitted) (quoting Fed. R. Civ. P. 35)); *Cutting v. U.S.*, No. 07-cv-02053-PAB-MEH, 2008 U.S. Dist. LEXIS 100723, at *3–4, 2008 WL 5064267 (D. Colo. Nov. 24, 2008) ("Defendants have established, to the Court's satisfaction, the relevance and importance of genetic testing on the child's mother, Nevena Cutting. Nevertheless, the Court must recognize its own jurisdiction, which, under persuasive authority, rejects Federal Rule of Civil Procedure 35's reach to nonparties. The Court also rejects any argument that it has inherent authority to compel Neneva Cutting to submit to the requested procedures. Finally, the Court does not believe that, under [Federal] Rule 35's language, Nevena Cutting should be considered a party.") (citations omitted); *Caban ex rel. Crespo v. 600 E. 21st St. Co.*, 200 F.R.D. 176, 181 (E.D.N.Y. 2001) ("This Court therefore declines to expand the scope of [Federal] Rule 35 to include representatives and natural guardians of infant-plaintiffs. . . .").

Texas Rule 205.1 provides that "a party may compel discovery from a nonparty *only by obtaining a court order under Rules* 196.7, 202, or *204*, or by serving a subpoena compelling: (a) an oral deposition; (b) a deposition on written questions; (c) a request for production of documents or tangible things, pursuant to Rule 199.2(b)(5) or Rule 200.1(b), served with a notice of deposition on oral examination or written questions; and (d) a request for production of documents and tangible things under this rule." Tex. R. Civ. P. 205.1 (emphasis added). The Rule's reference to Texas Rule 204 relates to examinations of "a person in the other party's custody, conservatorship, or legal control" within in the meaning of Texas Rule 204.1(a)(2) and does not give a trial court the right to order a physical or mental examination of nonparties generally.

[7] Tex. R. Civ. P. 204.1(a) ("A party may—no later than 30 days before the end of any applicable discovery period—move for an order compelling another party to: (1) submit to a physical or mental examination by a qualified physician or a mental examination by a qualified psychologist; or (2) produce for such examination a person in the other party's custody, conservatorship or legal control.").

[8] Tex. R. Civ. P. 204.1(a); *see In re Ten Hagen Excavating, Inc.*, 435 S.W.3d 859, 865 (Tex. App.—Dallas 2014, orig. proceeding) (concluding that, because "[r]equests for mental or physical examinations are a form of discovery," the deadline for completing all discovery in the action was the "'applicable discovery deadline' for purposes of calculation of the thirty day time period for requesting a physical examination under [Texas R]ule 204.1").

[9] Tex. R. Civ. P. 191.1; *see In re Savoy*, 607 S.W.3d 120, 124–25 (Tex. App.—Austin 2020, orig. proceeding) (holding that a motion for a physical or mental examination was timely because it complied with the deadline for the filing of such motions in the agreed scheduling order); *In re Ten Hagen Excavating, Inc.*, 435 S.W.3d 859, 865 (Tex. App.—Dallas 2014, orig. proceeding) (holding that the defendant properly considered a motion for a physical

allows a party to file a motion for a physical or mental examination after the expert-designation deadline, as that deadline often is more than thirty days before discovery closes. No Texas case has considered the interplay between Texas Rule 204.1(a) and expert-designation deadlines. Federal courts are divided regarding whether physical and mental examinations must be completed before the expert-designation deadline.[10] It is prudent to include deadlines in the case's Texas Rule 190 discovery control plan regarding when Texas Rule 204 physical or mental examinations must be requested and completed and when the Texas Rule 204.2(a) reports must be provided.

The party moving for the physical or mental examination must serve both "[t]he motion and notice of hearing [on the motion] . . . on [(1)] the person to be examined[,] and [(2)] all parties."[11] As with other discovery types, Texas Rule 21a provides the permissible methods of service for the motion and the hearing notice.[12] Because Texas Rule 21a(a) allows motions and notices to be served on a party's attorney instead of the party,[13] service on the opposing party's attorney is sufficient both for a physical or

---

examination of the plaintiff filed ten days before the discovery close because of the defendant's expert's untimely death). See also Chapter 3, section 3-3 (addressing discovery-procedure modifications).

[10] Nothing in the 2021 Amendments to the Texas Rules of Civil Procedure addresses whether Texas Rule 204 examinations are expert discovery and, therefore, are governed by Texas Rule 195.5's expert disclosure and report deadlines. Unlike Texas Rule 204.1(a), neither Federal Rule 35 nor any other Federal Rule of Civil Procedure contains a deadline for moving for a physical or mental examination. Federal courts have split regarding whether such examinations must be completed before the expert-designation deadline of Federal Rule 26(a)(2). *E.g.*, *Buffington v. Nestle Healthcare Nutrition Inc.*, No. SACV1800106JVSJDEX, 2019 U.S. Dist. LEXIS 130969, at *6, 2019 WL 3063516 (C.D. Cal. Apr. 18, 2019) ("[Federal] Rule 35 does not specify a deadline for conducting an independent medical examination. . . . 'District courts are split as to whether the party seeking a [Federal] Rule 35 examination must make the request before the [Federal] Rule 26 deadline to designate experts expires.'" (quoting *Mailhoit v. Home Depot U.S.A., Inc.*, 2013 U.S. Dist. LEXIS 201990, at *12, 2013 WL 12122580 (C.D. Cal. Jan. 24, 2013))); *Garayoa v. Miami-Dade Cty.*, No. 16-Civ-20213, 2017 U.S. Dist. LEXIS 103855, at *9–11, 2017 WL 2880094 (S.D. Fla. July 6, 2017) ("[T]here is no doubt that there is varying treatment among the district courts on the relationship between the expert disclosure deadline in [Federal] Rule 26 and the timing for a [Federal] Rule 35 examination and report. Some courts have ruled that [Federal] Rule 26 and [Federal] Rule 35 operate independently. On the other hand, many more courts have considered the [Federal] Rule 26 deadline when determining the timing of a [Federal] Rule 35 report. . . . Despite these differences, we are not persuaded that [Federal] Rules 26 and 35 operate independently as most courts that have considered this question have persuasively found that [Federal] Rules 26 and 35 must be read in conjunction with each other."); *Diaz v. Con-Way Truckload*, 279 F.R.D. 412, 416–17 (S.D. Tex. 2012) (recognizing split and discussing cases).

[11] Tex. R. Civ. P. 204.1(b); *see* Tex. R. Civ. P. 191.5 ("Every disclosure, discovery request, notice, response, and objection required to be served on a party or person must be served on all parties of record.").

[12] Tex. R. Civ. P. 21a(a) (providing the methods of service for "[e]very notice required by these rules, and every . . . motion[] or other form of request required to be served under Rule 21"). See also Chapter 3, section 3-7 (discussing service of discovery materials, including the permissible service methods).

[13] Tex. R. Civ. P. 21a(a) ("Every notice required by these rules, and every pleading, plea, motion, or other form of request required to be served under Rule 21, other than the citation to be served upon the filing of a cause of action and except as otherwise expressly

mental examination of the party or a person in the party's "custody, conservatorship, or . . . legal control"[14] unless that person has separate counsel.

Because the order granting a motion for a physical or mental examination "must specify . . . the person or person by whom [the examination] is to be made,"[15] the motion for the examination should suggest a physician or psychologist—typically the movant's expert—to conduct the examination.[16]

12-2:1.3 The Motion's Grounds

Texas Rule 204.1(c) allows a trial court to issue an order permitting a physical or mental examination (1) for "good cause shown," and (2) when either "the mental or physical condition (including blood group)" of the person sought to be examined is "in controversy" or, except in cases arises under Titles II or III of the Family Code, when "the party responding to the motion has designated a psychologist as a testifying expert or has disclosed a psychologist's records for possible use at trial."[17] "These requirements cannot be satisfied 'by mere conclusory allegations of the pleadings—nor by mere relevance to the case.'"[18] Nonetheless, there are circumstances when a party's pleading alone is sufficient to meet the requirements for a physical or mental examination. As explained by the United States Supreme Court in construing Federal Rule 25: "A plaintiff in a negligence action who asserts mental or physical injury, places that mental or physical injury clearly in controversy and provides the defendant with good cause for an examination to determine the existence and extent of such asserted injury. This is not only true as to a plaintiff but applies equally to a defendant who asserts his mental or physical condition as a defense to a claim, such as, for example, where insanity is asserted as a defense to a divorce action."[19]

12-2:1.3a Good Cause

Texas Rule 204.1(c)'s "good-cause" requirement "recognizes that competing interests come into play when a party's mental or physical condition is implicated in a lawsuit—the party's right of privacy and the movant's right to a fair trial. A balancing of the

---

provided in these rules, may be served by delivering a copy to the party to be served, or the party's duly authorized agent or attorney of record. . . .").

14 Tex. R. Civ. P. 204.1(a), (c).

15 Tex. R. Civ. P. 204.1(d).

16 The selection and qualification of the physician and psychologist are discussed in Chapter 12, sections 12-2:2 and 12-7.

17 Tex. R. Civ. P. 204.1(c); *accord In re Estabrook*, No. 10-20-00175-CV, 2020 Tex. App. LEXIS 8328, at *5, 2020 WL 6192923 (Tex. App.—Waco Oct. 21, 2020, orig. proceeding) (mem. op.); *In re Soc'y of Our Lady of the Most Holy Trinity*, 622 S.W.3d 1, 11 (Tex. App.—Corpus Christi 2019, orig. proceeding).

18 *In re H.E.B. Grocery Co.*, 492 S.W.3d 300, 303 (Tex. 2016) (orig. proceeding) (per curiam) (quoting *Coates v. Whittington*, 758 S.W.2d 749, 751 (1988) (orig. proceeding) (citing *Schlagenhauf v. Holder*, 379 U.S. 104 (1964)).

19 *Schlagenhauf v. Holder*, 379 U.S. 104, 119 (1964); *accord In re Ten Hagen Excavating, Inc.*, 435 S.W.3d 859, 867–68 (Tex. App.—Dallas 2014, orig. proceeding).

two interests is thus necessary to determine whether a compulsory examination may properly be ordered."[20]

Establishing "good cause" requires the party moving for the physical or mental examination to: (1) "'show that the requested examination is relevant to issues in controversy and will produce or likely lead to relevant evidence,' (2) 'establish a reasonable nexus between the requested examination and the condition in controversy,' and (3) 'demonstrate that the desired information cannot be obtained by less intrusive means.'"[21]

Texas courts have provided guidance about each of these requirements. With respect to the first one—relevance—courts have held that (1) an expert's ability to "formulate an opinion without requesting or conducting an examination" does not undermine the physical or mental examination's relevance,[22] (2) a requested physical or mental examination is not rendered irrelevant by virtue of the fact that it is "sought for the purpose of litigation[,]"[23] (3) a plaintiff whose petition alleges "physical and mental injuries to several parts of his body . . . cannot dispute that a physical or neurological exam would be 'relevant to issues' that are genuinely in controversy,

---

[20] *Coates v. Whittington*, 758 S.W.2d 749, 753 (Tex. 1988) (orig. proceeding) (construing former Texas Rule 167a); *accord In re H.E.B. Grocery Co.*, 492 S.W.3d 300, 303 (Tex. 2016) (orig. proceeding) (per curiam); *In re Savoy*, 607 S.W.3d 120, 125 (Tex. App.—Austin 2020, orig. proceeding); *In re Soc'y of Our Lady of the Most Holy Trinity*, 622 S.W.3d 1, 11 (Tex. App.—Corpus Christi 2019, orig. proceeding); *In re Gonzalez*, No. 04-15-00553-CV, 2015 Tex. App. LEXIS 10368, at *4, 2015 WL 5837896 (Tex. App.—San Antonio Oct. 7, 2015, orig. proceeding) (mem. op.); *In re Thuesen*, No. 14-13-00174-CV, 2013 Tex. App. LEXIS 4617, at *7–8, 2013 WL 1461790 (Tex. App.—Houston [14th Dist.] Apr. 11, 2013, orig. proceeding) (mem. op.).

[21] *In re Savoy*, 607 S.W.3d 120, 125 (Tex. App.—Austin 2020, orig. proceeding) (quoting *In re H.E.B. Grocery Co.*, 492 S.W.3d 300, 303 (Tex. 2016) (orig. proceeding) (per curiam)); *accord Coates v. Whittington*, 758 S.W.2d 749, 753 (Tex. 1988) (orig. proceeding) (construing former Texas Rule 167a); *In re Soc'y of Our Lady of the Most Holy Trinity*, 622 S.W.3d 1, 11 (Tex. App.—Corpus Christi 2019, orig. proceeding); *In re Phx. Servs., LLC*, No. 04-18-00446-CV, 2018 Tex. App. LEXIS 8887, at *4–5, 2018 WL 5622049 (Tex. App.—San Antonio Oct. 31, 2018, orig. proceeding) (mem. op.); *In re AutoZone Parts, Inc.*, No. 01-17-00559-CV, 2017 Tex. App. LEXIS 10292, at *2–8 (Tex. App.—Houston [1st Dist.] Nov. 2, 2017, orig. proceeding) (mem. op.); *In re Advanced Powder Sols., Inc.*, 496 S.W.3d 838, 849–51 (Tex. App.—Houston [1st Dist.] 2016, orig. proceeding); *In re Offshore Marine Contractors, Inc.*, 496 S.W.3d 796, 800 (Tex. App.—Houston [1st Dist.] 2016, orig. proceeding); *In re Ten Hagen Excavating, Inc.*, 435 S.W.3d 859, 868–71 (Tex. App.—Dallas 2014, orig. proceeding); *In re Bell Hot Shot Co.*, No. 14-13-00877-CV, 2014 Tex. App. LEXIS 300, at *4–5, 2014 WL 260116 (Tex. App.—Houston [14th Dist.] Jan. 9, 2014, orig. proceeding) (mem. op.).

[22] *In re H.E.B. Grocery Co., L.P.*, 492 S.W.3d 300, 303 (Tex. 2016) (per curiam) (orig. proceeding) (per curiam).

[23] *In re AutoZone Parts, Inc.*, No. 01-17-00559-CV, 2017 Tex. App. LEXIS 10292, at *5, 2017 WL 4974559 (Tex. App.—Houston [1st Dist.] Nov. 2, 2017, orig. proceeding) (mem. op.) ("Maturey argued to the trial court that the requested exam is 'not relevant discovery' because the purpose of the exam would be for litigation, not treatment. But Maturey failed to provide any authority that [Texas] Rule 204 limits medical examinations to those experts who are treating the plaintiff. On the contrary, the rule specifically provides that physical exams may be sought for the purpose of litigation. Maturey's proposed limitation, thus, directly conflicts with the allowance of such exams under the rules.").

namely his claimed physical or mental injuries[,]"[24] and (4) if a plaintiff offers expert testimony relating to his or her future medical expenses, a requested examination that is designed to elicit opinions relating to the plaintiff's injuries and anticipated future medical treatment for the purpose of challenging the plaintiff's expert's opinions, is relevant to issues genuinely in controversy in the case.[25]

As to the second requirement—reasonable nexus—courts have held that (1) "a substantive description of the precise nature of the [requested] examination or expected outcome of the examination" is unnecessary to establish the reasonable nexus between the condition in controversy and examination, particularly when other case materials (such as pleadings and a competing expert's notes) demonstrate the nexus,[26] and (2) "a 'reasonable nexus' exists between the condition in controversy and the examination sought if the purpose of the requested exam . . . is to determine the existence, nature and extent of the plaintiff's injuries and . . . those injuries make up the 'condition in controversy.'"[27]

Finally, as to the third requirement—less intrusive means:

> Texas courts have identified a number of avenues that could, in appropriate cases, potentially provide less intrusive means for obtaining medical information

---

[24] *In re Reliable Commercial Roofing Servs., Inc.*, No. 01-15-00450-CV, 2016 Tex. App. LEXIS 5429, at *16, 2016 WL 3345483 (Tex. App.—Houston [1st Dist.] May 24, 2016, orig. proceeding) (mem. op.).

[25] *In re Advanced Powder Sols., Inc.*, 496 S.W.3d 838, 850 (Tex. App.—Houston [1st Dist.] 2016, orig. proceeding).

[26] *In re Ten Hagen Excavating, Inc.*, 435 S.W.3d 859, 869 (Tex. App.—Dallas 2014, orig. proceeding).

[27] *In re AutoZone Parts, Inc.*, No. 01-17-00559-CV, 2017 Tex. App. LEXIS 10292, at *5–6 (Tex. App.—Houston [1st Dist.] Nov. 2, 2017, orig. proceeding) (mem. op.); *see In re H.E.B. Grocery Co.*, 492 S.W.3d 300, 303 (Tex. 2016) (orig. proceeding) (per curiam) ("HEB has also established a reasonable nexus between the requested examination and the condition in controversy. Again, the purpose of the examination is to determine the existence, nature, and extent of the injuries Rodriguez sustained on HEB property. The condition in controversy is Rodriguez's physical health—his past, present, and future injuries related to the fall and other causes, and the extent of his damages. The requested examination thus directly relates to the condition in controversy and satisfies the nexus requirement.") (citations omitted); *In re Savoy*, 607 S.W.3d 120, 126 (Tex. App.—Austin 2020, orig. proceeding) (concluding that the defendant established that a reasonable nexus existed between the requested physical examination and the condition because its orthopod proposed to examine the plaintiff regarding his alleged "cervical and lumbar injuries" arising from the traffic accident at issue); *In re Phx. Servs., LLC*, No. 04-18-00446-CV, 2018 Tex. App. LEXIS 8887, at *11, 2018 WL 5622049 (Tex. App.—San Antonio Oct. 31, 2018, orig. proceeding) (mem. op.) (holding that a reasonable nexus existed between the requested mental examination and the condition because the defendant engaged a neuropsychologist to examine the plaintiff regarding his alleged traumatic brain injury suffered in the automobile accident at issue); *In re Reliable Commercial Roofing Servs., Inc.*, No. 01-15-00450-CV, 2016 Tex. App. LEXIS 5429, at *16, 2016 WL 3345483 (Tex. App.—Houston [1st Dist.] May 24, 2016, orig. proceeding) (mem. op.) ("[G]iven that Presson has admitted to suffering head injuries and ongoing hearing and memory loss, and that he designated fourteen healthcare providers, including a neurologist, as potential expert medical witnesses to testify regarding Presson's alleged physical injuries and his need for future medical care, we conclude that the 'reasonable nexus' between Presson's claimed injuries and Reliable's requested neurological exam is satisfied.").

> without an examination. For instance, less intrusive measures might include deposing the opposing party's doctors and attempting to obtain copies of medical records, or relying on existing expert witness reports already filed in the case. The adequacy of these measures must still be evaluated in light of the fair trial standard, however. In general, and particularly where the intended examination is not intrusive, invasive or unnecessarily physically uncomfortable, parties are permitted to explore matters not covered by the opposing party's examinations, make their own observations, and attempt to discover facts that may contradict the opinions of the opposing party's expert witnesses. In many cases the treating physician's notes, the medical records of the complaining party, and expert witness reports filed by other parties cannot serve these legitimate purposes. In addition, where the information already available through less intrusive means is inadequate, a party may obtain a physical examination for which good cause is otherwise shown.[28]

There are no "less intrusive means," and "good cause" generally exists, for a physical or mental examination when an opposing party intends to use expert medical or psychological testimony to establish his or her physical or mental condition.[29] This because "[o]rdinarily, a moving party's expert should be allowed the 'same opportunity' as the opposing party's expert to 'fully develop and present [his or her] opinion, ensuring a fair trial.'"[30]

---

[28] *In re Ten Hagen Excavating, Inc.*, 435 S.W.3d 859, 869–70 (Tex. App.—Dallas 2014, orig. proceeding) (citations omitted); *accord In re Phx. Servs., LLC*, No. 04-18-00446-CV, 2018 Tex. App. LEXIS 8887, at *6, 2018 WL 5622049 (Tex. App.—San Antonio Oct. 31, 2018, orig. proceeding) (mem. op.); *In re Advanced Powder Sols., Inc.*, 496 S.W.3d 838, 850–51 (Tex. App.—Houston [1st Dist.] 2016, orig. proceeding).

[29] *Coates v. Whittington*, 758 S.W.2d 749, 753 (Tex. 1988) (orig. proceeding) ("If, however, a plaintiff intends to use expert medical testimony to prove his or her alleged . . . condition, that condition is placed in controversy and *the defendant would have good cause for an examination under [former] Texas Rule 167a.*") (emphasis added); *accord In re Phx. Servs., LLC*, No. 04-18-00446-CV, 2018 Tex. App. LEXIS 8887, at *6, 2018 WL 5622049 (Tex. App.—San Antonio Oct. 31, 2018, orig. proceeding) (mem. op.); *In re Advanced Powder Sols., Inc.*, 496 S.W.3d 838, 850–51 (Tex. App.—Houston [1st Dist.] 2016, orig. proceeding); *In re Offshore Marine Contrs., Inc.*, 496 S.W.3d 796, 802 (Tex. App.—Houston [1st Dist.] 2016, orig. proceeding).

[30] *In re Redbird Trails Apartments*, No. 05-20-00284-CV, 2020 Tex. App. LEXIS 4676, at *10, 2020 WL 3445811 (Tex. App.—Dallas June 24, 2020, orig. proceeding) (mem. op.) (quoting *In re H.E.B. Grocery Co.*, 492 S.W.3d 300, 304–05 (Tex. 2016) (orig. proceeding) (per curiam)); *accord In re Ten Hagen Excavating, Inc.*, 435 S.W.3d 859, 870 (Tex. App.—Dallas 2014, orig. proceeding) ("In general, and particularly where the intended examination is not intrusive, invasive or unnecessarily physically uncomfortable, parties are permitted to explore matters not covered by the opposing party's examinations, make their own observations, and attempt to discover facts that may contradict the opinions of the opposing party's expert witnesses."); *see In re Kirby Inland Marine, LP*, No. 01-18-00383-CV, 2018 Tex. App. LEXIS 5475, at *7–8, 2018 WL 3468476 (Tex. App.—Houston [1st Dist.] July 18, 2018, orig. proceeding) (mem. op.) (concluding that, because the "time and advance notice limitations imposed by the trial court" denied the defendant the ability to conduct full neuropsychological evaluation, limitations violated fundamental fairness and fair-trial standard and constituted abuse of discretion); *In re AutoZone Parts, Inc.*, No. 01-17-00559-CV, 2017 Tex. App. LEXIS 10292, at *4–5, 2017 WL 4974559 (Tex. App.—Houston [1st Dist.] Nov. 2, 2017, orig. proceeding) (mem. op.) (explaining that because the plaintiff had "designated multiple medical providers" as testifying expert witnesses the defendant's expert

12-2:1.3b Mental or Physical Condition in Controversy

Texas Rule 204.1 most often is litigated with respect to mental examinations.[31] Texas cases suggest that the "in-controversy" requirement depends on whether a physical or mental examination is requested.[32] "Physical injuries have been held to be in controversy when a party (1) places the condition into controversy by employing it either in support of, or in defense of, a claim or (2) a party affirmatively shows that the condition is in controversy."[33]

Mental examinations, however, "are subject to a more rigorous standard due to their sensitive nature."[34] "[A] routine allegation of mental anguish or emotional distress does not place the party's mental condition in controversy. The plaintiff must assert

---

witness disadvantaged without examining the plaintiff); *In re Advanced Powder Sols., Inc.*, 496 S.W.3d 838, 851 (Tex. App.—Houston [1st Dist.] 2016, orig. proceeding) (concluding that "fundamental fairness" required allowing the defendant's expert to examine the plaintiff because his expert's report included "at least four pages and multiple 'diagnostic conclusions' . . . based exclusively upon [the expert's] examination of [the plaintiff]," and not his "medical records or other sources"); *In re Offshore Marine Contractors, Inc.*, 496 S.W.3d 796, 801-02 (Tex. App.—Houston [1st Dist.] 2016, orig. proceeding) (holding that the defendant met its burden of showing that less intrusive means were inadequate when its neuropsychological expert provided a "detailed explanation" why he could not "confidently rely on [the plaintiff's] previous examinations and medical records," stating that the findings were "inconsistent with typical symptoms of concussion and there [were] indications of test score errors and possible misrepresentations by [plaintiff] of his symptoms").

31 *In re Ten Hagen Excavating, Inc.*, 435 S.W.3d 859, 867 n.2 (Tex. App.—Dallas 2014, orig. proceeding) (noting that Texas "Rule 204.1 is rarely litigated with regard to physical examinations, as opposed to mental examinations" (citing *In re Caballero*, 36 S.W.3d 143, 145 (Tex. App.—Corpus Christi 2000, orig. proceeding))).

32 *In re AutoZone Parts, Inc.*, No. 01-17-00559-CV, 2017 Tex. App. LEXIS 10292, at *3–4, 2017 WL 4974559 (Tex. App.—Houston [1st Dist.] Nov. 2, 2017, orig. proceeding) (mem. op.) ("The 'in controversy' requirement varies according to whether physical or mental medical exams are at issue." (citing *In re Medina*, No. 01-07-00747-CV, 2007 Tex. App. LEXIS 9547, at *4, 2007 WL 4279171 (Tex. App.—Houston [1st Dist.] Dec. 6, 2007, no pet.) (mem. op.)); *accord In re Reliable Commer. Roofing Servs., Inc.*, No. 01-15-00450-CV, 2016 Tex. App. LEXIS 5429, at *12, 2016 WL 3345483 (Tex. App.—Houston [1st Dist.] May 24, 2016, orig. proceeding) (mem. op.). *But see In re Ten Hagen Excavating, Inc.*, 435 S.W.3d 859, 867 n.2 (Tex. App.—Dallas 2014, orig. proceeding) ("We need not consider here whether the 'in controversy' requirement varies according to whether physical or mental examinations are at issue.") (citation omitted).

33 *In re AutoZone Parts, Inc.*, No. 01-17-00559-CV, 2017 Tex. App. LEXIS 10292, at *3–4, 2017 WL 4974559 (Tex. App.—Houston [1st Dist.] Nov. 2, 2017, orig. proceeding) (mem. op.); *In re Reliable Commer. Roofing Servs., Inc.*, No. 01-15-00450-CV, 2016 Tex. App. LEXIS 5429, at *12, 2016 WL 3345483 (Tex. App.—Houston [1st Dist.] May 24, 2016, orig. proceeding) (mem. op.); *In re Medina*, No. 01-07-00747-CV, 2007 Tex. App. LEXIS 9547, at *4, 2007 WL 4279171 (Tex. App.—Houston [1st Dist.] Dec. 6, 2007, no pet.) (mem. op.); *Williams v. Sanderson*, 904 S.W.2d 212, 214–15 (Tex. App.—Beaumont 1995, no writ) (applying former Texas Rule 167a).

34 *In re AutoZone Parts, Inc.*, No. 01-17-00559-CV, 2017 Tex. App. LEXIS 10292, at *3–4, 2017 WL 4974559 (Tex. App.—Houston [1st Dist.] Nov. 2, 2017, orig. proceeding) (mem. op.) (citing *In re Medina*, No. 01-07-00747-CV, 2007 Tex. App. LEXIS 9547, at *4, 2007 WL 4279171 (Tex. App.—Houston [1st Dist.] Dec. 6, 2007, no pet.) (mem. op.)).

mental injury that exceeds the common emotional reaction to an injury or loss."[35] Moreover, "sweeping examinations of a party who has not affirmatively put his mental condition in issue may not be routinely ordered simply because the party brings a personal injury action."[36] Rather, a party "must assert mental injury that exceeds the common emotional reaction to an injury or loss"—e.g., a specific, persistent medical condition.[37] If the party is only claiming a past physical or mental pain and suffering, the party's physical or mental condition generally is not in controversy.[38]

A party generally cannot place another party's mental condition in controversy simply by alleging that the other party's mental condition contributed to, or caused, the incident in question.[39] Nor does an issue about a party's state of mind place the party's

---

[35] *In re Estabrook*, No. 10-20-00175-CV, 2020 Tex. App. LEXIS 8328, at *5–6, 2020 WL 6192923 (Tex. App.—Waco Oct. 21, 2020, orig. proceeding) (mem. op.) (quoting *Coates v. Whittington*, 758 S.W.2d 749, 753 (Tex. 1988) (orig. proceeding)); *cf. Nolan v. Int'l Bhd. of Teamsters Health & Welfare & Pension Funds, Local 705*, 199 F.R.D. 272, 275 (N.D. Ill. 2001) ("[T]he clear weight of authority on this issue shows that a simple claim of emotional distress does not automatically justify a [Federal] Rule 35 order compelling an examination.").

[36] *In re Estabrook*, No. 10-20-00175-CV, 2020 Tex. App. LEXIS 8328, at *6, 2020 WL 6192923 (Tex. App.—Waco Oct. 21, 2020, orig. proceeding) (mem. op.) (quoting *Coates v. Whittington*, 758 S.W.2d 749, 751 (Tex. 1988) (orig. proceeding)).

[37] *Coates v. Whittington*, 758 S.W.2d 749, 753 (Tex. 1988) (orig. proceeding) (applying former Texas Rule 167a); *accord In re Estabrook*, No. 10-20-00175-CV, 2020 Tex. App. LEXIS 8328, at *5–6, 2020 WL 6192923 (Tex. App.—Waco Oct. 21, 2020, orig. proceeding) (mem. op.); *In re Offshore Marine Contractors, Inc.*, 496 S.W.3d 796, 799, 802, 802 n.5 (Tex. App.—Houston [1st Dist.] 2016, orig. proceeding); *In re Thuesen*, No. 14-13-00174-CV, 2013 Tex. App. LEXIS 4617, at *6–7, 2013 WL 1461790 (Tex. App.—Houston [14th Dist.] Apr. 11, 2013, orig. proceeding) (mem. op.); *In re Williams*, No. 10-08-00364-CV, 2009 Tex. App. LEXIS 1561, at *13–14, 2009 WL 540961 (Tex. App.—Waco Mar. 4, 2009, orig. proceeding) (mem. op.); *In re Medina*, No. 01-07-00747-CV, 2007 Tex. App. LEXIS 9547, at *5–6, 2007 WL 4279171 (Tex. App.—Houston [1st Dist.] Dec. 6, 2007, orig. proceeding) (mem. op.); *In re Trimac Transp., Inc.*, No. 09-08-270 CV, 2008 Tex. App. LEXIS 5329, at *2–3, 2008 WL 2758793 (Tex. App.—Beaumont July 17, 2008, orig. proceeding) (mem. op.).

[38] *Cf. Winters v. Travia*, 495 F.2d 839, 840–41 (2nd Cir. 1974) ("Thus plaintiff is willing to abandon any claim that any present or anticipated physical or mental disability or condition was caused by [Defendants' actions.] Under these circumstances we do not see what purpose could be served by a [Federal] Rule 35 examination."); *Coca-Cola Bottling Co. v. Torres*, 255 F.2d 149, 153 (1st Cir. 1958) (holding that the district court's denial of a [Federal] Rule 35 motion for examination on basis of plaintiff's assertion that he was not seeking damages for any present suffering but only for past physical injury and emotional disturbance was "sound"); *Cotten v. Burt*, No. 04-CV-73508-DT, 2007 U.S. Dist. LEXIS 113636, at *4, 2007 WL 9811293 (E.D. Mich. Mar. 19, 2007) ("[A] a plaintiff who alleges only past, rather than current, injuries or disturbances should not be forced to submit to an examination under [Federal] Rule 35(a).").

[39] *See, e.g., Coates v. Whittington*, 758 S.W.2d 749, 752 (Tex. 1988) (orig. proceeding) ("Drackett also contends that Mrs. Coates' mental condition has been placed in controversy by virtue of its contributory negligence claim. With regard to that claim, it is Mrs. Coates' *conduct* that is in controversy. The jury will be asked to decide whether Mrs. Coates was negligent in her use of the oven cleaner. Whatever mental processes underlay her conduct, it is the nature of that conduct, not the reasons for it, that is in issue. [Former Texas] Rule 167a clearly does not contemplate that a plaintiff would be subjected to a probing psychiatric incursion into his or her entire psychological past on the strength of a defendant's contributory negligence claim."); *In re Nance*, 143 S.W.3d 506, 512 n.5 (Tex. App.—Austin 2004,

mental condition in controversy.[40] When, however, a party "intends to use expert medical testimony to prove his or her alleged [mental] condition, that condition is placed in controversy. . . ."[41]

Texas Rule 204.1(c)(2) does away with the in-controversy requirement in cases in which the responding party "has designated a psychologist as a testifying expert or has disclosed a psychologist's records for possible use at trial."[42]

12-2:2 Order

Texas Rule 204.1(d) sets forth the requirements for an order compelling a physical or mental examination: "The order must be in writing and must specify the time, place, manner, conditions, and scope of the examination and the person or persons by whom it is to be made."[43] Although Texas courts of appeals require that the trial court's order meet the Rule's requirements,[44] those courts otherwise have given trial courts broad discretion in crafting orders under the Rule.[45] Nonetheless, an order that allows for an

---

orig. proceeding) ("[A] plaintiff's mental condition is in issue 'only if the plaintiff asserts a mental injury that exceeds the common emotional reaction to an injury or loss.' Unless the plaintiff seeks to recover for a 'permanent mental injury' or 'a deep seated emotional disturbance or psychiatric problem' her mental condition or history is not 'in controversy.' That a plaintiff had past mental problems is 'peripheral' to determining what is in controversy." (citations omitted) (quoting *In re Doe*, 22 S.W.3d 601, 606 (Tex. App.—Austin 1994, orig. proceeding))).

40 *Amis v. Ashworth*, 802 S.W.2d 374, 378 (Tex. App.— Tyler 1990, orig. proceeding) (holding that the defendant's assertion of self-defense as a defense to an assault claim did not his put mental condition in controversy).

41 *In re Redbird Trails Apartments*, No. 05-20-00284-CV, 2020 Tex. App. LEXIS 4676, at *6, 2020 WL 3445811 (Tex. App.—Dallas June 24, 2020) (mem. op.) (quoting *In re H.E.B. Grocery Co.*, 492 S.W.3d 300, 303 (Tex. 2016) (orig. proceeding) (per curiam)); *accord Coates v. Whittington*, 758 S.W.2d 749, 753 (Tex. 1988) (orig. proceeding) (construing former Texas Rule 167a).

42 Tex. R. Civ. P. 204.1(c)(2).

43 Tex. R. Civ. P. 204.1(d).

44 *In re Estabrook*, No. 10-20-00175-CV, 2020 Tex. App. LEXIS 8328, at *8–9, 2020 WL 6192923 (Tex. App.—Waco Oct. 21, 2020, orig. proceeding) (mem. op.) ("[Texas Rule] 204.1(d) requires the trial court to specify the time, place, manner, conditions, and scope of the mental examination. Texas courts have held that the failure to place any limitations on the scope of the mental examination, especially to the mental conditions specifically in controversy in the matter, constitutes an abuse of discretion. Because the trial court's order did not limit the neuropsychological examination to the mental conditions in controversy—Estabrook's depression and PTSD, we conclude that the trial court abused its discretion to the extent that it ordered the mental examination without proper limitations, as fairness requires.") (citations omitted); *In re Reyes*, No. 02-20-00071-CV, 2020 Tex. App. LEXIS 2298, at *3–4, 2020 WL 1294923 (Tex. App.—Fort Worth Mar. 19, 2020, orig. proceeding) (mem. op.) (same); *In re Sharaf*, 2018 Tex. App. LEXIS 9027, at *7–8, 2018 WL 5796977 (Tex. App.—Austin Nov. 5, 2018, orig. proceeding) (mem. op.) (same).

45 *See, e.g.*, *In re Offshore Marine Contractors, Inc.*, 496 S.W.3d 796, 803 (Tex. App.—Houston [1st Dist.] 2016, orig. proceeding) (explaining that an interview's length and quantity and duration of neuropsychological tests ordered by trial court "are matters for the trial court's discretion").

examination of conditions not in issue is improper,[46] as is one that fails to specify the time, place, manner, conditions, or scope of the examination or the person or persons by whom it is to be made.[47]

Several questions arise with respect to the order. *First*, can the trial court order that the examination either be observed by a third person, such as the examined person's attorney, physician, or psychologist, or videotaped or otherwise recorded? *Second*, can the trial court order the examination to be conducted by someone other than the requesting party's designated physician or psychologist? *Third*, can the trial court order that the examiner not communicate with the examined person during the examination? *Fourth*, who pays for the examination? *Finally*, where can the physical or mental examination be conducted?

A physical or mental examination cannot be observed or recorded unless the examined person shows good cause for the accommodation—that is, the examined person shows that special circumstances, unique to that party, requires the accommodation.[48]

---

[46] *In re Evans*, No. 03-20-00532-CV, 2021 Tex. App. LEXIS 637, at *15–16, 2021 WL 278944 (Tex. App.—Austin Jan. 28, 2021, orig. proceeding) (mem. op.) ("The order for the mental examination, which may be as long as five hours, does not limit the scope to the only conditions placed in controversy by Evans—PTSD, anxiety disorder, panic disorder, and major depressive disorder. Instead, the order broadly provides that 'the examination may also include having the Plaintiff complete standardized testing (using paper and pencil/pen) of the form that is typically and routinely used to assess an individual's mental health and/or mental diagnosis for conditions such as: depression, PTSD, etc.' The broad language of 'conditions such as,' followed by 'etc.,' combined with the lack of identification of the possible tests that Ticknor may administer, makes the order inadequately specific."); *In re Estabrook*, No. 10-20-00175-CV, 2020 Tex. App. LEXIS 8328, 2020 WL 6192923, at *4 (Tex. App.—Waco Oct. 21, 2020, orig. proceeding) (mem. op.) (holding that an order was too broad because it failed to limit the examination to mental conditions put in controversy by the plaintiff).

[47] *In re Estabrook*, No. 10-20-00175-CV, 2020 Tex. App. LEXIS 8328, at *9, 2020 WL 6192923 (Tex. App.—Waco Oct. 21, 2020, orig. proceeding) (mem. op.) ("Texas courts have held that the failure to place any limitations on the scope of the mental examination, especially to the mental conditions specifically in controversy in the matter, constitutes an abuse of discretion."); *In re Sharaf*, No. 03-18-00671-CV, 2018 Tex. App. LEXIS 9027, at *7–8, 2018 WL 5796977 (Tex. App.—Austin Nov. 5, 2018, orig. proceeding) (mem. op.) ("Although we agree with Liberty Mutual that the trial court was not required to list the specific tests that will be administered, the order does not limit the scope of the examination to the identified testing and interview or place other parameters on the examination, such as limiting the testing to standardized testing or placing a limitation on the duration of the testing and interview."); *In re Reyes*, No. 02-20-00071-CV, 2020 Tex. App. LEXIS 2298, at *3–4, 2020 WL 1294923 (Tex. App.—Fort Worth Mar. 19, 2020, orig. proceeding) (mem. op.) ("Here, on its face, Respondent's order does not set out the place, manner, conditions, or scope of the examination, or by whom it is to be made. . . . Because the order demonstrates a clear failure to comply with [Texas] Rule 204.1's requirements, we sustain the relevant portions of Reyes's four issues and conditionally grant partial relief so that Respondent may tailor the order to comply with Rule 204.1's requirements, thereby limiting the order to that which fairness requires.") (citations omitted).

[48] *In re Redbird Trails Apartments*, No. 05-20-00284-CV, 2020 Tex. App. LEXIS 4676, at *9–10, 2020 WL 3445811 (Tex. App.—Dallas June 24, 2020, orig. proceeding) (mem. op.) ("Relators also complain about the trial court's order requiring the exams to be videotaped and prohibiting Dr. Rosenfield from communicating with real party about the children's

Good cause for such an accommodation "may be shown by various special circumstances, including for instance, where the examinee is a minor, does not speak the relevant language, or suffers from a disability that might impair his or her ability to communicate to counsel what occurs during the examination, or where evidence otherwise suggests that recording would be advisable."[49]

"[G]eneralized concerns about accuracy, reliability, and methodology for the examination do not constitute good cause for recording. Thus, good cause for recording an examination is not established by the inherently adversarial nature of the examination, the fact that the examining physician was selected or paid for by opposing counsel, the theoretical potential for misconduct during the examination, the desire to obtain an accurate, dispute-free version of what was said, or the fear that the examination would become a de facto deposition."[50] In other words, good cause is determined on a "case-by-case basis according to evidence showing a particularized need, rather than by a categorical determination based on the underlying tort or cause of action, or the nature of the injury alleged."[51]

Although the requesting party does not have the absolute right to have the party examined by its designated doctor or psychologist, the trial court generally should allow that doctor or psychologist to conduct the examination. As explained by the Dallas Court of Appeals: "'[F]undamental fairness' dictates that a defendant's expert

---

medical history at the exams. Ordinarily, a moving party's expert should be allowed the 'same opportunity' as the opposing party's expert to 'fully develop and present [his or her] opinion, ensuring a fair trial.' Real party did not provide proof of any special circumstance that required videotaping the examinations, and does not suggest any such evidence exists in her reply to the petition for writ of mandamus. The examinations performed by real party's experts were not videotaped. Thus, in the absence of proof of special circumstances or a particularized need for videotaping or having an attorney present at the opposing party's examination, one party should not be required to videotape the examination when the other party did not. Thus, it was an abuse of discretion for the trial court to sua sponte require the exams be videotaped." (citation omitted) (quoting *In re H.E.B. Grocery Co.*, 492 S.W.3d 300, 304–05 (Tex. 2016) (orig. proceeding) (per curiam))); *In re Soc'y of Our Lady of the Most Holy Trinity*, 6622 S.W.3d 1, 13 (Tex. App.—Corpus Christi 2019, orig. proceeding) (collecting federal cases, and explaining that "[u]nder federal law, third-party observations and recordings of examinations are disfavored. This is because '[t]he introduction of a human or mechanical presence—whether a lawyer, a stenographer, a tape recorder, or other instrumentality—changes the nature of the proceeding.' . . . And further, allowing an observer or recording subverts the purpose of the rule allowing examinations, which is to put both the plaintiff and the defendant on an equal footing regarding the evaluation of the party's medical or psychological status. In other words—where one party has been examined by his or her doctors outside the presence of others or recording devices—the other party should be given the same equal opportunity. Under the majority viewpoint, the party requesting the presence of counsel or seeking to record or videotape the examination has the burden to show a factual basis establishing special circumstances which constitute good cause for the accommodation." (citations omitted) (quoting *Ornelas v. S. Tire Mart, LLC*, 292 F.R.D. 388, 397 (S.D. Tex. 2013))).

49 *In re Soc'y of Our Lady of the Most Holy Trinity*, 622 S.W.3d 1, 14 (Tex. App.—Corpus Christi 2019, orig. proceeding) (collecting federal cases).

50 *In re Soc'y of Our Lady of the Most Holy Trinity*, 622 S.W.3d 1, 15 (Tex. App.—Corpus Christi 2019, orig. proceeding) (citing federal cases).

51 *In re Soc'y of Our Lady of the Most Holy Trinity*, 622 S.W.3d 1, 16 (Tex. App.—Corpus Christi 2019, orig. proceeding).

be allowed to examine the plaintiff. Otherwise, the defendant will be at a significant disadvantage in the 'battle of the experts.'"[52] Because Texas Rule 204.1(a) requires the physician or psychologist to be "qualified,"[53] a valid objection to the requesting party's physician or psychologist is that the physician or psychologist is unqualified by reason of his or her training, skills, or experience (e.g., requesting that a psychiatrist conduct an orthopedic examination of a plaintiff).[54] Generalized claims that the proposed examining expert is biased because the expert regularly testifies for the requesting party should not be a sufficient objection to the expert.[55]

---

[52] *In re Redbird Trails Apartments*, No. 05-20-00284-CV, 2020 Tex. App. LEXIS 4676, at *7, 2020 WL 3445811 (Tex. App.—Dallas June 24, 2020, orig. proceeding) (mem. op.); *cf. Khobragade v. Covidien LP*, No. 16-cv-0468-WQH-AGS, 2018 U.S. Dist. LEXIS 50993, at *2–3 (S.D. Cal. March 27, 2018) ("[Federal] Rule 35 does not require that the examiner be uninterested: the proposed examiner need only be 'suitably licensed or certified.' Although the Court is not required to accept defendants' proposed examiner as the examining psychologist, only if plaintiff raises a valid objection will the Court appoint a different examiner.' Plaintiff has made no such showing, and in any event, plaintiff will have the opportunity to impeach the expert's opinions at trial with any evidence of bias." (quoting *Redon v. Ruiz*, No. 13cv1765-WQH(KSC), 2015 U.S. Dist. LEXIS 163797, at *11, 2015 WL 13238642 (S.D. Cal. Dec. 4, 2015), and *Ragge v. MCA/Universal Studios*, 165 F.R.D. 605, 609 (C.D. Cal. 1995))); *Livingston v. Union Par. Det. Ctr.*, No. 18-cv-0209, 2018 U.S. Dist. LEXIS 86762, at *3–4, 2018 WL 2347094 (W.D. La. May 22, 2018) ("Plaintiff also objects to attending an IME with Defendants' chosen psychologist, Dr. Simoneaux. Plaintiff cites some negative reviews regarding Dr. Simoneaux on the internet. . . . [T]he purported negative reviews on the internet are not credible evidence of Dr. Simoneaux's professional abilities or judgment. Of course, whether Dr. Simoneaux's opinions are admissible in evidence is a question for another day. And if the opinions are admitted, cross-examination can be used to explore such concerns and air them before the factfinder."); *Spencer v. Huron Cnty.*, No. 15-cv-12209, 2016 U.S. Dist. LEXIS 118814, at *4–5, 2016 WL 4578102 (E.D. Mich. Sept. 2, 2016) ("Although Defendants do not have an absolute right to compel an examination by a particular physician of their choosing, absent a showing of bias or prejudice, the Court will not disturb the Defendants' choice of medical examiner. The rationale for this approach is that, if a 'plaintiff may select his own doctor to testify as to his physical [or mental] condition, fundamental fairness dictates that a defendant shall have the same right[.]'" (citations omitted) (quoting 8B Charles A. Wright, Arthur R. Miller, & Richard L. Marcus, *Federal Practice and Procedure* § 2234.2 at 274 (2010))); *Redon v. Ruiz*, No. 13cv1765-WQH(KSC), 2015 U.S. Dist. LEXIS 163797, at *12, 2015 WL 13238642 (S.D. Cal. Dec. 4, 2015) ("The Court would only consider the appointment of a different examiner from the one proposed by defendants if plaintiff raised valid objections. 'The "valid objection" requirement provides defendants with the same opportunity as plaintiffs in choosing an expert witness. Defendants have absolutely no say in determining which physician a plaintiff chooses as a treating physician or an expert witness; likewise, a plaintiff should be limited in his ability to object to the selection of the defendant's expert witnesses.' The plaintiff in *Powell v. U.S.* [, 149 F.R.D. 122, 124 (E.D. Va. 1993),] argued that defendant's proposed examiner was biased, because he was regularly retained by insurance companies and defendants to perform medical examinations. The Court rejected this argument because the plaintiff did not demonstrate personal bias on the part of the proposed examiner." (citations omitted) (quoting *Powell v. U.S.*, 149 F.R.D. 122, 124 (E.D. Va. 1993))).

[53] Tex. R. Civ. P. 204.1(a)(1).

[54] See cases cited in note 52.

[55] See cases cited in note 52.

"A trial court may not deny a motion for an examination under [Texas R]ule 204.1 based on lack of qualification of the proposed examining doctor. . . . Thus, if a trial court finds the proposed examining physician to be unqualified, the remedy is to appoint a different physician of the trial court's choice rather than to deny the examination altogether."[56]

Further, a trial court cannot properly prohibit the examiner from communicating with the examined person.[57]

Absent agreement regarding the location of the physical or mental examination, the examined person generally will be required to come to the place where the lawsuit is pending.[58] The examined person generally pays his or her expenses for coming to

---

[56] *In re Ten Hagen Excavating, Inc.*, 435 S.W.3d 859, 871 (Tex. App.—Dallas 2014, orig. proceeding).

[57] *In re Redbird Trails Apartments*, No. 05-20-00284-CV, 2020 Tex. App. LEXIS 4676, at *10–11, 2020 WL 3445811 (Tex. App.—Dallas June 24, 2020, orig. proceeding) (mem. op.) ("We likewise conclude the trial court abused its discretion in prohibiting Dr. Rosenfield from communicating with real party about the children's medical history at the exams. Although real party argues that allowing Dr. Rosenfield to communicate with the mother or caregiver is tantamount to a 'back door means of questioning that would deprive mother of legal counsel,' we do not agree. As previously stated, the Texas Supreme Court has concluded that in the absence of any special circumstance, a movant for a [Texas R]ule 204 examination should have the same opportunity to fully develop and present his opinion as the opposing party's expert."); *cf. Hansen v. Savage Arms Co.*, No. 17-CV-3002-LTS, 2017 U.S. Dist. LEXIS 204937, at *9, 2017 WL 6376342 (N.D. Iowa Dec. 13, 2017) ("Plaintiff's final concern with respect to the examination is the potential waiver of plaintiff's attorney-client privilege. Specifically, plaintiff states that 'defendants (who are precluded from directly speaking with [plaintiff] without the presence of his attorneys) want their retained expert, Dr. Tyler, to be able to interview the plaintiff about his damage claim arising out of his hearing loss, out of the presence of his attorneys.' Dr. Tyler's examination is limited to the medical facts at issue. There is no reason to believe Dr. Tyler would ask any questions of plaintiff about communication he has had with his attorneys. Plaintiff has failed to articulate any other means by which defendants may seek to obtain protected information by way of the examination, and the Court is not convinced that such means exist. However, should potentially privileged information be revealed during the examination, plaintiff may petition the Court to prevent the use of that information, as plaintiff sees fit.").

[58] *Cf. Knuth v. Reg'l Transit Auth. of New Orleans*, No. 20-396, 2020 U.S. Dist. LEXIS 214647, at *5–6, 2020 WL 6742800 (E.D. La. Nov. 7, 2020) ("[M]ost judges have, in the usual case, ordered the plaintiff to appear for examination at the place where the trial would be held—that is, at the venue selected initially by the plaintiff. This allows the examining physician to be available conveniently for testimony. However, the burden is not on the defendant to demonstrate that a satisfactory examination cannot be had a nearer locale to the plaintiff; rather, 'the burden is on the plaintiff to show that traveling to the examination poses undue burden or hardship.' And given the inability to compel an out of district IME to appear in the forum for trial, ordering an IME outside the district should not be done absent evidence of hardship or burden." (footnotes omitted) (quoting *Baird v. Quality Foods, Inc.*, 47 F.R.D. 212, 212–13 (E.D. La. 1969), and *Thomas v. W & T Offshore, Inc.*, No. 16-14694, 2018 U.S. Dist. LEXIS 9600, at *4, 2018 U.S. Dist. LEXIS 9600 (E.D. La. Jan. 22, 2018))); *Richardson v. Prisoner Transp. Servs. of Am.*, No. 3:15-CV-01061, 2017 U.S. Dist. LEXIS 70710, at *4, 2017 WL 1902170 (M.D. Pa. May 17, 2017) ("The general rule is that a plaintiff who brings suit in a particular forum may not avoid appearing for an examination in that forum."); *Ornelas v. S. Tire Mart, LLC*, 292 F.R.D. 388, 399–400 (S.D. Tex. 2013) ("The general rule is that a

the examination and bears any lost income from it.[59] The examining party generally pays the expense of the examination itself.[60]

12-3 Report of Examining Physician or Psychologist

Texas Rule 204.2(a) requires the examining party, upon the "request of" the examined person, to "deliver to the person a copy of a detailed written report of the examining physician or psychologist setting out the findings, including results of all tests made, diagnoses and conclusions, together with like reports of all earlier examinations of the same condition."[61] If the examining party delivers the report and requests "a like report of any examination made before or after the ordered examination of the same condition[,]" then the other party must produce any such reports "unless the person examined is not a party[, that is, the examined person is in the custody, conservatorship or under the legal control of a party,] and the party shows that the party is unable to obtain it."[62] Texas Rule 204.2(a)'s disclosure requirements are mandatory and apply even if the report at issue is privileged because, for example, the examiner is a consulting expert rather than a testifying one.[63]

---

plaintiff who brings suit in a particular forum may not avoid appearing for an examination in that forum. In the case of physical or mental examinations, this rule ensures that the examining specialist is available as an expert witness at trial. Logic also dictates such a result, because the facilities and equipment an examiner needs are likely at his place of practice. 'For an exception to be made [to this general rule], the burden is not on the defendant to demonstrate that a satisfactory examination cannot be had a nearer locale to the plaintiff, but rather on the plaintiff to show that traveling to the examination poses undue burden or hardship.'" (footnote omitted) (citations omitted) (quoting *McDonald v. Southworth*, No. 1:07-cv-217-JMS-DFH, 2008 U.S. Dist. LEXIS 52830, at *15, 2008 WL 2705557 (S.D. Ind. July 10, 2008))).

59 *Cf. Richardson v. Prisoner Transp. Servs. of Am.*, No. 3:15-CV-01061, 2017 U.S. Dist. LEXIS 70710, at *4, 2017 WL 1902170 (M.D. Pa. May 17, 2017) ("[T]he party being examined, with limited exception, must pay his or her own travel expenses to an examination in the forum state. An exception to the general rule is made if the part being examined will suffer undue financial hardship by fronting the travel expenses or if the travel expenses could have been avoided by better planning."); *Spencer v. Huron Cnty.*, No. 15-cv-12209, 2016 U.S. Dist. LEXIS 118814, at *5–6, 2016 WL 4578102 (E.D. Mich. Sept. 2, 2016) (same); *McCloskey v. UPS Gen. Servs. Co.*, 171 F.R.D. 268, 270 (D. Or. 1997) (same).

60 *Cf. Strosin v. J.M. Smucker Co.*, No. 5:14-cv-07085, 2015 U.S. Dist. LEXIS 142824, at *8 (E.D. Pa. Oct. 20, 2015) (holding that the examining party bears the expense of the examination itself); *Duarte v. Wong*, No. C 05-01374, 2007 U.S. Dist. LEXIS 73678, at *26 n.4, 2007 WL 2782940 (N.D. Cal. Sept. 24, 2007) ("The party who requested the examination must pay for it.").

61 Tex. R. Civ. P. 204.2(a); *see In re Commitment of Hatchell*, 343 S.W.3d 560, 562–63 (Tex. App.—Beaumont 2011, no pet.) (Texas "Rule 204.2 provides that a person subject to court order under [Texas] Rule 204.1 has the right to 'a detailed written report of the examining physician or psychologist setting out the findings, including results of all tests made, diagnoses and conclusions, together with like reports of all earlier examinations of the same condition.'" (quoting Tex. R. Civ. P. 204.2(a))).

62 Tex. R. Civ. P. 204.2(a).

63 *Shulin v. Werner Enters.*, No. 1:15CV95, 2017 U.S. Dist. LEXIS 231777, at *4–5, 2017 WL 10379220 (N.D.W. Va. Jan. 9, 2017) ("While Federal Rule of Civil Procedure 26(b)(4)(D) protects against disclosure of 'facts known or opinions held' by a non-testifying expert

Several questions arise regarding the provision of reports, only some of which are answered by Texas Rule 204(a). *First,* is Texas Rule 204(a)'s requirement that the examining party deliver to the examined person "like reports of all earlier examinations of the same condition" limited to reports related to examinations of the examined person or does it include all reports of examinations of any person with the same condition as that of the examined person? *Second,* can the trial court order the examining party or the examined person to prepare a report and, if not, what happens if the examining party or the examined person fails to provide the required report? *Third,* can the examined person depose the examiner if the examiner is not disclosed as a testifying expert for the examining party? *Finally,* can the examined person obtain protection from the disclosure of extraneous information in the required reports?

No Texas case has considered whether the examining party's obligation under Texas Rule 204.2(a) to produce "like reports of all earlier examinations of the same condition"[64] includes reports about the examination of persons examined in other cases or circumstances with the same condition. The issue has not been conclusively decided by federal courts construing Federal Rule 35(b)(1)'s identical language.— One federal court has construed the language as requiring the production of such reports, while another court has limited the language to other reports of the examined person.[65]

---

retained specifically to assist a party prepare for trial, it provides an exception pursuant to Rule 35(b). Federal Rule of Civil Procedure 35(b)((1) clearly entitles Kennedy to receive a copy of Dr. Coburn's report and psychometric testing data. In short, Defendants have failed—after being given multiple opportunities to do so otherwise—to provide to Kennedy, Dr. Coburn's report and psychometric testing data thus impeding his ability to effectively address his severe emotional distress claims.") (citation omitted); *Delgado v. GGNSC Grand Island Lakeview LLC*, No. 4:15CV3124, 2016 U.S. Dist. LEXIS 130507, at *4, 2016 WL 5339535 (D. Neb. Sept. 23, 2016) (explaining that that the examiner's report has to be produced even if the examiner is a consulting-only expert because Federal Rule 35(b)(1) "does not distinguish between examinations by testifying or non-testifying experts and the rule has generally been interpreted to mean that the person examined has an absolute right to a copy of the examining physician's report"); *Decristo v. Sw. Motor Transp., Inc.*, Civil Action No. 89-6080, 1990 U.S. Dist. LEXIS 13617, at *2–3 (E.D. Pa. Oct. 12, 1990) ("Defendants argue that under Federal Rules of Civil Procedure 26(b)(4) and 35(b) they may not be compelled to produce the report of Dr. Nordone because Dr. Nordone was a 'consulting expert' who they do not intend to call to testify at trial. Defendants further contend that under [Federal] Rule 35, plaintiff's remedy is limited to the entry of an order precluding Dr. Nordone's testimony. . . . Historically, [Federal] Rule 35(b) has been interpreted to mean that the person examined has an absolute right to a copy of the report of the examining physician.").

64 Tex. R. Civ. P. 204.2(a).

65 *Compare Clark v. Wilkin*, No. 2:06cv00693, 2008 U.S. Dist. LEXIS 14861, at *3–4, 2008 WL 1787657 (D. Utah Feb. 7, 2008) (holding that Federal Rule 35(b)(1) does not require the production of reports of other persons examined who suffer from the same condition as the examined person), *with Bryant v. Dillon Real Estate Co.*, No. 18-cv-00479-PAB-MEH, 2019 U.S. Dist. LEXIS 140944, at *11, 2019 WL 3935174 (D. Colo. Aug. 20, 2019) ("The Court finds that the plain language of [Federal] Rule 35(b)(1), together with the [advisory] committee's notes, demonstrate that an examined party is entitled to production by the examiner of 'all' reports, to which the examiner has access, regarding examinations of the same condition(s) suffered by the examined party ('like reports'). Accordingly, here, Dr. Gutterman is ordered to produce reports in accordance with the rule and as (potentially) limited by the Plaintiff, which the Court construes as: the last twenty 'like reports' prepared

Texas Rule 204.2(a) does not permit the trial court to order the examining party or the examined person's examiner to prepare a report if the *examiner* fails or refuses to prepare one.[66] Texas Rule 204.2(a), however, permits the exclusion of testimony of an examiner who fails or refuses to prepare a report of the examination, providing: "If a physician or psychologist fails or refuses to make a report the court may exclude the testimony if offered at the trial."[67] On its face, the Rule gives the trial court discretion in deciding whether to exclude such testimony for noncompliance. In other words, exclusion is not automatic.[68]

Whether the examiner can be deposed depends on whether the examiner is a testifying expert or a consulting expert whose mental impressions or opinions have been reviewed by a testifying expert. If the examiner is such an expert, the examiner can be deposed. If the examiner is a consulting-only expert, the examiner cannot be deposed. This is made clear by the fact that Texas Rule 204.2 does not expressly permit the examiner to be deposed. Rather, it provides that "[t]his subdivision does not preclude . . . the taking of a deposition of the physician or psychologist in accordance with the provisions of any *other* rule."[69] As noted by one federal court in discussing the similar language of Federal Rule 35(b):[70]

> The specific language of [Federal] Rule 35 indicates that if a party is subjected to a physical examination, the party is entitled to a detailed written report of that examination, but no more. The Rule could have stated that the party is also entitled to depose the examiner, but it does not, and there is no indication in the rule that participating in a physical examination entitles the examined party to a deposition of the examiner as well as a report of the examination. Furthermore, while [Federal] Rule 35 does not preclude depositions of examiners, it limits depositions to those which are permitted in accordance with the provisions of other rules. The examined party's entitlement, therefore, is limited to the examiner's report of the examination. We find, therefore, that while [Federal] Rule 35

---

by Dr. Gutterman for the defense counsel's firm, the last twenty 'like reports' prepared by Dr. Gutterman for any defendant, and the last twenty 'like reports' prepared by Dr. Gutterman for anyone.").

66 Tex. R. Civ. P. 204.2(a); *cf. Delgado v. GGNSC Grand Island Lakeview LLC*, No. 4:15CV3124, 2016 U.S. Dist. LEXIS 130507, at *4, 2016 WL 5339535 (D. Neb. Sept. 23, 2016) (noting that, if the examiner is a consulting expert nothing in Federal Rules 26 or 35 requires such an expert to create an expert report). *But see Salvatore v. Am. Cyanamid Co.*, 94 F.R.D. 156, 157–59 (D.R.I. 1982) (ordering the examining party to provide the report because there was no evidence that the examiner refused to prepare one).

67 Tex. R. Civ. P. 204.2(a); *see In re Commitment of Hatchell*, 343 S.W.3d 560, 563 (Tex. App.—Beaumont 2011, no pet.) ("'If a physician or psychologist fails or refuses to make a report the court may exclude the testimony if offered at the trial.'" (quoting Tex. R. Civ. P. 204.2(a))).

68 *See In re Commitment of Hatchell*, 343 S.W.3d 560, 563 (Tex. App.—Beaumont 2011, no pet.) (noting in *dicta* that "even if [Texas] Rule 204 did govern here, the [R]ule does not require the trial court to strike expert testimony for failure to comply with [Texas] Rule 204.2; it merely gives the trial court discretion to do so"); *cf. Kerns v. Consol. Rail Corp.*, 90 F.R.D. 134, 138 (E.D. Pa. 1981) (Federal "Rule 35(b) permits, but does not require, the Court to exclude the testimony of a doctor if the doctor fails or refuses to deliver a report to the other party.").

69 Tex. R. Civ. P. 204.2(b) (emphasis added).

70 Federal Rule 35(b)(6) provides that the Federal Rule 35(b) "does not preclude . . . deposing an examiner under other rules." Fed. R. Civ. P. 35(b)(6).

will allow a deposition that does not contravene any other rule, the limitations of other rules will control the taking of depositions of examination-conducting expert witnesses.[71]

On motion, a trial court "may limit delivery of a report on such terms as are just."[72] Thus, if the report contains extraneous material unrelated to the examination, a motion for protective order asking for the redaction of such information should be filed, and the trial court should examine the report in camera to determine if such relief should be granted.

---

[71] *Carroll v. Praxair, Inc.*, No. 05-0307, 2007 U.S. Dist. LEXIS 9212, at *6, 2007 WL 437697 (W.D. La. Feb. 7, 2007); *accord Chet Morrison Contractors, Inc. v. Medco Energi US LLC*, No. 08-1638, 2009 U.S. Dist. LEXIS 83093, at *10–11 (E.D. La. 2009) ("[W]here an expert will not be a witness at trial, the parties are limited in their discovery practices to those methods referred to in [Federal] Rule 35(b)—which limits the discovery to the examiner's report of the examination."). Unlike the Texas discovery rules, which categorically precludes discovery from consulting-only experts, Tex. R. Civ. P. 192.3(e) ("The identity, mental impressions, and opinions of a consulting expert whose mental impressions and opinions have not been reviewed by a testifying expert are not discoverable."); Tex. R. Civ. P. 195 cmt. 1 to 199 Change ("Information concerning purely consulting experts, of course, is not discoverable."), the federal discovery rules allow a party to depose an opposing party's consulting-only expert "on showing exceptional circumstances under which it is impracticable for the party to obtain facts or opinions on the same subject by other means[,]" Fed. R. Civ. P. 26(b)(4)(D)(1). Federal courts have taken three approaches regarding whether an examiner who is a consulting-only expert can be deposed or called as a trial witness. "Some courts have adopted an 'entitlement' standard, finding that by submitting to a [Federal] Rule 35 examination, a plaintiff is entitled to 'call an opposing party's [Federal] Rule 35 expert, despite the opposing party's desire not to have the expert testify.' Other courts have relied on a 'discretionary' or 'balancing' standard, which 'involv[es] a balancing of the interests of the party and the court against the potential for prejudice to the party who hired the expert, but who does not wish to use that expert at trial.' A third group of courts utilizes the 'exceptional circumstances approach, which 'recognize[s] interests weighing against allowing an opposing party to depose or to call at trial a consultative, non-testifying expert witness' absent exceptional circumstances." *Bankr. Estate of Lee v. Burlington N. Santa Fe R.R.*, No. 07 C 5829, 2010 U.S. Dist. LEXIS 21465, at *7, 2010 WL 894056 (N.D. Ill. 2010) (quoting *Lehan v. Ambassador Programs, Inc.*, 190 F.R.D. 670, 671, 672 (E.D. Wash. 2000))); *see Rawers v. United States*, 488 F. Supp. 3d 1059, 1085 n.29 (D.N.M. 2020) (discussing different approaches and adopting the "exception circumstances" test); *Anderson v. Metro-North Commuter R.R.*, No. 3:14cv452 (JBA), 2016 U.S. Dist. LEXIS 62708, at *3–10 (D. Conn. May 11 2016) (noting that entitlement approach is the "minority" one and adopting the balancing approach).

[72] Tex. R. Civ. P. 204.2(a); *see also In re Offshore Marine Contractors, Inc.*, 496 S.W.3d 796, 800 (Tex. App.—Houston [1st Dist.] 2016, orig. proceeding) (after concluding that the trial court abused its discretion in not permitting the defendant's neuropsychologist expert to conduct a neuropsychological examination of a plaintiff who put his neuropsychological condition in controversy, noting that, under Texas Rule 204.1(d), the trial court "retain[ed] discretion to place reasonable limits on" the contemplated examination); *In re Trimac Transp., Inc.*, No. 09-08-270 CV, 2008 Tex. App. LEXIS 5329, at *3, 2008 WL 2758793 (Tex. App.—Beaumont July 17, 2008, no pet.) (mem. op.) ("The trial court may place reasonable conditions on the manner and scope of the examination.").

12-4 Examination by Agreement

Under Texas Rules 191.1 and 204.2(b), parties may enter an agreement for, and establish the terms of, a physical or mental examination of a party or a person in a party's custody, conservatorship, or legal control.[73] Unless such an "agreement expressly provides otherwise[,]" the examination-report discovery permitted by Texas Rule 204.2(a) "applies to examinations made by agreement of the parties[.]"[74] In other words, to avoid the default Texas Rule 204.2(a) discovery, parties need to state expressly in their agreement relating to the examination that such discovery will not be permitted in the case.

12-5 Effect of No Examination

Texas Rule 204.3 prohibits parties from commenting at trial about a party's willingness to submit to a physical or mental examination, stating: "If no examination is sought either by agreement or under this subdivision [allowing court-ordered examinations], the party whose physical or mental condition is in controversy must not comment to the court or jury concerning the party's willingness to submit to an examination, or on the right or failure of any other party to seek an examination."[75] The Rule's purpose is to "to prevent an adverse party from being forced to seek a medical evaluation or risk opening his failure to do so to comment before the jury."[76] It also prevents a party from using Texas Rule 204 generally to challenge the opposing party's medical evidence on the basis that an independent medical examination was neither sought nor conducted.[77]

12-6 Actions Arising Under Titles II or V, Family Code (No Motion Required)

Texas Rule 204.4 contains unique standards for actions arising under Title II of the Texas Family Code, regarding children in relation to the family,[78] or Title V of the Texas Family Code, regarding the parent-child relationship and suits affecting the parent-child relationship (or SAPCRs).[79] Under the Rule, mental examinations of children and paternity testing may be prompted by a party's motion or the trial court's own initiative. The Rule provides:

---

[73] *See* Tex. R. Civ. P. 191.1 ("Except where specifically prohibited, the procedures and limitations set forth in the rules pertaining to discovery may be modified in any suit by the agreement of the parties . . . . An agreement of the parties is enforceable if it complies with [Texas] Rule 11 or, as it affects an oral deposition, if it is made a part of the record of the deposition."), 204.2(b) (addressing "examinations made by agreement of the parties"). See also Chapter 3, section 3-3 (discussing agreed-upon modifications to discovery procedures and limitations).

[74] Tex. R. Civ. P. 204.2(b).

[75] Tex. R. Civ. P. 204.3.

[76] *Parkway Hosp. v. Lee*, 946 S.W.2d 580, 585 (Tex. App.—Houston [14th Dist.] 1997, writ denied), *overruled on other grounds, Roberts v. Williamson*, 111 S.W.3d 113, 120 (Tex. 2003).

[77] *Parkway Hosp. v. Lee*, 946 S.W.2d 580, 585 (Tex. App.—Houston [14th Dist.] 1997, writ denied), *overruled on other grounds, Roberts v. Williamson*, 111 S.W.3d 113, 120 (Tex. 2003).

[78] *See* Tex. Fam. Code §§ 31.001–47.001(c).

[79] *See* Tex. Fam. Code §§ 101.001–266.013.

In cases arising under Family Code Titles II or V, the court may—*on its own initiative or on motion of a party*—appoint:

(a) one or more psychologists or psychiatrists to make any and all appropriate mental examinations of the children who are the subject of the suit or of any other parties, and may make such appointment irrespective of whether a psychologist or psychiatrist has been designated by any party as a testifying expert; [and]

(b) one or more experts who are qualified in paternity testing to take blood, body fluid, or tissue samples to conduct paternity tests as ordered by the court.[80]

To date, no Texas court has answered the question of whether, or to what extent, Texas Rule 204.1's requirements apply to mental examinations under Texas Rule 204.4(a).[81] Texas Rule 204.1(c)(2) expressly addresses its relationship to Texas Rule 204.4, providing that "except as provided in [Texas] Rule 204.4, an examination by a psychologist may be ordered when the party responding to the motion has designated a psychologist as a testifying expert or has disclosed a psychologist's records for possible use at trial." The remainder of Texas Rule 204.1, however, is silent regarding its interplay with Texas Rule 204.4. In the absence of explicit guidance, the prudent course of action is to assume that Texas Rule 204.1's requirements apply to examinations under Texas Rule 204.4, except as expressly provided otherwise.

12-7 Number of Examinations

Texas Rule 204 does not limit the number of independent medical examinations that may be ordered. Whether multiple examinations are appropriate depends upon the case's facts.[82] "Courts have found that a second examination is justified when: (1) 'separate injuries call[] for examination by distinct medical specialties'; (2) 'a physician requires

80 Tex. R. Civ. P. 204.4 (emphasis added).

81 *See In re Brown*, 277 S.W.3d 474, 478 (Tex. App.—Houston [14th Dist.] 2009, orig. proceeding) ("Darlina asserts that these requirements of Texas Rule . . . 204.1 do not apply to the trial court's orders because they are governed by Texas Rule . . . 204.4. For the purpose of this analysis, it is presumed, without deciding, that the requirements of [Texas] Rule 204.1 apply in the instant case [under Title V of the Texas Family Code].") (footnotes omitted); *see also In re Brown*, 277 S.W.3d 474, 478 n. 4 (Tex. App.—Houston [14th Dist.] 2009, orig. proceeding) ("In *In re N.R.C.*, [94 S.W.3d 799 (Tex. App.—Houston [14th Dist.] 2002, pet. denied),] no party argued that the requirements of Texas Rule . . . 204.1 do not apply to trial court orders that are governed by Texas Rule . . . 204.4, and the court did not determine that the party requesting the examination had invoked [Texas] Rule 204.4. Furthermore, the *N.R.C.* court did not need to address the issue presented in this case because it concluded the trial court abused its discretion by denying the ex-wife's request for a psychological examination of her ex-husband and children under the standards of [Texas] Rule 204.1. Therefore, the *N.R.C.* court's holding did not resolve the issue raised by the parties in this proceeding.") (citations omitted).

82 *Cf. Louviere v. W&T Offshore Inc.*, No. 6:16-cv-00724, 2017 U.S. Dist. LEXIS 189097, at *2 (W.D. La. Nov. 15, 2017) ("[Federal] Rule 35 does not establish a limitation on the number of examinations to which a party may be subjected; each request for an independent medical examination must turn on its own facts and depends solely on the circumstances underlying the request.").

assistance of other consultants before he can render a diagnosis'; (3) the first examination was inadequate or incomplete; or (4) there has been a 'substantial time lag . . . between the initial examination and the trial.'"[83]

12-8 Eligible Examiners

Texas Rule 204 identifies the types of healthcare providers authorized to conduct physical and mental examinations. Texas Rule 204.1 authorizes "a qualified physician" to conduct a physical examination[84] and a "qualified physician or . . . a qualified psychologist" to conduct a mental examination.[85] A physical examination only can be conducted by a "qualified" physician. Neither Texas Rule 204 nor the case law define "qualified."[86] Presumably the same standard used to determine whether an expert is qualified to render an opinion under Texas Rule of Evidence 702 applies to the

---

[83] *Cf. Guidry v. Noble Drilling Servs.*, No. 16-4135, 2018 U.S. Dist. LEXIS 88965, at *4–5, 2018 WL 2418835 (E.D. La. May 29, 2018) (quoting *Moore v. Calavar Corp.*, 142 F.R.D. 134, 135 (W.D. La. 1992)); *see Chandler v. Escobar*, No. 4:10-CV-00591, 2010 U.S. Dist. LEXIS 112323, at *6, 2010 WL 4256151(N.D. Ohio Oct. 21, 2010) ("A second physical examination is permitted under certain circumstances provided that the 'court should require a stronger showing of necessity before it will order such repeated examination.' Several district courts have refused a second examination generally because 'there ha[s] been no showing of a change in the situation." (quoting *Vopelak v. Williams*, 42 F.R.D. 387, 387, 389 (N.D. Ohio 1967))).

[84] Tex. R. Civ. P. 204.1(a)(1), (c). The federal rule permits a physical examination to be conducted by "a suitably licensed or certified examiner[.]" Fed. R. Civ. P. 35(a)(1).

[85] Tex. R. Civ. P. 204.1(c)(2). The federal rule permits a physical examination to be conducted by "a suitably licensed or certified examiner[.]" Fed. R. Civ. P. 35(a)(1).

Former Texas Rule 167a(a) permitted a trial court to order an examination by a psychologist "only when the opposing party designated a psychologist as an expert witness." Tex. R. Civ. P. 167a(a), ***repealed*** 1998. Texas Rule 204.1's language is more liberal with respect to mental examinations by psychologist, providing that "an examination by a psychologist may be ordered when the party responding to the motion has designated a psychologist as a testifying expert or has disclosed a psychologist's records for possible use at trial[,]" The federal rule permits a physical examination to be conducted by "a suitably licensed or certified examiner[.]" Fed. R. Civ. P. 35(a)(1).

[86] The case law is clear that (1) the party opposing a motion for a physical or mental examination can object to it because the proposed physician or psychologist is unqualified, *see In re Redbird Trails Apartments*, No. 05-20-00284-CV, 2020 Tex. App. LEXIS 4676, at *8, 2020 WL 3445811 (Tex. App.—Dallas June 24, 2020, orig. proceeding) (mem. op.) (implication); *In re Ten Hagen Excavating, Inc.*, 435 S.W.3d 859, 871 (Tex. App.—Dallas 2014, orig. proceeding) (implication); (2) the trial court cannot sua sponte reject the proposed examiner, *In re Redbird Trails Apartments*, No. 05-20-00284-CV, 2020 Tex. App. LEXIS 4676, at *8, 2020 WL 3445811 (Tex. App.—Dallas June 24, 2020, orig. proceeding) (mem. op.) ("Here, real party never objected to or challenged the qualifications of Dr. Rosenfield in the trial court. Unless the patient involved has a valid objection to the movant's selection of an examiner, the examination should be conducted by a physician of the movant's choosing. Accordingly, we conclude that the trial court abused its discretion in sua sponte rejecting relators' examining physician."); and (3) "if a trial court finds the proposed examining physician to be unqualified, the remedy is to appoint a different physician of the trial court's choice rather than to deny the examination altogether[.]" *In re Ten Hagen Excavating, Inc.*, 435 S.W.3d 859, 871 (Tex. App.—Dallas 2014, orig. proceeding).

determination of whether a physician or psychologist is "qualified" under Texas Rule 204.1.[87]

Texas Rule 204.4 authorizes "psychologists or psychiatrists" to conduct mental examinations of children[88] and "one or more experts who are qualified in paternity testing to take blood, bodily fluid, or tissue samples to conduct paternity testing as ordered by the court."[89]

Texas Rule 204.5 defines "psychologist" as "a person licensed or certified by a state or the District of Columbia as a psychologist."[90] "Physician" is not defined in the Rule but has been defined in case law to mean "'a practitioner of medicine' who is skilled in medicine and surgery."[91] "Psychiatrist" is not defined in Rule 204 or in any case addressing it.[92] Because psychiatrists are physicians, however, the case law's definition of "physician" should apply to "psychiatrist." Moreover, consistent with statutory rules of construction, "psychiatrist" should be given its plain or literal meaning[93]—that is, "a physician specializing in psychiatry."[94]

Texas courts have strictly construed Texas Rule 204's examiner requirements. For example, in *Coates v. Whittington*,[95] the Texas Supreme Court, applying former Texas Rule 167a, which like Texas Rule 204 authorized physicians *and* psychologists to conduct mental examinations, held that a trial court abused its discretion by ordering a plaintiff to "undergo a mental examination with a court appointed examining *psychologist* [because former Texas] Rule 167a expressly require[d] that a mental examination be conducted by a physician" and "[a] psychologist is not a physician."[96] Similarly, in

---

[87] "Texas Rule of Evidence 702 permits a witness qualified as an expert by 'knowledge, skill, experience, training, or education' to testify on 'scientific, technical, or other specialized' subjects if the testimony 'will assist the trier of fact to understand the evidence or to determine a fact in issue.'" *Volkswagen of Am., Inc. v. Ramirez*, 159 S.W.3d 897, 904 (Tex. 2004) (quoting Tex. R. Evid. 702); *accord Whirlpool Corp. v. Camacho*, 298 S.W.3d 631, 637 (Tex. 2009).

[88] Tex. R. Civ. P. 204.4(a).

[89] Tex. R. Civ. P. 204.4(b).

[90] Tex. R. Civ. P. 204.5.

[91] *Coates v. Whittington*, 758 S.W.2d 749, 751 (Tex. 1988) (orig. proceeding) (quoting 42 Tex. Jur. 3d *Healing Arts and Institutions* § 1 (1985), and *Black's Law Dictionary* 1033 (5th ed. 1979)).

[92] Federal Rule 35 does not refer to psychologists, physicians, or psychiatrists; it more broadly allows "a suitably licensed or certified examiner" to conduct a physical or mental examination. Fed. R. Civ. P. 35(a)(1).

[93] *See In re Christus Spohn Hosp. Kleberg*, 222 S.W.3d 434, 437 (Tex. 2007) (orig. proceeding) ("We begin by examining the discovery rules in dispute, applying the same rules of construction that govern the interpretation of statutes. When a rule of procedure is clear and unambiguous, we construe the rule's language according to its plain or literal meaning.") (citations omitted).

[94] Merriam-Webster Medical Dictionary, https://www.merriam-webster.com/medical/psychiatrist (last visited Apr. 17, 2021).

[95] *Coates v. Whittington*, 758 S.W.2d 749 (Tex. 1988) (orig. proceeding).

[96] *Coates v. Whittington*, 758 S.W.2d 749, 751 (Tex. 1988) (orig. proceeding); *accord Exxon Corp. v. Starr*, 790 S.W.2d 883, 886–87 (Tex. App.—Tyler 1990, orig. proceeding). Under Texas Rules 204.1(a)(1) and 204.4(a), psychologists are expressly authorized to conduct mental examinations. Thus, the specific holding in *Coates v. Whittington*, 758 S.W.2d 749, 751 (Tex. 1988) (orig. proceeding), no longer applies; however, the fact that the Texas

Moore v. Wood,[97] the First Court of Appeals, applying former Texas Rule 167a, held that a trial court abused its discretion by ordering a vocational-rehabilitation interview.[98] Finally, in *In re Advanced Power Solutions, Inc.*,[99] the First Court of Appeals held that a movant failed to meet its burden under Texas Rule 204 with respect to a requested "functional capacity evaluation and impairment rating" by Ergonomic Rehabilitation of Houston, in part because the motion was "silent regarding who would perform the [evaluation]" and "whether it would be performed by a 'qualified physician.'"[100]

A movant has "no absolute right to appointment of a physician of its own choosing to conduct the examination" under Texas Rule 204.1.[101] Nonetheless, it generally should allow the movant's expert to conduct the examination if the expert is qualified.[102]

A movant also has no "absolute right to have a physician of his own choosing conduct the independent examination of [a child]" under Texas Rule 204.4.[103]

> Family court judges may on their own initiative or on the motion of a party, appoint psychologists or psychiatrists to make any and all appropriate mental examinations of the children who are the subject of the suit or of any other parties. The family court judge may make such an appointment irrespective of whether a psychologist or psychiatrist has been designated by any party as a testifying expert.[104]

Supreme Court was strict in its construction of eligible examiners continues to have precedential value.

97 *Moore v. Wood*, 809 S.W.2d 621 (Tex. App.—Houston [1st Dist.] 1991, no writ).

98 *Moore v. Wood*, 809 S.W.2d 621, 624 (Tex. App.—Houston [1st Dist.] 1991, no writ) ("Some of the areas to be covered in the vocational rehabilitation interview are the same as those usually covered in a physical or mental examination. However, under [former Texas R]ule 167a and the reasoning in *Coates [v. Whittington*, 758 S.W.2d 749 (Tex. 1988) (orig. proceeding)], a plaintiff can be compelled to submit to a physical or mental examination only if conducted by a doctor or a psychologist . . . . [A]n involuntary vocational rehabilitation interview and assessment of the plaintiff is not permitted by the Texas Rules . . . . Therefore, we hold that Judge Wood has no authority to order such an interview and assessment.").

99 *In re Advanced Powder Sols., Inc.*, 496 S.W.3d 838 (Tex. App.—Houston [1st Dist.] 2016, orig. proceeding).

100 *In re Advanced Powder Sols., Inc.*, 496 S.W.3d 838, 852 (Tex. App.—Houston [1st Dist.] 2016, orig. proceeding) (quoting Tex. R. Civ. P. 204.1(a)(1)).

101 *In re Ten Hagen Excavating, Inc.*, 435 S.W.3d 859, 871 (Tex. App.—Dallas 2014, orig. proceeding); *cf. Simpson v. Univ. of Colo.*, 220 F.R.D. 354, 363 (D. Colo. 2004) ("While Defendant is entitled to a [Federal] Rule 35 examination of the Plaintiff, this court retains considerable discretion to establish the manner, conditions and scope of the examination. For example, the court is not bound by Defendant's selection of a particular examining physician or psychologist.") (citations omitted).

102 See cases cited in note 52.

103 *In re Weisinger*, No. 14-12-00558-CV, 2012 Tex. App. LEXIS 7643, at *5, 2012 WL 3861960 (Tex. App.—Houston [14th Dist.] Sept. 6, 2012, orig. proceeding) (mem. op.) (holding that the trial court did not abuse its discretion by appointing a different examiner than the one requested by the movant).

104 *In re N.R.C.*, 94 S.W.3d 799, 813–14 (Tex. App.—Houston [14th Dist.] 2002, pet. denied) (citations omitted); *see In re Scheller*, 325 S.W.3d 640, 645 (Tex. 2010) (per curiam) ("In SAPCRs [suits affecting the parent-child relationship], a trial court may appoint a psychologist or psychiatrist to conduct a mental examination of the parties and children subject to the suit." (citing Tex. R. Civ. P. 204.4(a)).

In addition, in a suit affecting the parent-child relationship, a judge does not necessarily abuse his or her discretion by appointing the same psychologist to serve as the child's guardian ad litem and as "an expert psychologist to examine the parties and children to make recommendations to the court."[105]

But, "[d]espite considerable discretion vested in courts to issue temporary orders 'for the safety and welfare of the child,' a court cannot act to infringe on a party's constitutional rights" in issuing such orders.[106] Thus, for example, a court cannot make a Texas Rule 204 appointment that infringes on the "fundamental liberty interest" of "[p]arental control and autonomy[.]"[107]

12-9 Examiners' Derived Judicial Immunity

Under certain circumstances, examiners appointed under Texas Rule 204.4 are entitled to derived judicial immunity. "When entitled to the protection of [such] immunity, an officer of the court receives the same immunity as a judge acting in his or her official judicial capacity—absolute immunity from liability for judicial acts performed within the scope of jurisdiction."[108] Judicial immunity not only protects the judges, but it also protects "the public 'whose interest it is that the judges should be at liberty to exercise their functions with independence, and without fear of consequences.'"[109]

---

105 *In re Scheller*, 325 S.W.3d 640, 644 (Tex. 2010) (orig. proceeding) (per curiam); *see In re Scheller*, 325 S.W.3d 640, 644 (Tex. 2010) (orig. proceeding) (per curiam) (noting that "[t]he role of the psychologist in evaluating the children and parties is consistent with the role of a guardian ad litem because the psychologist gives the court recommendations about the children's best interests[,]" and concluding that "the trial court's appointment of an evaluative [psychologist] expert [did] not infringe on [a parent's] rights because such an appointment is allowed by law; the order entered by the [c]ourt [did] not interfere with the parental relationship, but rather [sought] to determine the best interests of the children; and no conflict exists between appointing the evaluating psychologist as guardian ad litem").

106 *In re Scheller*, 325 S.W.3d 640, 644 (Tex. 2010) (orig. proceeding) (per curiam) (quoting Tex. Fam. Code § 105.001(a)).

107 *In re Scheller*, 325 S.W.3d 640, 644 (Tex. 2010) (orig. proceeding) (per curiam) (quoting *In re Derzapf*, 219 S.W.3d 327, 335 (Tex. 2007)).

108 *Dall. Cnty. v. Halsey*, 87 S.W.3d 552, 554 (Tex. 2002); *accord Wilder v. Merritt*, No. 02-16-00477-CV, 2017 Tex. App. LEXIS 10810, at *6, 2017 WL 5494258 (Tex. App.—Fort Worth Nov. 16, 2017, no pet.) (mem. op.) ("An officer of a court who is entitled to the protection of derived judicial immunity 'receives the same immunity as a judge acting in his or her official judicial capacity—absolute immunity from liability for judicial acts performed within the scope of jurisdiction.'" (quoting *Dall. Cnty. v. Halsey*, 87 S.W.3d 552, 554 (Tex. 2002))); *Glasstex, Inc. v. Arch Aluminum & Glass Co. Inc.*, No. 13-07-00483-CV, 2016 Tex. App. LEXIS 1869, at *9, 2016 WL 747893 (Tex. App.—Corpus Christi Feb. 25, 2016, no pet.) (mem. op.) ("When entitled to the protection of derived judicial immunity, an officer of the court receives the same immunity as a judge acting in his or her official judicial capacity—absolute immunity from liability for judicial acts performed within the scope of jurisdiction.") (citation omitted); *see B.K. v. Cox*, 116 S.W.3d 351, 357 (Tex. App.—Houston [14th Dist.] 2003, no pet.) ("[O]nce an individual is cloaked with derived judicial immunity because of a particular function being performed for a court, every action taken with regard to that function—whether good or bad, honest or dishonest, well-intentioned or not—is immune from suit.").

109 *Dall. Cnty. v. Halsey*, 87 S.W.3d 552, 554 (Tex. 2002) (quoting *Bradley v. Fisher*, 80 U.S. (13 Wall.) 335, 349 n.16 (1871)).

The derived-judicial-immunity doctrine recognizes that "[t]he policy reasons for judicial immunity are also implicated when a judge delegates or appoints another person to perform services for the court or when a person otherwise serves as an officer of the court. In this circumstance, the immunity attaching to the judge follows the delegation, appointment, or court employment."[110]

Texas courts, like federal courts, use a "functional approach" in determining whether an individual is entitled to the protection of derived judicial immunity.[111] This approach "focuses on whether the person seeking immunity is 'intimately associated with the judicial process and if that person exercises discretionary judgment

---

[110] *Dall. Cnty. v. Halsey,* 87 S.W.3d 552, 554 (Tex. 2002) ("The person acting in such a capacity also enjoys absolute immunity, known as derived judicial immunity.") (citations omitted); *accord Wilder v. Merritt,* No. 02-16-00477-CV, 2017 Tex. App. LEXIS 10810, at *6 (Tex. App.—Fort Worth Nov. 16, 2017, no pet.) (mem. op.) ("Judicial immunity can attach to certain nonjudges because the policy reasons for judicial immunity—to protect the individual judge as well as the public's interest in an independent judiciary—are also implicated when judges delegate or appoint a person to perform services for the court or when a person serves as an officer of the court. In those circumstances, the immunity attaching to the judge follows the delegation, appointment, or court employment. The person acting in such a capacity thus also enjoys absolute immunity, derivatively.") (citations omitted); *Glasstex, Inc. v. Arch Aluminum & Glass Co. Inc.*, No. 13-07-00483-CV, 2016 Tex. App. LEXIS 1869, at *9–10, 2016 WL 747893 (Tex. App.—Corpus Christi Feb. 25, 2016, no pet.) (mem. op.) (same); *Delcourt v. Silverman*, 919 S.W.2d 777, 781 (Tex. App.—Houston [14th Dist.] 1996, writ denied) ("When judges delegate their authority or appoint others to perform services for the court, the judicial immunity that attaches to the judge may follow the delegation or appointment. . . . The policy underlying derived judicial immunity that protects participants in judicial and other adjudicatory proceedings is sound. Not only does the policy guarantee an independent, disinterested decision-making process, these immunities prevent the harassment and intimidation that might otherwise result if disgruntled litigants could vent their anger by suing either the person who presented the decision maker with adverse information, or the person or persons who rendered an adverse opinion.") (citations omitted).

[111] *See Dall. Cnty. v. Halsey*, 87 S.W.3d 552, 556–57 (Tex. 2002) ("The United States Supreme Court's explication of the functional approach to derived judicial immunity in *Antoine [v. Byers & Anderson, Inc.*, 508 U.S. 429 (1993),] comports with our decision in *Clements [v. Barnes*, 834 S.W.2d 45, 46 (Tex. 1992),] and the analysis that has been applied by our courts of appeals in varying contexts. Thus, we conclude that the functional approach should similarly guide our analysis in this case as we consider whether court reporters enjoy derived judicial immunity for the preparation of a reporter's record when requested by a party.") (citations omitted); *Wilder v. Merritt*, No. 02-16-00477-CV, 2017 Tex. App. LEXIS 10810, at *6, 2017 WL 5494258 (Tex. App.—Fort Worth Nov. 16, 2017, no pet.) (mem. op.) ("Texas uses a functional approach to determine whether someone is entitled to derived judicial immunity."); *Logsdon v. Owens*, No. 02-15-00254-CV, 2016 Tex. App. LEXIS 6171, at *6–7, 2016 WL 3197953 (Tex. App.—Fort Worth June 9, 2016, no pet.) (mem. op.) (same); *B.W.D. v. Turnage*, No. 05-13-01733-CV, 2015 Tex. App. LEXIS 1947, at *9, 2015 WL 869289 (Tex. App.—Dallas Mar. 2, 2015, pet. denied) (mem. op.) (same); *Wilkinson v. USAA Fed. Sav. Bank Tr. Servs.*, No. 14-13-00111-CV, 2014 Tex. App. LEXIS 7091, at *29–30, 2014 WL 3002400 (Tex. App.—Houston [14th Dist.] July 1, 2014, pet. denied) (mem. op.) (same); *City of Hous. v. W. Capital Fin. Servs. Corp.*, 961 S.W.2d 687, 690 (Tex. App.—Houston [1st Dist.] 1998, pet. dism'd w.o.j.) (applying the functional approach to conclude that a court clerk was not entitled to derived judicial immunity for the conduct at issue, which was not judicial in nature).

comparable to that of the judge'"[112] and "on the nature of the function performed, not the identity of the actor"; thus, in assessing whether derived judicial immunity applies to conduct in question, courts "consider[] whether the conduct is like that of the delegating or appointing judge."[113] "Officers of the court who are integral parts of the judicial process, 'such as court clerks, law clerks, bailiffs, constables issuing writs, and court-appointed receivers and trustees are entitled to [derived] judicial immunity *if they actually function as an arm of the court.*'"[114] Likewise, court-appointed examiners

---

112 *Alpert v. Gerstner*, 232 S.W.3d 117, 126 (Tex. App.—Houston [1st Dist.] 2006, pet. denied) (quoting *Dall. Cnty. v. Halsey*, 87 S.W.3d 552, 554 (Tex. 2002)); *see Wilder v. Merritt*, No. 02-16-00477-CV, 2017 Tex. App. LEXIS 10810, at *6–7, 2017 WL 5494258 (Tex. App.—Fort Worth Nov. 16, 2017, no pet.) (mem. op.) ("This [functional] approach 'looks to whether the person seeking immunity is intimately associated with the judicial process' and to whether that person 'exercises discretionary judgment comparable to that of the judge,' as opposed to whether that person engages in ministerial or administrative tasks." (quoting *Dall. Cnty. v. Halsey*, 87 S.W.3d 552, 554, 557 (Tex. 2002))); *Logsdon v. Owens*, No. 02-15-00254-CV, 2016 Tex. App. LEXIS 6171, at *6–11, 2016 WL 3197953 (Tex. App.—Fort Worth June 9, 2016, no pet.) (mem. op.) (same); *B.W.D. v. Turnage*, No. 05-13-01733-CV, 2015 Tex. App. LEXIS 1947, at *9, 2015 WL 869289 (Tex. App.—Dallas Mar. 2, 2015, pet. denied) (mem. op.) ("Under the functional approach, courts determine whether the activities of the person seeking immunity are intimately associated with the judicial process and whether the person exercised discretionary judgment comparable to a judge, as opposed to ministerial or administrative tasks."); *Wilkinson v. USAA Fed. Sav. Bank Tr. Servs.*, No. 14-13-00111-CV, 2014 Tex. App. LEXIS 7091, at *29–30, 2014 WL 3002400 (Tex. App.—Houston [14th Dist.] July 1, 2014, pet. denied) (mem. op.) (same).

113 *B.W.D. v. Turnage*, No. 05-13-01733-CV, 2015 Tex. App. LEXIS 1947, at *9–10, 2015 WL 869289 (Tex. App.—Dallas Mar. 2, 2015, pet. denied) (mem. op.) (quoting *Davis v. W.*, 317 S.W.3d 301, 307 (Tex. App.—Houston [1st Dist.] 2009, no pet.)); *accord Wilkinson v. USAA Fed. Sav. Bank Tr. Servs.*, No. 14-13-00111-CV, 2014 Tex. App. LEXIS 7091, at *29–30, 2014 WL 3002400 (Tex. App.—Houston [14th Dist.] July 1, 2014, pet. denied) (mem. op.); *see Wilder v. Merritt*, No. 02-16-00477-CV, 2017 Tex. App. LEXIS 10810, at *11, 2017 WL 5494258 (Tex. App.—Fort Worth Nov. 16, 2017, no pet.) (mem. op.) ("But under *Halsey's* functional approach, the focus is not on the actor's identity but on the function that the actor performs; the question is whether the actor is 'intimately associated with the judicial process' and 'exercises discretionary judgment comparable to that of the judge.'" (quoting *Dall. Cnty. v. Halsey*, 87 S.W.3d 552, 554 (Tex. 2002))); *Logsdon v. Owens*, No. 02-15-00254-CV, 2016 Tex. App. LEXIS 6171, at *7, 2016 WL 3197953 (Tex. App.—Fort Worth June 9, 2016, no pet.) (mem. op.) ("'The functional approach looks to the nature of the function performed, not the identity of the actor, and considers whether the court officer's conduct is like that of the delegating or appointing judge.'" (quoting *Conner v. Guemez*, No. 02–10–00211–CV, 2010 Tex. App. LEXIS 9383, at *7, 2010 WL 4812991 (Tex. App.—Fort Worth Nov. 24, 2010, no pet.) (mem. op.))).

114 *Alpert v. Gerstner*, 232 S.W.3d 117, 126 (Tex. App.—Houston [1st Dist.] 2006, pet. denied) (quoting *Delcourt v. Silverman*, 919 S.W.2d 777, 781 (Tex. App.—Houston [14th Dist.] 1996, writ denied)); *see Wilder v. Merritt*, No. 02-16-00477-CV, 2017 Tex. App. LEXIS 10810, at *11, 2017 WL 5494258 (Tex. App.—Fort Worth Nov. 16, 2017, no pet.) (mem. op.) ("Because the District Clerk's tabulation and taxation of costs are ministerial duties belonging to the clerk—and not to the trial-court judge—Wilder was not exercising discretionary judgment comparable to that of a judge. Judicial immunity thus does not bar Merritt's equitable-reimbursement claim against the District Clerk."); *B.W.D. v. Turnage*, No. 05-13-01733-CV, 2015 Tex. App. LEXIS 1947, at *10–11, 2015 WL 869289 (Tex. App.—Dallas Mar. 2, 2015, pet. denied) (mem. op.) (supporting the following statement with multiple examples: "Derived judicial immunity has been extended to court officers and appointees for acts they

who conduct mental or physical examinations of individuals are entitled to derived judicial immunity while functioning as an arm of the court.

In *Delcourt v. Silverman*,[115] a case arising under Title II of the Texas Family Code, the court of appeals extended derived judicial immunity to a psychologist appointed by the trial court under former Texas Rule 167a(d)(1).[116] In doing so, the court reasoned:

> A psychologist who is appointed by the court is entitled to absolute immunity if he or she is appointed to fulfill quasi-judicial functions intimately related to the judicial process. The focus is on the nature of the function performed, not the identity of the actor. The question is whether the psychologist's activity is such an integral part of the judicial process that to deny immunity would disserve the broader public interest that non-judicial officers act without fear of liability.
>
> Numerous courts have extended absolute immunity to psychiatrists and other mental health experts assisting the court in criminal cases. The consistent reasoning given by the courts in these cases is that the psychiatrist or mental health professional performed a special task closely related to the judicial process pursuant to a court directive.
>
> We believe this reasoning also applies to mental health experts appointed to provide psychological expertise in child custody suits. Many courts recognize that psychiatrists and psychologists performing court-ordered custody evaluations perform a judicial function and enjoy absolute immunity. When a court appoints a mental health professional to examine the child and the parents in a custody proceeding, the professional is acting as a fact finder for the court. The court relies on the professional to provide information essential to the decision-making process. Without the protection of absolute immunity, such professionals would be, at the very least, reluctant to accept these appointments. This would in turn inhibit judges from performing their duties.[117]

---

are required to do under court order or at a judge's direction."); *B.K. v. Cox*, 116 S.W.3d 351, 357 (Tex. App.—Houston [14th Dist.] 2003, no pet.) ("Texas protects non-judges who have been appointed by a court as an arm of the court when (1) their function is intimately associated with the judicial process, and (2) they exercise discretionary judgment like a judge.").

[115] *Delcourt v. Silverman*, 919 S.W.2d 777, 783 (Tex. App.—Houston [14th Dist.] 1996), writ denied), *cited with approval in Dall. Cnty. v. Halsey*, 87 S.W.3d 552, 554–57 (Tex. 2002).

[116] *Delcourt v. Silverman*, 919 S.W.2d 777, 783 (Tex. App.—Houston [14th Dist.] 1996), writ denied); *see Dall. Cnty. v. Halsey*, 87 S.W.3d 552, 555 n.1 (Tex. 2002) (noting that former Texas Rule 167a(d)(1) "was repealed in 1998 and is now found in substantially the same form at Texas Rule of Civil Procedure 204.4(a))").

[117] *Delcourt v. Silverman*, 919 S.W.2d 777, 782–83 (Tex. App.—Houston [14th Dist.] 1996), writ denied) (citations omitted).

The Texas Supreme Court has analyzed *Delcourt* extensively and approvingly.[118] Thus, *Delcourt* provides a useful guide in determining when derived judicial immunity applies to examiners appointed under Texas Rule 204.4.[119]

12-10 Challenging Orders Under Texas Rule 204

An order granting or denying a physical or mental examination is an interlocutory one that, generally, cannot be appealed.[120] Such an order generally is reviewable pursuant to writ of mandamus.[121]

---

118 *See Dall. Cnty. v. Halsey*, 87 S.W.3d 552, 554–57 (Tex. 2002).

119 *E.g., B.W.D. v. Turnage*, No. 05-13-01733-CV, 2015 Tex. App. LEXIS 1947, at *9–10, 2015 WL 869289 (Tex. App.—Dallas Mar. 2, 2015, pet. denied) (mem. op.) (relying on *Dall. Cnty. v. Halsey*, 87 S.W.3d 552 (Tex. 2002), and *Delcourt v. Silverman*, 919 S.W.2d 777 (Tex. App.—Houston [14th Dist.] 1996, writ denied), among other cases, in concluding that an individual and his company were entitled to derived judicial immunity as a matter of law for their actions in connection with the random urinalysis testing that they conducted pursuant to a court order in a divorce proceeding involving a child); *B.K. v. Cox*, 116 S.W.3d 351, 356–57 (Tex. App.—Houston [14th Dist.] 2003, no pet.) (relying on *Delcourt v. Silverman*, 919 S.W.2d 777 (Tex. App.—Houston [14th Dist.] 1996, writ denied), to hold that doctors and a hospital performing psychological evaluations and examinations of family members pursuant to a court order were entitled to derived judicial immunity because they "were to help the trial judge perform a judicial function of evaluating this family in an effort to determine custody issues. The only other question to ask in determining if immunity attaches was if [the doctors and hospital] were acting within the scope of this appointment when they allegedly neglected to report suspected child abuse. [One of the doctor's] affidavit establishes that they were within the scope of the order because their acts—whether negligent or not—related to the family's evaluation.").

120 *Triplett v. Greenway*, No. 03-00-00363-CV, 2000 Tex. App. LEXIS 4000, at *1 (Tex. App.—Austin June 15, 2000, no pet.) (per curiam) (mem. op.) ("Triplett has filed her interlocutory appeal from a trial court order denying her motion to compel plaintiff in the underlying suit to submit to a mental examination. Such a discovery order is interlocutory and not immediately appealable in the absence of express statutory authority."); *Barnett v. Tankersley*, No. A14-85-591-CV, 1985 Tex. App. LEXIS 12073, at *2 (Tex. App.—Houston [14th Dist.] Aug. 29, 1985, no writ) (not designated for publication) (same).

121 *In re H.E.B. Grocery Co.*, 492 S.W.3d 300, 304 (Tex. 2016) (orig. proceeding) (per curiam); *In re Evans*, No. 03-20-00532-CV, 2021 Tex. App. LEXIS 637, at *19, 2021 WL 278944 (Tex. App.—Austin Jan. 28, 2021) (mem. op.); *In re Estabrook*, No. 10-20-00175-CV, 2020 Tex. App. LEXIS 8328, at *3–4, 2020 WL 6192923 (Tex. App.—Waco Oct. 21, 2020, orig. proceeding) (mem. op.); *In re Soc'y of Our Lady of Most Holy Trinity,* 622 S.W.3d 1, 10-11 (Tex. App.—Corpus Christi 2019, orig. proceeding).

CHAPTER 13

Discovery from Nonparties—Texas Rule 205

13-1 Text of Rule 205

RULE 205. DISCOVERY FROM NON-PARTIES

205.1. Forms of Discovery; Subpoena Requirement

A party may compel discovery from a nonparty—that is, a person who is not a party or subject to a party's control—only by obtaining a court order under Rules 196.7, 202, or 204, or by serving a subpoena compelling:

(a) an oral deposition;

(b) a deposition on written questions;

(c) a request for production of documents or tangible things, pursuant to Rule 199.2(b)(5) or Rule 200.1(b), served with a notice of deposition on oral examination or written questions; and

(d) a request for production of documents and tangible things under this rule.

205.2. Notice

A party seeking discovery by subpoena from a nonparty must serve on the nonparty and all parties, a copy of the form of notice required under the rules governing the applicable form of discovery. A notice of oral or written deposition must be served before or at the same time that a subpoena compelling attendance or production under the notice is served. A notice to produce documents or tangible things under Rule 205.3 must be served at least 10 days before the subpoena compelling production is served.

205.3. Production of Documents and Tangible Things Without Deposition

(a) **Notice; subpoena.** A party may compel production of documents and tangible things from a nonparty by serving—a reasonable time before the response is due but no later than 30 days before the end of any applicable discovery period—the notice required in Rule 205.2 and a subpoena compelling production or inspection of documents or tangible things.

(b) **Contents of notice.** The notice must state:

(1) the name of the person from whom production or inspection is sought to be compelled;

(2) a reasonable time and place for the production or inspection; and

(3) the items to be produced or inspected, either by individual item or by category, describing each item and category with reasonable particularity, and, if applicable, describing the desired testing and sampling with sufficient specificity to inform the nonparty of the means, manner, and procedure for testing or sampling.

(c) **Requests for production of medical or mental health records of other non-parties.** If a party requests a nonparty to produce medical or mental health records of another nonparty, the requesting party must serve the nonparty whose records are sought with the notice required under this rule. This requirement does not apply under the circumstances set forth in Rule 196.1(c)(2).

(d) **Response.** The nonparty must respond to the notice and subpoena in accordance with Rule 176.6.

(e) **Custody, inspection and copying.** The party obtaining the production must make all materials produced available for inspection by any other party on reasonable notice, and must furnish copies to any party who requests at that party's expense.

(f) **Cost of production.** A party requiring production of documents by a nonparty must reimburse the nonparty's reasonable costs of production.

Comments

Comment to 1999 change: Under this rule, a party may subpoena production of documents and tangible things from nonparties without need for a motion or oral or written deposition.

13-1:1 2021 Amendments to the Texas Rules of Civil Procedure

The 2021 amendments to the Texas Rules of Civil Procedure did not modify Texas Rule 205 regarding discovery from nonparties in any respect.

13-2 Discovery from Nonparties in General

Texas Rule 205 governs discovery from nonparties and sets forth the discovery methods that can be used to obtain materials and information from nonparties.[1] It limits

[1] Tex. R. Civ. P. 205.1; *In re Sun City Gun Exch., Inc.*, 545 S.W.3d 1, 6 (Tex. App.—El Paso 2017, orig. proceeding) ("[Texas] Rule 205.1 limits what the trial court may order in relation to discovery from a non-party. A party may obtain discovery from a non-party only by obtaining a court order under [Texas] Rules 196.7, 202, or 204, or by serving a subpoena compelling an oral deposition, a deposition on written questions, a request for production of documents or tangible things, or a request for production of documents and tangible things.") (citation omitted); *In re Univ. of Tex. Health Ctr.*, 198 S.W.3d 392, 396 (Tex. App.—

nonparty discovery to seven specified methods that are more formal than party discovery. Three of them require a court order: (1) entry on a nonparty's property under Texas Rule 196.7;[2] (2) a presuit deposition under Texas Rule 202;[3] and (3) a physical or mental examination under Texas Rule 204.[4] The four other discovery methods require a subpoena's service:[5] "(a) an oral deposition;"[6] "(b) a deposition on written questions;"[7] "(c) a request for production of documents or tangible things [served with an oral- or written-deposition notice under Texas Rules 199.2(b)(5) and 200.1,

---

Texarkana 2006, orig. proceeding) ("Discovery from nonparties is governed by [Texas] Rule 205."); *see In re Univ. of Tex. at San Antonio*, No. 04-20-00439-CV, 2021 Tex. App. LEXIS 365, at *9, 2021 WL 185529 (Tex. App.—San Antonio Jan. 20, 2021, orig. proceeding) (mem. op.) ("Texas Rule of Civil Procedure 205 governs discovery from nonparties, including a request for production of a document or tangible thing.").

2 Tex. R. Civ. P. 205.1. Texas Rule 196.7 provides, in relevant part:

> A party may gain entry on designated land or other property to inspect, measure, survey, photograph, test, or sample the property or any designated object or operation thereon by serving—no later than 30 days before the end of any applicable discovery period—
>
> . . . .
>
> (2) a motion and notice of hearing on all parties and the nonparty if the land or property belongs to a nonparty. . . .

Tex. R. Civ. P. 196.7(a). Motions for entry on property are discussed in Chapter 8, section 8-7.

3 Tex. R. Civ. P. 205.1. Texas Rule 202 provides, in relevant part:

> A person may petition the court for an order authorizing the taking of a deposition on oral examination or written questions either:
>
> (a) to perpetuate or obtain the person's own testimony or that of any other person for use in an anticipated suit; or
>
> (b) to investigate a potential claim or suit.

Tex. R. Civ. P. 202.1. Presuit depositions are discussed in Chapter 11, section 11-5.

4 Tex. R. Civ. P. 205.1. Texas Rule 204 provides, in relevant part:

> A party may—no later than 30 days before the end of any applicable discovery period—move for an order compelling another party to:
>
> (1) submit to a physical or mental examination by a qualified physician or a mental examination by a qualified psychologist; or
>
> (2) produce for such examination a person in the other party's custody, conservatorship or legal control.

Tex. R. Civ. P. 204.1(a). Texas Rule 205.1's reference to Texas Rule 204 relates to examinations of "a person in the other party's custody, conservatorship, or legal control" within in the meaning of Texas Rule 204.1(a)(2) and does not give a trial court the right to order a physical or mental examination of nonparties generally. Physical and mental examinations are discussed in Chapter 12.

5 *See In re K & L Auto Crushers, LLC*, 627 S.W.3d 239, 259 n.2 (Tex. 2021) (orig. proceeding) (Huddle, J., concurring) ("Discovery from a nonparty requires service of a subpoena." (citing Tex. R. Civ. P. 205.1)).

6 Tex. R. Civ. P. 205.1(a). Oral depositions are discussed in Chapter 11, section 11-2.

7 Tex. R. Civ. P. 205.1(b). Depositions upon written questions are discussed in Chapter 11, section 11-3.

respectively];"[8] and "(d) a request for production of documents and tangible things" under Texas Rule 205.3 served without an oral- or written-deposition notice.[9]

The last discovery method—a production request served without a deposition notice—is based on Federal Rule 45, which also allows parties to obtain documents from nonparties without a deposition,[10] and was first introduced into Texas discovery practice by the 1999 amendments to the Texas discovery rules. Before those amendments, a party could obtain documents and other tangible things from a nonparty only with a subpoena duces tecum served in connection with an oral- or written-deposition notice.

As noted above, under Texas Rule 205, a party can obtain documents and other tangible things from a nonparty either with or without a deposition and without filing a motion for production with the trial court.[11] The methods of obtaining a nonparty's documents and tangible things and nonparty depositions are discussed below.

13-3 Who Is a Nonparty?

As noted above, Texas Rule 205 governs discovery from "nonparties."[12] The Rule defines a "nonparty" in the negative—i.e., as "a person who is *not* a party or subject to a party's *control*."[13] Nothing in the Rule or any other Texas discovery rule, however,

[8] Tex. R. Civ. P. 205.1(c); *see In re Perrilloux*, No. 05-19-01584-CV, 2020 Tex. App. LEXIS 3737, at *9, 2020 WL 2092483 (Tex. App.—Dallas May 1, 2020, orig. proceeding) (mem. op.) (Texas "Rule 205, which governs discovery of non-parties, permits a party to compel discovery from a non-party by serving a subpoena requesting 'production of documents or tangible things . . . served with a notice of deposition on oral examination or written questions.' Accordingly, the plain language of the rules permits a petition seeking a pre-suit deposition under [Texas] Rule 202 to request the production of documents as well." (quoting Tex. R. Civ. P. 205.1(c))); *In re United Fire Lloyds*, 578 S.W.3d 572, 578 (Tex. App.—Tyler 2019) ("Texas Rule of Civil Procedure 205.1 authorizes a party to compel discovery from a nonparty by serving a subpoena compelling a request for production of documents or tangible things, pursuant to [Texas] Rule 199.2(b)(5) or Rule 200.1(b), served with a notice of deposition on oral examination or written questions."). Production requests served with oral- and written-deposition notices are discussed in Chapters 11, sections 11-2:2 and 11-3:3, respectively.

[9] Tex. R. Civ. P. 205.1(d); *see In re Skyhawk Sec., LLC*, No. 09-20-00146-CV, 2021 Tex. App. LEXIS 852, at *14, 2021 WL 377691 (Tex. App.—Beaumont Feb. 4, 2021, orig. proceeding) (per curiam) (mem. op.) (Texas "Rule 205.1[(d)] . . . authorizes a party to compel discovery from a non-party by serving a subpoena compelling a request for production of documents."); *In re Univ. of Tex. at San Antonio*, No. 04-20-00439-CV, 2021 Tex. App. LEXIS 365, at *9, 2021 WL 185529 (Tex. App.—San Antonio Jan. 20, 2021, orig. proceeding) (mem. op.) ("Texas Rule of Civil Procedure 205 governs discovery from nonparties, including a request for production of a document or tangible thing.").

[10] *See* Fed. R. Civ. P. 45(a)(1)(C) ("A command to produce documents, electronically stored information, or tangible things or to permit the inspection of premises may be included in a subpoena commanding attendance at a deposition, hearing, or trial, or may be set out in a separate subpoena.").

[11] Tex. R. Civ. P. 205 cmt. to 1999 change ("Under this rule, a party may subpoena production of documents and tangible things from nonparties without need for a motion or oral or written deposition.").

[12] Tex. R. Civ. P. 205.

[13] Tex. R. Civ. P. 205.1 (emphasis added).

defines "control."[14] Because undefined words in procedural rules generally are given their plain or ordinary meaning,[15] "control" as used in Texas Rule 205.1 should be given its plain or ordinary meaning—"[t]he power or authority to manage, direct, or oversee[.]"[16] Thus, whether an individual or entity is subject to a party's control is a fact question.[17] For example, a business entity controls its officers, employees, and

---

14 The word "control" appears (outside of the phrase "discovery control plan") in the following discovery rules: Texas Rules 190.3(b)(2), 192.3(b), 192.3(h), 192.7(b), 194.2(b)(6), 195.3(a)–(b), 195.5(a)(3)–(a)(4), 195.6, 196.3(a), 199.2(b)(5), 199.3, 200.2, 204.1(a)(2), 204.1(c)(1), and 205.1. Texas Rule 192.7(b) comes the closest to defining "control," providing: "Possession, custody, or control of an item means that the person either has physical possession of the item or has a right to possession of the item that is equal or superior to the person who has physical possession of the item." Tex. R. Civ. P. 192.7(b).

15 *E.g., In re Tex. Educ. Agency*, 619 S.W.3d 679, 687 (Tex. 2021) ("We apply the plain meaning of statutory language unless (1) the Legislature has prescribed definitions, (2) the words have acquired a technical or particular meaning, (3) a contrary intention is apparent from the context, or (4) a plain-meaning construction leads to nonsensical or absurd results.") (footnote omitted) (citation omitted); *In re Silver*, 540 S.W.3d 530, 534 (Tex. 2018) (orig. proceeding) ("[W]hen determining a rule's meaning we typically rely on the ordinary meaning of the words used, unless the text or relevant definitions indicate a different meaning. When determining the ordinary meaning of a word, we frequently consult dictionaries.") (citation omitted); *In re Bridgestone Ams. Tire Operations, LLC*, 459 S.W.3d 565, 569 (Tex. 2015) (orig. proceeding) ("When we analyze Texas's procedural rules, we apply the same rules of construction that govern the interpretation of statutes. That is, we look first to the rule's language and construe it according to its plain meaning.") (citation omitted); *In re Christus Spohn Hosp. Kleberg*, 222 S.W.3d 434, 437 (Tex. 2007) (to determine the meaning of a procedural rule, a court "appl[ies] the same rules of construction that govern the interpretation of statutes").

16 *Control, Black's Law Dictionary* (11th ed. 2019). *But see In re Saddles Blazin, LLC*, No. 09-20-00209-CV, 2021 Tex. App. LEXIS 853, at *2, 4-5, 2021 WL 377247 (Tex. App.—Beaumont Feb. 4, 2021, orig. proceeding) (per curiam) (mem. op.) ("We have observed that 'control' of a nonparty witness for purposes of [Texas] Rule 199.3 requires control of the same kind, class, or nature as that a party would have over an employee or a retained expert.") (applying *In re Reaud*, 286 S.W.3d 574, 580 (Tex. App.—Beaumont 2009, orig. proceeding) (per curiam)). Chapter 11, section 11-2:4 discusses when a witness is "subject to the control of a party" for purposes of Texas Rule 199.3 so that a deposition notice is sufficient to compel the witness's attendance for a deposition.

17 *In re Saddles Blazin, LLC*, No. 09-20-00209-CV, 2021 Tex. App. LEXIS 853, at *2–4, 2021 WL 377247 (Tex. App.—Beaumont Feb. 4, 2021, orig. proceeding) (per curiam) (mem. op.) (holding that a passive minority member of a limited liability company was not in the company's control "[a]bsent some evidence that [the company's] governing documents granted the limited liability company the power to adversely affect [the member's] status or compensation as a member if he refused to attend the deposition" (applying *In re Reaud*, 286 S.W.3d 574, 580–82 (Tex. App.—Beaumont 2009, orig. proceeding) (per curiam))); *In re Reaud*, 286 S.W.3d 574, 581–82 (Tex. App.—Beaumont 2009, orig. proceeding) (per curiam) (holding that there was "no evidence in the record to support the trial court's implied finding that [the plaintiff corporation] could control [its independent director's] appearance at a deposition as a person subject to the control of a party"); *cf. Founding Church of Scientology v. Webster*, 802 F.2d 1448, 1453 (D.C. Cir. 1986) (holding that the trial court properly required the Church of Scientology to produce its founder, L. Ron Hubbard, for deposition as a "managing agent" because Hubbard still exercised "ultimate control" over the church despite his ostensible resignation from his official position at it).

agents; a principal controls its agents; and a corporation or other entity controls its subsidiaries.[18]

The burden of establishing control is on the requesting party.[19] However, once it makes a prima facie showing of control, the burden shifts to responding party to show why it lacks control.[20]

---

[18] *See, e.g., Imagine Auto. Grp. v. Boardwalk Motor Cars, Ltd.*, 430 S.W.3d 620, 641 (Tex. App.—Dallas 2014, pet. denied) (holding that an individual who was a company's CEO was under the company's control); *In re Summersett*, 438 S.W.3d 74, 82 (Tex. App.—Corpus Christ 2013, orig. proceeding) (holding that the president and chief medical officer of a hospital was under the hospital's control); *In re Williams*, 328 S.W.3d 103, 112–13 (Tex. App.—Corpus Christi 2010, orig. proceeding) (holding that an individual who was the president of a corporation was under the corporation's control); *Valley Forge Ins. Co. v. Jones*, 733 S.W.2d 319, 321–22 (Tex. App.—Texarkana 1987, no writ) (holding that a controlling shareholder had control of corporations that he owned); *cf. U. S. v. Int'l Union of Petroleum & Indus. Workers, AFL-CIO*, 870 F.2d 1450, 1452 (9th Cir. 1989) (holding that a corporation has control over its subsidiaries); *Wiand v. Wells Fargo Bank, N.A.*, No. 8:12-CV-557-T-27EAJ, 2013 U.S. Dist. LEXIS 174768, at *10–11, 2013 WL 12156100 (M.D. Fla. Dec. 13, 2013) (holding that a principal has control over its agent); *Twentieth Century Fox Film Corp. v. Marvel Enters.*, No. 01 Civ. 3016 (AGS) (HBP), 2002 U.S. Dist. LEXIS 14682, at *12–13, 2002 WL 1835439 (S.D.N.Y. Aug. 8, 2002) (holding that a corporation has control over its subsidiaries). *But see In re Saddles Blazin, LLC*, No. 09-20-00209-CV, 2021 Tex. App. LEXIS 853, at *2–4, 2021 WL 377247 (Tex. App.—Beaumont Feb. 4, 2021, orig. proceeding) (per curiam) (mem. op.) (holding that a passive minority member of a limited liability company was not in the company's control "[a]bsent some evidence that [the company's] governing documents granted the limited liability company the power to adversely affect [the member's] status or compensation as a member if he refused to attend the deposition") (applying *In re Reaud*, 286 S.W.3d 574, 580–82 (Tex. App.—Beaumont 2009, orig. proceeding) (per curiam)); *In re Reaud*, 286 S.W.3d 574, 581–82 (Tex. App.—Beaumont 2009, orig. proceeding) (per curiam) (holding that there was "no evidence in the record to support the trial court's implied finding that [the plaintiff corporation] could control [its independent director's] appearance at a deposition as a person subject to the control of a party").

[19] *Cf. In re Summersett*, 438 S.W.3d 74, 81 (Tex. App.—Corpus Christ 2013, orig. proceeding) ("The party seeking production has the burden of proving that the relator has constructive possession or the right to obtain possession of the requested documents."); *In re U-Haul Int'l*, 87 S.W.3d 653, 656 (Tex. App.—San Antonio 2002, orig. proceeding) ("The plaintiffs had the burden of proving UHI had constructive possession or the right to obtain possession of the requested documents from Republic."); *see GTE Commc'ns Sys. Corp. v. Tanner*, 856 S.W.2d 725, 729 (Tex. 1993) (orig. proceeding) ("Likewise, there is no evidence that GCSC had constructive possession of the document or a right to compel its production. Plaintiffs adduced no evidence regarding the corporate relationship between GTFL and GCSC, or any right of the latter to control the former. In fact, the only testimony regarding control was James' speculation regarding the ability of GCSC's parent to control its subsidiaries, assuming both GCSC and GTFL were subsidiaries of the same parent. There is no evidence that GCSC ever actually did exercise control of any type over GTFL."); *cf. Norman v. Young*, 422 F.2d 470, 472–73 (10th Cir. 1970) ("There is no doubt that the moving party is charged with establishing possession, custody or control. . . ."); *Union Home Mortg. Corp.* v. *Jenkins*, No. 1:20cv2690, 2021 U.S. Dist. LEXIS 54129, at *28, 2021 WL 1110440 (N.D. Ohio 2021) (same); *Hawley Ins. Co. v. Felman Prod., Inc.*, 269 F.R.D. 609, 620 (S.D. W. Va. 2010) (same); *N. Y. ex rel. Boardman v. Nat'l R.R. Passenger Corp.*, 233 F.R.D. 259, 268 (N.D.N.Y. 2006) (same).

[20] *Cf. In re Nat'l Century Fin. Enters., Inc. Fin. Inv. Litig.*, No. 2:03-md-1565, 2009 U.S. Dist. LEXIS 92237, at *31, 2009 WL 10687963 (S.D. Ohio Sept. 1, 2009) ("The fact remains,

13-4 Nonparty Production Requests Without a Deposition

Texas Rule 205.3 governs a nonparty's production of documents and tangible things without a deposition. To obtain such material from a nonparty without a deposition, the requesting party must serve (1) the nonparty and all other parties with a notice,[21] and (2) the nonparty with a subpoena.[22]

13-4:1 Service of the Notice

Under Texas Rule 205.2, "[a] notice to produce documents or tangible things under [Texas] Rule 205.3 [without a deposition] must be served at least 10 days before the subpoena compelling production is served."[23] The 10-day notice requirement's purpose is to give the other parties time to seek protection from the requested nonparty production.[24] Without the notice requirement, a nonparty who received a notice and subpoena simultaneously might immediately produce its documents even if the

---

however, that it was Pharos' burden to demonstrate that the email was not in its possession, custody, or control, and it failed to do so."); *Banff Ltd. v. Ltd., Inc.*, No. 93 Civ. 2514 (CSH) (RLE), 1994 U.S. Dist. LEXIS 1779, at *5, 1994 WL 66069 (S.D.N.Y. Feb. 22, 1994) ("[Federal Rule 34] requires a party to produce things which are in its 'possession, custody or control.' Items which have been lost cannot be deemed to fit this description. The party claiming this situation would, of course, have the burden of demonstrating that the items are lost or should be considered lost.").

21 Tex. R. Civ. P. 205.2, 205.3(a); *In re State*, 599 S.W.3d 577, 597–98 (Tex. App.—El Paso 2020, orig. proceeding) ("With respect to parties seeking production of documents and tangible things from nonparties without deposition, the Rules impose the requirements that, *inter alia*, '[a] notice to produce documents or tangible things under [Texas] Rule 205.3 must be served at least 10 days before the subpoena compelling production is served. . . .'" (quoting Tex. R. Civ. P. 205.2)).

22 Tex. R. Civ. P. 205.3(a), *see In re State*, 599 S.W.3d 577, 597–98 (Tex. App.—El Paso 2020, orig. proceeding) ("With respect to parties seeking production of documents and tangible things from nonparties without deposition, the Rules impose the requirements that, *inter alia*, '[a] notice to produce documents or tangible things under [Texas] Rule 205.3 must be served at least 10 days before the subpoena compelling production is served. . . .'" (quoting Tex. R. Civ. P. 205.2)); *In re Mosser Mallers PLLC*, No. 05-08-00259-CV, 2008 Tex. App. LEXIS 2589, at *5, 2008 WL 963170 (Tex. App.—Dallas Apr. 9, 2008, orig. proceeding) (mem. op.) ("Production of documents from a non-party is available by serving a subpoena compelling a request for production of documents under [Texas R]ule 205."); *In re Diversicare Gen. Partner, Inc.*, 41 S.W.3d 788, 794 (Tex. App.—Corpus Christi 2001, orig. proceeding) (same), *overruled on other grounds*, *In re Arriola*, 159 S.W.3d 670, 677 (Tex. App.—Corpus Christi 2004, orig. proceeding).

23 Tex. R. Civ. P. 205.2; *In re State*, 599 S.W.3d 577, 597–98 (Tex. App.—El Paso 2020, orig. proceeding) ("With respect to parties seeking production of documents and tangible things from nonparties without deposition, the Rules impose the requirements that, *inter alia*, '[a] notice to produce documents or tangible things under [Texas] Rule 205.3 must be served at least 10 days before the subpoena compelling production is served' . . . . Plainly, pursuant to [Texas] Rule 205.3, a day's notice is not reasonable, especially when Rule 205.2 requires at least 10 days' notice between a request for production and a subpoena compelling production to allow a nonparty to determine if they wish to withhold privileged information, lodge objections, or seek protective orders." (quoting Tex. R. Civ. P. 205.2)).

24 *See In re State*, 599 S.W.3d 577, 598 (Tex. App.—El Paso 2020, orig. proceeding) (Under Texas "Rule 205.3, a day's notice is not reasonable, especially when Rule 205.2 requires at least 10 days' notice between a request for production and a subpoena compelling

subpoena did not require immediate production simply to be finished with the matter, thereby depriving the other parties of their right to move for protection with respect to the production request.

Both the notice and subpoena for a nonparty production request without a deposition must be served no later than thirty days (and in some cases thirty-one or thirty-three days) before the discovery period ends.[25] Texas Rule 205.3 also requires that service be "a reasonable time before the response is due."[26] Of course, what constitutes a "reasonable time" will depend on the facts of the case.

Texas Rule 205.3 does not indicate how the notice must be served on the nonparty. Because Texas Rule 21a applies to "[e]very notice required by" the civil procedure rules,[27] compliance with one of Texas Rule 21a's service methods should suffice.[28]

Unlike written-discovery requests under Texas Rules 196, 197, and 198 (i.e., production requests, interrogatories, and requests for admission, respectively), the notice and subpoena must be filed with the trial court.[29]

13-4:2 The Notice's Contents

The notice's contents are set forth in Texas Rule 205.3(b), which requires the notice to "state: (1) the name of the person from whom production or inspection is sought to be compelled; (2) a reasonable time and place for the production or inspection; and (3) the items to be produced or inspected[.]"[30] Each item in the notice must be "described" either individually or by category and "with reasonable particularity[.]"[31] These requirements are identical to those in Texas Rule 196.1(b),[32] which relates to production requests to parties, and the principles regarding them apply to Texas Rule 205.3 production requests.[33] Of course, the general rules regarding discovery's scope also apply to Texas Rule 205.3 production requests.[34]

---

production to allow a nonparty to determine if they wish to withhold privileged information, lodge objections, or seek protective orders.").

[25] Tex. R. Civ. P. 205.3(a). If the notice is served by mail, it must be served at least thirty-three days before the discovery period ends. *See* Tex. R. Civ. P. 21a(c). If it is served by fax after 5:00 p.m. local time of the recipient, the request must be served at least thirty-one days before the discovery period ends. *See* Tex. R. Civ. P. 21a(b)(2).

[26] Tex. R. Civ. P. 205.3(a).

[27] Tex. R. Civ. P. 21a(a).

[28] Texas Rule 21a allows service on the nonparty or its duly authorized agent "in person, by mail, by commercial delivery service, by fax, by email, or by such other manner as the court in its discretion may direct." Tex. R. Civ. P. 21a(a)(2).

[29] Tex. R. Civ. P. 191.4(b)(1) ("The following discovery materials must be filed: . . . discovery requests, deposition notices, and subpoenas required to be served on nonparties[.]").

[30] Tex. R. Civ. P. 205.3(b).

[31] Tex. R. Civ. P. 205.3(b). If the requesting party intends to test or sample items, the notice must "describ[e] the desired testing and sampling with sufficient specificity to inform the nonparty of the means, manner, and procedure for testing or sampling." Tex. R. Civ. P. 205.3(b)(3).

[32] *Compare* Tex. R. Civ. P. 205.3(b), *with* Tex. R. Civ. P. 196.1(b).

[33] See Chapter 8, section 8-2 (discussing description and particularity requirement for Texas Rule 196 production requests).

[34] See Chapter 4, section 4-3 (discussing discovery's scope).

13-4:3 The Subpoena

Texas Rule 176 governs the form and other requirements of the subpoena compelling the production of the documents and other tangible things.[35]

13-4:3.1 The Subpoena's Form

Texas Rule 176.1 specifies the subpoena's form. It "must be issued in the name of 'The State of Texas'" and "state:" (1) the action's style and number; (2) the court in which the action is pending; (3) the subpoena's issuance date; and (4) that the subpoenaed nonparty is to produce and permit inspection and copying of the designated documents and tangible things in its possession, custody, or control, at a specified time and place.[36] In addition, the subpoena must identify the person subpoenaed and the party and its attorney, if any, at whose instance the subpoena was issued.[37] Finally, the subpoena must be signed by the person issuing it and contain the text of Texas Rule 176.8(a),[38] which provides that "[f]ailure by any person without adequate excuse to obey a subpoena served upon that person may be deemed a contempt of the court from which the subpoena is issued or a district court in the county in which the subpoena is served, and may be punished by fine or confinement, or both."[39] The production requests in the subpoena must be identical to those in the earlier-served notice.

13-4:3.2 Persons Who Can Issue the Subpoena

Under Texas Rule 176.4, an attorney, a court clerk, and "an officer authorized to take depositions in this State" (i.e., a court reporter) can issue subpoenas.[40]

13-4:3.3 Service of the Subpoena

Texas Rule 176.5 allows a sheriff, constable, or any person who is at least eighteen years of age and is not a party to the action to serve the subpoena "at any place within the State of Texas."[41] Thus, a party's attorney can both issue and serve a subpoena.[42]

The subpoena "must be served by delivering a copy to the witness and tendering to that person any fees required by law."[43] It can require the nonparty's production of documents and things "in a county" that is not more than 150 miles from where the

---

[35] Tex. R. Civ. P. 176.1–176.5.

[36] Tex. R. Civ. P. 176.1(a)–(c), (e), 176.2(b). If the notice and subpoena also require the nonparty to appear for an oral or written deposition, the subpoena should so state. Tex. R. Civ. P. 176.1(e), 176.2(a).

[37] Tex. R. Civ. P. 176.1(d), (f).

[38] Tex. R. Civ. P. 176.1(g)–(h).

[39] Tex. R. Civ. P. 176.8(a).

[40] Tex. R. Civ. P. 176.4.

[41] Tex. R. Civ. P. 176.5(a).

[42] Tex. R. Civ. P. 176.4(b), 176.5(a).

[43] Tex. R. Civ. P. 176.5(a); *see In re Berry*, 578 S.W.3d 173, 178–79 (Tex. App.—Corpus Christi 2019, orig. proceeding) (holding that a trial court erred in allowing a party to serve a deposition notice and subpoena on a nonparty by substituted service).

The failure to pay the fee prevents the subpoena's enforcement by fines or attachments. Tex. R. Civ. P. 176.8(b). There is only a fee for a subpoena requiring the nonparty's appearance at an oral or written deposition. With respect to the production of documents and nonparty "resides or is served."[44] Thus, for example, if the action is pending in Dallas County, and the subpoenaed nonparty lives 175 miles from the Dallas County courthouse, but within 150 miles of the Dallas County line, the nonparty can be required to produce its documents in Dallas County.

Under Texas Rule 176.5, proof of the subpoena's service must be filed with the trial court.[45]

13-4:4 Response to the Notice and Subpoena

A nonparty served with a notice and subpoena for the production of documents and other tangible things without a deposition must respond to them in accordance with Texas Rule 176.6.[46] Under Texas Rule 176.6(c), the nonparty can, but need not, appear in person at the production.[47]

With respect to the documents and other tangible things requested by the notice and the subpoena, the nonparty has three options. ***First,*** it simply can comply with the request and produce the requested documents and other tangible things at the time and place specified in the subpoena. In such event, the nonparty "must produce documents as they are kept in the usual course of business or must organize and label them to correspond with the categories in the demand."[48] Moreover, "[a] nonparty's production of a document authenticates the document for use against the nonparty to the same extent as a party's production of a document is authenticated for use against the party under Texas Rule 193.7."[49]

---

other tangible things, a nonparty is entitled to recover its "reasonable costs of production." See Chapter 13, section 13-8.

44 Tex. R. Civ. P. 176.3(a). This provision is consistent with Section 22.002 of the Texas Civil Practice and Remedies Code, which provides that "[a] witness who is represented to reside 150 miles or less from a county in which a suit is pending or who may be found within that distance at the time of trial on the suit may be subpoenaed in the suit."

45 Tex. R. Civ. P. 176.5(b) ("Proof of service must be made by filing either: (1) the witness's signed written memorandum attached to the subpoena showing that the witness accepted the subpoena; or (2) a statement by the person who made the service stating the date, time, and manner of service, and the name of the person served."); Tex. R. Civ. P. 191.4(b)(1) ("The following discovery materials must be filed: . . . discovery requests, deposition notices, and subpoenas required to be served on nonparties[.]").

46 Tex. R. Civ. P. 205.3(d) ("The nonparty must respond to the notice and subpoena in accordance with [Texas] Rule 176.6."), 176.6(e) ("A person commanded . . . to produce and permit inspection and copying of designated documents and things, and any other person affected by the subpoena, may move for a protective order under [Texas] Rule 192.6(b)[.]"); ***see In re Diversicare Gen. Partner, Inc.***, 41 S.W.3d 788, 794 (Tex. App.—Corpus Christi 2001, orig. proceeding) ("The nonparty must then respond in accordance with [Texas R]ule 176 which provides the nonparty with an opportunity to make objections to the production and to move for a protective order."), ***overruled on other grounds, In re Arriola***, 159 S.W.3d 670, 677 (Tex. App.—Corpus Christi 2004, orig. proceeding).

47 Tex. R. Civ. P. 176.6(c) ("A person commanded to produce documents or tangible things need not appear in person at the time and place of production unless the person is also commanded to attend and give testimony, either in the same subpoena or a separate one.").

48 Tex. R. Civ. P. 176.6(c). See Chapter 8, section 8-4:3.2 for a discussion of this requirement.

49 Tex. R. Civ. P. 176.6(c). Texas Rule 193.7 provides:

> A party's production of a document in response to written discovery authenticates the document for use against that party in any pretrial proceeding or at trial unless—

Second, the nonparty, "*before* the time specified for compliance," can object to either the time or place specified for the production and/or the notice's and subpoena's production requests in whole or in part.[50] If the objection is to the time or place of the production, the nonparty should state a reasonable time and place for production.[51] The objecting nonparty need not produce the documents or other tangible things that are subject to the objections unless the trial court orders it to do so.[52] Permissible objections to a nonparty production request are the same as those to a party production request under Texas Rule 196 and include a lack of relevance, overbreadth, undue burden or expense, vagueness, ambiguity, and unreasonably cumulative or duplicative.[53] A nonparty that fails to timely object (or move for protection) generally waives its objections to the notice and subpoena.[54]

Texas Rule 176.6(d), which sets forth the objection procedure, does not provide for privilege assertions. Texas Rule 193, which relates to "written discovery," however, does so.[55] Because the term "written discovery" does not include subpoenas,[56]

> within 10 days or a longer or shorter time ordered by the court, after the producing party has actual notice that the document will be used—the party objects to the authenticity of the document, or any part of it, stating the specific basis for objection. An objection must be either on the record or in writing and must have a good faith factual and legal basis. An objection made to the authenticity of only part of a document does not affect the authenticity of the remainder. If objection is made, the party attempting to use the document should be given a reasonable opportunity to establish its authenticity.

Tex. R. Civ. P. 193.7. See Chapter 5, section 5-7 for a discussion regarding Texas Rule 193.7.

50 Tex. R. Civ. P. 176.6(d) (emphasis added); *accord In re Yamin*, No. 14-20-00280-CV, 2020 Tex. App. LEXIS 6676, at *10, 2020 WL 4873021 (Tex. App.—Houston [14th Dist.] Aug. 20, 2020, orig. proceeding) (mem. op.) (Texas "Rule 176.6(d) provides that the person commanded to produce documents may serve written objections 'before the time specified for compliance.' Under Rule 193.2, a party must make an objection to written discovery in writing 'within the time for response' Thus, the Yamins contend that either under [Texas] Rule 176.6 or [Texas] Rule 193.2 objections are timely if made before the time for the response. The subpoena stated: 'RECORDS NEEDED BY 2/15/20.' The Yamins made their objections on February 12, 2020, before Hardy was required to produce the tax returns and documents related to the returns. The Yamins' objections were timely." (quoting Tex. R. Civ. P. 176.6(d), 193.2)); *In re Univ. of Tex. Health Ctr.*, 198 S.W.3d 392, 395 (Tex. App.—Texarkana 2006, orig. proceeding) ("Any objections to a subpoena must be made 'before the time specified for compliance' with the subpoena." (quoting Tex. R. Civ. P. 176.6(d)–(e)).

51 *Cf.* Tex. R. Civ. P. 192.6(a) ("If a person seeks protection regarding the time or place of discovery, the person must state a reasonable time and place for discovery with which the person will comply.").

52 Tex. R. Civ. P. 176.6(d).

53 See Chapter 8, section 8-5 (discussing proper objections to Texas Rule 196 production requests).

54 *In re Univ. of Tex. Health Ctr.*, 198 S.W.3d 392, 395 (Tex. App.—Texarkana 2006, orig. proceeding) ("Because the objections were filed after subpoena compliance was due, and because the Hospital failed to explain or justify its three-month delay in objecting to the subpoena, the Hospital waived its objections to the subpoena.").

55 See Chapter 5, sections 5-3 and 5-4 (discussing objections and privilege assertions to written-discovery requests, respectively).

56 Tex. R. Civ. P. 192.7 (defining "written discovery" as "required disclosures, requests for production and inspection of documents and tangible things, requests for entry onto property, interrogatories, and requests for admission").

arguably Texas Rule 193.3 does not apply to subpoenas served under Texas Rule 176. Nonetheless, Texas Rule 176.6(c) provides that a nonparty "may withhold material or information claimed to be privileged but must comply with [Texas] Rule 193.3[,]"[57] and Texas Rule 176.7 requires the trial court to provide the nonparty with "protection from disclosure of privileged material or information[.]"[58] Thus, a nonparty, who wants to withhold privileged material, should follow the withholding-statement procedure of Texas Rule 193.3.[59] If the requesting party requests the identification of the material withheld, the nonparty should follow the privilege-log procedure of Texas Rule 193.3(b).[60] Under Texas Rule 193.3, a nonparty who improperly interposes privilege objections to a production request instead of following the Rule's withholding statement procedure, does not waive the privilege, but rather "must comply with [Texas] Rule 193.3 when the error is pointed out."[61]

Third, a non-requesting party or any other person affected by the Texas Rule 176 and 205 notice and subpoena, "*before* the time specified for compliance," may move for protection under Texas Rule 192.6(b) either in the court where the action is pending or in a district court in the county where the subpoena was served.[62] A nonparty movant must serve the motion on all the parties in accordance with Texas Rule 21a and "need

---

[57] Tex. R. Civ. P. 176.6(c).

[58] Tex. R. Civ. P. 176.7.

[59] See Chapter 5, section 5-4 (discussing privilege assertions to written-discovery requests).

[60] See Chapter 5, section 5-4 (discussing privilege assertions to written-discovery requests).

[61] Tex. R. Civ. P. 193.2(f). See also Chapter 5, section 5-4 (discussing privilege assertions to written-discovery requests). Texas Rule 193.3(d)'s snap-back right should apply to nonparties. *See In re Sw. Airlines Co.*, No. 02-12-00179-CV, 2012 Tex. App. LEXIS 5613, at *6–7, 2012 WL 2864507 (Tex. App.—Fort Worth July 12, 2012, orig. proceeding) (mem. op.) (applying Texas Rule 193.3's snap-back provision to nonparties); *In re Certain Underwriters at Lloyd's London*, 294 S.W.3d 891, 903 (Tex. App.—Beaumont 2009, orig. proceeding) ("By employing the term 'party who produces,' we do not perceive any intent by the drafters of [Texas] Rule 193.3(d) to constrict the Rule's application solely to those that are named as parties in a suit.").

Applying the snap-back provision to nonparties is consistent with the principles of both the discovery rules and the rules regarding privilege waivers because (1) the Texas Rules of Evidence governing privileged material indicate that "the right to assert the existence of a privilege is not generally dependent upon physical possession of a document[;]" (2) a restrictive reading of Texas Rule 193.3(d) would "effectively negate the privilege holder's enforcement rights when nonparties to the suit produce privileged information[,]" which is problematic when the rules permit the sharing of such privileged material with non-parties under certain circumstances; and (3) "[p]rivileges like the work-product privilege . . . extend beyond documents physically in the party's possession, and may often extend to information in the possession of nonparties as well." *In re Certain Underwriters at Lloyd's London*, 294 S.W.3d 891, 902–03 (Tex. App.—Beaumont 2009, orig. proceeding). Nonetheless, the Houston (Fourteenth) Court of Appeals in *In re Ortuno*, No. 14-08-00227-CV, 2008 Tex. App. LEXIS 3396, at *5, 2008 WL 2339800 (Tex. App.—Houston [14th Dist.] May 6, 2008, orig. proceeding) (mem. op.), reached the opposite conclusion and held that Texas Rule 193.3(d) could not be used to remedy the production of privileged patient records by a nonparty to the suit. See Chapter 5, section 5-4:3 (discussing the snap-back right).

[62] Tex. R. Civ. P. 176.6(e) (emphasis added); *see In re Univ. of Tex. Health Ctr.*, 198 S.W.3d 392, 395 (Tex. App.—Texarkana 2006, orig. proceeding) ("Any objections to a subpoena must be made 'before the time specified for compliance' with the subpoena." (quoting Tex. R. Civ. P. 176.6(d)–(e))).

not comply with that part of the subpoena from which protection is sought . . . unless ordered to do so by the court."[63] An affected person who fails to timely move for protection (or object) waives its objections to the notice and subpoena.[64]

A motion for a protective order filed by anyone other than the subpoenaed nonparty does *not* prevent the nonparty from producing the requested documents and other tangible things.[65] Rather, such a movant should obtain an order staying production until a ruling on its motion for protective order is made. In other words, the other affected person has the burden to obtain a ruling on its motion.

In response to an objection or motion for protective order, the requesting party can move for an order compelling production.[66] The requesting party, and not the nonparty (or other party who has moved for protection), has the burden of obtaining a ruling on the objection or motion. This is because Texas Rules 176.6(d) and (e) *only* require the nonparty to object or move for protection before the time specified by the subpoena for the production, and not to obtain a ruling on its objection or motion before that time.[67]

The trial court can sustain the objections, grant protection, or impose reasonable conditions on compliance with the Texas Rule 176 and 205 notice and subpoena. Also, "[i]n ruling on objections or motions for protection, the court must provide [the nonparty] with an adequate time for compliance, protection from disclosure of privileged material or information, and protection from undue burden or expense."[68]

13-4:5 The Subpoena's Enforcement

Under Texas Rule 176.8, subpoenas are enforceable by attachment, contempt, fines, and imprisonment. The requesting party seeking enforcement can seek relief either in the court that issued the subpoena or in a district court in the county where the subpoena was served.[69] To ensure that the nonparty understands the subpoena's import and the consequences of failing to comply with it, Texas Rule 176.1(g) requires every subpoena to warn that "[f]ailure by any person without adequate excuse to obey a subpoena served upon that person may be deemed a contempt of the court from which

---

[63] Tex. R. Civ. P. 176.6(e). A party who moves for protection also must serve the motion on the nonparty.

[64] *See In re Univ. of Tex. Health Ctr.*, 198 S.W.3d 392, 395 (Tex. App.—Texarkana 2006, orig. proceeding) ("Because the objections were filed after subpoena compliance was due, and because the Hospital failed to explain or justify its three-month delay in objecting to the subpoena, the Hospital waived its objections to the subpoena.").

[65] *See* Tex. R. Civ. P. 176.6(e) (providing only that the responding party "need not," rather than that it "shall not," "comply with the part of a subpoena from which protection is sought").

[66] Tex. R. Civ. P. 176.6(e)–(f).

[67] Tex. R. Civ. P. 176.6(d)–(e).

[68] Tex. R. Civ. P. 176.7; *see also In re K & L Auto Crushers, LLC*, 627 S.W.3d 239, 252 (Tex. 2021) (orig. proceeding) ("Although sheer volume does not make discovery overbroad as a matter of law, Alford, 997 S.W.2d at 180 n.1, proportionality requires a fact-intensive, complex balancing of many relevant factors, particularly where discovery is sought from non-parties whom trial courts 'must' protect from undue burden or expense in answering subpoenas. . . . (citation omitted) (quoting Tex. R. Civ. P. 176.7).

[69] Tex. R. Civ. P. 176.8(a).

the subpoena is issued or a district court in the county in which the subpoena is served, and may be punished by fine or confinement, or both."[70] The requesting party seeking a subpoena's enforcement must establish by affidavit that all witness fees were paid or tendered.[71]

13-5 Nonparty Production Requests with a Deposition

The discussion in Chapter 13, section 13-4, relates to Texas Rule 205's most useful method of securing a nonparty's documents—production without an oral or written deposition. As pointed out in Chapter 13, section 13-2, Texas Rule 205 also authorizes the use of subpoenas to obtain documents in another way: a production request served in connection with an oral or written deposition notice.[72] As with a nonparty production request without a deposition, to obtain a nonparty's documents and other tangible things with a deposition, a party must serve: (1) the nonparty and all other parties with a notice[73] and (2) the nonparty with a subpoena.[74]

---

[70] Tex. R. Civ. P. 176.1(g), 176.8(a).

[71] Tex. R. Civ. P. 176.8(b); *cf. Onkst v. Onkst*, No. 03-15-00636-CV, 2017 Tex. App. LEXIS 5514, at *6, 2017 WL 2628245 (Tex. App.—Austin June 16, 2017, no pet.) (mem. op.) ("Without such proof [that all fees due the subpoenaed witness were paid or tendered], the trial court has no authority to hold a witness in contempt or issue a writ of attachment to force the witness to appear at trial.").

[72] Tex. R. Civ. P. 205.1; *In re Perrilloux*, No. 05-19-01584-CV, 2020 Tex. App. LEXIS 3737, at *9, 2020 WL 2092483 (Tex. App.—Dallas May 1, 2020, orig. proceeding) (mem. op.) (Texas "Rule 205, which governs discovery of non-parties, permits a party to compel discovery from a non-party by serving a subpoena requesting 'production of documents or tangible things . . . served with a notice of deposition on oral examination or written questions.' Accordingly, the plain language of the rules permits a petition seeking a pre-suit deposition under Rule 202 to request the production of documents as well." (quoting Tex. R. Civ. P. 205.1(c)); *In re United Fire Lloyds*, 578 S.W.3d 572, 578 (Tex. App.—Tyler 2019) ("Texas Rule of Civil Procedure 205.1 authorizes a party to compel discovery from a nonparty by serving a subpoena compelling a request for production of documents or tangible things, pursuant to Rule 199.2(b)(5) or Rule 200.1(b), served with a notice of deposition on oral examination or written questions."). Production requests served with oral- and written-deposition notices are discussed in Chapters 11, sections 11-2:2 and 11-3:3, respectively.

[73] Tex. R. Civ. P. 199.2(a) ("A notice of intent to take an oral deposition must be served on the witness and all parties a reasonable time before the deposition is taken."); Tex. R. Civ. P. 200.1(a) ("A notice of intent to take [a] deposition [on written questions] must be served on the witness and all parties at least 20 days before the deposition is taken."); Tex. R. Civ. P. 205.2 ("A party seeking discovery by subpoena from a nonparty must serve, on the nonparty and all parties, a copy of the form of notice required under the rules governing the applicable form of discovery.").

[74] Tex. R. Civ. P. 176.5, 205.1(c); *see In re Diversicare Gen. Partner, Inc.*, 41 S.W.3d 788, 794 (Tex. App.—Corpus Christi 2001, orig. proceeding) (Texas "Rule 205 mandates that a party may compel discovery from a nonparty by order of the court under [Texas R]ule 196.7 (entry upon property), [Texas R]ule 202 (deposition before suit or to investigate claims), or [Texas R]ule 204 (physical and mental examinations), or by serving a notice on the nonparty and all parties pursuant to [Texas R]ule 205.2 and a subpoena compelling production of documents."), *overruled on other grounds, In re Arriola*, 159 S.W.3d 670, 677 (Tex. App.—Corpus Christi 2004, orig. proceeding).

13-5:1 Service of the Notice and Subpoena

Unlike the notice for a nonparty production request without a deposition, which must be served at least ten days before the subpoena,[75] the notice for an oral or written deposition can be served "before or at the same time that a subpoena compelling attendance or production under the notice is served."[76]

The timing of the subpoena's service depends on the type of deposition. A subpoena for an oral deposition "must be served on the witness and all parties a reasonable time before the deposition is taken."[77] In contrast, a subpoena for a deposition on written questions "must be served on the witness and all parties at least 20 days before the deposition is taken."[78] Moreover, both types of depositions must be noticed and completed before the discovery period closes absent agreement of the parties or leave of court.[79]

Texas Rule 205.2 does not indicate how the notice must be served on the nonparty. Because Texas Rule 21a applies to "[e]very notice required by" the civil procedure rules,[80] compliance with one of Texas Rule 21a's service methods should suffice.[81] Moreover, because Texas Rule 205.2 allows the notice to be served with the subpoena, the best practice is to serve both documents simultaneously. Finally, the notice must be filed with the trial court.[82]

13-5:2 The Notice's and Subpoena's Contents

Texas Rule 199.2(b) governs the contents of both the oral- or written-deposition notice and any production request contained in it.[83] That Rule provides that "the request must comply with [Texas] Rule 205 and the designation of materials required to be identified in the subpoena must be attached to, or included in, the notice."[84]

---

[75] Tex. R. Civ. P. 205.2.

[76] Tex. R. Civ. P. 205.2.

[77] Tex. R. Civ. P. 199.2(a).

[78] Tex. R. Civ. P. 200.1(a).

[79] Tex. R. Civ. P. 199.2(a) ("An oral deposition may be taken outside the discovery period only by agreement of the parties or with leave of court."); Tex. R. Civ. P. 200.1(a) ("A deposition on written questions may be taken outside the discovery period only by agreement of the parties or with leave of court.").

[80] Tex. R. Civ. P. 21a(a).

[81] Texas Rule 21a allows service on the nonparty or its duly authorized agent: "in person, by mail, by commercial delivery service, by fax, by email, or by such other manner as the court in its discretion may direct." Tex. R. Civ. P. 21a(a)(2).

[82] Tex. R. Civ. P. 191.4(b)(1) ("The following discovery materials must be filed: . . . discovery requests, deposition notices, and subpoenas required to be served on nonparties[.]").

[83] Tex. R. Civ. P. 199.2(b)(5) ("A notice may include a request that the witness produce at the deposition documents or tangible things within the scope of discovery and within the witness's possession, custody, or control."); Tex. R. Civ. P. 200.1(b) ("The notice [for a deposition on written questions] also may include a request for production of documents as permitted by [Texas] Rule 199.2(b)(5), the provisions of which will govern the request, service, and response.").

[84] Tex. R. Civ. P. 199.2(b)(5). See Chapter 13, section 13-4:2, which discusses the requirements of a Texas Rule 205 production request.

13-5:3 The Subpoena

The subpoena must comply with Texas Rule 176, which governs subpoenas generally and is discussed in Chapter 13, section 13-4:3.[85] The nonparty's response to the notice's and subpoena's production requests likewise is governed by Texas Rules 176 and 205 and is discussed in Chapter 13, section 13-4:4.[86]

13-6 Requests for Medical or Mental-Health Records About Nonparties

Texas Rule 205.3(c) relates to the medical or mental-health records of a nonparty in the possession of the nonparty from whom discovery is sought. If the requesting party asks a nonparty to produce medical or mental-health records of another nonparty, the requesting party must serve the Texas Rule 205.3(a) notice on the nonparty whose records are sought.[87] This requirement parallels Texas Rule 196.1(c)(1)'s requirement, which applies when discovery of a nonparty's medical or mental-health is sought by one party from another.[88] As under Texas Rule 196.1(c), notice to the nonparty whose records are sought is excused when (1) the nonparty has signed a release for his or her records, (2) the production will not disclose the identity of the nonparty whose records are sought, or (3) the court, on a showing of good cause by the requesting party, orders that service is not required.[89]

---

[85] Tex. R. Civ. P. 176.2 ("A subpoena must command the person to whom it is directed to do either or both of the following: (a) attend and give testimony at a deposition, hearing, or trial; (b) produce and permit inspection and copying of designated documents or tangible things in the possession, custody, or control of that person.").

[86] Tex. R. Civ. P. 199.2(b)(5) ("The nonparty's response to the request is governed by [Texas] Rules 176 and 205."). If the notice is for an oral deposition, the nonparty "may object to the time and place designated for an oral deposition by motion for protective order or by motion to quash the notice of deposition. If the motion is filed by the third business day after service of the notice of deposition, an objection to the time and place of a deposition stays the oral deposition until the motion can be determined." Tex. R. Civ. P. 199.4. Such a motion will also stay the nonparty's production of documents and tangible things.

[87] Tex. R. Civ. P. 205.3(c) ("If a party requests a nonparty to produce medical or mental health records of another nonparty, the requesting party must serve the nonparty whose records are sought with the notice required under this rule.").

[88] Tex. R. Civ. P. 191.6(c). Texas Rule 191.6(c)(1) provides that "[i]f a party requests another party to produce medical or mental health records regarding a nonparty, the requesting party must serve the nonparty with the request for production under [Texas] Rule 21a." Tex. R. Civ. P. 191.6(c)(1).

[89] Tex. R. Civ. P. 205.3(c) (The notice required by Texas Rule 205.3(c) "does not apply under the circumstances set forth in [Texas] Rule 196.1(c)(2)."). Texas Rule 196.1(c)(2) provides: "A party is not required to serve the request for production on a nonparty whose medical records are sought if: (A) the nonparty signs a release of the records that is effective as to the requesting party; (B) the identity of the nonparty whose records are sought will not directly or indirectly be disclosed by production of the records; or (C) the court, upon a showing of good cause by the party seeking the records, orders that service is not required." Tex. R. Civ. P. 196.1(c)(2).

13-7 Providing Copies to Other Parties

The requesting party who served the notice and issued the subpoena must make the produced materials available to the other parties for inspection on reasonable notice.[90] Such parties, at their own expense, may obtain copies of the materials from the requesting party.[91]

13-8 The Nonparty's Document-Production's Costs

Under Texas Rule 205.3(f), the requesting party must reimburse the nonparty's "reasonable costs of production,"[92] but not its attorneys' fees.[93] One recent case suggests that such costs include compensation for the time spent by the nonparty and its employees in locating and reviewing the requested documents.[94]

13-9 Nonparty Depositions

The discussion in Chapter 13, sections 13-4 and 13-5, relates to Texas Rule 205's most useful application—nonparty production requests. As discussed in Chapter 13, section 13-2, Texas Rule 205 also authorizes subpoenas for discovery from nonparties in three other ways: oral depositions, depositions on written questions, and production requests served in connection with an oral or written deposition.[95] Subpoenas served

---

90 Tex. R. Civ. P. 205.3(e).

91 Tex. R. Civ. P. 205.3(e).

92 Tex. R. Civ. P. 205(f); *see Wichita Cnty. v. Envtl. Eng'g & Geotechnics, Inc.*, 576 S.W.3d 851, 860 (Tex. App.—Austin 2019, no. pet.) (noting that the cost reimbursement is "mandatory—i.e., that the requesting party 'must reimburse' the nonparty—distinguishing this rule from other contexts in which a trial court may or may not make an award or reach a certain conclusion" (quoting Tex. R. Civ. P. 205.3(f)). *See also In re K & L Auto Crushers, LLC*, 627 S.W.3d 239, 254 (Tex. 2021) (noting that Texas Rule 205.3's purpose is to address the third party's burden in responding to the subpoena).

93 *BASF Fina Petrochemicals L.P. v. H.B. Zachry Co.*, 168 S.W.3d 867, 872–73 (Tex. App.—Houston [1st Dist.] 2004, pet. denied) (holding that "costs of production" under Texas Rule 205.3(f) does not include attorney's fees), *cited with approval in Wichita Cnty. v. Envtl. Eng'g & Geotechnics, Inc.*, 576 S.W.3d 851, 862 (Tex. App.—Austin 2019, no. pet.).

94 In *Wichita County v. Environmental Engineering & Geotechnics, Inc.*, 576 S.W.3d 851 (Tex. App.—Austin 2019, no. pet.), the trial court awarded a nonparty $11,283.89 as "reasonable costs" for the production of documents in response to the County's document subpoena with most of the costs related to the search for, and review of, documents responsive to the subpoena. *Wichita Cnty. v. Envtl. Eng'g & Geotechnics, Inc.*, 576 S.W.3d 851, 854–56 (Tex. App.—Austin 2019, no. pet.). On appeal, the Austin Court of Appeals reversed the award and remanded the determination of the amount of such costs to the trial court because the nonparty's invoice improperly included time spent before the subpoena was issued and block-billed its employees' time under the notation "document production," thereby preventing the court or appeals from determining the specific activities in which the nonparty's employees engaged and whether the amount of time spent on them was reasonable. *Wichita Cnty. v. Envtl. Eng'g & Geotechnics, Inc.*, 576 S.W.3d 851, 863–77 (Tex. App.—Austin 2019, no. pet.). The court did not, however specifically hold that a nonparty can bill for its or its employees' time in locating and reviewing responsive documents. Nor did it provide any guidance regarding what constitutes a reasonable charge for such activities if they constitute "reasonable costs" of production.

95 Tex. R. Civ. P. 205.1.

for such discovery must comply with Texas Rule 176, which governs subpoenas generally. In addition, the party seeking the nonparty deposition must serve on the nonparty and all other parties the notice required by the rule governing the applicable deposition type.[96] "A notice of oral or written deposition must be served before or at the same time that a subpoena compelling attendance or production under the notice is served."[97] Finally, the noticing party must comply with the rules governing the type of deposition sought (i.e., an oral one or one on written questions).[98]

---

[96] Tex. R. Civ. P. 205.2 ("A party seeking discovery by subpoena from a nonparty must serve on the nonparty and all parties, a copy of the form of notice required under the rules governing the applicable form of discovery.").

[97] Tex. R. Civ. P. 205.2.

[98] Tex. R. Civ. P. 199, 200. Oral depositions and depositions on written questions are discussed in Chapter 11, sections 11-2 and 11-3, respectively.

CHAPTER 14

Sanctioning Discovery Abuse and Compelling Discovery—Texas Rule 215

This Chapter addresses the procedures governing motions for sanctions and orders compelling discovery, recoverable expenses relating to such motions, and procedural and substantive issues relating to sanctions for discovery abuses in Texas proceedings.[1] It focuses primarily on Texas Rule 215 and cases construing that Rule.[2]

14-1 Text of Rule 215

RULE 215. ABUSE OF DISCOVERY; SANCTIONS

[1] Other types of sanctions are addressed in other Texas rules and in statutes. *See, e.g.*, Tex. Civ. Prac. & Rem. Code Ann. §§ 9.011-9.014 (providing for sanctions for pleadings that are groundless and brought in bad faith, groundless and brought for harassment, or groundless and interposed for any improper purpose); Tex. Civ. Prac. & Rem. Code Ann. §§ 10.001-10.006 (addressing sanctions for frivolous pleadings and motions); Tex. Civ. Prac. & Rem. Code Ann. §§ 105.001-105.004 (addressing sanctions for frivolous claims by state agencies); Tex. R. Civ. P. 13 (addressing sanctions relating to pleadings, motions, and other papers that are groundless and brought in bad faith or groundless and brought for purpose of harassment); Tex. R. Civ. P. 18a(h) (addressing sanctions for recusal motions that are "groundless and filed in bad faith or for the purpose of harassment" or "clearly brought for unnecessary delay and without sufficient cause"); Tex. R. Civ. P. 21b (addressing sanctions for failure to properly serve or deliver any pleading, plea, motion, or other application).

[2] Texas Rule 215 was patterned after Federal Rule 37. *Firestone Photographs, Inc. v. Lamaster*, 567 S.W.2d 273, 277 (Tex. Civ. App.—Texarkana 1978, no writ) (Texas "Rule 215a was patterned after Rule 37 of the Federal Rules of Civil Procedure and was designed to give the trial court an expeditious procedure for insuring the effectiveness of pre-trial discovery and for dealing with recalcitrant or contumacious parties and witnesses. The authorized sanctions are not intended to be arbitrary and exclusive, but flexible and plural, vesting in the trial court broad discretion to fashion a remedy which will secure compliance with its orders and deter future non-compliance."); *Downer v. Aquamarine Operators, Inc.*, 701 S.W.2d 238, 242 (Tex. 1985) ("To determine the trial judge's guiding rules and principles in imposing sanctions for discovery abuse, we must look to the Texas Rules of Civil Procedure as promulgated and amended by this Court as well as the decisions of appellate courts of this State and of the United States."). Federal Rule 37(a) and (e) were amended effective December 1, 2015. Those amendments are discussed in Chapter 14, sections 14-2:4 and 14-3:4.5.

215.1. Motion for Sanctions or Order Compelling Discovery

A party, upon reasonable notice to other parties and all other persons affected thereby, may apply for sanctions or an order compelling discovery as follows:

(a) **Appropriate court.** On matters relating to a deposition, an application for an order to a party may be made to the court in which the action is pending, or to any district court in the district where the deposition is being taken. An application for an order to a deponent who is not a party shall be made to the court in the district where the deposition is being taken. As to all other discovery matters, an application for an order will be made to the court in which the action is pending.

(b) **Motion**

(1) If a party or other deponent which is a corporation or other entity fails to make a designation under Rules 199.2(b)(1) or 200.1(b); or

(2) If a party, or other deponent, or a person designated to testify on behalf of a party or other deponent fails:

(A) to appear before the officer who is to take his deposition, after being served with a proper notice; or

(B) to answer a question propounded or submitted upon oral examination or upon written questions; or

(3) If a party fails:

(A) to serve answers or objections to interrogatories submitted under Rule 197, after proper service of the interrogatories; or

(B) to answer an interrogatory submitted under Rule 197; or

(C) to serve a written response to a request for inspection submitted under Rule 196, after proper service of the request; or

(D) to respond that discovery will be permitted as requested or fails to permit discovery as requested in response to a request for inspection submitted under Rule 196; the discovering party may move for an order compelling a designation, an appearance, an answer or answers, or inspection or production in accordance with the request, or apply to the court in which the action is pending for the imposition of any sanction authorized by Rule 215.2(b) without the necessity of first having obtained a court order compelling such discovery.

When taking a deposition on oral examination, the proponent of the question may complete or adjourn the examination before he applies for an order.

If the court denies the motion in whole or in part, it may make such protective order as it would have been empowered to make on a motion pursuant to Rule 192.6.

(c) **Evasive or incomplete answer.** For purposes of this subdivision an evasive or incomplete answer is to be treated as a failure to answer.

(d) **Disposition of motion to compel: award of expenses.** If the motion is granted, the court shall, after opportunity for hearing, require a party or deponent whose conduct necessitated the motion or the party or attorney advising such conduct or both of them to pay, at such time as ordered by the court, the moving party the reasonable expenses incurred in obtaining the order, including attorney fees, unless the court finds that the opposition to the motion was substantially justified or that other circumstances make an award of expenses unjust. Such an order shall be subject to review on appeal from the final judgment.

If the motion is denied, the court may, after opportunity for hearing, require the moving party or attorney advising such motion to pay to the party or deponent who opposed the motion the reasonable expenses incurred in opposing the motion, including attorney fees, unless the court finds that the making of the motion was substantially justified or that other circumstances make an award of expenses unjust.

If the motion is granted in part and denied in part, the court may apportion the reasonable expenses incurred in relation to the motion among the parties and persons in a just manner.

In determining the amount of reasonable expenses, including attorney fees, to be awarded in connection with a motion, the trial court shall award expenses which are reasonable in relation to the amount of work reasonably expended in obtaining an order compelling compliance or in opposing a motion which is denied.

(e) **Providing person's own statement.** If a party fails to comply with any person's written request for the person's own statement as provided in Rule 192.3(h), the person who made the request may move for an order compelling compliance. If the motion is granted, the movant may recover the expenses incurred in obtaining the order, including attorney fees, which are reasonable in relation to the amount of work reasonably expended in obtaining the order.

215.2. Failure to Comply with Order or with Discovery Request

(a) **Sanctions by court in district where deposition is taken.** If a deponent fails to appear or to be sworn or to answer a question after being directed to do so by a district court in the district in which the deposition is being taken, the failure may be considered a contempt of that court.

(b) **Sanctions by court in which action is pending.** If a party or an officer, director, or managing agent of a party or a person designated under Rules 199.2(b)(1) or 200.1(b) to testify on behalf of a party fails to comply with proper discovery requests or to obey an order to provide or permit discovery, including an order made under Rules 204 or 215.1, the court in which the action is pending may, after notice and hearing, make such orders in regard to the failure as are just, and among others the following:

(1) an order disallowing any further discovery of any kind or of a particular kind by the disobedient party;

(2) an order charging all or any portion of the expenses of discovery or taxable court costs or both against the disobedient party or the attorney advising him;

(3) an order that the matters regarding which the order was made or any other designated facts shall be taken to be established for the purposes of the action in accordance with the claim of the party obtaining the order;

(4) an order refusing to allow the disobedient party to support or oppose designated claims or defenses, or prohibiting him from introducing designated matters in evidence;

(5) an order striking out pleadings or parts thereof, or staying further proceedings until the order is obeyed, or dismissing with or without prejudice the action or proceedings or any part thereof, or rendering a judgment by default against the disobedient party;

(6) in lieu of any of the foregoing orders or in addition thereto, an order treating as a contempt of court the failure to obey any orders except an order to submit to a physical or mental examination;

(7) when a party has failed to comply with an order under Rule 204 requiring him to appear or produce another for examination, such orders as are listed in paragraphs (1), (2), (3), (4) or (5) of this subdivision, unless the person failing to comply shows that he is unable to appear or to produce such person for examination.

(8) In lieu of any of the foregoing orders or in addition thereto, the court shall require the party failing to obey the order or the attorney advising him, or both, to pay, at such time as ordered by the court, the reasonable expenses, including attorney fees, caused by the failure, unless the court finds that the failure was substantially justified or that other circumstances make an award of expenses unjust. Such an order shall be subject to review on appeal from the final judgment.

(c) **Sanction against nonparty for violation of Rules 196.7 or 205.3.** If a nonparty fails to comply with an order under Rules 196.7 or 205.3, the court which made the order may treat the failure to obey as contempt of court.

215.3. Abuse of Discovery Process in Seeking, Making, or Resisting Discovery

If the court finds a party is abusing the discovery process in seeking, making or resisting discovery or if the court finds that any interrogatory or request for inspection or production is unreasonably frivolous, oppressive, or harassing, or that a response or answer is unreasonably frivolous or made for purposes of delay, then the court in which the action is pending may, after notice and hearing, impose any appropriate sanction authorized by paragraphs (1), (2), (3), (4), (5), and (8) of Rule 215.2(b). Such order of sanction shall be subject to review on appeal from the final judgment.

215.4. Failure to Comply with Rule 198

(a) **Motion.** A party who has requested an admission under Rule 198 may move to determine the sufficiency of the answer or objection. For purposes of this subdivision an evasive or incomplete answer may be treated as a failure to answer. Unless the court determines that an objection is justified, it shall order that an answer be served. If the court determines that an answer does not comply with the requirements of Rule 198, it may order either that the matter is admitted or that an amended answer be served. The provisions of Rule 215.1(d) apply to the award of expenses incurred in relation to the motion.

(b) **Expenses on failure to admit.** If a party fails to admit the genuineness of any document or the truth of any matter as requested under Rule 198 and if the party requesting the admissions thereafter proves the genuineness of the document or the truth of the matter, he may apply to the court for an order requiring the other party to pay him the reasonable expenses incurred in making that proof, including reasonable attorney fees. The court shall make the order unless it finds that (1) the request was held objectionable pursuant to Rule 193, or (2) the admission sought was of no substantial importance, or (3) the party failing to admit had a reasonable ground to believe that he might prevail on the matter, or (4) there was other good reason for the failure to admit.

215.5. Failure of Party or Witness to Attend or to Serve Subpoena; Expenses

(a) **Failure of party giving notice to attend.** If the party giving the notice of the taking of an oral deposition fails to attend and proceed therewith and another party attends in person or by attorney pursuant to the notice, the court may order the party giving the notice to pay such other party the reasonable expenses incurred by him and his attorney in attending, including reasonable attorney fees.

(b) **Failure of witness to attend.** If a party gives notice of the taking of an oral deposition of a witness and the witness does not attend because of the fault of the party giving the notice, if another party attends in person or by attorney because he expects the deposition of that witness to be taken, the court may order the party giving the notice to pay such other party the reasonable expenses incurred by him and his attorney in attending, including reasonable attorney fees.

215.6. Exhibits to Motions and Responses

Motions or responses made under this rule may have exhibits attached including affidavits, discovery pleadings, or any other documents.

Comments to Texas Rule 215

Comment to 1990 change:

To require notice and hearing before an imposition of sanctions under paragraph 3 [of Texas Rule 215.2], and to specify [in Texas Rule 215.3] that such sanctions be appropriate.

Comment to 1999 change:

The references in this rule to other discovery rules were changed to reflect the revisions in those rules and former Rule 203 is added as Rule 215.5 in place of the former provisions, which is superseded by Rule 193.6.

14-1:1 2021 Amendments to the Texas Rules of Civil Procedure

The 2021 amendments to the Texas Rules of Civil Procedure did not modify Texas Rule 215 regarding sanctions in any respect.

14-2 Motions for Sanctions or Order Compelling Discovery

Texas Rule 215 addresses discovery failures that warrant a motion for sanctions or to compel discovery.[3] It contains procedures that apply equally to both types of motions, as well as procedures unique to each type of motion.[4] A party can seek sanctions without first moving to compel discovery; likewise, a party can move to compel discovery without seeking sanctions.[5] Regardless, the party must follow the Texas Rule 215.1 procedures.

14-2:1 Notice and Hearing Requirements

Under Texas Rule 215.1, a party may move for sanctions or an order compelling discovery, "upon reasonable notice to other parties and all other persons affected" by the relief sought.[6] Oral notice of a sanctions hearing has been deemed "insufficient as a

---

[3] *See* Tex. R. Civ. P. 215.1(b), Tex. R. Civ. P. 215.1(e), Tex. R. Civ. P. 215.4(a).

[4] *Compare, e.g.*, Tex. R. Civ. P. 215.1(a)–(b) (applying to both types of motions), *and* Tex. R. Civ. P. 215.6 (same), *with* Tex. R. Civ. P. 215.1(d)–(e) (applying to motions to compel), *and* Tex. R. Civ. P. 215.2–215.3 (applying to motions for sanctions). See also Chapter 10, section 10-9 (discussing procedures under Texas Rule 215.4 for testing the sufficiency of answers, objections, and privilege assertions to requests for admission).

[5] Tex. R. Civ. P. 215.1(b) (providing that, if one party commits one or more of the discovery abuses enumerated in Texas Rule 215.1(b), "the discovering party may move for an order compelling a designation, an appearance, an answer or answers, or inspection or production in accordance with the request, *or* apply to the court in which the action is pending for the imposition of any sanction authorized by [Texas] Rule 215.2(b) without the necessity of first having obtained a court order compelling such discovery") (emphasis added); *Horizon Health Corp. v. Acadia Healthcare Co., Inc.*, 520 S.W.3d 848, 884 (Tex. 2017) ("[S]anctions may be appropriate even when a party eventually complies with a discovery request."); *City of Richardson v. Cannon*, No. 05-18-00181-CV, 2018 Tex. App. LEXIS 9376, at *5 (Tex. App.—Dallas Nov. 16, 2018, no pet.) (mem. op.) ("A party may apply for sanctions or an order compelling discovery if the other party fails to respond to discovery requests."); *Adkins Servs., Inc. v. Tisdale Co., Inc.*, 56 S.W.3d 842, 844 (Tex. App.—Texarkana 2001, no pet.) ("In applying the predecessors to these rules, appellate courts have uniformly held that [Texas] Rule 215.1 means what it says: that a party may pursue sanctions instead of filing a motion to compel.") (citations omitted).

[6] Tex. R. Civ. P. 215.1 ("A party, upon reasonable notice to other parties and all other parties affected thereby, may apply for sanctions or an order compelling discovery. . . ."); *see Horizon Health Corp. v. Acadia Healthcare Co., Inc.*, 520 S.W.3d 848, 884 (Tex. 2017) ("Sanctions may be imposed, *after notice and a hearing*, on parties who refuse to respond, or who give inadequate responses, to valid discovery requests or orders.") (emphasis added); *Koslow's v. Mackie*, 796 S.W.2d 700, 704 (Tex. 1990) ("It is an abuse of discretion for the trial court to impose sanctions when the defaulting party has inadequate notice or no notice of the sanctions hearing."); *In re First Transit Inc.*, 499 S.W.3d 584, 596 (Tex. App.—Houston [14th Dist.] 2016, orig. proceeding) ("The imposition of sanctions requires that 'notice reasonably calculated, under the circumstances, to apprise interested parties of the pendency of the action and afford them the opportunity to present their objections.' The motion for sanctions must provide notice of the conduct that the movant seeks to sanction so that the respondent may attempt to prepare a defense." (citation omitted) (quoting *Greene v. Young*, 174 S.W.3d 291, 298 (Tex. App.—Houston [1st Dist.] 2005, pet. denied))); *Low v. State*, No. 2-03-347-CV, 2005 Tex. App. LEXIS 3657, at *4, 2005 WL1120013, (Tex. App.—Fort Worth May 12, 2005, no pet.) ("Proceedings for sanctions must meet due process requirements, giving a person reasonable notice and an adequate opportunity to be heard."); *Seckers v.*

matter of law[.]"[7] Accordingly, a party who files a motion for sanctions should ensure that all other parties, as well as all other persons affected by the sanctions sought, receive written notice of the sanctions hearing.

A court must provide an opportunity for a hearing regarding a sanctions motion and a motion to compel discovery.[8] But the hearing need not be oral; written submissions will suffice.[9]

Ocean Chems., Inc., 845 S.W.2d 317, 318 (Tex. App.—Houston [1st Dist.] 1992, no writ) (holding that "a misleading notice is equal to no notice" and that the trial court abused its discretion by dismissing the action as a discovery sanction because the sanctioned party did not receive notice of the dismissal motion); *Zep Mfg. Co. v. Anthony*, 752 S.W.2d 687, 689–90 (Tex. App.—Houston [1st Dist.] 1988, orig. proceeding) ("Without a motion before the trial court that asked for sanctions for discovery abuse, the relator had no notice that the hearing scheduled on other discovery motions would result in respondent's spontaneous striking of its pleadings. Notice is essential for the proper imposition of sanctions.").

7 *Low v. State*, No. 2-03-347-CV, 2005 Tex. App. LEXIS 3657, at *4, 2005 WL1120013, (Tex. App.—Fort Worth May 12, 2005, no pet.) (mem. op.) ("Oral notice of a sanctions hearing is insufficient as a matter of law; written notice is required."); *In re Acceptance Ins. Co.*, 33 S.W.3d 443, 451 (Tex. App.—Fort Worth 2000, orig. proceeding) (same).

8 Tex. R. Civ. P. 215.1(d) (referring to a motion's disposition "after opportunity for hearing"); *see Horizon Health Corp. v. Acadia Healthcare Co., Inc.*, 520 S.W.3d 848, 884 (Tex. 2017) ("Sanctions may be imposed, *after notice and a hearing*, on parties who refuse to respond, or who give inadequate responses, to valid discovery requests or orders.") (emphasis added); *In re Sw. Pub. Serv. Co.*, No. 13-19-00111-CV, 2020 Tex. App. LEXIS 3212, at *33, 2020 WL 1887762 (Tex. App. —Eastland Apr. 16, 2020,orig. proceeding) (mem. op.) ("Sanctions may be imposed, after notice and a hearing, on parties who refuse to respond, or who give inadequate responses, to valid discovery requests or orders."); *Alma Invs., Inc. v. Bahia Mar Co-Owners Ass'n, Inc.*, 497 S.W.3d 137, 142 (Tex. App.—Corpus Christi 2016, pet. denied) ("[W]hichever permissible sanction is ordered by a trial court under [Texas] Rule 215.2(b), it must be done after notice and hearing. . . ."); *Low v. State*, No. 2-03-347-CV, 2005 Tex. App. LEXIS 3657, at *4, 2005 WL1120013, (Tex. App.—Fort Worth May 12, 2005, no pet.) (mem. op.) ("Proceedings for sanctions must meet due process requirements, giving a person reasonable notice and an adequate opportunity to be heard."); *Bedding Component Mfrs., Ltd. v. Royal Sleep Prods.*, 108 S.W.3d 563, 564 (Tex. App.—Dallas 2003, no pet.) ("Without a hearing on the motion for sanctions, the trial court has no evidence before it to determine that a pleading is sanctionable."); *In re Acceptance Ins. Co.*, 33 S.W.3d 443, 451 (Tex. App.—Fort Worth 2000, orig. proceeding) ("Like contempt proceedings, proceedings for sanctions must comport with due process, affording a party an adequate opportunity to be heard."); *Davila v. World Car Five Star*, 75 S.W.3d 537, 544 (Tex. App.—San Antonio 2002, no pet.) ("By refusing to allow Davila to introduce evidence of the facts available and circumstances in existence at the time he filed [his petition], the trial court denied Davila an opportunity to be heard in a meaningful manner.").

9 *E.g., Cire v. Cummings*, 134 S.W.3d 835, 843–44 (Tex. 2004) ("[T]here is no oral hearing requirement in the rules. [Texas] Rule 215.3, which authorizes a trial court to impose sanctions, does require notice and hearing before sanctions are imposed. However, nothing in the rule indicates that this must be an oral hearing. A hearing does not necessarily contemplate a personal appearance before the court or an oral presentation to the court."); *Hicks v. Hicks*, No. 01-15-01011-CV, 2016 Tex. App. LEXIS 4597, at *7–8 n.4, 2016 WL 2342913, (Tex. App.—Houston [1st Dist.] May 3, 2016, no pet.) (mem. op.) ("To the extent that Larry contends that the trial court erred in denying a hearing on his discovery motion, we note that the decision 'to hold an oral hearing on a motion to compel is a matter within the discretion of the trial court.' And 'there is no "oral hearing" requirement in the rules.'" (citation omitted) (quoting *Cire v. Cummings*, 134 S.W.3d 835, 843–44 (Tex. 2004))); *McCollum v. Bank of*

14-2:2 Where and What to File

Texas Rule 215.1(a) identifies the appropriate court in which to file a motion for an order directed to a party deponent, a motion for an order directed to a nonparty deponent, and a motion for an order regarding "all other discovery matters."[10] A motion relating to a party deponent must be filed in "the court in which the action is pending, or . . . any district court in the district where the deposition is being taken."[11] A motion relating to a nonparty deponent, however, must be filed in "the court in the district where the deposition is being taken."[12] Finally, "[a]s to all other discovery matters," the motion must be filed in "the court in which the action is pending."[13]

A motion or response filed in any court, pursuant to Texas Rule 215.6, "may have exhibits attached including affidavits, discovery pleadings, or any other documents."[14] Thus, in the context of discovery motions and responses, there is an exception to the general rule against filing discovery materials served on or by parties.[15] Even though Texas Rule 215.6 does not require the filing of exhibits with a motion or response, movants and respondents should attach all discovery materials and other items of import as exhibits because (1) the trial court may rule on the motion without an oral hearing,[16] and (2) the exhibits will be part of the record if either the movant or respondent seeks review of the trial court's ruling on appeal or by mandamus.[17]

Although Texas Rule 215.6 expressly permits affidavits as exhibits to motions and responses, some courts have excluded such affidavits as hearsay.[18] Thus, movants

N.Y. Mellon Tr. Co., 481 S.W.3d 352, 358 (Tex. App.—El Paso 2015, no. pet.) (same); ***Melasky v. Warner***, No. 09-11-00447-CV, 2012 Tex. App. LEXIS 9760, at *6–7, 2012 WL 5960310 (Tex. App.—Beaumont Nov. 29, 2012, pet. denied) (mem. op.); ***Van Es v. Frazier***, 230 S.W.3d 770, 776 (Tex. App.—Waco 2007, pet. denied) (same).

[10] Tex. R. Civ. P. 215.1(a).

[11] Tex. R. Civ. P. 215.1(a).

[12] Tex. R. Civ. P. 215.1(a).

[13] Tex. R. Civ. P. 215.1(a).

[14] Tex. R. Civ. P. 215.6.

[15] Tex. R. Civ. 9. 215.6; *see* Tex. R. Civ. P. 191.4(b)(2) (requiring "motions and responses to motions pertaining to discovery matters" to be filed); Tex. R. Civ. P. 191.4(c)(2) (providing that "a person may file discovery materials in support of or in opposition to a motion or for other use in a court proceeding").

[16] See Chapter 14, section 14-2:1 (addressing hearing requirements).

[17] *E.g.*, ***Otis Elevator Co. v. Parmelee***, 850 S.W.2d 179, 181 (Tex. 1993) ("Here, the trial court heard no evidence but expressly based its decision on the papers filed and the argument of counsel. Under these circumstances, there are no factual resolutions to presume in the trial court's favor. The court of appeals should have looked to the record to determine whether the case-determinative sanctions imposed by the trial court are just. . . .").

[18] *E.g.*, ***Kugle v. DaimlerChrysler Corp.***, 88 S.W.3d 355, 363 (Tex. App.—San Antonio 2002, pet. denied) ("The trial court sustained hearsay objections to each of the affidavits. In response, the appellants argued that [Texas R]ule 215.6 . . . permits testimony by affidavit. . . . [A]ppellants liken a sanctions hearing to a summary judgment hearing and argue that since the sanctions rule contemplates the use of affidavits as exhibits to a response to a sanctions motion, the affidavits are admissible at the sanctions hearing in the same manner as such exhibits are admissible at a summary judgment hearing. However, unlike a sanctions hearing, a summary judgment hearing is 'an exception to the usual and traditional form of procedure wherein witnesses are heard in open court and documentary evidence is offered and received in evidence.' In order to assess sanctions in this case, the trial court

and respondents should not assume that affidavits in this context will be treated like affidavits in the summary judgment context. When evidence is provided with a sanctions motion or a response thereto, the most prudent course is to treat the hearing on the motion as a traditional evidentiary hearing.

14-2:3 Timeliness of Motions

Texas Rule 215 contains no filing deadline for motions for sanctions or to compel discovery.[19] Nonetheless, a party should not lay behind the log and complain about alleged discovery abuse long after it has occurred. Delay may result in denial of the motion during pretrial proceedings.[20] And "the failure to obtain a pretrial ruling on discovery disputes that exist before commencement of trial constitutes a waiver of any claim for sanctions based on that conduct."[21]

The trial court has the authority to sanction discovery abuse that is discovered during trial.[22] But any motion seeking sanctions for discovery abuse discovered during trial must be filed before the trial court loses plenary power over its judgment.[23]

---

was required to conduct an *evidentiary* hearing to which the rules of evidence necessarily apply. Therefore, although [Texas R]ule 215.6 allows affidavits to be attached to a response to a sanctions motion, in order for the trial court to consider such affidavits, they must be admitted in compliance with the rules of evidence at the evidentiary hearing." (citations omitted) (quoting *IKB Indus. (Nigeria) Ltd. v. Pro-Line Corp.*, 938 S.W.2d 440, 441 (Tex. 1997))). *But see Horizon Health Corp. v. Acadia Healthcare Co., Inc.*, 520 S.W.3d 848, 886 (Tex. 2017) (holding that the trial court did not abuse its discretion in imposing discovery sanctions and noting that it "based its sanctions decision on a host of discovery misconduct by [the sanctioned party] that was established through multiple hearings and motions and supported *by affidavit testimony and other evidence*.") (emphasis added).

[19] *In re City of Hous.*, No. 14-12-00861-CV, 2013 Tex. App. LEXIS 21, at *13, 2013 WL 85097 (Tex. App.—Houston [14th Dist.] 2013, orig. proceeding) (mem. op.) ("The rule contains no filing deadline.").

[20] *E.g., Piazza v. Cinemark, USA, Inc.*, 179 S.W.3d 213, 216 (Tex. App.—Eastland 2005, pet. denied) (holding that trial court did not abuse its discretion in denying a motion to compel discovery because, among other reasons, the motion was filed two days before a rescheduled summary judgment hearing that had been continued previously to give the movant more time for discovery and because the movant "had more than ample time to conduct discovery" before filing motion); *cf. Brandt v. Vulcan, Inc.*, 30 F.3d 752, 756 (7th Cir. 1994) ("Although [Federal] Rule 37(b)(2) does not establish any time limits within which a motion for sanctions must be filed, Brandt does not dispute that unreasonable delay may render such a motion untimely.").

[21] *Remington Arms Co. v. Caldwell*, 850 S.W.2d 167, 170 (Tex. 1993); *cf. Butler v. Pettigrew*, 409 F.2d 1205, 1207 (7th Cir. 1969) (holding that a party that waited until after judgment was entered to request sanctions for the opposing party's failure to fully answer interrogatories waived its rights under Federal Rule 37(b) and (d)). As discussed in Chapter 10, section 10-10, this waiver rule should not apply under Texas Rule 215.4(b)—the "admit or pay" rule for requests for admission.

[22] *Remington Arms Co. v. Caldwell*, 850 S.W.2d 167, 170 (Tex. 1993) (affirming the exclusion of a party's expert's testimony during trial based on the party's failure to disclose such testimony, noting that "[u]nquestionably, the trial court has the power during trial to sanction nondisclosure of information requested during discovery").

[23] *In re Bennett*, 960 S.W.2d 35, 38 (Tex. 1997) (original proceeding) ("[A] trial court is free to impose sanctions while it retains plenary jurisdiction even when a motion is filed after the notice of nonsuit is filed. It is only after plenary jurisdiction has expired that a trial

14-2:4 Motion's Grounds

Under Texas Rule 215.1(b), "the discovering party may move for an order compelling a designation, an appearance, an answer or answers, or inspection or production in accordance with [a discovery] request, or apply to the court in which the action is pending for the imposition of any sanction authorized by Texas Rule 215.2(b)" for the following reasons:

(1) If a party or other deponent which is a corporation or other entity fails to make a designation under [Texas] Rules 199.2(b)(1) or 200.1(b); or

(2) if a party, or other deponent, or a person designated to testify on behalf of a party or other deponent fails:

(A) to appear before the officer who is to take his deposition, after being served with a proper notice; or

(B) to answer a question propounded or submitted upon oral examination or upon written questions; or

(3) if a party fails:

(A) to serve answers or objections to interrogatories submitted under [Texas] Rule 197, after proper service of the interrogatories; or

(B) to answer an interrogatory submitted under Rule 197; or

(C) to serve a written response to a request for inspection submitted under [Texas] Rule 196, after proper service of the request; or

(D) to respond that discovery will be permitted as requested or fails to permit discovery as requested in response to a request for inspection submitted under [Texas] Rule 196[.][24]

When assessing whether a party has failed to answer a discovery request as provided in Texas Rule 215.1(b), "an evasive or incomplete answer is to be treated as a failure to answer."[25]

---

court may not sanction counsel for pre-judgment conduct."); *Scott & White Mem'l Hosp. v. Schexnider*, 940 S.W.2d 594, 596 (Tex. 1996) (same). "Generally, a trial court loses plenary jurisdiction thirty days after entry of final judgment." *In re Bokeloh*, 21 S.W.3d 784, 787 (Tex. App.—Houston [14th Dist.] 2000,orig. proceeding); *accord Lane Bank Equip. Co. v. Smith S. Equip., Inc.*, 10 S.W.3d 308, 310 (Tex. 2000).

[24] Tex. R. Civ. P. 215.1(b)(1)–(3).

[25] Tex. R. Civ. P. 215.1(c); *see Horizon Health Corp. v. Acadia Healthcare Co., Inc.*, 520 S.W.3d 848, 884 (Tex. 2017) ("For purposes of these provisions[,Texas Rules 215.1 through 215.5], evasive or incomplete answers are treated as a failure to answer."); *In re Sw. Pub. Serv. Co.*, No. 13-19-00111-CV, 2020 Tex. App. LEXIS 3212, at *33, 2020 WL 1887762 (Tex. App.—Eastland Apr. 16, 2020,orig. proceeding) (mem. op.) (same); *Hernandez v. Mid-Loop, Inc.*, 170 S.W.3d 138, 143 (Tex. App.—San Antonio 2005, no pet.) ("Hernandez contends the evidence is insufficient to support the conclusion he was intentionally evasive. We disagree. Hernandez repeatedly blamed his failure to answer questions on memory problems, but could not produce any conclusive medical evidence of memory deficit. Moreover, the record reveals Hernandez knew he had been ordered to produce his medical records and the names of his medical providers since 1987, but failed to do so. Hernandez implied that he was able to produce such records, however, as he continuously asked if he could provide the list at a later time. Hernandez also provided

In addition, sanctions may also be appropriate even when a party eventually complies with a discovery request.[26] For example, in *Drozd Corporation v. Capitol Glass & Mirror Company*, the plaintiff moved for sanctions when the defendant failed to answer Plaintiff's interrogatories.[27] The defendant did not appear at the hearing but instead filed its responses two days later.[28] The trial court granted the plaintiff's motion on the same day, and the trial court's order was upheld on appeal.[29]

Although the prefatory language to Texas Rule 215.1(b) provides for a motion "compelling . . . production," the Rule does not list a failure to produce documents as a ground for a motion to compel discovery. Federal Rule 37(a)(3)(B) contained a similar disconnect until December 1, 2015, when it was amended to provide: "A party seeking discovery may move for an order compelling an answer, designation, production, or inspection. This motion may be made if . . . a party fails to produce documents or fails to respond that inspection will be permitted—or fails to permit inspection—as requested under [Federal] Rule 34."[30] The Advisory Committee explained the amendment as follows: Federal "Rule 37(a)(3)(B)(iv) is amended to reflect the common practice of producing copies of documents or electronically stored information rather than simply permitting inspection. This change brings item (iv) into line with paragraph (B), which provides a motion for an order compelling "production, or inspection."[31] Texas Rule 215.1(b) would be clearer with a similar amendment, but case law leaves no doubt that a party's failure to produce responsive documents or responsive electronically stored information is a proper ground for a motion to compel production in Texas state-court proceedings.[32]

---

incomplete answers regarding his prior accidents. The evidence is sufficient to support the trial court's conclusion Hernandez violated [Texas] Rule 215.1(c).").

26 *Horizon Health Corp. v. Acadia Healthcare Co.*, 520 S.W.3d 848, 884 (Tex. 2017) ("[S]anctions may be appropriate even when a party eventually complies with a discovery request."); *In re Sw. Pub. Serv. Co.*, No. 13-19-00111-CV, 2020 Tex. App. LEXIS 3212, at *33, 2020 WL 1887762 (Tex. App.—Eastland Apr. 16, 2020, orig. proceeding) (mem. op.) (same).

27 *Drozd Corp. v. Capitol Glass & Mirror Co.*, 741 S.W.2d 221, 223 (Tex. App.—Austin 1987, no writ).

28 *Drozd Corp. v. Capitol Glass & Mirror Co.*, 741 S.W.2d 221, 223 (Tex. App.—Austin 1987, no writ).

29 *Drozd Corp. v. Capitol Glass & Mirror Co.*, 741 S.W.2d 221, 223 (Tex. App.—Austin 1987, no writ) (explaining that, because a basis of sanctions is deterrence of violations by other litigants, party's eventual compliance with discovery request does not preclude imposition of sanctions).

30 Fed. R. Civ. P. 37(a)(3)(B)(iv).

31 Fed. R. Civ. P. 37(a)(3)(B)(iv), Advisory Committee Note to 2015 Amend.

32 *E.g.*, *In re Weekley Homes, L.P.*, 295 S.W.3d 309, 315 (Tex. 2009) (orig. proceeding) ("Weekley additionally complains that HFG's 'Motion for Limited Access to [Weekley's] Computers' is not a permissible discovery device. We agree with HFG, however, that the motion was, in effect, a motion to compel and the trial court properly treated it as such."); *In re Sabine Valley Ctr.*, 986 S.W.2d 612, 613–14 (Tex. 1999) (orig. proceeding) (per curiam) (holding that the trial court abused its discretion in granting a motion to compel the production of a government unit's insurance policies); *Contractors Source, Inc. v. Amegy Bank Nat'l Ass'n*, 462 S.W.3d 128, 140 (Tex. App.—Houston [1st Dist.] 2015, no pet.) (holding that the trial court did not abuse its discretion in denying a motion to compel the production of documents); *In re Select Energy Servs., LLC*, No. 04-14-00693-CV, 2014 Tex. App. LEXIS 11387, at *1–2, 2014 WL 5242133 (Tex. App.—San Antonio Oct. 15, 2014, orig. proceeding) (mem. op.) (denying a mandamus petition complaining about the trial court's order granting the plaintiffs'

Texas Rule 215.1(e) provides an additional basis for a motion to compel, relating to witness statements, providing: "If a party fails to comply with any person's written request for the person's own statement as provided in [Texas] Rule 192.3(h), the person who made the request may move for an order compelling compliance."[33]

Texas Rule 215.2(b) enables a movant to seek certain enumerated sanctions orders and other sanctions "orders . . . as are just" if "a party or an officer, director, or managing agent of a party or a person designated under [Texas] Rules 199.2(b)(1) or 200.1(b) to testify on behalf of a party fails to comply with proper discovery requests or to obey an order to provide or permit discovery."[34] Also, Texas Rule 215.3 provides more generally that, "[i]f the court finds a party is abusing the discovery process in seeking, making or resisting discovery or if the court finds that any interrogatory or request for inspection or production is unreasonably frivolous, oppressive, or harassing, or that a response or answer is unreasonably frivolous or made for purpose of delay," then the court may impose any appropriate sanction under Texas Rule 215.2(b)(1)–(5) and (8).[35]

As discussed in Chapter 10, sections 10-8 and 10-9, Texas Rule 215.4 also provides a procedure for motions relating to a party's failure to comply with Texas Rule 198, regarding requests for admission.

14-2:5 Conference and Cooperation Requirements for Motions

As explained in Chapter 3, section 3–3, motions for sanctions and motions to compel discovery are subject to the conference and cooperation requirements of Texas Rule 191.2 and applicable local rules.[36] Movants and respondents should also heed any applicable standing orders relating to conference and cooperation requirements. Although such orders cannot be applied to determine the merits of any matter,[37] they generally warrant attention and adherence.

---

motion to compel the production of documents); *Mayfield v. Fullhart*, 444 S.W.3d 222, 226 (Tex. App.—Houston [14th Dist.] 2014, pet. denied) ("Mayfield argues that appellees failed to respond to her discovery requests with documents that would defeat the statute-of-limitations ground. Mayfield has waived her complaint because the record does not indicate she filed a motion to compel production of any documents before the hearing, much less obtained a ruling."); *In re Staff Care, Inc.*, 422 S.W.3d 876, 883–85 (Tex. App.—Dallas 2014, no pet.) (holding that the trial court did not abuse its discretion in denying two motions to compel the production of documents); *Hagerman v. Wells Fargo*, No. 03-03-00769-CV, 2006 Tex. App. LEXIS 7559, at *32, 2006 WL 2448598 (Tex. App.—Austin Aug. 25, 2006, no pet.) (mem. op.) ("[B]ecause Hagerman was proceeding *pro se* and because the sanctions were imposed in connection with motions to compel production of the documents that she continually failed to produce, there is no question that a direct relationship existed between the improper conduct and the sanction imposed.").

[33] Tex. R. Civ. P. 215.1(e).

[34] Tex. R. Civ. P. 215.2(b).

[35] Tex. R. Civ. P. 215.3.

[36] See Chapter 3, section 3-4 (discussing conference and cooperation requirements).

[37] *See* Tex. R. Civ. P. 3a ("[N]o local rule, order, or practice of any court, other than local rules and amendments which fully comply with all requirements of this [Texas] Rule 3a, shall ever be applied to determine the merits of any matter.").

14-2:6 Award of Reasonable Expenses, Including Attorney's Fees

Texas Rule 215.1(d) provides for an award of reasonable expenses, including attorney's fees, incurred in pursuing or opposing a motion to compel discovery.[38] The rule provides that such expenses may be awarded against a party or an "advising" attorney, and it contains varying standards for determining the award depending on whether the motion is (1) granted, (2) denied, or (3) granted in part and denied in part:

> If the motion is granted, the court *shall*, after opportunity for hearing, require a party or deponent whose conduct necessitated the motion or the party or attorney advising such conduct or both of them to pay, at such time as ordered by the court, the moving party the reasonable expenses incurred in obtaining the order, including attorney fees, *unless* the court finds that the opposition to the motion was substantially justified or that other circumstances make an award of expenses *unjust*. Such an order shall be subject to review on appeal from the final judgment.
>
> If the motion is denied, the court *may*, after opportunity for hearing, require the moving party or attorney advising such motion to pay to the party or deponent who opposed the motion the reasonable expense incurred in opposing the motion, including attorney fees, *unless* the court finds that the making of the motion was substantially justified or that other circumstances make an award of expenses *unjust*.
>
> If the motion is granted in part and denied in part, the court *may* apportion the reasonable expenses incurred in relation to the motion among the parties and persons in a *just* manner.[39]

---

38 Tex. R. Civ. P. 215.1(d); *see Bowling v. Dahlheimer*, No. 05-16-01196-CV, 2017 Tex. App. LEXIS 10393, at *9–10, 2017 WL 5166998 (Tex. App.—Dallas Nov. 7, 2017, pet. denied) (mem. op.) (concluding that the trial court did not abuse its discretion in awarding attorney's fees, pursuant to Texas Rule 215.1(d), to the prevailing party on a motion to compel); *Hood v. Edward D. Jones & Co.*, 277 S.W.3d 505, 509–10 (Tex. App.—El Paso 2009, pet. denied) (affirming award of attorney's fees to a party opposing a Texas Rule 215 motion); *Rammah v. Abdeljaber*, 235 S.W.3d 269, 274 (Tex. App.—Dallas 2007, no pet.) (same); *Blake v. Dorado*, 211 S.W.3d 429, 434 (Tex. App.—El Paso 2006, no pet.) (affirming an award of attorney's fees to a successful Texas Rule 215 movant); *In re White*, 227 S.W.3d 234, 237 (Tex. App.—San Antonio 2007, orig. proceeding) (holding that a successful movant under Texas Rule 215 was entitled to an award of attorney's fees for expenses incurred in obtaining a discovery order).

39 Tex. R. Civ. P. 215.1(d) (emphasis added); *see In re Nat'l Lloyds Ins. Co.*, 507 S.W.3d 219, 226 (Tex. 2016) (orig. proceeding) (per curiam) (emphasizing the mandatory nature of Texas Rule 215.1(d)'s first paragraph); *Clark v. Clark*, 546 S.W.3d 268, 273 (Tex. App.—El Paso 2017, no pet.) ("Under its plain terms, a trial court is required to award expenses for a necessary motion unless the court finds the opposition to the motion was 'substantially justified' or other circumstances make the award 'unjust.'" (quoting Tex. R. Civ. P. 215.1(d)); *MacDonald Devin, PC v. Rice*, No. 05-14-00938-CV, 2015 Tex. App. LEXIS 10992, at *16, 2015 WL 6468188 (Tex. App.—Dallas Oct. 27, 2015, no pet.) (mem. op.) (Texas "Rule 215.1(d) requires that in determining the amount of reasonable expenses, including attorney's fees, to be awarded in connection with a motion, the trial court shall award expenses which are reasonable in relation to the amount of work reasonably expended in obtaining an order compelling compliance."); *In re White*, 227 S.W.3d 234, 236 (Tex. App.—San Antonio 2007,

Texas Rule 215.1(d) also provides the following guidance for "determining the amount of reasonable expenses . . . to be awarded in connection with a motion[:] the trial court shall award expenses which are reasonable in relation to the amount of work reasonably expended in obtaining an order compelling compliance or in opposing a motion which is denied."[40] Thus, attorneys dealing with such a motion should keep clear records of the time spent on the motion.

As discussed in Chapter 10, section 10-8, pursuant to Texas Rule 215.4(a), "[t]he provisions of [Texas] Rule 215.1(d) apply to the award of expenses incurred in relation to [a] motion" to determine the sufficiency of an answer or objection to a request for admission under Texas Rule 198.[41] And as discussed in Chapter 10, section 10-9, a party that has requested admissions may invoke the "admit-or-pay" rule of Texas Rule 215.4(b) for a responding party's unjustified refusal to "admit the genuineness of any document or the truth of any matter as requested under [Texas] Rule 198[.]"[42] If the requirements of Texas Rule 215.4(b) are met, then the requesting party is entitled to

---

orig. proceeding) ("By its terms, [Texas] Rule 215.1 authorizes the trial court . . . to award expenses against both party and nonparty deponents."); *Blake v. Dorado*, 211 S.W.3d 429, 434 (Tex. App.—El Paso 2006, no pet.) (noting that Texas Rule 215.1(d) "functions to reimburse the movant for the expenses incurred in obtaining the order" to compel and that "[a]n award under Texas Rule 215.1(d) is not a penalty").

It is unclear whether an order issued under Texas Rule 215.1(d) is properly considered a sanctions order. *Compare In re Nat'l Lloyds Ins. Co.*, 507 S.W.3d 219, 226 (Tex. 2016) (orig. proceeding) (per curiam) (referring to an order issued under Texas Rule 215.1(d) as a "sanctions order"), *with Bowling v. Dahlheimer*, No. 05-16-01196-CV, 2017 Tex. App. LEXIS 10393, at *9 n.7, 2017 WL 5166998 (Tex. App.—Dallas Nov. 7, 2017, pet. denied) (mem. op.) ("An award of expenses including attorney's fees to obtain an order compelling discovery pursuant to [Texas R]ule 215.1(d) is not a sanction."), *and Jones v. Carlos & Parnell, M.D., P.A.*, No. 05-17-00329-CV, 2017 Tex. App. LEXIS 10216, at *10 n.5, 2017 WL 4930896 (Tex. App.—Dallas Oct. 31, 2017, pet. denied) (mem. op.) ("[W]e note an award of expenses including attorney's fees to obtain an order compelling discovery is authorized by rule of civil procedure 215.1(d) and is not a sanction."), *and Clark v. Clark*, 546 S.W.3d 268, 273 (Tex. App.—El Paso 2017, no pet.) ("[A]n award under [Texas] Rule 215.1(d) is not a penalty. Rather, the rule functions to reimburse the movant for the expenses incurred in advancing the motion.") (citations omitted), *and MacDonald Devin, PC v. Rice*, No. 05-14-00938-CV, 2015 Tex. App. LEXIS 10992, at *11–12, 2015 WL 6468188 (Tex. App.—Dallas Oct. 27, 2015, no pet.) (mem. op.) ("[W]hile appellants refer to the order as a sanction, we conclude it was an award of expenses on a motion to compel under Texas Rule of Civil Procedure 215.1(d) and not a 'traditional discovery sanction.' . . . The rule functions as a method to reimburse a party for the expenses incurred in obtaining the order on a motion to compel. As this Court has previously explained, it is not designed to be used as a 'penalty.'" (citations omitted) (quoting *Blake v. Dorado*, 211 S.W.3d 429, 434 (Tex. App.—El Paso 2006, no pet.))).

[40] Tex. R. Civ. P. 215.1(d); *see In re White*, 227 S.W.3d 234, 237 (Tex. App.—San Antonio 2007, orig. proceeding) (holding that the trial court erred in ordering a nonparty to pay court reporter's fees in connection with the continuance of the nonparty's deposition because Texas "Rule 215.1(d) cannot reasonably be construed to include the actual cost of a deposition not yet conducted").

[41] Tex. R. Civ. P. 215.4(a).

[42] Tex. R. Civ. P. 215.4(b); *see Medina v. Zuniga*, 593 S.W.3d 238, 245 (Tex. 2019) (denying a request for admission regarding the merits of a case is not sanctionable because "[t]hat is not how our system works").

"an order requiring the other party to pay him the reasonable expenses [including attorney's fees] incurred in" proving the genuineness of the document or the truth of the matter requested.[43]

Texas Rules 215.2(b)(8), 215.3, and 215.5 also allow for the imposition of discovery sanctions in the form of reasonable expenses, including attorney's fees. These types of discovery sanctions, among many others, are explained further in section 14-3 below.

14-3 Discovery Sanctions

14-3:1 General Objectives of and Limits on Discovery Sanctions

Discovery sanctions are intended to serve three legitimate purposes: "(1) secure the parties' compliance with the rules of discovery, (2) deter other litigants from violating the discovery rules, and (3) punish parties that violate the rules of discovery."[44] The Texas Supreme Court has made it clear, however, that "discovery sanctions are *primarily* intended to remedy discovery abuse and [thus] should be tailored to serve their remedial purpose."[45]

Although a trial court has broad discretion in assessing sanctions, the sanctions it imposes must further one of the purposes discovery sanctions are intended

---

[43] Tex. R. Civ. P. 215.4(b); *see Medina v. Zuniga*, 593 S.W.3d 238, 245 (Tex. 2019) (denying a request for admission regarding the merits of a case is not sanctionable because "[t]hat is not how our system works").

[44] *Bodnow Corp. v. Hondo*, 721 S.W.2d 839, 840 (Tex. 1986); *accord Horizon Health Corp. v. Acadia Healthcare Co., Inc.*, 520 S.W.3d 848, 884 (Tex. 2017); *Cire v. Cummings*, 134 S.W.3d 835, 839 (Tex. 2004); *Remington Arms Co. v. Caldwell*, 850 S.W.2d 167, 171 (Tex. 1993); *Chrysler Corp. v. Blackmon*, 841 S.W.2d 844, 849 (Tex. 1992); *Downer v. Aquamarine Operators, Inc.*, 701 S.W.2d 238, 242 (Tex. 1985); *In re Sw. Pub. Serv. Co.*, No. 13-19-00111-CV, 2020 Tex. App. LEXIS 3212, at *34, 2020 WL 1887762, (Tex. App.—Eastland Apr. 16, 2020, orig. proceeding) (mem. op.); *Span Inv. Grp. LLC v. Cameron Appraisal Dist.*, No. 13-19-00329-CV, 2020 Tex. App. LEXIS 10119, at *9, 2020 WL 7549887 (Tex. App.—Corpus Christi Dec. 22, 2020, no pet.) (mem. op.); *McAlister v. Grabs*, No. 11-17-00148-CV, 2019 Tex. App. LEXIS 2510, at *9, 2019 WL 1428623 (Tex. App.—Eastland Mar. 29, 2019, no pet.) (mem. op.); *McKeithan v. Condit*, No. 13-16-00348-CV, 2018 Tex. App. LEXIS 9707, at *4, 2018 WL 6219624 (Tex. App.—Corpus Christi Nov. 29, 2018, no. pet) (mem. op.); *In re 7677 Real St., LLC*, No. 01-16-00683-CV, 2017 Tex. App. LEXIS 9299, at *6, 2017 WL 4366033 (Tex. App.—Houston [1st Dist.] Oct. 3, 2017, orig. proceeding) (mem. op.); *Ring & Ring v. Sharpstown Mall Tex., LLC*, No. 01-16-00341-CV, 2017 Tex. App. LEXIS 6873, at *18, 2017 WL 3140121 (Tex. App.—Houston [1st Dist.] July 25, 2017, no pet.) (mem. op.); *Wilson v. Shamoun & Norman, LLP*, 523 S.W.3d 222, 231 (Tex. App.—Dallas 2017, pet. denied); *England v. Kolbe*, No. 03-15-00409-CV, 2017 Tex. App. LEXIS 2680, at *12, 2017 WL 1228884 (Tex. App.—Austin Mar. 30, 2017, no pet.) (mem. op.).

[45] *Paradigm Oil, Inc. v. Retamco Operating, Inc.*, 372 S.W.3d 177, 187 (Tex. 2012) (emphasis added), *quoted in Primo v. Rothenberg*, No. 14-13-00794-CV, 2015 Tex. App. LEXIS 6173, at *53, 2015 WL 3799763 (Tex. App.—Houston [14th Dist.] June 18, 2015, pet. struck) (mem. op.), and *Wiegand v. Sky King Found. Inc.*, No. 05-12-00020-CV, 2013 Tex. App. LEXIS 10005, at *6, 2016 WL 1238183 (Tex. App.—Dallas Aug. 9, 2013, no pet.) (mem. op.).

to further[46] and must be "just."[47] "Two factors mark the bounds of the trial court's discretion in order for sanctions to be just:"[48] (1) "a direct relationship must exist

---

[46] *E.g., Horizon Health Corp. v. Acadia Healthcare Co., Inc.*, 520 S.W.3d 848, 884 (Tex. 2017) ("[T]he broad discretion granted to trial courts to impose discovery sanctions is not unlimited; the award must further one of the recognized purposes of discovery sanctions."); *Bodnow Corp. v. City of Hondo*, 721 S.W.2d 839, 840 (Tex. 1986) ("A trial court abuses its discretion if the sanction it imposes does not further one of the purposes that discovery sanctions were intended to further."); *Caron v. Smaby*, No. 01-15-00528-CV, 2017 Tex. App. LEXIS 5244, at *35, 2017 WL 2471101 (Tex. App.—Houston [1st Dist.] June 8, 2017, no pet.) (mem. op.) ("[A] sanction imposed for discovery abuse should be no more severe than necessary to satisfy its legitimate purposes, which include securing compliance with discovery rules, deterring other litigants from similar misconduct, and punishing violators."); *Guerrero-McDonald v. Nassour*, 516 S.W.3d 198, 213 (Tex. App.—Eastland 2017, no pet.) (same); *Sheffield Dev. Co., Inc. v. Carter & Burgess, Inc.*, No. 02-11-00204-CV, 2012 Tex. App. LEXIS 10599, at *14, 2012 WL 6632500 (Tex. App.—Fort Worth Dec. 21, 2012, pet. dism'd) (mem. op.) ("Trial courts have broad discretion to impose discovery sanctions to secure compliance with discovery rules, to deter other litigants from similar misconduct, and to punish violators."); *Brushy Creek Enters., Inc. v. Heller First Capital Corp.*, 03-07-00542-CV, 2012 Tex. App. LEXIS 10599, at *14, 2010 WL 2698750 (Tex. App.—Austin July 7, 2010, no pet.) (mem. op.) (same); *Varner v. Howe*, 860 S.W.2d 458, 463 (Tex. App.—El Paso 1993, no writ) (same).

[47] Tex. R. Civ. P. 215(2)(b) (allowing trial courts to make such sanctions orders "as are just"); *see Horizon Health Corp. v. Acadia Healthcare Co., Inc.*, 520 S.W.3d 848, 884 (Tex. 2017) ("[T]he sanctions imposed must be 'just,' no more severe than required to further their legitimate purposes, and specifically related to the harm done by the condemned conduct."); *Petroleum Sols., Inc. v. Head*, 454 S.W.3d 482, 489 (Tex. 2014) ("Texas Rule of Civil Procedure 215.2 allows a trial court to impose 'just' sanctions for discovery abuse."); *Paradigm Oil, Inc. v. Retamco Operating, Inc.*, 372 S.W.3d 177, 184 (Tex. 2012) (same); *Chrysler Corp. v. Blackmon*, 841 S.W.2d 844, 849 (Tex. 1992) (same); *TransAmerican Nat. Gas Corp. v. Powell*, 811 S.W.2d 913, 917 (Tex. 1991) (same); *Centennial Psychiatric Assocs., LLC v. Cantrell*, Nos. 14-17-00391-CV, 14-17-00380-CV, 2017 Tex. App. LEXIS 11909, at *29, 2017 WL 6544283 (Tex. App.—Houston [14th Dist.] Dec. 21, 2017, no pet.) (mem. op.) (same); *In re Nueces Hosp. GP, LLC*, No. 13-17-00453-CV, 2017 Tex. App. LEXIS 10691, at *10, 2017 WL 5474514 (Tex. App.—Corpus Christi Nov. 14, 2017, orig. proceeding) (mem. op.) (same); *In re 7677 Real St., LLC*, No. 01-16-00683-CV, 2017 Tex. App. LEXIS 9299, at *6, 2017 WL 4366033 (Tex. App.—Houston [1st Dist.] Oct. 3, 2017, orig. proceeding) (mem. op.) (same).

[48] *Chrysler Corp. v. Blackmon*, 841 S.W.2d 844, 849 (Tex. 1992) (relying on *TransAmerican Nat. Gas Corp. v. Powell*, 811 S.W.2d 913, 917 (Tex. 1991)); *accord In re Nat'l Lloyds Ins. Co.*, 507 S.W.3d 219, 226 (Tex. 2016) (orig. proceeding) (per curiam); *Paradigm Oil, Inc. v. Retamco Operating, Inc.*, 372 S.W.3d 177, 184 (Tex. 2012); *In re Sw. Pub. Serv. Co.*, No. 13-19-00111-CV, 2020 Tex. App. LEXIS 3212, at *34–35, 2020 WL 1887762 (Tex. App.—Eastland Apr. 16, 2020, orig. proceeding) (mem. op.); *McAlister v. Grabs*, No. 11-17-00148-CV, 2019 Tex. App. LEXIS 2510, at *9, 2019 WL 1428623, at *4 (Tex. App.—Eastland Mar. 29, 2019, no pet.) (mem. op.); *Hernandez v. Rockwater Energy Sols., Inc.*, No. 02-17-00302-CV, 2018 Tex. App. LEXIS 7722, at *5, 2018 WL 4496149 (Tex. App.—Fort Worth Sep. 20, 2018, no pet.) (mem. op.); *McKeithan v. Condit*, No. 13-16-00348-CV, 2018 Tex. App. LEXIS 9707, at *5, 2018 WL 6219624 (Tex. App.—Corpus Christi Nov. 29, 2018, no. pet) (mem. op.); *Wilson v. Shamoun & Norman, LLP*, 523 S.W.3d 222, 229 (Tex. App.—Dallas 2017, pet. denied); *In re Nueces Hosp. GP, LLC*, No. 13-17-00453-CV, 2017 Tex. App. LEXIS 10691, at *10 (Tex. App.—Corpus Christi Nov. 14, 2017, orig. proceeding) (mem. op.); *In re 7677 Real St., LLC*, No. 01-16-00683-CV, 2017 Tex. App. LEXIS 9299, at *6 (Tex. App.—Houston [1st Dist.] Oct. 3, 2017, orig. proceeding) (mem. op.).

between the offensive conduct, the offender, and the sanction imposed[,]"[49] and (2) "the sanction imposed must not be excessive. In other words, the punishment should fit the crime."[50] To meet the first "requirement, a sanction must be directed against the wrongful conduct and toward remedying the prejudice suffered by the innocent party."[51] To meet the second requirement, the sanction "should be no more severe than necessary to satisfy its legitimate purposes."[52]

---

[49] *Petroleum Sols., Inc. v. Head*, 454 S.W.3d 482, 489 (Tex. 2014); *accord Altesse Healthcare Sols., Inc. v. Wilson*, 540 S.W.3d 570, 572 (Tex. 2018); *Nath v. Tex. Children's Hosp.*, 446 S.W.3d 355, 363 (Tex. 2014); *Cire v. Cummings*, 134 S.W.3d 835, 839 (Tex. 2004); *Chrysler Corp. v. Blackmon*, 841 S.W.2d 844, 849 (Tex. 1992); *TransAmerican Nat. Gas Corp. v. Powell*, 811 S.W.2d 913, 917 (Tex. 1991); *In re Sw. Pub. Serv. Co.*, No. 13-19-00111-CV, 2020 Tex. App. LEXIS 3212, at *34, 2020 WL 1887762, at *12 (Tex. App.—Eastland Apr. 16, 2020, orig. proceeding) (mem. op.); *Hernandez v. Rockwater Energy Sols., Inc.*, No. 02-17-00302-CV, 2018 Tex. App. LEXIS 7722, at *5, 2018 WL 4496149 (Tex. App.—Fort Worth Sep. 20, 2018, no pet.) (mem. op.); *In re Nueces Hosp. GP, LLC*, No. 13-17-00453-CV, 2017 Tex. App. LEXIS 10691, at *10 (Tex. App.—Corpus Christi Nov. 14, 2017, orig. proceeding) (mem. op.).

[50] *Chrysler Corp. v. Blackmon*, 841 S.W.2d 844, 849 (Tex. 1992); *accord Altesse Healthcare Sols., Inc. v. Wilson*, 540 S.W.3d 570, 572 (Tex. 2018); *Paradigm Oil, Inc. v. Retamco Operating, Inc.*, 372 S.W.3d 177, 187 (Tex. 2012); *Cire v. Cummings*, 134 S.W.3d 835, 839 (Tex. 2004); *TransAmerican Nat. Gas Corp. v. Powell*, 811 S.W.2d 913, 917 (Tex. 1991); *In re Sw. Pub. Serv. Co.*, No. 13-19-00111-CV, 2020 Tex. App. LEXIS 3212, at *35, 2020 WL 1887762, (Tex. App.—Eastland Apr. 16, 2020,orig. proceeding) (mem. op.); *Hernandez v. Rockwater Energy Sols., Inc.*, No. 02-17-00302-CV, 2018 Tex. App. LEXIS 7722, at *5, 2018 WL 4496149 (Tex. App.—Fort Worth Sep. 20, 2018, no pet.) (mem. op.); *In re Nueces Hosp. GP, LLC*, No. 13-17-00453-CV, 2017 Tex. App. LEXIS 10691, at *11; (Tex. App.—Corpus Christi Nov. 14, 2017, orig. proceeding) (mem. op.); *Scarbrough v. Purser*, No. 03-13-00025-CV, 2016 Tex. App. LEXIS 13863, at *59, 2016 WL 7583546 (Tex. App.—Austin Dec. 30, 2016, pet. denied) (mem. op.). *Associated Air Ctr. LP v. Tary Network Ltd.*, No. 05-13-00685-CV, 2015 Tex. App. LEXIS 2069, at *15–16, 2015 WL 970664 (Tex. App.—Dallas Mar. 4, 2015, no pet.) (mem. op.).

[51] *Petroleum Sols., Inc. v. Head*, 454 S.W.3d 482, 489 (Tex. 2014); *accord Christus Health Gulf Coast v. Carswell*, 505 S.W.3d 528, 541 (Tex. 2016);); *Spohn Hosp. v. Mayer*, 104 S.W.3d 878, 882 (Tex. 2003) (per curiam); *In re Sw. Pub. Serv. Co.*, No. 13-19-00111-CV, 2020 Tex. App. LEXIS 3212, at *34, 2020 WL 1887762 (Tex. App.—Eastland Apr. 16, 2020,orig. proceeding) (mem. op.); *Span Inv. Grp. LLC v. Cameron Appraisal* Dist., No. 13-19-00329-CV, 2020 Tex. App. LEXIS 10119, at *9, 2020 WL 7549887 (Tex. App.—Corpus Christi Dec. 22, 2020, no pet.) (mem. op.); *Centennial Psychiatric Assocs., LLC v. Cantrell*, Nos. 14-17-00391-CV, 14-17-00380-CV, 2017 Tex. App. LEXIS 11909, at *29, 2017 WL 6544283 (Tex. App.—Houston [14th Dist.] Dec. 21, 2017, no pet.) (mem. op.); *In re Nueces Hosp. GP, LLC*, No. 13-17-00453-CV, 2017 Tex. App. LEXIS 10691, at *10 (Tex. App.—Corpus Christi Nov. 14, 2017, orig. proceeding) (mem. op.) (same); *Ring & Ring v. Sharpstown Mall Tex., LLC*, No. 01-16-00341-CV, 2017 Tex. App. LEXIS 6873, at *17–18, 2017 WL 3140121 (Tex. App.—Houston [1st Dist.] July 25, 2017, no pet.) (mem. op.).

[52] *TransAmerican Nat. Gas Corp. v. Powell*, 811 S.W.2d 913, 917 (Tex. 1991); *accord Altesse Healthcare Sols., Inc. v. Wilson*, 540 S.W.3d 570, 572 (Tex. 2018); *Petroleum Sols., Inc. v. Head*, 454 S.W.3d 482, 489 (Tex. 2014); *Paradigm Oil, Inc. v. Retamco Operating, Inc.*, 372 S.W.3d 177, 187 (Tex. 2012); *PR Invs. & Specialty Retailers, Inc. v. State*, 251 S.W.3d 472, 480 (Tex. 2008); *In re Sw. Pub. Serv. Co.*, No. 13-19-00111-CV, 2020 Tex. App. LEXIS 3212, at *35, 2020 WL 1887762 (Tex. App.—Eastland Apr. 16, 2020, orig. proceeding) (mem. op.); *Centennial Psychiatric Assocs., LLC v. Cantrell*, Nos. 14-17-00391-CV, 14-17-00380-CV, 2017 Tex. App. LEXIS 11909, at *30 (Tex. App.—Houston [14th Dist.] Dec. 21, 2017, no pet.) (mem. op.); *In re Nueces Hosp. GP, LLC*, No. 13-17-00453-CV, 2017 Tex. App. LEXIS

14-3:2 Heightened Standards Applicable to Death-Penalty Sanctions

In a case in which discovery abuse has occurred, heightened standards apply, and due-process concerns are implicated, when a court imposes sanctions that preclude a presentation on the merits (i.e., "death-penalty" sanctions):[53]

10691, at *11 (Tex. App.—Corpus Christi Nov. 14, 2017, orig. proceeding) (mem. op.); *Young v. Young*, No. 03-14-00720-CV, 2016 Tex. App. LEXIS 13254, at *7, 2016 WL 7339117 (Tex. App.—Austin Dec. 15, 2016, no pet.) (mem. op.); *see Spohn Hosp. v. Mayer*, 104 S.W.3d 878, 882 (Tex. 2003) (per curiam) ("[J]ust sanctions must not be excessive. In other words, a sanction imposed for discovery abuse should be no more severe than necessary to satisfy its legitimate purposes, which include securing compliance with discovery rules, deterring other litigants from similar misconduct, and punishing violators.") (citation omitted).

[53] *E.g., GTE Commc'ns Sys. Corp. v. Tanner*, 856 S.W.2d 725, 732 (Tex. 1993) (describing case-determinative sanctions as "death-penalty" sanctions); *In re Sw. Pub. Serv. Co.*, No. 13-19-00111-CV, 2020 Tex. App. LEXIS 3212, at *36, 2020 WL 1887762 (Tex. App.—Eastland Apr. 16, 2020, orig. proceeding) (mem. op.) ("There are due process limitations on merits preclusive sanctions. In short, there are constitutional limitations upon the power of courts, even in aid of their own valid processes, to dismiss an action without affording a party the opportunity for a hearing on the merits of his cause.") (citations omitted); *In re Nueces Hosp. GP, LLC*, No. 13-17-00453-CV, 2017 Tex. App. LEXIS 10691, at *11 (Tex. App.—Corpus Christi Nov. 14, 2017, orig. proceeding) (mem. op.) ("A death penalty sanction is any sanction that adjudicates a claim or defense and precludes the presentation of the merits of a case."); *Ring & Ring v. Sharpstown Mall Tex., LLC*, No. 01-16-00341-CV, 2017 Tex. App. LEXIS 6873, at *18 (Tex. App.—Houston [1st Dist.] July 25, 2017, no pet.) (mem. op.) ("A death-penalty sanction is a severe form of sanction that prevents a party from contesting liability and allows for the determination of liability based on the party's discovery conduct rather than the dispute's merits."); *Young v. Young*, No. 03-14-00720-CV, 2016 Tex. App. LEXIS 13254, at *8 (Tex. App.—Austin Dec. 15, 2016, no pet.) (mem. op.) ("Courts have described those sanctions as 'death penalty' or 'case determinative' sanctions because they have the effect of adjudicating claims, not on their merits, but for the failure of a party or his attorney to comply with discovery requirements or court orders. Such severe sanctions may be necessary to prevent an abusive party from thwarting the administration of justice by concealing the merits of a case. But because they inhibit or terminate the presentation of the merits of a party's claim, they are further limited by constitutional due process.") (citations omitted); *Exergy Dev. Grp. of Idaho, LLC v. Higher Power Energy, LLC*, No. 14-14-00788-CV, 2016 Tex. App. LEXIS 105, at *19 (Tex. App.—Houston [14th Dist.] Jan. 7, 2016, pet. denied) (mem. op.) ("The imposition of severe sanctions is further limited by constitutional due process."); *Hoa Dao v. Md. Cas. Co.*, No. 09-13-00353-CV, 2015 Tex. App. LEXIS 4893, at *21, 2015 WL 2255263 (Tex. App.—Beaumont May 14, 2015, no pet.) (mem. op.) ("A court order striking pleadings is commonly referred to as a 'death-penalty sanction.'"); *Charles v. Crouch*, No 04-02-00372-CV, 2003 Tex. App. LEXIS 8050, at *3, 2003 WL 22134615 (Tex. App.—San Antonio Sept. 17, 2003, no pet.) (mem. op.) ("A trial court may grant 'death penalty' sanctions, or sanctions that terminate or inhibit the presentation of the merits of a party's claims, under Texas Rule of Civil Procedure 215."); *Perez v. Murff*, 972 S.W.2d 78, 81 (Tex. App.—Texarkana 1998, pet. denied) ("A death penalty sanction is any sanction that adjudicates a claim and precludes the presentation of the merits of the case."). Whether the exclusion of evidence constitutes a death-penalty sanction is determined on a case-by-case basis. *E.g., Centennial Psychiatric Assocs., LLC v. Cantrell*, Nos. 14-17-00391-CV, 14-17-00380-CV, 2017 Tex. App. LEXIS 11909, at *31, 2017 WL 6544283 (Tex. App.—Houston [14th Dist.] Dec. 21, 2017, no pet.) (mem. op.) ("'Although death-penalty sanctions most often are thought of in

Discovery sanctions cannot be used to adjudicate the merits of a party's claims or defenses unless a party's hindrance of the discovery process justifies a *presumption that its claims or defenses lack merit*. . . . Although punishment and deterrence are legitimate purposes for sanctions, they do not justify a trial by sanctions. Sanctions which are so severe as to preclude presentation of the merits of the case should not be assessed absent a *party's flagrant bad faith or counsel's callous disregard for the responsibilities of discovery* under the rules.[54]

---

the context of striking pleadings or rendering a default judgment, any sanctions that are case determinative may constitute death-penalty sanctions, including those that exclude essential evidence.'" (quoting *In re First Transit Inc.*, 499 S.W.3d 584, 592 (Tex. App.—Houston [14th Dist.] 2016, orig. proceeding))); *In re First Transit Inc.*, 499 S.W.3d 584, 593 (Tex. App.—Houston [14th Dist.] 2016, orig. proceeding) ("Dr. James is Defendants' only retained expert on negligence and causation and the exclusion of all of his testimony will effectively preclude the presentation of Defendants' defense. Thus, we conclude that the trial court's exclusion of all of Dr. James's testimony equates to a death-penalty sanction to which the above-discussed requirements for a death-penalty sanction apply."); *In re Namdarkhan*, No. 05-16-01410-CV, 2017 Tex. App. LEXIS 2386, at *6, 2017 WL 1075640 (Tex. App.—Dallas Mar. 21, 2017, orig. proceeding) (mem. op.) ("Where the exclusion of testimony is only an inconvenience that impairs the presentation of a party's case but does not preclude a trial on the merits, the exclusion of evidence is not a death penalty sanction. A death penalty sanction is any sanction that adjudicates a claim and precludes the presentation of the merits of a case.") (citation omitted); *In re Ramsey*, No. 10-16-00003-CV, 2016 Tex. App. LEXIS 6857, at *5, 2016 WL 3564407 (Tex. App.—Waco June 29, 2016, orig. proceeding) (mem. op.) ("The trial court's sanction is a de facto adjudication of Ramsay's claims in his counterpetition—it prohibits him from supporting his claims, and it prohibits him from introducing any evidence in support of those claims.").

54 *TransAmerican Natural Gas Corp. v. Powell*, 811 S.W.2d 913, 918 (Tex. 1991) (emphasis added) (citations omitted); *accord Cire v. Cummings*, 134 S.W.3d 835, 839 (Tex. 2004); *see also Paradigm Oil, Inc. v. Retamco Operating, Inc.*, 372 S.W.3d 177, 187 (Tex. 2012) ("[S]anctions that adjudicate the merits of a party's claim or defense cannot be imposed as mere punishment but rather are appropriate only when the sanctioned party's conduct justifies a presumption that an asserted claim or defense lacks merit."); *Chrysler Corp. v. Blackmon*, 841 S.W.2d 844, 849 (Tex. 1992) ("Sanctions that by their severity, prevent a decision on the merits of a case cannot be justified absent a party's flagrant bad faith or counsel's callous disregard for the responsibilities of discovery under the rules.") (citations omitted); *In re Sw. Pub. Serv. Co.*, No. 13-19-00111-CV, 2020 Tex. App. LEXIS 3212, at *36–37, 2020 WL 1887762 (Tex. App.—Eastland Apr. 16, 2020, orig. proceeding) (mem. op.) ("In rare cases, extreme bad faith alone might justify extreme sanctions." (citing *Altesse Healthcare Sols., Inc. v. Wilson, 540 S.W.3d 570, 576 (Tex. 2018))); Duncan v. Park Place Motorcars, Ltd.*, 605 S.W.3d 479, 490 (Tex. App.—Dallas 2020, pet. withdrawn) (stating that the defendant engaged in various forms of discovery abuse that "took the trial court and [plaintiffs] down an ugly and protracted road" and concluding: "[T]he imposition of death penalty sanctions was just because it related directly to the conduct at issue in the case—specifically, Duncan's failure to appear for the completion of his deposition, and generally, Duncan's continuing violation of the trial court's orders and hindrance of the discovery process for appellees; the trial court imposed lesser sanctions to no avail; and Duncan's conduct throughout the long history of the case reasonably justified a presumption his affirmative claims lacked merit."); *Hernandez v. Rockwater Energy Sols., Inc.*, No. 02-17-00302-CV, 2018 Tex. App. LEXIS 7722, at *5, 2018 WL 4496149 (Tex. App.—Fort Worth Sep. 20, 2018, no pet.) (mem. op.) ("A trial court may dismiss a plaintiff's claims as a discovery sanction—sometimes referred to as a death-penalty sanction—if the plaintiff abuses the discovery process."); *McKeithan v. Condit*, No. 13-16-00348-CV, 2018 Tex. App. LEXIS 9707, at *4, 2018 WL 6219624 (Tex.

The Texas Supreme Court has recognized, for example, that "[m]ultiple violations of the discovery rules and court orders relating to discovery may be a factor authorizing imposition of [a death-penalty] sanction, even when the offending party offers justifications and excuses."[55]

App.—Corpus Christi Nov. 29, 2018, no. pet) (mem. op.) ("Although punishment, deterrence, and securing compliance continue to be valid reasons for imposing sanctions, these considerations alone will not justify 'trial by sanctions.'"); *In re Nueces Hosp. GP, LLC*, No. 13-17-00453-CV, 2017 Tex. App. LEXIS 10691, at *11 (Tex. App.—Corpus Christi Nov. 14, 2017, orig. proceeding) (mem. op.) ("Discovery sanctions that are so severe as to inhibit presentation of the merits of a case should be reserved to address a party's flagrant bad faith or counsel's callous disregard for the responsibilities of discovery under the rules.") (citations omitted); *Caron v. Smaby*, No. 01-15-00528-CV, 2017 Tex. App. LEXIS 5244, at *35, 2017 WL 2471101 (Tex. App.—Houston [1st Dist.] June 8, 2017, no pet.) (mem. op.) ("[S]anctions that by their severity, prevent a decision on the merits of a case cannot be justified absent a party's flagrant bad faith or counsel's callous disregard for the responsibilities of discovery under the rules.") (citations omitted); *England v. Kolbe*, No. 03-15-00409-CV, 2017 Tex. App. LEXIS 2680, at *13, 2017 WL 1228884 (Tex. App.—Austin Mar. 30, 2017, no pet.) (mem. op.) ("[T]he severe sanctions imposed here are not appropriate unless the offensive conduct justifies a presumption that the party's claims or defenses lack merit."); *Scarbrough v. Purser*, No. 03-13-00025-CV, 2016 Tex. App. LEXIS 13863, at *60, 2016 WL 7583546 (Tex. App.—Austin Dec. 30, 2016, pet. denied) (mem. op.) ("Actions that callously disregard the rules of discovery warrant a presumption that the actor's claims are meritless because the very purpose of discovery is to seek the truth, so that disputes may be decided by what the facts reveal, not by what facts are concealed.") (citations omitted); *Imagine Auto. Grp. v. Boardwalk Motor Cars, Ltd.*, 430 S.W.3d 620, 633 (Tex. App.—Dallas 2014, pet. denied) ("The offensive conduct must justify a presumption that the offending party's claims or defenses lack merit before the trial court may impose 'death penalty' sanctions.").

[55] *Koslow's v. Mackie*, 796 S.W.2d 700, 704 (Tex. 1990) (citing *Med. Protective Co. v. Glanz*, 721 S.W.2d 382, 388 (Tex. App.—Corpus Christi 1986, writ ref'd)); *accord Duncan v. Park Place Motorcars, Ltd.*, 605 S.W.3d 479, 490 (Tex. App.—Dallas 2020, pet. withdrawn) (affirming a death-penalty sanction where the defendant failed to produce court-ordered documents, preserve ESI, and appear at a court-ordered deposition and produced a computer without its hard drive); *see Downer v. Aquamarine Operators, Inc.*, 701 S.W.2d 238, 241–43 (Tex. 1985) (holding that the trial court did not abuse its discretion by imposing the ultimate (i.e., death-penalty) sanction of striking the answer of a party that had engaged in a pattern of discovery abuse); *Hoa Dao v. Md. Cas. Co.*, No. 09-13-00353-CV, 2015 Tex. App. LEXIS 4893, at *25, 2015 WL 2255263 (Tex. App.—Beaumont May 14, 2015, no pet.) (mem. op.) ("If, after the imposition of lesser sanctions, a party continues to refuse to produce material evidence, the court may presume that an asserted claim or defense lacks merit and take action to dispose of it."); *Ricks v. Quality Carriers, Inc.*, No. 14-14-00431-CV, 2015 Tex. App. LEXIS 11773, at *6, 2015 WL 7258697 (Tex. App.—Houston [14th Dist.] Nov. 17, 2015, no pet.) (mem. op.) ("The court ordered Ricks to comply with discovery on multiple occasions and sanctioned her for refusing to do so. However, these lesser sanctions and orders did nothing to secure Ricks's compliance. Despite the court's orders, Ricks continued her noncompliance up until the time that the trial court dismissed her case—over two full years after the court's first order compelling production. This protracted refusal to produce evidence was enough to support the trial court's presumption that Ricks's claims lacked merit. The death penalty sanction in this case, although severe, is not excessive under *TransAmerican [Nat. Gas Corp. v. Powell*, 811 S.W.2d 913 (Tex. 1991)]. The trial court did not abuse its discretion when it dismissed Ricks's case with prejudice.") (citations omitted); *In re Malone*, 336 S.W.3d 860, 864–65 (Tex. App.—Beaumont 2011, pet. denied) (affirming a trial court's imposition of death-penalty sanctions against a litigant who continuously refused to answer questions at

"Case determinative sanctions may be imposed in the first instance only in exceptional cases when they are clearly justified and it is fully apparent that no lesser sanctions would promote compliance with the rules."[56] Thus, before imposing a death-penalty sanction, a trial court "must consider the availability of less stringent sanctions and whether such lesser sanctions would fully promote compliance."[57] The "record

---

depositions despite the trial court's multiple orders and warnings that the litigant's pleadings would be struck); *Valdez v. Progressive Cty. Mut. Ins. Co.*, No. 04-11-00254-CV, 2011 Tex. App. LEXIS 9773, at *14, 2011 WL 6208702 (Tex. App.—San Antonio Dec. 14, 2011, no pet.) (mem. op.) ("Valdez was . . . obligated to comply with the trial court's orders compelling production of the returns. His subsequent disobedience of numerous court orders constituted blatant disrespect for the trial court and the rules of discovery. Valdez's continued obstruction led the trial court to dismiss his lawsuit with prejudice. Accordingly, we hold the trial court's imposition of a death penalty sanction was not abuse of discretion.").

[56] *GTE Commc'ns Sys. Corp. v. Tanner*, 856 S.W.2d 725, 729 (Tex. 1993); *accord Nath v. Tex. Children's Hosp.*, 446 S.W.3d 355, 363 (Tex. 2014); *Spohn Hosp. v. Mayer*, 104 S.W.3d 878, 882 (Tex. 2003) (per curiam); *Centennial Psychiatric Assocs., LLC v. Cantrell*, Nos. 14-17-00391-CV, 14-17-00380-CV, 2017 Tex. App. LEXIS 11909, at *30, 2017 WL 6544283 (Tex. App.—Houston [14th Dist.] Dec. 21, 2017, no pet.) (mem. op.); *In re K.R.*, No. 02-14-00275-CV, 2016 Tex. App. LEXIS 3631, at *8–9 (Tex. App.—Fort Worth Apr. 7, 2016, no pet.) (mem. op.); *Hoa Dao v. Md. Cas. Co.*, No. 09-13-00353-CV, 2015 Tex. App. LEXIS 4893, at *24, 2015 WL 2255263 (Tex. App.—Beaumont May 14, 2015, no pet.) (mem. op.); *Shops at Legacy (Inland) Ltd. P'ship v. Fine Autographs & Memorabilia Retails Stores, Inc.*, 418 S.W.3d 229, 233 (Tex. App.—Dallas 2013, no pet.); *Dibco Underground, Inc. v. JCF Bridge & Concrete, Inc.*, No. 03-09-00255-CV, 2010 Tex. App. LEXIS 2531, at *8, 2010 WL 1413071 (Tex. App.—Austin Apr. 8, 2010, no pet.) (mem. op.).

[57] *TransAmerican Nat. Gas Corp. v. Powell*, 811 S.W.2d 913, 917 (Tex. 1991); *accord PR Invs. & Specialty Retailers, Inc. v. Tex.*, 251 S.W.3d 472, 480 (Tex. 2008); *Cire v. Cummings*, 134 S.W.3d 835, 839 (Tex. 2004); *Spohn Hosp. v. Mayer*, 104 S.W.3d 878, 882 (Tex. 2003); *see Chrysler Corp. v. Blackmon*, 841 S.W.2d 844, 849 (Tex. 1992) ("A permissible sanction should, therefore, be no more severe than required to satisfy legitimate purposes. This means that a court must consider relatively less stringent sanctions first to determine whether lesser sanctions will fully promote compliance, deterrence, and discourage further abuse."); *McKeithan v. Condit*, No. 13-16-00348-CV, 2018 Tex. App. LEXIS 9707, at *5, 2018 WL 6219624 (Tex. App.—Corpus Christi Nov. 29, 2018, no. pet) (mem. op.) ("[E]ven in those cases where death penalty sanctions can be justified, a trial court must first consider less stringent sanctions and if those lesser sanctions would adequately promote compliance, deterrence, and punishment."); *Centennial Psychiatric Assocs., LLC v. Cantrell*, Nos. 14-17-00391-CV, 14-17-00380-CV, 2017 Tex. App. LEXIS 11909, at *30 (Tex. App.—Houston [14th Dist.] Dec. 21, 2017, no pet.) (mem. op.) ("Before issuing death-penalty sanctions, a trial court must consider lesser sanctions."); *Mullins v. Mullins*, No. 02-16-00449-CV, 2017 Tex. App. LEXIS 7035, at *10, 2017 WL 3184676 (Tex. App.—Fort Worth July 27, 2017, no pet.) (mem. op.) ("[B]efore a trial court may order death-penalty sanctions, the court must both consider lesser sanctions and provide a reasoned explanation concerning the appropriateness of the greater sanction imposed."); *Ring & Ring v. Sharpstown Mall Tex., LLC*, No. 01-16-00341-CV, 2017 Tex. App. LEXIS 6873, at *18–19, 2017 WL 3140121 (Tex. App.—Houston [1st Dist.] July 25, 2017, no pet.) (mem. op.) ("Before imposing death-penalty sanctions, 'courts must consider the availability of less stringent sanctions and whether such lesser sanction would fully promote compliance.'" (quoting *TransAmerican Nat. Gas Corp. v. Powell*, 811 S.W.2d 913, 917 (Tex. 1991))); *In re First Transit Inc.*, 499 S.W.3d 584, 591 (Tex. App.—Houston [14th Dist.] 2016, orig. proceeding) (same); *Hoa Dao v. Md. Cas. Co.*, No. 09-13-00353-CV, 2015 Tex. App. LEXIS 4893, at *24, 2015 WL 2255263 (Tex. App.—Beaumont May 14, 2015, no pet.) (mem. op.) (same).

must reflect that the court considered the availability of lesser sanctions."[58] This requirement can be met, for example, with a sanctions order containing "an extensive, reasoned explanation of the appropriateness of the sanction imposed, demonstrating that the trial court considered the availability of less stringent sanctions."[59] But the trial court is not required "to list each possible lesser sanction in its order and then explain why each would be ineffective."[60] Instead, the trial court is simply required to "analyze the available sanctions and offer a reasoned explanation as to the appropriateness of the sanction imposed."[61] This analysis may be done on the record at the sanctions hearing or in the written sanctions order.[62]

In addition to considering lesser sanctions, "in all but the most exceptional cases, [the trial court must] actually test the lesser sanctions" before determining they are insufficient to promote compliance.[63] Exceptional cases include, for example, a party

---

[58] *GTE Commc'ns Sys. Corp. v. Tanner*, 856 S.W.2d 725, 729 (Tex. 1993); *accord Spohn Hosp. v. Mayer*, 104 S.W.3d 878, 883 (Tex. 2003); *Otis Elevator Co. v. Parmelee*, 850 S.W.2d 179, 181 (Tex. 1993); *TransAmerican Nat. Gas Corp. v. Powell*, 811 S.W.2d 913, 918 (Tex. 1991); *McKeithan v. Condit*, No. 13-16-00348-CV, 2018 Tex. App. LEXIS 9707, at *5, 2018 WL 6219624 (Tex. App.—Corpus Christi Nov. 29, 2018, no. pet) (mem. op.); *Centennial Psychiatric Assocs., LLC v. Cantrell*, Nos. 14-17-00391-CV, 14-17-00380-CV, 2017 Tex. App. LEXIS 11909, at *30, 2017 WL 6544283 (Tex. App.—Houston [14th Dist.] Dec. 21, 2017, no pet.) (mem. op.); *In re Ramsey*, No. 10-16-00003-CV, 2016 Tex. App. LEXIS 6857, at *7, 2016 WL 3564407 (Tex. App.—Waco June 29, 2016, orig. proceeding) (mem. op.); *Mullins v. Mullins*, No. 02-16-00449-CV, 2017 Tex. App. LEXIS 7035, at *7–8, 2017 WL 3184676 (Tex. App.—Fort Worth July 27, 2017, no pet.) (mem. op.); *Hoa Dao v. Md. Cas. Co.*, No. 09-13-00353-CV, 2015 Tex. App. LEXIS 4893, at *24, 2015 WL 2255263 (Tex. App.—Beaumont May 14, 2015, no pet.) (mem. op.).

[59] *Cire v. Cummings*, 134 S.W.3d 835, 842 (Tex. 2004) ("The discussion in the trial court's order goes beyond simply stating that lesser sanctions would not be effective; the order contains an extensive, reasoned explanation of the appropriateness of the sanction imposed, demonstrating that the trial court considered the availability of less stringent sanctions as we have required."); *accord GTE Commc'ns Sys. Corp. v. Tanner*, 856 S.W.2d 725, 730 (Tex. 1993) (orig. proceeding); *Trishe Res., Inc. v. Hilliard Energy, Ltd.*, No. 11-18-00086-CV, 2019 WL 4232226, at *5 (Tex. App.—Eastland Sept. 6, 2019, pet. denied) (mem. op.) (affirming the trial court's death-penalty sanctions after it had imposed lesser sanctions to no avail and the withheld evidence was material to the amount of plaintiff's damages).

[60] *Cire v. Cummings*, 134 S.W.3d 835, 842 (Tex. 2004).

[61] *Cire v. Cummings*, 134 S.W.3d 835, 842 (Tex. 2004); *see Spohn Hosp. v. Mayer*, 104 S.W.3d 878, 883 (Tex. 2003) ("This Court has noted that the record should contain some explanation of the appropriateness of the sanctions imposed.") (citing *GTE Commc'ns Sys. Corp. v. Tanner*, 856 S.W.2d 725, 729 (Tex. 1993), *Otis Elevator Co. v. Parmelee*, 850 S.W.2d 179, 181 (Tex. 1993), and *Chrysler Corp. v. Blackmon*, 841 S.W.2d 844, 852–53 (Tex. 1992))); *Imagine Auto. Grp. v. Boardwalk Motor Cars, Ltd.*, 430 S.W.3d 620, 634 (Tex. App.—Dallas 2014, pet. denied) (providing that "the trial court 'must analyze the available sanctions and offer a reasoned explanation as to the appropriateness of the sanction imposed'" (quoting *Shops at Legacy (Inland) Ltd. Pp. v. Fine Autographs & Memorabilia Retails Stores, Inc.*, 418 S.W.3d 229, 233 (Tex. App.—Dallas 2013, no pet.))).

[62] *See Cire v. Cummings*, 134 S.W.3d 835, 843 (Tex. 2004) (concluding that the trial court considered using a lesser sanction before striking the plaintiff's pleadings because the "sanctions hearing record reflects that the trial court considered using a spoliation instruction as a sanction even though it ultimately chose not to do so").

[63] *Cire v. Cummings*, 134 S.W.3d 835, 841 (Tex. 2004); *accord Chrysler Corp. v. Blackmon*, 841 S.W.2d 844, 849 (Tex. 1992);); *In re Sw. Pub. Serv. Co.*, No. 13-19-00111-CV, 2020 Tex. App. LEXIS 3212, at *35, 2020 WL 1887762 (Tex. App.—Eastland Apr. 16, 2020, orig. proceeding)

deliberately destroying dispositive evidence after being asked and ordered repeatedly to produce it,[64] a party fabricating critical evidence and then lying about it during a deposition,[65] and a party leaving the country with no intent to appear in the action again.[66]

(mem. op.); *McKeithan v. Condit*, No. 13-16-00348-CV, 2018 Tex. App. LEXIS 9707, at *5, 2018 WL 6219624 (Tex. App.—Corpus Christi Nov. 29, 2018, no. pet) (mem. op.) ("In all but the most exceptional cases, before the trial court may strike a party's pleadings, the record must show that the trial court considered and tested less stringent sanctions."); *Ring & Ring v. Sharpstown Mall Tex., LLC*, No. 01-16-00341-CV, 2017 Tex. App. LEXIS 6873, at *19, 2017 WL 3140121 (Tex. App.—Houston [1st Dist.] July 25, 2017, no pet.) (mem. op.) (same); *Exergy Dev. Grp. of Idaho, LLC v. Higher Power Energy, LLC*, No. 14-14-00788-CV, 2016 Tex. App. LEXIS 105, at *20, 2016 WL 109859 (Tex. App.—Houston [14th Dist.] Jan. 7, 2016, pet. denied) (mem. op.) (same); *see Hernandez v. Polley*, No. 03-15-00384-CV, 2016 Tex. App. LEXIS 11116, at *11, 2016 WL 6068259 (Tex. App.—Austin Oct. 13, 2016, no pet.) (mem. op.) ("The trial court does not need to test the effectiveness of all available lesser sanctions by actually imposing them before issuing the death penalty but must 'analyze the available sanctions and offer a reasoned explanation as to the appropriateness of the sanction imposed.'" (quoting *Cire v. Cummings*, 134 S.W.3d 835, 841 (Tex. 2004))); *In re First Transit Inc.*, 499 S.W.3d 584, 595 (Tex. App.—Houston [14th Dist.] 2016, orig. proceeding) ("In the November 2 Order, the trial court warned that Defendants' failure to comply would result in the exclusion all of Dr. James's testimony. That warning, however, does not justify the imposition of a death-penalty sanction. Regardless of the warning, the trial court still had a duty to impose a punishment that fit the transgression and to consider lesser sanctions."); *Hoa Dao v. Md. Cas. Co.*, No. 09-13-00353-CV, 2015 Tex. App. LEXIS 4893, at *30–31, 2015 WL 2255263 (Tex. App.—Beaumont May 14, 2015, no pet.) (mem. op.) ("No threat of sanctions, much less death-penalty sanctions, for noncompliance with the court's orders was made prior to the entry of those sanctions here. Thus, we conclude the trial court abused its discretion in entering death-penalty sanctions against appellants and that 'lesser sanctions must first be tested to determine whether they are adequate to secure compliance, deterrence, and punishment of the offender.'" (quoting *Chrysler Corp. v. Blackmon*, 841 S.W.2d 844, 849 (Tex. 1992))).

64 *See Cire v. Cummings*, 134 S.W.3d 835, 841 (Tex. 2004) (upholding death penalty sanctions imposed against a legal-malpractice plaintiff that deliberately destroyed audiotapes of conversations with lawyers at defendant law firm after being requested to produce them and "being thrice ordered to produce them"); *Duncan v. Park Place Motorcars, Ltd.*, 605 S.W.3d 479, 490 (Tex. App.—Dallas 2020, pet. withdrawn) (affirming a death-penalty sanction where the defendant failed to produce court-ordered documents, preserve ESI, and appear at a court-ordered deposition and produced a computer without its hard drive).

65 *See JNS Enter., Inc. v. Dixie Demolition, LLC*, 430 S.W.3d 444, 456 (Tex. App.—Austin 2013, no pet.) ("[A]lthough the district court properly explained in its order that it had considered lesser sanctions against JNS and Leesboro, it was not necessary under the circumstances here for the district court to first employ lesser sanctions against JNS and Leesboro. JNS and Leesboro fabricated the contracts and performance guarantee that formed the basis of their claims. This was certainly an egregious act and an exceptional case.") (citation omitted); *JNS Enter., Inc. v. Dixie Demolition, LLC*, 430 S.W.3d 444, 453 (Tex. App.—Austin 2013, no pet.) ("While it may be true that death-penalty sanctions cases in Texas usually involve discovery orders under [Texas R]ule 215, the absence of such orders does not necessarily preclude the imposition of death-penalty sanctions where, as here, the objectionable discovery conduct is fabricating evidence and lying about that evidence in deposition.").

66 *See Sharpe v. Kilcoyne*, 962 S.W.2d 697, 702 (Tex. App.—Fort Worth 1998, no pet.) ("Kilcoyne moved for sanctions after Sharpe missed the first deposition and his motion was denied. Kilcoyne's second motion came after Sharpe missed another deposition and, through the evidence presented at the hearing, it became evident that Sharpe had left the country and was not going to appear for any case related proceedings. Thus, in this limited

In cases involving parental-rights determinations, "the trial court must also consider the child's best interest when ruling on death-penalty sanctions."[67] This additional requirement reflects the legislative mandate to make the best interest of the child the court's primary consideration in such cases.[68]

14-3:3 Persons Who May Be Sanctioned—Parties, Attorneys, and Nonparties

A discovery "sanction should be visited upon the offender[,]"[69] which may be a party, its attorney, or both a party and its attorney.[70] The Texas Supreme Court has

---

factual situation, we find that imposition of lesser sanctions would have been futile. Lesser sanctions would merely have postponed the inevitable as evidenced by Sharpe's complete failure to appear for any subsequent proceedings.").

67 *Young v. Young*, No. 03-14-00720-CV, 2016 Tex. App. LEXIS 13254, at *9, 2016 WL 7339117 (Tex. App.—Austin Dec. 15, 2016, no pet.) (mem. op.).

68 *Young v. Young*, No. 03-14-00720-CV, 2016 Tex. App. LEXIS 13254, at *9–10, 2016 WL 7339117 (Tex. App.—Austin Dec. 15, 2016, no pet.) (mem. op.) ("[C]ourts have observed that discovery sanctions in cases involving determination of parental rights may be 'difficult to reconcile with the legislative mandate that 'the best interest of the child shall always be the primary consideration of the court in determining the issues of conservatorship and possession of and access to the child.' . . . This Court has similarly recognized that, with regard to the best interest of the child, '[i]t is in the court's primary interest to have as much evidence before it as possible.'" (quoting *Taylor v. Taylor*, 254 S.W.3d 527, 534–35 (Tex. App.—Houston [1st Dist.] 2008, no pet.), Tex. Fam. Code § 153.002, and *Spurck v. Tex. Dep't of Family & Protective Servs.*, 396 S.W.3d 205, 215 (Tex. App.—Austin 2013, no pet.))).

69 *Spohn Hosp. v. Mayer*, 104, S.W.3d 878, 882 (Tex. 2003); *accord Nath v. Tex. Children's Hosp.*, 446 S.W.3d 355, 363 (Tex. 2014); *TransAmerican Nat. Gas Corp. v. Powell*, 811 S.W.2d 913, 917 (Tex. 1991); *see In re 7677 Real St., LLC*, No. 01-16-00683-CV, 2017 Tex. App. LEXIS 9299, at *16–17, 2017 WL 4366033 (Tex. App.—Houston [1st Dist.] Oct. 3, 2017, orig. proceeding) (mem. op.) ("Absent evidence of piercing the corporate veil or some other legal doctrine or reason that the parties should be treated as one for discovery purposes, a trial court must consider discovery sanctions against each party separately when the basis for the sanction is separate misconduct by each of the parties. It does not further the purposes of discovery sanctions to impose sanctions against a party due to a co-party's misconduct.") (citation omitted); *Hernandez v. Polley*, No. 03-15-00384-CV, 2016 Tex. App. LEXIS 11116, at *12, 2016 WL 6068259 (Tex. App.—Austin Oct. 13, 2016, no pet.) (mem. op.) ("Here, there is nothing in the record to show that the trial court adhered to the first prong of the *TransAmerican* test, which requires a direct relationship among the conduct, the offender, and the sanction imposed. There is nothing in the record to indicate, and the trial court did not inquire, whether Hernandez or her attorney was responsible for the incomplete discovery responses, and there is therefore no evidence that the sanctions were visited on the actual offender. Rather, the trial court here appeared only to assume that Hernandez and not her attorney was the problem, as indicated by its reference to 'herding' clients. While 'a lawyer cannot shield his client from sanctions, . . . a party should not be punished for counsel's conduct in which it is not implicated apart from having entrusted counsel its legal representation.'" (citations omitted) (quoting *TransAmerican Nat. Gas Corp. v. Powell*, 811 S.W.2d 913, 917 (Tex. 1991))).

70 *E.g.*, *Am. Flood Research, Inc. v. Jones*, 192 S.W.3d 581, 584 (Tex. 2006) (per curiam) (Texas "Rule 215.2 provides that the trial court may impose sanctions against the party or the attorney advising the party when the party fails to comply with an order to permit discovery."); *TransAmerican Nat. Gas Corp. v. Powell*, 811 S.W.2d 913, 918 (Tex. 1991) ("In the present case, it is not clear whether TransAmerican or its counsel or both should be faulted for [TransAmerican's president's] failure to attend his deposition."); *Flores v. Garcia*, No.

recognized that "apportioning blame between an attorney and a represented party 'will not be an easy matter in many instances.'"[71] Nonetheless, a trial court is required to "attempt to determine whether the offensive conduct is attributable to counsel only, to the party only, or to both."[72]

A party cannot hide behind its attorney to avoid sanctions if the party engaged in, or was complicit in allowing, the discovery abuse. For example, a party may be sanctioned if it has been personally involved in the discovery abuse,[73] if it has destroyed evidence,[74] if it has refused to produce evidence,[75] or if it was or should have been aware of its attorney's discovery abuses.[76] Further, "a lawyer cannot shield his client from sanctions; a party must bear some responsibility for its counsel's discovery abuses when it is or should be aware of counsel's conduct and the violation of discovery rules."[77] A party should not be sanctioned, however, where there is evidence that it was *not* personally involved with, or aware of, the discovery abuse.[78]

13-15-00047-CV, 2015 Tex. App. LEXIS 10383, at *16, 2015 WL 5895087 (Tex. App.—Corpus Christi Oct. 8, 2015, no. pet.) (mem. op.) ("A just sanction 'should be visited upon the offender. The trial court must attempt to determine whether the offensive conduct is attributable to counsel only, to the party only, or to both.'") (quoting *Spohn Hosp. v. Mayer*, 104, S.W.3d 878, 883 (Tex. 2003))); *Galindo v. Prosperity Partners, Inc.*, 429 S.W.3d 690, 698 (Tex. App.—Eastland 2014, pet. denied) (same); *Katy Intern., Inc. v. Jinchun Jiang*, 451 S.W.3d 74, 96 (Tex. App.—Houston [14th Dist.] 2014, pet. denied) (same).

71 *Nath v. Tex. Children's Hosp.*, 446 S.W.3d 355, 363 (Tex. 2014) (quoting *TransAmerican Nat. Gas Corp. v. Powell*, 811 S.W.2d 913, 917 (Tex. 1991)); *accord Clark v. Clark, 546 S.W.3d 268, 276* (Tex. App.—El Paso 2017, no pet.).

72 *Spohn Hosp. v. Mayer*, 104, S.W.3d 878, 882 (Tex. 2003); *accord Nath v. Tex. Children's Hosp.*, 446 S.W.3d 355, 363 (Tex. 2014); *TransAmerican Nat. Gas Corp. v. Powell*, 811 S.W.2d 913, 917 (Tex. 1991); *Clark v. Clark*, 546 S.W.3d 268, 276 (Tex. App.—El Paso 2017, no pet.); *Caron v. Smaby*, No. 01-15-00528-CV, 2017 Tex. App. LEXIS 5244, at *33–35, 2017 WL 2471101 (Tex. App.—Houston [1st Dist.] June 8, 2017, no pet.) (mem. op.); *Imagine Auto. Grp. v. Boardwalk Motor Cars, Ltd.*, 430 S.W.3d 620, 633 (Tex. App.—Dallas 2014, pet. denied).

73 *E.g.*, *Nath v. Tex. Children's Hosp.*, 446 S.W.3d 355, 366–69 (Tex. 2014) (holding that the trial court did not abuse its discretion in striking the party's pleading because there was some evidence of the party's involvement with sanctionable conduct).

74 *E.g.*, *In re Dynamic Health, Inc.*, 32 S.W.3d 876, 885–86 (Tex. App.—Texarkana 2000, orig. proceeding) (affirming a sanctions order because the sanctioned party was found to have "flagrantly disregard[ed]" the Texas discovery rules).

75 *See TransAmerican Nat. Gas Corp. v. Powell*, 811 S.W.2d 913, 918 (Tex. 1991) ("[I]f a party refuses to produce material evidence, despite the imposition of lesser sanctions, the court may presume that an asserted claim or defense lacks merit and dispose of it.").

76 *See Nat'l Land Records, LLC v. Peirson Patterson, LLP*, No. 12-16-00205-CV, 2017 Tex. App. LEXIS 6033, at *15, 2017 WL 2829331 (Tex. App.—Tyler June 30, 2017, no pet.) (mem. op.) ("A trial court may impose sanctions on a party when the party 'is or should be aware of counsel's conduct[.'] There is sufficient indication in the record that NLR should have been aware of its attorney's derelict performance. Accordingly, the trial court's imposition of sanctions equally between NLR and its former attorneys was just under the circumstances." (citation omitted) (quoting *TransAmerican Nat. Gas Corp. v. Powell*, 811 S.W.2d 913, 917 (Tex. 1991))).

77 *TransAmerican Nat. Gas Corp. v. Powell*, 811 S.W.2d 913, 917 (Tex. 1991); *accord Elec. Data Sys. Corp. v. Tyson*, 862 S.W.2d 728, 737–78 (Tex. App.—Dallas 1993, orig. proceeding).

78 *E.g.*, *TransAmerican Nat. Gas Corp. v. Powell*, 811 S.W.2d 913, 917 (Tex. 1991) ("[A] party should not be punished for counsel's conduct in which it is not implicated apart from having entrusted to counsel its legal representation."); *In re Garza*, 544 S.W.3d 836, 842–43 (Tex.

"Sanctions may be visited exclusively on the attorney if the evidence demonstrates that the offensive conduct is attributable to counsel alone."[79] Moreover, "a party should not be punished for counsel's conduct in which it is not implicated apart from having entrusted to counsel its legal representation."[80] Where an attorney alone is sanctioned, the trial court must consider the effect of the sanction on the party when fashioning a sanction.[81] Multiple attorneys who engage in discovery abuse may be sanctioned jointly and severally.[82]

2018) (orig. proceeding) (holding that the trial court abused its descretion in imposing discovery sanctions on party for a nonparty's failure to produce documents in response to a subpoena absent evidence that the party was involved in the failure); *Lott v. McCain*, No. 12-15-00244-CV, 2016 Tex. App. LEXIS 3796, at *5, 2016 WL 1446069 (Tex. App.—Tyler Apr. 13, 2016, no pet.) (mem. op.) ("Because the trial court did not determine whether Lott or his counsel is responsible for the offending conduct, we cannot conclude on this record that Lott's failure to comply with the discovery order justifies the presumption that his claim lacks merit. Thus, the record does not show a direct relationship between Lott's conduct and the sanction imposed by the trial court. Therefore, the sanction was not just, and the trial court abused its discretion by imposing it.") (citations omitted); *Galindo v. Prosperity Partners, Inc.*, 429 S.W.3d 690, 698 (Tex. App.—Eastland 2014, pet. denied) (same); *Gunn v. Fuqua*, 397 S.W.3d 358, 374–75 (Tex. App.—Dallas 2013, pet. denied) (holding that sanctions were "excessive" because "[t]here is no indication in the record of this case that [the party] had any knowledge of, or role in, the failure of her counsel to timely provide a complete designation of expert witnesses and produce expert reports" and the "trial court made no finding that [the party] was personally responsible for the failure of her counsel to fully comply with discovery rules and the scheduling orders in this case"); *Prize Energy Res., L.P. v. Cliff Hoskins, Inc.*, 345 S.W.3d 537, 576 (Tex. App.—San Antonio 2011, no pet.) ("Although a party should not be punished for counsel's conduct in which the party is not implicated apart from having entrusted its legal representation to counsel, a party must bear some responsibility for its counsel's discovery abuses when it is or should be aware of counsel's conduct and the violation of the discovery rules."); *Thompson v. Woodruff*, 232 S.W.3d 316, 321–22 (Tex. App.—Beaumont 2007, no pet.) (reversing sanctions because the "record of this appeal provides no indication that the Thompsons were personally responsible for the discovery abuse or even aware that their attorney had failed to produce the expert witness for deposition").

79 *Am. Flood Research, Inc. v. Jones*, 192 S.W.3d 581, 584 (Tex. 2006) (per curiam); *accord TransAmerican Nat. Gas Corp. v. Powell*, 811 S.W.2d 913, 917 (Tex. 1991).

80 *TransAmerican Nat. Gas Corp. v. Powell*, 811 S.W.2d 913, 917 (Tex. 1991).

81 *E.g.*, *McKeithan v. Condit*, No. 13-16-00348-CV, 2018 Tex. App. LEXIS 9707, at *4, 2018 WL 6219624 (Tex. App.—Corpus Christi Nov. 29, 2018, no. pet) (mem. op.) ("Absent . . . counsel's callous disregard for the responsibilities of discovery under the rules, sanctions that prevent a decision on the merits of a case cannot be justified."); *In re Harvest Cmtys. of Houston, Inc.*, 88 S.W.3d 343, 348 (Tex. App.—San Antonio 2002, orig. proceeding) ("Except under the most extreme circumstances, a party should not be denied its Constitutional right to a trial by jury simply because its attorney misbehaved and ignored the [Texas] Rules of Civil Procedure. Lesser sanctions were possible in this case, and we appreciate the candor evidenced by the Mennellas' attorney in oral argument in agreeing that the record does not reflect that the trial court considered a lesser sanction."); *Chrysler Corp. v. Blackmon*, 841 S.W.2d 844, 849 (Tex. 1992) ("Sanctions that by their severity, prevent a decision on the merits of a case cannot be justified absent a party's flagrant bad faith or counsel's callous disregard for the responsibilities of discovery under the rules. Even then, lesser sanctions must first be tested to determine whether they are adequate to secure compliance, deterrence, and punishment of the offender.").

82 *E.g.*, *Kugle v. DaimlerChrysler Corp.*, 88 S.W.3d 355, 365 (Tex. App.—San Antonio 2002, pet. denied) ("[T]he trial court did not abuse its discretion in ordering that the sanctions be

When the party and its attorney acted together and both knew about the discovery abuse, the sanctioning of both is proper.[83]

Finally, trial courts may impose sanctions on a nonparty when, for example, it is subject to a Texas Rule 196.7 request or motion for entry upon property or a Texas Rule 205.3 production request without a deposition and fails to comply with an order under Texas Rules 196.7 or 205.3.[84] But the type of sanctions available is limited. Specifically, a trial court may not impose sanctions on nonparties under Texas Rule 215.2(b).[85] Rather, the sanction relating to nonparties is specified in Texas Rule 215.2(c): "If a nonparty fails to comply with an order under [Texas] Rules 196.7 or 205.3, the court which made the order may treat the failure to obey as ***contempt of court.***"[86]

14-3:4 Sanctionable Discovery Conduct

Texas Rule 215 describes types of discovery abuses that call for discovery sanctions. In addition, Texas case law defines and addresses "spoliation" for which discovery sanctions may be imposed. The following sections address each type of conduct for which a trial court may impose discovery sanctions.

14-3:4.1 Conduct That Warrants Motion for Sanctions by Discovering Party

As discussed in section 14-2:4 of this Chapter, Texas Rule 215.1(b) addresses a wide variety of conduct warranting a sanctions motion by "the discovering party."[87] For example, Texas Rule 215.1(b)(1) provides that a discovering party may move for sanctions "if a party or other deponent which is a corporation or other entity fails to make a designation under [Texas] Rules 199.2(b)(1) or 200.1(b)[.]"[88] And Texas Rule 215.1(b)(2) entitles a discovering party to move for sanctions if "a party, or other

---

paid jointly and severally by the three attorneys.").

[83] *E.g., In re Zenergy, Inc.*, 968 S.W.2d 1, 11 (Tex. App.—Corpus Christi 1997, orig. proceeding) (affirming sanctions imposed against a party and its attorney, jointly and severally, for "interwoven conduct").

[84] *See* Tex. R. Civ. P. 215.2(c).

[85] *See In re Perrilloux*, No. 05-19-01584-CV, 2020 WL 2092483, at *5 (Tex. App.—Dallas May 1, 2020, orig. proceeding) (mem. op.) (holding that a person deposed under Texas Rule 202 is not a "party" for purposes of imposing sanctions under Texas Rule 215.2(b)); *In re White*, 227 S.W.3d 234, 236 (Tex. App.—San Antonio 2007, orig. proceeding) ("By its terms, [Texas] Rule 215.1 authorizes the trial court to compel discovery and to award expenses against both party and nonparty deponents. . . . However, [Texas] Rule 215.2(b) only authorizes the trial court to impose sanctions for discovery abuses committed by 'a party or an officer, director, or managing agent of a party or a person designated . . . to testify on behalf of a party.' [Texas] Rule 215.2(b) does not authorize the trial court to impose sanctions on nonparty deponents.").

[86] Tex. R. Civ. P. 215.2(c) (emphasis added). See also case cited in note 85.

[87] Tex. R. Civ. P. 215.1(b)(3).

[88] Tex. R. Civ. P. 215.1(b)(1). Texas Rule 199.2(b)(1) governs the procedure for noticing oral depositions, and Texas Rule 200.1(b) governs the procedure for noticing depositions upon written questions. *See* Tex. R. Civ. P. 199.2(b)(1), 200.1(b). See also Chapter 11, section 11-2:4 and 11-3:4 (respectively discussing the notice requirements for oral depositions and depositions upon written questions).

deponent, or a person designated to testify on behalf of a party or other deponent," after being served with proper notice, fails "to appear before the officer who is to take his deposition,"[89] or fails "to answer a question propounded or submitted upon oral examination or upon written questions."[90] A discovering party may also move for sanctions if a party fails to object to or answer interrogatories pursuant to Texas Rule 197[91] or fails to respond properly to requests for inspection pursuant to Texas Rule 196.[92] For motions made under this section, Texas Rule 215.1(c) provides that "an evasive or incomplete answer is to be treated as a failure to answer."[93]

14-3:4.2 Failure to Comply with an Order or with a Discovery Request

Texas Rule 215.2 addresses conduct that is sanctionable by the trial court, with or without a motion.[94] Texas Rule 215.2(a) provides for sanctions (specifically, contempt of court) for the failure of a deponent "to appear or to be sworn or to answer a question after being directed to do so by a district court in the district in which the deposition is being taken[.]"[95] Texas Rule 215.2(b) provides for sanctions for the failure of a (1) party, (2) an officer, director, or managing agent of a party, or (3) a person designated under the deposition rules to testify on behalf of a party, "to comply with proper discovery requests or to obey an order to provide or permit discovery."[96] Finally, as

---

89 *See Stromberger v. Turley Law Firm*, 315 S.W.3d 921, 925 (Tex. App.—Dallas 2010, no pet.) (holding that the trial court did not abuse its discretion in imposing monetary sanctions against a party for his failure to appear for his deposition and produce documents); *Min Rong Zheng v. Bridgestone Firestone N. Am. Tire, L.L.C.*, 284 S.W.3d 890, 893–94 (Tex. App.—Eastland 2009, no pet.) (concluding that the imposition of a death-penalty sanction for plaintiffs' failure to appear for deposition was unjust because nothing in the record suggested that they were aware that their depositions had been noticed); *cf. Black Horse Lane Assoc., L.P. v. Dow Chem. Corp.*, 228 F.3d 275, 302–04 (3d Cir. 2000) (holding that an unprepared representative deponent fails to appear at the organization's deposition).

90 Tex. R. Civ. P. 215.1(b)(2)(A)–(B); *see In re White*, 227 S.W.3d 234, 235 (Tex. App.—San Antonio 2007, orig. proceeding) (concluding that a deponent abused the discovery process by failing to answer questions during her deposition).

91 Tex. R. Civ. P. 215.1(b)(3)(A), (B); *see Swain v. Sw. Bell Yellow Pages*, 998 S.W.2d 731, 732–33 (Tex. App.—Fort Worth 1999, no pet.) (affirming a sanction precluding the counter-plaintiff defendant from testifying about his damages because he failed to respond to interrogatories and production requests regarding them).

92 Tex. R. Civ. P. 215.1(b)(3)(C), (D).

93 Tex. R. Civ. P. 215.1(c). Texas Rule 215(c) does not apply to a party's failure to verify interrogatory answers. *State Farm Fire & Cas. Co. v. Morua*, 979 S.W.2d 616, 620 (Tex. 1998) (holding that an interrogatory with a "missing verification" was not an "evasive or incomplete answer"). See *also* Chapter 14, section 14-2:4 (discussing grounds for motions for sanctions and to compel discovery).

94 Tex. R. Civ. P. 215.2 (containing no motion requirement).

95 Tex. R. Civ. P. 215.2(a).

96 Tex. R. Civ. P. 215.2(b); *see Jardon v. Pfister*, 593 S.W.3d 810, 826 (Tex. App.—El Paso 2019, no pet.) (affirming the trial court's exclusion of documents and evidence at trial because they were not produced in discovery); *Lesikar v. Moon*, No. 14-16-00299-CV, 2017 Tex. App. LEXIS 10172, at *12, 2017 WL 4930851 (Tex. App.—Houston [14th Dist.] Oct. 31, 2017, no pet.) (mem. op.) ("Texas Rule of Civil Procedure 215.2 allows a trial court to sanction a party for failure to comply with a discovery order or request."); *Young v. Young*, No. 03-14-00720-CV, 2016 Tex. App. LEXIS 13254, at *6–7, 2016 WL 7339117 (Tex. App.—Austin

discussed in section 14-3:3, Texas Rule 215.2(c) provides for sanctions (specifically, contempt of court) for the failure of a nonparty to comply with an order under Texas Rules 196.7 or 205.3.

A number of Texas courts have held that the sanctions provided by Texas Rule 215.2(b) *cannot* be imposed against a nonparty.[97] In so holding, the courts have

---

Dec. 15, 2016, no pet.) (mem. op.) (same); *Schmidt v. BPC Corp.*, No. 05-14-00653-CV, 2015 Tex. App. LEXIS 11203, at *8, 2015 WL 6538038 (Tex. App.—Dallas Oct. 29, 2015, pet. denied) (mem. op.) ("[T]he record is clear the trial court ordered Schmidt to produce board minutes, which he failed to do. He admitted to violating the court's order. As such, the trial court was authorized under Texas Rule of Civil Procedure 215.2 to impose sanctions for abusing the discovery process by failing to comply with a proper discovery request and disregarding a discovery order."); *Christus Health Gulf Coast v. Carswell*, 433 S.W.3d 585, 614 (Tex. App.—Houston [1st Dist.] 2013), *rev'd in part and vacated in part on other grounds*, 505 S.W.3d 528 (Tex. 2016) (affirming a trial court's judgment finding that a hospital engaged in sanctionable conduct when it improperly concealed a deceased individual's heart tissue, failed to supplement its response to a discovery request in a timely manner, and violated the court's ruling denying its motion for leave to inspect the heart tissue); *Trahan v. Lone Star Title Co. of El Paso, Inc.*, 247 S.W.3d 269, 279–84 (Tex. App.—El Paso 2007, pet. denied) (upholding sanctions against a party for failing to produce audio recordings in response to a request for disclosure asking for "witness statements"); *Fethkenher v. Kroger Co.*, 139 S.W.3d 24, 35 (Tex. App.—Fort Worth 2004, no pet.) (concluding that it was sanctionable for a party's attorney to fail to produce the party for deposition and to respond to letters seeking supplemental discovery responses); *Adams v. Allstate Cty. Mut. Ins. Co.*, 199 S.W.3d 509, 513–14 (Tex. App.—Houston [1st Dist.] 2006, pet. denied) (affirming the striking of the a chiropractor's assistant's affidavit about the reasonableness and dollar amount of certain of the plaintiff's chiropractic services as a sanction for the assistant's attempts to evade his deposition); *In re Lavernia Nursing Facility, Inc.*, 12 S.W.3d 566, 571–72 (Tex. App.—San Antonio 1999, no pet.) (holding that a trial court did not abuse its discretion when it sanctioned a defendant employer for failing to produce its employee's records in response to a discovery request for the employee's personnel files, even though the employer claimed the disciplinary records were privileged, when the employer did not follow procedures available to challenge the discovery request). Texas Rule 215.2(b) also provides a nonexhaustive list of the sanctions that a court can impose to address the discovery abuses described in Texas Rule 215.2(b). See also Chapter 14, section 14-4 (discussing permissible discovery sanctions).

[97] *E.g.*, *In re Perrilloux*, No. 05-19-01584-CV, 2020 WL 2092483, at *5 (Tex. App.—Dallas May 1, 2020, orig. proceeding) (mem. op.) (holding that a person deposed pursuant to Texas Rule 202 is not a "party" for purposes of imposing sanctions under Texas Rule 215.2(b)); *In re White*, 227 S.W.3d 234, 236–37 (Tex. App.—San Antonio 2007, orig. proceeding) (holding that the trial court abused its discretion in ordering a deponent to pay, as sanctions, the court reporter's fees to continue the deposition); *In re Prince*, No. 14-06-00895-CV, 2006 Tex. App. LEXIS 10558, at *12, 2006 WL 3589484 (Tex. App.—Houston [14th Dist.] Dec. 12, 2006, orig. proceeding) (mem. op.) ("[A] court's power to impose sanctions on non-parties is limited to its contempt power."); *see City of Hous. v. Chambers*, 899 S.W.2d 306, 309 (Tex. App.—Houston [14th Dist.] 1995, orig. proceeding) (holding that the trial court abused its discretion in ordering a nonparty deponent, as sanctions, to pay the court reporter's fees to continue the deposition). In so holding, the courts in *White* and *Prince* relied on the fact that Texas "Rule 215.2(b) only authorizes the trial court to impose sanctions for discovery abuses committed by 'a party or an officer, director, or managing agent of a party or a person designated . . . to testify on behalf of a party.'" *In re White*, 227 S.W.3d 234, 236 (Tex. App.—San Antonio 2007, orig. proceeding); *In re Prince*, No. 14-06-00895-CV, 2006 Tex. App. LEXIS 10558, at *12, 2006 WL 3589484 (Tex. App.—Houston [14th Dist.] Dec. 12,

relied on the fact that Texas "Rule 215.2(b) only authorizes the trial court to impose sanctions for discovery abuses committed by 'a party or an officer, director, or managing agent of a party or a person designated . . . to testify on behalf of a party.'"[98] Texas Rule 215.1(a), however, provides that if "a party[] *or other deponent* . . . fails to answer a question propounded or submitted upon oral examination or upon written questions . . . the discovering party may . . . apply to the court in which the action is pending for the imposition of any sanction authorized by [Texas] Rule 215(b) without the necessity of first having obtained a court order compelling such discovery." (Emphasis added.) This language is inconsistent with Texas Rule 215.2(b), and the conflict has not been addressed by the courts that have held that Texas Rule 215.2(b) sanctions cannot be imposed against a nonparty. Thus, it is unclear whether, under Texas Rule 215.2(b)(2), sanctions can be imposed against a nonparty or the nonparty's attorney for not answering or evasively answering a deposition question.

14-3:4.3 Abuse of the Discovery Process in Seeking, Making, or Resisting Discovery

Texas Rule 215.3 allows a court to sanction a party that "is abusing the discovery process in seeking, making or resisting discovery" or if the court "finds that any interrogatory or request for inspection or production is unreasonably frivolous, oppressive, or harassing, or that a response or answer is unreasonably frivolous or for purposes of delay."[99] While this Rule gives a trial court wide latitude in identifying and sanctioning discovery abuse,[100] it limits the sanctions available to the sanctions authorized

---

2006, orig. proceeding) (mem. op.).

[98] *In re White*, 227 S.W.3d 234, 236 (Tex. App.—San Antonio 2007, orig. proceeding); *accord, e.g.*, *In re Prince*, No. 14-06-00895-CV, 2006 Tex. App. LEXIS 10558, at *12 (Tex. App.—Houston [14th Dist.] Dec. 12, 2006, orig. proceeding) (mem. op.) (citing Texas Rules 215(b)–(c)).

[99] Tex. R. Civ. P. 215.3; *see In re Garza*, 544 S.W.3d 836, 840 (Tex. 2018) (orig. proceeding) (permitting a court to impose appropriate sanctions if the court finds that a party is abusing the discovery process in seeking, making, or resisting discovery); *Centennial Psychiatric Assocs., LLC v. Cantrell*, Nos. 14-17-00391-CV, 14-17-00380-CV, 2017 Tex. App. LEXIS 11909, at *28, 2017 WL 6544283 (Tex. App.—Houston [14th Dist.] Dec. 21, 2017, no pet.) (mem. op.) (Texas "Rule 215.3 authorizes a trial court to impose sanctions on a party who abuses the discovery process in seeking, making, or resisting discovery."); *England v. Kolbe*, No. 03-15-00409-CV, 2017 Tex. App. LEXIS 2680, at *10, 2017 WL 1228884 (Tex. App.—Austin Mar. 30, 2017, no pet.) (mem. op.) (same); *Knoderer v. State Farm Lloyds*, 515 S.W.3d 21, 33 (Tex. App.—Texarkana 2017, pet. denied) (Texas "Rule 215.3 authorizes the trial court to 'impose any appropriate sanction authorized by paragraphs (1), (2), (3), (4), (5), and (8) of [Texas R]ule 215.2(b)' on a party abusing discovery. This includes charging all discovery expenses, reasonable expenses, and court costs on the abusing party." (citation omitted) (quoting Tex. R. Civ. P. 215.3)); *Scarbrough v. Purser*, No. 03-13-00025-CV, 2016 Tex. App. LEXIS 13863, at *58, 2016 WL 7583546 (Tex. App.—Austin Dec. 30, 2016, pet. denied) (mem. op.) ("A trial court may impose sanctions on any party that abuses the discovery process in seeking, making, or resisting discovery."); *In re K.R.*, No. 02-14-00275-CV, 2016 Tex. App. LEXIS 3631, at *6, 2016 WL 1393392 (Tex. App.—Fort Worth Apr. 7, 2016, no pet.) (mem. op.) ("When a party abuses the discovery process by resisting discovery (such as by failing to attend a deposition), a trial court may impose sanctions." (citing Tex. R. Civ. P. 215.3)).

[100] *See JNS Enter., Inc. v. Dixie Demolition, LLC*, 430 S.W.3d 444, 452–56 (Tex. App.—Austin 2013) (upholding sanctions against plaintiffs who fabricated contracts and a performance

by Texas Rule 215.2(b)(1)-(5) and (8).[101] The omission of the sanction authorized by Texas Rule 215.2(b)(6) is logical, as it pertains specifically to "contempt of court [for] the failure to obey [court] orders[.]"[102] The omission of the sanction authorized by Texas Rule 215.2(b)(7) is also logical, but for a different reason—it simply refers back to and incorporates "such orders as are listed in paragraphs (1), (2), (3), (4), or (5)" of the Rule.[103]

---

guarantee and gave false deposition testimony about them); *Prize Energy Res., L.P. v. Cliff Hoskins, Inc.*, 345 S.W.3d 537, 577 (Tex. App.—San Antonio 2011, no pet.) (upholding monetary sanctions for discovery abuses by the plaintiff's counsel, which included "witness tampering, misrepresentation of counsel's identity, securing documents under false pretenses, contacting represented witnesses in the absence of their counsel, and falsely threatening witnesses with criminal prosecution"); *Buck v. Estate of Buck*, 291 S.W.3d 46, 55–60 (Tex. App.—Corpus Christi 2009, no pet.) (upholding a trial court's striking of a testator's grandson's pleadings for abuse of discovery because the grandson had failed to appear for depositions, failed to provide a sworn accounting, and failed to pay fees); *Scott Bader, Inc. v. Sandstone Prods., Inc.*, 248 S.W.3d 802, 811–14 (Tex. App.—Houston [1st Dist.] 2008, no pet.) (holding that a trial court did not err in finding that a party abused the discovery process by producing invoices in a manner calculated to conceal customer information, altering invoices to conceal such information, and failing to timely produce relevant documents); *Fertic v. Spencer*, 247 S.W.3d 242, 245–47 (Tex. App.—El Paso 2007, pet. denied) (concluding that a party's failure to provide adequate responses to discovery requests for designated witness list, despite explanations of deficiencies and repeated warnings to comply, was sanctionable); *Clark v. Bres*, 217 S.W.3d 501, 508 (Tex. App.—Houston [14th Dist.] 2006) (agreeing with the trial court that a lawyer's behavior at a deposition was sanctionable because it was "conducted for the purposes of harassment, intimidation of the witness, and unfair tactical advantage and was inconsistent with the conduct required of an officer of the court"); *Aguilar v. Morales*, 162 S.W.3d 825, 831–34 (Tex. App.—El Paso 2005, pet. denied) (upholding sanctions against an attorney acting pro se because he hired an expert retained by opposing counsel in violation of Texas Disciplinary Rule of Professional Conduct 4.02(b)); *Magnuson v. Mullen*, 65 S.W.3d 815, 824–28 (Tex. App.—Fort Worth 2002, pet. denied) (holding that a trial court did not abuse its discretion in sanctioning a former employee in a defamation suit for repeatedly refusing to provide disclosures, answer written-discovery requests, and appear for his deposition).

[101] Tex. R. Civ. P. 215.3 ("[T]he court in which the action is pending may, after notice and hearing, impose any appropriate sanction authorized by paragraphs (1), (2), (3), (4), (5), and (8) of [Texas] Rule 215.2(b)."); *Centennial Psychiatric Assocs., LLC v. Cantrell*, Nos. 14-17-00391-CV, 14-17-00380-CV, 2017 Tex. App. LEXIS 11909, at *28–29, 2017 WL 6544283 (Tex. App.—Houston [14th Dist.] Dec. 21, 2017, no pet.) (mem. op.) ("If a court finds that a party is abusing the discovery process in seeking discovery or if a court finds a request for inspection or production of documents is unreasonably frivolous, oppressive, or harassing, it may impose any appropriate sanction authorized by [Texas R]ules 215.2(b)(1), (2), (3), (4), (5), and (8).").

[102] Tex. R. Civ. P. 215.2(b)(6) (providing that, "in lieu of any of the foregoing orders [in Texas Rule 215.2(b)] or in addition thereto, [a court may issue] an order treating as a contempt of court the failure to obey any orders except an order to submit to a physical or mental examination").

[103] Tex. R. Civ. P. 215.2(b)(7) (providing fully that, "when a party has failed to comply with an order under [Texas] Rule 204 requiring him to appear or produce another for examination, [a court may issue] such orders as are listed in paragraphs (1), (2), (3), (4) or (5) of [Texas Rule 215.2(b)], unless the person failing to comply shows that he is unable to appear or to produce such person for examination").

14-3:4.4 Failure of a Party or Witness to Attend a Deposition or to Serve a Subpoena on the Witness

Under Texas Rule 215.5(a),[104] "the party giving the notice of the taking of an oral deposition" may be sanctioned if it fails to attend and proceed with the deposition and another party attends pursuant to the notice.[105] Sanctions in this context include payment of "the reasonable expenses incurred by" the other party and that party's attorney "in attending, including reasonable attorney fees."[106]

Additionally, under Texas Rule 215.5(b), "if a party gives notice of the taking of an oral deposition of a witness and the witness does not attend because of the fault of the party giving the notice, if another party attends in person or by attorney because he expects the deposition of that witness to be taken, the court may order the party giving the notice to pay such other party the reasonable expenses incurred by him and his attorney in attending, including reasonable attorney fees."[107]

14-3:4.5 Spoliation of Evidence

Texas Rule 215 neither defines nor addresses spoliation.[108] Although a detailed discussion of spoliation is beyond this book's scope, a brief discussion of it is warranted because

---

[104] Texas Rule 193.6 formerly was Texas Rule 215.5. *See Best Indus. Unif. Supply Co., Inc. v. Gulf Coast Alloy Welding, Inc.*, 41 S.W.3d 145, 147 (Tex. App.—Amarillo 2000, pet. denied) ("The progenitor of [Texas Rule 193.6] was [Texas] Rule . . . 215.5."). Although the rule was renumbered in 1999, some post-1999 opinions inadvertently refer to the former Rule. *E.g.*, *Ceasar v. Rodriguez*, No. 01-02-00027-CV, 2003 Tex. App. LEXIS 749, at *7, 2003 WL 164463 (Tex. App.—Houston [1st Dist.] Jan. 23, 2003, no pet.) (mem. op.) ("[W]e hold that former [Texas R]ule 215.5 controls the sanction imposed by the trial court."); *Brehm v. Brehm*, No. 14-99-00055-CV, 2000 Tex. App. LEXIS 2079, at *3, 2000 WL 330076 (Tex. App.—Houston [14th Dist.] Mar. 30, 2000, no pet.) (mem. op.) ("When witnesses are not identified timely, or are not identified at all, the trial court must exclude them unless it finds the failure to file a timely response was supported by good cause. *See* Tex. R. Civ. P. 215.5.").

[105] Tex. R. Civ. P. 215.5(a); *cf.* Fed. R. Civ. P. 30(g)(1) ("A party who, expecting a deposition to be taken, attends in person or by an attorney may recover reasonable expenses for attending, including attorney's fees, if the noticing party failed to: (1) attend and proceed with the deposition. . . ."); *Detsch & Co. v. Am. Prods. Co.*, 141 F.2d 662, 663 (9th Cir. 1944) (affirming an award of expenses incurred by a party who attended a noticed deposition that did not occur); *In re K.R.*, 02-14-00275-CV, 2016 Tex. App. LEXIS 3631, at *6, 2016 WL 1393392 (Tex. App.—Fort Worth Apr. 7, 2016, no pet.) (mem. op.) ("When a party abuses the discovery process by resisting discovery (such as by failing to attend a deposition), a trial court may impose sanctions." (citing Tex. R. Civ. P. 215.3)).

[106] Tex. R. Civ. P. 215.5(a).

[107] Tex. R. Civ. P. 215.5(b); *cf.* Fed. R. Civ. P. 30(g)(2) ("A party who, expecting a deposition to be taken, attends in person or by an attorney may recover reasonable expenses for attending, including attorney's fees, if the noticing party failed to: . . . (2) serve a subpoena on a nonparty deponent, who consequently did not attend.").

[108] *See Brookshire Bros., Ltd. v. Aldridge*, 438 S.W.3d 9, 18 (Tex. 2014) ("Neither the Texas Rules of Evidence nor the Texas Rules of Civil Procedure specifically address spoliation."). Federal Rule 37 was amended effective December 1, 2015 to address the spoliation of electronically stored information, as follows:

> If electronically stored information that should have been preserved in the anticipation

the Texas Supreme Court has made clear that spoliation is a discovery abuse that may justify a wide array of sanctions, some of which are listed in Texas Rule 215.2(b).[109]

In *Brookshire Brothers, Ltd. v. Aldridge*,[110] the Texas Supreme Court held that a trial court (rather than a jury) determines whether spoliation has occurred,[111] and it provided a two-part test for making that determination: "To conclude that a party spoliated evidence, the court must find that (1) the spoliating party had a duty to reasonably preserve evidence, and (2) the party intentionally or negligently breached that duty by failing to do so."[112] The court then applied an anticipation-of-litigation

---

or conduct of litigation is lost because a party failed to take reasonable steps to preserve it, and it cannot be restored or replaced through additional discovery, the court:

(1) upon finding prejudice to another party from loss of the information, may order measures no greater than necessary to cure the prejudice; or

(2) only upon finding that the party acted with the intent to deprive another party of the information's use in the litigation may:

(A) presume that the lost information was unfavorable to the party;
(B) instruct the jury that it may or must presume the information was unfavorable to the party; or
(C) dismiss the action or enter a default judgment.

Fed. R. Civ. P. 37(e); *see* Fed. R. Civ. P. 37(e), Advisory Committee's Note to 2015 Amend. (providing a detailed explanation regarding the need for, and intended construction of, amended Federal Rule 37(e)); Fed. R. Civ. P. 16(b)(3)(B)(iii) (also amended effective December 1, 2015 to provide that a scheduling order may "provide for . . . preservation of electronically stored information); Fed. R. Civ. P. 26(f)(3)(C) (also amended effective December 1, 2015 to require a discovery plan to "state the parties' views and proposals on . . . any issues about . . . preservation of electronically stored information, including the form or forms in which it should be produced").

109 *E.g., Brookshire Bros., Ltd. v. Aldridge*, 438 S.W.3d 9, 18 (Tex. 2014) ("Texas courts necessarily enjoy wide latitude in remedying acts of discovery abuse, including evidence spoliation."); *accord, e.g., In re Advanced Powder Sols., Inc.*, 496 S.W.3d 838, 853 (Tex. App.—Houston [1st Dist.] 2016, orig. proceeding); *Telesis/Parkwood Ret. I, Ltd. v. Anderson*, 462 S.W.3d 212, 253 (Tex. App.—El Paso 2015, no pet.).

110 *Brookshire Bros., Ltd. v. Aldridge*, 438 S.W.3d 9 (Tex. 2014).

111 *Brookshire Bros., Ltd. v. Aldridge*, 438 S.W.3d 9, 20 (Tex. 2014) ("[T]he trial court, rather than the jury, must determine whether a party spoliated evidence and, if so, impose the appropriate remedy. The trial court may hold an evidentiary hearing to assist the court in making spoliation findings, but not in the presence of the jury.") (citation omitted); *see Wackenhut Corp. v. Gutierrez*, 453 S.W.3d 917, 921 (Tex. 2015) ("Whether a party spoliated evidence and whether a particular remedy is appropriate are questions of law for the trial court."); *Petroleum Sols., Inc. v. Head*, 454 S.W.3d 482, 488 (Tex. 2014) ("[W]hether a party spoliated evidence and whether a particular remedy is appropriate are questions of law for the trial court. Because the trial court bears this responsibility, evidence of the circumstances surrounding alleged spoliation is generally inadmissible at trial, as such evidence is largely irrelevant to the merits and unfairly prejudicial to the spoliating party.") (citations omitted); *Knoderer v. State Farm Lloyds*, 515 S.W.3d 21, 34 (Tex. App.—Texarkana 2017, pet. denied) ("[I]t is the trial court, not the jury, that determines whether spoliation of evidence has occurred and, if it has, that imposes the appropriate remedy.").

112 *Brookshire Bros., Ltd. v. Aldridge*, 438 S.W.3d 9, 14 (Tex. 2014); *accord Christus Health Gulf Coast v. Carswell*, 505 S.W.3d 528, 540 (Tex. 2016); *Petroleum Sols., Inc. v. Head*, 454 S.W.3d 482, 488 (Tex. 2014); *In re Sw. Pub. Serv. Co.*, No. 13-19-00111-CV, 2020 Tex. App. LEXIS 3212, at *40–41, 2020 WL 1887762 (Tex. App.—Eastland Apr. 16, 2020,orig. proceeding) (mem. op.); *Knoderer v. State Farm Lloyds*, 515 S.W.3d 21, 35 (Tex. App.—Texarkana 2017,

standard for assessing when a duty to preserve arises:

> The standard governing the duty to preserve resolves two related inquiries: when the duty is triggered, and the scope of that duty. Specifically, we observed in *Wal–Mart Stores [v. Johnson*, 106 S.W.3d 718, 722 (Tex. 2003),] that "[s]uch a duty arises only when a party knows or reasonably should know [1] that there is a substantial chance that a claim will be filed and [2] that evidence in its possession or control will be material and relevant to that claim." In turn, a "substantial chance of litigation" arises when "litigation is more than merely an abstract possibility or unwarranted fear."[113]

To obtain a spoliation remedies, the party seeking them "must demonstrate that the other party breached its duty to preserve material and relevant evidence."[114] Such a breach occurs when the party possessing a duty to preserve evidence fails to exercise reasonable care to do so. "[T]he breach may be either intentional or negligent."[115] As explained in section 14-4:3 of this Chapter, whether the breach is negligent or intentional can have a significant impact on the type of discovery sanctions that are warranted for the breach (i.e., spoliation) at issue.

14-3:4.6 Pattern of Discovery Abuse

In determining whether to impose discovery sanctions and the degree of such sanctions to impose, "[t]he trial court is not limited to considering only the specific violation for which sanctions are finally imposed, but may consider everything that has occurred during the history of the litigation."[116] A pattern of discovery abuse can be

---

pet. denied); *Scarbrough v. Purser*, No. 03-13-00025-CV, 2016 Tex. App. LEXIS 13863, at *49, 2016 WL 7583546 (Tex. App.—Austin Dec. 30, 2016, pet. denied) (mem. op.); *In re First Transit Inc.*, 499 S.W.3d 584, 596 n.3 (Tex. App.—Houston [14th Dist.] 2016, no pet.); *In re Advanced Powder Sols., Inc.*, 496 S.W.3d 838, 853 (Tex. App.—Houston [1st Dist.] 2016, orig. proceedings); *In re J.H. Walker, Inc.*, No. 05-14-01497-CV, 2016 Tex. App. LEXIS 483, at *8, 2016 WL 819592 (Tex. App.—Dallas Jan. 15, 2016, orig. proceeding) (mem. op.).

113 *Brookshire Bros., Ltd. v. Aldridge*, 438 S.W.3d 9, 20 (Tex. 2014) (quoting *Nat'l Tank Co. v. Brotherton*, 851 S.W.2d 193, 204 (Tex. 1993)); *accord In re Advanced Powder Sols., Inc.*, 496 S.W.3d 838, 853 (Tex. App.—Houston [1st Dist.] 2016, orig. proceedings); *In re J.H. Walker, Inc.*, No. 05-14-01497-CV, 2016 Tex. App. LEXIS 483, at *8 (Tex. App.—Dallas Jan. 15, 2016, orig. proceeding) (mem. op.). See also Chapter 4, section 4-5:2.2 (discussing the application of the anticipation-of-litigation test in relation to the work-product doctrine in Texas).

114 *Brookshire Bros., Ltd. v. Aldridge*, 438 S.W.3d 9, 20 (Tex. 2014).

115 *Brookshire Bros., Ltd. v. Aldridge*, 438 S.W.3d 9, 20 (Tex. 2014); *accord Petroleum Sols., Inc. v. Head*, 454 S.W.3d 482, 488 (Tex. 2014) ("A party cannot breach its duty without at least acting negligently.").

116 *McKeithan v. Condit*, No. 13-16-00348-CV, 2018 Tex. App. LEXIS 9707, at *5, 2018 WL 6219624 (Tex. App.—Corpus Christi Nov. 29, 2018, no. pet) (mem. op.) ("Absent a party's flagrant bad faith or counsel's callous disregard for the responsibilities of discovery under the rules, sanctions that prevent a decision on the merits of a case cannot be justified."); *White v. Bath*, 825 S.W.2d 227, 230 (Tex. App.—Houston [14th Dist.] 1992, writ denied), *cert. denied*, 507 U.S. 1039 (1993); *see ABN Amro Mortg. Grp., Inc. v. Rabalais*, No. 13-06-00598-CV, 2008 Tex. App. LEXIS 9423, at *24–25, 2008 WL 5248880 (Tex. App.—Corpus Christi Dec. 18, 2008, no pet.) (mem. op.) ("Based on the course of litigation, which indicated a general and continuing pattern of discovery abuse, a lengthy delay, and attorney's fees incurred by the Rabalaises in pursuing the discovery at issue, . . . we hold the trial court did not abuse its

considered in crafting sanctions.[117]

14-4 Permissible Discovery Sanctions

A trial court has several options when deciding how to respond to discovery abuse.[118] For example, Texas Rules 215.2 and 215.3 specify orders a court may impose as sanctions.[119] In addition, Texas Rule 215.2 authorizes a trial court to craft its own sanctions orders "as are just."[120] A trial court also has inherent power to impose sanctions

---

discretion in assessing $100,000 in sanctions for discovery abuse or bad faith abuse of the judicial process."); *Sharpe v. Kilcoyne*, 962 S.W.2d 697, 702 (Tex. App.—Fort Worth 1998, no pet.) ("In determining whether to impose discovery sanctions, the trial court is not limited to considering only the specific violation for which sanctions are finally imposed, but may consider everything that has occurred during the history of the litigation.").

117 *E.g., Ayati-Ghaffari v. Farmers Ins. Exch.*, No. 05-17-00864-CV, 2018 Tex. App. LEXIS 10178, at *14–17, WL 6498643 (Tex. App.—Dallas Dec. 11, 2018) (mem. op.) (finding a pattern of discovery abuse, including a party's refusal to comply with a trial court's discovery orders to produce material evidence, can give rise to a presumption that the party's claims lack merit and justify the trial court striking plaintiff's pleading, dismissing the case with prejudice, and awarding attorneys' fees); *NRG & Assocs., LLC v. Serv. Transfer, Inc.*, No. 05-16-01375-CV, 2017 Tex. App. LEXIS 11999, 2017 WL 6523396, at *5 (Tex. App.—Dallas Dec. 21, 2017, no pet.) (mem. op.). *ABN Amro Mortg. Grp., Inc. v. Rabalais*, No. 13-06-00598-CV, 2008 Tex. App. LEXIS 9423, at *24–25 (Tex. App.—Corpus Christi Dec. 18, 2008, no pet.) (mem. op.) ("Based on the course of litigation, which indicated a general and continuing pattern of discovery abuse, a lengthy delay, and attorney's fees incurred by the Rabalaises in pursuing the discovery at issue, . . . we hold the trial court did not abuse its discretion in assessing $100,000 in sanctions for discovery abuse or bad faith abuse of the judicial process."); *Vela v. Wagner & Brown, Ltd.*, 203 S.W.3d 37, 59 (Tex. App.—San Antonio 2006, no pet.) ("A trial court may impose sanctions based on a general pattern of discovery abuse[.]"); *In re Harvest Cmtys. of Houston, Inc.*, 88 S.W.3d 343, 347 (Tex. App.—San Antonio 2002, no pet.) ("Harvest takes the position that by limiting its motion to reconsider to the striking of Dr. Watson, the discovery abuse that occurred with respect to and during Dr. Silverman's deposition no longer has any relevance. The history of Dr. Silverman's deposition, however, could be considered by the trial court in its overall consideration of the appropriate sanction and can be considered by this court in our review of that sanction."). See also Chapter 14, section 14-3:2 (discussing how a pattern of discovery abuse can justify death-penalty sanctions).

118 *Brookshire Bros., Ltd. v. Aldridge*, 438 S.W.3d 9, 18 (Tex. 2014) ("Texas courts necessarily enjoy wide latitude in remedying acts of discovery abuse. . . ."); *In re Sw. Pub. Serv. Co.*, No. 13-19-00111-CV, 2020 Tex. App. LEXIS 3212, at *33, 2020 WL 1887762 (Tex. App.—Eastland Apr. 16, 2020, orig. proceeding) (mem. op.) ("Rule 215 of the Texas Rules of Civil Procedure enumerates a wide array of remedies available to a trial court in addressing discovery abuse, such as an award of attorney's fees or costs to the harmed party, the exclusion of evidence, striking a party's pleadings, or dismissing a party's claims."). See also Chapter 14, section 14-4:1 (discussing sanctions orders authorized under Texas Rule 215.2(b)).

119 Tex. R. Civ. P. 215.2(b). See also Chapter 14, section 14-4:1 (discussing permissible sanctions orders).

120 Tex. R. Civ. P. 215.2(b); *see In re Sw. Pub. Serv. Co.*, No. 13-19-00111-CV, 2020 Tex. App. LEXIS 3212, at *34, 2020 WL 1887762 (Tex. App.—Eastland Apr. 16, 2020,orig. proceeding) (mem. op.) ("[T]he punishment must fit the crime."); *Altesse Healthcare Sols., Inc. v. Wilson*, 540 S.W.3d 570, 575 (Tex. 2018) ("[Texas] Rule 215's simple requirement that discovery sanctions must be 'just.'"); Christus Health Gulf Coast v. Carswell, 505 S.W.3d 528, 540 (Tex. 2016) (Texas "Rule 215.2 allows a trial court to . . . make such orders regarding the failure [to obey a discovery order] as are just. But to be just, a sanction must be based on

for discovery abuses. Finally, in remedying the spoliation of evidence, a trial court may impose the sanctions orders listed in Texas Rule 215.2(b) or "craft other remedies it deems appropriate in light of the particular facts of the individual case, including the submission of a spoliation instruction to the jury."[121]

Although the trial court has broad discretion in determining whether to impose discovery sanctions and which sanctions to impose, its discretion is bounded by the parameters addressed in sections 14-3:1 and 14-3:2 of this Chapter. Moreover, spoliation sanctions (sometimes called "spoliation remedies") are subject to the unique considerations addressed in section 14-4:3 of this Chapter.

14-4:1 Sanctions Orders Specified in Texas Rule 215

Texas Rule 215.2(b) sets forth a nonexclusive list of sanctions orders that a trial court can issue,[122] with respect to certain specified discovery abuses,[123] after "notice and hearing [:]"[124]

- an order disallowing any further discovery of any kind or of a particular kind by

---

a direct relationship between the particular offensive conduct and the sanction imposed, and the sanction must not be excessive vis-a-vis that conduct.") (citations omitted); *Lott v. McCain*, No. 12-15-00244-CV, 2016 Tex. App. LEXIS 3796, at *3, 2016 WL 1446069 (Tex. App.—Tyler Apr. 13, 2016, no pet.) (mem. op.) ("A trial court may impose sanctions for violations of discovery orders or abuse of the discovery process. However, the sanctions imposed must be 'just.' If the sanctions are not just, a trial court abuses its discretion in imposing them." (citation omitted) (quoting Tex. R. Civ. P. 215.2(b))). See also Chapter 14, section 14-3:1 (discussing the requirement for "just" sanctions).

121 *Brookshire Bros., Ltd. v. Aldridge*, 438 S.W.3d 9, 21 (Tex. 2014); *see Altesse Healthcare Sols., Inc. v. Wilson*, 540 S.W.3d 570, 572 (Tex. 2018).

122 Texas Rule 215.2(b) ("[T]he court in which the action is pending may, after notice and hearing, make such orders in regard to the failure as are just, *and among others* [the ones listed in Texas Rule 215.2(b)(1)-(8).]") (emphasis added); *see Young v. Young*, No. 03-14-00720-CV, 2016 Tex. App. LEXIS 13254, at *23–24, 2016 WL 7339117 (Tex. App.—Austin Dec. 15, 2016, no pet.) (mem. op.) ("Although [Texas] Rule 215.2 does not expressly grant trial courts authority to strike a jury demand as a sanction for discovery violations, the rule appears to grant courts broad general discretion in issuing orders to address discovery abuse. We conclude, however, that the order striking the jury demand in this case does not satisfy discovery-sanction standards.") (citations omitted); *Ashmore v. JMS Constr., Inc.*, No. 05-15-00537-CV, 2016 Tex. App. LEXIS 13201, at *17 n.6, 2016 WL 7217256 (Tex. App.—Dallas Dec. 13, 2016, no pet.) (mem. op.) ("A trial court may impose any appropriate sanction under rule 215.2 of the Texas Rules of Civil Procedure, including striking out pleadings or parts thereof, if a party is abusing the discovery process."); *Hoa Dao v. Md. Cas. Co.*, No. 09-13-00353-CV, 2015 Tex. App. LEXIS 4893, at *14, 2015 WL 2255263 (Tex. App.—Beaumont May 14, 2015, no pet.) (mem. op.) (Texas "Rule 215.2 allows a trial court to impose a number of sanctions, including disallowing further discovery; charging certain expenses, costs, or attorney's fees of one party against the offending party; ordering certain facts to be established as true; limiting a party's ability to defend against or bring certain claims; striking pleadings or parts of pleadings; or finding a party in contempt of court. A trial court is not limited to the list of sanctions specifically identified in [Texas] Rule 215.2.") (citation omitted).

123 See Chapter 14, sections 14-3:4.1–14-3:4.3 (describing sanctionable conduct under Texas Rule 215.2(b)).

124 Tex. R. Civ. P. 215.2(b). See also Chapter 14, section 14-2:1 (addressing notice and hearing requirements).

the disobedient party;[125]

- an order charging all or any portion of the expenses of discovery or taxable court costs or both against the disobedient party or the attorney advising him;[126]
- an order that matters regarding which the order was made or any other designated facts shall be taken to be established for the purposes of the action in accordance with the claim of the party obtaining the order;[127]
- an order refusing to allow the disobedient party to support or oppose designated claims or defenses, or prohibiting him from introducing designated matters in evidence;[128]
- an order striking out pleadings or parts thereof or dismissing with or without prejudice the action or proceedings or any part thereof, or rendering a judgment by default against the disobedient party;[129]

---

125 Tex. R. Civ. P. 215.2(b)(1).

126 Tex. R. Civ. P. 215.2(b)(2); *see Lopez v. La Madeleine of Tex., Inc.*, 200 S.W.3d 854, 865 (Tex. App.—Dallas 2006, no pet.) (holding that an award under Texas Rule 215.2(b)(2) is "designed to remedy the abuse by compensating the aggrieved party for expenses incurred in litigation" and that any "monetary sanctions available for abuse of discovery are limited to reasonable expenses, including attorney's fees, caused by the abuse").

127 Tex. R. Civ. P. 215.2(b)(3); *see Spohn Hosp. v. Mayer*, 104 S.W.3d 878, 883 (Tex. 2003) (holding that a trial court abused its discretion in ordering, pursuant to Texas Rule 215.2(b)(3), that specified portions of witness statements be taken as established fact at trial); *Van Es v. Frazier*, 230 S.W.3d 770, 782–84 (Tex. App.—Waco 2007, pet. denied) (affirming Texas Rule 215.2(b)(3) sanctions).

128 Tex. R. Civ. P. 215.2(b)(4). Such sanctions also must be carefully weighed to ensure that they are just in relation to the discovery abuse. *See Paradigm Oil, Inc. v. Retamco Operating, Inc.*, 372 S.W.3d 177, 187–87 (Tex. 2012) ("[A] trial court should have discretion to bar a defendant's participation, such as at the damages hearing in this case, if such a sanction is necessary to remedy the abuse. Even so, such an extreme sanction must be carefully tailored to comport with the requirements . . . due process. Sanctions that preclude the admission of evidence intrude upon the fact-finding process of a trial just as much as a default judgment on liability. In the latter instance, sanctions that adjudicate the merits of a party's claim or defense cannot be imposed as mere punishment but rather are appropriate only when the sanctioned party's conduct justifies a presumption that an asserted claim or defense lacks merit. The justification for also barring the defaulted party from the ensuing evidentiary trial on damages must go beyond that presumption because the damages issue is materially different."); *accord In re Sw. Pub. Serv. Co.*, No. 13-19-00111-CV, 2020 Tex. App. LEXIS 3212, at *34–35, 2020 WL 1887762 (Tex. App.—Eastland Apr. 16, 2020, orig. proceeding) (mem. op.); *McKeithan v. Condit*, No. 13-16-00348-CV, 2018 Tex. App. LEXIS 9707, at *4, 2018 WL 6219624 (Tex. App.—Corpus Christi Nov. 29, 2018, no. pet) (mem. op.); *Jardon v. Pfister,* 593 S.W.3d 810, 826 (Tex. App.—El Paso 2019, no pet.). *See also* Chapter 5, section 5-7 (discussing Texas Rule 193.6 and the consequences for failing to timely respond or amend or supplement written discovery).

129 Tex. R. Civ. P. 215.2(b)(5); *see Shops at Legacy (Inland) Ltd. P'ship v. Fine Autographs & Memorabilia Retails Stores, Inc.*, 418 S.W.3d 229, 232 (Tex. App.—Dallas 2013, no pet.) ("Among the sanctions available under Texas R]ule 215.2 are orders 'striking out pleadings or parts thereof,' 'dismissing with or without prejudice the actions or proceedings or any part thereof,' and 'rendering a judgment by default against the disobedient party.' These sanctions, that adjudicate a claim and preclude presentation of the merits of the case, are often referred to as 'death penalty' sanctions." (quoting Tex. R. Civ. P. 215.2(b)(5))). See also Chapter 14, section 14-3:2 (discussing standards governing death-penalty sanctions).

- an order staying further proceedings until the order is obeyed;[130]
- an order treating as a contempt of court the failure to obey any orders;[131] and
- an order requiring the party failing to obey the order or the attorney advising him, or both, to pay, at such time as ordered by the court, the reasonable expenses, including attorney fees, caused by the failure, unless the court finds that the failure was substantially justified or that other circumstances make an award of expenses unjust.[132]

Several of these orders may also be an "appropriate sanction" pursuant to Texas Rule 215.3 if the court finds that "a party is abusing the discovery process in seeking, making or resisting discovery or if the court finds that any interrogatory or request

---

130 Tex. R. Civ. P. 215.2(b)(5).

131 Tex. R. Civ. P. 215.2(b)(6). Texas Rule 215.2(b)(6) does not apply to an order to submit to a physical or mental examination. Moreover, a contempt order cannot require the contemnor to pay costs or fees, including attorney's fees, as a condition of release from the contempt. *Ex parte Dolenz*, 893 S.W.2d 677, 680–81 (Tex. App.—Dallas 1995, orig. proceeding) ("A trial court shall not imprison a person for debt. Nor does our law allow collection of attorney's fees by contempt proceedings.").

132 Tex. R. Civ. P. 215.2(b)(8); *see Christus Health Gulf Coast v. Carswell*, 505 S.W.3d 528, 539–40 (Tex. 2016) ("Texas Rule of Civil Procedure 215.2(b)(8) authorizes a trial court to charge the party abusing the discovery process with the reasonable expenses, including attorney's fees, caused by the failure to obey discovery orders. These sanctions are designed to rectify discovery abuse by compensating the aggrieved party for expenses incurred. Consequently, when a party seeks attorney's fees as sanctions, the burden is on that party to put forth some affirmative evidence of attorney's fees incurred and how those fees resulted from or were caused by the sanctionable conduct.") (citations omitted); *Porretto v. Tex. Gen. Land Office*, 448 S.W.3d 393, 403 (Tex. 2014) (holding that a "trial court's award of $19,349.52 in attorney fees and expenses as discovery sanctions against the defendants" was "well within the trial court's discretion," reasoning in part that (1) the trial court could have found that the defendants "made no reasonable effort to locate responsive documents[,]" (2) the defendants "did not seek a more specific process for production in response to the request" they contended came late in the litigation and was broad, and (3) the defendants "did not even respond to the motions for sanctions"); *Quick Change Artist, LLC v. Iris T. Accessories*, No. 05-14-01562-CV, 2017 Tex. App. LEXIS 1220, at *13, 2017 WL 563340 (Tex. App.—Dallas Feb. 13, 2017, no pet.) (mem. op.) ("A trial court may award attorney's fees on a party's abuse of the discovery process. . . . As to the amount of attorney's fees awarded, the supreme court has held that the amount of attorney's fees awarded as sanctions for discovery abuse is solely within the sound discretion of the trial judge and will only be set aside upon a showing of clear abuse of discretion." (citing *Brantley v. Etter*, 677 S.W.2d 503, 504 (Tex. 1984) (per curiam))); *Chevron Phillips Chem. Co. LP v. Kingwood Crossroads, L.P.*, 346 S.W.3d 37, 74–78 (Tex. App.—Houston [14th Dist.] 2011, pet. denied) (holding that the trial court did not abuse its discretion in awarding attorney's fees as sanctions against a party that failed to produce all requested emails on a subject, violated an order regarding email discovery, and made known at the outset of the search for emails that it did not intend to comply fully with the discovery order); *Hagerman v. Wells Fargo*, No. 03-03-00769-CV, 2006 Tex. App. LEXIS 7559, at *32–33, 2006 WL 2448598 (Tex. App.—Austin Aug. 25, 2006, no pet.) (mem. op.) ("[T]he imposition of sanctions to compensate for the attorneys' fees of a party that has suffered delay as a result of the disobedient party's discovery abuse is expressly permitted by [Texas] Rule 215.2(b). In fact, subpart (b)(8) mandates that the court shall impose such monetary sanctions unless there are contrary reasons for not doing so.") (citation omitted).

for inspection or production is unreasonably frivolous, oppressive, or harassing, or that a response or answer is unreasonably frivolous or made for purposes of delay."[133] But, as indicated above, Texas Rule 215.3—unlike Texas Rule 215.2(b)—provides an *exclusive* list of the appropriate sanctions.[134]

14-4:2 A Trial Court's Inherent Power to Impose Sanctions

In addition to being able to impose the sanctions listed in Texas Rule 215, trial courts may impose sanctions pursuant to their inherent power to sanction abusive conduct.[135]

---

[133] Tex. R. Civ. P. 215.3; *see JNS Enter., Inc. v. Dixie Demolition, LLC*, 430 S.W.3d 444, 453 (Tex. App.—Austin 2013, no pet.) ("[Texas] Rule 215.3 authorizes a trial court to impose a variety of sanctions 'if the court finds a party is abusing the discovery process in seeking, making or resisting discovery.' . . . Producing false documents in discovery and then lying about those documents in deposition undoubtedly qualifies as an abuse—flagrant, in fact—of the discovery process, whose ultimate goal is, after all, a search for the truth." (quoting Tex. R. Civ. P. 215.3)).

[134] Texas Rule 215.3 lacks the nonexclusive "among others" language of Texas Rule 215.2(b) regarding available sanctions. Thus, the appropriate sanctions for the abuse of discovery in seeking, making, or resisting discovery as set forth in Texas Rule 215.3 are limited to those listed in Texas Rules 215.2(b)(1), (2), (3), (4), (5), and (8). *See Clone Component Distribs., Inc. v. State*, 819 S.W.2d 594, 597 (Tex. App.—Dallas 1991, no writ) ("Appropriate sanctions for abuse of discovery are specifically limited by [Texas] Rule 215(3). Any monetary sanctions available for abuse of discovery are limited to reasonable expenses, including attorney's fees, caused by the abuse."); *Owens-Corning Fiberglas Corp. v. Caldwell*, 807 S.W.2d 413, 415 (Tex. App.—Houston [1st Dist.] 1991, orig. proceeding) (holding that the predecessor to Texas Rule 215.3 limited sanctions and "does not contain the broad encompassing language 'such orders as are just'"). *But see Braden v. S. Main Bank*, 837 S.W.2d 733, 739–40 (Tex. App.—Houston [14th Dist.] 1992, writ denied) (holding that monetary fines are an appropriate sanction under Texas Rule 215.3).

[135] *E.g., In re Bennett*, 960 S.W.2d 35, 40 (Tex. 1997) ("A court has the inherent power to impose sanctions on its own motion in an appropriate case."); *Scarbrough v. Purser*, No. 03-13-00025-CV, 2016 Tex. App. LEXIS 13863, at *58–59, 2016 WL 7583546 (Tex. App.—Austin Dec. 30, 2016, pet. denied) (mem. op.) ("A trial court also has inherent power to sanction to the extent necessary to deter, alleviate, and counteract bad faith abuse of the judicial process."); *Union Carbide Corp. v. Martin*, 349 S.W.3d 137, 147–48 (Tex. App.—Dallas 2011, no pet.) (recognizing a trial court's ability to impose sanctions under Texas Rule 215 and its inherent powers); *Ezeoke v. Tracy*, 349 S.W.3d 679, 685 (Tex. App.—Houston [14th Dist.] 2011, no pet.) ("Trial courts have inherent power to impose sanctions for bad-faith abuse of the judicial process even when the targeted conduct is not expressly covered by a rule or statute."); *Prize Energy Res., L.P. v. Cliff Hoskins, Inc.*, 345 S.W.3d 537, 575 (Tex. App.—San Antonio 2011, no pet.) ("Prize and the Rutherfords were not required to specifically plead for monetary damages because '[c]ourts possess inherent powers to discipline attorney behavior through the imposition of sanctions sua sponte in appropriate cases.'" (quoting *Roberts v. Rose*, 37 S.W.3d 31, 33 (Tex. App.—San Antonio 2000, no pet.))); *Metzger v. Sebek*, 892 S.W.2d 20, 50–51 (Tex. App.—Houston [1st Dist.] 1994, writ denied) ("Trial courts also have inherent powers on which they may call to administer justice and preserve their dignity and integrity. This power includes the ability to sanction bad faith conduct that occurs during the course of litigation."); *Kutch v. Del Mar College*, 831 S.W.2d 398, 510 (Tex. App.—Corpus Christi 1992, no writ) ("The power to compel compliance with valid orders incident to the administration of justice is fundamental, and closely related to the core functions of the judiciary. We expressly recognize this power today. Consequently, we hold that Texas Courts have the inherent power to sanction for abuse of the judicial process which may not

But "[t]he scope of a trial court's discretion in this context is limited by the recognition that this power 'exists to the extent necessary to deter, alleviate, and counteract bad faith abuse of the judicial process, such as any significant interference with the traditional core functions of Texas courts.'"[136] Thus, "'for inherent power to apply, there must be some evidence and factual findings that the conduct complained of significantly interfered with the court's legitimate exercise of one of these powers.'"[137]

Texas courts have used their inherent power to impose monetary sanctions[138] and community-service requirements against attorneys.[139] The Texas Supreme Court also has recognized that, under certain circumstances, the production of attorney-work product may be an appropriate sanction for discovery abuse.[140]

---

be covered by rule or statute. This power includes the power to sanction appropriately for failure to comply with a valid court order incident to one of the core functions of the judiciary.").

136 *Ezeoke v. Tracy*, 349 S.W.3d 679, 685 (Tex. App.—Houston [14th Dist.] 2011, no pet.) (quoting *McWhorter v. Sheller*, 993 S.W.2d 781, 788–89 (Tex. App.—Houston [14th Dist.] 1999, pet. denied)).

137 *Stacey v. Shadd*, No. 03-20-00126-CV, 2020 Tex. App. LEXIS 10202, at *16 (Tex. App.—Austin Dec. 23, 2020, no pet.) (mem. op.) (holding that the trial court abused its discretion in granting discovery sanction in the absence of any evidence of discovery abuse); *Ezeoke v. Tracy*, 349 S.W.3d 679, 685 (Tex. App.—Houston [14th Dist.] 2011, no pet.) (quoting *McWhorter v. Sheller*, 993 S.W.2d 781, 788–89 (Tex. App.—Houston [14th Dist.] 1999, pet. denied)); *see Kutch v. Del Mar Coll.*, 831 S.W.2d 506, 510–11 (Tex. App.—Corpus Christi 1992, no writ) (holding "that trial courts have an inherent power to sanction for certain conduct which affects the core functions of the judiciary" and describing core functions as "hearing evidence, deciding issues of fact raised by the pleadings, deciding questions of law, entering final judgment and enforcing that judgment").

138 *Braden v. Downey*, 811 S.W.2d 922, 924 (Tex. 1991) (considering a sanctions order requiring a party to pay $10,000 to the party seeking discovery); *Ismail v. Ismail*, 702 S.W.2d 216, 224–25 (Tex. App.—Houston [1st Dist.] 1985, writ ref'd n.r.e.) (affirming monetary sanctions for failures to comply with a discovery order compelling the production of a sworn inventory in a divorce action). Monetary sanctions must be supported by the record. *See Hanley v. Hanley*, 813 S.W.2d 511, 521 (Tex. App.—Dallas 1991, no writ) (reversing order awarding monetary sanctions because the record did not reflect that it "was anything more than an arbitrary amount").

139 *Braden v. Downey*, 811 S.W.2d 922, 924 (Tex. 1991) (considering a sanctions order requiring an attorney to perform ten hours of community service); *Hill & Griffith Co. v. Bryant*, 139 S.W.3d 688, 697 (Tex. App.—Tyler 2004, pet. denied) (upholding a community-service sanction even though "as a general rule we do not view community service for discovery abuse with much favor"); *Cap Rock Elec. Co-op., Inc. v. Tex. Utils. Elec. Co.*, 874 S.W.2d 92, 97–98 (Tex. App.—El Paso 1994, no writ) (holding that the trial court did not abuse its discretion in ordering party to perform 200 hours of community service as a sanction for its violation of the trial court's order for discovery of documents); *Braden v. S. Main Bank*, 837 S.W.2d 733, 742–43 (Tex. App.—Houston [14th Dist.] 1992, writ denied) (affirming a sanctions order requiring an attorney to perform five hours of community service).

140 *Occidental Chem. Corp. v. Banales*, 907 S.W.2d 488, 490 (Tex. 1995) (per curiam) ("Even though [R]ule 215 of the Texas Rules of Civil Procedure does not expressly mention production of work product or other privileged documents as a sanction for discovery abuse, we cannot agree with OxyChem that the latter type of work product production can never be imposed as a sanction. Orders that privileged documents be produced must be an option for discovery abuse, if the court correctly finds the abuse has waived or otherwise invalidated the privilege.").

14-4:3 Spoliation

To remedy the spoliation of evidence, a trial court may impose any of the sanctions listed in Texas Rule 215.2(b) or "craft other remedies it deems appropriate in light of the particular facts of the individual case, including the submission of a spoliation instruction to the jury."[141] But as with other discovery sanctions, a spoliation sanction "must relate directly to the conduct giving rise to the sanction and may not be excessive."[142] Relying on federal precedent, the Texas Supreme Court set forth the following specific standards for spoliation sanctions:

> Upon finding that spoliation occurred, the trial court must exercise its discretion in imposing a remedy. In determining what remedy, if any, is appropriate, the court should weigh the spoliating party's culpability and the prejudice to the nonspoliating party. Prejudice is evaluated based on [(1)] the spoliated evidence's relevancy to key issues in the case, [(2)] whether the evidence would have been harmful to the spoliating party's case (or, conversely, helpful to the nonspoliating party's case), and [(3)] whether the spoliated evidence was cumulative of other competent evidence that may be used in its stead.[143]

---

141 *Brookshire Bros., Ltd. v. Aldridge*, 438 S.W.3d 9, 21 (Tex. 2014); *see Petroleum Sols., Inc. v. Head*, 454 S.W.3d 482, 488 (Tex. 2014) ("Upon finding that spoliation occurred, the trial court must exercise its discretion in imposing a remedy.").

142 *Brookshire Bros., Ltd. v. Aldridge*, 438 S.W.3d 9, 14 (Tex. 2014) ("Upon a finding of spoliation, the trial court has broad discretion to impose a remedy that, as with any discovery sanction, must be proportionate; that is, it must relate directly to the conduct giving rise to the sanction and may not be excessive."); *see Brookshire Bros., Ltd. v. Aldridge*, 438 S.W.3d 9, 21 (Tex. 2014) ("In accordance with our well-settled precedent on remedying discovery abuse, . . . the remedy must have a direct relationship to the act of spoliation and may not be excessive."); *In re Advanced Powder Sols., Inc.*, 496 S.W.3d 838, 853 (Tex. App.—Houston [1st Dist.] 2016, orig. proceeding) (providing that, "'[w]hile the trial court's discretion to remedy an act of spoliation is broad, it is not limitless'" and that courts must follow the two-part test for assessing whether the sanction imposed is just. (quoting *Petroleum Sols., Inc. v. Head*, 454 S.W.3d 482, 489 (Tex. 2014))); *In re J.H. Walker, Inc.*, No. 05-14-01497-CV, 2016 Tex. App. LEXIS 483, at *9, 2016 WL 819592 (Tex. App.—Dallas Jan. 15, 2016, orig. proceeding) (mem. op.) ("After the trial court determines a party spoliated evidence by breaching its duty to preserve such evidence, it may impose an appropriate remedy under Texas Rule of Civil Procedure 215.2, which includes striking the parties pleadings. The remedy, however, must have a direct relationship to the act of spoliation and may not be excessive.") (citation omitted). See also Chapter 14, section 14-3:1 (discussing limits on a trial court's discretion regarding discovery sanctions).

143 *Petroleum Sols., Inc. v. Head*, 454 S.W.3d 482, 488–89 (Tex. 2014) (citations omitted); *accord Brookshire Bros., Ltd. v. Aldridge*, 438 S.W.3d 9, 21–22 (Tex. 2014) (after adopting the three-factor test for evaluating prejudice to the nonspoliating party and noting that the test is "similar to the test followed by federal courts[,]" holding that "the remedy crafted by the trial court must be proportionate when weighing the culpability of the spoliating party and the prejudice to the nonspoliating party. . . . This logically follows from the remedial purpose undergirding the imposition of a spoliation remedy under Texas law, which is to restore the parties to a rough approximation of their positions if all evidence were available."); *In re Sw. Pub. Serv. Co.*, No. 13-19-00111-CV, 2020 Tex. App. LEXIS 10202, at *36, 2020 WL 1887762 (Tex. App.—Eastland Apr. 16, 2020,orig. proceeding) (mem. op.) ("The purpose of the sanction must be to impose an appropriate remedy so that the parties are restored to a rough approximation of what their positions would have been were the evidence available."); *Knoderer v. State Farm Lloyds*, 515 S.W.3d 21, 35 (Tex. App.—

As discussed in section 14-3:4.5 of this Chapter, an assessment of culpability entails determining whether the spoliating party acted negligently or intentionally. "Intentional" spoliation, which is often referred to as "bad faith" or "willful" spoliation, means "that the party acted with the subjective purpose of concealing or destroying discoverable evidence. This includes the concept of 'willful blindness,' which encompasses the scenario in which a party does not directly destroy evidence known to be relevant and discoverable, but nonetheless 'allows for its destruction.'"[144]

"In light of the difficulty of conducting a prejudice analysis based on evidence that is no longer available for review, . . . a party's intentional destruction of evidence may, '[a]bsent evidence to the contrary,' be sufficient by itself to support a finding that the spoliated evidence is both relevant and harmful to the spoliating party."[145] This finding "flows from the common-law spoliation presumption that all things are presumed against the wrongdoer."[146] On the other hand, "negligent spoliation [is not] enough to support such a finding without 'some proof about what the destroyed evidence

---

Texarkana 2017, pet. denied) ("If the trial court finds that spoliation has occurred, it must then determine the appropriate remedy. In determining the appropriate remedy, the trial court should consider 'both the culpability of the spoliating party and the prejudice to the other party. In evaluating prejudice, courts consider the relevance of the spoliated evidence to key issues in the case, the harmful effect of the evidence on the spoliating party's case (or, conversely, whether the evidence would have been helpful to the nonspoliating party's case), and whether the spoliated evidence was cumulative of other competent evidence that may be used instead of the spoliated evidence.'" (citations omitted) (quoting *Brookshire Bros., Ltd. v. Aldridge*, 438 S.W.3d 9, 21–22 (Tex. 2014), and *Smith v. Williams*, No. 06-14-00040-CV, 2015 Tex. App. LEXIS 5461, at *20, 2015 WL 3526089 (Tex. App.—Texarkana May 29, 2015, no pet.) (mem. op.))); *cf. Schmid v. Milwaukee Elec. Tool Corp.*, 13 F.3d 76, 79 (3d Cir. 1994) (holding that, in crafting a remedy for spoliation, a trial court should assess (1) the degree of fault of party who failed to preserve evidence, (2) the degree of prejudice suffered by the opposing party, and (3) whether there is a lesser sanction that will avoid substantial unfairness to the opposing party).

144 *Brookshire Bros., Ltd. v. Aldridge*, 438 S.W.3d 9, 24 (Tex. 2014) (quoting Andrew Hebl, *Spoliation of Electronically Stored Information, Good Faith, and Rule 37(e)*, 29 N. Ill. U.L. Rev. 79, 97–98 (2008)); *accord In re N. Hous. Pole Line, L.P.*, No. 09-19-00384-CV, 2020 Tex. App. LEXIS 196, at *8, 2020 WL 97579 (Tex. App.—Beaumont Jan. 9, 2020, no pet.) (mem. op.) ("A finding of bad-faith spoliation requires evidence that the party acted with the subjective purpose of concealing or destroying discoverable evidence."); *Scarbrough v. Purser*, No. 03-13-00025-CV, 2016 Tex. App. LEXIS 13863, at *49, 2016 WL 7583546 (Tex. App.—Austin Dec. 30, 2016, pet. denied) (mem. op.); *In re J.H. Walker, Inc.*, No. 05-14-01497-CV, 2016 Tex. App. LEXIS 483, at *9 (Tex. App.—Dallas Jan. 15, 2016, orig. proceeding) (mem. op.).

"The issue of willful blindness is especially acute in the context of automatic electronic deletion systems. A party with control over one of these systems who intentionally allows relevant information to be erased can hardly be said to have only negligently destroyed evidence. . . . " *Brookshire Bros., Ltd. v. Aldridge*, 438 S.W.3d 9, 25 n.17 (Tex. 2014). But the Texas Supreme Court has acknowledged "the complexities of these determinations when a potential litigant who controls massive volumes of electronic data is attempting to determine, prelitigation, which information is likely to be discoverable" and, thus, has suggested that leniency in the application of the standard may be warranted in certain cases. *Brookshire Bros., Ltd. v. Aldridge*, 438 S.W.3d 9, 25 n.17 (Tex. 2014).

145 *Brookshire Bros., Ltd. v. Aldridge*, 438 S.W.3d 9, 22 (Tex. 2014) (quoting *Trevino v. Ortega*, 969 S.W.2d 950, 958 (Tex. 1998) (Baker, J., concurring)).

146 *Brookshire Bros., Ltd. v. Aldridge*, 438 S.W.3d 9, 22 (Tex. 2014).

would show.'"[147] In any event, a trial court should "consider all evidence bearing on the factors associated with evaluating prejudice to the nonspoliating party."[148] The trial court should, however, "exercise caution in evaluating the final prejudice factor, which accounts for the existence of cumulative evidence[,]" and be cognizant of the fact that "difference[s] in kind and quality between the available evidence and the spoliated evidence will . . . be a key factor in analyzing prejudice to the nonspoliating party."[149]

The distinction between intentional versus negligent spoliation is critical in assessing whether a trial court may impose spoliation remedies that are akin to death-penalty sanctions, such as striking a party's claims or defenses or submitting "an instruction to the jury to presume that the missing evidence would have been unfavorable to the spoliator."[150] A trial court may impose such remedies "only if it finds (1) the spoliating party acted with intent to conceal discoverable evidence, or (2) the spoliating party acted negligently and caused the nonspoliating party to be irreparably deprived of any meaningful ability to present a claim or defense."[151]

---

[147] *Brookshire Bros., Ltd. v. Aldridge*, 438 S.W.3d 9, 22 (Tex. 2014) (quoting *Trevino v. Ortega*, 969 S.W.2d 950, 958 (Tex. 1998) (Baker, J., concurring)).

[148] *Brookshire Bros., Ltd. v. Aldridge*, 438 S.W.3d 9, 22 (Tex. 2014).

[149] *Brookshire Bros., Ltd. v. Aldridge*, 438 S.W.3d 9, 22 (Tex. 2014).

[150] *Brookshire Bros., Ltd. v. Aldridge*, 438 S.W.3d 9, 22 (Tex. 2014).

[151] *Petroleum Sols., Inc. v. Head*, 454 S.W.3d 482, 489 (Tex. 2014) (extending the holding in *Brookshire Bros., Ltd., v. Aldridge*, 438 S.W.3d 9, 23–26 (Tex. 2014), which applied specifically to spoliation instructions, to all "other remedies akin to death-penalty sanctions, such as striking a party's claims or defenses"); *see Wackenhut Corp. v. Gutierrez*, 453 S.W.3d 917, 921 (Tex. 2015) (per curiam) (applying *Brookshire Bros., Ltd. v. Aldridge*, 438 S.W.3d 9, 23–26 (Tex. 2014), and holding that the trial court abused its discretion by submitting a spoliation instruction to a jury, as the spoliation of evidence was at most negligent and did not deprive the nonspoliating party of a meaningful ability to present its claims "in light of the abundance of available evidence"); *Cire v. Cummings*, 134 S.W.3d 835, 841–42 (Tex. 2004) (affirming the striking of the plaintiff's pleadings in a legal-malpractice case because she deliberately destroyed dispositive evidence—audiotapes of recorded conversations with her former lawyers relating to key issues); *In re N. Hous. Pole Line, L.P.*, No. 09-19-00384-CV, 2020 Tex. App. LEXIS 196, at *7–8, 2020 WL 97579 (Tex. App.—Beaumont Jan. 9, 2020, no pet.) (mem. op.) ("A party's intentional destruction of evidence may, absent evidence to the contrary, be enough by itself to support a finding that the spoliated evidence is both relevant and harmful to the non-spoliating party, but negligent spoliation could not be enough to support such a finding without some proof about what the destroyed evidence would show."); *In re First Transit Inc.*, 499 S.W.3d 584, 596 n.3 (Tex. App.—Houston [14th Dist.] 2016, no pet.) ("Before a trial court may submit a spoliation instruction or impose a death-penalty sanction for spoliation, the trial court must find that (1) the spoliating party acted with intent to conceal discoverable evidence, or (2) the spoliating party acted negligently and caused the nonspoliating party to be irreparably deprived of any meaningful ability to present a claim or defense."); *Scarbrough v. Purser*, No. 03-13-00025-CV, 2016 Tex. App. LEXIS 13863, at *49, 2016 WL 7583546 (Tex. App.—Austin Dec. 30, 2016, pet. denied) (mem. op.) ("A spoliation instruction is an appropriate remedy when a party's spoliation of evidence is intentional."); *In re Advanced Powder Sols., Inc.*, 496 S.W.3d 838, 857 (Tex. App.—Houston [1st Dist.] 2016, orig. proceeding) ("Even if APS's spoliation qualifies as merely negligent and not intentional, it nonetheless deprived Hewitt of a meaningful opportunity to present his claims. The trial court had before it Baker's testimony, including 'some proof about what the destroyed evidence would show,' as required for a spoliation instruction based on negligent spoliation. Because APS has availed itself of the video in defending the case while depriving Hewitt of the right on a central element of the case—causation—

Texas case law addressing spoliation instructions has flourished since the Supreme Court's 2014 opinion in *Brookshire Brothers*.[152] And, in the fall of 2015, the State Bar of Texas Pattern Jury Charge Oversight Committee approved the following instruction on spoliation, "recommended for the adverse inference resulting from spoliation": "*[Name of spoliating party] [destroyed/failed to preserve/destroyed or failed to preserve] [describe evidence]*. You *[must/may]* consider that this evidence would have been unfavorable to *[name of spoliating party]* on the issue of *[describe issue(s) to which evidence would have been relevant]*."[153] In comments relating to the instruction, the

---

we hold that this case meets the 'narrow exception' allowing for a spoliation instruction for negligent spoliation." (quoting *Brookshire Bros., Ltd. v. Aldridge*, 438 S.W.3d 9, 22 (Tex. 2014))).

152 *Brookshire Bros., Ltd. v. Aldridge*, 438 S.W.3d 9 (Tex. 2014); *see, e.g., Wackenhut Corp. v. Gutierrez*, 453 S.W.3d 917, 918–22 (Tex. 2015) (per curiam); *Petroleum Sols., Inc. v. Head*, 454 S.W.3d 482, 488–89 (Tex. 2014); *In re N. Hous. Pole Line, L.P.*, No. 09-19-00384-CV, 2020 Tex. App. LEXIS 196, at *7–8, 2020 WL 97579 (Tex. App.—Beaumont Jan. 9, 2020, no pet.) (mem. op.); *Saavedra v. State*, No. 04-16-00747-CR, 2017 Tex. App. LEXIS 10950, at *13–15, 2017 WL 5615577 (Tex. App.—San Antonio Nov. 22, 2017, no pet.) (mem. op.); *Knoderer v. State Farm Lloyds*, 515 S.W.3d 21, 35 (Tex. App.—Texarkana 2017, pet. denied); *Scarbrough v. Purser*, No. 03-13-00025-CV, 2016 Tex. App. LEXIS 13863, at *48–58 (Tex. App.—Austin Dec. 30, 2016, pet. denied) (mem. op.); *Nat'l Sec. Fire & Cas. Co. v. Lampson*, No. 09-15-00299-CV, 2016 Tex. App. LEXIS 12766, at *33–35, 2016 WL 7018302 (Tex. App.—Beaumont Dec. 1, 2016, pet. denied) (mem. op.); *In re Advanced Powder Sols., Inc.*, 496 S.W.3d 838, 853–58 (Tex. App.—Houston [1st Dist.] 2016, orig. proceeding); *In re A.H.J.*, No. 05-15-00501-CV, 2015 Tex. App. LEXIS 10440, at *23–25, 2015 WL5866256 (Tex. App.—Dallas Oct. 8, 2015, pet. denied) (mem. op.); *Smith v. Williams*, No. 06-14-00040-CV, 2015 Tex. App. LEXIS 5461, at *18–37, 2015 WL 3526089 (Tex. App.—Texarkana May 29, 2015, no pet.) (mem. op.); *Telesis/Parkwood Ret. I, Ltd. v. Anderson*, 462 S.W.3d 212, 251–55 (Tex. App.—El Paso 2015, no pet.); *Nat'l Lloyds Ins. Co. v. Lewis*, No. 09-13-00413-CV, 2015 Tex. App. LEXIS 1635, at *37–39, 2015 WL 690807 (Tex. App.—Beaumont Feb. 19, 2015, pet. denied) (mem. op.); *Flagstar Bank, FSB v. Walker*, 451 S.W.3d 490, 506–07 (Tex. App.—Dallas 2014, no pet.).

153 *See* Comm. On Pattern Jury Charges, State Bar of Tex., Texas Pattern Jury Charges—Family & Probate, PJC 200.12 cmt. (Instruction on Spoliation) (2020). The comments to the instruction explain the "must/may" alternative as follows:

> In *Brookshire Bros.*, [*Ltd. v. Aldridge*, 438 S.W.3d 9 (Tex. 2014),] the majority does not articulate the specific language that should be included in the instruction, particularly whether the jury "may" or "must" consider that the missing evidence would have been unfavorable to the spoliator. The dissent in *Brookshire Bros.* interpreted the majority as requiring the use of the term *must*. *Brookshire Bros., [Ltd. v. Aldridge*, 438 S.W.3d 9, 34 (Tex. 2014)]. The overarching guideline, as with any sanction, remains proportionality. "Upon a finding of spoliation, the trial court has broad discretion to impose a remedy that, as with any discovery sanction, must be proportionate; that is, it must relate directly to the conduct giving rise to the sanction and may not be excessive." *Brookshire Bros., [Ltd. v. Aldridge*, 438 S.W.3d 9, 14 (Tex. 2014)]. Whether *may* or *must* is used should be based on the facts applied to the standards articulated above.

PJC 200.12 cmt. The spoliation instruction and comment now appear in other parts of the Pattern Jury Charge. *E.g.*, Texas Pattern Jury Charges—General Negligence & Intentional and Personal Torts, PJC 1.13, (Instruction on Spoliation) (2021); Texas Pattern Jury Charges—Malpractice, Premises & Products, PJC 40.13, (Instruction on Spoliation) (2018); Texas Pattern Jury Charges—Business, Consumer, Insurance & Employment, PJC 100.13, (Instruction on Spoliation); Texas Pattern Jury Charges—Oil & Gas, PJC 300.13, committee attributed the ambiguous "must/may" option to a lack of sufficient guidance in *Brookshire Brothers* as to the language that should be used and asserted that, "[w]hether *may* or *must* is used should be based on the facts applied to the standards articulated" elsewhere in the comments.[154]

(Instruction on Spoliation).

154 *See* Texas Pattern Jury Charges—Family & Probate, PJC 200.12 cmt. (Instruction on Spoliation) (2020).

APPENDIX 1

FORMER TEXAS DISCOVERY RULES EFFECTIVE PRIOR TO JANUARY 1, 2021 AMENDMENTS

RULE 190. DISCOVERY LIMITATIONS

190.1. Discovery Control Plan Required

Every case must be governed by a discovery control plan as provided in this Rule. A plaintiff must allege in the first numbered paragraph of the original petition whether discovery is intended to be conducted under Level 1, 2, or 3 of this Rule.

190.2. Discovery Control Plan—Expedited Actions and Divorces Involving $50,000 or Less (Level 1)

(a) **Application.** This subdivision applies to:

(1) any suit that is governed by the expedited actions process in Rule 169; and

(2) unless the parties agree that Rule 190.3 should apply or the court orders a discovery control plan under Rule 190.4, any suit for divorce not involving children in which a party pleads that the value of the marital estate is more than zero but not more than $ 50,000.

(b) **Limitations.** Discovery is subject to the limitations provided elsewhere in these rules and to the following additional limitations:

(1) **Discovery period.** All discovery must be conducted during the discovery period, which begins when the suit is filed and continues until 180 days after the date the first request for discovery of any kind is served on a party.

(2) **Total time for oral depositions.** Each party may have no more than six hours in total to examine and cross-examine all witnesses in oral depositions. The parties may agree to expand this limit up to 10 hours in total, but not more except by court order. The court may modify the deposition hours so that no party is given unfair advantage.

(3) **Interrogatories.** Any party may serve on any other party no more than 15 written interrogatories, excluding interrogatories asking a party only to identify or authenticate specific documents. Each discrete subpart of an interrogatory is considered a separate interrogatory.

(4) **Requests for production.** Any party may serve on any other party no more than 15 written requests for production. Each discrete subpart of a request for production is considered a separate request for production.

(5) **Requests for admissions.** Any party may serve on any other party no more than 15 written requests for admissions. Each discrete subpart of a request for admission is considered a separate request for admission.

(6) **Requests for disclosure.** In addition to the content subject to disclosure under Rule 194.2, a party may request disclosure of all documents, electronic information, and tangible items that the disclosing party has in its possession, custody, or control and may use to support its claims or defenses. A request for disclosure made pursuant to this paragraph is not considered a request for production.

(c) **Reopening discovery.** If a suit is removed from the expedited actions process in Rule 169 or, in a divorce, the filing of a pleading renders this subdivision no longer applicable, the discovery period reopens, and discovery must be completed within the limitations provided in Rules 190.3 or 190.4, whichever is applicable. Any person previously deposed may be redeposed. On motion of any party, the court should continue the trial date if necessary to permit completion of discovery.

190.3. Discovery Control Plan—By Rule (Level 2)

(a) **Application.** Unless a suit is governed by a discovery control plan under Rules 190.2 or 190.4, discovery must be conducted in accordance with this subdivision.

(b) **Limitations.** Discovery is subject to the limitations provided elsewhere in these rules and to the following additional limitations:

(1) **Discovery period.** All discovery must be conducted during the discovery period, which begins when suit is filed and continues until:

(A) 30 days before the date set for trial, in cases under the Family Code;

(B) in other cases, the earlier of

(i) 30 days before the date set for trial, or

(ii) nine months after the earlier of the date of the first oral deposition or the due date of the first response to written discovery.

(2) **Total time for oral depositions.** Each side may have no more than 50 hours in oral depositions to examine and cross-examine parties on the opposing side, experts designated by those parties, and persons who are subject to those parties' control. "Side" refers to all the litigants with generally common interests in the litigation. If one side designates more than two experts, the opposing side may have an additional six hours of total deposition time for each additional expert designated. The court may modify the deposition hours and must do so when a side or party would be given unfair advantage.

(3) **Interrogatories.** Any party may serve on any other party no more than 25 written interrogatories, excluding interrogatories asking a party only to identify or authenticate specific documents. Each discrete subpart of an interrogatory is considered a separate interrogatory.

190.4. Discovery Control Plan—By Order (Level 3)

(a) **Application.** The court must, on a party's motion, and may, on its own initiative, order that discovery be conducted in accordance with a discovery control plan tailored to the circumstances of the specific suit. The parties may submit an agreed order to the court for its consideration. The court should act on a party's motion or agreed order under this subdivision as promptly as reasonably possible.

(b) **Limitations.** The discovery control plan ordered by the court may address any issue concerning discovery or the matters listed in Rule 166, and may change any limitation on the time for or amount of discovery set forth in these rules. The discovery limitations of Rule 190.2, if applicable, or otherwise of Rule 190.3 apply unless specifically changed in the discovery control plan ordered by the court. The plan must include:

(1) a date for trial or for a conference to determine a trial setting;

(2) a discovery period during which either all discovery must be conducted or all discovery requests must be sent, for the entire case or an appropriate phase of it;

(3) appropriate limits on the amount of discovery; and

(4) deadlines for joining additional parties, amending or supplementing pleadings, and designating expert witnesses.

190.5. Modification of Discovery Control Plan

The court may modify a discovery control plan at any time and must do so when the interest of justice requires. Unless a suit is governed by the expedited actions process in Rule 169, the court must allow additional discovery:

(a) related to new, amended or supplemental pleadings, or new information disclosed in a discovery response or in an amended or supplemental response, if:

(1) the pleadings or responses were made after the deadline for completion of discovery or so nearly before that deadline that an adverse party does not have an adequate opportunity to conduct discovery related to the new matters, and

(2) the adverse party would be unfairly prejudiced without such additional discovery;

(b) regarding matters that have changed materially after the discovery cutoff if trial is set or postponed so that the trial date is more than three months after the discovery period ends.

190.6. Certain Types of Discovery Excepted

This rule's limitations on discovery do not apply to or include discovery conducted under Rule 202 ("Depositions Before Suit or to Investigate Claims"), or Rule 621a ("Discovery and Enforcement of Judgment"). But Rule 202 cannot be used to circumvent the limitations of this rule.

RULE 191. MODIFYING DISCOVERY PROCEDURES AND LIMITATIONS; CONFERENCE REQUIREMENT; SIGNING DISCLOSURES, DISCOVERY REQUESTS, RESPONSES, AND OBJECTIONS; FILING REQUIREMENTS

191.1. Modification of Procedures

Except where specifically prohibited, the procedures and limitations set forth in the rules pertaining to discovery may be modified in any suit by the agreement of the parties or by court order for good cause. An agreement of the parties is enforceable if it complies with Rule 11 or, as it affects an oral deposition, if it is made a part of the record of the deposition.

191.2. Conference

Parties and their attorneys are expected to cooperate in discovery and to make any agreements reasonably necessary for the efficient disposition of the case. All discovery motions or requests for hearings relating to discovery must contain a certificate by the party filing the motion or request that a reasonable effort has been made to resolve the dispute without the necessity of court intervention and the effort failed.

191.3. Signing of Disclosures, Discovery Requests, Notices, Responses, and Objections

(a) **Signature required.** Every disclosure, discovery request, notice, response, and objection must be signed:

(1) by an attorney, if the party is represented by an attorney, and must show the attorney's State Bar of Texas identification number, address, telephone number, and fax number, if any; or

(2) by the party, if the party is not represented by an attorney, and must show the party's address, telephone number, and fax number, if any.

(b) **Effect of signature on disclosure.** The signature of an attorney or party on a disclosure constitutes a certification that to the best of the signer's knowledge, information, and belief, formed after a reasonable inquiry, the disclosure is complete and correct as of the time it is made.

(c) **Effect of signature on discovery request, notice, response, or objection.** The signature of an attorney or party on a discovery request, notice, response, or objection constitutes a certification that to the best of the signer's knowledge, information, and belief, formed after a reasonable inquiry, the request, notice, response, or objection:

(1) is consistent with the rules of civil procedure and these discovery rules and warranted by existing law or a good faith argument for the extension, modification, or reversal of existing law;

(2) has a good faith factual basis;

(3) is not interposed for any improper purpose, such as to harass or to cause unnecessary delay or needless increase in the cost of litigation; and

(4) is not unreasonable or unduly burdensome or expensive, given the needs of the case, the discovery already had in the case, the amount in controversy, and the importance of the issues at stake in the litigation.

(d) **Effect of failure to sign.** If a request, notice, response, or objection is not signed, it must be stricken unless it is signed promptly after the omission is called to the attention of the party making the request, notice, response, or objection. A party is not required to take any action with respect to a request or notice that is not signed.

(e) **Sanctions.** If the certification is false without substantial justification, the court may, upon motion or its own initiative, impose on the person who made the certification, or the party on whose behalf the request, notice, response, or objection was made, or both, an appropriate sanction as for a frivolous pleading or motion under Chapter 10 of the Civil Practice and Remedies Code.

191.4. Filing of Discovery Materials

(a) **Discovery materials not to be filed.** The following discovery materials must not be filed:

(1) discovery requests, deposition notices, and subpoenas required to be served only on parties;

(2) responses and objections to discovery requests and deposition notices, regardless on whom the requests or notices were served;

(3) documents and tangible things produced in discovery; and

(4) statements prepared in compliance with Rule 193.3(b) or (d).

(b) **Discovery materials to be filed.** The following discovery materials must be filed:

(1) discovery requests, deposition notices, and subpoenas required to be served on nonparties;

(2) motions and responses to motions pertaining to discovery matters; and

(3) agreements concerning discovery matters, to the extent necessary to comply with Rule 11.

(c) **Exceptions.** Notwithstanding paragraph (a)

(1) the court may order discovery materials to be filed;

(2) a person may file discovery materials in support of or in opposition to a motion or for other use in a court proceeding; and

(3) a person may file discovery materials necessary for a proceeding in an appellate court.

(d) **Retention requirement for persons.** Any person required to serve discovery materials not required to be filed must retain the original or exact copy of the materials during the pendency of the case and any related appellate proceedings begun within six months after judgment is signed, unless otherwise provided by the trial court.

(e) **Retention requirement for courts.** The clerk of the court shall retain and dispose of deposition transcripts and depositions upon written questions as directed by the Supreme Court.

191.5. Service of Discovery Materials

Every disclosure, discovery request, notice, response, and objection required to be served on a party or person must be served on all parties of record.

RULE 192. PERMISSIBLE DISCOVERY: FORMS AND SCOPE; WORK PRODUCT: PROTECTIVE ORDERS; DEFINITIONS

192.1. Forms of Discovery

Permissible forms of discovery are:

(a) requests for disclosure;

(b) requests for production and inspection of documents and tangible things;

(c) requests and motions for entry upon and examination of real property;

(d) interrogatories to a party;

(e) requests for admission;

(f) oral or written depositions; and

(g) motions for mental or physical examinations.

192.2. Sequence of Discovery

The permissible forms of discovery may be combined in the same document and may be taken in any order or sequence.

192.3. Scope of Discovery

(a) **Generally.** In general, a party may obtain discovery regarding any matter that is not privileged and is relevant to the subject matter of the pending action, whether it relates to the claim or defense of the party seeking discovery or the claim or defense of any other party. It is not a ground for objection that the information sought will be inadmissible at trial if the information sought appears reasonably calculated to lead to the discovery of admissible evidence.

(b) **Documents and tangible things.** A party may obtain discovery of the existence, description, nature, custody, condition, location, and contents of documents and tangible things (including papers, books, accounts, drawings, graphs, charts, photographs, electronic or videotape recordings, data, and data compilations) that constitute or contain matters relevant to the subject matter of the action. A person is required to produce a document or tangible thing that is within the person's possession, custody, or control.

(c) **Persons with knowledge of relevant facts.** A party may obtain discovery of the name, address, and telephone number of persons having knowledge of relevant facts, and a brief statement of each identified person's connection with the case. A person has knowledge of relevant facts when that person has or may have knowledge of any discoverable matter. The person need not have admissible information or personal knowledge of the facts. An expert is "a person with knowledge of relevant facts" only if that knowledge was obtained first-hand or if it was not obtained in preparation for trial or in anticipation of litigation.

(d) **Trial witnesses.** A party may obtain discovery of the name, address, and telephone number of any person who is expected to be called to testify at trial. This paragraph does not apply to rebuttal or impeaching witnesses the necessity of whose testimony cannot reasonably be anticipated before trial.

(e) **Testifying and consulting experts.** The identity, mental impressions, and opinions of a consulting expert whose mental impressions and opinions have not been reviewed by a testifying expert are not discoverable. A party may discover the following information regarding a testifying expert or regarding a consulting expert whose mental impressions or opinions have been reviewed by a testifying expert:

(1) the expert's name, address, and telephone number;

(2) the subject matter on which a testifying expert will testify;

(3) the facts known by the expert that relate to or form the basis of the expert's mental impressions and opinions formed or made in connection with the case in which the discovery is sought, regardless of when and how the factual information was acquired;

(4) the expert's mental impressions and opinions formed or made in connection with the case in which discovery is sought, and any methods used to derive them;

(5) any bias of the witness;

(6) all documents, tangible things, reports, models, or data compilations that have been provided to, reviewed by, or prepared by or for the expert in anticipation of a testifying expert's testimony;

(7) the expert's current resume and bibliography.

(f) **Indemnity and insuring agreements.** Except as otherwise provided by law, a party may obtain discovery of the existence and contents of any indemnity or insurance agreement under which any person may be liable to satisfy part or all of a judgment rendered in the action or to indemnify or reimburse for payments made to satisfy the judgment. Information concerning the indemnity or insurance agreement is not by reason of disclosure admissible in evidence at trial.

(g) **Settlement agreements.** A party may obtain discovery of the existence and contents of any relevant portions of a settlement agreement. Information concerning a settlement agreement is not by reason of disclosure admissible in evidence at trial.

(h) **Statements of persons with knowledge of relevant facts.** A party may obtain discovery of the statement of any person with knowledge of relevant facts—a "witness statement"—regardless of when the statement was made. A witness statement is (1) a written statement signed or otherwise adopted or approved in writing by the person making it, or (2) a stenographic, mechanical, electrical, or other type of recording of a witness's oral statement, or any substantially verbatim transcription of such a recording. Notes taken during a conversation or interview with a witness are not a witness statement. Any person may obtain, upon written request, his or her own statement concerning the lawsuit, which is in the possession, custody or control of any party.

(i) **Potential parties.** A party may obtain discovery of the name, address, and telephone number of any potential party.

(j) **Contentions.** A party may obtain discovery of any other party's legal contentions and the factual bases for those contentions.

192.4. Limitations on Scope of Discovery

The discovery methods permitted by these rules should be limited by the court if it determines, on motion or on its own initiative and on reasonable notice, that:

(a) the discovery sought is unreasonably cumulative or duplicative, or is obtainable from some other source that is more convenient, less burdensome, or less expensive; or

(b) the burden or expense of the proposed discovery outweighs its likely benefit, taking into account the needs of the case, the amount in controversy, the parties' resources, the importance of the issues at stake in the litigation, and the importance of the proposed discovery in resolving the issues.

192.5. Work Product

(a) **Work product defined.** Work product comprises:

(1) material prepared or mental impressions developed in anticipation of litigation or for trial by or for a party or a party's representatives, including the party's attorneys, consultants, sureties, indemnitors, insurers, employees, or agents; or

(2) a communication made in anticipation of litigation or for trial between a party and the party's representatives or among a party's representatives, including the party's attorneys, consultants, sureties, indemnitors, insurers, employees, or agents.

(b) **Protection of work product**

(1) **Protection of core work product—attorney mental processes.** Core work product—the work product of an attorney or an attorney's representative that contains the attorney's or the attorney's representative's mental impressions, opinions, conclusions, or legal theories—is not discoverable.

(2) **Protection of other work product.** Any other work product is discoverable only upon a showing that the party seeking discovery has substantial need of the materials in the preparation of the party's case and that the party is unable without undue hardship to obtain the substantial equivalent of the material by other means.

(3) **Incidental disclosure of attorney mental processes.** It is not a violation of subparagraph (1) if disclosure ordered pursuant to subparagraph (2) incidentally discloses by inference attorney mental processes otherwise protected under subparagraph (1).

(4) **Limiting disclosure of mental processes.** If a court orders discovery of work product pursuant to subparagraph (2), the court must—insofar as possible— protect against disclosure of the mental impressions, opinions, conclusions, or legal theories not otherwise discoverable.

(c) **Exceptions.** Even if made or prepared in anticipation of litigation or for trial, the following is not work product protected from discovery:

(1) information discoverable under Rule 192.3 concerning experts, trial witnesses, witness statements, and contentions;

(2) trial exhibits ordered disclosed under Rule 166 or Rule 190.4;

(3) the name, address, and telephone number of any potential party or any person with knowledge of relevant facts;

(4) any photograph or electronic image of underlying facts (e.g., a photograph of the accident scene) or a photograph or electronic image of any sort that a party intends to offer into evidence; and

(5) any work product created under circumstances within an exception to the attorney-client privilege in Rule 503(d) of the Rules of Evidence.

(d) **Privilege.** For purposes of these rules, an assertion that material or information is work product is an assertion of privilege.

192.6. Protective Orders

(a) **Motion.** A person from whom discovery is sought, and any other person affected by the discovery request, may move within the time permitted for response to the discovery request for an order protecting that person from the discovery sought. A person should not move for protection when an objection to written discovery or an assertion of privilege is appropriate, but a motion does not waive the objection or assertion of privilege. If a person seeks protection regarding the time or place of discovery, the person must state a reasonable time and place for discovery with which the person will comply. A person must comply with a request to the extent protection is not sought unless it is unreasonable under the circumstances to do so before obtaining a ruling on the motion.

(b) **Order.** To protect the movant from undue burden, unnecessary expense, harassment, annoyance, or invasion of personal, constitutional, or property rights, the court may make any order in the interest of justice and may—among other things—order that:

(1) the requested discovery not be sought in whole or in part;

(2) the extent or subject matter of discovery be limited;

(3) the discovery not be undertaken at the time or place specified;

(4) the discovery be undertaken only by such method or upon such terms and conditions or at the time and place directed by the court;

(5) the results of discovery be sealed or otherwise protected, subject to the provisions of Rule 76a.

192.7. Definitions

As used in these rules

(a) *Written discovery* means requests for disclosure, requests for production and inspection of documents and tangible things, requests for entry onto property, interrogatories, and requests for admission.

(b) *Possession, custody, or control* of an item means that the person either has physical possession of the item or has a right to possession of the item that is equal or superior to the person who has physical possession of the item.

(c) A *testifying expert* is an expert who may be called to testify as an expert witness at trial.

(d) A *consulting expert* is an expert who has been consulted, retained, or specially employed by a party in anticipation of litigation or in preparation for trial, but who is not a testifying expert.

RULE 193. WRITTEN DISCOVERY: RESPONSE; OBJECTION; ASSERTION OF PRIVILEGE; SUPPLEMENTATION AND AMENDMENT; FAILURE TO TIMELY RESPOND; PRESUMPTION OF AUTHENTICITY

193.1. Responding to Written Discovery; Duty to Make Complete Response

A party must respond to written discovery in writing within the time provided by court order or these rules. When responding to written discovery, a party must make a complete response, based on all information reasonably available to the responding party or its attorney at the time the response is made. The responding party's answers, objections, and other responses must be preceded by the request to which they apply.

193.2. Objecting to Written Discovery

(a) **Form and time for objections.** A party must make any objection to written discovery in writing—either in the response or in a separate document—within the time for response. The party must state specifically the legal or factual basis for the objection and the extent to which the party is refusing to comply with the request.

(b) **Duty to respond when partially objecting; objection to time or place of production.** A party must comply with as much of the request to which the party has made no objection unless it is unreasonable under the circumstances to do so before obtaining a ruling on the objection. If the responding party objects to the requested time or place of production, the responding party must state a reasonable time and place for complying with the request and must comply at that time and place without further request or order.

(c) **Good faith basis for objection.** A party may object to written discovery only if a good faith factual and legal basis for the objection exists at the time the objection is made.

(d) **Amendment.** An objection or response to written discovery may be amended or supplemented to state an objection or basis that, at the time the objection or response initially was made, either was inapplicable or was unknown after reasonable inquiry.

(e) **Waiver of objection.** An objection that is not made within the time required, or that is obscured by numerous unfounded objections, is waived unless the court excuses the waiver for good cause shown.

(f) **No objection to preserve privilege.** A party should not object to a request for written discovery on the grounds that it calls for production of material or information that is privileged but should instead comply with Rule 193.3. A party who objects to production of privileged material or information does not waive the privilege but must comply with Rule 193.3 when the error is pointed out.

193.3. Asserting a Privilege

A party may preserve a privilege from written discovery in accordance with this subdivision.

(a) **Withholding privileged material or information.** A party who claims that material or information responsive to written discovery is privileged may withhold the privileged material or information from the response. The party must state—in the response (or an amended or supplemental response) or in a separate document—that:

(1) information or material responsive to the request has been withheld,

(2) the request to which the information or material relates, and

(3) the privilege or privileges asserted.

(b) **Description of withheld material or information.** After receiving a response indicating that material or information has been withheld from production, the party seeking discovery may serve a written request that the withholding party identify the information and material withheld. Within 15 days of service of that request, the withholding party must serve a response that:

(1) describes the information or materials withheld that, without revealing the privileged information itself or otherwise waiving the privilege, enables other parties to assess the applicability of the privilege, and

(2) asserts a specific privilege for each item or group of items withheld.

(c) **Exemption.** Without complying with paragraphs (a) and (b), a party may withhold a privileged communication to or from a lawyer or lawyer's representative or a privileged document of a lawyer or lawyer's representative

(1) created or made from the point at which a party consults a lawyer with a view to obtaining professional legal services from the lawyer in the prosecution or defense of a specific claim in the litigation in which discovery is requested, and

(2) concerning the litigation in which the discovery is requested.

(d) **Privilege not waived by production.** A party who produces material or information without intending to waive a claim of privilege does not waive that claim under these rules or the Rules of Evidence if—within 10 days or a shorter time ordered by the court, after the producing party actually discovers that such production was made—the producing party amends the response, identifying the material or information produced and stating the privilege asserted. If the producing party thus amends the response to assert a privilege, the requesting party must promptly return the specified material or information and any copies pending any ruling by the court denying the privilege.

193.4. Hearing and Ruling on Objections and Assertions of Privilege

(a) **Hearing.** Any party may at any reasonable time request a hearing on an objection or claim of privilege asserted under this rule. The party making the objection or asserting the privilege must present any evidence necessary to support the objection or privilege. The evidence may be testimony presented at the hearing or affidavits served at least seven days before the hearing or at such other reasonable time as the court permits. If the court determines that an *in camera* review of some or all of the requested discovery is necessary, that material or information must be segregated and produced to the court in a sealed wrapper within a reasonable time following the hearing.

(b) **Ruling.** To the extent the court sustains the objection or claim of privilege, the responding party has no further duty to respond to that request. To the extent the court overrules the objection or claim of privilege, the responding party must produce the requested material or information within 30 days after the court's ruling or at such time as the court orders. A party need not request a ruling on that party's own objection or assertion of privilege to preserve the objection or privilege.

(c) **Use of material or information withheld under claim of privilege.** A party may not use—at any hearing or trial—material or information withheld from discovery under a claim of privilege, including a claim sustained by the court, without timely amending or supplementing the party's response to that discovery.

193.5. Amending or Supplementing Responses to Written Discovery

(a) **Duty to amend or supplement.** If a party learns that the party's response to written discovery was incomplete or incorrect when made, or, although complete and correct when made, is no longer complete and correct, the party must amend or supplement the response:

(1) to the extent that the written discovery sought the identification of persons with knowledge of relevant facts, trial witnesses, or expert witnesses, and

(2) to the extent that the written discovery sought other information, unless the additional or corrective information has been made known to the other parties in writing, on the record at a deposition, or through other discovery responses.

(b) **Time and form of amended or supplemental response.** An amended or supplemental response must be made reasonably promptly after the party discovers the necessity for such a response. Except as otherwise provided by these rules, it is presumed that an amended or supplemental response made less than 30 days before trial was not made reasonably promptly. An amended or supplemental response must be in the same form as the initial response and must be verified by the party if the original response was required to be verified by the party, but the failure to comply with this requirement does not make the amended or supplemental response untimely unless the party making the response refuses to correct the defect within a reasonable time after it is pointed out.

193.6. Failing to Timely Respond—Effect on Trial

(a) **Exclusion of evidence and exceptions.** A party who fails to make, amend, or supplement a discovery response in a timely manner may not introduce in evidence the material or information that was not timely disclosed, or offer the testimony of witness (other than a named party) who was not timely identified, unless the court finds that:

(1) there was good cause for the failure to timely make, amend, or supplement the discovery response; or

(2) the failure to timely make, amend, or supplement the discovery response will not unfairly surprise or unfairly prejudice the other parties.

(b) **Burden of establishing exception.** The burden of establishing good cause or the lack of unfair surprise or unfair prejudice is on the party seeking to introduce the evidence or call the witness. A finding of good cause or of the lack of unfair surprise or unfair prejudice must be supported by the record.

(c) **Continuance.** Even if the party seeking to introduce the evidence or call the witness fails to carry the burden under paragraph (b), the court may grant a continuance or temporarily postpone the trial to allow a response to be made, amended, or supplemented, and to allow opposing parties to conduct discovery regarding any new information presented by that response.

193.7. Production of Documents Self-Authenticating

A party's production of a document in response to written discovery authenticates the document for use against that party in any pretrial proceeding or at trial unless—within 10 days or a longer or shorter time ordered by the court, after the producing party has actual notice that the document will be used—the party objects to the authenticity of the document, or any part of it, stating the specific basis for objection. An objection must be either on the record or in writing and must have a good faith factual and legal basis. An objection made to the authenticity of only part of a document does not affect the authenticity of the remainder. If objection is made, the party attempting to use the document should be given a reasonable opportunity to establish its authenticity.

RULE 194. REQUESTS FOR DISCLOSURE

194.1. Request

A party may obtain disclosure from another party of the information or material listed in Rule 194.2 by serving the other party—no later than 30 days before the end of any applicable discovery period—the following request: "Pursuant to Rule 194, you are requested to disclose, within 30 days of service of this request, the information or material described in Rule [state rule, *e.g.*, 194.2, or 194.2(a), (c), and (f), or 194.2(d)—(g)]."

194.2. Content

A party may request disclosure of any or all of the following:

(a) the correct names of the parties to the lawsuit;

(b) the name, address, and telephone number of any potential parties;

(c) the legal theories and, in general, the factual bases of the responding party's claims or defenses (the responding party need not marshal all evidence that may be offered at trial);

(d) the amount and any method of calculating economic damages;

(e) the name, address, and telephone number of persons having knowledge of relevant facts, and a brief statement of each identified person's connection with the case;

(f) for any testifying expert:

(1) the expert's name, address, and telephone number;

(2) the subject matter on which the expert will testify;

(3) the general substance of the expert's mental impressions and opinions and a brief summary of the basis for them, or if the expert is not retained by, employed by, or otherwise subject to the control of the responding party, documents reflecting such information;

(4) if the expert is retained by, employed by, or otherwise subject to the control of the responding party:

(A) all documents, tangible things, reports, models, or data compilations that have been provided to, reviewed by, or prepared by or for the expert in anticipation of the expert's testimony; and

(B) the expert's current resume and bibliography;

(g) any indemnity and insuring agreements described in Rule 192.3(f);

(h) any settlement agreements described in Rule 192.3(g);

(i) any witness statements described in Rule 192.3(h);

(j) in a suit alleging physical or mental injury and damages from the occurrence that is the subject of the case, all medical records and bills that are reasonably related to the injuries or damages asserted or, in lieu thereof, an authorization permitting the disclosure of such medical records and bills;

(k) in a suit alleging physical or mental injury and damages from the occurrence that is the subject of the case, all medical records and bills obtained by the responding party by virtue of an authorization furnished by the requesting party;

(l) the name, address, and telephone number of any person who may be designated as a responsible third party.

194.3. Response

The responding party must serve a written response on the requesting party within 30 days after service of the request, except that:

(a) a defendant served with a request before the defendant's answer is due need not respond until 50 days after service of the request, and

(b) a response to a request under Rule 194.2(f) is governed by Rule 195.

194.4. Production

Copies of documents and other tangible items ordinarily must be served with the response. But if the responsive documents are voluminous, the response must state a reasonable time and place for the production of documents. The responding party must produce the documents at the time and place stated, unless otherwise agreed by the parties or ordered by the court, and must provide the requesting party a reasonable opportunity to inspect them.

194.5. No Objection or Assertion of Work Product

No objection or assertion of work product is permitted to a request under this rule.

194.6. Certain Responses Not Admissible

A response to requests under Rule 194.2(c) and (d) that has been changed by an amended or supplemental response is not admissible and may not be used for impeachment.

RULE 195. DISCOVERY REGARDING TESTIFYING EXPERT WITNESSES

195.1 Permissible Discovery Tools

A party may request another party to designate and disclose information concerning testifying expert witnesses only through a request for disclosure under Rule 194 and through depositions and reports as permitted by this rule.

195.2 Schedule for Designating Experts

Unless otherwise ordered by the court, a party must designate experts—that is, furnish information requested under Rule 194.2(f)—by the later of the following two dates: 30 days after the request is served, or—

(a) with regard to all experts testifying for a party seeking affirmative relief, 90 days before the end of the discovery period;

(b) with regard to all other experts, 60 days before the end of the discovery period.

195.3 Scheduling Depositions

(a) **Experts for party seeking affirmative relief.** A party seeking affirmative relief must make an expert retained by, employed by, or otherwise in the control of the party available for deposition as follows:

(1) **If no report furnished.** If a report of the expert's factual observations, tests, supporting data, calculations, photographs, and opinions is not produced when the expert is designated, then the party must make the expert available for deposition reasonably promptly after the expert is designated. If the deposition cannot—due to the actions of the tendering party—reasonably be concluded more than 15 days before the deadline for designating other experts, that deadline must be extended for other experts testifying on the same subject.

(2) **If report furnished.** If a report of the expert's factual observations, tests, supporting data, calculations, photographs, and opinions is produced when the expert is designated, then the party need not make the expert available for deposition until reasonably promptly after all other experts have been designated.

(b) **Other experts.** A party not seeking affirmative relief must make an expert retained by, employed by, or otherwise in the control of the party available for deposition reasonably promptly after the expert is designated and the experts testifying on the same subject for the party seeking affirmative relief have been deposed.

195.4 Oral Deposition

In addition to disclosure under Rule 194, a party may obtain discovery concerning the subject matter on which the expert is expected to testify, the expert's mental impressions and opinions, the facts known to the expert (regardless of when the factual information was acquired) that relate to or form the basis of the testifying expert's mental impressions and opinions, and other discoverable matters, including documents not produced in disclosure, only by oral deposition of the expert and by a report prepared by the expert under this rule.

195.5 Court-Ordered Reports

If the discoverable factual observations, tests, supporting data, calculations, photographs, or opinions of an expert have not been recorded and reduced to tangible form, the court may order these matters reduced to tangible form and produced in addition to the deposition.

195.6 Amendment and Supplementation

A party's duty to amend and supplement written discovery regarding a testifying expert is governed by Rule 193.5. If an expert witness is retained by, employed by, or otherwise under the control of a party, that party must also amend or supplement any deposition testimony or written report by the expert, but only with regard to the expert's mental impressions or opinions and the basis for them.

195.7 Cost of Expert Witnesses

When a party takes the oral deposition of an expert witness retained by the opposing party, all reasonable fees charged by the expert for time spent in preparing for, giving, reviewing, and correcting the deposition must be paid by the party that retained the expert.

RULE 196. REQUESTS FOR PRODUCTION AND INSPECTION TO PARTIES; REQUESTS AND MOTIONS FOR ENTRY UPON PROPERTY

196.1 Request for Production and Inspection to Parties

(a) **Request.** A party may serve on another party—no later than 30 days before the end of the discovery period—a request for production or for inspection, to inspect, sample, test, photograph and copy documents or tangible things within the scope of discovery.

(b) **Contents of request.** The request must specify the items to be produced or inspected, either by individual item or by category, and describe with reasonable particularity each item and category. The request must specify a reasonable time (on or after the date on which the response is due) and place for production. If the requesting party will sample or test the requested items, the means, manner and procedure for testing or sampling must be described with sufficient specificity to inform the producing party of the means, manner, and procedure for testing or sampling.

(c) **Requests for production of medical or mental health records regarding nonparties**

(1) **Service of request on nonparty.** If a party requests another party to produce medical or mental health records regarding a nonparty, the requesting party must serve the nonparty with the request for production under Rule 21a.

(2) **Exceptions.** A party is not required to serve the request for production on a nonparty whose medical records are sought if:

(A) the nonparty signs a release of the records that is effective as to the requesting party;

(B) the identity of the nonparty whose records are sought will not directly or indirectly be disclosed by production of the records; or

(C) the court, upon a showing of good cause by the party seeking the records, orders that service is not required.

(3) **Confidentiality.** Nothing in this rule excuses compliance with laws concerning the confidentiality of medical or mental health records.

196.2 Response to Request for Production and Inspection

(a) **Time for response.** The responding party must serve a written response on the requesting party within 30 days after service of the request, except that a defendant served with a request before the defendant's answer is due need not respond until 50 days after service of the request.

(b) **Content of response.** With respect to each item or category of items, the responding party must state objections and assert privileges as required by these rules, and state, as appropriate, that:

(1) production, inspection, or other requested action will be permitted as requested;

(2) the requested items are being served on the requesting party with the response;

(3) production, inspection, or other requested action will take place at a specified time and place, if the responding party is objecting to the time and place of production; or

(4) no items have been identified—after a diligent search—that are responsive to the request.

196.3 Production

(a) **Time and place of production.** Subject to any objections stated in the response, the responding party must produce the requested documents or tangible things within the person's possession, custody or control at either the time and place requested or the time and place stated in the response, unless otherwise agreed by the parties or ordered by the court, and must provide the requesting party a reasonable opportunity to inspect them.

(b) **Copies.** The responding party may produce copies in lieu of originals unless a question is raised as to the authenticity of the original or in the circumstances it would be unfair to produce copies in lieu of originals. If originals are produced, the responding party is entitled to retain the originals while the requesting party inspects and copies them.

(c) **Organization.** The responding party must either produce documents and tangible things as they are kept in the usual course of business or organize and label them to correspond with the categories in the request.

196.4 Electronic or Magnetic Data

To obtain discovery of data or information that exists in electronic or magnetic form, the requesting party must specifically request production of electronic or magnetic data and specify the form in which the requesting party wants it produced. The responding party must produce the electronic or magnetic data that is responsive to the request and is reasonably available to the responding party in its ordinary course of business. If the responding party cannot—through reasonable efforts—retrieve the data or information requested or produce it in the form requested, the responding party must state an objection complying with these rules. If the court orders the responding party to comply with the request, the court must also order that the requesting party pay the reasonable expenses of any extraordinary steps required to retrieve and produce the information.

196.5 Destruction or Alteration

Testing, sampling or examination of an item may not destroy or materially alter an item unless previously authorized by the court.

196.6 Expenses of Production

Unless otherwise ordered by the court for good cause, the expense of producing items will be borne by the responding party and the expense of inspecting, sampling, testing, photographing, and copying items produced will be borne by the requesting party.

196.7 Request or Motion for Entry upon Property

(a) **Request or motion.** A party may gain entry on designated land or other property to inspect, measure, survey, photograph, test, or sample the property or any designated object or operation thereon by serving—no later than 30 days before the end of any applicable discovery period—

  (1) a request on all parties if the land or property belongs to a party, or

  (2) a motion and notice of hearing on all parties and the nonparty if the land or property belongs to a nonparty. If the identity or address of the nonparty is unknown and cannot be obtained through reasonable diligence, the court must permit service by means other than those specified in Rule 21a that are reasonably calculated to give the nonparty notice of the motion and hearing.

(b) **Time, place, and other conditions.** The request for entry upon a party's property, or the order for entry upon a nonparty's property, must state the time, place, manner, conditions, and scope of the inspection, and must specifically describe any desired means, manner, and procedure for testing or sampling, and the person or persons by whom the inspection, testing, or sampling is to be made.

(c) **Response to request for entry**

  (1) **Time to respond.** The responding party must serve a written response on the requesting party within 30 days after service of the request, except that a defendant served with a request before the defendant's answer is due need not respond until 50 days after service of the request.

  (2) **Content of response.** The responding party must state objections and assert privileges as required by these rules, and state, as appropriate, that:

    (A) entry or other requested action will be permitted as requested;

    (B) entry or other requested action will take place at a specified time and place, if the responding party is objecting to the time and place of production; or

    (C) entry or other requested action cannot be permitted for reasons stated in the response.

(d) **Requirements for order for entry on nonparty's property.** An order for entry on a nonparty's property may issue only for good cause shown and only if the land, property, or object thereon as to which discovery is sought is relevant to the subject matter of the action.

RULE 197. INTERROGATORIES TO PARTIES

197.1. Interrogatories

A party may serve on another party—no later than 30 days before the end of the discovery period—written interrogatories to inquire about any matter within the scope of discovery except matters covered by Rule 195. An interrogatory may inquire whether a party makes a specific legal or factual contention and may ask the responding party to state the legal theories and to describe in general the factual bases for the party's claims or defenses, but interrogatories may not be used to require the responding party to marshal all of its available proof or the proof the party intends to offer at trial.

197.2 Response to Interrogatories

(a) **Time for response.** The responding party must serve a written response on the requesting party within 30 days after service of the interrogatories, except that a defendant served with interrogatories before the defendant's answer is due need not respond until 50 days after service of the interrogatories.

(b) **Content of response.** A response must include the party's answers to the interrogatories and may include objections and assertions of privilege as required under these rules.

(c) **Option to produce records.** If the answer to an interrogatory may be derived or ascertained from public records, from the responding party's business records, or from a compilation, abstract or summary of the responding party's business records, and the burden of deriving or ascertaining the answer is substantially the same for the requesting party as for the responding party, the responding party may answer the interrogatory by specifying and, if applicable, producing the records or compilation, abstract or summary of the records. The records from which the answer may be derived or ascertained must be specified in sufficient detail to permit the requesting party to locate and identify them as readily as can the responding party. If the responding party has specified business records, the responding party must state a reasonable time and place for examination of the documents. The responding party must produce the documents at the time and place stated, unless otherwise agreed by the parties or ordered by the court, and must provide the requesting party a reasonable opportunity to inspect them.

(d) **Verification required; exceptions.** A responding party—not an agent or attorney as otherwise permitted by Rule 14—must sign the answers under oath except that:

(1) when answers are based on information obtained from other persons, the party may so state, and

(2) a party need not sign answers to interrogatories about persons with knowledge of relevant facts, trial witnesses, and legal contentions.

197.3 Use

Answers to interrogatories may be used only against the responding party. An answer to an interrogatory inquiring about matters described in Rule 194.2(c) and (d) that has been amended or supplemented is not admissible and may not be used for impeachment.

RULE 198. REQUESTS FOR ADMISSIONS

198.1 Request for Admissions

A party may serve on another party—no later than 30 days before the end of the discovery period—written requests that the other party admit the truth of any matter within the scope of discovery, including statements of opinion or of fact or of the application of law to fact, or the genuineness of any documents served with the request or otherwise made available for inspection and copying. Each matter for which an admission is requested must be stated separately.

198.2 Response to Requests for Admissions

(a) **Time for response.** The responding party must serve a written response on the requesting party within 30 days after service of the request, except that a defendant served with a request before the defendant's answer is due need not respond until 50 days after service of the request.

(b) **Content of response.** Unless the responding party states an objection or asserts a privilege, the responding party must specifically admit or deny the request or explain in detail the reasons that the responding party cannot admit or deny the request. A response must fairly meet the substance of the request. The responding party may qualify an answer, or deny a request in part, only when good faith requires. Lack of information or knowledge is not a proper response unless the responding party states that a reasonable inquiry was made but that the information known or easily obtainable is insufficient to enable the responding party to admit or deny. An assertion that the request presents an issue for trial is not a proper response.

(c) **Effect of failure to respond.** If a response is not timely served, the request is considered admitted without the necessity of a court order.

198.3 Effect of Admissions; Withdrawal or Amendment

Any admission made by a party under this rule may be used solely in the pending action and not in any other proceeding. A matter admitted under this rule is conclusively established as to the party making the admission unless the court permits the party to withdraw or amend the admission. The court may permit the party to withdraw or amend the admission if:

(a) the party shows good cause for the withdrawal or amendment; and

(b) the court finds that the parties relying upon the responses and deemed admissions will not be unduly prejudiced and that the presentation of the merits of the action will be subserved by permitting the party to amend or withdraw the admission.

RULE 199. DEPOSITIONS UPON ORAL EXAMINATION

199.1 Oral Examination; Alternative Methods of Conducting or Recording

(a) **Generally.** A party may take the testimony of any person or entity by deposition on oral examination before any officer authorized by law to take depositions. The testimony, objections, and any other statements during the deposition must be recorded at the time they are given or made.

(b) **Depositions by telephone or other remote electronic means.** A party may take an oral deposition by telephone or other remote electronic means if the party gives reasonable prior written notice of intent to do so. For the purposes of these rules, an oral deposition taken by telephone or other remote electronic means is considered as having been taken in the district and at the place where the witness is located when answering the questions. The officer taking the deposition may be located with the party noticing the deposition instead of with the witness if the witness is placed under oath by a person who is present with the witness and authorized to administer oaths in that jurisdiction.

(c) **Nonstenographic recording.** Any party may cause a deposition upon oral examination to be recorded by other than stenographic means, including videotape recording. The party requesting the nonstenographic recording will be responsible for obtaining a person authorized by law to administer the oath and for assuring that the recording will be intelligible, accurate, and trustworthy. At least five days prior to the deposition, the party must serve on the witness and all parties a notice, either in the notice of deposition or separately, that the deposition will be recorded by other than stenographic means. This notice must state the method of nonstenographic recording to be used and whether the deposition will also be recorded stenographically. Any other party may then serve written notice designating another method of recording in addition to the method specified, at the expense of such other party unless the court orders otherwise.

199.2 Procedure for Noticing Oral Deposition

(a) **Time to notice deposition.** A notice of intent to take an oral deposition must be served on the witness and all parties a reasonable time before the deposition is taken. An oral deposition may be taken outside the discovery period only by agreement of the parties or with leave of court.

(b) **Content of notice.**

(1) **Identity of witness; organizations.** The notice must state the name of the witness, which may be either an individual or a public or private corporation, partnership, association, governmental agency, or other organization. If an organization is named as the witness, the notice must describe with reasonable particularity the matters on which examination is requested. In response, the organization named in the notice must—a reasonable time before the deposition—designate one or more individuals to testify on its behalf and set forth, for each individual designated, the matters on which the individual will testify. Each individual designated must testify as to matters that are known or reasonably available to the organization. This subdivision does not preclude taking a deposition by any other procedure authorized by these rules.

(2) **Time and place.** The notice must state a reasonable time and place for the oral deposition. The place may be in:

(A) the county of the witness's residence;

(B) the county where the witness is employed or regularly transacts business in person;

(C) the county of suit, if the witness is a party or a person designated by a party under Rule 199.2(b)(1);

(D) the county where the witness was served with the subpoena, or within 150 miles of the place of service, if the witness is not a resident of Texas or is a transient person; or

(E) subject to the foregoing, at any other convenient place directed by the court in which the cause is pending.

(3) **Alternative means of conducting and recording.** The notice must state whether the deposition is to be taken by telephone or other remote electronic means and identify the means. If the deposition is to be recorded by nonstenographic means, the notice may include the notice required by Rule 199.1(c).

(4) **Additional attendees.** The notice may include the notice concerning additional attendees required by Rule 199.5(a)(3).

(5) **Request for production of documents.** A notice may include a request that the witness produce at the deposition documents or tangible things within the scope of discovery and within the witness's possession, custody, or control. If the witness is a nonparty, the request must comply with Rule 205 and the designation of materials required to be identified in the subpoena must be attached to, or included in, the notice. The nonparty's response to the request is governed by Rules 176 and 205. When the witness is a party or subject to the control of a party, document requests under this subdivision are governed by Rules 193 and 196.

199.3 Compelling Witness to Attend

A party may compel the witness to attend the oral deposition by serving the witness with a subpoena under Rule 176. If the witness is a party or is retained by, employed by, or otherwise subject to the control of a party, however, service of the notice of oral deposition upon the party's attorney has the same effect as a subpoena served on the witness.

199.4 Objections to Time and Place of Oral Deposition

A party or witness may object to the time and place designated for an oral deposition by motion for protective order or by motion to quash the notice of deposition. If the motion is filed by the third business day after service of the notice of deposition, an objection to the time and place of a deposition stays the oral deposition until the motion can be determined.

199.5 Examination, Objection, and Conduct During Oral Depositions

(a) **Attendance**

(1) **Witness.** The witness must remain in attendance from day to day until the deposition is begun and completed.

(2) **Attendance by party.** A party may attend an oral deposition in person, even if the deposition is taken by telephone or other remote electronic

means. If a deposition is taken by telephone or other remote electronic means, the party noticing the deposition must make arrangements for all persons to attend by the same means. If the party noticing the deposition appears in person, any other party may appear by telephone or other remote electronic means if that party makes the necessary arrangements with the deposition officer and the party noticing the deposition.

(3) **Other attendees.** If any party intends to have in attendance any persons other than the witness, parties, spouses of parties, counsel, employees of counsel, and the officer taking the oral deposition, that party must give reasonable notice to all parties, either in the notice of deposition or separately, of the identity of the other persons.

(b) **Oath; examination.** Every person whose deposition is taken by oral examination must first be placed under oath. The parties may examine and cross-examine the witness. Any party, in lieu of participating in the examination, may serve written questions in a sealed envelope on the party noticing the oral deposition, who must deliver them to the deposition officer, who must open the envelope and propound them to the witness.

(c) **Time limitation.** No side may examine or cross-examine an individual witness for more than six hours. Breaks during depositions do not count against this limitation.

(d) **Conduct during the oral deposition; conferences.** The oral deposition must be conducted in the same manner as if the testimony were being obtained in court during trial. Counsel should cooperate with and be courteous to each other and to the witness. The witness should not be evasive and should not unduly delay the examination. Private conferences between the witness and the witness's attorney during the actual taking of the deposition are improper except for the purpose of determining whether a privilege should be asserted. Private conferences may be held, however, during agreed recesses and adjournments. If the lawyers and witnesses do not comply with this rule, the court may allow in evidence at trial statements, objections, discussions, and other occurrences during the oral deposition that reflect upon the credibility of the witness or the testimony.

(e) **Objections.** Objections to questions during the oral deposition are limited to "Objection, leading" and "Objection, form." Objections to testimony during the oral deposition are limited to "Objection, nonresponsive." These objections are waived if not stated as phrased during the oral deposition. All other objections need not be made or recorded during the oral deposition to be later raised with the court. The objecting party must give a clear and concise explanation of an objection if requested by the party taking the oral deposition, or the objection is waived. Argumentative or suggestive objections or explanations waive objection and may be grounds for terminating the oral deposition or assessing costs or other sanctions. The officer taking the oral deposition will not rule on objections but must record them for ruling by the court. The officer taking the oral deposition must not fail to record testimony because an objection has been made.

(f) **Instructions not to answer.** An attorney may instruct a witness not to answer a question during an oral deposition only if necessary to preserve a privilege, comply with a court order or these rules, protect a witness from an abusive question or one for which any answer would be misleading, or secure a ruling pursuant to paragraph (g). The attorney instructing the witness not to answer must give a concise, nonargumentative, nonsuggestive explanation of the grounds for the instruction if requested by the party who asked the question.

(g) **Suspending the deposition.** If the time limitations for the deposition have expired or the deposition is being conducted or defended in violation of these rules, a party or witness may suspend the oral deposition for the time necessary to obtain a ruling.

(h) **Good faith required.** An attorney must not ask a question at an oral deposition solely to harass or mislead the witness, for any other improper purpose, or without a good faith legal basis at the time. An attorney must not object to a question at an oral deposition, instruct the witness not to answer a question, or suspend the deposition unless there is a good faith factual and legal basis for doing so at the time.

199.6 Hearing on Objections

Any party may, at any reasonable time, request a hearing on an objection or privilege asserted by an instruction not to answer or suspension of the deposition; provided the failure of a party to obtain a ruling prior to trial does not waive any objection or privilege. The party seeking to avoid discovery must present any evidence necessary to support the objection or privilege either by testimony at the hearing or by affidavits served on opposing parties at least seven days before the hearing. If the court determines that an in camera review of some or all of the requested discovery is necessary to rule, answers to the deposition questions may be made in camera, to be transcribed and sealed in the event the privilege is sustained, or made in an affidavit produced to the court in a sealed wrapper.

RULE 200. DEPOSITIONS UPON WRITTEN QUESTIONS

200.1 Procedure for Noticing Deposition Upon Written Questions

(a) **Who may be noticed; when.** A party may take the testimony of any person or entity by deposition on written questions before any person authorized by law to take depositions on written questions. A notice of intent to take the deposition must be served on the witness and all parties at least 20 days before the deposition is taken. A deposition on written questions may be taken outside the discovery period only by agreement of the parties or with leave of court. The party noticing the deposition must also deliver to the deposition officer a copy of the notice and of all written questions to be asked during the deposition.

(b) **Content of notice.** The notice must comply with Rules 199.1(b), 199.2(b), and 199.5(a)(3). If the witness is an organization, the organization must comply with the requirements of that provision. The notice also may include a request for production of documents as permitted by Rule 199.2(b)(5), the provisions of which will govern the request, service, and response.

200.2 Compelling Witness to Attend

A party may compel the witness to attend the deposition on written questions by serving the witness with a subpoena under Rule 176. If the witness is a party or is retained by, employed by, or otherwise subject to the control of a party, however, service of the deposition notice upon the party's attorney has the same effect as a subpoena served on the witness.

200.3 Questions and Objections

(a) **Direct questions.** The direct questions to be propounded to the witness must be attached to the notice.

(b) **Objections and additional questions.** Within ten days after the notice and direct questions are served, any party may object to the direct questions and serve cross-questions on all other parties. Within five days after cross-questions are served, any party may object to the cross-questions and serve redirect questions on all other parties. Within three days after redirect questions are served, any party may object to the redirect questions and serve recross questions on all other parties. Objections to recross questions must be served within five days after the earlier of when recross questions are served or the time of the deposition on written questions.

(c) **Objections to form of questions.** Objections to the form of a question are waived unless asserted in accordance with this subdivision.

200.4 Conducting the Deposition Upon Written Questions

The deposition officer must: take the deposition on written questions at the time and place designated; record the testimony of the witness under oath in response to the questions; and prepare, certify, and deliver the deposition transcript in accordance with Rule 203. The deposition officer has authority when necessary to summon and swear an interpreter to facilitate the taking of the deposition.

RULE 201. DEPOSITIONS IN FOREIGN JURISDICTIONS FOR USE IN TEXAS PROCEEDINGS; DEPOSITIONS IN TEXAS FOR USE IN FOREIGN PROCEEDINGS

201.1 Depositions in Foreign Jurisdictions for Use in Texas Proceedings

(a) **Generally.** A party may take a deposition on oral examination or written questions of any person or entity located in another state or a foreign country for use in proceedings in this State. The deposition may be taken by:

(1) notice;

(2) letter rogatory, letter of request, or other such device;

(3) agreement of the parties; or

(4) court order.

(b) **By notice.** A party may take the deposition by notice in accordance with these rules as if the deposition were taken in this State, except that the deposition officer may be a person authorized to administer oaths in the place where the deposition is taken.

(c) **By letter rogatory.** On motion by a party, the court in which an action is pending must issue a letter rogatory on terms that are just and appropriate, regardless of whether any other manner of obtaining the deposition is impractical or inconvenient. The letter must:

(1) be addressed to the appropriate authority in the jurisdiction in which the deposition is to be taken;

(2) request and authorize that authority to summon the witness before the authority at a time and place stated in the letter for examination on oral or written questions; and

(3) request and authorize that authority to cause the witness's testimony to be reduced to writing and returned, together with any items marked as exhibits, to the party requesting the letter rogatory.

(d) **By letter of request or other such device.** On motion by a party, the court in which an action is pending, or the clerk of that court, must issue a letter of request or other such device in accordance with an applicable treaty or international convention on terms that are just and appropriate. The letter or other device must be issued regardless of whether any other manner of obtaining the deposition is impractical or inconvenient. The letter or other device must:

(1) be in the form prescribed by the treaty or convention under which it is issued, as presented by the movant to the court or clerk; and

(2) must state the time, place, and manner of the examination of the witness.

(e) **Objections to form of letter rogatory, letter of request, or other such device.** In issuing a letter rogatory, letter of request, or other such device, the court must set a time for objecting to the form of the device. A party must make any objection to the form of the device in writing and serve it on all other parties by the time set by the court, or the objection is waived.

(f) **Admissibility of evidence.** Evidence obtained in response to a letter rogatory, letter of request, or other such device is not inadmissible merely because it is not a verbatim transcript, or the testimony was not taken under oath, or for any similar departure from the requirements for depositions taken within this State under these rules.

(g) **Deposition by electronic means.** A deposition in another jurisdiction may be taken by telephone, videoconference, teleconference, or other electronic means under the provisions of Rule 199.

201.2 Depositions in Texas for Use in Proceedings in Foreign Jurisdictions

If a court of record of any other state or foreign jurisdiction issues a mandate, writ, or commission that requires a witness's oral or written deposition testimony in this State, the witness may be compelled to appear and testify in the same manner and by the same process used for taking testimony in a proceeding pending in this State.

RULE 202. DEPOSITIONS BEFORE SUIT OR TO INVESTIGATE CLAIMS

202.1 Generally

A person may petition the court for an order authorizing the taking of a deposition on oral examination or written questions either:

(a) to perpetuate or obtain the person's own testimony or that of any other person for use in an anticipated suit; or

(b) to investigate a potential claim or suit.

202.2 Petition

The petition must:

(a) be verified;

(b) be filed in a proper court of any county:

(1) where venue of the anticipated suit may lie, if suit is anticipated; or

(2) where the witness resides, if no suit is yet anticipated;

(c) be in the name of the petitioner;

(d) state either:

(1) that the petitioner anticipates the institution of a suit in which the petitioner may be a party; or

(2) that the petitioner seeks to investigate a potential claim by or against petitioner;

(e) state the subject matter of the anticipated action, if any, and the petitioner's interest therein;

(f) if suit is anticipated, either:

(1) state the names of the persons petitioner expects to have interests adverse to petitioner's in the anticipated suit, and the addresses and telephone numbers for such persons; or

(2) state that the names, addresses, and telephone numbers of persons petitioner expects to have interests adverse to petitioner's in the anticipated suit cannot be ascertained through diligent inquiry, and describe those persons;

(g) state the names, addresses and telephone numbers of the persons to be deposed, the substance of the testimony that the petitioner expects to elicit from each, and the petitioner's reasons for desiring to obtain the testimony of each; and

(h) request an order authorizing the petitioner to take the depositions of the persons named in the petition.

2023 Notice and Service

(a) **Personal service on witnesses and persons named.** At least 15 days before the date of the hearing on the petition, the petitioner must serve the petition and a notice of the hearing—in accordance with Rule 21a—on all persons petitioner seeks to depose and, if suit is anticipated, on all persons petitioner expects to have interests adverse to petitioner's in the anticipated suit.

(b) **Service by publication on persons not named.**

(1) **Manner.** Unnamed persons described in the petition whom the petitioner expects to have interests adverse to petitioner's in the anticipated suit, if any, may be served by publication with the petition and notice of the hearing. The notice must state the place for the hearing and the time it will be held, which must be more than 14 days after the first publication of the notice. The petition and notice must be published once each week for two consecutive weeks in the newspaper of broadest circulation in the county in which the petition is filed, or if no such newspaper exists, in the newspaper of broadest circulation in the nearest county where a newspaper is published.

(2) **Objection to depositions taken on notice by publication.** Any interested party may move, in the proceeding or by bill of review, to suppress any deposition, in whole or in part, taken on notice by publication, and may also attack or oppose the deposition by any other means available.

(c) **Service in probate cases.** A petition to take a deposition in anticipation of an application for probate of a will, and notice of the hearing on the petition, may be served by posting as prescribed by Section 33(f)(2) of the Probate Code. The notice and petition must be directed to all parties interested in the testator's estate and must comply with the requirements of Section 33(c) of the Probate Code insofar as they may be applicable.

(d) **Modification by order.** As justice or necessity may require, the court may shorten or lengthen the notice periods under this rule and may extend the notice period to permit service on any expected adverse party.

202.4 Order

(a) **Required findings.** The court must order a deposition to be taken if, but only if, it finds that:

(1) allowing the petitioner to take the requested deposition may prevent a failure or delay of justice in an anticipated suit; or

(2) the likely benefit of allowing the petitioner to take the requested deposition to investigate a potential claim outweighs the burden or expense of the procedure.

(b) **Contents.** The order must state whether a deposition will be taken on oral examination or written questions. The order may also state the time and place at which a deposition will be taken. If the order does not state the time and place at which a deposition will be taken, the petitioner must notice the deposition as required by Rules 199 or 200. The order must contain any protections the court finds necessary or appropriate to protect the witness or any person who may be affected by the procedure.

202.5 Manner of Taking and Use

Except as otherwise provided in this rule, depositions authorized by this rule are governed by the rules applicable to depositions of nonparties in a pending suit. The scope of discovery in depositions authorized by this rule is the same as if the anticipated suit or potential claim had been filed. A court may restrict or prohibit the use of a deposition taken under this rule in a subsequent suit to protect a person who was not served with notice of the deposition from any unfair prejudice or to prevent abuse of this rule.

RULE 203. SIGNING, CERTIFICATION AND USE OF ORAL AND WRITTEN DEPOSITIONS

203.1 Signature and Changes

(a) **Deposition transcript to be provided to witness.** The deposition officer must provide the original deposition transcript to the witness for examination and signature. If the witness is represented by an attorney at the deposition, the deposition officer must provide the transcript to the attorney instead of the witness.

(b) **Changes by witness; signature.** The witness may change responses as reflected in the deposition transcript by indicating the desired changes, in writing, on a separate sheet of paper, together with a statement of the reasons for making the changes. No erasures or obliterations of any kind may be made to the original deposition transcript. The witness must then sign the transcript under oath and return it to the deposition officer. If the witness does not return the transcript to the deposition officer within 20 days of the date the transcript was provided to the witness or the witness's attorney, the witness may be deemed to have waived the right to make the changes.

(c) **Exceptions.** The requirements of presentation and signature under this subdivision do not apply:

(1) if the witness and all parties waive the signature requirement;

(2) to depositions on written questions; or

(3) to nonstenographic recordings of oral depositions.

203.2 Certification

The deposition officer must file with the court, serve on all parties, and attach as part of the deposition transcript or nonstenographic recording of an oral deposition a certificate duly sworn by the officer stating:

(a) that the witness was duly sworn by the officer and that the transcript or nonstenographic recording of the oral deposition is a true record of the testimony given by the witness;

(b) that the deposition transcript, if any, was submitted to the witness or to the attorney for the witness for examination and signature, the date on which the transcript was submitted, whether the witness returned the transcript, and if so, the date on which it was returned.

(c) that changes, if any, made by the witness are attached to the deposition transcript;

(d) that the deposition officer delivered the deposition transcript or nonstenographic recording of an oral deposition in accordance with Rule 203.3;

(e) the amount of time used by each party at the deposition;

(f) the amount of the deposition officer's charges for preparing the original deposition transcript, which the clerk of the court must tax as costs; and

(g) that a copy of the certificate was served on all parties and the date of service.

203.3 Delivery

(a) **Endorsement; to whom delivered.** The deposition officer must endorse the title of the action and "Deposition of (name of witness)" on the original deposition transcript (or a copy, if the original was not returned) or the original nonstenographic recording of an oral deposition, and must return:

(1) the transcript to the party who asked the first question appearing in the transcript, or

(2) the recording to the party who requested it.

(b) **Notice.** The deposition officer must serve notice of delivery on all other parties.

(c) **Inspection and copying; copies.** The party receiving the original deposition transcript or nonstenographic recording must make it available upon reasonable request for inspection and copying by any other party. Any party or the witness is entitled to obtain a copy of the deposition transcript or nonstenographic recording from the deposition officer upon payment of a reasonable fee.

203.4 Exhibits

At the request of a party, the original documents and things produced for inspection during the examination of the witness must be marked for identification by the deposition officer and annexed to the deposition transcript or nonstenographic recording. The person producing the materials may produce copies instead of originals if the party gives all other parties fair opportunity at the deposition to compare the copies with the originals. If the person offers originals rather than copies, the deposition officer must, after the conclusion of the deposition, make copies to be attached to the original deposition transcript or nonstenographic recording, and then return the originals to the person who produced them. The person who produced the originals must preserve them for hearing or trial and make them available for inspection or copying by any other party upon seven days' notice. Copies annexed to the original deposition transcript or nonstenographic recording may be used for all purposes.

203.5 Motion to Suppress

A party may object to any errors and irregularities in the way the testimony is transcribed, signed, delivered, or otherwise dealt with by the deposition officer by filing a motion to suppress all or part of the deposition. If the deposition officer complies with [Texas] Rule 203.3 at least one day before the case is called to trial, with regard to a deposition transcript, or 30 days before the case is called to trial, with regard to a nonstenographic recording, the party must file and serve a motion to suppress before trial commences to preserve the objections.

203.6 Use

(a) **Nonstenographic recording; transcription.** A nonstenographic recording of an oral deposition, or a written transcription of all or part of such a recording, may be used to the same extent as a deposition taken by stenographic means. However, the court, for good cause shown, may require that the party seeking to use a nonstenographic recording or written transcription first obtain a complete transcript of the deposition recording from a certified court reporter. The court reporter's transcription must be made from the original or a certified copy of the deposition recording. The court reporter must, to the extent applicable, comply with the provisions of this rule, except that the court reporter must deliver the original transcript to the attorney requesting the transcript, and the court reporter's certificate must include a statement that the transcript is a true record of the nonstenographic recording. The party to whom the court reporter delivers the original transcript must make the transcript available, upon reasonable request, for inspection and copying by the witness or any party.

(b) **Same proceeding.** All or part of a deposition may be used for any purpose in the same proceeding in which it was taken. If the original is not filed, a certified copy may be used. "Same proceeding" includes a proceeding in a different court but involving the same subject matter and the same parties or their representatives or successors in interest. A deposition is admissible against a party joined after the deposition was taken if:

(1) the deposition is admissible pursuant to Rule 804(b)(1) of the Rules of Evidence, or

(2) that party has had a reasonable opportunity to redepose the witness and has failed to do so.

(c) **Different proceeding.** Depositions taken in different proceedings may be used as permitted by the Rules of Evidence.

RULE 204. PHYSICAL AND MENTAL EXAMINATION

204.1 Motion and Order Required

(a) **Motion.** A party may—no later than 30 days before the end of any applicable discovery period—move for an order compelling another party to:

(1) submit to a physical or mental examination by a qualified physician or a mental examination by a qualified psychologist; or

(2) produce for such examination a person in the other party's custody, conservatorship or legal control.

(b) **Service.** The motion and notice of hearing must be served on the person to be examined and all parties.

(c) **Requirements for obtaining order.** The court may issue an order for examination only for good cause shown and only in the following circumstances:

(1) when the mental or physical condition (including the blood group) of a party, or of a person in the custody, conservatorship or under the legal control of a party, is in controversy; or

(2) except as provided in Rule 204.4, an examination by a psychologist may be ordered when the party responding to the motion has designated a psychologist as a testifying expert or has disclosed a psychologist's records for possible use at trial.

(d) **Requirements of order.** The order must be in writing and must specify the time, place, manner, conditions, and scope of the examination and the person or persons by whom it is to be made.

204.2 Report of Examining Physician or Psychologist

(a) **Right to report.** Upon request of the person ordered to be examined, the party causing the examination to be made must deliver to the person a copy of a detailed written report of the examining physician or psychologist setting out the findings, including results of all tests made, diagnoses and conclusions, together with like reports of all earlier examinations of the same condition. After delivery of the report, upon request of the party causing the examination, the party against whom the order is made must produce a like report of any examination made before or after the ordered examination of the same condition, unless the person examined is not a party and the party shows that the party is unable to obtain it. The court on motion may limit delivery of a report on such terms as are just. If a physician or psychologist fails or refuses to make a report the court may exclude the testimony if offered at the trial.

(b) **Agreements; relationship to other rules.** This subdivision applies to examinations made by agreement of the parties, unless the agreement expressly provides otherwise. This subdivision does not preclude discovery of a report of an examining physician or psychologist or the taking of a deposition of the physician or psychologist in accordance with the provisions of any other rule.

204.3 Effect of No Examination

If no examination is sought either by agreement or under this subdivision, the party whose physical or mental condition is in controversy must not comment to the court or jury concerning the party's willingness to submit to an examination, or on the right or failure of any other party to seek an examination.

204.4 Cases Arising Under Titles II or V, Family Code

In cases arising under Family Code Titles II or V, the court may—on its own initiative or on motion of a party—appoint:

(a) one or more psychologists or psychiatrists to make any and all appropriate mental examinations of the children who are the subject of the suit or of any other parties, and may make such appointment irrespective of whether a psychologist or psychiatrist has been designated by any party as a testifying expert;

(b) one or more experts who are qualified in paternity testing to take blood, body fluid, or tissue samples to conduct paternity tests as ordered by the court.

204.5 Definition

For the purpose of this rule, a psychologist is a person licensed or certified by a state or the District of Columbia as a psychologist.

RULE 205. DISCOVERY FROM NONPARTIES

205.1 Forms of Discovery; Subpoena Requirement

A party may compel discovery from a nonparty—that is, a person who is not a party or subject to a party's control—only by obtaining a court order under Rules 196.7, 202, or 204, or by serving a subpoena compelling:

(a) an oral deposition;

(b) a deposition on written questions;

(c) a request for production of documents or tangible things, pursuant to Rule 199.2(b)(5) or Rule 200.1(b), served with a notice of deposition on oral examination or written questions; and

(d) a request for production of documents and tangible things under this rule.

205.2 Notice

A party seeking discovery by subpoena from a nonparty must serve, on the nonparty and all parties, a copy of the form of notice required under the rules governing the applicable form of discovery. A notice of oral or written deposition must be served before or at the same time that a subpoena compelling attendance or production under the notice is served. A notice to produce documents or tangible things under Rule 205.3 must be served at least 10 days before the subpoena compelling production is served.

205.3 Production of Documents and Tangible Things Without Deposition

(a) **Notice; subpoena.** A party may compel production of documents and tangible things from a nonparty by serving—a reasonable time before the response is due but no later than 30 days before the end of any applicable discovery period—the notice required in Rule 205.2 and a subpoena compelling production or inspection of documents or tangible things.

(b) **Contents of notice.** The notice must state:

(1) the name of the person from whom production or inspection is sought to be compelled;

(2) a reasonable time and place for the production or inspection; and

(3) the items to be produced or inspected, either by individual item or by category, describing each item and category with reasonable particularity, and, if applicable, describing the desired testing and sampling with sufficient specificity to inform the nonparty of the means, manner, and procedure for testing or sampling.

(c) **Requests for production of medical or mental health records of other nonparties.** If a party requests a nonparty to produce medical or mental health records of another nonparty, the requesting party must serve the nonparty whose records are sought with the notice required under this rule. This requirement does not apply under the circumstances set forth in Rule 196.1(c)(2).

(d) **Response.** The nonparty must respond to the notice and subpoena in accordance with Rule 176.6.

(e) **Custody, inspection and copying.** The party obtaining the production must make all materials produced available for inspection by any other party on reasonable notice, and must furnish copies to any party who requests at that party's expense.

(f) **Cost of production.** A party requiring production of documents by a nonparty must reimburse the nonparty's reasonable costs of production.

RULE 215. ABUSE OF DISCOVERY; SANCTIONS

215.1 Motion for Sanctions or Order Compelling Discovery

A party, upon reasonable notice to other parties and all other persons affected thereby, may apply for sanctions or an order compelling discovery as follows:

(a) **Appropriate court.** On matters relating to a deposition, an application for an order to a party may be made to the court in which the action is pending, or to any district court in the district where the deposition is being taken. An application for an order to a deponent who is not a party shall be made to the court in the district where the deposition is being taken. As to all other discovery matters, an application for an order will be made to the court in which the action is pending.

(b) **Motion**

(1) If a party or other deponent which is a corporation or other entity fails to make a designation under Rules 199.2(b)(1) or 200.1(b); or

(2) if a party, or other deponent, or a person designated to testify on behalf of a party or other deponent fails:

(A) to appear before the officer who is to take his deposition, after being served with a proper notice; or

(B) to answer a question propounded or submitted upon oral examination or upon written questions; or

(3) if a party fails:

(A) to serve answers or objections to interrogatories submitted under Rule 197, after proper service of the interrogatories; or

(B) to answer an interrogatory submitted under Rule 197; or

(C) to serve a written response to a request for inspection submitted under Rule 196, after proper service of the request; or

(D) to respond that discovery will be permitted as requested or fails to permit discovery as requested in response to a request for inspection submitted under Rule 196; the discovering party may move for an order compelling a designation, an appearance, an answer or answers, or inspection or production in accordance with the request, or apply to the court in which the action is pending for the imposition of any sanction authorized by Rule 215.2(b) without the necessity of first having obtained a court order compelling such discovery.

When taking a deposition on oral examination, the proponent of the question may complete or adjourn the examination before he applies for an order.

If the court denies the motion in whole or in part, it may make such protective order as it would have been empowered to make on a motion pursuant to Rule 192.6.

(c) **Evasive or incomplete answer.** For purposes of this subdivision an evasive or incomplete answer is to be treated as a failure to answer.

(d) **Disposition of motion to compel: award of expenses.** If the motion is granted, the court shall, after opportunity for hearing, require a party or deponent whose conduct necessitated the motion or the party or attorney advising such conduct or both of them to pay, at such time as ordered by the court, the moving party the reasonable expenses incurred in obtaining the order, including attorney fees, unless the court finds that the opposition to the motion was substantially justified or that other circumstances make an award of expenses unjust. Such an order shall be subject to review on appeal from the final judgment.

If the motion is denied, the court may, after opportunity for hearing, require the moving party or attorney advising such motion to pay to the party or deponent who opposed the motion the reasonable expenses incurred in opposing the motion, including attorney fees, unless the court finds that the making of the motion was substantially justified or that other circumstances make an award of expenses unjust.

If the motion is granted in part and denied in part, the court may apportion the reasonable expenses incurred in relation to the motion among the parties and persons in a just manner.

In determining the amount of reasonable expenses, including attorney fees, to be awarded in connection with a motion, the trial court shall award expenses which are reasonable in relation to the amount of work reasonably expended in obtaining an order compelling compliance or in opposing a motion which is denied.

(e) **Providing person's own statement.** If a party fails to comply with any person's written request for the person's own statement as provided in Rule 192.3(h), the person who made the request may move for an order compelling compliance. If the motion is granted, the movant may recover the expenses incurred in obtaining the order, including attorney fees, which are reasonable in relation to the amount of work reasonably expended in obtaining the order.

215.2 Failure to Comply with Order or with Discovery Request

(a) **Sanctions by court in district where deposition is taken.** If a deponent fails to appear or to be sworn or to answer a question after being directed to do so by a district court in the district in which the deposition is being taken, the failure may be considered a contempt of that court.

(b) **Sanctions by court in which action is pending.** If a party or an officer, director, or managing agent of a party or a person designated under Rules 199.2(b)(1) or 200.1(b) to testify on behalf of a party fails to comply with proper discovery requests or to obey an order to provide or permit discovery, including an order made under Rules 204 or 215.1, the court in which the action is pending may, after notice and hearing, make such orders in regard to the failure as are just, and among others the following:

(1) an order disallowing any further discovery of any kind or of a particular kind by the disobedient party;

(2) an order charging all or any portion of the expenses of discovery or taxable court costs or both against the disobedient party or the attorney advising him;

(3) an order that the matters regarding which the order was made or any other designated facts shall be taken to be established for the purposes of the action in accordance with the claim of the party obtaining the order;

(4) an order refusing to allow the disobedient party to support or oppose designated claims or defenses, or prohibiting him from introducing designated matters in evidence;

(5) an order striking out pleadings or parts thereof, or staying further proceedings until the order is obeyed, or dismissing with or without prejudice the action or proceedings or any part thereof, or rendering a judgment by default against the disobedient party;

(6) in lieu of any of the foregoing orders or in addition thereto, an order treating as a contempt of court the failure to obey any orders except an order to submit to a physical or mental examination;

(7) when a party has failed to comply with an order under Rule 204 requiring him to appear or produce another for examination, such orders as are listed in paragraphs (1), (2), (3), (4) or (5) of this subdivision, unless the person failing to comply shows that he is unable to appear or to produce such person for examination.

(8) In lieu of any of the foregoing orders or in addition thereto, the court shall require the party failing to obey the order or the attorney advising him, or both, to pay, at such time as ordered by the court, the reasonable expenses, including attorney fees, caused by the failure, unless the court finds that the failure was substantially justified or that other circumstances make an award of expenses unjust. Such an order shall be subject to review on appeal from the final judgment.

(c) **Sanction against nonparty for violation of Rules 196.7 or 205.3.** If a nonparty fails to comply with an order under Rules 196.7 or 205.3, the court which made the order may treat the failure to obey as contempt of court.

215.3 Abuse of Discovery Process in Seeking, Making, or Resisting Discovery

If the court finds a party is abusing the discovery process in seeking, making or resisting discovery or if the court finds that any interrogatory or request for inspection or production is unreasonably frivolous, oppressive, or harassing, or that a response or answer is unreasonably frivolous or made for purposes of delay, then the court in which the action is pending may, after notice and hearing, impose any appropriate sanction authorized by paragraphs (1), (2), (3), (4), (5), and (8) of Rule 215.2(b). Such order of sanction shall be subject to review on appeal from the final judgment.

215.4 Failure to Comply with Rule 198

(a) **Motion.** A party who has requested an admission under Rule 198 may move to determine the sufficiency of the answer or objection. For purposes of this subdivision an evasive or incomplete answer may be treated as a failure to answer. Unless the court determines that an objection is justified, it shall order that an answer be served. If the court determines that an answer does not comply with the requirements of Rule 198, it may order either that the matter is admitted or that an amended answer be served. The provisions of Rule 215.1(d) apply to the award of expenses incurred in relation to the motion.

(b) **Expenses on failure to admit.** If a party fails to admit the genuineness of any document or the truth of any matter as requested under Rule 198 and if the party requesting the admissions thereafter proves the genuineness of the document or the truth of the matter, he may apply to the court for an order requiring the other party to pay him the reasonable expenses incurred in making that proof, including reasonable attorney fees. The court shall make the order unless it finds that (1) the request was held objectionable pursuant to Rule 193, or (2) the admission sought was of no substantial importance, or (3) the party failing to admit had a reasonable ground to believe that he might prevail on the matter, or (4) there was other good reason for the failure to admit.

215.5 Failure of Party or Witness to Attend or to Serve Subpoena; Expenses

(a) **Failure of party giving notice to attend.** If the party giving the notice of the taking of an oral deposition fails to attend and proceed therewith and another party attends in person or by attorney pursuant to the notice, the court may order the party giving the notice to pay such other party the reasonable expenses incurred by him and his attorney in attending, including reasonable attorney fees.

(b) **Failure of witness to attend.** If a party gives notice of the taking of an oral deposition of a witness and the witness does not attend because of the fault of the party giving the notice, if another party attends in person or by attorney because he expects the deposition of that witness to be taken, the court may order the party giving the notice to pay such other party the reasonable expenses incurred by him and his attorney in attending, including reasonable attorney fees.

215.6 Exhibits to Motions and Responses

Motions or responses made under this rule may have exhibits attached including affidavits, discovery pleadings, or any other documents.